A History of the Desire for Christian Unity, Volume I

A History of the Desire for Christian Unity

Ecumenism in the Churches (19th–21st Century)

Directed by Alberto Melloni
Edited by Luca Ferracci

Volume 1

Dawn of Ecumenism

BRILL

LEIDEN | BOSTON

A project realized thanks to the contribution of Ministero dell'Università e della Ricerca (MUR), Ministero della Cultura (MiC) and Regione Emilia-Romagna.

The Library of Congress Cataloging-in-Publication Data is available online at http://catalog.loc.gov

Typeface for the Latin, Greek, and Cyrillic scripts: "Brill". See and download: brill.com/brill-typeface.

ISBN 978-90-04-44669-4 (hardback volume I)
ISBN 978-90-04-44851-3 (hardback volume II)
ISBN 978-90-04-44852-0 (hardback volume III)
ISBN 978-90-04-47241-9 (hardback volume IV)

This book is printed on acid-free paper and produced in a sustainable manner.

Contents

List of Acronyms   IX
List of Archives   XII
List of Journals, Lexicons, and Sources   XIII
Notes on Contributors   XVII

Introduction
Premises for a History of the Desire for Christian Unity   1
   Alberto Melloni

PART 1
Preamble: Long Term Issues

1   From Division to the Search for Unity: Difficulties and Horizons in a History Still
   Underway   21
     John D. Zizioulas

2   Before Ecumenism, at the Dawn of Modernity: Historical-Political Causes and
   Effects of the Revolutions of the 18th Century   42
     Mathijs Lamberigts

3   Historiography of the Ecumenical Movement: The State of the Question   66
     Étienne Fouilloux and Luca Ferracci

PART 2
Prehistory: The Challenges of Modernity

4   A Theological Geography of Confessions and Churches in the 19th Century   87
     Sandra Mazzolini

5   The Search for an Orthodox Christian Identity: Orthodoxy, Nation, and
   Ecumenism between 19th and 20th Century   110
     Vasilios N. Makrides

6   Newman and the Oxford Movement: A Prehistory of Ecumenism (1833–1870)   132
     Peter B. Nockles

7   Ignaz von Döllinger and the Bonn Reunion Conferences of 1874–1875   164
     Franz Xaver Bischof

8   The Slavophiles: From Khomyakov to Solovyov   187
      Jeremy Pilch

9   Unions, Alliances and World Communions in 19th-Century Protestant World   211
      Martin Friedrich

10   The 1893 World's Parliament of Religions: Striving for Religious Unity   224
      Arie L. Molendijk

11   Pontifical Unionism from Pius IX to Pius X   244
      Laura Pettinaroli

12   The Origins of Anglican Ecumenical Theology, the Chicago-Lambeth
      Quadrilateral, and the Question of Anglican Orders   264
      Paul Avis

13   Scholarship and Unity in the 19th and 20th Century: Johann Adam Möhler and
      Adolf von Harnack Compared   300
      Michel Fédou, s.j.

14   The World Student Christian Federation and John R. Mott   320
      Sarah Scholl

15   The Origins of Kimbanguism: Charismatic Autonomy and Narrative Unity in the
      Congo Sources   340
      Silvia Cristofori

16   Liberal Theology and Its Aftermath   371
      Mark D. Chapman

17   The American Social Gospel: Christian Socialism, Neo-Abolitionism, and
      Ecumenism   390
      Gary Dorrien

18   The World Missionary Conference at Edinburgh in 1910, and the Role of the
      Protestant Missionary Movement   412
      Brian Stanley

19   The Historical Turn: World War I   430
      Frédéric Gugelot

PART 3
Beginnings: Movements Become a Movement

20   The Catholic Biblical Movement between Fear and Hope   453
        Mathijs Lamberigts

21   The Role of Liturgical Movements in Developing an Ecumenical Awareness in
        Catholicism and Orthodoxy   474
        Benedikt Kranemann and Adalberto Mainardi

22   The Second Liturgical Movement in the German Protestant Churches:
        The "Catholicization" of the Liturgy and the Development of the Ecumenical
        Process   501
        Martin Cyprian Lenz

23   The Role of the Peace Movements in the Ecumenical Encounter (1907–1919)   523
        Gerhard Besier

24   Latin American Rebound Effect: The Panama Congress on Christian Work   541
        Juan Sepúlveda

25   Unto the Churches of Christ Everywhere: The Ecumenical Patriarchate's 1920
        Encyclical   565
        Stylianos Tsompanidis

26   The Life and Work of Nathan Söderblom   585
        Dietz Lange

27   Charles Brent and the Faith and Order Project: From Its Origins to the Lausanne
        Conference of 1927   615
        Luca Ferracci

28   The Malines Conversations   640
        Bernard Barlow and Martin Browne

29   The Beginnings of Ecumenism in Germany: From the Hochkirche Movement
        to the Development of the Una Sancta Groups   659
        Paul Metzlaff

30   Dom Lambert Beauduin, Founder of the Monastery of Amay-Chevetogne:
        A Prelude to Ecumenism in the Catholic Church   679
        André Haquin

31   The Positioning of the Roman Catholic Church in the Interwar Period:
     The Encyclical *Mortalium Animos*   703
       Marie Levant

32   The International Missionary Council between 1910 and 1961   722
       Kenneth R. Ross

     Index of Names   745

Acronyms

ABCFM	American Board of Commissioners for Foreign Missions
ABFMS	American Baptist Foreign Mission Society
ABMU	American Baptist Missionary Union
ABS	American Bible Society
ACIP	Association du Consistoire israélite de Paris
ACK	Arbeitsgemeinschaft Christlicher Kirchen
ACS	Anglo-Continental Society
AEA	American Economic Association
AEF	American Expeditionary Forces
AFL	American Federation of Labor
AFSC	American Friends Service Committee
AHMS	American Home Missionary Society
AIMO	Affaires Indigenes et de la Main d'Œuvre
AME	African Methodist Episcopal
AMEZ	African Methodist Episcopal Zion Church
APUC	Association for the Promotion of the Unity of Christendom
ARCIC	Anglican-Roman Catholic International Commission
ASSU	American Sunday School Union
AUA	American Unitarian Association
AWSA	American Woman Suffrage Association
BAdW	Bayerische Akademie der Wissenschaften (Bavarian Academy of Sciences)
BFBS	British and Foreign Bible Society
BFSS	British and Foreign School Society
BMS	Baptist Missionary Society
BSVMU	British Student Volunteer Missionary Union
BWA	Baptist World Alliance
CAM	Central American Mission
CANF	Comité d'Alimentation du Nord de la France
CBL	Colloquium Biblicum Lovaniense
CCEQ	Catholic Conference for Ecumenical Questions
CCJ	Council of Christians and Jews (UK)
CCPFE	Comité Catholique de Propagande Française à l'Etranger
CCLA	Committee on Cooperation on Latin America
CCWLA	Congress on Christian Work in Latin America
CEO	Corps expeditionnaire d'Orient (Oriental Expeditionary Force)
CFC	Christian Frontier Council
CIMADE	Comité inter-mouvements auprès des évacués
CNEWA	Catholic Near East Welfare Association
CMA	Christian and Missionary Alliance
CMS	Church Missionary Society
CPL	Centre de Pastoral Liturgique (Paris)
CPU	Church Peace Union
CSU	Christian Social Union
CWBM	Christian Woman's Board of Missions
CWS	Church World Service
DEKA	Deutscher Evangelischer Kirchenausschuss (German Evangelical Church Committee)
DEMA	Deutscher Evangelischer Missions-Ausschuß (German Protestant Missions Committee)
DRAC	Ligue des Droits des Religieux Ancien Combattant
EA	Evangelical Alliance
EBAF	École biblique et archéologique française
ECA	Eastern Churches Association
ECM	Ecumenical Missionary Conference
EJCSK	Église de Jésus Christ sur la terre par le prophète Simon Kimbangu (Church of Jesus Christ on Earth through the Prophet Simon Kimbangu)
EPS	Ecumenical Press Service
ERE	Union nationale des Églises Réformées Évangeliques de France (National Union of Reformed Evangelical Churches of France)
ERF	Union nationale des Églises Réformées de France (National Union of Reformed Churches of France)
ESK	Evangelisch-Soziale Kongress (Evangelical Social Congress)

FCCC	Federal Council of Churches of Christ (in United States)	PCB	Pontificia Commissione Biblica (Pontifical Biblical Commission)
FES	Foreign Evangelical Society, New York	PIB	Pontificio Istituto Biblico (Pontifical Biblical Institute)
FMCNA	Foreign Missions Conference of North America	PIO	Pontificio Istituto Orientale (Pontifical Oriental Institute)
FNC	Fédération Nationale Catholique	RBMU	Regions Beyond Missionary Union
FPF	Fédération Protestante de France (Protestant Federation of France)	RFSP	Reverenda Fabrica Sancti Petri (Sacred Congregation for the Fabric of St. Peter's)
ICC	International Congregational Council	RSCM	Russian Student Christian Movement
ICCLA	International Committee on Christian Literature for Africa	RTS	Religious Tract Society
ICP	Institut catholique de Paris	SAMS	South American Missionary Society
IMC	International Missionary Council	SCM	Student Christian Movement (of Great Britain and Ireland)
IRC	International Red Cross		
IRO	International Refugee Organization	SEA	Schweizerische Evangelische Allianz (Swiss Evangelical Alliance)
ISCE	International Society of Christian Endeavour	SFS	Seamen's Friends Society
ISP	Institut supérieur de philosophie	SMF	Swedish Missionary Alliance (Svenska Missionsförbundet)
ITC	International Theological Commission		
IWW	Industrial Workers of the World	SNTS	Studiorum Novi Testamenti Societas
JDC	Joint Distribution Committee	SOTS	Society for Old Testament Study
JOC	Jeunesse ouvrière chrétienne	SPbDA	Sankt-Peterburgskaya Dukhovnaya Akademiya (Saint Petersburg Theological Academy)
KETI	Kongo Evangelical Training Institution		
LIM	Livingstone Inland Mission		
LMS	London Missionary Society	SPCK	Society for Promoting Christian Knowledge
LN	League of Nations		
LRCS	League of Red Cross Societies	SPG	Society for the Propagation of the Gospel in Foreign Parts
LSPCJ	London Society for Promoting Christianity amongst the Jews	SVM	Student Volunteer Movement for Foreign Missions
LWF	Lutheran World Federation		
MEC	Methodist Episcopal Church	SWV	Sint-Willibrordvereniging (Society of Saint Willibrord)
MEMB	Methodist Episcopal Missionary Board		
NAACP	National Association for the Advancement of Colored People	UMCA	Universities' Mission to Central Africa
		UN	United Nations
NBG	Nederlands Bijbelgenootschap (Dutch Bible Society)	UNRRA	United Nations Relief and Rehabilitation Administration
NCC	National Council of Churches	WA	World Alliance for Promoting International Friendship through the Churches
NCCJ	National Conference of Christians and Jews (US)		
NCWC	National Catholic Welfare Conference	WARC	World Alliance of Reformed Churches
NECC	Near East Council of Churches	WCC	World Council of Churches
NINS	National Institute for Newman Studies	WCCE	World Council of Christian Education
OMS	Orthodox Missionary Society, Moscow	WCCY	World Conference of Christian Youth
PBFM	Presbyterian Board of Foreign Mission	WCRC	World Communion of Reformed Churches

WILPF	Women's International League for Peace and Freedom	WSSA	World Sunday School Association
WJC	World Jewish Congress	YPSCE	Young People's Society of Christian Endeavor
WMC	World Missionary Conference	YMCA	Young Men's Christian Association
WSCF	World Student Christian Federation	YWCA	Young Women's Christian Association

Archives

AAA	Archiv des Auswärtigen Amtes, Berlin (Archives of the German Foreign Office)	ASV	Archivio Segreto Vaticano
AAC	Archives d'Amay-Chevetogne	BAB	Bundesarchiv Berlin
AAM	Archives de l'Archevêché de Malines	BIA	Borthwick Institute for Archives, University of York
AAR	Archives of the Archdiocese of Rheims	BL	British Library
AAV	Archivio Apostolico Vaticano	BSB	Bayerische Staatsbibliothek, Munich
ACDF	Archives of the Congregation for the Doctrine of the Faith	CUL	Cambridge University Library
		EAM	Erzbischöfliches Archiv München
ACO	Archives of the Congregation for the Oriental Churches	HAAP	Historical Archives of the Archdiocese of Paris (Archives historiques de l'archevêché de Paris)
ADPSJ	Archiv der Deutschen Provinz der Jesuiten, Munich		
AFSJ	Archives of the French Jesuits in Vanves	MLR	Missionary Research Library Collection
AMC	Archives du Mont-César, Leuven	NCL	New College Library, University of Edinburgh
AMT	Archives de l'Abbaye ss. jean et Scholastique de Maredet	NSS	Nathan Söderbloms samling
		PHL	Pusey House Library, Oxford
ASA	Archives de Sint-Andriesabdij, Saint-André, Loppem-Bruges	UTS	Union Theological Seminary, New York
		UUB	Uppsala universitetsbibliotek (Uppsala University Library)
ASFT	Acta Sacrae Facultatis Theologiae Lovaniensis		
		WCCA	WCC Library and Archives, Ecumenical Center, Geneva
ASRS	Archivio Storico della Sezione per i Rapporti con gli Stati della Segreteria di Stato	YDSL	Yale Divinity School Library

Journals, Lexicons, and Sources

Journals

AAS	Acta apostolicae sedis	CMRS	Cahiers du monde russe et soviétique
AEH	Anglican & Episcopal History	ColMechl	Collectanea mechliniensia
AELKZ	Allgemeine evangelisch-lutherische Kirchenzeitung	CQR	Church Quarterly Review
		CrSt	Cristianesimo nella storia
AER	The American Economic Review	CSS	Canadian-American Slavic Studies
AHC	Annuarium Historiae Conciliorum	CSSH	Comparative Studies in Society and History
AHR	The American Historical Review		
AHRF	Annales historiques de la Révolution française	DtPfrBl	Deutsches Pfarrerblatt
		EGO	Europäische Geschichte Online
AJT	The American Journal of Theology	EcRev	The Ecumenical Review
AKBMS	Archiv für Kirchengeschichte von Böhmen-Mähren-Schlesien	EHK	Eine heilige Kirche
		EIA	Ethics & International Affairs
ALH	American Literary History	EJST	European Journal of Social Theory
ALw	Archiv für Liturgiewissenschaft	ENDS	Endowment Studies
AR	Archiv für Religionswissenschaft	EtBalk	Études balkaniques
ArH	Archivium Hibernicum	ETL	Ephemerides Theologicae Lovanienses
ASSR	Archives de sciences sociales des religions [1973–2018] before Archives de Sociologie des Religions [1956–1972]	ETR	Études théologiques et religieuses
		EvTh	Evangelische Theologie
		ExpTim	The Expository Times
ASR	Annali di scienze religiose	FoiVie	Foi et vie
ASS	Acta sanctae sedis	FWWS	First World War Studies
AThR	Anglican Theological Review	FZPhTh	Freiburger Zeitschrift für Philosophie und Theologie
BL	Bibel und Liturgie		
BQ	Baptist Quarterly	GC	La gerarchia cattolica
BS	Balkan Studies	GG	Geschichte und Gesellschaft
BSHPF	Bulletin de la Société de l'Histoire du Protestantisme Français	GOTR	The Greek Orthodox Theological Review
Bull. Cl. lett. sci. morales polit. (Acad. r. Belg.)	Bulletin de la Classe des lettres et des sciences morales et politiques (Académie royale de Belgique)	Greg	Gregorianum
		HID	Heiliger Dienst
		HKi	Die Hochkirche
BWKG	Blätter für württembergische Kirchengeschichte	HR	History of Religions
		HTR	Harvard Theological Review
CBQ	Catholic Biblical Quarterly	IBMR	International Bulletin of Mission Research
CEJ	Christian Education Journal		
CEMOTI	Cahiers d'Études sur la Méditerranée Orientale et le monde Turco-Iranien	IKZ	Internationale kirchliche Zeitschrift
		Irén	Irénikon
CH	Church History	IRM	International Review of Mission
Chm	The Churchman	ITQ	Irish Theological Quarterly
CHR	The Catholic Historical Review	JAH	The Journal of American History
ChW	Die Christliche Welt	JCH	Journal of Contemporary History
CivCatt	La Civiltà Cattolica	JEastCS	The Journal of Eastern Christian Studies

JEH	The Journal of Ecclesiastical History	*QO*	Quaderni di O Odigos
JES	Journal of Ecumenical Studies	*RAR*	Revue Anglo-Romaine
JHMTH	Journal for the History of Modern Theology / Zeitschrift für Neuere Theologiegeschichte	*RB*	Revue biblique
		RdT	Rassegna di teologia
		RESEE	Revue des études sud-est européennes
JMGS	Journal of Modern Greek Studies	*RESlav*	Revue des études slaves
JRH	Journal of Religious History	*RevScRel*	Revue des sciences religieuses
JTS	The Journal of Theological Studies	*RHE*	Revue d'histoire ecclésiastique
JWCS	Journal of War and Culture Studies	*RHEF*	Revue d'histoire de l'Église de France
KD	Kerygma und Dogma	*RHPR*	Revue d'histoire et de philosophie religieuses
KiO	Kirche im Osten		
KZG	Kirchliche Zeitgeschichte / Contemporary Church History	*RSCI*	Rivista della Storia della Chiesa in Italia
LJ	Liturgisches Jahrbuch	*RSPT*	Revue des sciences philosophiques et théologiques
MEFRIM	Mélanges de l'École français de Rome – Italie et Méditerranée	*RSR*	Recherches de science religieuse
MIH	Modern Intellectual History	*RTL*	Revue théologique de Louvain
MR	Methodist Review	*RusR*	The Russian Review
MThZ	Münchener Theologische Zeitschrift	*SCH*	Studies in Church History
N&N	Nations and Nationalism	*SEER*	Slavonic & East European Review
NBf	New Blackfriars	*ST*	Studia theologica
NRT	Nouvelle revue théologique	*StSp*	Studies in Spirituality
NSJ	Newman Studies Journal	*StZ*	Stimmen der Zeit
NTT JTSR	NTT Journal for Theology and the Study of Religion	*SVTQ*	St Vladimir's Theological Quarterly
		ThLZ	Theologische Literaturzeitung
NYRB	The New York Review of Books	*ThQ*	Theologische Quartalschrift
OCP	Orientalia Christiana Periodica	*TS*	Theological Studies
OiC	One in Christ	*USCH*	U.S. Catholic Historian
OM	Oriente Moderno	*Vestnik RSChD*	Vestnik Russkogo Studenchenskogo Khristianskogo Dvizheniya
ÖR	Ökumenische Rundschau		
OrChrAn	Orientalia Christiana Analecta	*WoHR*	Women's History Review
OS	Ostkirchliche Studien	*WPKG*	Wissenschaft und Praxis in Kirche und Gesellschaft
POC	Proche-Orient chrétien		
PTR	Princeton Theological Review	*ZfB*	Zeitschrift für Balkanologie
QFIAB	Quellen und Forschungen aus italienischen Archiven und Bibliotheken	*ZKG*	Zeitschrift für Kirchengeschichte
		ZRGG	Zeitschrift für Religions- und Geistesgeschichte
QL	Questions Liturgiques / Studies in Liturgy	*ZThK*	Zeitschrift für Theologie und Kirche

Lexicons and Sources

BBKL	Biographisch-Bibliographisches Kirchenlexikon, ed. F.W. Bautz, Hamm 1,1975ff.	*BNB*	Biographie nationale de Belgique, Brussels, 1,1866–44,1986.

Catholicisme	*Catholicisme: Hier Aujourd'hui Demain*, ed. G. Jacquemet, Paris, Letouzey et Ané, 1,1948–15,1998–2000.	*EnchBib*	*Enchiridion biblicum: Documenta ecclesiastica sacram scripturam spectantia*, Rome, 1927.
CC SL	*Corpus Christianorum: Series latina*, Turnhout, Brepols, 1,1954ff.	*ERE*	*Encyclopedia of Religion and Ethics*, ed. J. Hastings, Edinburgh, T&T Clark, 1,1908–13,1926; reprint, 7 vols., 1951.
CHC	*The Cambridge History of Christianity*, Cambridge, Cambridge University Press, 1,2005–9,2009.	*Fliche-Martin*	*Histoire de l'Église depuis les origines jusqu'à nos jours*, ed. A. Fliche & V. Martin, Paris, Bloud et Gay, 1,1946–21,1952.
COGD	*Corpus Christianorum Conciliorum Oecumenicorum Generaliumque Decreta*, ed. A. Melloni & G. Alberigo, 5 vols., Turnhout, Brepols, 2006–.	*GKH*	*Geschiedenis van de Kerk in tien delen*, ed. L.J. Rogier, R. Aubert, M.D. Knowles, Hilversum, Paul Brand, 1964.
DaS	*Divino afflante Spiritu*	*HC*	*Histoire du Christianisme des origines à nos jours*, ed. J.-M. Mayeur, Paris, Desclée, 1,1990–14,2000.
DBI	*Dizionario Biografico degli Italiani*, Rome, Treccani, 1,1960ff.		
DDC	*Dictionnaire de droit canonique*, dir. R. Naz, Paris, Letouzey et Ané, 1,1924–7,1965.	*HCF*	*Histoire du catholicisme en France*, ed. Latreille & others, Paris, Spes, 1,1957–3,1962.
DEM	*Dictionary of the Ecumenical Movement*, ed. N. Lossky & others, Geneva, WCC Publications, 1991; ²2002.	*HistCh*	*History of the Church*, ed. H. Jedin, London, Burns & Oates.
		HistDog	*Histoire des dogmes*, dir. B. Sesboué, Paris, Desclée, 1,1994–4,1996.
DHGE	*Dictionnaire d'histoire et de géographie ecclésiastique*, dir. A. Baudrillart, Paris, Letouzey et Ané, 1,1912ff.	*Hist. eccl.*	*Historia ecclesiastica*, Eusebius of Caesarea [ET: Paul L. Maier, ed., *Eusebius: The Church History; A New Translation with Commentary*, Grand Rapids MI, Kregel, 1999.]
DSAM	*Dictionnaire de spiritualité ascétique et mistique, doctrine et histoire*, ed. M. Viller, Paris, Beauchesne, 1,1937ff.		
DThC	*Dictionnaire de théologie catholique*, ed. A. Vacant & others, Paris, Letouzey et Ané, 1,1903–15,1950; tables générales, ed. B. Loth & A. Michel, 3 vols., 1951–1972.	*HKG*	*Handbuch der Kirchengeschichte*, ed. H. Jedin, Freiburg i.Br. etc., Herder, 1,1962–7,1979; supplement 1970.
		HThK Vat.II	*Herders Theologischer Kommentar zum Zweiten Vatikanischen Konzil*, ed. B.J. Hilberath & P. Hünermann, 5 vols., Freiburg i.Br, Herder.
EDCE	*Encyclopedic Dictionary of the Christian East*, ed. E.G. Farrugia, Rome, PIO, ²2015.		
EGO	*Europäische Geschichte Online*, ed. Institut für Europäische Geschichte, Mainz.	*LThK*	*Lexikon für Theologie und Kirche*, ed. M. Buchberger & others, Freiburg i.Br., Herder, 1,1930–10,1938.
		MD	*Mediator Dei*
EKL	*Evangelisches Kirchenlexikon*, ed. E. Fahlbusch & others, Göttingen, Vandenhoeck & Ruprecht, ³1,1986ff.	*NBN*	*Nouvelle Biographie Nationale*, Brussels, 1,1988ff.

NCE	*New Catholic Encyclopedia*, ed. W.J. McDonald & others, Washington DC, CUA Press, 1–15,1967; supplement 16,1974–17,1979; [2]2002.	RGG	*Die Religion in Geschichte und Gegenwart*, ed. K. Galling & others, Tübingen, Mohr Siebeck, [3]1,1957–6,1962; index vol. 1965
NDB	*Neue deutsche Biographie*, Berlin, 1,1953ff.	SgV	Sammlung Gemeinverständlicher Vorträge und Schriften aus dem Gebiet der Theologie und
OCE	*Old Catholic Encyclopedia*, ed. C.G. Herbermann & others, New York NY, Robert Appleton Company, 1,1907–16,1914	SM	Religionsgeschichte *Sacramentum mundi: Theologisches Lexikon für die Praxis*, ed. K. Rahner & others, Freiburg i.Br. etc., Herder, 1,1967–4,1969
OHA	*The Oxford History of Anglicanism*, 5 vols., Oxford, Oxford University Press, 2017	Storia teol.	*Storia della teologia*, Piemme, Casale Monferrato, 1,1993–4,2001
PD	*Providentissimus Deus*	Tracts	*Tracts for the Times*, ed. J.H.
Pdg	*Pascendi dominici gregis*		Newman & others, London,
PG	*Patrologiae Cursus Completus: Series Graeca*, ed. J.-P. Migne, Paris, Imprimerie Catholique, [1]1,1856–81,1861; [2]1,1857–166,1866	TRE	J.G.F & J. Rivington, 1840 *Theologische Realenzyklopädie*, ed. G. Krause, G. Müller & H. Balz, Berlin, De Gruyter, 1,1976–36,2004.
PL	*Patrologiae cursus completus: Series Latina*, ed. J.-P. Migne, Paris, 1st series 1,1844–73,1849; 2nd series 74,1849–217,1855	WA	*D. Martin Luthers Werke: Kritische Gesamtausgabe* (*Weimarer Ausgabe*), Weimar, 1,1883ff.

Notes on Contributors

Paul Avis, *University of Exeter*
Bernard Barlow, *University of St. Andrews*
Gerhard Besier, *TU Dresden*
Franz Xaver Bischof, *University of Munich*
Martin Browne, *Glenstal Abbey*
Mark D. Chapman, *University of Oxford*
Silvia Cristofori, *Link Campus University of Rome*
Gary Dorrien, *Columbia University*
Michel Fédou, *Centre Sèvres – Paris*
Luca Ferracci, *FSCIRE Bologna*
Étienne Fouilloux, *Université Lumière Lyon II*
Martin Friedrich, *Elstal Theological University*
Fréderic Gugelot, *University of Reims Champagne-Ardenne*
André Haquin, *Université catholique de Louvain*
Benedikt Kranemann, *University of Erfurt*
Mathijs Lamberigts, *KU Leuven*
Dietz Lange, *University of Göttingen*
Martin Cyprian Lenz, *University of Bonn*
Marie Levant, *Gerda Henkel Stiftung of Germany*
Adalberto Mainardi, *Monastery of Bose*
Vasilios N. Makrides, *University of Erfurt*
Sandra Mazzolini, *Pontifical Urbanian University, Rome*
Alberto Melloni, *FSCIRE Bologna*
Paul Metzlaff, *University of Erfurt*
Arie L. Molendijk, *University of Groningen*
Peter Nockles, *The University of Manchester*
Laura Pettinaroli, *Institut Catholique de Paris*
Jeremy Pilch, *St Mary's University*
Kenneth R. Ross, *The University of Edinburgh*
Sarah Scholl, *University of Geneva*
Juan Sepúlveda, *University of Santiago, Chile*
Brian Stanley, *The University of Edinburgh*
Stylianos Tsompanidis, *Aristotle University of Thessaloniki*
John Zizioulas, *Academy of Athens*

Premises for a History of the Desire for Christian Unity

Alberto Melloni

1   Foreword

The experience of Christianity does not and *cannot* claim to be immune to history. It cannot because it has inherited from Israel the principle of the narratability of its past (what the biblical Greek calls λόγος),[1] and that instance of the intelligibility of its unfolding in time has even entered the New Testament canon (Luke's διήγησις).[2] It cannot do so moreover because, in the encounter with the cultures of the peoples in which the claim for the universality of the gospel of Jesus and the gospel about Jesus was honed, that link between the Christian life and the construction of traditions has become reality in an ever-varying and equally intrinsic manner.

What we have always called Christianity since the gospel of Jesus until today, is in its factual dimension an intrinsically plural, transcultural, and rationally comprehensible event (*res gestae*), another present-time to be entrusted to others,[3] not because an academic discipline (*historia rerum gestarum*) has constituted it as the object of its investigation, but rather thanks to a dynamism of its own, because it is what places in history a gaze like that of Klee's angel: "Where we see a series of events, he sees a single catastrophe" from

which emanates the expectation "to reunite the shattered."[4]

This is such that at every stage – even in its current situation as a salaried university discipline within the liberal-bourgeois *paideia* of the West – history reveals itself to be an instrument to which Christian experience reacts as if the discipline, which has an entirely modern critical physiognomy, could recognize it *per quandam connaturalitatem*.[5] This is seen in the fact that, throughout its entire tradition, the history of Christianity has elaborated epistemological paradigms that have changed in the course of time,[6] becoming an apologetics of

---

1   For this aspect, I refer readers to Giuseppe Ruggieri, *Della fede: La certezza, il dubbio, la lotta*, Rome, Carocci, [2]2015.

2   See David P. Moessner, "The Lukan Prologues in the Light of Ancient Narrative Hermeneutics: Παρηκολουθηκότι and the Credentials of the Author," in: Joseph Verheyden, ed., *The Unity of Luke-Acts*, Leuven, Leuven University Press, 1999, 399–418.

3   On this problem, see François Dosse, *Michel De Certeau: Le marcheur blessé*, Paris, La Découverte, 2007, 262–277; on the question of alterity in history posed by Certeau, see his *La Fable mystique: XVIème–XVIIème siècle*, 2 vols., Paris, Gallimard, 1987–2013.

4   See Walter Benjamin, *On the Concept of History*, in: Howard Eiland & Michael W. Jennings, eds., *Walter Benjamin: Selected Writings*, vol. 4, *1938–1940*, Cambridge MA, Harvard University Press, 2006, 389–400.

5   I do not use here the Thomist category (*Summa Theologiae* I, q. 1, a. 6, ad 3; *Summa Theologiae* II–II, q. 45, a. 2, c; *In de divinis nominibus*, c. II, lect. IV, nn. 191–192, from the corpusthomisticum.org editions) to say that on the part of history there may be a "non-ratiocinative cognitive judgment that determines the goodness of a concrete object by virtue of the convergence of the apprehension of the object and of the appetitive inclination directed toward it" (according to the proposal in Marco D'Avenia, *La conoscenza per connaturalità in S. Tommaso d'Aquino*, Bologna, Edizioni Studio Domenicano, 1992, 177) but to indicate the opposite process. On Maritain's contribution, see Pierre-Antoine Belley, *Connaître par le cœur: La connaissance par connaturalité dans les œuvres de Jacques Maritain*, Paris, Tequi, 2006.

6   See Hans-Werner Goetz, *Geschichtsschreibung und Geschichtsbewußtsein im hohen Mittelalter*, Berlin, Akademie Verlag, 1999, and Jean-Philippe Genet, ed., *L'historiographie médiévale en Europe: Actes du colloque organisé par la Fondation Européenne de la Science au Centre de Recherches Historiques et Juridiques de l'Université Paris I du 29 mars au 1er avril 1989*, Paris, Éditions du CNRS, 1991.

Christian power,[7] a controversial *argumentum*,[8] or part of the *loci communes*,[9] or of erudition.[10] Yet, after the secularization of theodicy became grafted onto historical-critical knowledge,[11] Christianity itself has discovered in history a way of being understood and of understanding itself as a non-theological object. This has triggered hostile reactions to, aroused diffidence towards, and suggested domestication of, trust in a relationship that has in any case been so fertile that today no one, not even the most bigoted integralist, can do without it entirely.[12]

The relationship has been a fertile one because history unmasks the providentialist shortcuts that exempt themselves from the hard work of understanding objects and causes, appealing to a "sense" that resembles a pietist amulet rather than Christian faith. History reveals the symmetrical phobias of those who think that belonging to a faith, and even more, to the Christian faith, constitutes an impediment to a fully "secularized" history,[13] requiring an ideological auto-da-fé as a prerequisite for methodological rigor, which is incompatible with a scholarly approach.[14] History produces an understanding that claims to attain a certain degree of truth,[15] able to be built upon or judged by that "more than" of a knowledge and of an awareness of things that has no other effect than to entrust such knowledge (like any other knowledge) to responsibility. With that "more than," lost hopes, retrograde mechanisms, reformative potentialities, even nostalgia, which only become a critical asset if soundly identified, are made to resurface; and only if they are sound can they be essential to the gospel's journey through time,[16] that is, to the way in which the subject receiving the gospel has historically surrendered to every possible interpretation (theological, sociological, philosophical, etc.).[17]

Every experience that aspires to be Christian, therefore, "exposes" itself to being known in space

---

7   See Claudia Rapp, "Imperial Ideology in the Making: Eusebius of Caesarea on Constantine as 'Bishop,'" *JTS* 49, 1988, 685–695; and Manlio Simonetti, "L'esegesi di Eusebio e la figura di Costantino," in: Alberto Melloni & others, eds., *Costantino I: Enciclopedia costantiniana sulla figura e l'immagine dell'imperatore del cosiddetto Editto di Milano (313–2013)*, vol. 2, Rome, Treccani, 2013, 129–134.

8   See Franco Motta, *Bellarmino: Una teologia politica della Controriforma*, Brescia, Morcelliana, 2005.

9   See John R. Schneider, *Philip Melanchthon's Rhetorical Construal of Biblical Authority: Oratio Sacra*, Lewiston NY, Edwin Mellen Press, 1990, 233–235.

10   It is still seminal the essay by Eric Cochrane, "Muratori: The Vocation of a Historian," *CHR* 51/2, 1965, 153–172, as well as the more recent studies mentioned in Antonello Mattone, "Il modello muratoriano e la storiografia sardo-piemontese del Settecento," *Rivista storica italiana* 12/1, 2009, 67–120.

11   See the principal contributions of Odo Marquard, *Abschied vom Prinzipiellen: Philosophische Studien*, Stuttgart, Reclam, 1981, and Alberto Melloni & Odo Marquard, *La storia che giudica, la storia che assolve*, Bari, Laterza, 2008.

12   See Reinhart Koselleck, *Vergangene Zukunft: Zur Semantik geschichtlicher Zeiten*, Frankfurt a.M., Suhrkamp, 1979; ET: *Futures Past: On the Semantics of Historical Time*, trans. Keith Tribe, New York NY, Columbia University Press, 2005.

13   Geoffrey R. Elton, *Return to Essentials: Some Reflections on the Present State of Historical Study*, Cambridge, Cambridge University Press, 1991, already saw the mere belonging to a faith, even worse if it were a true adherence, as a danger. He confuses the survey of a formula with an approach: Daniele Menozzi, "La secolarizzazione della storia della chiesa: Giuseppe Alberigo da una proposta al ripensamento," *Rivista di storia del cristianesimo* 12/1, 2015, 165–183.

14   The analogy of the nonexistence of two mathematics (a Catholic and a non-Catholic one) remains illuminating. Roger Aubert, "Les nouvelles frontières de l'historiographie ecclésiastique," *RHE* 95/3, 2000, 757–781.

15   This is the main point of the classic by Henri-Irénée Marrou, *De la connaissance historique*, Paris, Éditions du Seuil, 1954; ET: *The Meaning of History*, trans. Robert J. Olsen, Baltimore MD, Helicon, 1966; on him, see Pierre Riché, *Henri Irénée Marrou historien engagé: Préface par R. Rémond*, Paris, Cerf, 2003.

16   Marie-Dominique Chenu, *Une école de théologie: le Saulchoir: Avec les études de with essays by Giuseppe Alberigo, Étienne Fouilloux, Jean Ladrière et Jean-Pierre Jossua*, Paris, Cerf, 1985, (first edition: 1937, Kain-Lez-Tournai, Le Saulchoir).

17   See Christoph Theobald, *La révélation*, Paris, Les Éditions de l'Atelier, 2006, 214–224.

and time, by analytically examined roots and developments, by rigorously dated regresses and progresses, through the history of texts and figures, cults and doctrines, and institutions and conceptions understood by adhering to the sources. In short, this experience must be able to be known historically "in the calm telling of a tale, in the resurgence and denial of the origin, the unfolding of a dead past and result of a present practice."[18]

The Christian desire for unity that is the object of this historical oeuvre belongs to the same order of problems. It is *not* the history of ecumenism, *not* another history of ecumenism, nor the history of another ecumenism,[19] *not* the history of a splinter of historicizable ecumenism, distinguished by an adjective, *not* the history of a phenomenon that can be postulated as historicizable only because it is glorified by its triumphs or imprisoned by its aporias.[20]

2 On the History of Ecumenism

This work, however, intends to be a work of history. It therefore searches in history and in its sources its proper object, taking into account the seasons, the narratives, and the articulations that have constructed a vast historiography of the movements, figures, doctrines, experiences, institutions, and processes for which the adjective "ecumenical"

can be legitimately used according to its common meaning.[21]

2.1 Seasons of Ecumenical Historiography

In this historiography, belonging to the 20th century by production or culture, we can distinguish infinite variations and an irreducible variety of epistemological approaches.[22] This is a vast

---

18 Michel de Certeau, *The Writing of History*, trans. Tom Conley, New York NY, Columbia University Press, 1988, 47. On de Certau, other than the already cited Dosse, *Michel De Certeau*, see also Hervé Martin, "À propos de 'L'opération historiographique,'" in: Christian Delacroix & others, eds., *Michel de Certeau: Les chemins d'histoire*, Paris, Éditions Complexe/IHTP-CNRS, 2002, 107–124, and Pierre-Antione Fabre, "Postérités mystiques de Michel de Certeau," in: Philippe Artières, ed., *Après Certeau: Histoire, archives et psychanalyse, Sociétés et représentations* 43, 2017, 17–27.

19 For example, Peter Neuner, *Théologie œcuménique: La quête de l'unité des Églises chrétiennes*, Paris, Cerf, 2005.

20 Giuseppe Ruggieri, "Il vicolo cieco dell'ecumenismo," *CrSt* 7/3, 1988, 563–615.

21 The history of the adjective "ecumenical" can be gleaned, e.g., through encyclopedias. After the 1920s, every great work of this kind includes an entry on "ecumenism," even if the content and object has changed over time, up to the definition given by *Encyclopedia Britannica* online in the 21st century, which reads: "Movement or tendency toward worldwide Christian unity or cooperation," with a rather eloquent option ("or"!). There have been those who recognized the crisis stemming from the unattainability of the goal of unity, such as Thomas Torrance in Appendix IV of the *Enciclopedia Italiana* (1978). At the end of the 20th century, Günther Gassmann, a leading ecumenical figure, recalled, in his contribution to that work, the universalistic connotation of the word and its cognates. The term "oecumene" (which appears for the first time in Herodotus in the 5th century BC) was adopted by Christian authors to denote the supralocal character as well as the universal validity and authority of the decisions expressed in the "ecumenical" councils, or to designate the three main creeds (Apostles, Nicaean, and Athanasian) called "ecumenical symbols." Gassman continues: "The terms 'oecumene' and 'ecumenical' were taken up again in the 19th century with a new and wider meaning. In Christian associations such as the Evangelical Alliance (1846) and the Federation of Christian Youth Associations (1855) – which can be considered precursors of the ecumenical movement – an awareness developed that all Christians and all churches were part of the same household. In this context, the term 'ecumenical' was used to denote an attitude, a communion, and a cooperation capable of overcoming political and confessional divisions. The idea of an ecumenical spirit, conscience, and will, therefore, was added to the geopolitical meaning and the idea of universal validity and, with that, the foundations were laid for the current use of the concepts of 'oecumene' and 'ecumenical' in this century's 'ecumenical movement.'" This entry first appeared in Italian in *Enciclopedia del Novecento*, vol. 2, *Supplemento*, Rome, Treccani, 1998.

22 Étienne Fouilloux, "Ecumenismo," in Alberto Melloni, ed., *Dizionario del sapere storico-religioso del Novecento*, vol. 1, Bologna, Il Mulino, 2019, 842–851.

bibliographic ocean where many seasons can be identified. I shall mention only three, ignoring many nuances, because they are useful in order to reveal some tendencies to which the path we would like to undertake is much indebted.

2.1.1 The Victorious Historiography of the Prophets

In the 20th century, in point of fact, there was a militant season of historiography, written by figures who were prophets – or almost like prophets – of church unity. The season of 1954 was personified by Ruth C. Rouse and Stephen C. Neill, the editors of *A History of the Ecumenical Movement*.[23] It was a generation of people convinced – and rightly so – of living at a time when the overwhelming four decades that separated the Edinburgh Missionary Conference from the first assembly of the WCC in Amsterdam in 1948 had shone a light on an effort of which, among other things, they had been the blessed protagonists, hence capable of bringing into focus – in an effort that was neither overly nor solely historiographical – the framework of the historical problem that saw harbingers, impulses, moments of discontent, and, in the end, a dawn. They were figures with an ecumenical life beyond their function as historians of ecumenism.

The first female student admitted to Girton College, Cambridge, Ruth Rouse (1872–1954) was a proponent of the women's student movement and its leading figure in a vibrant season of *evangelical* Anglicanism.[24] In 1899, she went as a missionary to India and returned, in ill health, to England two years later: she became secretary of the WSCF[25] from 1905 to 1924 at the insistence of John R. Mott,[26] and was one of the female protagonists[27] who would continue to exert an influence by establishing the European Student Relief in 1920 in a postwar utopia of reconciliation.[28] Rouse remained the educational secretary of the missionary body of the National Assembly of the Church of England until 1939. A member of the executive committee of the YWCA from 1908 – that is, during the time of the greatest fervor of interdenominationalism – she was its president from 1938 to 1946 and, after her retirement, earned recognition not only for her works in the missionary apostolate[29] but also for editing that *History of the Ecumenical Movement* which, beyond the historical-critical relevance of each single section, was to establish a way of conceiving as a unified "movement" a process that, at that moment in time, was an infra-Protestant fact to which Orthodoxy was extraneous and Roman Catholicism hostile.[30]

Its coeditor was a generation younger. Bishop Stephen C. Neill (1900–1984)[31] was born into a family of Anglican missionaries in India. He was a student of Trinity College, Cambridge, and arrived

---

26   This is recounted in Ruth C. Rouse, *The World's Student Christian Federation: A History of the First Thirty Years*, London, SCM Press, 1948, with a preface by John Mott.

27   See Jenny Daggers, "The Victorian Female Civilising Mission and Women's Aspirations Towards Priesthood in the Church of England," *WoHR* 10/4, 2001, 651–670.

28   Ruth C. Rouse, *Rebuilding Europe: The Student Chapter in Post-War Reconstruction*, London, SCM, 1925.

29   Ruth Franzén, *Ruth Rouse Among Students: Global, Missiological, and Ecumenical Perspectives*, Uppsala, Uppsala University, 2008.

30   Ruth Franzén also wrote the entry on Rouse in: Anderson, ed., *Biographical Dictionary*, 580–581, as well as the essay "The Legacy of Ruth Rouse," *IBMR* 17/10, 1993, 154–156.

31   See Dyron B. Daughrity, *Bishop Stephen Neill: From Edinburgh to South India*, New York NY, Peter Lang, 2008; concise treatments can be found in Eleanor M. Jackson, "The Continuing Legacy of Stephen Neill," *IBMR* 19/2, 1995, 77–80; Charles Lamb, "Stephen Neill," in: Gerald H. Anderson & others, eds., *Mission Legacies: Biographical Studies of Leaders of the Modern Missionary Movement*, Maryknoll NY, Orbis Books, 1994, 445–451.

---

23   Ruth Rouse & Stephen C. Neill, eds., *A History of the Ecumenical Movement (1517–1948)*, London, SPCK, ¹1954.

24   Eleanor M. Jackson, "Neill, Stephen Charles," in: Gerald H. Anderson, ed., *Biographical Dictionary of Christian Missions*, New York NY, Macmillan Reference USA, 1998, 488.

25   Rouse wrote *John R. Mott: An Appreciation*, Geneva, WSCF, 1929, on the American Methodist and future Nobel Prize winner.

in India in 1924 with his parents, coming into conflict with the legendary *Amma* (mother) Amy Carmichael[32] who ran a large refuge for children who had been orphaned or entrusted to the temples in Dohnavur. After joining the CMS, Neill became a professor of Tamil in Palayankottai, in southern Tamil Nadu, and was elected bishop of Tinnevelly in 1939. He was forced to resign in 1944, accused of having beaten an Indian leader.[33] From 1947 to 1954, Neill worked at the WCC where he edited the first volume of the history of the ecumenical movement with Rouse. His academic career continued, however, first in Hamburg, as a professor of missiology (1962–1967) and then in Nairobi (1969–1973), before he retired to Oxford. He was thus able to add to his bibliography[34] an updated edition of the history of the ecumenical movement in 1967 and the editorship of its continuation, together with Harold E. Fey, from 1948 to 1968.[35] Published under the patronage of the Committee on Ecumenical History in Geneva, that volume was joined by a further continuation edited by John Briggs, Mercy Amba Oduyoye, and Georges Tsetsis for the years up to 2000.[36] From

Ruth Rouse onward, the work maintained its unity because, volume after volume, one expiry date after another, it reposed the same working hypothesis: the existence of *one* powerful, historical, and spiritual impetus driving towards unity, the protagonist of which was an active and multifaceted movement, inflamed by a "consecrated" ardor, in which will, dedication, and ability produced results. Both internally and externally, it was a culture unlike that of research, which, while placing its sterile scalpel on those facts and processes, could not fail to recognize in that living historiography, pulsing with Christian passion, the clues and insights which question the provincialism of this age that believes it has become globalized.

32   Her best biography, which however omits the conflict with Neill, is still that of Elisabeth Elliot, *Amy Carmichael: A Chance to Die*, Old Tappan NJ, Revell, 1987.

33   Eleanor M. Jackson, ed., *God's Apprentice: The Autobiography of Stephen Neill*, London, Hodder & Stoughton, 1991; see also Lamb, "Stephen Neill."

34   Neill wrote *A History of Christian Missions*, Harmondsworth, Penguin Books, 1964; *History of Christianity in India (1707–1858)*, Cambridge, Cambridge University Press, 1985; and many scholarly articles.

35   *A History of the Ecumenical Movement*, vol. 1, Ruth Rouse & Stephen C. Neill, eds., *1517–1948*, London, SPCK, ²1967; *A History of the Ecumenical Movement*, vol. 2, Harold E. Fey, ed., *The Ecumenical Advance (1948–1968)*, London, SPCK, 1970, and as displayed in the frontispiece "published on behalf of the Committee on Ecumenical History". Fey was a minister of the Disciples of Christ from 1937 and editor of *Christian Century* from 1956 to 1964. On him, see his own work, Harold E. Fey, "Seventy Years of the Century," *The Christian Century*, Oct 11, 1978, 950–954.

36   Its third volume, *1968–2000*, edited by John H.Y. Briggs, Mercy A. Oduyoye, and Georges Tsetsis, was published

in 2004 by the WCC. On John Briggs, scholar and practicing Baptist, first Convenor of the Free Churches Group of Churches Together in England from 2001 to 2009, see Anthony R. Cross, ed., *Ecumenism and History: Studies in Honour of John H.Y. Briggs*, Milton Keynes, Paternoster Press, 2003. Briggs worked on important studies such as *The English Baptists of the Nineteenth Century*, Didcot, Baptist Historical Society, 1994, he is the editor of the entry on the World Baptist Alliance for the forthcoming COGD 7, and wrote on "Baptists and Ecumenical Engagement," *Baptistic Theologies* 5/1, 2013, 84–102. Mercy Amba Oduyoye, a Ghanaian Methodist theologian, directs the Institute of African Women in Religion and Culture at Trinity Theological Seminary in Accra, Ghana, after having taught at Harvard University; she was deputy secretary general of the WCC from 1987 to 1994. She is the author of important contributions, including *Introducing African Women's Theology*, Cleveland OH, The Pilgrim Press, 2001. On her, see Pui-lan Kwok, "Mercy Amba Oduyoye and African Women's Theology," *Journal of Feminist Studies in Religion* 20/1, 2004, 7–22. Georges Tsetsis, has been active in the WCC since 1965 and, from 1984 to 1999, was the representative of the Ecumenical Patriarchate. He has written "What is the World Council's Oikoumene?," *EcRev* 43/1, 1991, 86–96. A small example of his political role is given in Tobias Rupprecht, "Orthodox Internationalism: State and Church in Modern Russia and Ethiopia," *CSSH* 60, 2018, 212–223.

2.1.2   The Historiography of the Professional
          Historians

A new, but shorter and more sparsely populated,
season in ecumenical historiography was one in
which the protagonists were historians *tout court*.
They studied the path of Christian unity when
the hope of a possible ecumenical surprise was
still felt and some of the great figures of Christian
unity were still on the scene, although disappoint-
ments had marred the surface of the utopia; it was
a period, therefore, when a historical maturity
demanded a place for itself.

It was a season exemplified by Étienne
Fouilloux's monumental work in 1982 on *Les
catholiques et l'unité chrétienne du XIXème au XXème
siècle*, which was published only in French.[37] It did
not take into consideration the ecumenical movement as such. The Genevan experience was not
its institutional or emotional epicenter, nor did it
aim to look at the entirety of Catholicism following the path that had led the Church of Rome from
antagonist to protagonist in the development of
ecumenism. Nevertheless, it constituted a historiographical landmark that, in some ways, remains
unsurpassed.[38]

This is because, first of all, Fouilloux practiced
a methodological distancing from the world of
active ecumenism and from the "concrete objective" that Jedin made famous. With regard to that
world, however, he knew how to objectify its tensions as well as how *to comprehend*[39] its deepest
motivations, using the tools of historical research.
His was the certainty of a scholar hailing from the
school of René Rémond[40] that transformed such

a mega-thesis into an unprecedented contribution
to the historicization of ecumenism. To Fouilloux
we owe the acquisition of the hiatus that separated unionism from ecumenism, the knowledge
of the channels through which the unionist erudition of the Leonine age had paved the way to
surpassing an ideology of return, and the role of
the French *nouvelle théologie*, so despised in Rome,
in the construction of a turning point that would
require Vatican II in order to be imposed.[41]

Secondly, Fouilloux's work became a touchstone because, thanks to his intellectual sensitivity,
he was able to historicize the intentions of peoples, communities, and circles that constitute a
challenge for historians: in order to understand
rigorously lives burning with the desire for unity,
willing to accept marginalization or persecution
within their own denominational context, mere
dexterity in using the historian's toolbox to catalogue ideas in competition with other ideas,
to apply categories manneristically, or to allude to
long time spans constituted by thoughts, words,
deeds, and omissions is not enough. Neither is it
enough to reject clerical simplification in facing
the strangleholds of history with the absolvitory
suffering that witnesses the institution doing
what it cannot but do. Understanding the lives
seduced (פתה, Jer 20:7) by the passion for unity
requires descending into intentionality and gratu-
ity, self-justifications and mandates, foretastes and
conflicts that constitute the legacy (or Michel de
Certeau's "absence," perhaps) that every generation

37   Étienne Fouilloux, *Les catholiques et l'unité chrétienne
     du XIXème au XXème siècle*, Paris, Le Centurion, 1982.

38   One exception may be Silvia Scatena, *Taizé, una
     parabola di unità: Storia della comunità dalle origini al
     concilio dei giovani*, Bologna, Il Mulino, 2018.

39   To cite the aphorism of Marc Bloch in *Apologie pour
     l'histoire* "un mot, pour tout dire, domine et illu-
     mine nos études: comprendre"; ET: *The Historian's
     Craft*, trans. Peter Putnam, Manchester, Manchester
     University Press, 1992, 118.

40   For the autobiography of Fouilloux, a student of René
     Rémond, and his conversion to Catholicism with Fr.

Congar, see "Un historien et la foi," *Annali di storia
dell'educazione e delle istituzioni scolastiche* 20, 2013,
265–326.

41   See Jean-Dominique Durand, "La 'Furia francese' vue de
     Rome: Peurs, suspicions et rejets des années 1950," in:
     Michel Lagrée & Nadine-Josette Chaline, eds., *Religions
     par-delà les frontières*, Paris, Beauchesne, 1997, 15–35.
     For the connection with the world of worker priests
     and the Lyon cenacle, see François Leprieur, *Quand
     Rome condamne: Dominicains et prêtres-ouvriers*, Paris,
     Cerf, 1989; Étienne Fouilloux, *La collection «Sources
     chrétiennes»: Éditer les Pères de l'Église au XXe siècle*,
     Paris, Cerf, 1995.

that has experienced that call passes down to another time and another generation.

2.1.3   The Historiography of the Negotiators
The historiography of ecumenism also saw a third season, in which the central figures were not the heroes of the 20th century epic and its institutionalization in Geneva, nor were they historians *tout court*, but scholars who lived a different ecumenical professionalism, one shaped by the time of dialogues – a summit as well as an abyss in the passion for unity. Professionals of a negotiatory ecumenism, its authors proposed a global vision of the problems by using a metre that reassessed individual and collective specificities.

The *Personenlexikon Ökumene*, published in 2010 by the Johann-Adam-Möhler-Institut für Ökumenik in Paderborn and edited by Wolfgang Thönissen and Jörg Ernesti,[42] can be considered a significant product of this season.

Its meaning can be understood comparing it to the even more restricted *Dictionary of the Ecumenical Movement* on which the leading figures of the season of dialogues had worked. The dictionary's editors were Nicolas Lossky, José Miguez Bonino, John Pobee, Thomas F. Stransky, and Geoffrey Wainwright. It was first published in 1991, it was then revised in 2002 and produced by the WCC. The dictionary offered thematic entries (such as that on "Authority" by Bernard Sesboüé) as well as entries on the interreligious dialogue by Seevaratham Wesley Ariarajah, biographical entries such as that on Pierre Duprey by Tom Stransky and one on the integration of ecology in the work on justice and peace by D. Preman Niles, Mary Tanner's entry on the ordination of women and those on prayer and liturgy by Teresa Berger.[43] Therefore, it had greater breadth than the Paderborn *Personenlexikon*, but already indicated

the need for subdivisions that, in the work edited by one of Walter Kasper's best students, would become a true biographical dictionary.

It was no coincidence that Thönissen – confirmed in the field of ecumenical theology with his 1994 work that had provided an analysis of the criteria of tradition and Vatican II in ecumenical matters[44] – should turn his attention to this biographical dictionary. It was equally relevant that a member of the Paderborn institute such as Ernesti, born after Vatican II, professor at Augsburg and a scholar of the ecumenical parable during the Third Reich and, who had tried his hand at a brief but meticulous history of ecumenism, also worked on it.[45]

This biographical dictionary, indeed, more than its competitors,[46] was a work of scholarship that masterfully marked the passage to a season in which those who were aware of ecumenism as a long-term phenomenon felt the need to enter the easier terrain of pure erudition as an alternative to the history of dialogues or a triumphalistic display of their results in a paradoxical reproposal of an ecumenical *Denzingertheologie*.[47]

---

42 See Jörg Ernesti & Wolfgang Thönissen (eds.), *Personenlexikon Ökumene*, Freiburg i.Br., Herder, 2010.

43 Nicolas Lossky & others, eds., *Dictionary of the Ecumenical Movement*, Geneva, WCC Publications, ²2003 with internal variations in respect to the ¹1991 edition published in Geneva.

44 Wolfgang Thönissen, *Gemeinschaft durch Teilhabe an Jesus Christus: Ein katholisches Modell für die Einheit der Kirchen*, Freiburg i.Br., Herder, 1996 (originally his Habilitationsschrift, Freiburg i.Br., 1994), later developed in his *Dogma und Symbol: Eine ökumenische Hermeneutik*, Freiburg i.Br., Herder, 2008.

45 Jörg Ernesti, *Ökumene im Dritten Reich*, Paderborn, Bonifatius, 2007 and *Kleine Geschichte der Ökumene*, Freiburg i.Br., Herder, 2007.

46 Pantelis Kalaitzidis & others, eds., *Orthodox Handbook on Ecumenism: Resources for Theological Education*, Oxford, Regnum Books International, 2014, was prepared at the same time for educational use.

47 The prounione.it and wcc.org websites have the collections of the online versions of the dialogues. In Italy, the *Enchiridion Oecumenicum*, which now numbers ten volumes, has been published since 1984. For Canada, see *The Margaret O'Gara Ecumenical Dialogue Collection*, available at <https://ecumenical-dialogue .ca> (accessed Dec 2, 2020). For Rahner's position on *Denzingertheologie*, see, for example, "Zur momentanen Situation der katholischen Theologie," in: Karl Rahner, *Schriften zur Theologie*, vol. 15, Zürich, Benziger, 1983, 76–83. See also Bernard J.F. Lonergan,

It was therefore a meritorious condensation that inevitably, however, raised the question of the very possibility of attempting a vision of the whole, not a synthesis but one capable of historically giving voice to a historical reality marked by nonlinear time, one consisting of urgencies and delays, of premature acts and lost opportunities, of heightened formations and unexpected conversions.

2.2 *Narratives and Privileges*

In these historiographical seasons, recalled here extremely briefly, hundreds of works could be included that would produce the infinite nuances in the library of ecumenical historiography to which I referred above. This immense library has had access to various, growing sources produced both by individuals and by institutions, disseminated with or without academic intent, admitting varying degrees of access.[48] Different narratological currents have acted and continue to act upon the historical knowledge of ecumenical experience in it. I restrict myself here to mentioning only three narratives that serve as examples.

2.2.1 Competing Narratives

The *narrative of return* is the first that the ecumenical movement applied to itself and which historiography took up as the description of a "must."[49] It posits unity as a past fact to which to turn in an analeptic procedure that, from a papist viewpoint, has clear unionist connotations and

which, in the name of a lost authenticity, has a tone recognized as such throughout the post-Reformation world.[50]

This type of narrative can be found not only in the sources. It belongs to an original instance of Christianity since, already at the time of John 17:21, the community was aware of its own division.[51] Throughout the history of the exegesis of that passage – besides that of the other ecclesiological archetypes such as Acts 4:32 or Acts 9:31,[52] or the hermeneutics of the notes on the Nicene-Constantinopolitan Creed – the narrative of return inscribes κοινωνία[53] as an objective that lies behind those waiting for it. It is a reverse paradigm that came down to the 20th century, embraced by both those responsible for the ecumenical *inventio* and by a historiography seeking intermediate stages. For example, it is seen in the study of the estrangement between East and West in the 9th and 10th centuries that prepared the 1054 schism that separated those worlds during the Gregorian era[54] and in the study of the

---

Method in Theology, Toronto, University of Toronto Press, 1972, 330–331.

48   The catalogue of the papers from Geneva (https://archives.oikoumene.org/en) comes to mind, or the digital edition of all of the documents published by the Faith and Order Commission (https://archive.org/details/faithandorderpapersdigitaledition).

49   See Jacques Derrida's 1986 essay "Comment ne pas parler: Dénégations," in: Jacques Derrida, *Psyché: Inventions de l'autre*, vol. 2, Paris, Galilée, 2003; ET: "How to Avoid Speaking: Denials," in: Jacques Derrida, *Psyche: Inventions of the Other*, ed. and trans. Peggy Kamuf & Elizabeth Rottenberg, vol. 2, Palo Alto CA, Stanford University Press, 2008, 143–195.

50   See Stephen J. Barnett, "Where Was Your Church Before Luther? Claims for the Antiquity of Protestantism Examined," *CH* 68/1, 1999, 14–41, or, for a pastoral reading, Glen L. Thompson, "The Daughter of The Word: What Luther learned from the Early Church and the Fathers," *Perichoresis* 17/4, 2019, 41–56.

51   Jean Zumstein, *Das Johannesevangelium*, Göttingen, Vandenhoeck & Ruprecht, 2016, 650–659, on the second hand aspect of prayer.

52   On Acts 9, see again Jacques Dupont, *Nouvelles Études sur les Actes des Apôtres*, Paris, Cerf, 1984; for an example of a theological reading from an Orthodox perspective, see, for example, Anatoly A. Alexeev, Christos Karakolis & Ulrich Luz, eds., *Einheit der Kirche im Neuen Testament*, Heidelberg, Mohr Siebeck, 2008; for the recent studies, see Daniel Marguerat, *Les Actes des Apôtres (1–12)*, Geneva, Labor et Fides, 2007.

53   Pier Cesare Bori, *Koinonia: L'idea della comunione nell'ecclesiologia recente e nel Nuovo Testamento*, Brescia, Paideia, 1972. For the recent developments in different sources, see Julien M. Ogereau, "A Survey of Κοινωνία and Its Cognates in Documentary Sources," *Novum Testamentum* 57/3, 2015, 275–294.

54   To understand its significance, it is enough to review the fortunes of the studies on Photius by Francis Dvornik, Harvard professor from 1948 to 1965, and author of

union council of 1438–1439 that preceded the fall of Constantinople into Turkish hands and that historicized the Latin ideology of the *reductio* of the "schismatics"[55] when unionism was still the prevailing culture in the Roman Catholic Church. It is this looking backward that is the driving force behind a search in history for the code of fallibility of a unity lost and of a restored Eucharistic communion.[56]

The *narrative of suffering* is a second thread that runs through the sources and enters the ecumenical *fabula*. It distances itself from an admiration of controversial virtuosity, from an epic recollection[57] of religious violence, whether suffered or practiced, in the "dutiful commitment to defend the truth,"[58] and from everything that anesthetizes the scandal of division, adopting instead a

view that sees the rupture of unity as a fatal error that strives for healing. Biblical tradition and the history of exegesis supplied this narrative with a lexicon of reference, too,[59] and Greco-Hellenistic philosophy furnished a filter laden with historical-political consequences on the meaning of being-one.[60] This narrative also "calls upon" historical research to narrate the pain of the laceration, for example, the misunderstandings that generated the theological rifts between the great church and the non-Constantinopolitan East, or the tragedy of the sack of Constantinople in the Fourth crusade in 1204.[61]

The *narrative of urgency* is a third thread that operates in the sources and which historiography

---

The Photian Schism: History and Legend, Cambridge, Cambridge University Press, 1948, the French edition, *Le Schisme de Photius: Histoire et légende*, Paris, Cerf, 1950, has a preface by Yves Congar.

55   Fr. Joseph Gill was a student at the PIO in the 1930s. He spent the war in Oxford where he worked on a history of the Anglican Church and began work on the Council of Ferrara-Florence with Georg Hofmann. He later returned to Rome and became Rector of the PIO. See Joseph A. Munitiz, "Joseph Gill s.j. (8 IX 1901–15 X 1989)," *OCP* 57, 1991, 5–10.

56   See Federico Fatti, "Il seme del diavolo: La parabola della zizzania e i conflitti politico-dottrinali a Bisanzio (IV–V sec.)," *CrSt* 26/1, 2005, 123–172. For a bibliography on intercommunion, see Alberto Melloni, *Tempus visitationis: L'intercomunione inaccaduta fra Roma e Costantinopoli*, Bologna, Il Mulino, 2019. On Piet Frans Fransen's insight into the mutual obligations arising from the condemnations, see Alberto Melloni, "La chiesa fra comunione e scomunica," in: Giuseppe Alberigo, Giuseppe Ruggieri & Roberto Rusconi, eds., *Il cristianesimo, grande Atlante*, vol. 2, *Ordinamenti, gerarchie, pratiche*, Turin, Utet, 2006, 501–515.

57   Erika Kuijpers & others, eds., *Memory Before Modernity: Practices of Memory in Early Modern Europe*, Leiden, Brill, 2013.

58   This is the expression used during the *mea culpa* of the Roman Catholic Church used by Joseph Ratzinger in the Jubilee of 2000, for which the ITC had prepared a document entitled *Memory and Reconciliation: The Church and the Faults of the Past*. On this issue, see Giuseppe Alberigo, *Chiesa santa e peccatrice*, Magnano, Qiqajon, 1997.

59   On the problem of the principle of union in the earliest Christian communities, see Bruce D. Chilton & Craig A. Evans, eds., *James the Just and Christian Origins*, Leiden, Brill 2014; Claudio Gianotto, *Pietro: Il primo degli apostoli*, Bologna, Il Mulino, 2018.

60   Today it is less common to encounter the extreme position that claims a perpetual and irrevocable right for the philosophy of saying the Christian faith as that of Joseph Ratzinger, *Einführung in das Christentum: Vorlesungen über das Apostolische Glaubensbekenntnis*, Munich, Kösel, 1968; ET: *Introduction to Christianity*, San Francisco, Ignatius Press, 1990. This thesis was also reiterated in his 2006 Regensburg lecture *Glaube, Vernunft und Universität: Erinnerungen und Reflexionen*, available at <http://www.vatican.va/content/benedict-xvi/en/speeches/2006/september/documents/hf_ben-xvi_spe_20060912_university-regensburg.html> (accessed Dec 4, 2020), which quotes from the essay of Aloys Grillmeier, "Hellenisierung – Judaisierung des Christentums als Deuteprinzipien der Geschichte des kirchlichen Dogmas," in: Aloys Grillmeier, *Mit ihm und in ihm: Christologische Forschungen und Perspektiven*, Freiburg i.Br., Herder, 1975, 423–488. For the Plotinian filter, see Christian Tornau, "Qu'est-ce qu'un individu? Unité, individualité, et conscience de soi dans la métaphysique Plotinienne de l'âme," *Les Études philosophiques* 3, 2009, 333–360. On the ontological and henological question from Origen to Pico, see Jean-Marc Narbonne, *La métaphysique de Plotin*, Paris, Vrin, 2001, 162–163.

61   See Alfred J. Andrea, *Contemporary Sources for the Fourth Crusade*, Leiden, Brill, 2008, and Alfred J. Andrea, *The Capture of Constantinople: The "Hystoria Constantinopolitana" of Gunther of Pairis*, Philadelphia PA, University of Pennsylvania Press, 1997.

finds itself facing because, for many, what must be committed to the record is the conviction of living not a linear but a "steep" time, inclined toward a καιρός whereby it seems objective situations internal or external to ecclesial dynamism cannot be escaped. For the pioneers of ecumenism, it was the missionary urgency in the early age of colonialist globalization at the end of the 19th century that led them to set aside their hesitations and self-understand themselves as *the* ecumenical movement (one should recall Rouse and Neill's title), even in the absence of factual evidence of the extensive participation on which they wagered. Yet the same sense of urgency leads back to Constantinople immediately after World War I, and again when ecumenism had to measure up to the success of atheism, or, after World War II, to the threat of Soviet imperialism. One finds it again in the growth of antinuclear pacifism in the 1960s, under the banner of rebellion against racial discrimination, in the struggle against the structural sin of capitalist society, and in calls for the defense of the environment at the end of the 20th century.

These historical contingencies become the reason for overcoming ancient divisions and for believing that "visible" unity is necessary, and is the sole guarantee with respect to spiritualist shortcuts that have never been silenced.[62] This narrative also calls on historiography to explore the weight of divided Christianity in the great twists of history, as demonstrated, for example, by research on the Third Reich[63] or the Council of Ferrara-

Florence and the instrumentalization of the occasion leading up to the catastrophe of 1453.[64]

2.2.2 The Privileged Viewpoint

This complex historiography,[65] written like all the others in the conviction of being able to distinguish prehistory from history, constructed like all the others in the conviction of being accorded a privileged viewpoint by time and sources, has provided a profound understanding of the beginnings of what would come to be called "ecumenism," of its changing self-consciousness, of its institutions, of its leading figures, of the astuteness and the crises that have led many churches to avoid or use adjectives for a term with a very particular history. It is precisely the extension of this historiography that permits us today to understand that the expectation of unity[66] consists of precise, imaginable, and possible articulations that must be clarified and studied.

However, it is precisely the vastness of this effort that makes it possible to hypothesize that the expectation constitutes a *sum of meanings* that exceed the individual articulations. There is no doubt that all those who constitute the history of the ecumenical movement are true articulations – trailblazers moved by the passion for unity,[67]

---

62   See Walter Kasper, *A Handbook of Spiritual Ecumenism*, Hyde Park NY, New City Press, 2007, and the review of the 2002 collection of Kasper's essays by Ingolf Dalferth, "Cardinal Kasper on Ecumenism," *Ecclesiology* 2/1, 2005, 131–137.

63   Other than the previously cited work by Ernesti, see, for example, the theme of the impossibility of excommunication (in regard to the Arian paragraph) as an obstacle to an ecumenical council in the work of Bonhoeffer, see *Ökumenische Ungeduld: Das Drängen Dietrich Bonhoeffers auf die Einheit der Kirche im Geiste Jesu Christi*, forthcoming, and Norbert Greinacher, *Von der Wirklichkeit zur Utopie: Der Weg eines Theologen*, Frankfurt a.M., Peter Lang, 2010, 91–93.

64   Giuseppe Alberigo, ed., *Christian Unity: The Council of Ferrara-Florence: 1438/39–1989*, Leuven, Peeters, 1991.

65   Fouilloux, "Ecumenismo."

66   See the introductory essay by Antonella Cavazza in the critical edition that she edited of *"La Chiesa è una" di A.S. Chomjakov: Edizione documentario-interpretativa*, Bologna, Il Mulino, 2006.

67   The category of "trailblazer" was already widely used by the mid-1950s, as shown by the book by Hermann Maas, *Wegbereiter der Ökumene: Nathan Söderblom, John Mott, Marc Boegner, W.A. Visser't Hooft, Begegnungen und Erinnerungen*, Stuttgart, Junge, 1954, whose title inspired the collection published fifty years later, Christian Möller & others, eds., *Wegbereiter der Ökumene im 20. Jahrhundert (Transkulturelle Perspektiven)*, Göttingen, Vandenhoeck & Ruprecht, 2005. This is a type of approach that emerges in other biographical works of great significance, for example, Charles Howard Hopkins, *John R. Mott (1865–1955): A Biography*, Grand Rapids MI, Eerdmans, 1979; Jonas

environments that have safeguarded their seeds,[68] figures hidden in the folds of spiritual intuition or ecclesiastical institutions. They are linked back to distant expectations and, as in other 19th and pre-20th century Christian movements, they create relationships that are equipped with both old and new instruments, both typically ecclesial ones and those from the political and cultural context.

But is there anything beyond a theory of articulations that is not the adoption of a narrative or the adherence to a trend?

3 For a History of the Christian Desire for Unity

The working hypothesis proposed here is that that "thing" (*res oecumenica*) exists, that it changes and that it can be traced throughout the passage between the generations that experienced two world wars, a Cold War, the clash of civilizations, colonizations, true and fictitious decolonizations, the globalization of markets, and the spirituality market in the whirlwinds of demographic changes. It is a Christian *quid*, thus a historical fact; it would be a defection to attempt to circumvent it with

ritual formulas of complexity and is what will be called here *desire*.

It is a *desiderium unitatis*,[69] and the desire for an ecclesial *unitas corporis*[70] of which history can be made. It is the history – that is to say "not controversy or the setting of concrete objectives, but an act through which to retain the image of the past that is created [in me] through studying the sources"[71] – of the Christian desire for the unity of the churches, the history of the churches' desire for the unity of Christians, the history of the desire for the unity for Christians.[72] It is the history of a κρίσις that truly runs through all the churches, which, in every person who embraces it, defines the priorities and doctrines, compromises and deeds, convictions and evaluations of which historical research has much to say. This is because they are parts of a story that has seen a collective subject such as Christianity – whose social dangerousness has been documented by religious wars – turn to thoughts and deeds of peace, not on the basis of an extrinsic, pluralist or,

---

Jonson, *Nathan Soderblom: Called to Serve*, Grand Rapids MI, Eerdmans, 2016; Dietz Lange, *Nathan Soderblom und seine Zeit*, Göttingen, Vandenhoeck & Ruprecht, 2011; Jacques Mortiau & Raymond Loonbeek, *Dom Lambert Beauduin visionaire et précurseur (1873–1960): Un moine au cœur libre*, Paris, Cerf, 2005; Jan Schubert, *Willem Adolph Visser 't Hooft (1900–1985): Ökumene und Europa*, Göttingen, Vandenhoeck & Ruprecht, 2017; Jurjen Albert Zeilstra, *Visser 't Hooft. Een leven voor de oecumene – Biografie (1900–1985)*, Middelbourg, Skandalon, 2018 (ET: *Visser 't Hooft, 1900–1985: Living for the Unity of the Church*, Amsterdam, Amsterdam University Press, 2020); Saretta Marotta, *Gli anni della pazienza: Bea, l'ecumenismo e il Sant'Uffizio di Pio XII*, Bologna, Il Mulino, 2020; Valeria Martano, *Athenagoras, il patriarca (1886–1972): Un cristiano fra crisi della coabitazione e utopia ecumenica*, Bologna, Il Mulino, 1996.

68   See Scatena, *Taizé*, and, on Chevetogne, Mortiau & Loonbeek, *Dom Lambert Beauduin*.

69   Thus John Cassian, *Conferences* 3.23.5.3; I note *per transennam* that the expression comes from the 1962 Ratzinger-Frings schema on the church, *Dominus noster Jesus Christus*, cited in: Jerard Wicks, "Six Texts by Prof. Joseph Ratzinger," *Gregorianum* 89/2, 2008, 233–311, here 295. On this see Giuseppe Alberigo, ed., *Storia del concilio Vaticano II*, 5 vols., Bologna/Leuven, Il Mulino/Peeters, ²2015, *ad indicem*.

70   Cyprian, *De Ecclesiae catholicae unitate*, cited in John XXIII's opening speech at Vatican II, *Gaudet mater ecclesia*; on this see Alberto Melloni, *Papa Giovanni: Un cristiano e il suo concilio*, Turin, Einaudi 2008, 258–273.

71   I like the formula inscribed in the preface to volume 2 of the history of the Council of Trent: "Auch dieser Band verfolgt mithin keine konkreten Ziele, weder ökumenische noch kontroverstheologische. Er will nur darstellen, d. h. jenes Bild der Vergangenheit festhalten, das sich in mir durch das Studium der Quellen geformt hat," Hubert Jedin, *Geschichte des Konzils von Trient*, vol. 2, Freiburg i.Br., Herder, 1957, v–vi.

72   On this, see Alberto Melloni, "Per una storia del desiderio cristiano di unità," in: Jean-Dominique Durand & others, *Nel mare aperto della storia: Studi in onore di Andrea Riccardi*, Rome, Laterza, 2021, 120–142.

as some pope has said, "irenicist"[73] instance, but as a response to an obedience that has been heard and accepted.

It is the history not of concepts or models, but that of men and women who, starting from the irreplaceable contribution supplied by the historiography of ecumenism, make of ecumenism a subtitle. This does not downplay the factual breadth of a process that, nevertheless, is not recognized or is no longer recognized in the term "ecumene" imported into Christianity by Eusebius of Caesarea,[74] yet cannot divorce itself from the grasp of the call to unity. It is a history that studies concrete men and women. Often without knowing one another, and at times not even being aware of the existence of one another, in quite separate confessional and cultural spheres, they embodied what many of them understood to be obedience to the Word and the discovery of a *potentia oboedientalis*.[75] In virtue of that inner dimension (from which historical understanding is precluded in its exploration but not in its effects), they set in motion historical processes that went beyond their categorization as a "movement," and which can be the object of a historical investigation that is thus neither anachronistic nor finalistic.

3.1   *Methodological Caveats*

Like every operation of historical knowledge, this one also has such a large body of research behind it that it can express its own particular approach and the caveats that set its course.

The "biographical" presentation so often imagined for ecumenism is neither sufficient nor necessary in a history of the Christian desire for

---

73   In a certain sense, one can say that the formula used in the Catholic condemnations of the 1920s ("false irenicism") paradoxically evoked a conception arising from Erasmus and François du Jon the Elder (Franciscus Junius) and then from the irenicists of the 17th and 18th centuries. On this, see Michael B. Lukens, "Witzel and Erasmian Irenicism in the 1530s," *JTS* 39/1, 1988, 134–136. On some of the principal figures, see Nick Thompson, "The Long Reach of Reformation Irenicism: The Considerationes Modestae et Pacificae of William Forbes (1585–1634)," in: Ian Breward, ed., *Reforming the Reformation: Essays in Honour of Principal Peter Matheson*, Melbourne, Australian Scholarly Press, 2004, 124–147; Tobias Sarx, *Franciscus Junius d. Ä. (1545–1602): Ein reformierter Theologe im Spannungsfeld zwischen späthumanistischer Irenik und reformierter Konfessionalisierung*, Göttingen, Vandenhoeck & Ruprecht, 2007; Christiaan de Jonge, *De irenische Ecclesiologie van Franciscus Iunius (1545–1602)*, Nieuwkoop, De Graaf, 1980; François Gaquère, *Le dialogue irénique Bossuet-Leibniz: La réunion des Églises en échec (1691–1702)*, Paris, Beauchesne, 1966; Christiane Berkvens-Stevelinck, Jonathan Irvine Israel & Guillaume H.M. Posthumus Meyjes, eds., *The Emergence of Tolerance in the Dutch Republic*, Leiden, Brill, 1997; Graeme Murdock, "The Boundaries of Reformed Irenicism: Royal Hungary and the Transylvania in Howard Louthan," in: Randall Zachman, ed., *From Conciliarism to Confessional Church (1400–1618)*, South Bend IN, Notre Dame Press, 2004; Daphne M. Wedgbury, "Protestant Irenicism and the Millennium: Mede and the Hartlib Circle," in: Jeffrey K. Jue, ed., *Heaven Upon Earth: Joseph Mede (1586–1638) and the Legacy of Millenarianism*, Dordrecht, Springer, 2006.

74   It was, as mentioned, Eusebius of Caesarea who borrowed Herodotus's term for the inhabited "world/home" – οἰκυμηνικός – to indicate the entire "world/church/empire" of Constantine, as the court of the new

Rome understood it. On this, see Giuseppe Ruggieri, "Il dibattito sulla teologia politica, prima e dopo Peterson," in: Melloni, *Costantino I*, vol. 3, 407–415, which dicusses the theological-political question posed by Eric Peterson, *Monotheismus als politisches Problem: Ein Beitrag zur Geschichte der politischen Theologie, im Imperium Romanum*, Leipzig, Jakob Hegner, 1935 and by the reaction of Carl Schmitt, *Politische Theologie II: Die Legende von der Erledigung jeder Politischen Theologie*, Berlin, Duncker & Humblot, 52008. On this see Michele Nicoletti, "Erik Peterson e Carl Schmitt: Ripensare un dibattito," in: Giancarlo Caronello, ed., *Erik Peterson: La presenza teologica di un outsider*, Vatican City, Libreria Editrice Vaticana, 2012, 517–537. On using adjectives for the council, see Alberto Melloni, "Concili, ecumenicità e storia: Note di discussione," *CrSt* 28/3, 2007, 509–542, and on the conciliar "peace," see Thomas Graumann, "Frieden schließen auf Konzilien? Zwei Beispiele aus dem vierten Jahrhundert," *AHC* 48, 2018, 53–69. The metrics of the symbol that uses the rhythm of the One (One God, One Son, One Spirit, One Church, One Baptism) need to be studied.

75   Karl Rahner & Herbert Vorgrimler, eds, *Kleines Theologisches Wörterbuch*, Freiburg i.Br., Herder, 1961, *ad vocem*.

unity. The idea of reading a trajectory of unity along a path of infancy, maturity, old age (and death) has sustained much research, but it leaves the historical problem of what prepared the adherence to a previously unheard of perspective intact[76] and also leaves even more unsolved the problem of the distancing from multilateral ecumenism and the dialogues that characterize relevant sectors of each great denomination today.

Indeed, it is precisely this aspect that confirms the inadequacy of a methodology that condenses the ecumenical relationship into dialogues and sees the engineering of dialogues as the best product of "mature" ecumenism. This is not because the experience that connects national and supranational, multilateral and bilateral dimensions is insignificant but because it has shown how it is now possible for theologians to reach an understanding on almost any question of dogma, while internal divisions make it impossible to understand one another's points of view as far as moral issues are concerned.

On the other hand, as in any other history of global and transgenerational dimensions, it is not a pseudo-erudite segmentation of the object that solves the problem. The history of the desire for unity, therefore, poses questions that are identical, e.g., to those of a history of France. It would be foolish to say it were unadvisable merely because biographies of all the French individuals do not exist, or it should be postponed until after accumulating all the monographs that could be written: because the mountain of analytical excavation and painstaking research – if, by some absurdity, such did exist – would not constitute a precondition for a research that has already been fulfilled but rather its negation.

This also holds for the, albeit essential, analysis of lexical items. The origin of identifying oneself as "ecumenical," which arose from the combination

of the theological approach of Faith and Order with the practical one of Life and Work, has since developed into a lexicon that accompanied the evolution and then involution that always corresponded to actual events.

A geography that is content with, or that excludes, the relevance of the Old World in the divisions and agenda of what would come to be perceived as a movement is neither enough for, nor of any help to, a history of the Christian desire for unity. Those lacerations and expectations of unity that were exported by diasporas and colonialism travel along a two-way street where particular conceptions/experiences pose universal problems/solutions and vice versa. Likewise, a thematic list of key problems – generational leaps, the role of youth and student groups, female protagonists, the role of research centers or monasteries, the practice of *communicatio in sacris*, declarations of double communion, and practices of intercommunion, or the identification of key figures – is neither enough nor of any help if it is limited to being a mere inventory.

Neither can the evident exchange among political cultures – starting with those which think of unity as a common subjugation to cultures of multinational imperialism or of federalism – or the conceptions that the churches express within or under those cultures – for example, those of papist absolutism or the Victorian world – be reduced to a mere inventory. Likewise, we cannot restrict ourselves to observing the parallels between the "ecumenical" approaches and the instruments of international or diplomatic relations. From the 1920 encyclical letter written on behalf of St. Andrew's throne by Germanos of Seleucia to the "Churches of Christ," inviting them to be no less audacious than the states which established the League of Nations,[77] to the ecumenical question

---

76 See, for example, the above-cited Marotta, *Gli anni della pazienza*, which poses the problem of the non-ecumenism of a future ecumenist within the repressive Roman apparatus.

77 The letter of Jan 1, 1920, *Enkyklios Synodike tes Ekklesias Konstantinoupòleos pros tas apantachoù Ekklesias tou Christoù*; ET: "Encyclical of the Ecumenical Patriarchate, 1920: *Unto the Churches of Christ Everywhere*," in: Gennadios Limouris, ed., *Orthodox Visions of Ecumenism: Statements, Messages, and*

posed by the Helsinki Accords in order to achieve the ecumenical versions of "minilateralism,"[78] it is clear that there is an osmosis between politics and ecumenism that, at times, has been understood at a political level by figures who were hostile to religion as such,[79] and which sometimes remained invisible to the theologians who themselves were politically aligned with the political implications of inter-ecclesial agreements.[80]

3.2 *Requiem for a Modern Desire?*

What then does a history of the Christian desire for unity require? In order to answer this question, we can perhaps start from a study that is far from the discussion we would like to tackle. When Harold J. Berman published *Law and Revolution: The Formation of the Western Legal Tradition* in

1983,[81] some scholars found it seriously flawed due to its second-hand access to the sources and to a very limited interpretation of the studies on the turning point of the 11th century.[82] The haste of some passages, the gaps in the bibliography, and the superficiality of certain interpretations were easy to detect. For others, however, precisely due to its hasty judgements and negligence in categorizing the aporias of its discourse, Berman afforded a reflection upon what the West became after the Gregorian reform – and therefore after the break with the East sanctioned by the excommunications of 1054. Some aspects were appreciated by a historian of medieval canon law such as Brian Tierney because it confirmed the idea that "juridical" modernity (even that of papal infallibility) had medieval roots, and therefore his research on 13th and 14th century canonical foundations and origins of traits commonly held to be the most typical product of modernity was of specific worth.[83] It was also esteemed by a historian of the Tridentine era such as Paolo Prodi who, on discussing the book, began a series of studies on the "dualisms" that he saw opening up precisely thanks to the Gregorian shift and the founding of the profile of the West. The dualism in justice, in the conception of state and ecclesial power, of market and morality is thought to have initiated an entirely modern trajectory that he saw ending with the 20th century. This, for him, included Vatican II, the final throes of a world in

Reports on the Ecumenical Movement (1902–1992), Geneva, WCC publications, 1994, 1–8.

78 See Moisés Naim, "Minilateralism," *Foreign Policy*, June 21, 2009, at foreignpolicy.com (accessed 4 Dec, 2020): "By minilateralism, I mean a smarter, more targeted approach: We should bring to the table the smallest possible number of countries needed to have the largest possible impact on solving a particular problem." So, if minilateralism is the opening of non-bilateral and non-universal dialogues from which exemplary solutions are expected, the BEM can be conceived along these lines. See, in this regard, Luca Ferracci, *Battesimo Eucaristia Ministero: Genesi e destino di un documento ecumenico*, Bologna, Il Mulino, 2021.

79 See Mikhail V. Shkarovsky, *Russkaya pravoslavnaya tserkov pri Staline i Khrushcheve: gosudarstvenno-tserkovnye otnosheniya V SSSR V 1939–1964 godach* [The Russian Orthodox Church under Stalin and Krushchev: State-Church Relations in the USSR from 1939 to 1964], Moscow, Graal, ⁴2005, and Alberto Melloni, "Chiese sorelle – diplomazie nemiche: Il Vaticano II e Mosca fra ecumenismo, propaganda ed Ostpolitik," in Alberto Melloni, ed., *Vatican II in Moscow (1959–1965): Acts of the Colloquium on the History of Vatican II. Moscow, March 30–April 2, 1995*, Leuven, Bibliotheek van de Faculteit Godgeleerdheid, 1997.

80 If Joseph Ratzinger had not objected to and blocked the signing of the ARCIC I agreement as early as 1983 – before *glasnost* – the oldest and most represented Christian components in NATO countries would have achieved a unity that did not lack general implications.

81 Harold J. Berman, *Law and Revolution: The Formation of the Western Legal Tradition*, Cambridge MA, Harvard University Press, 1983.

82 The great master Peter Landau severely criticized it in *The University of Chicago Law Review*, 51, 1984, 937–943, showing how Berman had made no reference to Italian or Spanish literature and reproaching him for having happily ignored the three volumes of *Das Recht der Gnade* by Hans Dombois, the result of twenty years of study (*Das Recht der Gnade: Ökumenisches Kirchenrecht*, 3 vols., Witten, Luther-Verlag, 1961–1983).

83 For all of these, see the Wiles Lectures collected in Brian Tierney, *Religion, Law and the Growth of Constitutional Thought (1150–1650)*, Cambridge, Cambridge University Press, 1983.

agony, as opposed to a reading of the council as an epochal turning point, which was Giuseppe Alberigo's interpretation and is my own.[84]

The controversial vigor of Prodi's thesis, which saw a concept of state, of law, of the West, and of Christianity come to an end, was irredeemably fragile. Precisely because it struggled to "keep everything" in an act of intellectual voluntarism shored up by an immense historical culture, his theory does not stand up to an examination of conscience and the bad conscience of the West. Yet, as with Berman's archetype, it is not the summation of Prodi's incongruities that avoids the question, which concerns nothing less than the existence of a "second millennium" and the locating of the Christian desire for unity within that space; because, in Prodi's philosophy of history, ecumenism could be yet another phenomenon that, precisely between the 11th and 20th centuries, experienced its entire existence, consumed its entire energy, and collapsed along with the utopia of real socialism, the concept of the state, and the culture of market regulation.

Could not the pallid ecumenism of the 21st century – one that requires third-party themes, be they ecological or migratory, to express a convergence that on a doctrinal level has been hijacked by theologians, on a hierarchical level is driven by media, and on a spiritual level has lost its voice – be used as proof of a season in which tendencies toward integralism, Pentecostal digressions, doctrinal supremacies, and identity traditionalisms prevail in every church?

3.3 *A Working Hypothesis*

For a historian who does not prove but reveals the answer is that it could not, because in that imaginary trajectory there is something that is not quite right. Saying that the desire for Christian unity belongs, heart and soul, to "modernity" and thus

is considered to end along with it, would be nothing more than a more sophisticated repetition of a *topos* of the history of "classical" ecumenism, which legitimized its own point of view by maintaining that the process of growth, or the process *tout court*, to which study is dedicated, has been exhausted, having been overtaken by facts.

It is enough to ask oneself one question: in a global Christianity, increasingly evangelical and fragmented, in which division is no longer seen as a scandal but as the multiplication of religious offers in a new union with autocratic right-wing forces, what should reveal that the desire for Christian unity has run its course and that its fated dissolution has begun to push the pendulum of history towards a season of identity conflict and violence?

The answer is simple: matters would seem to suggest a negative response to this question and a different working hypothesis, starting exactly from Berman's controversial theory on the 11th century because it is precisely the ecclesiological, juridical, and political legitimacy accorded at the time to the original schismatic fracture that the desire for unity calls into question. And it is precisely the inexorability of post-Tridentine confessionalization that is jolted by the vibration of the desire that makes one think of the *visible* unity of the churches as a real goal.

Instead of collapsing along with the utopias of the second half of the 20th century, the ferment of Christian unity took a different path. The ecumenical effort had used everything that postmodernity has swept away: historical finalism, the unifying *Weltanschauung* of the Enlightenment, the anthropology of civilization; but then it had already experienced all the aporias. In the disenchantment of the 1970s, the desire for unity discovered that it was not the vanguard of a process towards a compulsory end, the expression of a therapeutic rationality, or the protagonist of the turning point that intellectualistically sees more unity in the churches' lack of unity today than in the unity of the churches of the 4th century. Those who awaited the appearance on earth of a *homo*

---

84 See, at the conclusion to the new edition, Alberto Melloni, "Post scriptum alla storia del Vaticano II," in: Alberigo, ed., *Storia del concilio Vaticano II*, vol. 5, ix–xix.

œcumenicus, endowed with hitherto unknown thoughts and abilities, have had to acknowledge that, without that turning point, however, the bloodthirsty horrors of infra-Christian antagonism have been eradicated. The scandal of division, but not division itself, has been eroded, generating a practice of ecumenical courtesy that is not unity, but seems to be rather the glass partition that separates the churches from it. All this is thanks to a long series of figures of varying interior and cultural stamp, from whose hands we receive more than one testimony, the baton in a relay race that deceives those who would like there to be only one.

It is a process that escapes (ברח Sg 8:14) the ideologies of modernity and the West and demands to be studied, known and narrated exactly for what it is, on the basis of a heuristic consideration, a hermeneutic criterion, and the postulate typical of every historical work.

The *heuristic consideration* is that the history of this desire leaves an interminable documentary trail, as in so much of the contemporary history of the pre-digital age. It is so vast that it can be used by a journalist or a judge as a deposit that can be mined with a rigor that, even if passed off as meticulousness, remains an arbitrary concatenation of proofs. Or it can be used by historians as a shimmering firmament from which to draw hypotheses whose truth can be seen by all, reconstructed by all, and rediscussed by all.

The *hermeneutic criterion* is also common to every historical piece of work. In order to know that lost present that is the past, the historian must be wary of the siren that gives it a "concrete purpose" which, if accepted, would render that fragment of historical truth a servant of this purpose. It may, however, have a function in virtue of the understanding it generates. The Christian desire for unity may disappear forever from the horizon, by itself or along with Christianity (Jesus' πλήν in Luke 18:8b concerning the matter is rather pessimistic). But for the historian, what will remain will be the significance of an experience that has changed the religious landscape and – let

a comparison with the confessional divisions of Islam suffice – has changed it in a way favorable to peace.

The *postulate* is linked to this aspect and harkens back to Jean-Pierre Jossua's intuition concerning post-Kantian Christianity. Once the duty of establishing ethics was concluded, Christianity could have regained its kerygmatic dimension (and it did not do so).[85] Today's ecumenical trajectory has certainly exhausted the idea that the unity of the churches is "useful": useful in improving missionary performance, useful in ending atheist communism, useful in combating Nazi idolatry, useful for living in a postwar society, useful in improving religious life, useful to migrants, the environment, or to post-Covid world. No *utilitas* has survived. Rather, the rise to predominance, at least in the political sphere, of churches (in Brazil, the United States) that are disinterested and hostile to an ecumenical course and the tumultuous growth of interreligious dialogue makes the desire for unity today a completely gratuitous act, embraced by its servants who are useless but nevertheless still capable of trusting in the delays, convinced that only what arrives late will some time take place.

If one intends to understand this, it means being aware that, all things considered, what is needed to produce a historical knowledge worthy of such an object is the careful examination of the multidimensionality of every single articulation[86]

---

85   Jean-Pierre Jossua, "De foi en foi: Hommage à Pierre-André Liégé," *RSPT* 97/1, 2013, 95–107.

86   This can be explained through recourse to the figure of the parallelogram used by Giuseppe Alberigo in his "Criteri ermeneutici per una storia del Vaticano II," in Giuseppe Alberigo, ed., *Il Vaticano II fra attese e celebrazione*, Bologna, Il Mulino, 1995, 9–26. There are four sides, on which presses and along which runs all the energy of experience and intelligence that emanates from the Christian desire for unity in the last two centuries. It has two horizontal sides: on the one hand, the dimensions of ecclesiastical government and, on the other, political dimensions. Along the vertical sides are, on the one hand, theologies (not in the abstract but in the debate produced by a theological class of

of an object that is exposed to history and historical knowledge, thanks to a certain connaturality. Because it is a fact, and because it is Christian.

Translated from Italian to English by Susan Dawson Vásquez and David Dawson Vásquez.

Bibliography

Alberigo, Giuseppe, ed., *Christian Unity: The Council of Ferrara-Florence: 1438/39–1989*, Leuven, Peeters, 1991.

Anderson, Gerald H. & others, eds., *Mission Legacies: Biographical Studies of Leaders of the Modern Missionary Movement*, Maryknoll NY, Orbis Books, 1994.

Berman, Harold J., *Law and Revolution: The Formation of the Western Legal Tradition*, Cambridge MA, Harvard University Press, 1983.

Bori, Pier Cesare, *Koinonia: L'idea della comunione nell'ecclesiologia recente e nel Nuovo Testamento*, Brescia, Paideia, 1972.

Cavazza, Antonella, *"La Chiesa è una" di A.S. Chomjakov: Edizione documentario-interpretativa*, Bologna, Il Mulino, 2006.

de Certeau, Michel, *The Writing of History*, trans. Tom Conley, New York NY, Columbia University Press, 1988.

Fouilloux, Étienne, *Les catholiques et l'unité chrétienne du XIXème au XXème siècle*, Paris, Le Centurion, 1982.

Karakolis, Christos & Ulrich Luz, eds., *Einheit der Kirche im Neuen Testament*, Heidelberg, Mohr Siebeck, 2008.

Koselleck, Reinhart, *Futures Past: On the Semantics of Historical Time*, trans. Keith Tribe, New York NY, Columbia University Press, 2005.

Marguerat, Daniel, *Les Actes des Apôtres (1–12)*, Geneva, Labor et Fides, 2007.

Marrou, Henri-Irénée, *The Meaning of History*, trans. Robert J. Olsen, Baltimore MD, Helicon, 1966.

Melloni, Alberto, *Tempus visitationis: L'intercomunione inaccaduta fra Roma e Costantinopoli*, Bologna, Il Mulino, 2019.

Thönissen, Wolfgang, *Dogma und Symbol: Eine ökumenische Hermeneutik*, Freiburg i.Br., Herder, 2008.

Tierney, Brian, *Religion, Law and the Growth of Constitutional Thought (1150–1650)*, Cambridge, Cambridge University Press, 1983.

specialized "professionals") and, on the opposite side, spiritualities in which prophetic figures and early intuitions are rooted and which find clear expression in realities such as ecumenical monasticism. The sides are connected by diagonals representing the great figures, such as Athenagoras, in whom the spiritual and ecclesiastical are joined, or Frère Roger Schutz, whose *Ostpolitik* constitutes a spiritual diplomacy, or an all-around theologian such as Dietrich Bonhoeffer, who thinks of church unity as a possible rupture in ecclesiastical unity.

PART 1

Preamble: Long Term Issues

∵

From Division to the Search for Unity: Difficulties and Horizons in a History Still Underway

John D. Zizioulas

1 Communion and Otherness: The Knots in an Ancient Problem

Any attempt to address the question of church unity in a theologically rigorous way leads to a discussion of the relationship between unity and diversity within the church itself. A glance at ecclesiastical history would be enough to show how crucial this has been in the course of the centuries. During the apostolic period, the issue dominated the debate on the acceptance of Gentile Christians into the body of the church. The question of whether or not to require everyone to observe certain articles of Jewish law, such as circumcision, was a problem that well illustrated the significance that the question of diversity had assumed from the outset.[1] A similar problem emerged in the 2nd century, in the form of a debate on the observance of fasting in connection to the celebration of Easter, when St. Irenaeus famously asserted that "the divergence in the fast emphasizes the unanimity of our faith."[2] It is also well known how fundamental the question was at the time of the first great dispute between Rome and Constantinople when, in the 9th century, Photius had to insist that the Eastern section of the church had always maintained customs different from the West concerning, among other things, the election of bishops.[3]

The entire conflict between the two sees, which then led to the schism of 1054, besides the controversy that accompanied and followed it for a long time during the Middle Ages, concerned differences between East and West. A few examples were the celebration of the Lord's Supper with unleavened bread, the clergy's beards, and so on, which some considered essential for church unity. It could be said that the wider the gap between the two churches became, the more difficult any reconciliation between the two sides was, due to the legitimacy of their differences. Each side tried to assert its own particular identity by minimizing internal differences as much as possible. Even today, differences in matters such as the date of Easter and the clergy's beards are emphasized and used to define ecclesial identities and to solidify and strengthen division; traditions take the place of Tradition and the deeper the rift, the more difficult it is to distinguish between the two.[4]

---

1 The bibliography on the subject is very extensive. See, for example, Ernst Käsemann, "Begründet der neutestamentliche Kanon die Einheit der Kirche?," *EvTh* 11, 1951, 13–21, for a radical prodiversity point of view. See also, James D.G. Dunn, *Unity and Diversity in the New Testament*, London, SCM Press, 1990, and John Charlot, *New Testament Disunity: Its Significance for Christianity Today*, New York NY, E.P. Dutton, 1970.

2 "Ἡ διαφωνία τῆς νηστείας τὴν ὁμόνοια τῆς πίστεως συνίστησιν"; Eusebius, *Hist. eccl.*, 5.24; ET: Eusebius, *The History of the Church from Christ to Constantine*, trans. G.A. Williamson, ed. Andrew Louth, London, Penguin, 1989, 173.

3 See Photius, "Second Letter to Pope Nicholas I," *PG* 102, cols. 593–618, in particular 604–605 and 616. See also the acts of the council of 879–880 in: Mansi 17a, cols. 373–524, and *COGD* 2/1, 2013, 49–71.

4 This distinction was proposed, elaborated upon, and discussed in detail during the fourth World Conference on Faith and Order in Montreal in 1963. See Lukas Vischer & Patrick C. Rodger, eds., *The Fourth World Conference on Faith and Order: The Report from Montreal 1963*, London, SCM Press, 1964.

The same issue has been raised not only with regard to customs but also as far as the faith is concerned. Can there be a legitimate diversity in matters of faith? To what extent can there be a difference of opinion on dogmatic issues? The "comprehensiveness" that is typical of the Anglican tradition, for example, presents more than a few difficulties for the faithful of other confessions, particularly with the lack of clear, recognizable limits to diversity. How can such limits be established? Is it simply a matter of distinguishing between "faith" and its "formulation" or "expression," as Roman Catholic theologians say? To what extent are the formulations of faith intimately tied to the unity of the church?

Similar problems also arise regarding the "order" of the ministry and the structure of the church. What elements, in church structure and ministry, are essential and therefore immutable? Is everything that pertains to "order" mutable, since it relates to the church's *bene esse*, or is it organically correlated to its *esse*?

In the area of ecumenism there have been, needless to say, various attempts to address the question of unity and diversity, especially in the work of the Faith and Order commission.[5] There has, however, been no attempt to establish theological criteria by which to judge what, theologically, constitutes legitimate diversity or what is theologically necessary for the *esse* of the unity of the church.

Such criteria can only be established with the help of the fundamental principles of the Christian faith. Indeed, unity and diversity are linked, particularly in Trinitarian theology, Christology, and pneumatology, doctrines in which the philosophical issues of unity and otherness, of the "one" and the "many" are implicit, issues that have occupied human thought since the time of Plato.[6]

Diversity, therefore, is essential to church unity for profoundly theological reasons. Monolithic unity is not ecclesial unity. The one church is made up of many churches: this is the true *esse* of church. This affirmation, however, needs to be justified.

The ecumenical movement today has endeavored to unite churches mainly understood as confessions. From the emergence of confessionalism in the 17th century, the term church has acquired a further meaning that it did not have until then, that is, of being a "confessional family." In ecumenical circles, therefore, it has become common to speak of the "Orthodox Church," the "Roman Catholic Church," the "Old Catholic Church," of "Anglican" and "Lutheran" Churches, and so on. In the period before the Reformation, however the term church had a strictly geographical meaning, that is, it indicated the "church (singular) of a particular city."[7] Without entering a debate concerning the causes of such an evolution, I shall restrict myself here to analyzing the effects that this type of "confessionalist" ecclesiology has had on the ecumenical movement.

When introduced into ecumenical dialogue, the idea of the "confessional church" has made it possible to speak of the diversity of churches as a diversity of confessions. From the oldest idea of a branch theory to the most recent idea of reconciled diversity, models of unity have been proposed, essentially conceived of as the variety and diversity of confessions that, while reconciled to

---

5   For a recent overview of the models of unity at the heart of ecumenical dialogue, see Gesa Elsbeth Thiessen, ed., *Ecumenical Ecclesiology: Unity, Diversity, and Otherness in a Fragmented World*, London, T&T Clark, 2009, in particular the editor's essay on method, "Seeking Unity: Reflecting on Method in Contemporary Ecumenical Dialogue," 35–48, as well as that of Miriam Haar, "The Struggle for an Organic, Conciliar and Diverse Church: Models of Church Unity in Earlier Stages of the Ecumenical Dialogue," 49–61. Also noteworthy is the reconstruction in Konrad Raiser, "Modelle kirchlicher Einheit: Die Debatte der siebziger Jahre und die Folgerungen für heute," *ÖR* 36, 1987, 195–216. Günther Gassmann, instead, has studied the models of unity at the first two world conferences of Faith and Order in his *Konzeptionen der Einheit in der Bewegung für Glauben und Kirchenverfassung (1910–1937)*, Göttingen, Vandenhoeck & Ruprecht, 1979.

6   See, in particular, his *Parmenides*.

7   Rom 16:1, 1 Cor 1:2, 2 Cor 1:1, Col 4:16, 1 Thess 1:1. See also John D. Zizioulas, *Eucharist, Bishop, Church: The Unity of the Church in the Divine Eucharist and the Bishop during the First Three Centuries*, Brookline MA, Holy Cross Orthodox Press, 2001, 45.

one another, nevertheless maintained their distinct doctrinal heritage almost intact. All this occurred until the world assembly of the WCC in Nairobi in 1975 proposed the achievement of a true and visible unity of local churches rooted in the three classical cornerstones of organic unity, namely, the sharing of the chalice, the common profession of apostolic faith, and the mutual acceptance of ministers.

Which of these two models then should be followed? If we opt for the model of reconciled diversity, which many of the Reformation churches chose and which was the basis for the 1973 Leuenberg Agreement, it is then necessary to focus on which of the Christian truths should be confessed together and which, instead, can be held as *adiaphora* or *theologoumena*, that is, issues where disagreement is allowed while still maintaining communion. The latter model, albeit with significant variants, has been the main method used in ecumenical dialogue so far, promoted by the WCC and its theological commission. The question remains, however, whether or not this approach is satisfactory for the unity we seek.

However, if we consider, for example, intra-Orthodox ecumenical dialogue or that between Orthodox, Old Catholic, and Oriental Orthodox, it becomes evident how this method is problematic. In fact, although in both cases almost complete agreement has been reached concerning which doctrinal points are to be considered essential for unity and which instead could fall under a framework of legitimate diversity in confessional terms, it still has not been possible to reestablish full communion, the desired objective.

This is because the crucial problem that keeps the churches separate is not so much their inability to profess together the same apostolic faith, as many, Orthodox included, have maintained and continue to do, but rather the lack of agreement on how to form a united church visibly and organically at the local level, to use the words of the Nairobi assembly. In terms of the unity of the faith, therefore, the classification of doctrinal points as essential and secondary should never be separated from the question of which ecclesial structure is required for the unity of all Christians, at both a local and a universal level.

In conclusion, it is certainly not my intent to affirm that the confessional aspect of Christian division should take a back seat to ecclesial questions but rather that the ultimate plan of ecumenical unity cannot be one of a diversity of confessions understood as a diversity of churches. The diversity of confessional perspectives or positions, in essence, can only be admitted within a single local church in the form of theological opinions, of *theologoumena*. It is ultimately the community that has to decide what is *adiaphoron* and what is *anagkaion* (necessary) in the confession of faith.

2   The Notion of Local Church and Its Fruits in the Ecumenical Movement

Much discussion has taken place regarding the local church and how it might and should form the original nucleus of a unity of faith and order that could be experienced and replicated by Christians on the universal level. At this point, it is as well to introduce this concept better and to demonstrate its historical development as well as its potential for ecumenism.

First of all, it needs to be said that the catholicity of the local church may seem to many today a challenge to be faced or a project for the future. For the Christians of the patristic period, it was an evident fact. They could not have contemplated a local church that was not catholic. It was Ignatius of Antioch who first used the expression "Catholic Church," and he did so in a Eucharistic context: "You should regard that Eucharist as valid which is celebrated either by the bishop or by someone he authorizes. Where the bishop is present, there let the congregation gather, just as where Jesus Christ is, there is the Catholic Church."[8] Here, catholicity

---

8   Ignatius of Antioch, *Letter to the Smyrneans*, 8 in: Cyril C. Richardson, ed., *Early Christian Fathers*, New York NY, Simon & Schuster, 1996, 112–116, here 115.

defines the "integrity," "fullness," and "totality" of the church as described in the local church's Eucharistic community. Almost all Orthodox theologians insist on this point. According to Georges Florovsky: "The Church is catholic, because it is the one Body of Christ; it is union in Christ."[9]

Orthodox ecclesiology is rooted in the idea that the Eucharist is the place where the church is present in its fullness as the Body of Christ.[10] Catholicity, therefore, is fundamentally a Christological reality. The church is catholic because it is the Body of Christ. Since Christ in his entirety is tied to the church in the Eucharist, the church in its fullness, or catholicity (ἡ καθόλου ἡ καθολικη Ἐκκλησία), is present where the Eucharist and the bishop are present.[11] The tendency to pit the local church against the universal one, therefore, is wrong. In the early church, every local church

> was a concretization and localization of the general ... The local eucharistic assembly understood itself as the revelation of the eschatological unity of all in Christ. This meant that *no mutual exclusion* between the local and the universal was possible in a eucharistic context, but the one was automatically involved in the other.[12]

In this case, the analogy with Trinitarian theology helps explain the relationship between local and universal church. "The faith in 'one' God who is at the same time 'three,' i.e. 'many' implies that unity and diversity coincide in God's very being."[13]

It is essentially thanks to the contribution of Orthodox theology that the concept of church as Eucharistic communion has been taken up by the ecumenical movement, thus making its own contribution to the cause of Christian unity.[14] In the 1960s and 1970s, the ecclesiology of communion between local churches, at times, seemed to become the grounds for a possible meeting between the Roman Catholic Church and large sections of the Protestant world. Indeed, if Vatican II had rediscovered the value of the local church in the universal communion, Protestant theology certainly could not reject an ecclesiological conception that considered each local community a "church" in all respects.

The issue of the *episkopos* is more complicated. It has been previously noted that the ecclesiological requisite for the Eucharist is an assembly, a synaxis (σύναξις), of people in one place. However, for such a meeting to take place, it is necessary

---

9   *The Collected Works of Georges Florovsky*, vol. 1, Georges Florovsky, *Bible, Church, Tradition: An Orthodox View*, Belmont MA, Nordland, 1972, ch. 3, "The Catholicity of the Church," 37–55, here 41, and ch. 4, "The Church: Her Nature and Task," 57–72.

10   John D. Zizioulas, "The Local Church in a Eucharistic Perspective: An Orthodox Contribution," in: *In Each Place: Towards a Fellowship of Local Churches Truly United*, Geneva, WCC Publications, 1977, 50–61.

11   See John D. Zizioulas, *Being as Communion: Studies in Personhood and the Church*, Crestwood NY, St. Vladimir's Seminary Press, 1993, ch. 4, "Eucharist and Catholicity," 143–169, here 157; originally published with the title "Eucharistic Community and the Catholicity of the Church," *OiC* 6, 1970, 314–337, here 329.

12   Zizioulas, "Eucharist and Catholicity," 154–155 (italics original).

13   "The Church is the mystery of the 'One' and the 'Many,' i.e. the realisation of the event of Christ constituted by the Spirit in space and time ... Just as in the Holy Trinity and in Christology the 'many' are as primary ontologically as the 'one,' unity in the Church is inconceivable without multiplicity. The Church is not first one Church and then many Churches. She is one by being many, and many by being one"; John D. Zizioulas, "Uniformity, Diversity, and the Unity of the Church," *IKZ* 91, 2001, 44–59, here 47, 48–49.

14   For the most significant contributions from Orthodox theology on Eucharistic theology, see Georges Florovsky, "The Eucharist and Catholicity," in: Richard S. Haugh, ed., *The Collected Works of Georges Florovsky*, vol. 13, Georges Florovsky, *Ecumenism I: A Doctrinal Approach*, Vaduz, Büchervertriebsanstalt, 1989, 46–57; Nikolai Afanasev, *Trapeza Gospodnja*, Paris, Izdanie Religiozno-Pedagogičeskogo Kabineta pri Pravoslavnom Bogoslovskom Institute v Pariže, 1952, and John D. Zizioulas, "Verité et communion dans la perspective de la pensée patristique grecque," *Irén* 50, 1977, 451–510. In the vein of Eucharistic ecclesiology, see Hervé Legrand, "L'ecclésiologie eucharistique dans le dialogue actuelle entre l'Église catholique et l'Église orthodoxe," *Istina* 51, 2006, 354–374.

for a bishop to be present. The bishop, therefore, can be considered "the ecclesial presupposition *par excellence* of the Eucharist."[15] In this case, the key category of "one and many" clarifies not only the relationship between Christ and the church but also the reality of the communion between the bishop and the community. Just as Christ (one) cannot be conceived of without the church (many), neither can the bishop (one) be conceived of without his community (many). As far as the local church is concerned, communion, the intimate relationship between one and many, is ontologically constitutive.

Consequently, the local bishop's fundamental function with regard to his community is to express in himself the "multitude" of the faithful who constitute the church entrusted to his care. He is the only one "through whose hands the whole community would have to pass in its being offered up to God in Christ, i.e., in the highest moment of the Church's unity."[16] In essence, the figure of the bishop sums up in himself the entire multiplicity of his people, and it is in the relationship of interdependence with the Eucharistic community that episcopal authority finds its basis, since the "one" (the bishop) cannot exist without the "many" (the community) and neither can the "many" exist without the "one." Bishop and community exist and cooperate in solidarity in order to bring the church into being.

How, then, can such a perspective be reconciled with the Eucharistic community's subdivision into orders, that is, into categories and classes of people? History shows us that we are faced with a real problem here because the divisions, often formed on this very basis, run so deep that the church still suffers from them.[17]

In order to find a possible solution to this problem, it is necessary to start from a given fact, which is that it is not possible to conceive of any type of ministry that might exist in parallel to that of Christ, the founder of the church, of the ministry that it carries out, and of every charism that arises from it. As the Body of Christ, in fact, the church exists only as a manifestation of the ministry instituted directly by Christ in the world and in history. Moreover, it is no coincidence that the early church attributed all the existing forms of ministry to Christ.[18] Understood Christologically, therefore, ministry transcends all the categories of precedence and separation that might be created in history by the act of ordination and election.

What applies to the bishop is also valid for any other person called upon to carry out a task in the church; this means that no ministry can be conceived of outside the context of the community. There is no room for interpreting it in terms of representation or delegation of authority because such terms, due to their fundamentally juridical nature, ultimately lead to a separation between the ordained person and the community. Acting in the name of the community means being outside it because it means acting in its stead.[19] Hence, what is rejected by the communal dimension highlighted here is the possibility of exercising a ministry outside, or above, the community.

Affirming that the ministry belongs to the community ultimately means ruling out that there is a division between "ontology" and "function" in ordination. The question of whether ordination confers something indelible on the ordained person, something that constitutes their individual

---

15   John D. Zizioulas, "The Ecclesiological Presuppositions of the Holy Eucharist," *Nicolaus* 10, 1982, 333–349, here 345.

16   Zizioulas, "Eucharist and Catholicity," 153.

17   Think of the issues of clericalism and anticlericalism that have been a real problem, especially in the West. The East, having maintained for centuries a Eucharistic ecclesiology, did not have this problem. Only recently,

following the replacement of this perspective with later ecclesiological theories, has this problem emerged in a serious way in some Orthodox countries.

18   He was the apostle (see Heb 3:1), the teacher (see Matt 23:8, John 13:13), the priest (see Heb 2:17, 5:6, and 10:21), the bishop (see 1 Pet 2:25, 5:4) and the deacon (see Rom 15:8, Luke 22:27, and Phil 2:7).

19   In this sense, terms like "vicar," applied to the episcopate or ministry in general, may suggest the idea of someone who is "outside" or "in the place of" an absentee.

possession (either permanently or temporarily), or whether it simply gives them the authority to act toward a certain end, has been discussed at length.[20] In light of the Eucharistic community, that dilemma loses all meaning and leads to a dead end since the reference points of such a perspective are essentially existential in nature. There is no charism that can be possessed individually and, consequently, there is no charism that can be conceived of or exercised by individuals alone. Outside this existential bond with the community, the ministry is destined to die, just as the Spirit that once donated this charism and continually sustains it cannot dwell outside that community, for it is the bond of love. It is in this sense that the Spirit is possessed exclusively by the church[21] and that every ministry is a gift of the Spirit.

All this implies surpassing the divisions created by the variety of ministries and the dimension of a distinction of orders in the church. The bishop's exclusive right to confer ordination should be seen in this context. Should he have such a right, it is thanks to his status as head of the community (from which it follows that he cannot ordain outside that community) and in relation to his role as

the "one" who offers the entire community to God in the Eucharist, as stated above.

The implications of such a conception of the ministry, in particular of the episcopate, are clear for the understanding of apostolic succession. Speaking of apostolic succession as a concatenation of episcopal ordinations dating back to the apostolic period, without the indispensable prerequisite of their link with the community in the Eucharistic assembly in which they were celebrated, would be to absolutize the ministry.[22] If it is not purely by chance that the early church never saw an episcopal ordination outside the Eucharistic context, or without the specific mention of the place to which the bishop would be bound, we must conclude that there is no apostolic succession that does not pass through the concrete community.

Affirming that apostolic succession passes through a concrete community gathered around the bishop frees us from enslavement to the idea of historicity and places the entire question within the broader context of the church in history. It would be impossible and irrelevant to discuss here the problems associated with the emergence of the idea of apostolic succession tied to the attempts to reconstruct episcopal lists, which means that, from the 2nd to the 3rd century, the concern

---

20   This refers to a problem (of ordination and the status that it confers on the minister) that was discussed at length by Faith and Order in the late 1960s, as lines of agreement on the issue of the ministry emerged. Reference here is made in particular to the preparatory study, "The Meaning of Ordination: A Study Paper of the Faith and Order Commission," *Study Encounter* 4/4, 1968, 166–189, and the document, "The Ordained Ministry in Ecumenical Perspective," *Study Encounter* 8/4, 1972, 1–22, which formed the basis for the chapter on ministry in the Accra Document of 1974: *One Baptism, One Eucharist, and a Mutually Recognized Ministry: Three Agreed Statements*, Geneva, WCC Publications, 1975, and then for the BEM: *Baptist, Eucharist and Ministry*, Geneva, WCC Publications, 1982.

21   See, for example, Cyprian of Carthage, *Epistle* 69.11; 75.14. In this perspective, the *extra ecclesiam nulla salus* is something more than a negative statement. The fundamental truth contained in such an affirmation is the impossibility of an individualistic conception of salvation: *Unus christianus, nullus christianus.*

22   It is hard to deny the importance of the contribution made by Edmund Schlink, a Lutheran theologian from Heidelberg, to the development of the theme of apostolic succession from an ecumenical perspective. Starting from the panorama of divergent conceptions of apostolic succession and measuring the theological value of each of them, Schlink came to the conclusion that, in dogmatic terms, apostolic succession should be considered in relation to the apostolicity of the church, identifying both the church as a whole and its ministers as successors of the apostles. See Edmund Schlink, "Die apostolische Sukzession," *KD* 7, 1961, 79–114. From the World Conference in Montreal of 1963 onwards, this definition of apostolic succession offered by Schlink has formed the backbone of many ecumenical documents on the ministry drawn up by Faith and Order (of which Schlink had been a member since the 1950s), and of BEM, which was published in 1982.

was ensuring the survival of orthodox teaching by means of a strictly historical reconstruction. However, whatever the case, the fact that the lists of succession were exclusively episcopal shows that the underlying idea was broader than the concern for the survival of orthodoxy or, in other words, that the concern for the survival of orthodoxy was not isolated from the wider reality of the life of the church as a community with the bishop as its guide. Bishops, as successors of the apostles, were not guardians of ideas like the masters of philosophical schools,[23] nor doctors like the presbyters, but leaders of communities whose life and thoughts were expected to express themselves in the exercise of their duty.[24]

Their apostolic succession, therefore, should be seen neither as an uninterrupted chain of ordinations nor as a transmission of truth, but rather as a sign and an expression of the continuity of the church's historical life as a whole in the way it has unfolded in each community. Apostolic succession thus represents a sign of the historical dimension of the church's catholicity. It serves to unite the historical dimension with the charismatic one and transcend the divisions caused by time. In an understanding of apostolic succession rooted in the Eucharistic community, in which past and future are perceived through the Holy Spirit in the one reality of the present,[25] history and time are assumed in their fullness, and eternal life does not oppose them but penetrates and transcends them to the extent that they have a role in the destiny and salvation of the human person. The church thus manifests itself in time to be what it is eschatologically, that is to say, a catholic church that is present in history as a transcendence of all division in the unity of all in Christ.

These ideas have found discrete resonance in the ecumenical movement, thanks especially to the work of the Dombes Group, the Catholic-Protestant interdenominational group founded in 1937 by Abbé Paul Couturier. Since the late 1950s, it has been charged with developing significant texts of agreement on issues of ministry, to which the Faith and Order commission will long be indebted in the years to come.[26] By way of example, in 1959, they published one of the first series of theses on pastoral authority in the church. In it, the theologians of Dombes reaffirmed the close interdependence between the minister invested with authority and the Christian people, with the aim of converging toward a kind of "Christocracy" that would counteract extreme understandings. It is assumed that these are, on the one hand, the Catholic temptation towards an authoritarian and top-down theory in the conception of ecclesial life and, on the other, an almost "democratic" interpretation of the synodal-presbyterian system on the part of the Protestant Churches that adopted it as a structure of governance.[27]

Regarding the episcopal ministry, toward the end of the 1960s, both in theology more sensitive

23 See, for example, Pseudo-Hippolytus, *Refutation of All Heresies (Élenchos)*, 9.12.

24 On this matter, see in particular my contribution "Episkopé and Episkopos in the Early Church: A Brief Survey of the Evidence," in the short collection of the contributions to a day of study organized by Faith and Order in Chambésy in February of 1979: *Episkopé and Episcopate in Ecumenical Perspective*, Geneva, WCC Publications, 1980, 30–42.

25 "Remembering, therefore, this saving commandment and all that has been done for our sake: the Cross, the tomb, the Resurrection on the third day, the Ascension into heaven, the enthronement at the right hand, and the second and glorious coming again: Your own of Your own we offer to You, in all and for all"; *The Divine Liturgy of Saint John Chrysostom*, <www.goarch

.org/-/the-divine-liturgy-of-saint-john-chrysostom> (accessed June 5, 2020).

26 On Couturier and the foundation of the Dombes Group, see Étienne Fouilloux's contribution in the second volume of this work. On the contribution that the group has made in theology to the progress of ecumenical dialogue from the mid-20th century to the present, see Catherine E. Clifford's contribution in the same volume.

27 "L'Autorité pastorale dans l'Église," in: Dombes Group, *Pour la communion des Églises: L'Apport du Groupe des Dombes (1937–1987)*, Paris, Le Centurion, 1988, 16–18.

to ecumenical concerns and in the discussions promoted by Faith and Order, the need was felt to start from the episcopal function existing concretely in all the churches in order to overcome the dead end resulting from concentrating on the normative character of the episcopal-presbyteral-diaconate triad. The decisive leap, therefore, was made by extracting the concept of *episkopé*, as a distinct function, from the concrete forms of its denomination and the subjects exercising it. Up to that moment, in fact, there had simply been talk of the "episcopate" or of the "bishop" without being able to escape the temptation of speaking of the superiority, or lack thereof, of the episcopate in regard to the other ministries.

The emphasis placed on function, regardless of name (even if, in fact, it was decided to maintain the word *episkopé*, given that an indicative term was still necessary), has opened the way to an alternative path toward achieving an ecumenical understanding of the figure and ministerial exercise of the bishop. For example, it was possible to point out that the *episkopé* has, in fact, always existed, at least in a certain way, even in those churches without an episcopate, and to urge churches endowed with an episcopal structure to improve the expression of this function by better harmonizing the two ways of exercising it, that is, the "personalized" and the "collegial" ways, rather than highlighting one to the detriment of the other.

For some time, Orthodox and Catholics have made such a conception of the episcopal ministry a point of encounter, particularly after Vatican II recognized the plurality of charisms operating within the church, reequilibrating the internal polarity between hierarchy and community, and finally placing Christ at the origin of the bishops' apostolic mandate. On the other hand, there was great resistance on the part of the Protestant world, although many Reformed churches, beginning with the Presbyterian ones, spoke out in favor of the way in which the BEM urged churches to become aware of the historical evolution of ecclesiastical structures and, on that basis, to arrive at a new understanding of the different functions and denominations assumed by the ministries in the various churches and denominations.[28]

The question seems to have run aground at this precise point and does not, for the moment, seem to promise positive developments in the short term. This means that Catholics and Orthodox still have much to do in order to purify definitively the concept of *episkopos* of all those accretions that are still unacceptable on the part of the Protestants, starting with the monarchical conception of its nature, so that the original figure of the bishop as the ordinary minister of the Eucharist may be reestablished, a symbol of unity *par excellence*, which Protestants may rediscover and Catholics and Orthodox may recover under centuries of institutional stratification.[29]

---

28   *Baptist, Eucharist and Ministry*; par. 19–25 of the chapter on ministry (pp. 24–26 of the English edition) are dedicated to the description of the historical evolution of ministries according to the principle that the New Testament does not actually contain any normative description of the ministry valid for every Christian era. In the final commentary on this part of the text (p. 26), the Lima Document thus urges churches to ask themselves how much of the very essence of ministry has been preserved from abuse and historical stratification. The responses of the churches to BEM are collected in Max Thurian, ed., *Churches Respond to BEM: Official Responses to the "Baptism, Eucharist and Ministry" Text*, 6 vols., Geneva, WCC Publications, 1986–1988. For a historical analysis of the editing process and the reception of BEM, see Luca Ferracci *Battesimo Eucaristia Ministero: Genesi e destino di un documento ecumenico*, Bologna, Il Mulino, 2021.

29   I have dedicated many pages to the relation between the bishop and the ecclesial community, both in my *L'Eucharistie, l'évêque et l'Église Durant les trois premiers siècles*, Desclée de Bouwer, Paris, 1994, and in *Being as Communion: Studies in Personhood and the Church*, Crestwood NY, St. Vladimir's Seminary Press, 1985, evaluating both the Catholic and the Protestant conceptions. In 1993, Faith and Order held an important meeting on the concept of *koinonia*, and on that occasion I had the opportunity to introduce the work with an address entitled "The Church as Communion," which received the unanimous applause of the other delegates. I could thus see how there was great agreement on the idea that ecclesial ministries are "relational" and not juridical, and that they should be included in the church as a communion enlivened by the Spirit.

The main path to unity, or at least the one capable of ensuring some concrete progress in ecumenical dialogue, passes through reform, that is, through a profound rethinking of the ecclesiological patterns that have crystallized in the course of time. Protestants have every right to exhort Catholics and Orthodox to continue along this route with greater commitment and conviction. For a long time and in many quarters, in fact, it has been affirmed that the church is in constant need of reform. We now know, however, that this reform can only take place on the basis of an apparently simple concept, which at the same time is rich in implications, including ecumenical ones, for the life of our communities: the church is, in its essence, a communion. Accordingly, this leads us to questions of Christian eschatology, since there can be no *eschaton* without communion in Christ, who is the supreme root of all eschatology. It is communion with Christ, in fact, which holds together, in faith, the present and the future of humanity, in the sense that communion with the Risen One is a real but open communion. It is a communion already present but not yet accomplished, as is the unity of the church, which is the image and anticipation of the kingdom.

3   The Recovery of an Eschatological View of Christian Unity and the Challenges of Hermeneutics

The topic of eschatology has become central to the theology of our times and has indeed been a typical trait of Christian theology since the beginning of the 20th century. It was in about 1900 that the German theologian and biblical scholar Johannes Weiss published his revolutionary work *Die Predigt Jesu vom Reiche Gottes*[30] in which he affirmed that the essence of Christ's preaching, and, by extension, the essence of Christianity itself, was not to be found in Jesus's ethical teaching, as liberal Protestant theologians of the 19th century (Adolf von Harnack and Paul Sabatier, among others) thought. Rather, it lay in the proclamation of the coming of the Kingdom of God. As Weiss pointed out, Christ and the first Christians awaited the imminent arrival of the last days and the Kingdom of God, and that expectation ended up marking all the faiths, starting from their relationship to the world. St. Paul, as Albert Schweitzer expressly emphasized 20 years after Weiss, shared this same eschatological expectation, reflected as much in his thinking as in his frenetic missionary activity. In fact, it was not uncommon for Paul to advise Christians not to marry if they could avoid it, given that the time before the Parousia was, so to speak, "condensed." The concern with which he hastened to take the Gospel to many hitherto unknown corners of the world testifies to his conviction that the Lord's return was imminent.[31]

The Sermon on the Mount, which according to liberal theologians prior to Weiss contained the moral principles through which humanity could bring about the Kingdom of God in history, in the eyes of this new generation of theologians ceased to be a mere code of conduct and became the description of the new world that God had foretold by sending his only begotten Son.

See John D. Zizioulas, "The Church as Communion: A Presentation on the World Conference Theme," in: Thomas F. Best & Günther Gassmann, eds., *On the Way to Fuller Koinonia: Official Report of the Fifth World Conference on Faith and Order, Santiago di Compostela, August 1993*, Geneva, WCC Publications, 1994, 103–111.

30   The writings of Johannes Weiss should be seen as the starting point for this "rediscovery"; see his *Die Predigt Jesu vom Reiche Gottes*, Göttingen, Vandenhoeck & Ruprecht, 1892. In some sense, however, the forerunner of this new sensitivity had already appeared: Franz Overbeck, *Über die Christlichkeit unserer heutigen Theologie*, Leipzig, E.W. Fritzsch, 1873. Overbeck influenced both Albert Schweitzer, in his *Vom Reimarus zu Wrede: Eine Geschichte der Leben-Jesu-Forschung*, Tübingen, J.C.B. Mohr (Paul Siebeck), 1906, as well as the young Karl Barth. See Sigurd Hjelde, *Das Eschaton und die Eschata: Eine Studie über Sprachgebrauch und Sprachverwirrung in protestantischer Theologie von der Orthodoxie bis zur Gegenwart*, Munich, Kaiser, 1987.

31   Schweitzer, *Vom Reimarus zu Wrede*.

It is, therefore, difficult not to believe, along with Weiss and Schweitzer, that this eschatological orientation dominated the New Testament Church, at least in its early days. If, in the 1930s, Charles Harold Dodd[32] still insisted on the concept of a "realized eschatology," according to which the Kingdom of Christ had already arrived with the coming of the Savior, others such as Oscar Cullmann spoke more cautiously of "already and not yet," arguing, on the contrary, that there was a strong projection towards the future in the life of the early Christians. Hardly anyone since Weiss has ever doubted that eschatology, that is, the expectation of the kingdom, lies at the very heart of the Gospel and that Christianity, faithful to its Jewish origins, turned toward the *eschaton* from its outset.

While this theory may be applied easily to the first apostolic communities, it remains undeniable that, with the passage of time and the need for the church to come to terms with the delay of the Parousia, things have changed considerably, and it is precisely these changes, which mainly occurred during the first four centuries of Christian history, that interest us directly here, since they have left a decisive mark on our churches.

Once the church gradually reconciled itself with the delayed arrival of the Parousia, considered imminent by the early Christians, it became inevitable for it to concentrate its efforts on finding ways of adapting to history. All this has led to the radical rethinking on the part of the church of the very concept of eschatology. In the West in particular, and especially during the Middle Ages, a tendency to reassign the place assigned to the expectation of the last days in the life of Christians has developed, and the Reformation, for its part, did nothing to overturn that tendency. Eschatology, therefore, has become a kind of final chapter of

dogmatics, one dealing with the "last things" such as life after death and the end of the world. The church has thus ceased to have an ontological relationship with the kingdom and has instead begun to understand itself as a historical entity living between the Christ event and the coming kingdom. The direct, and in some ways more serious, consequence of this historicization of the church has been the tendency to compete with secular power and to influence, as far as possible, world affairs.[33] This has led to numerous conflicts between the church and secular authorities, at the height of which the Reformation proclaimed the separation of the two spheres, that of church and that of state, on the basis of Augustine's "two cities." Again, eschatology played no role. Protestantism, in fact, has taken the role of the church to be a moral and spiritual force in the world, whose purpose is to impose its moral values on society, both in regard to the spirituality of its members, and by making use of the state's power, while also leaving the latter to pursue its own objectives as though they were the expression of God's will, based on a literal interpretation of Romans 13.

The WCC, which is basically a Protestant institution in its ecclesiological orientation, seems to have conceived of its role as that of a secular force attempting to influence political decisions and events without an overall conception of what the church is, precisely because it lacks an eschatological understanding of its nature. This may be one of the reasons that eschatology, despite its rediscovery by 20th century theology, has so far only been a marginal theme in the ecumenical movement, particularly in the dialogue promoted by

---

32   In 1935, Dodd published *The Parables of the Kingdom*, London, Nisbet, 1935, and, a year later, *The Apostolic Preaching and its Development: With an Appendix on Eschatology and History*, London, Hodder & Stoughton, 1936.

33   See Werner Verbeke, Daniel Verhelst & Andries Welkenhuysen, eds., *The Use and Abuse of Eschatology in the Middle Ages*, Leuven, Leuven University Press, 1988; Ovidio Capitani & Jürgen Miethke, eds., *L'attesa della fine dei tempi nel medioevo*, Bologna, Il Mulino, 1990; Giuseppe Ruggieri, ed., *La cattura della fine: Variazioni dell'escatologia in regime di cristianità*, Genoa, Marietti, 1992.

the WCC American Board of Commissioners for Foreign Missions.[34]

Today it seems, rather, that it is up to hermeneutics to set the ecumenical process in motion again, providing theology with the horizon within which to try to understand and solve many of the questions that still divide the churches on matters of Christian doctrine and tradition. This evaluation must be clarified and deepened.

It is now well-known and agreed that hermeneutics can be considered a kind of common language, not only for philosophy, but also theology and Christian history. The universalization of the hermeneutical problem implies two fundamental understandings, namely, that there is a plurality of hermeneutical processes that vary according to the contexts in which they are formulated, and that the act of interpretation is always characterized by a "receptive" disposition towards what is to be interpreted, by an openness of the subject to the object, by dialogue that implies mutual change.[35] This permitting oneself to become involved in the encounter with the other, even leading to one's own transformation, is probably the greatest contribution that hermeneutics can make to ecumenical dialogue in order for it to be authentic and bring lasting fruit to the churches.

Adopting a hermeneutical perspective can, in fact, cure the theologies of the churches of those doctrinal fixations that prevent us from grasping the hermeneutical structuring in the history of Christian truth. As such, this implies that the churches, renouncing a defensive attitude towards their own doctrinal heritage, express a conception

of ecclesial identity in essentially relational terms, both in an individualistic and collective sense, and that they accept the partiality that constitutes their own particular identity. Christian communities would thus open themselves up to the possibility of discovering the fruitfulness of Christian division, which can be expressed in the possibility of carrying out a common search for unity starting from the perception that each tradition has its own limits and, above all, a recognition of those of other traditions. The different churches can help one another fraternally both to identify what is transient or secondary and to grasp more fully than each one can do on its own what is essential to the faith and what must be valued by all, so that nothing is lost of what has been manifested of God's greatness (see Acts 2:7–11) in each great Christian experience.

4 Potentials and Pitfalls of the Principle of *Oikonomia*

The problem of hermeneutics leads us to address more closely the so-called principle of *oikonomia*, generally considered to be one of Orthodox theology's main contributions to ecumenical dialogue.[36] In the Orthodox tradition, the theme

---

34   Perhaps the following three-author publication is an exception to this picture: John D. Zizioulas, Jean-Marie Roger Tillard & Jean-Jacques von Allmen, eds., *L'eucharistie*, Paris, Mame, 1970.

35   Hans-Georg Gadamer, *Gesammelte Werke*, vol. 1, *Hermeneutik I: Wahrheit und Methode: Grundzüge einer philosophischen Hermeneutik*, Tübingen, Mohr Siebeck, [7]2010. A decisive contribution to a pluralistic understanding of hermeneutics can certainly be acknowledged in Paul Ricœur's work, *Le Conflit des interprétations: Essais d'herméneutique*, Paris, Éditions du Seuil, 1969.

36   Yves Congar, "Propos en vue d'une théologie de l'économie dans la tradition latine," *Irén* 45, 1972, 155–206. Beginning with the classic monograph by Hamilcar Alivisatos, *Ī oikonomia kata to Kanonikon Dikaion tīs Orthodoxou Ekklīsias* [Oikonomia in the Canon Law of the Orthodox Church], Athens, Astīr, 1949 (see also its German translation: *Die Oikonomia: Die Oikonomia nache dem kanonischen Recht der Orthodoxen Kirche*, Frankfurt a.M., Lembeck 199), there has been much attention dedicated to the theological and canonical concept of *oikonomia*, even in recent years: Will Adam, *Legal Flexibility and the Mission of the Church: Dispensation and Economy in Ecclesiastical Law*, Farnham, Ashgate, 2011; Gerhard Richter, *Oikonomia: Der Gebrauch des Wortes Oikonomia im Neuen Testament, bei den Kirchenvätern und in der theologischen Literatur bis ins 20. Jahrhundert*, Berlin, De Gruyter, 2005; Florian Schuppe, *Die pastorale Herausforderung – Orthodoxes Leben zwischen Akribeia und Oikonomia: Theologische*

of ecclesiastical *oikonomia* is intimately connected with the problem of the interpretation and observance of the canons. It is a very important subject, but also one of considerable complexity whose understanding requires considerations of a juridical, theological, and historical nature. What can be said here is that,

> in general ecclesiastical usage οἰκονομία is a term of very many meanings. In its broadest sense "economy" embraces and signifies the whole work of salvation (cf. *Colossians* 1:25; *Ephesians* 1:10; 3, 2, 9). The Vulgate usually translates it by *dispensatio*. In canonical language "economy" has not become a technical term. It is rather a descriptive word, a kind of general characteristic; οἰκονομία is opposed to ἀκρίβεια as a kind of relaxation of church discipline, an exemption or exception from the "strict rule" (*ius strictum*) or from the general rule.[37]

The value of the concept of ecclesiastical economy, however, is instead measured on a pastoral level. As Florovsky continues, in fact: "'Economy' can be and should be employed by each individual pastor in his parish, still more by a bishop or council of bishops. For 'economy' is pastorship and pastorship is 'economy.'"[38] Indeed, every *oikonomia* can be considered the application of an extreme interpretation to a concrete case, that is, when, whatever the interpretation of the canon, its literal execution is suspended, and the pastor seeks a way in that circumstance that is more in favor of the

salvation of the people concerned. However, the boundary between legitimate flexibility and the illegitimate transgression of the canons has never been clearly defined. The history of the Byzantine Church is studded with disputes between supporters of *oikonomia* and those of *akribeia*, especially over questions of marriages, the acceptance of irregularly ordained clergy, and, in the late Middle Ages, relations with the Latin West.

In the second half of the 19th century, the concept of *oikonomia* was very popular in Orthodox theology, particularly Greek theology, but it created several problems when attempts were made to ensure that it might be applied in practice within the area of ecumenism. Florovsky, for example, believed that even if a baptism or ordination by a Protestant Church were recognized as valid *kat'oikonomian*, that is by virtue of the principle of *oikonomia*, it would still be necessary for the two churches to recognize one another as sacramental realities in order to avoid everything remaining on a purely formal level. Florovsky indeed believed it more useful to insist on the distinction between ecclesial and canonical boundaries, stressing the concept that the former were more extensive than the latter, as taught by Vatican II magisterium itself, which recognized elements of ecclesial reality even outside the boundaries of the Roman Catholic Church.

Florovsky was inspired by St. Augustine when he maintained that, even when two churches separated owing to a schism, an indissoluble and perpetual bond of love continues to keep them together and, by virtue of that bond, the sacraments and ecclesiastical ordinances of the one continue to apply to the other. Unfortunately, the numerous asymmetries still existing among the churches on questions of ecclesiology prevent churches from holding a dialogue based on a single, shared hierarchy of fundamental articles or truths, to use Catholic terminology. In the present state of ecumenical dialogue and agreements, an incautious use of the principle of *oikonomia* would run the risk of leading the churches astray or of producing

---

Grundlagen, Praxis und ökumenische Perspektiven, Würzburg, Augustinus-Verlag, 2006.

37 Georges Florovsky, "The Boundaries of the Church," in: Haugh, ed., *The Collected Works*, vol. 13, 36–45, here 38. The concepts expressed in this essay, originally published in *CQR* 47, 1933, 117–131, were proposed again in similar form seventeen years later in: Georges Florovsky, "The Doctrine of the Church and the Ecumenical Problem," *EcRev* 2/3, 1950, 152–161.

38 Florovsky, "The Boundaries," 38.

results that are only a distant and fragile echo of the unity that Christians have been striving to achieve for a century.

5 Primacy in the Church: A Historical and Theological Approach

The issue of primacy is at the very heart of Catholic-Orthodox relations. Historically, it was the problem that led to the gradual estrangement and then separation between East and West, ratified by the Great Schism of 1054. The same theme also lies at the root of the division between Rome and the Reformation churches, even if the theological divergences that led to the birth of Protestantism were much wider in nature. Truly, the same can also be said for Catholic-Orthodox relations, where other theological questions soon took over, the principle one being that of the *Filioque*,[39] but pontifical primacy remains the most important and most difficult problem to solve.

There are two ways of approaching the matter. The first is the historical method, which was widely used in the past without, however, achieving the desired results. This method presupposes the existence *ab origine* of Peter's primacy in the apostolic college, which is accepted even by many Protestant biblical scholars, including Oscar Cullmann.[40] Yet despite this, it remains difficult to recognize any biblical foundation to the connection between the Petrine ministry and that of the bishop of Rome. Moreover, while accepting that the apostle Peter suffered his martyrdom and was buried in Rome, it would be difficult to prove the existence of any connection between his primacy and that of the pope based solely on that fact, however obvious and commonly accepted it may be. Apart from Peter, the apostle Paul also died in Rome, as did many other martyrs of the church, but no Roman pontiff has ever made claims on the basis of those facts. As can be seen from the controversy in the 2nd century concerning the celebration of Easter, several churches in Asia Minor boasted the honor of hosting the tombs and relics of the apostles in their regions, but none of them have ever attempted to exploit this circumstance to claim the apostolic succession of their sees. As Francis Dvornik has shown, it was only in medieval times that the use of this argument became widespread in the individual churches in order to demonstrate and defend their own apostolicity, using mostly spurious testimonies, as has recently been proven by research into the sources.[41] This approach has proved to be essentially inconclusive in the theological debate and is really of little use in the context of ecumenical discussions of primacy.

Besides this, there is also the theological method, which has been adopted in the official dialogue between the Roman Catholic and Orthodox Churches, and which can instead lead to concrete results. This approach focuses on ecclesiology, with all its questions concerning the problem of the nature of the church. In order to bear fruit on an ecumenical level, however, ecclesiology must not be approached in a sterile way, as if it were an isolated object of dogmatics, but rather as part of a broader Christian doctrine, in a harmony integrated with

---

39 Ecumenical dialogue has made significant progress on the issue of the *Filioque*. On the matter, I here refer to the document: Pontifical Council for Promoting Christian Unity, ed., *Les traditions grecque et latine concernant la procession du Saint-Esprit*, Vatican City, Tipografia Poliglotta Vaticana, 1996. Originally published in French and Italian in *L'Osservatore Romano* on Sept 13, 1995, this small booklet was later translated and republished in Greek, English, and Russian.

40 See, Oscar Cullmann, *Petrus: Jünger, Apostel, Märtyrer: Das historische und das theologische Petrusproblem*, Zürich, Zwingli Verlag, 1952.

41 Francis Dvornik, *The Idea of Apostolicity in Byzantium and the Legend of the Apostle Andrew*, Cambridge MA, Harvard University Press, 1958. As far as the Petrine primacy of the See of Rome is concerned, it was formulated and applied as early as late antiquity, as testified by a study of the orations of popes Leo and Gregory the Great. On this matter, see George E. Demacopoulos, *The Invention of Peter: Apostolic Discourse and Papal Authority in Late Antiquity*, Philadelphia PA, University of Pennsylvania Press, 2013.

the study of the Trinity, Christology, and pneumatology. Let us begin with the latter. If the church is "the church of God," we must ask ourselves "what kind of God" the church is of. Only in this way can the biblical expressions "Body of Christ" and "temple of the Spirit" be fully understood, since pneumatology conditions Christology on a fundamental level. Indeed, pneumatology is far more than a condition of Christology. It is linked to the latter in a relationship of simultaneity and, precisely for that reason, becomes an ontological category of ecclesiology. In other words, the understanding of the church as the Body of Christ is not possible without that of eschatological communion as the work of the Holy Spirit.

If, ultimately, the church is revealed in its fullness in the sacrament of the Holy Eucharist, we cannot imagine its structures and ministries without taking into account the very essence of the Eucharist. All these considerations are the fundamental prerequisite for a correct theological approach to the question of primacy.

Similarly, Trinitarian theology also provides a fundamental principle for the affirmation and foundation of every type of primacy in the church. In fact, it places the ministry of the "one" and the "many" in a close and simultaneous relationship. The Holy Trinity, in which the oneness of the divine substance and the plurality of the persons are simultaneous, containing and expressing each other, is a norm for the nature of the church as communion. The church is conceived as a communion of people and local communities in the image of the Holy Trinity. A primatial ministry is therefore necessary in the church, since it is an icon of Trinitarian communion. Just as the persons of the Trinity find the principle of their unity in the person of the Father and believers of a local church in the person of the bishop, so the universal communion of local churches must possess a ministry of unity that expresses the oneness of the church. Primacy, therefore, derives as a necessary consequence from the concept of the universal unity of the church and the catholicity of the local churches. The local and universal dimensions of

the church, in fact, are not in opposition to each other but stand in a very close relationship. The local churches cannot isolate themselves in their self-sufficiency but are inserted into an organic and structural communion.

Without any shadow of doubt, it can be said that by perceiving the question of primacy as essentially a mystery of ecclesial communion, it can be transformed from a problem that divides the church into a common article of faith. In this way, primacy does not represent a purely functional or occasional reality but has a profound theological and ecclesial significance, first and foremost in expressing the will of God. Only a primacy of relationship, which depends upon and expresses the church as communion, does not lead to a self-justifying authority.

6   The Primacy of Love for a True *Koinonia* of Local Churches

Until the 1960s, the arguments raised by Orthodox theologians against the primacy of Rome centered, more or less, on the reasoning that the church is, by its nature, "democratic," which, in terms of canonical constitution, means that it is conciliar. There can, therefore, be no authority assigned to an individual that could be superior to that of the conciliar synod. Therefore, there is no universal primacy other than that of the ecumenical council.

After Vatican II in the 1960s, all ecclesiological debate started to move in another direction. The question that had already dominated the discussion during the long period that paved the way for the council, thanks to leading figures such as Yves Marie-Joseph Congar, Karl Rahner, Joseph Ratzinger, and Henri-Marie de Lubac, concerned the fullness of the church, its catholicity, and how that coincided with its universal structure. The challenge had come from Orthodox theology, especially from the so-called Eucharistic ecclesiology of the Russian theologian Nikolai Afanasev, who had proposed the axiom "wherever the Eucharist is, there is the church."[42] This meant that each local church where the Eucharist is celebrated must be considered a church in the full and catholic sense. Roman Catholic theologians who influenced Vatican II took Afanasev's challenge seriously, and it was thanks to them that a theology of the local church became part of the council's decisions, initiating a considerable number of studies on the subject.[43]

The shift in ecclesiological debate has had significant repercussions for the question of primacy. If each local church is a catholic church, is it still necessary to talk about universal primacy or even a universal church? On the Orthodox side, the debate was continued first by Russian émigré theologians living in Paris and then in the United States.[44] Four of these theologians, Nikolai Afanasev, John Meyendorff, Alexander Schmemann, and Nicholas Koulomzine joint authored a volume entitled *La Primauté de Pierre dans l'Église orthodoxe*,[45] in which the debate on primacy was placed within the context of the debate that arose around Vatican II. It is interesting to note that there is a considerable divergence among the different positions of the four.

Afanasev insisted that a universal ecclesiology was unknown to the early church before St. Cyprian, and that the idea of primacy was a juridical notion capable of contradicting the evangelical idea of grace. In this he echoed Aleksey Khomyakov and to some extent also liberal Protestant theologians (Rudolph Sohm, Paul Sabatier, etc.). Afanasev did not like the term primacy and therefore proposed instead that of "priority." If every church is catholic, then the only form of primacy on a universal level that could satisfy Afanasev was that of the "church that presides in love," as Ignatius said in his letter to the Church of Rome.

Now, the difference between primacy and priority remains ambiguous. Why should priority necessarily signify grace and primacy, instead, legalism? Yet the heart of this question, the true problem created by Afanasev's position, is another, namely, the danger of opening a path to an isolationist ecclesiology that leads local churches to perceive themselves as self-sufficient and independent in relation to their sister churches. Nicolas Lossky[46] was among the first to observe a causal link between a certain form of "autocephaly" and the refusal of many Orthodox Churches to admit the importance of Orthodox unity on a universal level, although this should not be considered a direct consequence of Afanasev's thought. The fact that many of these very same churches are marked by a particularly pronounced nationalism, continues Lossky, is further proof that such positions regarding autocephaly may easily lead to the infiltration of nationalist sentiments into Orthodoxy.[47]

Afanasev's thoughts on primacy do not seem to be entirely shared by other Russian diaspora theologians. Florovsky, Meyendorff, and Schmenmann all demonstrated a different approach to the problem. Schmemann, for example, in the abovementioned volume on Petrine primacy, concluded that the definitive and highest form of primacy was "universal primacy." He wrote:

---

42   Nicolas Afanassieff "Le sacrement de l'assemblée," *IKZ* 46, 1956, 200–213, here 205.

43   In particular, see Emmanuel Lanne, "The Local Church: Its Catholicity and Apostolicity," *OiC* 3, 1970, 288–313, and especially the following works by Jean-Marie Roger Tillard, "What is the Church of God?" *Mid-Stream* 23, 1984, 28–40; *Eglise d'Eglises: L'ecclesiologie de communion*, Paris, Cerf, 1987; "L'universel et le local: Reflexion sur Église universelle et Églises locales," *Irén* 60, 1987, 483–494.

44   For a history of Russian emigration to France and its contribution to the debate on the unity of the church, see Adalberto Mainardi's contribution in the second volume of this work.

45   Nikolai Afanas'ev & others, *La Primauté de Pierre dans l'Église orthodoxe*, Neuchâtel, Delachaux & Niestlé, 1960; ET: *The Primacy of Peter in the Orthodox Church*, London, Faith Press, 1963.

46   Nicolas Lossky, "Conciliarity – Primacy in a Russian Orthodox Perspective," in: James F. Puglisi, ed., *Petrine Ministry and the Unity of the Church: Toward a Patient and Fraternal Dialogue*, Collegeville MN, Liturgical Press, 1999, 127–135.

47   On the theologico-political roots of Orthodox nationalism, see the contribution by Vasilios N. Makrides in this volume.

An age-long anti-Roman prejudice has led some Orthodox canonists simply to deny the existence of such primacy in the past or the need for it in the present. But an objective study of the canonical tradition cannot fail to establish beyond any doubt that, along with local "centers of agreement" or primacies, the Church had also known a universal primacy.[48]

Unlike Ioannis Karmiris and other theologians who deny any *iure divino* origin of primacy, for Schmemann, primacy is part of the church's *esse*.

A local church cut off from this universal "koinonia" is indeed a *contradictio in adjecto*, for this koinonia is the very essence of the Church. And it has, therefore, its *form* and *expression*: primacy. Primacy is the necessary expression of the unity in faith and life of all local churches, of their living and efficient koinonia.[49]

Meyendorff has similar opinions on the matter. It is worthwhile quoting from his *The Byzantine Legacy in the Orthodox Church* of 1982:

The very *idea* of primacy was very much a part of ecclesiology itself: the provincial episcopal synods needed a president, without whose sanction no decision was valid ... Such is indeed an inevitable requirement of the very existence of the Church in the world ... It is a fact ... that there has never been a time when the Church did not recognize a certain "order" among first the apostles, then the bishops, and that, in this order, one apostle, St. Peter, and later, one bishop, heading a particular church, occupied the place of a

"primate" ... I would venture to affirm here that the universal primacy of one bishop ... was not simply a historical accident, reflecting "pragmatic" requirements ... The function of the "first bishop" is *to serve* that unity on the world scale, just as the function of a regional primate is to be the agent of unity on a regional scale.[50]

The latter argument reveals how, in the final analysis, the problem of universal primacy depends on the relationship between the local church and the universal church. Is the local church part of the universal church or a complete and catholic church? Does the universal church have ecclesiological priority over the local church or is it a *koinonia* of local churches? These questions must be answered before any theological formulation of universal primacy can take shape.

While incomplete, this brief review of the discussions on primacy during the last century reveals how Orthodox theology is ready to accept primacy as ecclesiologically justifiable at all levels of church structure, including the universal one. The problem that remains in the context of dialogue between Roman Catholics and Orthodox is *what kind of primacy* needs to be kept in mind. Fortunately, dialogue between the two churches was officially renewed in 2005 with the specific purpose of discussing this issue, eleven years after John Paul II, in *Ut unum sint*, spoke of the need to find ways of exercising primacy in the context of the new ecumenical situation that had opened up with the 21st century.[51]

After the plenary meeting of the Joint International Commission for Theological Dialogue between the Catholic Church and the Orthodox Church in Belgrade in 2006, an agreement was reached the following year in Ravenna with the

---

48   Alexander Schmemann, "The Idea of Primacy in Orthodox Theology," in: John Meyendorff, ed., *The Primacy of Peter: Essays in Ecclesiology and the Early Church*, Crestwood NY, St. Vladimir's Seminary Press, 1992, 145–171, here 163.

49   Schmemann, "The Idea of Primacy," 165 (italics original).

50   John Meyendorff, *The Byzantine Legacy in the Orthodox Church*, Crestwood NY, St. Vladimir Seminary Press, 1982, 243–245 (italics original).

51   On John Paul II's ecumenism, see the contribution by Enrico Galavotti in the third volume of this work.

publication of a document entitled *The Ecclesiological and Canonical Consequences of the Sacramental Nature of the Church: Ecclesial Communion, Conciliarity and Authority* (hereafter referred to as the Ravenna Document).[52] Unfortunately, representatives of the Patriarchate of Moscow did not attend the meeting, having abandoned it due to the presence of delegates of the autonomous Estonian Apostolic Orthodox Church, which is not recognized by Moscow. The Ravenna Document describes synodality as a form of responsibility shared by all the baptized for the church's communal life and, in a particular way, as the bond that keeps the bishops who lead it united (par. 5). In par. 43, the document also establishes two key principles: (1) that there has been and must be some kind of primacy, leadership, or authority at all three levels of the life of the church: episcopal at the local, metropolitan or patriarchal at the regional, and a universal primacy and that (2) primacy and synodality are "mutually interdependent."

With regard to the question of the relationship between synodality and primacy, the Ravenna Document recognizes that Rome has always been first in the ancient order, or *taxis*, of the major sees (par. 35, 41), and cites the famous statement of Ignatius of Antioch, referred to above, that the local church of Rome "presides in love" (par. 41). The document concludes by stating that "it remains for the question of the role of the bishop of Rome in the communion of all the Churches to be studied in greater depth" (par. 45).

A historical study of the role of the bishop of Rome during the first millennium was prepared for the plenary session in Vienna in 2010 but was not approved. A second document, this time of a strictly theological nature, on synodality and primacy, was then prepared for the plenary session in Amman in 2014, but it also failed to win approval. The commission's working session that took place in Chieti in September 2016, on the other hand, ended with the unanimous approval of a document entitled *Synodality and Primacy during the First Millennium: Towards a Common Understanding in Service to the Unity of the Church*.[53] Of course, this is not a binding text for the churches, but its unanimous approval remains a positive sign of the willingness of both sides to remove a major obstacle from the path towards unity.

There is still a long way to go, and the debate on universal primacy is unlikely to be concluded by a true agreement as long as the traditional dichotomy is kept alive between an extreme defense of the autonomy of the local church that goes so far as to obscure the importance of Orthodox unity on a universal level, on the one hand, and, on the other, a medieval universalism that tends, on the contrary, to underline the preeminence of the universal church over particular churches. Few so far, however, have considered the hypothesis that these two principles can coexist instead of excluding each other. Without local churches there can be no universal church that expresses communion in Christ. A universal church that does not give voice to the local churches and that does not even recognize their ecclesial fullness denies, in essence, their very existence.

Can the practice of synodality, accompanied by theological consensus on ecclesiology, constitute an adequate means for rediscovering unity in the context of contemporary ecumenical dialogue? And if this is the case, how will it be possible for all the different models of unity in the Christian

---

52 Available at <www.christianunity.va/content/unitacristiani/it/dialoghi/sezione-orientale/chiese-ortodosse-di-tradizione-bizantina/commissione-mista-internazionale-per-il-dialogo-teologico-tra-la/documenti-di-dialogo/2007-documento-di-ravenna/testo-in-inglese.html> (accessed June 5, 2020). The original document was discussed and edited in English. For an analysis of the text, see Joseph Famerée, "Communion ecclésiale, conciliarité, et autorité: Le document de Ravenne," *RTL* 40, 2009, 236–247.

53 Available at <www.christianunity.va/content/unitacristiani/en/dialoghi/sezione-orientale/chiese-ortodosse-di-tradizione-bizantina/commissione-mista-internazionale-per-il-dialogo-teologico-tra-la/documenti-di-dialogo/2016-sinodalita-e-primato-nel-primo-millennio-verso-una-comune-/testo-in-inglese.html> (accessed June 5, 2020).

traditions to be united? How can the Protestant model of reconciled diversity coexist with the Petrine primacy claimed by the bishop of Rome or, even further, with the Orthodox claim of considering themselves the sole true owners and witnesses of the faith and tradition of a single universal church? How can separated Christians face the third millennium together, discovering and appreciating their common roots in the historical conditions of the contemporary world?

More and more Christians today believe that the golden age of the ecumenical movement lies behind us and that the divided churches are left with nothing but days of darkness and isolation ahead of them. The causes can be retraced in a society that has become as "liquid" as the ecclesial boundaries, in the elimination of a sense of guilt about the continued division, or, more specifically, in the excessive institutional structuring assumed in the course of time by the ecumenical movement. It is still evident, however, that the occasional interest of the Orthodox Churches, and not theirs alone, in a type of ecumenism that is systematically confined to academic circles and curbed by purely bureaucratic matters, has contributed decisively to dampening the desire and search for true unity for many Christians.

7   The Question of Inculturation

If there is one thing the ecumenical movement of the past century has taught us clearly, it is that, however sincere, the churches' efforts to analyze and solve their doctrinal differences are not always duly rewarded by some form of progress along the path to unity. Very frequently, in fact, ecumenical impulses have occurred without a sound awareness of the current historical context and the challenges it poses to each Christian community engaged in ecumenical dialogue. Church unity cannot be achieved in a kind of vacuum of a historical or cultural nature. It has meaning and significance only if it is part of the historical reality in which Christians are immersed.

Having said that, it is necessary to specify that the examination of the historical context in which the problem of the unity of the church arises, or in which it is intended to be effected, cannot and must not be separated from careful theological reflection. Without a theological criterion, in fact, the history of cultures would be irrelevant to the path towards the unity of the church. There is no doubt that the church is not only a historical or cultural entity but that it claims to have an eternal, metahistorical value, if you like, and to be able to relate to history and culture by transcending them in a critical way. If it is indeed correct to say that culture always precedes the church, it is equally correct to say that it also, somehow, follows it. Both these statements can be proven on both a historical and a theological level. From a historical point of view, it is undeniable that the Gospel, from the very beginning, had to confront specific cultures, to face them, take a critical stance towards them, embrace them, and finally influence and transform them. From a theological point of view, however, the church has always considered itself as part of the world, even though it is not of this world, in order to remain faithful to the eschatological plan envisaged by the annunciation of the Kingdom. Yet, at the same time, the announcer as well as content of the Gospel, Jesus Christ, is God incarnate, that is God who has taken upon his shoulders all that is human, which includes culture. This dialectical affinity between the church and culture, which paradoxically allows for both a positive and a negative relationship between the two, is one of the most delicate and demanding tasks that the church must constantly face. Frequently, more weight is placed on one arm of these scales than on the other. For example, the Protestant theological liberalism of the 20th century, which had eminent representatives such as von Harnack, often identified the essence of Christianity with prevailing cultural values, while the Neoorthodoxy of the century's end, by contrast, drew too rigid a boundary between faith and culture. In both cases, these were exaggerations that contemporary theology is endeavoring to correct.

In short, the problem of inculturation is one of the most critical issues facing the church today. What can ecumenical theology contribute? The answer to that question can only be found in historical experience and theological teaching. The Christian Gospel, while being the product of a Semitic culture from a historical point of view, assumed a universal character from the very beginning, intending to transcend the geographical and cultural limits of Palestine and spread its message to the Greco-Roman world and beyond. Christianity thus had to face a culture that was not only different, but which could, at times, be defined as completely antagonistic. Academically, one may discuss at length to what extent the Judaism that heard Jesus's preaching was already sufficiently Hellenistic, but it remains a fact, accepted by a large number of patristic studies, that the inculturation of the Gospel in the Greco-Roman world of late antiquity proved a far from simple mission. At stake were not only religious issues, that is to say, the replacement of polytheism with faith in a single God in accordance with biblical teaching, but the ethos and mentality of the entire Mediterranean civilization or, in other words, the "worldview" of Greek culture. One could not expect, after all, that key concepts of the Christian message, such as the incarnation and resurrection of the flesh, would simply be peacefully accepted by Greek philosophers such as Celsus or the Neoplatonists within the cultured and intellectual elite of the first centuries of the Christian era.

On the other hand, at a more fundamental level, the widespread philosophical mentality of the Greco-Roman world, which gave priority to the "one," to the unity of the universe and its circular, well-ordered movements, to the detriment of the "many," that is the particular entities that had ended up being identified with decadence and evil, was itself an obstacle to the inculturation of Christianity.

In other words, the Gospel, which carried inscribed in its essence an eschatological dimension and considered the end of history more important than its beginning, ended up measuring itself against a culture that had among its distinctive features those of distrusting history and of considering origins to be more important than the *eschaton*. It was sufficient to render the inculturation of Christianity a mission with an outcome that was anything but obvious. Yet it was successful. Certainly, scholars have not failed and do not fail to have diverging judgments concerning the degree of this success, but whether it is considered genuine or the result of an "acute Hellenization" (von Harnack) or a betrayal of the Bible in favor of Aristotelian metaphysics (Schweitzer), it remains evident how, at least as far as the orthodox tradition is concerned, inculturation has succeeded in preserving the Gospel's original message and how, for this reason, it is not so much a model to follow as a valuable example from which to draw lessons for the contemporary situation.

Essentially, what the church should realize, that is to say, in the world today at the end of a historical culture modelled on the Enlightenment, is that the Gospel must be presented as an alternative. If the church fails in this task, others will find the answers to human needs and questions in this period of transition. In patristic times, the fact that the church had immediately entered into an intense dialogue with the culture in which it was immersed prevented others in late antiquity from replacing it in this undertaking of cultural transformation. The lesson we must draw from this is that today, as then, the church must necessarily play a key role in the dialogue with contemporary Western culture if it is to avoid marginalization. In particular, such an encounter must take place within the idealistic scope of the Enlightenment, whose values are in such a critical state today. Ideas such as the sovereignty of human reason, the pursuit of individual happiness, and the very notion of the individual, are, in fact, being progressively challenged by an increasingly cosmic and relational approach to human relations, which the churches must defend and carry forward with ever-increasing conviction, to the point of making it a central theme of contemporary cultural debate.

If, on the other hand, Christian theology remains on the margins of society, without being able to influence contemporary culture institutionally, it will remain so because it has adopted an antiquated and obsolete ethic, unable to articulate an alternative proposal to the crisis of Western values or to give meaning to life in the world, to humanity, or to history. In a society that is becoming increasingly open and pluralistic, Christian theology is called upon to exert a beneficial influence on the different cultural and religious forms of the contemporary world. In order to do so, it will be necessary for churches to overcome the ancient temptations of sectarianism and fanaticism, the only true dangers threatening the survival of an authentic religious life in every corner of the world today.

Having said this, however, the question of whether there is a value commonly called "Christian culture," a culture to be applied universally in Christ's name, should be answered in the negative. Great harm has been done to the Gospel whenever the church's mission has been understood as the promotion, and often imposition, of a specific culture. Needless to say, this does not mean that the Gospel must be completely separated from all cultural forms in order to be preached. Rather, it means that the mission of evangelization should respect people's freedom to express their faith in the way that suits them best, provided that the fundamental perspective of their "worldview" remains that of the Gospel. Inculturation, therefore, requires discernment, a discernment that the Spirit provides through theological consciousness, "orthodoxy" in the original sense of the term.

Nevertheless, the church does not draw its being and inspiration from the cultural realities of the past alone, but from the end of history, from its relationship with the Kingdom of God announced in the Gospel. Thinking in images, this means that the church should not turn, like Lot's wife, to the past, nostalgic for cultural autonomy, or for a history of successes, glories, and conquests. On the other hand, it is also pointless, and disappointing, for the church to present itself to the world as imprisoned within itself owing to an unfortunate theological aphasia, flaunting an embarrassed defensive attitude and often armed with an inexplicable polemical predisposition towards new cultural and social realities. Rather, everyone expects it to engage in a fruitful and creative dialogue with the present, whatever that may be, precisely thanks to its eschatological perspective.

The provisional and transitory nature of history leaves no margin for the church to identify its vision of a new city of God, of persons, and of the world, as the precise expression of any particular community, be it an empire, an ethnic group, a Christian state, a race, or a particular culture. The experience of the early church that, despite being the victim of serious persecution, was able to blend different civilizations and peoples shows how a theology of otherness can, in the final analysis, substantiate the realization of the church's eschatological perspective without falling into a comparative theological approach, which tends, on the contrary, to reduce everything to a common denominator of universal value in time and space.

The unity of the church remains an imperative for the world today, and its realization cannot be achieved by avoiding the great contemporary issues or by permitting churches to be towed by cultural fashions. The confessional pluralism to which the churches seem to have resigned themselves today should not be the equivalent of the cultural pluralism that dominates unchallenged as the social model. Accepting oneself without any effort, in an attempt to smooth out the differences that still keep the churches apart, or being content with the introduction of "good behavior" among religious leaders, would mean giving in to an excessively simplistic approach to the problem of Christian unity that risks leading, in the long run, to an inconclusive kind of ecumenism.

That is why possessing and manifesting to the world a shared vision of ultimate realities is an indispensable prerogative, so that we may rediscover a form of unity that will once again make the churches capable of acting as a communion and of influencing human cultural life. The church is, must be, and always will be, made up of many churches, just as the world is made up of many nations and a multitude of cultures. The goal of Christian unity, which reflects the unity of God's life itself in the communion of churches, can only be achieved by providing the world with an ultimate meaning, in theological terms, an *eschaton*, which gives meaning and a perspective to human history. It will be on this ground that the challenge of tomorrow's ecumenism will be played out.

Translated from Italian to English by Susan Dawson Vásquez and David Dawson Vásquez.

Bibliography

Alivisatos, Hamilcar, *Ī oikonomia kata to Kanonikon Dikaion tīs Orthodoxou Ekklīsias*, Athens, Astīr, 1949.

Charlot, John, *New Testament Disunity: Its Significance for Christianity Today*, New York NY, E.P. Dutton, 1970.

Dunn, James D.G., *Unity and Diversity in the New Testament*, London, SCM Press, 1990.

Dvornik, Francis, *The Idea of Apostolicity in Byzantium and the Legend of the Apostle Andrew*, Cambridge MA, Harvard University Press, 1958.

Hjelde, Sigurd, *Das Eschaton und die Eschata: Eine Studie über Sprachgebrauch und Sprachverwirrung in protestantischer Theologie von der Orthodoxie bis zur Gegenwart*, Munich, Kaiser, 1987.

Meyendorff, John, ed., *The Primacy of Peter: Essays in Ecclesiology and the Early Church*, Crestwood NY, St. Vladimir's Seminary Press, 1992.

Ricœur, Paul, *Le Conflit des interpretations: Essais d'herméneutique*, Paris, Éditions du Seuil, 1969.

Schweitzer, Albert, *Vom Reimarus zu Wrede: Eine Geschichte der Leben-Jesu-Forschung*, Tübingen, J.C.B. Mohr (Paul Siebeck), 1906.

Zizioulas, John D., *Being as Communion*, Crestwood NY, St. Vladimir's Seminary Press, 1993.

Zizioulas, John D., *L'Eucharistie, l'évêque et l'Église Durant les trois premiers siècles*, Desclée de Bouwer, Paris, 1994; ET: *Eucharist, Bishop, Church: The Unity of the Church in the Divine Eucharist and the Bishop during the First Three Centuries*, Brookline MA, Holy Cross Orthodox Press, 2001.

Zizioulas, John D., *The One and the Many: Studies on God, Man, the Church, and the World Today*, Alhambra CA, Sebastian Press, 2010.

CHAPTER 2

Before Ecumenism, at the Dawn of Modernity: Historical-Political Causes and Effects of the Revolutions of the 18th Century

Mathijs Lamberigts

1   Introduction

In his preface to *Les défis de la modernité*, which he edited for Jean-Marie Mayeur's *Histoire du Christianisme*, the master of French religious historiography Bernard Plongeron asserted that no diachronic synthesis or reconstruction of the Christian experience can avoid dealing with certain "hot spots"[1] in the history of the churches, even when it is not tempted to be an *histoire événementielle* and when it permits itself to go beyond the usual sphere of institutional history. It must treat those problematic and conflictual moments in the relationship with modernity that generation after generation, within a well-determined temporal and political space, have modified the interpretive categories with which Christians have reabsorbed the ruptures and continuities of history, to use a phrase popular in current historiography.

In the present chapter, I argue that the revolutions in the 18th century offer to the reader an outline of the problems that serve to introduce the heart of the ecumenical matter that is explored in the following chapters. These stand out among the vast choice of crucial moments that have characterized the encounter between the church and the modern world, having arisen along that stable historiographical axis born between the poles of revolution and modernity.[2] An analogous experiment could also demonstrate the same problematic concerning themes such as colonialization, war, racial hatred, or globalization.

My purpose, therefore, is to offer to the reader, without overburdening the pages of this work, a thorough synthesis of the events as a guide to a critical reflection on the similarities and differences between France's recognized centrality in the disintegration of medieval Christianity and the North American experience, which – in the same period but with radically different solutions – posed the problem of Christian freedom in civil society. Suffice it to say here that in the United States religious diversity discovered a cohesion in the universal concept of citizenship, albeit in different ways, making the most of the possibilities of a public sphere free from attachments to religious confessions. In France, however, which was predominantly Catholic, the distinction between the faithful and the citizen was sanctioned by the Revolution but – bloodied by the infamy of religious persecution – was seen as dangerous and anarchic by Catholic apologetics and the legitimist rearguard that reescorted the sovereigns to their thrones. Religious freedom in the United States soon gave rise to an experimentalism in terms of Christian forms and practices that did

---

1   *HC* 10, 13.

2   Among the more general studies, which are also useful for a methodological reflection on the theme of the church in modernity after the revolutions, it suffices to mention here: Giovanni Miccoli, *Fra mito della cristianità e secolarizzazione: Studi sul rapporto chiesa-società nell'età contemporanea*, Casale Monferrato, Marietti, 1985 and Daniele Menozzi, *La Chiesa cattolica e la secolarizzazione*, Turin, Einaudi, 1993. For more general works on the history of the church during the revolutionary period, see Timothy Tackett, "The French Revolution and Religion to 1794," *CHC* 7, 536–555 and Roger Aubert, "Die katholische Kirche und die Revolution," *HKG* 6/1, 3–104; ET: "The Catholic Church and the Revolution," *HistCh* 7, 3–84.

not fail to bear fruit, even in ecumenical actions. In France, the shock of Revolution and the end of the Napoleonic era reanimated the myth of a papist and Roman Christian unity where the other was (almost) always the enemy.

2 The American Revolution

As is well known, the principal objective of the American Revolution was to expel the British from the thirteen colonies in North America. They had been founded by Great Britain along the Atlantic coast to the disadvantage of the native peoples who had occupied those lands since time immemorial.[3] The Franco-Indian War, which ended in 1763 with the annexation of the Canadian territories by the British Empire, can be considered the driving force of the uprising. In order to compensate for the great costs of the war, the British crown decided to increase the financial pressure on the emerging economies of the American colonies, thus antagonizing its overseas subjects. The union of the forces that emerged between colonists, who wanted freedom and independence from the motherland, and Christian preachers, convinced that sooner or later the injustices of the English colonial system would be vindicated by the Lord, inflamed people's spirits and created a broad front of opposition to England. This allowed the revolutionaries to set aside their internal religious disagreements (which, however, were not completely forgotten). For this reason, America was not permeated and shaken by such a strong, generalized anti-Christian fervor as France was to be shortly thereafter. Nothing prevented leaders who criticized dogmatic religion and struggled for a religion based on the principles of reason[4] (such as Thomas Jefferson, who claimed that his mind was his only church) from collaborating with others committed to their denominations, especially when they were also openly in conflict with the British establishment.[5] In the early days of the crisis, however, the Christian response to the cry of the patriots varied considerably according to social class and the interests in play. If the laborers, dockworkers, and owners of small estates, or those who had arrived in the New World with the hope of beginning a new life far from England, were always ready to cut the ties that still bound them to the Anglican Church, the merchants and large landholders were more lenient towards the Anglican establishment for fear of compromising their business with the empire. Moreover, it was the lower strata of the population who suffered most from the British military occupation and were thus the first, in 1768, to push for a break with England, followed only in 1776 by the wealthier rungs of society.[6] The colonial militias, poorly trained and badly armed, nevertheless managed to stand up to the British army, or at least to hold their own against it, while waiting for France to come to their rescue, turning the tide of the war and internationalizing the crisis.

We turn now to the situation of the churches in the period preceding the Revolution. Already before the war, the multifaceted Christian landscape

---

3 There are abundant historiographical contributions on this topic. See, for example, Jack P. Greene, "The American Revolution," *AHR* 105, 2000, 93–102; Jack P. Greene, *The Constitutional Origins of the American Revolution*, Cambridge, Cambridge University Press, 2010; Frances II. Kennedy, ed., *The American Revolution: A Historical Guidebook*, Oxford, Oxford University Press, 2014; Jonathan I. Israel, *The Expanding Blaze: How the American Revolution Ignited the World*, Princeton NJ, Princeton University Press, 2017.

4 Vincent Phillip Muñoz, *God and the Founders: Madison, Washington, and Jefferson*, Cambridge, Cambridge University Press, 2009, 70–116.

5 See Martin E. Marty, "The American Revolution and Religion (1765–1815)," *CHC* 7, 497–516, here 506–507, referencing Sidney E. Mead, *The Lively Experiment: The Shaping of Christianity in America*, New York NY, Harper and Row, 1963, 45–48, 57–59.

6 See Guy Lemarchand, "À propos des révoltes et révolutions de la fin du XVIIIe siècle: Essai d'un bilan historiographique," *AHRF* 340, 2005, 145–174, in particular § 19 (text consulted on line).

of the colonies was arranged along a fault line that opposed it to the attempts of the Church of England to impose an Anglican episcopate on the colonial territories. The fiercest in resisting any Episcopalian drift were the churches that were labeled as "dissenters" in the home country by the High Church establishment. These were followed by the Anglicans in the southern colonies who had long been "accustomed to running parish affairs to their own lay tastes,"[7] and by Presbyterians and Congregationalists, who had vivid memories of the harassment suffered in England at the hands of the Anglican hierarchy and who had no intention of giving up such a precious good as the autonomy of their local communities.

Congregationalists and Presbyterians thus found themselves allies against the English ambitions to establish a hierarchical church in the New World based on the Anglican model, significantly increasing their chance of success.[8] Between 1766 and 1775, the Presbyterians of the Middle Colonies joined the Congregationalists of Connecticut in a series of antiepiscopal conventions and managed – thanks also to support garnered in the home country – to keep the English Parliament from going ahead with its project of establishing an episcopal system in America that would be the image and likeness of the Anglican one.[9]

This description, we concede, is only a rough outline of a far more complex Christian reality on which the outbreak of the Revolution acted as a detonator of the long-smoldering anti-British resentment, catalyzing the energies of an evangelical fermentation that, less than thirty years earlier, had thoroughly redesigned the nature and confessional form of North American Christianity.

2.1   *A Contentious Religious Diversity*

The idea that the American Revolution was also partly the consequence of the Great Awakening is commonly accepted. This movement of the 1730s and 1740s took place everywhere from Nova Scotia to Georgia and induced many churches to cooperate, at least for a short time, in the great evangelizing enterprise that Providence had entrusted to the Protestants of the American colonies.[10] A good example of interdenominational collaboration is to be found in the churches of Pennsylvania, where William Penn, the founder of the colony, managed in the 16th century to attract adherents of all kinds of denomination, thanks to a liberal policy on religion. English and Welsh Quakers, along with Anglicans, Baptists, Roman Catholics, and Scottish-Irish Presbyterians arrived from the British Isles, while from the Rhineland, which he had visited in 1677, mainly Lutherans and Reformed Christians (the so-called Church People) emigrated, along with Mennonites, Amish, and Moravian Brethren (also known as the Plain People).[11]

While Pennsylvania's name and religious diversity come from Penn, it was thanks to the Moravian missionary Nikolai Ludwig Graf von Zinzendorf, founder of the Herrnhut community, that a certain openness to inter-Christian collaboration was cultivated. Between 1742 and 1748, at the Brethren's urging, a series of synods were held in Pennsylvania in which nearly all the denominations present in the colony participated. They launched a kind of spiritual union known as the Congregation of God in the Spirit. Those who participated maintained intact their denominational affiliations and developed methods of cooperation in the evangelization of the Native Americans, having an exchange of pastors and devotional writings and, even, intercommunion.[12] Sabotaged by increasing confessional rivalries, Zinzendorf's experiment did not

---

7   Don Herbert Yoder, "Christian Unity in Nineteenth-Century America," in: *A History of the Ecumenical Movement*, vol. 1, Ruth Rouse & Stephen C. Neill, eds., *1517–1948*, London, SPCK, ²1967, 221–262, here 231.

8   Yoder, "Christian Unity in Nineteenth-Century America," 226–228.

9   Yoder, "Christian Unity in Nineteenth-Century America," 233.

10   See Marty, "The American Revolution and Religion," 500.

11   See Yoder, "Christian Unity in Nineteenth-Century America," 228.

12   Yoder, "Christian Unity in Nineteenth-Century America," 229.

actually go much further. However, in time, it did bear ecumenical fruit: the churches that took part in the activities of the Congregation refined their sensitivity and capacity for action in regard to those problems, which encouraged them to work beyond confessional barriers and helped various confessions, especially the Lutherans, to create a stronger organizational structure through the establishment of local synods, not unlike the reformed congregations in Pennsylvania.[13]

Elsewhere, missionary attempts such as the SPG, led by Anglicans, proved far less successful. It should be remembered, in fact, that nine of the thirteen colonies had a kind of state-subsidized ecclesiastical establishment. Many of these "official churches" used a strongly anti-British language due partly to the perennial suspicion that the Anglican Church, through missionary societies like the SPG, were attempting to place religious control in the hands of bishops – and it is well known how much the members of the Congregationalist churches perceived this as a symbol of English repression.[14] On the other hand, the Anglican clergy were in a difficult situation. They had been ordained in the home country and found themselves caught between loyalty to the English establishment and adherence to the principles of the Great Awakening, which instead wanted to orient religious life in the colonies towards a form of Christianity far removed from the institutional tradition imposed by London. At the outbreak of hostilities in 1775, therefore, England expected the loyalty of these clergymen, and the revolutionaries suspected them of being English collaborators. This explains the reason why, during the War of Independence, many Anglicans fled to Canada or returned to England, while others simply joined the rebels, as did the most illustrious

figure of those christened into the Church of England on American soil, George Washington.

The immediate result of the Revolution, therefore, was that the churches were confronted with the choice of whether or not to support the cause of independence advocated by American patriots. While the Quakers, a substantial group in Pennsylvania, refused to take up arms, the Scottish-Irish immigrants, coming from Calvinist contexts – and for that reason susceptible to the influence of the Presbyterians – soon convinced themselves that God's Providence had called them to fight for freedom, which explained their greater willingness to enroll in the colonial army.[15] The Methodists, instead, born from the side of Anglicanism, at times found themselves sharing its sympathy for the British crown. They thus did not play an important role during the Revolution. This did not detract from the fact that, once the war was over, the Methodists became supporters of the republic and a reality of some importance in the public life of the new country.[16]

2.2 Catholics and the Quebec Act (1774)

Thanks to the confessional diversity and the climate of tolerance that permeated the colonies, the situation of Catholics in North America, paradoxically, was better than in England. Before the Revolution, their status was still rather problematic since Catholics were forbidden to receive or impart confessional education according to the dictates of their church and, until 1718, were denied the right to vote everywhere except in Pennsylvania.[17] The turning point seemed to arrive with the annexation of Canada to the British Empire when the English parliament approved the Quebec Act in 1774, guaranteeing the numerous Catholics in the new territories a position as

---

13 Yoder, "Christian Unity in Nineteenth-Century America," 229–230.

14 Marty, "The American Revolution and Religion," 500–501. The Anglican Church was also very committed to the conversion of the natives.

15 Marty, "The American Revolution and Religion," 502–503.

16 Marty, "The American Revolution and Religion," 503–504.

17 Ludovicus Jacobus Rogier, *De kerk in het tijdperk van verlichting en revolutie*, Hilversum, Brand, 1964 (= GKH 7), 231ff.

subjects of the crown. In the rest of the colonies, however, the decision was not well received by the American patriots who saw extending political rights to Catholics as a threat to the Protestant faith of the majority. This gave them a further motive to protest against England,[18] almost triggering anti-papist crusades, particularly in New England. It should be remembered that, in the thirteen colonies before the Revolution, Catholics were only a small minority of 25,000 persons, corresponding to 0.6% of the population.[19] Most of these were concentrated in Pennsylvania (7,000) and Maryland (16,000), with no other colony having more than 1,000 Catholics.[20] With the exception of Pennsylvania, where Catholics could live in relative tranquility,[21] in the other territories of the original United States – New Hampshire, Massachusetts, Rhode Island, Connecticut, New York, New Jersey, Delaware, Maryland, Virginia, North Carolina, South Carolina, and Georgia – it was only with the Revolution that they received religious liberty.

In any case, Catholics proved to be loyal supporters of the revolutionary cause, as evidenced by the events connected to some members of the Carroll family. Charles Carroll of Carrollton, for example, a wealthy Catholic from Maryland, was one of the most convinced advocates of the independence of the colonies and, as the representative of Maryland in the First Continental Congress, he was one of the authors of the Declaration of Independence in 1776, as well as the only Catholic to sign it.[22] Likewise, his cousin Daniel represented Maryland in the legislative session of 1787 when the Constitution was drafted, while his brother John, an ex-Jesuit ordained in 1789, was the first Catholic bishop of the first diocese in the United States, Baltimore, and was entrusted by Congress with a mission to Canada to convince the French colonies to join in the war against Great Britain.[23] John Carroll can be said to have been as deeply Catholic as he was a convinced American.[24] He had studied in Europe with the Jesuits of Saint-Omer, where he acquired all the tools necessary to engage in dialogue with Enlightenment thought, in which he recognized both risks and opportunities. In regard to the US Constitution, in particular he appreciated its open and tolerant character, and was convinced that liberal legislation in regard to religion – as much as it was disliked by the confessional states of old Europe – was an opportunity full of promise for American Catholics.[25] Carroll was proved right by the example of Elizabeth Bayley Seton, who converted to Catholicism from the Episcopalian Church, founded the Sisters of Charity, and was the first Catholic saint in American history. This showed how religious freedom became an unexpected grace for Catholics. In a short time, Seton became the principal supporter of Bishop Carroll's work, founding an impressive number of parochial schools where even men and women of the lower classes could have access to a free Catholic education.[26]

18   Marty, "The American Revolution and Religion," 504–505.
19   *GKH* 7, 231; see also Roger Aubert, "Die katholische Kirche und die Restauration," *HKG* 6/1, 3–104; ET: "The Catholic Church and the Restoration," *HistCh* 7, 85–257, here 171.
20   Maryland was founded in 1632 by a Catholic convert, George Calvert, who, because of persecutions of Catholics on the Isles, wanted to provide a religious free place for those persecuted. Calvert promoted a policy of toleration, reason why other denominations would also find hospitality in this state and Catholics always would remain a minority. See *GKH* 7, 233.
21   Theodore Maynard, *The Story of American Catholicism*, New York NY, Macmillan, 1942, 91.
22   *GKH* 7, 235–236.
23   Marty, "The American Revolution and Religion," 507–509; on John Carroll, see also Guillaume de Bertier de Sauvigny, *De kerk in het tijdperk van de restauratie (1801–1848)*, Hilversum, Brand, 1965 (= *GKH* 8), 142–143.
24   Aubert, "The Catholic Church and the Restoration," 171, and Bernard Plongeron, "Le grand refus nord-américain," *HC* 10, 479–538, here 495.
25   See Plongeron, "Le grand refus nord-américain," 495–503.
26   See, for example, Judith Metz, "Elizabeth Bayley Seton: Animator of the Early American Catholic Church," *USCH* 22, 2004, 49–65.

In the immense task of organizing the pastoral life of a diocese that initially included the whole of the United States, Carroll counted on the assistance of several French priests who had fled their home country after the first anti-Catholic measures had been adopted by the revolutionary government there. It was also thanks to the help of two of them, a couple of Sulpicians, that the bishop was able to open the first Catholic seminary in the United States in Baltimore in 1792.[27] Protected by the freedom of religion, of which Carroll was an ardent supporter, US Catholicism grew rapidly in the course of a few years (a trend that the first waves of immigrants from Europe in the 19th century only augmented, making the Catholic Church one of immigrants and, ethnically, of a minority);[28] in 1815, there were about 150,000 Catholics and 100 priests. The number of dioceses also quickly increased: four were founded in 1808 and another twenty were proposed between 1820 and 1837.[29] The rapid expansion of US Catholicism did not fail, however, to preoccupy the Congregation for the Propagation of the Faith. It considered the United States a mission territory or, as one American bishop put it, a papal colony, and it tended to look with distrust on the autonomous development of a national church in North America.[30]

Its exponential growth, in demographic terms, presented Catholicism with one of its greatest challenges during its early years in the new nation: the shortage of priests.[31] This problem was aggravated by the fact that most of the priests (about 80%) came from Europe and, moreover, from countries with very different religious traditions. While the French clergy, for example, were educated in the Sulpician manner, according to ascetic principles based on a rather severe lifestyle, the Irish clergy,

instead, manifested a lively and energetic temperament and were at times "boisterous."[32] It soon became clear that the rigid French approach, despite the solid intellectual preparation of its clergy, was not well adapted to the American spirit, which was far removed from the European mentality and its cultural parameters. On the contrary, the Irish priests, because they came from a reality marked by oppression and religious persecution, were more able than the French to deal with a society dominated by Protestant leaders and, thus, more able to organize the life of their church in difficult conditions without state support. In the long run, this sort of *ante litteram* "ecclesiastical Darwinism" would produce a progressive "Irishizing" of the Catholic clergy in the United States.

Despite the gradual institutionalization of American Catholicism initiated by the provincial councils of Baltimore (which began to be held in 1829)[33] and the slow normalization of relations with the Protestant Churches, the latter, between the 1830s and 1840s, had no liking either for the growing influence of Catholics in organizational terms or for the related massive influx of Irish and German immigrants into the large industrial cities, which swelled the ranks of cheap labor, threatening the skilled labor of many Protestants. This was one of the reasons why American Catholics sometimes ended up as the target of violent acts. In the eyes of the Protestants, the greatest fear was that of risking the delicate confessional equilibrium guaranteed by religious freedom and threatened by what many held to be a conspiracy coordinated by the pope and the Holy Alliance, which in Europe had united the crowns of Russia, Austria, and Prussia.[34] In order to defend Catholics and to make clear what they stood for, the Catholic Press was founded. Also, the organization of provincial councils like those of Baltimore would help

---

27 *GKH* 7, 237.
28 *GKH* 8, 138.
29 Aubert, "The Catholic Church and the Restoration," 172.
30 See *GKH* 8, 143.
31 European priests were often sent to America by their superiors for having been a cause of problems in Europe. See Aubert, "The Catholic Church and the Restoration," 173.

32 The term is used in Aubert, "The Catholic Church and the Restoration," 174.
33 Aubert, "The Catholic Church and the Restoration," 175.
34 For a vivid description of these increasing tensions, see *GKH* 8, 148–149.

to normalize the situation. In any case, the growth of Catholicism would continue, orders and congregations would come, for men and women, the latter actively involved in education and care.

2.3 A New Constitution for a New Nation

It is worth repeating that nearly all the key figures of the Revolution, besides the authors of the Constitution (drafted in 1787 and ratified in 1789), were for the most part members of some church, despite the fact that some of them considered themselves devoted to Reason rather than to God.[35] This feeling, in reality, was combined with a religious-like devotion to the state and the nation and a rigorous and disciplined lifestyle marked by a Christian ethics.[36] If this were not enough to demonstrate the true extent of the role played by religion in the struggle for independence and in the creation of the American nation,[37] consider the many examples of political and military leaders who, during the Revolution, directly asked Providence to lead them to victory and to enlighten them in the drafting of the documents that were to be the basis of a free and independent American society. One of these was George Washington, the undisputed leader of the young republic for a quarter of a century (1775–1799), a living personification of the Revolution, advocate for the Constitution, father of the nation, and a political figure capable of generating a consensus across denominations. He played a fundamental role in the promotion of an American civil religion,[38] despite the fact that his personal religious convictions – closer to theistic rationalism than Christianity[39] – were called into question.[40]

What the US Constitution says in regard to religion, however briefly worded, is a surprising innovation: "No religious Test shall ever be required as a Qualification to any Office or public Trust under the United States" (art. 6). In a state characterized by a variety of Christian denominations, even minorities such as "Jews, Turks, and infidels" were to enjoy the same rights as Christians.[41] Furthermore, the document made it clear that Congress could not pass any legislation restricting the exercise of any religion, a principle that was confirmed in 1789 with the Bill of Rights. Both these documents were inspired by Enlightenment principles[42] permeated by an intense American spirit.[43] The First Amendment also prohibited Congress from passing any laws that would accord to a specific religion or church a privileged position or, again, prohibit its exercise. The freedoms of speech, of the press, of peaceful assembly, and of petitioning the government on the basis of grievances were also affirmed.

---

35 See Marty, "The American Revolution and Religion," 498.

36 Marty, "The American Revolution and Religion," 498.

37 See Catherine L. Albanese, *Sons of the Fathers: The Civil Religion of the American Revolution*, Philadelphia PA, Temple University Press, 1976.

38 Gary Scott Smith, "The Faith of George Washington," in: Mark J. Rozell & Gleaves Whitney, eds., *Religion and the American Presidency*, New York NY, Palgrave Macmillan, ³2018, 13–44, here 14–15.

39 See Paul F. Boller, *George Washington and Religion*, Dallas TX, Southern Methodist University Press, 1963, 3–23, here 5; see also Muñoz, *God and the Founders*, 49–69.

40 Smith, "The Faith of George Washington," 27.

41 See Morton Borden, *Jews, Turks, and Infidels*, Chapel Hill NC, The University of North Carolina Press, 1984.

42 The literature on the topic is vast: see Henry F. May, *The Enlightenment in America*, New York NY, Oxford University Press, 1976; Robert A. Ferguson, *The American Enlightenment (1750–1820)*, Cambridge MA, Harvard University Press, 1997. On the way in which the relationship between Protestantism and the Enlightenment continued to play a role in American history, see Andrew Finstuen, "The Search for a Plural America: Protestant and Enlightenment Authority in American History," *HTR* 109, 2016, 144–155. An excellent review of the many studies on American Enlightenment context can be found in Nathalie Caron & Naomi Wulf, "American Enlightenments: Continuity and Renewal," *JAH* 99, 2013, 1072–1091.

43 See Jennifer Greeson, "American Enlightenment: The New World and the Modern Western Thought," *ALH* 25, 2013, 6–17.

The effects of these decisions did not take long to be felt in the American churches. The different religious groups indeed began to grow, even if in a disorderly and often competitive way. Churches with a less rigid structure (such as the Baptists and Methodists) proved to be the most successful, while the protection and promotion of individual rights contributed to the advancement of "individual" churches. The decision to prohibit any type of coordination between church and state, however, opened the door to all kinds of experiments. Without limits or obligations imposed by the government, experimentalism in religion became the rule, giving rise to the founding of Christian groups which quickly established themselves on the North American religious scene, for example the Mormons in the 1820s, or the Adventists in the 1840s. We should not forget, moreover, the birth of several Black churches. The first of these was AUMP, established in 1813, soon followed by AME in 1816.

However, the benefits of the Revolution for Protestant religiosity in the United States would not have reached this extent if they had not been intertwined with the Second Great Awakening that spread across America between 1790 and 1840, contributing more than any other political or social phenomenon to exalting the emotional and experiential characteristics of Christianity.[44] It was, in fact, a season of vast evangelization in which conversions to Christianity increased significantly, with a revival of ecclesial life.

The Awakening focused solely on the Bible and was characterized by a certain lack of interest in, if not actual discontent with, institutional churches, which led to the rise, for example, of Mormons and the Wesleyan Methodists in New York, and the growth of Methodists and Baptists in Kentucky and Tennessee. The institutional churches also felt the impact of the constant and considerable migratory flow towards the west. This was an impressive movement of peoples that, from the ecclesial

point of view, represented real challenges, on the one hand, to keeping their own faithful in the fold, and, on the other, to welcoming new ones. In some cases, rivalries between churches exploded. In others, forms of collaboration were attempted, as in the case of the Plan of Union between Presbyterians and Congregationalists (1801–1852), a project aimed particularly at evangelization.[45] In the colonial period, the two denominations had already worked together and had progressively adopted very similar structures of self-government, so much so that the Congregationalists, it seems, sometimes called themselves Presbyterians.[46] The Plan of Union would later also be adopted by the Congregationalist Associations of Vermont, New Hampshire, and Massachusetts, allowing for the exchange of ministers and the promotion of new relationships, with the approval of both clergy and laity. The bond between the two denominations would last until the middle of the 19th century, when the Congregationalists realized that they had been, so to speak, "Presbyterianized" and had lost their own identity. This form of collaboration met with opposition even within the Presbyterian Church, which, from 1837 and 1838, saw the Presbyterian General Assembly split between Old School and New School, becoming reconciled only in the 1860s.[47]

During the Second Awakening, and at least until the beginning of the Civil War, the revival of ecclesial life stimulated the foundation of many interdenominational societies[48] that, active at the national level, stimulated a vision of missionary activity that embraced the whole nation. This attempt explains why, at one point, the ABS had to publish the Bible without any commentary in order not to risk offending any church.

---

44 See Marty, "The American Revolution and Religion," 498.

45 Yoder, "Christian Unity in Nineteenth-Century America," 231–232.

46 Yoder, "Christian Unity in Nineteenth-Century America," 233–234.

47 Yoder, "Christian Unity in Nineteenth-Century America," 234.

48 For an exhaustive treatment, see Yoder, "Christian Unity in Nineteenth-Century America," 241–247.

Indeed there was cooperation, but not yet the search for compromise on doctrine. It must be said that these societies were supported mainly by Congregationalists and Presbyterians, by the Dutch and German Reformed churches, and by general synod Lutherans; they never managed to represent North American Protestant Christianity in its entirety. The Methodist churches, for example, were among the denominations that chose not to participate in these "ecumenical" missionary endeavors and formed, instead, their own missionary societies.[49]

3   The French Church and the French Revolution

At the dawn of the French Revolution, the church in France was one of the largest assets of Louis XVI's kingdom.[50] In 1789, 625 of the 740 abbeys in France were assigned as emoluments without the beneficiaries being required to perform any related ecclesiastical duties. Moreover, the large Catholic majority of the French population and the great number of monastic communities scattered throughout the country guaranteed France a prominent place in the Christian geography of the Old World.[51] Truth be told, however, it must be pointed out that not all the 135 dioceses

that constituted the church in France enjoyed an equal degree of wealth. In general, the smaller ones, concentrated mainly in the south, were rather poor, while those in the north, larger and wealthier, received most of the benefits.[52] The same kind of gap also applied to the clergy, since in northern France priests and religious generally enjoyed a far better quality of life than those in the southeast of the kingdom. The distribution of goods also varied considerably: while in the north these were shared among the clergy who cared for the faithful, in the south, particularly the southeast, it was the religious and the episcopal class who garnered most of them.[53] In the church in France, the clergy's prosperity essentially depended on the particular region and on the scale of the position of power held by notables of that region, the interests of the local clergy being, of course, strongly dependent upon the balance of power that regulated the relations between the nobles and absolute sovereign and between the latter and the pope in Rome.

At first glance, even from the point of view of popular religiosity, religion in France was a flourishing reality. In the countryside, people regularly fulfilled their "Easter duties" and as to catechetical precepts, Catholic books were printed and disseminated in large quantities. Until the middle of the 18th century, vocations remained numerous, only experiencing a slight decline in the second half of the century, especially among the urban elite, that is, in those circles where there was a gradual loss of interest in religious literature. In time, that disaffection would make France, particularly rural France, a mission country, as the followers of Louis-Marie Grignion de Montfort were well aware.

---

49   Yoder, "Christian Unity in Nineteenth-Century America," 243–244.

50   See, for example, John McManners, *Church and Society in Eighteenth-Century France*, vol. 1, *The Clerical Establishment and Its Social Ramifications*, Oxford, Clarendon Press, 1998, 3.

51   Some figures: in the parishes, there were around 50,000 priests active, dedicated primarily to the care for the poor and the education of the youth; there were instead between 15,000 and 18,000 canons who populated the cities of France, even though their contribution was less visible to the faithful, while the number of monks was around 20,000 to 25,000 and sisters between 30,000 and 40,000. Despite the fact that a certain decline in the number of priests and religious is documented between 1768 and 1789, on the eve of the taking of the Bastille, the Catholic Church still represented, in the France of the Ancien Régime, a power of

the highest magnitude. Aubert, "The Catholic Church and the Revolution," 13–14.

52   In the diocesan geography of France at the time, Strasbourg, for example, was part of the ecclesiastical province of Mainz; Metz, Toul, and Verdun, part of Trier.

53   Tackett, "The French Revolution and Religion to 1794," 537–538.

Behind such reassuring statistics and these impressions of power, however, lay the reality of an effective power that had long been losing ground on both the moral and the political fronts. Already in 1682, the four articles of the Declaration of the Clergy of France had limited papal authority to spiritual matters alone and had, at the same time, affirmed the inviolability of the French national church's particular freedoms, which even Rome had to respect. Since the concordat of 1516, three centuries before the outbreak of the French Revolution, the king had wielded a significant power in the life of the church through the granting of benefices, including abbeys and episcopates. Obviously, the crown continued to need the pope's support in order to reign with full legitimacy but, in fact, all requests sent to Rome were almost invariably accepted by the pontiff. The king's increased power in religious matters explains the pact of loyalty that bound the French high clergy to the monarchy along with, in part, the popularity that Gallican doctrines encountered in the lands ruled under the emblem of the fleur-de-lis.

The system of ecclesiastical appointments, in which the role played by the monarch had become predominant, therefore assumed a prevailingly political importance,[54] given the aristocratic origin of the ecclesiastical leadership and also the fact that most of the candidates for the episcopate, while generally well-educated, were not always adequately prepared from a theological or spiritual point of view. Essentially, one became a bishop more by birthright than by personal merit and, according to this logic, the king's favor became an indispensable requirement. This did not, however, mean that no parish priest or ecclesiastical dignitary took his pastoral responsibilities seriously. There were many bishops who strove to become good administrators or who, if absent too frequently from their dioceses, chose to rely on prepared vicars-general to carry out the ordinary

duties of government.[55] The lower diocesan clergy, for their part, continued to care for their flock by improving the material and spiritual conditions of the faithful,[56] often blaming the episcopal hierarchies for the state of abandonment in which dioceses languished. In their work of caring for souls, priests demanded the reestablishment of diocesan synods and the initiation of spiritual reform while acting to remedy the injustices that the perpetuation of the status quo imposed on the poorest sections of the population.[57]

However, it also bears mentioning that, in view of the privileged position held by the church – which paid less than 2% in taxes to the crown – there was nevertheless a considerable investment in educational and charitable activities. The church's commitment to these two crucial areas of outreach, in fact, had the advantage of gaining great appreciation among the population, together with increasing the ranks and prestige of the numerous religious congregations active in the territory, although this fueled competitiveness and, at times, conflict between the diocesan clergy and the religious orders. The latter, in many cases consisting of men and women who were driven to enter by their families of origin rather than by a desire for a life consecrated to the faith, not infrequently demonstrated a moral standard that was much lower than that required by the order, thus helping to shape the outsider's image of a Christian life in decline.[58]

On the threshold of the Revolution, therefore, behind a prevailing impression of strength and power, the church in France was a building as majestic as its foundations were fragile. Several factors contributed to undermining it from the inside and making it as vulnerable as ever to external attacks, such as that achieved by a joint venture of philosophers, encyclopedists, Jansenists, and members

---

54   Aubert, "The Catholic Church and the Revolution," 17.

55   Tackett, "The French Revolution and Religion to 1794," 538.

56   Aubert, "The Catholic Church and the Revolution," 14.

57   See André Latreille in *HCF* 3, 51.

58   Aubert, "The Catholic Church and the Revolution," 16.

of the Gallican clergy against the Society of Jesus that, in 1764, was expelled from the Kingdom of France and its territories. If, at a theological level, Jansenism questioned the hierarchy of the church itself,[59] at a social one, the evident disproportion of income between high and low clergy often provoked clashes, disputes, and a growing acrimony that then led, in 1789, to an unparalleled institutional crisis within the church. Envious of the patrimony upon which the wealth of abbeys and monasteries was based, even the diocesan clergy soon began to question the *raison d'être* of those traditionally better-off and more powerful religious orders, finally joining the democratic thrust of the Third Estate.

The ideas of the Enlightenment exacerbated the situation, like fanning the coals in a brazier, further polarizing French society and feeding the disaffection of many Catholics towards the church with a merciless anti-religious criticism, unable in the long term, however, to predict Catholicism's regenerative capacity and its degree of resistance to the attempt to eradicate it from France.[60]

---

59 See Catherine Maire, ed., *Jansénisme et Révolution: Actes du colloque de Versailles tenu au Palais des congrès les 13 et 14 octobre 1989*, Paris, Bibliothèque Mazarine, 1990. Many of the contributions to this volume offer interesting reflections regarding the way in which the Jansenists gradually became increasingly opposed to the power of the monarchy.

60 See, for example, the work of Darrin M. McMahon, *Enemies of the Enlightenment: The French Counter-Enlightenment and the Making of Modernity*, Oxford, Oxford University Press, 2001. Not all of the Catholic Church, however, proved to be against the Enlightenment. A portion of the episcopate was, instead, attracted or even inspired by it, like Pope Benedict XIV or the prince-bishop François-Charles de Velbrück, two good examples of an attitude of dialogue that Catholicism, too, was able to offer to the claims of the *Aufklärung*. See Ulrich L. Lehner, *The Catholic Enlightenment: The Forgotten History of a Global Movement*, New York NY, Oxford University Press, 2016 and Rebecca M. Messbarger, *Benedict XIV and the Enlightenment: Art, Science, and Spirituality*, Toronto, University of Toronto Press, 2016.

3.1 The Economic Crisis and Attempts to Resolve It

The direct causes of the French Revolution were mainly economic in nature. Forced into action by the country's persistent financial deficit, in 1789 Louis XVI convoked the Estates General at Versailles. Among the items on the agenda was also the discussion of a series of complaints about church privileges and the degeneration of monasticism. For the most part, however, it cannot be said that the assembly's main objective was to question the Catholic Church's position in the state or the way it conducted its educational and charitable activities in the realm.[61]

It was not long, however, before the process set in motion that fateful summer of 1789 began to take a rather unfavorable turn against the Catholic Church. Clerical privileges were abolished on Aug 4, 1789, ecclesiastical property was secularized on Nov 2, 1789, and religious orders were suppressed on Feb 13, 1790. These first three legislative interventions in the ecclesiastical field, approved by the Constituent Assembly, paved the way for the progressive separation between revolutionary France and Catholicism, which then resulted in an open persecution of the religion professed by the majority of the citizens. Although they had a detrimental effect on the French church, none of these three measures, however, was motivated by the desire to launch a lethal attack on Catholicism. For example, the abolition of feudalism decided in August was intended by the revolutionaries to put an end to certain abuses by the clergy, not to strike at the church in its entirety, which is why an ad hoc committee was set up to ensure that parishes, convents, and religious congregations were provided with sufficient financial means to cover their expenses and continue their assistance to the poor. The same sensitivity was shown for those regular orders and religious congregations that zealously carried out philanthropic activities and

---

61 On this topic, see Bernard Plongeron, "Affirmations et contestations du chrétien-citoyen (1789–1792)," *HC* 10, 301–362, esp. 307–310.

that were therefore spared dissolution and forced secularization.[62] Additionally, it should be considered that, with 568 votes in favor and 346 votes against, the law of the nationalization of ecclesiastical property was passed thanks to the support of many Christian legislators who were convinced that the measure, however drastic, was a necessary cure for the country's financial collapse and, at the same time, an unprecedented opportunity to correct the distortions of the Catholic Church and to integrate it into the great process of national regrowth triggered by the Revolution.[63]

3.2 Catholicism: From National Religion to one of the State Controlled Religions

The course of events was soon bound to change very quickly, and with it also the fortunes of the Catholic Church in the Revolution. In the summer of 1790, the conviction that Catholicism was still an indispensable moral component of the nation began to show its first cracks, besieged as it was by the idea slowly making its way into the revolutionary governing body that the rebirth of France – desired by all good citizens, Christians and non-Christians alike – would instead occur thanks to a form of civil religion guaranteeing the unity of national worship.[64] The bankruptcy of the state and the rapid enkindling of an evangelical patriotism that believed it was possible to achieve social happiness on earth were two concomitant factors that accelerated the process of separation between the Revolution and the Catholic Church. The first effects of this reorientation were manifested in the radical manner in which the Constituent Assembly proceeded to reform the features and functioning of the Catholic Church, as it did with all the other institutions that the end of the Ancien Régime had bequeathed to the new revolutionary state.

After about two months of debate, on July 12, 1790, the decree on the Civil Constitution of the Clergy was approved, organized into four distinct sections. The first redesigned the geography of ecclesiastical offices in France, aligning the boundaries of the dioceses with those of the administrative units, with one diocese and one bishop for each department. Only those benefices caring for souls were maintained. Chapters and collegiate churches disappeared. Vicars general (replaced by the episcopal vicars of the cathedral churches), extra-urban vicars, and seminary rectors were abolished. The dioceses were reduced from a number of 135 to 83, one per department. Instead of 18 archbishops, there were 10 metropolitans. Cities with fewer than 6,000 inhabitants were granted only one parish while in towns and country villages exceeding this number, a reorganization according to the needs of the population and local necessities was carried out.

The second section regulated the way in which benefices were granted. The department's electoral body would elect the bishops; that of the district the parish priests. Bishops and parish priests would be free to choose their own vicars, but not to dismiss them without the consent of the majority of the councils formed to assist them in governing the diocese and the parish. It was also decided that each parish priest would receive his canonical institution exclusively from the bishop, and the bishop from the metropolitan. The third section established that bishops, pastors, and vicars would receive a state salary and established the amount for each category, while the fourth section obliged all clergy in the care of souls – from bishops to country pastors – to reside in their diocese or parish or be subject to losing their salary.

All these measures were intended to clarify a very simple principle, namely that the state was responsible for ecclesial life as a whole. Favored by the Gallican clergy, who saw it as a synthesis of the cornerstones of ecclesiastical Gallicanism, this new legislation did not meet with the favor of the bishops, who saw in the new system a disregard of the church's character as a perfect and

---

62   Plongeron, "Affirmations et contestations du chrétien-citoyen," 321.

63   Plongeron, "Affirmations et contestations du chrétien-citoyen," 325.

64   Plongeron, "Affirmations et contestations du chrétien-citoyen," 321.

independent society as required by its spiritual mission. In its defense, the assembly maintained that the Constitution of the Clergy intervened to modify only ecclesiastical discipline, that is, the institutions' functioning, and that it left doctrine intact. The already serious situation deteriorated when the Left began to consider the bishops' resistance to the new religious policy proof of a conspiracy between the aristocracy and the ecclesiastical upper echelons.[65]

The breaking point was reached when, on Nov 27, 1790, the oath of allegiance to the nation, to the king, and to the Constitution was also made obligatory for priests, as had already been the case for public officials, since by now the clergy of every order and rank were seen as such. By law, refusing to take the oath would lead to the loss of salary and pension, even imprisonment in the case of contestation:[66] any evading would be accused of rebellion against the state. Supported by many bishops, who claimed the inapplicability of the oath's formula to spiritual matters,[67] Louis XVI attempted an ephemeral and useless opposition with the sole outcome being the division of the French clergy into *insermentés* (nonjuring), those who refused to swear the oath, and *assermentés* (juring), those who subscribed to the formula.[68] Naturally, several bishops preferred exile to taking the oath while, surprisingly, the number of priests who agreed to vow obedience to the state, on the condition that their spiritual rights would

be respected, was equally as great.[69] The dreaded schism had essentially taken place: the French Catholic Church now consisted of constituent and refractory priests.

No less insidious were the ideological attacks on the Catholic Church that the Constituent Assembly was conducting. The Declaration of the Rights of Man and of the Citizen approved on Aug 26, 1789 – a new "national catechism" in the words of Antoine Barnave – had introduced the principle of indifferentism in religious matters into French legislation, prescribing tolerance towards all forms of worship and religious opinion but maintaining Catholicism as the national religion. The Catholic Church thus received the exclusive right to teach. For the moment, the danger that Protestants and Jews would be placed on equal footing with Catholics was averted – an equality that would be progressively granted to Protestants in December 1789, to the Jews of Bordeaux and the South in 1790, and those of Alsace in 1791. However, the church was still aware of damage that the new Constitution of the Clergy had done to centuries of political theology based on the sacredness of the bond between throne and altar.

Although many members of the lower clergy initially declared themselves in favor of the National Assembly's religious policy – the same ones who were indifferent to the nationalization of ecclesiastical property and the closure of monasteries and convents – the secularization measures had a great impact on the Catholic Church and on the very same 295 ecclesiastical legislators who had, on Apr 13, 1790, opposed the Assembly's refusal to declare Catholicism the state religion. From that moment on, particularly in the South, the conviction that the Revolution had launched

---

65   Plongeron, "Affirmations et contestations du chrétien-citoyen," 328–329.

66   Aubert, "The Catholic Church and the Revolution," 25.

67   Plongeron, "Affirmations et contestations du chrétien-citoyen," 330–332.

68   There is still a debate about the exact number of those who accepted or refused the oath, but it is more or less agreed that slightly more than 50% of those concerned swore fidelity. However, it should be remembered that the numbers vary from region to region. For details, see Plongeron, "Affirmations et contestations du chrétien-citoyen," 338–344; the map on page 339 is particularly interesting.

---

69   It must be said, however, that the number of objectors varied greatly from region to region. Greater resistance was in fact encountered in the cities, villages, and border areas that had previously belonged to Habsburg domains and for that reason had a more ultramontane outlook. For details, see Tackett, "The French Revolution and Religion to 1794," 545–546.

an open attack on Catholicism[70] spread unhindered, and hundreds of priests, once supporters of the revolutionary cause, wound up disassociating themselves from the new political order in France.

3.3 *Growing Conflicts with Rome*

Many of the bishops who refused to swear allegiance to the Constitution chose the Papal States as their land of exile. From there, with the pope's support and protection, they could continue in safety to fight against the usurpers of legitimate power in France. It was to be expected, of course, that Rome, under Pius VI, would soon become one of the main centers of resistance to the Revolution. It was rumored in the papal court that, after having split the French church in two, confiscated ecclesiastical property, destroyed monasteries, and proclaimed religious freedom, the Revolution was about to raze Christianity itself to the ground.

Rome, in particular, awaited the National Assembly's deliberation on the delicate issue of the nomination of bishops. The auspicious occasion arrived at the beginning of 1791. New bishops, elected by the people, had to be attributed their jurisdiction by canonical investiture and their episcopal character through consecration. It was a matter of choosing which of the constituent bishops who were already in office before the Revolution would confer these. Charles-Maurice de Talleyrand-Périgord, Ancien Régime bishop of Autun, who had adhered to the Civil Constitution, stepped forward, agreeing to set the process in motion by personally consecrating the first two new constituent bishops, Claude Marolles and Louis-Alexandre Expilly. Following the example set by Talleyrand, the constituent archbishop of Paris, Jean-Baptiste Gobel, consecrated 26 others in the following two months.[71]

In the pontiff's eyes, therefore, the time had come for action. In the breve *Quod alinquantum* of Mar 10, 1791, Pius VI condemned the Civil Constitution of the Clergy for having overturned the divine order of the church by giving the state the right to consecrate bishops, appoint parish priests, and establish episcopal synods. In his next breve, on Apr 13, 1791, the pope was even harsher with *Charitas quae*, which declared sacrilegious the consecration of those bishops who had been forbidden by Rome to assume their offices. It made the penalty of suspension for those who refused to retract their oath and denounced outright the Declaration of the Rights of Man and of the Citizen.

Pius VI's condemnations and appeals did not fall on deaf ears. The loyalty that broad swaths of French Catholics nurtured towards the pope and the Church of Rome was a factor that the revolutionaries had long underestimated. Indeed, despite the fact that many constituent bishops and priests were proving to be honest and capable pastors, genuinely convinced that the Revolution had brought about a necessary change of pace in the life of the church and the nation, their credibility was constantly undermined by refractory priests who, in the increasingly chaotic climate, played upon the doubt of the validity of the sacraments administered by priests who had gone over to the state's side.[72]

In the following months, the situation continued to deteriorate. The Legislative Assembly, which met on Oct 1, 1791, in the wake of the Constituent Assembly, in no way followed the liberal and pacifying policy that, in religious matters, had characterized the latest months of the Constituent Assembly's efforts but, on the contrary, set out on a path of the legalized persecution of Catholicism. This development can primarily be explained by the composition of the second chamber, consisting entirely in new men who lacked political experience and were almost all imbued

---

70   Tackett, "The French Revolution and Religion to 1794," 544.

71   For more information on this personality in French ecclesial history, who ended up being a victim of the Revolution, see Bernard Plongeron, "Gobel (Jean-Baptiste)," DHGE 21, cols. 359–362.

---

72   Aubert, "The Catholic Church and the Revolution," 25–29.

with an anti-religious and anticlerical sentiment. A second revolutionary generation was coming to power, composed mostly of young men of petit-bourgeois extraction who were instilled with the modern philosophical principles of the day. They were, therefore, totally unwilling to compromise with those who still represented a dangerous legacy of obscurantism, unlike the constituents who wanted to incorporate the church into the state and make church reform the basis for the general reform of the kingdom.

Under the control of the Girondins – the name the new masters of the fate of the nation had chosen for themselves, taken from that of the Gironde Department where they had been elected – the Legislative Assembly helplessly witnessed the September massacres and the first Terror. Then, caught in the undertow of events and popular movements, it decreed a series of provisions that affected not only the refractory clergy – whose religious cause had by then become fused with the political cause of the king and aristocrats in revolt against the nation – but also the constituent church itself. In the eyes of the refractory clergy, the Revolution became more and more a movement aimed at attacking Christianity in general and Catholicism in particular by violent means.[73]

3.4   The Terrible 1792

When Jean-Sifrein Maury, a priest who had taken refuge in Rome after refusing to take the oath, was appointed papal legate to Germany with the task of convincing the German emperor to renounce his Febronianist and Josephinist principles, the French – who had entered the war against Austria and Russia in May 1792 – protested against the clear evidence that refractory priests sought the collaboration of the enemies of France and the Revolution. In the grip of a conspiracy mania, the Girondins waited no longer to raise the level of their clash with the church and ensnare the war saboteurs and on May 27, 1792, the

Legislative Assembly thus ordered the deportation of refractory priests, who were suspected of uprising against the homeland.

The situation of the church in France swiftly deteriorated after the arrest, deposition, and imprisonment of Louis XVI on Aug 10, by the Jacobins and the insurrectional Commune of Paris, and after a National Convention was called to give the country a new republican constitution – as the monarchy would be completely abolished by the Convention on Sept 21, 1792. On Aug 14, galvanized by the king's expulsion, the assembly approved the deportation of all refractory priests to Guyana and, four days later, the suppression of the regular congregations and prohibition of donning an ecclesiastical habit. A new wave of exiles was therefore preparing to leave France (it is estimated that 35,000 priests and religious left the country after 1792, including many women),[74] while a fair number of priests chose to go into hiding, often winding up executed on charges of conspiracy.[75]

The summer of 1792, however, was only a step away from the height of the crisis. On Sept 2, more than 300 churchmen and 3 bishops, mostly belonging to the clergy of the capital, were slaughtered in Paris during what would go down in history as the September Massacres, a killing spree of unclear motives that continued into the following days and which, by November, had led to the death of between 2,000 and 3,000 persons.[76]

On Sept 20, a law was passed that exclusively recognized the validity of civil marriages, and, as a corollary, the possibility of marrying was extended to priests, disconcerting several constituent bishops who, at least in this instance, ended up creating a united front with their refractory adversaries. The number of priests who abandoned the habit or were forced to do so was not counted, nor were those who freely or under coercion took a wife

---

73   Tackett, "The French Revolution and Religion to 1794," 547.

74   Tackett, "The French Revolution and Religion to 1794," 550.

75   Tackett, "The French Revolution and Religion to 1794," 549.

76   For a more detailed treatment, see Plongeron, "Affirmations et contestations du chrétien-citoyen," 354–355.

(it is estimated that this type of defection affected about 80% of the French clergy active in 1792).[77]

In short, the Terror was just around the corner, announced by the iconoclastic fury that fell upon the Christian symbols of France when the congressional deputy Jacques-René Hébert, known in the Commune of Paris for his fierce antagonism against the monarchy and the church,[78] urged the French people to throw off the past by replacing Christian rites with new civil ones, renaming streets and squares, transforming churches into barracks, and melting bells to make cannons. Then, in April 1794, the payment of wages to constituent priests was stopped and, on Sept 18, the religious budget was eliminated.[79] With the refractory clergy already reduced to operating in secrecy, it was the constituent church that suffered the consequences of these new measures approved by a political faction that made no distinction whatsoever between rebellious and republican clergy.[80] Not even Protestants, Jews, or Freemasons were sheltered from the anti-religious fury of the Jacobins. Temples, synagogues, and lodges were closed. Names and religious symbols were removed from the streets in order to show how the new republican state's genetic code included no religion other than the civil one.

3.5 After Robespierre

Aware of the risks that an unbridled iconoclastic policy would entail for the stability of French society, which had already been tested by the war, Maximilien Robespierre had intervened to correct the problem. First, he made sure that the freedom of religion affirmed in the Declaration of the Rights of Man was respected. Then, he arrested Hébert

and condemned him to beheading, the execution being carried out on Mar 16, 1794. Neither of these two acts, however, contributed decisively to curbing the dechristianization in progress.[81] In truth, neither the Terror nor the persecution of the clergy ended, not even with the fall of Roberspierre himself. In fact, in July 1794 the Thermidorians condemned him to the guillotine with the accusation, among others, that he had reawakened fanaticism by replacing the religion of the Revolution with a spiritualist creed (that is the institution of the Festival of the Supreme Being that ended up uniting the refractory and constituent factions of the French church, in addition to being Robespierre's political triumph). The National Convention had, in fact, tried to revive and promote civic worship on a national scale before being dissolved in October of 1795 and replaced by a Directory on Nov 2, of that year. The new Constitution of Year III (1795) granted the Directory executive power, which it exercised until the end of 1799.[82]

Despite everything, from the spring of 1795 to the autumn of 1797, Christian churches experienced a gradual return to some form of religious freedom.[83] As a gesture of détente towards the reactionary forces in turmoil in the west, and mainly towards the Catholic powers of the First Coalition with which France was entering into peace negotiations, on Feb 21, 1795, four days after the signing of the first truce in the Vendée, the Thermidorian Convention solemnly declared that it no longer considered religious practices crimes against society, resigning itself to overseeing what it had hitherto endeavored in vain to repress. The new law, however, granted very little to the churches: the withdrawal of financial support for any religion or Christian church in France was confirmed, churches remained reserved for declining worship, and Catholics were forbidden to form associations,

---

77 Similar incidents occurred also between Protestant ministers in areas with a more marked Protestant presence. See Bernard Plongeron, "Gouvernement révolutionnaire contre chrétienté," HC 10, 363–426, here 386.

78 For greater detail, see Plongeron, "Gouvernement révolutionnaire contre chrétienté," 372–377.

79 Aubert, "The Catholic Church and the Revolution," 34.

80 The situation naturally might be different in each department.

81 For a general overview, see Suzanne Desan, "The French Revolution and Religion (1795–1815)," CHC 7, 556–574.

82 Aubert, "The Catholic Church and the Revolution," 33.

83 Desan, "The French Revolution and Religion," 557.

hold demonstrations, receive donations from private individuals, or post any religious signs outside places of worship.[84]

What remained unchanged was the condition of decline to which the separation from the state had condemned the constituent church, depriving it of its official character and reducing it, in theory, to the same condition as the refractory Roman clergy. The Catholic Church, which had remained faithful to Rome, on the other hand, even though it saw the door shut on the possibility of some kind of reestablishment of the order in force prior to the Revolution, took advantage of the new climate of tolerance to gather its forces. In fact, many refractory priests returned from exile, settling first in the border regions and then, gradually, also within the country, while the bishops who had emigrated abroad began sending vicars general to France, often to carry out clandestine missions in support of the clergy that was still persecuted or in difficulty. Likewise, the Roman rites had to adapt to the new situation of semi-clandestineness. Very often, the lack of priests or their frequent inability to celebrate Mass drove the laity to organize forms of Eucharistic celebrations that were semi-official. Worship practices of the Ancien Régime were recovered in secret and promoted, despite opposition from the republican bodies and, at times, even the clergy themselves.[85]

3.6   The Anti-Christian Policies of the Directory

While the Directory ruled in Paris, in the Vendée, the royalists' revolt raged, at times revealing its partial nature as a religious conflict. Faced with the danger that the pauperist war would turn into a Catholic crusade to revive the papacy's ancient privileges, many Protestants chose to enlist in the republican army.[86] Once famine had been averted and the Vendée uprising had been settled in bloodshed, on Sept 4, 1797, a coup d'état changed the balance of the Directory, reversing the tempering of certain restrictive measures against the refractory clergy. From the autumn of that year, therefore, the decrees of 1792 and 1793 came back into effect, and priests who were obedient to Rome that remained or returned to France became liable to execution if they did not submit to the constitutional oath or if they were not expatriated within two weeks of being denounced.[87]

This revival of anticlericalism, however, had the opposite effect to that hoped for by the Directory. Priests and lay persons, who had developed a greater awareness of their ecclesial responsibilities than in the past,[88] gave rise to an unexpected religious revival in which women often played a central role.[89] In rural areas, in particular, where the precepts of faith were transmitted in families from generation to generation, traditional practices and devotions took on a special attraction precisely because of their forbidden and clandestine nature. Although the republican authorities attempted to obstruct it or prevent it from spreading, this underground, "catacombic" faith continued to maintain France's dissenting Catholicism alive for a long time to come. It should be borne in mind, moreover, that, both in France and other countries with a Catholic majority subject to the republic, such as Belgium, the force of government countermeasures was regularly weakened by the inertia of the administrative machine and by the

---

84   See Claude Langlois & Timothy Tackett, "A l'épreuve de la Révolution (1770–1830)," in: François Lebrun, ed., *Histoire des Catholiques en France du XVe siècle à nos jours*, Toulouse, Privat, 1980, 239–320, in particular 264–265.

85   See Desan, "The French Revolution and Religion," 562–563.

86   Plongeron, "Gouvernement révolutionnaire contre chrétienté," 396. The war proved to be a bloodbath for both Catholics and Protestants. The year 1796 saw the cessation of hostilities and the surrender of the rebels, with the respective populations dramatically reduced in number. Plongeron, "Gouvernement révolutionnaire contre chrétienté," 397–406.

87   See Bernard Plongeron, "L'impossible laïcité de l'État républicain," *HC* 10, 427–478, in particular 430–431, and Desan, "The French Revolution and Religion," 558.

88   Aubert, "The Catholic Church and the Revolution," 37.

89   Aubert, "The Catholic Church and the Revolution," 37; Desan, "The French Revolution and Religion," 560.

clergy's clandestine activities, and this despite the deportation of many priests and faithful.[90]

It is surprising to note that, in many cases, this new wave of persecution also aroused the disapproval of republican political circles and even civil servants themselves who, in various regions of France, worked to mitigate the severity of the sanctions and reduce state pressure on the clergy and the faithful. However, it is no less surprising that these abuses also generated tensions between Catholics and Protestants as well as between Lutherans and Reformed, who accused one another of being responsible for the violence that befell all of them without distinction.[91]

Undermined in its authority by the military upheavals suffered by the French armies in Egypt and, by then, without popular support, on 18 Brumaire, Year VIII of the Revolution (Nov 9, 1799), Napoleon Bonaparte definitively liquidated the Directory in a coup d'état, putting an end to the French Revolution and the republic that it had generated in such a radically anti-Christian manner.

3.7 The Concordat and the Relaunching of French Catholicism

Unlike his predecessors, Napoleon well understood the resilient nature of Catholicism. For this reason, as soon as he came to power, he launched a series of measures aimed at easing political pressure on the church. At the end of 1799, deportations ceased; the churches were restored to the faithful; the oath of allegiance to the Constitution became the sole requirement for the practise of religion; and, on Dec 30, to seal the new course of things, it was decided to render public honor to the remains of Pius VI. He had died a prisoner at the end of August in the fortress of Valence-sur-Rhône, to

where he had been deported after the occupation of Rome by the Napoleonic army at the end of its Italian campaign. It was to all intents and purposes a détente that the new first consul of France sought with Rome, aware of how only an agreement with the pope could guarantee the religious peace that the nation's prosperity (and his own personal rise to power) required. Having said that, what Napoleon needed at the time was a solution that would bring the entire Catholic Church, both the constituent and the refractory one, under state control. This truce with the pope, however, did not require the restitution of the ecclesiastical patrimony confiscated during the Revolution, which would have risked antagonizing the entire class of landowners whose support was no less important than that of the bishops.[92]

The new pope, Pius VII, elected in Venice under the protection of the Austrians after a three-month conclave and in a far from harmonious atmosphere, was for his part well aware of his disadvantage and the fact that Napoleon held the power to decide the fate of the Catholic Church in many parts of Europe.[93] He was, needless to say, primarily concerned with the restitution of the papal territories but, at the same time, he was convinced that a renewal of the ecclesiastical institutions was necessary, even though this was opposed by most of the Roman Curia.[94] Encouraged by the signs of peace arriving from France, the pope therefore enthusiastically accepted Bonaparte's invitation to reconciliation, hoping in this way also to put a brake on internal tensions within the French church.

After lengthy negotiations, the concordat between Napoleon and Pius VII was signed on

---

90   Plongeron, "L'impossible laïcité de l'État républicain," 431. It should be added that the measures adopted proved to be less effective in Belgium, where the vast majority of priests and religious refused to accept a salary from a state that had confiscated all ecclesiastical property.

91   See Plongeron, "L'impossible laïcité de l'État républicain," 439.

92   Aubert, "The Catholic Church and the Revolution," 57, offers a detailed analysis of Napoleon's motivations.

93   For more information, see GKH 8, 18–19, while for an intellectual and spiritual profile of Pius VII, see Aubert, "The Catholic Church and the Revolution," 51–53.

94   Aubert, "The Catholic Church and the Revolution,", 53–54.

July 15, 1801.[95] The agreement consisted of a com-promise that gave the French government the right to control important sectors of church life and that recognized Catholicism as the confession of the majority of the French, although it did not proclaim it the state religion. In exchange for loy-alty to the government, Catholics were guaranteed freedom of religion, while the church renounced claims to the property confiscated during the Revolution. In compensation, however, the state would assure a salary for the clergy and once again grant private citizens the right to donate to the church. Finally, cathedrals, churches, and other buildings of worship were returned to the clergy and to their original uses. To the pope's great relief, the experiment of separation between church and state had thus come to an end, but the fact that the legal recognition of Protestants and Jews re-mained valid relativized this success of the legal primacy that the Church of Rome once again ex-ercised in France.

However, there was still the matter of ecclesi-astical jurisdiction that caused the church major difficulties with the concordat: the conditions dic-tated by Napoleon provided that both the refrac-tory and constituent bishops would resign their respective offices (in the case of refusal, the pope would see to their replacement), that the first con-sul would have the power to nominate bishops (something that would give Napoleon the power to impede both Gallican and pro-Roman adversar-ies) whom the Holy Father would invest canoni-cally, and that the bishops would themselves be able to nominate parish clergy with the approval of the government.[96]

In the treaty, moreover, nothing was said about the restoration of religious orders; the Protestant denominations continued to be accepted by the state; the number of dioceses were dramatically reduced from over 130 to 50, which then rose to 60 (when Belgium, Savoy, and the Catholic regions of the Rhineland annexed by Napoleon became, for all intents and purposes, considered part of France).[97] To this should be added that, in obe-dience to the provisions of the concordat, about 40% of the bishops refused to resign and a small number of them formed the schismatic church Petite Église.[98]

This, however, was not enough to satisfy the more anticlerical faction, which accused Napoleon of giving in to the pope too easily. In response, when it was time for the parliament to approve the concordat, Bonaparte ordered a vote on the so-called Organic Laws of the clergy to be added to the agenda. These were a kind of executive reg-ulation aimed at increasing state control over the church. They established that any papal document had to obtain the government's approval in order to be published in France, that the declaration of the four articles of the French clergy, dear to the Gallican tradition, would be once again taught in the seminaries, and that civil marriage services would precede religious ones. The bishops, more-over, under the control of the Minister of Religion, could no longer act as a collective body but as prefects of their dioceses with discretional pow-ers over their priests, while the cathedral chapters, which had once been powerful, were now deprived of all of their prerogatives and reduced to a purely decorative function. Nevertheless, Napoleon did not fail to gain the sympathies of the bishops, who saw their power increased, as well as of those of the clergy in general, who were at least guaranteed

---

95   For more details, see *GKH* 8, 20–22; see also Desan, "The French Revolution and Religion," 564–565 and Bernard Plongeron, "De Napoléon à Metternich: Une modernité en état de blocus," *HC* 10, 635–738, here 670–689, which emphasizes the important role played by Cardinal Consalvi in the pontificate.

96   Desan, "The French Revolution and Religion," 565. *GKH* 8, 22–23, offers a detailed review of the articles. See also Joseph F. Byrnes, *Priests of the French Revolution: Saints and Renegades in a New Political Era*, University

Park PA, The Pennsylvania State University Press, 2014, 211–214.

97   For Napoleon's motivations, see Aubert, "The Catholic Church and the Revolution," 60–61.

98   For more details on the Petite Église, see Aubert, "The Catholic Church and the Revolution," 61–62.

a fixed salary by the state.[99] Financial support was also granted to the two major Protestant denominations, Lutherans and Calvinists, who were officially recognized by the regime, although this progress required that the Reformed church of France renounce its pyramidal system of synods that governed it locally.[100] Finally, there was also room for Jews, who gradually received greater benefits, despite the fact that state control had caused several tensions between the central government and those communities, accustomed as they were to self-management.[101]

As was to be expected, Rome objected to the organic articles, considering them to be a stratagem to make the concordat more favorable to France than it already was, but the lack of valid alternatives forced Pius VII to concede. It must be said, however, that despite Napoleon's evident and overwhelming victory over the pope, the concordat proved to be advantageous in the long run for the Catholic Church as well, which was slowly able to regain the splendors of the past, enjoying much more favorable treatment than the Protestants. It is sufficient to point out that for the latter, state subsidies were accorded only if a community consisted of 6,000 souls, a completely unrealistic number given the political and social conditions of the time. In theory, Catholics and Protestants enjoyed equal rights in the eyes of the state, but in fact delays and the organizational difficulties of the Protestants put them at a clear disadvantage, thus fueling a continual confessional rivalry.[102]

Be that as it may, the challenges that the Catholic Church in France had to face after signing the concordat were enormous, starting with the reorganization of the dioceses, which often resulted in artificial constructs. In the aftermath of Napoleon's seizure of power, the composition of the French episcopate was, to say the least, diversified. The fracture between refractory and constituent bishops was still intact, and to these two groups had been added that of the schismatic bishops of the Petite Église. The reorganization of the parishes was also a far from easy task, particularly due to the lack of personnel. Most of the French clergy were elderly (more than 30% were over 60 years old), many priests had married in the meantime, there were few ordinations of priests for many years, and monks continued to be either uneducated or unwilling to engage in pastoral work, or both. As a result, in 1808, more than 20% of the French parishes were vacant.[103]

Years passed before the bishops could reopen the seminaries, as provided for by the concordat, due mainly to the lack of funds. There was also a shortage of sufficiently prepared professors, and the effects of dechristianization began to manifest themselves in the scarcity of vocations. In the long run, however, both the exemption from military service and the security of a decent salary were two sufficient reasons to drive many young men into the priesthood, thus raising the curve in regard to vocations, although the situation varied from region to region and according to the work of prefects and individual bishops.

Unlike most congregations and religious orders, missionary groups engaged in caring for the poor: for example, the Vincentians (who in the eyes of the state had the merit of not demanding any salary), were immediately allowed to reorganize and operate again. A similar support was immediately granted to women religious who were involved in education and caring for the sick, and many orders were founded *ex novo*, such that, in 1809, more than 16,000 sisters were active in a total of 2,000

---

99   Aubert, "The Catholic Church and the Revolution," 58–59.
100   Desan, "The French Revolution and Religion," 566–567.
101   Desan, "The French Revolution and Religion," 567.
102   *GKH* 8, 24–25. For example, during the hundred days between the return of the emperor from exile on Elba and his defeat at Waterloo in 1815, Catholics were responsible for several episodes of violence against the Protestant communities. See Desan, "The French Revolution and Religion," 567.

---

103   There is a detailed description in Aubert, "The Catholic Church and the Revolution," 63–64.

convents.[104] It was certainly not one of Napoleon's intentions to provoke a rebirth of the Catholic Church in France, but that was in fact what happened, due to a great extent to the contribution of women at a time when women were still excluded from teaching in state schools.[105]

3.8   *New Conflicts*

The peace between Pius VII and Napoleon was, however, destined to last only a short while; it was disturbed by new tensions in 1808–1809. Parish missions, which had achieved a certain success, were banned on Sept 25, 1809.[106] It did not take long for the French emperor to realize that the means chosen to regain control over the affairs of the church had in reality been more beneficial to the pope, to whom many of his subjects and all the clergy had returned in search of guidance and consolation. These were also the years in which an influential essay by François-René de Chateaubriand, *Le génie du christianisme*,[107] circulated in France. It offered an apologetic defense of the church and of the idea of a universal Catholicism able to embrace even contemporary secular values like liberty, progress, and the emancipation of the dispossessed. Announcing the imminent return to prominence of religion after the revolutionary parenthesis, Chateaubriand's essay ended up giving Catholicism an aura of respectability, restoring its citizenship in European intellectual circles.[108] On the wave of this Catholic resurgence, for which the concordat and spiritual stature of Pius VII had in a certain sense prepared the way, the autonomist aspirations of the French Gallican Church soon gave way to a sort of ultramontane passion. This was especially true after the

pope's visit to Paris for the coronation of Napoleon had rekindled the enthusiasm of many Catholics. Pilgrimages thus flourished again, and confraternities made their return to the public sphere. In short, in the space of a few years, Catholicism once again became a strong and visible component of public life in France.[109]

However, before all of this could take shape, one of Napoleon's primary concerns even as emperor of the French, when he was not leading his armies on the battlefields of Europe, was to exploit Catholicism to consolidate his own power, linking adoration of his person with the adoration of God. The much coveted consent of the Catholic masses was slow in coming, and the religious tolerance sanctioned by the Organic Laws, if it was well received by Protestants, Jews, and other religious minorities in the empire, also aroused unrest, criticism, and opposing demonstrations in France and Italy, theaters of clerical opposition that did not spare Napoleon the label of antichrist.[110] When Pius VII refused to increase the number of transalpine cardinals in the Sacred College to one third of the total, as requested by Napoleon, the situation began to deteriorate, resulting first in the occupation of Rome by French troops in February 1808 and then, in the following year, in the annexation of the Papal States to the empire, which marked the end of the temporal power of the popes. In response, Pius VII excommunicated Napoleon, who in turn confined the pope to Savona, where he was kept in isolation until 1812. The news of the emperor's excommunication by the pope quickly spread throughout Europe, raising feelings of opposition to France among Catholics everywhere.

The French bishops, on the other hand, remained silent, aware of the harmful consequences for the church of opening hostilities with a state far more powerful than the government of the Directory. Yet the collaborationist line taken by the French episcopate, while it proved useful in avoiding the retaliation of the emperor, was not

---

104   Aubert, "The Catholic Church and the Revolution," 66–67.
105   See Desan, "The French Revolution and Religion," 568.
106   Aubert, "The Catholic Church and the Revolution," 69.
107   The complete title was *Le génie du christianisme, ou Beatués de la religion chrétienne.*
108   See also his *Les martyrs ou le triomphe de la religion*, Paris, Le Normant, 1809. Naturally, anti-Catholic attitudes continued to exist.

---

109   Desan, "The French Revolution and Religion," 568–569.
110   Desan, "The French Revolution and Religion," 570–572.

as effective in appeasing the displeasure of the clergy. In fact, beginning in 1810, when the bishops appointed by the government but not yet canonically installed by the pope took possession of their respective dioceses, they had to face the opposition of their own clergy, firmly united on the side of Pius VII. A synod organized in Paris on June 17, 1811, also defended the prerogatives of the pope. The synod, openly challenging the will of Napoleon, decreed that no act or decision, even a conciliar one, concerning episcopal appointments would be valid without the approval of the pope.

The matter thus ended up on the desk of Pius VII, who paid for his refusal to concede canonical investiture to the bishops appointed by the government with his forced transfer to Fontainebleau where, weakened by illness and the pressure of the events, on 25 Jan, 1813, he agreed to sign a draft agreement that was to remain secret. The agreement was then made public by Napoleon. The betrayal of the secrecy clause by the emperor convinced the pope, already plagued by second thoughts, to retract the agreement of Mar 25, a decision that had the effect of greatly increasing his popularity to the point of consecrating him a savior of the faith and of the freedom of the church.[111] It was a success in terms of public support and affection that the pope was able to experience personally when, after the fall of Napoleon, he returned to a Rome scarred by the unpleasant French occupation yet celebrating the vicar of Christ retaking possession of his chair.[112] It cannot be denied that Napoleon's excommunication was a decision that required courage and a willingness to be sacrificed.

4 Conclusions

The American Revolution was a rebellion of colonists with roots firmly planted in Europe. From Boston to Atlanta, everyone battled to achieve freedom and independence, even though the way that these two concepts were interpreted varied according to the social groups and to their immediate objectives. If from a strictly economic and political perspective the freedom sought by most of the colonists was freedom from the control of the British crown, religious minorities, such as Catholics, Jews, and also dissident English churches, who had not forgotten the harassment suffered in the homeland by the Anglican Church, associated this type of claim with the hope for a kind of freedom that did not recognize religious or denominational fences.

Supported by a rich mixture of Christian denominations and driven by the effluence of faith during the Great Awakening, which had profoundly changed the physiognomy and essence of North American Protestantism, the American Revolution never had to tackle an anti-religious movement aimed at expunging the Christian faith from the public sphere. The founding fathers of the United States were, in any case, well aware of how important the support of religion was in a process of nation building and, for this reason, all involved, from military commanders to the drafters of the Constitution, were at least nominally affiliated with a church. The positive attitude toward religious freedom and tolerance would partly change only after the massive immigration of European Catholics in the 1830s, but it never degenerated into a systematic persecution of minorities, nor suffered an intrusion of the state into religious issues.

The French Revolution had causes of a different nature. What lit the fire there was an unprecedented economic-financial crisis due to the concentration of wealth in the hands of the nobility and higher ecclesial ranks. The latter reflected, along with many religious orders, an affluent church in a famished country held in check by social imbalances. These imbalances existed within the church itself. If the bishops became such by birthright, and not by Christian merit or virtue, the rest of the French clergy often came from more disadvantaged social classes. It is not surprising, therefore,

---

111   Aubert, "The Catholic Church and the Revolution," 75–76.
112   On the situation in Rome, see Plongeron, "De Napoléon à Metternich," 685–686.

that many priests caring for souls, already in close contact with the material needs of the population, initially supported the Revolution. The oath of allegiance imposed on the clergy in 1790, which in fact equated the clergy with civil servants, ended up dividing the Catholic Church and generating discord even in the few clergymen sympathetic to the revolutionaries. The decision to declare Catholicism no longer the state religion, thus separating the church from the state, was the misstep that lost the Revolution the support of large sections of the population, initiating a process that first the abolition of the freedom of religion sanctioned by the Legislative Assembly and later the anti-Catholic persecutions carried out under the Terror only made irreversible. The anti-religious policy that accompanied the various phases of the Revolution, in fact, was not seen by the vast majority of French Catholics as a necessary expedient to free people and the modern state from ecclesiastical constraints but as an attempt to destroy Christianity and the church by removing the latter from the public sphere and depriving it of the main worldly instruments that guaranteed the effectiveness of its apostolate.

Napoleon only gave back to the church a vague shadow of the splendor of the Ancien Régime, inscribing it with his ephemeral neo-Constantinian design, while only the Restoration was able to lull it into the dream of a reconstituted Christianity that would relegate the traumas of the Reformation and Revolution to an unrepeatable past.

Historiography has always treated the American Revolution and the French Revolution, despite their evident incommensurability, as two fundamental genetic stages in that complex of ideals, doctrines, ruptures, and political experiences that is called modernity, and which forced all Christian forms, no longer assumed to be determining elements in an organic conception of society and the world, to redefine their own relationship with otherness profoundly. This process had very different outcomes on either side of the Atlantic.

As far as the United States is concerned, it should first of all be pointed out that, contrary to a stubborn conviction, the scope of the First Amendment to the Constitution was not to institute a separation between church and state – perhaps even to the point of attaining a *republique laïque* in the French manner – but rather to guard against the birth of a state church, as had been the case in England and in the Catholic and Lutheran countries of Europe. Resisting the voices that rose up in favor of a direct or indirect constitutionalizing of the Christian Protestant character of the new republic, the First Amendment sanctioned the freedom of religious expression, whether private or public, and, while reducing the churches to private associations, guaranteed the presence of faith – or, more correctly, faiths – in that which today is called the "public square."[113]

Leaving aside the extent to which this choice seems to be the root of the alleged American eccentricity in matters relating to religion and politics, in terms of the relations between the churches, the First Amendment had the effect of unleashing in the confessional space all the potential of Christian creativity that would have otherwise been absorbed by forms of competition for access to a dominant position in the state. Although the absence of a dominant church and the impossibility of invoking the intervention of political power in order to reestablish the rights of the majority confession in the case of schism proved in the short term to be two factors of little use in healing the denominational multiplicity which affected American Christianity, one fact speaks eloquently.

---

113   The issue is still the subject of bitter debate, caused above all by the resurgence of conservatism in recent years that argues for a Christian interpretation of the Constitution in order to enable a re-Christianization of the United States. For two divergent points of view on the issue, see Richard John Neuhaus, *The Naked Public Square*, Grand Rapids MI, Eerdmans, ²1986 (which defends the constitutionality of political religious discourse) and Isaac Kramnick & R. Laurence Moore, *The Godless Constitution: The Case Against Religious Correctness*, New York NY, Norton, 1997. A recent historical analysis favorable to the presence of faith in American public debate is that of Jon Meacham, *American Gospel: God, the Founding Fathers, and the Making of the Constitution*, New York NY, Random House, 2006.

While in Europe a practical ecumenism was born in the 1920s from the scandalously basic need to prevent another generation of Christians from going to war against other Christians in the future, in the United States, where the last religious blood-soaked division dated back to the War of Secession, churches were already beginning to raise the stakes of the ecumenical challenge, betting on their readiness to transfer that cooperation that had been thus far experienced only at the practical level to a theological level.

It is hard to imagine anything more distant from the American situation than the model of the relationship between church and state that prevailed in the course of the 19th century within the European Catholic world as a response to the problems posed by the French Revolution. That Revolution, it is often said, in the light of the principles of 1789 and its bloody results during the Terror, was seen as a constant threat to the whole of Christianity, and, as a consequence, to Western society as a whole. In the famous "genealogy of errors," Protestants – long blamed for having started, with the Reformation, "that age of degeneration that led, with the revolutionary apostasy of society from the church, to the period of the final apocalyptic clash between good and evil that the year Eighty-Nine had opened"[114] – were especially ensnared in the intransigent scheme.

Translated from Italian to English by Susan Dawson Vásquez and David Dawson Vásquez.

---

114   Menozzi, *La Chiesa cattolica e la secolarizzazione*, 25.

Bibliography

Albanese, Catherine L., *Sons of the Fathers: The Civil Religion of the American Revolution*, Philadelphia PA, Temple University Press, 1976.

Aubert, Roger, "Die katholische Kirche und die Revolution," *HKG* 6/1, 3–104; ET: "The Catholic Church and the Revolution," *HistCh* 7, 3–84.

Byrnes, Joseph F., *Priests of the French Revolution: Saints and Renegades in a New Political Era*, University Park PA, The Pennsylvania State University Press, 2014.

de Bertier de Sauvigny, Guillaume, *De kerk in het tijdperk van de restauratie (1801–1848)*, Hilversum, Brand, 1965.

Lehner, Ulrich L., *The Catholic Enlightenment: The Forgotten History of a Global Movement*, New York NY, Oxford University Press, 2016.

Marty, Martin E., "The American Revolution and Religion (1765–1815)," *CHC* 7, 497–516.

McMahon, Darrin M., *Enemies of the Enlightenment: The French Counter-Enlightenment and the Making of Modernity*, Oxford, Oxford University Press, 2001.

Mead, Sidney E., *The Lively Experiment: The Shaping of Christianity in America*, New York NY, Harper and Row, 1963.

Menozzi, Daniele, *La Chiesa cattolica e la secolarizzazione*, Turin, Einaudi, 1993.

Miccoli, Giovanni, *Fra mito della cristianità e secolarizzazione: Studi sul rapporto chiesa-società nell'età contemporanea*, Casale Monferrato, Marietti, 1985.

Plongeron, Bernard, "Affirmations et contestations du chrétien-citoyen (1789–1792)," *HC* 10, 301–362.

CHAPTER 3

Historiography of the Ecumenical Movement: The State of the Question

Étienne Fouilloux and Luca Ferracci

Strictly defined as the attempt to bring separated Christians together in order to restore the unity that has been lost over time, ecumenism barely goes back any further than the beginning of the 20th century, when it becomes one of the most significant religious phenomena. Indeed, the word and the reality appeared during the years from 1910 to 1920 in the Anglican and Protestant worlds in Europe and the United States, designating the movement that arose from the first meetings among non-Catholic Christians: the missionary Conference of Edinburgh in 1910; the Stockholm Conference in 1925 on "practical" divergences; and the Lausanne Conference in 1927 on doctrinal disputes. Thus defined, ecumenism has, since its emergence, given rise to a considerable body of literature, mainly in theology and spirituality; these kinds of studies are not the concern of the present review. Only a small section of that literature will be treated, that studying the ecumenical movement with the methods of the social sciences, mainly history and sociology. Furthermore, only the most important published texts and articles will be mentioned, not the memoirs or unpublished dissertations, with a few exceptions.

The historiography of ecumenism is distributed rather unevenly in the half century of its emergence. While the ecumenical euphoria of the 1960s generated a considerable amount of work in the attempt to explain such success, its later stagnation, or what was judged as such, often discouraged further progress on this bumpy road, until a new generation of scholars, who were too young to have known its heroic times, took hold of ecumenism as just one subject among others, without too many prejudices and with much better access to sources than their predecessors. Hence a new burst of works of sound academic quality has emerged since the beginning of the third millennium, which the present *History of the Desire for Christian Unity* seeks to assess.

1 Initial Approaches

Until the movement's consecration in the early 1960s, when the Eastern Churches under Soviet rule and the IMC joined the WCC at its third World Assembly in New Delhi in 1961, and by the Roman Catholic Church's official endorsement with Vatican II's decree *Unitatis redintegratio* in 1964, the historiography of the nascent ecumenism unsurprisingly played an instrumental role. From within the movement, some of its promoters became its chroniclers, wishing to justify its creation and growth. Thus the WCC – established in 1948 at the Amsterdam assembly and based in Geneva – during its first half century of prehistory and history, between 1954 and 1970, produced a multi-authored synthesis that remains a reference point,[1] even though it has been corrected and completed along the way on more than one point.[2]

---

1 *A History of the Ecumenical Movement*, vol. 1, Ruth Rouse & Stephen C. Neill, eds., *1517–1948*, London, SPCK, [2]1967; *A History of the Ecumenical Movement*, vol. 2, Harold E. Fey, ed., *The Ecumenical Advance (1948–1968)*, London, SPCK, 1970.

2 See, for example, Nils Karlström, *Ökumene in Mission und Kirche: Entwicklungslinien der heutigen ökumenischen Bewegung*, Munich, Claudius, 1962 (original Swedish

Two renowned Catholic theologians also made their contribution.[3]

At the same time, "brief histories" of ecumenism sought to acclimate the idea to Protestant circles.[4] They reflect its origins well, without any particular indulgence towards the Roman Church, which at the time stubbornly refused to associate itself with the movement. A comparison between the two volumes of the famous collection Que sais-je?, published by the Presses Universitaires de France, successively dedicated to ecumenism with the same title, is highly instructive in this respect. Berthe Gavalda provided a first, balanced synthesis, making room for confessional reticence whether liberal or, contrarily, evangelical or fundamentalist. Less than ten years later, the synthesis of Madeleine Barot, an ecumenist who had long been a permanent presence in Geneva, exalted the work accomplished and somewhat minimized its weaknesses in the ecumenical euphoria of the 1960s.[5]

During the time when Rome shunned the movement, the position of Catholic historiography towards it remained ambiguous. There were "Catholic ecumenists," to use a tautological expression of the time, but they were few in number and were often suspect within a church that was little inclined to open a dialogue of equals with those whom it reproached for having once detached themselves from it. It was therefore necessary to prove that Rome, far from being indifferent to the division among Christians, had not ceased to feel sorry for it and to call for unity, according to its own conception of the term. It was for this reason that collections of documents from the papal magisterium were produced by Roger Aubert in 1947 and Gregory Baum in 1958.[6] For the same reason, Catholic "brief histories" of ecumenism were also generated, such as those of Georges Tavard in 1960, François Biot in 1963, and Henri Daniel-Rops in 1965 for the French-speaking world,[7] and more recently those of Paul M. Minus Jr., in 1976 for the English-speaking world[8] and of Jörg Ernesti in 2007 for the German-speaking world.[9]

It was in this same context that ecumenism made its appearance, in a significant way, in dictionaries and encyclopedias but, since specialists in the field were rare, they were often called upon repeatedly. Beginning in 1954, Fr. Gabriel Jacquemet entrusted Fr. Yves Congar with dozens of entries on separated Christians for his encyclopedia Catholicisme: Hier, aujourd'hui, demain,[10] published in Paris by Letouzey et Ané. Fr. Congar also wrote the article "Ökumenische Bewegung" for the second edition of the Lexikon für Theologie und Kirche published in 1962 in Freiburg by Herder.[11] Willem Adolph Visser 't Hooft, for his part, contributed the entry "Ökumenische Bewegung" in the Protestant encyclopedia Religion in Geschichte und Gegenwart in 1960.[12]

version, 1960); David P. Gaines, The World Council of Churches: A Study of its Background and History, Peterborough, Richard R. Smith, 1966.

3 Gustave Thils, Histoire doctrinale du mouvement œcuménique, Paris, Desclée de Brouwer, ²1963; Bruno Chenu, La signification ecclésiologique du Conseil œcuménique des Églises (1945–1963), Paris, Beauchesne, 1972.

4 For France, André Paul, L'unité chrétienne: Schismes et rapprochements, Paris, Rieder, 1930; Paul Conord, Brève histoire de l'œcuménisme, Paris, Les Bergers et les Mages, 1958.

5 Madeleine Barot, Le Mouvement oecuménique, Que sais-je? 841, Paris, PUF, 1959 and 1967.

6 Respectively, Roger Aubert, Le Saint-Siège et l'union des Églises, Brussels, Éditions Universitaires, 1947; Gregory Baum, That They May Be One: A Study of Papal Doctrine (Leo XIII–Pius XI), London, Bloomsbury, 1958.

7 Georges Tavard, Petite histoire du mouvement œcuménique, Paris, Fleurus, 1960; François Biot, De la polémique au dialogue, 2 vols., Paris, Cerf, 1963; Henri Daniel-Rops, Ces chrétiens nos frères, Paris, Fayard, 1965.

8 Paul M. Minus Jr., The Catholic Rediscovery of Protestantism: A History of Roman Catholic Ecumenical Pioneering, New York NY, Paulist Press, 1976.

9 Jörg Ernesti, Kleine Geschichte der Ökumene, Freiburg i.Br., Herder, 2007.

10 Gabriel Jacquemet & others, eds., Catholicisme: Hier, aujourd'hui, demain, 15 vols., Paris, Letouzey et Ané, 1948–2000.

11 LThK, ²7, 1128–1137.

12 RGG, ³4, 1517–1586.

2   The Viewpoint of Sociology

A decisive epistemological split in the history of
the ecumenical movement occurred in the second
half of the 1960s, at the precise moment when triumphant ecumenism was suffering the first attacks
of a protest that no longer saw itself as a rearguard,
as a defense of threatened confessional identities,
but as a vanguard in its uncompromising criticism
of a movement that had lost its dynamism and
had become, in its eyes, an ecclesiastical institution as open to criticism as the others. This rupture was the work of sociologists who, considering
the events of ecumenical rapprochement as part
of the general history of the 20th century, stressed
the importance of nontheological and even nonreligious factors in its emergence. This gave rise
to two types of interpretation that are not mutually exclusive. In the first case, the ecumenical
movement was seen as the convergent and simultaneous reaction of the great historical churches
threatened by secularization in Europe and North
America or by the proselytism of the practitioners
of the new movements in the Third World. In the
second, it was a form of regulating the market for
religious goods, tending to substitute peaceful
emulation for brutal competition, now considered
ruinous, especially in mission countries.[13] These
theses by the Anglo-Saxon scholars Peter Berger,
Robert Currie, Thomas Luckmann, and Bryan
Wilson were disseminated, discussed, and extended in France by Jean Séguy of the Sociology of
Religions Group of the CNRS, whose contribution,
summarized in *Les conflit du dialogue* in 1973,[14] is
central here. With conviction and talent, he pleaded for a nontheological ecumenology that would
break the umbilical cord linking it to its object of
study in order to explore its multiple facets better.

Without establishing such distance, there could be
no truly scientific approach to ecumenism.

Such an objectification was not well received
by the movement's protagonists, the most experienced of whom then felt that the time had come
to publish memoirs of their struggles in order to
give ecumenism a legitimate place in their respective churches: the Reformed pastors Marc Boegner
and Willem Adolph Visser 't Hooft, who were
key players in the WCC,[15] and the philosopher
Jean Guitton, the Dominican Yves Congar, and
the Marist Maurice Villain, who were central figures of French-speaking "Catholic ecumenism."[16]
These testimonials in the historical record have
thus swelled the growing emission of theological
and spiritual works on ecumenism, boosted by the
movement's successes, at the forefront of which
was Vatican II's preferential option for ecumenism.

3   Between the East and England

This epistemological rupture has borne less fruit
in sociology than in history due to new access to
certain archival collections and the testimonies
of witnesses. As the origins began to recede, anamnesis could begin. The work then unfolded
in two distinct, though complementary directions. With their eyes in the rearview mirror,
some researchers set out to discover the early
signs of rapprochement, and ended up showing
its distance in relation to the paths that opened
up later. In this vein, the main areas of research

---

13   Maurice Cheza, Monique Costermans & Jean Pirotte,
       eds., *Œcuménisme et pratiques missionnaires*, Paris,
       Karthala, 2002.

14   Jean Séguy, *Les conflits du dialogue*, Paris, Cerf, 1973.

15   Marc Boegner, *L'exigence œcuménique: Souvenirs et
       perspectives*, Paris, Albin Michel, 1968; Willem Adolph
       Visser 't Hooft, *Memoirs*, London, SCM Press, 1973.

16   Jean Guitton, *Dialogue avec les précurseurs: Journal œcu-
       ménique (1922–1962)*, Paris, Aubier, 1962; Yves Congar,
       *Chrétiens en dialogue: Contributions catholiques à
       l'œcuménisme*, Unam Sanctam 50, Paris, Cerf, 1964, ix–
       lxiv (preface reprinted and expanded in Yves Congar,
       Une passion: L'unité, Réflexions et souvenirs (1929–1973),
       Paris, Cerf, 1974); Maurice Villain, *Vers l'unité: Itinéraire
       d'un pionnier (1935–1975)*, Dinard, Groupement pour le
       Service Œcuménique, 1986.

concern the efforts made at the turn of the 20th century to bridge the gap between Rome, Eastern Orthodoxy, and Anglicanism, efforts that were facilitated by the opening of the Vatican archives, first for the pontificate of Leo XIII and then for those of Pius X and Benedict XV, and finally for that of Pius XI. In the East, the pioneering work of Angelo Tamborra[17] and Vittorio Peri[18] must be joined by the considerable and dedicated work of the Greek-Melkite historian Joseph Hajjar. Starting from a concern with defending the prerogatives of his community and Eastern-rite Catholicism as a whole, faced with Latinization and Romanization, he reconstructed the entire fabric of unequal political-religious exchanges between Western Europe, Eastern Europe, and the Near East in the 19th century at the crossroads of a history of interconfessional and international relations.[19] Claude Soetens's work on the Eastern initiatives of the Eucharistic Congress of Jerusalem in 1893[20] and Giuseppe Croce's work on those of Grottaferrata

Abbey at the time of Pius X[21] are more modest in their purpose, if not in their size and scope, and are milestones in their own right.

There is also a well-advanced body of work concerning the three "Anglo-Roman campaigns" of the 1860s, 1890s, and 1920s, which were failures. Mark Chapman reported on the APUC, an offshoot of the Oxford Movement in which English Catholics rubbed shoulders with Anglicans, an association condemned by Rome in texts from 1864 to 1865 that set a precedent until the 1928 encyclical *Mortalium animos*.[22] From the second campaign – which saw the French Vincentian Fernand Portal and the head of the English High Church Lord Halifax attempt to obtain Roman recognition of the validity of Anglican ordinations – we have Régis Ladous's two works on French religious[23] based on Jacques de Bivort de La Saudée's premature study.[24] Moreover, the hope that the Holy See would reexamine its negative decision of 1896 gave rise to works on new sources,[25] reaching its completion in the publication and analysis of the

---

17   Angelo Tamborra, *Studi storici sull'Europa orientale*, Rome, Edizioni dell'Ateneo, 1987; Angelo Tamborra, *Chiesa cattolica e Ortodossia russa: Due secoli di confronto e dialogo: Dalla Santa Alleanza ai nostri giorni*, Cinisello Balsamo, Edizioni Paoline, 1992; more recently in the same perspective: Rita Tolomeo, *La Santa Sede e il mondo danubiano-balcanico: Problemi nazionali e religiosi (1875–1921)*, Rome, La Fenice, 1996; and Giorgio Del Zanna, *Roma e l'Oriente: Leone XIII e l'Impero ottomano (1878–1903)*, Milan, Guerini, 2003.

18   Vittorio Peri, *Orientalis varietas: Roma e le Chiese d'Oriente – Storia e Diritto canonico*, Rome, PIO, 1994.

19   On Joseph Hajjar's journey, see the collection of his *membra disjecta*, *Antioche: Entre Rome, Byzance et La Mecque*, 3 vols., Beirut, Éditions al-Mourad, 1998, (as well as its review by Roger Aubert in *RHE* 94, 1999, 98–102, which cites the major steps).

20   Claude Soetens, *Le Congrès eucharistique international de Jérusalem (1893) dans le cadre de la politique orientale du pape Léon XIII*, Leuven, Nauwelaerts, 1977. On Soetens and Hajjar, see the critical note by Étienne Fouilloux, "Religion et politique en Méditerranée orientale (1878–1914)," *ASSR* 50/2, 1980, 167–175, reprinted in Étienne Fouilloux, *Au cœur du XXᵉ siècle religieux*, Paris, Éditions Ouvrières, 1993, 117–128.

21   Giuseppe Croce, *La badia greca di Grottaferrata e la rivista "Roma e l'Oriente": Cattolicesimo e ortodossia fra unionismo ed ecumenismo (1799–1923)*, Vatican City, Libreria Editrice Vaticana, 1990.

22   Mark D. Chapman, "The Fantasy of Reunion: The Rise and Fall of the Association for the Promotion of the Unity of Christendom," *JEH* 58, 2007, 49–74; and, more broadly, his book *The Fantasy of Reunion: Anglicans, Catholics and Ecumenism (1833–1882)*, Oxford, Oxford University Press, 2014.

23   Régis Ladous, *L'abbé Portal et la campagne anglo-romaine (1890–1912)*, Lyon, Centre d'Histoire du Catholicisme, 1973; Régis Ladous, *Monsieur Portal et les siens (1855–1926)*, Paris, Cerf, 1985.

24   Jacques de Bivort de La Saudée *Anglicans et catholiques*, vol. 1, *Le problème de l'union anglo-romaine (1833–1933)*, Paris, Plon, 1949.

25   Among these, John Jay Hughes, *Absolutely null and utterly void: The Papal Condemnation of Anglican Orders, 1896*, London, Sheed & Ward, 1968; William Franklin, ed., *Anglican Orders: Essays on the Centenary of Apostolicae Curae (1896–1996)*, Harrisburg PA, Morehouse Publishing, 1996, and, in Italy, Giuseppe Rambaldi, *Ordinazioni anglicane e sacramento dell'ordine nella Chiesa: Aspetti storici e teologici, a cento*

documents preserved in the archives of the Holy Office.[26] As for the Malines Conversations held under the auspices of the Belgian Cardinal Désiré-Joseph Mercier between 1921 and 1926, these have long attracted the attention of historians: documents published by Bivort de La Saudée,[27] and the pioneering studies of Roger Aubert and R.J. Lahey.[28] "Revisited" by John A. Dick's study, which gives a plausible version of their failure,[29] it was nevertheless necessary to wait for the archives of the pontificate of Pius XI, now accessible, to reveal their last secrets.

4   On the Ecumenical Movement

The other major direction in research concerns ecumenism itself, as it emerged between 1910 and 1920. The centenary of the Edinburgh Missionary Conference, which had given it its decisive impetus, was greeted with a burst of scholarly production.[30]

The centenaries of 1925 and 1927 are thus also awaited with curiosity. Will the same hold true for Life and Work and Faith and Order, after the pioneering but old work of Karl-Christoph Epting on the origins of the movement's doctrinal branch, which has given rise to more literary output than its practical branch?[31] The history of the "ecumenical movement," in the Genevan sense of the term, has received little attention from historians, no doubt because the *History of the Ecumenical Movement* seemed solid and copious enough to discourage possible vocations among historians. It owes much, however, to the great biographies of some of the "movements" founders, such as Bengt Sundkler's on the Lutheran Archbishop of Uppsala Nathan Söderblom,[32] Keith Clements's on Joseph H. Oldham, Secretary of the IMC,[33] or that of Charles Howard Hopkins on the American Methodist layman John R. Mott,[34] which provide much useful information (for "practical Christianity," in the first case; for missionary and scholarly sources of ecumenism, in the second and third case).

_____

anni dalla bolla Apostolicae curae di Leone XIII, Rome, Pontificia Università Gregoriana, 1995.

26   André-François von Gunten, ed., *La validité des ordinations anglicanes: Les documents de la commission préparatoire à la lettre "Apostolicae curae"*, vol. 1, *Les dossiers précédents*, Florence, Leo S. Olschki, 1997, and especially Alejandro Cifres, *La condena de las ordenaciones anglicanas: Los documentos del Santo Oficio y la bula "Apostolica curae"*, Rome, Pontificia Università Gregoriana, 2011.

27   Jacques de Bivort de La Saudée, *Anglicans et catholiques*, vol. 2, *Documents sur le problème de l'union anglo-romaine (1911–1927)*, Paris, Plon, 1949.

28   On the first, see the two articles in: Roger Aubert, *Le cardinal Mercier (1851–1926): Un prélat d'avant-garde: Publications du professeur Roger Aubert rassemblées à l'occasion de ses 80 ans*, eds. Jean-Pierre Hendrickx, Jean Pirotte & Luc Courtois, Louvain-la-Neuve, Presses Universitaires de Louvain, 1994, 393–459; on the second, "The Origins and Approval of the Malines Conversations," *CH* 43, 1974, 366–384.

29   John A. Dick, *The Malines Conversations Revisited*, Leuven, Leuven University Press, 1989 (reviewed by Roger Aubert, in *RHE* 88, 1993, 294–296).

30   *La Conférence missionnaire mondiale Édimbourg 1910*, special issue of *Histoire et Missions chrétiennes* 13, March 2010 (bibliography, 173–175, to which can be added Ian M. Ellis, *A Century of Mission and Unity:*

_____

A Centenary Perspective on the 1910 Edinburgh World Missionary Conference, Dublin, Columba Books, 2010).

31   Karl-Christoph Epting, *Ein Gespräch beginnt: Die Anfänge der Bewegung für Glauben und Kirchenverfassung in den Jahren 1910–1920*, Zürich, Theologischer Verlag, 1972 (following Reinhard Frieling, *Die Bewegung für Glauben und Kirchenverfassung (1910–1937)*, Göttingen, Vandenhoeck & Ruprecht, 1970, less close to the sources). Also to be noted is Lukas Vischer, ed., *A Documentary History of the Faith and Order Movement (1927–1963)*, Saint Louis MO, Bethany Press, 1963.

32   Bengt Sundkler, *Nathan Söderblom: His Life and Work*, Lund, Gleerup, 1968. It has since given rise to several others: Dietz Lange, *Nathan Söderblom und seine Zeit*, Göttingen, Vandenhoeck & Ruprecht, 2011 (whose Swedish translation was edited by Erik Aurelius and Ludvig Berggren for Artos, Skellefteå, in 2014) and, last by date, Jonas Jonson, *Nathan Söderblom: Called to Serve*, Grand Rapids MI, Eerdmans, 2016.

33   Keith Clements, *Faith on the Frontier: A Life of J.H. Oldham*, Edinburgh, T&T Clark, 1999.

34   Charles H. Hopkins, *John R. Mott (1865–1955): A Biography*, Grand Rapids MI, Eerdmans, 1979.

More recently, the Dutch Reformed pastor Willem Adolph Visser 't Hooft, the principal architect of the WCC, has been the inspiration for two biographies, in addition to the publication of his extensive correspondence with the Anglican Bishop George Bell,[35] on whom an important monograph is also available.[36] For the whole period, but from a unique perspective, Gabriel Mützenberg's *L'éthique sociale dans l'histoire du mouvement œcuménique*, has long been an isolated figure.[37] Even more recently, Matthias Haudel has studied the impact of the biblical movement on the ecumenical movement.[38] In her doctoral thesis, Hanne Lamparter analyzed how the WCC has developed its own liturgical practice throughout its history.[39] Lucian Leustean has reconstructed the way in which a certain type of ecumenical dialogue, gravitating mainly around Geneva, interacted with the process of European integration.[40] Thomas Herwig has examined the complex attitude of the great Reformed theologian Karl Barth towards ecumenism.[41] Keith Clements has conducted an equally successful study on the no less complex case of Dietrich Bonhoeffer.[42]

5   Rome: from Mission to Ecumenism

Much research has focused on the phenomenon that seemed the most surprising, namely, the Catholic Church's conversion to ecumenism. The paradox is all the more striking because the Catholic Church has long restricted access to its archives while the WCC and several of its member churches were more liberal. Can we use the word "conversion"? The term does not seem an exaggeration when comparing two of the magisterium's documents that are less than 40 years apart. On Jan 6, 1928, Pius XI strongly condemned the nascent ecumenical movement as "pan-Christianity" in his encyclical *Mortalium animos*, forbidding Catholics to participate in it. For a long time, it was thought that this text was a rejection of the movement's first international conferences. The Roman archives prove instead that it was meant to put a halt to the attempts at dialogue between Protestants and Catholics in the Germany of the Weimar Republic.[43] The decree *Unitatis*

35   Jan Schubert, *Willem Adolph Visser 't Hooft (1900–1985): Ökumene und Europa*, Göttingen, Vandenhoeck & Ruprecht, 2017; Jurjen A. Zeilstra, *Visser 't Hooft (1900–1985): Een leven voor de oecumene*, Middelbourg, Skandalon, 2018; ET: *Visser 't Hooft, 1900–1985: Living for the Unity of the Church*, trans. Henry Jansen, Amsterdam, Amsterdam University Press, 2020. In Italian: Franco Giampiccoli, *Willem A. Visser 't Hooft: La primavera dell'ecumenismo*, Turin, Claudiana, 2015. See also Filippo Maria Giordano & Stefano Dell'Acqua, eds., *"Die Welt war meine Gemeinde": Willem A. Visser 't Hooft: A Theologian for Europe between Ecumenism and Federalism*, New York NY, Peter Lang, 2014. The correspondence with Bell was published by Gerhard Besier, *"Intimately Associated for Many Years": George K.A. Bell's and Willem A. Visser 't Hooft's Common Life-Work in the Service of the Church Universal, Mirrored in their Correspondence*, 2 vols., Newcastle upon Tyne, Cambridge Scholars Publishing, 2015.

36   Andrew Chandler, *George Bell, Bishop of Chichester: Church, State and Resistance in the Age of Dictatorship*, Grand Rapids MI, Eerdmans, 2016.

37   Gabriel Mützenberg, *L'éthique sociale dans l'histoire du mouvement œcuménique*, Geneva, Labor et Fides, 1992.

38   Matthias Haudel, *Die Bibel und die Einheit der Kirche: Eine Untersuchung der Studien von "Glauben und Kirchenverfassung"*, Göttingen, Vandenhoeck & Ruprecht, ³2012.

39   Hanne Lamparter, *Gebet und Gottesdienst: Praxis und Diskurs in der Geschichte des Ökumenischen Rates der Kirchen*, Leipzig, Evangelische Verlagsanstalt, 2019.

40   Lucian N. Leustean, *The Ecumenical Movement & the Making of the European Community*, Oxford, Oxford University Press, 2014.

41   Thomas Herwig, *Karl Barth und die ökumenische Bewegung: Das Gespräch zwischen Karl Barth und Willem Adolf Visser 't Hooft auf der Grundlage ihres Briefwechsels (1930–1968)*, Neukirchen-Vluyn, Neukirchener, 1998.

42   Keith Clements, *Dietrich Bonhoeffer's Ecumenical Quest*, Geneva, WCC, 2015.

43   Manuela Barbolla, "La genesi della *Mortalium animos* attraverso lo spoglio degli archivi vaticani," *Rivista di storia della chiesa in Italia* 64, 2012, 495–538 and Philippe Chenaux, "Le Saint-Siège et les débuts du

redintegratio, adopted by an overwhelming majority of the council fathers in November 1964, instead identified ecumenism as a sign of the Holy Spirit's action in the world. Certainly, the ecumenism of 1964 was no longer the ecumenism of 1928, the new spirit strongly imbued with theological liberalism or social Christianity. However, does such a "conversion" not deserve close observation?[44]

The clearest effect of the epistemological break reported above was the clear distinction among its three roughly successive stages. As earlier studies of the Roman documents had shown, the Catholic Church did not wait for the first conferences of the ecumenical movement to develop its own model for the reunification of Christianity. Under Leo XIII, at the end of the 19th century, this model moved from being one of *mission*, of seeking to convert individual "schismatics" and other "heretics" to Latin Catholicism, to one of *unity*, which advocated a "return to the body" by the "dissidents" who were least distant from Rome, by means of bridges to be strengthened or built, such as the Uniate Eastern Churches or a hypothetical Unitatism with Anglicans. The search for individual conversions nevertheless remained attractive until the middle of the 20th century in ecumenical circles in Germany, the Netherlands, and the Anglo-Saxon world.

The ecumenical movement of Anglo-Protestant origin competed with Roman unity, particularly in the Middle East, in about the time of World War I,[45] the challenge being the rapproche-

ment with Orthodoxy that both advocated, but in different ways. In addition to doctrinal reasons, this was enough to justify the condemnation of 1928. The Fellowship of St. Alban and St. Sergius, focusing on the rapprochement between Anglicans and Orthodox in the West, is the subject of a recent work.[46] With the rally of a part of Orthodoxy to the ecumenical movement, Rome feared the birth of a non-Roman catholicity that would, in fact, be an anti-Roman catholicity. This fear was rekindled at the end of the 1950s by the rapprochement between Geneva and Moscow that gave the WCC – sometimes tempted to consider itself a "super-church" – unequalled representativeness: only conservative evangelical churches maintained a mistrust of it.

Within Catholicism, however, some theologians and spiritual leaders precociously doubted the viability of a uniate solution. They thus invented a "Catholic ecumenism," that is, a Catholic contribution to the single ecumenism, one that works toward the reconciliation of all separated Christians within the same church without surrendering to one another, through an effort of common prayer highlighting convergences and working patiently on differences. One of the present authors, Fouilloux, formalized the tripartition between mission, unity, and ecumenism for the first time in 1977 in the encyclopedia *2000 ans de*

Mouvement œcuménique: La conférence de Lausanne (1927)," in: Andreas Gottsmann, Pierantonio Piatti & Andreas E. Rehberg, eds., *Incorrupta monumenta Ecclesia defendunt, studi offerti a Mgr Sergio Pagano*, vol. 1, Vatican City, Archivio Segreto Vaticano, 2018, 213–226.

44 A suggestive path is given by Roger Aubert, "Les étapes de l'oecuménisme catholique depuis le pontificat de Léon XIII jusqu'à Vatican II," in: Laurence K. Shook & Guy M. Bertrand, *La théologie du renouveau*, vol. 1, Paris, Cerf, 1968, 291–307.

45 Anastassios Anastassiadis, "Un 'Vatican anglicano-orthodoxe' à Constantinople? Relations interconfessionnelles, rêves impériaux et enjeux de pouvoir en

Méditerranée orientale à la fin de la Grande Guerre," in: Anastassios Anastassiadis, ed., *Voisinages fragiles: Les relations interconfessionnelles dans le Sud-Est européen et la Méditerranée orientale (1854–1923): Contraintes locales et enjeux internationaux*, Athens, École Française d'Athènes, 2013, 283–302; Pandora Dimanopoulou, *Rendez à César ce qui est à César et à Dieu ce qui est à Dieu? Le rapprochement entre les Églises anglicane et orthodoxe grecque (1903–1930)*, Paris, Cerf, 2016.

46 Dimitrios Filippos Salapatas, *The Fellowship of St Alban and St Sergius: Orthodox and Anglican Ecumenical Relations (1927–2012)*, Newcastle upon Tyne, Cambridge Scholars Publishing, 2018. On Anglican-Orthodox dialogue in the interwar period, see Bryn Geffert, *Eastern Orthodox and Anglicans: Diplomacy, Theology, and the Politics of Interwar Ecumenism*, Notre Dame IN, University of Notre Dame Press, 2010.

christianisme.[47] This was confirmed and developed in defense of his thesis three years later.[48]

6　Roman Uniatism

Now considered incompatible with studies on ecumenism, the work on the second wave of Roman uniatism after the Bolshevik Revolution has progressed considerably since the fall of communism, in spite of the lack of access, until 2002–2006, to the Vatican archives on Pius XI's pontificate, in particular, to those of the Congregation for the Oriental Churches: some Russian aspects that it would have been dangerous to unveil before 1989 take on a prophetic guise. These studies describe the origins, foundation, and first developments of the Vatican Uniate apparatus under Benedict XV and Pius XI: the Pontifical Oriental Institute[49] and the Russian College[50] in particular. Mainly, however, they focus on the relations between Rome and Moscow or the Vatican and Moscow, to use the titles of the works of Antoine Wenger and Andrea Riccardi, at the risk of giving precedence to international relations over strictly religious ones or of overlooking the rest of the Christian East. In both a political and a religious vein, for the period after 1940,[51] Riccardi extended and examined in greater depth Hansjakob Stehle's investigation into the Vatican's *Ostpolitik* since 1917.[52] For his part, Roberto Morozzo Della Rocca focused on the unprecedented political-religious situation created by the collapse of the Ottoman and Russian Empires in Eastern Europe and the Balkans.[53] As for Antoine Wenger, he sought above all to retrace the Russian adventure of his congregation, the Augustinians of the Assumption, from the beginning of the 20th century,[54] an adventure which was then revisited more broadly in two conferences.[55] More recently, the Dominicans have undertaken the same exercise on their own behalf.[56] Wenger's conclusions were less pessimistic than those emerging from the work of Léon Tretjakewitsch, dedicated to the key figure of Roman Uniatism between the two wars, the French Jesuit Michel d'Herbigny, who restored an ephemeral Catholic hierarchy in Russia in the mid-1920s.[57]

47　Étienne Fouilloux, "L'oecuménisme contemporain," in André Mandouze &others, eds., *2000 ans de christianisme*, vol. 10, Paris, Société d'Histoire Chrétienne, 1977, dossier 28.

48　Étienne Fouilloux, "Un historien devant l'œcuménisme," *Irén* 53, 1980, 314–330 (reprinted in Fouilloux, *Au cœur du XXᵉ siècle religieux*, 47–61); completed by Étienne Fouilloux, "Un historien devant l'œcuménisme (suite)," in: *Historiens et sociologues aujourd'hui: Journées d'études annuelles de la Soc. Française de Sociologie*, Paris, Éditions du CNRS, 1986, 121–125 (reprinted in Fouilloux, *Au cœur du XXᵉ siècle religieux*, 63–69).

49　Edward G. Farrugia, ed., *The Pontifical Oriental Institute: The First Seventy-five Years (1917–1992)*, Rome, PIO, 1993; Vincenzo Poggi, *Per la storia del Pontificio Istituto Orientale: Saggi sull'istituzione, i suoi uomini e l'Oriente Cristiano*, Rome, PIO, 2000.

50　Constantin Simon, *Russicum: Pioneers and Witnesses of the Struggle for Christian Unity in Eastern Europe*, 2 vols., Rome, Opere Religiose Russe, 2001–2002.

51　Andrea Riccardi, *Il Vaticano e Mosca (1940–1990)*, Bari, Laterza, 1992.

52　Hansjakob Stehle, *Die Ostpolitik des Vatikans (1917–1975)*, Munich, Pipen, 1975; ET: *Eastern Politics of the Vatican (1917–1979)*, trans. Sandra Smith, Athens OH, Ohio University Press, 1981 (expanded version).

53　Roberto Morozzo Della Rocca, *Le nazioni non muoiono: Russia rivoluzionaria, Polonia indipendente e Santa Sede*, Bologna, Il Mulino, 1992.

54　Antoine Wenger, *Rome et Moscou (1900–1950)*, Paris, Desclée de Brouwer, 1987; then Antoine Wenger, *Catholiques en Russie d'après les archives du KGB (1920–1960)*, Paris, Desclée de Brouwer, 1998.

55　Bernard Holzer, ed., *Mgr Petit, assomptionniste, fondateur des "Échos d'Orient," archevêque latin d'Athènes (1868–1927): Actes du Colloque, Rome, 15–17 décembre 1997*, Rome, PIO, 2002; Bernard Holzer, ed., *Les assomptionnistes et la Russie (1903–2003): Actes du Colloque d'Histoire, Rome, 20–22 novembre 2003*, Paris, Bayard, 2005.

56　Viliam Š. Dóci & Hyacinthe Destivelle, eds., *I Domenicani e la Russia*, Rome, Angelicum University Press, 2019.

57　Léon Tretjakewitsch, *Bishop Michel d'Herbigny SJ and Russia: A Pre-Ecumenical Approach to Church Unity*, Würzburg, Augustinus-Verlag, 1990.

The entire dossier was masterfully taken up by Laura Pettinaroli in her monumental work on *La politique russe du Saint-Siège (1905–1939)* and her many subsequent works. In the first comprehensive research using Russian or Soviet and Vatican archives, she did not overturn what was already known but completed it on more than one point and, above all, offered a synthesis that will make history on the Vatican's reservations toward Russia before and after the Revolution.[58] Her thesis, however, does not render previous works obsolete, among which should be mentioned the studies compiled in the second part of the present author's collection *Au coeur du XXe siècle religieux*, which tries to disentangle the three Catholic strategies implemented in Central Europe (*Mitteleuropa*) between undeniably Germanic and undeniably Slavic lands: Latin missions, Russian or Ukrainian Uniatism,[59] and ecumenical dialogue. Also, and above all, Giuseppe Croce's critical and monumental edition of the autobiography of Cyrille Korolevskij, a French priest who converted to the Slavic rite, with its wealth of supporting documents, sheds light on many aspects of Uniatism.[60] Élisabeth Behr-Sigel's heartfelt biography dedicated to Lev Gillet, the "monk of the Eastern Church," a French Benedictine who converted to Orthodoxy in 1928, also offers an original insight into the Orthodox reactions to these undertakings, which – in her opinion – were tainted by Uniatism.[61]

7   "Catholic Ecumenism"

Progress on the study of ecumenism itself before Vatican II was, until recently, very uneven. "Catholic ecumenism" was born in two main geographical areas, the German-speaking one and the French-speaking one. The doctoral thesis of Fouilloux, examined the depths of French-speaking Catholic contexts,[62] preceded by some useful biographical essays,[63] and accompanied by the surveys gathered in the first part of *Au cœur du XXe siècle religieux*.[64] He showed how an ecumenism with a more theological resonance, such as that of an Yves Congar, and more spiritual than that of a Paul Couturier, had been nourished by previous experiences, notably that of the Belgian Benedictine priory in Amay-sur-Meuse. This took shape before gaining a true audience, thanks to the annual occasion of the January Week of Prayer for Christian Unity,[65] encountering Roman distrust. For the most part, the panorama thus sketched has barely been contested.[66]

To these were added, on the one hand, studies on a series of experiments in encounter at

---

58   Laura Pettinaroli, *La politique russe du Saint-Siège (1905–1939)*, Rome, École Française de Rome, 2015.

59   Fouilloux, *Au cœur du XXe siècle religieux*, 115–201; see also *Santa Sede e Russia da Leone XIII a Pio XI: Atti del Simposio organizzato dal Pontificio Comitato di Scienze Storiche e dall'Istituto di Storia Universale dell'Academia delle Scienze di Mosca, Mosca, 23–25 giugno 1998*, Vatican City, Libreria Editrice Vaticana, 2002.

60   Cyrille Korolevskij, *Kniga bytija moego: Le livre de ma vie: Mémoires autobiographiques*, ed. Giuseppe Maria Croce, 5 vols., Vatican City, Archives secrètes vaticanes, 2007.

61   Élisabeth Behr-Sigel, *Un moine de l'Église d'Orient: Le père Lev Gillet*, Paris, Cerf, 1993.

62   Étienne Fouilloux, *Les catholiques et l'unité chrétienne du XIXe au XXe siècle: Itinéraires européens d'expression française*, Paris, Le Centurion, 1982.

63   Although unequally satisfying for the historian: Maurice Villain, *L'abbé Paul Couturier*, Paris, Casterman, 1957 [⁴1964]; Sonya A. Quitslund, *Beauduin: A Prophet Vindicated*, New York NY, Newman Press, 1973 (completed by Jean-Jacques von Allmen & others, ed., *Veilleur avant l'aurore: Colloque Lambert Beauduin*, Chevetogne, Éditions de Chevetogne, 1978). Rather more recent, instead, is the biography of Louis Bouyer by Bertrand Lesoing, *Vers la plénitude du Christ: Louis Bouyer et l'œcuménisme*, Paris, Cerf, 2017.

64   Fouilloux, *Au cœur du XXe siècle religieux*, 25–114.

65   There are few specific studies on this development: Dominique Beloeil, "L'apparition et le développement de la Semaine de l'Unité dans l'ouest de la France: L'exemple de la Bretagne (1945–1959)," *RHE* 100, 2005, 124–145.

66   Corrections and replies to certain objections in Étienne Fouilloux, "L'œcuménisme d'avant-hier à aujourd'hui," *Les Quatre Fleuves* 20, 1984, 7–31 (reprinted in Fouilloux, *Au cœur du XXe siècle religieux*, 71–97).

the monastery of Chevetogne,[67] heir of Amay, at the Cistercian monastery of Les Dombes,[68] and at the meetings of the Catholic Conference on Ecumenical Questions, a Dutch initiative that, beginning in 1952,[69] gathered together the principal specialists yearly, with Rome's approval. The ongoing work of Peter De Mey and Saretta Marotta in the Chevetogne archives will provide renewed syntheses on the weeks of the monastery and on the conferences. On another note are the bibliographical approaches from which emerge the work dedicated to the founder of Amay-Chevetogne, Dom Lambert Beauduin,[70] and the first biography of Fr. Congar.[71] There is, however, no history of the Belgian monastery comparable to Silvia Scatena's study of Taizé, which departs from the beaten path of Roger Schutz's biographies in order to reconstruct the beginnings of this other union monastery.[72]

In contrast, the important German-speaking ecumenical area had, until recently, only the valuable but secondhand and already dated work of Leonard J. Swidler.[73] While it is true that Armin

Boyens had studied the support of the WCC for the formation of the German Confessing Church in its struggle against Nazism,[74] it was not until over 30 years later that Jörg Ernesti presented the Catholic counterpart to such resistance, the Una Sancta movement led by Fr. Max Joseph Metzger.[75] Since then, at the insistence of Ernesti and of Wolfgang Thönissen, in addition to an important collection of studies,[76] two reference works, *Lexikon der Ökumene und Konfessionskunde* and *Personenlexikon Ökumene*, were published by Herder in Freiburg in 2007 and 2010, respectively. Saretta Marotta's book on the ecumenical initiation of the future Cardinal Augustin Bea provides a rich documentation on the confessional rapprochement in Germany between the end of the war and the council.[77] Other recent research, such as that of Leonhard Hell on the Archbishop of Mainz, Albert Stohr, who worked to provide spiritual assistance to evangelical pastors converts to Catholicism,[78] or that of Karl Heinz Voigt

67   Albert Verdoodt, *Les colloques œcuméniques de Chevetogne (1942–1983) et la réception par l'Église catholique des charismes d'autres communions chrétiennes*, Chevetogne, Éditions de Chevetogne, 1986.

68   Catherine E. Clifford, *The Groupe des Dombes: A Dialogue of Conversion*, New York NY, Peter Lang, 2005.

69   Jan Jacobs, *"Naar één oecumenische beweging,"* De Katholieke Conferentie voor Oecumenische Vragen: Een leerschool en gids (1951–1965), Tilburg, Tilburg University Press, 1991; Giuseppe Alberigo, "Agli albori dell'ecumenismo cattolico," in: Emanuele Curzel, ed., *In factis mysterium leggere: Miscellanea di studi in onore di Iginio Rogger in occasione del suo ottantesimo compleanno*, Bologna, EDB, 1999, 209–233.

70   Raymond Loonbeek & Jacques Mortiau, *Un pionnier Dom Lambert Beauduin (1873–1960): Liturgie et unité des chrétiens*, 2 vols., Louvain-la-Neuve, Collège Erasme, 2001.

71   Étienne Fouilloux, *Yves Congar: Une vie*, Paris, Salvator, 2020.

72   Silvia Scatena, *Taizé, una parabola di unità: Storia della comunità dalle origini al concilio dei giovani*, Bologna, Il Mulino, 2018.

73   Leonard J. Swidler, *The Ecumenical Vanguard: The History of the Una Sancta Movement*, Pittsburgh PA, Duquesne University Press, 1966.

74   Armin Boyens, *Kirchenkampf und Ökumene*, 2 vols., Munich, Chr. Kaiser Verlag, 1969–1973. On this crucial period of World War II, see also Uta Gerdes, *Ökumenische Solidarität mit christlichen und jüdischen Verfolgten: Die CIMADE in Vichy-Frankreich (1940–1944)*, Göttingen, Vandenhoeck & Ruprecht, 2005. On the Cold War and the attitude of the German churches, see instead Gerhard Besier, Armin Boyens & Gerhard Lindemann, eds., *Nationaler Protestantismus und Ökumenische Bewegung: Kirchliches Handeln im Kalten Krieg (1945–1990)*, Berlin, Duncker & Humblot, 1999.

75   Jörg Ernesti, *Ökumene im Dritten Reich*, Paderborn, Bonifatius, 2007, which, completing the work of Boyans cited above, has highlighted the Catholic contribution to German ecumenism in the 1930s and 40s, using mainly the archives of Friedrich Heiler and the secret police of the Third Reich.

76   Jörg Ernesti & Wolfgang Thönissen, *Die Entdeckung der Ökumene: Zur Beteiligung der katholischen Kirche an der Ökumenischen Bewegung*, Paderborn/Frankfurt a.M., Bonifatius/Lembeck, 2008.

77   Saretta Marotta, *Gli anni della pazienza: Bea, l'ecumenismo e il Sant'Uffizio di Pio XII*, Bologna, Il Mulino, 2020.

78   Leonhard Hell, "Unio ecclesiae – materia primaria: Bischof Albert Stohrs Einbindung in den entstehenden internationalen katholischen Ökumenismus und in die Vorbereitung des Zweiten Vatikanischen Konzils," in:

on the formation in the postwar years of the ACK in Deutschland completes the picture.[79] In Germany, just as in the French-speaking world at the same period but in a more conflictual manner, we find a dualism between the theological dialogue of the upper levels, centered around the Archbishop of Paderborn, Lorenz Jaeger,[80] and a more popularized spiritual ecumenism in the Una Sancta[81] movement and the Benedictine abbey of Niederaltaich.

There is a lack of similar work from other countries and geographical areas. Pastor Visser 't Hooft and Cardinal Willebrands's biographies provide as much information on the Dutch situation as a monograph on the SWV, between conversion and

ecumenism.[82] In Italy, an initial survey was carried out by Riccardo Burigana.[83] It is important to note the absence of a general work on ecumenism from the British Isles, except from Wales,[84] as well as the biographies of two great protagonists of national Anglicanism and leading players in the ecumenical movement such as the Archbishops of Canterbury William Temple and Michael Ramsey.[85] As far as Scandinavia and Finland are concerned, we limit ourselves to mentioning the works of Gunnar Heiene and Jaakko Rusama.[86]

From North America, the most comprehensive overview of ecumenism of the 19th century remains the work by Don Herbert Yoder in the first volume of *A History of the Ecumenical Movement* edited by Ruth Rouse and Stephen Charles Neill,[87] although, for the 20th century, there are studies dedicated to the interweaving of the desire for

Karl Lehmann, ed., *Dominus fortitudo: Bischof Albert Stohr (1890–1961*, Mainz, Publikationen Bistum Mainz, 2012, 99–120.

79 Karl Heinz Voigt, *Ökumene in Deutschland: Von der Gründung der ACK bis zur Charta Oecumenica (1948–2001)*, Göttingen, Vandenhoeck & Ruprecht, 2015.

80 On the birth and evolution of the theological ecumenical dialogue group promoted in Paderborn in the post World War II period by Bishop Jaeger and Wilhelm Stählin, Landesbischof of Oldenburg, see Barbara Schwahn, *Der Ökumenische Arbeitskreis evangelischer und katholischer Theologen von 1946 bis 1975*, Göttingen, Vandenhoeck & Ruprecht, 1996. Note the inauguration in 2017 of an important research project on the figure of Lorenz Jaeger, archbishop from 1941 to 1973 and cardinal from 1965, at the University of Paderborn, which by 2022 plans to organize a cycle of five international conferences followed by the publication of their proceedings. See the already published ones: Nicole Priesching & Gisela Fleckenstein, eds., *Lorenz Jaeger Als Theologe: Eine Publikation Der Kommission Fur Kirchliche Zeitgeschichte Paderborn*, Schonigh, 2019 and Nicole Priesching & Arnold Otto, *Lorenz Jaeger als Okumeniker: Eine Publikation der Kommission fur kirchliche Zeitgeschichte im Erzbistum Paderborn*, Paderborn, Schonigh, 2020.

81 The vicissitudes of the Una Sancta movement, such as Niederaltaich's itinerary, after the death of Metzger at the hands of the Gestapo in 1944 have not received much study. Some information about this is provided by Saretta Marotta in "'Ökumene von unten': Augustin Bea di fronte alle attività del movimento Una Sancta," *CrSt* 37/3, 2016, 541–611.

82 Jan Jacobs, *Nieuwe visies op een oud visoen: Een portret van de Sint Willibrord Vereniging (1948–1998)*, Tilburg, Valkhof Pers, 1998.

83 Riccardo Burigana, *Una straordinaria avventura: Storia del Movimento ecumenico in Italia (1910–2010)*, Bologna, EDB, 2013.

84 Noel A. Davies, *A History of Ecumenism in Wales (1956–1990)*, Cardiff, Wales University Press, 2008.

85 Edward Loane, *William Temple and Church Unity: The Politics and Practice of Ecumenical Theology*, Basingstoke, Palgrave Macmillan, 2016, and Owen Chadwick, *Michael Ramsey: A Life*, Oxford, Oxford University Press, 1991. Northern Ireland is a case apart; for that, see Maria Power, *From Ecumenism to Community Relations: Inter-Church Relationships in Northern Ireland (1980–1999)*, Dublin, Irish Academic Press, 2007.

86 Gunnar Heiene, "Den norske kirke og økumenikken i etterkrigstiden," in: Jens Holger Schjørring, ed., *Nordiske folkekirker i opbrud: National identitet og international nyorientering efter 1945*, Aarhus, Aarhus Universitetsforlag, 2001, 385–398; Jaakko Rusama, *Ecumenical Growth in Finland: The History of the Finnish Ecumenical Council (1917–1999)*, Tampere, The Research Institute of the Evangelical Lutheran Church in Finland, 2002.

87 Don Herbert Yoder, "Christian Unity in Nineteenth-Century America," in: *A History of the Ecumenical Movement*, vol. 1, 221–259.

unity with the challenges of war[88] and the history of institutional theological dialogue.[89] The story of Canada's most successful ecumenical experience, the United Church of Canada of 1925, was reconstructed in 2013 by Phyllis D. Airhart.[90] From Latin America, we are still awaiting the publication of the proceedings of the international conference "Recuperando la historia del ecumenismo en América Latina y el Caribe," which was sponsored by the Catholic Theology Faculty of Santiago de Chile in 2017, bearing witness to the interest that this subject is also attracting in the South American continent. There are two volumes of work on the history of the ecumenical movement in Asia, edited by Ninan Koshy,[91] while the academic production on African ecumenism is more fragmented and dispersed.[92]

Despite the shortcomings that remain in the initial works, ecumenism now has its place in dictionaries and reference material intended for an educated audience. Proof of this, among many others, is the article "Œcuménisme chrétien" (1972) by the Jesuit Charles Boyer in the *Dictionnaire de théologie catholique*,[93] Francis Frost's large article "Œcuménisme" (1984) in the encyclopedia *Catholicisme*,[94] and the successive updates of its

equivalent in the *Encyclopaedia universalis*.[95] At the same time, the "problem of Christian unity" has been appearing in the general histories of Christianity. If it had still been merely a question of Catholicism's relationship with the East in volume V of the *Nouvelle Histoire de l'Église*, edited by Roger Aubert and published by the Éditions du Seuil in 1975,[96] by 1979, the issue received its own treatment in the *Handbuch der Kirchengeschichte* published by Hubert Jedin and Konrad Repgen for Herder.[97] The same is true in the pages Fouilloux devoted to the subject in Desclée's *Histoire du christianisme*, and especially in his article for *Storia della Chiesa*, the Italian version of the great undertaking of Augustin Fliche and Victor Martin.[98]

8   Vatican II

The turn negotiated by the Roman Church at Vatican II has not yet revealed all its secrets, although it has given rise to many studies. There is still a lack of in-depth research on the ecumenical path of John XXIII, from his discovery of the Christian East in Bulgaria and Turkey up until his pontificate. Was not one of the main objectives that the new pope set for the council, which he announced on Jan 25, 1959, the closing day of the Week of Prayer for Christian Unity, the bringing together of separated Christians? Nonetheless,

88   Jill K. Gill, *Embattled Ecumenism: The National Council of Churches, the Vietnam War, and the Trials of the Protestant Left*, DeKalb IL, Northern Illinois University Press, 2011.

89   William A. Norgren, *Faith and Order in the USA: A Brief History of Studies and Relationships*, Grand Rapids MI, Eerdmans, 2011.

90   Phyllis D. Airhart, *A Church with the Soul of a Nation: Making and Remaking the United Church of Canada*, Montreal, McGill-Queens University Press, 2013.

91   Ninan Koshy, *A History of the Ecumenical Movement in Asia*, 2 vols., Hong Kong, WSCF, Asia Pacific Alliance of YMCAS & Christian Conference of Asia, 2004.

92   Here we mention only James Amanze, *A History of the Ecumenical Movement in Africa*, Gaborone, Pula Press, 1999, and Christopher Byaruhanga, *History and Theology of the Ecumenical Movement in East Africa*, Kampala, Fountain Publishers, 2015.

93   "Œcuménisme chrétien," *DThC* tables, 3 (1972), 3343–3362.

94   "Œcuménisme," *Catholicisme* 9, 1501–1536 and 10, 1–21, the article has been reprinted in an independent

       volume: *Œcuménisme*, Paris, Letouzey et Ané, 1984.

95   Initially begun by Georges Casalis, the article has been supplemented by Jean Baubérot and Étienne Fouilloux (*Encyclopaedia universalis* 16, 649–651, in the 2002 edition).

96   Joseph Hajjar, "Les Églises orientales catholiques," in: Roger Aubert, ed., *Nouvelle Histoire de l'Église*, vol. 5, *L'Église dans le monde moderne: 1848 à nos jours*, Paris, Éditions du Seuil, 1975, 479–580.

97   Erwin Iserloh, "Die Geschichte der ökumenischen Bewegung," *HKG* 7, 458–466.

98   See *HC* 12, 232–239, and Étienne Fouilloux, "Il cammino dell'ecumenismo," in: Maurilio Guasco, Elio Guerriero & Francesco Traniello, eds., *Storia della Chiesa*, vol. 23, *I cattolici nel mondo contemporaneo (1922–1958)*, Cinisello Balsamo, Edizioni Paoline, 1991, 495–526.

some recent studies provide convincing portraits of two of the men he trusted in interconfessional rapprochement. Emulating other scholars, Saretta Marotta has sketched the decisive role of the German situation of 1945–1960 in the ecumenical initiation of future cardinal Augustin Bea, which she proves was significant in the creation of the Secretariat for Christian Unity.[99] His deputy, Msgr. Jan Willebrands, coming from the Catholic Conference on Ecumenical Questions, has been the object of a documented biography, following some preparatory work on him.[100]

Mauro Velati's work on the ecumenical contribution of Vatican II is essential, drawing on accounts such as that of Fr. Maurice Villain, which were published immediately after the council's conclusion.[101] Starting from the present author's typology, he first retraced Rome's "difficult transition" from Uniatism to ecumenism between 1952 and 1965. This was marked by the creation of the Secretariat for Promoting Christian Unity entrusted to Cardinal Bea, whose idea it was, and the merging, after the first session of the council, of the schema by the Commission for the Eastern Churches, the chapter on unity in the early *De Ecclesia*, and a document prepared by the Bea secretariat, under the trustworthy care of the latter.[102] He has published the minutes of the secretariat's meetings during the preparatory phase.[103] Finally,

he has also published what can be considered a definitive account of the role of the non-Catholic observers, whose presence was a major innovation of the council.[104]

From a more general perspective, the preparatory work for the *History of Vatican II*, published in seven languages and edited by Giuseppe Alberigo,[105] cannot fail to stimulate interest in this important episode in the rise of ecumenism that the council was. One need only to open the proceedings of the colloquium *Vatican II in Moscow (1959–1965)* to be convinced of this.[106] However, the edifice lacks one major brick: a reconstitution of the documents on the writing of the decree *Unitatis redintegratio*, which was the keystone of the council's ecumenical work. In regard to its writing and a commentary, we have only the studies that Werner Becker and Johannes Feiner effected for the supplement of *Lexikon für Theologie und Kirche*.[107] The volume on the decree for Fr. Congar's collection Unam Sanctam, which was given to the Benedictine from Chevetogne Emmanuel Lanne, was never published. Further, *Unitatis redintegratio* has not benefited from a major study from the Secretariat for Promoting Christian Unity,[108] one of those exhaustive monographs published by the "Officina bolognese," such as that dedicated to the declaration on religious liberty. This is a lacuna that needs to be filled.[109]

99 Marotta, *Gli anni della pazienza*; Jerome Michael Vereb, *"Because He was a German!": Cardinal Bea and the Origins of Catholic Engagement in the Ecumenical Movement*, Grand Rapids MI, Eerdmans, 2006.

100 Karim Schelkens, *Johannes Willebrands: Een leven in gesprek (1909–2006)*, Amsterdam, Boom, 2020; Adelbert Denaux & Peter De Mey, eds., *The Ecumenical Legacy of Johannes Cardinal Willebrands (1909–2006)*, Leuven, Peeters, 2012.

101 Maurice Villain, *Vatican II et le dialogue œcuménique*, Paris, Casterman, 1966.

102 Mauro Velati, *Una difficile transizione: Il cattolicesimo tra unionismo ed ecumenismo (1952–1964)*, Bologna, Il Mulino, 1996.

103 Mauro Velati, *Dialogo e rinnovamento: Verbali e testi del Segretariato per l'unità dei cristiani nella preparazione del concilio Vaticano II (1960–1962)*, Bologna, Il Mulino, 2011.

104 Mauro Velati, *Separati ma fratelli: Gli osservatori non cattolici al Vaticano II (1962–1965)*, Bologna, Il Mulino, 2014.

105 Giuseppe Alberigo & Joseph Komonchak, eds., *History of Vatican II*, 5 vols., Leuven/Maryknoll NY, Peeters/Orbis Books, 1995–2006.

106 Alberto Melloni, ed., *Vatican II in Moscow (1959–1965): Acts of the Colloquium on the History of Vatican II, Moscow, March 30–April 2, 1995*, Leuven, Bibliotheek van de Faculteit Godgeleerdheid, 1997.

107 *Das Zweite Vatikanisch Konzil: Dokumente und Kommentare*, LThK, ²13, 11–39 and 40–126.

108 Silvia Scatena, *La fatica della libertà: L'elaborazione della dichiarazione sulla libertà religiosa del concilio Vaticano II*, Bologna, Il Mulino, 2004.

109 Although it did not intend to offer an exhaustive history of the drafting of this document and its reception in ecumenical dialogue after Vatican II, it is worth

9 Repercussions

The consecration of ecumenism, during the 1960s, as a major phenomenon of the religious evolution of the 20th century introduced a new rupture in its historiography. Manageable only when the movement remained fragile and the purview of a minority, the literary production that followed its success became both pervasive and unsatisfactory from the point of view of the history and sociology of religion. These kinds of studies of ecumenism are few and far between, and they pale in comparison with the theological and spiritual work in full swing. This lack is all the more significant because, from the end of the 1960s, ecumenism experienced a challenge to its institutionalization even before the resurgence of confessional identities ten or fifteen years later. This has not encouraged research on an object now considered partially obsolete by both the "left" and the "right." For the former, this is because it did not move quickly enough or far enough towards the hoped-for unity. For the latter, it is because it too readily sacrificed doctrinal questions in favor of questionable social cooperation. Since the movement seemed to be losing momentum, what would be the point of scrutinizing its most recent developments, which are also the most difficult to study objectively, given they are still so fresh and given the difficult access to sources? The few indications that follow, therefore, should not afford any illusion of completeness. From a scholarly point of view, the history of ecumenism since the 1970s essentially still needs to be written.

It is true that a third volume of the *History of the Ecumenical Movement*, from the years 1968 to 2000, has been published.[110] Prior to this major publication, the WCC, then wracked by multiple tensions and abandoned by the Orthodox Churches of Bulgaria and Georgia, had been content to produce reference works of a documentary nature, such as the *Dictionary of the Ecumenical Movement*, soon followed by the beginnings of a prosopography, *Ecumenical Pilgrims*, published in 1991 and 1995, respectively.[111] On the other hand, it seems to us that little was said about the working group of the Catholic Church and the WCC, which has been in existence since 1965, or about the evolution of the Faith and Order Commission, in which Catholic theologians have fully participated since 1968, before Luca Ferracci's study on *Baptism, Eucharist, and Ministry*, a major document adopted in Lima in 1982 that has not had much practical effect.[112]

As for bilateral and multilateral dialogues, which have been increasing for over half a century and which constitute the best response of ecumenists to criticisms from all sides, they have resulted in exhaustive compilations which are, however, only raw material awaiting analysis, such as the *Dokumente wachsender Übereinstimmung*[113]

consulting the collection of studies edited by Wolfgang Thönissen to celebrate its 40th anniversary: *"Unitatis redintegratio": 40 Jahre Ökumenismusdekret – Erbe und Auftrag*, Paderborn, Bonifatius, 2005. See also Peter De Mey, "Preparing the Ground for Fruitful Dialogue with the Orthodox. An Important Motivation of the Ecumenical 'Avant-garde' during the Redaction History of *Lumen Gentium, Unitatis redintegratio and Orientalium Ecclesiarum* (1959–1964)," in: Benoît Bourgine, ed., *Le souci de toutes les Églises: Hommage à Joseph Famerée*, Leuven, Peeters, 2020, 57–86.

110 John Briggs, Mercy Amba Oduyoye & George Tsetsis, eds., *A History of the Ecumenical Movement*, vol. 3, *1968–2000*, Geneva, WCC, 2004.

111 Nicolas Lossky & others, eds., *Dictionary of the Ecumenical Movement*, Geneva, WCC Publications, 1991; Ion Bria & Dagmar Heller eds., *Ecumenical Pilgrims. Profiles of Pioneers in Christian Reconciliation*, Geneva, WCC Publications, 1995.

112 Luca Ferracci, *Battesimo, Eucaristia, Ministero: Genesi e destino di un documento ecumenico*, Bologna, Il Mulino, 2021.

113 The collection *Dokumente wachsender Übereinstimmung: Sämtliche Berichte und Konsenstexte interkonfessioneller Gespräche auf Weltebene* today comprises 4 volumes, published from 1983 to 2012 by the Evangelische Verlangstalt (Leipzig) and Bonifatius (Paderborn). The first volume covers the years 1931–1982; the second 1982–1990; the third 1990–2001; and the fourth 2001–2010. The corresponding English edition is *Growth in Agreement: Reports and Agreed Statements of Ecumenical Conversations on a World Level*, Geneva/Grand Rapids MI, WCC/Eerdmans, 1984–2007; this has

in Germany (translated into English by the WCC) or the *Enchiridion Œcumenicum* in Italy.[114] Among the rare Orthodox contributions to the historiography of ecumenism is the valuable *Orthodox Handbook on Ecumenism*,[115] which as a reference work offers a general overview of the themes and the encounters that have characterized the Orthodox presence in the ecumenical movement. In that vein, three collections of dialogue documents also deserve to be mentioned,[116] along with a German study by Stylianos Tsompanidis[117] and two recent collections of essays.[118] The abundant bibliography of a theological nature that has arisen from these attempts at rapprochement after decades or centuries of mutual ignorance and even bitter polemics is well known. However, for historians and sociologists, it is a matter of one source

among many, even if some of these theological works are well anchored in history.[119]

It is important, moreover, to note the symbolic importance for the resumption of relations between Rome and Constantinople of the *Tomos Agapis Vatican-Phanar (1958–1970)*, in which the two parties published the proceedings of their meetings.[120] Father Hyacinthe Destivelle, a participant in this "dialogue of charity" as a member of the Pontifical Council for Promoting Christian Unity, has recently identified some of its major steps.[121] Although it has not reached a decisive conclusion, the dialogue between the Anglican Communion and the Catholic Church is old enough[122] to have received, beyond the publication of its principal documents, a first evaluation of a partly historical nature.[123]

---

also reached four volumes and is organized substantially along the same lines as the German edition in terms of the choice of materials and the time period covered.

114   Giovanni Cereti & others, eds., *Enchiridion Œcumenicum: Documenti del dialogo teologico interconfessionale*, 10 vols., Bologna, EDB, 1986–2010.

115   Pantelis Kalaitzidis & others, *Orthodox Handbook on Ecumenism: Resources for Theological Education*, Oxford, Regnum Books International, 2014.

116   Constantin G. Patelos, ed., *The Orthodox Church in the Ecumenical Movement: Documents and Statements (1902–1975)*, Geneva, WCC, 1978, followed by Gennadios Limouris, ed., *Orthodox Visions of Ecumenism: Statements Messages and Reports on the Ecumenical Movement (1902–1992)*, Geneva, WCC, 1994, updated, in German, by Athanasios Basdekis, ed., *Orthodoxe Kirche und Ökumenische Bewegung: Dokumente – Erklärungen – Berichte (1900–2006)*, Frankfurt a.M., Lembeck, 2006.

117   Stylianos Tsompanidis, *Orthodoxie und Ökumene: Gemeinsam auf dem Weg zu Gerechtigkeit, Frieden und Bewahrung der Schöpfung*, Münster, LIT, 1999.

118   Reinhard Flogaus & Jennifer Wasmuth, eds., *Orthodoxie im Dialog: Historische und Aktuelle Perspektiven*, Berlin, De Gruyter, 2015. For reflections on the patristic and theological arguments related to dialogue between the Chalcedonian and non-Chalcedonian Orthodox, see the collection Christine Chaillot, ed., *The Dialogue between Eastern Orthodox and Oriental Orthodox Churches*, Volos, Volos Academy Publications, 2016, which also includes an appendix with documents.

119   See, for example, Bernard Sesboüé, *Hors de l'Église pas de salut: Histoire d'une formule et problèmes d'interprétation*, Paris, Desclée de Brouwer, 2004 (which could not take into account the work of Maria Carosio, "Extra ecclesiam nulla salus: Il caso Feeney," *CrSt* 25/3, 2004, 833–876).

120   *Tomos Agapis: Vatican-Phanar (1958–1970)*, Rome/ Istanbul, Imprimerie polyglotte vaticane, 1971. On the theological dialogue that followed, see Dimitri Salachas, *Il dialogo teologico ufficiale tra la chiesa cattolico-romana e la chiesa ortodossa: Iter e documentazione*, Bari, Centro Ecumenico S. Nicola, 1994, and Patrice Mahieu, *Se préparer au don de l'unité: La commission internationale catholique-orthodoxe (1975– 2000)*, Paris, Cerf, 2016.

121   Hyacinthe Destivelle, *Conduis-la vers l'unité parfaite: Œcuménisme et synodalité*, Paris, Cerf, 2018.

122   See historical overviews by Bernard C. Pawley & Margaret Pawley, *Rome and Canterbury through Four Centuries: A Study of the Relations between the Church of Rome and the Anglican Churches (1530–1973)*, London, Mowbray, 1974; or Wolfgang Haase, ed., *Rome and the Anglicans: Historical and Doctrinal Aspects of Anglican-Roman Catholic Relations*, Berlin, De Gruyter, 1982.

123   Christopher Hill & Edward Yarnold, *Anglicans and Roman Catholics: The Search for Unity*, London, SPCK, 1994; Adelbert Denaux & John A. Dick, eds., *From Malines to ARCIC: The Malines Conversations Commemorated*, Leuven, Leuven University Press, 1997. An interesting reconstruction of the Catholic-Anglican dialogue is found in the biography of the Dominican Jean-Marie Tillard, who was involved for a long time

As far as Rome is concerned, the situation is in many ways paradoxical. Since John XXIII, all the popes have affirmed the irrevocable nature of the ecumenical commitment of the Catholic Church, yet every single pope has also had both a positive and a negative attitude towards the matter. For instance, Paul VI increased symbolic gestures, notably toward the East,[124] but he also endowed ecumenism with a "directory" that restricted its development.[125] And it was during his pontificate, at the beginning of the 1970s, that two blows were struck against the wildest hopes of the earlier ecumenical euphoria: Rome would not seek membership in the WCC[126] and intercommunion would not be achieved with Constantinople.[127] In regard to the Ecumenical Institute in Tantur desired by the pope, it was not long before it did not live up to the hopes placed in it.[128]

As for John Paul II, on the one hand, he did more for ecumenism than all his predecessors. In his encyclical *Ut unum sint* of 1995, he went so far as to offer to put his mandate on the line if interconfessional rapprochement required it. Moreover, following the advice of Cardinal Joseph Ratzinger, in 1999 he approved the signing of an agreement on justification by faith with the LWF On the other hand, the very same Ratzinger, in the declaration

Dominus Iesus of 2000, called into question the ecclesiality of the Protestant denominations. As Pope Benedict XVI, he promulgated the constitution *Anglicanorum coetibus* in 2009, which initiated a sort of Uniatism in England, at odds with a half century of ecumenism.[129]

10 Some Footholds

Understandably, the most recent developments in the movement towards unity appear as the poor cousins in historiography. As valuable as they are, the few reported firsthand works are only isolated sparks of light on a predominantly dark horizon. A single example will suffice: the lack of works on the opposition to ecumenism, which is perhaps the greatest obstacle to the ecumenical project, voiced by the most conservative sectors of Catholicism,[130] by the burgeoning evangelical Protestantism, and especially by Orthodoxy, where ecumenism has occasionally been called a 20th-century heresy. The available materials are too rare, or too controversial, to permit anything other than highly hypothetical attempts. Among these, three tentative footholds, from three different disciplines, can be identified.

In the path sketched by Jean Séguy and others, some sociologists have endeavored here and there to place ecumenism within the rapidly changing religious and social context. The proceedings of the colloquium held in Strasbourg in 1987, published two years later under the title *Vers de nouveaux œcuménismes*,[131] bear witness to this effort.

in the work of ARCIC; see Pascale Watine Christory, *Dialogue et Communion: L'itinéraire œcuménique de Jean-Marie R. Tillard*, Leuven, Peeters, 2015.

124 *Paolo VI e l'ecumenismo: Colloquio Internazionale di Studio (Brescia, 25–27 settembre 1998)*, Brescia, Istituto Paolo VI, 2001; Patrice Mahieu, *Paul VI et les orthodoxes*, Paris, Cerf, 2012. See also Philippe Chenaux, "Paul VI, un cheminement oecuménique," in: Bourgine, ed., *Le souci de toutes les Églises*, 15–28.

125 Bruno Cherubini, *Non un trattato né un manuale: Il direttorio ecumenico (1961–1970)*, Bologna, Il Mulino, 2021.

126 Jan Grootaers, *Rome et Genève à la croisée des chemins (1968–1972): Un ordre du jour inachevé*, Paris/Geneva, Cerf/WCC, 2005.

127 Alberto Melloni, *Tempus visitationis: L'intercomunione inaccaduta fra Roma e Costantinopoli*, Bologna, Il Mulino, 2019.

128 Alberto Guasco, "L'Istituto ecumenico di Tantur (1963–1978): Appunti e problemi per una storia," *CrSt* 38/1, 2017, 221–246.

129 Giuseppe Ruggieri, ed., *La Costituzione "Anglicanorum coetibus" e l'ecumenismo*, Bologna, EDB, 2012.

130 See the recent curious book by Pierre-Marie Berthe, *Les dissensions ecclésiales, un défi pour l'Église catholique: Histoire et actualité*, Paris, Cerf, 2019, and also the reflections offered in Thomas Bremer & Maria Wernsmann, eds., *Ökumene – überdacht: Reflexionen und Realitäten im Umbruch*, Freiburg i.Br., Herder, 2014.

131 Jean-Paul Willaime, ed., *Vers de nouveaux œcuménismes: Les paradoxes contemporains de l'œcuménisme: Recherches d'unité et quêtes d'identité*, Paris, Cerf, 1989; as well as his "L'ambivalence œcuménique de Jean Paul

Ideally situated from a chronological point of view, this meeting was able to take note of the uneven record of the dialogues that had taken place, to measure the effects of the challenge to official ecumenism by various networks, and to perceive the return in force of confessional identities. After this, Jean-Paul Willaime took up the charge, seeing in the multiple "new ecumenisms" of the current religious panorama one of the aspects of its "ultramodernity."[132] It is truly regrettable that the thesis defended in 2014 at the Protestant Faculty of Theology in Strasbourg by the sociologist and ethnologist Françoise Lautman has not been published. Entitled "L'œcuménisme local: Catholiques et Protestants en France (1976–1986 et 2002–2012)," it provides a new perspective on interconfessional relations as seen "from below" for the two time periods covered. The project deserves to be taken up in other national contexts.

Historians have rarely ventured beyond the 1970s. It took the inauguration of this *History of the Desire for Christian Unity* to launch research into the evolution of ecumenism after the 1960s.[133] Previously, when driven to abandon the reserve that he intended to maintain in regard to contemporary religious history, Fouilloux gave three summarizing perspectives on ecumenism at the end of the 20th century. Written in the 1980s, the first two revealed certain salient traits of the opposition that had appeared before the upheavals of 1968: the primacy of the social, even the political, over

the religious.[134] The third, in 2000,[135] put forth the dual hypothesis of the obscuring of convergences by a new demand for differentiation and the surpassing of ecumenism, in the strictest sense of the term, by interreligious dialogue, whose growth in power is one of the characteristics of the early 21st century. Faced with the challenge to the various branches of Christianity by the progress of Islam or Buddhism, the historical differences among these branches that had separated them tend to lose, if not their sharpness, at least their immediate interest, although the continuity too frequently displayed between interreligious and interconfessional dialogue is debatable.[136] Some recent works no longer make any distinction between the two.[137]

Finally, sociologists and historians of religion can only welcome the fact that some of the most active theologians in the field of ecumenism have returned, in renewed conceptual frameworks, to the question of the "nontheological factors" in ecumenical debate, factors that were somewhat forgotten in the euphoria of the 1960s.[138] The context in which they now have to operate has changed too

---

II: Entre la restauration catholique et la promotion des dialogues," in: René Luneau & Patrick Michel, eds., *Tous les chemins ne mènent plus à Rome: Les mutations actuelles du catholicisme*, Paris, A. Michel, 1995, 191–224.

132   Jean-Paul Willaime, "L'ultramodernité sonne-t-elle la fin de l'œcuménisme?," *RSR* 89/2, 2001, 177–204.

133   Other than the works already cited by Bruno Cherubini and Luca Ferracci, see the explorative summary Luca Ferraci, ed., *Toward a History of the Desire for Christian Unity*, Zürich, LIT, 2015.

134   Fouilloux, *L'œcuménisme d'avant-hier à aujourd'hui*; and its reprinting: "L'ecumenismo da Giovanni XXIII a Giovanni Paolo II," in: *Storia della Chiesa*, vol. 25/2, *La Chiesa del Vaticano II (1958–1978)*, 1994, 249–270.

135   Étienne Fouilloux, "Les voies incertaines de l'œcuménisme," *Vingtième siècle: Revue d'histoire* 66/2, 2000, 133–145.

136   See for example Thom Sicking, "Dialogue interreligieux et dialogue œcuménique, différences et similitudes," *POC* 54, 2004, 98–116.

137   Acts from a conference at the Université du Mans in 2013: Nicolas Breton, Thomas Guillemin & Frédéric Lunel, eds., *Les dialogues interreligieux: Lieux et acteurs (XVIᵉ–XXIᵉ siècle)*, Rennes, Presses Universitaires de Rennes, 2018; it thus includes texts on both types of encounter.

138   See for example Joseph Famerée, "De l'affrontement à la reconnaissance: Petite 'phénoménologie' du dialogue œcuménique," *ETL* 74, 1998, 344–363; or Hervé Legrand, "Où en est l'œcuménisme? Quarante ans après la promulgation d'*Unitatis redintegratio*," *Istina* 50, 2005, 353–384.

much for them not to incorporate some of the salient features of such development into their work: renewed secularization in the Western world, renewed nationalism in the Orthodox lands, the exponential growth of evangelical Protestantism, or the challenge of Islam and Eastern religions in Africa and Asia, to name just a few. Notable evidence of such renewed interest can be seen in: (1) "L'œcuménisme en question(s)," a collection of articles in *Recherches de Science Religieuse*;[139] (2) the colloquium at the Institut Supérieur d'Études Œcuméniques of Paris, whose proceedings were published as *Nouveaux territoires de l'œcuménisme: Déplacements depuis 50 ans et appels pour l'avenir*;[140] and (3) the colloquium of the Accademia Internazionale di Scienze Religiose held in Bologna, Mar 6–8, 2019, whose proceedings were published in *Istina*.[141]

Looking back at over half a century of scattered research, the balance sheet may appear meagre or substantial, depending on the lenses through which one looks. Scanty, because historians and sociologists of ecumenism have been and remain few in number, and because certain gaps remain significant, whether they be persistent confessional reticence toward the ecumenical movement in the past and its revival today, or Orthodox participation in the movement and its infamous limits.[142] While the ecumenism born at the beginning of the 20th century has rapidly given rise to an imposing bibliography, there are not many disinterested accounts. At the intersection of sociology and history, this movement has above all engendered a method that will have to be refined and strengthened in order to resist the ecumenical or confessional sirens better: rigorous equal treatment of the different partners in dialogue, fair evaluation of its results without triumphalism or gloom, and consideration of all parameters without either privileging or denigrating strictly religious or institutional aspects.

Translated from French to English by Susan Dawson Vásquez and David Dawson Vásquez.

---

139   "L'œcuménisme en question(s)," *RSR* 89/2, 2001.

140   *Nouveaux territoires de l'œcuménisme: Déplacements depuis 50 ans et appels pour l'avenir*, Paris, Cerf, 2019.

141   "L'Avenir de l'œcuménisme," *Istina* 64/1–2, 2019. See in this regard: Hans-Christoph Askani, "Pour un œcuménisme autrement ouvert," in: Bourgine, ed., *Le souci de toutes les Églises*, 113–130.

142   Despite Valeria Martano, *Athenagoras il patriarca (1886–1972): Un cristiano fra crisi della coabitazione e utopia ecumenica*, Bologna, Il Mulino, 1996 and, from a theological perspective, Razvan Porumb, *Orthodoxy and Ecumenism: Towards an Active Metanoia*, Oxford, Peter Lang, 2019.

PART 2

Prehistory: The Challenges of Modernity

∵

A Theological Geography of Confessions and Churches in the 19th Century

Sandra Mazzolini

1 Preliminary Remarks

There are some significant factors that shape the theological geography of the confessions and churches in the 19th century, a transitional century in which the results of the previous period converge and which prelude further developments in the 20th century.[1] These were internal and external factors that, in general terms, affected the theology and implementation, whether thematized or not, of a renewed theological methodology, belonging both to the dynamics of ecclesial life and mission and to contemporary historical-cultural developments. Hence, there is a need to pay attention, first of all, to a wider chronological period, which considers both the term *a quo* and the term *ad quem*, secondly, to the relationship between theological thought and contemporary cultural instances as understood and carried out in the various confessions and churches, and, thirdly, to the question of the sources of theology and their analysis. These rapid brushstrokes introduce a complex picture, of which this contribution aims to sketch out only some fundamental elements, though not exhaustively.

The thorny question of the relationship between theology and the coeval cultural instances is also a crucial question on the theological agenda today. In the 19th century, this question touched on the recovered critique of the results of prior theological reflection roughly during the first half of the century (these are results that can be collected under the double figure of specialization and fragmentation); and the search for new forms and methods in the second half of the same century.[2] It is in this complex framework that "the Christian theology of the modern era found itself, similar to the churches in the tension between the claim of Christian tradition over the universal truth for all humanity and the challenge itself to such a claim by the modern limitation of the Christian faith based on private faith convictions."[3] The need for a more congruent foundation for theology and that of seeking more suitable methods of investigation and systematization is thus derived. In short, it was a research that aimed to overcome the gap between reason and faith, as well as to reconcile

---

1 Pannenberg's affirmation can be shared, for which the diversity of today's theological orientations is not rooted only in current issues "which often evolve quickly, but – more profoundly and frequently – in the past and in the entire situation of theology and Christianity which gradually took shape in the modern era"; Wolfhart Pannenberg, *Problemgeschichte der neueren evangelischen Theologie in Deutschland*, Göttingen, Vandenhoeck & Ruprecht, 1997, 14 (from here onwards, the English translation is the author's).

2 See Yves Congar, "Théologie," *DThC* 15/1, cols. 341–502, here 411; Giuseppe Angelini, "L'unica teologia e le sue molte articolazioni," *Storia teol.* 4, 491–508, here 494–505; Franco Giulio Brambilla, "Il neotomismo fra restaurazione e rinnovamento," *Storia teol.* 4, 399–490, here 453.

3 Pannenberg, *Problemgeschichte*, 32. A similar problem also concerned 18th-century theology, set before two different options for sustaining the plausibility of the Gospel's claim to truth, brought up by opposite cultural tendencies: (1) to concentrate on the motives for which the authority over Christian revelation merits trust; (2) to render such authority plausible through an explanation of the contents of revelation, in critical confrontation with the contemporary consciousness of the truth; see Pannenberg, *Problemgeschichte*, 32–33.

tradition, prior to its critical examination that is meant to free it of the accumulated incrustations over time, and instances of modernity in its various declinations. This research, which could/did not want to completely avoid the comparison with what came from outside it, had taken on specific features within the confessions and churches, achieving different results, whose impact could be found even outside the socio-cultural contexts proper to its own development.

The 19th century was therefore a complex period in which different positions coexisted despite being opposing and sometimes incompatible. It may seem reductive to categorize them in terms of defensive and opposing closure or, contrarily, of an uncritical assumption of new instances. Such categorization does not in fact account for the complexity of the issues at stake and for the variety of positions taken by individual scholars, nor by schools of thought, nor – perhaps, above all – by confessions and churches. Although we cannot deny the existence of verifiably extreme positions, they do not, however, fully account for the overall picture, which is rather rich in nuances and the presence of a variety of approaches even within the same ecclesial tradition, influencing not only within it, but also in inter-ecclesial relations. Subsequently, from this point of view, for example, it would be "a stretch to pretend to resolve the thematic polarization of faith and reason in the corresponding opposition between fideism and rationalism; as it would analogously be to bring back the debate that characterized the first half of the 19th century to simple choices of fields between one philosophical current or another."[4] Similarly, the assertion would be equally forced that, on the one hand, unlike Protestant thought, "Catholic theology and spirituality seemed to stand in opposition to 'modernity'";[5] and, on the

other, that the Orthodox world was characterized by an anachronistic immobility. The crystallization in stereotypes prevents the grasp of complex dynamics of the accomplished path; it is necessary, therefore, to proceed more so with founded approximations than with precise categorizations, because the former allow us to focus more adequately on the fundamental perspectives of the theological geography of the 19th century while respecting the nuances.

2   The Path of Catholic Theology between Renewal and Restoration

The confrontation with the world of human knowledge, which proceeds regardless of revelation, with the detachment from the harmonious relationship between philosophy and theology and with the evolving world, radically configures the Catholic theological structure of the epoch. In more specific terms, this confrontation translates into a commitment towards the reconstruction and renewal of theology.[6] It unfolds along a path which is less than easy, influenced among other things, by the fact that the church understands itself substantially as a community constrained by adverse positions to assume defensive attitudes. Such attitudes characterize coeval theology in an apologetic sense,[7] and at times even in a

---

4   Paolo Colombo, "La scuola di Tübingen," *Storia teol.* 4, 301–338, here 302 (from here onwards, the English translation is the author's).

5   Jacques Gadille, "Grands courants doctrinaux et de spiritualité dans le mond catholique," *HC* 11, 113–136, here 113 (the English translation is the author's).

6   See Congar, "Théologie," cols. 435–439.

7   "The question of the relationships between reason and faith is precisely the crucial point around which the Catholic response revolves in philosophy; a response that will become inevitably apologetic. Starting from the premise of the reciprocal irreducibility between the Christian and the philosopher, one encounters the challenge of presenting faith and reason in all their fullness and with the originality proper to each of them. At the same time, one finds oneself faced with the necessity of tracing a certain form of relationship between the two, in such a way that, respecting their identity, a possible communication may be rendered in which faith may remain legitimate before reason, and that reason may act within the possible comprehension of faith"; Karl H. Neufeld, "Le nuove sfide," *Storia teol.* 3, 113–143, here 115 (from here onwards, the English translation is the author's).

controversial one.[8] It deals with a path that follows more or less different directions,[9] summarized as follows by Karl Neufeld:

> 1. To face the modern critique of the Christian faith and to seek to respond and to overcome this critique according to its own method to the point of achieving a synthesis or agreement. 2. To confront modern thought and to exercise a critique on reason to the point of denying the possibility of it being a foundation of truth and certainty. In this case, it does not deal with responding to the critique of reason, but with seeking the authentic foundation of faith beyond that [sic] which is rational. 3. To offer the alternative of a system of philosophical thought different from that of modern thought as the only way out to overcome the critique of Christianity and to render theology possible.[10]

This brief enunciation of the possible directions for theology refers to a rather articulated theological geography, given also the inevitable connections between the different Christian traditions; from here flows the choice to focus on two moments which are significant not only for their temporal positioning but also for their representativeness in the historical-cultural climate of the time, namely the Tübingen School (1817) and the encyclical *Pastor aeternus* of Leo XIII (1879). While the first takes place in the first part of the 19th century, an era that Bernhard Welte describes

in terms of "spiritual genius, unparalleled in our history in terms of richness and splendor,"[11] the second is attributable to a different period characterized by "a completely changed spiritual climate, of much lesser genius, but superior in its diligence, work, and performance – in any case, different in interests and in the entire lifestyle."[12] In this framework, the Tübingen School, which is distinguished for the peculiarity of its proposal, is emblematic of the profuse commitment and effort to offer an authentic alternative and a valid critique of modern thought. Whether it is to rethink the relationship between faith and reason in the perspective of their unity, founded on the principle of revelation, or to accentuate the historicity of theological research that opposes the hypothesis of a perennial theological paradigm, the Tübingen School confronts itself by placing itself in a tight relationship with modern thought.[13] Following the direction already authoritatively traced by *Dei Filius*,[14]

---

8   It is sufficient to recall the debates regarding the vindication of freedom; see Jacques Gadille, "Libertés publiques: Question sociale," *HC* 11, 11–43.

9   "These three directions are respectively represented by the so-called semi-rationalism, by fideism and by the scholastic renaissance. These have their own, though not exclusively, geographical ambits: semi-rationalism that is developed especially in German lands, fideism in France and in Mediterranean territories, and the scholastic renaissance in Italy and in Spain, though having no lack of illustrious scholastics in Germany"; Neufeld, "Le nuove sfide," 116 (see also 116–143).

10 Neufeld, "Le nuove sfide," 116.

11 Bernhard Welte, *Auf der Spur des Ewigen: Philosophische Abhandlungen über verschiedene Gegenstände der Religion und der Theologie*, Freiburg i.Br., Herder, 1965, 381–382 (from here onwards, the English translation is the author's).

12 Welte, *Auf der Spur des Ewingen*, 382. The pause between the first and the second half of the 19th century had its preludes "in 1831, with the death of Hegel caused by the foreign power of cholera, whose suddenness makes it seems like a great symbol"; Welte, *Auf der Spur des Ewingen*, 381. This pause also affected the development of theological thought and method; see Welte, *Auf der Spur des Ewingen*, 383–409.

13 See Elmar Klinger, "Tübinger Schule," *SM* 4, cols. 1032–1037; Josef Rupert Geiselmann, *Die katholischer Tübinger Schule: Ihre theologische Eigenart*, Freiburg i.Br., Herder, 1964. For an in-depth study of thought of Johann Adam Möhler, a leading figure of Catholic Tübingen School, and for a comparison with another major protagonist of German religious life between the 19th and 20th centuries, see Michel Fédou's contribution in this volume.

14 Refer to the concise analysis by Christoph Theobald, "La Constitution dogmatique *Dei Filius* du concile de Vatican I," *HistDog* 4, 259–313; Annibale Zambarbieri, "'Ratio fide illustrata': La figura di teologia nel Vaticano I," *Storia teol.* 4, 339–398. For an overview of the orientations of theologians before Vatican I, see Gadille, "Grands courants doctrinaux," 113–123.

Aeterni Patris is located instead at the apex of a difficult path, in which Thomism was gradually re-evaluated, "retaining – in continuity with tradition, but without any yielding to traditionalism – able to mediate perennially valid perspectives of resolution regarding the theological question even in the evolution of historical epochs."[15]

The Tübingen School falls under the theological renewal action of romantic inspiration which rediscovers the sense of development and history, as Yves Congar points out, also through an appreciation of that past that is represented by the Fathers and Scholasticism. In this way, the Tübingen School retakes "the request that is constantly renewed over the years: that of a theology linked to life, and even a theology where life is expressed; the request that theology may be linked to the gift made by God to humanity of a new and supernatural life, one that pursues its work in an environment of faith and piety, and one that may inspire life in its turn."[16] In 1817, the Catholic Faculty of Theology that was founded in 1812 in the town of Ellwangen, one of Catholic majority and hardly touched by the Enlightenment spirit, moved to Tübingen. This passage

> therefore meant the essential possibility of greater inter-confessional and intercultural dialogue. ... The dialogue with the evangelical theological world, with the resulting demands of ecumenical openness, on the one hand, and the breath of contemporary idealistic philosophy which may end up overlapping the more traditional matrix of Scholastic and Manualistic thought, on the other, provide the unequivocal keys to understand the margin of novelty that the recent foundation brought with it.[17]

Although it may be difficult to bring the diverse theological elaborations of the School back to unity,[18] it is nevertheless possible to indicate a point of convergence in the procedure adopted by the various authors, namely, the relevance attributed to the historical profile of theological research, which places itself at the crossroads between reason and faith. While having to record a substantial differentiation with respect to the idealistic reference model,[19] there is here an echo of the historical lesson of Idealism:

> If in Hegel, faith represents a *moment* in the process through which the spirit attains full self-awareness, and revelation is understood as the anticipation of the truth that, in any case, is accessible to rational reflection, the role of theology would be to deal with defining the conditions of the possibility of the believer's access to revealed data. These conditions, while safeguarding the otherness and the gratuity of revelation, may exhibit the character of co-possibility with the instance of a reason that, in an already net manner, is understood as essentially historical. Here, the difference with respect to the structuring of the previous theology stands out.[20]

Subjected to the typical evolution of every phenomenon of consciousness, the task of theology would be that

---

15   Colombo, "La scuola di Tübingen," 303.

16   Congar, "Théologie," col. 436 (from here onwards, the English translation is the author's).

17   Colombo, "La scuola di Tübingen," 305.

18   Such a difficulty depends substantially on the fact that the definition of "Tübingen School" does not refer immediately to a thought that was universally shared by the various authors; it alludes, rather, to a thematic proximity and a sharing of viewpoints. For a brief profile of some authors, see Colombo, "La scuola di Tübingen," 320–338.

19   For Congar, instead, there was not – comprehensively speaking – a sufficient freedom from German theological and philosophical Idealism; see Congar, "Théologie," col. 436.

20   Colombo, "La scuola di Tübingen," 307.

of rethinking the foundational process of faith, with the awareness that the inadequacy of the Thomist-scholastic perspective lies not merely in the intrinsic errors, but in its ahistorical structure. In a parallel vein, the instance of overcoming the ultimately dualistic scheme of manuals becomes decisive. It is a scheme that resolves the "theological" paradigm in the supernatural with excessive simplicity, and configures as "natural" the profile of reflection that is properly historical-human.[21]

From this point of view, the decision to take the concept of revelation as a starting point for theological reflection is decisive. Naturally, "even revelation will ask to expose the criteria of its own credibility, yet these criteria do not precede it by placing themselves at a level external to it, as happens in relation to the *preambula fidei*, but accompany it in a connatural manner, so to speak."[22] This distances us from the framework of the anti-deist apologetics, in which "the course of philosophy explained the value of human knowledge and illustrated the proofs of the existence of a personal God and the immortality of the soul; in the strict sense of the term, apologetics was then asked to show the need for supernatural revelation and to explain the criteria for its recognition."[23]

There is the traditional scheme of the relationship between "nature" and "super-nature" in the setting of this approach, one that is coherent because it is supported by an analogous articulation between natural religion and revealed religion. In fact, the connection between these two levels is more complex if we consider it in the context of the historicity of the relationship between human beings and reality. This complexity would extend to the consequential theological system. From this point of view, the main reference would be the extension of faith even to the natural moment. Thus, faith does not begin where reason ends, but constitutes a datum inscribed in the very nature of the human being. From here, a recomprehension of the relationship between anthropology and revelation is derived, which cannot, from this point of view, be understood as a simple extension of rational inquiry. Consequently, the way of understanding the relationship between philosophy, defined in reference to the field of nature, and theology, which refers instead to revelation, is also modified. The difficulty of the issue is evident if we consider the aporetic profile of the proposed solutions or the various questions left open. Moreover, as Paolo Colombo points out, there is both a necessary redetermination of categories such as reason, faith and revelation, and an equally necessary rethinking of their mutual correlation. "Thus, the dynamics of the relationship between reason and faith tend to be replaced by that between human beings and revelation, in the framework of the common reference to the historical datum as an essential qualification of both realities."[24]

In addition, it is worth mentioning the commitment regarding the development of a system, understood as a concise representation of the theological approaches developed by the authors of the Tübingen School, who confronted themselves, on the one hand, with the encyclopedic project[25] and, on the other, with the specific claim of German Idealism to bring the whole order of knowledge back to completeness. It is an attempt, so to speak, to reorganize all theological subject matter, an attempt that is no longer followed from

---

21   Colombo, "La scuola di Tübingen," 308.

22   Colombo, "La scuola di Tübingen," 309.

23   Colombo, "La scuola di Tübingen," 310. Characteristic features of classical apologetics are: (1) being directly against deism, without taking into account that it deals with a result or residue of laicized Christianity; (2) except for Pascal, the separation of the meaning and fact, maintaining that the fact of the revelation may be established independently from its meaning and demonstrated with external arguments; (3) the position that faith is imposed "due to the authority of God who reveals Godself"; see Henri Bouillard, *Vérité du christianisme*, Paris, Desclée de Brouwer, 1989, 131–147.

---

24   Colombo, "La scuola di Tübingen," 313 (see also 311–317).

25   See Congar, "Théologie," col. 434.

the middle of the century. In the perspective of the Tübingen School, the system is articulated from the principle of revelation, in which the basic ideas that allow theologians to give unity to the set of theological truths are to be found. The idea of the system is variously elaborated within the same school by the different authors;[26] and in addition, next to it, another scheme develops, that is

> the organicist model, much more open to the understanding of the individual as it is, more flexible in welcoming the dynamic quality of the concrete-historical events. Here the progressive growth of the ecclesial and theological tradition does not result as aprioristically drawn to a univocal systematic nucleus. Greater space is given to creativity, to innovativeness that only history, in its unsurpassable concreteness, is capable of producing. The history of the Church – particularly referring to the history of dogmas – represents a living body in constant evolution and at the same time guided by God, the result of which, in coherence with Christological foundation, does not depend on the eventual process of its rationalization, but on its being supported and oriented by God himself.[27]

The questions, touched on by the Tübingen School in the perspective of a critical rethinking of the theological method and of problems within its contemporary context, are also taken up in another perspective, that of ecclesiastical teaching. Against the backdrop of *Aeterni Patris*, there are both the results of the debate in progress and the stances already taken and elaborated, which are now received by the pope's magisterium. At the same time, elements for further development can be glimpsed.[28] The encyclical must be included in what Congar describes as the renewal of Scholasticism. The 17th and 18th centuries, as the Dominican theologian points out, did not eliminate Scholasticism, but it seems to have been deprived little by little of its object or contents, having at least progressively slackened – if not lost – its reference to what animated it in the proper sense, that is, Christian philosophy.[29] The popes tried to restore it first through teaching, then with doctrinal interventions and, finally, with a series of documents whose peak point was represented by *Aeterni Patris*. A philosophy that had the Fathers and the great authors of the Christian Middle Ages as its points of reference, one that led to proposing St. Thomas as the safest teacher, who had expressed Christian philosophy in the most perfect, elevated and universal way.

In this framework, the notions of Neo-Scholasticism and Neo-Thomism need to be collocated. The two phenomena are not coincident but correlated, so that this double notion is sometimes used in a synonymous way, even if in reality it could be more correct to consider Neo-Thomism as a particular phenomenon that fits into the wider framework of Neo-Scholasticism. Both Neo-Scholasticism[30] and Neo-Thomism are articulated in successive phases. The latter, with its slightly different emphasis from previous ones, surpasses the 19th century and assumes a function that is prodromal to other complex and sometimes painful events through

---

26   If Johann Sebastian von Drey radically upholds the idea and identifies the Kingdom of God as the guiding idea to achieve unity in theological data, contrarily, Johann Adam Möhler pays a greater attention to the limits of the system that can never be fully completed, in that history receives even the fragmentary and the contradictory (as such, the rigidly univocal results of a system are made relative); Franz Anton Staudenmaier observes the irreducibility of the particular, of the personal, not in order to discard the idea of systematics, but rather to sketch a system of individuality; Johannes Evangelist von Kuhn applies the perspective of the system to the history of dogmas.

27   Colombo, "La scuola di Tübingen," 318–319.

28   To the developments of Thomism is added the retaking of philosophical currents different from Thomist philosophy; see Jacques Gadille, "Courants de théologie et de spiritualité dans le monde catholique," *HC* 11, 349–366, here 362–366.

29   See Congar, "Théologie," col. 437.

30   For a concise overview, see Otto Muck, "Neuscholastik," *SM* 3, cols. 749–754.

20th-century theology. It is a long wave that will stretch till the conciliar season of Vatican II and beyond.

The first phase of Neo-Scholasticism, prior to the promulgation of the encyclical *Aeterni Patris*, is characterized first of all by the affirmation concerning the plausibility of a Catholic philosophy and theology in reference to tradition, specifically to that of the 13th century; secondly, by the ancillary function attributed to philosophy (perennial), subject to the competence of the magisterium; thirdly, by the opposition to modern philosophy, as derived by Protestantism; fourthly, by the use of the notion of "nature," substantially considered in the perspective of redemption operated by grace. The second phase, following *Aeterni Patris*, is configured by the commitment "to bring ancient Scholasticism to maturity through the maturation of his thought (*vetera novis augere et perficere*). Hence, the expression *ad mentem sancti Thomae* or *ad sancti Thomae sapientiam*, that is, a knowledge that is confronted with every thought, in the conviction that the guidance of St. Thomas may help to discern whether it is compatible or assumable by faith."[31]

A more complex operation is to delineate the physiognomy of Neo-Thomism and its periodization; what is certain is that after the promulgation of *Aeterni Patris* and its differentiated reception, Neo-Thomism becomes a widespread phenomenon, although its early harbingers precede the encyclical itself.[32] *Aeterni Patris* is not a programmatic document of the pontificate of Leo XIII; but as Franco Giulio Brambilla notes, it is an intuition or pastoral vision consisting of various elements

that "merge into a design to which 'Thomism' provides a dynamic reference model, rather than a rigid system to be applied in the practice."[33] Leo XIII did not therefore assume the "Thomism of professors"; the encyclical, in fact, distinguishes between the principles and the historical figure of a certain Thomistic philosophy, canonizing only a *genius philosophandi* – a way of philosophizing,[34] proposed as paradigmatic and which, in reality, has given rise to different forms of application and even bringing results that its initiators did not expect, distinguished among which is the rediscovery of a much richer and more complex Middle Ages than had initially been thought of.

The question of the renewal of theology[35] and its method is not thematized in the encyclical, because it is more interested in pointing out the service that philosophy must render to faith, a service that could be qualified as giving structure.[36] From this point of view, theology would be a science of conclusions, because it would be none other than a philosophy applied to mysteries; in addition,

---

31 Brambilla, "Il neotomismo," 404 (from here onwards, the English translation is mine).

32 See Brambilla, "Il neotomismo," 416–443; Roger Aubert, "Le context historique et le motivations doctrinales de l'enciclique *Aeterni Patris*," in: Benedetto D'Amore, ed., *Tommaso d'Aquino nel I centenario dell'enciclica "Aeterni Patris": Atti del Convegno organizzato a Roma dalla Società Internazionale Tommaso d'Aquino e dalla Pontificia Università "San Tommaso d'Aquino": Roma, 15–16–17 novembre 1979*, Rome, Società Internazionale Tommaso d'Aquino, 1981, 15–33.

33 Brambilla, "Il neotomismo," 448. For an overview, see Christoph Theobald, "La raison et la cité: De la canonisation du thomisme à l'affirmation du fondement divin du droit," *HistDog* 4, 423–433.

34 See Theobald, "La raison et la cité," 432.

35 It should be indicated that there are seven occurrences of the term "theology," three of which are in association with the adjective "scholastic." The term is declined in an adjective form ("theological") once, while in another instance the word "theologians" is adopted, accompanied by the adjective "scholastic." A certain relevance is attributed to the problem of the renewal of theology only in two occurrences, the first inserted in the part on theoretical consideration and the second in the historical verification; see Giuseppe Colombo, "Filosofia e teologia nell'*Aeterni Patris*," *RdT* 22/1, 1981, 1–11. Leo XIII borrowed the concept of theology from the contemporary context and sketched an ideal model of the same, individuating it in "that scholastic, highlighted by the double characterization of the structure and the goal. The structure is that which is derived from the connection between the respective forces of revelation and reason. The goal is that of defending the faith"; Colombo, "Filosofia e teologia," 5 (from here onwards, the English translation is the author's).

36 See Colombo, "Filosofia e teologia," 7–8.

focusing on the reform of philosophy in terms of an almost exclusive assumption of the Thomistic one, the renewal of theology would consequently be derived in a conforming way. A renewal that would not have concerned the structure of theology as such, but rather the content to be applied to revealed truth, a content taken from scholastic philosophy in general and, specifically, from Thomist philosophy. This is an operation that is out of date, "not because St. Thomas was no longer current, but because no longer current – in the living and vital sense – was philosophy,"[37] considering the growing interest in history.

Meanwhile the historical-critical method is developing elsewhere; the theological production within the Catholic Church following the promulgation of the encyclical is actually a positive-scholastic theology, which develops theological demonstration proceeding *ex Scriptura, traditione et ratione*. This scheme proposes a simplified procedure of *De locis theologicis* by Melchor Cano, whose theology develops under the sign of authority.[38] With the goal of establishing the sense of the *auctoritates*, leaving reason in second place to defend, prepare and make explicit each and every statement, this methodology also characterizes the theological manuals, where *auctoritas* and *ratio* coexist without actually meeting. A Thomism elevated to the level of system transforms theology into a definitive and immutable form, preventing an effective confrontation with history and almost immunizing itself from it.

3   Protestant Theology in Germany and beyond: Subjectivity as Theological Foundation

Protestant theology underwent a great renewal especially in the first decades of the 19th century (around 1800–1860), a renewal in which conceptual and methodological innovations were intertwined, such as the introduction of the concept of "religious ethical experience," the development of the historical-critical method, etc., which were taken up and deepened in the following decades. Hence, as André Encrevé notes, the development of 19th-century theology appears to be marked by the scientific spirit.[39] Furthermore, there is another particular datum which is nevertheless relevant for a comprehensive understanding of the Protestant theological geography of the 19th century, namely, the internationally significant contribution that German Protestant theology of the 19th century offered to the development of the self-understanding of Christianity in the modern world.

In this regard, Wolfhart Pannenberg investigates the reasons that led to this contribution, elaborating his analysis in a double approach. The first, of a more general character, focuses on the peculiar and critical reception of the concentration on the human being and human reason, as it was configured in a widespread way in 18th-century Europe and by 19th-century German theologians. In fact, they assumed this anthropocentric approach as the basis for carrying out their attempts in view of a renewed and significant foundation of Christian theology.[40] The second and more specific approach explains why "the need for a new foundation of theology imposed itself precisely in Germany, at least in such a decisive and

---

37   Colombo, "Filosofia e teologia nell'*Aeterni Patris*," *RdT* 22/2, 1981, 98.

38   See Zambarbieri, "'Ratio fide illustrata,'" 339–349.

39   Already in the 16th century, there is a noted will, though not yet systematic, to integrate new developments of modern thought into a personal reflection; in the 19th century, such a will would be expressed in a more precise way, confronting itself with that modernity which configures a world in constant change and which distinguishes itself from the past precisely because it is penetrated by scientific knowledge; see André Encrevé, "La pensée protestante," *HC* 11, 45–112, 367–426, here 46.

40   "In other words, it can be said that, in the German Evangelical theology of the 19th century, the subjectivity of the human person and the affirmation of its constitution that is untied from the link with God, became the structural model of theological thought"; Pannenberg, *Problemgeschichte*, 23.

consequent manner."[41] An answer to this question cannot leave out a preliminary step, consisting in a reflection regarding the reasons for which this anthropocentric tendency has been so pervasive in previous European thought. Regarding this tendency, Karl Barth offers a precise description,[42] which is shared by Pannenberg, though he proceeds further.[43] In fact, Pannenberg identifies the reasons behind the anthropological change, which had arisen since the dawn of the modern era, particularly in political history, such that they are not ultimately reasons of an exclusively religious, anti-religious or historical-spiritual nature. In other words, these reasons can be attributed to the Reformation, although it must be specified that they cannot be totally ascribed to Reformation thought as such (for example, regarding the insistence on individual conscience) as much a derived consequence of the political-ecclesiastical order.

Particular attention is paid to the religious wars of the 16th and 17th centuries, more specifically to the consequences that derive from them; mostly concluded with compromises, these determined a new situation for the relationship between Christianity and society in Europe, whose long wave rolled on till the 19th and 20th centuries. The fundamental consequences are namely three: "(1) The autonomizing of state and law, with reference to the concept of the 'nature' of the human being; (2) the privatization of religious confession (or at least the demarcation of religion to a particular area of social life); (3) the self-determination of the specific sphere of society and, connected to it, the formation of a cultural-secular conscience."[44]

As an outcome of the religious wars, a new situation is therefore created for the relationship between Christianity and European society, one that also impacts theology, and the theological framework of the 18th century, whose fundamental coordinates certify that Protestant theology developed in the meaning and direction of its time. Although the comparison with the contemporary context always took place a little late,[45] is a necessary presupposition to understand the theological development of the 19th century in which previous questions that were still open were taken up and to which it was sought to respond in a new way. Among them, two main epistemological questions can be noted which permeated the 19th-century German Protestant theology in various ways;[46] while the first concerns the nature

---

41   Pannenberg, *Problemgeschichte*, 23.

42   See Karl Barth, *Protestant Theology in the Nineteenth Century: Its Background and History*, Grand Rapids MI, Eerdmans, 2002, 19–65. In such a framework, Barth firstly introduces the problem of theology in the 18th century, that is, the humanization of Christianity according to four main orientations: its humanization in a tangible, political form; its incorporation into bourgeois morality; its philosophical "reduction"; its attempt to make Christianity a more individual, more inward matter. Then, he focuses in a triple motive (internal weaknesses, contradictions and persistent reference to the Bible) for which this attempt of humanizing does not fully succeed; see Barth, *Protestant Theology*, 66–121.

43   In fact, Barth is limited to ascertaining "the emergence of the 'absolute man' as a *fact* that manifests itself in various areas of life, that which still has reasons and historical premises not deepened by Barth. According to him, therefore, the appearance of the anthropocentric way of thought is somewhat unexpected, unexplainable, since the phenomenon is considered an expression of a sort of human revolt against God, and of a sort of revolt that is not fully conscious, even for Barth"; Pannenberg, *Problemgeschichte*, 23.

44   Pannenberg, *Problemgeschichte*, 26 (see also 26–32).

45   In general terms, this is a theology that "sees itself confronted with particular facts in the Church, or rather in the Christianity of its time: with new interests, aims and attitudes, with obvious changes in disposition, thought and taste, with new convictions and new doctrines. It feels that both it and the concerns it represents by virtue of its office are isolated over and against this new situation, and feels threatened in its isolation. On the one hand it would like to break through the isolation and yet on the other it recognizes that there may be all sorts of good things in the changes that have come about without it. It feels competent, indeed obliged, and technically capable of bringing about corresponding changes in its own sphere also, and so, rather late, there is theological progress"; Barth, *Protestant Theology*, 122 (see also 122–159).

46   In the 19th century, the theological development was neither linear, nor homogeneous; beyond the already

and the forms of the knowledge of God which are accessible to the human spirit, the second deals with the type of knowledge which the Scriptures allow one to reach, given the role of the Bible in the expression of faith.[47] These two issues outline the plot of a very articulated picture, not always easy or immediate to decipher; in it are included the following authors, namely Immanuel Kant, Friedrich Schleiermacher and August Tholuck, among whom there are points of contact, starting from a shared, though different commitment to a theological foundation that values the anthropological data.

A point of distinction between the theological heritage of the 18th century and its development in the 19th is that of Kant's thought. He stands at the turn of an era in a more interesting and significant way compared to other authors; in fact, "he lent the eighteenth-century spirit a pregnancy of expression which, for all the connexions he has here, makes of him an incomparable figure."[48] This significance is determined by the fact that, according to Barth, "it was in this man and in this work [*Critique of Pure Reason*, 1781] that the 18th century saw, understood and affirmed itself in its own limitations."[49] It is a critique of reason radically understood in the sense of the reason that comprehends itself,[50] a critique that also impacts theological knowledge, because "[f]rom now on theology would no longer be able to formulate its tenets, no matter on what foundation it might base them, without having acquired a

clear conception of the method of reason, which it also uses in the construction of its tenets."[51]

An analogously significant work is that of *Religion Within the Limits of Reason Alone* (1793), whose title cannot be interpreted in the sense that religion exists only within the limits of reason, but rather, in that in which the religious fact should also be considered within the limits of simple reason.[52] "In this it must be borne in mind that 'reason alone' must in no circumstances be confused with 'pure' reason, the capacity for knowledge of ideas, but stands in contrast to the reason illuminated by revelation, the reason which believes positively and concretely."[53] Kant develops his reflection by placing himself in the viewpoint of the philosophy of religion, specifying its object at the same time: "It is this religion of reason as such, or the inner circle of positive religion, where it too is comprehensible as a religion of reason, and only in so far as it is here comprehensible as a religion of reason too, which interested philosopher."[54] As a corollary of this clarification, Kant also justifies the apparent intrusion of philosophy into theological questions, noting that on principle, for example, when it concerns itself with Christianity and its original

---

mentioned differences between the first and second half of the century, it is necessary to consider the spectrum of theological orientations and tendencies in all its complexity; see Encrevé, "La pensée protestante," 83–112, 367–426; Barth, *Protestant Theology*, 411–647; Pannenberg, *Problemgeschichte*, 46ff.

47   See Encrevé, "La pensée protestante," 49–67.

48   Barth, *Protestant Theology*, 252.

49   Barth, *Protestant Theology*, 252.

50   It is essentially "criticism of knowledge itself and of knowledge as such"; Barth, *Protestant Theology*, 255. See also Barth, *Protestant Theology*, 255–256.

51   Barth, *Protestant Theology*, 259.

52   Kant "wants on the one hand, as a philosopher, i.e. as the advocate of human reason in the general sense – which is seeking to understand itself and is thus self-critical – to remind religion, too, and theology as religion's mouth-piece, of the significance of the fact that it too is a matter in which reason plays its part, an additional part, at all events, just as certainly as it too at least *makes use* of reason in the establishment of its propositions. And on the other hand, once again as philosopher, he wants to assess religion as a phenomenon of reason, as a cultural manifestation, in so far at least as it is these things; he wants to make it intelligible within the frame-work of all the other phenomena of reason, to construct it by applying the general principles pertaining to all civilization. The theological propositions are at all events also, those of reason. And reason for its part has the 'idea of a religion' as something which is, at all events, also peculiar to it"; Barth, *Protestant Theology*, 265 (italics original).

53   Barth, *Protestant Theology*, 266.

54   Barth, *Protestant Theology*, 266.

testimonies, it does so to explain the universal truth of religion in this way.[55]

Against the background of his work, the results of the Kantian critique of reason are generally recognizable in relation to the ideal character and practical character of every pure knowledge of reason.[56] These results, however, can also be referred to Kant's attempt to interpret religion

> as a necessary phenomenon of reason, in pursuance of his general undertaking of the critique of reason; an attempt, that is to say, to reduce it to a capacity *a priori* and measure its concretely empirical content against this capacity as if this were its inner law. ... Since it is reason itself which has alone been able to perform the critique of reason and has thus supplied those results of the critique of reason which have now become criteria, it is already taken for granted by the very starting-point of this philosophy of religion, and by the conception of the problem it is supposed to involve, that it is the agent of reason, man, that is, who, just as he is the measure of all things, is here thought of and provided for as the measure of religion, too: of its practical and theoretical possibilities, and also, and in particular, as God's measure.[57]

Barth observes that "[t]his conception of the problem proves itself faultlessly in execution for precisely as long as it is merely a matter of

its own development, of drawing the limits, that is, between it and the notion of a revealed positive religion, between it and the authority of the Bible when this authority is conceived as a merely historical one, and between it and the merely historically conceived instance of a Word of God made flesh confronting man."[58] Contrarily, from the point of view of its applicability, so to speak, it is possible to find a certain discrepancy[59] which could be indicative either of the need to improve the Kantian presupposition, as Kant has put it, or for another presupposition that is completely different, but necessary, to be put forward, beside or before it.

From this point of view, one can read the subsequent development of theology and its method. Schleiermacher is representative of that theological line which affirms the Kantian presupposition from a methodological view point, though subjecting it to an immanent criticism, aimed at widening and enriching "the conception of reason which forms the premise by pointing out that there is another capacity which is part of the necessities of human reason, apart from the theoretical and practical ones: the capacity of feeling, as Schleiermacher put it, or that of 'presentiment,' as de Wette preferred to express it, linking up with the philosophers Jacobi and Fries."[60] The central theme of Schleiermacher's research is the turning point of a new theological foundation within the universally human, that of subjectivity; a research carried out without reaching a systematic presentation in the strict sense of his thought, which developed in two phases. The first phase found its thematization above all in *On Religion: Speeches to Its Cultured Despisers* (1799);[61] the second refers

---

55   See Barth, *Protestant Theology*, 266.

56   "Beginning from the demands of criticism or doubt that brings us to the foundation of knowledge – influence of Descartes – and from the necessity of sensible experience – Hume –, the pure Kantian reason does not reach the proper knowing of the idea of God, of the soul and of the world, because it is not possible to have a representation of it. In this way, even the so-called *preambula fidei* fail. The practical reason, instead, *demands* God, the freedom and immortality of the soul, and receives, within itself, the faith as its own form of knowledge"; Neufeld, "Le nuove sfide," 115–116 (italics original). See also Barth, *Protestant Theology*, 359–264.

57   Barth, *Protestant Theology*, 290.

---

58   Barth, *Protestant Theology*, 290.

59   See Barth, *Protestant Theology*, 266–292.

60   Barth, *Protestant Theology*, 292. This is a characterizing orientation of 19th-century theology, be it the so-called positive conservative, or the liberal one.

61   The work has had an echo that "went far beyond the *theology* of its time, in which the *Speeches* were perceived as the end of the Enlightenment period and a theological break towards totally new platforms.

to the work *The Christian Faith* (1821–1822) which, unlike the *Speeches*, did not receive much attention outside the theological circle.[62] Between one work and the other, an undoubted development in Schleiermacher's thought becomes evident because he deals with the changing contemporary cultural instances,[63] assuming results and, at the same time, taking critical distances, as it is possible to verify, for example, in two interrelated fundamental themes: the autonomy of religion (Second *Speech*) and the originality of the historical-positive religion (Fifth *Speech*).[64]

With regards to the new foundation of theology, useful guidelines can be recovered in the question of the autonomy of religion and its corollaries. To overcome the difficulties arising in none too few theologians from the Kantian epistemology, Schleiermacher does not define religion in the framework of a philosophical system, but recognizes that it belongs to human nature and constitutes its third original factor, together with knowledge and action.[65] This gives rise to

the autonomy of religion, compared to the other two constitutive factors of human nature, an autonomy that Schleiermacher proves by establishing a correlation between the concept of religion and the idea of infinity. The correlation with the idea of infinity obviously also concerns the sphere of knowledge (metaphysics) and of action (morality), but in the case of religion it is connoted in a different and specific way: while metaphysics and morality assume the finite as a starting point, which they overcome in the infinite, religion captures the infinite in the finite, since its starting point is the infinite which manifests itself in the finite individuals.[66] Religion is therefore described "as the moment of unity between intuition and feeling, which takes place beyond all thought and action. Intuition is the receptive, and feeling the spontaneous, side of the act of awareness, in which man in his finite quality comes to partake, as Schleiermacher put it at the time, of the infinite quality of the universe."[67] Intuition and feeling, therefore, contribute to describing religion; both represent a moment of passivity, beyond which there is no longer intuition, but knowledge, no longer feeling, but action. "Both derive from a conceptually undefined moment, but described metaphorically by Schleiermacher as a sort of carnal union between the soul and the universe"[68] understood as the infinite, but the infinite bound to the human person. The universe is neither the world, nor humanity, nor the ego; rather, it is what ensures their mutual correspondence.

Also from the *philosophical* movement of the epoch, above all from Schelling and from Hegel, the *Speeches* were seen as a contribution to the development of Idealistic and transcendental philosophy on the way of great systems in mature Idealism"; Pannenberg, *Problemgeschichte*, 46–47 (italics original).

62   See Pannenberg, *Problemgeschichte*, 47.

63   "In brief, the speaker on religion seeks an admission from the educated people to whom he is speaking that religion in general and the Christian religion in particular is the highest value in life, something which is not only possible, but real and necessary beside science, art, the Fatherland, etc., something which is already existing in latent form, and only requiring their correct recognition; and that civilization without religion, without the Christian religion, is not a complete civilization"; Barth, *Protestant Theology*, 247–248.

64   See Pannenberg, *Problemgeschichte*, 49.

65   In adopting such a stand, Schleiermacher takes up a distance both from rationalism that, in fact, reduces religion to two elements (Providence and immortality); and from supernaturalism, that confuses religion and theology. With respect to Kant, there is, instead, the commitment to place religion in an ambit that is substantially inaccessible to criticism; see Encrevé, "La pensée protestante," 68.

66   See Pannenberg, *Problemgeschichte*, 50. Regarding the origin of the constitutive elements of the concept of religion formalized by Schleiermacher, there are different assessments; Pannenberg, *Problemgeschichte*, 50–52.

67   Barth, *Protestant Theology*, 439. In the *Speeches*, Schleiermacher, in order to avoid misunderstanding, associates the term "feeling" with that of intuition, which is on the first level "being destined to describe the contents and the particular individuality of the religious conscience"; Pannenberg, *Problemgeschichte*, 52.

68   Encrevé, "La pensée protestante," 70 (the English translation is the author's).

Later, given also the development of Friedrich Schelling's philosophy,[69] Schleiermacher will no longer attribute the concept of intuition to religion in order to describe its essence, because this concept has become too contiguous with philosophical knowledge, and will rather use a modified concept of feeling, understood as "a form of the idealistic theory of self-consciousness, precisely as an original variation of this theory. ... Such a feeling is ... characterized by Schleiermacher, at least implicitly, as a consciousness of God."[70] Moreover, in the fourth paragraph of *The Christian Faith*, the content of feeling will be presented with the keyword of dependence, a dependence that not only refers to the relationship of humanity with the world – since in this relationship there is neither pure freedom, nor pure dependence – but rather to the fact that all human self-activity is justified by an "elsewhere." "The feeling of dependence constitutes here ... the reason why we 'bring up' our being dependent on an 'origin.' ... The 'from where' (*Woher*) of our dependence is called 'God' by us, so that the representation of God already presupposes the feeling of dependence and is the result of a 'more immediate reflection of the same.'"[71] The feeling of dependency, which is intuitive, does not derive from an intellectual reasoning or from a philosophical doctrine; in other words, immediate knowledge of God and the feeling of absolute dependence are, in reality, synonymous.[72] Despite possible objections to the conceptual value of the argumentation, the considerations reached by Schleiermacher represent "a considerable effort of theoretical-subjective foundation and justification of the religious consciousness as consciousness of God."[73]

Without going into the debate as to whether or not we may speak of a theology of the Awakening,[74] it should however be noted that Schleiermacher's theological thought, be it for the presence of pietistic motifs found in his concept of religion, or for the strong emphasis on religious sentiment and to its connection to ethical life, had an echo in the Awakening movement. In addition, the theologians of the Awakening perceived its strong affinity with Schleiermacher's thought with much caution.[75] The Awakening movement represents the late anti-rationalist phase of Pietism,[76] with a decisive emphasis on personal spiritual experience (the individual conversion of the heart) and a new life characterized by a joyful and optimistic activity based on the efficacy of the Gospel message, intended as a perfect guide for daily life. In a context of clear opposition to rationalism, this religious interiority is also assumed as the starting point for a new foundation of faith in revelation.[77]

In theology, the impact of the Awakening was more indirect than direct, so much so that Barth recognizes Tholuck[78] as the only "pure theologian

---

69 See Pannenberg, *Problemgeschichte*, 62.

70 Pannenberg, *Problemgeschichte*, 66; see also Barth, *Protestant Theology*, 439–440.

71 Pannenberg, *Problemgeschichte*, 67. On possible objections, see Pannenberg, *Problemgeschichte*, 68–69.

72 See Encrevé, "La pensée protestante," 70–71.

73 Pannenberg, *Problemgeschichte*, 69.

74 See Encrevé, "La pensée protestante," 80–83. See the entry "Risveglio, Teologia del," in: Pietro Bolognesi, Leonardo De Chirico & Andrea Ferrari, eds., *Dizionario di teologia evangelica*, Marchirolo, EUN, 2007, 624–625.

75 See Pannenberg, *Problemgeschichte*, 77–78, 80–81.

76 The link between the first Pietism and the incipient Enlightenment did not last long, entering into crisis during the 18th century because of the progressive rationalist dissolution of not only ecclesiastical doctrine, but even of the authority of Scripture. In England, the reaction against deism was expressed in a strongly anti-rationalist preaching, ending in conversion, in the fight for expiation and in the reception of divine grace in one's own life. The Pietist reaction came much later in Germany, characterized both by the formation of circles of Awakening and by the relationship with irrationalism and Romantic nationalism. In such circles, Pietism and conservative orthodox theology came together, since from them a conservative renewal was derived both in the churches and in theology; see Pannenberg, *Problemgeschichte*, 78–79.

77 See Pannenberg, *Problemgeschichte*, 79–80.

78 For Barth, there are two contributions of the Awakening to theology, of which Tholuck is representative: (1) the affirmation that the contents of each theological

of the awakening."[79] In relation to Schleiermacher, there is a radicalization of the principle of subjectivity in him, in that he attributes a decisive place to moral experience, which every human being can carry out and which they in fact do, and in which the fundamental principle of the truth of revelation is recovered.[80] However, the reference to moral experience, as a test tool or criterion that allows the person to evaluate between many alleged revelations, is not without problems, if one considers, in addition to the rest, that human beings are able to assimilate only as much as, in its turn, is absolutely certain. While on the one hand, what a person more certainly possesses is his or her self, that is, their moral nature (in the Kantian sense), on the other hand, there is in them a split between their egoistic nature and their own ethical determination, a split that needs to be resolved and that man or woman cannot solve on their own. It follows that if "the experience of the liberating action of the remission of moral guilt becomes the criterion of the truth of revelation,"[81] its occurrence is given only through "a reconciliation of guilt rendered possible by God through vicarious satisfaction and, in this sense, through a divine revelation."[82] In this way, Tholuck combines the theological problematic of founding the need for divine revelation, moving through the moral

self-understanding of man, with the doctrine of reconciliation through the death of Jesus.[83]

The Awakening, however, certainly meant much for other aspects of ecclesial life; as an example, it is sufficient to recall the commitment to the external and internal mission, because "among the Christians touched by the Awakening, there was a tremendous sense of gratitude for what they had received and an urgent desire to share with others, both at home and abroad, the blessings so freely shed upon them."[84] The key to all this commitment is love for Christ and for people, which manifests itself in absolute dedication, not infrequently accompanied by an element of sacrifice, of self-denial, of willingness to suffer for Christ.[85] Three elements characterize the Awakening movement everywhere: "International Christian intercourse and action; a missionary awakening showing itself in the formation of missionary societies; efforts directed to social reform."[86] In this regard, it should be noted that these

---

proposition is, in any case, also condithioned by a determined human situation which it expresses; (2) the recovery of a part of the traditional questions related, for example, to the doctrine of sin and grace; see Barth, *Protestant Theology*, 500–503.

79　Barth, *Protestant Theology*, 495. "For precisely as a pure theologian of the Revival, he stands out above others to whom one can give this name in that one can hardly say much about his theology other than he did it as a revived and a reviving man"; Barth, *Protestant Theology*, 495. For Pannenberg, just as for Barth, the systematic profile of the reflection of Tholuck should not be undervalued; see Pannenberg, *Problemgeschichte*, 82.

80　See Pannenberg, *Problemgeschichte*, 86–87.

81　Pannenberg, *Problemgeschichte*, 83.

82　Pannenberg, *Problemgeschichte*, 85.

83　"Tholuck seemed to repropose the Anselmic doctrine [the doctrine of satisfaction of Anselm of Aosta] in modern theology, justifying it again in the area of Kantian ethics, as the only way out of the moral split in man"; Pannenberg, *Problemgeschichte*, 84. Pannenberg observes that, from this point of view, the theology of the Awakening of Tholuck is close to that of the Reformers, particularly that of Luther and Melanchthon, even overturning the position, given the emergence of new problems; see Pannenberg, *Problemgeschichte*, 85 (see also 85–86).

84　David J. Bosch, *Transforming Mission: Paradigm Shifts in Theology of Mission*, Maryknoll NY, Orbis, 2011, 293. The Awakening is one of the factors that has had a great influence on the missionary world; Bosch, *Transforming Mission*, 283–287; Stephen B. Bevans & Roger P. Schroeder, *Constants in Context: A Theology of Mission for Today*, Maryknoll NY, Orbis, 2004, 209–219. The presence of women in this process of missionary expansion should also be noted; see Bevans & Schroeder, *Constants in Context*, 218–219.

85　See Bosch, *Transforming Mission*, 292–297.

86　Ruth Rouse, "Voluntary Movements and the Changing Ecumenical Climate," in: *A History of the Ecumenical Movement*, vol. 1, Ruth Rouse & Stephen C. Neill, eds., *1517–1948*, London, SPCK, 1954, 309–349, here 310.

societies and movements were pioneers, albeit unconscious pioneers, of the movement for Christian unity which was to come. They were not ecumenical in objective. Each had some specific aim of its own – missionary work or social reform –, but, though not ecumenical in aim, they were ecumenical in result. They were not called into existence to promote Christian unity; but they created a consciousness of that unity, a "sense of togetherness" amongst Christians of different churches. Though rarely formulated, the fundamental conception of Christian unity which lay beneath their common striving was that all true Christians share the life in Christ, that they are one by virtue of that sharing, and that this oneness is the essential Christian unity.[87]

4 Russian Theology of the 19th Century: The Complex Search for a Russian Identity

1453, the year of the fall of Constantinople, decided a new situation for the Christian East. The Ecumenical Patriarchate was juridically extended, comprising all the Christians of the Ottoman Empire; this was, however, "a despised presence barely tolerated by the conquerors and one seriously compromised in the eyes of the Christians of the empire, to the point that from the 19th century, after the reawakening of nationhood and the birth of the independent states, followed the fate of the Ottoman Empire in that both lost their territories: with independence in the former and autocephaly in the latter."[88] From this moment, differentiated

theological forms begin to take shape,[89] a development by no means homogeneous, given moreover their different contextualization. 19th-century Russian theology presents elements of particular interest also with reference to the analysis conducted so far; as such, the final part of this contribution is dedicated to some of its salient aspects.

An approach to the Russian Orthodox theological thought of the time also involves both a positioning over a wider time span,[90] and the acknowledgment of the actual impact of specific external factors, such as the geopolitical changes for example, as well as of internal ones, on the development of theology.[91] A linear schematization of Russian Orthodox theology is not an easy operation, given the greater number of theologians compared to previous epochs, the intertwining of different currents, the difficulty at times to distinguish religious philosophy from theology.[92] In addition, it is necessary to consider, on the one

---

89   "There are so many different theological positions in the East, at times in open conflict with one other, that it would be more accurate to speak of theologies in the plural. However, the particular theologies betray a common origin or background, whereas the various historical periods underline the differences in time and space"; Edward G. Farrugia, "Theology, Eastern," *EDCE*, 1810–1814, here 1811 (the English translation is the author's); Edward G. Farrugia, "Theology, Orthodox Sources of," *EDCE*, 1818–1820.

90   See John Meyendorff, *The Orthodox Church: Its Past and Its Role in the World Today*, Crestwood NY, St. Vladimir's Seminary Press, ³1981, 83–120; Nicolas Zernov, *Eastern Christendom: A Study of the Origin and Development of the Eastern Orthodox Church*, New York NY, G.P. Putnam's Sons, 1961, 133–201; Santi Cucinotta, "L'apporto della teologia," 579–580.

91   See in particular Vasilios N. Makrides's contribution in this volume.

92   See Gerardo Cioffari, "Breve storia della teologia russa," *QO* 3, 1987, 5–100, here 23. The work of Georges Florovsky presents an interesting cross-analysis, see Richard S. Haugh, ed., *The Collected Works of Georges Florovsky*, vol. 5, Georges Florovsky, *Ways of Russian Theology: Part One*, Belmont MA, Nordland Publishing Company, 1979, and Haugh, ed., *The Collected Works*, vol. 6, Georges Florovsky, *Ways of Russian Theology: Part Two*, Vaduz, Büchervertriebsanstalt, 1987. Hence, there are no few derived problems regarding the

---

87   Rouse, "Voluntary Movements," 309–310. Useful cues with reference also to the Awakening in Henry R.T. Brandreth, "Approaches of the Churches towards Each Other in the Nineteenth Century," in: *A History of the Ecumenical Movement*, vol. 1, 263–306.

88   Filippo Santi Cucinotta, "L'apporto della teologia delle Chiese d'Oriente," *Storia teol.* 3, 577–598, here 580 (from here onwards, the English translation is the author's).

hand, that its framework is that of Orthodox the-ology as a complex whole,[93] even though, from the initial phase, "there exist specificities that distin-guish the Russian tradition from the Byzantine one";[94] and on the other, the influence of Western thought.[95] With a certain approximation, even well founded, it can be said that the 19th century was characterized by the search for an identity of its own, within the overall framework of the Orthodox tradition, a search that mirrored an inevitable multifaceted confrontation with the thought of the Christian West.

This is a research that has meant, first of all, the reappropriation of the Orthodox concept of the-ology, according to which it is not fundamentally a system of axioms and concepts, deduced "from 'revealed' premises, i.e. from Scripture or from the statements of an ecclesiastical magisterium; rather, it was a vision experienced by the saints, whose authenticity was, of course, to be checked against the witness of Scripture and Tradition."[96] Thus understood, theology has an indispensable reference to the personal experience of God,[97] founded however "upon a sacramental, and there-fore hierarchically structured, ecclesiology, which gives a Christological and pneumatological basis to personal experience and presupposes that Christian theology must always be consistent with

the apostolic and patristic witness;"[98] such experi-ence, therefore, "is a continuous process of growth and maturation, a progress within the experience of the Church,"[99] that is within the multiple forms of ecclesial life (liturgy, spiritual and ascetic life, missionary life).

Secondly, the aforementioned research could not dispense itself of a critical comparison with motives, forms and stages of the complex process of Westernization of Russian Orthodox theology, whose outcomes were summarized by Georges Florovsky with the term *pseudomorphosis*: an ap-parently Orthodox theological form, while the expressed concepts and underlying thought struc-ture are not.[100] It was an altogether ambivalent comparison, given the interweaving of explicit and well-founded distancing from Western theolo-gy and persistent forms of influence that may con-dition theology, even if this reference was ideal.[101] Even theology was not exempt from Western in-fluence, from the day after the rupture of the re-ligious and theological unity of the Latin Church (16th century), when Western ideas, Catholic or

---

subjects and contents; see Santi Cucinotta, "L'apporto della teologia," 585.

93   The individual Oriental theologies share some fun-damental theological assertions, which characterize the Orthodox theology as a whole, and, as highlighted by Bremer, that it shares from the patristic times; see Thomas Bremer, *Kreuz und Kreml: Kleine Geschichte der orthodoxen Kirchen in Russland*, Freiburg i.Br., Herder, 2007, 143.

94   Bremer, *Kreuz und Kreml*, 143 (see also 143–146) (from here onwards, the English translation is the author's).

95   See Bremer, *Kreuz und Kreml*, 147–154.

96   John Meyendorff, *Byzantine Theology: Historical Trends and Doctrinal Themes*, New York NY, Fordham University Press, 1974, 8–9.

97   On the theological relevance of experience, see Karl Christian Felmy, *Die Orthodoxe Theologie der Gegen-wart: Eine Einführung*, Darmstadt, Wissenschaftliche Buchgesselschaft, 1990, 1–24.

98   Meyendorff, *Byzantine Theology*, 9. In comparison with other possible interpretations, this ecclesial profile dis-tinguishes the Orthodox understanding of the concept of experience; see Felmy, *Die Orthodoxe Theologie*, 3–5 (the English translation is the author's).

99   Felmy, *Die Orthodoxe Theologie*, 5. The particular de-rived meaning of the concept of development and growth is attributed not to the truth in itself (this truth is God himself), but to the conceptual elaboration of the Christian doctrine or to the refusal of heresy; see Meyendorff, *Byzantine Theology*, 10–11. It is also worth mentioning the apophatic character of theology; see Meyendorff, *Byzantine Theology*, 12–14.

100   See Haugh, ed., *The Collected Works*, vol. 5, Florovsky, *Ways of Russian Theology*, 85.

101   It is also to be noted that such a process was not a homogenous phenomenon, either in the diachronic and/or synchronic sense, or in reference to the differ-ent protagonists of this stage, of which it represents, moreover, an aspect recurring in various ambits, the editorial, the political, the monastic life, teaching of theology, theology itself and its method, etc., among which exist various forms of intersection; see Haugh, ed., *The Collected Works*, vol. 5–6, Florovsky, *Ways of Russian Theology*, passim.

Reformed, penetrated the East. "Deprived of a genuine Orthodox schooling, the theologians of the seventeenth and eighteenth centuries not infrequently used Roman arguments against the Protestants and Protestant arguments against the Roman Catholics."[102]

In addition, such a confrontation also recurs in the thorny question of the reform of ecclesiastical studies which, in the 19th century, translates into a series of incompatible projects *de facto*, underlying which there is a different appreciation of either the relationship with the Western theological world, or of theology as such.[103] Among the many, two data seem to be interesting. The first concerns the difficult transition to the Russian language; only in the middle of the century do they distance themselves from the use of Latin as a language in ecclesiastical studies. As Florovsky has accurately pointed out, such linguistic dissolution is not necessarily equivalent to a full distancing from Latin Scholasticism.[104] To do this, it would have been necessary to autonomously elaborate their own theological thought and method, assuming "three fundamental factors such as a new direct critical approach to biblical-patristic sources, the

replacement of Latin with Russian and the consequent neutralization of Western Scholastic influence also mediated by the linguistic style."[105] In fact, for a good part of the century, this elaboration marked the pace; while the assumption of the aforementioned three factors was not linear,[106] the academies, within which theology was confined, were not able to promote an autonomous and significant theological development, despite having achieved some undeniable results.[107] The second datum, only mentioned here, consists of the contribution of philosophical-religious thought which, given the particular attention progressively placed on philosophy and the condition of freedom of research (certainly greater than that found in the theological field), is also reflected in the theological works and which "will generate an extraordinary religious-cultural flowering between the end of the 19th and beginning of the 20th centuries."[108]

Theological scholarship was brought to Russia from the West. Having been a stranger to Russia for too long, it stubbornly spoke in its own peculiar and foreign tongue – instead of in the language of daily life or the language of prayer – and remained a foreign element in the church organism. Theology in Russia developed in an artificial and excessively limited environment. It began as, and remained, an academic subject, and as such it ceased to be a quest for truth or a confession of faith.[109]

---

102 Meyendorff, *The Orthodox Church*, 91. Particularly emblematic is the *Confessio orthodoxa* (1640) of Peter Mogila that "made a strong imprint on Orthodoxy; in this way, however, he brought it down to the forms of Western thought. This methodical adaptation to the situation of his time … seemed something necessary to him"; Bremer, *Kreuz und Kreml*, 149 (from here onwards, the English translation is mine). Regarding such adaptation, see Basilio Petrà, *L'etica ortodossa: Storia, fonti, identità*, Assisi, Cittadella, 2010, 18.

103 The long history of the reform of the religious educational system, to which concur ecclesiastic and non-ecclesiastical actors and that deals with such aspects as the curriculum of studies, the titles, the courses taught, the teachers and students, etc., is documented in detail by Florovsky, see Haugh, ed., *The Collected Works*, vol. 5, Florovsky, *Ways of Russian Theology*, 175–181, 238–265 and vol. 6, Florovsky, *Ways of Russian Theology*, 128–137, 190–191, 262–267.

104 See Haugh, ed., *The Collected Works*, vol. 5, Florovsky, *Ways of Russian Theology*, 211–212.

105 Santi Cucinotta, "L'apporto della teologia," 586.

106 See, for example, the question of the translation of the Bible into Russian, or of that related to historical-critical studies; Haugh, ed., *The Collected Works*, vol. 5, Florovsky, *Ways of Russian Theology*, 181–201 and vol. 6, Florovsky, *Ways of Russian Theology*, 122–128, 138–150.

107 See Haugh, ed., *The Collected Works*, vol. 5, Florovsky, *Ways of Russian Theology*, 265–268.

108 Petrà, *L'etica ortodossa*, 19 (the English translation is the author's).

109 Haugh, ed., *The Collected Works*, vol. 6, Florovsky, *Ways of Russian Theology*, 290.

The 16th century

marked the falling-out of Russian thought from the patristic tradition. ... Recovery of the patristic style is the primary and fundamental postulate for Russia's theological renaissance. Renaissance does not mean some sort of "restoration" or some repetition of or return to the past. "Following the fathers" always means moving forwards, not backwards; it means fidelity to the patristic spirit and not just to the patristic letter. One must be steeped in the inspiration of the patristic flame and not simply be a gardener pottering around amongst ancient texts. *Unde ardet, inde lucet*! One can follow in the path of the fathers only through creativity, not through imitation.[110]

Traces of such reintegration, or at least of attempts at it, can also be found in the framework of the so-called synodal period of the Russian Church (1721–1917).[111] The 19th century is inscribed in this problematic period, whose lights and shadows deserve an objective assessment. The ministry of spiritual paternity, the missionary expansion and the Slavophile movement are three fragments of a broader history. They can be considered representative, each in its own way and yet not without ambiguity or limits, of the reintegration of the patristic style from a creative point of view, which is consistent with the contemporary context, as well as an essential condition for a theological rebirth.[112] They are three fragments of a more complex history and are disconnected only in appearance. In reality, there are various correlation

elements among them, subjective (for example, the actors involved, their influence in their lifetime and beyond) and objective (among others, the tradition, the sources, the reference to the context and its cultural, social implications).

The ministry of spiritual paternity has to be understood in the context of monasticism, a significant expression of spiritual life, although it does not coincide with it.[113] Monasticism, in full expansion in the 19th century,[114] became a reference point for Russian society,

not only because of the hundreds of thousands of pilgrims who went to the monasteries annually, but because of the intense charitable activity that took place there (schools, hospices and hospitals, assistance to the disowned), and which had a non-secondary role (especially after the abolition of serfdom in 1861) in the mitigation of social conflict, in supporting the population in the difficult conditions of a time of transition, in strengthening the "principles of religion, of good and of justice."[115]

Although the evaluation of the influence of monasticism on Russian society and culture may be

---

110   Haugh, ed., *The Collected Works*, vol. 6, Florovsky, *Ways of Russian Theology*, 294.

111   In 1589, the metropolitan of Moscow became a patriarch; the Patriarchate was abolished by Peter the Great (tsar between 1682 and 1725) and the Holy Synod was established. In this way, the synodal period begins.

112   On the return to Patristicism in the Orthodox field, see Nikolaos Asproulis's contribution in the second volume of this work, while as regards the Slavic movement, see Jeremy Pilch's contribution in this volume.

113   Regarding other aspects of spiritual life, see Bremer, *Kreuz und Kreml*, 181–194.

114   For a concise look at Russian monasticism, see Bremer, *Kreuz und Kreml*, 166–181. In the synodal period, the fidelity to the monastic ideal is also highly important "because it was largely this which made possible the survival of Russian spirituality by acting as a counterweight to the process of statism, the attempt of the state to make the Church in its own image and reduce it to the role of a mere servant. It was in monasteries that the great Russian saints of the period made their appearance and carried on their apostolate"; Meyendorff, *The Orthodox Church*, 114.

115   Adalberto Mainardi, "La riforma possibile: Società e monachesimo in Russia nel XIX secolo: Il fenomeno dello 'starčestvo,'" in: Eduardo López-Tello García & Benedetta Selene Zorzi, eds., *Church, Society and Monasticism: Acts of the International Symposium, Rome, May 31–June 3, 2006*, Rome, Pontificio Ateneo S. Anselmo, 2009, 509–529, here 510 (from here onwards, the English translation is the author's).

different, there is, on the other hand, a substantial agreement in indicating the importance assumed by the exercise of the ministry of spiritual paternity, the so-called *starčestvo*.

What is emblematic in this regard is the experience of the monastery of Optina Pustyn', aimed at promoting a fruitful interaction between the *starčestvo* and contemporary Russian society, characterized by an undoubted novelty, which arose "in the wake of tradition, because it is watered at the patristic and biblical sources – [and which] one can grasp especially in three aspects: (1) attention to interior life in a community context; (2) the study of the Fathers and publishing activity;[116] (3) openness to the laity."[117] In this framework, one can understand the "spiritual and existential exchange between Optina's *starsy* and some great protagonists of Russian culture, over several generations, from Kireyevsky to Gogol, from Dostoevsky to Tolstoy, from Solovyov to Florensky."[118] This exchange would "draw nourishment from the deep terrain of the foundations of spiritual life,"[119] the search for which, in conformity with a profound interior demand, was transversal through the different strata of Russian society, since the question of the individual journey and Christian personality progressively acquired more and more substance. Hence, Optina Pustyn' became "a meeting place for the bearers of the authentic patristic tradition of Eastern Orthodoxy

and of Westernized intellectuals in search of Christian teaching unpolluted by bureaucratic interventions or Western controversies."[120]

Probably, the least known is the missionary season of the Russian Orthodox Church in the 19th century. "While not comparable in scale to the missionary work of the Protestant and Catholic churches, the nineteenth century can also be considered the 'Great Century' for the Orthodox Church, since it marked the beginning of a new period of mission."[121] The peculiarity of the subjects involved (monks, lay people, etc.), often men of great intellect, knowledgeable of the Bible and of the tradition of the Fathers, endowed with good linguistic skills and able to adapt to the harsh life of the environment in which they carried out their evangelizing activity; the breadth and distances of the evangelized areas, inside and outside the Russian Empire (Siberia, Alaska and East Asia) in line with the Russian colonial expansion;[122] the Moscow foundation of an Orthodox Missionary Society (1870) to coordinate and to finance Russian missionaries and their activities; the creation in the Kazan Academy of a department of missionary studies and for the translation of texts into dozens of languages are only some significant elements of this time of missionary rebirth.[123]

Anastasios Yannoulatos remarks that the Russian missionaries were inspired by the principles of Byzantine Orthodoxy, which they developed in a bold and creative way. In this regard, it is sufficient to mention

---

116   In the 1840s, the publication of translated works of the Fathers is undertaken. Although handwritten, they were already sufficiently known; circulating a series of published edifying books and reflections, a real spiritual demand of the epoch is responded to in this way; see Haugh, ed., *The Collected Works*, vol. 6, Florovsky, *Ways of Russian Theology*, 164–166.

117   Mainardi, "La riforma possibile," 517 (see also 513–528). For deepening, see Adalberto Mainardi, ed., *Optina Pustyn' e la paternità spirituale: Atti del X convegno ecumenico di spiritualità ortodossa, sezione russa: Bose, 19–21 settembre 2002*, Magnano, Qiqajon, 2003.

118   See Mainardi, "La riforma possibile," 521. See also Meyendorff, *The Orthodox Church*, 115–116; Haugh, ed., *The Collected Works*, vol. 6, Florovsky, *Ways of Russian Theology*, 164–165.

119   Mainardi, "La riforma possibile," 521.

120   Zernov, *Eastern Christendom*, 179.

121   Bevans & Schroeder, *Constants in Context*, 227. For further information, see Adalberto Mainardi, ed., *Le missioni della Chiesa ortodossa russa: Atti del XIV convegno ecumenico di spiritualità ortodossa, sezione russa: Bose: 18–20 settembre 2006*, Magnano, Qiqajon, 2007.

122   See Meyendorff, *The Orthodox Church*, 120.

123   See Zernov, *Eastern Christendom*, 180–184; Meyendorff, *The Orthodox Church*, 118–120; Bevans & Schroeder, *Constants in Context*, 227–228; Anastasios Yannoulatos, "Orthodox Mission: Past, Present, Future," in: Petros Vassiliadis, ed., *Orthodox Perspectives on Mission*, Oxford, Regnum, 2013, 15–33, here 18.

the creation of an alphabet for unwritten languages; the translation of biblical and liturgical texts into new tongues; the celebration of liturgy in local dialects, with systematic philological care; the preparation of a native clergy as quickly as possible; the joint participation of clergy and laity, with an emphasis on the mobilization of the faithful; care for the educational, agricultural, and artistic or technical development in the tribes and people drawn to the Orthodoxy. Continuing the Orthodox tradition, they gave importance to liturgical life, to the harmonious architecture of the churches, to the beauty of worship and to its social consequences.[124]

An overview of the contemporary Orthodox mission, as Stephen Bevans and Roger Schroeder observe, "points to an incarnational approach with importance placed on vernacular, cultural understanding and indigenous church leadership in developing local churches. ... However, in most situations the Orthodox church followed a more holistic approach to mission, which was characteristic of Protestant and Catholic mission as well."[125]

The third reference experience is that of the Slavophile movement and its instances. In the 40s of the 19th century, new groups were formed and for the first time all the differences between Westernists and Slavophiles were drawn out, differences that, in the middle of the decade, evolved into real and properly opposite positions. The two above-mentioned orientations – Slavophiles (*slavjanofily*) and Westernists (*zapadniki*) – are decisive for 19th-century Russian philosophy. In them, among other things, "the ancient question of Russia's orientation, that is, the type of attitude that Russia should have assumed towards Western influences, emerges again. With the growing contacts with the West, the question became more

heated,"[126] and was made more acute by the fact that it also threw on the rug the difficult problem of placing Russia in the context of universal history.

The historiosophic theme of Russia's destiny also became fundamental for the newly awakening philosophical thought in Russia. And on this historical plane the religious question was again posed, with complete clarity, in Russian cultural and social consciousness. The uniqueness of Russia became ever more apparent as, through trial and doubt, it was historically counterposed to "Europe." From the outset the difference was analyzed as a difference in religious destiny.[127]

In this way, Petr Yakovlevich Chaadayev[128] sets the question in his *Philosophical Letters* (1836). Setting himself at the viewpoint of human history in relation to spiritual progress, to civilization, he emphasizes the role of religion in this regard, maintaining that each religion must be evaluated not only according to the purity of its doctrine, but also with reference to its civilizing impact. It follows, on the one hand, an appreciation for Western values and for the socio-cultural action of the Church of Rome; and on the other, a severe evaluation both of Russian religiosity, excessively impregnated with ascetic and spiritual values, and the passivity of the Orthodox Church towards

124   Yannoulatos, "Orthodox Mission," 18.
125   Bevans & Schroeder, *Constants in Context*, 228. For an overview of the missionary paradigm of the Eastern Church, see Bosch, *Transforming Mission*, 195–218.
126   Bremer, *Kreuz und Kreml*, 155. "Here, the fact that the critical orientation regarding the West was by itself inspired by Western ideas and established on Western concepts was not considered. One such phenomenon was neither new in history nor in Russian thought. Generally, it is not possible to trace a dividing line between the two orientations, because the concepts are often used in an imprecise way, and in many thinkers there are approaches that could be attributed to one or another of the orientations"; Bremer, *Kreuz und Kreml*, 115.
127   Haugh, ed., *The Collected Works*, vol. 6, Florovsky, *Ways of Russian Theology*, 14.
128   On Chaadayev, see Haugh, ed., *The Collected Works*, vol. 6, Florovsky, *Ways of Russian Theology*, 14–16.

the state.[129] Generally considered to be the first Westernist, Chaadayev was in effect only *sui generis*, given the religious nature of his thought. In reality, the Westernists, because they maintained that for Russia there was a possibility of salvation "only in the openness to Western thought, did not nourish a great interest in religious matters and among them there was no exponent who could make his own imprint on theological thought."[130]

Slavophiles had a greater impact, envisaging an opposition that does not remain confined to the psychological or nationalistic sphere, but which is also culturally creative. A complex movement, "which was characterized both by the strong reaction to the Westernism of the *intellighenzia* that went back to the project of Peter the Great, and by the re-proposal of the resurgent Russian messianism, the soul of religious pan-Slavism,"[131] thus arises as a decisive reaction to all that appeared to be Western. Also nourished by the development of monasticism, it promotes as a matter of fact

> the emancipation of Orthodoxy from every form of dependence on the West and the recovery of authentic sources of Orthodox thought identified around some fundamental thematic points, such as the assumption of apophatic and mystic theology, the eucharistic dimension of ecclesiology, the re-proposition of the traditional ascetic source, through the Philocalia, and that iconic,

through the *theology of images* of the Russian ethos.[132]

Under the influence of German Romanticism and Idealism, the Slavophiles refer to the Russian people, to the ancient-Russian and Slavic values, while the question of the destiny of Russia becomes central. From their perspective, the tendency developed in Western Europe to overvalue the human person, a verifiable tendency in humanism, in the Enlightenment and rationalism, involved, on the one hand, a progressive distancing from the old and right Christian principles and, on the other,

> produced an emphasis on the individual in which the human community loses every value. This was shown as particularly evident in Protestantism, where there would be no bond for the individual Christian. But for Slavophiles, even within Catholicism, where the individual element is hidden by the absolute authority of the papacy, the problem of the Western Christian is manifested.[133]

Contrarily, Orthodoxy emphasizes the value of the religious community that is realized in it. From this point of view, the Slav is conceived as a person inserted in a community, in which one does not renounce his or her true destiny; indeed, that they find it (in this regard, a certain idealization of the Slavic forms of coexistence, for example of that of the rural village communities, should be noted).

The same applies to the religious community, in which the identity of the individual finds its fulfillment. "The central category of this idea is the word *sobornost*, which was coined later. This concept, difficult to translate, according to its very etymology contains the meaning of terms like "conciliarity" or "synodality" or "catholicity." In the religious sphere it indicates the conviction that the entire

---

129 See Cioffari, "Breve storia," 23–24.
130 Bremer, *Kreuz und Kreml*, 160. "Many exponents of Western philosophy radicalize and create the presuppositions of Russian anarchism, also for the various socialist and communist currents that characterize the political life of Russia until the 19th and beginnings of the 20th centuries"; Bremer, *Kreuz und Kreml*, 160. Also Florovsky affirms that "Russian Westernism in those years usually led to atheism, realism, positivism"; Haugh, ed., *The Collected Works*, vol. 6, Florovsky, *Ways of Russian Theology*, 15.
131 Santi Cucinotta, "L'apporto della teologia," 586.
132 Santi Cucinotta, "L'apporto della teologia," 586 (italics original). The figures working in this field came both from philosophical and from theological backgrounds.
133 Bremer, *Kreuz und Kreml*, 156.

church should make its contribution in important decisions and in the search for truth."[134] From the consideration attributed to *sobornost* as the community of all within the church, derives the great interest shown by Slavophiles in religious matters, on the one hand, and, on the other, the fact that

> the Slavic culture, conceived as orthodox, has no interest in the hierarchy or structure of the Church, but rather, in the community of *sobornost*. Starting from this idea of community, even questions such as those regarding religious authority and of the power of decision-making in the Church, are interpreted, with the result that the conciliar decisions of the hierarchy always have a relative character and have to be confirmed by the entire Church for approval (or for disapproval) in an informal process.[135]

The three above-mentioned experiences represent, as previously noted, three parts of a broader itinerary of research into Russian identity, including the theological one; an itinerary that was concluded in an ambivalent way, both due to the forceful and forced interruption caused by the 1917 revolution, and to the unpredictable and original continuation elsewhere, given the work of the so-called theologians of the Diaspora, a characteristic phenomenon of the 20th century and of none too simple reading. As noted by Filippo Santi Cucinotta, "[t]hese Orthodox theologians realize the first significant encounter with Western Christianity, favoring the rise of creative directions of research both in Orthodox theology and in those Catholic and Protestant."[136]

This alternation between interruption and continuation is, in some way and by analogy, a figure of the theological geography of the confessions and churches of the 19th century, which can be interpreted as a complex whole in the light of four intricacies that are not always synchronic: (1) that of common background questions and the elaboration of plural answers, not necessarily always conflicting; (2) that of different attitudes, ranging from an aprioristic closeness to an openness that is not always critical; (3) that of premises for further developments and of lost opportunities of encounter with the socio-cultural context of the epoch, but also within the confessions and churches and between the confessions and churches; (4) that of history and prehistory, because drafted or thematized perspectives in the 19th century, the aspects once praised in the climate in which they were elaborated and depended upon, would be received and further thematized in the 20th century.

Translated from Italian to English by Michael Cheong.

Bibliography

Angelini, Giuseppe, Giuseppe Colombo & Marco Vergottini, eds., *Storia della teologia*, vol. 4: *Età moderna*, Casale Monferrato (AL), Piemme, 2011.

Barth, Karl, *Protestant Theology in the Nineteenth Century: Its Background and History*, Grand Rapids MI, Eerdmans, 2002.

Bremer, Thomas, *Kreuz und Kreml: Kleine Geschichte der orthodoxen Kirchen in Russland*, Freiburg i.Br., Herder, 2007.

Congar, Yves, "Théologie," *DThC* 15/1, 341–502.

Encrevé, André, "La pensée protestante," *HC* 11, 45–112, 367–426.

---

134   Bremer, *Kreuz und Kreml*, 156–157. The most important theorist of *sobornost* has been Aleksey Khomyakov; see Cioffari, "Breve storia," 25–28. On Khomyakov, see also Haugh, ed., *The Collected Works*, vol. 6, Florovsky, *Ways of Russian Theology*, 38–48. For a comparison with the ecclesiological thought of Johann Adam Möhler, see Haugh, ed., *The Collected Works*, vol. 6, Florovsky, *Ways of Russian Theology*, 46–48.

135   Bremer, *Kreuz und Kreml*, 157.

---

136   Santi Cucinotta, "L'apporto della teologia," 588.

Felmy, Karl Christian, *Die Orthodoxe Theologie der Gegenwart: Eine Einführung*, Darmstadt, Wissenschaftliche Buchgesselschaft, 1990.

Fisichella, Rino, *Storia della teologia*, vol. 3: *Da Vitus Pichler a Henri de Lubac*, Bologna, EDB, 2015.

Gadille, Jacques, "Grands courants doctrinaux et de spiritualité dans le mond catholique," *HC* 11, 113–136.

Gadille, Jacques, "Courants de théologie et de spiritualité dans le monde catholique," *HC* 11, 349–366.

Haugh, Richard S., ed., *The Collected Works of Georges Florovsky*, vol. 5, Georges Florovsky, *Ways of Russian Theology: Part One*, Belmont MA, Nordland Publishing Company, 1979. Haugh, Richard S., ed., *The Collected Works*, vol. 6, Georges Florovsky, *Ways of Russian Theology: Part Two*, Vaduz, Büchervertriebsanstalt, 1987.

Meyendorff, John, *Byzantine Theology: Historical Trends and Doctrinal Themes*, New York NY, Fordham University Press, 1974.

Meyendorff, John, *The Orthodox Church: Its Past and Its Role in the World Today*, Crestwood NY, St. Vladimir's Seminary Press, ³1981.

Pannenberg, Wolfhart, *Problemgeschichte der neueren evangelischen Theologie in Deutschland*, Göttingen, Vandenhoeck & Ruprecht, 1997.

Sesboüé, Bernard, "2ᵉ Phase. De Trente à Vatican I. Un nouvel âge de la theologie. De l'apologétique à l'émergence du "magistère vivant," *HistDog* 4, 133–226.

Theobald, Christopher, "Troisième phase. De vatican I aux annés 1950: révélation, foi et raison, inspiration, dogme et magistère infallible," *HistDog* 4, 227–470.

CHAPTER 5

The Search for an Orthodox Christian Identity: Orthodoxy, Nation, and Ecumenism between 19th and 20th Century

Vasilios N. Makrides

1 Introduction: The Orthodox Christian World in the Modern Era

One of the most important challenges facing the Orthodox Christian world has been the inevitable encounter with modernity in its many and peculiar facets. In historical terms, modernity initially originated in Western Europe in close connection with the radical transformations, also in the religious sphere, that took place there with the advent of the Reformation. These transformations extended beyond their original geographical boundaries and exerted strong, even catalytic influences, on the rest of Western and non-Western societies. They naturally also affected Orthodox Christianity, which was forced in the situation to face unexpected developments as well as intricate issues, and to formulate plans and strategies for the future. These were problems that, despite all the differences of context, are still relevant today, starting with the question of defining a common Orthodox identity that takes into account the national fragmentation that has characterized Orthodoxy over the last two centuries. This problem frames past and present ecumenical efforts to build a common Orthodox terrain and identity and is the context in which the Patriarchate of Constantinople has taken on a prominent role from the outset.

Indeed, it should be noted here that the progressive expansion of the various Orthodox nationalisms, which led to the foundation of national Orthodox Churches from the 19th century onwards, had an immediate impact on the authority and prestige of the Constantinopolitan Patriarchate. This process of nationalization was also intrinsically connected with turbulent political and social transformations, most significantly the growing secularization that spread quickly and in different forms from Western Europe to the Eastern hemisphere of the Old Continent. Taken together, these factors struck at the heart of Constantinople's primacy in the Orthodox ecumene as well as its territorial and jurisdictional integrity, prompting it to undertake various initiatives aimed, in an ecumenical sense, at preserving a type of pan-Orthodox unity that still looked to the Phanar as its political and spiritual point of reference. These actions, it should be recalled, were not only directed towards the other Orthodox Churches but frequently also towards the rest of the Christian world.

It was certainly not the first time that the Orthodox world found itself engaged in activities related to the ecumenical cause. However, it was historically significant that the impulse toward unity arose in response to the political upheavals that had changed the face of European societies from the 19th century to the beginning of the 20th. They also badly affected the Orthodox world as a whole, compelling it to react.

This is the reason that, in continuing this analysis, more emphasis will be placed on the sociopolitical context of that tormented historical period than on the religious developments that were at the background of the ecumenical undertakings that we shall consider, such as the contacts that had been established in the late 19th century between the Old Catholics and the Orthodox,[1] and between the Orthodox and Anglicans.[2]

2 The Changing Socio-Political Context and the National Transformation of the Orthodox World

The numerous connections between nationalist unrest and the Orthodox world in general have produced an enormous number of studies in recent decades. It was not, after all, an insignificant or marginal phenomenon since it has radically changed the structure of Orthodoxy and shaped its development over the last two centuries. The heart of the matter lies in understanding how and why traditional concepts of the Christian Church, and more specifically of Eastern Orthodoxy, such as universality, ecumenicity, and catholicity, soon diminished in importance on coming into contact with the phenomenon of 19th-century nationalism, leading Orthodoxy towards a process of fragmentation not unlike the one that was slowly disintegrating the Ottoman Empire. This problem

acquires greater weight if observed in the light of the present day, when many Orthodox Churches (with rare exceptions such as the Ecumenical Patriarchate of Constantinople) still claim they are proud to serve the interests of their respective states, letting the universal character and vocation that have historically defined Orthodoxy be passed over in silence and forgetting how, on several occasions, the Orthodox Christian tradition expressed itself at the highest level of authority against both nationalism and the nationalization of the churches, rejecting both these phenomena on theological and ecclesiological levels.[3]

Looking more closely at the phenomenon of nationalism for a moment, it must be said that it was basically a product of 18th-century Western Europe, which drew mainly on two sources. On the one hand, there was the civic and political tradition of the Enlightenment and the French Revolution, which identified the nation with the state and expressed the national sovereignty of the citizens residing in that state, to whose government and laws they owed obedience. On the other hand, it drew on the cultural tradition of German Romanticism, which considered the nation as an organic community of people united by certain characteristics and constitutive elements of a society, such as language and customs. This shows how, inevitably, there was much continuity between the national identities of the modern era and earlier ethnic identities or identifications, but there were also crucial differences. Contrary to the modern model of the nation-state, for example, the imperial model of political organization provided for the coexistence within it of many distinct ethnic groups, usually being more pluralistic, flexible, malleable, and heterogeneous than the nation-states that would follow it. The ethnic variety that characterized the great multicultural empires would be lost in the nation-states of the modern era, which by constitution aspired

---

1 See LeRoy Albrecht Boerneke, *The Dawn of the Ecumenical Age: Anglican, Old Catholic, and Orthodox Reunion Negotiations of the 1870's*, Ph.D thesis, University of Minnesota, 1977; Eugen Hämmerle, "Wahrnehmung und Begegnung: Altkatholiken und Orthodoxe in der Frühzeit des Evangelischen Bundes," in: Gottfried Maron, ed., *Evangelisch und ökumenisch: Beiträge zum 100jährigen Bestehen des Evangelischen Bundes*, Göttingen, Vandenhoeck & Ruprecht, 1986, 497–511; Harald Rein, *Kirchengemeinschaft: Die anglikanisch-altkatholisch-orthodoxen Beziehungen von 1870 bis 1990 und ihre ökumenische Relevanz*, 2 vols., Bern, Peter Lang, 1993–1994.

2 See Bryn Geffert, *Eastern Orthodox and Anglicans: Diplomacy, Theology, and the Politics of Interwar Ecumenism*, Notre Dame IN, University of Notre Dame Press, 2010; Pandora Dimanopoulou, *Rendez à César ce qui est à César et à Dieu ce qui est à Dieu?: Le rapprochement entre les Églises anglicane et orthodoxe grecque (1903–1930)*, Paris, Cerf, 2016; Dimitrios Filippos Salapatas, *The Fellowship of St. Alban and St. Sergius: Orthodox and Anglican Ecumenical Relations (1927–2012)*, Newcastle upon Tyne, Cambridge Scholars Publishing, 2018. See also Dimitri Salapatas's contribution in this work.

3 See, for example, Ioannes N. Karmiris, "Nationalism in the Orthodox Church," *GOTR* 26/3, 1981, 171–182.

to cultural homogeneity and uniformity. It is well known, moreover, that within their borders repressive policies were usually pursued against minorities who were urged, at times forcibly, to comply with the normative and dominant national narrative.

A multiform and multifaceted phenomenon, the process of nationalization that began at the end of the 18th century did not fail to spread rapidly to eastern and southeastern Europe and the Near East, where the majority of the Orthodox population had lived for a very long time. Eastern and southeastern Europeans, in particular, considered nationalism to be the best path towards the modernization of the state and, in many cases, it revealed a facet partly inclined towards the religious aspect. In this respect, it should be added that the historic politicization of the Orthodox Church had created a singularly favorable backdrop for the spread of nationalism in the Orthodox region of Christianity, paving the way for the emergence of national churches within the borders of the respective independent states.[4] Historically limited to the Patriarchates of Constantinople, Jerusalem, Alexandria, and Antioch, from the 19th century the autonomous structures of the Orthodox Church experienced in fact an unprecedented proliferation, creating considerable problems in maintaining pan-Orthodox unity and cooperation. With the passage of time, further difficulties were added, such as those related to the type of ecclesiastical and jurisdictional status to be assigned to the numerous diasporic communities born during the 20th century in various parts of the world owing to the great migratory flows.

Within this process, the Russian Orthodox Church presents some specific features. Historically, it was under Constantinople's jurisdiction, given Byzantium's initial Christianization of the Kievan Rus'. After 1453, mainly due to the fall of Byzantium and the fact that it had a strong and politically organized state behind it, the Russian Church enjoyed *de facto* independence, receiving later formal recognition by being elevated to a patriarchate status by Constantinople and the other Orthodox Churches (1589–1593) that were under Ottoman rule and control at the time. As an integral part of the nascent and ambitious Tsarist Empire, the Russian Orthodox Church grew in strength, influence, and importance, becoming a fundamental instrument of the tsars' imperial ideology and gradually claiming the legacy and leadership in the Orthodox world that had once belonged to Byzantium (it is sufficient to recall the confidence with which the idea of Moscow as the "Third Rome" was promoted).[5] Further developments, such as the Council of a Hundred Chapters (Stoglavy Sobor) held in Moscow in 1551 and the great ecclesiastical reforms called for by Tsar Peter the Great at the beginning of the 18th century, led to an increased "Russification" of the Orthodox Church within the confines of the empire and its control by the government. All this contributed to strengthening the link between Orthodoxy and Russian ethnic identity, even though this took place in a context that could still be defined as "pre-national." In other words, it was not yet a question of nationalization in the modern sense. That only occurred in the 19th century when Orthodoxy was officially declared one of the three pillars of Russian imperial ideology, along with autocracy and national consciousness.

It was at this point that the Tsarist imperial design placed Russian Orthodoxy in direct opposition to the Greek Orthodoxy of Constantinople and against which the combination of nationalism and political messianism that is usually labeled pan-Slavism was unleashed.[6] In terms of international politics, pan-Slavism was translated into forms of military and diplomatic support for the

---

4 See Vasilios N. Makrides, "Why Orthodox Churches are Particularly Prone to Nationalization and even to Nationalism?," *SVTQ* 54/4, 2013, 325–352.

5 See Edgar Hösch, "Die Idee der Translatio Imperii im Moskauer Russland," *EGO* Dec 3, 2010, <www.ieg-ego.eu/hoesche-2010-de> (accessed July 4, 2019).

6 See Lora Gerd, *Russian Policy in the Orthodox East: The Patriarchate of Constantinople (1878–1914)*, Berlin, De Gruyter, 2014.

Slavic peoples of the Balkans in their struggle for political independence from the Ottoman Empire, which was slowly but steadily declining, and Russia also aspired to take control of its straits once and for all. This strategy foresaw the necessary reversal of Greek Orthodox influence over the Balkan region in favor of the Slavic influence sponsored by St. Petersburg. There are those who have read pan-Slavism as a reaction to the Hellenization imposed by Constantinople on non-Greek peoples in previous centuries (this will be discussed below) and, at the same time, as the ideological basis of a much broader political project aimed at building a cultural and linguistic tradition that would gather all the Slavic peoples of the East under the wing of the Russian Empire.

The other geographical area that was a good indication of how the 19th century was the turning point in the growing nationalization of the Orthodox world[7] was the Ottoman Empire, where various peoples formed together the Orthodox millet (*millet-i Rûm*, "Rum/Rhomeic Millet"), which recognized the patriarch of Constantinople as its religious and civil leader. This patriarchate was mainly in "Greek hands," especially given the spontaneous process of Hellenization to which some Orthodox ethnic groups in the Balkans submitted themselves by virtue of their preference for Greek culture, which was seen as superior. The framework within which this occurred, however, did not yet present the typical features

of nationalism and therefore did not lead to serious ethnic divisions. On the contrary, it must be said that, at the time, there was a kind of common Orthodox culture in the Balkans, which managed to hold the ethnic differences of the peoples it represented together.[8] The situation, however, began to change from the second half of the 18th century, when the revolutionary winds blowing in from France awakened nationalist stirrings in the Balkan peoples as well, with a gradual aspiration to political self-determination and the founding of independent nation-states on linguistic and cultural grounds.[9] This inevitably provoked the disintegration of the millet system.[10] The first to rise up against the Ottoman Empire were the Serbs (1804–1813, 1815–1817), followed by the Greeks (1821–1829). After this, emerging from the wave of subsequent revolts, the national Balkan states were born, but a situation of perennial tension between opposing nationalisms arose that would long undermine the balance of peace both in the Balkans and in the rest of Europe.[11]

Although these uprisings were supported by many members of the Orthodox clergy, the Patriarchate of Constantinople was generally ill-disposed towards such developments. This attitude was dictated not only by the fact that it was under the full control of the central Ottoman

---

7   See Paschalis M. Kitromilides, *Enlightenment, Nationalism, Orthodoxy: Studies in the Culture and Political Thought of South-Eastern Europe*, Aldershot, Ashgate Variorum, 1994, ²2003; Victor Roudometof, *Nationalism, Globalization and Orthodoxy: The Social Origins of Ethnic Conflict in the Balkans*, Westport CT, Greenwood Press, 2001; Sia Anagnostopoulou, *The Passage from the Ottoman Empire to the Nation-States. A Long and Difficult Process: The Greek Case*, Istanbul, Isis Press, 2004; Benjamin C. Fortna & others, eds., *State-Nationalisms in the Ottoman Empire, Greece and Turkey: Orthodox and Muslims (1830–1945)*, London, Routledge, 2012; Dimitri Gondicas & Charles Issawi, eds., *Ottoman Greeks in the Age of Nationalism: Politics, Economy, and Society in the Nineteenth Century*, Princeton NJ, Darwin Press, 1999.

8   See Paschalis M. Kitromilides, "'Balkan Mentality': History, Legend, Imagination," *N&N* 2/2, 1996, 163–191; Paschalis M. Kitromilides, "Orthodox Culture and Collective Identity in the Ottoman Balkans during the Eighteenth Century," *OM* n.s., 18/1, 1999, 131–145; Paschalis M. Kitromilides, *An Orthodox Commonwealth: Symbolic Legacies and Cultural Encounters in Southeastern Europe*, Aldershot, Ashgate Variorum, 2007.

9   See Paschalis M. Kitromilides, "The Legacy of the French Revolution: Orthodoxy and Nationalism," *CHC* 5, 229–250.

10 See Victor Roudometof, "From Rum Millet to Greek Nation: Enlightenment, Secularization, and National Identity in Ottoman Balkan Society, 1453–1821," *JMGS* 16/1, 1998, 11–48.

11 See Paschalis M. Kitromilides, *Religion and Politics in the Orthodox World: The Ecumenical Patriarchate and the Challenges of Modernity*, London, Routledge, 2019, 25–59.

administration, but also by the early awareness of the imminent national disintegration that the common Orthodox body was facing. This was indeed what happened at different stages throughout the 19th century, when insurrectionary events inevitably led to the formation of national and independent Orthodox Churches and to the states to which they belonged. The Greeks were the first, after the founding of their state in 1830 and under the Bavarian regime of King Otto of Greece (1833–1862), proceeding in 1833 to the unilateral establishment of an autocephalous Orthodox Church, breaking ties with Constantinople and causing a temporary schism with that patriarchate that was only resolved in 1850 with Constantinople's formal recognition of the Greek Church.[12] The incident clearly demonstrated how obtaining ecclesiastical independence by a national church was a complex process that, in most cases, resulted in conflict with Constantinople. This, however, did not stop the process of nationalization that redesigned the statehood of the Balkans in the 19th century, nor did it prevent the new national churches from claiming full autonomy from the Patriarchate of Constantinople. It can be argued that, in many cases, the enterprise was largely successful.

For example, in regard to the Serbian people, it can be said that the process of nationalization took place quite smoothly. Following two uprisings, the Orthodox Church of the Principality of Serbia obtained autonomy in 1831 as Metropolitanate of Belgrade, while remaining under the jurisdiction of Constantinople. It was only in 1878, when the principality gained full political independence from the Ottoman Empire as the Kingdom of Serbia, that the Patriarchate of Constantinople granted autocephaly to the new territorial church (1879), while keeping the other Serbian eparchies under its jurisdiction. Finally, in 1920, through the

unification of the Metropolitanate of Belgrade and the Patriarchate of Karlovci, the Patriarchate of Belgrade was created.[13]

The matter was more complicated in the case of Romania. When, in 1859, the Principalities of Wallachia and Moldavia united to form the first modern Romanian state, so did their respective churches, that is, the Metropolitanates of Ungro-Wallachia and Moldavia, both existing under the jurisdiction of Constantinople since 1359 and 1401 respectively. In 1865, the churches of the Romanian Principalities of Moldavia and Wallachia unilaterally proceeded to declare independence from Constantinople with the support of Prince Alexandru Ioan Cuza and, in 1872, they united to form the autocephalous Romanian Orthodox Church. Once the two principalities were politically recognized as the independent Romanian state in 1878, the Patriarch of Constantinople Joachim IV, seven years later, also granted autocephaly to the Romanian Church, which however only received the status of patriarchate in 1925.[14]

Far more troubled was the process that led to the autocephaly of the Bulgarian Orthodox Church,[15] supported by Russia that was willing to take advantage of any opportunity to weaken Constantinople's authority over the Orthodox communities in the Balkans and, as a result, Ottoman control over that strategically key region. It is a fact that Bulgarian nationalism became particularly virulent from the 1860s when the creation

---

12   See Dimitris Stamatopoulos, "The Orthodox Church of Greece," in: Lucian N. Leustean, ed., *Orthodox Christianity and Nationalism in Nineteenth-Century Southeastern Europe*, New York NY, Fordham University Press, 2014, 34–64.

13   See Bojan Aleksov, "The Serbian Orthodox Church," in: Leustean, ed., *Orthodox Christianity*, 65–100.

14   See Lucian N. Leustean, "The Romanian Orthodox Church," in: Leustean, ed., *Orthodox Christianity*, 101–163.

15   See Dimitris Stamatopoulos, "Bulgarian Patriarchs and Bulgarian Neophanariotes: Continuities and Discontinuities in the Ecumenical Patriarchate during the Age of Revolution," in: Michel De Dobbeleer & Stijn Vervaet, eds., *(Mis)understanding the Balkans: Essays in Honour of Raymond Detrez*, Ghent, Academia Press, 2013, 45–57; Daniela Kalkandjieva, "The Bulgarian Orthodox Church," in: Leustean, ed., *Orthodox Christianity*, 164–201.

of an autonomous state was married to the aspiration to establish a church that was independent of the Patriarchate of Constantinople in spite of the latter's lukewarm concessions (such as in regard to the use of Church Slavonic in worship). As in every move involving the patriarchate and the individual, budding national churches, here, too, the sultan played a decisive role. In order to overcome the stalemate reached in the Bulgarian crisis, he decided to bypass the patriarchate by issuing a firman (royal decree) in 1870 that allowed Bulgarians to establish a separate and autonomous exarchate, with relative dioceses, whose jurisdiction overlapped in part with that of Constantinople, which maintained a voice in various issues; for example, in matters of faith or the election of the exarch. As was to be expected, the reaction from Constantinople, which considered the intervention of the Ottoman authority in the church's internal affairs a blatant violation of Orthodox canonical order, was not long in arriving. After his request to convene a pan-Orthodox council on the matter had been rejected, Patriarch Gregory VI, who, owing to conflicts with the sultan, reigned for two terms, the first from 1835 to 1840 and the second from 1867 to 1871, tendered his resignation. In response, in 1872, the Bulgarian Assembly elected the Metropolitan of Vidin Anthim I as the first exarch. Contrary to the actions of the Sublime Porte, however, Constantinople recognized neither the new exarch's authority nor the legitimacy of the synod that had elected him. Taking advantage of the chaotic situation, the Bulgarian exarchate proceeded unilaterally and officially to proclaim complete independence from Constantinople, thus prompting the Patriarchal Synod to respond first with ecclesiastic penalties for the Bulgarian exarch and bishops, and second, through the convocation of a Great Council in Constantinople in 1872, with a condemnation of the Bulgarian actions and the declaration of the exarchate as schismatic. This decision was based, first of all, on the ecclesiological principle that prohibited two bishops from serving in the same city or geographical area. It was the beginning of a lengthy schism that lasted until 1945

and which led to the elevation of the Bulgarian Church to a patriarchate only in 1953. It must be mentioned that, in the course of the 20th century, similar problems of a jurisdictional nature have appeared in much more widespread form for the Orthodox diaspora communities throughout the world, but, unlike the Bulgarian case, the involved actors are still in search of viable and permanent solutions today.[16]

The Great Council of 1872 was not only historically important for its having condemned the Bulgarian exarchate as schismatic. It also openly condemned "phyletism" (φυλετισμός), literally "racialism," but the word can also mean "nationalism," as ecclesiological heresy – the term (and the variant "ethnophyletism") has since entered Orthodox vocabulary, recalling even today the council's decision – as it was considered contrary to canonical tradition. It was said that such a principle constituted a serious threat to the unity of the Orthodox body and was the primary cause of the division of the church and the consequent shattering of Christian universality on the basis of ethnic, national, linguistic, racial, and cultural differences.[17] Phyletism and the creation, in its name, of "parasitic" national churches such as the Bulgarian one were considered unprecedented innovations, disrespectful of the Orthodox canonical tradition and therefore problematic ("καὶ φυλετισμοῦ καινήν τινα δόξαν ... πρωτοφανῆ ... φυλετικὴν παρασυναγωγὴν ... νεωτερικῆς λύμης"),[18] as they introduced racial differences, national disputes, and worldly disagreements into the Body of Christ's church.[19]

16   See Sebastian Rimestad, *The Establishment of Religious Authority: A Case Study of Orthodox Christians in Western Europe*, Postdoctoral thesis (habilitation), University of Erfurt, 2019.

17   See Maximos, metropolitan of Sardes, *Das ökumenische Patriarchat in der orthodoxen Kirche*, Freiburg i.Br., Herder, 1980, 395–408.

18   *COGD* 4/1, 2016, 371, 373.

19   See Ioannis N. Karmiris, *Dogmatica et symbolica monumenta Orthodoxae Catholicae Ecclesiae*, vol. 2, Graz, Akademische Druck- und Verlagsanstalt, ²1968, 930ε–930ζ [1014–1016].

The council's decision was ratified by the Patriarch of Constantinople Anthimus VI, who reigned for three periods, first from 1845 to 1848, then between 1853 and 1855, and finally from 1871 to 1873, and several other patriarchs, archbishops, and metropolitans. Not all the local Orthodox Churches followed suit, however, including many that followed the Greek tradition and considered themselves close to Constantinople. Not surprisingly, the Russian Church, which supported the Bulgarian side for strategic reasons, refrained from sending its representatives to the synod in Constantinople. It is interesting to note that the independence of the Bulgarian Church (1870) preceded by eight years that of the Bulgarian state established by the Treaty of San Stefano, which put an end to the Russo-Turkish War in 1878 and which, meeting Russian expansionist designs on the warm seas of southern Europe, did not place any obstacles to the creation of a "Greater Bulgaria" with access to the Aegean Sea. Although the situation changed within the space of a few months, thanks to the Treaty of Berlin in July 1878, which partly rectified Bulgaria's borders and brought the young state back under Ottoman influence, these events show how hard the battle over the Eastern Question was at the time. Needless to say, the Patriarchate of Constantinople was at the very heart of these many conflicting interests, as its overall policies varied and depended heavily on the changing international balances and the hegemonic powers that took turns in controlling the European concord.

3   Hellenization and Nationalism

As mentioned above, Constantinople's official condemnation of nationalism occurred in 1872 with the council held to bring the Bulgarian separatist church back to obedience and thus heal the rift between the Greek and Slavic Orthodox traditions fueled by the fierce competition between Russia and the Ottoman Empire for hegemonic control of the Balkan area. This again highlights the role

of the Greek tradition within the Patriarchate of Constantinople, which until then had managed not to compromise itself politically with any national cause.[20] It should be pointed out that, contrary to what one might expect, at that time the patriarchate's interests did not directly coincide with those of the state and the Church of Greece, that is to say, with the two entities that had, in fact, begun the process of nationalization in the Orthodox world. It was not so much the patriarchate's traditional Greek character that created embarrassment in the already tense relations between the Phanar and the Ottoman authorities as the growing irredentist operations that the Greek nationalists, whose ranks often included clergy and bishops, carried out in the Ottoman territories of Epirus, Macedonia, and Thrace, that is to say, in regions belonging to Constantinople's ecclesiastical jurisdiction, which lasted until the defeat that the Kemalist Turks inflicted on the Greeks in 1922. Although it disassociated itself from Greece's irredentist aspirations, Constantinople was neither able to considerably lighten the yoke imposed upon it by the Ottoman authorities nor to prevent the Slavic Orthodox families from continuing to see it as a Greek institution with an oppressive character at the exclusive service of Greek objectives and interests.

In all truth, it must be remembered that the process of Hellenization of the Orthodox millet under the Ottoman government promoted by Constantinople had been perceived by non-Greeks in the past not as a burden or harassment, but, on the contrary, as a necessary path for the improvement of the political conditions and the cultural progress of their Orthodox minorities in the Ottoman Empire. However, during the 19th century, with the rise of nationalism, the situation

---

20   See Vasilios N. Makrides, "Orthodoxie, griechische Ethnie und Nation, griechischer Nationalstaat und Nationalismus: Mythen und Realitäten," in: István Keul, ed., *Religion, Ethnie, Nation und die Aushandlung von Identität(en): Regionale Religionsgeschichte in Ostmittel- und Südosteuropa*, Berlin, Frank & Timme, 2005, 67–92.

changed radically, and Hellenization came to co-incide with the extreme attempt to prevent an autonomous political, religious, and cultural development for the non-Greek peoples. In spite of this and in line with what had been effected in the past, the Patriarchate of Constantinople continued to promote the Hellenization of the Orthodox minorities in the empire under the conviction that it was not serving the cause of the irredentist Greeks (who had in effect everything to gain from the spread of their language and their culture in the body of a state that they were trying to overthrow), but to slow down, or at best completely stop, the disintegration of Orthodox unity that immediately threatened the inviolability of the ecclesiastical jurisdiction headed by the patriarchate. The decision to keep Greek bishops at the head of the Bulgarian Orthodox communities was in line with this, along with the insistence on the use of Greek as the language of worship despite the fact that the non-Greek Orthodox had long been asking to be able to celebrate the liturgy in their own national languages. Paradoxically, in the pre-modern era the Byzantine tradition had been far more liberal in matters of worship, permitting the translation of the Bible and other texts into the local languages and recognizing the right of the Christianized peoples to use their own language in worship (one thinks of the missionary work of Cyril and Methodius among the Slavic peoples in the 9th century). This stood in open contrast to the more centralizing policies that the Latin Church was adopting in liturgical matters during the same years.[21]

One understands well, therefore, how the non-Greek peoples, once they had obtained their coveted political independence from the Sublime Porte and ecclesiastical independence from Constantinople, had been in a hurry to free

themselves of the obligation to pray in Greek. The first to do this were the Bulgarians, who requested not only the possibility to celebrate the liturgy in the Slavic language, but also the ability to name their own bishops. Needless to say, both requests were rejected by the patriarchate at a synod convened already in 1858, and this decision resulted in a further intensification of the Bulgarians' animosity. Shortly thereafter, in fact, the Greek bishops were expelled from dioceses that had a Bulgarian majority, while, on Easter Sunday 1860, the liturgy was celebrated in the Church of St. Stephen in Constantinople without commemorating the name of the then reigning patriarch, Cyril VII.

The Bulgarians were not the only ones to oppose Constantinople, and like them many other Slavic peoples involved in this kind of conflict with the patriarchal see tried to maintain the tie between their autonomist demands and their claim of Byzantine heritage. It was an ideological position rich in political advantages to their eyes (it was a way of placing themselves on the same level as Constantinople in terms of the antiquity of religious tradition), and the national histories of the Balkan peoples were often put at the service of this ideology with efforts to trace the national roots of their communities back to medieval Byzantium.[22] It is therefore understandable how, in this picture, any attempt to reintroduce the old idea of Hellenization would be seen quite critically, as an obstacle, in essence, to the autonomous growth of the non-Greek national identities. One such example is the case of the Danubian principalities of Wallachia and Moldova. These had enjoyed a certain autonomy for many centuries under the

---

21   See Vasilios N. Makrides, "The 'Individuality of Local Cultures': Perceptions, Policies and Attitudes in the Context of Orthodox Christian Missions," in: Martin Fuchs, Antje Linkenbach & Wolfgang Reinhard, eds., *Individualisierung durch christliche Mission?*, Wiesbaden, Harrassowitz, 2015, 152–169.

22   See Dimitris Stamatopoulos, *To Vyzantio meta to ethnos: To problima tis synecheias stis valkanikes istoriographies* [Byzantium after the nation: The question of continuity in Balkan historiography], Athens, Alexandreia, 2009; Diana Mishkova, "The Afterlife of a Commonwealth: Narratives of Byzantium in the National Historiographies of Greece, Bulgaria, Serbia and Romania," in: *Entangled Histories of the Balkans*, vol. 3, Roumen Daskalov & Alexander Vezenkov, eds., *Shared Pasts, Disputed Legacies*, Leiden, Brill, 2015, 118–273.

formal Ottoman *suzeraineté*, but had been largely Hellenized between 1711 and 1821 under the Phanariot regime. The latter was formed of a group of rich, well-educated, and influential families who, even though they were not all of Greek origin, strongly supported the promotion of Hellenic education in their territories to the point of making Bucharest and Jassy the two main centers of Greek culture in the Danube region. Incidentally, the same had partly happened in these areas before the Phanariots, thanks to other political leaders, who were themselves not of Greek origin, among whom the name of Vasile Lupu, the Voivode of Moldavia, stands out. It goes without saying that the political ambitions of these people supported this process. They aspired to assume, in some form, the legacy of the Byzantine Empire and for this reason usually maintained good relations with the Patriarchate of Constantinople, which was the only institution of the old empire to have survived. With the outbreak of the irredentist movement and the spread of nationalism, this heritage began to appear in a very negative light. Romanian historiography, for example, was for a long time critical of the Phanariot period and its Hellenization efforts, which were considered detrimental to the development of the Romanian national identity.[23]

The Patriarchate of Constantinople, as has just been recounted, was considered *nolens volens* to be an institution at the service of the national Greek interests, or at least very close to them. Although this argument was in the main wrong, various events seemed to affirm it in the eyes of the Slavic peoples. One example is the Patriarchate of Constantinople's reaction to the unilateral Greek declaration of ecclesiastical autocephaly in 1833, which was far milder than the condemnation of the Bulgarian exarchate in 1872. Certainly, the historical context was not the same. In the 1870s, the deterioration of the Greek-Slavic relations had made the issue of the independence of the Church

of Bulgaria a crucial concern for Constantinople. In contrast, the relative ease with which relations with the Church of Greece were established a few years after 1833, when compared to the length and harshness of the Bulgarian schism, indicates a closeness that was lacking in Constantinople's relations with the non-Greek Orthodox peoples who sought the same ecclesiastical independence.[24] All this inevitably had serious effects on the impartiality with which the Patriarchate of Constantinople sought, in those difficult circumstances, to call the Orthodox family to unity.

4   The Ottoman Empire between Reform
         Attempts and the Assault of Pan-Slavism

The changes in ecclesiastical matters discussed so far must be seen in relation to the equally radical transformations that took place in those years in the structure of the Ottoman Empire, particularly with regard to the treatment and rights of the ethno-religious communities that traditionally formed the various millets. A first wave of reforms took place in the so-called Tanzimat period, between 1839 and 1876, during which an attempt was made to modernize the empire in order to halt its gradual decline and put an end to the growing internal tensions by incorporating non-Muslim ethnic groups into a centralized administration and system of control. Among the reformist measures adopted at that time, some included equal freedoms and rights for both Muslims and people of other religions, including freedom of conscience for Christians, as established by the imperial decrees *Hatt-ı-Şerif* of 1839 and *Hatt-ı Hümayun* of 1856. The objective was to avoid further conflicts between Muslims and non-Muslims, which were considered harmful to the political and social integrity of the empire (the same objective led to

---

23   See Christina Ion, "The Present Creates the Past: The 'Phanariots' in the Romanian Textbooks during the Second Half of the 19th Century," RESEE 33/1–2, 1995, 41–47.

24   See Paraskevas Matalas, *Ethnos kai Orthodoxia: Oi peripeteies mias schesis, Apo to "Elladiko" sto Voulgariko Schisma* [Nation and Orthodoxy: The adventures of a relationship, from "Greek" to Bulgarian schism], Heraklion, University of Crete Press, ²2003.

the passing in 1869 of the law on nationality that extended Ottoman citizenship to all the inhabitants of the empire, regardless of their religious or ethnic differences). These reforms inevitably ended up in altering the millet system in which communities, organized according to religious criteria, were accustomed to maintaining their external boundaries, operating autonomously in regard to other communities, and enjoying particular privileges. It was understandable, therefore, that Christians in particular were far from happy with a governmental decree that elevated them to the rank of citizens with the sole purpose of assimilating them. Encouraged by the nascent nationalist climate, they therefore sought to use the Tanzimat reforms, more as the basis for claiming full national autonomy and independence than for improving their integration into Ottoman society as envisioned in the spirit of the new laws.

This was the case, in fact, of the Christian middle class, which, thanks to its superior level of education, managed to make more progress than the Muslim majority and thus to play a key role in such a decisive sector as the economy to the benefit of its own interests. Weakened by an evident internal contradiction, deriving from the fact of having proclaimed the legal equality of all of its subjects while preserving the millet system as the central organizing principle of the multiethnic Ottoman society, the Tanzimat reforms paradoxically ended up in producing the opposite effect to what had been sought, making the millet the principal vehicle for the dissemination of claims for autonomy throughout the empire. To this must be added that, particularly after the Crimean War, certain powers, including England and France, preyed on these contradictions, hoping to see the ethno-religious communities of the Ottoman Empire acquire a greater sovereignty in order to further undermine the "sick man" in Europe, thus minimizing the possibility of further Russian interference in the Balkan regions. The numerous wars that followed, such as the Russo-Turkish War of 1877–1878, and the continual interventions of foreign powers in what everyone called the Eastern

Question certainly did not help to shore up the empire's already precarious situation.

In regard to the internal political dimension, not even the introduction of an Ottoman Constitution in 1876 as an instrument of control over the autocratic power of the sultan bore the fruits anticipated because it was unable, in its short lifespan, to prevent the growing nationalism of the Balkan peoples and block their path to political independence. Interestingly enough, the same nationalist waves that stirred up the Orthodox peoples in the Balkans soon began to spread even among the Ottoman Muslims (for example, the Young Turks movement), which after World War I would prove decisive in the political transition to modern Turkey. What the Muslim nationalists reproached in the Tanzimat reforms was that they had favored the social rise of non-Muslims, who until then had constituted groups subject to the Islamic majority and who now repaid the sultan by waging war against him for the foundation of autonomous states, and that they had not actually been able to put a stop to the interference of foreign powers in the internal affairs of the Sublime Porte. It was considerations of this kind that led the nationalist Turks, once they had come to power, to engage in a bloody chain of wars against the young Balkan nations and opened the door to the policies of genocide that would accompany the imperial dissolution after World War I.[25]

It goes without saying here, too, that the Tanzimat reforms and the turbulent political climate they generated in Turkish territories had a direct impact on the Patriarchate of Constantinople

---

25   On these reforms, see Roderic H. Davison, *Reform in the Ottoman Empire (1856–1876)*, Princeton NJ, Princeton University Press, 1963; Fatma Müge Göçek, *Rise of the Bourgeoisie, Demise of Empire: Ottoman Westernization and Social Change*, New York NY, Oxford University Press, 1996; Selim Deringil, *The Well-Protected Domains: Ideology and the Legitimation of Power in the Ottoman Empire (1876–1909)*, London, I.B. Tauris, 1998; James J. Reid, "Was There a Tanzimat Social Reform?," BS 40/1, 1999, 173–208.

in regard to both its internal administrative structure and its relations with the Ottoman government. For example, there were among the reform measures some that promoted the reorganization of the empire's population through "special assemblies" which, under the supervision of the state and with the involvement of the laity (in particular in the management of finances and the fight against corruption), were to facilitate the implementation of reforms within the respective ethno-religious communities. This led to greater intervention by the Ottoman authorities in the internal affairs of the Orthodox millet in order to find support for their reform policy. It also justified the diverse currents in the patriarchal court, including one that was openly pro-Russian, supporting divergent interests and objectives that, in any case, were not always in line with the Ottoman authorities' *desiderata*.

The first National Assembly called to implement these reforms within the Orthodox millet was held from 1858 to 1860 and produced a constitutional text entitled "General Regulations," subsequently ratified by the Sublime Porte, which in this way carved out for itself a decisive role in the election of future patriarchs. Moreover, the patriarchate's new administrative model gave increased rights to various neo-Phanariot circles and emerging social groups (such as merchants and bankers) both in the management of the patriarchate's "material affairs" and in the process of electing the patriarch. Furthermore, the Patriarchal Synod was restructured in such a way as to limit the rights and prestige of the elder metropolitans (Γέροντες) who had hitherto been accustomed to cooperating closely with the patriarch. The ultimate aim of these reforms, it is worth remembering, was to protect the affairs of the patriarchate from feared Russian intervention, although at the time the greatest threat to the unity of the Orthodox millet came from the demands for independence by the Bulgarian Church set forth precisely during this first National Assembly.

Subsequent political developments did not lead to any improvements because Ottoman constitutionalism failed to establish itself fully, leaving the field free for the pan-Islamist ideology of Sultan Abdülhamid II that dominated unchallenged until the Young Turks revolution of 1908. This was yet another change of scene that led, among other things, to the restriction of the privileges that the patriarchate and the Orthodox communities had inherited from the Tanzimat period, while the rift between the nationalist Orthodox clergy and the more ecumenical ones widened. In order to limit the damage, Patriarch Joachim III, who was deposed by the sultan in 1884 and reigned again from 1901 to 1912, sought to oppose the irredentist policies of Greece, attempting in this way to reestablish the impartiality of the patriarchate in an extremely agitated imperial context and to maintain the trust of the Ottoman political authorities. His was an ecumenical-imperial, pan-Orthodox project that called, in the first place, for the creation of a unified Greco-Ottoman empire on the model of Austria-Hungary as an extreme bulwark against the national and ecclesiastical separatism that for decades had been ravaging the Orthodox universe under his jurisdiction. This did not impede Joachim III, who contrary to his internal opponents in the patriarchate did not hide his esteem for Tsarist Russia, from promoting a political rapprochement between Constantinople and St. Petersburg as an indispensable condition for a pan-Orthodox unity in the full sense of the term.[26]

Joachim III's project, however, was strongly opposed by Greece and its nationalist circles that did not understand the patriarch's resistance to becoming an instrument and spokesman for their irredentist pretentions to the Sublime Porte.[27]

---

26   See Dimitris Stamatopoulos, *The Eastern Question or Balkan Nationalism(s): Balkan History Reconsidered*, Göttingen, Vandenhoeck & Ruprecht, 2018.

27   See Evangelos Kofos, "Patriarch Joachim III (1878–1884) and the Irredentist Policy of the Greek State," *JMGS* 4/2, 1986, 107–120; Christos Kardaras, *To Oikoumeniko Patriarcheio kai o alytrotos ellinismos tis Makedonias, Thrakis, Ipeirou: Meta to sinedrio tou Verolinou (1878)* [The Ecumenical Patriarchate and Hellenism in the

Be that as it may, the Greek authorities did not oppose the reelection of Joachim in 1901, thanks also to the fact that Greece, after their defeat in the war against the Ottomans in 1897, was in diplomatic isolation and therefore strongly in need of the political support of the patriarchate. The exacerbation of nationalism, in turn, led Joachim to attenuate the imperial aspects of his pan-Orthodox idea, becoming open, as we shall see, to more ecumenical solutions.[28]

It is as well to remember, however, that in this period Constantinople was not alone in nurturing imperial ambitions in regard to Orthodoxy. Following the defeat that it suffered in the Crimean War, Russian foreign policy, in point of fact, began to diversify its objectives, concentrating less on defending the Orthodox populations of the Ottoman Empire and more on defending the Slavic peoples of the Balkans in the name of the ideology of pan-Slavism. It soon began to incorporate into its objectives the control of important religious sites of Orthodox Christianity that were, historically, "in the hands of the Greeks," including the most ancient patriarchal sees and other significant places, such as Mount Athos. Jerusalem itself became the object of interest of Russian foreign policy, which, in order to ensure control of the patriarchate, sparked repeated conflicts with the Greek hierarchy in the Holy Land (it is sufficient to think of the role played in these events by Archimandrite Porphyrius Uspensky and the founding of the Imperial Orthodox Palestine Society in 1882). In 1898, the Russians even succeeded in ousting the Greeks from the Patriarchate of Antioch, which after the resignation of Spyridon, the last Greek patriarch, was definitively brought under Arab-Orthodox influence. Following in the footsteps of the universalist political ideology of Byzantium, in essence, Tsarist Russia intended to accredit itself, both in the Balkans and in the East, as the heir to the Byzantine tradition and thus to its imperial and pan-Orthodox ambitions. These policies continued until the beginning of the 20th century, when the military defeats on the Eastern Front in the Great War and the outbreak of the Revolution in 1917 for a while extinguished Russian imperial ambitions.[29]

---

irredentist territories of Macedonia, Thrace, and Epirus after the congress of Berlin, 1878], Athens, Epikairotita, 1996; Christos Kardaras, *Ioakeim III – Charilaos Trikoupis: I antiparathesi apo tin anekdoti allilographia tou Oikoumenikou Patriarchi (1878–1884)* [Joachim III – Charilaos Trikoupis: The conflicts reflected in the unpublished correspondence of the Ecumenical Patriarchate (1878–1884)], Athens, Trochalia, 1998.

28   On the Patriarchate of Constantinople in the 19th Century, see Paraskevas Konortas, *Othomanikes theoriseis gia to Oikoumeniko Patriarcheio: veratia gia tous prokathimenous tis Megalis Ekklisias (17ᵒˢ arches 20ᵒᵘ aiona)* [Ottoman views on the Ecumenical Patriarchate: Berats to the primates of the Great Church, from the 17th century to the beginning of the 20th century], Athens, Alexandreia, 1998; Dimitris Stamatopoulos, *Metarrythmisi kai ekkosmikeusi: Pros mia anasunthesi tis Istorias tou Oikoumenikou Patriarcheiou ton 19ᵒ aiona* [Reform and secularization: Towards a reconstruction of the history of the Ecumenical Patriarchate in the 19th century], Athens, Alexandreia, 2003; Dimitris Stamatopoulos, "From Millets to Minorities in the 19th-Century Ottoman Empire: An Ambiguous Modernization," in: Steven G. Ellis, Gudmundur Hálfadanarson & Ann Katherine Isaacs, eds., *Citizenship in Historical Perspective*, Pisa, Plus – Pisa University Press, 2006, 253–273; Murat Çağlayan, "Das griechisch-orthodoxe Patriarchat von Konstantinopel im Konfliktfeld der Reformen im Osmanischen Reich," *ZfB* 52/2, 2016, 171–195. See also the old but still valuable study by Ivan Sokolov, published in Russian in 1904 and translated as *The Church of Constantinople in the Nineteenth Century: An Essay in Historical Research*, trans. Hieromonk Nikolai Sakharov, Oxford, Peter Lang, 2013.

---

29   See Theofanis G. Stavrou, *Russian Interests in Palestine (1882–1914): A Study of Religious and Educational Enterprise*, Thessaloniki, Institute for Balkan Studies, 1963; Derek Hopwood, *The Russian Presence in Syria and Palestine (1843–1914): Church and Politics in the Near East*, Oxford, Clarendon Press, 1969; Jelena Milojković-Djurić, *Panslavism and National Identity in Russia and in the Balkans (1830–1880): Images of the Self and Others*, Boulder CO, East European Monographs, 1994; Lora Gerd, *Konstantinopol' i Peterburg: Cerkovna-ja politika Rossii na Pravoslavnom Vostoke (1878–1898)* [Constantinople and Petersburg: Ecclesiastical Policies of Russia in the Orthodox East (1878– 1898)], Moscow, Indrik, 2006; Lora Gerd, *Russkij Afon (1878–1914): Očerki*

5   The Birth of Official Orthodox Ecumenical Initiatives

It is not surprising, therefore, that the Patriarchate of Constantinople attempted to tackle and control this series of changes that profoundly altered the traditional universalist profile of Orthodoxy and threatened its internal unity since the patriarchate was the institution most affected on diverse levels by these developments. In the first place, it lost significant parts of its ecclesiastical jurisdiction to the new national churches. Secondly, it saw its authority undermined by growing Russian Orthodox influence and pan-Slavism. Thirdly, it faced the threat of a reinforced Turkish nationalism and the concomitant hostile sociopolitical environment. All this forced the patriarchate to develop new strategies and new plans for the future, without ruling out eventual initiatives in the field of ecumenism.

The first to move in this direction was Patriarch Joachim III[30] during his second reign (1901–1912);[31]

his initiative may in some way have been influenced by the unionist policy promoted by Pope Leo XIII that was expressly directed toward the Eastern Orthodox Christians.[32] Since his particular pan-Orthodox aims with ecumenical-imperial hues did not materialize politically, it is in fact plausible that Joachim III, on his return to the Phanar, tried to initiate a second ecumenical attempt, this time with purely religious connotations, towards the other Orthodox Churches and, more generally, toward the entire Christian ecumene. It was to this end that, in 1902, taking the opportunity of his recent reelection to the patriarchal throne, he promoted, together with the Holy Synod, an encyclical addressed to "their Beatitudes and Holinesses the Patriarchs of Alexandria and Jerusalem, and to the most holy autocephalous sister-Churches in Christ, in Cyprus, Russia, Greece, Romania, Serbia and Montenegro."[33] This was enough to make this encyclical the first of its kind to display a clear pan-Orthodox character in that it was also addressed to all the local churches born during the nationalist movements (without prejudice to the primacy of the patriarch over the rest of the Orthodox Churches).[34] It also had an ecumenical aspect in the sense that it aspired to achieve a broader unity within the Christian world.[35]

cerkovno-političeskoj istorii [Russian Athos (1878–1914): Essays in political-ecclesiastical history], Moscow, Indrik, 2010; Gerd, *Russian Policy*; Denis Vovchenko, *Containing Balkan Nationalism: Imperial Russia and Ottoman Christians (1856–1914)*, New York NY, Oxford University Press, 2016.

30   On Patriarch Joachim III, see also Athanasios E. Karathanasis, ed., *Epistimoniko Symposio: Christianiki Makedonia, O apo Thessalonikis Oikoumenikos Patriarchis Ioakeim III o Megaloprepis* [Scholarly symposium: Christian Macedonia, the ecumenical Patriarch Joachim III the Great of Thessaloniki], Thessaloniki, Kentro Historias Thessalonikis, 1994; Theodoros I. Dardavesis, ed., *Ioakeim III o Megaloprepis: O apo Thessalonikis Oikoumenikos Patriarchis kai i epoki tou* [Joachim III the Great: The ecumenical patriarch from Thessaloniki and his time], Thessaloniki, Philoptochos Adelphotis Andron Thessalonikis, 2012.

31   See Dimitris Stamatopoulos, "Ecumenical Ideology in the Orthodox Millet (19th–20th c.)," in: Lorans Tanatar Baruh & Vangelis Kechriotis, eds., *Economy and Society on Both Shores of the Aegean*, Athens, Alpha Bank Historical Archives, 2010, 201–247; Dimitris Stamatopoulos, "'… den ginetai na min einai Phanariotis stin psychi tou …': Oikoumenismos kai Ethnikismos apo tin proti sti deuteri Patriarcheia tou Ioakeim III" ["… it is not possible that he is not a Phanariot in his soul …": Ecumenism and nationalism

from the first to the second term of Patriarch Joachim III], in: Dardavesis, ed., *Ioakeim III o Megaloprepis*, 189–224; Dimitris Stamatopoulos, "Orthodox Ecumenicity and the Bulgarian Schism," *EtBalk* 51/1, 2015, 70–86; Spyridon Sfetas, "Anamesa stin oikoumeniki politiki kai to ethniko sympheron: O Ioakeim III kai to zitima tis arsis tou voulgarikou schismatos" [Between ecumenical politics and the national interests: Joachim III and the question relative to the revocation of the Bulgarian schism], in: Dardavesis, ed., *Ioakeim III o Megaloprepis*, 225–247.

32   See also the essay by Laura Pettinaroli in this volume.

33   Constantin G. Patelos, ed., *The Orthodox Church in the Ecumenical Movement: Documents and Statements (1902–1975)*, Geneva, WCC Publications, 1978, 27.

34   Stamatopoulos, "Ecumenical Ideology," 236.

35   The text of the 1902 encyclical can be found in Constantin G. Patelos, ed., *The Orthodox Church in the Ecumenical Movement: Documents and Statements (1902–1975)*, Geneva, WCC Publications, 1978, 27–33; Gennadios Zervos, *Il contributo del patriarcato ecumenico per l'unità dei cristiani*, Rome, Città Nuova, 1974,

The encyclical was thus an occasion to touch on the various issues that were at the heart of relations among the Christian Churches as well as on the theme of pan-Orthodox unity, which still presented many unresolved problems, such as the possibility of adopting a common calendar with the West. If nothing else, Joachim found a way to highlight the "ancient and unbreakable bond" that, despite difficulties, still existed among the Orthodox; "this appearance of brethren praying together in Christ and united in a sacred harmony" raised "greater hopes of a more fruitful cultivation of mutual relations among Churches sharing in the same opinion."[36] He also specifically cited the message of congratulations with which the Russian Orthodox Church had greeted his reelection as patriarch, affirming his willingness to continue to cultivate pan-Orthodox love, unity, and cooperation, despite past and present difficulties:

> Divided by reasons of history and differences of language and nationality, the local holy Churches of God find their unity in mutual love and their courage in close fellowship with one another; and they derive power to make progress in faith and devotion, rejecting the crafts of hostility and proclaiming the Gospel universally.[37]

Encouraged by the words of the Russian Church, quoted faithfully in the encyclical, Joachim proceeded to outline his program, which had already been discussed at the Patriarchal Synod, "towards bringing together the Orthodox people" and to illustrate his considerations "on the subject of our present and future relations with the two great growths of Christianity, viz. the Western Church and the Church of the Protestants."[38] Moved by a genuine interest in the cause of Christian unity, the patriarch was nevertheless frank in pointing out the historical problems that still divided the Orthodox and Western Churches and that, with the passage of time, had inevitably become even more serious. Nothing indeed could convince Joachim of the need for Orthodoxy to abandon the principle that the Orthodox Church possessed Christian truth in its fullness on the basis of what was established by the seven ecumenical councils in regard to dogmas of faith and ecclesiastical governance. Nevertheless, the patriarch remained firmly convinced that with God's help even pan-Christian unity would one day become possible:

> If, as in every matter which is impossible with men but possible with God, we cannot yet hope for the union of all as ever being a possibility, yet because divine grace is constantly active and men are being guided in paths of evangelical love and peace, one must consider very carefully whether it might be possible to prepare the (at present) anomalous way which leads to such a goal and to find points of encounter and contact, or even to turn a blind eye to certain irregularities until the completion in due course of the whole task, whereby might be fulfilled to our joint satisfaction and benefit our Lord and God and Savior Jesus Christ's saying about one flock and one shepherd. Wherefore, if it might be acceptable to the holy brethren to follow up this suggestion, we are bold to add this fraternal question: whether the present is judged to be the right time for a preliminary conference on this, to prepare a level ground for a fraternal approach and to determine, by common agreement of members

---

27–33. See also Gennadios Limouris, ed., *Orthodox Visions of Ecumenism: Statements, Messages and Reports on the Ecumenical Movement (1902–1992)*, Geneva, WCC Publications, 1994, 1–5; Athanasios Basdekis, ed., *Orthodoxe Kirche und Ökumenische Bewegung: Dokumente, Erklärungen, Berichte (1900–2006)*, Frankfurt a.M., Lembeck, 2006, 1–8. See also the essay by Stylianos Tsompanidis in this volume.

36   Patelos, ed., *The Orthodox Church in the Ecumenical Movement*, 28.

37   Patelos, ed., *The Orthodox Church in the Ecumenical Movement*, 28.

38   Patelos, ed., *The Orthodox Church in the Ecumenical Movement*, 30.

of the whole of our Orthodox Church, what might be considered the best bases, ways and means.[39]

It is at this point that Joachim III made specific reference to Old Catholics, who for some time had sought union and communion with the Orthodox Church, even though there was not yet a unanimous opinion on the issue. If a complete communion of faith with the Old Catholics could be achieved, concluded Joachim, it would certainly represent "an auspicious first-fruit of the hoped-for and longed-for unity of all Christians."[40]

There was also room in the encyclical for the delicate question of the reform of the calendar, whether, that is, the Orthodox Churches should adopt the more scientifically correct Gregorian calendar in place of the defective Julian calendar, without forgetting the consequences that such a choice would have on the determination of the date of Easter. Joachim was indeed aware of the problems and the reactions that such a reform might trigger in the immediate future and which, in fact, did occur when, twenty years later, intentions turned into facts. But no matter how controversial and delicate the issue of the calendar, he considered it necessary to address it in the hope of bringing the Churches of East and West closer to reconciliation. It was with this in mind that the patriarch revealed himself to be open to a compromise solution combining scientific accuracy and the maintenance of the beloved Orthodox tradition.[41]

It is worth remembering that not all, but several, local Orthodox Churches responded to the 1902 encyclical, including those in Jerusalem, Russia, Greece, Romania, Serbia, and Montenegro.[42] In

their responses, the churches recognized the encyclical's proposals as reasonable, feasible, and in a certain sense realistic, but at the same time none of them showed that they underestimated the potential problems that might arise, starting with the thorny question of the reform of the calendar. Many churches, moreover, highlighted the difficulties that they still had with Western missionaries of various origins operating within their canonical jurisdictions who were putting East-West relations to the test.

In essence, most of the Orthodox Churches that reacted to the patriarch's letter were of the opinion that the encyclical's proposals could be put into practice, but maintained the condition that any action decided be preceded by consultations and careful preparations in a systematic manner, involving representatives of all the Orthodox Churches concerned.

Taking these opinions into account, Joachim proceeded, together with the Patriarchal Synod, to draw up a second encyclical in 1904, addressed to the Orthodox sister-Churches, which aimed to clarify various issues and establishing a possible program for launching pan-Orthodox cooperation.[43] Using, this time, a more critical tone compared to that of the previous encyclical, Joachim pointed precisely to nationalism, which had always been

---

39   Patelos, ed., *The Orthodox Church in the Ecumenical Movement*, 30–31

40   Patelos, ed., *The Orthodox Church in the Ecumenical Movement*, 31.

41   Patelos, ed., *The Orthodox Church in the Ecumenical Movement*, 31–32 and 32–33.

42   All these responses (together with the 1902 and 1904 encyclicals) were published in Greek in a single

booklet by the Patriarchate of Constantinople: *I peri ton scheseon ton autokephalon Orthodoxon Ekklision kai peri allon genikon zitimaton Patriarchiki kai Synodiki Egkyklios tou 1902: Ai eis autin apantiseis ton agion autokephalon Orthodoxon Ekklision kai i antapantisis tou Oikoumenikou Patriarcheiou* [The relations of the autocephalous Orthodox Churches and other general issues in the patriarchal and synodal encyclical of 1902: The replies of the holy autocephalous Orthodox Churches and the response of the Ecumenical Patriarchate], Constantinople, Patriarchal Printing Press, 1904, 13–72.

43   The text of the 1904 encyclical can be found in Patelos, ed., *The Orthodox Church in the Ecumenical Movement*, 34–39; Limouris, ed., *Orthodox Visions of Ecumenism*, 5–8; Zervos, *Il contributo*, 233–236; Basdekis, ed., *Orthodoxe Kirche*, 9–15. On this issue, see also the essay by Tsompanidis in this volume.

lurking even in ecclesiastical circles, as the greatest obstacle to unity:

> Especially in recent days when ambitions and calculations have a more secular and nationalist character and are opposed to the holy Apostolic and Conciliar canons: they are foreign to the holy Churches of God and to their godly pastors, and they are pursued under the guise of a zealous provision for and protection of the interests of Orthodoxy, and by stirring up proselytizing societies among her suffering children. These things are done in open breach and violation of the rights of the local Churches which have pertained since time immemorial and which were ratified by ecumenical canons; and they create misunderstandings and suspicions among the sister-Churches, to the confusion and incalculable harm of Christian people and to the disruption and fragmentation of the one Catholic Church of Christ into parts and sections recognizable by national traditions and linguistic particularities. They forget usually their kinship in faith and provoke one another for the sake of worldly goods, and envy one another.[44]

It was therefore an explicit condemnation of nationalism, even that of an ecclesial nature, which the new encyclical defined in terms of a "strange and cunning spirit"; it aimed "to make the Church of Christ nothing but a handmaid and instrument of worldly ambitions and political programmes."[45] Since nationalism gravely threatened "the peace and health of the holy Churches of God,"[46] it was of the utmost importance that these churches consult one another on this matter, in the light of the venerable Orthodox tradition. In short, Joachim III

did everything in his power to show how ecclesiastical nationalism was totally contrary to the tradition of the faith and the ecclesiastical structure of Orthodoxy and that it therefore constituted a significant deviation from the true Christian path. It was the patriarch's conclusion that the Orthodox nationalists had "set worldly goods and their own glory above the authority of the ecclesiastical and canonical order and doctrine."[47]

Moreover, the new encyclical recognized how the intense proselytizing activity carried out in the Orthodox territory by Roman Catholics and Protestants greatly contributed to the deterioration of the situation, exacerbating the struggle, discord, and conflicts among the Orthodox. It was therefore considered absolutely necessary to resist the pressures of the present, to overcome localism, and to work for greater unity, both in pan-Orthodox and pan-Christian terms.[48]

In this context, the patriarch paid particular attention to the efforts that Old Catholics and Anglicans were making to approach the Orthodox Church in a spirit of genuine respect, entrusting the Orthodox Churches with the responsibility to help these Christians achieve their desire to join Orthodoxy. Naturally this was not to occur at the expense of sacred tradition, but by working together to articulate a common Orthodox policy in regard to these two Western Churches. For the first time, moreover, the scope of Joachim's appeal was also extended to the Oriental Orthodox Churches. In various respects, he viewed these churches as very close to the traditional Orthodox Churches and that they should therefore be included in future ecumenical reflections and contacts. As far as the issue of the common calendar was concerned, Joachim III expressed himself in the encyclical in a much more pragmatic manner. While recognizing the problems of the inaccuracy of the Julian calendar, this time he stood firmly in defense of

---

44   Patelos, ed., *The Orthodox Church in the Ecumenical Movement*, 35.

45   Patelos, ed., *The Orthodox Church in the Ecumenical Movement*, 35.

46   Patelos, ed., *The Orthodox Church in the Ecumenical Movement*, 35.

47   Patelos, ed., *The Orthodox Church in the Ecumenical Movement*, 36.

48   Patelos, ed., *The Orthodox Church in the Ecumenical Movement*, 36–37.

the Orthodox tradition and considered any desire to reform the calendar to be premature and superfluous, given the historical moment. Once again, however, these were issues that all Orthodox Churches could decide together.[49]

Among all the reactions that the Phanar received in the aftermath of this second encyclical, that of the Russian Orthodox Church was certainly one of the most interesting. In full agreement with what Patriarch Joachim said, the Russians not only condemned the nationalistic fragmentation of the Orthodox world as contrary to the tradition of the church and merely at the service of worldly powers; they also claimed that the nationalism of the 19th century was only an ephemeral interlude and that the division of the Orthodox Churches called for other solutions. It is also worth recalling that, with its response, the Russian Church effectively accepted the Patriarchate of Constantinople's precedence in initiating the process of pan-Orthodox rapprochement. This shows that Joachim's pro-Russian tendency had very probably once again won him the support of the Holy Synod in St. Petersburg.[50]

It is evident that there are significant differences between the encyclicals of 1902 and 1904, besides a considerable distance that separates these from those of the 19th century (for example, the encyclicals of 1836, 1838, 1848, and 1895).[51] The latter, in fact, were far more critical of Western Christianity, whose innovations and intense missionary campaigns in the Orthodox East were condemned. For this reason, it is difficult to see in these encyclicals an ecumenical spirit analogous to that found in the first two of the 20th century.[52] The clear dis-

continuity between the patriarchal documents of the 19th century and those of the early 20th century can be explained by the radical deterioration of the sociopolitical environment in which the Patriarchate of Constantinople was forced to operate at the turn of the century. As proof of this, it is enough to mention here the outbreak in rapid succession of the Ilinden Uprising of 1903, which initiated the struggle in Macedonia between Greek and Bulgarian partisans (1904–1908), the Revolution of the Young Turks in 1908 with the consequent strengthening of Turkish nationalism, the two Balkan Wars (1912–1913) and World War I, the unrest and social conflicts in Tsarist Russia and the October Revolution, and, last but not least, the repeated clashes between Turkey and Greece that led to the war of 1919–1922, which erupted because the Greeks, guided by their strong pan-Hellenic nationalism, tried to assimilate the Orthodox Rum populations of Asia Minor.[53] In addition, we must add the frequent interior crises in the patriarchal court, such as the one that in 1910 saw a clash between supporters and opponents of Joachim III.[54] It goes without saying that all this did not help the ecumenical plans of Constantinople and its supporters who dreamed of "reconnecting the 'imperial' and 'pan-Orthodox' perspectives or even of reuniting the Orthodox world of the Ottoman Empire with the Orthodox world of the Slavs."[55]

The fact remains that the Patriarchate of Constantinople was always well aware of how precarious its position was on the tumultuous international scene that brought the *belle époque* to a close, and for this reason it tried in every way to strengthen its status through the authoritativeness

---

49   Patelos, ed., *The Orthodox Church in the Ecumenical Movement*, 36–39.

50   See Stamatopoulos, "Ecumenical Ideology," 237–239.

51   See Karmiris, *Dogmatica et symbolica monumenta*, 871–925 [951–1005], 930ζ–946α [1016–1032].

52   See Sotirios L. Varnalidis, "Oi scheseis metaxy Oikoumenikou Patriarcheiou kai Vatikanou kata tin periodo tis Patriarcheias Ioakeim III" [The relations between the Ecumenical Patriarchate and the Vatican during the reign of Joachim III], in: Karathanasis, ed., *Epistimoniko Symposio*, 251–273.

53   See Sia Anagnostopoulou, *Mikra Asia 19os ai.–1919: Oi Ellinorthodoxes Koinotites, Apo to Millet ton Romion sto Elliniko Ethnos* [Asia Minor from the 19th Century to 1919: The Greek Orthodox Communities, from the Rum Millet to the Greek Nation], Athens, Ellinika Grammata, 1997.

54   See Nobuyoshi Fujinami, "The Patriarchal Crisis of 1910 and Constitutional Logic: Ottoman Greeks' Dual Role in the Second Constitutional Politics," *JMGS* 27/1, 2009, 1–30.

55   Stamatopoulos, "Ecumenical Ideology," 241.

of appeals that began to cross the boundaries of Orthodoxy and of the religious sphere. The patriarchate's ecumenical commitment did not stop, therefore, in 1904, and continued even in critical moments such as the almost three years' vacancy of the Patriarchal Throne (1918–1921).

It was in this period, in January 1920 to be precise, that the most famous encyclical was issued, that to "the Churches of Christ everywhere,"[56] the first that can be defined as ecumenical in the true sense of the term.[57] Drafted by a special committee, this encyclical was approved by the Patriarchal Synod and by the *locum tenens* of the Patriarchal Throne, Metropolitan Dorotheos of Bursa. It was a call to establish a rapprochement between the Christian Churches in East and West and to overcome the problems, prejudices, difficulties, and doctrinal differences that still existed.

> Our own church holds that rapprochement between the various Christian Churches and fellowship between them is not excluded by the doctrinal differences which exist between them. In our opinion such a rapprochement is highly desirable and necessary. It would be useful in many ways for the real interest of each particular church and of the whole Christian body, and also for the preparation and advancement of that blessed union which will be completed in the future in accordance with the will of God. We therefore consider that the present time is most favorable for bringing forward this important question and studying it together.[58]

The central idea was to reestablish relations among the churches and take the first steps towards their rapprochement, relying on the good will of all parties involved and their readiness to leave aside the negative aspects that in the past had regulated relations between the divided Christians. The model which the Constantinopolitan Patriarchate had in mind, and which it considered particularly promising for the ecumenical movement, was that of the League of Nations, born after the end of the long period of war that had brought bloodshed to Europe in the first two decades of the 20th century.[59]

According to the encyclical, two measures were necessary to promote this inter-Christian rapprochement:

> *First*, we consider as necessary and indispensable the removal and abolition of all the mutual mistrust and bitterness between the different churches which arise from the tendency of some of them to entice and proselytize adherents of other confessions. For nobody ignores what is unfortunately happening today in many places, disturbing the internal peace of the churches, especially in the East. So many troubles and sufferings are caused by other Christians and great hatred and enmity are aroused, with such insignificant results, by this tendency of some to

---

56 The text of the 1920 encyclical can be found in Patelos, ed., *The Orthodox Church in the Ecumenical Movement*, 40–43; Limouris, ed., *Orthodox Visions*, 9–11; Zervos, *Il contributo*, 236–238; Basdekis, ed., *Orthodoxe Kirche*, 16–20.

57 On this issue, see the essay by Tsompanidis in this volume.

58 Patelos, ed., *The Orthodox Church in the Ecumenical Movement*, 40.

59 Patelos, ed., *The Orthodox Church in the Ecumenical Movement*, 40–41. The Patriarchate of Constantinople was certainly not the first or only church to be attracted, in the aftermath of World War I, by diplomatic models in the development of their external relations. Recall, for example, the intense diplomatic activity in favor of peace exerted by Pope Benedict XV during and after the war, which earned for the Holy See completely new prestige on the international stage. On this, see the various contributions in Giovanni Cavagnini & Giulia Grossi, eds., *Benedict XV: A Pope in the World of the "Useless Slaughter" (1914–1918)*, dir. Alberto Melloni, 2 vols., Turnhout, Brepols, 2020, and Cormac Shine, "Papal Diplomacy by Proxy? Catholic Internationalism at the League of Nations' International Committee on Intellectual Cooperation (1922–1939)," *JHE* 69/4, 2018, 785–805.

proselytize and entice the followers of other Christian confessions.

After this essential re-establishment of sincerity and confidence between the churches, we consider,

Secondly, that above all, love should be rekindled and strengthened among the churches, so that they should no more consider one another as strangers and foreigners, but as relatives, and as being a part of the household of Christ and "fellow heirs, members of the same body and partakers of the promise of God in Christ" (Eph. 3:6).

For if the different churches are inspired by love, and place it before everything else in their judgments of others and their relationships with them, instead of increasing and widening the existing dissensions, they should be enabled to reduce and diminish them. By stirring up a right brotherly interest in the condition, the well-being and stability of the other churches; by readiness to take an interest in what is happening in those churches and to obtain a better knowledge of them, and by willingness to offer mutual aid and help, many good things will be achieved for the glory and the benefit both of themselves and of the Christian body.[60]

The encyclical then set out issues and ways in which mutual friendship and respect among Christians could be reestablished. Some of these were: the adoption of a common calendar; the exchange of friendly correspondence between churches on special occasions such as the great Christian feast days; the regular and mutual exchange of representatives, professors of theology, and publications; the convening of pan-Christian conferences on topics of common interest; the impartial and in-depth historical study of doctrinal differences; respect for the diversity of customs and practices; mutual cooperation regarding the

believers of other churches and confessions who died in foreign lands; the solution to the question of mixed marriages; and finally, collaboration in efforts to advance the Christian religion and charity.[61]

Naturally, there had to be a reference to the bloodbath from which humanity had just emerged after World War I and that represented, the encyclical said, a serious threat to Christian life itself. Modernity, with its corollary of evils, was called into question: secularization, individualism, materialism, liberalism, consumerism, and immanentism, all challenges that the churches needed to tackle together and that rendered cooperation between Christians imperative, if not inevitable.[62] The encyclical also warned the churches against becoming pawns in the political interests of the states and their ideologies, beginning with nationalism, the motive for which the patriarch praised the recent establishment of the League of Nations, whose aim was precisely to defend justice and international order, as the direct realization of the spirit of the Gospel and the teaching of Christ.[63]

Ecumenical attempts intensified in the 1920s, especially during the innovative but controversial patriarchal period of Meletios IV (Metaxakis), who was supported by the Greek government and who shared its irredentist aspirations. Previously, Meletios had been archbishop of Athens, had served in the Greek Orthodox Archdiocese of North and South America, and was an ardent opponent of pan-Slavism.[64] He had excellent relations with the Western Churches (in particular with the Anglicans) and was very active ecumenically throughout his long and diversified

---

60   Patelos, ed., *The Orthodox Church in the Ecumenical Movement*, 41.

61   Patelos, ed., *The Orthodox Church in the Ecumenical Movement*, 41–42.

62   Patelos, ed., *The Orthodox Church in the Ecumenical Movement*, 43.

63   Patelos, ed., *The Orthodox Church in the Ecumenical Movement*, 43.

64   See Meletios Metaxakis, metropolitan of Kition, *To Agion Oros kai i Rosiki politiki en Anatoli* [The Holy Mountain and Russian politics in the East], Athens, P.D. Sakellariou, 1913.

ecclesiastical career.[65] As patriarch, he convened a pan-Orthodox Council (May 10–June 8, 1923) in Constantinople, even though this did not obtain the participation of all of the local churches, which proceeded to adopt the new Gregorian calendar (without, however, changing the calculation of the date of Orthodox Easter).[66] These initiatives provoked major controversy in the rest of the Orthodox world and led to very serious disagreements that are even today still in need of a solution (one can think, for example, of the subsequent schism of the Old Calendarists in Greece).

As just mentioned, with the ascent of Meletios IV to the throne, the policies of the Patriarchate of Constantinople were intertwined for better or for worse with the destinies of Greek nationalism.[67] This was evident when the failure of the military expedition to Asia Minor in 1922 put an end to the "Megali Idea" that had long inspired Greece's irredentist policy,[68] leaving the patriarchate to face alone the growing threat of Turkish nationalism aimed in every way at reducing the prestige and international authority of the patriarchate, even

expelling it from Istanbul.[69] One of the moments of greatest tension in this struggle was in 1924, when the Kemalist government openly challenged the Phanar by creating a parallel autocephalous "Turkish Orthodox Patriarchate" supported by the political authority.[70]

It was understandable that, finding itself in such a precarious situation and in such an unpredictably changed scenario, Constantinople needed not only to define a long-term survival policy, but also to exploit all the advantages that could be derived from its increased international role. This explains why the patriarchate chose to intensify its activities in favor of inter-Orthodox cooperation and rapprochement with the Western Churches. It was in this spirit that the Patriarchate of Constantinople participated in the preparatory conference in Geneva in 1920 and then in the First World Conference on Faith and Order held in Lausanne in 1927, whose ecumenical aims were not far removed from those of the patriarchal encyclical of 1920.[71] The position taken by the Orthodox delegation at the Lausanne Conference did not fail to emphasize the profound differences and disagreements that still divided the churches on many points of doctrine, but at the same

65   See Andreas Nanakis, *I chireia tou Oikoimenikou Thronou kai i eklogi tou Meletiou Metaxaki (1918–1921)* [The vacant ecumenical throne and the election of Meletios Metaxakis, 1918–1921], Ph.D. thesis, University of Thessaloniki, 1991.

66   See Patrick Viscuso, *A Quest for Reform of the Orthodox Church: The 1923 Pan-Orthodox Congress: An Analysis and Translation of Its Acts and Decisions*, Berkeley CA, InterOrthodox Press, 2006.

67   See Sia Anagnostopoulou, "1919–1922: O ethnarchismos tou Oikoumenikou Patriarcheiou sto plaisio tis Megalis Ideas" [1919–1922: The ethnarchismos of the Ecumenical Patriarchate in the context of the Megali Idea], *Ta Istorika* 47, 2007, 373–420.

68   See Ioannis Zelepos, *Die Ethnisierung griechischer Identität (1870–1912): Staat und private Akteure vor dem Hintergrund der "Megali Idea"*, Munich, R. Oldenburg, 2002; Anastasia Stouraiti & Alexander Kazamias, "The Imaginary Topographies of the Megali Idea: National Territory as Utopia," in: Nikiforos P. Diamandouros, Thalia Dragonas & Çaglar Keyder, eds., *Spatial Conceptions of the Nation: Modernizing Geographies in Greece and Turkey*, London, I.B. Tauris, 2010, 11–34.

69   See Georgios-Spyridon Mamalos, *To Patriarcheio Konstantinoupoleos kata tin periodo (1918–1972): Diethnis politiki kai oikoumenikos prosanatolismos* [The Patriarchate of Constantinople in the period 1918–1972: International politics and ecumenical orientations], Athens, Ant. N. Sakkoulas, 2011; Evangelos Yfantidis, *Oikoumeniko Patriarcheio kai politikes dunameis: Apo ti dundiaskepsi tis Lozannis eos tin eklogi tou patriarchi Vasileiou* [The Ecumenical Patriarchate and political forces: From the Lausanne Conference to the election of Patriarch Basil], Kavala/Venice, Patriarchal Institute for Patristic Studies, 2014; Kitromilides, *Religion and Politics*, 60–71.

70   See Michael Knüppel, *Die Türkisch-Orthodoxe Kirche: Ein Beitrag zur türkischen Religionspolitik*, Göttingen, Pontus, 1996; Xavier Luffin, "Baba Eftim et l'Église orthodoxe turque: De l'usage politique d'une institution religieuse," *JEastCS* 52/1–2, 2000, 73–95; Giorgos T. Printzipas, *Oi Tourkorthodoxoi* [The Turkish-Orthodox], Athens, Saitis, 2018.

71   On Faith and Order, see the essay by Luca Ferracci in this volume.

time it reaffirmed the strong Orthodox interest in working for the ecumenical cause.[72] These efforts went hand in hand with the persistent commitment to strengthen cooperation among Orthodox Churches in the hope of one day succeeding in convening a truly pan-Orthodox council, the preparation of which had already begun in 1930.[73]

6   Concluding Remarks

Political processes such as the nationalist irredentism of the mid-19th century and the consequent birth of autonomous ecclesiastical identities on an ethnic and national basis, not to mention the encounter with Western modernity and its secularism, profoundly shaped the form that the Orthodox world presented at the dawn of the 20th century and which it preserved for much of the century. The Orthodox institution most affected by these changes was the Patriarchate of Constantinople which gradually lost ground, in terms of ecclesiastical jurisdiction, in favor of the nascent nation-states and their independent churches, while the antagonism between Greek and Slavic (especially Russian) Orthodoxy made internal unity and cooperation increasingly difficult and precarious. At the dawn of the 20th century, then, other tragic developments, such as the extensive and continual clashes between nationalisms in southeastern Europe, World War I, foreign interference in the Levant territories, the Bolshevik Revolution, the crumbling of the Ottoman Empire, and the

creation, from its ashes, of Atatürk Kemal's modern Turkey, contributed not a little to putting the patriarchate under continuous pressure. In response, Constantinople launched a series of messages and dialogue initiatives that would become the ground upon which Orthodox participation in the contemporary ecumenical movement would be based in the future. This explains why, should one wish to trace the origins of the ecumenical movement or to outline the reasons why the Orthodox Churches decided in great measure to align themselves with it, it is necessary to take into consideration factors that appear to be exquisitely socio-political and to study their interaction with the religious framework of the time.[74]

This applies as much to the modern history of Constantinople[75] as it does to the contemporary situation, now that the Ecumenical Patriarchate once again finds itself caught between the discriminatory pressures of the Turkish government and the unrelenting rise, in terms of political prestige, of the Patriarchate of Moscow, which has found in the heirs to communist Russia no less valuable allies than the tsars once were. It is in the light of these considerations and of the continuity linking the Orthodox present to its modern history that we should read, for example, the complex ecumenical policy of Patriarch Athenagoras in the years of the Cold War, when the projects of the Phanar could hardly have been executed without the approval of the contemporary foreign superpower, in that

72   The text of this message can be found in Patelos, ed., *The Orthodox Church in the Ecumenical Movement*, 79–82; Limouris, ed., *Orthodox Visions*, 12–14; Zervos, *Il contributo*, 241–243; Basdekis, ed., *Orthodoxe Kirche*, 21–26.

73   Preparations were launched on the initiative of Patriarch Photius II, who called the first inter-Orthodox commission at the monastery of Vatopedi on Mount Athos. Many other meetings and consultations followed in the next decades, leading only in 2016 to the Council of Crete. See Anastasios Kallis, *Auf dem Weg zu einem Heiligen und Großen Konzil: Ein Quellen- und Arbeitsbuch zur Orthodoxen Ekklesiologie*, Münster, Theophano, 2013.

74   For more details, see Vasilios Stavridis, *Istoria tis Oikoumenikis Kiniseos* [History of the ecumenical movement], Thessaloniki, Patriarchal Institute for Patristic Studies, 1985; Evangelia Varella, *Diorthodoxoi kai oikoumenikai scheseis tou Patriarcheiou Konstantinoupoleos kata ton XX Aiona* [Intra-Orthodox and ecumenical relations of the Patriarchate of Constantinople in the 20th Century], Thessaloniki, Patriarchal Institute for Patristic Studies, 1994. See also Antonios M. Papadopoulos, *Ἡ Ἐκκλησία τῆς Ἑλλάδος ἔναντι θεμάτων πανορθοδόξου ἐνδιαφέροντος κατὰ τὸν εἰκοστὸν αἰῶνα*, Postdoctoral thesis (habilitation), University of Thessaloniki, 1975.

75   See Gunnar Hering, *Oikoumeniko Patriarcheio kai Eyropaïkï Politiki (1620–1638)* [Ecumenical Patriarchate and European politics, 1620–1638], Athens, MIET, 2003.

case, of the United States government, and in any case regardless of the equilibrium of the blocs.[76]

It should not be forgotten, however, that while the aim of these first ecumenical initiatives was to create a new common Orthodox identity that would extend beyond local nationalisms, they also prematurely triggered various contrary, one might say anti-ecumenical,[77] reactions, which still persist in the Orthodox world at large.[78] Curiously enough, these kinds of responses are largely rooted in the contradictions of the historical period examined here, demonstrating once again how multifaceted and varied the history of Orthodox Christianity's involvement in the birth of the contemporary ecumenical movement is.

Translated from Italian to English by Susan Dawson Vásquez and David Dawson Vásquez.

Bibliography

Basdekis, Athanasios, ed., *Orthodoxe Kirche und Ökumenische Bewegung: Dokumente, Erklärungen, Berichte (1900–2006)*, Frankfurt a.M., Lembeck, 2006.

Gerd, Lora, *Russian Policy in the Orthodox East: The Patriarchate of Constantinople (1878–1914)*, Berlin, De Gruyter, 2014.

Kalaitzidis, Pantelis & others, eds., *Orthodox Handbook on Ecumenism: Resources for Theological Education*, Oxford, Regnum, 2014.

Kitromilides, Paschalis M., *An Orthodox Commonwealth: Symbolic Legacies and Cultural Encounters in Southeastern Europe*, Aldershot, Ashgate Variorum, 2007.

Kitromilides, Paschalis M., *Religion and Politics in the Orthodox World: The Ecumenical Patriarchate and the Challenges of Modernity*, London, Routledge, 2019.

Leustean, Lucian N., ed., *Orthodox Christianity and Nationalism in Nineteenth-Century Southeastern Europe*, New York NY, Fordham University Press, 2014.

Limouris, Gennadios, ed., *Orthodox Visions of Ecumenism: Statements, Messages and Reports on the Ecumenical Movement (1902–1992)*, Geneva, WCC Publications, 1994.

Patelos, Constantin G., ed., *The Orthodox Church in the Ecumenical Movement: Documents and Statements (1902–1975)*, Geneva, WCC Publications, 1978.

Roudometof, Victor, *Nationalism, Globalization and Orthodoxy: The Social Origins of Ethnic Conflict in the Balkans*, Westport CT, Greenwood Press, 2001.

Roudometof, Victor, *Globalization and Orthodox Christianity: The Transformations of a Religious Tradition*, New York NY, Routledge, 2014.

Sokolov, Ivan, *The Church of Constantinople in the Nineteenth Century: An Essay in Historical Research*, trans. Hieromonk Nikolai Sakharov, Oxford, Peter Lang, 2013.

Stamatopoulos, Dimitris, *Metarrythmisi kai ekkosmikeusi: Pros mia anasunthesi tis Istorias tou Oikoumenikou Patriarcheiou ton 19° aiona*, Athens, Alexandreia, 2003.

Stamatopoulos, Dimitris, *The Eastern Question or Balkan Nationalism(s): Balkan History Reconsidered*, Göttingen, Vandenhoeck & Ruprecht, 2018.

Vovchenko, Denis, *Containing Balkan Nationalism: Imperial Russia and Ottoman Christians (1856–1914)*, New York NY, Oxford University Press, 2016.

Yfantidis, Evangelos, *Oikoumeniko Patriarcheio kai politikes dunameis: Apo ti dundiaskepsi tis Lozannis eos tin eklogi tou patriarchi Vasileiou*, Kavala/Venice, Patriarchal Institute for Patristic Studies, 2014.

---

76   See Pavlos Serapheim, *To Oikoumeniko Patriarcheio sti dini tou Psykrou Polemou: I eklogi tou Patriarchi Athenagora (1948)* [The Ecumenical Patriarchate in the vortex of the Cold War: The election of Patriarch Athanagoras (1948)], Thessaloniki, Barbounakis, 2017.

77   See Dimitri Kitsikis, "Les anciens calendaristes depuis 1923 et la montée de l'intégrisme en Grèce," CEMOTI 17/1, 1994, 17–51.

78   See Pantelis Kalaitzidis, "Theological, Historical, and Cultural Reasons for Anti-Ecumenical Movements in Eastern Orthodoxy," in: Pantelis Kalaitzidis & others, eds., *Orthodox Handbook on Ecumenism: Resources for Theological Education*, Oxford, Regnum, 2014, 134–152.

CHAPTER 6

Newman and the Oxford Movement: A Prehistory of Ecumenism (1833–1870)

Peter B. Nockles

1 Birth of the Oxford Movement

John Henry Newman has been commonly acknowledged as the leader, if not the main inspiration for that religious revival within the Church of England from the early 1830s onwards known as the Oxford or Tractarian Movement. Normative beliefs are shaped by particular historical contexts and circumstances and the Oxford Movement was no exception to this rule. The Movement's origins partly lay in opposition to the liberalizing and pluralizing trends of the later 1820s which culminated in the repeal of the Test and Corporation Acts in 1828, Roman Catholic Emancipation in 1829, and the Parliamentary Reform Act in 1832. Forged in the traditional Anglican clerical and academic milieu of the University of Oxford and in particular Oriel College, it represented a concerted reaction to the undermining of the hegemony of the established church implicit in these landmark reforms of the British Protestant Constitution and to the general challenge posed by liberalism, utilitarianism, political Whiggery, Protestant Dissent or Nonconformity, as well as by a reinvigorated Roman Catholicism. The removal of the old constitutional props for the established Church of England forced Newman and the Oxford divines to look beyond any mere defense of a threatened temporal establishment with its traditional rallying cry of "the Church in Danger!" to deeper and more enduring doctrinal, ecclesial, and spiritual grounds of security.

This was the message which John Keble famously delivered in an impassioned sermon on "National Apostasy" from the pulpit of the Church of St. Mary the Virgin in Oxford on July 14, 1833, which Newman regarded as the Movement's defining birth date. Assuming that the English Church was the sole representative on English soil of a divinely constituted supernatural society and not simply a national religious establishment, the Oxford Movement, as proclaimed by Newman, Keble, Richard Hurrell Froude and others, sought to recover the church's apostolic basis and "primitive" Catholic character, of which Newman claimed sight had been lost. In short, there was a new focus on the very nature of the English Church, its self-understanding *qua* church and of its proper relationship with and to the state. However, while the emphasis was new and while Tractarianism was to be characterized by a distinctive *ethos*,[1] Tractarian ecclesiology drew heavily upon a pre-existing High Church Anglican tradition of privileging the church's apostolic and patristic roots. This was to have important implications for future ecumenical and reunionist endeavors. Newman's own Tractarian religious journey in itself also needs to be recognized as important in ecumenical terms, not least his abandonment in the later 1820s of an early Evangelicalism with its inherent somewhat loose ecclesiology wherein the invisible church was prioritized over the visible.[2]

The Oxford Movement under Newman's evolving leadership was never a static phenomenon and was to have an increasingly international

---

1   For an excellent discussion of this aspect of the Movement, see James Pereiro, *"Ethos" and the Oxford Movement: At the Heart of Tractarianism*, Oxford, Oxford University Press, 2008.

2   Joseph Andrew Komonchak, *John Henry Newman's Discovery of the Visible Church (1816 to 1828)*, Ph.D. thesis, Union Theological Seminary, 1976, 347.

dimension and context, especially *vis-à-vis* continental Roman Catholicism. An Anglo-centric bias in the literature, fueled by an abundance and ready availability of English sources, is only now being re-addressed by a new generational wave of Newman scholarship, partly fostered by the NINS at Pittsburgh. These scholarly developments are helping to break down "artificial divisions between national, linguistic, and ecclesiastical boundaries"[3] and drawing heavily on hitherto neglected continental archives. This has profound implications for viewing Newman and the Oxford Movement in relation to the prehistory and early history of ecumenism.

2 Some Questions of Terminology and Methodology

The modern ecumenical movement, with its organized expression of concern for the cause of Christian unity, is normally regarded as a product or outcome of 19th-century Evangelical missionary movements culminating in the famous Edinburgh WMC of 1910. That conference and its declarations represented the culmination of years of thaw between the various Protestant denominations which had been competing in the overseas mission field. This chapter looks at another earlier strand in the background or genesis of modern ecumenism, focusing instead on a different religious and theological tradition to that of the Evangelical missionary movement, viz., Anglo-Catholicism/ High Church Anglicanism emanating from the Oxford Movement. The "desire" for ecumenism (insofar as it existed) within this tradition is better characterized by the terms reunion or reunionism – given that it involved an acceptance of or accommodation between certain common ecclesial forms and thus envisaged an authoritative or semi-structural rather than individualistic

relationship between churches. In short, insofar as there was an ecumenical awareness in the history of the Oxford Movement, it was mainly one which faced in a particular direction – namely that of churches conforming to the historic three-fold ministry of deacon, priest, and bishop. Yet while there was a distinctive ecclesiology or theology of the church which underpinned Oxford Movement-inspired ecumenical developments, the resulting reunionist endeavors tended to be mainly the work of individuals or groups of individuals confronting particular crises involving relationships with other churches.

Another caution as to the slippery nature of terminology is also necessary. The desire for Christian unity flowed naturally from the dominical precepts of Christ himself. While it may seem an obvious truism, nonetheless, we need reminding that ecumenism could mean very different things to different sides in ecumenical dialogue and religious controversy. Models of Christian unity could be very varied. On the one hand they could imply formal organic union involving either an accommodation or submission, or on the other hand they might constitute merely fellowship, community, and consensus. They could be predicated on a high doctrine of a hierarchical visible church or merely represent an aspiration to a spiritual union based on an invisible church of "true believers" with ministerial succession and ecclesiological issues sidelined or omitted – this was the "Ultra Protestant" model rejected by Anglo-Catholic partisans. Even if we cannot provide a definitive answer, we also need to ask ourselves whose "desire," whose voice do we listen to in the history of ecumenical dialogues? How do we detect a "desire" for ecumenism? What publications and activities evoke it? Is there such a thing as anti-ecumenism? We need to be aware of confessional factors, cultural as well as theological. For instance, one might argue that what really drove 19th-century High Church Anglican or Anglo-Catholic ecumenical efforts was the desire for self-validation of the Anglican Communion itself and in particular of the Anglican so-called "branch theory."

---

3 C. Michael Shea, *Newman's Early Roman Catholic Legacy (1845–1854)*, Oxford, Oxford University Press, 2017, 2–3.

3   Pre-Tractarian High Church Anglican
       Ecclesiology: The "Branch Theory"

As formulated by the Caroline Divines in the 17th
century, the theory of Anglican[4] Catholicity cited
scriptural and patristic (notably St. Cyprian) testimonies to unity being a key mark or note of the
true church. On the one hand, the Roman Catholic
theory of church unity based on papal supremacy
was repudiated as a usurpation and deviation from
antiquity. On the other hand, the pan-Protestant
Evangelical and continental Protestant traditions
(both Lutheran and Reformed) were considered
to have erred in a contrary direction by interpreting church unity primarily in terms of an invisible body of true believers (the Reformer William
Tyndale notoriously translated the word "church"
as "congregation" in his translation of the New
Testament). Anglican Catholicity implied a federation of separate territorial entities that each upheld certain notes or "fundamentals" of Catholic
faith and apostolic order. By this rationale, the
Church of England was not in itself the Catholic
or universal church, as Anglican controversialists
charged the Church of Rome with professing itself
to be. Rather, from the Anglican viewpoint, it was
a branch of the universal church, its claim resting
on its preservation of apostolic order through an
orderly and unbroken episcopal and ministerial
succession as well as through its adherence to the
doctrine of the primitive church as enshrined in

the Creeds and early ecumenical councils. As a
notable pre-Tractarian High Churchman, Charles
Daubeny, put it: "Every Christian society, pos-
sessing the characteristic marks of the Church of
Christ, I consider to be a separate branch of the
Catholic or universal visible church upon earth."[5]

Pre-Tractarian Anglican High Churchmen argued that the unity of the church did not entail
the dependence of one branch of the church upon
another but was rather a coexistence of federated
branches or parts resting on an equal or not so
equal basis. The unity of the church did not even
depend on a "necessary communion between
all branches of the Catholic church," as Roman
Catholic apologetics maintained. As John Hume
Spry explained,

> as Christian unity is not merely a union of
> hearts and opinions, so neither does it con-
> sist in, or require an entire union of opin-
> ion ... or we shall destroy the possibility of
> unity, by making that essential to it, which
> never can be obtained.[6]

The Church of England's apparent breach of the
unity of the church by its separation from Rome at
the Reformation was defended as a restoration of
apostolic purity and order. The Church in England
remained the same church, shorn of corruptions
and abuses. As Daubeny explained, the Church of
England had simply exercised

> the right which one independent branch of
> the Church of Christ claims, of protesting,
> in its collective character, against the errors
> of another branch of it; with which, from

---

4   However, the terms "Anglican" and "Anglicanism" were
    later constructs and usage is an anachronism if ap-
    plied to the period prior to the 19th century. See Peter B.
    Nockles, *The Oxford Movement in Context: Anglican High
    Churchmanship (1760–1857)*, Cambridge, Cambridge Uni-
    versity Press, 1994, 39–41; Anthony Milton, "Introduction:
    Reformation, Identity, and 'Anglicanism' (c. 1520–1662),"
    OHA 1, 1–27, here 7–8; Paul Avis, "What is 'Anglicanism'?,"
    in: Stephen Sykes, John E. Booty & Jonathan Knight, eds.,
    The Study of Anglicanism, London, SPCK, ²1998, 459–476,
    here 460–462; Stephen Sykes, *Unashamed Anglicanism*,
    London, Darton, Longman & Todd, 1995, xiv. See also Colin
    Podmore, *Aspects of Anglican Identity*, London, Church
    House, 2005, 26–42.

5   Charles Daubeny, *An Appendix to the Guide to the Church*,
    London, J. Hatchard, 1799, 106–107.
6   John Hume Spry, *Christian Unity Doctrinally and
    Historically Considered, in Eight Sermons Preached before
    the University of Oxford, in the Year MDCCCXVI, at the
    Lecture Founded by the Late Rev. John Bampton*, Oxford,
    Oxford University Press, 1817, 10–11.

local circumstances, it may, or may not hold communion.[7]

Unity appeared to be treated differently from communion.[8]

This High Church Anglican ecclesiology with its focus on "primitive order" as well as "apostolic truth" encouraged a certain ecclesial insularity which contrasted with the Protestant internationalism of many leaders of the early Reformed Church of England in the Edwardian and Elizabethan eras with their close ties with the churches of Strasbourg, Zurich, Geneva and continental Reformed divines such as Martin Bucer and Heinrich Bullinger. Later Anglican Evangelicals and latitudinarians continued to retain an enthusiastic sense of theological kinship with, and openness towards, Protestant Nonconformist as well as non-episcopal continental Protestant Churches. They claimed to hold the closest affinity with their Reformation inheritance, and this distinguished them from many later High Church Anglicans for whom fidelity to episcopal order and ministerial continuity was paramount. The ecumenical spirit of early 19th-century Anglican Evangelicals was reflected in their support for the nondenominational and ecumenical BFBS, an outlook which characterized the then Evangelical young John Henry Newman himself in the early and mid-1820s, the young Newman at that time holding the BFBS's ecumenical character to be a benefit, rather than the drawback which High Churchmen and he himself later held it to be.[9]

For pre-Tractarian High Churchmen, like their Caroline forebears, the status of continental Protestant Churches was considered to be quite distinct from that of English Protestant Dissent or Nonconformist bodies. The former were deemed to have abandoned episcopacy unwillingly and were able to urge the plea of "necessity" while the latter were regarded as schismatic by having willfully and deliberately separated from a doctrinally pure episcopal church. In fact, the Church of England was even defended from the objections of English Dissenters in at least one work of apologetic by recourse to the principles and teaching of continental Reformed Churches.[10] For most pre-Tractarian High Churchmen, any reconciliation with English Protestant Dissenters could only be on the basis of their unconditional individual submission to the church. In contrast, even Archbishop William Laud had accepted the validity of German Lutheran orders, maintaining that the Lutheran system of superintendency preserved the substance, though not the name, of episcopacy. As Norman Sykes argued, by formulating such an accommodation to their theory, Anglican High Churchmen were able to preserve their solidarity with the rest of the Reformation world, and to avoid the potentially embarrassing isolation that would have resulted from its unqualified application, not least in its implication for the status of Britain's 18th-century Hanoverian monarchs.[11] For instance, in 1689 the future archbishop of Canterbury, the moderate High Churchman William Wake, preached "An Exhortation to Mutual Charity and Union among Protestants."[12] As archbishop in 1719 Wake initiated terms of mutual conciliation with the

---

7   Charles Daubeny, *A Guide to the Church*, London, T. Cadell, Jun. & W. Davies, 1798, 149–150.

8   On the apparent inconsistencies in Daubeny's ecclesiology, see George H. Tavard, *The Quest for Catholicity: A Study in Anglicanism*, London, Burns & Oates, 1963, 145.

9   I owe this insight to Geertjan Zuijdwegt of KU Leuven; see Geertjan Zuijdwegt, *An Evangelical Adrift: The Making of John Henry Newman's Theology*, Ph.D. thesis, KU Leuven, 2019, 245–246.

10 Joseph Bingham, *The French Churches Apology for the Church of England: or The Objections of Dissenters against the Articles, Homilies, Liturgy and Canons of the English Church, Considered and Answered upon the Principles of the Reformed Church of France*, London, R. Knaplock, 1706.

11 Norman Sykes, *Old Priest and New Presbyter: Episcopacy and Presbyterianism since the Reformation with Especial Relation to the Churches of England and Scotland*, Cambridge, Cambridge University Press, 1956, 30–84.

12 William Wake, *An Exhortation to Mutual Charity and Union among Protestants in Sermon Preach'd before the King and Queen at Hampton-Court, May 21, 1689*, London, R. Chiswell and W. Rogers, 1689.

non-episcopal Reformed Churches on the continent and carried on an energetic correspondence with Jean Leclerc of Amsterdam and Jean-Alphonse Turrettini of Geneva.[13] Wake's hope was that they might embrace "a moderate episcopal government." Similarly, in 1707 the archbishop of York, John Sharp, had entered into correspondence with the Lutheran divines of the court of Frederick I of Prussia with the aim of finding an accommodation based on acceptance of a common liturgy and moderate episcopacy. On this evidence, for pre-Tractarian High Churchmen episcopacy was part of the *bene esse* of the church, rather than the *esse*. Lutherans and Calvinists had Christian churches but second-rate ones – "German silver was good, though worth less than episcopal gold."[14]

Nonetheless, Sykes's argument is open to qualification and has been questioned.[15] The Tractarian emphasis on *jure divino* episcopacy had Jacobean and Caroline precedents. The Laudian divines had increasingly distanced the Church of England from foreign Reformed Churches. As early as the 1620s, anxiety was being expressed that intercommunion with the foreign Reformed Churches might undermine the Church of England's claim to Catholicity. In the 1630s Laud's disciple Viscount Scudamore refused to receive communion with the French Protestants at Charenton. Once in exile in France in the 1650s, the Laudian John Cosin appears to

have adopted a softer stance and endorsed intercommunion with the French Huguenot Church there but there is no evidence that he personally attended French Protestant services.[16] Meanwhile, Laudian polemicists such as Peter Heylyn retold the history of the English Reformation as one of primarily English renewal and renovation of the medieval church with the involvement of continental divines dismissed as an alien intrusion. After 1662, non-episcopal continental Protestant ministers had to seek re-ordination in order to serve in the Church of England.[17] The Tractarians would identify with this harder line position.[18]

There was some affinity between pre-Tractarian High Churchmen and the Greek Church with examples of cordial ecumenical contact dating back to the early 17th century, as witnessed by the correspondence dating from 1612 between George Abbot, archbishop of Canterbury, and Cyril Lucaris, patriarch of Alexandria and afterwards Constantinople. These contacts were strengthened by the reunionist hopes of King James I and bore some fruit in the later foundation of the so-called Greek college in Oxford.[19] These links continued into the 18th century. The nonjuror bishops of Scotland and England who refused to recognize the Hanoverian title to the throne were at the forefront of such contacts. Between 1716 and 1725 they conducted a theological correspondence with representatives of the Russian and Greek Churches, but negotiations came to nothing.

13   Paul Avis, *Anglicanism and the Christian Church: Theological Resources in Historical Perspective*, London, T&T Clark, 2002, 121–129.

14   Stephen Sykes & Sheridan Gilley, "'No Bishop, No Church!': The Tractarian Impact on Anglicanism," in: Geoffrey Rowell, ed., *Tradition Renewed: The Oxford Movement Conference Papers*, London, Darton, Longman & Todd, 1986, 120–39, here 123.

15   Arthur L. Peck, *Anglicanism and Episcopacy: A Re-Examination of Evidence: With Special Reference to Professor Norman Sykes's "Old Priest and New Presbyter"*, London, Faith Press, 1958, 40–41. See also John Pinnington, "Anglican Openness to Foreign Protestant Churches in the Eighteenth Century," *AThR* 51, 1969, 320–332, and Anthony Milton, *Catholic and Reformed: The Roman and Protestant Churches in English Protestant Thought (1600–1640)*, Cambridge, Cambridge University Press, 1995, 377–528.

16   Milton, *Catholic and Reformed*, 526.

17   Tony Claydon, "The Church of England and the Churches of Europe," *OHA* 2, 314–331, here 317.

18   See Peter B. Nockles, "Survivals or New Arrivals?: The Oxford Movement and the Nineteenth Century Historical Construction of Anglicanism," in: Stephen Platten, ed., *Anglicanism and the Western Christian Tradition: Continuity, Change and the Search for Communion*, Norwich, Canterbury Press, 2003, 144–191.

19   William B. Patterson, "Cyril Lucaris, George Abbot, James VI and I, and the Beginning of Orthodox-Anglican Relations," in: Peter M. Doll, ed., *Anglicanism and Orthodoxy 300 years after the "Greek College" in Oxford*, Oxford, Peter Lang, 2006, 39–55.

Instances of ecumenical overtures with the Roman Catholic Church were more limited but some are noteworthy. Beginning shortly after his accession in England in 1603 King James I initiated moves towards closer relations between the Church of England and the Roman Catholic Church as well as other churches which continued throughout his reign as part of attempts to achieve a lasting European peace.[20] Under Charles I, ecumenical contact with Roman Catholicism increased further. In 1635 the Caroline bishop of Chichester, Richard Montagu, had written a tract which appeared to be designed to entice English Catholics to conform to the Church of England by minimizing doctrinal and devotional differences between Rome and Canterbury. An anonymous annotation made at the end of the tract proclaims, "It is the same way from Rome to London, which is from London to Rome; why then may not a Protestant go to the Popish Mass"; this is apparently indicative of the irenic intent of the document.[21] Moreover in 1635–1636 secret but direct communications took place between the Court of Charles I and two papal emissaries, the Benedictine Father Leander a Sancto Martino and the Oratorian Father Gregorio Panzani, involving meetings between Montagu and Panzani[22] – a dialogue which later Anglo-Catholic reunionists in the Oxford Movement tradition picked up

on as a source of inspiration during the 1860s.[23] However, later ecumenical initiatives, such as that of Archbishop Wake and Louis Ellies du Pin from 1717 to 1720, focused on interaction with the French Gallican Church, which was perceived as sitting more loosely in regard to its Roman obedience. In fact, Wake's discussions over potential unity with the Gallican Church were based on the assumption that the latter would break with Rome. This ecumenical trend reached a climax with the enthusiastic Anglican response to the Gallican divine Pierre François Le Courayer's controversial defense of Anglican ordinations (1727) and his being honored by the University of Oxford.

The impact of the French Revolution with the degradation of the Gallican Church in France and the emigration to Britain of a large number of French clergy in the 1790s helped weaken the barriers of anti-Catholic prejudice at least among High Church Anglicans.[24] It would lead to a modest increase of interest at least in the abstract concept of reunion between the Churches of England and Rome. On the French Catholic side this was exemplified in a work by Jean François-Marie Le Pappe de Trévern, a one-time émigré priest and later bishop of Strasbourg, in his *Discussion amicale sur l'Église Anglicane* (1817).[25] However, as Jeremy Morris notes, Trévern's treatise, for all its amicable arguments, shows that the assistance given to French Catholic exiles during the Revolutionary and Napoleonic era did not diminish

---

20 See William B. Patterson, *King James VI and I and the Reunion of Christendom*, Cambridge, Cambridge University Press, 1997.

21 Richard Montagu, "Concerning Recusancie of Communion with the Church of England", ed. Anthony Milton & Alexandra Walsham, in: Stephen Taylor, ed., *From Cranmer to Davidson: A Church of England Miscellany*, Woodbridge, Boydell, 1999, 69–102, here 101. However, Dr. Milton has kindly drawn my attention to the fact that the anonymous annotation at the end of the Montagu manuscript only survives on copies that seem to have been made by hostile sources. Therefore, caution needs to be observed in interpreting Montagu's precise intentions.

22 Anthony Milton, *Richard Montagu and Reunion with Rome*, in: Milton, *Catholic and Reformed*, 353–373.

23 Frederick George Lee, "1636 and 1866," in: Frederick George Lee, ed., *Essays on the Re-Union of Christendom*, London, J.T. Hayes, 1868, 118–142.

24 Dominic Bellenger, "The Émigré Clergy and the English Church (1789–1815)," *JEH* 34, 1983, 392–410; Dominic Bellenger, *The French Exiled Clergy in the British Isles after 1789: An Historical Introduction and Working List*, Bath, Downside Abbey, 1986, 28–46; James J. Sack, *From Jacobite to Conservative: Reaction and Orthodoxy in Britain (c. 1760–1832)*, Cambridge, Cambridge University Press, 1993, 217–251.

25 Jean François-Marie Le Pappe de Trévern, *Discussion amicale sur l'établissement et la doctrine de l'église anglicane et en général sur la Réformation rédigée en forme de lettres écrites en 1812 et 1813*, London, R. Juigné, 1817.

"the critical eye they cast on the Anglicanism they encountered."[26] Moreover, on the Anglican side any diminution of anti-Catholic feeling could be offset by a lingering prophetical tradition even among some High Churchmen according to which Rome was a seat of the Antichrist,[27] though the exile of Pope Pius VI and the fall of Rome to Napoleonic armies, while triggering some Protestant triumphalism and millenarian expectations, also created a wave of sympathy for the exiled Holy Father amid claims that the Antichrist should really be associated with Napoleon Bonaparte rather than Pius VI.[28]

Pre-Tractarian High Churchmen always felt the need to justify the causes of the Church of England's break with Rome at the Reformation, precisely because they acknowledged the Church of Rome to be a branch, albeit a corrupt one, of the universal church. In breaking with Rome, it was claimed that the British churches had merely returned to their original independence and "primitive character." It was because of the Anglican High Church claim that the British churches had preserved apostolic continuity at the Reformation that Roman Catholicism within the British Isles could be portrayed as an alien "usurpation" and schism. It was because pre-Tractarian High Churchmen regarded schism as "a sin" or even "heinous crime" that Roman Catholic doctrinal corruption had to be emphasized.[29] As Shute Barrington, bishop of Durham, argued, this was

necessary "because we are not contending for trifles; because they are not slight matters which first separated the Church of England from the Romish Church."[30] Therefore, when it came to potential reunion with the Roman Catholic Church, the essential precondition laid down was that Rome must renounce her supposed "corruptions" and accretions and return to what was portrayed as a "primitive" condition.[31] Otherwise the Church of Rome was deemed, according to Thomas Burgess, bishop of Salisbury, incapable of union with the Church of England.[32] Even those two Irish pre-Tractarian High Churchmen, John Jebb (from 1823 bishop of Limerick) and the layman and mystic Alexander Knox, who have been rightly claimed as precursors of the Oxford Movement with Knox viewing the Church of England as a conduit for "prospective unity,"[33] yet insisted that any accommodation with Rome must be on the basis of that church abandoning "the monstrous doctrine of transubstantiation" and the "the tenet of infallibility."[34]

A rare exception to this standard Protestant High Church viewpoint was represented by two High Church Anglican proponents of proposals for a

---

26   Jeremy Morris, *The High Church Revival in the Church of England: Arguments and Identities*, Leiden, Brill, 2016, 135–169, here 148–152.

27   William H. Oliver, *Prophets and Millennialists: The Use of Biblical Prophecy in England from the 1790s to the 1840s*, Auckland, Auckland University Press, 1978, 50–51; John A. Oddy, *Eschatological Prophecy in the English Theological Tradition (c. 1700–c. 1840)*, Ph.D. thesis, University of London, 1982, ch. 3; Nockles, *The Oxford Movement in Context*, 70, 167.

28   Nigel Aston, *Christianity and Revolutionary Europe (c. 1750–1830)*, Cambridge, Cambridge University Press, 2002, 235.

29   Ralph Churton, *An Answer to a Letter from Francis Eyre of Warkworth*, London, Fletcher & Hanwell, 1796, 14.

30   Shute Barrington, *Grounds of Union between the Churches of England and Rome, Considered, in a Charge Delivered to the Clergy of the Diocese of Durham, at the Ordinary Visitation of that Diocese, in the Year 1810*, London, T. Payne, Pall Mall & C., 1811, 8.

31   Charles Daubeny, *The Protestant Companion: or A Seasonable Preservative against the Errors, Corruptions, and Unfounded Claims of a Superstitious and Idolatrous Church*, London, C. & J. Rivington, 1824, vii–viii.

32   See Thomas Burgess, *Popery Incapable of Union with a Protestant Church: And not a Remedy for Schism, nor an Exemplar of Unity, Sanctity, or Christian Verity: A Letter in Reply to the Rev. Samuel Wix*, Carmarthen, J. Harris, 1820.

33   Alexander Knox, "Letter to the Rev. James Dunn, on the Impossibility of Union between the Churches of England and of Rome," in: Alexander Knox, *Remains of Alexander Knox, Esq.*, vol. 3, London, Duncan & Malcolm, 1844, 314–330, here 326.

34   J. Jebb to A. Knox, July 10, 1811, in: Charles Forster, ed., *Thirty Years' Correspondence between John Jebb, D.D.F.R.S., Bishop of Limerick, Ardfert and Aghadoe and Alexander Knox, Esq. M.R.I.A.*, vol. 2, London, Duncan & Cochran, 1836, 41.

qualified reunion with the Church of Rome: Samuel Wix, then vicar of St. Bartholomew-the-less, and John Oxlee, then rector of Scawton, near York. Wix, against whom Bishop Burgess's *Popery Incapable of Union* pamphlet was a direct response, proposed a council between the two churches to settle differences, guardedly advocating an accommodation with a potential for reunion on condition that Rome reformed certain "abuses."[35] The argument ran that there could be no objection to such an attempt at reunion because "the Church of Rome is acknowledged by the Church of England to be a true apostolical church."[36] Moreover, those who would "disclaim our Romish parentage," it was claimed, "causes us to approach to the degraded and precarious condition of dissenters."[37] It is also significant that Wix's plea for unity was restricted to the Churches of England and Rome, and excluded those who in his view were not "within the pale of the visible church."[38] Wix also cited the precedent of Archbishop Wake's dialogue with du Pin, but as Bishop Burgess pointed out, Wake in that earlier dialogue had only envisaged reunion with the Gallican Church and not the Church of Rome as a whole.[39]

On the Roman Catholic side, the lawyer Charles Butler in 1816 published a comparative study of the Roman, Eastern, and Protestant liturgical and confessional standards of faith in which he adopted a broadly reunionist position,[40] while in 1824 James Doyle, bishop of Kildare and Leighlin, advocated the possibility for a future reunion between Rome and the Church of England. Doyle observed: "They are pride and points of honor which keep us divided on many subjects, not a love of Christian humility, charity, and truth."[41] Doyle even conceded that some of the doctrinal differences amounted to differing forms of words that could be reconciled with each other.[42] Bishop Doyle's proposals met with a mixed response from both sides of the theological divide, though an Anglican divine, Thomas Newenham, engaged the bishop in friendly correspondence and supported his suggestion. Nothing came of this offer, and hostile voices were raised against any such accommodation. It has been suggested that Bishop Doyle's overtures were a later embarrassment for Ultramontanes,[43] with Archbishop Paul Cullen, of the next generation, privately criticizing him for "Gallicanism." In fact, while Doyle may have been politically a Gallican, he was also a theological Ultramontane. Moreover, later reunionists made more of the episode than was probably warranted, and it is an open question, as some later plausibly argued, that had Bishop Doyle's proposal been made thirty or forty years later in the wake of the

35 Samuel Wix, *Reflections Concerning the Expediency of a Council of the Church of England and the Church of Rome Being Holden, with a View to Accommodate Religious Differences*, London, F.C. & J. Rivington, 1818. For further discussion of the controversy between Wix and Bishop Burgess, see Peter B. Nockles, "Recreating the History of the Church of England: Bishop Burgess, the Oxford Movement and Nineteenth-Century Reconstructions of Protestant and Anglican Identity," in: Nigel Yates, ed., *Bishop Burgess and His World: Culture, Religion and Society in Britain, Europe, and North America in the Eighteenth and Nineteenth Centuries*, Cardiff, University of Wales Press, 2007, 233–289, here 240–246.

36 Samuel Wix, *Christian Union without the Abuses of Popery: A Letter to the Right Reverend the Lord Bishop of St. David's, in reply to his Lordship's letter, entitled "Popery incapable of union with a Protestant Church"*, London, F.C. & J. Rivington, 1820, 16–17.

37 Stephen Hyde Cassan, *Lives of the Bishops of Winchester*, vol. 2, London, C. & J. Rivington, 1827, 16.

38 Tavard, *The Quest for Catholicity*, 150.

39 Burgess, *Popery Incapable of Union with a Protestant Church*, 37–38.

40 Charles Butler, *An Historical and Literary Account of the Formularies, Confessions of Faith, or Symbolical Books of the Roman Catholic, Greek, and Principal Protestant Churches*, London, A.J. Valpy, 1816.

41 James Doyle & others, *Letters on a Re-Union of the Churches of England and Rome from and to the Rt. Revd. Dr. Doyle, R.C. Bishop of Kildare, John O'Driscol, Alexander Knox, and Thomas Newenham, Esqrs.*, Dublin, R. Moore Tims, 1824, 9.

42 Doyle & others, *Letters on a Re-Union of the Churches*, 9.

43 Elizabeth Bridget Stuart, *Roman Catholic Reactions to the Oxford Movement and Anglican Schemes for Reunion: From 1833 to the Condemnation of Anglican Orders in 1896*, Ph.D. thesis, University of Oxford, 1983, 72.

Oxford Movement, whether it would have been more warmly received.[44]

4   The Ecclesiology of the Early Oxford Movement

The necessity of holding the doctrine of the unity or oneness of the church was central to the Oxford Movement but was predicated upon holding a right understanding of the nature of the church. For as Henry Manning put it, if an honest inquirer did not know "where the Church is, how shall they [all Christians] partake of the salvation which is enshrined in it?"[45] The Oxford Movement's evolving model of union and reunion needs to be viewed within this conceptual framework. It involved selectivity in the use of foundational sources and was predicated on a certain rewriting of history.[46] It was in the interest of second- and third-generation Tractarians to create the legend of the Oxford Movement as an ecumenical endeavor *ab initio*.[47] A contrast was drawn between the English Caroline Revival which had been concerned merely to complete the healing of "national insular divisions" in the Church of England while neglecting "the loss of intercommunion with foreign Catholics," and the current Catholic Revival with its active concern to restore the union of Christendom.[48] Yet even the "failures" of ecumenism and the idiosyncrasies of its individual practitioners deserve a place in this history. Moreover, even some later reunionists on the Anglican side recognized that in the early days of the Oxford Movement its leaders had other more immediate

priorities – the establishment of elementary foundational doctrinal principles. As one candid commentator later observed:

> Mr. Keble had compiled "Prayers for Unity," and Mr. Wackerbarth had done the same: here and there a sermon indistinctly hinting at the need of a more complete unity than existed was preached and printed; otherwise little was attempted.[49]

The Oxford Movement's concept of the universal church with its three main branches and sense of an Anglican identity linked to a wider Christendom in theory should have made the re-establishment of a lost original unity a leading priority.[50] In practice this was not the case, and ecumenical endeavor took time to emerge. As late as 1842, Newman, echoing Manning's point above, could observe, "while the Catholic Church is broken up into fragments, it will always be a most perplexing question, what and where is the Church?"[51] As for Edward Bouverie Pusey, his primary interest at this time was the internal reform of the Church of England and he was against premature reunion. In fact, the early Oxford Movement was not initially directly motivated by an overarching ecumenical vision. Its immediate concerns were more insular and Anglo-centric – to strengthen the sense of the supremacy of the Church of England as the only legitimate embodiment of the church in Britain by reference to its apostolical foundations, order, and continuity. This was in line with the relative insularity inherent in Caroline and traditional pre-Tractarian High Church ecclesiology.

---

44   Thomas G. McGrath, "The Historiography of the Papers of Bishop James Doyle O.S.A. (1766–1834) in the Kildare and Leighlin Diocesan Archives," *ArH* 43, 1988, 85–94, here 90–91.

45   Henry Edward Manning, *The Unity of the Church*, London, J. Murray, 1842, 3.

46   Nockles, "Survivals or New Arrivals," 144–191.

47   See Frederick George Lee, *The Progress of the Church*, London, J. Masters, 1857, and "Introduction," in: Lee, ed., *Essays on the Re-Union*, ix–x.

48   Lee, ed., *Essays on the Re-Union*, ix.

49   "Essays on Re-Union," *Union Review* 5, 1867, 474–486, here 474.

50   E. Charles Miller, *Toward a Fuller Vision: Orthodoxy and the Anglican Experience*, Wilton CT, Morehouse Barlow, 1984, 61.

51   J.H. Newman to J.C. Wynter, July 16, 1842, in: John Henry Newman, *The Letters and Diaries of John Henry Newman*, vol. 9, ed. Francis J. McGrath, Oxford, Oxford University Press, 2006, 44.

In Tractarian apologetic the English Church was deemed to be one and the same church as the Church of the Apostles. The deposit of faith was fixed in apostolic times and had been handed down to the Church of England, and this notwithstanding the Reformation of the 16th century. Apostolic succession and its preservation were the key to sacramental validity that had survived the English Reformation and which was recast as a mere "purification" of the worst corruptions of "Romanism" and in deference to antiquity. Continuity was also provided by retention of the threefold order of ministry, the creeds, and the *Book of Common Prayer*. This was the message of the early numbers of the series published by leaders of the Oxford Movement, the *Tracts for the Times*, the majority of the early numbers of which, published in 1833 and 1834, were primarily concerned with the apostolical succession and the doctrine of the church and ministry. As John Keble put it in *Tract* 4, the Church of England was "the only church in this realm which has a right to be quite sure that she has the Lord's Body to give his people."[52]

Although the identity of the Oxford Movement under Newman's leadership was initially grounded on opposition to threats to the unity of church and state in England, the more fundamental question of the unity of the church *qua* church as a whole was not entirely ignored. Of course, the divine imperative of unity was recognized but the Anglican Newman and early Tractarians understood unity and Catholicity largely in terms of apostolicity. The contemporary church was representative of the undivided church of the early fathers. The early Tractarian Newman's vision of history was, as Kenneth Parker has demonstrated, an essentially successionist metanarrative of the Christian past, linking the absolute and changeless nature of Christian truth claims with the apostolic succession of bishops in defense of the doctrinal continuity of the English Church with primitive Christian

teaching.[53] As a consequence, the Tractarian emphasis on the Catholicity of the Church was temporal in the sense that it was the past that gave the church its underlying identity.[54] Catholicity was primarily established by continuity with apostolic teaching and the early church as enshrined in the doctrines of the creeds and primitive councils of the church. On the other hand, in contrast to its later ecumenical understanding, the early Oxford Movement's notion of Catholicity was not primarily spatial in being tied to a particular interest in or focus upon the unity of Christians across the world. For there was no easy way of overcoming the practical reality of a divided Christendom as represented by the breach between East and West and most notably by the continental Reformations. Catholic doctrine and discipline comprised what was taught before the division of the Eastern and Western Churches, including the first six general councils. This meant that the Tractarian sense of Catholic identity stood opposed to alternative expressions of Christianity, including that of the Roman Catholic Church, which was deemed to have "added to" the faith once delivered to the saints, as well as to non-episcopal continental Protestant Churches and English Nonconformist bodies which were deemed to have subtracted or deviated from apostolic faith and order notably by abandoning episcopacy and apostolical succession. This inevitably restricted the potential for ecumenical engagement in relation to continental Protestantism.

In the early numbers of the *Tracts for the Times*, Newman on the surface struck a robustly anti-Roman tone. There was nothing ecumenical about them. He even referred to "Papistical corruptions

---

52   *Tracts* 4, 5.

53   Kenneth L. Parker, "Historiography," in: Frederick D. Aquino & Benjamin J. King, eds., *The Oxford Handbook of John Henry Newman*, Oxford, Oxford University Press, 2018, 557–577, here 558.

54   See Mark D. Chapman, "Temporal and Spatial Catholicism: Tensions in Historicism in the Oxford Movement," in: Colby Dickinson, ed., *The Shaping of Tradition: Context and Normativity*, Leuven, Peeters, 2013, 17–26.

of the Gospel."[55] Moreover, in his controversy with a French priest of the diocese of Nancy, the Abbé Jean-Nicolas Jager, and in his *Lectures on the Prophetical Office of the Church* (1836),[56] Newman set out the Anglican theory of Catholicity as a basis for refuting Roman Catholic claims and notably the papal supremacy.[57] Added to this, Newman toyed with the notion of the Church of Rome as Antichrist – a view that had been a feature of a Protestant prophetical tradition stretching back to the Reformation and associated with John Bale, John Foxe, Joseph Mede, and Thomas Newton,[58] and as we have seen, included even the High Churchman Charles Daubeny.

Newman's *Lectures on the Doctrine of Justification* (1838),[59] with its clear attempt to mediate between extreme Protestant and Catholic views on Justification, have been hailed as a "pioneering classic of ecumenical theology," with, according to Louis Bouyer, "enormous consequences for ecumenism."[60] It has been cited as paving the way for later convergences on this issue to be found in the *Joint Declaration on the Doctrine of Justification* in 1999. Others have questioned this claim and argued that Newman seriously distorted the true character of the Protestant doctrine of Justification and that he indulged in a myopic misreading of Luther, implying that the work was deliberately anti-ecumenical.[61] However, as Austin Wilson argues, posing such questions in this context misses

the point. Ecumenism was not at the forefront of Newman's mind at this stage, either in favor or against. Newman was essentially concerned in the *Lectures* to overturn the Protestant interpretation of private judgment with its apparent undermining of the role of the visible church and its sacramental ordinances as being incompatible with the doctrine of justifying faith.[62]

Newman also kept his distance from the first Roman Catholic overtures in England towards unity. This included an Association of Prayers for the Conversion of England to the Roman faith drawn up by Father Ignatius (the Hon. & Rev. George Spencer) in 1838,[63] "all Catholic Europe" being apparently "enrolled in the Crusade of Prayer,"[64] with Spencer recently being called "a Pioneer of Ecumenical Prayer."[65] Spencer's reunion model was strictly predicated upon the basis of individual submissions to Rome.

Newman may have kept his distance, but he allowed his curate at St. Mary the Virgin in Oxford and fellow of Magdalen College, John Rouse Bloxam, to play something of a surrogate ecumenical role. Bloxam corresponded and met in Oxford with the Roman Catholic convert and ecumenical and visionary enthusiast, Ambrose Phillipps de Lisle. De Lisle with his love of the medieval, eschatological and mystical preoccupations has been portrayed as an example of "Romantic ecumenism" and his efforts as "little more than

---

55   *Tracts* 20, 1.

56   John Henry Newman, *Lectures on the Prophetical Office of the Church, Viewed Relatively to Romanism and Popular Protestantism*, London, Rivington & J.H. Parker, 1836.

57   See Louis Allen, ed., *John Henry Newman and the Abbé Jager: A Controversy on Scripture and Tradition (1834–1836)*, Oxford, Oxford University Press, 1975.

58   See Paul Misner, "Newman and the Tradition Concerning the Papal Antichrist," *CH* 42, 1973, 377–395.

59   John Henry Newman, *Lectures on the Doctrine of Justification*, London, Rivington, 1838.

60   Louis Bouyer, "Preface," in: Thomas L. Sheridan, *Newman on Justification*, New York NY, Alba, 1967, 12.

61   Alister E. McGrath, "The Emergence of the Anglican Tradition on Justification," *Chm* 98/1, 1984, 28–43, here 40–41.

62   Austin Wilson, "Ecclesiology and the Problem of Private Judgment," in Newman's *Lectures on the Doctrine of Justification*," *NSJ* 15/1, 2018, 29–43.

63   Father Pius, *Life of Father Ignatius of St. Paul, Passionist (the Hon. & Rev. George Spencer)*, London, J. Duffy, 1866, 248.

64   Edmund Sheridan Purcell, *Life and Letters of Ambrose Phillipps de Lisle*, ed. Edwin de Lisle, vol. 1, London, Macmillan & Co., 1900, 177.

65   The Hon. & Rev. George Spencer, son of the second Earl Spencer, rector of Brighton, and chaplain to James Blomfield, bishop of London, converted to Roman Catholicism in 1830, and later became superior of the Passionist Order. See also Jozef Vanden Bussche, *Ignatius (George) Spencer, Passionist (1799–1864): Crusader of Prayer for England Pioneer of Ecumenical Prayer*, Leuven, Leuven University Press, 1991.

instances of a passionate Romanticism that developed as a reaction to the rapid social change of the nineteenth century."[66] Nonetheless, de Lisle deserves to be regarded as part of a broader Oxford Movement culture shaped by these forces, and not outside it. De Lisle's own almost obsessive campaign for reunion directly flowed, as he later confided, from his first reading of the *Tracts for the Times*: "I then said thank God for this, a movement has begun that will bring back the English Church to unity."[67] It was not merely that de Lisle envisaged that the "only logical issue for the principles avowed in those Tracts" lay in "the return of England to Catholic unity," but that he regarded both the Oxford Movement itself and the movement towards reunion as the fulfilment of a prophecy made to him by a holy man, Marco Carrichia, whom he had met in Rome in 1831.[68] De Lisle was tireless in touring Europe promoting Spencer's prayer crusade. However, Newman remained highly suspicious of both English and foreign Catholic overtures and only dealt with them reluctantly through intermediaries. As Louis Allen has put it, Newman was "almost conspiratorially prudent" in this matter.[69] He refused to dine with Spencer whom he regarded as a "schismatic" when he visited Oxford in 1840, though he later repented of this and greeted him warmly. As he told his friend Bloxam in 1841: "If Mr. Phillipps wishes to extinguish the Catholic movement among us,

he cannot take a better way than by introducing foreign divines to Oxford."[70] Although he was persuaded by Bloxam to begin a correspondence with de Lisle which touched on the subject of reunion in April 1841, Newman made clear that he "did not expect the reunion of our churches in our time, and [I] have discouraged the notion of all sudden proceedings with a view to it."[71] His list of the obstacles involved made reunion seem a chimera at this time. As he put it in a letter to de Lisle via Bloxam in February 1841:

> Why should we be separate, except that there is a strong body in both churches whose antipathies are more powerful still, and because this body has the governing authorities on its side? I cannot wonder that our authorities should feel as they do, considering what the Church of Rome practically is.[72]

In another letter to de Lisle, Newman was even more dismissive, claiming that de Lisle had over-optimistic hopes for what the Oxford Movement could achieve on the matter of reunion and injecting a realistic note based on historical perspective.

> You overrate our exertions, our influence, our tendencies. We are but a few, and we are what we are. Many times before now in the course of the last three hundred years has a hope of concord arisen among Christians, but as yet it has ever come to nothing. When was a great schism ever healed? Why should ours cease, if that between East and West has continued for so long?[73]

---

66 Mark D. Chapman, *The Fantasy of Reunion: Anglicans, Catholics, and Ecumenism (1833–1882)*, Oxford, Oxford University Press, 2014, 9.

67 A.P. de Lisle to F.G. Lee (editor of the *Union Newspaper*), Feb 16, 1857, in: PHL, F.G. Lee Papers, 2/3 and 2/5.

68 PHL, F.G. Lee Papers, 2/3. According to de Lisle, Carrichia prophesied in answer to his question "How will the conversion of England come?" that "There will be a great movement of the learned of that kingdom, and this shall be the sign of the near accomplishment of the event. God has chosen you to work with them"; A.P. de Lisle to Canon Macdonnell, Aug 31, 1859, in: Purcell, *Life and Letters of Ambrose Phillipps de Lisle*, vol. 1, 31.

69 Louis Allen, "Ambrose Phillipps de Lisle (1809–1878)," *CHR* 40/1, 1954, 1–26, here 14.

70 Cited in Margaret Pawley, *Faith & Family: The Life and Circle of Ambrose Phillipps de Lisle*, Norwich, Canterbury Press, 1993, 124.

71 J.H. Newman to A.P. de Lisle, June 28, 1841, in: Robert Dudley Middleton, *Newman and Bloxam: An Oxford Friendship*, Oxford, Oxford University Press, 1947, 150.

72 Purcell, *Life and Letters of Ambrose Phillipps de Lisle*, vol. 1, 205.

73 Cited in: Allen, "Ambrose Phillipps de Lisle," 18.

It seems that Newman at even this late stage retained something of the older High Church Anglican insistence that Rome must reform herself before any meaningful reunion discussion could take place.

In his *Lectures on the Prophetical Office of the Church*, Newman had emphasized a unity of the church that was multi-centered, distinguishing between the prophetical tradition, "which gives the church life," and the episcopal tradition, "which gives the church form."[74] For the Tractarian Newman, it was not that the unity of the church had been lost *per se* but that it had been "impaired" and weakened. For Newman and the Tractarians, unlike earlier Protestant High Churchmen, loyalty to Anglicanism was defined as loyalty to the portion of the church universal they identified with rather than primarily to the "particular" Church of England. This was implicit of a subtle but significant shift of emphasis away from traditional High Church Anglicanism. Earlier High Church Anglican ecclesiology when translated into ecumenical endeavor insisted that Rome, as a corrupt Church, was entirely to blame for the division of Christendom and its adherents in the British Isles in a state of schism, and that any prospect of reunion had to be predicated on Rome reforming herself and abjuring the Tridentine decrees. Newman himself had held this line and, as we shall see, was slow to abandon it, but the trend was towards a new emphasis on Anglican "imperfections."

5   Newman, the Oxford Movement, and Ecumenism

The leaders and followers of the Oxford Movement initially shared the insular presuppositions of pre-Tractarian High Churchmen. In *Tract* 15, co-authored by Newman and William Palmer of Worcester College, it was denied that the Church of England had initiated the schism with Rome. The claim was made that the Church of England was one and the same body that had subsisted in England since before the Reformation. In a sermon in 1829, Newman made his own the "branch theory": "We are the English Catholics, abroad are the Roman Catholics, some of whom are also among ourselves, elsewhere are the Greek Catholics."[75] Palmer, in his classic two-volume *Treatise on the Church of Christ* (1838),[76] gave the classical exposition of the "branch theory," identifying the church with three branches or great episcopal communions, the Anglican, the Eastern Orthodox, and the Roman Catholic. Palmer's was essentially a territorial statement of Catholicity based on shared apostolic roots. Far from accepting any Anglican blame for the divisions of Christendom, Palmer insisted that at the Reformation the Church of England did not "by any voluntary act whatever, *separate herself from the communion of the universal* church."[77]

Others sought to make the "branch theory" a practical and guiding principle and even a plan of ecumenical action. Palmer of Worcester's namesake but no relation, William Palmer of Magdalen, not only adhered to this concept of the church as coexisting in three branches, each with a triple presence, but made it the basis for his own lifelong ecumenical endeavors which were especially directed towards the Eastern Churches. Writing many years later, in his preface to his own edition of Palmer of Magdalen's *Notes of a Visit to the Russian Church in the Years 1840, 1841* (1882), Newman explained that for Palmer the distinctions between the three branches were essentially secondary,

---

74   Michael J.G. Pahls, *School of the Prophets: John Henry Newman's Anglican Schola and the Ecclesial Vocation of the Theologian*, Ph.D. thesis, Saint Louis University, 2014, 8.

75   John Henry Newman, *Parochial and Plain Sermons*, vol. 3, London, Rivingtons, 1885, 198ff.

76   William Palmer [of Worcester College], *Treatise on the Church of Christ*, 2 vols., London, J.G.F. & J. Rivington, ³1842.

77   Palmer [of Worcester College], *Treatise on the Church of Christ*, vol. 1, part 2, ch. 2, sect. 7, 339–342 (italics original).

fortuitous, and local.[78] The consequence, Newman maintained, was that when Anglicans were in Rome they recognized Rome as the branch of the one church subsisting there, and likewise when Anglicans were in Moscow they recognized the Orthodox Church – to do otherwise was "nothing short of setting up altar against altar, that is the heinous sin of schism, and a sacrilege."[79] Thus, unlike his 18th-century nonjuror predecessors in ecumenical dialogue, Palmer of Magdalen did not seek reunion with the Eastern Church, believing in defiance of reality that communion between the two churches had never been lost.[80] Palmer's aim was to prove "that the doctrine of the Anglican divines was no mere theory, and that an Anglican Christian was *ipso facto* an Oriental Orthodox also."[81] The whole church in its fullness consisted of its Anglican, Greek, and Latin branches, and therefore the three could not have relations with each other, as if they were three substantive bodies, there being no real difference between them except the external accident of place.[82] Newman explained that he conceived Palmer of Magdalen's view "to be the formal teaching of Anglicanism; this is what we held and professed in Oxford forty years ago."[83] However, was it?

In fact, while Newman's comment that Palmer of Magdalen's position was normative of Anglicanism may have been true for some in a later generation of Anglo-Catholics, it is clear that this was not what Palmer of Worcester and other moderate early Tractarians, with all their qualifications about the "corrupt" state of both the Churches

of Rome and the East, actually had in mind. The whole history of Anglican chaplaincies in continental Europe (especially after the foundation of the see of Gibraltar in 1842 to establish jurisdiction over "the Clergy and Laity of the communion of the United Church of England and Ireland resident within Gibraltar and Malta and diverse places within the islands and countries situated in and around the Mediterranean")[84] negated a neat and tidy interpretation of the "branch theory." In 1845 the German-born moderate High Churchman George Edward Biber, then vicar of Roehampton, with the sanction of Charles James Blomfield, bishop of London, carried out a survey of the Anglican continental chaplaincies which recorded a huge growth of such provision since 1815, especially in France and Germany.[85] These developments highlighted the ambiguities in the situation of Anglicanism outside England and in continental Europe. Newman's comment therefore is revealing and begs the question: how far was the Oxford Movement, under his leadership, focused on a broad-based ecumenism?

The Tractarian converts to Rome later commented on the ignorance of both Anglican and Roman Catholics of each other's true religious state during the early phase of the Oxford Movement.[86] Nonetheless, there were notable exceptions, and the Oxford of the 1830s was less insular than sometimes supposed.[87] Mutual knowledge and comprehension grew, aided by French priests living in England acting as channels of information,

78   William Palmer [of Magdalen], *Notes of a Visit to the Russian Church in the Years 1840, 1841*, ed. John Henry Newman, London, Kegan Paul & Co., 1882, vi.

79   Palmer [of Magdalen], *Notes of a Visit to the Russian Church*, vi–vii.

80   Robin Wheeler, *Palmer's Pilgrimage: The Life of William Palmer of Magdalen*, Oxford, Peter Lang, 2006, 86.

81   Palmer [of Magdalen], *Notes of a Visit to the Russian Church*, vii.

82   Palmer [of Magdalen], *Notes of a Visit to the Russian Church*, vi.

83   Palmer [of Magdalen], *Notes of a Visit to the Russian Church*, vii.

84   Henry J.C. Knight, *The Diocese of Gibraltar: A Sketch of Its History, Work and Tasks*, London, SPCK, 1917, 43, cited in: *OHA* 3, 38.

85   George Edward Biber, *The English Church on the Continent: or An Account of the Foreign Settlements of the English Church*, London, F. & J. Rivington, 1846, 3–8. For fuller discussion of this issue see John Wolffe, "British and European Anglicanism," *OHA* 3, 24–44, here 36–42.

86   Thomas W. Allies, *Journal in France in 1845 and 1848: With Letters from Italy in 1847: Of Things and Persons Concerning the Church and Education*, London, Longman, Brown, Green & Longmans, 1849, 2–3.

87   Allen, ed., *John Henry Newman and the Abbé Jager*, 1.

foreign travels, and the visits to Oxford of leading French Catholics, such as Jules Gondon,
Charles de Montalembert, Canon Hilaire Lorain,
and the Abbé Henri-Dominique Lacordaire, who
then conveyed their impressions of the Oxford
Movement and Anglicanism back to their native literary audience.[88] Newman and Hurrell
Froude were deeply marked and influenced by
their Mediterranean journey of 1832–1833, which
included a visit to Rome. Froude was also impressed by the anti-Erastian views on the alliance
of throne and altar espoused by the French cleric
Félicité de La Mennais in his newspaper *L'Avenir* in
the early 1830s.[89] Newman's correspondence with
the Abbé Jager, through the medium of his friend
and associate Benjamin Harrison while in Paris,
has already been noted. Moreover, from as early
as 1833 onwards Palmer of Magdalen had been as
much involved with the French church as he was
to be with the Russian Church, travelling in France
and staying and corresponding with various
French Catholic priests.[90] Other Tractarian foreign
contacts included that of Pusey with the German
Catholic theologian, Ignaz von Döllinger,[91] and

from an earlier date Pusey's friendship and correspondence with the German Lutheran divine,
Friedrich Augustus Tholuck.[92]

The Tractarian Newman gradually entertained
reservations about the theoretical basis as well as
the practical application of the "branch theory."
Newman's review of Palmer of Worcester's work
in the High Church *British Critic* in 1838 was less
commendatory than a first reading might suggest. Newman may have found it a useful contribution to the *via media*, claiming it to be a theory
"at once conformable to the ancient doctrine on
the subject and to the necessities of the modern English communion."[93] However, Newman
also questioned the apparent limitations of this
"static" conception of Catholicity based on mere
apostolicity. In his review, he implicitly criticized
Palmer's apparent detachment of Catholicity
from doctrinal questions. "What," Newman asked,
"becomes of the Notes of the Church? What purpose do they serve? What relief and guidance
is afforded to the inquiring mind, if the church
thus indicated preaches Popery in Rome and
Zwingli-Lutheranism in England? The difficulty is
certainly considerable."[94] It might here be suggested that this was already a difficulty for Newman
but not for Palmer of Worcester and other moderate early Tractarians closer to the old High Church
tradition. However, Newman had highlighted the
Achilles heel of the "branch theory" that did not
appear to offer a secure *locus standi* against Rome.
As Christopher Dawson observed:

> In the eyes of a man like Palmer, to leave
> the Church of England for the Church of
> Rome was a damnable act of apostasy, but
> considered in the light of his own theory
> it would seem to be a very small matter

88 See Jeremy Morris, "French Catholics and the Oxford Movement," in: Stewart J. Brown & Peter B. Nockles, eds., *The Oxford Movement: Europe and the Wider World (1830–1930)*, Cambridge, Cambridge University Press, 2012, 203–220. Gondon, the author of an influential book, *Du mouvement religieux en Angleterre: ou Les progrès du catholicisme et le retour de l'Église anglicane a l'unité*, Leuven, C.-J. Fonteyn, 1844, has been claimed as "probably the first Catholic on the Continent to have seriously studied the Oxford Movement"; Jan De Maeyer & Karel Strobbe, "The Oxford Movement in Nineteenth-Century Belgium," in: Brown & Nockles, eds., *The Oxford Movement*, 185–202, here 188.
89 Marvin R. O'Connell, "Politics and Prophecy: Newman and Lamennais," in: Ian T. Ker & Alan G. Hill, eds., *Newman after a Hundred Years*, Oxford, Clarendon Press, 1990, 176–191, here 184. See also, Eric Lafferty, "A Channel Apart: Contrasting John Henry Newman and Félicité Lamennais on the Dilemna of Church and State in the Nineteenth Century," *Newman Studies Journal* 16/1, 2019, 28–50.
90 Wheeler, *Palmer's Pilgrimage*, 43–63.
91 See Angela Berlis, "Ignaz von Döllinger and the Anglicans," in: Brown & Nockles, eds., *The Oxford*

Movement, 236–248.
92 Albrecht Geck, "Pusey, Tholuck and the Reception of the Oxford Movement in Germany," in: Brown & Nockles, eds., *The Oxford Movement*, 168–184.
93 [John Henry Newman,] "Palmer's *Treatise on the Church of Christ*," *British Critic* 24, 1838, 347–372.
94 [Newman,] "Palmer's *Treatise*," 203.

indeed – nothing more, in fact, than a mere change of perch, from one branch to another.[95]

Elsewhere, Newman had already begun to inject a less narrow and insular perspective into Tractarian discourse. Thus, as Newman put it in no. 71 of the *Tracts for the Times*, the *sacramentum unitas* which he defined as essential to preservation of the purity of the faith had been "shattered in the great schism of the sixteenth century." In consequence, Newman argued that "since that era at least, Truth has not dwelt simply and securely in any visible Tabernacle." The divisions between East and West meant that the church no longer retained the gift of indefectibility. Moreover, Newman even conceded that the Church of England was "in a measure in that position which we fully ascribe to her Latin sister, in captivity."[96] More traditional High Churchmen took offence and Newman was criticized for "instilling a habit of viewing our church … from above, and from without."[97]

Newman's move towards a Roman Catholic vision of the church was a product of his wrestling with finding a necessary balance between the center and periphery of authority and unity within the church.[98] His misgivings about the essentially territorial and non-doctrinal nature of the traditional High Church Anglican ecclesiology enshrined in the "branch theory" surfaced in 1839. His doubts were first raised through his study of the history of the Monophysite controversy of the 5th century and secondly the impact on him of an article in the *Dublin Review* by Nicholas Wiseman, a spearhead of the Roman Catholic Revival in England at the time, in which he suggested that according to St. Augustine's principle of Catholicity,

securus judicat orbis terrarium, the orb of the whole Catholic Church judges securely. By this reading, High Church Anglicans were, like St. Augustine's opponents, the North African Donatists, guilty of upholding a false local position against a universal Catholicism.[99] Moreover, Wiseman, archbishop of Westminster and appointed cardinal in 1850, argued that a breach of unity of schism inevitably led to or was accompanied by heresy and heterodoxy. Far from being merely heterodox elements within the Church of England as Newman at this time assumed, they were an inevitable expression of the Church of England's inherently schismatic nature. For Newman, the Oxford Movement's original preoccupation with apostolicity was thus undermined by an appeal to Catholicity or universality, and his theory of the *via media* was, in his own words, "absolutely pulverized."[100]

Newman continued a rear-guard defense of Anglicanism, notably in an article "The Catholicity of the Church" in the *British Critic* in 1840. In spite of the body blows his ecclesiastical theory had received in the previous year, he still restated a muted form of the "branch theory" of the church. Thus, he still presented the Anglican theory that "each church is naturally independent of every other and that each bishop was a complete channel of grace, and ultimate center of unity."[101] In fact, descent from the primitive church – apostolicity – conferred an invisible unity which made visible unity a secondary consideration, the view which Daubeny and Palmer of Worcester had upheld. Yet in the article one finds Newman in effect arguing with himself and seeking to resolve his own growing doubts. The "Anglican view" was presented in a detached way indicative of its increasingly tenuous hold on him. Newman needed a new balance in grappling with the issue of the basis of both the unity and authority of the

95   Christopher Dawson, *The Spirit of the Oxford Movement and Newman's Place in History*, London, Saint Austin Press, 2001, 104.

96   *Tracts* 3, 29.

97   George Ayliffe Poole, *The Present State of Parties in the Church of England*, London, Burns, 1842, 22.

98   See C. Michael Shea, "Ecclesiology: The Polycentric Church," in: Aquino & King, eds., *The Oxford Handbook of John Henry Newman*, 318–334.

99   [Nicholas Wiseman,] "The Anglican Claim of Apostolical Succession," *Dublin Review* 7, 1839, 138–180.

100   John Henry Newman, *Apologia pro vita sua*, London, Longman, Green, Longman, Roberts & Green, 1864, 212.

101   [John Henry Newman,] "The Catholicity of the English Church," *British Critic* 27, January 1840, 40–88, here 74.

church and to rein in some of his younger more "Romanizing" followers such as William George Ward and Oakeley. The latter were soon making visits to the English Roman Catholic seminary at Oscott near Birmingham. They were vulnerable to the blandishments and overtures of Wiseman, now a bishop, especially thanks to his influential *Letter on Catholic Unity* addressed to the Earl of Shrewsbury (1841).[102] Generally speaking, the literature on what has been called "Continental Church Tourism" reveals by the 1840s the susceptibility of this group to the devotional and liturgical richness of European Catholicism when they encountered it.[103] Frederick William Faber's *Sights and Thoughts in Foreign Churches* (1842) and Thomas Allies' *Journal in France* (1850) were classics of this genre.[104]

Michael Shea has revealed the extent of the Vatican's Propaganda Fide Congregation's interest in and the knowledge of the Oxford Movement thanks to English Roman Catholic reports from Wiseman and Charles Baggs[105] and articles in French and Italian religious journals, notably the *Annali delle scienze religiose.* Wiseman was following events closely, and Shea shows that Wiseman probably tipped the scales and made the Oxford Movement a priority in the Vatican despite the lack of enthusiasm from the four heads of the English vicariates or Irish ordinaries.[106] In short, as Shea argues, this evidence suggests "a reason why authorities in Rome began to privilege Oxford converts in their missionary strategy."[107] However, of course for Wiseman and Baggs there was a clear assumption and expectation that an approximation towards Catholic union among the Oxford divines

meant submission to Rome. According to Baggs in an article in the *Annali* in 1842,[108] Newman and his school "do not know how to discover another way to avoid the growing misbelief of Protestant rationalism, other than by the rapprochement of the Anglican Church with Rome."[109]

On the other hand, for most Anglican High Churchmen, any such approximation "meant a reconciliation of all Christians, Roman, Greek, English, Protestant, on the basis of the primitive church, before it was unhappily split into rival communions."[110] In short, "Catholic union" meant different things to Roman Catholic and High Church Anglican controversialists.

Newman's new attempt at striking and resetting the balance between unity and authority would prove a crucial step towards the final death knell of his *via media* hypothesis. In Newman's eyes the crucial test for the tenability of the *via media* and "branch theory" hypotheses came with his publication in 1841 of *Tract* 90, in which he attempted to reconcile "Catholic" teaching, that is the faith of the primitive church as he viewed it, with the Church of England's Thirty-Nine Articles (1563). Newman drew on an earlier ecumenical attempt to reconcile the Tridentine Decrees with the Thirty-Nine Articles formulated by the Franciscan convert Christopher Davenport, also known as Franciscus a Sancta Clara, chaplain to Queen Henrietta Maria at the court of King Charles I. The close parallels between *Tract* 90 and Sancta Clara's *Paraphrastica expositio articulorum confessionis*

---

102   N.P. Wiseman, *A Letter on Catholic Unity, Addressed to the Right Hon. the Earl of Shrewsbury*, London, Dolman, 1841.

103   Morris, *The High Church Revival*, 107–134.

104   Frederick William Faber, *Sights and Thoughts in Foreign Churches and among Foreign Peoples*, London, J.G.F. & J. Rivington, 1842; Allies, *Journal in France.*

105   Charles Baggs was later bishop of the Western District.

106   Shea, *Newman's Early Roman Catholic Legacy*, 37.

107   Shea, *Newman's Early Roman Catholic Legacy*, 38.

108   Charles Baggs, "Some Answer to the Inquiry: Why do you Become a Catholic? etc., cioè: Alcuna risposta alla domanda: Perché voi siete divenuto cattolico? In una lettera indirizzata a un amico Riccardo Waldo Sibthorp," *Annali delle Scienze Religiose* 14, 40, 1842, 61–85.

109   Baggs, "Some Answer to the Inquiry," cited in: Shea, *Newman's Early Roman Catholic Legacy*, 44–45.

110   Robert Owen, *An Apology for the "High Church" Movement on Liberal Principles: Containing a Reply to Some Statements Made in Parliament, in a Letter to John Williams Esq.*, Oxford, J.H. Parker, 1851, 8.

Anglicanae (1636)[111] have been explored by Kenneth Parker and Michael J.G. Pahls. Parker has shown how Newman's use of a copy of Sancta Clara's treatise in the library of Oriel College, Oxford, confirms Newman's knowledge and use of the commentary.[112] Parker and Pahls demonstrate that the affinities between the two works reveal Newman's debt to this 17th-century Roman Catholic divine for his own exposition of the Thirty-Nine Articles in 1841.

The real relevance of Newman's *Tract* 90 for ecumenical history however lies in whether *Tract* 90, as Parker and Pahls postulate, represented Newman's last best effort to uphold Anglicanism – the standard interpretation – or whether it was a new venture and challenge to force his own university and the Anglican episcopate to acknowledge his creative vision of Anglican Catholicity which was open to reunion with the Roman Catholic Church.[113] Whichever it was, and Parker and Pahls suggest that it could have been both, there is no doubt that the hostile reaction to *Tract* 90 represented a damaging blow to Newman's residual faith in Anglicanism and one which had implications for Newman's ecumenical outlook. Apostolicity had to be matched by Catholicity. Newman had sought to test and prove to himself whether the Church of England retained the content of Catholicism as well as retaining apostolicity. The negative reaction to the *Tract* fatally undermined that claim. However, the impact of that hostile reaction on Newman and his personal religious journey can be overestimated. Certainly, some of his "Romanizing" followers took it as a green light for ecumenical dialogue with continental Catholics. William George Ward

wrote anonymously to the French Ultramontane paper *L'Univers*, claiming that the eyes of Catholic Europe were focused on England and that there was a general expectation "that the hour of her reunion is at hand."[114] Newman, on the other hand, was much less sanguine. For even in the wake of the condemnation of *Tract* 90 he still assumed that any rapprochement with Rome must involve the precondition of Rome reforming itself. As he told the Irish Catholic priest and professor of church history at Maynooth, Charles Russell, who was to play a part in his eventual conversion to Rome,

> my only anxiety is lest your branch of the Church should not meet us by those reforms which surely are *necessary*. It never could be, that so large a portion of Christendom should have split off from the communion of Rome, and kept up a protest for 300 years for nothing.[115]

It is significant in ecclesiological terms that even in *Tract* 90 Newman still used the term "Church of Rome." The Roman Catholic ecumenist de Lisle took great exception to this. De Lisle admitted that the Church of Rome was indeed "the Mother and Mistress of all Churches" but insisted that "it would be as absurd to call the Church of France the Church of Rome, as it would be to say that a man's head was the same as his arms or legs."[116]

---

111 A new edition of *Paraphrastica Expositio Articulorum Confessionis Anglicanae* edited by Frederick George Lee was published in 1865 by J.T. Hayes.

112 Michael J.G. Pahls & Kenneth L. Parker, "Tract 90: Newman's Last Stand or a Bold New Venture," in: Stewart J. Brown, Peter B. Nockles & James Pereiro, eds., *The Oxford Handbook of the Oxford Movement*, Oxford, Oxford University Press, 2017, 304–319, here 305.

113 Pahls & Parker, "Tract 90," 317.

114 Wilfrid Ward, *William George Ward and the Oxford Movement*, London, Macmillan & Co., 1989, 187. Whereas Wilfrid Ward attributed this letter to his father William George Ward, Henry R.T. Brandreth argues that the more likely and plausible correspondent was Newman's disciple John Dobree Dalgairns. See Henry R.T. Brandreth, *The Œcumenical Ideals of the Oxford Movement*, London, SPCK, 1947, 2.

115 J.H. Newman to C. Russell, Apr 26, 1841, in: Newman, *The Letters and Diaries of John Henry Newman*, vol. 8, ed. Gerard Tracey, Oxford, Clarendon Press, 1999, 82.

116 Ambrose Phillipps de Lisle, *Some Remarks on a Letter Addressed to the Reverend R.W. Jelf, D.D., Canon of Christ Church, in Explanation of No. 90*, London, C. Dolman, 1841, 6.

The Oxford Movement's ecumenical model, focused as it was on the historic three branches of the universal church with episcopacy as its binding prerequisite, left little space for or even interest in non-episcopal continental Protestant Churches let alone English Nonconformist bodies. In fact the Oxford Movement's rallying in defense of what were called "church principles" meant a defense of them against Protestant Dissent or Nonconformity and the continental Protestant Churches.[117] The Tractarians dissociated themselves from and repudiated any previous rapport which the 18th-century Evangelical revival had established between certain elements in the Church of England and Protestant Dissent, as exemplified in the nondenominational BFBS. Pre-Tractarian High Churchmen had already distanced themselves from it on the basis of their view of the lack of ecclesial credentials of Protestant Dissent. The Tractarians would take this further. One of the signs of Newman's move from his own early Evangelicalism and relative lack of concern over ecclesiological issues to a more High Church position where such concerns became paramount had been represented by his own withdrawal from the BFBS in 1830.[118]

Not surprisingly, Tractarian championship of an exclusivist model of church unity and of the "branch theory", as for example by Robert Wilberforce in his *Tract on Christian Unity* (1842)[119] and Henry Manning in his *The Unity of the Church* (1842)[120] met with a vigorous Low Church and Evangelical response.[121] In his preface to his own archidiaconal charge, also entitled *The Unity of the Church* (1840),[122] Julius Charles

Hare, archdeacon of Lewes, argued against his friend and neighboring archdeacon Manning's position that conformity to specific beliefs and external ordinances was essential to church unity, and against identifying the unity of the church with mere uniformity, arguing instead for a spirit of Catholic "comprehension."[123] Hare's insistence that the unity of the church should not be equated or confounded with uniformity and was not dependent on external church organization or government, became a familiar Broad Church trope but one which resonated also with moderate High Churchmen.[124] One anti-Tractarian polemicist, clearly affronted by the Tractarian "unchurching" of non-episcopal churches, listed its doctrine of the "Unity of the Church" as one of the eight "Scripture Truths" most undermined by the teaching of the Oxford Movement.[125]

Continental non-episcopal Protestants particularly seized upon the Tractarian doctrine of the church as a basis for unity in their strictures. As the Genevan Calvinist theologian and pastor Jean-Henri Merle d'Aubigné argued in a lecture on Tractarianism, unity and holiness were marks of the invisible church but not of its visible or external form. A divine institution and a divine authority were indeed attributes pertaining to the essence of the church "but by no means to its form," the latter being dismissed as a "narrow bigotry."[126] The pan-Protestant ecumenical EA, in

117   Brandreth, *The Œcumenical Ideals*, 60.
118   Zuijdwegt, *An Evangelical Adrift*, 246.
119   R. Wilberforce, *Christian Unity*, London, Burns, 1842.
120   Manning, *The Unity of the Church*.
121   William Hamilton Turner, *The Tractarian Doctrine of Christian Unity Not the Doctrine of the Gospel: A Reply to the Rev. H.W. Wilberforce's Tract on Christian Unity*, London, J. Nisbet & Co., 1842.
122   Julius Charles Hare, *The Unity of the Church: A Sermon Preacht at St. Peter's Church, Brighton on Thursday, December 10, 1840*, London, J.W. Parker, 1845, bound

with Julius Charles Hare, *The Duty of the Church in Times of Trial*, London, J.W. Parker, 1848.
123   Mary Louise McIntyre, "Julius Charles Hare on the Catholic Revival: 'Signs of Hope,'" *AEH* 75, 2006, 224–244, here 240–241.
124   For example, see Lewis Borrett White, *The Unity of the Church: A Sermon Preached before the University of Oxford, on Sunday, June 21, 1868*, London, T. Fellowes, 1868, 14–15.
125   John Eliot Howard, *Eight Lectures on the Scriptural Truths Most Opposed by Puseyism*, London, Longman, Brown, Green & Longmans, 1845.
126   Jean-Henri Merle d'Aubigné, *Geneva and Oxford: A Discourse Delivered at the Opening Meeting of the Theological School of Geneva, October 3, 1842*, London, W.H. Dalton, 1842, 60.

which d'Aubigné was a leading light and which had many Anglican Evangelical adherents, was predicated on a model of church unity that privileged the invisible over the visible church. It sought to unite in alliance all those whose heritage was the Protestant Reformation and who upheld the principle of *sola scriptura*, along with the doctrines of the atonement, incarnation, salvation by faith alone, and the agency of the Holy Spirit.[127] It cut across ecclesiastical and denominational boundaries, but its primary aim was Evangelical spiritual unity. This was interpreted as unity against Roman Catholicism and all that the Oxford Movement was perceived to stand for. As d'Aubigné put it in a letter to the archbishop of Canterbury, union between the Church of England and continental Protestant Churches had to be on "the basis of our common Protestantism" and in a spirit of "unity against Popery and its incursions." The unity of the church, he insisted, against Tractarians and Roman Catholics, was spiritual and invisible, not external and hierarchical, representing "the church of the New Testament," whereas the Tractarian and Roman model, he claimed, "produces a legal church, which reverts to the principles of the Old Testament dispensation."[128]

6   The Oxford Movement and the Jerusalem Bishopric: An Ecumenical Test Case

In this context, the Jerusalem bishopric, an Anglo-Prussian venture, the brainchild of Christian Karl Josias Baron von Bunsen, the Prussian ambassador to Great Britain and his evangelical monarch King Frederick William IV, was established in late 1841. Bunsen, who had an almost utopian ecumenical vision, had long been concerned about the religious divisions among Christian nations, and his scheme was designed to heal division. The measure provided for the nomination, alternatively by the Crowns of England and Prussia, of a bishop to minister to members of the Church of England and German Protestants in Jerusalem and the Holy Land, including Syria, Chaldea, Egypt, and Abyssinia, with the archbishop of Canterbury having an absolute right of veto with regard to those nominated by the Prussian crown.[129] In fact, the original official document establishing the bishopric bore an air of Anglican triumphalism, which was clearly resented by German Lutherans who feared an attempt to "episcopalianize the Church of Prussia." For it was stated that, "we may reasonably hope that it may lead the way to an essential unity of discipline, as well as of doctrine, between our own church and the less perfectly constituted churches of Europe."[130]

Many Anglican High Churchmen supported the scheme because of its potential for extending episcopacy in Protestant Europe, with the confident expectation that it might lead to "a joyful and ready adoption of more regular church government on the part of the German Protestants."[131] It was hoped that this development in turn might encourage German Roman Catholics to meet "us … halfway in intercommunion" after undergoing a reformation themselves.[132] Even the Tractarian Pusey initially hoped that the Jerusalem bishopric might allow for the purification of the Prussian Church through the restoration of episcopacy, arguing that

---

127 William Richey Hogg, *Ecumenical Foundations: A History of the International Missionary Council and Its Nineteenth-Century Background*, New York NY, Harper, 1952, 36.

128 Jean-Henri Merle d'Aubigné, *A Letter to the Archbishop of Canterbury on the Grounds of Union between the Church of England and Foreign Churches Holding the Essentials of Christian Truth*, London, Seeleys, 1851, 7–10.

129 John Mason Neale, ed., *Documents Connected with the Foundation of the Anglican Bishopric at Jerusalem, and with the Protest against Bishop Gobat's proselytism*, London, J. Masters, 1853, 7.

130 Neale, ed., *Documents Connected with the Foundation*, 6.

131 John Hamilton Gray, *Letter to the Right Hon. and Rev. the Lord Bishop of London: On the State of Anglican Congregations in Germany*, London, J.G.F. & J. Rivington, 1843, 7.

132 Gray, *Letter to the Right Hon. And Rev. the Lord Bishop of London*, 32.

"it may be, that through us what is lacking in them to the full gifts of a church is to be supplied."[133] The Broad Churchman, Archdeacon Julius Hare, a friend and correspondent of Bunsen, shared this vision, expressing the hope that "our church might be enabled to aid in perfecting the discipline and constitution of the Reformed Churches on the Continent."[134] There was an attempt to reconcile the scheme with the Anglican "branch theory." Thus for Walter Farquhar Hook, the placing of "a Bishop of our own Church in Jerusalem" was not an act of usurpation but merely the sending of "a Representative of the English Church, in a land where such conduct is tolerated with respect to other branches of the Catholic Church."[135]

Tractarian concerns focused on the apparent novelty and violation of traditional ecclesiastical order which they eventually detected in Bunsen's scheme. For Newman's friend and correspondent James Hope (later Hope-Scott), it represented "a plan for gathering up the scraps of Christendom and making a new church out of them."[136] Tractarians were alarmed because they sensed that for Bunsen the proposed bishopric was "the foundation of a new body which was to supplant eventually all the other portions of the Church."[137] This was a view which was to receive its fullest expression in Bunsen's *The Constitution of the Church of the Future* (1847).[138]

On the other hand, Anglican Evangelicals holding a Christian Zionist eschatological perspective regarded the scheme as a means of converting Jews to Christianity as well as a check on what they regarded as Tractarian pretensions.[139] Furthermore, Anglican latitudinarians, echoing Bunsen himself, viewed it as potentially realizing an ideal of an undogmatic Broad Church. Archdeacon Hare's vision of "unity not uniformity" in church relations was at one with that of Bunsen.[140]

While the foundational documents of the Jerusalem bishopric show that it was not established with the intention of proselytizing Christians from the ancient churches of the area,[141] its later history reveals that precisely this charge was levelled against Samuel Gobat, a successor to the first Anglican bishop, Michael Solomon Alexander, including by the High Church bishop of Exeter, Henry Phillpotts.[142] In fact, Hare had envisaged as much when he expressed the hope that the opportunities afforded for communication and connection with the ancient Churches of the East might become means of imparting to them "a purer doctrine and ritual and a more spiritual faith."[143] It was precisely the fears of this eventuality and what he deplored as the unholy alliance with nonepiscopal Protestants, Lutherans, and Calvinists

---

133   Edward Bouverie Pusey, *The Articles Treated on in Tract 90 Reconsidered and Their Interpretation Vindicated in a Letter to the Rev. R.W. Jelf, D.D.*, Oxford, J.H. Parker, 1841, 27.

134   Julius Charles Hare, *The Means of Unity: A Charge to the Clergy of the Archdeaconry of Lewes, Delivered at the Ordinary Visitation in 1842*, London, J.W. Parker, 1847, 38.

135   Walter Farquhar Hook, *Reasons for Contributing Towards the Support of an English Bishop at Jerusalem: Stated in a Letter to a Friend*, London, J.G.F. & J. Rivington, 1842, 11.

136   Robert Ornsby, *Memoirs of James Robert Hope-Scott of Abbotsford*, vol. 1, London, J. Murray, 1884, 305.

137   Henry P. Liddon, *Life of Edward Bouverie Pusey*, vol. 2, London, Longmans & Green, 1894, 256–257.

138   C.C.J. von Bunsen, *The Constitution of the Church of the Future: A Practical Explanation of the Correspondence*

with the Right Honourable William Gladstone, on the German Church, Episcopacy, and Jerusalem*, London, Longmans, Brown, Green, & Longmans, 1847.

139   Geoffrey Best, *Shaftesbury*, London, Batsford, 1964, 69–70.

140   Bunsen congratulated Hare on his sermon "Unity and Uniformity" as a complete refutation of the Tractarian theory of church unity; C.C.J. Bunsen to J.C. Hare, Nov 27, 1844, in: Christian Karl Josias von Bunsen, *A Memoir of Baron Bunsen Drawn Chiefly from Family Papers by His Widow, Frances Baroness Bunsen*, ed. Frances Bunsen, vol. 2, London, Longman, Green & Co., 1868, 77.

141   "Statement of Proceedings Relating to the Establishment of a Bishopric of the United Church of England and Ireland in Jerusalem" (Dec 9, 1841), in: Neale, ed., *Documents Connected with the Foundation*, 5–9.

142   H. Phillpotts to W.H. Mill, Oct 24, 1853, in: Neale, ed., *Documents Connected with the Foundation*, 36.

143   Hare, *The Means of Unity*, 38.

NEWMAN AND THE OXFORD MOVEMENT

that led Newman to anathematize the scheme from the start, and for Pusey soon to change his mind for the same reason.[144] Newman's reaction has been branded as "disproportionate, extreme, and vehement"[145] but it was entirely in accord with his own evolving ecclesiological principles and vision of what real church unity embodied. Already in 1840 Newman had commented that a "serious observer" would have more reason to say "let my soul be found with Wesley" than "with Luther" or "with Calvin,"[146] and in his Protest against the Jerusalem Bishopric[147] he referred to Lutheranism and Calvinism as "heresies."

For Newman, to form "a special league" with "foreign Protestants" was not a brand of ecumenism which he had any wish to promote. He felt that the archbishop of Canterbury's sanctioning of the scheme was "to prejudice our title to be a branch of the Apostolic Church."[148] Newman's vision of Anglican Catholicity was rendered dead by the public endorsement of the scheme. What Newman also deplored was the fact that the German liturgy was to be allowed, and in order to be ordained by the bishop any Germans would have to signify their acceptance of the Lutheran Confession of Augsburg. This went against the original idea pushed by High Church Anglican supporters of the project that German Lutheran pastors laboring in the Holy Land would have to accept Anglican ordination. It was Bunsen who rescinded this proposal in favor of an insistence that the Lutheran service and Confession of Augsburg were to be used by German Lutheran congregations and converts. Bunsen had made clear to the Anglican side "that they must act in a *catholic* and

not in an *Anglican* sense," and that they ought to adhere to the principle of "unity in principle with national individuality."[149] Radically alternative views of ecumenical relations and church unity clashed here. Hare took a similar view to Bunsen's and privately criticized Newman's letter of protest to the bishop of Oxford against the Jerusalem bishopric as "the hateful fruit" of "episcopolatry," expressing astonishment at Newman's "audacity" in labelling "those doctrines heretical which almost all the great divines of our church" had considered to be "among the best expositions of the truth."[150]

7   The Oxford Movement without Newman, and Ecumenism (1845–1857)

Historians have debated as to how far the Oxford Movement "died" in 1845 with Newman's departure for Rome or in 1850/1851 after the Gorham Judgment and Manning's defection.[151] For some contemporaries, notably Richard William Church, the loss of Newman represented a "catastrophe," and for many others, notably the converts to Rome, this marked the culmination and *denouement* of the Oxford Movement. Its providential work as paving the way for its followers to join the Roman Catholic fold was apparently complete. The Oxford Movement converts to Rome had decisively rejected the Anglican "branch theory" as untenable and claimed it to be a mere theoretical construct and one not realized in fact or reality.

144   Mark D. Chapman, "The Oxford Movement, Jerusalem and the Eastern Question," in: Brown & Nockles, eds., *The Oxford Movement*, 221–235.

145   Frank M. Turner, *John Henry Newman: The Challenge to Evangelical Religion*, New Haven CT, Yale University Press, 2002, 395.

146   [John Henry Newman,] "Memoirs of the Countess of Huntingdon," *British Critic* 56, 1840, 264.

147   See Newman, *Apologia*, 265ff.

148   Newman, *Apologia*, 250.

149   C.C.J. Bunsen to F. Bunsen, July 13, 1841, in: Christian Karl Josias von Bunsen, *Memoirs of Baron Bunsen*, ed. Frances Bunsen, vol. 1, London, Longmans, Green & Co., 1868, 608 (italics original).

150   N. Merrill Distad, *Guessing at Truth: The Life of Julius Charles Hare (1795–1855)*, Shepherdstown WV, Patmos Press, 1979, 164. For discussion of Hare's rejection of what Paul Avis calls Newman's "Apostolic Paradigm" in determining church relations, see Avis, *Anglicanism and the Christian Church*, 280–287, esp. (for Hare's attack on Newman) 283–286.

151   See James Pereiro, "Did the Oxford Movement Die in 1851?," in: Brown, Nockles & Pereiro, eds., *The Oxford Handbook of the Oxford Movement*, 557–570.

The Anglican Church *qua* church, it was claimed, could not *as a whole* "deliver to men any belief as to where the Catholic Church at this moment is."[152] In fact, from the standpoint of the converts, the position of Low Churchmen, for whom doctrine provided the invisible but real spiritual bond and basis of union regardless of denomination, was actually more tenable than that of High Churchmen and Tractarians who remained loyal to the Church of England.[153] Moreover, many of the Tractarian converts were consumed by disdain and bitterness against the Anglican Communion which they had left, an attitude which did not always characterize continental Catholics who lacked personal knowledge of the Church of England. As Newman put it in a letter to Thomas Allies, when the latter was contemplating this step,

> the position of those who leave it in the only way in which I think it justifiable to leave it, is necessarily one of *hostility* to it. To leave it merely as a branch of the Catholic Church, for another which I liked better, would have been to desert without reason the post where Providence put me. It is impossible, then, but that a convert, if justifiable in the grounds of his conversion, must be an enemy of the communion he has left, and more intensely so than a foreigner who knows nothing about that communion at all.[154]

For Newman at this time and a majority of the recent converts, Ultramontane ideas prevailed, and the concept of corporate reunion was shunned.

However, for a majority of his followers, there was life after Newman. For them, the Oxford Movement had merely entered a new phase, with its ecumenical dimension eventually becoming more rather than less evident. Newman's own relationship to Anglican High Churchmanship and Tractarianism was regarded by some as always provisional and tangential, and his "loss" was readily explained away by those he left behind, with a few in a later generation even making the farfetched claim that the Oxford Movement would have happened without him or that he "captured" a preexisting movement.[155] The most recent scholarship debunks this myopic view and also points to the endurance of Tractarianism beyond Newman's departure.[156] In fact, Newman himself privately acknowledged that the Oxford Movement would outlive his own Anglican life. As he candidly conceded to de Lisle in a letter of July 1857: "I perfectly agree with you in thinking that the movement of 1833 is not over in the country, whatever be the state of Oxford itself."[157]

In the immediate aftermath of Newman's secession, which had been preceded by that of William George Ward, there was a temporary lull in Tractarian Anglican support for de Lisle's reunionist scheme, while on the Roman Catholic side any enthusiasm also waned.[158] The Tractarian party in the Church of England was preoccupied in holding its ground and reassembling. There were intra-church controversies such as the protest

152   Thomas W. Allies, *The See of St. Peter: The Rock of the Church, the Source of Jurisdiction, and the Centre of Unity*, London, Burns & Lambert, 1850, 152.

153   William Dodsworth, *Anglicanism Considered in its Results*, London, W. Pickering, 1851, 19.

154   J.H. Newman to T.W. Allies, Feb 20, 1849, in: Thomas W. Allies, *A Life's Decision*, London, Kegan Paul & Co., 1880, 176.

155   This was the extraordinary claim made by Frederick Meyrick, one of the founders of the ecumenical ACS. See Frederick Meyrick, *Memories of Life at Oxford: And Experiences in Italy, Greece, Turkey, Germany, Spain and Elsewhere*, London, J. Murray, 1903, 26; Frederick Meyrick, *Old Anglicanism and Modern Ritualism*, London, Skeffington, 1901, 231.

156   See George Herring, *The Oxford Movement in Practice: The Tractarian Parochial World from the 1830s to the 1870s*, Oxford, Oxford University Press, 2016; Peter B. Nockles, "Newman's Tractarian Receptions," in: Frederick D. Aquino & Benjamin J. King, eds., *Receptions of Newman*, Oxford, Oxford University Press, 2015, 137–155, here 148.

157   J.H. Newman to A.P. de Lisle, July 1, 1857, in: Purcell, *Life and Letters of Ambrose Phillipps de Lisle*, vol. 1, 368.

158   Elizabeth Bridget Stuart, "'Unjustly Condemned?' Roman Catholic Involvement in the APUC (1857–1864)," *JEH* 41, 1990, 44–63.

against Renn Dickson Hampden's appointment to the see of Hereford (1847), the Gorham Judgment (1850), restoration of Convocation (1854) and the Eucharistic controversy and legal case triggered by George Anthony Denison. On the Anglican side, it was only from the mid to late 1850s onwards that the impulse to ecumenical initiative revived.

With the demise of the overt "Romanizers" among Newman's followers, there was initially a renewed emphasis among some Tractarians on the need for Rome to undergo reform prior to any Anglican moves towards reunion being likely to bear fruit. Pusey's view that Newman had merely been called to another "vineyard" of the Lord, as expressed in a letter to the *English Churchman*, was not widely shared. In contrast, the Tractarian vicar of St. Paul's Knightsbridge, William James Early Bennett, in another letter in the same issue of the *English Churchman*, expressed his indignation at Newman's departure. In the immediate wake of the conversion of Newman and others, some Tractarian former followers recycled an older High Church rhetoric which maintained that the Roman Catholic Church in England was in schism according to a strict interpretation of the "branch theory," and that any Roman Catholic episcopal consecrations that for England would involve "perpetuating schism," were "illegitimate and confer no canonical mission or jurisdiction."[159] Bennett argued that "what may be a true Church in the patriarchate over which the Bishop of Rome holds lawful and canonical jurisdiction, still may be schismatic when it makes an aggression into a country where such Bishop has no jurisdiction."[160]

The renewed Tractarian reunionist endeavor took an Eastward or Orthodox turn, a trend encouraged by the gradual breakdown of the

Ottoman Empire in Europe and Asia Minor but one which was also an increasing corollary of a Tractarian desire to take issue with the view that the Church of England was a Protestant Church and child of the Reformation while at the same time being cautious about drawing too close to Rome.[161] Yet not all approved of the Don Quixote-like endeavors of Deacon William Palmer, as perhaps befitted Palmer's own ambiguous relationship with the Oxford Movement. It has been argued that pursuing a closer relationship with the Eastern Orthodox Churches was not an attractive option for many.[162] There was the example of Frederick William Faber who in 1842 thought that "the Greek Church in Greece is in very disadvantageous circumstances" with "shabby dirty edifices and ill-clothed priests."[163] Faber conceded that years of Turkish oppression was largely to blame, but his pro-Roman orientation – characteristic of Newman's Tractarian disciples – showed itself in his view that the Greek Church could not compare with the Roman in the quality of its liturgy.[164] While the post-convert Roman Catholic Newman admitted that the "Greek Church" had valid sacraments and authentic orders, it had in his eyes become passive and superstitious, and the Russian Church was merely national or local and thus constituted no objection to the Catholicity of the Roman communion.[165]

By the mid-1840s, however, John Mason Neale as well as Palmer of Magdalen had reoriented Tractarian ecumenical priorities in an eastward direction. Palmer had embarked on a

---

159 Palmer, *Treatise on the Church of Christ*; William Palmer [of Worcester College], *A Letter to N. Wiseman, D.D., Calling Himself Bishop of Melipotamus, Containing Remarks on His Letter to Mr. Newman*, Oxford, J.H. Parker, 1841, 4.

160 William J.E. Bennett, *The Schism of Certain Priests and Others, Lately in Communion with the Church: A Sermon*, London, W.J. Cleaver, 1845, 17.

161 Michael Hughes, "The English Slavophile: W.J. Birkbeck and Russia," *SEER* 82, 2004, 680–706, here 685.

162 Nigel Yates, "Anglicans, Old Catholics and Reformed Catholics in Late Nineteenth-Century Europe," in: Brown & Nockles, eds., *The Oxford Movement*, 249–265, here 249.

163 Faber, *Sights and Thoughts in Foreign Churches*, 583.

164 Faber, *Sights and Thoughts in Foreign Churches*, 590.

165 John Henry Newman, *Lectures on Certain Difficulties Felt by Anglicans in Submitting to the Catholic Church*, London, Burns & Lambert, 1850, lecture XI, "Heretical and Schismatical Bodies No Prejudice to the Catholicity of the Church," 269–294.

correspondence with the Russian Orthodox divine Aleksey Khomyakov with the aim of forging ever closer ties with the Orthodox Churches.[166] It was Neale who drew up and signed a circular letter addressed to the "Most Holy Governing Synod of All the Russia's and to the Holy Kingdom of the Kingdom of Greece" protesting "against the proselytizing proceedings of Bishop Gobat at Jerusalem."[167] For Neale and Palmer, the condescension towards the ancient Eastern Churches by a Broad Churchman like Archdeacon Hare was unacceptable. The eastward ecumenical trend culminated in Palmer's most important contribution to Anglican-Orthodox ecumenical relations, *A Harmony of Anglican Doctrine with the Doctrine of the Catholic and Apostolic Church of the East* (1846).[168] Unfortunately, Palmer was seeking endorsement not so much from mainstream Anglican doctrine but from an unrepresentative minority, the Episcopal Church in Scotland. A more substantial Anglo-Catholic contribution emanated in the following year with Neale's *History of the Holy Eastern Church* (1847).[169] Anglo-Catholic interest in the Eastern Church also took concrete and practical form with the formation of the ECA and the later Oriental ecumenical endeavors of William John Birkbeck, a prominent Anglo-Catholic Russophile and like Palmer coming from Magdalen College, Oxford. Nonetheless, the ecumenical focus of Anglo-Catholics continued primarily to be one of healing divisions within Western Christendom.

8   The APUC and the *Eirenicon* Controversy (1857–1870)

The APUC founded in 1857 by the Rev. Frederick George Lee, a second-generation Tractarian, in conjunction with the Catholic layman de Lisle was the most significant product of renewed Oxford Movement-inspired ecumenical enthusiasm. Mark Chapman, author of the definitive analysis of the rise and fall of the APUC, has described it as "one of the most successful of the eccentric and idiosyncratic private ecumenical initiatives of the mid-nineteenth century."[170] Closely associated with the *Union Newspaper*, and then its replacement the *Union Review*, the APUC was founded by Lee "in the interests of Anglo-Catholicism and Union with Rome."[171] It was born out of a quest for the recovery of the united Christendom of the medieval era. The sidelining of Protestant denominations was intentional. Its Anglo-Catholic protagonists made clear that the society was aiming at "a visible reunion of visible Christendom, and of course we must begin with those who believe in a visible church."[172] Protestant Nonconformists were shunned because, it was argued, they did not understand the nature of a visible church and had rebuffed any overtures made to them – theirs was "the act of the invited guest who scorned the official banquet."[173]

---

166   See William J. Birkbeck, ed., *Russia and the English Church during the Last Fifty Years*, vol. 1, *Containing a Correspondence between Mr. William Palmer, Fellow of Magdalen College, Oxford, and M. Khomiakoff, in the Years 1844–1854*, London, Rivington, Percival & Co., 1895.

167   Neale, ed, *Documents connected with the Foundation*, 7.

168   *A Harmony of Anglican Doctrine with the Doctrine of the Catholic and Apostolic Church of the East*, Aberdeen, A. Brown, 1846.

169   J.M. Neale, *History of the Holy Eastern Church*, 3 vols., London, J. Masters, 1847.

---

170   Mark D. Chapman, "The Fantasy of Reunion: The Rise and Fall of the Association for the Promotion of the Unity of Christendom," *JEH* 58, 2007, 49–73, here 49. See also, Stuart, *Roman Catholic Reactions*, esp. ch. 9.

171   J.H. Newman to J.M. Capes, Apr 6, 1857, in: Newman, *The Letters and Diaries of John Henry Newman*, vol. 18, ed. Charles S. Dessain, Oxford, Oxford University Press, 1968, 12.

172   William H.P. Ward & others, *Corporate Re-Union, not Individual Secession: Two Sermons Preached at the Eleventh Anniversary of the Foundation of the Association for the Promotion of the Unity of Christendom, to which is Added a Report of the Progress of the Association from the Year 1857 to the Year 1868*, London, J.T. Hayes, 1868, 24.

173   Ward & others, *Corporate Reunion, not Individual Session*, 24.

The whole reunionist endeavor was inspired by a rejection of the Protestant polemics of the Reformation era and a belief that disunity was proving the handmaid of religious skepticism. As one protagonist of reunion put it, "common sense was teaching men, that, so long as the apostles of peace were squabbling over trifles and mutually condemning each other as emissaries of the devil, the world would practically decide the disputes by repudiating the claims of all."[174] Reunion was not only presented as a necessary antidote to rising modern skepticism but as a concomitant of holiness. It was a common trope of advocates of reunion that unity and sanctity were linked on one side against anti-doctrinal liberalism and disunion on the other.[175] Nonetheless, Anglican representation in unionist endeavors represented a distinct minority within the Church of England, and even Bishop Alexander Forbes admitted they lacked a definite organization.[176] Moreover, Forbes and Keble withdrew their support for the *Union Newspaper*, Keble on the ground that it was "undutiful to the Church of England."[177]

The APUC contained several English Roman Catholic adherents, notably the converts Henry Nutcombe Oxenham and Edmund Salusbury Ffoulkes as well as de Lisle, who convinced themselves that the George Cornelius Gorham and Denison cases, far from weakening the Oxford Movement and its impetus towards unity, had

given it "new strength."[178] However, the organization was from the first discountenanced by the Ultramontane wing of the Catholic Church, earning the strictures of the *Dublin Review*, which regarded it as a manifestation of Tractarianism, which was "a mockery of its own former self" with Lee as editor of the *Union Review* representing "the forlorn hope of Tractarianism."[179] Moreover, though the APUC regarded itself as a direct descendant of Spencer's Prayer Crusade movement of 1838, and Lee himself described it modestly as but one of "united prayer that visible unity may be restored to Christendom,"[180] Spencer himself refused to join it on the grounds that it appeared to advocate *communicatio in sacris* and because it would lead to a retarding of individual conversions in favor of corporate reunion.[181] In moderating the more overtly pro-Roman tone of the *Union Newspaper*, its successor the *Union Review* antagonized Roman Catholics by its apparent opposition to individual conversions.[182] The *Union Review* remained pro-Roman in its ecumenical outlook, but any transition between communions was downplayed – anyone seeking salvation should go the branch that was most compatible with that individual's conscience.[183] Rather than allowing Newman's conversion to be viewed as a signal for others to follow into the Roman Communion, his example was relativized – one could be as much a Catholic by staying in the Church of England as by going to Rome. It was claimed he was "much more with us than the Newman of 1844" and it was even stated that "Dr. Newman has found the rest which

---

174   "Intercommunion and Reunion," *Union Review* 10, 1872, 18–40, here 21.

175   Alexander P. Forbes, *The Notes of Unity and Sanctity in Reference to Modern Scepticism: A Charge*, London, J. Masters & Son, 1864, 10. On the link between ecumenism and anti-liberalism, see Mark D. Chapman, "An Ecumenical Front against Liberalism: Bishop Alexander Penrose Forbes of Brechin and *An Explanation of the Thirty-Nine Articles*," *JHMTH* 17, 2010, 147–161.

176   A.P. Forbes to V. de Buck, Apr 10, 1869, in: PHL, Liddon Bound Volume 5.

177   Brandreth, *The Œcumenical Ideals*, 33. See Rowan Strong, *Alexander Forbes of Brechin: The First Tractarian Bishop*, Oxford, Clarendon Press, 1995, 196–197.

178   A.P. de Lisle to F.G. Lee, Feb 16, 1857, in: PHL, F.G. Lee Papers, 2/6.

179   See "Catholic Unity and English Parties," *Dublin Review* 43, 1857, 193.

180   Frederick George Lee, *Sermons on the Reunion of Christendom*, London, J.T. Hayes,1864, xi.

181   Stuart, *Roman Catholic Reactions*, 50.

182   Vincent Alan McClelland, "Corporate Reunion: A Nineteenth-Century Dilemma," *TS* 43, 1982, 3–29, here 25.

183   Erik Sidenvall, *After Anti-Catholicism?: John Henry Newman and Protestant Britain (1845–c. 1890)*, London, T&T Clark, 2005, 143.

the Catholic faith alone can give, whether learnt in our own Communion or in that of Rome."[184]

De Lisle was definitely in a minority on the Roman Catholic side in preferring corporate re-union over individual conversion, largely because of his view that the existing Church of England had retained a degree of organic continuity with the church founded by Pope Gregory the Great. Along with Oxenham, he appears to have believed in the validity or at least genuineness of Anglican orders,[185] which Wiseman and others decidedly did not.[186] It has also been claimed that on the doctrine of the Eucharist (Transubstantiation) de Lisle was prepared to give away more than had the Gallican Louis du Pin in his correspondence with Archbishop Wake in the previous century.[187] Moreover, de Lisle conducted a friendly personal correspondence with Bishop Forbes, address-ing him as "my dear and venerated Bishop of Brechin."[188] De Lisle's enthusiasm on the subject of reunion also owed much to the continuing influence of prophecy upon him. However, for Wiseman as for most Catholics de Lisle was suffer-ing from delusion on the subject. As a result of the representations of Wiseman and later of Manning, Catholics were forbidden from membership in the APUC in 1864. This was followed by a rescript from the papal Congregation of the Holy Office against it in 1865 in which the notion of a "branch theo-ry" was condemned,[189] with Manning as Roman

Catholic archbishop of Westminster later fol-lowing up with a pastoral letter on the subject in 1866.[190]

Further ecumenical episodes, notably the de-bate between the Roman Catholic Newman and Anglo-Catholic Pusey over Pusey's three instal-ments of *Eirenica* (1865–1870) and discussions between Bishop Alexander Forbes and the Dutch Jesuit Victor de Buck in the run up to Vatican I, have been more fully treated elsewhere.[191] In his first *Eirenicon*, Pusey restated the traditional Anglican view of the *via media* and the "branch theory" not as a mere insular self-validation but as a means of "restoring visible unity."[192] While he did not expect external unity of communion to be restored in his own lifetime, he urged that it was "an end to be wished for, and prayed for."[193] He was also keen to establish the compatibility of the Anglican Thirty-Nine Articles with the Roman Catholic decrees of the Council of Trent, in part not only echoing the then Anglican Newman's argument in *Tract* 90 but in some respects going beyond it. Pusey's ecumenical approach was pre-mised on his belief that the impaired commu-nion between the Churches of England and Rome might be restored without sacrificing the claim of either to antiquity.[194]

---

184   "Dr. Newman's Apology," *Union Review* 2, 1864, 506–517, here 515.

185   Allen, "Ambrose Phillipps de Lisle," 21. Oxenham re-tained this belief to the last. See Henry Nutcombe Oxenham, *Recollections of an Old Friend*, Manchester, Guardian Printing Works, 1888, 19.

186   Wilfrid Ward, *The Life and Times of Cardinal Wiseman*, vol. 1, London, Longmans, Green & Co., 1897, 300.

187   Ward, *The Life and Times of Cardinal Wiseman*, vol. 1, 16.

188   A.P. de Lisle to A.P. Forbes, Dec 9, 1869, in: PHL, Liddon Bound Volume 5, letter no. 13.

189   Manning appears to have been unfairly blamed by Anglo-Catholic reunionists for the rescript. See James Pereiro, *Cardinal Manning: An Intellectual Biography*, Oxford, Clarendon Press, 1998, 191–193; Chapman, "The Fantasy of Reunion," 66.

190   Henry Edward Manning, *The Reunion of Christendom: A Pastoral Letter to the Clergy*, London, Longmans, Green, 1866.

191   See Roderick Strange, "Reflections on a Controversy: Newman and Pusey's *Eirenicon*," in: Perry Butler, ed., *Pusey Rediscovered*, London, SPCK, 1983, 332–348; Chapman, *The Fantasy of Reunion*, chs. 3–4, 6–7.

192   See Edward Bouverie Pusey, *An Eirenicon, in a Letter to the Author of "The Christian Year"*, Oxford, J.H. & J. Parker, 1865, i.

193   Pusey, *An Eirenicon*, 98. For developments in Pusey's ecclesiology and ecumenical outlook towards Rome, see Robert H. Greenfield, "Such a Friend to the Pope," in: Butler, ed., *Pusey Rediscovered*, 162–184, here 173–182.

194   Michael J.G. Pahls, "Canterbury's Rejoinder: Pusey, Gladstone, and the Neo-Ultramontanism of Manning," in: Kenneth L. Parker & Michael J.G. Pahls, eds., *Authority, Dogma, and History: The Role of the Oxford Movement Converts in the Papal Infallibility Debates*, Bethesda MD, Academica Press, 2010, 115–128, here 123.

Pusey's *Eirenicon* had been partly a response to the convert Manning's denial of the validity of Anglican orders and of the Church of England to be a true church[195] and Manning's subsequent claim in *The Temporal Mission of the Holy Ghost* (1865) that the infallibility of the once undivided church of the first six centuries, which Pusey himself upheld, was only "infallible to those who lived in those ages, but is not infallible to us."[196] In his own response to Pusey, Newman again put the Anglican "branch theory" on trial, pointing out to his French Catholic correspondent Archbishop Félix-Antoine-Philibert Dupanloup that the Anglo-Catholics represented "just one part of three factions or parties in [the Anglican Communion] which are at present disputing amongst themselves."[197] Since Catholicity for Pusey continued to be defined primarily in terms of a return to the teaching of the early undivided church, this meant that for him it was a second order activity which should only take place after a purification process within all the churches.[198] It was the same for Pusey's disciple Bishop Forbes for whom there had to be a dogmatic as well as organic identity between the Church of England before and after the Reformation, with any future reunion predicated upon the basis of the doctrinal formularies of the once undivided church prior to the separation between East and West.[199] Forbes's *An*

Explanation of the Thirty-Nine Articles (first edition 1867–1868) has been seen as intended "to provide a Catholic interpretation of the standard Anglican formularies in the light of the prospective Vatican Council."[200] Forbes went further than Pusey in apparent moves towards Roman Catholicism, especially in acceptance of the primacy of St. Peter. Pusey made it clear that he did not like the idea – for a time considered – of Forbes attending the forthcoming council.[201]

The Roman Catholic response to the reunion projects of Pusey and Forbes, as illustrated by that of Thomas Allies and Frederick Oakeley remained uncompromising, and the complaint was made that while at one moment the *Eirenicon* was "a profession of peace," it was "at another a declaration of war."[202] Objection was raised to the very notion "of restoring unity in the Church of Christ" as a false admission because, it was claimed, the restoration was not mutual: "When the sheep who have wandered away are brought back by the Good Shepherd, it is they are restored to the Fold, and not the Fold to them."[203] Allies divided those Anglicans who were advocating reunion into two classes. There were those for whom such an advocacy was just a stage or phase in their own conversion process. For these, he argued, unionism represented "a healthy and hopeful stage, in their journey from the bad extreme of contented isolation to the good extreme of humble submission."[204] In fact, Oakeley conceded, all the earlier Tractarian converts to Rome, with the exception of Newman himself, took up the theory of corporate reunion for a time and hoped for "something like a combined movement" before each took their own

---

195 Henry Edward Manning, *The Workings of the Holy Spirit in the Church of England: A Letter to the Rev. E.B. Pusey, D.D.*, London, Longman, Green, Longman, Roberts & Green, 1864, 8. For fuller discussion of Manning's contribution to the controversy over the APUC and Pusey's *Eirenica*, see James Pereiro, "Crossed Visions: The Anglican Manning's Opinion of Rome and the Catholic Manning's Thoughts on Canterbury," in: Vincent Alan McClelland, ed., *By Whose Authority?: Newman, Manning and the Magisterium*, Bath, Downside Abbey, 1996, 204–243, here 224–235.

196 Henry Edward Manning, *The Temporal Mission of the Holy Ghost*, London, Longmans, Green & Co., 1865, 78–79.

197 Cited in Chapman, *The Fantasy of Reunion*, 93.

198 Chapman, "The Oxford Movement," 230.

199 See Alexander P. Forbes, *An Explanation of the Thirty-Nine Articles*, vol. 1, Oxford, J. Parker, ²1871, i–xliii, esp. xl.

200 Strong, *Alexander Forbes of Brechin*, 202.

201 E.B. Pusey to A.P. Forbes, Mar 15, 1869, in: PHL, Liddon Bound Volume 5, letter no. 5.

202 Gerald Molloy, *Doctor Pusey's Eirenicon: A Review*, London, Longmans, Green, Reader & Dyer, 1866, 9.

203 Molloy, *Doctor Pusey's Eirenicon*, 15.

204 [Thomas W. Allies,] "Dr. Pusey's Project of Union," *Dublin Review* 58, 1866, 412–449, here 415.

independent step.[205] The Tractarian Charles Seager, fellow of Worcester College, Oxford, who in 1844 edited the Gallican Pierre François Le Courayer's 18th-century treatise in defense of Anglican orders, prior to his own conversion to Rome, was one example.[206] Francis Diedrich Wackerbarth, author of a plea for church unity composed on the eve of his own conversion to Rome in 1842, was another.[207] Moreover, it seems that Newman's onetime disciple Mark Pattison, fellow of Lincoln College, drew back from Rome as soon as it had become clear that mass corporate conversions to Rome were not a viable option in the febrile atmosphere of 1845.[208] However, there was another class of person, Allies argued, for whom "the project of Union seems a pretext, for ignoring the consequences legitimately deducible from their Church's frightful corruptions; and for shutting their eyes to the peremptory obligation, of fleeing for safety to the Ark of God."[209] Allies clearly had in mind the Anglo-Catholic reunionist supporters of the APUC and *Union Review*. Oakeley made another pertinent point when he argued that corporate reunion presupposed a union of bodies, and that implied a "substantive existence on the part of both the bodies so uniting."[210]

Oakeley maintained that while the presence of this condition was evident on the Roman side, there was no clear principle of cohesion or mark of organization "in the communion with which the Holy See would be invited to enter into ecclesiastical relations" – was its denomination to be "the Established Church, the Anglo-Catholic Church, or the National Church"?[211] Manning was even blunter in highlighting the unrepresentative character of the APUC in relation to the Church of England. Not only did the Church of England itself only represent half the English people, but Manning maintained "that the Anglican school represents only a portion of the Church of England, and that the Anglo-Catholic movement represents only a section of the Anglican school, and that the Unionist movement represents only a fraction of that section."[212] Another Roman Catholic critic of the reunion movement argued that

> no individual in the Anglican Church is competent to accept any terms of Union, except for himself alone. Neither is there any corporate body whose decision, upon such a question, would have any binding force, except for the individuals who compose that body.[213]

The "principle of private judgment," it was claimed, characterized "the Anglican Unionist."[214] Nonetheless, Manning did concede that the impulse to promote reunion among Anglicans was an "impulse of sacramental grace" and was itself "a wonderful reaction from the days within living memory when fidelity to the Church of England was measured by repulsion from the Church of Rome."[215]

---

205   Frederick Oakeley, *The Leading Topics of Dr. Pusey's Recent Work: Reviewed in a Letter Addressed (by Permission) to the Most Rev. H.E. Manning, D.D.*, London, Longmans, Green & Co., 1865, 46–48.

206   Pierre François Le Courayer, *A Dissertation on the Validity of the Ordinations of the English, and of the Succession of the Bishops of the Anglican Church*, Oxford, J.H. Parker, 1844.

207   Wackerbarth was the author of *The Egyptian Bondage: or A Second Call to Union: On the Principles of the Holy Catholic Church, and the Everlasting Gospel of Christ*, London, C. Dolman, 1842, written as he stated in his "Preface" with the "sole object of promoting church unity, while a member of the established Church" (Wackerbarth, *The Egyptian Bondage*, 6) but only published after he had become a Roman Catholic.

208   Fergal Nolan, *A Study of Mark Pattison's Religious Experience (1813–1850)*, Ph.D. thesis, University of Oxford, 1977, 256.

209   [Allies,] "Dr. Pusey's Project of Union," 415–416.

210   Oakeley, *The Leading Topics of Dr. Pusey's Recent Work*, 48.

211   Oakeley, *The Leading Topics of Dr. Pusey's Recent Work*, 48.

212   Manning, *The Reunion of Christendom*, 13.

213   Molloy, *Doctor Pusey's Eirenicon*, 13.

214   [Allies,] "Dr. Pusey's Project of Union," 448.

215   Manning, *The Reunion of Christendom*, 12.

9 Epilogue

Later chapters in the history of Oxford Movementinspired ecumenism, including the role of Frederick Meyrick and the ACS after 1870, the development of Anglican relations with the so-called Old Catholics and Reformed Catholics, and in particular the Bonn union conferences of 1874 and 1875, with their vision for a possible future reorientation of European Christianity, have been ably treated elsewhere.[216] This later period was one of a redefinition of ecumenism away from a focus on Rome and in favor of intercommunion among national churches. The notion of the Anglican Communion comprising a communion of national churches rather than satellite churches of the Church of England took shape.[217] These developments were exemplified by the rise in prominence of anti-Roman and long-term critics of the Tractarian Newman, such as Christopher Wordsworth[218] and Frederick Meyrick, in Anglican ecumenical discussions. Another crucial development was the formulation of the so-called Chicago-Lambeth Anglican Quadrilateral in 1888, originating from the American Episcopalian William Reed Huntington and first defined in his *The Church-Idea: An Essay Towards Unity* (1870) which sought to divest Anglicanism of its inessential Englishness and globalize it.[219] All these ecumenical reorientations, along with the virtual eclipse of Anglican discussion with Roman Catholics for a generation following Vatican I, of which the rapprochement with Old Catholics was a byproduct, lie beyond the chronological scope of this contribution.[220]

10 Conclusions

My treatment of the period from the early modern era down to 1870 has shown that the issue of Anglican and Catholic identity lay at the heart of Newman and the Oxford Movement's ecumenical vision or lack thereof. This contribution has also demonstrated that only in a highly qualified sense can Charles Miller's claim that the "Oxford Movement was an ecumenical movement" be accepted.[221] The movement's later protagonists may have regarded it as such, and its later *Union Review* wing went to some lengths to reconnect with ecumenical overtures from earlier centuries, though sometimes in a highly selective way.[222] Ecumenical overtures tended to be focused on the need for Anglican self-validation with the non-episcopal Reformed and Lutheran continental Churches as well as English Nonconformists effectively "unchurched" and largely ignored, leaving endeavors in that direction mainly to Evangelical and liberal Anglican churchmen. With the exception of the Jerusalem bishopric episode involving the Church of Prussia and its enthusiastic advocacy by Archdeacon Hare and others, any sustained and meaningful High Church Anglican ecumenical engagement with continental Protestants or English Nonconformists postdated the end of the

---

216 Chapman, *The Fantasy of Reunion*, 220–262; Yates, "Anglicans, Old Catholics," 249–265.

217 Mark D. Chapman, "Ecumenism, Mariology and the Papacy," in: Aquino & King, eds., *The Oxford Handbook of John Henry Newman*, 355–372, here 370–371.

218 Christopher Wordsworth, bishop of Lincoln from 1869, had been the author of *Union with Rome: Is not the Church of Rome the Babylon of the Book of Revelation?*, London, Rivington, 1850.

219 Stephen Sykes, "Newman, Anglicanism, and the Fundamentals," in: Ker & Hill, eds., *Newman after a Hundred Years*, 353–374, here 356–357. See Paul Avis's contribution in this volume.

220 See Franz X. Bischof's contribution in this volume.

221 Miller, *Toward a Fuller Vision*, 61.

222 For example, Oxenham in 1877–1879 edited an apparent plea for reunion in 1704 by someone he identified as an Anglican minister, Joshua Bassett, though the authorship and the intentions of the author were disputed by others. See Henry Nutcombe Oxenham, ed., *An Eirenicon of the Eighteenth Century: A Proposal for Catholic Communion, by a Minister of the Church of England*, London, Rivingtons, 1879. Similarly, in 1865 the founder of the APUC, Frederick George Lee, edited Christopher Davenport's *Paraphrastica expositio articulorum confessionis Anglicanae*.

period under review.[223] As late as the 1880s it was being lamented that the Church of England and continental Lutheran Churches had receded from even the aspiration of a unity of sympathy which had characterized the 16th and 17th centuries.[224] While the Oxford Movement was from the start certainly keen to rise above the limitations of a national church and establishment, the basis of its desire for unity was restricted to encompassing only those who adhered to the doctrinal standards of the early and undivided church. There was the practical reality of concrete division within Christendom which remained an obstacle to surmount. The Eastern Churches eventually became a more attractive focus for ecumenical endeavor for many Tractarians, especially when attempted overtures towards Rome stalled. Ultimately reunion foundered on an apparently unbridgeable gulf between an Anglo-Catholic quest for reunion on the basis of a patristic consensus from the once undivided church[225] and a Roman Catholic vision of unity based on allegiance to the papacy as the doctrinal basis and center of authority.

There were relatively few advocates of corporate reunion on the Roman Catholic side to match the preponderance of Anglo-Catholic reunionists in the APUC, with even this small number declining after the papal intervention of 1864/1865.[226] Moreover, the Tractarian converts, Newman included, who came to regard Rome as both the necessary center of unity and seat of a living

infallibility and submission to her as the logical and providential outcome of the Oxford Movement could only ever regard the desire for corporate reunion as a temporary phase on the path to full individual communion with Rome. Ambrose Phillipps de Lisle, however, stands out not only as an enthusiast for corporate reunion with the Church of England but as one who private suggested visionary schemes for the reunion of all Christendom which even encompassed those bodies and pastors which lacked the episcopate and apostolic succession,[227] thus going beyond what Anglo-Catholic reunionists could countenance. De Lisle and Oxenham, nonetheless, were unrepresentative of the great mass of Roman Catholic converts. The Roman Catholic Newman regarded the Protestant and Anglican Churches as cut off from true communion, and he was increasingly doubtful about the validity of Anglican ordinations. He was insistent that the providential direction of the Oxford Movement had not been towards "a branch church."[228] On the other hand, he later speculated that some Anglo-Catholics may providentially have been "kept where they were, with no more light than they have" so that the harvest would be richer when one day it came.[229] One might conclude that Newman's own personal religious journey and lived experience through "the varieties of Christianity" gave a providential ecumenical flavor to his theological outlook as a Catholic,[230] conscious as he always was that "the absence of visible unity between ... different communions is so great a triumph, and so great an advantage to

---

223   A rare exception was Charles Wordsworth's *Reunion of the Church in Great Britain: A Bicentenary Address Delivered at Kidderminster, August 22, 1862*, Edinburgh, R. Grant & Son, 1862.

224   William Ince, *The Luther Commemoration and the Church of England: A Sermon Preached Before the University of Oxford, on Sunday, November 11, 1883*, London, Rivingtons, 1883, 25–27.

225   For Pusey, going beyond even this position, this came to mean "all that was held in common by the Roman Catholic and Eastern Orthodox Churches"; E.B. Pusey to H.E. Manning, Aug 12, 1845, in: PHL, Pusey Papers.

226   See bound volumes "A List of Members" and "Signed Declarations of Membership, 1857 to 1863," in: PHL, APUC Papers.

---

227   A.P. de Lisle to A.P. Forbes, Dec 9, 1869, in: PHL, Liddon Bound Volume 5, letter no. 13.

228   Newman, *Lectures on Certain Difficulties*, lecture VI, "The Providential Direction of the Movement of 1833 not towards a Branch Church," 135–163.

229   J.H. Newman to an unknown correspondent, c. 1871, in: Newman, *The Letters and Diaries of John Henry Newman*, vol. 25, ed. Charles S. Dessain & Thomas Gornall, Oxford, Oxford University Press, 1973, 260.

230   Ian T. Ker, *Newman and the Fullness of Christianity*, Edinburgh, T&T Clark, 1993, 1–9.

the enemies of the Cross."[231] Moreover, Newman's influence on a later generation of Nonconformist and Evangelical writers such as the Scottish Presbyterian divine Alexander Whyte was such that Wilfrid Ward even referred to "a cultus of Cardinal Newman outside the Church."[232] The aged Newman himself regarded this as hopeful sign that, "in spite of the sad divisions of Christendom, a great work is going on in the hearts of serious men tending towards the restoration of the scattered members of Christ, even though not in our day, yet in the future, in the "times and seasons which He has appointed."[233]

As relations and prospects of reunion on any terms with the Latin Western Church declined, other than on the basis of individual submission, so Tractarian Anglican cultivation of relations with the Eastern Churches waxed. However, at the end of our period (Vatican I, 1869–1870), with the declaration of papal infallibility appearing to dash the hopes of Pusey and corporate reunionists, the desire for the reunion of Christendom seemed as far away from realization as it had been at the beginning. Yet we must avoid the condescension of history from a present-centered vantage point. The past can be "another country" and needs to be understood on its own terms and in context, even while the issues raised were for all time. Many of the protagonists in the ecumenical cause may have been visionary enthusiasts whose efforts bore little apparent concrete fulfilment or realization, fighting for a final victory that never came. Nonetheless for them and for those who steered the issue away from corporate reunion to individual submission, deep principles of faith were at stake, while the transition away from an era of religious wars to at least a degree of peaceful understanding and coexistence was a triumph in itself. The hope remained alive that, as Newman put it, the healing of Christendom's divisions would one day arrive in the "times and seasons which He has appointed."

Bibliography

A *History of the Ecumenical Movement*, vol. 1, Ruth Rouse & Stephen C. Neill, eds., 1517–1948, London, SPCK, 1954.

Brandreth, Henry R.T., *The Œcumenical Ideals of the Oxford Movement*, London, SPCK, 1947.

Chapman, Mark D., *The Fantasy of Reunion: Anglicans, Catholics, and Ecumenism (1833–1882)*, Oxford, Oxford University Press, 2014.

Lee, Frederick George, ed., *Essays on the Re-Union of Christendom*, London, J.T. Hayes, 1868.

Palmer [of Magdalen], William, *Notes of a Visit to the Russian Church in the Years 1840, 1841*, ed. John Henry Newman, London, Kegan Paul & Co., 1882.

Pawley, Margaret, *Faith & Family: The Life and Circle of Ambrose Phillipps de Lisle*, Norwich, Canterbury Press, 1993.

---

231 Cited in Avery Dulles, "Newman, Conversion, and Ecumenism," *TS* 51, 1990, 717–731, here 729.

232 Gordon Rupp, "Newman through Nonconformist Eyes," in: John Coulson & Arthur Macdonald Allchin, eds., *The Rediscovery of Newman: An Oxford Symposium*, London, SPCK, 1967, 195–212.

233 Rupp, "Newman through Nonconformist Eyes," 204.

CHAPTER 7

Ignaz von Döllinger and the Bonn Reunion Conferences of 1874–1875

Franz Xaver Bischof

1   Introduction

The reunion conferences that were held in Bonn in 1874–1875 on the initiative and under the chairmanship of Ignaz von Döllinger are among the founding events of the modern ecumenical movement. These conferences were unique on account of their multilateral orientation and met with a wide response, especially in the English-speaking world. Since they were not followed up and failed to elicit any ecclesial response, they are little known today. In the following contribution, they will be described from the perspective of Döllinger's own ecumenical awakening and within the context of the confessional developments of the 19th century, which will be briefly outlined.

The 16th-century reformations entailed the division of Western Christendom and its fragmentation into various confessions, almost all of which went their own ways until the 20th century. Nevertheless, repeated attempts were made to overcome the schism and to regain the lost unity. The 17th and 18th centuries witnessed several attempts at reunion that made considerable progress to a certain extent but remained isolated and failed to gain the agreement of the respective church leaderships.[1] Only under the influence of

the Enlightenment began an irenic phase that was characterized by a decrease in reciprocal polemics and a relative easing of religious tensions. One of the most prominent representatives of such an irenic attitude in Catholic Germany was the moral and pastoral theologian Johann Michael Sailer. With his openness towards devout Protestantism, his cultivation of friendships beyond confessional borders, and his efforts to overcome confessional biases in order to view the confessions primarily from the standpoint of Christ and not from that of the churches, he provided the first "building blocks for an ecumenical path,"[2] even though Sailer himself, who would later become bishop of Regensburg, never really doubted that the Church of Christ could be found only in the Roman Catholic Church.[3] Sailer and his numerous disciples and followers in southern Germany, Austria, and Switzerland, such as the church reformer Ignaz Heinrich von Wessenberg, contributed to the spread of this attitude[4] and exerted a

---

& Kathrin Paasch, eds., *Zwischen theologischem Dissens und politischer Duldung: Religionsgespräche der Frühen Neuzeit*, Göttingen, Vandenhoeck & Ruprecht, 2018.

2   Bertram Meier, *Die Kirche der wahren Christen: Johann Michael Sailers Kirchenverständnis zwischen Unmittelbarkeit und Vermittlung*, Stuttgart, Kohlhammer, 1990, 373.

3   In addition to Meier, see also Franz Georg Friemel, "Johann Michael Sailer und die getrennten Christen," in: Georg Schwaiger & Paul Mai, eds., *Johann Michael Sailer und seine Zeit*, Regensburg, Verlag des Vereins für Regensburger Bistumsgeschichte, 1982, 331–349.

4   For an exemplary case, see Ignaz Heinrich von Wessenberg & Heinrich Zschokke, *Der Briefwechsel (1806–1848) zwischen Ignaz Heinrich von Wessenberg und Heinrich Zschokke*, ed. Rudolf Herzog & Othmar Pfyl, Basel, Krebs, 1990. On the period, see Georg Schwaiger, ed., *Zwischen Polemik und Irenik: Untersuchungen zum Verhältnis der*

---

1   See Hans Otte & Richard Schenk, eds., *Die Reunionsgespräche im Niedersachsen des 17. Jahrhunderts: Rojas y Spinola, Molan, Leibniz*, Göttingen, Vandenhoeck & Ruprecht, 1999; Heinz Duchhardt & Gerhard May, eds., *Union, Konversion, Toleranz: Dimensionen der Annäherung zwischen den christlichen Konfessionen im 17. und 18. Jahrhundert*, Mainz, Philipp von Zabern, 2000; Harm Klueting, ed., *Irenik und Antikonfessionalismus im 17. und 18. Jahrhundert*, Hildesheim, Olms, 2003; Irene Dingel, Volker Leppin

decisive influence on the interconfessionally open religious climate which arose in this area in the late 18th and early 19th centuries.

In the wake of the Reformation jubilee of 1817, which was exploited for political and national purposes, and under the influence of a widespread polarization of church politics, a new wave of reciprocal demarcations and exclusions arose from the 1820s on. The confessional antagonism between Catholics and Protestants in 19th-century Germany was not only a historical fact but also "a defining reality of German life, thinking, and self-understanding," and equally "a defining reality of politics."[5] The early changes in this attitude, which belong to the formative history of the modern ecumenical movement, remained the exception. On the Catholic side, they are found especially in the works of Johann Adam Möhler, church historian in Tübingen. His work *Symbolik: oder Darstellung der dogmatischen Gegensätze der Katholiken und Protestanten nach ihren öffentlichen Bekenntnisschriften*,[6] first appeared in 1832, was written in the light of the Reformation jubilees of 1817 and 1830 and of the controversial theological interests associated therewith. In this work, he adopted the perspective of confessional studies and effected a first historical-critical comparison among the "various religious parties opposed to each other, in consequence of the ecclesiastical

revolutions of the sixteenth century,"[7] along with their doctrinal differences, on the basis of their official confessional statements. In so doing, he dispensed with the confessional apologetics that had been exchanged for centuries and reminded Catholics of the question of unity, although he still abstained from pursuing any ecumenical goal.[8] Drawing on the understanding of the church in his 1825 early work *Die Einheit in der Kirche: oder, Das Prinzip des Katholizismus dargestellt im Geiste der Kirchenväter der ersten drei Jahrhunderte*,[9] which influenced generations of Catholics decisively, Möhler proposed that "the question of truth was resolved *a priori* on the Catholic side." In his view, all that really mattered was, "essentially, to expose the contradiction of all non-Catholic Christian confessions to the 'principle of Catholicism.'"[10] Regardless, Möhler's theological œuvre and his main work, *Symbolik*, in particular, have influenced the later development of Catholic theology in many ways and continued to do so until Vatican II (1962–1965); even the modern ecumenical movement owes him important impulses.[11]

Konfessionen im späten 18. und frühen 19. Jahrhundert, Göttingen, Vandenhoeck & Ruprecht, 1977.

5   Thomas Nipperdey, *Deutsche Geschichte*, 3 vols., Munich, Beck, 1983–1992, vol. 2, *Machtstaat vor der Demokratie*, 528–530, here 529. See also Olaf Blaschke, "Das 19. Jahrhundert: Ein zweites konfessionelles Zeitalter?," *GG* 26, 2000, 38–75.

6   Johann Adam Möhler, *Symbolik: oder Darstellung der dogmatischen Gegensätze der Katholiken und Protestanten nach ihren öffentlichen Bekenntnisschriften*, Mainz, F. Kupferberg, 1832; ET: *Symbolism: or Exposition of the Doctrinal Differences Between Catholics and Protestants, as Evidenced by Their Symbolical Writings*, trans. James Burton Robertson, London, C. Dolman, 1843. A two-volume reprint of the original edition with an introduction and commentary by Josef Rupert Geiselmann was published by the latter in Cologne, Hegner, 1960–1961.

7   Möhler, *Symbolism*, 1.

8   Quite to the contrary, as Möhler confided to a friend, this work was intended to "deal a blow to Protestantism such as had not been dealt to it in a long time, [albeit] with the greatest leniency and the mildest of judgments"; J.A. Möhler to A. Gengler, June 25, 1830, in: Stefan Lösch, *Prof. Dr. Adam Gengler (1799–1866): Die Beziehungen des Bamberger Theologen zu J.J.J. Döllinger und J.A. Möhler: Ein Lebensbild mit Beigabe von 80 bisher unbekannten Briefen darunter 47 neuen Möhler-Briefen: Zugleich ein Beitrag zur Gelehrtengeschichte Bambergs im XIX. Jahrhundert*, Würzburg, Schöningh, 1963, 64.

9   Johann Adam Möhler, *Die Einheit der Kirche: oder Das Prinzip des Katholizismus: Dargestellt im Geiste der Kirchenväter der ersten drei Jahrhunderte*, Tübingen, Laupp, 1825; new edition ed. Josef Rupert Geiselmann, Darmstadt, Wissenschaftliche Buchgesellschaft, 1957; ET: *Unity in the Church: or The Principle of Catholicism, Presented in the Spirit of the Church Fathers of the First Three Centuries*, Washington DC, The Catholic University of America Press, 1996.

10 Manfred Weitlauff, "Möhler, Johann Adam," *NDB* 17, 616–620, here 620.

11 See Paul-Werner Scheele, *Johann Adam Möhler*, Graz, Styria, 1969, 54–63; Harald Wagner, "Johann Adam

In the second half of the 19th century, only two notable pioneers of ecumenism can be found on the Roman Catholic side: the English theologian John Henry Newman[12] and the abovementioned Ignaz von Döllinger – two of the most outstanding personalities in the entire 19th-century European Catholicism.

2   Döllinger, an Ecumenist *avant la lettre*

As a professor of church history at the University of Munich from 1826 to 1871, excommunicated in 1871 due to his rejection of the new dogmas on papal primacy and papal infallibility, president of the BAdW from 1873 to 1890, and a scholar of European standing,[13] Döllinger soon expressed

his strict disapproval of the other confessions during the first decades of his confessional polemics, although he was never indifferent towards them. From the late 1840s, his theological orientation gradually began to shift from confessional demarcation to ecumenical openness. This development was rooted in different but convergent causes. It was a reaction to the social democracy that had been emerging in Germany since the middle of the century, in which Döllinger recognized a threat to the Christian faith, as well as the consequence of his identification with the German intellectual and cultural life arising after 1850. Moreover, it had also been prompted by his exchanges with non-Catholic personalities since the 1840s, notably with the English Prime Minister William Ewart Gladstone, with whom he had corresponded since 1845, but also with leading theologians of the Oxford Movement, above all Edward Bouverie Pusey and Henry Parry Liddon.[14] Yet another factor coming into play from the 1860s on was his increasingly critical stance on the Catholic Church's tendency toward uniformity under the sign of Ultramontanism, which strove to focus all aspects of church life on the pope alone.

Döllinger's first speech in favor of a mutually respectful coexistence of Catholicism and Protestantism in Germany was delivered in 1848 at the Frankfurt National Assembly, where he expressed his hope that the ecclesial schism might still be overcome.[15] However, ecumenical issues did not yet feature prominently in his theological and historical works, although they were to

Möhler: Die Kirche als Organ der Inkarnation," in: Peter Neuner & Gunther Wenz, eds., *Theologen des 19. Jahrhunderts: Eine Einführung*, Darmstadt, Wissenschaftliche Buchgesellschaft, 2002, 59–74, here 67; Jörg Ernesti & Wolfgang Thönissen, eds., *Die Entdeckung der Ökumene: Zur Beteiligung der katholischen Kirche an der ökumenischen Bewegung*, Paderborn, Bonifatius, 2008, 13. See also Michel Fédou's contribution in this volume.

12   See Peter Nockles's contribution in this volume.

13   On Döllinger, see Franz Xaver Bischof, *Theologie und Geschichte: Ignaz von Döllinger (1799–1890) in der zweiten Hälfte seines Lebens: Ein Beitrag zu seiner Biographie*, Stuttgart, Kohlhammer, 1997; Victor Conzemius, "Ignaz von Döllinger (1799–1890): Una Sancta Catholica auf dem Prüfstand," in: Victor Conzemius, *Gottes Spurensucher: Zwanzig christliche Profile der Neuzeit*, Freiburg i.Br., Herder, 2002, 83–104; Peter Neuner, "Ignaz von Döllinger, Katholizität und Antiultramontanismus," in: Neuner & Wenz, eds., *Theologen des 19. Jahrhunderts*, 75–93; Franz Xaver Bischof, "John Henry Newman und Ignaz von Döllinger: Papstdogmen und Gewissen," in: Mariano Delgado, Volker Leppin & David Neuhold, eds., *Ringen um die Wahrheit: Gewissenskonflikte in der Christentumsgeschichte*, Stuttgart, Kohlhammer, 2011, 271–286; Thomas Albert Howard, *The Pope and the Professor: Pius IX, Ignaz von Döllinger, and the Quandary of the Modern Age*, Oxford, Oxford University Press, 2017; Manfred Weitlauff, *Das Erste Vatikanum (1869/70) wurde ihnen zum Schicksal: Der Münchener Kirchenhistoriker Ignaz von Döllinger (1799–1890) und sein englischer Schüler John Lord Acton (1834–1902): Ein Beitrag*

zum 150-Jahr-"Jubiläum" dieses Konzils, 2 vols., Munich, Bayerischen Akademie der Wissenschaften, 2018.

14   Döllinger's correspondence with Gladstone, Liddon, and Plummer is included in the edition *Ignaz von Döllinger: Briefwechsel (1830–1890): Englische und französische Korrespondenz*, which is being prepared by the present author and will appear soon.

15   "Rede, gehalten in der 64. Sitzung der deutschen konstituierenden Nationalversammlung zu Frankfurt am 22. August 1848," in: Franz Heinrich Reusch, ed., *Kleinere Schriften, gedruckte und ungedruckte, von Joh. Jos. Ign. v. Döllinger*, Stuttgart, J.G. Cotta, 1890, 23–41, here 38f.

be found there. In 1861, he referred to a conference that had been held in Erfurt on Sept 21–22, 1860 in a letter to an old friend from his youth, the Protestant social reformer Victor Aimé Huber. At this conference, Catholics and Protestants had proposed, as private citizens, the possibility of a rapprochement between the confessions, primarily on the political and social level: on the path towards the reunion of the churches, it was important to emphasize the unifying aspects rather than the dividing ones and to learn from one another in spite of all confessional polemics.[16]

Referring to the Erfurt Conference, the preface to Döllinger's work *Kirche und Kirchen, Papstthum und Kirchenstaat* (1861) formulated 17 propositions pertaining to the reunion of the churches. However, his realistic assessment of the situation on both the Protestant and the Catholic side led him to believe that there was little prospect of achieving this in the foreseeable future.[17] However, the subject had nevertheless been broached. Döllinger formulated a kind of theory of ecumenical principles in this first clearly accentuated and, in today's meaning of the word, ecumenical statement.[18] Among the preparatory steps for a future reunion, he mentioned the removal of mutual prejudices, the focus on the common Christian heritage in all confessions, and the self-reform of each individual church.[19] In doing so, he picked up objectives Johann Michael Sailer had already posited before him. Even Johann Adam Möhler, whose last essay Döllinger published posthumously in 1839, had already spoken of the conciliatory coexistence of the different confessions as a prerequisite for a "return to the former unity,"[20] although he did not expect

it to occur soon. The particularly new and convincing element in Döllinger's idea was the option of placing "the great salvific truths in the center of all doctrine at all times" while treating "the minor matters not as the main issue in doctrine as well as in life."[21] In his preface, Döllinger pointed the way for future ecumenical church work and outlined the structure of an ecumenical theology that was well in advance of his time. Later in his life, as he once wrote to his friend Gladstone, he could rightly boast that "in terms of concessions, he had gone as far as, or even farther than, any notable Catholic theologian of recent times."[22] In substance, which must be seen as highly significant, his conception may be said to have anticipated the recognition of the "hierarchy of truths"[23] which Vatican II would later place at the center of Catholic ecumenical work independently of Döllinger, who did not know the concept.[24]

Döllinger went one step further in his famous speech *Rede über Vergangenheit und Gegenwart der katholischen Theologie*,[25] held in 1863 at the Conference of Catholic Scholars in Munich. In

---

16 I. von Döllinger to V.A. Huber, January 1861, in: Hans-Joachim Schoeps, "Die Erfurter Konferenz von 1860 (Zur Geschichte des katholisch-protestantischen Gesprächs)," *ZRGG* 5, 1953, 135–159, here 147f.

17 Ignaz von Döllinger, *Kirche und Kirchen, Papstthum und Kirchenstaat: Historische-politische Betrachtungen*, Munich, J.G. Cotta, 1861, xxi–xxxii.

18 Döllinger, *Kirche und Kirchen*, xxi–xxiv.

19 Döllinger, *Kirche und Kirchen*, xxix–xxx.

20 *Dr. J.A. Möhler's, ernannten Domdecans zu Würzburg und Ritters des kgl. bayerischen St. Michael-Ordens,*

ehedem ord. Professors der Theologie zu München, Gesammelte Schriften und Aufsätze, ed. Ignaz von Döllinger, vol. 2, Regensburg, G.J. Manz, 1839, 226–243, here 236.

21 Döllinger, *Kirche und Kirchen*, xxix.

22 I. von Döllinger to W.E. Gladstone, Munich, Jan 19, 1862, in: BL, Gladstone Papers, Add. 44398.

23 *Unitatis redintegratio* §11.

24 On the "hierarchy of truths" see Karl Rahner's "Der Glaube der Christen und die Lehre der Kirche," in: Karl Rahner, *Schriften zur Theologie*, vol. 10, Zürich, Benziger, 1972, 262–285, esp. 276–278; Bernd Jochen Hilberath, "Theologischer Kommentar zum Dekret über den Ökumenismus: *Unitatis redintegratio*," *HThK Vat.II* 3, 69–223, here 146–157.

25 Ignaz von Döllinger, "Rede über Vergangenheit und Gegenwart der katholischen Theologie," in: Pius Bonifacius Gams, ed., *Verhandlungen der Versammlung katholischer Gelehrten in München vom 28. September bis 1. Oktober 1863*, Regensburg, G.J. Manz, 1863, 25–69; unchanged reprint in: Franz Xaver Bischof & Georg Essen, eds., *Theologie, kirchliches Lehramt und öffentliche Meinung: Die Münchener Gelehrtenversammlung von 1863 und ihre Folgen*, Stuttgart, Kohlhammer, 2015, 11–33, here 24f.

this speech, he elaborated an ecumenical program, though still with a one-sided concentration on the German situation based on a strong sense of national identity. He assigned the specific task of overcoming the ecclesial schism to German theology, since German theologians had caused the schism in the first place. With this innovative approach to an ecumenical theology, Döllinger remained an isolated voice. However, the stance taken by him reflected his ecumenical optimism, which he had also recognized in the Oxford Movement in the 1860s and particularly in Pusey's work *Eirenicon*[26] calling upon a reunion of the churches, especially within the Anglican Church. Döllinger stated in a letter to Gladstone on Mar 15, 1870[27] that the consideration shown for the non-Catholic churches, whose reunion with Rome he believed had been made more difficult, or even impossible, by new dogmas, was also a reason for his struggle against the resolutions on papal primacy and papal infallibility of Vatican I (1869–1870), which he rejected, thus leading to his excommunication by the Archbishop of Munich Gregor von Scherr in 1871.[28]

3   The Lectures on the Reunion of the Christian Churches (1872)

The issue of the reunion of the Christian churches gained greater priority for Döllinger after Vatican I, his excommunication, and the founding of the German Reich in 1871.[29] In his speech as rector of the University of Munich in December 1871, he had singled out this concern as the most urgent task on the theological agenda of both confessions.[30]

From January to March 1872, he delivered seven further speeches on the topic of the reunion of the Christian churches (*Über die Wiedervereinigung der christlichen Kirchen*).[31] The chief motive cited by Döllinger in support of Christian unity was the commission of Christ, who, as the founder of the church, desired and commanded its unity. According to him, the church's credibility towards the world depended on its unity, the latter being the precondition for a successful mission and for the civilizing of the non-Christian peoples. Church divisions, on the other hand, "have an opposite impact on the non-Christian peoples and even more on many Christians,"[32] as this gives them reason for anger and doubts regarding the truthfulness of the Christian teaching. It is indeed true that Döllinger, like nearly all European missionaries of the time, was convinced of the superiority of European culture and largely equated Christianity with European civilization, an attitude that is no longer comprehensible.[33] Yet, the credibility of

---

26   Edward Bouverie Pusey, *The Church of England: A Portion of Christ's One Holy Catholic Church, and a Means of Restoring Visible Unity: An Eirenicon, in a Letter to the Author of "The Christian Year"*, Oxford, J.H. & J. Parker, 1865. This volume was followed by two others: *First Letter to the Very Rev. J.H. Newman, D.D.: In Explanation Chiefly in Regard to The Reverential Love Due to the Ever-Blessed Theotokos and the Doctrine of Her Immaculate Conception*, Oxford, J. Parker, 1869, and *Is Healthful Reunion Impossible?: A Second Letter to the Very Rev. J.H. Newman, D.D.*, Oxford, J. Parker, 1870.

27   "In a broader perspective, the author conceived the idea and the hope of a future reunion of the churches that could be achieved on the basis of the necessary reforms and of mutual concessions. But of course: only in a distant time, which, however, should already be prepared and initiated today by *the wise and loving ones*, and not cast aside as something utterly impossible or wholly undesirable"; I. von Döllinger to W.E. Gladstone, Munich, Mar 15, 1870, in: BL, Gladstone Papers, Add. 44425.

28   For a detailed account of Döllinger's position prior to, during, and after Vatican I and his excommunication, see Bischof, *Theologie und Geschichte*, 122–383.

29   See I. von Döllinger to W.E. Gladstone, Munich, Apr 2, 1874, in: BL, Gladstone Papers, Add. 44443.

30   Ignaz von Döllinger, "Die Bedeutung der großen Zeitereignisse für die deutschen Hochschulen," in: Ignaz von Döllinger, *Akademische Vorträge*, vol. 3, Nördlingen, Beck, 1891, 11–38, here 33f.

31   Ignaz von Döllinger, *Über die Wiedervereinigung der christlichen Kirchen: Sieben Vorträge gehalten zu München im Jahr 1872*, Nördlingen, Beck, 1888.

32   Döllinger, *Über die Wiedervereinigung*, 13. The first two speeches dealt with the international situation of religion (*Ueberblick über die religiöse Weltlage*) and formed a thematic whole. The partitioning was merely the consequence of time limitations.

33   See Döllinger, *Über die Wiedervereinigung*, 19–20, 23.

the Christian mission was precisely what led to the first WMC in Edinburgh in 1910, which marked the beginning of the modern ecumenical movement in the 20th century.[34]

Compared to *Kirche und Kirchen* (1861) and to his *Theologierede* (1863), the views expressed by Döllinger in 1872 with regard to the restoration of church unity were characterized by a greater degree of reservation. Indeed, two churches cannot "suddenly throw themselves into each other's arms like two friends who meet again after a long separation."[35] Concretely, he called on the churches to make every effort to improve their relationship and, as he had already stated in the 1860s, to place greater emphasis on the unifying aspects than on the dividing ones. Dogmas and doctrinal positions were to be interpreted by all churches in such a way as to remove misunderstandings and overcome biases, thereby permitting the common heritage to reemerge in full clarity. Negotiations in view of a union, if they were to take place, should not be conducted bilaterally between two churches or communities but always with due regard for the other particular churches if the latter could not be induced to participate in the negotiations.[36] The risk that the union of two churches might widen the gap with a third one could only be avoided in this manner. In his view, the precondition for a mutual recognition of churches lies in their continuity with the early church of apostolic doctrine and constitution: "Its basis would be: 'the

Holy Scripture with the three ecumenical symbols, interpreted according to the doctrine of the still undivided church of the first three centuries.'"[37] The ecclesiological model of the reunited church of the future as outlined by Döllinger was thus, in today's terms, that of a reconciled diversity that would find its unifying core in the *Una sancta catholica et apostolica* of the creed.

With a view to the individual churches, Döllinger outlined the respective tradition as well as the specific constitutional and doctrinal developments of each individual church, along with the causes that had led to the separation, and listed the conditions under which the conformity with the early church could, in his opinion, be regained. As far as the Orthodox Church was concerned, he saw little need for reform, as he believed that its doctrine and constitution largely corresponded to that of the early church. However, it would be necessary to get rid of its superstitious practices, reform the training of its priests, and free itself of its dependency on the state. Likewise, the Anglican Church would have to emancipate itself from the state and, furthermore, overcome the Calvinistic tendencies exhibited by the Presbyterian wing of the Anglican Church, the Low Church, in contrast to the Catholicizing High Church. It would need to give priority to its Catholic tradition following the example of the Oxford Movement, with an emphasis on the episcopal office and an interpretation of the Thirty-Nine Articles in the Catholic sense. The Roman Catholic Church, Döllinger stated, was the one that conformed most fully to the doctrine and constitution of the early church. However, he further maintained that the papal dogmas of Vatican I had brought about a fundamental ecclesiological change and had currently destroyed all hope of achieving a union of the churches. Nevertheless, as Döllinger still optimistically believed in 1872, these dogmas would not win acceptance and would

---

34   See Brian Stanley's contribution in this volume.

35   Döllinger, *Über die Wiedervereinigung*, 28.

36   "It is, in any case, indispensable that the members of the Latin Catholic Church, as soon as they enter into henotic negotiations with Protestants, always proceed with due regard for the Anatolian Church, or, better still, always go about their work in consultation with members of the latter church; otherwise, the desire to bridge a gap might lead to the widening and deepening of another, the disappearance of which is no less desirable, no less bidden from on high. And were we to leave the English Church aside in our efforts, the golden chain that we seek to mend and reassemble would lack an equally indispensable and precious middle link"; Döllinger, *Über die Wiedervereinigung*, 33f.

---

37   Döllinger, *Über die Wiedervereinigung*, 139. For Döllinger, the three *Symbola* included the Niceno-Constantinopolitan Creed, the Apostles' Creed, and the Athanasian Creed.

thus, in the long run, not be able to prevent the churches from drawing closer to the Roman Catholic Church. On the other hand, Döllinger believed that massive reforms were needed in the Protestant Churches. Protestantism in both its Lutheran and Reformed variants, he argued, did not stand within the continuity of the apostolic tradition, which he viewed as an indispensable criterion of catholicity. It thus needed to restore the episcopal office according to the statutes of the early church.

The lectures aroused enormous interest in the public. The domestic and foreign press published nonauthorized excerpts, notably in England, where the speeches were read "with eagerness."[38] The Anglican theologian, Alfred Plummer, who had been corresponding with Döllinger since 1870 and regularly visited him in Munich, wrote to him from Oxford the following comment on the speeches, which were held on Wednesday evenings: "Before the week is out your words have found an echo in hearts all over Europe. Over and over again I say to myself your noble words 'It must be possible for it is duty.' Never have the dry bones of Kant's famous dictum seemed to have been so instinct with life and power."[39] An English edition of the lectures appeared in the very same year, 1872, in a translation by the theologian Henry Nutcombe Oxenham, who had converted from Anglicanism to Catholicism in 1857 and formed a lifelong friendship with Döllinger during a longer stay in Germany. Döllinger had sent him the manuscript of the lectures in order to translate them. Oxenham wrote a preface to this edition and provided the footnotes.[40] In 1880, Emily Meriman, an American who had been married to the former

Dominican theologian Hyacinthe Loyson since 1872, used Oxenham's translation as a reference text for her French translation.[41] The German edition of the lectures did not appear until 1888, when, as Döllinger wrote in his preface, "the hopes of understanding and union" that had still spurred him on in 1872 had proved to be "illusions."[42] So these illusions had been fueled to a considerable extent by the outcome of the Bonn reunion conferences, which had been initiated and organized by Döllinger.[43]

4 The Bonn Reunion Conferences of 1874–1875

The strong response evoked by the lectures *Über die Wiedervereinigung der christlichen Kirchen* in Germany and in Europe was the actual reason why Döllinger decided to convene two reunion conferences in Bonn.[44] He first discussed his plans in the summer of 1872 with Liddon, Pusey's disciple and the leading theologian of the Oxford revival, during a stroll through the English Garden in Munich. According to Liddon's later testimony, Döllinger had apparently told him:

---

38   J. Acton to I. von Döllinger, Aldenham, Mar 21, 1872, in: Ignaz von Döllinger, *Briefwechsel (1850–1890)*, ed. Victor Conzemius, vol. 3, *Briefwechsel mit Lord Acton (1871–1890)*, Munich, Beck, 1971, 55–60 (no. 369), esp. 58.

39   A. Plummer to I. von Döllinger, Oxford, Feb 26, 1872, in: BSB, Döllingeriana II.

40   Ignaz von Döllinger, *Lectures on the Reunion of the Churches*, trans. Henry Nutcombe Oxenham, London, Rivingtons, 1872. See also Döllinger's correspondence with Oxenham, included in my *Ignaz von Döllinger: Briefwechsel (1830–1890)*.

41   Ignaz von Döllinger, *Conférences sur la réunion des Églises chrétiennes*, eds. Emilie Jayne Loyson & Henry Nutcombe Oxenham, Paris, G. Fischbacher, 1880.

42   Döllinger, *Über die Wiedervereinigung*, iv.

43   The Bonn reunion conferences have been variously described, often in a very concise manner. For a selection of bibliographical references, see Peter Neuner, *Döllinger als Theologe der Ökumene*, Paderborn, Schöningh, 1979, 181–211; Owen Chadwick, "Döllinger and Reunion," in: Gillian Rosemary Evans, ed., *Christian Authority: Essays in Honour of Henry Chadwick*, Oxford, Clarendon Press, 1988, 296–334; Bischof, *Theologie und Geschichte*, 404–437; Mark D. Chapman, "Liddon, Döllinger and the Bonn Conferences of 1874 and 1875: A Case Study in Nationalism and Ecumenism," *IKZ* 92, 2002, 21–59; Howard, *The Pope and the Professor*, 190–213; Weitlauff, *Das Erste Vatikanum*, vol. 1, 374–382.

44   See A. Plummer to I. von Döllinger, Oxford, June 4, 1872, in: BSB, Döllingeriana II.

When so many threatening forms of infidelity are attacking our Christian belief on one side, and Vaticanism is putting forth its altogether new propositions about the constitution and faith of the Church of Christ on the other, ought not all we, who profess to follow the ancient Catholic Church as the keeper and unfolder of the Holy Scriptures, to be able to come to an understanding with each other? Surely this should not be impossible, unless we are rather stupid, or, perhaps, even self-willed.[45]

The expectations expressed herein of what could be achieved in the near future went far beyond what Döllinger had deemed possible only a few months earlier in his lectures *Über die Wiedervereinigung der christlichen Kirchen.* The generally unionistic mood that prevailed in his thinking in the years 1872–1875 and found euphoric expression in these words was hardly realistic. Quite to the contrary, Döllinger very soon realized that churches, once separated, are incapable or unwilling to effect a quick rapprochement even when Christianity itself is at stake, as he believed it to be. How the church historian from Munich assessed the situation at the time is revealed by his letter to Gladstone from Apr 2, 1874:

> As you well know, the question of the church, which is now more than ever a world-encompassing issue and, as such, intertwined with the grand course of world history, is of greatest concern to me, and I would like to devote myself to it with the last vital energy that God has given me. While the churches of Eastern rite have, on the one hand, awakened to new life and moved much closer to Western Christianity, the West, on

the other hand, is witnessing a large-scale religious and ecclesial decomposition, and on the continent, particularly in Germany, neither the Protestant nor the Catholic Church will be able to endure over the long term in their present form. New ecclesial ties or unions (and any union would simultaneously need to be a new formation) are bound to happen. Even in England, there is a growing desire and hope that the insular status of the church can be overcome in favor of belonging to greater, truly Catholic (i.e. of the early Church) whole.[46]

Indeed, the widely expressed wish not to be content with theoretical considerations strengthened Döllinger in taking concrete steps. Anglican support of this course of action came especially from the ACS (founded in 1853), whose founder and secretary Frederick Meyrick entertained a broad network and sought to enter into contact with Döllinger and the Old Catholic movement after 1870;[47] additional encouragement came from the clergyman William Chauncy Langdon, a representative of the North American Episcopal Church who had established a first parish in Rome in 1859 and supported Old Catholic tendencies in Italy following Vatican I. He had conferred with Döllinger in Munich in August 1871 and appealed to him once again in a public letter in August 1872, but failed to enlist Döllinger's support for an Anglican/

---

45 Liddon's preface, in: *Report of the Proceedings at the Reunion Conference: Held at Bonn on September 14, 15, and 16, 1874,* ed. Henry Parry Liddon, London, Rivingtons, 1875, iii.

46 I. von Döllinger to W.E. Gladstone, Munich, Apr 2, 1874, in: BL, Gladstone Papers, Add. 44443.

47 On the ACS, its goals, and Meyrick's role, see Ralph Ruhtenberg, "Gesellschaften und Vereinigungen für Interkommunion zwischen den Anglikanischen und Orthodoxen Kirchen," in: Robert Stupperich, ed., *Kirche im Osten: Studien zur osteuropäischen Kirchengeschichte und Kirchenkunde,* vol. 15, Göttingen, Vandenhoeck & Ruprecht, 1972, 48–73, here 65–67; Frederick Meyrick, *Memories of Life at Oxford, and Experiences in Italy, Greece, Turkey, Germany, Spain and Elsewhere,* London, J. Murray, 1905.

Old Catholic conference.[48] Nevertheless, his appeal seemed to have had a certain impact. On the Russian Orthodox side, the Society of the Friends of Spiritual Enlightenment, which had been founded in Saint Petersburg, strove to eliminate Western prejudices against Orthodoxy. In particular, the archpriest Johannes Janyshev, the rector of the SPbDA at Saint Petersburg, together with Ivan T. Osinin, professor of theology at the same academy, and the secretary of the aforementioned society, Aleksandr Kireev, closely monitored the developments after Vatican I. Since 1871, they had been in contact with Döllinger, as had the nascent Old Catholic movement with the ACS.

The Old Catholics also joined the group. The second Old Catholic congress, which took place in Cologne in 1872, had made interconfessional dialogue one of the Old Catholic Church's chief tasks and instructed a commission to bilaterally explore the possibilities of a cooperation with the ACS as well as with the Society of the Friends of Spiritual Enlightenment.[49] By dispatching Bishop Harold Edward Browne of Ely (from 1873 of Winchester) along with Janyshev and Kireev as observers, both organizations had sent prominent representatives to the congress in Cologne. They were supported by presence of the bishops Christopher Wordsworth of Lincoln, and William R. Whittingham of Maryland, the presiding bishop of the North American Episcopal Church. However, Döllinger as president of the commission remained inactive. In his lectures *Über die Wiedervereinigung der*

christlichen Kirchen, he had already made it clear that he rejected the bilateral negotiations with the individual churches that had formally been agreed upon at the Old Catholic congress of 1873. Moreover, it seems as if he wished to detach his union plans from the like-minded initiatives of the Old Catholics, probably because he feared that the whole matter would otherwise escape his control. Moreover, he might have also wished to create a distance between his own ecclesial position as an excommunicated Catholic and the formation of the Old Catholic Church, which was finalized in 1873 with the consecration of the Breslau church historian Joseph Hubert Reinkens as the first Old Catholic bishop.[50]

4.1 The Reunion Conference of 1874

In late July 1874, Döllinger finally convened a first union conference in Bonn under the name of the Comité zur Beförderung kirchlicher Unionsbestrebungen (Committee for the Advancement of Reunion in the Church), despite the opposition of leading Old Catholics, such as Friedrich Michelis, Johann Friedrich von Schulte, and his student and faculty colleague Johann Friedrich.[51] As stated in the invitation, the conference was to be a meeting of theological experts from different churches "who meet in the desire and hope of a future great union of devout Christians." The basis and guiding principle of all debates and negotiations were to be sought both in the creeds of the church's early centuries and in those "doctrines and institutions" that "were regarded as fundamental and indispensable in the

48   W.C. Langdon to I. von Döllinger, Munich, Aug 24, 1871, in: BSB, Döllingeriana II; I. von Döllinger to J. Acton, Munich, Aug 24, 1871, in: Döllinger, *Briefwechsel*, vol. 3, 25–27 (no. 357), here 26f. See also Döllinger's comment on the corresponding wishes of the North American Episcopal Church, in: *Stenographischer Bericht über die Verhandlungen des Katholiken-Congresses abgehalten vom 22. bis 24. September 1871 in München: Mit einer historischen Einleitung und Beilagen*, Munich, Ackermann, 1871, 29f.

49   See Urs Küry, *Die altkatholische Kirche: Ihre Geschichte, ihre Lehre, ihr Anliegen*, Frankfurt a.M., Evangelisches Verlagswerk, ³1982, 461f.

50   For a detailed study of this topic, see Bischof, *Theologie und Geschichte*, 404–410.

51   Döllinger had already notified Gladstone and Plummer of the upcoming conference on Apr 2, 1874; I. von Döllinger to W.E. Gladstone, Munich, Apr 2, 1874, in: BL, Gladstone Papers, Add. 44443; I. von Döllinger to A. Plummer, Munich, Apr 2, 1874, in: Alfred Plummer, *Conversations with Dr. Döllinger (1870–1890)*, ed. Robrecht Boudens & Leo Kenis, Leuven, Leuven University Press, 1985, 99.

mainstream churches of the East and West prior to the great schisms."[52] The goal of the negotiations was not to be an "absorptive union or total amalgamation" of churches but, as already advocated by Döllinger in his series of lectures, "the creation of a church fellowship on the basis of *unitas in necessariis*"[53] in conjunction with the preservation and retention of those distinctive features of the individual churches that have no bearing on the substance of the early Christian creed.

The invitation, which was also published in the daily press in Germany and England, was greeted with an overwhelming response on account of Döllinger's international prestige. A total of 56 participants from 8 countries (Denmark, Germany, England, France, Greece, Russia, Switzerland, and the United States) participated in this first multilateral confessional dialogue in the modern era, which was held in the premises of the University of Bonn from Sept 12 to 14, 1874, and brought together theologians from the East and the West. The number of academic theologians, who alone played an important role in the conference due to the complex theological nature of the topics under discussion, was limited to about a dozen people. The Old Catholics were represented by Franz Heinrich Reusch, Joseph Langen, Franz Peter Knoodt, Bishop Reinkens, and Eugène Michaud, who had come from Paris. The five representatives of Orthodoxy included Janyshev and the Athenian professor Zikos Rosis, both influential theologians. The largest delegation was that of the Anglicans. Bishop Browne of Ely, who had to leave on the first day due the death of a relative,[54] had come to Bonn in the company of (partly very prominent) theologians from the High Church, namely Liddon, Plummer, and Edward Stuart Talbot, all of whom

were personally acquainted with Döllinger.[55] John Saul Howson, the dean of Chester, represented the Low Church. Robert Jenkins Nevin, the rector of the North American Episcopal Church in Rome, headed a group of six Americans, including Bishop John Barrett Kerfoot from Pittsburgh and Langdon. The Anglican Bishop Alexander Penrose Forbes of Brechin had excused himself. The "Scottish Pusey," as Forbes was also called, realized that his hopes for a reunion of the Catholic and Anglican Churches on the basis of a moderate interpretation of the Council of Trent by the conciliar decrees of 1870 had been dashed but nevertheless welcomed any well-thought-out attempt to overcome "the chronic state of separation."[56] Furthermore, the Scottish

---

52 Letter of invitation, printed in: Franz Heinrich Reusch, ed., *Bericht über die am 14., 15. und 16. September zu Bonn gehaltenen Unions-Conferenzen, im Auftrage des Vorsitzenden Dr. von Döllinger*, Bonn, P. Neusser, 1874 (hereafter *Bericht 1874*), 1.

53 Reusch, ed., *Bericht 1874*, 1.

54 Reusch, ed., *Bericht 1874*, 4; Plummer, *Conversations with Dr. Döllinger*, 100.

55 See E.S. Talbot to I. von Döllinger, Freiburg i.Br., Sept 7, 1874, in: BSB, Döllingeriana II.

56 "The hope of the Reunion of Christendom has been in my heart ever since I thought deeply on theological subjects. For years I hoped that such reconciliation might be effected on the basis of the Canons of the Council of Trent interpreted in a benign sense. ... The unfortunate action of the Vatican Council has destroyed all hopes of an immediate union on such a basis as this. I wish to do justice to the sincerity of those who promoted it. I believe that they acted as they thought for the best, but I do not the less deplore the result. No immediate advantage in the way of consolidating the hierarchical power, no short and easy method for the settlement of controversies can counterbalance the injury to Christianity which a break with history on the part of its largest section occasions, and such a break with history has been effected by the late Vatican decrees. If the Personal Infallibility of the Pope, and the consequent proposition that his determinations are in themselves, and not on account of any consent of the Church, irreformable, be part of the original depositum, the central truth of the faith once delivered to the saints, then the history of the Church is a tissue of inconsequences, and men for eighteen centuries have been in error as to the nature and conditions of the tradition and interpretation of Divine Truth. Thrown back in this wise on ourselves, with hopes crushed, one cannot fail to hail with satisfaction such an effort as yours. Whatever difficulties may arise in attempting to adjust terms of ecclesiastical communion between those who hold to Apostolic succession and those who repudiate it, one must rejoice in every well considered attempt to break up the chronic state of separation which does more to retard the final triumph of Christianity than the fellest

clergyman Malcolm MacColl and Frederick Meyrick were prevented from coming due to unforeseen circumstances, although they did attend the follow-up conference.[57] Pusey failed to appear. He did not attend either of the two conferences but assured Döllinger of his "devoted affection" and "unceasing sympathy"[58] and indirectly influenced the conference through the presence of Liddon. Numerous Protestant Christians from Germany and Denmark also attended the first conference. However, these participants consisted mainly of interested pastors; not a single theologian of note was among them. Döllinger was disappointed and explained their absence by stating that the reasons for the Protestant alienation were of fundamental nature, precisely those from which everything depended.[59] The attendance of Catholic theologians was not to be expected under the given circum-

stances. At the time, they would have not been able to do so anyway, at least not without having to fear personal consequences and running the risk of being accused of heresy. The sole exception was Henry Nutcombe Oxenham. The former Tractarian considered his Anglican ordination to be valid even after his conversion to Catholicism and had therefore refused to submit to the required Catholic ordination procedure. According to Catholic canon law, he was thus considered a layman and escaped excommunication in spite of his decidedly anti-infallible stance.

Franz Heinrich Reusch, at the time rector of the University of Bonn, opened the conference in his capacity as host. At Döllinger's behest, he declared that none of the participants held a mandate from a church. From the outset, it was thus clear that the gathering was of a strictly private nature and, as Döllinger added, only strove "to promote ... religious harmony and church union."[60] Accordingly, the proceedings were recorded neither in minutes nor in shorthand. However, the bilingual conference secretaries, Reusch and George Edgar Broade, the English chaplain of Düsseldorf, took notes on the overall progression of the negotiations and informed the interested press. Broade simultaneously acted as correspondent for the

---

assaults of open or concealed enemies. May the Holy Ghost, the Life Giver, the Illuminator, guide and direct you!"; A.P. Forbes to I. von Döllinger, Dundee, Sept 4, 1874, in: Reusch, ed., *Bericht 1874*, 63f.

57   F. Meyrick to I. von Döllinger, Aylsham, Sept 5, 1874, in: Reusch, ed., *Bericht 1874*, 60f. (with the suggestion that special commissions be formed for the negotiations, a proposal which Döllinger rejected as "unpractical"); M. MacColl to I. von Döllinger, Glamis Castle, Sept 11, 1874, in: Reusch, ed., *Bericht 1874*, 66–68.

58   "Dr. Pusey wishes me to express his devoted affection to you, and his unceasing sympathy with you"; A.P. Forbes to I. von Döllinger, Dundee, Sept 4, 1874, in: Reusch, ed., *Bericht 1874*, 64.

59   "They both [Döllinger and Reinkens] appeared to be disappointed at the non-appearance of distinguished Protestant theologians. I asked the reason of their non-appearance. 'Oh, they are various,' said the bishop [Reinkens]. 'In some cases prejudice keeps them away. Some of the so-called orthodox Lutherans are as fast bound by the wording of their formularies as any Ultramontane can be by utterances of the Pope. Then again they are so divided among themselves. To take a single instance. Here in Bonn we have some five or six theological professors, and among them there are at least three entirely distinct schools of thought, schools utterly at variance with each other. That in a single faculty in a single university!' 'And moreover,' added Dr. Döllinger, 'the points of difference are the most fundamental; those on which all the rest depend'"; Plummer, *Conversations with Dr. Döllinger*, 101.

60   Reusch, ed., *Bericht 1874*, 6. "Prof. Reusch of the University of Bonn opened the proceedings by stating what the wishes of the Germans, who had taken the initiative in the matter, were: (1) The Conference was not a *public* one, although the invitation to it had been very general. It was not intended that detailed reports should be published; and it would be well if reports sent to newspapers were brief and couched in general terms. (2) No one was present in any *official* capacity. Each member was to be understood as stating only his own personal convictions, not anything which could bind others. We were there to suggest, and discuss, and prepare the way for agreement, not to determine the exact terms. He concluded by proposing (3) that Dr. Döllinger be asked to preside; which was carried of course unanimously"; Plummer, *Conversations with Dr. Döllinger*, 100. See also I. von Döllinger to C.J. Blennerhassett, Munich, June 4, 1874, in: Ignaz von Döllinger & Charlotte Julia Blennerhassett, *Briefwechsel (1865–1886)*, ed. Victor Conzemius, Munich, Beck, 1981, 562–564 (no. 342), here 563f.

London *Guardian*. After the two conferences, Reusch used these notes to draw up a memorandum of each conference that claimed to be "not official" but "at least substantially reliable."[61] These memoranda were then translated into English and, in each case, published with a preface written by Liddon.[62] The memorandum of the conference of 1875 also appeared in the United States with an introduction by Nevin[63] – an indication of the widespread interest the conferences elicited in the English-speaking world. The Russian participants reported on the conferences in the Saint Petersburg press and in the journal *Byzantis*, which was published in Constantinople. Although Reusch rendered the discussion items in direct speech as if they had actually been spoken that way and made ample use of editorial license,[64] no one formally complained that he had been misunderstood.[65] It can therefore be assumed that the memoranda offer a fairly accurate description of the negotiations, even though the progression of the conferences and the individual contributions to the discussions cannot be fully reconstructed. Additionally, the conference memoranda need to

be supplemented with private notes, such as those written by Alfred Plummer.[66]

Döllinger was elected chairman at the very beginning of the conference,[67] and was indeed the linchpin. In addition to a widely recognized erudition, he also held the necessary authority to guarantee an efficient negotiation process, never losing sight of the prime objective even when the various parties had different opinions (particularly during the follow-up conference), at times not shrinking from public rebukes[68] and, as one critic put it, occasionally behaving "like a professor in front of his students in the lecture hall."[69] The sources document the masterly way in which the 75-year-old Döllinger determined the course of negotiations, the perseverance to expound the most difficult theological issues (not infrequently in monologues that could last for hours), and

---

61   Reusch, ed., *Bericht 1874*, preface, not paginated.

62   Reusch, ed., *Bericht 1874*; Reusch, ed., *Report 1874*; *Bericht über die vom 10. bis 16. August 1875 zu Bonn gehaltenen Unions-Conferenzen, im Auftrage des Vorsitzenden Dr. von Döllinger*, Bonn, P. Neusser, 1875 (hereafter *Bericht 1875*); ET: *Report of the Proceedings at the Reunion Conference: Held at Bonn between the 10th and 16th of August, 1875*, ed. Henry Parry Liddon, London, Basil Montagu Pickering, 1876 (hereafter *Report 1875*).

63   Franz Heinrich Reusch, ed., *Report of the Union Conferences Held from August 10 to 16, 1875, at Bonn: Under the Presidency of Dr. von Döllinger*, trans. Samuel Buel with a preface by Robert J. Nevin, New York NY, T. Whittaker, 1876.

64   See Reusch, ed., *Bericht 1874*, preface, not paginated.

65   Liddon confirmed that Reusch's summary was generally accurate, even if numerous issues had either been treated too concisely or not mentioned at all; see Chadwick, "Döllinger and Reunion," 319f.

66   Plummer's very informative notes are a valuable addition to the two conference memoranda; see Plummer, *Conversations with Dr. Döllinger*, 99–116, 126–145.

67   Reusch, ed., *Bericht 1874*, 6.

68   As happened in the case of the objections raised by Philip Schaff, a member of the North American Presbyterian Church, in the context of the *Filioque* issue, when the latter argued against the basis of the doctrine of the undivided church that had been adopted by the second conference. Döllinger's answer is not recorded in the conference memorandum but is documented in Plummer, *Conversations with Dr. Döllinger*, 134: "As soon as he [Schaff] had finished, Dr. Döllinger came forward and said, 'The last speaker, not being a member of those Churches which have preserved the episcopate, has no claim to be heard at this Conference. But as a matter of courtesy I thought it well to allow him to speak. If his opinions are shared by the other members of the Conference, it follows that we all of us should have done far more wisely if we had remained at home.'" Plummer commented this as follows: "I have seldom seen a man so quietly, and at the same time so effectually, snuffed out as Dr. Schaff was by this remark from Dr. Döllinger."

69   Thus the criticism voiced by Schaff in his conference memorandum; quoted according to Matthias Joseph Scheeben, "Die zweite Unionsconferenz zu Bonn," *Periodische Blätter zur wissenschaftlichen Besprechung der großen religiösen Fragen der Gegenwart* 4, 1875, 529–544, here 533.

the energy to translate between the German and English-speaking participants. After the end of the second conference and still influenced by it, Broade wrote that Döllinger had been the soul of the conference from beginning to end, for which reason his memorandum should actually carry the title "Dr. von Döllinger at Bonn."[70]

During the preparations for the conference, the Anglicans, Old Catholics, and Orthodox had drawn up lists of issues that were to be addressed at the conference and in which the main points of dissent among the churches were believed to be. The doctrine of the undivided church, which was not disputed by any side, was to serve as the basis for all discussions. As a result, both the Thirty-Nine Articles of the English Church and the decrees of the Council of Trent were ruled out as binding doctrinal clauses, as was the recognition of the Council of Trent as an ecumenical council.[71]

From the outset, it proved extremely difficult to discuss the issue that was to take up so much time in the first conference and almost completely dominated the follow-up conference of 1875: the dogmatic question of the *Filioque*, the Latin creed's assertion that the Holy Spirit proceeds from Father *and* Son (*qui ex patre filioque procedit*) and not, as taught by the Orthodox Church in accordance with the First Council of Constantinople (381), from the Father alone. Döllinger had already initiated the debate on this highly complex issue in the separate meeting of Anglicans and Old Catholics, as he believed its clarification to be the *conditio sine qua non* of successful negotiations with the representatives of Orthodoxy.[72] The discussion at the conference of 1874 initially revolved around the question as to whether or not the insertion of the *Filioque* formula into the creed of the Latin Church by Pope Benedict VIII in the year 1014 had been legitimate. Döllinger began the discussion by describing the historical development that had, in his opinion, contributed to the schism between the Eastern and Western churches.[73] He pleaded in favor of a sweeping concession and proposed that the conference should make a declaration implying that the insertion of the *Filioque* into

---

70 "Patient, forbearing, untiring with an eloquent word of praise ever ready for a timely suggestion, and a kindly setting-down for every empiric in theology, Dr. Döllinger was the soul of the conference from beginning to end. The way in which he addressed the Easterns on the community of interest which bound them to us in resistance against Papal encroachment, and the wonderfully eloquent review of the religious state of the world with which he closed the conferences, together with his keen application of historical fact and his deep knowledge of theological science, were simply marvels. I ought to have headed this report as 'Dr. von Döllinger at Bonn'"; [George Broade,] "The Second Reunion Conference at Bonn," supplement no. 1051 to *The Guardian*, Aug 25, 1875, 1081–1084, here 1081.

71 See Reusch, ed., *Bericht 1874*, 8.

72 "Dr. Döllinger thought it best to begin with the *Filioque* question. We must come to some understanding about that before meeting the members of the Greek Church at six o'clock. He briefly stated the history of the controversy. All parties, he believed, would now agree that the *Filioque* was introduced into the Nicene Creed in an unlawful manner. The creed drawn up at Nicaea, completed and confirmed at other Councils, ought never to have been changed. No such addition as the *Filioque* could be rightly made except by a General Council. Pope Leo III had pointedly refused to consent to the addition, when requested do to do so by Charles the Great. The Bishop of Rome, Leo said, had no power to change anything in the creed or to add anything to it. (In strong contrast, we may remark by the way, said Dr. Döllinger, to the claims of the Pope at the present time.) The words *Filioque* were not introduced into the Western creed generally until the eleventh century (?); and the time of their introduction coincides pretty nearly with the time of separation between the Eastern and Western Churches. They inflicted a wound which has festered ever since; which has never been healed and never will be healed so long as this stumbling-block remains. Orientals said with justice that a creed, to which three Councils had declared that no addition must be made, had been interpolated by one portion of the Church. We ought to endeavour to redress this wrong that the wound might be healed"; see Plummer, *Conversations with Dr. Döllinger*, 102.

73 See Reusch, ed., *Bericht 1874*. On the background of the relationship between East and West, see Hans-Georg Beck, "Die Ostkirche vom Anfang des 10. Jahrhunderts bis Kerullarios," *HKG* 3/1, 462–484.

the creed had been "unlawful"; it was therefore "in the interest of harmony and unity" to restore "the original form of the creed"[74] as established by the councils of the undivided church.

This proposal met with massive opposition from the Anglican side. The Bishops Browne and Kerfoot (the latter is said to have sworn beforehand that he would under no circumstances relinquish the Western creed),[75] Liddon with explicit reference to his mentor Pusey as well as Oxenham, made it clear that the participants from the British isles were, for the most part, quite prepared to admit that the insertion of the *Filioque* into the Latin creed had taken place in an "unlawful manner" but that they would never agree to a removal of the *Filioque*. They would readily acknowledge that the creed of the Orthodox Church contained the whole truth and could be left in its original form. However, they were equally adamant that the creed of the Western Church also contained the whole truth and that the *Filioque* did not contradict Orthodox doctrine.[76] They maintained the credo "proceeding from the Father and the Son" was in agreement with the New Testament and its interpretation by the early church. Furthermore, and in spite of all criticism of Vatican I, Liddon (here again in accordance with Pusey) and Oxenham, in particular, did not wish to widen the gap between Canterbury and Rome, which had already been deepened by the Council. Finally, they agreed upon a compromise formula proposed by Bishop Browne in response to Döllinger's objection that it would be pointless to enter into negotiations with the Orthodox Church if the *Filioque* could not be "surrendered":[77]

We agree that the way in which the *Filioque* was inserted into the Nicene Creed was illegal, and that, with a view to future peace and unity, it is much to be desired that the whole church should set itself seriously to consider whether the Creed could possibly be restored to its primitive form, without sacrifice of any true doctrine expressed in the present Western form.[78]

As was to be expected, the discussion with the Orthodox delegates was tumultuous.[79] It made little difference that Döllinger gave a detailed account of the history of the schism between the Eastern and Western churches in his very comprehensive introductory address, in which he argued that mistakes by both sides had led to the schism and to mutual alienation, but most of the blame was to be placed on the Latin Church.[80] The Saint Petersburg theologian, Johannes Janyshev, was

---

74   Reusch, ed., *Bericht 1874*, 9; Döllinger's appeal is recorded in nearly the same words in: Plummer, *Conversations with Dr. Döllinger*, 102.

75   Plummer, *Conversations with Dr. Döllinger*, 102.

76   Bishop Browne's statement in: Plummer, *Conversations with Dr. Döllinger*, 10.

77   "Dr. Döllinger said that no question of principle was involved. It was the rectification of a wrong, which all parties acknowledged to be a wrong. If members of

the English Church there present were seriously of the opinion that the *Filioque* could not now be surrendered, he conceived that the present negotiations, so far as they had reference to members of the Greek Church, were at an end. It would be useless to meet them with a view of approximation, if we had already made up our minds that the *Filioque* must in any case be retained"; Plummer, *Conversations with Dr. Döllinger*, 102f.

78   Reusch, ed., *Bericht 1874*, 14; original wording of the compromise formula, taken from Howard, *The Pope and the Professor*, 201.

79   See Plummer, *Conversations with Dr. Döllinger*, 104.

80   "It was the Latins who, from the first and for many centuries, ceaselessly endeavored to impose the forgeries and fictions authorized by their hierarchy, and the innovations and claims based on them, upon the Orientals. An imperious despotism, attended by the fear that the sight of the free Eastern Church might produce an unfavorable feeling towards Papal monarchy in the West, an evil ignorance of Christian antiquity, and especially of Greek tradition and ecclesiastical literature, on the part of the Westerns – these were the real causes of the schism. But for these, the doctrinal difference concerning the Holy Ghost would never have assumed such dimensions, nor have been branded by both parties as a soul-destroying heresy"; Reusch, ed., *Bericht 1874*, 19.

doubtlessly pleased with this "Western confession of penitence towards the Eastern Churches,"[81] especially with the acknowledgment expressed therein that the Orthodox Church had preserved the genuine character of Catholicity. However, the representatives of Eastern Orthodoxy were totally unwilling to engage in a debate on the *Filioque*. They categorically rejected the proposed declaration. Since it constituted a dogmatic statement, the *Filioque* had to be rejected if the negotiations were, as already agreed, to be conducted on the basis of the doctrine of the undivided church.[82] Döllinger was barely able to limit the scope of the discussion to the "historical fact"[83] upon which he had wished to focus from the very outset, namely the question as to whether or not the insertion of the *Filioque* into the Nicene Creed had been lawful. Following a protracted debate that lasted well into the second day of the negotiations, all sides finally agreed on a preliminary statement in which the insertion of the *Filioque* into the credo was said to have been "unlawful" and in which the participants, in a nonbinding formulation, expressed the wish to consider a restoration of the original form of the credo, albeit "without sacrificing any true doctrine expressed in the current Western form."[84] The clarification of the Trinitarian statement on the origin of the Holy Spirit was to be dealt with at a follow-up conference.

The question of the validity of Anglican episcopal consecrations and, accordingly, the question of a recognition of the apostolic succession in the Anglican Church, also remained controversial. Döllinger was strongly in favor of recognizing the validity of the Anglican ordinations, arguing that this was a historical problem that could only

be solved by assessing the historical evidence – or, more specifically, by determining whether or not the consecration of Matthew Parker as archbishop of Canterbury in the year 1559 had been valid. Döllinger held the view that this question was all the easier to answer inasmuch as the validity of this episcopal consecration had not been doubted before the early 17th century; moreover, double standards should not be applied when assessing the criteria for its validity: "In the Western Church before the Reformation, things took place that may potentially raise far more serious objections to the unbroken succession and validity of many ordinations than anything which has been brought against the English consecration."[85] Speaking quite bluntly, he told the representatives of Eastern Orthodoxy that they lacked information and knowledge in this matter.[86] The Orthodox theologians nevertheless qualified the validity of the Anglican episcopal consecrations as at least "very doubtful" and "still undecided,"[87] for which reason the reservations regarding their validity could not be dropped until the problem had been solved by the respective churches.

The question of the invocation of saints was postponed. In adherence to the doctrinal resolutions of the Council of Trent, Döllinger had argued in favor of the current, still valid, Catholic view that the veneration of saints is not a necessary prerequisite for salvation and, consequently, not mandatory for all Christians. The Orthodox representatives, on the other hand, insisted that the veneration of saints constituted a religious duty. Since no agreement could be reached on this

---

81   This is how Chadwick characterized Döllinger's address; see Chadwick, "Döllinger and Reunion," 321.

82   The arguments that were put forth in the discussion are recorded in: Reusch, ed., *Bericht 1874*, 23–32.

83   Reusch, ed., *Bericht 1874*, 23–32. On the discussion, see also Plummer, *Conversations with Dr. Döllinger*, 104.

84   Plummer, *Conversations with Dr. Döllinger*, 32.

85   Döllinger's contribution to the discussion can be found in: Reusch, ed., *Bericht 1874*, 35f.

86   Reusch, ed., *Bericht 1874*, 37.

87   Reusch, ed., *Bericht 1874*, 35, 37. On the question of the validity of Anglican consecrations, see Jean-Marie Tillard, "Anglikanische Weihen," *LThK* 1, 668–670 (bibl.); David Reed, "Anglikanische Kirche," *RGG* 1, 484–488. On the annulment of the Anglican consecrations by Pope Leo XIII in 1896, see also Paul Avis's contribution in this volume.

matter (as Döllinger seems to have expected),[88] the dispute was temporarily set aside.[89]

A fierce dispute arose over the issue of the dogma of the Immaculate Conception. The verbal exchange over this "new Roman doctrine"[90] can only be reconstructed on the basis of Plummer's notes. Döllinger recommended to reject this dogma altogether. The corresponding doctrine stood in contradiction to the tradition of the first 13 centuries, according to which Christ alone had been conceived without sin, and was not part of the Catholic faith. Oxenham vehemently objected to this characterization, as did Liddon in more moderate terms. Oxenham stated that he had already believed in the doctrine of the Immaculate Conception prior to its dogmatization in 1854 and "it would be suicidal, with a view to union with other Christians, to pronounce such a belief false."[91] Doing so would be tantamount to setting up one's own new dogma. Liddon declared that

although he believed the doctrine was wrong, he did not wish to reject it as it had been attested since the 13th century and had undoubtedly been believed by many in the sense of a pious opinion since then. Döllinger countered that this doctrine was *fons et origo malorum* to him and the Old Catholic theologians.[92] The purpose of this dogma of 1854, he argued (here in agreement with current scholarly opinion), had been "to prepare the way of the later dogma of papal infallibility: the dogma of 1854 was not merely a feeler; it virtually initialized the dogma of 1870."[93] As Oxenham wrote after the conference, this had been "the first open break with the tradition of the older church."[94] Following a turbulent discussion, the dogma of the Immaculate Conception was rejected by 25 to 9 votes on the grounds of contradicting the doctrine of the first 13 centuries. Because Bishop Kerfoot, who condemned the doctrine as heretical, had apparently personally attacked Oxenham during the discussion and due to a proceeding of the controversy in *The Guardian* after the end of the conference, Oxenham did not attend the reunion conference of 1875.[95]

Although central issues such as the *Filioque* and its theological relevance, the validity of the

---

88   "Dr. Döllinger pointed out that it was nowhere commanded in Scripture; that it was not commanded in the canons of the Councils of the Church; that in the first five or six Councils the subject was never even mentioned. Could it then be said to be a '*duty necessary* to salvation for *every* Christian'? Would a duty of such importance have been passed over in silence for so long? … But the Orientals had the greatest objection to admitting, even in the most qualified form, that the invocation of saints was not of paramount importance for man's spiritual welfare. 'I expected this,' said Dr. Döllinger to Liddon: 'the Orientals attach almost as great importance to the acts of Councils as to the canons, and consider them almost as binding; and certainly in the acts of the Council referred to there is a great deal about the invocation of saints.' He then resumed his place as President and said, 'I suppose then that we can do no more than leave this article unpassed, as one on which the gentlemen of the English Church agree with us Germans, but in which our brethren from the East find themselves unable to go along with us.' And no subsequent appeal moved the Orientals to yield"; Plummer, *Conversations with Dr. Döllinger*, 110.

89   See Reusch, ed., *Bericht 1874*, 44–46.

90   Plummer, *Conversations with Dr. Döllinger*, 107f., here 107. A harmonizing description can be found in: Reusch, ed., *Bericht 1874*, 38–41.

91   Oxenham's objection can be found in: Plummer, *Conversations with Dr. Döllinger*, 107.

92   Reusch, ed., *Bericht 1874*, 39; also cited in: Plummer, *Conversations with Dr. Döllinger*, 107.

93   Plummer, *Conversations with Dr. Döllinger*, 107. It was well known that this dogma had been made to prepare the way of the later dogma of papal infallibility. The dogma of 1854 was not merely a feeler; it virtually included the dogma of 1870. On the Marian dogma as a "test case" for the definition of papal infallibility in 1870, see for instance Giacomo Martina, *Pio IX*, vol. 2, Rome, Pontificia Università Gregoriana, 1986, 278f.; Klaus Schatz, *Vaticanum I (1869–1870)*, vol. 1, Paderborn, Schöningh, 1992, 24–26.

94   I. von Döllinger to H.N. Oxenham, Munich, Nov 16, 1874, privately owned letter, soon to be printed in my *Ignaz von Döllinger: Briefwechsel (1830–1890)*.

95   H.N. Oxenham to I. von Döllinger, Aug 6, 1875, and I. von Döllinger to H.N. Oxenham, Nov 16, 1874, privately owned letter, soon to be printed in my *Ignaz von Döllinger: Briefwechsel (1830–1890)*. On the controversy following the conference and on Oxenham's statement in *The Guardian*, Sept 30, 1874, 1238f., see Chadwick, "Döllinger and Reunion," 325; Chapman, "Liddon," 33.

Anglican consecrations, or the invocation of saints had not been solved, the conference had achieved more than could have been generally expected in such a short time. In a series of important and hitherto controversial questions, the theologians, at least, believed that they had achieved a basic consensus, although the Orthodox representatives repeatedly expressed reservations. Anglicans and Old Catholics were able to agree on matters of Scripture (the original text is always normative, not the translation), Bible reading, the canon of Scripture, the use of the vernacular in liturgy, the doctrine of the sacraments (the main sacraments being baptism and Holy Communion), and the doctrine of justification (the means and the precondition of justification lying in the faith that is active in love, a definition that was compatible with the doctrine of the Council of Trent). Negotiations with the representatives of Eastern Orthodoxy led to agreements on questions of tradition (along with Holy Scripture, a source of faith is also seen in tradition, i.e. "the unbroken, partly oral and partly written transmission of the doctrine that was first set forth by Christ and the apostles,"[96] which was said to be a binding and God-willed source of knowledge for all successive generations of Christians), the dogma of the Immaculate Conception, the sacrament of penance (the early Christian practice of communal penance might be retained alongside the private confession, albeit only in a form that has been cleansed of improper usages), the system of indulgences, the prayer for the deceased, and the Eucharist (emphasis on the meal-like and communal character of the Eucharistic celebration).[97]

According to Plummer's account, the participants in the conference gained the impression that the hope for a reunion between the Eastern and Western Churches had suddenly moved into the realm of possibility.[98] Döllinger himself was extremely satisfied with the outcome. Eyewitnesses reported that the strenuous conference work seemed to have literally awakened him to new life.[99] These testimonies document the euphoric unionist mood that had taken hold of Döllinger and of many of the conference participants at this time and explain the high, albeit overoptimistic, expectations which they attached to these negotiations.

4.2   The Reunion Conference of 1875

It had been agreed that the unresolved questions were to be resumed at a follow-up conference, which convened from Aug 12 to 16, 1875, once again in Bonn. Döllinger's invitation was dated July 20, 1875 and formulated the goal of the conference as the "establishment of an intercommunion and church confederation, that is, a mutual recognition" of the churches.[100] In spite of the fact that the invitation was sent at short notice, over 100 persons attended the conference, more than in the previous year.

Prior to the conference, Döllinger had appealed to Constantinople[101] and Saint Petersburg[102] to send qualified theologians; in mid-July 1875, he conferred with Liddon and Plummer in Munich.[103]

---

96   On this particular point, the compromise represented a step backwards in relation to the Council of Trent, which, in its fourth session of Apr 8, 1546, did not employ *partim ... partim* but *et* in its dogmatic statement on Scripture and tradition as the sources of faith.

97   On the discussion, see Neuner, *Döllinger als Theologe*, 185–190 (with a reprint of the approved propositions).

98   "The last solemn act of the Conference was some evidence that a bridge, frail possibly and far from secure, had really been thrown across the abyss"; Plummer, *Conversations with Dr. Döllinger*, 116.

99   "Dr. Döllinger's face quite beamed with satisfaction. The very severe work of these three days seemed positively to have refreshed him, so encouraging had been the outcome"; Plummer, *Conversations with Dr. Döllinger*, 115.

100 Reusch, ed., *Bericht 1875*, 1.

101 Döllinger's invitation from Mar 18, 1875 was personally delivered to the patriarch of Constantinople by a delegation headed by the Munich professor of philosophy Johann Nepomuk Huber. Printed in: Reusch, ed., *Bericht 1875*, 117f.

102 I. von Döllinger to A. Kireev, Munich, June 2, 1875, in: Reusch, ed., *Bericht 1875*, 118f.

103 See Plummer, *Conversations with Dr. Döllinger*, 117–128; Chapman, "Liddon," 40f.

Eastern Orthodoxy was now represented by 21 delegates, including prominent theologians. The Greek delegation was headed by the Archbishop Alexandros Lykourgos of Syros, Melos, and Tenos; the patriarch of Constantinople had sent the Archimandrites Ioannis Anastasiadis and Philoteos Bryennios, the autocephalous Church of Romania was represented by the Bishops Ghenadie of Argeş and Melchizedek of Lower Danube, that of Serbia by the Archimandrite Sabbas of Belgrade. The Russian Orthodox Church was represented by the theologians Janyshev and Osinin as well as by Julian Joseph Overbeck, a German-born, former Catholic priest living in Cambridge UK, who had married and converted to the Lutheran faith, then to Anglicanism, and finally, in 1865, to Russian Orthodoxy. With over 60 participants, the Anglicans from England and the United States formed the largest delegation. Bishop Charles Waldegrave Sandford of Gibraltar had traveled to Bonn at the behest of the archbishop of Canterbury. Among the theologians, Liddon was again the most important representative of the English High Church. The Bishops Forbes of Brechin, Browne of Winchester, and Wordsworth of Lincoln sent their apologies, as did Bishop Gregory Thurston Bedell of Ohio, who was following a cure in Switzerland.[104] As in the preceding year, Gladstone declined to attend the conference out of consideration for his political office. With regard to the *Filioque* issue, however, he had pleaded in favor of a statement that would allow both sides "to move significantly and effectively closer to each other, without touching upon the last and cardinal question of a change in the

'occidental' formula."[105] The Old Catholics were represented by Eduard Herzog, the first Christian Catholic bishop of Switzerland. Protestant and Catholic theologians were once again absent, but seven Evangelical pastors from Germany were present.[106]

The *Filioque* issue determined almost the entire course of the conference. Speaking in the name of the Orthodox participants, who had already discussed the issue with Döllinger on the two preceding days,[107] Osinin opened the negotiations by drawing a red line that had not to be crossed. He declared that the Orthodox doctrine and praxis as laid down in the seven ecumenical councils and in the corresponding teachings of the church fathers was nonnegotiable. It was "complete and forever unalterable."[108] Although later doctrinal developments should not be ignored, they could not claim the same authority.

Subsequently, the Trinitarian theological debate over the doctrine of the procession of the Holy Spirit turned out to be extremely difficult. During the conference of 1875, Döllinger no longer pleaded in favor of deleting the *Filioque* but strove to harmonize the different views.[109] However, it

---

104 See A.P. Forbes to I. von Döllinger, Dundee, Aug 4, 1875, in: BAB, NL, Reusch 7/43; H.E. Browne to I. von Döllinger, London, Aug 3, 1875, in: Reusch, ed., *Bericht 1875*, 119–122, 126f. (with a detailed statement on the three unresolved questions regarding the *Filioque*, the validity of the Anglican episcopal consecrations, and the veneration of saints); G.T. Bedell to I. von Döllinger, Thusis, Aug 11, 1875, in: BSB, Döllingeriana II.

105 W.E. Gladstone to I. von Döllinger, Aug 2, 1875, in: Reusch, ed., *Bericht 1875*, 34–36. See also W. E. Gladstone to I. von Döllinger, London, June 5, and I. von Döllinger to W.E. Gladstone, Munich, July 21, and Aug 2, 1875, in: BL, Gladstone Papers, Add. 44140, 44447.

106 List of participants in: Reusch, ed., *Bericht 1875*, 3–5.

107 On these talks, see Reusch, ed., *Bericht 1875*, 6–18.

108 Reusch, ed., *Bericht 1875*, 7.

109 See Plummer's notes in Plummer, *Conversations with Dr. Döllinger*, 121f., recording the following conversation with Döllinger on July 14, 1875: "We talked also of the approaching Conference at Bonn. The *Filioque* was to be the great question to be discussed: not, as last year, whether it was to be retained in the formula; that might very well be left an open question, each Church retaining its own use. The doctrine itself is to be discussed this year. I asked him whether he considered the Greek position with regard to the Procession a strong one. Dr. Döllinger said that he believed that, as regards mere *wording*, the Greek position, based upon their own fathers, was *unattackable*. There can be no doubt that in the passages in which the Greek fathers treat of the subject they are quite silent about the

proved very difficult to convince the Orthodox participants of the necessity to distinguish between dogma and theological doctrine, something they were very reluctant to accept. This led to endless discussions on the meaning of theological concepts, especially with regard to whether the Latin word *procedere* (*qui procedit a Patre Filioque*), as understood by the Latin Church, could also be understood in a broader sense than the Greek ἐκπορεύεσθαι, and thus be harmless in its relationship to the *Filioque*.

After eight exhausting sessions that repeatedly threatened to end without any results,[110] and only after the conference had been extended to four days[111] (instead of the originally planned three days), the breakthrough was finally achieved. Döllinger, who remained strictly oriented to the doctrine of the church fathers, was able to convince all sides that in the matter of the *Filioque*, the point of contention between the Eastern and the Western churches was largely the consequence of a terminological misunderstanding. In substance, both meant the same thing.[112] Under

his guidance, six propositions regarding the Holy Spirit were agreed upon on the basis of the teaching of John of Damascus, the last church father of the undivided church, who had summarized the doctrinal development on this issue up to the Council of 680. With the main proposal that the Spirit proceeds from the Father *through* the Son, the doctrine was also viewed as legitimate by the Latin Church, as already expressed at the Council of Florence (1439), and therefore allowed a sustainable basis for further debates.[113]

Just when the agreement appeared to be within reach, it was once again jeopardized when Overbeck, who wished to prevent an agreement with the Anglicans, insisted that the conference should first specify the exact number of councils encompassed by the old undivided church: the first seven ecumenical councils which the Orthodox Church cannot renounce or only the first six councils recognized by the Anglicans? Döllinger was only barely able to convince the Orthodox representatives that the negotiated topic was not dependent on the recognition of the ecumenicity of the seventh ecumenical council (787) as it had not pronounced itself on the doctrine of the procession of the Holy Spirit.[114]

Owing to the dominance of the *Filioque* issue, the unresolved questions concerning the validity of the Anglican episcopal consecrations and the veneration of saints had receded into the background. The latter was not addressed, while the Anglicans categorically rejected a debate on the validity of their consecrations in order not to create an opportunity for eventual doubts. Döllinger took it upon himself to explain the Anglican

---

Procession of the Spirit from the Son. But he believed that if these passages were thoroughly sifted, and the quintessence of thought expressed from them, it would be found possible to bring them into harmony with the belief of the West."

110 See Plummer, *Conversations with Dr. Döllinger*, 117–135, esp. 133f. The passion with which the different opinions collided and partly led to tumultuous scenes was only hinted at in the conference report but is quite palpable in the notes of the participants.

111 The conference was extended by one day, or more precisely by two since Aug 15 was a Sunday, and ended on Monday 16, 1875.

112 "I now recognize more clearly than before that there is no real contradiction with regard to the dogma. The existing contrast mainly arose as a result of the fact that two different terminologies were developed and that the difference between the latter was artificially reinforced. I believe that we will reach a full understanding, perhaps even this year. In any case, it is no little feat that we are now moving closer to an understanding. Indeed, it would already be quite an achievement if you, the Orientals, could tell your homeland: At this conference, we have seen that the Occidentals recognize our churches as true Catholic churches and find

no dogmatic error in our exposition of the doctrine of the Holy Spirit and no Western contradiction to their own doctrinal formulation"; Reusch, ed., *Bericht 1875*, 90.

113 Text of the six proposals in: Reusch, ed., *Bericht 1875*, 92f.; reprinted in: Neuner, *Döllinger als Theologe*, 202. On the Trinitarian theological discussion: Neuner, *Döllinger als Theologe*, 200–203.

114 On the dispute: Reusch, ed., *Bericht 1875*, 83–86; Plummer, *Conversations with Dr. Döllinger*, 140f.

position to the Orthodox, who shared the views of the Roman Catholic Church on this issue. Arguing historically, he spoke out strongly in favor of recognizing the validity of the Anglican orders. The English Church had "carried out its Reformation" in the 16th century, "without forsaking the old episcopal constitution" and without interrupting the apostolic succession at the controversial ordination of Matthew Parker as archbishop of Canterbury.

> The fact that Parker was consecrated by four legitimately consecrated bishops *rite et legitime*, by laying on of hands and the words which are to be regarded as essential, is confirmed by such ample testimony that if one should wish to doubt these facts, one might with the same right doubt 100,000 facts, or, as someone has jokingly done after the publication of the *Life of Jesus* by Strauss, describe the history of the first Napoleon as a myth.[115]

The matter was laid to rest and no pertinent resolutions were adopted.

Döllinger concluded the conference on Aug 16, 1875, with a five-hour speech that was delivered, with interruptions, over the course of the day. In a historical outline, he examined the situation of the churches in past and present. After sharply criticizing the influence of the Roman "papal system on the individual Catholic nations"[116] and the confessional discord throughout the Christian world, he went on to encourage the participants in the conference to continue in their efforts "to promote the work of Christian reunion."[117] He himself was highly satisfied with the results that had been achieved. In his concluding remarks, he spoke of an "understanding" that went far beyond anything that he had hoped for. He expressed his belief that "at least among us Westerners," the conviction prevailed "that at the core of the matter, there is a real

consensus with regard to what an article of faith should be."[118] He hoped to be able to continue the international conference in the following year, and stated optimistically: "How joyful the day when the Orientals can tell us: our bishops, synods, and churches have accepted our agreement."[119] Even before leaving Bonn, he wrote the following words to Gladstone: "The conference was quite successful and met with general approval, and has exceeded my expectations."[120]

5   The Legacy of the Bonn Reunion Conferences

The third conference announced by Döllinger never took place. Although the conferences were widely acknowledged in church circles, especially in the English-speaking world, they also elicited much criticism. On the Orthodox side, Overbeck in particular strongly opposed the resolutions of the Bonn conferences. With the zeal of a convert, he took the view that the Orthodox Church was the only true Church of Christ and that the Old Catholics should break with Rome and Canterbury and convert to Orthodoxy. The true intention behind this rhetoric was the establishment of a Western Orthodoxy – an initiative the Russian Orthodox Church initially welcomed and which it did not definitively reject until the Saint Petersburg synod of 1892. After the conference of 1875, he sought to discredit the results of the conferences in several publications; with his appeal

---

115   Reusch, ed., *Bericht 1875*, 86.
116   Reusch, ed., *Bericht 1875*, 91–113, here 100; Plummer, *Conversations with Dr. Döllinger*, 143f.
117   Reusch, ed., *Bericht 1875*, 113.

118   Reusch, ed., *Bericht 1875*, 91.
119   Reusch, ed., *Bericht 1875*, 94.
120   I. von Döllinger to W.E. Gladstone, Bonn, Aug 20, 1875, in: BL, Gladstone Papers, Add. 44140. See the detailed account of the conference written by the correspondent George E. Broade: "So closed the second conference at Bonn, as the first had closed, with praise. It has been longer, more perplexed, and more anxious, but at last concord has been achieved. People will doubtless talk of theologians playing at a council, but we did what did no assembly for centuries has done – namely, passed in common formula of doctrinal expression, to which Easterns and Western alike subscribed"; [Broade,] "The Second Reunion Conference at Bonn," 1084.

to the patriarchs and holy synods of the Orthodox Catholic Church, he managed to sow distrust in the Eastern Churches and convinced them to oppose the Bonn reunion plans.[121]

In the English-speaking realm, the results of the Bonn reunion conferences were widely debated and positively received. However, Pusey's opposition proved a serious obstacle in the aftermath. Although the influential leader of the Oxford Movement in England had abandoned his decade-long hope of reaching an understanding with Rome due to the resolutions of Vatican I,[122] he was nevertheless unwilling to cut all ties to the Catholic Church and actually told Döllinger that he was critical, or even aloof, towards the Old Catholics.[123] He had stayed away from the reunion conferences in order not to compromise himself in any way, but closely followed their progress nonetheless. After the first conference, he still expressed his satisfaction at the present course of the negotiations,[124] but warned of efforts to sacrifice the *Filioque* for the

sake of a union with Orthodoxy, a warning that was undoubtedly also addressed to Döllinger. When the ECA, following the second Bonn Conference, again demanded that the *Filioque* should be removed from the credo and Meyrick also gave his consent, Pusey turned to the public. In two letters addressed to his disciple Liddon published in the London *Times* on Dec 27, 1875 and Jan 10, 1876, he vehemently rejected the notion that the insertion of the *Filioque* into the Nicene Creed had been unlawful.[125] It was his conviction, he declared, that the *Filioque* finds as much confirmation – if not even more – in the Holy Scripture and the majority of the Greek church fathers than in the Eastern form of the credo. Moreover, it expressed the same truth, albeit in different terms. He criticized the resolutions of Bonn as "unhappy"[126] and described the recourse to John of Damascus as misleading. Döllinger, he wrote to Newman, had attempted the impossible with his conciliatory formula, namely to make the message of the Western creed fit into the words of John of Damascus, who had himself rejected this creed.[127] The controversy reached its climax on Feb 18, 1876, when Pusey informed Liddon that he would convert to Catholicism or at least leave the Church of England if the Anglican Church should, as isolated voices had demanded, remove the *Filioque* from the confession of faith at the Lambeth Conference of 1878.[128] Liddon at-

121 Julian Joseph Overbeck, *Die Bonner Unions-Konferenzen: oder Altkatholicismus und Anglikanismus in iherm Verhältnis zur Orthodoxie: Eine Appellation an die Patriarchen und Heiligen Synoden der orthodox-katholischen Kirche*, Halle, H.W. Schmidt, 1876. On Overbeck's plans for a Western Orthodoxy and his role in the second reunion conference, see Wilhelm Kahle, *Westliche Orthodoxie: Leben und Ziele Julian Joseph Overbecks*, Leiden, Brill, 1968; Neuner, *Döllinger als Theologe*, 211–217; Bischof, *Theologie und Geschichte*, 430–432.

122 Pusey changed the tile of the third volume of *Eirenicon* to *Healthful Reunion: As Conceived Possible before the Vatican Council*. On Aug 26, 1870, he wrote to Newman: "I have done what I could, and now have done with controversy and Eirenica"; cited in: Henry Parry Liddon, *Life of Edward Bouverie Pusey*, vol. 4, London, Longmans, Green & Co., 1897, 193.

123 E.B. Pusey to I. von Döllinger, Reichenhall, Sept 6, 1872, and Milan, Oct 9, 1872, in: BSB, Döllingeriana II; E.B. Pusey to H.P. Liddon, Reichenhall, Sept 13, 1872, in: Liddon, *Life of Edward Bouverie Pusey*, vol. 4, 292f.

124 "I was glad too that you had no definite plan of union, but only wished 'arbores serere, quae alteri prosint saeculo.' I have been made very anxious by the eagerness of some (especially Americans) for proximate union with the Greek Church and the readiness to sacrifice the *Filioque*"; E.B. Pusey to I. von Döllinger, [Oxford,] Dec 30, 1874, in: BSB, Döllingeriana II.

125 Edward Bouverie Pusey, *On the Clause "And the Son," in Regard to the Eastern Church and the Bonn Conference: A Letter to the Rev. H.P. Liddon, D.D., Ireland Professor of Exegesis, Canon of S. Paul's*, Oxford, J. Parker, 1876.

126 This important letter from Pusey to Liddon, dated Dec 27, 1875, may be found in: Liddon, *Life of Edward Bouverie Pusey*, vol. 4, 297–299, here 299. On the whole controversy, see also John Octavius Johnston, *Life and Letters of Henry Parry Liddon*, London, Longmans, Green & Co., [3]1905, 185–204; Chadwick, "Döllinger and Reunion," 331–333; Chapman, "Liddon," 48–54.

127 Pusey's letter to Newman from Jan 11, 1876 may be found in: Liddon, *Life of Edward Bouverie Pusey*, vol. 4, 300: "Döllinger, of course, attempted an impossibility – to squeeze the principle of our Western Confession into the words of St. John Damascene, who rejected it."

128 As recorded in Liddon's diary on Feb 18, 1876; see Johnston, *Life and Letters*, 189: "Dr. Pusey told me that if the English Church gave up the *Filioque*, he must either

tempted to remedy the situation by assuring the public, also through *The Times*, that the English Church would not remove the *Filioque* and that the Anglican representatives in Bonn had not voted in favor of declaring that the *Filioque* had been inserted into the credo in an unlawful manner – a claim that was evidently false, as Liddon undoubtedly knew.[129]

A continuation of the reunion conferences was inconceivable under these circumstances.[130] External political events created additional obstacles. In the summer of 1876, the Balkan crisis (1875–1878) escalated among the European powers. The crisis, in which the respective churches were also implicated, was linked to the efforts of the Balkan peoples to gain independence from the Ottoman Empire. It led to the outbreak of the Russo-Turkish War (1877–1878) with long-lasting tensions between England and Russia. Due to English reservations in the so-called Eastern Question, Döllinger (who may have followed Liddon's advice in this)

finally abandoned his plans to convene a third reunion conference, which had been scheduled to take place in 1878 in spite of all adversity.[131]

The project of the Bonn reunion conferences had failed. Even the numerous expressions of gratitude and solidarity Döllinger received – mainly from England and the United States – could not conceal the reality.[132] Moreover, it had become abundantly clear that all church factions viewed the Bonn reunion conferences with skepticism or even with disbelief. Since they had taken place without a church mandate, their resolutions had no binding force, were not taken into consideration, and could be forgotten. German Protestantism, in any case, had stood aloof from Döllinger's idea of reunion on the basis of the tradition of the early church, as had the Roman Catholic Church. Then, and for many years afterwards, the latter could not conceive of church union as anything other than a return to the Catholic Church – not to mention the fact that its representatives were under no circumstances prepared to view the initiative of an excommunicated theologian in a positive light.[133] Döllinger's efforts to restore church unity, or at

shut his eyes and go to Rome, or trust that God would save him out of any Church at all. He could have no part in it."

129 See Chadwick, "Döllinger and Reunion," 333. See also Liddon's preface in: Reusch, ed., *Report of the Proceedings at the Reunion Conference: Held at Bonn between the 10th and 16th of August, 1875*, iii–li, esp. xl–li (critical analysis of Pusey's arguments).

130 I. von Döllinger to J. Acton, Munich, June 29, 1876, in: Döllinger & Acton, *Briefwechsel*, vol. 3, 165–167 (no. 421), here 166f.; "We regret this very much indeed; but I can quite understand that, under present circumstances, no other decision was possible"; Liddon to Döllinger, Oxford, June 23, 1876, in: BSB, Döllingeriana II. "After general conversation for a time he [Döllinger] spoke of the Reunion Conferences, and stated why he thought it would have been useless to have had one this year. (1) The troubled state of the East, where some of the bishops were taking part in the political struggle. (2) The divisions among the Orientals themselves, especially the jealousies and heart-burnings among the Greeks respecting the Slavic populations. (3) The mischief done by Overbeck, who has been working to prevent any union of Orientals with Anglicans. (4) The mischief done by Dr. Pusey in the line which he had taken about the *Filioque*"; Plummer, *Conversations with Dr. Döllinger*, 146.

131 Johnston, *Life and Letters*, 190. See also F. Meyrick to I. von Döllinger, Aylsham, June 24, 1879, in: BSB, Döllingeriana II: "I am afraid that the world is not ready for the third session of the Bonn Conference."

132 In September 1876, Döllinger received an *Address of Thanks to Dr. von Döllinger, and the Other Promoters of the Bonn Conference, 1875, from Clergy and Lay Communicants in Communion with the Church of England: Clerical & Selected Lay Signatures* that had originally been initiated by the politician Alexander Beresford-Hope and had been signed by 38 bishops, 3,800 clerics and deacons, as well as 4,170 laypeople belonging to the Anglican Church of England, Scotland, Northern Ireland, and India; see BSB, Döllingeriana I.7. For the solidarity statement of the bishops of the Protestant Episcopal Church of the United States of America from July 7, 1876, see BSB, Döllingeriana I.8.

133 By way of example, see Scheeben, "Die zweite Unionsconferenz," 529: "In the autumn holidays, an old scholar plays pope by assembling a number of self-proclaimed representatives of all the world's churches at the foot of his lectern in order to found, in fantasy or on paper, a church illuminated by his wisdom, gathered around him as its sun."

least to pave the way for it, had proved illusory. He had greatly overestimated the possibilities of mutual theological understanding and its importance for the respective churches. In 1878, having by now resigned himself to the facts of reality, he summed up the results of the conferences as follows: "We theologians have done what we set out to do. Everything depends on how the church authorities position themselves. However, some do nothing out of habitual indolence, the others out of political considerations."[134]

The Bonn reunion conferences were nonetheless "the most important ecumenical conversations in the 19th century";[135] even in their failure, they stand as a beacon for the future. For the first time in centuries, Eastern and Western theologians had taken a seat at the same table in order to discuss, in all ecumenical openness and with some prospect of success, the various questions associated with the reunion of divided Christendom. That the hope for the future prevailed in spite of all resignation was made abundantly clear by Döllinger in 1888, on the occasion of the publication of the German edition of his course of lectures entitled *Über die Wiedervereinigung der christlichen Kirchen*. In the preface, he looked back at the Bonn reunion conferences and wrote that they may "perhaps ..., if a politically less unfavorable constellation should one day arise in Europe, serve as a means of orientation and as a foundation on which one can then continue to build."[136]

Translated from German to English by Robert Meyer.

---

[134] Johann Friedrich, *Ignaz von Döllinger: Sein Leben auf Grund seines schriftlichen Nachlasses*, vol. 3, *Von der Rückkehr aus Frankfurt bis zum Tod, 1849–1890*, Munich, Beck, 1901, 649f.

[135] Victor Conzemius, "Ignaz v. Döllinger: The Development of a XIXth Century Ecumenist," in: *Hundert Jahre Christkatholisch-theologische Fakultät der Universität Bern*, supplement of *IKZ* 64, 1974, 110–127, here 125.

[136] Döllinger, *Über die Wiedervereinigung*, v.

Bibliography

Bischof, Franz Xaver, *Theologie und Geschichte: Ignaz von Döllinger (1799–1890) in der zweiten Hälfte seines Lebens: Ein Beitrag zu seiner Biographie*, Stuttgart, Kohlhammer, 1997.

Chadwick, Owen, "Döllinger and Reunion," in: Gillian Rosemary Evans, ed., *Christian Authority: Essays in Honour of Henry Chadwick*, Oxford, Clarendon Press, 1988, 296–334.

Chapman, Mark D., "Liddon, Döllinger and the Bonn Conferences of 1874 and 1875: A Case Study in Nationalism and Ecumenism," *IKZ* 92, 2002, 21–59.

Conzemius, Victor, "Ignaz von Döllinger (1799–1890): Una Sancta auf dem Prüfstand," in: Victor Conzemius, *Gottes Spurensucher. Zwanzig christliche Profile*, Freiburg – Basel – Wien 2002, 83–104.

Howard, Thomas Albert, *The Pope and the Professor: Pius IX, Ignaz von Döllinger, and the Quandary of the Modern Age*, Oxford, Oxford University Press, 2017.

Neuner, Peter, *Döllinger als Theologe der Ökumene*, Paderborn, Schöningh, 1979.

Plummer, Alfred, *Conversations with Dr. Döllinger (1870–1890)*, ed. Robrecht Boudens & Leo Kenis, Leuven, Leuven University Press, 1985.

Reusch, Franz Heinrich, ed., *Bericht über die am 14., 15. und 16. September zu Bonn gehaltenen Unions-Conferenzen, im Auftrage des Vorsitzenden Dr. von Döllinger*, Bonn, P. Neusser, 1874; ET: *Report of the Proceedings at the Reunion Conference: Held at Bonn on September 14, 15, and 16, 1874*, ed. Henry Parry Liddon, London, Rivingtons, 1875.

Reusch, Franz Heinrich, ed., *Bericht über die vom 10. bis 16. August 1875 zu Bonn gehaltenen Unions-Conferenzen, im Auftrage des Vorsitzenden Dr. von Döllinger*, Bonn, P. Neusser, 1875; ET: *Report of the Proceedings at the Reunion Conference: Held at Bonn between the 10th and 16th of August, 1875*, ed. Henry Parry Liddon, London, Basil Montagu Pickering, 1876.

Weitlauff, Manfred, *Das Erste Vatikanum (1869/70) wurde ihnen zum Schicksal: Der Münchener Kirchenhistoriker Ignaz von Döllinger (1799–1890) und sein englischer Schüler John Lord Acton (1834–1902): Ein Beitrag zum 150-Jahr-"Jubiläum" dieses Konzils*, 2 vols., Munich, Bayerischen Akademie der Wissenschaften, 2018.

CHAPTER 8

The Slavophiles: From Khomyakov to Solovyov

Jeremy Pilch

1 Introduction

Considered purely in terms of its 19th-century political and social influence, Slavophilism as a major force in 19th-century Russian life was rather short-lived. The two most notable Slavophiles, Aleksey Stepanovich Khomyakov (1804–1860) and Ivan Vasilyevich Kireyevsky (1806–1856), both died relatively young. Konstantin Sergeyevich Aksakov (1817–1860), another of the original Slavophiles who had met regularly in Moscow from the late 1830s, died in the same year as Khomyakov, leaving just Yuri Fyodorovich Samarin (1819–1876) as the main representative of the group. Samarin lived to see some of the reforms he had argued for enacted when Tsar Alexander II authored the Emancipation Edict in 1861. By the time of his death, the age of the first generation of Slavophiles was over; the leading Russian scholar of the subject, Nikolai Tsimbaev, has suggested that by the mid-1870s, Slavophilism was outdated and ceased to exist as a special direction of Russian social movement.[1]

Nonetheless, precisely because Slavophile social and political thought tried to articulate what was distinctive about Russian culture and history, it has continued to be seen as a significant living force in shaping Russian national identity, and contemporary Western scholars have approached this topic through the lens of Slavophilism.[2] The significance of Slavophilism in ecclesial terms, especially with regard to church unity, retains a particularly powerful contemporary resonance, not least because many current points of ecumenical tension were first brought into sharp relief in the debate and polemics in which the Slavophiles and their ecclesial heirs engaged.

2 Ivan Vasilyevich Kireyevsky

The figure most typically associated with Slavophilism, especially its ecclesiological dimension, is Aleksey Stepanovich Khomyakov. He is known for the idea of *sobornost* (synodality) and his treatise "Tserkov odna" ("The Church is One")[3] is a natural starting point for any understanding of the Slavophile contribution to the desire for Christian unity. However, notable scholars of the Slavophile movement, in particular the Orthodox priest,

---

1   Nikolai I. Tsimbaev, *Slavyanofilstvo: Iz istorii russkoj obschestvenno-politicheskoj mysli XIX veka* [Slavophilism: from the history of twentieth century's Russian social-political thought], Moscow, MGU, [2]2013 [[1]1986], 115. Tsimbaev's very thorough historical survey of the Slavophiles considers the movement in four stages: 1838/39–1848; 1848–1855; 1855–1861; 1861–1875. It is overwhelmingly written from a social and political perspective, though the second edition does acknowledge the religious and ecclesial aspect of Slavophile thought.

2   See, for example: Judith Devlin, *Slavophiles and Commissars: Enemies of Democracy in Modern Russia*, New York NY, St. Martin's Press, 1999; Susanna Rabow-Edling, *Slavophile Thought and the Politics of Cultural Nationalism*, Albany NY, State University of New York Press, 2007; Laura Engelstein, *Slavophile Empire: Imperial Russia's Illiberal Path*, Ithaca NY, Cornell University Press, 2009, and Patrick Michelson, "Slavophile Religious Thought and the Dilemma of Russian Modernity," *MIH* 7/2, 2010, 239–267.

3   Aleksey S. Khomyakov "Tserkov odna" ["The Church is One"], in: Aleksey S. Khomyakov, *Polnoe sobranie sochinenij* [Complete collected works], vol. 2, Moscow, Universitetskaya tipografiya na Strastnom bulvare, [5]1907; ET: "The Church is One," in: Boris Jakim & Robert Bird, eds., *On Spiritual Unity: A Slavophile Reader: Aleksei Khomiakov, Ivan Kireevsky, with essays by Yury Samarin, Nikolai Berdiaev and Pavel Florensky*, Hudson NY, Lindisfarne Books, 1998, 29–54.

theologian, and historian of Russian thought, Vasily Zenkovsky and the French Jesuit Slavist, François Rouleau, have seen fit to give a certain precedence to Ivan Kireyevsky. For Rouleau, Kireyevsky was "the most gifted and the most qualified of the Slavophiles" and was "in effect, the grand theoretician of the Slavophile group."[4] While Kireyevsky's writings are not as numerous as Khomyakov's, the two main essays of his mature years, "O kharaktere prosveshceniya Evropy i o ego otnoshenii k prosveshceniyu Rossii" ("On the Nature of European Culture and on Its Relationship to Russian Culture") and "O neobkhodimosti i vozmozhnosti novykh nachal dlya filosofij" ("On the Necessity and Possibility of New Principles in Philosophy")[5] are essential expressions of the Slavophile perspective, a kind of intellectual manifesto.[6] Furthermore, of all the Slavophile figures, he was the closest to the Orthodox Church; indeed so intimate was his relationship with the monastery at Optina Pustyn that he was buried, with his wife and brother Pyotr, next to the great Elders of Optina, Leonid, Macarius, and Ambrose.[7] Kontzevich observed "of all the lay people who spent time in Optina Monastery, Kireyevsky was closer than anyone to its spirit."[8] Similarly Zenkovsky has explained:

His was a genuine and profound religious *experience*, and in giving it meaning he drew very close to the immense spiritual wealth that was opened to him in the Optina Cloister. In this sense, Kireyevski, more than anyone else, must be looked upon as an exponent of what had been preserved within the ecclesiastical consciousness. If Khomyakov drew more from the depths of his own *personal* ecclesiastical consciousness, Kireyevski rested predominantly on what he found among the *Startsy* and in the monasteries. Kireyevski was, in a sense, closer to the Church than Khomyakov; he was in constant touch with people in the Church, especially the *Startsy* of the Optina Cloister. And, if the idea of the Church was central for Khomyakov – in philosophy as well as theology – the idea of *spiritual life* was central for Kireyevski.[9]

A good grasp of Kireyevsky's thought is essential in order to understand the philosophical perspective underpinning Slavophilism. Kireyevsky's acute criticism of European culture and the rationalism of the West, the Catholic Church, and secular culture alike, undoubtedly help to fuel Khomyakov's polemical works. Moreover, Kireyevsky's attempts to offer a renewed Christian anthropology in the tradition of the church fathers of the East and his overall philosophy of integral knowledge offer valuable insights which flesh out and enrich Khomyakov's principal contribution to ecclesiology, namely his idea of *sobornost*. As Slezkine writes, "if Khomyakov was the first to speak of 'sobornost,' there is no doubt that he had been very largely inspired by his friend, Ivan Kireyevsky, who revealed to the Russian philosophical conscience the principal of integrality, the

4   François Rouleau, *Ivan Kiréievski et la naissance du Slavophilisme*, Namur, Culture et vérité, 1990, 84 (the English translation is the author's).

5   Ivan V. Kireyevsky, "O kharaktere prosveshceniya Evropy i o ego otnoshenii k prosveshceniyu Rossii" ["On the Nature of European Culture and on Its Relationship to Russian Culture"], *Moskovskij Sbornik* 1, 1852; Ivan V. Kireyevsky, "O neobkhodimosti i vozmozhnosti novykh nachal dlya filosofij" ["On the Necessity and Possibility of New Principles in Philosophy"], *Russkaya Beseda* 3, 1856.

6   An English version of Kireyevsky's essays can be found in Jakim & Bird, eds., *On Spiritual Unity*, 187–232 and 233–274.

7   Leonid Kavelin, *Elder Macarius of Optina*, Platina CA, St. Herman of Alaska Brotherhood, 1995, 306.

8   Kavelin, *Elder Macarius of Optina*, 297. Kontzevich's brief biography is part of his larger work: Ivan M. Kontzevich,

Optina pustyn i eyo vremya [Optina monastery and its era], Jordanville NY, Holy Trinity Monastery, 1970.

9   Vasilii V. Zenkovskii, *A History of Russian Philosophy*, vol. 1, London, Routledge & Kegan Paul, 1953, 213 (italics original).

'totalizing vision.'"[10] Furthermore, it was in explicit continuity with the positions espoused by Kireyevsky, that the young Vladimir Sergeyevich Solovyov established himself as a philosophical and religious voice in the Slavophile tradition in the 1870s.

Born in Moscow on 3 Apr, 1806, Kireyevsky grew up on the family estate at Dolbino to the south of Moscow. In 1821, the family moved to Moscow and their home became a salon to the city's intellectual elite. Indeed, here were the origins of the first Slavophile-Westerners debates – Pyotr Yakovlevich Chaadayev was present, as were Khomyakov, Aleksandr Ivanovich Herzen, Nikolai Vasilievich Gogol, Konstantin Dmitrievich Kavelin and the brothers Konstantin Sergeyevich and Ivan Sergeyevich Aksakov. Kireyevsky also become part of a secret society of philosophers, the Obschestvo Lyubomudriya (Society for the Love of Wisdom), when he enrolled at Moscow University in 1822. In 1830, Kireyevsky's youthful discussions of German philosophers were crowned by a trip to Germany during which time he heard lectures by Hegel and Schelling. On returning to Russia Kireyevsky resumed his literary activities again and with his friends made the decision to establish and edit a journal, *Evropeets* (The European) which he hoped would reflect the culture of the times and European intellectual research. His own article, entitled "Devyatnadtsatyj vek" (The nineteenth century), contributed significantly to the success of the journal. Unfortunately, it also caught the eye of the authorities and was immediately suppressed. Even the censor, Sergey Timofeyevich Aksakov (father of Ivan and Konstantin, the two Slavophiles) was severely reprimanded, and it was only the intervention of Vasily Andreyevich Zhukovsky, tutor to the tsar's wife and once tutor to the young Kireyevsky, which prevented Kireyevsky from being banished from Moscow. Kireyevsky was devastated and would suffer psychologically

from this blow for the rest of his life; nor would this be the only time he would experience the hand of censorship.

For the next decade, Kireyevsky wrote little but intellectually and inwardly his life changed significantly. The months and years immediately following were marked by some psychological inner developments and a decisive change in his views. His thoughts moved towards the Slavophile position, and influences included his younger brother, Pyotr Kireyevsky, whose own intellectual interests centered on Russian folk traditions, and also the distinct figure of Khomyakov.[11] However, the most significant influence on him at this time was that of his wife Natalya Petrovna Kireyevksaya (née Arbeneva), whom he married on 18 Apr, 1834. She was a devout Orthodox Christian who had had St. Seraphim of Sarov as her spiritual leader until his death in 1833. After this, she became the spiritual child of the Elder Philaret, a monk of Moscow's Novospassky Monastery. A year into their marriage, responded to her husband's enthusiasm for the philosophy of the German Idealists with the reproach that such ideas were far better expressed by the fathers of the Eastern Church. Kireyevsky came to embrace the faith wholeheartedly.[12] On the death of the Elder Philaret, his wife became the disciple of the Elder Macarius of Optina Pustyn, near the Dolbino estate where the couple began to reside regularly from about 1840. Kireyevsky also came to adopt the Elder as his spiritual leader and confessor. In 1846 he supported the Elder in a major project of translating patristic texts into Russian; in the last decade of

---

10   Hélène Slezkine, *Kiréievski et Optino Poustyne*, Lavardac, Éditions Saint-Jean le Roumain, 2001, 22 (the English translation is the author's).

11   On the younger Kireyevsky brother and the Slavophile movement see: Michael Hughes, "Peter Kireevskii and the Development of Moscow Slavophilism," *Slavonica* 14/2, 2008, 89–107.

12   In his 1852 essay, Kireyevsky reiterates the essential point his wife had made to him before his conversion arguing that the "profound writings" of the church fathers, "filled with supreme theological and philosophical speculations, may even today test the wisdom of any German professor of philosophy (though none of them is likely to admit this)." See Jakim & Bird, *On Spiritual Unity*, 215.

his life, his own writings would increasingly reflect this influence although there is no doubt he was still "in formation" at the time of his death and this thought was still maturing. In this sense, the legacy of Kireyevsky to Slavophile thought was embryonic, awaiting further development, a point very noticeable in the posthumously published fragments,[13] which have the same pithy style as the spiritual writings contained in the *Philokalia*, and on occasion, also reflect the best of them in terms of spiritual insight and luminosity.[14]

Kireyevsky's 1852 essay "On the Nature of European Culture and on Its Relationship to Russian Culture," published in *Moskovskyj Sbornik* (Moscow miscellany) is notable for a sustained critique of Western culture, a critique which is intimately linked to schism in the church. The West is characterized by a one-sided rationalism, which Kireyevsky sees particularly embodied in St. Augustine. He writes that "of all the Church Fathers, both early and late, surely no one had so marked a predilection for the logical concatenation of truths as St. Augustine, most often called the Teacher of the West. Some of his works are like an iron chain of syllogisms, each link fitting seamlessly into the next."[15] Kireyevsky sees the whole of the West as suffering from this excessive rationality and sees it as principle cause of the schism which divided the church: "It may even be that this Roman peculiarity, this isolated rationality, this excessive inclination toward the formal coherence of ideas, had itself been one of the main reason for Rome's defection."[16]

When Kireyevsky speaks of Rome's defection, he is referring to the issue of the *Filioque*: "The actual pretext for defection – the new addition of a dogma to the earlier creed, an addition that, contrary to the ancient tradition and shared consciousness of the Church, was justified only by the logical deductions of the Western theologians."[17] Instead of addressing theological aspects of the *Filioque* or the historical circumstances in which it was introduced, Kireyevsky considers it solely in terms of Western one-sided rationalism. He considers that this planted "the inescapable seed of the Reformation" as early as the 9th century and, moreover, in terms of the original East-West schism, it was this "same moral cause, the same bias toward one-sided logic, which gave rise to the doctrine of the necessary external unity of the Church, [and] was bound to produce also the doctrine of the infallibility of its visible head."[18] Such sweeping statements are characteristic of the broader approach of Kireyevsky and the Slavophiles to history and we are left to blame human rationality, purportedly an exclusively negative characteristic of the Western Church alone, as the principle cause of all the factors which caused the division in the churches.

Kireyevsky sees the Western Church as split between its spiritual activities and its relations with the world. A Western Christian culture is tacitly acknowledged, though only in so far as Scholasticism, which is viewed negatively, contributed to its downfall: "Reason's disintegration into particular faculties, this predominance of rationality over other activities of the spirit, would ultimately destroy the entire edifice of European medieval civilization."[19] He also makes the rather far-reaching claim that "when, with the conquest of Constantinople, the fresh, uncontaminated air of Greek thought poured in from the East and thinkers in the West began to breathe more easily and freely, the entire edifice of Scholasticism collapsed instantaneously."[20] Kireyevsky devotes the rest of this essay to presenting authentic Christian

---

13   Ivan V. Kireyevsky, "Otryvki" [Fragments], *Russkaya Beseda* 5, 1857.

14   The *Philokalia* are a collection of writings from the Eastern Christian tradition compiled on Mount Athos in the 18th century. The monks at Optina played a significant role in the dissemination of these teachings throughout Russia in the 19th century.

15   Jakim & Bird, *On Spiritual Unity*, 202.

16   Jakim & Bird, *On Spiritual Unity*, 202.

17   Jakim & Bird, *On Spiritual Unity*, 203.

18   Jakim & Bird, *On Spiritual Unity*, 203.

19   Jakim & Bird, *On Spiritual Unity*, 206.

20   Jakim & Bird, *On Spiritual Unity*, 208–209.

culture and civilization – in other words Russian culture. Of particular importance for Kireyevsky is

> the spiritual philosophy of the Eastern Church Fathers who wrote after the tenth century was openly and purely Christian. It was profound, alive, elevating the reason from the status of rationalistic mechanism to higher, morally free speculation, a philosophy that even an unbelieving thinker could well find instructive because of the remarkable wealth, depth, and subtlety of its psychological observations.[21]

It was under the guidance of the Fathers of the East, says Kireyevsky, "that the authentic Russian mind, which lies at the foundation of Russian life, was formed."[22] This understanding of the Christian nature of old Russian culture is very important for it is from this source that Kireyevsky seeks the renewal of modern philosophy and ultimately the unity of humanity in the church.

Kireyevsky offers some important clues to the key influences on his thought. Among these are the figures whom he is reading through his contact with the Elder Macarius and his participation in Optina Pustyn's patristic translation project. He highlights the high culture of aspects of medieval Russian life, both princely and monastic, and points out that

in some of the compositions that survive from the fifteenth century, we find excerpts from Russian translations of Greek works that not only were unknown in Europe, but had been lost in Greece itself during its decline and have only recently been rediscovered with great effort in the uncatalogued treasure troves of Athos.[23]

This spiritual influence had a decisive effect on the Russian mind and personality according to Kireyevsky. In contrast to the West, where "people fragment their lives into separate aspirations; and though they then unite them into a coherent plan by means of rationalistic understanding, at each moment of life the individual is like a different person," the Russian people possess a "constant striving for the combined wholeness of all moral faculties."[24] It is this principle, "the special, living, integral philosophy of the Holy Fathers of the Church" which Kireyevsky presents as the remedy for the questions of modernity, and concludes his essay with the desire that the wholeness of being that we observe in ancient Russia should forever be the destiny of our present and future Orthodox Russia.[25]

In his final essay, "On the Necessity and Possibility of New Principles in Philosophy," published in *Russkaya Beseda* (The Russian colloquy) shortly after his death in 1856, Kireyevsky, primarily addressing philosophical matters, also offers significant reflections about church unity. The first of these points is linked to the place and importance of tradition in the church. "Sacred tradition," writes Kireyevsky, "is the repository of the common consciousness of the whole Christian

---

21   Jakim & Bird, *On Spiritual Unity*, 212. Kireyevsky names no specific figures, and he argues that the West was not able to understand this philosophy, admitting Thomas à Kempis as a possible exception. Who, therefore, are these Eastern church fathers from the 10th century onwards who are clearly major influences on Kireyevsky's? They are figures that remain very little known to Western Christians, presumably those who feature in the third and fourth volume of the *Philokalia*. Among the most significant of these who are regularly cited in the correspondence of the Elder Macarius are St. Peter of Damascus, Niketas Stethatos, St. Symeon Metaphrastis, and St. Gregory of Sinai.

22   Jakim & Bird, *On Spiritual Unity*, 214.

23   Jakim & Bird, *On Spiritual Unity*, 215. The 15th-century writings referred to are very likely those of Nil Sorsky (1433–1508) whose spirituality was in direct continuity with the Eastern patristic tradition and, of course, was formally rejected in the mid-16th century with the victory of St. Joseph of Volokolamsk and the landed monasteries over Sorsky and the "Non-Possessors."

24   Jakim & Bird, *On Spiritual Unity*, 222–223.

25   Jakim & Bird, *On Spiritual Unity*, 232.

world and holds the Universal Church together in a living, indissoluble unity."[26] In Kireyevsky's view, Catholicism prefers reason to tradition, and only upheld the latter over the former when forced to do so in opposition to Protestantism. He repeats this assertions about Western rationalism and the consequent defection of the West, albeit offering more historical context: out of "excessive zeal against the Arians," influenced by "superficially logical thought," the West "created a new dogma concerning the Godhead in direct opposition to the Arians"; hence "as a result of the Western peoples' ignorance, their very striving for church unity tore them from it, and their very striving for Orthodoxy tore them away from Orthodoxy."[27] An "illegitimate addition to the Creed" required popular ignorance and "papal love of power" to be realized – and, as a result, Kireyevsky emphasizes, the *Filioque* became "the permanent obstacle to the return of the West to the Church."[28] Kireyevsky is reluctant to seek ways of understanding the *Filioque* sympathetically since for him it is integrally connected to the West's predilection for rationality and papal primacy and thus to his whole critique of Western Christianity.[29] The result is a perverse insistence upon the permanence of ecclesial division. Certainly these three themes which Kireyevsky introduces with regard to the West – rationality, doctrinal additions, and papal power – become part of the Slavophile world view and remain decisive issues which continue to impede the work of ecclesial reunion.

Yet despite the dead-end which Kireyevsky appears to have created in a historical narrative which is built on ecclesial disunity, one can discern a way out of this *impasse* in his work. He acknowledges that the East suffers from the schism because "the fate of all humanity is in a state of living and sympathetic reciprocity."[30] Hence he argues that the development of social civilization was halted in the East because this was beyond the power of the East alone, which was thus left to preserve divine truth in purity and holiness, while being unable to embody it.[31] Furthermore, Kireyevsky's own philosophical system forces him to acknowledge the need for church unity. In terms of how this might occur, Kireyevsky observes that "it is hard to see what European civilization may come to if some sort of inner change does not occur among the European peoples."[32] Thus an interior change, a recalibrating of Western thought towards wholeness is for Kireyevsky the solution. It is the philosophical path of integral knowledge which is the route by which ecclesial unity may be reestablished.

Kireyevsky's philosophy of integral knowledge was never developed fully, but his final work offers valuable examples of the direction his thought would follow. This is the collection of short, "philokalic" spiritual reflections, published posthumously by Khomyakov as "Fragments" and described by its modern editor as "Kireevsky's most definitely religious work."[33] In it Kireyevsky stresses the centrality of the heart and religious faith in the human endeavor for true knowledge. Moreover, the author clearly presents his philosophical conception of unity as situated in and through the church. Kireyevsky's emphasis of wholeness now assumes an ecclesial form, and as such his philosophical reflections incorporate and illuminate the idea of *sobornost* which is the central ecclesial legacy of the Slavophiles. Most commonly associated with Khomyakov, it is in Kireyevsky that we find the fuller conceptual and philosophical expression of it.

Kireyevsky also adds an important anthropological dimension to his philosophical ideas. The

---

26   Jakim & Bird, *On Spiritual Unity*, 236.

27   Jakim & Bird, *On Spiritual Unity*, 251.

28   Jakim & Bird, *On Spiritual Unity*, 251.

29   In contrast, Solovyov proposed a clear way out of the problem of the *Filioque* through the work of St. Maximus the Confessor. See Vladimir S. Solovyov, *O khristianskom edinstve* [On Christian unity], Brussels, Zhizn s Bogom, 1967, 188–189.

30   Jakim & Bird, *On Spiritual Unity*, 251.

31   One of Solovyov's severest criticisms of the Russian Orthodox Church focuses precisely on this inability to embody Christian principles in society.

32   Jakim & Bird, *On Spiritual Unity*, 256–257.

33   Jakim & Bird, *On Spiritual Unity*, 275.

idea of integrality he proposes is nothing other than the ecclesial interconnectedness of human beings. "Each Christian," he writes, "is in spiritual communion with the fullness of the entire Church."[34] Thus Kireyevsky emphasizes the corporate dimension of salvation:

> Christians know that in the inner disorder of the soul they act not alone and for themselves only; they know that they perform the common task of the entire Church and of the entire human race, for which the redemption was completed and of which they are only a part. Only together with the entire Church and in living communion with her can Christians be saved.[35]

In terms of Kireyevsky's contemporary significance, one should point out that his ecclesial thinking here resonates distinctly with that of the *communio* school of 20th-century Catholic theologians, many of whom were clearly influenced by the Greek fathers and *ressourcement* more broadly.

Another, perhaps more surprising link with Catholic theology, may be considered in the light of one of the most wonderful passages in all of Kireyevsky writings. Naturally integrating moral theology within ecclesiology, Kireyevsky argues that, "each moral victory hidden within a single Christian soul is a spiritual victory for the entire Christian world. Each spiritual force created within a single person invisibly attracts the forces of the moral world to itself and emboldens them."[36] What Kireyevsky expresses here is a concrete expression of what *sobornost* means in practice. At the heart of this aspect of Orthodox ecclesiology, which the Slavophiles helped highlight so well, is a recognition that an individual's actions have consequences well beyond their immediate environment and, most significantly, at a supernatural level. There is a clear awareness of the redemptive value of our actions, both in terms of our own salvation and of those of others. Indeed, Kireyevsky recognizes such a spirituality as having been lived by the Elder Macarius to whom he wrote in July 1855, congratulating him on receiving the pectoral cross: "We have always seen how you bear within your heart the Cross of the Lord and co-suffer with Him in His love for sinners. Now this sanctity which is within your loving heart will be visible for all on your breast."[37]

3   Aleksey Stepanovich Khomyakov

If Kireyevsky played a pioneering philosophical role among the Slavophiles, the dominant theological figure among the group was Aleksei Stepanovich Khomyakov. Khomyakov was a landowner with a large estate in the Tula province, to the south of Moscow. His interests were varied, he had a lasting affection for England, and his collected writings run to eight volumes, including an extensive historiosophical account of world history.[38] Underpinning all his activities was a deep piety instilled in him from his youth by his mother, and his profound Orthodox faith lay at the heart of his marriage and domestic life. Zernov writes that "he was exceptionally happy in his marriage. His wife shared his convictions and gave him unfailing support in all his work. They had four sons and five daughters."[39] Although his theological writings only amount to one of the eight volumes

34   Jakim & Bird, *On Spiritual Unity*, 287.
35   Jakim & Bird, *On Spiritual Unity*, 287.
36   Jakim & Bird, *On Spiritual Unity*, 288.

37   Kavelin, *Elder Macarius of Optina*, 304.
38   The major study of Khomyakov remains: Albert Gratieux, *A.S. Khomiakov et le Mouvement Slavophile*, 2 vols., Paris, Cerf, 1939. For Khomyakov's ecclesiology see Serge Bolshakoff, *The Doctrine of the Unity of the Church in the Works of Khomiakov and Moehler*, London, SPCK, 1946. Recent studies of Khomyakov include Vladimir Tsurikov, ed., *A.S. Khomiakov: Poet, Philosopher, Theologian*, Jordanville NY, Holy Trinity Seminary Press, 2004, and Artur Mrówczyński-Van Allen, Teresa Obolevitch & Paweł Rojek, eds., *Alexei Khomiakov: The Mystery of Sobornost'*, Eugene OR, Pickwick, 2019.
39   Nicolas Zernov, *Three Russian Prophets: Khomiakov, Dostoevsky, Soloviev*, London, SCM Press, 1944, 50.

of his collected works, they are sufficient for him to be considered Russia's first lay theologian. As such, Khomyakov's legacy is primarily linked to his work on the church, which was expressed in two ways: firstly in his brief but seminal essay "The Church is One" and secondly in his sometimes bitterly polemical engagement with non-Orthodox Christians. Both these aspects of Khomyakov's ecclesial writings remain significant with regard to church unity.

Khomyakov's essay "O Tserkvi" ("On the Church") first appeared in print after his death, published in *Pravoslavnoe Obozrenie* (The Orthodox review) in 1864.[40] It is uncertain exactly when he wrote it, although he did try unsuccessfully to have the work published in French and Greek translation between 1846 and 1848.[41] It is therefore one of his earliest pieces of theological writing and it is markedly his least polemical work, partly because it was not written directly in response to a Catholic or Protestant publication.

The key focus of this essay is not primarily that of doctrinal differences but rather an exposition of Khomyakov's Orthodox understanding of the church, centered predominantly on the themes of unity and love. Khomyakov emphasized the pneumatological over the Christological in his ecclesiology, and it is this dimension of his work which underpins claims that the idea of *sobornost* helped shape the ecclesiology of Vatican II.[42] There are a number of key themes which Khomyakov develops in the opening part of this essay and among the most central are those of unity and grace: "The unity of the Church follows necessarily from the unity of God, for the Church is not a multiplicity of persons in their personal separateness, but the unity of God's grace, living in the multitude of rational creatures who submit themselves to God's grace."[43] It is important to recognize that this is an ideal unity, for Khomyakov highlights that "those who live on earth, those who have completed their earthly paths, those who are not created for earthly paths (such as angels), those who have not yet begun their earthly paths (the future generations), all are united in the one Church – in the one grace of God." It is this "essential unity," the "fullness and perfection of the entire Church" toward which the visible earthly Church advances in time and which "the Lord appointed to be made manifested at the Last Judgement of the entire creation."[44] Although Khomyakov openly states that the primary focus of ecclesial unity is eschatological, his delineation of the distinction between this ideal and the reality of the life of the church on earth is not clearly made.

For Khomyakov the liturgy plays a significant role in manifesting ecclesial unity, for "only one who understands the liturgy can understand the Church. Above all else is unity of holiness and love."[45] This, "the unity of Church rituals," is particularly significant for the local churches – he refers to the Greek, Russian, and Syrian – "for it is here that the unity of spirit and doctrine is made visibly manifest."[46] In distinct contrast to counter-Reformation Catholic ecclesiology, Khomyakov highlights the fact that: "The visible Church is not the visible society of Christians but the Spirit of God and the grace of the sacraments living in the society."[47] He places a strong emphasis on the

---

40   Aleksey S. Khomyakov, "O Tserkvi" ["On the Church"], *Pravoslavnoe Obozrenie* 13, 1864, 233–258.

41   "The Church is One" first appeared in an English translation by William J. Birkbeck as an accompaniment to his edition of the correspondence between Khomyakov and the English theologian William Palmer: William J. Birkbeck, ed., *Russia and the English Church during the Last Fifty Years*, vol. 1, *Containing a correspondence between Mr. William Palmer, fellow, of Magdalen College, Oxford and M. Khomiakoff, in the years 1844–1854*, London, Rivington, Percival & Co. 1895, 192–222. In this chapter I have used the more recent translation by Robert Bird in *On Spiritual Unity*, 29–54.

42   Yves Congar, *Je crois en l'Esprit Saint*, Paris, Cerf, 1979; ET: *I Believe in the Holy Spirit*, vol. 1, trans. David Smith, New York NY, Crossroad, 2013, 171.

43   Jakim & Bird, *On Spiritual Unity*, 31.

44   Jakim & Bird, *On Spiritual Unity*, 31.

45   Jakim & Bird, *On Spiritual Unity*, 51.

46   Jakim & Bird, *On Spiritual Unity*, 34.

47   Jakim & Bird, *On Spiritual Unity*, 39.

communal nature of salvation and the unity of the faithful in prayer:

> We know that those among us who fall, fall by themselves, but that no one is saved by oneself. Those who are saved are saved in the Church as her member and in unity with all her other members. When someone believes, that person is in a community of faith; when someone loves, that person is in a community of love; when someone prays, such a person is in a community of prayer.[48]

The interdependence of believers is further emphasized: "If you are a member of the Church, your prayer is needed by all her members. ... The Church prays for all, and we all together pray for all. ... True prayer is true love."[49] Although he does not use the actual word in this essay, it is this unity of believers in the Holy Spirit, in prayer and love, which constitutes the essence of *sobornost* and Khomyakov's distinctive contribution to 19th-century Russian Orthodox ecclesiology.

In the second half of his essay, Khomyakov offers an exposition of the Creed of Nicaea-Constantinople and the seven sacraments of the church. Although the tone is not overtly polemical, this part of the work shows most clearly that his positive account of the nature and life of the church is nonetheless conditioned by what it is not – i.e. it is distinct from various errors of the West. Thus "the addition of the word *filioque* contains such illusory dogma unknown to any of the God-pleasing writers, bishops, or apostolic successors in the first centuries of the Church, nor was it spoken by Christ the Saviour";[50] "the Holy Church ... does not reject also the word 'transubstantiation,' but does not ascribe to it the material sense attributed to it by the teachers of the churches that have fallen away";[51] writing of a baptism

of desire, Khomyakov notes that "Cornelius also received the Holy Spirit without having received Baptism [Acts 10] ... For God can glorify the sacrament of Baptism before it is accomplished, just as after it. Thus the difference between *opus operans* and *opus operatum* disappears."[52] Regarding reception of the sacraments, Khomyakov keenly attacks the custom of the Catholic Church:

> Baptism, Chrismation, and Communion of the holy gifts have been taken away from infants by those who, inheriting the blind wisdom of blind paganism, have not grasped the greatness of God's sacraments and have demanded that everything yield reason and utility and, subordinating the teaching of the Church to scholastic interpretations, do not desire even to pray if they do not see in the prayer a direct goal and profit.[53]

This criticism of the sacramental practice of the Latin-rite Catholic Church is followed in the rest of the essay by similar remarks highlighting what Khomyakov sees as false teachings and beliefs of the Catholic Church. In particular, the idea of the Immaculate Conception, soon to be dogmatized in 1854, is refuted – "we glorify ... the most-pure Mother of Lord Jesus, without considering her to be either sinless by birth or perfect."[54] Other distinctly Catholic teachings, such as purgatory, the redemptive value of good works, and the notions of sufficient and efficient grace, are also sharply criticized by Khomyakov. With regard to the theology of grace, his distaste for Tridentine scholasticism appears to draw him closer to a strong Augustinian position and away from the Eastern patristic emphasis on synergy. The decisively unirenic position towards Catholicism continues into the conclusion, where Khomyakov marks the very bold statement that:

---

48   Jakim & Bird, *On Spiritual Unity*, 48.
49   Jakim & Bird, *On Spiritual Unity*, 49–50.
50   Jakim & Bird, *On Spiritual Unity*, 38.
51   Jakim & Bird, *On Spiritual Unity*, 41–42.

52   Jakim & Bird, *On Spiritual Unity*, 47 (italics original).
53   Jakim & Bird, *On Spiritual Unity*, 47.
54   Jakim & Bird, *On Spiritual Unity*, 48.

By the will of God, after the falling away of many schisms and of the Roman patriarchate, the Holy Church was preserved in the Greek eparchies and patriarchates, and only those communities can recognize themselves as fully Christian that preserve or come into unity with the Eastern patriarchates.[55]

Thus for all of Khomyakov's emphasis on the unity of the church and his positive reception among some Catholic ecclesiologists in the 20th century, Khomyakov's work, paradoxically, is profoundly hostile to the desire for church unity as understood in a contemporary sense. For him, the universal church is to be found exclusively in the Eastern Orthodox Church. Moreover, the majority of Khomyakov's theological writing was polemical in nature, and his intra-denominational exchanges mark an important stage in ecumenical relations. As Nicolas Zernov observed, "it was one of the greatest paradoxes of Khomiakov's life that the man who attacked most bitterly the Western Christians was at the same time the first Eastern theologian who felt a genuine concern for the Churches of the West and realized the grave sin of divisions."[56]

The best-known of Khomyakov's "foreign correspondence" was a long-standing exchange of letters with the Anglican theologian William Palmer.[57] The correspondence began in 1844 sparked by Palmer's interest in the Eastern Churches, an interest which would grow into an exploration of the possibility of becoming Orthodox. Eventually he was received into the Catholic Church in Rome in 1855, by which time Khomyakov had written, in 1854 at the start of the Crimean War, the last of

his letters to his friend. A learned deacon of the Anglican Church who was, at the outset of their correspondence, open to the possibility of becoming Orthodox, Palmer was a perfect foil for Khomyakov, who enabled him to express and develop his theological ideas freely, something not practicable in Russia.[58]

In his first letter, after disavowing calumnies which appeared against him, Khomyakov distinguishes between the idea of union and unity, arguing that "Union cannot be understood by any Orthodox otherwise than as the sequence of a complete harmony, or of a *perfect Unity of Doctrine*. ... Union is possible with Rome. Unity alone is possible with Orthodoxy."[59] Yet, crucially, Khomyakov also adds that the obstacle to doctrinal unity is not actually doctrinal but the fact that, since the time of the addition of the *Filioque*,

> the Western communities have nurtured a deep enmity and an incurable disdain for the unchanging East. These feelings have become traditional and, as it were, innate, to the Roman-German world, and England has all the time partaken of that spiritual life. Can it tear itself away from the past? There stands, in my opinion, the great and invincible obstacle to Unity.[60]

Khomyakov responds to Palmer's considered response to the issues raised dismissively – "this explanation seems to me quite arbitrary" – preferring once again to put the problem in terms of psychological permanence:

> The reluctance of the West to admit the simple truth of the Church arises neither from ignorance nor from rational objections, but from a *moral obstacle* which no human

---

55   Jakim & Bird, *On Spiritual Unity*, 52.

56   Zernov, *Three Russian Prophets*, 68.

57   Robin Wheeler, *Palmer's Pilgrimage: The Life of William Palmer of Magdalen*, Bern, Peter Lang, 2006. Wheeler devotes only one brief chapter to this correspondence: see ch. 12, 289–302. See also Richard J. Mammana, Jr., "Not a Harmony of Discords: Ecclesiology in the Correspondence of Aleksei Khomiakov and William Palmer (1844–1854)," in: Tsurikov, ed., *A.S. Khomiakov*, 98–128.

58   The correspondence can be found in: Birkbeck, ed., *Russia and the English Church*, vol. 1.

59   Birkbeck, ed., *Russia and the English Church*, vol. 1, 6–8 (italics original).

60   Birkbeck, ed., *Russia and the English Church*, vol. 1, 8–9.

efforts can conquer, if it is not conquered by the better feelings of the better part of human nature, in those who can know the truth but do not wish to confess it.[61]

A certain intransigence marks Khomyakov's side of the correspondence, an unwillingness to admit the possibility that theological issues which divide may be resolved. In this respect, Khomyakov mirrors the position of Kireyevsky: for all their theoretical emphasis on the principle of unity, their thought also appears founded on a necessary opposition between Russia and the West.

The rest of the correspondence reflects Palmer's ongoing faith journey, Khomyakov's response to it, and reactions to ecclesial and political events. In the hope of Palmer's entry into the Orthodox Church, Khomyakov spoke with a number of prominent Russian Orthodox churchmen, including Metropolitan Philaret of Moscow, and was particularly encouraged by the openness and hopefulness of the latter. With regard to Khomyakov's ecclesiology, his comments on the 1848 letter of the Eastern patriarchs to Pope Pius IX are significant. This letter had been written by the Orthodox patriarchs in response to what Aidan Nichols has described as "the first 'unionist' encyclical of the modern papacy,"[62] namely his encyclical of Jan 6, 1848, *In suprema Petri apostoli sede*. Much of the resentment this papal letter caused was due to the fact that it was distributed directly to the Orthodox faithful, bypassing their bishops. Hence the swift response from the four Oriental patriarchs which Khomyakov described as "important in itself as being the only instance for more than a hundred years of a declaration of Faith coming so near to an ecumenical act, and as giving a splendid example of Unity."[63] Khomyakov sees the patriarchs as having affirmed his own view

that division between the "Eastern Church and all the Western communities ... consists in the different manner of considering the Church itself."[64] In particular, he highlights two related points made in response to Rome, namely that "the knowledge of truth is given to mutual love" and that "the unvarying constancy and the unerring truth of Christian dogma does not depend on any Hierarchical Order: it is guarded by the totality, by the whole *people* of the Church, which is the Body of Christ."[65] These are points which Khomyakov also makes elsewhere in his polemical brochures of the 1850s. Palmer highlights the potential danger of Khomyakov's position on authority in the church, explaining that "your idea of the Christian people being the guardians of the faith of the Church is in a sense and degree very true, but, if carried too far and put absolutely, a very mischievous error; for the Hierarchy are sent to teach all nations, with the promise of Christ's presence in doing so, even to the end, and the nations are thereby required to submit to the teaching of the united Apostolate."[66] This crucial point is left without answer by Khomyakov in subsequent correspondence.

Much of the rest of Khomyakov's correspondence with Palmer is marked by Palmer's journey toward full communion with the Catholic Church, accelerated by the differing messages he received from the Russian and Greek Orthodox Churches on the necessity of rebaptism.[67] As Solovyov put it: "No one could solve his dilemma ... he became a Roman Catholic."[68] Another factor for Palmer's decision, acknowledged by Khomyakov, was the evident government control over the Orthodox Church. Khomyakov urges Palmer not to convert, writing "that the Roman Church is independent I will concede; but that it has anything like ecclesiastical freedom, the liberty of the Spirit, I totally

61   Birkbeck, ed., *Russia and the English Church*, vol. 1, 56–57 (italics original).
62   Aidan Nichols, *Rome and the Eastern Churches: A Study in Schism*, San Francisco CA, Ignatius, [2]2010, 352.
63   Birkbeck, ed., *Russia and the English Church*, vol. 1, 93.
64   Birkbeck, ed., *Russia and the English Church*, vol. 1, 94.
65   Birkbeck, ed., *Russia and the English Church*, vol. 1, 94 (italics original).
66   Birkbeck, ed., *Russia and the English Church*, vol. 1, 155.
67   Birkbeck, ed., *Russia and the English Church*, vol. 1, 109.
68   Vladimir S. Solovyov, *Russia and the Universal Church*, London, G. Bles, 1948, 69.

deny"; he adds further that "the examples of Mr. Newman and Mr. Allies are ... conclusive. They were certainly better Christians formerly that they are now; their openheartedness is gone forever; they have crippled themselves instead of expanding."[69] After defending the Greek and Russian Churches, Khomyakov refers to the brochure he sends, summarizing some of its points, and also suggesting that Palmer might have acted differently in approaching the Russian Church. The personal friendship remains but the theological engagement between the two has now, effectively, run its course, with Khomyakov summing up his position explicitly: "My firm conviction, most reverend sir, is, that Romanism is nothing but Separatism, and that humanity has only one choice: Catholic Orthodoxy or infidelity. All middle terms are nothing but preparatory steps towards the latter."[70] In a subsequent letter of 1853 he repeats the point, urging Palmer: "Do not shut your eyes to the evident *separatism of the Roman west, which is the only true plague of humanity*, as I hope to have shown in my Essay."[71] The essay Khomyakov was referring to is the first in a series of polemical brochures he wrote in French in the 1850s, and it is these which provide the final aspects of Khomyakov's Slavophile ecclesial thought.[72]

The brochure Khomyakov sent Palmer was his 1853 article, "Quelques mots par un Chrétien Orthodoxe sur les Communions Occidentales à l'occasion d'une brochure de M. Laurentie,"[73] was written to refute Pierre-Sébastien Laurentie's 1852 response to an article in *Revue des Deux Mondes* by the Russian diplomat and poet Fyodor Ivanovich Tyutchev, which was critical of papal supremacy and the mixture of spiritual and temporal interests of the papacy. Essentially he developed with greater confidence his earlier points about authority in the church, arguing that authority is something external while all that is truly of the church, including truth itself, is interior, and therefore exists on a completely different epistemic and ontological plane. He describes the response of the Eastern patriarchs to Pope Pius IX as "the most remarkable fact of ecclesiastical history in recent centuries," and adds that "infallibility resides solely in the universality of the Church united by mutual love; and that the protection of both the constancy of dogma and the purity of rite was entrusted not to any hierarchy but to the people of the Church as a whole, which is the body of Christ."[74] Khomyakov believes that the Catholic Church and the Protestant communion are both divided by their affirmation of a "teaching Church," arguing that "there is no teaching Church in the true Church."[75] Moreover, he claims "the Church does not recognize a teaching Church other than herself in her totality."[76]

Khomyakov follows up this article with another in 1855, written in response to a letter by the Catholic archbishop of Paris, Marie Dominique-Auguste Sibour, at the outset of the Crimean War. Khomyakov acknowledges that the tragedy of the conflict is that "a religious hatred has certainly poisoned the quarrel," and paraphrases the words of Archbishop Sibour as typical, albeit bolder, of widely shared sentiments among Catholics: "The war France is going to wage against Russia is not a political war at all but a holy war; ... solely a war of religion; ... that the true cause of this war, the sacred cause, the cause agreeable to God, is the

---

69   Birkbeck, ed., *Russia and the English Church*, vol. 1, 124.

70   Birkbeck, ed., *Russia and the English Church*, vol. 1, 134.

71   Birkbeck, ed., *Russia and the English Church*, vol. 1, 160 (italics original).

72   These French articles were published posthumously in Lausanne, Switzerland in 1872: Aleksey Khomyakov, *L'Église latine et le Protestantisme au point de vue de l'Église d'Orient*, Lausanne, B. Benda, 1872.

73   Aleksey S. Khomyakov, *Quelques mots par un Chrétien Orthodoxe sur les Communions Occidentales à l'occasion d'une brochure de M. Laurentie*, Paris, Imprimerie de Ch. Meyrueis et compagnie, 1853.

74   Jakim & Bird, *On Spiritual Unity*, 59.

75   Jakim & Bird, *On Spiritual Unity*, 59.

76   Jakim & Bird, *On Spiritual Unity*, 62. In the French original, he does qualify this statement with a footnote explaining that "this does not prevent/deny that the clergy are more particularly chargé/committed to the service of the Word." Khomyakov, *L'Église latine et le Protestantisme*, 92.

necessity of expunging the error of Photius."[77] Such a view fuels Khomyakov's argument that the moral fratricide committed by the West in adding the *Filioque* to the Creed, this "Western heresy against the dogma of Church unity," leads directly to bloodshed.[78] Moral fratricide leads inevitably to "the desire for *material fratricide*" expressed by Archbishop Sibour.[79] Moreover, such a view is not simply that of one extreme archbishop but universal: "In the Western confessions, there is at the bottom of every soul a profound hostility against the Eastern Church."[80] In this context Khomyakov introduces the theme of papal infallibility, which he sees as "a question that the curia of Rome does not yet dare approach."[81] In Khomyakov's view, papal infallibility was unknown in the early church but was necessitated because of the *Filioque*. It is, for him, "a conditional principle accepted retrospectively and by necessity – in order to justify an illegal act prior to it."[82] Thus Khomyakov sees the individualism of Protestantism, the rationalism of the West *per se*, the doctrine of papal infallibility, the moral animosity of the Christian West towards the East and the Crimean War as all being caused by the moral fratricide which he claims is embodied in the *Filioque*.

Khomyakov wrote a final polemical brochure in 1858 and, in 1860, prior to his death from cholera in the summer, was also able to see published a response to ideas of the significant Russian convert to Catholicism, Ivan Gagarin, author of the provocative 1856 book *La Russie sera-t-elle catholique?*. Khomyakov's engagement with Gagarin is prompted by a speech the latter made on Jan 27, 1860 at Our Lady of Victories Church in Paris, and especially by two of his brochures, "De le Réunion de l'Église orientale avec l'Église romaine" and "Réponse d'un Russe à un Russe".[83] Khomyakov's short but important letter in response to Gagarin's brochures focuses particularly on the Jesuit's treatment of the term *sobornyj*, the adjectival root of *sobornost*. Essentially, Gagarin is critical of the Slavonic translation of the creed where "the word *catholic* has been replaced by an *obscure and vague* expression that does not give the idea of universality" and suggests as a result that Orthodox faithful, "instead of saying, 'I believe in the Catholic Church,' say: 'I believe in the synodal Church.'"[84] In response, Khomyakov points out that alternatives were available which would have expressed the concept of universality, namely *vsemirnyj* and *vselenskij*, the first of which, he says, "occurs in very old homilies," and the second, "is indisputably ancient and is used to render the idea of the universal Church (*vselenskaia tserkov*) or in the ecumenical sense (*vselenskii sobor* = ecumenical council)."[85] For Khomyakov, the whole point is that saints Cyril and Methodius chose *sobornyj* to translate the Greek term *katholikos* and this expresses something essential about the meaning of the church. Indeed, Khomyakov wants "to emphasize that the word *sobornyi* contains a profession of faith."[86]

This article is especially significant because for Khomyakov *sobornyj* suggests something essential about the meaning of the church, "the idea of an assembly ... unity in plurality ... the Church of free unanimity, of perfect unanimity."[87] Here Khomyakov comes closest to giving a definition of the term *sobornost*, usually associated with Slavophile ecclesiology but in fact never

---

77 Jakim & Bird, *On Spiritual Unity*, 65.

78 Jakim & Bird, *On Spiritual Unity*, 66.

79 Jakim & Bird, *On Spiritual Unity*, 66 (italics original).

80 Jakim & Bird, *On Spiritual Unity*, 67.

81 Jakim & Bird, *On Spiritual Unity*, 69.

82 Jakim & Bird, *On Spiritual Unity*, 69.

83 Ivan S. Gagarin, *De la réunion de l'Eglise orientale avec l'Eglise romaine*, Paris, Bureau de l'Oeuvre et R. Peaucelle, 1860 and Ivan S. Gagarin, *Réponse d'un Russe à un Russe*, Paris, Librairie ecclésiastique et classique d'Eugene Belin, 1860. See Jeffrey Bruce Beshoner, *Ivan Sergeevich Gagarin: The Search for Orthodox and Catholic Union*, Notre Dame IN, University of Notre Dame Press, 2002, 113.

84 Jakim & Bird, *On Spiritual Unity*, 135 (italics original).

85 Jakim & Bird, *On Spiritual Unity*, 138.

86 Jakim & Bird, *On Spiritual Unity*, 139.

87 Jakim & Bird, *On Spiritual Unity*, 139.

used by Khomyakov or Kireyevsky. In the essay that accompanied the first Russian edition of Khomyakov's collected works, published in Prague in 1867, Samarin helps to cement Khomyakov's place in Orthodox theology and ecclesiology, famously saying that he "was a teacher of the Church."[88] Khomyakov, emphasizes Samarin, "lived in the Church" and "for him the Church was a living center in which all his thoughts originated and to which they all returned."[89] Samarin argues that Khomyakov brought something original to Russian thought and theology, which he also communicated to Western Christians, suggesting that in Khomyakov the West first encountered Orthodoxy. In terms of ecclesiology he highlights the fact that Khomyakov showed that "the Church is a living organism, an organism of truth and love, or more precisely: *truth and love as an organism*."[90]

4 The Second Generation

If Khomyakov sought to show Western Christians an Orthodox ecclesiology that highlighted an interior mystical union of believers, it should be acknowledged that Khomyakov's teaching was not the only encounter with Orthodoxy and Slavophilism experienced in the West. A far more concrete and politicized expression of it can be found in the ideas of the poet and diplomat Fyodor I. Tyutchev who shared the Slavophiles' profoundly critical view of the West. He regarded the 1848 revolutions as the death throes of a civilization crippled by individualism. In April 1848 he sent a memorandum on the situation to Tsar Nicholas I presenting the crisis as a struggle to the death between the idolatrous anti-Christian forces of revolution and the Christian Empire of Russia. Although order had been restored by the summer of 1849, Tyutchev's apocalyptic view of a doomed West remained unshaken, and in the autumn of 1849, he expressed his views more fully in a much larger work "Rossiya i Zapad" (Russia and the West).[91] Here he expressed a pan-Slavist ideology, centered on a messianic role for Russia, the Slavic race, and Orthodox faith, as the leader of a great Eastern empire, thus rekindling Moscow's claim to be the "Third Rome." The empire would also bring about ecclesial unity, as explained in the second chapter of this work which addressed "the Roman Question." Here Tyutchev provocatively proposed the return of the Catholic Church to Orthodoxy. Overall, his vision is almost the inverse of Khomyakov's, and in its embrace of temporal power it seems to embody one aspect of the criticism that the Slavophiles directed at the Catholic Church. He is also far removed from Khomyakov's advocacy of freedom and mutual love.

Yet Tyutchev certainly admired the Slavophiles. His recent biographer John Dewey notes that

> Tyutchev acknowledged Khomyakov as his intellectual equal and described his theological writings as "the most intelligent glorification of the Orthodox Church and doctrine"; of Samarin he asserted that none could match his intellect, while the political writings of Ivan Aksakov displayed in his opinion a "superiority to everything without exception written and printed in our country."[92]

When he was in Moscow, which became more accessible after the St. Petersburg-Moscow railway line was opened on Nov 1, 1851, he enjoyed the

---

88   Jakim & Bird, *On Spiritual Unity*, 183.

89   Jakim & Bird, *On Spiritual Unity*, 162.

90   Jakim & Bird, *On Spiritual Unity*, 171 (italics original). Khomyakov statement that "The Church as a living organism of truth, entrusted to mutual love; that is, as freedom in unity and unity in freedom; that is, as freedom in the harmony of its manifestations" is identified by Samarin as the "single, dominant theme" of his work; Jakim & Bird, *On Spiritual Unity*, 182.

91   Fyodor I. Tyutchev, "Rossiya i Zapad" [Russia and the West], in: Fyodor I. Tyutchev, *Polnoe sobranie sochinenij i pisma, v shesti tomakh* [Complete collected works and letters, in six volumes], vol. 3, *Publitsisticheskie proizvedeniya*, Moscow, Klassika, 2003, 179–200.

92   John Dewey, *Mirror of the Soul: A Life of the Poet Fyodor Tyutchev*, Shaftesbury, Brimstone Press, 2010, 507.

intellectual company of leading Slavophile figures who welcomed him as a supporter of their cause. Indeed, Tyutchev's criticism of the West, rationalism, and individualism, his advocacy of the unity of the Slav peoples, his championing of Orthodoxy and of a special Russian mission in world history are central themes of Slavophile thought. Dewey considers "it would be most appropriate to think of him as the movement's unofficial and always independent-minded adviser and spokesman in foreign affairs."[93]

Tyutchev's provocative vision of church unity subsumed within an Eastern empire expressed in the second chapter of the work was also separately published in Paris in *Revue des Deux Mondes* under the title "La Papauté et la question romaine au point de vue de Saint-Pétersbourg."[94] One of the respondents was the friend who had helped establish him as a recognized poet, namely the recently ordained Jesuit priest, Fr. Ivan Gagarin, Samarin's cousin, who has been described as a Catholic Slavophile.[95] At the heart of his response to Tyutchev was his own vision of Russia's conversion to Catholicism, which would guarantee the independence of the church from the state and prevent revolution occurring in Russia. This vision became Gagarin's lifework and he established the journal *Études* in 1856 to publicize his ideas. A small group of other Russians converted to Catholicism and the priesthood, collaborated with Gagarin and continued his work after his death in 1876. Of significance for the subsequent development of the Slavophile movement are Fr. Paul Pierling and Jean Martynov, both of whom corresponded with Vladimir Solovyov in the 1880s as the latter moved from a Slavophile religious and philosophical position to writing bitter criticisms of it.

The ideas of these Russian Catholic priests entered Russia indirectly through the Slavophile journal *Den* edited by Ivan Aksakov. Following the Polish uprising of 1863, anti-Catholic sentiment and Russian nationalism increased, and Samarin took up Khomyakov's mantle as a critical interlocutor with Western confessions. Aksakov had published an editorial critical of the Jesuits, which led to the publication of a letter in response from the Russian-born Jesuit, Fr. Martynov: it was something of a success for freedom of speech in Russia.[96] This letter of Martynov's then led to Samarin's epistolary work on the Jesuits, where, "his outstanding polemical gifts ... were most brilliantly displayed."[97] This rather overlooked work, published as a whole in 1865 as *Iezuity i ikh otnoshenie k Rossii*,[98] was important, not just as an expression of Russian and Slavophile anti-Jesuit polemics, but also as a fuller Slavophile response to the challenge which Ivan Gagarin posed to Orthodoxy.[99]

Whether Samarin was effective in this is a moot point. Vladimir Solovyov, who as a young philosopher in the late 1870s was seen as the great hope and intellectual future of the Slavophile movement, writes that reading Samarin's work actually helped him begin to consider Catholicism positively. In the early spring of 1887, Solovyov had delivered a public lecture on "Slavyanofilstvo i russkaya ideya" (Slavophilism and the Russian idea) during which he expresses one of the central ideas of his mature thought, namely that for

---

93   Dewey, *Mirror of the Soul*, 364.

94   Fyodor I. Tyutchev, "La Papauté et la question romaine au point de vue de Saint-Pétersbourg," *Revue des deux mondes* 20/5, 1850, 117–133.

95   Raymond T. McNally, "Two Catholic Slavophiles?: Ivan S. Gagarin and August von Haxthausen in Search of Church Reconciliation (1857–1860)," *CSS* 34/3, 2000, 251–309.

96   Ekaterina N. Tsimbaeva, *Russkij ekumenizm: Poisk osnov mezhkonfessionalnogo edinstva v Rossii XIX veka* [Russian ecumenism: A quest for the interconfessional basis of unity in nineteenth-century Russia], Moscow, URSS, 2015, 146.

97   Zenkovsky, *A History of Russian Philosophy*, vol. 1, 229.

98   Yuri F. Samarin, *Iezuity i ikh otnoshenie k Rossii: Pisma k iezuitu Martynovu* [Jesuits and their attitude towards Russia: Letters to the Jesuit Martynov], Moscow, Lazarevskij Inst., 1866.

99   The text can be found in: Yuri F. Samarin, *Sobranie sochinenij v piati tomakh* [Collected works in five volumes], vol. 2, *Tserkov i obschestvo* [Church and society], St. Petersburg, Rostok, 2014, 388–594.

Russia to fulfil her mission, the unification of the churches was required. For Solovyov, in order for this to happen meant Russian recognition of the pope. The Slavophile public were indignant on hearing him, and some began sending copies of Samarin's text about the Jesuits, which had been recently published in Samarin's collected works. Writing to Fr. Martynov in July 1887 in this regard, Solovyov explains that:

> My venerable friends do not know, that the said work, which I read for the first time eight years ago, acted significantly in forming my sympathies for the Catholic Church. Crude logical blunders and a clear lack of conscientiousness on the part of a generally speaking upright and intelligent man like Yu. Samarin led me to think seriously over our relationship to Catholicism.[100]

Solovyov's intellectual and spiritual journey in the ten years leading up to this letter had been significant. His early work stands very clearly in the Slavophile tradition and his ecclesial sensibilities appeared to bring new life to this dimension of the movement. As a whole, although the two preeminent Slavophile figures, Kireyevsky and Khomyakov, died in 1856 and 1860 respectively, the movement as a whole remained significant in Russian culture and politics, and the second generation of Slavophiles had a very influential figurehead in Ivan Aksakov, editor of Slavophile journals such as *Den* and subsequently *Rus*. Aksakov was a younger brother of Konstantin Aksakov and was a living connection with the first generation of Slavophile thinkers. At the same time, he was much more distant from the church than Kireyevsky and Khomyakov and emphasized Slavophilism's nationalist element, thereby providing a bridge with the pan-Slavist movement

which was centered around the work of Nikolay Yakovlevich Danilevsky. Slavophile thought also influenced Dostoevsky, particularly in terms of his high regard for the Russian people. The most significant inheritor and adaptor of the work of the first generation of Slavophiles, however, is Vladimir Solovyov who also responded significantly to all three of these figures. It is also in Solovyov that the genuine concern for church union is most fully developed.

5 Vladimir Sergeyevich Solovyov

Vladimir Solovyov's early work stands very clearly in the Slavophile tradition. His master's thesis, published in 1874, *Krizis zapadnoj filosofii (protiv pozitivistov)* (*The Crisis of Western Philosophy (Against the Positivists)*) is not only a critique of the contemporary positive philosophy that was widely influential in Russia at the time, but also a critical survey of the development of philosophy in the West in which the strong rationalist current is exposed. Interestingly, Solovyov suggests that a little-known Slavophile figure, Nikita Petrovich Gilyarov-Platonov, is his primary influence here[101] and concludes this work by arguing that the "ultimate necessary results of the *Western* philosophical development affirm, in the form of *rational knowledge*, the *same* truths that have been affirmed in the form of *faith* and *spiritual contemplation* by the great theological teachers of

100 Vladimir S. Solovyov, *Pisma* [Letters], vol. 3, St. Petersburg, Obschestvennaya Polza, Vremya, 1908–1923; repr. Brussels, Zhizn s Bogom, 1970, 25 (the English translation is the author's).

101 "Only the general basis of Hegel's system is expounded here. A more detailed exposition (especially of the point of departure and method) of this system, and a very substantial critique of it, can be found in N. G-v's articles in *Russkaya Beseda*, 1859, vol 3. Besides this remarkable work, a just, though too general, criticism of philosophical rationalism can be found in certain articles of Khomyakov and I. Kireyevsky." Vladimir S. Solovyov, *The Crisis of Western Philosophy (Against the Positivists)*, Hudson NY, Lindisfarne, 1996, 172. Although he was buried next to Solovyov, this figure is not mentioned in any of the existing studies of Solovyov. Gilyarov-Platonov helped prepare the Russian edition of Khomyakov's works.

the *East* (in part the ancient East and especially the Christian East)." He believes that a synthesis of science, philosophical, and religion must be achieved, arguing that "the attainment of this goal will be the restoration of the complete inner *unity of the intellectual world*."[102] With such a conclusion Solovyov appears to seal himself as the heir apparent to the Slavophiles.

Furthermore, Solovyov became an immediate sensation on defending his thesis. The historian Konstantin Nikolayevich Bestuzhev-Ryumin remarked afterwards, "if to-day's hopes are fulfilled in the future, Russia possesses a new genius, who in manner and style resembles his father, although he will surpass him. I have never been conscious of such prodigious intellectual force at the reading of any other thesis."[103] Indeed, after this great success, Slavophile figures seek him out. Strémooukhoff relates that

> the wife of I.S. Aksakov, the daughter of Tiutchev, came to the Sologub's to see this astonishing young man. Iu. Samarin – uncle Iusha, as Soloviev calls him – confides in him the sources of Khomyakov's works. Finally, he visits M.N. Katkov and N.A. Liubimov; he is welcomed with open arms in these conservative Slavophile circles where his "childish babbling," as he will later say, was very seriously listened to.[104]

Solovyov follows this up with further works of religious philosophy which show him to be very much the heir of Kireyevsky and the Slavophile movement. In 1877 *Filosofskie nachala tselnogo znaniya* (*The Philosophical Principles of Integral Knowledge*)[105] was published, a work which self-consciously reflects Kireyevsky's call for a new philosophical path in his final work. Particularly significant were the public lectures he delivered in 1878 in St. Petersburg which drew huge crowds and are a landmark in the history of Russian thought. These lectures were revised and published independently in *Pravoslavnoe Obozrenie* – and then collected with the title *Chteniya o bogochelovechestve* (*Lectures on Divine Humanity*) – and reflect a transition in Solovyov's thought from a philosophical to a theological register.[106]

At the end of this work, lectures 11 and 12, significantly revised and published in March 1881, Solovyov sets out clearly his teaching about divine humanity (*bogochelovechestvo*) a term etymologically rooted in late Greek patristic Christology and that Solovyov introduced into Russian thought to express the church fathers' teaching about deification.[107] Besides representing patristic teaching here, Solovyov was also using a different language to articulate his philosophical thought. The idea of all-unity, the inter-connectedness of all human beings, and indeed, all that exists, so central to his more strictly philosophical work (and to Kireyevsky's, of course) is now expressed in ecclesial terms. In this way, Solovyov shows how all-unity is to be realized, namely through the church. In this he remains within the parameters of Slavophile thought, and *Lectures* is also still more a theoretical work rather than a guide to the

102 Solovyov, *The Crisis of Western Philosophy*, 149 (italics original).

103 Cited in Michel D'Herbigny, *Vladimir Soloviev: A Russian Newman (1853–1900)*, London, R. & T. Washbourne, 1918, 69.

104 Dimitri Strémooukhoff, *Vladimir Soloviev and His Messianic Work*, Belmont MA, Nordland, 1980, 45.

105 Now in: Vladimir S. Solovyov, *Sobranie sochinenij* [Collected works], vol. 1, *1873–1877*, St. Petersburg, Prosveschenie, 1911, pp. 250–406; ET: Vladimir S. Solovyov, *The Philosophical Principles of Integral Knowledge*, Grand Rapids MI, Eerdmans, 2008.

106 Published in the journal *Pravoslavnoe Obozrenie* between 1878 and 1881, these lectures where collected in Vladimir S. Solovyov, *Chteniya o bogochelovechestve*, ed. Mikhail Katkov, Moscow, Universitetskaya tipografiya, 1881; ET: *Lectures on Divine Humanity*, ed. Boris Jakim, trans. Peter Zouboff, Hudson, New York, Lindisfarne, 1995.

107 For a detailed exposition of this, see Jeremy Pilch, *"Breathing the Spirit with Both Lungs": Deification in the Work of Vladimir Solov'ev*, Leuven, Peeters, 2018, 57–111.

realization of this project in practice. What is new, however, is the Christological origins of Solovyov's ecclesiology, a dimension noticeably absent in Khomyakov's work.

The most strikingly Slavophile aspect of *Lectures* is Solovyov's presentation of church history and the way in which ecclesial union, embracing ultimately all humanity, is the preserve of the Orthodox Church. Solovyov argues that during the Middle Ages the Western Church, led by Rome, tried to compel belief in Christ, and "succumbed to the temptation of the religious lust for power."[108] For Solovyov such an attitude ultimately suggests a lack of belief in the power of Christ's truth. In Catholicism this unbelief was at first embryonic but later revealed clearly: "In Jesuitism, an extreme and pure expression of the Roman Catholic principle, the motive force was an outright lust for power, not Christian zeal."[109] Protestantism recognized the falsity of the Catholic path, and emphasized the interior act of faith, says Solovyov. However, the subjective interpretation of Holy Scripture in Protestantism elevates "the activity of a *personal reason* ... to be the actual source of religious truth. Protestantism thus naturally passes into rationalism" and as such, in it "Western humankind succumbed to the second temptation."[110] Solovyov notes that "reason turned out to be impotent against passions and interests, and the kingdom of reason proclaimed by the French Revolution ended in a wild chaos of insanity and violence."[111] Ultimately, the dominance of reason ended in empty abstractions and led the West to succumb to the third and last temptation, resulting in the dominance of materialism and empiricism.

It is in this context that Solovyov proposes his vision of a full acceptance and realization of Christ's truth. Besides this Slavophile interpretation of history, Solovyov also sees the West as the embodiment of the spontaneous human principle, while the East is the preserve of the divine. For the realization of divine humanity in the church, the two need to come together.[112] It is this awareness that East and West need each other that compels Solovyov to overcome the traditional Slavophile rejection of the West in favor of a search for reconciliation and union.

Solovyov's desire to see the realization of this Christian society required a reunited Christian Church. His project of "free theocracy," i.e. a society which voluntary submits itself to the will of God, received new impetus following the shocking assassination of Tsar Alexander II in 1881. This event marks a decisive shift in Russian political history and a hardening and distortion of the Westerner-Slavophile positions. Conservative and Slavophile circles were profoundly perturbed by the assassination, which was carried out by the radical "nihilist" Narodnaya Volya group, one easily characterized as the fruit of Western ideas. Solovyov gave two public lectures after the event and, along with reiterating the Slavophile ideas about the destiny and mission of the Russian people in whom Christian truth resides, he also calls for Christian action in response to the regicide, namely that the new tsar, Alexander III, forgive the murderers of his father. As a result, Solovyov lost his position at university and was subsequently compelled to make a living by means of his writing.

One of the first of his explicitly ecclesial works is an article published in the summer of 1881 in *Rus*, entitled "O duchovnoj vlasti v Rossii" (On spiritual authority in Russia).[113] In this excoriating criticism

---

108   Solovyov, *Lectures*, 166.

109   Solovyov, *Lectures*, 167. Solovyov's portrayal of Catholicism reflects something of Dostoevsky's views expressed in *The Brothers Karamazov*, especially in the famous depiction of the Grand Inquisitor. Solovyov knew Dostoevsky well, and accompanied the novelist to Optina Pustyn in 1878, during which time they discussed the future novel.

110   Solovyov, *Lectures*, 168 (italics original).

111   Solovyov, *Lectures*, 168.

---

112   Solovyov, *Lectures*, 172–74.

113   Vladimir S. Solovyov, "O duchovnoj vlasti v Rossii" [On spiritual authority in Russia], *Rus* 56, 1881; now in: Solovyov, *Sobranie sochinenij*, vol. 3, *1877–1884*, 227–242; for an English translation see Vladimir Wozniuk, ed., *Freedom, Faith, and Dogma: Essays by V.S. Soloviev on*

of the Russian Orthodox Church, he seeks answers to queries about why the Church in Russia has failed to transform society in a truly Christian way. Here he differs from the Slavophiles by blaming the destruction of the sacred traditions of Holy Russia on Patriarch Nikon, who presided over the schism (*raskol*), in the Russia Church in 1667, when the Old Believers were anathematized; or as Solovyov puts it, "a significant part of the Russian people suddenly feel that it was not possible to live during the 'quiet' reign of Alexei Mikhailovich, when they plunged in despair into forests and wilderness, and scaled mountains to live in log cabins."[114] He argues that while "Patriarch Nikon did not go over to Latinism … the fundamental error of Latinism was instinctively adopted by him."[115] The schism is still important says Solovyov because "the Russian hierarchy has still not repudiated the Latin principle of religious coercion brought into it by Nikon."[116] The subject of the Old Believers, so often overlooked in consideration of the Orthodox Church in regard to Christian unity, thus emerges as a practical starting point from which Solovyov is drawn towards seeking Christian unity through an engagement with Catholicism and a recognition of the positive role of the papacy.

Solovyov continued to publish articles in Aksakov's *Rus* focusing on the cause of disunity in the church, namely a series of essays examining the roots of the alienation of East and West entitled *Velikij spor i khristianskaya politika* (The great controversy and Christian politics).[117] Published in 1883, this was a work he was never able to see published in its entirety in his lifetime. It also marked the beginning of his split with the Slavophiles. Aksakov himself refused to publish any more of Solovyov's work after the final instalment of *The Great Controversy*. Both Aksakov and the scholarly

priest Ivantsov-Platonov had been particularly irked by the fourth article "Razdelenie tserkvej" (The division of the churches), and when Aksakov received the sixth article "Papstvo i papizm. Smysl Protestantstva" (The papacy and papism: The meaning of Protestantism) from Solovyov, he abbreviated it and published it only with additional notes by Ivantsov-Platonov. Essentially, Solovyov now saw that the role of papacy was crucial to the unity of the church, and such a view was unpalatable to Aksakov. Solovyov pointed out exactly where the problem lay in a letter to Aksakov of March 1883:

> It seems to me that you are looking *only* at papism, but I see first of all the great, holy and eternal Rome, the foundational and integral part of the universal Church. I believe in this Rome, I bow down before it, I love it with my whole heart, and with all the forces of my soul I desire its restoration for the unity and wholeness of the world-wide Church.[118]

Although this marks his exit from the somewhat narrow Moscow Slavophile world, Solovyov may still be considered a Slavophile thinker. Indeed he now finds inspiration in the 17th-century Croatian Catholic priest, Juraj Križanić, who had visited Russia in the 17th century and had developed significant pan-Slavist and theocratic ideas. Works of his were (re)published in the mid-19th century and Russia Slavophiles adopted his pan-Slavism. Strémooukhoff argues that for Solovyov, whose father, the great historian, had first spoken to him of Križanić as one who embodied a great contradiction, namely that of being a Slavic patriot and a Catholic, Križanić was "the first and the purest of the Slavophiles," and he also notes that Solovyov develops the point made by Križanić that the Russian *raskol* made Slavic union difficult.[119]

     Christianity and Judaism, Albany NY, State University of New York Press, 2008, 17–31.

114   Wozniuk, ed., *Freedom, Faith, and Dogma*, 21.
115   Wozniuk, ed., *Freedom, Faith, and Dogma*, 21.
116   Wozniuk, ed., *Freedom, Faith, and Dogma*, 24.
117   Now in: Solovyov, *Sobranie sochinenij*, vol. 4, *1883–1887*, 1–114.

118   Solovyov, *Pis'ma*, vol. 4, 20–21 (the English translation is the author's; italics original).
119   Strémooukhoff, *Vladimir Soloviev and His Messianic Work*, 153.

Committed to the work of church union, Solovyov now develops friendships with the Catholic Croatian clergymen who share his ideal, Bishop Josip Juraj Strossmayer and Canon Franjo Rački. He also embarks to a major written work, *Istoriya i buduschnost teokratii* (The history and future of theocracy), published in Zagreb owing to Russian censorship.[120] The first part of this addresses the theme of the development of dogma in the early church. Solovyov initially published this section as a separate booklet in Moscow in 1885 with the subtitle "in liaison with the question about the reunion of the Churches," and it sold out immediately. He prepared a second edition, the only copy of which was mysteriously lost at the publishers. The subject of dogmatic development remains an understudied topic in Catholic-Orthodox relations, and it is perhaps little surprise that Solovyov's manuscript disappeared.[121] His work on this subject is extremely lucid and rich, centered on expounding the way in which church dogma concerning the Christ and the Trinity developed in the writings of the church fathers and the first seven ecumenical councils.[122] Moreover, he shows how integral this theme is, if the church is ever to attain the fullness of divinized humanity. Interestingly, Strémooukhoff points out that Solovyov received inspiration from

Samarin who had sketched out in correspondence a doctrine of the evolution of dogmas.[123]

Although he was alienated from Moscow Slavophile circles, Solovyov's ideas were still well received within the Russian Orthodox Church. In December 1886, having spent much of the summer in Croatia, the St. Petersburg Spiritual Academy invited him to speak about the union of the church. Here he was able to develop and share his ideas with prominent figures in the Russian Orthodox Church, including Archimandrite Anthony Vadkovsky (later metropolitan of St. Petersburg), Antony Khrapovitsky (later metropolitan of Kiev) and Rev. Innocent Figurovsky (later metropolitan of China). He subsequently wrote to Archimandrite Anthony: "Yesterday, I felt myself to be in a truly Christian society, primarily devoted to the work of God. This encourages me and gives me hope and from my part I can give you peace, for *I will never pass over* to Latinity."[124] In saying this, Solovyov happily uses the old Slavophile term for the Catholic Church. At the same time, he remains true to his actions earlier in the year in Croatia where, when pressed about becoming a Catholic, he responded by confessing to an Orthodox priest and receiving Communion in the Orthodox Church in Zagreb. Needless to say, Solovyov's point was that, unlike his friend Princess Elizabeth Volkonskaia who was received into the Catholic Church in 1887, he did not consider conversion from Orthodoxy to Catholicism to be necessary. Solovyov could see no grounds for those Orthodox who would accuse Catholics of heresy and asked if they could call an ecumenical council to pronounce this. He supported his views with reference to Orthodox teaching authorities:

> In any case, we believe with the metropolitan of Moscow, Philaret, that this situation

120   Vladimir S. Solovyov, *Istoriya i buduschnost teokratii* [The history and future of theocracy], Zagreb, Akcionernaja Tipografija, 1887.

121   See Andrew Louth, "Is Development of Doctrine a Valid Category for Orthodox Theology?," in: Valerie Hotchkiss & Patrick Henry, eds., *Orthodoxy and Western Culture: A Collection of Essays Honoring Jaroslav Pelikan on His Eightieth Birthday*, Crestwood NY, St. Vladimir's Seminary Press, 2005, 45–63.

122   Solovyov's work in this area has received little attention, see: Kazimierz Kupiec, *La théorie du développement dogmatique de Pavel Svetlov comparée avec la théorie de Vladimir Solov'ev*, Rome, Pontificia Universitas Gregoriana, 1972, and Bernard Marchadier, "L'Idée de développement dogmatique de l'Église chez John Henry Newman et Vladimir Soloviev," *Solovevskie issledovaniya* 32/4, 2012, 125–145.

123   Strémooukhoff, *Vladimir Soloviev and His Messianic Work*, 154. Subsequently, Solovyov learns of Newman's work on this subject from Fr. Martynov.

124   Solovyov, *Pisma*, vol. 3, 187 (the English translation is the author's, italics original).

cannot be subjected to any specific jurisdiction, and like the metropolitan of Kiev,
Platon, we view the Churches of the West
and the East as two sisters who have fallen
into a cruel dispute which can and must
be appeased, although this appeasement,
precisely because of the proximity of the
two quarrelling parties, presents particular
difficulties.[125]

This view of Solovyov is further reinforced by his
actions in 1896 in Moscow, when he recited the
Tridentine Creed and received communion from
a Byzantine-rite Catholic priest. At this time,
of course, there was no Byzantine-rite Russian
Catholic Church in Russia, so there is a certain canonical ambiguity or irregularity about Solovyov's
actions. Nonetheless, he clearly stands as the seminal figure behind the desire to see the Russian
Orthodoxy exist in union with Rome while maintaining its liturgical and spiritual traditions.

Solovyov's final work on the question of church
union was published in France in 1889. *La Russie
et L'Église Universelle*[126] contains a striking defense
of the papacy in the second part and a speculative Sophianic third part which alienated Solovyov
from his Jesuit friends in Paris. The first part of
this work is notable for the way in which Solovyov
makes extensive use of Slavophile writings to address the topic "État religieux de la Russie et de
l'Orient chrétien." For Solovyov, the challenge for
the Eastern Church is "to recognize unreservedly
the elementary truth that we of the East are but a
part of the Universal Church"[127] and that the West
has qualities lacking in the East. He argues that
advocates of the notion of Moscow as the Third
Rome "would reduce the ultimate historical objective of Christianity and the *raison d'être* of the

human race to the existence of a single nation";[128]
moreover advocates of a great mission for Russia,
including the old Slavophiles, have not clearly articulated what this means in practice. Solovyov begins to address directly the polemics surrounding
church union in 19th-century Russia in a chapter
entitled "L'orthodoxie véritable du peuple russe
et la pseudo-orthodoxie des théologiens anti-
catholiques." He argues that the straightforward
Orthodox faith of the Russian people is shared by
Catholics in the West, noting in particular a shared
Marian piety in the veneration of miraculous images, particularly in evidence at the shrine of the
Holy Virgin of Częstochowa in Poland.[129] Hence
a crucial part of his vision of church union centers on the fact that there does still exist a certain
union between the churches of the East and West
in the evidence of piety and holiness.

For Solovyov, division in the Church can be
traced to the Greeks, who "after the temporary
schism of Photius, were already imbued with national particularism."[130] Solovyov suggests that
the Russian Church received this inheritance
from Byzantium leading to a fundamental distortion emerging in theology in Russia, namely
its negative basis, constructed in opposition to
perceived Western error. He suggests that these
"pseudo-Orthodox" should "declare openly that
the religious ideal of Russia consists in denying
the *Filioque*, the Immaculate Conception, and the
authority of the Pope."[131] Solovyov views the papacy as a positive principle; he also recognizes it
as the issue most problematic for some. To these
fellow Orthodox who object to papal authority he
addresses the pointed, semi-rhetorical question:

---

125 Vladimir S. Solovyov, *Le Dévelopment Dogmatique de
     l'Église*, Paris, Desclée, 1991, 62–63 (the English transla-
     tion is the author's, italics original).
126 Vladimir S. Solovyov, *La Russie et L'Église Universelle*,
     Paris, Savine, 1889; ET: *Russia and the Universal Church*.
127 Solovyov, *Russia and the Universal Church*, 42.
128 Solovyov, *Russia and the Universal Church*, 43.
129 Among the basic elements of being Orthodox Solovyov
     includes "to pray to the Blessed Virgin most immacu-
     late," including a note stating: "'Most immaculate'
     or 'all-immaculate' (*vseneporochnaya*) is the epithet
     regularly added to the name of the Blessed Virgin in
     our liturgical books, being the translation of the Greek
     παντάμωμος and other kindred words." Solovyov, *Russia
     and the Universal Church*, 47.
130 Solovyov, *Russia and the Universal Church*, 47–48.
131 Solovyov, *Russia and the Universal Church*, 49.

"Why has not the East set up a *true* ecumenical council in opposition to those of Trent or the Vatican?"[132] Ultimately, if the Eastern Church cannot call an ecumenical council, Solovyov suggests it lacks something fundamentally constitutive of the life of the universal church. In addition, Solovyov finds that this idea of a universal church is lacking in Russian ecclesiology, both with regard to the Old Believers and especially in the works of theologians of the official church; in this respect he presents "the theory of the Church expounded by Archbishop Philaret, the able Metropolitan of Moscow, in one of his most important works,"[133] *Razgovory mezhdu ispytuyuschim i uverennym o pravoslavii vostochnoj Greko-rossiskoj Tserkvi* (Conversations of an inquirer and a believer on the truth of the Eastern Greek-Russian Church).[134] Solovyov sees the vision of unity presented here, centered on a basic belief in the dogma of the Incarnation, as "a unity based on a broad but hollow indifference, implying no organic bond and requiring no effective fellowship between particular Churches."[135]

Solovyov devotes the fifth chapter to some critical observations on the Russian Slavophiles and their ideas concerning the church ("Les slavophiles russeset leurs idées sur l'Église. Remarques critiques") He recognizes the positive aspect of their teaching, that the Church, "in its free and living unity founded on divine grace and Christian charity," is perfectly true and meritorious. Equally, he argues that they "confine themselves too much to vague generalizations" and that such ideas have been expressed more effectively by Catholic theologians "especially by the famous Möhler in

his admirable work, *Die Symbolik der christlichen Kirche*"; Solovyov also notes that this work has been "commended and frequently quoted" by Fr. Giovanni Perrone, "the official dogmatic theologian of the Latin Church."[136] He has some measured praise for Khomyakov's "The Church is One" which "though insignificant in itself deserves notice as the only attempt on the part of the Slavophiles to fix and systematize their theological ideas." After all, he asks, "what objection can there be to such an ideal?"[137] Now Solovyov highlights the shortcomings of Slavophile ecclesiology: that the ideal is presented as existing now rather than being the goal towards which the "divine-human organism of the Church"[138] is a journey. Moreover, he points out the tendency to identify this ideal with the Russian Church, claiming this alone to be the one true church and "other communions as nothing but anti-Christian associations,"[139] in this way denying in practice the universality they purport to uphold.

The question of religious and ecclesiastical freedom is also a crucial issue covered by Solovyov. He contrasts the situation in the Catholic Church "which has always enjoyed a measure of ecclesiastical freedom and has never been a State Church," with the established church in Russia in which the interests of the state are paramount and guarantee the church's "existence against the menace of dissent."[140] Solovyov suggests that the Slavophiles confuse the matter here by suggesting that periods of religious intolerance in the history of the Catholic Church point to an exclusively despotic Roman Church. Thus they ignore "the great prerogative of ecclesiastical freedom which Catholicism alone of all Christian communions has always maintained." Worse than confusing the two freedoms, however, Solovyov adds, is the fact the "we

132   Solovyov, *Russia and the Universal Church*, 49 (italics original).

133   Solovyov, *Russia and the Universal Church*, 54.

134   Philaret (Drozdov), *Razgovory mezhdu ispytuyuschim i uverennym o pravoslavii vostochnoj Greko-rossijskoj Tserkvi* [Conversations of an inquirer and a believer on the truth of the Eastern Greek-Russian Church], Moscow, Sinodalnaya Tipografiya, 1815.

135   Solovyov, *Russia and the Universal Church*, 55.

136   Solovyov, *Russia and the Universal Church*, 56.

137   Solovyov, *Russia and the Universal Church*, 56.

138   Solovyov, *Russia and the Universal Church*, 57.

139   Solovyov, *Russia and the Universal Church*, 58.

140   Solovyov, *Russia and the Universal Church*, 60.

possess neither," which is a "melancholy truth" that he says no one highlighted more forcefully than "the late I. Aksakov, the last notable representative of the old school of Slavophiles."[141] Solovyov actually devotes a chapter to examining the contemporary Russian Orthodox Church through the lens of the writings of Aksakov and this is one of the most powerful chapters of his book. He notes that Aksakov was once censored but that he recently gained, "with Katkov, the privilege of free speech – a privilege which was peculiar to these two men and has not survived them."[142] Solovyov cites abundantly from Aksakov to show that ecclesiastical freedom does not exist in Russia, concluding powerfully:

> We have not forgotten that the Slavophiles see in our Church the one true Church of Christ and the living synthesis of freedom and unity in the spirit of charity. And this is the conclusion reached by the latest representative of that party after an impartial enquiry into the state of the Church: "It is the spirit of truth, the spirit of charity, the spirit of life, the spirit of freedom, of whose invigorating breath the Church of Russia stands in need." Thus, according to the unimpeachable testimony of an eminent Russian Orthodox priest and patriot, our national Church has been deserted by the Spirit of Truth and Charity and is not the true Church of God.[143]

Solovyov's treatment here of the ecclesiastical situation in Russia in the 1880s, presented through the prism of Slavophile ideology and commentary, amounts to a decisive condemnation of the official Russian Orthodox Church as well as a pointed exposure of the ineffectual and contradictory core of Orthodox ecclesiology as presented by Khomyakov.

La Russie et l'Église universelle remains a stimulating and controversial work not least because of the directness with which it approaches both the Orthodox Church and the matters which divide her from the Catholic Church. On balance, Solovyov is far more critical of the Russian Church than he is of the Slavophiles. Indeed, his primary engagement with the Slavophiles in this work is to use their words and ideas to expose the weakness of the established church in Russia. He does, however, expound his criticisms of the Slavophiles themselves in a lengthy article of 1889, "Slavyanofilstvo i ego vyrozhdenie" (Slavophilism and its degeneration), published in the second volume of his work *Natsionalnyj vopros v Rossi* (The national question in Russia).[144] In some ways, through his recognition of some of the true limitations of the thought of the first generation of Slavophiles, Solovyov can be fruitfully understood as an genuine heir to them, creating in his own work an honest vision of ecclesial unity. The problem with such an understanding of Solovyov, needless to say, is that the developments to their ecclesiology which he saw as necessary, particularly his recognition of Catholicism and the role of the papacy, are difficult to accommodate within the Russian exclusivity of Slavophile Orthodoxy.

Bibliography

Gratieux, Albert, *A.S. Khomiakov et le Mouvement Slavophile*, 2 vols., Paris, Cerf, 1939.

Jakim, Boris & Robert Bird, eds., *On Spiritual Unity: A Slavophile Reader: Aleksei Khomiakov, Ivan Kireevsky, with essays by Yury Samarin, Nikolai Berdiaev and Pavel Florensky*, Hudson NY, Lindisfarne Books, 1998.

---

141 Solovyov, *Russia and the Universal Church*, 60.
142 Solovyov, *Russia and the Universal Church*, 60. Aksakov died in 1886, Katkov in 1887. Aksakov's collected works appeared the year following his death.
143 Solovyov, *Russia and the Universal Church*, 67.

---

144 See Vladimir S. Solovyov, *Natsionalnyj vopros v Rossii* [The national question in Russia], Moscow, AST, 2007, 220–314.

Khomyakov, Aleksey S., *Polnoe sobranie sochinenij*, 8 vols., Moscow, Universitetskaya Tipografiya na Stransom Bulvare, 1886–1906.

Mrówczyński-Van Allen, Artur, Teresa Obolevitch & Paweł Rojek, eds., *Alexei Khomiakov: The Mystery of Sobornost'*, Eugene OR, Pickwick, 2019.

Samarin, Yuri F., *Sobranie sochinenij v piati tomakh*, 5 vols., Rostok, St. Petersburg, 2013–2020.

Solovyov, Vladimir S., *Pisma*, 4 vols., St. Petersburg, Obschestvennaya Polza, Vremya, 1908–1923.

Solovyov, Vladimir S., *Sobranie sochinenij*, 10 vols., St. Petersburg, Prosveschenie, 1911–1914.

Tsimbaev, Nikolai I., *Slavyanofilstvo: Iz istorii russkoj obschestvenno-politicheskoj mysli XIX veka*, Moscow, MGU, [2]2013 [[1]1986].

Tsimbaeva, Ekaterina N., *Russkij ekumenizm: Poisk osnov mezhkonfessionalnogo edinstva v Rossii XIX veka*, Moscow, URSS, 2015.

Tsurikov, Vladimir, ed., *A.S. Khomiakov: Poet, Philosopher, Theologian*, Jordanville NY, Holy Trinity Seminary Press, 2004.

Tyutchev, Fyodor I., *Polnoe sobranie sochinenij i pisma, v shesti tomakh*, 6 vols., Moscow, Klassika, 2002–2005.

CHAPTER 9

Unions, Alliances and World Communions in 19th-Century Protestant World

Martin Friedrich

1   Introduction

The Reformation, which had once set out to renew the one (Western) Church, not only led to a schism between Catholics and Protestants but also to further separations and divisions among the latter. Even before Luther's death, the division into a Lutheran and Reformed wing had already become firmly established. The "radical" (i.e. non-magisterial) Reformation of the 16th century also led to the emergence of distinct confessions and churches. The subsequent period witnessed further divisions, especially within the Free Churches as well as in Reformed Protestantism. The causes were partly linked to theological issues and partly to disagreements in matters of church constitution, as in the case of the separation of Presbyterians and Congregationalists in the 17th century. Since the Lutheran and Reformed churches relied on the territorial states, they were also bound to specific regions and generally lacked any form of organization, even within their own confessional family.

Along with the first divisions, there were also the first attempts to restore the unity. Especially the Reformed churches, which mainly spread in environments that were hostile to them, were more interested in forging an alliance with the Lutherans, whereas the Lutherans of the 17th century considered the gap between them and the Reformed churches to be as wide as the one that separated them from the Catholics. The efforts of "irenicism" during the age of confessionalism were thus unsuccessful. It was not until the advent of Pietism and the age of Enlightenment that theological differences in doctrinal matters became

less harsh. In most cases, however, this did not give rise to alliances or even unions – and where they did take place, they made no significant impact.[1]

The situation did not change until the 19th century, the first quarter of which already witnessed the founding of union churches, followed by the establishment of worldwide interdenominational alliances of Christians in the middle of the century and, finally, by worldwide communions of individual Protestant confessional groups/families in the last quarter of the century. Largely independently of one another, these three different paths expressed the desire for a community that went beyond the individual church. Even though the modern ecumenical movement has its own distinct roots, these initiatives were nevertheless important in that they created the prerequisites for the efforts to achieve Christian unity in the 20th century. Owing to its 19th-century legacy, Protestantism was well prepared to assume a leading role in ecumenism over a considerable period of time.

2   Lutheran-Reformed Unions

In many European countries, early 19th-century Protestantism formed a homogeneous whole: Lutheran in Scandinavia and the Baltic regions, and Reformed in Switzerland, Scotland and to a large extent in the Netherlands. Where its status was

---

1   See Martin Friedrich, *Von Marburg bis Leuenberg: Der lutherisch-reformierte Gegensatz und seine Überwindung*, Waltrop, Spenner, 1999, 83–140.

that of a minority religion, the Reformed Protestants were usually the dominant group; Lutheran churches of significant size existed only in the Habsburg Empire. Aside from the United States with its great confessional diversity, the problem of intra-Protestant antagonism was thus particularly pressing in Germany. Although more than 80% of the German Evangelical Christians were Lutheran, Reformed Protestants were also present in many territories. The situation was particularly virulent in Prussia, which had a Lutheran majority but a Reformed royal house. Owing to the extensive reorganization of territories in the Napoleonic period, the populations of nearly all the German states were now confessionally mixed.

A source of inspiration was the founding, in 1802, of the first united church congregation in Mainz, where neither Lutherans nor Reformed Protestants had hitherto been allowed to exercise their religion freely. Not until the French occupation had it been possible to establish a congregation, and in the spirit of the Enlightenment and of the Revolution, the decision was made that it should be a united congregation. A joint communion service was to ensure that the former separation was now a thing of the past.[2] In these years, united congregations also formed in other cities on the western side of the Rhine, for instance in Koblenz, Aachen, and Neuss.

Where German Evangelical congregations had already existed for centuries, this path was, of course, more difficult. But since governments had a vested interest in reducing the scope of public administration, administrative unions were formed. In the Kingdom of Bavaria, which was proclaimed in 1806, the Lutheran and Reformed congregations were brought together under a joint administrative authority (albeit only until 1818).[3] Developments were more momentous in the Grand Duchy of

Baden, which had acquired the eastern portion of the Electoral Palatinate with its large Reformed community in 1803. The Reformed and Lutheran consistories were dissolved in 1807 and replaced by a joint high consistory.[4] Prussia followed suit in 1809 by transferring the powers of the highest Lutheran and Reformed superintendence bodies to a newly formed department within the Ministry of the Interior.[5] Even when consistories were established again as church authorities from 1815 onwards, they held the joint responsibility for both the Lutheran and the Reformed congregations.

These administrative unions were an important step, since the Evangelical churches, apart from their integration into the state administration, hardly ever disposed of any institutions of their own. However, these unions were of no consequence for the congregations and their umbrella organizations, nor did they have any bearing on the supervision of the clergy proper. For this reason, the union churches that emerged in various German federal states following the Congress of Vienna are widely seen as the sole true unions. Nassau and Prussia took the lead in 1817, followed by the Palatinate in 1818, and because they set an example, they deserve closer examination.

In Prussia, in particular, several appeals for a union of Lutherans and Reformed Protestants had been voiced since the 18th century, notably on the part of Friedrich Schleiermacher (1804) and of the progressive court preacher, Friedrich Sack (1812).[6]

---

2 Gustav Adolf Benrath, *Reformation, Union, Erweckung: Beispiele aus der Kirchengeschichte Südwestdeutschlands*, Göttingen, Vandenhoeck & Ruprecht, 2012, 119–144.

3 Hartmut Böttcher, "Die Entstehung der evangelischen Landeskirche und die Entwicklung ihrer Verfassung (1806–1918)," in: Gerhard Müller, Horst Weigelt & Wolfgang

Zorn, eds., *Handbuch der Geschichte der Evangelischen Kirche in Bayern*, vol. 2, Sankt Ottilien, EOS, 2000, 1–29.

4 Benrath, *Reformation*, 196–198.

5 J.F. Gerhard Goeters, "Die Reorganisation der staatlichen und kirchlichen Verwaltung in den Stein-Hardenbergschen Reformen," in: J.F. Gerhard Goeters, Joachim Rogge & Rudolf Mau, eds., *Die Geschichte der Evangelischen Kirche der Union*, vol. 1, Leipzig, Evangelische Verlagsanstalt, 1992, 54–58.

6 On the Prussian Union, its background and subsequent history, see Friedrich, *Von Marburg*, 144ff.; Wilhelm Heinrich Neuser, "Die Entstehung des preußischen Unionsaufrufes vom 27. September 1817," in: Jürgen Kampmann, ed., *Preußische Union: Ursprünge, Wirkung und Ausgang: Einblick in vier Jahrhunderte evangelischer Kirchen- und*

However, it took a revival of piety such as that triggered by the "Wars of Liberations" of 1813–1815 to really set the union process in motion. The actual impulse came from the western provinces, where Lutherans and Reformed Protestants had already been developing a sense of togetherness for over a century. In 1815, the Reformed and Lutheran congregations of the Saarland came together to form a joint synod. In 1816, the two synods of the County of Mark decided to celebrate the Reformation jubilee of the following year with a joint communion.

The impact of these events was felt not only locally (this will be dealt with in greater detail below) but also elsewhere. In August 1817, in the Duchy of Nassau, a joint synod of Lutheran and Reformed pastors convened by the duke unanimously decided to implement the church union on the upcoming Reformation Day. Theological discussions barely took place as there was a shared conviction that "this union corresponded to a long-held and widely cherished wish among the judicious and educated coreligionists of both Protestant confessions."[7] Indeed, the members of the congregations enthusiastically approved of this decision. The ensuing harmonization of the rite of Holy Communion, the pooling of the churches' property, and the adoption of a uniform set of rules with regard to superintendence and theological training led to the formation of a true

union church. The following years saw the introduction of a new catechism, a new hymnal and a new book of liturgies for all congregations; earlier confessional idiosyncrasies soon vanished.

Just as Nassau is seen as an example of a "union from above," the Palatinate, in particular, may be seen as a "union from below."[8] After the congregations of several communities had merged in 1817, the responsible consistory held an election among all heads of households in February–March 1818. An overwhelming majority having voted in favor of the union, a general synod then proceeded to draw up a unification charter that took effect in Advent 1818. Adopting the position of Zwingli, it declared that the Last Supper was a memorial meal and put the various confessional writings into perspective. In the first draft, it had even intended to abolish them altogether and to accept only the New Testament as a doctrinal basis. Only thanks to the initiative of the Maximilian I Joseph was the entire Bible mentioned as the doctrinal norm. After protracted disputes between liberal and orthodox Protestants, the *Confessio Augustana Variata* of 1540, i.e. Melanchthon's adaptation of the most important Lutheran confessional document that was meant to mediate between the various Protestant factions, was finally recognized as the fundamental creed of the church.

The spirit of the Enlightenment also spurred the unions in Baden (1821) and in Rhenish Hesse (1822), where the rite of the Holy Communion and its interpretation also followed the Zwinglian tradition. From then on, all congregations shared the same order of worship. By contrast, the unions in Hanau, Anhalt, Waldeck and Bremen allowed the individual congregations to retain their confessional status.[9] In most territories, however, union service books and catechisms were introduced in the course of the 19th century. In terms of theology

---

Konfessionsgeschichte; Wilhelm Heinrich Neuser zum Gedenken, Bielefeld, Luther-Verlag, 2011, 45–78; Martin Friedrich, Wilhelm Hüffmeier & Jürgen Kampmann, *Gemeinsam evangelisch: 200 Jahre lutherisch-reformierte Unionen in Deutschland*, Hanover, UEK, 2016; Wilhelm Hüffmeier, "'Den großen Zwecken des Christentums gemäß': Der königliche Aufruf vom 27. September 1817 zur lutherisch-reformierten Kirchenunion in Preußen und seine Folgen," in: Jürgen Kampmann & Christian Peters, eds., *200 Jahre lutherisch-reformierte Unionen in Deustchland*, Bielefeld, Luther-Verlag, 2018, 481–497.

7   Wording of the synod's memorandum according to Gerhard Ruhbach, *Kirchenunionen im 19. Jahrhundert*, Gütersloh, Mohn, 1968, 13–15 (quote on 14); for the background of this decision, see Reiner Braun, "Die nassauische Union von 1817: Vortrag mit eingebettetem Historiolog als narrativ-interaktivem Zugang," in: Kampmann & Peters, *200 Jahre*, 75–91.

8   Benrath, *Reformation*, 165–181.
9   For an overview, see Andreas Metzing, "Unionen in außerpreußischen Staaten Deutschlands im 19. Jahrhundert," in: Friedrich, Hüffmeier & Kampmann, *Gemeinsam evangelisch*, 33–56.

and liturgy, the union churches represented a new type that emphasized the common legacy of the Reformation as opposed to the particularities of the various confessional writings that it had brought forth.

A special case is that of Württemberg, where the regional church, in spite of incorporating exiled communities of Waldensians in 1823, retained its Lutheran character;[10] and, of course, the great Protestant federal state of Prussia should not be forgotten. In a cabinet order issued on Sept 27, 1817, King Frederick William III called for a "unification of the two Protestant Churches, which were now only separated by external differences."[11] However, he did not wish to impose the union by decree but only to promote it; accordingly, he merely announced that the two court congregations would unite on Reformation Day in Potsdam and expressed the hope that this example would be followed everywhere in the country. Although this did take place, especially in the western provinces, other areas mostly limited themselves to a joint celebration of the Holy Communion without further legal consequences. In spite of a generally positive reception of the call for unification, the implementation of a binding union for the entire church was not achieved. There was a general lack of institutions that could have resolved to do so as the development of a presbyterial-synodal church constitution, though underway, had not yet been completed. The king finally interrupted this process in 1819, thereby precluding any possibility that the churches themselves might still ratify the union at a general synod.

The exact nature of the Prussian Union was thus unclear. In the royal proclamation of 1817 it had sounded as if the union were to be an absorptive union "in which the Reformed Church does not blend into the Lutheran Church and the latter does not blend into the former – but in which both become a revitalized Evangelical-Christian Church in the spirit of its holy founder."[12] What was actually achieved was at first no more than an administrative union, on the level not only of the administrative authorities but also of the church districts and of the general superintendents in charge of clerical supervision. The king's true interest lay in the liturgical union; he himself, therefore, created an order of worship that was presented to all congregations for approval in 1822. However, this order of worship, which was to be the visible expression of the union, was opposed by clerics and laypeople of all factions; the Lutherans complained about the lack of a clear statement concerning the real presence of Christ in the Eucharist, the rationalists found it too antiquated, and the Reformed Protestants too liturgical.

The conflict over the order of worship preoccupied the Prussian Church for over a decade. It not only alienated the supporters of the union from the protagonists of church politics but also gave rise to fierce resistance against the union. Beginning in Silesia, and later in the provinces of Saxony and Pomerania, thousands of Lutherans left the regional church. While some of them emigrated, the majority fought for acceptance as an autonomous Evangelical-Lutheran church in Prussia. However, the king and his minister of culture, Karl vom Stein zum Altenstein, took draconic steps against them.

In order to placate the situation, the king decided to revoke the original conception of the union. In 1834, he proclaimed that the union did not aim to "abandon the present confession of faith" and did not abrogate the authority of the respective confessional writings but only expressed the "spirit of moderation and leniency" that would allow for an "external church fellowship" in spite

---

10   Siegfried Hermle, "Das Ende der württembergischen Waldenserkirche im 19. Jahrhundert," *BWKG* 101, 2001, 70–113.

11   For the text of the proclamation, see Ruhbach, *Kirchenunionen*, 34f.

12   Ruhbach, *Kirchenunionen*, 34. On the history of the Prussian Union after 1817, see Friedrich, *Von Marburg*, 160–185, and Axel Noack, "Auseinandersetzungen um die Unionen im 19. Jahrhundert," in: Kampmann & Peters, eds., *200 Jahre*, 133–175.

of "differences on individual points of doctrine."[13] The union would thus be limited to a mere administrative union combined with a Eucharistic fellowship. In 1835, the western provinces of Rhenish Prussia and Westphalia did in fact obtain the king's approval for a church order that combined the Lutheran tradition of consistorial leadership with the Reformed tradition of self-determination through presbyteries and synods.

His son and successor, Frederick William IV, also failed to solve the problem. Like his father, he was more in favor of a High Church. In 1845, he accordingly granted state recognition to the "Old Lutherans" and, as early as 1841, paved the way for the establishment of a joint diocese of Jerusalem of both his regional church and the Church of England, which existed until 1886.[14] However, what is now considered to have been one of the most interesting ecumenical experiments in the 19th century met with widespread disapproval in its time, not only on the part of John Henry Newman and the Oxford Movement but also within his own church.[15] Although the king's initiative set a reform process in motion, he refused to approve the resolutions of the general synod convened by him in 1846, which had aimed to develop a presbyterial-synodal church constitution and to introduce a doctrinal order that would have given the union the confessional basis that it lacked. Quite to the contrary, in 1852, he decreed that the congregations, but also the civil servants in the Evangelical High Consistory, should decide whether they were Lutheran or Reformed, whereby the union would have been reduced to a mere

administrative union.[16] Although this decree was repealed in the following year, a broad movement now advocated a genuine Lutheranism, even within the regional church. This antagonism initially foiled all attempts to forge closer bonds of fellowship within German Protestantism; instead, the rise of Neo-Lutheranism fueled the efforts to organize the first international gathering of Lutheran churches (see par. 4).

In spite of this, the Prussian regional church also survived the upheavals of 1866 and 1918. This was partly due to the fact that its theological justification, which had still been rather weak in 1817, was gradually provided in the course of the century. Friedrich Schleiermacher had already developed his dogmatics from the very outset as a dogmatic theology of union. In the generation that succeeded him, the mediation theologians Karl Immanuel Nitzsch and Julius Müller published works in which they defended the union. For many, the central theological idea had been formulated by the rationalist general superintendent Karl Gottlieb Bretschneider in his doctrine of the two theological principles of Protestantism: the sole reliance on the Bible as its formal principle and the acceptance of justification by faith alone as its material principle.[17] In addition to the latter, private societies run by laypersons, such as the Gustav-Adolf-Verein (from 1841) and the Evangelischer Bund (from 1886), were the most important bearers of a pan-Protestant consciousness that grew increasingly nationalistic. Last but not least, the supplementing of the hitherto purely consistorial church order with presbyterial-synodal structures, as implemented in the second half of the century in Prussia and in numerous other regional churches, also led to an erosion of intra-Protestant antagonisms.

The ultimately unsolved question of its status, on the other hand, fueled the continuing struggle to define the relationship between confession

---

13   Ruhbach, *Kirchenunionen*, 37.

14   See most recently Charlotte van der Leest, *Conversion and Conflict in Palestine: The Missions of the Church Missionary Society and the Protestant Bishop Samuel Gobat*, Ph.D. thesis, Leiden University, 2008, 53–81.

15   Albrecht Geck, "Pusey, Tholuck and the Reception of the Oxford Movement in Germany," in: Stewart J. Brown & Peter Nockles, eds., *The Oxford Movement: Europe and the Wider World (1830–1930)*, Cambridge, Cambridge University Press, 2012, 168–184. See also Peter Nockles's contribution in this volume.

16   See Ruhbach, *Kirchenunionen*, 41f.; Friedrich, *Von Marburg*, 177f.

17   Friedrich, *Von Marburg*, 168.

and church as well as between unity and diversity. While the south German unions constituted something of a third confession, the Prussian Union, in particular, avoided taking a clear stance and worked towards a differentiated understanding.[18] In the 20th century, it was this church that provided the strongest impulses for the development of the model of church fellowship that was realized with the Leuenberg Agreement.[19]

German emigrants also took the union churches to other continents. This led to the establishment, in 1840, of the German Evangelical Synod of North America, one of the predecessor churches of the United Church of Christ.[20] In Europe, on the other hand, only variants of the union model were able to assert themselves. Thus, the initiatives for a unification of the churches met with failure in the Netherlands. In Hungary, the Lutheran and Reformed churches concluded agreements (in 1830 and 1833) for a mutual admission to Holy Communion and a reciprocal substitution of pastors.[21] In Austria, the Protestant Church of Augsburgian and Helvetic confession was formed in 1867, albeit only as a legal bracketing of the still autonomous Lutheran and Reformed churches.[22]

In the "free church" environment of the United States, in any case, the efforts to achieve unity took place under different conditions. The Restoration movement of the early 19th century, which sought to overcome divisions by returning to the teachings of the New Testament, only led to the founding of a new confessional family, the Disciples of Christ, which soon split into several churches.[23] Samuel Simon Schmucker's attempts to form a Lutheran-Reformed Union failed, as did the Plan of Union between Presbyterians and Congregationalists.[24] However, according to the theory of denominationalism that had been elaborated since the separation of church and state affirmed by the American constitution, the external organization of the churches was in any case not the starting point of ecumenism. Since no single church community could claim that it was identical with the true church, Christian unity had to be effected beyond the denominations. This is why the second main strand of intra-Protestant ecumenism arose in the Anglo-Saxon world.

3   Nondenominational Movements

The spiritual Reformers of the 16th and 17th centuries had already minimized the importance of the visible church in favor of a direct access to God. For the same reason, the Philadelphian movement of the years around 1700 sought the unity of Christians beyond the confessional churches, which were all considered to have forsaken the true faith. Radical Pietism, in particular, propagated the idea that true believers should form a spiritual community (like the congregation of Philadelphia according to Rev 3:7–13). Inspired by this, Nikolaus Ludwig, count von Zinzendorf, founded the Herrnhuter Brüdergemeine in 1727 as a congregation in which the Lutheran, Reformed and Hussite traditions were to be united. The individual confessions were seen as mere "tropes," that is, as educational instruments of God.[25]

---

18   For the context, see Henning Theißen, "Über Verwaltungs- und Konsensunion hinaus: Unierte Theologie im 19. und 20. Jahrhundert," in: Kampmann & Peters, *200 Jahre*, 201–224.

19   See also Elisabeth Parmentier's contribution in the second volume of this work.

20   Carl E. Schneider, *The German Church on the American Frontier: A Study in the Rise of Religion among the Germans of the West, Based on the History of the Evangelischer Kirchenverein des Westens (Evangelical Church Society of the West) (1840–1866)*, Eugene OR, Wipf & Stock, 2009 [¹1939].

21   Mihály Márkus, ed., *Három egyezmény: Drei Abkommen 1830–1833–1900*, Budapest, Kálvin, 2006.

22   Friedrich, *Von Marburg*, 181.

---

23   *A History of the Ecumenical Movement*, vol. 1, Ruth Rouse & Stephen C. Neill, eds., *1517–1948*, London, SPCK, 1954, 236ff.; James D. Murch, *Christians Only: A History of the Restoration Movement*, Eugene OR, Wipf & Stock, 2004.

24   *A History of the Ecumenical Movement*, vol. 1, 243–246.

25   Friedrich, *Von Marburg*, 131–133.

Zinzendorf influenced John Wesley, who combined Luther's accent on justification and the Reformed emphasis on sanctification in his theology and founded Methodism as a revival movement within the Church of England. As bridge-builders between the latter and the Reform-minded Dissenters, the Methodists in Great Britain were able to usher in an era of cooperation that transcended confessional boundaries. The Revival movement, which began in about 1790, was characterized by the founding of societies in which the members of different churches worked together in the fields of missionary work and Bible distribution (LMS in 1795, BFBS in 1804).[26] This was soon joined by an international cooperation, notably with the Basel Mission (1815). Through travels and correspondence, a network of relationships was established across state and confessional boundaries, also with the participation of Catholics.

However, this did not yet constitute an ecumenical movement in the proper sense, since the main purpose of these undertakings was not to achieve a closer fellowship among the churches or among Christians. Even the nondenominational prayer gatherings organized in Liverpool from 1825 onwards had more to do with the joint summoning of the Holy Spirit than with the promoting of unity.[27] On the other hand, the close links among the revivalists paved the way for the founding of the organization that is widely regarded as the forerunner of the ecumenical movement: the EA.

Paradoxically, the founding of the alliance came at a time when the nondenominational mood had already diminished. In Germany, opposition to the union and to the order of worship had promoted a return to confessionalism. In France and the Netherlands, the Christians who reflected the influence of the *Réveil* established their own free churches. In England, the members of the Broad Church and the High Church increasingly distanced themselves from the free churches. The Oxford Movement, in particular, increased the gap that separated it from the Nonconformists. While the latter gained self-confidence after the abolition of the Test Acts in 1828, a growing number of Anglicans spoke out in defense of the state church, which was threatened by liberalism. The conflicts were even greater in Scotland, where the dispute over the right of patronage led to a schism within the Reformed national church. The Free Church of Scotland was constituted in 1843 under the leadership of Thomas Chalmers because it insisted on the right of the presbyteries to appoint parish ministers.

Against this background, the founding of the EA was determined almost as strongly by the spirit of demarcation as by the spirit of fellowship.[28] In 1842, the Congregational Union of England and Wales called upon Protestants (explicitly including the "devout portion of the clergy" belonging to the Church of England and the Church of Scotland) to band together in an "Evangelical Union" in order to oppose indifferentism, but also Catholicism and the Oxford Movement. Numerous conferences, besides the publication of the volume *Essays on Christian Union* (1845), elicited a widespread response. From Lyon, there came the idea that nondenominational prayer groups should meet in as many places as possible in order to establish national and international ties. In 1845, a preparatory conference decided that the EA should not consist in churches but in individual Christians. Its main purpose was to testify to the Christian unity that already existed.

The inception[29] took place in early August 1846 in London, as was initially the case for nearly all

---

26   *A History of the Ecumenical Movement*, vol. 1, 311ff.; Norman E. Thomas, *Missions and Unity: Lessons from History (1792–2010)*, Eugene OR, Wipf & Stock, 2010, 13–15, 23f.

27   *A History of the Ecumenical Movement*, vol. 1, 346–347.

28   On the alliance in general, see *A History of the Ecumenical Movement*, vol. 1, 318–324; for a very detailed account, see Gerhard Lindemann, *Für Frömmigkeit in Freiheit: Die Geschichte der Evangelischen Allianz im Zeitalter des Liberalismus (1846–1879)*, Münster, LIT, 2011 (the EA's historical background is addressed on 23–60).

29   Lindemann, *Für Frömmigkeit*, 60–137.

the other international ecumenical organizations, and like the others, it primarily concerned the British Empire. Some 10% of the members were from North America and 6% from the European continent. Among the British, the members of free churches constituted the largest group, although the Anglicans were also well represented. An extensive debate was conducted in search of a basic formula that was to be signed by all members. It was not meant to replace the various confessions of faith but to allow for a broadest possible basis of cooperation. However, the emphasis on the Trinity excluded the Unitarians, while the divine institution of the Christian ministry left out the Quakers. The declared belief in biblical inspiration and in the original sin was also intended as a demarcation from liberal theology. The Alliance was thus clearly "Evangelical" in the current sense of the term and, from the outset, enjoyed stronger support in the free churches than in the national churches. Moreover, the conservatives in the state churches not only viewed the participating Baptists with great suspicion but also entertained grave doubts regarding the call for religious freedom that had been a core element of the EA from the very beginning. It was not until 1853 that affiliated societies were founded in Germany and Sweden.[30] In spite of the encouragement stemming from Frederick William IV, who took the EA's fourth international conference to Berlin in 1857, only a small minority of pastors were willing to cooperate in the activities of the alliance. It was not until the rise of the Gemeinschaftsbewegung, from 1880 onwards, that a broad cooperation began to take place.[31] In the United States, the first affiliated society was not established until 1867, that is, only after the long and controversially debated question of whether slaveholders were to be allowed to become members had been solved.

The EA was nevertheless instrumental in spreading the idea of ecumenism (a programmatic term that was already quite popular in those early days). The large international gatherings raised the awareness of a worldwide fellowship. This was fully in tune with the spirit of the times; it was thus no coincidence that the EA's second international conference took place in London in 1851, concomitant to the first world exposition. A modern innovation which many conservatives deemed offensive was the fact that "ladies' committees" were allowed to develop their own independent activities from 1850. At the local level, the prayer weeks that were organized in early January were of great importance, especially from 1861, in which all local Protestants were permitted to participate; at the national level, the journals published by individual affiliate societies were equally important. Founded in 1847, the organ published by the British branch, *Evangelical Christendom*, also served as that of the worldwide alliance and printed both the reports of correspondents from many countries and theological articles (for example, in the very first issue, there was an article that praised the EA's approach as "The Path to Christian Union").[32]

Although the EA adhered strictly to the principle that it should be no more than a fellowship of individuals, and accordingly did not participate in the efforts to achieve a union of churches, it did promote further institutional cooperation. There were regular exchanges concerning the work of the missionary societies; at the same time, there was an agreement on cooperation projects that eventually led to the WMC of 1910 in Edinburgh.[33] Another focus of activity was the work of Sunday schools, which ultimately led to the founding of an international federation, the WSSA, which later

---

30   Lindemann, *Für Frömmigkeit*, 487ff., 505.

31   Lindemann, *Für Frömmigkeit*, 371–441, 666–677, 919–922; Karl Heinz Voigt, *Ökumene in Deutschland: Internationale Einflüsse und Netzwerkbildung: Anfänge 1848–1945*, Göttingen, Vandenhoeck & Ruprecht, 2014, 47–61, 67f.

32   Lindemann, *Für Frömmigkeit*, 139f.

33   William R. Hogg, *Ecumenical Foundations: A History of the International Missionary Council and its Nineteenth-Century Background*, New York NY, Harper, 1952, 36ff.; Thomas, *Missions*, 30f.; see also Brian Stanley's contribution in this volume.

merged in the WCC as the WCCE.[34] The establishment of further organizations, partly of even greater importance, is also directly or indirectly linked to the EA. Henry Dunant, who founded the IRC in 1864, was a cofounder and for many years the secretary of the SEA. The founding of the WSCF in 1895[35] is also linked to the alliance via the YMCA.

The YMCAS deserve special mention.[36] The first nondenominational YMCA was established in London as early as 1844. The movement quickly spread to other countries, leading to the founding of the international association in 1855, in the margins of the EA's third international conference. The so-called Paris Basis[37] was also agreed upon on this occasion. Deliberately couched in more general terms than the basic formula of the alliance, it served as the basis for the WCC's principle formula in 1948. The national associations mainly adopted a nondenominational orientation. In Germany alone, the Jünglingsbünde were subordinated to the regional churches, while the free churches were excluded from them. In all countries, however, the full-time secretaries strove for a close collaboration with the churches in their region and localities, thereby greatly contributing to their rapprochement. Since the initially clear Christian profile gradually seemed to diminish as the focus on recreational activities increased, the YPSCE was established as an alternative, first in Portland ME in 1881, then as a world association with almost four million members in 1894.[38]

The EA itself was also able to increase its membership substantially towards the end of the century although it abandoned its open, ecumenical profile in favor of a more fundamentalist one. Although the Gemeinschaftsbewegung and the Holiness Movement that spread in Europe and America from 1875 was decidedly international and also nondenominational, it only appealed to a certain milieu and distanced itself from many other currents within the churches.[39] The original purpose of Christian fellowship receded into the background.

The strength of this approach, the sole focus on individual persons, was ultimately also its weakness. At a time when a new appreciation of the church began to manifest itself in many Evangelical churches, the individualistic approach alone could not lead to radical changes in the isolationist orientation of Protestantism. For this reason, a third strand was needed to lay the ground for the modern ecumenical movement. Only when the seed of the ecumenical idea had been sown in the confessional churches themselves, would it be able to change the latter.

4   The Founding of Worldwide Confessional Alliances

In as early as the 16th century, the Reformed churches actively engaged in work for the promotion of international solidarity. Several synods were organized and attended by representatives from many countries, for example in 1618/1619 in Dordrecht. However, the efforts to establish permanent transnational structures proved unsuccessful. From the 17th century, the Lutherans occasionally also spoke of the *one* Lutheran Church, but contented themselves with the thought that this unity was a spiritual one. When the first embracive structures emerged, they displayed tendencies that were as clearly limitative as they were unifying. This situation was less pronounced at the first Nordic church

---

34   Voigt, *Ökumene*, 75–77.

35   See Sarah Scholl's contribution in this volume.

36   *A History of the Ecumenical Movement*, vol. 1, 327; Thomas, *Missions*, 36f.

37   "The Young Men's Christian Associations seek to unite those young men who, regarding Jesus Christ as their God and Saviour, according to the Holy Scriptures, desire to be his disciples in their faith and in their life, and to associate their efforts for the extension of his Kingdom amongst young men"; cited in <http://www.ymca.int/who-we-are/mission/paris-basis-1855/> (accessed July 4, 2019); see also Voigt, *Ökumene*, 69.

38   Jason Lanker, "Francis E. Clark: Founder of Christian Endeavor," *CEJ* 11, 2014, 383–391.

---

39   Lindemann, *Für Frömmigkeit*, 945.

conferences from 1857, which belonged to the context of a general striving for Scandinavian political unity but were also influenced by the EA.[40] However, it was all the more conspicuous at the first General Evangelical Lutheran Conference in Germany in 1868.[41] It was motivated by the fear that Prussia might also extend the union to the regions that had been annexed after the Austro-Prussian War of 1866, including Hanover and Schleswig-Holstein. Representatives of the Lutheran regional churches and of the Old Lutheran free churches thus banded together in a joint effort to preserve the Lutheran heritage; the Lutherans within the Prussian State Church, on the other hand, were excluded. This conference was also conceived as an association of individual persons. The initial goal of establishing a Lutheran national church was not achieved, even though the conference convened on twenty-one occasions until 1930. On the other hand, the conference did broaden the horizon of the participants, and the idea of international cooperation gained importance. In 1901, the conference convened for the first time outside Germany, namely in Sweden, and now called itself Lutherisches Einigungswerk. Its work led to the creation of the Lutheran World Convention in 1923, the predecessor of the Lutheran World Federation.

Leaving the Anglican Communion aside, for which the first Lambeth Conference of 1867 was the decisive date,[42] we may thus regard the Alliance of the Reformed churches holding the Presbyterian System, founded in London in 1875, as the first worldwide confessional alliance.[43]

At first, its membership consisted exclusively of English-language churches; only later were they joined by Hungary and other churches from mainland Europe. Constituted as a strictly consultative body, its main purpose was to coordinate the collaborative work of the Reformed churches. Devoid of direct ecumenical initiatives, it nevertheless contributed significantly to rapprochement among churches. Just as the contacts within the EA had been the driving force behind its foundation, it was now itself one of the main protagonists of cooperation in the field of missionary work, which led to the WMC of 1910. Moreover, it also promoted the reunification of separated churches that followed the tradition of Presbyterianism. Its most important achievements in this respect were the formation of the United Free Church in Scotland in 1900[44] (which was largely reintegrated into the national church in 1929) and the affiliation, in 1906, of the Cumberland Presbyterian Church with the Presbyterian Church in the United States of America.

In London again, the similarly structured ICC was established in 1891. That the first proclamation of 1874 called for an "ecumenical council" of the Congregationalists is worthy of note.[45] Since the member congregations were all very small and met only every ten years or so, the impulses generated by this worldwide alliance were generally weaker. After several major alliances had united with Presbyterian churches in the 20th century, the worldwide alliances merged in 1970 to form the WARC, which was integrated into the WCRC in 2010.

Meanwhile, the Methodists also created their own international association. In 1881, 400 delegates from 28 Methodist churches met in London for the first Ecumenical Methodist conference. Here, too, the idea of an "Ecumenical Protestant

---

40   Hogg, *Ecumenical Foundations*, 53–60.

41   Wilhelm Kahle, "Wege zur Einheit im Luthertum von der ersten allgemeinen evangelisch-lutherischen Konferenz 1868 bis zum Vorabend des ersten lutherischen Weltkonvents," in: Wilhelm Kahle & others, *Wege zur Einheit der Kirche im Luthertum*, Gütersloh, Gütersloher Verlagshaus Mohn, 1976, 157–208.

42   See Paul Avis's contribution in this volume.

43   Odair Pedroso Mateus, *The World Alliance of Reformed Churches and the Modern Ecumenical Movement: A Selected, Chronological, Annotated Bibliography (1863–2004)*, Geneva, WARC, 2005; for the background

history, see Alan P.F. Sell, *A Reformed, Evangelical, Catholic Theology: The Contributions of the World Alliance of Reformed Churches (1875–1982)*, Grand Rapids MI, Eerdmans, 1991, 4–7.

44   *A History of the Ecumenical Movement*, vol. 1, 303.

45   Sell, *A Reformed, Evangelical, Catholic Theology*, 7f.

conference" was invoked but not followed by any concrete steps. In 1951, the conferences that were held once every ten years became the World Methodist Council. The conference of 1881 provided the decisive impulse for a reunification of four Methodist denominations in Canada, which was successfully accomplished in 1884. This became a model for further unions (Australia in 1901, Ireland in 1905, Great Britain and Japan in 1907); with the founding of the Methodist Church in Britain in 1932 and of the Methodist Church in 1938, from which the United Methodist Church emerged in 1968 as a result of yet another fusion, the extreme fragmentation of Methodism had largely been overcome again.[46]

Owing to the strong autonomy of the individual Baptist congregations, the efforts to achieve unity among the Baptists were subject to additional, very particular premises. In this case, the rapprochement at the national level preceded that at the international level. Only after 1891, when the unification of General and Primitive Baptists was successfully accomplished in Great Britain (the cradle of Baptism), did it become possible to found the BWA in 1905, once again in London. As an expression of the bond with other Christians, the Apostles' Creed was recited at the inaugural session, which was for many Baptists a wholly new experience.[47] Especially for the small and often persecuted Baptist congregations in continental Europe, the European conferences held from 1908 were of great importance.

The founding of the worldwide confessional alliances can be seen as a delaying factor on the path towards the ecumenical movement. In all cases,

they either led a new appreciation of confessional identity or were the result of its revaluation. Interdenominational links between the individual groups (occasionally between Presbyterians and Congregationalists) were the exception. The idea, at least, of a pan-Protestant alliance was occasionally mentioned but was not implemented until 1923 with the establishment of the International League for the Defence and Furthercome of Protestantism (although the latter only existed for 22 years).[48] The rapprochement with Catholics or Orthodox Christians, or even with Anglicans, did not stand on the agenda of the world alliances for many years. Not surprisingly, they had played little or no role in the formation of the WCC's earlier organizations, and even when bilateral talks between the world alliances and the Roman Catholic Church were finally initiated in the 1960s, their relationship to multilateral ecumenism was either parallel either competitive.

The world alliances nevertheless played an important role in the formative history of the modern ecumenical movement. In many of the churches participating, these alliances were the very first to cultivate an awareness of being part of a much broader international context. They frequently extended nationally restricted horizons, promoted theological exchanges and made the first attempts to engage in projects for international cooperation. In short, the world alliances contributed significantly to the rise of the ecumenical movement by laying the groundwork for the very acceptance of ecumenism in the Protestant Churches. Last but not least, it was through their influence that the churches created the very first structures that could truly meet the desire for a more comprehensive and closer unity. Although the quest for Christian fellowship had certain limitations, it now became an increasingly determining factor in the policies of the Protestant Churches.

46   Morris L. Davis, "Methodism: Consolidation and Reunion (1865–1939)," in: William Gibson, Peter Forsaith & Martin Wellings, eds., *The Ashgate Research Companion to World Methodism*, Farnham, Ashgate, 2013, 51–64, here 56–58; *A History of the Ecumenical Movement*, vol. 1, 300–302.

47   *A History of the Ecumenical Movement*, vol. 1, 268; Richard V. Pierard, ed., *Baptists together in Christ (1905–2005): A Hundred-Year History of the Baptist World Alliance*, Falls Church VA, BWA, 2005.

48   Walter Fleischmann-Bisten, "Der Protestantische Weltverband," in: Jörg Haustein & Gerhard Philipp Wolf, eds., *Kirche an der Grenze: Festgabe für Gottfried Maron zum 65. Geburtstag*, Darmstadt, Bogen, 1993, 91–112.

5   The Creation of Church Federations in
     Germany and in the United States

Finally, the extent to which the notion of Christian unity now prevailed in the churches, but also the limitations to which it was still subjected, can be illustrated by citing the example of two endeavors that had long been planned but were only effected in the early 20th century.

In the wake of the German Revolution, attempts were made to bring the regional churches closer together, initially within the context of church congresses (*Kirchentag*). However, these endeavors failed due to the Lutherans' opposition to the union. Instead, a discussion forum for the governing bodies of the churches of the whole German Confederation was created in 1852, the German Evangelical Church Conference (also known as the Eisenach Conference), but the biannual conferences were unable to pass binding resolutions. Although agreements were reached with regard to guidelines for church construction (the Eisenach Regulative of 1861) and to standardized textual forms of the Luther Bible and of the Small Catechism, closer forms of cooperation were impeded for many years.[49]

In 1903, on the initiative of Emperor William II, the decision was finally made to reinforce the church conference through the creation of the German Evangelical Church Committee.[50] The 15-member committee now met several times a year in Berlin, was recognized as a statutory body and was empowered to conduct its own negotiations and to issue statements. One of its great successes was the first joint German-language hymnal, which was published in 1915 (though initially only for Germans living abroad). When the state's sovereignty over the territorial churches came to an end due to the downfall of the monarchies in Germany, the church committee was able to guide the regional churches during the transition to ecclesial autonomy and simultaneously promoted the establishment of a federation of churches that encompassed all Lutheran, united and Reformed regional churches (along with the Herrnhuter Brüdergemeine) from 1922. The remaining Protestant free churches, on the other hand, were still barred from participating.[51]

In the United States, a branch society of the EA had already been founded in 1847 but had since then dissolved. Only after the end of the Civil War did it prove possible to reestablish an organization.[52] From 1867, this cooperation gave rise to an interdenominational cooperation, which, however, remained loose and sporadic. The main problem still remained, namely the fact that the work was carried out by individuals. Towards the end of the century, it was joined by further interdenominational committees for missionary work, pastoral care and other activities. The joint commitment to the Social Gospel, in particular, created bonds among various Protestant denominations.[53] For a long time, however, it remained unclear whether the latter would choose the path of a federative or of an organic union. It was the Congregationalist Elias Sanford who, from 1905, finally convinced the majority of the "mainline churches" to adopt his concept. After a number of preparatory conferences, the FCCC was founded in 1908 as an organization in which the churches themselves were members and sent delegates to the annual meetings.[54] The latter consisted mainly of Methodist, Baptist, Reformed, and united

---

49   Voigt, *Ökumene*, 18–47; Joachim Rogge, "Kirchentage und Eisenacher Konferenzen," in: Rogge & Ruhbach, eds., *Die Geschichte*, vol. 2, Leipzig, Evangelische Verlagsanstalt, 1994, 42–55.

50   Hartmut Sander, "Der Deutsche Evangelische Kirchenausschuss," in: Rogge & Ruhbach, eds., *Die Geschichte*, vol. 2, 355–373.

51   Voigt, *Ökumene*, 110–116.

52   Lindemann, *Für Frömmigkeit*, 174–177, 506–513, 923–928; *A History of the Ecumenical Movement*, vol. 1, 255.

53   See Gary Dorrien's contribution in this volume.

54   *A History of the Ecumenical Movement*, vol. 1, 256–258; Robert A. Schneider, "Voice of Many Waters: Church Federation in the Twentieth Century," in: William R. Hutchison, ed., *Between the Times: The Travail of the Protestant Establishment in America (1900–1960)*, Cambridge, Cambridge University Press, 1989, 95–121.

churches; even the Anglicans and Lutherans remained aloof from it for many years. A broader ecumenical community was not represented until the founding of the succeeding organization, the NCC, in 1950. However, the FCCC had already revealed that in the early 20th century most Evangelical churches had already recognized that the challenges of modern times required closer bonds of fellowship than those which Protestantism had hitherto been able to achieve.

Translated from German to English by Robert Meyer.

Bibliography

A History of the Ecumenical Movement, vol. 1, Ruth Rouse & Stephen C. Neill, eds., *1517–1948*, London, SPCK, 1954.

Beyer, Michael, Ferdinand R. Gahbauer, Wolf Friedrich Schäufele & others, "Unionen, Kirchliche," *TRE* 34, 311–331.

FitzGerald, Thomas E., *The Ecumenical Movement: An Introductory History*, Westport CT, Praeger, 2004.

Friedrich, Martin, *Von Marburg bis Leuenberg: Der lutherisch-reformierte Gegensatz und seine Überwindung*, Waltrop, Spenner, 1999.

Friedrich, Martin, Wilhelm Hüffmeier & Jürgen Kampmann, *Gemeinsam evangelisch: 200 Jahre lutherisch-reformierte Unionen in Deutschland*, Hanover, UEK, 2016.

Geschichte des Pietismus, vol. 3, Ulrich Gäbler, ed., *Der Pietismus im neunzehnten und zwanzigsten Jahrhundert*, Göttingen, Vandenhoeck & Ruprecht, 2000.

Goeters, J.F. Gerhard, Joachim Rogge & Gerhard Ruhbach, eds., *Die Geschichte der Evangelischen Kirche der Union*, 3 vols., Leipzig, Evangelische Verlagsanstalt, 1992–1999.

Kampmann, Jürgen & Christian Peters, eds., *200 Jahre lutherisch-reformierte Unionen in Deustchland*, Bielefeld, Luther-Verlag, 2018.

Lindemann, Gerhard, *Für Frömmigkeit in Freiheit: Die Geschichte der Evangelischen Allianz im Zeitalter des Liberalismus (1846–1879)*, Münster, LIT, 2011.

Marquardt, Manfred, "Methodism in the Nineteenth and Twentieth Centuries," in: James E. Kirby & William J. Abraham, eds., *The Oxford Handbook of Methodist Studies*, Oxford, Oxford University Press, 2009, 85–103.

Randall, Ian M. & David Hilborn, *One Body in Christ: The History and Significance of the Evangelical Alliance*, Carlisle, Paternoster, 2001.

Sell, Alan P.F., *A Reformed, Evangelical, Catholic Theology: The Contributions of the World Alliance of Reformed Churches (1875–1982)*, Grand Rapids MI, Eerdmans, 1991.

Voigt, Karl Heinz, *Die Evangelische Allianz als ökumenische Bewegung: Freikirchliche Erfahrungen im 19. Jahrhundert*, Stuttgart, Christliches Verlashaus, 1990.

Voigt, Karl Heinz, *Ökumene in Deutschland: Internationale Einflüsse und Netzwerkbildung: Anfänge 1848–1945*, Göttingen, Vandenhoeck & Ruprecht, 2014.

CHAPTER 10

The 1893 World's Parliament of Religions: Striving for Religious Unity

Arie L. Molendijk

1 Introduction

The first World's Parliament of Religions was held in Chicago in 1893 during the World's Columbian Exposition, which celebrated 400 years of America.[1] Conceived by the lawyer Charles Carroll Bonney, it convened in the main hall of the Chicago Art Institute and attracted 150,000 people, according to a generous count.

The 1893 parliament has been analyzed by present-day scholars from various angles, not only as a landmark in American religious history but also as a key element in a series of international interfaith meetings. The parliament is seen as a contribution to the emerging science of religion, or – diametrically opposed to this view – as a blending of faith and scholarship. The remarkable participation of women and their new public role as speakers at the parliament are also often highlighted. Yet it is wise to qualify such statements about what was achieved. The parliament was indeed a step forward in the emancipation of Christian women, but their role was defined in stereotyped ways. Furthermore, it is true that contributions were made to scholarship, but claims of religious superiority were never far away. The organizers themselves were to some extent aware of the precarious relationship between Christianity and the other religions invited. They tried to avoid controversies by stipulating strict rules of discussion that forbade, for instance, polemics against other positions.[2] The term "parliament" itself may raise false expectations, as in Chicago the participants assembled "for mutual conference, fellowship, and information, and not for controversy, for worship, for the counting of votes, or for the passing of resolutions."[3]

---

[1] This text is based on Arie L. Molendijk, "'To Unite Religion against All Irreligion': The 1893 World Parliament of Religion," *JHMTH* 18, 2011, 1–23, and Arie L. Molendijk, *The Emergence of the Science of Religion in the Netherlands*, Leiden, Brill, 2005, 223–255. Section 9 and some considerations on liberal theology in the conclusion have been added by the editors and approved by the author.

[2] Charles Carroll Bonney, "The World's Parliament of Religions," *The Monist* 5, 1895, 321–343, here 331.

[3] Bonney, "The World's Parliament of Religions," 331. Of special importance to the organizers was the documentation of the parliament. Actually, several records were published within a year after the parliament closed. The most authoritative and complete edition is that of John Henry Barrows, "chairman of the general committee on religious congresses of the World's Congress Auxiliary" (as is indicated at the title page of the collection), which comprised more than 1,500 pages. Its complete title runs as follows: John Henry Barrows, ed., *The World's Parliament of Religions: An Illustrated and Popular Story of the World's First Parliament of Religions, Held in Chicago in Connection with the Columbian Exposition of 1893*, Chicago IL, The Parliament Publishing Company, 1893. The second important collection was edited by "a corps of able writers" with Professor Walter R. Houghton as editor in chief and Frank Tennyson Neely as publisher. It counts some 1,000 pages and is entitled: Walter R. Houghton, ed., *Neely's History of the Parliament of Religions and Religious Congresses at the World's Columbian Exposition: Compiled from Original Manuscripts and Stenographic Reports*, Chicago IL, F.T. Neely, 1893. These two reports are quoted as, respectively, Barrows and Neely, followed by page number. Two other – less known and even less reliable – editions are those by John Wesley Hanson, *The World's Congress of Religions: The Addresses and Papers Delivered before the Parliament*, Chicago IL, W.B. Conkey, 1894, and Jenkin Lloyd Jones, *A Chorus of Faiths as Heard in the Parliament of Religions*, Chicago IL, Unity Publishing, 1893, a Unitarian who was the executive secretary of the general committee on religious congresses and the parliament in particular.

2 World Exhibitions

The most impressive and indeed spectacular context of the parliament was the 1893 Columbian Exposition. Yet world exhibitions or world trade fairs were major business in the second half of the 19th and the beginning of the 20th century. The fairs epitomized progress and made it very clear that not all nations had reached the same level of industry and civilization.[4] The educational and civilizing intentions of the organizers were evident. The explicit international character of the World's Columbian Exposition, in which various nations and peoples participated with their own pavilions, did not preclude an encouragement of nationalistic feelings. Relics of American history, such as a lock of Thomas Jefferson's red hair, were shown at the Chicago exhibition, and the text of the Pledge of Allegiance to the flag of the United States was framed for this occasion. At the opening ceremonies, school girls formed a living flag, whereas millions of children around the country pledged "allegiance to my flag, and the republic for which it stands, one nation indivisible, with liberty and justice for all."[5] The fairs provided the visitors with nationalistic images, reinforced by ritualistic practices.[6]

If one looks at the photographs of the great fairs, it is easy to imagine how the magnificent architecture of the buildings and the design of the huge exhibition spaces and amusement parks must have made a deep impression on the visitors.[7] At the Midway Plaisance (where the more "popular" attractions were assembled) of the Chicago exhibition, for instance, there were Javanese, Egyptian, Indian and Eskimo villages, German and Hungarian bands, camel drivers and donkey boys, dancing girls from countries ranging from Samoa to Brazil, and the Ferris Wheel, from which it was possible for visitors to enjoy a bird's-eye view of the attractions and the crowds below. The simulated native villages doubtless furthered prevailing racial stereotypes, which were largely underpinned by ethnological scholarship.[8] The contrast between the Midway Plaisance (a *rue des nations*) and the Court of Honor with Doric temples and other classically inspired forms of architecture could not have been greater. It lent an evolutionary and even utopian flavor to the whole event. Religious rhetoric was frequently used on these occasions. The construction of the 1893 Chicago exhibition was seen as the building of a New Jerusalem: "The city so holy and clean, / No sorrow can breathe in the air; / No gloom of affliction or sin, / No shadow of evil is there."[9]

3 The 1893 World's Parliament

It would be wrong to view these exhibitions solely in terms of material and economic progress and expansion. They also had a strong intellectual, even spiritual dimension. During the preparations for the Chicago exhibition, Charles Carroll Bonney, a Chicago lawyer and counselor of the Supreme Court, launched the idea to organize intellectual conferences for this occasion as well.[10] To

---

4 See Robert W. Rydell, *All the World's a Fair: Visions of Empire at American International Expositions (1876–1916)*, Chicago IL, University of Chicago Press, 1984, 45.

5 Quoted in Rydell, *All the World's a Fair*, 46. The clause "under God" was added in 1954 to distinguish the United States from the atheistic Soviet Union; see Joan Didion, "Fixed Opinions, or the Hinge of History," NYRB 50/1, 2003, 56.

6 Astrid Böger, *Envisioning the Nation: The Early American World's Fairs and the Formation of Culture*, Frankfurt a.M., Campus, 2010, 109–172.

7 Norman Bolotin & Christine Laing, *The World's Columbian Exposition: A 100-Year Retrospective*, Washington DC, Preservation Press, 1992.

8 See Burton Benedict, "Rituals of Representation: Ethnic Stereotypes and Colonized Peoples at World's Fairs," in: Robert W. Rydell & Nancy E. Gwinn, eds., *Fair Representations: World's Fairs and the Modern World*, Amsterdam, VU University Press, 1994, 28–62; Nicolas Bancel & others, eds., *Zoos humains: De la Vénus hottentote aux reality shows*, Paris, La Découverte, 2002.

9 Rydell, *All the World's a Fair*, 48. After a hymn of the Methodist Charles Wesley "Away with our Sorrows and Care."

10 Neely 15–16.

this end, a new committee was established, called the World's Congress Auxiliary, of which Bonney became the chairman. This committee appointed more than 200 working committees to organize the various special conferences. In the field of religion, the World's Parliament of Religions was by far the biggest event, but there were also other meetings. It was the explicit aim of the organizers "to have a presentation of the faith and creeds of every denomination in Christendom as well as ex-positions of the beliefs of peoples and sects outside its pale."[11] These were the so-called denomination-al congresses, 41 of which convened from Aug 27 till Oct 25, 1893. Most of them were meetings by Christian organizations or related groups, such as the Lutheran General Council, the Universalistic Church, the Disciples of Christ, the Friends' Or-thodox Church, the African Episcopal Church, the International Board of Young Women's Christian Associations, the Sunday-Rest Congress, and the EA. Furthermore, meetings and presentations of Jewish groups, Theosophists and Buddhists were held.[12] Many denominational congresses bore a clear Catholic mark. Examples are the Congress of Colored Catholics, the German Catholic Young Men's Guilds, the Catholic Benevolent Legion, the Catholic Young Men's National Union, the Catholic Press, the Reunion of the Students of the American College in Leuven (Belgium), the Catholic Young Men's Societies, and – above all – the Columbian Catholic Congress.[13] Important officials – includ-ing the archbishops of New York, Philadelphia, Chicago, and New Orleans – were present at "most of the sessions" of the Columbian Catholic Con-gress, and Pope Leo XIII signaled his approval by a letter, in which he "imparted [his] apostolic benediction."[14] Msgr. Satolli, the pope's delegate to the United States, made "a thrilling speech in his native tongue," which was translated by Arch-bishop John Ireland of Saint Paul Satolli stated

that it is the duty of Catholics and the Catholic Congress "to bring into the world the fullness of supernatural truth and supernatural life."[15] The Columbian Catholic Congress attracted huge crowds and expressed its loyalty and "unaltered attachment to our Holy Father, Pope Leo XIII." It was a meeting within the strict confines of the Catholic tradition, that established once again that "the Catholic Church, properly understood, is the light of the world, and the refuge of suffering humanity."[16]

The balance between Christian and non-Christian churches and groups was strikingly un-even, and neither was the whole of Christianity represented. Although there was a large repre-sentation of (American) Catholic organizations, the American Presbyterian General Assembly and the archbishop of Canterbury, of the Church of England, explicitly declined to go to Chicago. The criticism of the archbishop of Canterbury was aimed in particular at the (alleged) presumption that the Christian religion is principally on the same footing as other religions.[17] The chairman of the parliament, John Henry Barrows, pastor of the First Presbyterian Church of Chicago and author of the most authoritative and complete edition of the parliament's records, emphasized the point that invitations went primarily to individuals, not to organizations, and that the meeting stood out-side ecclesiastical control.[18]

Notwithstanding these critical voices, the World's Parliament of Religions was a huge suc-cess in the eyes of its organizers and attendants. It convened in the main hall (the Hall of Colum-bus) of the Chicago Art Institute near Lake Michi-gan, which could accommodate 4,000 people. This enormous venue was at times still not big enough so that people were invited to go to the adjacent hall – the Hall of Washington (people

11   Neely 865.
12   See Neely 865–970.
13   Neely 865.
14   Neely 891.

15   Neely 894.
16   Neely 898.
17   See Barrows 20–21.
18   Barrows 60, 1560; for a short curriculum vitae of Bar-rows, see Neely 972.

were listening to the same addresses in turns).[19] Barrows claimed that almost 150,000 people attended the meetings and boasted that the "splendors and wonders of the great Fair itself" seemed powerless to divert the attention of the visitors to the parliament.[20]

4 Objectives

What was the parliament about? It is not so easy to answer this simple question. The event was meticulously prepared by an American committee representing many Christian and Jewish groups. In June 1891 they sent out some 3,000 invitations throughout the world "to the religious leaders of mankind in many lands."[21] This "preliminary address" starts with the statement that God exists, and that he who fears God and works righteously is accepted by him. The key aim is presented in the following way:

> [W]e affectionately invite the representatives of all faiths to aid us in presenting to the world, at the Exposition of 1893, the religious harmonies and unities in humanity, and

also in showing forth the moral and spiritual agencies which are at the root of human progress.[22]

The address also shows differences of opinion within the organizing committee. Apart from the alleged beneficial moral effects of religion, one of the aims is also to show its dominance in institutions of higher learning and "to make prominent the value of the weekly rest-day on religious and other grounds."[23] This last issue at least was controversial, and the parliament would, as a matter of fact, convene on Sundays.

The goals of the committee are specified in somewhat more detail, to be precise, in ten points.[24] The first three items were quintessential for the organizers: the goals were (1) to bring together in conference "the leading representatives of the great Historic Religions of the world," (2) to show how many "important truths" these religions have in common, and (3) "to promote and deepen the spirit of human brotherhood among religious men of different faiths" (while neither promoting indifferentism nor formal unity). The basic idea was that the great historical religions have important things in common, and that an exchange of ideas would bring this further to light and stimulate mutual understanding. In a cautious formulation, the focus was exclusively on what the various religions and branches of Christianity considered to be their most important truths. It is worthwhile quoting this in full: (4) "To set forth, by those most competent to speak, what are deemed the important distinct truths held and taught by each Religion, and by the various chief branches of Christendom." The terminology is unashamedly elitist: competence, leadership and also scholarship are the prerequisites of the whole venture. The next goal specifies the minimum of what is expected: (5) "To indicate the impregnable foundation of Theism, and the reasons for man's faith

---

19 Barrows 110; see Eric Jozef Ziolkowski, "Introduction," in: Eric Jozef Ziolkowski, ed., *A Museum of Faiths: Histories and Legacies of the 1893 World's Parliament of Religions*, Atlanta GA, Scholars Press, 1993, 1–68, here 8. On Sept 27, the last day of the meeting, one of the main Chicago newspapers published an article, "Crowds Besiege Managers of Parliament for Tickets," *The Chicago*, Sept 27, 1893, 9, which informed its readers of the enormous interest in the closing session: "At 9 o'clock it had been announced that tickets for the closing session of the parliament to be held this evening would be given out. At that hour 1,500 people were packed in Hall 2, and every one of the halls and corridors was equally crowded. The demand for seats was apparently greater than for boxes at a grand opera opening"; cited in: Dorothea Lüddeckens, *Das Weltparlament der Religionen von 1893: Strukturen interreligiöser Begegnung im 19. Jahrhundert*, Berlin, De Gruyter, 2002, 182; see Barrows 158 about the black market for tickets.

20 Barrows 110, 111f, 158.

21 Barrows 11.

22 Barrows 10.

23 Barrows 10.

24 Barrows 18.

in Immortality, and thus to unite and strengthen the forces which are adverse to a materialistic philosophy of the universe."

One of the main oppositions structuring the whole event was that between the religious ("spiritual" was also a favorite term) and the material.[25] It is also evident that a certain level of religious development was presupposed, and that only representatives of developed and theistic forms of religion would be invited. To secure sound knowledge "leading scholars" were invited, representing (6) "the Brahman, Buddhist, Confucian, Parsee, Mohammedan, Jewish and other Faiths" as well as "representatives of the various Churches of Christendom."[26] In at least three objectives, the beneficial effects of religions on each other and on culture and society are mentioned, with particular emphasis on their contributions to issues such as temperance, labor, poverty, and education. The final objective was to (10) "bring the nations of the world into a more friendly fellowship, in the hope of securing permanent international peace." These were high hopes indeed. World peace was not achieved, but notwithstanding some moments of strife and dissent, the attendants thought that the parliament had succeeded in establishing a sphere of harmony and mutual understanding.

5   Opening Ceremony: Historic Faiths

The parliament was described (and this neatly summarizes the event) as the "invitation of Christianity to all historic faiths."[27] The opening of the assembly was proclaimed by ten strokes of the new Liberty Bell, upon which, according to Neely's report, were engraved the words: "A new commandment I give unto you that ye love one another."[28] According to the reports, the ten strokes represented the ten "chief religions of the world."[29] It is not a hundred percent clear which religions were meant. To some degree ten is a symbolic number. In another report it is said that on Sept 11 at 10 AM, "the representatives of a dozen world-faiths" marched down the aisle of the Hall of Columbus, "beneath the waving flags of many nations, and amid the enthusiastic cheering of the vast audience."[30] The national element was clearly in the mind of the organizers, which might also explain why they chose to call the assembly a parliament.[31] In his opening address, Charles Bonney first mentioned the states involved, and then the religions:

> The programme of this general Parliament of Religions directly represents England, Scotland, Sweden, Switzerland, France, Germany, Russia, Turkey, Greece, Egypt, Syria, India, Japan, China, Ceylon, New Zealand, Brazil, Canada, and the American States, and indirectly includes many other countries. This remarkable programme presents, among other great themes to be considered in this Congress, Theism, Judaism, Mohammedanism, Hinduism, Buddhism, Taoism, Confucianism, Shintoism, Zoroastrianism, Catholicism, the Greek Church, Protestantism in many forms, and also refers to the nature and influence of other religious systems.[32]

---

25   See the section on spiritualization below.

26   See James Edward Ketelaar, *Of Heretics and Martyrs in Meiji Japan: Buddhism and its Persecution*, Princeton NJ, Princeton University Press, 1993, esp. ch. 4; Judith Snodgrass, *Presenting Japanese Buddhism to the West: Orientalism, Occidentalism, and the Columbian Exposition*, Chapel Hill NC, University of North Carolina Press, 2003; Anna Sun, *Confucianism as a World Religion: Contested Histories and Contemporary Realities*, Princeton NJ, Princeton University Press, 2013.

27   Neely 24.

---

28   Neely 33 refers only to this text, John 13:34 in the King James Version, whereas two other texts were engraved on the Liberty Bell as well (Lev 25:10 and Luke 2:14).

29   Neely 33; see Barrows 58.

30   Barrows 62.

31   I have found no references explaining why this term was chosen.

32   Barrows 70, Neely 39, which present identical formulations in this case.

The invitation sent out by the organizing committee mentioned various Christian churches and the "Brahman, Buddhist, Confucian, Parsee, Mohammedan, Jewish and other Faiths."[33] Depending on how one counts, and on whether one lists various Christian denominations as separate religions or not, the parliament counted some ten major, allegedly theistic, religions.[34]

In this way, many religions and denominations were excluded. Mormons, for example, were not invited,[35] and Barrows explicitly discussed in his report the negative reactions from the leadership of his own synod of the Episcopal Church and of the sultan of Turkey. According to Max Müller, the refusal of the sultan (in his capacity as caliph) to send delegates helped explain the gross under-representation of Muslims at the parliament.[36] However, what was more surprising in Müller's view was how many representatives, especially from the religions from the Far East, made the trip to Chicago.

A close connection that could have hardly escaped the attention of the visitors to the parliament was that between national, in particular religious, affiliation, on the one hand, and particular modes of dress on the other. "There were strange robes, turbans and tunics, crosses and crescents, flowing hair and tonsured heads." In the center of the platform in the main hall was Cardinal James Gibbons, "magnificent in his robes of red," "Buddhist monks were attired in garments of white and yellow; an orange turban and robe made the Brahman conspicuous," and so on.[37] "Picturesque" was a word that was frequently used to characterize the event. Barrows' report ("an illustrated story") tries to convey an impression of this by including not only black-and-white pictures of organizers and representatives but also of places of worship. "These volumes are enriched with views of Eastern Temples, painted and tiled Pagodas, superb and stately Mosques, humble meeting-houses and all the beautiful forms of Christian architecture in Europe and America."[38] Interestingly enough, the book also included illustrations of "idolatrous" forms of religion, forms that were explicitly excluded by the objectives of the parliament.[39]

6   "Religion"

In his opening address, Charles Bonney thought it useful to give a kind of working definition of "religion" as "the love and worship of God and the love and service of man."[40] This definition – often summarized in the more catchy form of "the fatherhood of God and the brotherhood of men" – resonated throughout the congress. The theistic idea of God and the ideal of religious unity that were motivating the event are even more clearly expressed in the latter formulation. Bonney also

---

33   Quoted in Bonney, "The World's Parliament of Religions," 330.

34   Richard Hughes Seager included Jainism in his list of ten religions: Richard Hughes Seager, *The World's Parliament of Religions: The East/West Encounter, Chicago, 1893*, Bloomington IN, Indiana University Press, 1995.

35   However, according to Barrows 153 there were contributions on Mormon religion.

36   Friedrich Max Müller, "The Real Significance of the Parliament of Religions," *The Arena* 61, 1894, 1–14, reprinted in: Ziolkowski, ed., *A Museum of Faiths*, 149–162, here 156. Fifty volumes of the "Sacred Books" appeared between 1879 and 1910, most of them under Müller's supervision: Friedrich Max Müller, ed., *The Sacred Books of the East: Translated by Various Oriental Scholars*, Oxford, Clarendon Press, 50 vols., 1879–1910, <http://www.sacred-texts.com/sbe/index.htm> (accessed July 4, 2019); see Arie L. Molendijk, *Friedrich Max Müller and the Sacred Books of the East*, Oxford, Oxford University Press, 2016; Peter van der Veer, *Imperial Encounters: Religion and Modernity in India and Britain*, Princeton NJ, Princeton University Press, 2001, ch. 5.

37   Neely 34.

38   Barrows vii.

39   Barrows 553, 559, 615; see Barrows 1358–1362 for three contributions on nature religion, lower religions and superstitions, which were all included in the scientific section of the report.

40   Barrows 68; reprinted in Richard Hughes Seager, *The Dawn of Religious Pluralism: Voices from the World's Parliament of Religions (1893)*, La Salle IL, Open Court, 1993, 17–22, here 17.

referred to an earlier programmatic statement by the organizers which proclaimed that the goal of the parliament was "to unite all Religion against all irreligion; to make the golden rule the basis of this union; and to present to the world the substantial unity of many religions in the good deeds of the religious life."[41] Although the emphasis in this statement is on religious unity and common understanding between the various faiths, at the same time Bonney made it very clear that this does not imply "the least surrender or compromise of anything which we respectively believe to be truth or duty."[42] The unique and superior character of Christian doctrines and ethics was not endangered by this meeting, the organizers claimed – probably trying to soothe the minds of participants who shared the criticism of the archbishop of Canterbury that the parliament assumed the parity of religious positions.[43] Christian superiority was enacted ritually by reciting the Lord's Prayer, "known in the parliament as the 'universal prayer'" at the opening of the daily meetings.[44]

In the moving last words of his report Barrows, reflecting on the death of his 13-year-old son, who laid "unburied in [his] house," made this claim again and asked his readership to "join once more in the prayer of Him who is the unifier of humanity."[45] By claiming here that the Christian god can ultimately bring humanity together and thus be the god of all mankind, the World's Parliament of Religions is presented as an almost eschatological event in history. Neely's report describes the joint saying of the Lord's Prayer at the opening ceremony as "the supreme moment of the 19th century." "This harmonious use of the Lord's Prayer by Jews, Mohammedans, Buddhists, Brahmans, and all the divisions of Christians seemed a rainbow of promise pointing to the time when the will of God will 'be done on earth as it is

done in heaven.'"[46] The parliament was compared to what happened in Jerusalem on the day of Pentecost, although this was – as Barrows added – a much more provincial assembly in comparison to Chicago. It is said that a "holy intoxication" overcame the speakers and the audience. One of the participants was even reminded of the emotions he had felt in the great revival movements of Charles Finney and Dwight L. Moody.[47]

The parliament is described as an event which brought people together – physically, intellectually, and emotionally. The framework used by the Christian reporters is, notwithstanding the respect for the representatives of other religions, that of the ultimate triumph of their own God, who is universal, that is to say, inclusive. This discursive strategy (achieving unity by inclusion) was, of course, not acceptable to (most) outsiders, who were "reduced" to (potential) insiders and thereby denied their own particular religious identity. It is easy to criticize the fact that the non-Christian guests were not perceived in their own right, but as potentially *aufgehoben* into the inclusive (and, therefore, higher) Christian religion. Many authors writing about the World's Parliament of Religions do so, and in principle they are right.[48] Yet how far does this help us to really understand the organizers, who are consequently depicted as some kind of intellectual and moral villains who invited "natives" or "others" in order to underscore their own superiority? It is true that they were not interested in foreign religions in their own right, in the same sense as religious scholars nowadays are supposed to be, but does that imply that there was

---

41   Barrows 72.
42   Barrows 68.
43   Barrows 22.
44   Neely 73.
45   Barrows 1582.

46   Neely 35–36.
47   Barrows 1566.
48   Ketelaar, *Of Heretics*, 153; Lüddeckens, *Das Weltparlament der Religionen*, 175–176; Snodgrass, *Presenting Japanese Buddhism to the West*, 1, 47, *passim*, stresses the (American and Christian) aggressiveness of the event and the power relations involved; see Norman J. Girardot, *The Victorian Translation of China: James Legge's Oriental Pilgrimage*, Berkeley CA, University of California Press, 2002, 486–490.

no interest at all? Why should they have taken the trouble to hold this event at all?

It is important to pay attention to the – sometimes very outspoken – exclusions made by John Barrows and his colleagues. One of the explicit aims was to unite all religion against all irreligion. The positive connotation of this statement is clearer than the negative one. As has been noted above, the organizers wanted to bring together representatives of the great historic religions. What did they have in mind when they spoke of "all irreligion"? This point is not taken up explicitly in the programmatic text. However, in a general sense it is evident that the aim was to further religious faith – against a spirit of indifference, agnosticism or even atheism.[49] Equally important was the theistic aspect, which was presumed to be shared by all these historic religions and which excluded polytheism(s).[50]

In this respect, a revealing contribution was made by "the author, scientist, scholar, and traveler" Richard Henry Savage, whom Neely called "a man of worldwide experience," whose "comprehensive, poetic, and appropriate words" were given a prominent place at the very beginning of his report.[51] Savage presented the parliament first and foremost as a peaceful event, where the brotherly spirit of religious men and women was admired by skeptics, atheists, and "those of little faith." His whole text is pervaded by oppositions at different levels:

> Not in idle curiosity, led on by no mere desire of amusement, did the earnest-browed religious thinkers of the world gather here to heap up a pyramid of garnered golden grains of truth, in honor of the great Giver of All Good.
>
> In their temporary camps the children of fetishism, wide-eyed and speechless, have

gazed here upon this multitude of believers bearing palms, trooping hither from the uttermost parts of the earth and the islands of the great deep![52]

Earnestness versus idleness, thinking versus gazing, believers versus children of fetishism, earnest-browed versus wide-eyed, amusement versus acquiring the true gold of truth. It is clear which side of these juxtapositions were to be preferred by the author (and his readers). The visitors are addressed by Savage as "pilgrims" on their way to a more enlightened form of religion, which should outdo the "Old World of Intolerance, Narrowness, Bigotry and Persecution."[53] In the view of the conveners, the parliament was indeed a serious and noble cause, which had no place for "cranks" and sectarian propaganda.[54] The congress was intended to contribute to the mutual understanding of the great theistic religions (excluding fetishism, magic, and superstition), and in this process of mutual engagement it was thought to stimulate world peace.

7   Contested Claims

Not all participants were happy to be included in the grand narrative of the parliament. There were moments of serious criticism, which was sometimes met by approval, but also by booing. The most serious incident seems to have taken place when Mohammed Webb, an American convert to Islam, defended the practice of polygamy and even claimed that "a pure-minded man can be a polygamist and be a perfect and true Christian."[55] The "hisses and cries of 'Shame!' were so emphatic that the speaker seemed deterred from pursuing

---

49   Barrows 1577.
50   Barrows 1578.
51   Neely 25–31. This text is not included in Barrows' report.
52   Neely 27.
53   Neely 31.
54   Barrows 1561.
55   Mohammed Webb, "The Spirit of Islam," in: Neely 459–464, here 460; this remark is omitted from Barrows' report (989–996).

the line of discourse on which he had entered."[56] On another occasion, after Kinza Riuge M. Hirai, a Buddhist from Japan, had severely denounced the way Christians had treated the Japanese, he was greeted by loud applause.[57]

Speakers took the opportunity to celebrate the contribution of their own nation and faith. This is a major theme in itself, which has been addressed by some authors, especially by Richard Hughes Seager and Dorothea Lüddeckens, the former presenting the parliament as an encounter between East and West, and the latter paying a good deal of attention to the various contexts of the participants.[58] Nevertheless, it remains difficult to discern clear patterns of engagement, self-definition and "othering" in the gamut of speakers and texts. The aim here is simply to offer a couple of examples of stories which go against the grain of the parliament. The first "case study" is the contribution of Alexander Kohut, a rabbi in New York and a proponent of reformed Judaism. He eloquently showed "what the Hebrew scriptures have wrought for mankind" and defended the thesis that "[i]n religion the Hebrew genius was supreme."[59]

> Israel … gave the world a pure religion – a creed undominated by cumbrous tyranny, unembarrassed by dogmatic technicalities, unstrained by heavy self-sacrifice and extravagant ceremonialism – a religion sublime and unique in history, free from gaping superstitions, appalling idolatries, and vicious immoralities – a pure, taintless, lofty, elevating, inspiring, and love-permeating faith, originating in a monotheistic conception – a religion at whose sparkling fountain wells of ethical truths, the world's famed pioneers in

art, science, literature, politics, philosophy, and architecture slackened their thirst.[60]

The claims are almost as high as those of the organizing committee, but they are "transferred" to the Jewish religion.

The substantial representation from the Far East was all the more impressive as some of them were not able to express themselves in fluent English, the only language permitted at the conference. Many texts of delegates from the East had to be translated and were read by Barrows, the chairman of the parliament. The previously mentioned Kinza Riuge M. Hirai,[61] however, was clearly capable of presenting his contribution "The Real Position of Japan toward Christianity" himself. It was one of the more critical papers and caused a small sensation. The aim of the parliament, according to Hirai, was "to finally establish religious affinity all over the world," and he saw it as his task to point to a "vigorous obstacle" to this noble aim.[62] The most important hindrance was, he claimed, the unjust treaties between the West and Japan, and the blunt discrimination against Japanese people. He detailed a number of discriminatory acts, such as signs saying "No Japanese Allowed," which make us "unintelligent heathens" hesitant "to swallow the sweet and warm liquid of the heaven of Christianity."[63] If such was the ethics of Christians, "we are perfectly satisfied to be heathen."

He then went on – in a rhetorically brilliant move – to point out that he did not want to be a hypocrite (hinting at the point he was finally going to make, that is to say, that Christians sometimes

---

56   Barrows 127.
57   Barrows 115; see Ketelaar, *Of Heretics*, 169f.
58   Seager, *The World's Parliament of Religions*, and Lüddeckens, *Das Weltparlament der Religionen*.
59   Barrows 725.

60   Alexander Kohut, "What the Hebrew Scriptures Have Wrought for Mankind," in: Barrows 725. The speech is also printed in Neely 308–312.
61   For reasons of convenience I adopt the transcription used in Barrows.
62   Kinza Riuge M. Hirai, "The Real Position of Japan toward Christianity," in: Barrows 444–450, here 444. The same text is included in Neely 157–161; see Ketelaar, *Of Heretics*, 169f.
63   Barrows 449.

are), and that he would not hide from his audience the fact that he was the first in his country to attack Christianity. Again, trying to win over the sympathy of his listeners, Hirai maintained that his criticism was aimed at a false Christianity, which preaches one thing and does another. Finally he quoted extensively from the United States Declaration of Independence, before concluding:

> If any religion urges the injustice of humanity, I will oppose it … with my blood and soul. I will be the bitterest dissenter from Christianity or I will be the warmest admirer of its gospels. To [those] who are assembled here, I pronounce that your aim is the realization of religious union, not nominally, but practically. We, the forty million souls of Japan, standing firmly and persistently upon the basis of international justice, await still further manifestations as to the morality of Christianity.

The *Chicago Daily Times* called the speech "a voice out of darkness, a cry of oppression from a strange land. It came … as a thunderblast, and when [he] had finished, the peoples rose again to their feet and gave him three mighty cheers." This way – as one author summarized Hirai's performance – he "'out-Christianized' the Christians and 'out-Americanized' the Americans."[64]

Swami Vivekananda, who propagated a reformed Hindu spirituality and founded the Ramakrishna Mission, was deemed to be "the most popular and influential man in the parliament."[65] Newspapers pointed to his strong physiognomy, his "oriental" dress, his excellent command of English and, last but not least, his attraction to women:

> Ladies, ladies everywhere, filled the great auditorium. They gave no outward sign of impatience through the delivery of three classic essays which separated them from Vivekananda's eloquence, but it was evident from the applause which greeted the Oriental about 5 o'clock, as in his orange garb he arose to speak, that had he spoken first instead of last some of the great audience might not have been present at the close of the session.[66]

Vivekananda was an ardent disciple of Ramakrishna. He sanitized and spiritualized his teacher's ideas from aspects such as an explicit eroticism, which would have appalled his Chicago audience. As Peter van der Veer notes, Vivekananda's Hindu spirituality is devoid of any specific devotional content that would involve, for instance, temple worship and thus a theological and ritual position.[67]

In this way, Vivekananda was able to reach out to his predominantly Christian audience, addressing them as "brothers and sisters of America," whereupon "there arose a peal of applause that lasted several minutes."[68] He presented the Hindu religion and Hindu people as the cradle of tolerance and inclusion. He began by thanking the audience "in the name of the most ancient order of monks in the world," then dwelled on the tolerance and hospitality of his own people in sentences that all started with "I am proud":

> I am proud to tell you that I belong to a religion into whose sacred language, the Sanskrit, the

64   James Edward Ketelaar, "The Reconvening of Babel: Eastern Buddhism and the 1893 World's Parliament of Religions," in: Ziolkowski, ed., *A Museum of Faiths*, 251–304, here 299–300. For Hirai's vision – again artfully constructed – of the unity of religion see his second long speech "Synthetic Religion" (Neely 798–803, Barrows 1286–1288).

65   Seager, *The Dawn of Religious Pluralism*, 111; van der Veer, *Imperial Encounters*, esp. 46–48, 72–74.

66   *The Daily Inter Ocean*, Sept 20, 1893, cited in: Seager, *The Dawn of Religious Pluralism*, 337–338.

67   Van der Veer, *Imperial Encounters*, 73; see also Vivekananda's main speech "Hinduism [as a Religion]" (Barrows 968–978, Neely 438–445), reprinted in: Seager, *The Dawn of Religious Pluralism*, 421–432.

68   Barrows 101 = Neely 64.

word exclusion is untranslatable. I am proud to belong to a nation which has sheltered the persecuted and the refugees of all religions and all nations of the earth.[69]

Finally, Vivekananda presented the parliament as a vindication of the "wonderful doctrine preached in the Gita: 'Whosoever comes to me, through whatsoever form I reach him, they are all struggling through paths that in the end always lead to me.'" He expressed the hope that the congress might mark the end of sectarianism, bigotry, and fanaticism – things that were apparently firmly opposed to the tradition he himself represented.

This message was repeated again in his closing words, which, according to Barrows' report, were not very well received.[70] Vivekananda warned in particular against triumphalist tendencies and ventured his "own theory" of religious unity. Using organic imaginary he argued that everything developed according to its own substance and laws. Therefore, it was wrong to expect a Christian to become a Hindu or a Buddhist, or the other way around. "[E]ach must assimilate the others and yet preserve its [sic] individuality and grow according to its own law of growth."[71] Holiness, purity and charity – these are the key terms used by Vivekananda – are not the exclusive possession of one religion, but are shared by many. By learning from each other – by assimilation, as he called it, and not by destruction – the various beliefs are supposed to enrich each other or, probably more in line with Vivekananda's discourse, to cross-fertilize each other.

There was much admiration for the "wise men of the East," as they were often called.[72] Barrows made the biblical reference very explicit, as he said in his opening speech: "Welcome, most welcome, O wise men of the East and of the West. May the star which has led you hither be like unto that luminary which guided the men of old."[73] The contrast between East and West that pervaded the parliament enabled speakers to stress similarities and differences at the same time. A good example is the following address by Bonney (with a curious mixing of family metaphors): "Fathers of the contemplative East; sons of the executive West – Behold how good and how pleasant it is for brethren to dwell together in unity."[74] The contrast catches the eye immediately: the passivity of the East versus the activity of the West, the fathers of religions versus the sons, who finally dwell in unity as brothers.

Another example of the same strategy of opposing East and West is the end of Protap Chunder Mozoomdar's speech "World's Religious Debt to India."[75] Mozoomdar was a member of the Brahmo Samaj, a small movement that defended a universalistic kind of religion, based on the Vedanta.[76] The oppositions listed here may be stereotypes, but that does not make them less strong or persuasive:

> In the West you observe, watch, act, and speculate. In the East we contemplate, commune, and suffer ourselves to be carried away by the spirit of the universe.
>
> In the West you wrest from nature her secrets, you conquer her, she makes you wealthy and prosperous, you look upon her as your slave, and sometimes fail to realize her sacredness. In the East nature is our eternal sanctuary, the soul is our everlasting temple, and the sacredness of God's creation is only next to the sacredness of God himself.

---

69   Barrows 102 = Neely 64 (with almost identical wording).
70   Barrows 171.
71   Barrows 170 = Neely 853.
72   Barrows 179.

73   Neely 41.
74   Barrows 173.
75   P.C. Mozoomdar, "World's Religious Debt to Asia," in: Neely 596–601; Barrows 1083–1092, cited in: Seager, *The Dawn of Religious Pluralism*, 440–449. In modern transcription his name is spelled Protap Chunder Majumdar.
76   See van der Veer, *Imperial Encounters*, 44–45. Mozoomdar addressed the Brahmo Samaj itself in a speech "Voice from New India" at the parliament: see Neely 134–138 and Barrows 345–351.

In the West you love equality, you respect man, you seek justice. In the East, love is fulfillment of the law, we have hero worship, we behold God in humanity.

In the West you establish the moral law, you insist upon propriety of conduct, you are governed by public opinion. In the East we aspire, perhaps vainly aspire, after absolute self-conquest, and the holiness which makes God its model.

In the West you work incessantly, and your work is your worship. In the East we meditate and worship for long hours, and worship is [Neely: in] our work.[77]

These oppositions underline the contrast between being active and passive (even suffering), between working (for material goods) and worshipping (for spiritual goods), between subjugating and respecting nature and its creator, and between (formal) justice and love. Although Mozoomdar suggests a kind of synthesis to overcome these oppositions, the final message that religious truth is ultimately found in the East comes as no real surprise: "It has been some consolation [sc. for us] that we still retain some of our spiritual ground; to reflect on the prophecy of Ezekiel: 'Behold, the glory of the Lord cometh from the way of the East.'"[78]

8   Spiritualization

The organizers of the Columbian Exposition did not want to restrict the event to the display "of the material triumphs, industrial achievements, and mechanical victories of man." In the autumn of 1889, Charles Bonney, who would become the president of the World's Congress Auxiliary, already wrote that something "higher and nobler is demanded by the progressive spirit of the present age."[79] The many conferences that were organized by the auxiliary had the motto "not matter, but mind." The World's Parliament of Religions epitomized the opposition between the material and the spiritual. In his opening words John Henry Barrows had already referred to two motivating ideas of the parliament. First, he expressed his belief that "even in this capital of material wonders" there is "a spiritual root to all human progress."[80] Second, he expressed the hope that the parliament would be more "spiritual and moral than theological," thereby hinting at one important tendency of the meeting, the spiritualization of religion.[81]

The opposition between matter and spirit (often associated with the West and the East, respectively) was invoked by many speakers and was often used to criticize (Western) materialism. In the previous section, Mozoomdar's criticism of the Western work ethos and subjugation of nature was mentioned. Similarly, his compatriot Nagarkar pointed to the dangers of this mentality:

The ceaseless demand on your time and energy, the constant worry and hurry of your business activity and the artificial conditions of your Western civilization are all calculated to make you forgetful of the personal presence of God.[82]

On the other hand, speakers also saw opportunities to counter these Western tendencies, and Mozoomdar even went so far as to praise the parliament as the final rebuttal of the charge of materialism directed at America.[83] The Indian theosophist, Gyanendra Nath Chakravarti, detected beneath the "thickness of material luxury, a secret and mystic aspiration to something spiritual."

---

77   Seager, *The Dawn of Religious Pluralism*, 448–449; see Neely 596–601.

78   Seager, *The Dawn of Religious Pluralism*, 449. See also Ezekiel 43:2.

79   Neely 15f.

80   Barrows 42.

81   See also the penultimate paragraph of his opening address: Neely 44.

82   Barrows 1227, cited in: Lüddeckens, *Das Weltparlament der Religionen*, 217.

83   Neely 848.

These are the final words of Chakravarti's opening statement:

> I can see that even you are getting tired of your steam, of your electricity, and the thousand different material comforts that follow these two great powers. I can see that there is a feeling of despondency coming even here – that matter, pursued however vigorously, can be only to the death of all, and it is only through the clear atmosphere of spirituality that you can mount up to the regions of peace and harmony. In the West, therefore, you have developed this material tendency. In the East we have developed a great deal of the spiritual tendency; [but even in the West] ... I have observed an ever increasing readiness of people to assimilate spiritual ideas, regardless of the source from which they emanate.[84]

At the end of his speech, Chakravarti envisioned the union of East and West, "the West supplying the vigor, the youth, the power of organization, and the East opening up its inestimable treasures of a spiritual law."[85] The Light of Asia is here presented as the salvation of Western man from his indulgence in the comforts of material prosperity.

Participants from the West also stressed the importance of spiritual truth, and spoke about the "unity of the spirituality of God."[86] Laura Ormiston Chant, a British Protestant laywoman, claimed that religion is the principle of spiritual growth and "that God has no creed whatever," detected a "religiousness" inside and outside the churches and proclaimed a message of living a good life as children of God.[87] In a slightly more sophisticated fashion the "Rev. Walter Elliott, o.s.p.," an ordained American priest, spoke about the "infinite reality of the Supreme Being, the most loving God, calling his creature to union with himself."[88] He began his speech with the programmatic statement that the aim of religion is "to direct the aspirations of the soul toward an infinite good, and to secure a perfect fruition."[89] In line with this type of thought, Elliott finally stated that love or charity, rather than obedience, is the highest Christian virtue.[90] He used elements from mystical traditions to stress aspects common to very different religions. Spiritualizing religion was probably the most important device employed in the endeavor to reach religious unity.

9   Philip Schaff's Speech on "The Reunion of Christendom"

Many among those who attended the Chicago event would become leaders of the ecumenical movement or important voices on the European theological scene: John Mott – who was to establish, two years later, the WSCF – was called to present the North American Intercollegiate Association Movement;[91] Joseph Estlin Carpenter – a leading pioneer in the early days of what was then called comparative religion – would be selected in 1900 as the first president of the International Council of Unitarian and other Liberal Religious

---

84   Barrows 100 = Neely 63f.
85   Only in Neely 64.
86   Barrows 180.
87   Barrows 591–593. The title of her speech was "The Real Religion of To-day," mentioned in Neely 250–252 under the title "Duty of God to Man Inquired."
88   Walter Elliott, "The Supreme End and Office of Religion," in: Barrows 462–465, here 462; Neely 167–169.
89   Barrows 462.
90   Barrows 465.
91   Mott became the secretary of the movement in 1888. According to his biographer, his speech was "an unashamed proclamation of [the NAIAM's] evangelical motivation and its ethical, social, and ecumenical aims"; Charles Howard Hopkins, *John R. Mott (1865–1955): A Biography*, Grand Rapids MI, Eerdmans, 1979, 107–108. See Sarah Scholl's contribution in this volume. The biographer confirms that "although Mott said that he had 'attended and participated in' the Parliament (JRM-IV, p. 995 [John Raleigh Mott, *Addresses and Papers of John R. Mott*, vol. 4, New York NY, Association Press, 1947, 995]), his address is not to be found in any of the several compilations of the speeches given there"; Hopkins, *John R. Mott*, 710 (endnote no. 89).

Thinkers and Workers, and Charles William Wendté – a Unitarian minister from Boston – would become at the beginning of the new century a pivotal figure of liberal theology and for twenty years (1900–1920) the general secretary of the council headed by Carpenter.[92]

However, it was the elderly Swiss American scholar, Philip Schaff, a respected professor of church history at the Union Theological Seminary in New York City and one of the key figures in the process that led to the creation of the Alliance of the Reformed Churches holding the Presbyterian System in 1877, who delivered carefully crafted sentences under the title "The Reunion of Christendom."[93] The speech was the last public statement of Schaff who was to die before the year ended.

In point of fact, many had already spoken of uniting divided denominations: the American Episcopal Rector William Reed Huntington, for instance, set forth at the end of the 19th century what he called "the Quadrilateral of pure Anglicanism" – four points essential to reunion between, in this case, the Protestant Episcopal Church of the United States and other Protestant Churches in America:[94] "The Holy Scriptures as the Word of God"; "The Primitive Creeds as the Rule of Faith"; "The Two Sacraments ordained by Christ himself"; and "The Episcopate as the keystone of Governmental Unity." Here we have the origin of the Chicago Quadrilateral of 1886 and the Lambeth Quadrilateral of 1888 on which the Episcopal Church first and then the Anglican Communion as a whole, in 1886 and 1888 respectively, laid down their concept of church unity and the conditions that were necessary, in their view, for such unity to be realized.

The route that Schaff proposed to achieve the goal of unity was very different and a frankly pragmatic one: for him there would be no prior conditions of the sort required by Huntington and other Anglicans, no ultimatums, only the basic biblical principle that God was himself reconciling the world in Christ. All else – including Anglicanism's beloved doctrine of the historic episcopate dating back to the restoration period under Charles II – was to be secondary. The components of a reunited Christian church would be bound together, not by a uniformity of doctrine or a uniformity of liturgical texts and rites, but by a common basic religious belief in the divinity of Christ. Schaff's ecclesiology, indeed, was based on the principle that "variety in unity and unity in variety is the law of God" and those "who believe in the ultimate triumph of their own creed, or form of government and worship, *but they* are all mistaken, and indulge in a vain dream."[95]

Appealing to simplicity as the basis for unity, the reunion of Christendom, Schaff argued, presupposed "an original union which has been marred and obstructed, but never wholly destroyed."[96] He already noted the existence of such an agreement on fundamental articles of faith necessary for salvation: Christ, the head of the church; God manifested in Jesus Christ and, for Schaff, an already accepted consensus among scholars concerning the creeds, the exegesis of scripture, and historical studies. These three points, he insisted, encapsulated the essentials of unity and were "more and more carried on without prejudice, and with the sole object of ascertaining the meaning of the text

92   On Carpenter, Wendté and the International Council of Unitarian and other Liberal Religious Thinkers, see Mark D. Chapman's contribution in this volume.

93   Barrows 1192–1201. Among Schaff's literary production see in particular: Philip Schaff, *The Principle of Protestantism*, Chambersburg PA, Publication Office of the German Reformed Church, 1845, and Philip Schaff, *Harmony of the Reformed Confessions*, New York NY, Dodd, Mead & Co., 1877. On Schaff see: George W. Richards, "Philip Schaff: Prophet of Church Union," *Christendom* 10/4, 1945, 463–471.

94   See William Reed Huntington, *The Church-Idea: An Essay Toward Unity*, New York NY, E.P. Dutton, 1870; William Reed Huntington, *A National Church*, New York NY, C. Scribner's Sons, 1898; and Paul Avis's contribution in this volume.

95   Barrows 1194.

96   Barrows 1192.

and the facts of history."[97] Rather optimistically, he thought that historical exegesis would bring out the "real meaning of the writer instead of putting in the fancies of the reader."[98] This conviction was based on the idea that the study of history – if carried on "with malice toward none, but with charity for all" – consisted in "a means of correcting sectarian prejudices and increasing mutual appreciation."[99] Such an investigation would, he believed, bring the denominations closer together in "an humble recognition of their defects and a grateful praise for the good which the same Spirit has wrought in them and through them."[100]

Not differently from Huntington, Schaff found in the North American situation the kind of atmosphere most favorable to Christian union. On the one hand, he explained, in the United States there was religious "liberty and equality before the law";[101] on the other hand, the evil of divisions, antagonism, and competitive interferences at home and on the missionary fields abroad was "beginning to be felt more and more."[102] Starting with North America, where once the Europeans deeply implanted their schisms, Schaff predicted that the movement towards a future reunion would expand to include even the Greek and Roman Churches. He also suggested by a stretch of imagination that the pope, "under the inspiration of a higher authority, should infallibly declare his own fallibility in all matters lying outside of his own communion, and invite Greeks and Protestants to a fraternal pan-Christian council in Jerusalem, where the mother-church of Christendom held the first council of reconciliation and peace."[103] In a spirit of humility and of listening to the others Schaff called for "a restatement of all controverted points ... [that] shall remove misrepresentations, neutralize the anathemas pronounced upon imaginary heresies, and show the way to harmony."[104] In the meantime, before reunion, churches had to do their part by cultivating an irenic spirit, cooperating in philanthropic initiatives, and staying true to the "duty and privilege of prayer for Christian union, [...] that his [Christ's] disciples may all be one in him, as he is one with the Father."[105]

At another occasion Schaff urged the restitution of the undivided church in the form of a "federal or confederate union" resembling the "political confederation of Switzerland, the United States, and the modern German Empire." This great union would be charged with monitoring the doctrine of each church, but it would not be invested with disciplinary power or the capacity to interfere with the liberty and autonomy of the various communities that adhered to the union. This federation would be, as Schaff specified, "a voluntary association of different Churches in their official capacity, each retaining its freedom and independence in the management of its internal affairs, but all recognizing one another as sisters with equal rights, and co-operating in general enterprises, such as the spread of the gospel at home and abroad, the defense of the faith against infidelity, the elevation of the poor and neglected classes of society, works of philanthropy and charity, and moral reform."[106]

Although no open debate on issues dividing different religions, or even Christian denominations, took place in the Chicago parliament before and after Schaff's speech, this farewell address of the elderly ecumenical leader was in a certain way prophetic: a decade and a half later, in 1908, the Federal Council of the Churches of Christ in America was formed with 32 denominations, accounting for a total of 18 million Americans.

---

97   Barrows 1192.
98   Barrows 1198.
99   Barrows 1199.
100 Barrows 1198.
101 Barrows 1193.
102 Barrows 1193.
103 Barrows 1196.
104 Barrows 1196.
105 Barrows 1199.
106 Don Herbert Yoder, "Christian Unity in Nineteenth-Century America," in: *A History of the Ecumenical Movement*, vol. 1, Ruth Rouse & Stephen C. Neill, eds., *1517–1948*, London, SPCK, 1954, 221–259, here 256.

10   The Comparative Study of Religion

In his opening address, John Barrows said that "we" meet here "in a school of comparative theology"[107] and in his final evaluation he hailed the parliament's contribution to the "study of comparative religion."[108] Besides various contributions to this subject in the main meeting, the organizers also opened an "interesting overflow meeting in Hall 3 of the Art Palace,"[109] "where papers of a more scientific and less popular character were read."[110] Barrows gives a helpful overview of the papers that were presented there.[111] Nowadays two points of criticism are raised: first, that the focus was very much on ancient, tribal, or non-Western, non-Christian topics, and second, that these religions were mainly represented by their own practitioners (Hindus representing Hinduism, and so on).[112]

To some extent, the opening address of the "scientific section" held by its chairman Merwin-Marie Snell illustrates this second issue. In his speech "Service of the Science of Religions to Unity and Mission Enterprise,"[113] Snell claimed that the parliament itself was "a vast hierological museum, a working collection of religious specimens, having the same indispensable value for the hierologist that the herbarium has to the botanist."[114] The "science of religions" had to carry out its beneficial work, give a fair overview of the facts, and counter

religious prejudice and animosity.[115] This was not effected by professional scholars alone. "[T]he man of broadening culture and thought may study them [religions] with the practical end of a fuller self-enlightenment regarding his duties to God and the race; and the intelligent religious partisan may seek to master, by means of his science, the secret of religious variations, and to obtain such a knowledge of the relation of other religious systems to his own, their points of agreement and contradiction." By comparing religions, according to Snell, a "very powerful and fruitful propaganda" was possible, and this lent science of religion great importance for missionary work.[116]

Notwithstanding these "practical" inclinations on the part of Snell, it is clear that the organizers had a clear picture of the current situation of religious studies. Many key figures, such as Max Müller, Cornelis Petrus Tiele, Jean and Albert Réville and the previously mentioned Joseph Estlin Carpenter, had been invited, and although some of them declined to come, many of them sent a paper. Perhaps they feared that the parliament would be too much of a religious – or what would now be called "interfaith" – meeting. Snell's framing of the study of religion with clear reference to religious unity and missionary work was to confirm their uneasiness.

Scholarly papers, however, were also presented in the main hall, as was the case with Tiele's contribution on the study of comparative theology. In the text that was read for him, Tiele excused himself for not being able to attend due to his heavy work load and teaching obligations, and then gave a short exposition of the field, expressing his joy that there was such a great interest in the study of religion in America.[117] The next speaker, Laura Ormiston Chant, who was greeted "with a great outburst of enthusiasm,"[118] was not

---

107   Barrows 75.
108   Barrows 1571.
109   Neely 227.
110   Barrows 152.
111   Barrows 150–152; see Barrows 1317–1383 (with selected papers from the "scientific section").
112   Ziolkowski, "Introduction," 38f.
113   Barrows 1347, under a slightly different title also reproduced in Neely 259–261.
114   Neely 260. The term "hierologist" was, to the best of my knowledge, introduced by the Dutch scholar of religion Cornelis Petrus Tiele as *terminus technicus* to denote the scholars of the science of religion (*godsdienstwetenschap*); see Cornelis Petrus Tiele, *Outlines of the History of Religion*, London, Trübner, 1877, vii.

---

115   Neely 260.
116   Neely 260–261.
117   Cornelis Petrus Tiele, "On the Study of Comparative Theology," in: Barrows 583–590 and Neely 245–250.
118   Neely 250.

so enthusiastic. She started: "Dear Friends, after listening long enough to the science of religion, probably, as this is the last word this morning, it may be a little relief to run off, or leave the science of religion to take care of itself for a while and take a few thoughts on religion independent of its science. ... We have learned that religion, whatever the science of it may be, is the principle of spiritual growth."[119] Other participants were perhaps a little less skeptical, but if we try to balance scholarly and religious interests, we undoubtedly see the pendulum swinging heavily towards the latter.

11   Conclusions

Barrows' description of the parliament as "a school of comparative theology" which would be spiritual and ethical rather than theological[120] may nowadays sound paradoxical, but at the time the hope was still widespread that scholarly and spiritual goals could be combined. Contemporary scholars of religion may find it difficult to appreciate the Chicago event. What Eric J. Sharpe has to say about its merits in his still influential history of the field is telling:

> The parliament was an encouragement, and a danger, to the emerging science of religion. An encouragement, because it showed the extent to which earlier impatience and intolerance was being overcome. A danger, because it tended to associate at least some comparative religionists (those who dared to associate themselves with it) with an idealistic programme of world peace and understanding. Observers were right when they pointed out that this meeting could only have been held in brash, sentimental, pluralistic America.[121]

Aside from the anti-Americanism of such an evaluation, Sharpe also seems to be confused by the event. On the one hand, he apparently appreciates the parliament as a step in overcoming intolerance, but, on the other, he does not favor the association of the new science with the endeavor to achieve world peace and understanding. Why this association should be rejected is not explained. Scholars of religion tend to see the Chicago parliament as a false beginning in the series of truly scholarly conferences on the history of religions, which would start with the Premier Congrès International d'Histoire des Religions held in Paris in 1900.

Nevertheless, the parliament has continued to be remembered among scholars of religion. At about the time of its centennial in 1993, various papers presented at the parliament were republished and its impact on the academic study of religion was assessed in various studies. While the tone was mainly critical, chiefly on account of the dominance of a "presentist" standpoint (assessing the event by "our" present-day scholarly standards), this also serves to reveal its importance. Well over a century has passed since the 1893 Chicago parliament took place, during which time the scholarly study of religion, on the one hand, and confessional theology and interfaith dialogue, on the other, have grown apart.[122] The World's Parliament of Religions that came together in Chicago in 1993 was not devoted to the study of religion, but sought rather "to celebrate diversity and harmony and to explore religious and spiritual responses to critical issues that confront us all."[123]

By way of conclusion, it is interesting to look at the short presentation given by Julia Ward Howe at the parliament. Howe was an American abolitionist, social activist, founder of the AWSA, and

---

119   Barrows 591 = Neely 250.
120   Barrows 75.
121   Eric J. Sharpe, *Comparative Religion: A History*, London, Duckworth, 1984, 139.

122   On the process by which the early historians of religion defined themselves as *scholars* against those interested in religious dialogue and theology, see Arie L. Molendijk, "The First Conferences on the History of Religion," *NTT JTSR* 72, 2018, 211–224.
123   See <http://www.parliamentofreligions.org/index.cfm?n=1&sn=4> (accessed July 4, 2019).

author of the well-known patriotic "Battle Hymn of the Republic." The title of her speech was "What Is Religion?"[124] She stressed the fact that she was a woman and expressed the hope that the crowd could indeed hear her "little voice." Referring to previous addresses (by male speakers), she further said that "as a woman" she did not want "to dwell upon any traits of exclusiveness." That approach, she suggested, belonged to an earlier phase of history. Instead she sought to go back "to that great Spirit which contemplated a sacrifice for the whole of humanity."[125] That was in no way an act of exclusion, she claimed, but one "of an infinite and endless and joyous inclusion," for which she thanked God.

In accordance with this inclusivist point of view, which tends to place the various religions "all on one basis," Howe said that it would be good to come to an agreement "as to what is religion and as to what is not religion."[126] For her and her audience, she claimed, it was "aspiration, the pursuit of the divine in the human; the sacrifice of everything to duty for the sake of God and of humanity and of our own individual dignity." It is very much a liberal idea of religion, which places the emphasis on the relationship between the individual and his or her God – a relationship that is conceived as being based on the divine element in human beings. Howe also made it clear that religion is not to be equated with magic ("you do something that will bring you good luck"). Magic is something which is invented by and "for the advantage of the priesthoods." She is very outspoken in this respect, claiming that magic is the "most mischievous irreligion."

She took up the point of inclusion again at the end of her short speech, focusing on the position of women. Although Howe did not make an outspoken plea for the equality of men and women, she undoubtedly made a big step in this direction in the following subtle argumentation:

I think nothing is religion which puts one individual absolutely above others, and surely nothing is religion which puts one sex above another. Religion is primarily our relation to the Supreme, to God himself. … And any religion which will sacrifice a certain set of human beings for the enjoyment or aggrandizement or advantage of another is no religion. It is a thing which may be allowed, but it is against true religion. Any religion which sacrifices women to the brutality of men is no religion.[127]

While the issue of slavery is not directly addressed, it is certainly hinted at, and implicitly condemned by the comparison with the (brute) suppression of women. This must have been an extremely efficient rhetorical move, as the participants, above all the organizers, were so proud that women were represented at the parliament. Although condescending remarks with respect to women were not lacking (and Howe was permitted only a short speech of no more than ten minutes),[128] the participation of women was remarkable and certainly more than a mere ornament to the parliament.

The "inclusivist" rhetoric of many participants did not imply, needless to say, that nobody was excluded. The spiritualist tendency of many – by no means all – contributors excluded those who explicitly claimed the superiority of their own faith. In the closing chapters of his report, Barrows was less inclusive than in the opening chapters, claiming that this meeting took nothing away from the superior standing of Christianity. Participants from non-Christian religions did not accept the dominating discourse but argued that their religion was more spiritualized and tolerant than that of their hosts. Most Christian participants claimed the superiority of their own tradition, but did not argue for specific dogmatic truths. Christianity was defined in general terms of the fatherhood of God and the brotherhood of man. Within the

---

124   Barrows 1250–1251; Neely 764–766.
125   Barrows 1250.
126   Barrows 1251.

127   Barrows 1251.
128   Neely 764.

special denominational congresses, the identity of one's own church could be reaffirmed more easily, whereas the World's Parliament of Religions represented a form of ecumenism that went beyond the single Christian traditions, not only because the parliament had a strong ethical and spiritual orientation, fighting poverty, intemperance and materialism, but also because the parliament symbolized for many of the churches' representatives a unique opportunity to provide an answer to the need for dialogue which was perceived by many of them as a very urgent issue.

The event offered to many Christian participants the possibility to experience a human and spiritual proximity which strengthened the perception that the essence of Christianity rests in a humanistic universalism that moves beyond any form of doctrinal Christianity, variously articulated as Christ-mysticism or as the expression of love. The search for unity among the churches assumed here a non-dogmatic perspective, which would be expressed in a more incisive way by part of the liberal theology wherein Wendté and Carpenter, both attending the Chicago parliament, played a fundamental role. What is significant is that such a perspective in addressing the problem of Christian unity went against the received wisdom of the time: either voluntary federalism or organic church unity, but not both. Philip Schaff disagreed; he saw the value of exploring both paths simultaneously, indeed that the one anticipated the other, leaving in Chicago a kind of legacy to the next generation of theologians and pioneers, which was destined to produce the majority of the leadership of the modern ecumenical movement.

It is not possible to draw one final conclusion from this heterogeneous event, but perhaps one can say that the participants who somehow felt united and had a strong sense of togetherness were convinced of the ultimate meaning of "religion" – however defined – as a force against indulging in consumerism and materialism (which form the core of irreligion). That does not imply that the parliament had no attractive or even fascinating aspects of its own. As Julia Ward Howe said: "I have turned my back to-day upon the great show [of the Columbian Exposition] in order to see a greater spectacle [at the World's Parliament of Religions]."[129] The mixture of people of different races, nationalities and religions, combined with a rhetoric of respect, mutual understanding and even religious unity and world peace, was a powerful attraction for the crowds that gathered at that time in Chicago on the shores of Lake Michigan.

Bibliography

The Major Conference Reports

Barrows, John Henry, ed., *The World's Parliament of Religions: An Illustrated and Popular Story of the World's First Parliament of Religions, Held in Chicago in Connection with the Columbian Exposition of 1893*, Chicago IL, The Parliament Publishing Company, 1893.

Houghton, Walter R., ed., *Neely's History of the Parliament of Religions and Religious Congresses at the World's Columbian Exposition: Compiled from Original Manuscripts and Stenographic Reports*, Chicago IL, F.T. Neely, 1893.

Further Primary Literature

Barrows, John Henry, "Results of the Parliament of Religions" (1894), in: Eric Jozef Ziolkowski, ed., *A Museum of Faiths: Histories and Legacies of the 1893 World's Parliament of Religions*, Atlanta GA, Scholars Press, 1993, 132–147.

Bonney, Charles Carroll, "The World's Parliament of Religions," *The Monist* 5, 1895, 321–343.

Müller, Friedrich Max, "The Real Significance of the Parliament of Religions," *The Arena* 61, 1894, 1–14, reprinted in: Ziolkowski, ed., *A Museum of Faiths*, 149–162.

---

129   Barrows 1250.

Secondary Literature

Bolotin, Norman & Christine Laing, *The World's Columbian Exposition: A 100-Year Retrospective*, Washington DC, Preservation Press, 1992.

Braybrooke, Marcus, *Pilgrimage of Hope: One Hundred Years of Global Interfaith Dialogue*, London, SCM Press, 1992.

Lüddeckens, Dorothea, *Das Weltparlament der Religionen von 1893: Strukturen interreligiöser Begegnung im 19. Jahrhundert*, Berlin, De Gruyter, 2002.

Molendijk, Arie L., *The Emergence of the Science of Religion in the Netherlands*, Leiden, Brill, 2005.

Seager, Richard Hughes, *The Dawn of Religious Pluralism: Voices from the World's Parliament of Religions (1893)*, La Salle IL, Open Court, 1993.

Seager, Richard Hughes, *The World's Parliament of Religions: The East/West Encounter, Chicago, 1893*, Bloomington IN, Indiana University Press, 1995.

Snodgrass, Judith, *Presenting Japanese Buddhism to the West: Orientalism, Occidentalism, and the Columbian Exposition*, Chapel Hill NC, University of North Carolina Press, 2003.

Sun, Anna, *Confucianism as a World Religion: Contested Histories and Contemporary Realities*, Princeton NJ, Princeton University Press, 2013.

Ziolkowski, Eric Jozef, ed., *A Museum of Faiths: Histories and Legacies of the 1893 World's Parliament of Religions*, Atlanta GA, Scholars Press, 1993.

CHAPTER 11

Pontifical Unionism from Pius IX to Pius X

Laura Pettinaroli

1   Introduction

In 1856, when Fr. Jean-Xavier (Ivan Sergeyevich) Gagarin, a Russian Orthodox who had converted to Catholicism and become a Jesuit, chose primary sources for the appendices of his book, *La Russie sera-t-elle catholique?*, he could only publish old texts: the decree of union of the Council of Florence (1439), Clement VIII's bull on the reunion of Russian bishops (1595), and Benedict XIV's encyclical to missionaries assigned to the East, *Allatae sunt* (1755).[1] The situation was quite different on the eve of World War I. The magisterium's corpus of texts on the reunion of the churches had increased considerably, and Catholic practices integrated the concern for union.

In the wake of Vatican II, and the further rejection of the practice of Uniatism (Balamand Document, 1993), historians became interested in this "pontifical unionism," which appeared in the 19th century and can be defined as an effort to bring Christians together through a "return" of the "separated" churches to the Roman "flock." While unionism differs from ecumenism (a dialogue aimed at unity but without the conversion of individuals or the disappearance of the different churches), it nevertheless stands on its basis.[2] From

this point of view, Leo XIII's pontificate attracted a great deal of attention, even though several authors have stressed Pius IX's role in the emergence of the "first unionist attempts."[3] Indeed, it is necessary to note the continuity between the initiatives of Pius IX, Leo XIII, and even Pius X. In different styles, in various contexts, the Roman conception of Christian unity – that can be read in the pontifical texts and observed in curial practices – appears very coherent.

2   New Catholic Perspectives on Christian Confessions and Christian Unity

After the revolutionary and counter-revolutionary effervescences, the question of the union of the churches was posed – at the beginning of the 19th century – from a perspective that went beyond the usual religious and theological dimensions to include major political issues. This period was also marked by the emergence of individuals and small groups that disseminated a unionist concern within the Catholic Church.

---

1   Jean-Xavier Gagarin, *La Russie sera-t-elle catholique?*, Paris, C. Douniol, 1856, 89–169.

2   Étienne Fouilloux, *Les catholiques et l'unité chrétienne du XIXᵉ au XXᵉ siècle: Itinéraires européens d'expression française*, Paris, Le Centurion, 1982; Giuseppe Maria Croce, *La Badia Greca di Grottaferrata e la rivista "Roma e l'Oriente": Cattolicesimo e ortodossia fra unionismo ed ecumenismo (1799–1923)*, 2 vols., Vatican City, Libreria Editrice Vaticana, 1990; Mauro Velati, *Una difficile transizione: Il cattolicesimo tra unionismo ed ecumenismo (1952–1964)*, Bologna, Il Mulino, 1996.

3   *Fliche-Martin* 21, 478–485; Angelo Tamborra, "Pio IX, la lettera agli Orientali *In Suprema Petri Apostoli Sede* del 1848 e il mondo ortodosso," *Rassegna storica del Risorgimento* 56, 1969, 347–367; Angelo Tamborra, "Il concilio Vaticano I e gli Orientali 'ortodossi': Illusioni e disinganni (1868–1870)," *Rassegna storica del Risorgimento* 57, 1970, 507–519. On this point, however, Pius IX remains in the shadow of his successor and no comprehensive study of the relationship with the different Christian churches during his pontificate has yet been carried out.

2.1 Church Union: An Issue of Political Relevance in the 19th Century

The revolutionary period was a turning point. Many projects were conceived between the years 1790 and 1810, ranging from traditional union attempts on a theological basis – particularly with the Greek Church around the figure of the Abbé Grégoire, but more generally with the French constitutional episcopate[4] – to the practice of interconfessional worship, as in the Netherlands with the group Christo Sacrum.[5] The early years of the French Empire, marked by Napoleon's reorganization of the cults, also gave rise to plans for union between Catholics and Protestants, which raised both hopes and concerns. It was in this context that Mathieu-Mathurin Tabaraud – an Oratorian priest who had emigrated to England in 1792 and who played a significant role in the service of Napoleon – published a detailed history of the attempts at union (1808, reissued in 1824).[6] However, despite many exchanges among leaders of different churches, the Catholic Enlightenment maintained a policy of "dogmatic intransigence and never yield[ed] … to ecumenical discourse,"[7]

which would have implied the recognition of a Christian diversity. The schism was always defined as an accident that had to be repaired by a "return" of the "lost" ones.

At the same time, the counter-revolutionary movement also took up the issue of union, which then became marked by a "defensive" approach against the Revolution and its excesses. In 1806, the Catholic writer Louis de Bonald highlighted the interest of statesmen in bringing together the different denominations to "save the Christian religion in Europe and, with it, civilization and society."[8] Joseph de Maistre, Savoy's ambassador to St. Petersburg from 1802 to 1816, placed the religious question at the core of his project to restore Europe politically. As Olivier Rousseau noted, de Maistre was both against unionism – because of his rejection of Protestantism, defined as the source of the Revolution and as a factor in intellectual and social dissolution[9] – as well as "a great unionist," thanks to his contacts with the Orthodox world.[10] Considering that the pope's eminent position was not recognized there, de Maistre opposed – in 1815 – the political project of a Holy Alliance, proposed by Tsar Alexander I and supported by Austria and Prussia, which was based on the belonging to the "same Christian nation."[11]

Throughout the 19th century, the international situation renewed interest in church union. The missionary impetus, in fact, raised the problem

---

4   Joseph F. Byrnes, "Les évêques constitutionnels face à l'orthodoxie et au protestantisme à l'époque du Directoire," in: Paul Chopelin, ed., Gouverner une Église en révolution: Histoires et mémoires de l'épiscopat constitutionnel: Actes du colloque organisé par le Laboratoire de recherche historique Rhône-Alpes, Lyon, 8–9 juin 2012, Lyon, LARHRA, 2017, 179–191.

5   Bernard Plongeron, "Les projets de réunion des communions chrétiennes, du Directoire à l'Empire," RHEF 176, 1980, 17–49.

6   Mathieu-Mathurin Tabaraud, De la Réunion des communions chrétiennes: ou Histoire des négociations, conférences, correspondances qui ont eu lieu, des projets et des plans qui ont été formés à ce sujet, depuis la naissance du protestantisme jusqu'à présent, Paris, A. Leclerc, 1808; Mathieu-Mathurin Tabaraud, Histoire critique des projets formés depuis trois cents ans pour la réunion des communions chrétiennes, Paris, Gauthier Frères & Cie, 1824.

7   Plongeron, "Les projets de réunion," 33. A few years later, the disciples of Félicité de Lamennais, who also invoked the notion of the unity of the church, manifested too "a proprietary sentiment in regard to the true"; Jean-René Derré, "L'œcuménisme mennaisien," in: Jacques Gadille, ed., Les catholiques libéraux au XIXᵉ siècle: Actes du

Colloque international d'histoire religieuse de Grenoble, des 30 septembre–3 octobre 1971, Grenoble, Presses universitaires de Grenoble, 1974, 53–66, here 65.

8   Louis de Bonald, "De l'unité religieuse en Europe," in: Louis de Bonald, Œuvres complètes de M. de Bonald, ed. Jacques-Paul Migne, vol. 3, Paris, Ateliers catholiques du Petit-Montrouge, 1862, cols. 675–676.

9   According to him, a real restoration in Europe had to take "an indispensable preliminary" step: "Remove the fatal world 'Protestantism' from the European dictionary"; Joseph de Maistre, Du Pape, Lyons, J.B. Pélagaud, 1862 [¹1819], 469.

10   Olivier Rousseau, "Les attitudes de pensées concernant l'unité chrétienne au XIXᵉ siècle," RevScRel, 34, 1960, 351–373, here 354.

11   The Holy Alliance Treaty, Paris, Sept 26, 1815, art. 2.

of the division of the Christian "old world." Inter-denominational rapprochement in the Protestant world was fueled by the need to coordinate extra-European action[12] and the Catholics were also aware – as Pius IX affirmed in 1848 – that "new help to spread the true faith of Jesus Christ more and more among heathen nations could be found in unity."[13] The Eastern Question, in particular, increased interfaith relations: Anglican-Orthodox rapprochement during clergyman William Palmer's stay in Russia in 1840;[14] creation, in 1841, of a Lutheran-Anglican bishopric in Jerusalem.[15] But it also raised tensions, as on the occasion of the Crimean War[16] and, more generally, in the competition for supporting Eastern Christians (that stimulated the creation of the Œuvre d'Orient by French Catholics in 1856,[17] and of the Imperial Orthodox Palestine Society by Russians in 1882).[18]

Finally, the rise of secularism, atheism and socialism also encouraged closer ties from a defensive perspective. In 1910, Nicola Franco – an Eastern rite Catholic priest close to curial circles – proposed defending Christianity "through the union of the churches." In effect, he denounced the "universal ... war" waged by "Freemasonry, free thought,

Judaism, socialism, and anarchism, in politics by the radicals and the Combes republicans, and, in the sciences and in literature, the rationalists, hypercriticals," as well as the "Modernists who, while claiming to remain profoundly Christian, even Catholic, together shook the foundations of Christianity."[19]

2.2 The Unionists: Individuals and Groups, Academics and Activists

To understand Catholic unionism in the 19th century, it is necessary to present its protagonists. From the beginning of the century, in the major Western European countries, emerged various unionist groups, in which converts played a decisive role. These intra-Christian conversions – which reflected an extreme individual expression of the desire for unity[20] – were sporadic but had an impact on religious and cultural history because they often concerned brilliant personalities whose motivations were made public through autobiographical or biographical accounts.[21] In the Romantic atmosphere, propitious to interior quests and spiritual emotions, but also to

12 Some preliminary initiatives in this regard took place beginning in 1810: see Kenneth Scott Latourette, "Ecumenical Bearings of the Missionary Movement and the International Missionary Council," in: *A History of the Ecumenical Movement*, vol. 1, Ruth Rouse & Stephen C. Neill, eds., *1517–1948*, London, SPCK, 1954, 353–402, here 355.

13 Pius IX, *In suprema Petri Apostoli Sede*, Jan 6, 1848.

14 Robin Wheeler, *Palmer's Pilgrimage: The Life of William Palmer of Magdalen*, Oxford, Peter Lang, 2006, esp. 93–153.

15 Martin Lückhoff, *Anglikaner und Protestanten im Heiligen Land: Das gemeinsame Bistum Jerusalem (1841–1886)*, Wiesbaden, Harrassowitz, 1998.

16 Angelo Tamborra, "Crisi d'Oriente, guerra di Crimea e polemiche politico-religiose fra cattolici e ortodossi (1853–1856)," *Clio* 5, 1969, 169–191.

17 Hervé Legrand & Giuseppe Maria Croce, eds., *L'Œuvre d'Orient: Solidarités anciennes et nouveaux défis*, Paris, Cerf, 2010.

18 Elena Astafieva, "La Russie en Terre Sainte: Le cas de la Société Impériale Orthodoxe de Palestine (1882–1917)," *CrSt* 24, 2003, 41–68.

19 Nicola Franco, *La difesa del Cristianesimo per l'unione delle Chiese*, Rome, M. Bretschneider, 1910, notes 6 and 1, On Franco, see Giuseppe Maria Croce, "Franco, Nicola," *DBI* 50, 196–197.

20 Intra-Christian conversions were at times referred to as a "return to unity"; Jean-Joseph-François Poujoulat, *Le Père de Ravignan, sa vie, ses œuvres*, Paris, C. Douniol, 1859, 447.

21 Always apologetical (F.E. Banks, *Lettre d'un jeune Anglais converti à la religion catholique à son père, ministre protestant*, Montdidier, Radenez, 1825), sometimes collective (Jules Gondon, ed., *Motifs de conversion de dix ministres anglicans exposés par eux-mêmes, et rétractation du révérend J.H. Newman*, Paris, Sagnier & Bray, 1847), these (auto)biographical accounts were very successful. For example, *La Vie de Mme Swetchine* – dedicated to this Russian noblewoman who had converted from Orthodoxy to Catholicism in 1815 – first published in 1860 by the Comte de Falloux, was reprinted many times. More generally, see Frédéric Gugelot, "Les enjeux du récit de conversion au tournant des XIXe et XXe siècles," in: Didier Boisson, & Elisabeth Pinto-Mathieu, eds., *La conversion: Textes et réalités*, Rennes, Presses Universitaires de Rennes, 2014, 113–121.

questions regarding their country's political and cultural development, several Russian nobles converted to Catholicism in the first third of the century.[22] Shortly after, Gagarin, a former diplomat who had converted to Catholicism in 1842, became a Jesuit in France in 1843. He was soon joined by two other converts: Jean Martynov in 1845 and Eugène Balabin in 1852.[23] The other major incubator for individual conversions – Anglicanism, itself marked by the Oxford Movement from 1833 – also raised great enthusiasm in Catholic circles. Even beyond the exceptional career of Anglican priest John Henry Newman (converted in 1845, created cardinal in 1879), who played a central role in the history of Christian unity,[24] conversions to Catholicism affected English society.[25] From 1838, the French-speaking press took an interest in this movement, which reached its peak in 1844/1845, when a large-scale reunion seemed possible.[26]

These individual intra-Christian conversions, however, played a complex role in the history of unionism, often favoring it, but also accentuating various tensions. Catholicism registered some departures too, such as that of Fr. Wladimir Guettée, a French priest who converted to Russian Orthodoxy in about 1861[27] and founded the journal L'Union Chrétienne (1859–1870). That publication then fueled interdenominational competition, and it was to refute it that, in 1861, Pius IX encouraged Fr. Gagarin to create a Russian-language journal.[28]

However, beyond the individuals, whose personal backgrounds often lent a sensitivity to the question of union, institutional groups took shape so to form, at the turn of the 20th century,

---

22   Katia Dmitrieva, "Les conversions au catholicisme en Russie au XIXᵉ siècle: Ruptures historiques et culturelles," *RESlav* 67, 1995, 311–336; Lucjan Suchanek, "Les catholiques russes et les pro-catholiques en Russie dans la première moitié du XIXᵉ siècle," *CMRS* 29, 1988, 361–374. "Russian Catholicism" has been interpreted as a political criticism of absolutism (Ekaterina Nikolaevna Tsimbaeva, *Russkij katolitsizm: Zabytoe proshloe rossijskogo liberalizma*, Moscow, Éditorial URSS, 1999) and even as an alternative to the antinomy between Westernism and Slavophilia (Elena Astafieva, *L'Empire russe et le monde catholique: Entre représentations et pratiques (1772–1905)*, Ph.D. thesis, École Pratique des Hautes Études, 2006, 11).

23   On these individuals, see Robert Danieluk, *"Œcuménisme" au XIXᵉ siècle: Jésuites russes et union des Églises d'après les Archives romaines de la Compagnie de Jésus*, Rome, Institutum Historicum Societatis Iesu, 2009, especially 49–58, as well as Jeffrey Bruce Beshoner, *Ivan Sergeevich Gagarin: The Search for Orthodox and Catholic Union*, Notre Dame IN, University of Notre Dame Press, 2002.

24   Vladimir Pecherin (writer and political activist who became a Catholic priest) wrote his memoirs entitled *Apologia pro vita mea* with reference to Newman's work (*Apologia pro vita sua*, London, Longmans, 1864); see Vladimir Pecherin, *The First Russian Political Émigré: Notes from beyond the Grave, or Apologia pro vita mea*, ed. and trans. Michael R. Katz, Dublin, University College Dublin Press, 2008. Although he does not offer an in-depth comparison of the two men, the Jesuit d'Herbigny draws a parallel with Solovyov; see Michel d'Herbigny, *Un Newman russe, Vladimir Soloviev (1853–1900)*, Paris, Beauchesne, 1911.

25   Jean-Alain Lesourd, *Les catholiques dans la société anglaise (1765–1865): Évolution numérique, répartition géographique, structure sociale, pratique religieuse*, Paris, Champion, 1978, esp. 565–587. The author underlines the role of some 10,000 French priests who emigrated during the Revolution, such as Fr. Giraud, tutor of Ambrose Phillips de Lisle, who converted in 1825; see Lesourd, *Les catholiques*, 578–579.

26   See Jan De Maeyer & Karel Strobbe, "The Oxford Movement: Reception and Perception in Catholic Circles in Nineteenth-Century Belgium," in: Stewart J. Brown & Peter B. Nockles, eds., *The Oxford Movement: Europe and the Wider World (1830–1930)*, Cambridge, Cambridge University Press, 2012, 185–202. Among the testimonies of this peak of enthusiasm in 1844, we can mention Jules Gondon, *Du mouvement religieux en Angleterre: ou Les progrès du catholicisme et le retour de l'église anglicane à l'unité*, Paris, Sagnier & Bray, 1844.

27   Wladimir Guettée, *Souvenirs d'un prêtre romain devenu prêtre orthodoxe*, Paris, Fischbacher, 1889, esp. 356–358. See Sylvio Hermann De Franceschi, "Antiromanisme historiographique et gallicanisme jansénisant: René-François Guettée et la mise à l'Index de son *Histoire de l'Église de France*," in: Sylvio Hermann De Franceschi, ed., *Histoires antiromaines: Antiromanisme et critique dans l'historiographie catholique (XVIᵉ–XXᵉ siècles): Actes de la journée d'études de Lyon, 24 septembre 2010*, Lyon, LARHRA, 2011, 115–149.

28   Fr. P.-J. Beckx to Fr. J. Martynov, Rome, Aug 10, 1861, in: Danieluk, *"Œcuménisme" au XIXᵉ siècle*, 217 (doc. 77).

a genuine unionist constellation. The forms that these associations took varied, ranging from prayer movements to the foundation of libraries and journals.

Prayer associations were certainly the most prominent aspect of this blossoming unionism.[29] As early as 1832, Fr. Ignatius (George) Spencer, a former Anglican priest who had converted to Catholicism in 1830, founded a prayer association in Rome for the reunion with the Church of England.[30] This Passionist also convinced a number of French bishops – such as Antoine de La Grange de Pons, bishop of Moulins, in 1846 – to embark upon this path.[31] In 1847, he encouraged the pastor of Notre-Dame-des-Victoires in Paris to organize a Mass to be said every first Saturday of the month "for the conversion of England and the reunion of the separated churches."[32] The movement resumed in the late 1890s during the debate on the validity of Anglican orders.[33]

In 1897, an Archconfraternity dedicated to "Notre-Dame de la Compassion" was founded at the church and seminary of Saint-Sulpice in Paris "for the conversion of England;"[34] Cardinal Benoît-Marie Langénieux also instituted one at the seminary of Reims.[35] This archconfraternity prospered. In 1907, it claimed several thousand members (individuals and communities) linked by a quarterly newsletter and monthly meetings combining prayers and a lecture.[36] French Catholicism also hosted several initiatives for union with Eastern Christians. In 1856, the group of the Russian Jesuits founded the Œuvre des saints Cyrille et Méthode, aiming for "the conversion of Orientals, particularly Russians, to Catholic unity,"[37] especially through prayer. In 1862, the Barnabite Cesare Tondini de' Quarenghi – who was close to Gregory Petrovich Shuvalov, himself a convert from Orthodoxy who had entered the Barnabites as Augustinus Maria in 1856[38] – created an association of prayer in honor of Mary Immaculate for the union of the churches, in particular the Russian Church. He was encouraged by several letters from Pius IX and received the blessings of many bishops, from Italy and France, but also from England, Belgium, and the Netherlands.[39]

29   The movements of prayer for unity also increased among the Protestant world; see Ruth Rouse, "Voluntary Movements and the Changing Ecumenical Climate," in: *A History of the Ecumenical Movement*, vol. 1, 309–349.

30   Jean Guibert, *Le Réveil du catholicisme en Angleterre au XIXe siècle: Conférences prêchées dans l'Église Saint-Sulpice (1901–1906)*, Paris, C. Poussielgue, 1907, 146–172 ("Le Père Ignace Spencer et les associations de prières pour l'Angleterre"). See also Jozef Vanden Bussche, *Ignatius (George) Spencer, Passionist (1799–1864): Crusader of Prayer for England and Pioneer of Ecumenical Prayer*, Leuven, Leuven University Press, 1991.

31   Antoine de Pons de La Grange, *Mandement de Monseigneur l'évêque de Moulins, pour le saint temps de Carême de l'année 1846, et pour des Prières en faveur de l'Église d'Angleterre*, Moulins, P.A. Desrosiers, 1846. More broadly, see Olivier Rota, "Entre la France et l'Angleterre: La campagne catholique pour la conversion de l'Angleterre, des années 1830 jusqu'à la Grande Guerre," RHEF 104, 2018, 97–115.

32   *Lettre pastorale de Son Eminence le Cardinal Richard Archevêque de Paris ordonnant la publication de l'encyclique Fidentem piumque animum sur le mois du Saint Rosaire et prescrivant des prières pour la réunion de l'Angleterre et des Églises séparées*, Paris, F. Levé, 1896, 12–13.

33   See also the contribution in this volume by Paul Avis.

34   *Lettre pastorale de Son Eminence le Cardinal Richard Archevêque de Paris ordonnant la publication du Bref apostolique qui institue dans l'église et le séminaire Saint-Sulpice l'Archiconfrérie de N.-D. de Compassion pour la conversion de l'Angleterre*, Paris, F. Levé, 1897.

35   *Instruction pastorale de Son Eminence le Cardinal Langénieux, archevêque de Reims, sur les progrès de la foi catholique parmi les nations dissidentes et Mandement pour le Carême de l'an de grâce 1898 portant publication de l'Encyclique Divinum Illud en date du 9 mai 1897*, Reims, N. Monce, 1898.

36   Guibert, *Le Réveil du catholicisme en Angleterre*, iii–iv.

37   Statutes of the Œuvre des saints Cyrille et Méthode, in: AFSJ, Slavic Library, Gagarin 4a, doc. 1bis.

38   He himself, on the advice of Pius IX, offered his life to God three times a day "for the return of Russia, his country, to Catholic unity"; C. Tondini to Pius X, Rome, Good Friday, 1905, in: ASRS, AAEESS, III, Russia, pos. 898, fasc. 290, fol. 50. See also Augustinus Maria Shuvalov, *Ma conversion et ma vocation*, Paris, C. Douniol, 1859.

39   Cesare Tondini de' Quarenghi, *La prière et l'appui du Saint-Siège et de l'Épiscopat dans l'œuvre de la réunion*

In Germany, Baron August von Haxthausen, who had traveled to Russia and was in contact with Orthodox personalities, supported Fr. Gagarin's projects and also encouraged prayers for unity, in which he hoped the Orthodox would join. To this end, in 1857, he founded the *Petrusverein*, which received approval from the German bishops and, in 1858, a letter from Pius IX.[40]

There was plenty of initiatives in the Slavic world, even though they came a little later and constantly referred to Cyril and Methodius, who had already been the symbolic base for political pan-Slavism.[41] From the end of the 1850s, Bishop Josip Juraj Strossmayer, the Croatian bishop of Đakovo, supported the restoration of the ancient Slavic rite in the Roman liturgy, which was perceived as a bridge between Catholicism and Orthodoxy. He corresponded with the Russian philosopher Vladimir Solovyov – who authored *Russia and the Universal Church* in 1889 and considered a Catholic-Orthodox reunion in a positive light – and with the Barnabite Tondini de' Quarenghi.[42]

Beginning in 1892, St. Methodius's ancient Episcopal See, the village of Velehrad, Moravia,

became the headquarters of a confraternity, the Apostolate of Sts. Cyril and Methodius, which had nearly 60,000 members in 1895.[43] For their part, the Assumptionists of the Eastern mission favored the *ad tollendum scisma* votive Mass (a not compulsory Mass, left to the personal devotion of each priest) that had been composed at the end of the 14th century during the Great Occidental Schism.[44] They undertook to celebrate it at least once a month in the Archconfraternity of Our Lady of the Assumption, an "association of prayers and charitable works for the unity of the churches, established as an archconfraternity *prima primaria*" by Leo XIII on May 25, 1898 in the church of the Anastasis (Resurrection) in Constantinople.[45]

In Russia, under the influence of the French Assumptionists, an Archiconfrérie de Notre Dame de l'Assomption, pour l'Union des Églises was created in 1908 in St. Petersburg, bringing "zealots" together on the first Friday of each month for a Slavic rite Mass followed by talks on the theme of union.[46]

Outside the Old Continent, the Society of the Atonement was created in the United States by Lewis Thomas (Paul James) Wattson. In 1900, in Graymoor, this Episcopalian priest founded a community inspired by Franciscan spirituality and dedicated to prayer for Christian unity. It was not until 1909 that Wattson, with his group of about ten persons, officially joined the Catholic Church and the Franciscan third order. He was ordained a priest in 1910.[47] Wattson was at the origin of the octave of prayer for Christian unity celebrated

des églises: Notice historique sur l'association de prières et l'honneur de Marie Immaculée pour le retour de l'Église gréco-russe à l'unité catholique, Paris, E. Plon, 1876, esp. 100–119.

40 Albert Marie Ammann, "Über das Gebet für die Wiedervereinigung der Kirchen (Ein Briefwechsel)," *OCP* 24, 1958, 276–308 and 25, 1959, 114–126; S. Frederick Starr, "August von Haxthausen and Russia," *SEER* 46, 1968, 462–478.

41 Angelo Tamborra, "La riscoperta di Cirillo e Metodio nel secolo XIX e il suo significato," in: Edward G. Farrugia, Robert F. Taft & Gino Piovesana, eds., *Christianity among the Slavs: The Heritage of Saints Cyril and Methodius: Acts of the International Congress Held on the Eleventh Centenary of the Death of St. Methodius: Rome, October 8–11, 1985*, Rome, PIO, 1988, 315–342.

42 See especially Rita Tolomeo, "L'unione delle Chiese nei rapporti tra J.J. Strossmayer e il barnabita Cesare Tondini de' Quarenghi," in: Grgo Grbešić, Darija Damjanović Barišić & Tomislav Mrkonjić, eds., *Josip Juraj Strossmayer (1815–2015): Đakovo, 1.–2. listopada 2015*, Đakovo, Katolički bogoslovni fakultet u Đakovu, 2017, 235–249.

43 Franz Machilek, "Welehrad und die Cyrill-Method Idee im 19. und 20. Jahrhundert," *AKBMS* 6, 156–183, here 163.

44 Robert Amiet, "La messe pour l'unité des chrétiens," *RevScRel* 28, 1954, 1–35.

45 Séverien J. Salaville, *Messes votives pour l'Union des Églises et pour la propagation de la foi*, Paris, Desclée de Brouwer, 1922, 5.

46 Report of Fr. Bois "on the Catholic movement of the Russian-Greek rite in Petersburg" (1907–1909), 67, in: ASRS, AAEESS, Rapporti delle Sessioni, 1126, 1909, Ponenza, Sommario Num. V.

47 Titus Cranny, *Le Père Paul Wattson, apôtre de l'Unité*, Paris, M. Lévêque, 1956, esp. 34–36.

between Jan 18 and 25, each day of the octave being dedicated to a specific intention (the Eastern Churches, the Anglicans, etc.).[48] This special kind of prayer was first observed in 1908. The initiative received Pius x's blessing at the end of 1909 and was then officially encouraged by Benedict xv on Feb 25, 1916.[49] The Protestant Faith and Order commission recommended its adoption in 1915.[50]

Alongside these prayer associations, several institutions were created to nurture and disseminate the intellectual unionist work: libraries, journals, and conferences. In 1855, the Russian Jesuits planned a "Slavic library" in France that, at the beginning of the 20th century, thanks to the work of Fr. Paul Pierling and despite many relocations, became a unique instrument for scholars interested in Slavic ecclesiastical issues.[51] In Velehrad, a "Cyril and Methodius" library was established as a consequence of the widespread interest in gathering sources and material on other Christian confessions. In Rome, the Vatican Library, wishing "to obtain the best collection [of Russian works] for academics,"[52] entrusted Fr. Aurelio Palmieri (who was already recognized for his knowledge of Orthodoxy, even in Russian ecclesiastic circles)[53] with a collection mission. As for the Assumptionists, they established a library in

Constantinople that was focused on Eastern topics and unity.[54]

Journals completed the picture. They ensured the dissemination of knowledge and the structuring of the Catholic orientalist and unionist sphere.[55] Several journals were created in the 1890s: *Bessarione* (1896), *Revue de l'Orient Chrétien* (1896), and *Échos d'Orient* (1897). Between 1905 and 1910, other titles blossomed such as *Slavorum Litterae Theologicae* (Prague, 1905) and *Roma e l'Oriente* (1910). The Eastern focus was clear: questions related to Protestantism and more global approaches hardly emerged, apart from Abbé Fernand Portal's ephemerals *Revue Anglo-Romaine* (1895–1896) and *Revue Catholique des Églises* (1904–1908).

The structuring of the Eastern unionist sphere finally came about thanks to the Velehrad conferences.[56] The first was held in July 1907. It brought together 76 participants and joined "scholarly theological and historical essays" with a "discussion of practical ways to attract dissident

---

48   Cranny, *Le Père Paul Wattson*, 28.

49   Benedict xv, *Romanorum Pontificum*, in: AAS 9, 1917, 61–63.

50   Roger Aubert, ed., *Unité: La semaine de prière pour l'unité chrétienne*, Bruxelles, Pro Apostolis, 1959, 7.

51   See Laura Pettinaroli, "L'Opera dei SS. Cirillo e Metodio in Francia: Un'opera slava al di fuori del mondo slavo," in: Emília Hrabovec, Pierantonio Piatti & Rita Tolomeo, eds., *I santi Cirillo e Metodio e la loro eredità religiosa e culturale ponte tra Oriente e Occidente: Raccolta di studi in occasione del 1150° anniversario della missione dei santi Cirillo e Metodio nella Grande Moravia (863–2013)*, Vatican City, Libreria Editrice Vaticana, 2015, 235–250.

52   "Cronaca contemporanea: Cose romane," *CivCatt* 56/1, 1905, 479–481, here 480.

53   "Il 'Bessarione' e la 'Viera' i Tzerkov di Mosca," *Bessarione* 8/73, 1903, 129–132.

54   Matthieu Cassin, "Au milieu des livres: Constitution et fonctions de la bibliothèque de l'IFEB," in: Marie-Hélène Blanchet & Ionuț-Alexandru Tudorie, eds., *L'apport des Assomptionnistes français aux études byzantines: Une approche critique: Actes du colloque de Bucarest, 25–27 septembre 2014*, Paris, Institut français d'études byzantines, 2017, 65–167.

55   Olivier Poncet, "Les revues orientalistes à Rome sous Léon XIII: L'exemple du *Bessarione* (1896–1903)," in: Philippe Levillain & Jean-Marc Ticchi, eds., *Le pontificat de Léon XIII: Renaissances du Saint-Siège?*, Rome, École française de Rome, 2006, 379–388. See also Croce, *La Badia Greca*; Étienne Fouilloux, "Les Échos d'Orient (1897–1908)," in: Bernard Holzer, ed., *Mgr Petit, assomptionniste, fondateur des Échos d'Orient, archevêque latin d'Athènes (1868–1927)*, Rome, PIO, 2002, 69–85. More generally, see Aurélien Girard, "Connaître l'Orient chrétien au prisme de l'unionisme: Remarques sur le traitement des christianismes orientaux dans le *Dictionnaire de théologie catholique* (1899–1950)," in: Sylvio Hermann De Franceschi, ed., *Théologie et érudition de la crise moderniste à Vatican II: Autour du Dictionnaire de théologie catholique*, Limoges, PULIM, 2014, 131–148.

56   Peter Esterka, "Toward Union: The Congresses at Velehrad," *JES* 8, 1971, 10–51.

Slavs to the path of Catholicism."[57] The Holy See sent a telegram of encouragement.[58] Other conferences followed in 1909 and 1911, even welcoming some Orthodox participants such as the chaplain of the embassy in Berlin, Alexei Petrovich Maltsev, who, in 1909, called for a "rapprochement between East and West" in order to prevent "atheism" and "disbelief."[59]

In the few decades from the 1850s to 1914, the Western Catholic world endowed libraries and specialized journals focusing on the issue of unity, especially with Eastern Christians. It harbored a small group of militants, particularly scholars, who were the bearers of a profound concern for union.

2.3 Unionism: Between Catholic Apologetics and the Recognition of Christian Diversity

What exactly meant the desire of unity to these unionist groups? What was their idea of Christian diversity and unity?

One of the practices they used most – the prayer – is revealing in this respect. While prayers for unity are as old as the church and its first divisions, new forms emerged in the 19th century. As early as 1856, the Œuvre des Saints Cyrille et Méthode, sponsored by the Jesuits, proposed using the traditional prayers of the Our Father and the Hail Mary, but also "the invocation St. Cyril and St. Methodius Pray for Us" and the "solemn Mass on July 8, the feast of Sts. Cyril and Methodius, Apostles to the Slavs,"[60] thus integrating these spiritual figures appreciated by the Orthodox and who preceded the separation. Among the

Barnabites, a frequently used prayer addressed to Mary Immaculate consisted of texts from the Greek-Slavic liturgy.[61]

Beyond prayer *for* unity, the Eastern rites were envisaged as the concrete demonstration of the unity of the Catholic Church: a unity that did respect the diversity of Christian identities. Within the Society of Jesus, Fr. Gagarin planned to found a seminary for priests of the Eastern rite.[62] It was not until 1912, however, that another Jesuit, the Frenchman Michel d'Herbigny, succeeded in establishing the seminary of the Holy Angels in Enghien, Belgium, specifically dedicated to Russian priests.[63] Other congregations were committed to this vision, such as the Assumptionists, who wanted to "work for the union of the churches through respect for, and maintenance of, the ancient rites."[64] At the first Congress of Velehrad on July 27, 1907, a "pontifical" Mass in the Ruthenian rite was celebrated by Bishop Andrej Sheptytsky.[65]

The other great method of union – the scholarly study of the separated Christian churches – is also significant to understand the way the Catholic unionists of the 19th century conceived union. Traditionally, the study of the separated churches aimed, above all, at collecting arguments for the controversy. And even the irenic *Revue Anglo-Romaine* insisted on the need for reliable arguments concerning the debated issue of Anglican orders.[66] In a more subtle manner, Catholic scholars collected texts from the Orthodox tradition in order to demonstrate its involuntary and unconscious Catholicism. In the 1860s, Fr. Gagarin and Fr. Tondini used liturgical and patristic sources to highlight the Orthodox recognition of papal

57   "Velehrad, Moravia, Nostra corrispondenza," *CivCatt* 58/4, 1907, 122–126, here 124.

58   *Acta I, Conventus Velehradensis: Theologorum commercii studiorum inter Occidentem et Orientem cupidorum*, Prague, Rohlíček & Sievers, 1908, 7.

59   "Il secondo congresso cattolico dell'unione delle chiese," *CivCatt* 60/3, 1909, 605–610, here 606–607. On Alexei Petrovich Maltsev, see *BBKL* 5, 610–613.

60   Statutes of the Œuvre des saints Cyrille et Méthode, in: AFSJ, Slavic Library, Gagarin 4a, doc. 1bis.

61   Tondini de' Quarenghi, *La prière et l'appui du Saint-Siège*, doc. 7, 94–95.

62   Pettinaroli, "L'Opera dei SS. Cirillo e Metodio," 246.

63   Léon Tretjakewitsch, *Bishop Michel d'Herbigny SJ and Russia: A Pre-Ecumenical Approach to Christian Unity*, Wurzburg, Augustinus-Verlag, 1990, 48–51.

64   Vincent de Paul Bailly, "À nos lecteurs," *Échos d'Orient* 1, 1897, 1–2, here 2.

65   "Velehrad, Moravia, Nostra corrispondenza," 125.

66   Fernand Portal, "Pour l'union," *RAR* 1/1, 1895, 8.

primacy.[67] However, scholarly research on the history, doctrine, and liturgies of the Eastern Churches was not only considered from a controversial perspective, but also led to new perspectives of rapprochement.

The Italian Augustinian Aurelio Palmieri wrote an extensive essay in Latin presenting Orthodox systematic theology, thus illuminating the other's point of view in a Catholic philosophical language.[68] At times, other Christian traditions were seen as a source of inspiration. From 1902 to 1903, the Benedictine Dom Antoine Staerk published the diary of Fr. John of Kronstadt (also known as St. John of Kronstadt), a great Orthodox figure of piety and charity, in order to make accessible his spirituality, which had many "similarities" to Catholicism, even if it consisted of nothing "new."[69]

This kind of paradoxical formulations reveals the delicate balance of unionism, between the search for a common ground and the need to be different. It can also be explained by the caution required in undertaking any move toward unity. The specter of indifferentism, repeatedly condemned by the Roman authorities,[70] was never far off. Was there not a risk – in recognizing, even only occasionally, the equal dignity of Christian confessions – that the one and only Catholic way to salvation would be devalued? Indeed, some unionist initiatives aroused Rome's suspicion.

The essay of the Anglican convert Ambrose Phillipps – *The Future Unity of Christendom* (1857) – was threatened to be placed on the Index. The organization that he founded with Anglicans – the APUC, which had more than 7,000 members in 1864 and even received the support of the Patriarch of Constantinople Joachim – was condemned on Sept 16, 1864, in a letter from Cardinal Costantino Patrizi Naro. This condemnation was caused both by the pressure from English Catholics, who feared a decrease in individual conversions, and by the fact that common prayers with "dissidents" and the definition of Greek and Anglican Churches as "Catholic" posed grave problems to the Roman authorities.[71] Unionist caution, which manifested itself in a continual citing of the texts of the Roman magisterium,[72] became even more accentuated after the Modernist crisis began in 1908.

Finally, it should be noted that the unionist dynamic of the 19th century led to important changes in some Catholic practices, such as the way other Christians were named. As early as 1830–1840, French-speaking Catholics interested in the movement for unity with the Anglican Church, such as Gondon, readily used the terms "Anglo-Catholic" and "separated brethren," although these expressions, in this context, sometimes accentuated the distance (the expression "lost brothers" was also

---

67   Jean-Xavier Gagarin, *La primauté de saint Pierre et les livres liturgiques de l'Église russe*, Paris, C. Douniol, 1863; Cesare Tondini de' Quarenghi, *La primauté de S. Pierre prouvée par les titres que lui donne l'Église russe dans sa liturgie*, Paris, V. Palmé, 1867.

68   Aurelio Palmieri, *Theologia dogmatica orthodoxa (Ecclesiae Graeco-Russicae) ad lumen catholicae doctrinae examinata et discussa*, 2 vols., Florence, Libreria Editrice Fiorentina, 1911–1913.

69   Antoine Staerk, *Le P. Jean de Cronstadt, archiprêtre de l'Église russe*, vol. 2, *Sa doctrine dogmatique et son influence morale: Étude historique et critique*, Paris, P. Lethielleux, 1903, 169, 172–173, 186. More broadly, Nadieszda Kizenko, "Ioann of Kronstadt and the Reception of Sanctity (1850–1988)," *RusR* 57, 1998, 325–344.

70   A section of Pius IX's *Syllabus*, annexed to the encyclical *Quanta cura* (Dec 8, 1864), is dedicated to it (condemned propositions 15–18). Number 18 specifically condemns the statement that "Protestantism is nothing else than a different form of the same true Christian religion"; the text can be found at

<http://www.papalencyclicals.net/pius09/p9syll.htm> (accessed July 8, 2020).

71   Mark D. Chapman, "The Fantasy of Reunion: The Rise and Fall of the Association for the Promotion of the Unity of Christendom," *JEH* 58, 2007, 49–74, esp. 56–62. In this volume see the contribution by Peter Nockles.

72   The journal *Bessarione*, under the direction of Msgr. Niccolò Marini, stated that *Praeclara gratulationis* and *Orientalium dignitas* were the "guidelines" of this journal; "Il nostro programma," *Bessarione* 1, 1896, 2–3, here 2.

used).[73] In 1852, the Passionist Ignatius Spencer advised Pius IX to use the term "acatholic" instead of "heretical."[74] With regard to Eastern Christians, the term "Orthodox" was already well "received among Catholics in 1913 ... in reference to the schismatic Greek Church."[75] Finally, at the turn of the 20th century, the Catholic vocabulary had changed, using ever less the words "heretics" and "schismatics," and ever more the term of "dissidents." Unionists, such as Fernand Portal, for their part, went further and encouraged the use of the expression "separated brethren."[76]

In order to replace this unionist trend in the Catholic Church within the more general context of Romanization and the progress of Vatican centralization, let us now focus on the specific role of the popes and the magisterium.

3 The Roman Laboratory of Unionism: Doctrinal Corpus, Liturgical Expressions, and Administrative Practices

The magisterium got involved in the issue of Christian unity in the 1840s, addressing public appeals to the "dissidents" and to the Catholics but also, more discreetly, introducing new devotional and administrative practices.

3.1 Theological Keystones: The Pontifical Unionist Corpus

Theologians and historians have commented extensively on the great texts about union, especially those of Leo XIII.[77] However, the fundamental articulations of unionist discourse were already established during Pius IX's pontificate and remained stable until the middle of the 20th century. From one pope to another, the corpus remains coherent, whether it concerns the arguments put forward (the common origin with the East, defined as the birthplace of Christianity, the Apostolic See as the center of unity), the biblical references employed (John 10:16: "One flock, one shepherd"; John 17:21–23: "That they may all be one"; passages defining Peter's role), or the disciplinary disposals (maintaining Eastern liturgies and customs).

The first significant text was Pius IX's encyclical letter *In suprema Petri Apostoli Sede*, addressed to the heads of the Eastern Churches on Jan 6, 1848, the feast of the Epiphany, celebrating Jesus' manifestation to the nations.[78] Roger Aubert has shown that the text was written under the influence of a group formed by Princess Elizabeth Volkonskaia, a convert from Orthodoxy, Fr. Giovanni Corboli Bussi (who, in the late 1840s, played a role in negotiations with Russia), and Fr. Augustin Theiner (who worked at the Vatican Library and authored a study on Catholic persecutions in the Russian Empire), together with the founders of the Polish congregation of the Resurrectionists.[79]

---

73 Jeremy Morris, "'Separated Brethren': French Catholics and the Oxford Movement," in: Brown & Nockles, eds., *The Oxford Movement*, 203–220, esp. 219.

74 Tondini de' Quarenghi, *La prière et l'appui du Saint-Siège*, 36–37. During the pontificate of Gregory XVI – who was worried about the Bible societies that distributed the Scriptures –, the pontifical documents on Protestantism use both the terms of "heretics" and "acatholics." For example, Gregory XVI uses "heretics" in *Probe nostis*, Aug 15, 1840; the text can be found at <https://www.papalencyclicals.net/greg16/g16probe.htm> (accessed July 8, 2020), but "acatholics of various denominations" in *Inter praecipuas*, May 8, 1844; the text can be found at <https://www.papalencyclicals.net/greg16/g16inter.htm> (accessed July 8, 2020).

75 "Calendrier orthodoxe," *Annuaire pontifical catholique*, 1913, 17–38, here 17. In a text of Feb 2, 1898, Cardinal Langénieux referred to the "Orthodox feast days" without putting the term "Orthodox" into quotation marks; see *Instruction pastorale de Son Eminence le Cardinal Langénieux*, 8.

76 Fernand Portal, "Pour l'union."

77 Gregory Baum, *That They May Be One: A Study of Papal Doctrine (Leo XIII to Pius XII)*, London, Bloomsbury, 1958; Rosario Francesco Esposito, *Leone XIII e l'Oriente cristiano: Studio storico-sistematico*, Rome, Edizioni Paoline, 1961.

78 Pius IX, "Lettre de N.S.P. le Pape Pie IX," *Irén* 6, 1929, 666–678.

79 Roger Aubert, "Les relations entre les églises occidentales et les églises orthodoxes slaves aux XIXᵉ et XXᵉ siècles," in: Pontifical Lateran University, Catholic University of Lublin, ed., *The Common Christian Roots*

This call of Pius IX "to return to the true Church and to communion with the Holy See"[80] provoked a violent response in May 1848 from 4 patriarchs and 29 bishops gathered in Constantinople.[81] The result was exactly opposite to expectations: an increased opposition between the Eastern and Western churches.[82] Despite that failure, twenty years later, at the opening of Vatican I, Pius IX launched a new public appeal for unity, an encyclical addressed "to all the bishops of the Churches of the Eastern rite who are not in communion with the Apostolic See"[83] and another "to all Protestants and other acatholics."[84] Responses were again negative and the Council, which had opened on Dec 8, 1869, symbolized the peak – in the continuity of the bull *Reversurus* of 1867 – of the affirmation of the Roman hegemony on the Eastern Churches.[85] Despite the important liturgical and canonical work accomplished by the commission in charge of Eastern rites,[86] the Council remained uncompleted after it was suspended *sine die* due to the international situation and the entry of the Italian army in Rome. Furthermore, the definition of the dogma of papal infallibility in the constitution *Pastor aeternus* of July 18, 1870 was criticized by many bishops engaged in unionism, such as Bishop Strossmayer.[87] The schism of the Old

Catholics, which grew out of the radical criticism of infallibility and which was organized into a federation with the Union of Utrecht in 1889, aroused the interest of other Christian churches, particularly the Anglicans[88] and Russian Orthodox.[89]

Elected in 1878, when the weakening of the Ottoman Empire was confirmed after the Congress of Berlin,[90] Leo XIII also issued many texts on union. In the first two years of his reign, he intervened no fewer than twenty times on Eastern and Slavic issues, demonstrating that union with these churches had become a priority.[91] A few years later he revealed that his commitment on this question came from a "heavenly impulse."[92] The culmination of Leo XIII's Eastern policy occurred in the early 1890s with the Eucharistic Congress in Jerusalem which, from May 15 to 20, 1893, brought

of the European Nations: An International Colloquium in the Vatican, vol. 2, *Written Contributions to the Twelve Carrefours*, Florence, Le Monnier, 1982, 3–17, here 5.

80   Pius IX, "Lettre de N.S.P. le Pape Pie IX," 676–677.

81   Text in Hélène Auffret-Pignot & Démétrius Dallas, eds., *Encycliques des patriarches orthodoxes de 1848 et 1895*, Paris, Fraternité orthodoxe Saint Grégoire Palamas, 1986, 10–50.

82   Tamborra, "Pio IX, la lettera agli Orientali."

83   Pius IX, *Arcano divinae*, in: ASS 4, 1868, 129–131.

84   Pius IX, *Iam vos omnes*, in: ASS 4, 1868, 131–135.

85   Constantin G. Patelos, *Vatican I et les évêques uniates: Une étape éclairante de la politique romaine à l'égard des Orientaux (1867–1870)*, Louvain-la-Neuve, Collège Érasme, 1981, 55–77.

86   Patelos, *Vatican I et les évêques uniates*, 388–421.

87   Johannes Beumer, "Der Primat des Papstes und die Union mit den Kirchen des Ostens im Blickfeld des Ersten Vatikanischen Konzils," OS 19, 1970, 167–184; Andrija Šuljak, *Il Vescovo J.J. Strossmayer e il Concilio*

Vaticano I, Rome, Pontificia Universitas Gregoriana, 1995.

88   The contacts were immediate, and the Anglican Church showed its openness to a more formal relationship beginning in 1888. However, intercommunion was not established until 1931 with the Bonn agreement; see Colin Buchanan, "Old Catholics," in: Colin Buchanan, *Historical Dictionary of Anglicanism*, Lanham, Rowman & Littlefield, ²2015, 445–447. On the relations between Anglicans and the German speaking Old Catholics, see the contribution in the third volume of this work by Peter-Ben Smit.

89   John D. Basil, "The Russian Theological Academies and the Old Catholics (1870–1905)," in: Charles Timberlake, ed., *Religious and Secular Forces in Late Tsarist Russia: Essays in Honor of Donald W. Treadgold*, Seattle WA, University of Washington Press, 1992, 90–104. See also Eugène Michaud's interest in the East and Russia: Raoul Dederen, *Un réformateur catholique au XIXᵉ siècle: Eugène Michaud (1839–1917): Vieux-catholicisme, œcuménisme*, Genève, Droz, 1963.

90   Joseph Hajjar, *Le Vatican, la France et le catholicisme oriental (1878–1914): Diplomatie et histoire de l'Église*, Paris, Beauchesne, 1979; Giorgio Del Zanna, *Roma e l'Oriente: Leone XIII e l'Impero ottomano (1878–1903)*, Milano, Guerini e associati, 2003.

91   Esposito, *Leone XIII e l'Oriente cristiano*, 702–703.

92   Leo XIII, "Praecipui a sanctissimo domino nostro Leone pp. XIII habiti sermones anno MDCCCXCV – I. Die II Martii ad S.R.E. cardinales redeunte coronationis die," in: Leo XIII, *Leonis XIII: Pontificis Maximi Acta*, vol. 15, Rome, Ex Typographia Vaticana, 1896, 432.

together in the holy city many Eastern and Latin prelates around the figure of Cardinal Legate Benoît-Marie Langénieux.[93]

On June 20, 1894, his apostolic letter *Praeclara gratulationis*, addressed "to the rulers and peoples of the whole world," launched a broad appeal for international concord and "human brotherhood" but also relaunched the call to Eastern Christians and Protestants (here referred to as "the peoples who – in more recent times – [were] separated from the Roman Church") for "reconciliation and union with the Roman Church." Although this text appeared as a new charter of unionism, it contained themes that had recurred since 1848, such as the primacy of the bishop of Rome and its ancient recognition by the East.[94]

A few weeks later, on Nov 30, 1894, his apostolic letter *Orientalium dignitas* was published: it was the result of the patriarchal conferences held in the Vatican in October and November that year. Focused on the Eastern Question, it confirmed Rome's desire to preserve Eastern disciplines and rites, protecting them from the initiatives of the missionaries of the Latin rite.[95] Two texts from 1896 complete this corpus. The encyclical *Satis cognitum* from June 29, 1896 offered an in-depth synthesis on church unity. The issue of union was here replaced in a broader context: within a church defined as the "mystical body" of Christ, the pope emphasized the gravity of schism (an attack on the church) and of heresy (a rupture in doctrine), and recalled his own role as guarantor of unity.[96] Then, on Sept 13, 1896, the apostolic

letter *Apostolicae curae* was published, rejecting the validity of Anglican orders and renewing appeals to return to the "flock."[97]

While posterity acknowledges these initiatives by Leo XIII, which were rather appreciated in the Protestant world, the Orthodox world received them as badly as those of Pius IX. The Patriarchate of Constantinople responded curtly to the overtures of the *Praeclara* in a text dated August 1895 and published on Sept 21, 1895, which dramatized the differences between Orthodox and Catholics.[98] In Russia, the encyclical indeed was translated and distributed "in a small, affordable, easy to consult volume,"[99] but the response was hostile. Belyaev, a professor of systematic theology at the Moscow Theological Academy, defined the Latins as "schismatics" and "heretics"[100] and their commitment to the unity of the churches as a form of "propaganda

93   Claude Soetens, *Le Congrès eucharistique international de Jérusalem (1893): Dans le cadre de la politique orientale du pape Léon XIII*, Leuven, Éditions Nauwelaerts, 1977; Esposito, *Leone XIII e l'Oriente cristiano*, 373–379.

94   Leo XIII, *Praeclara gratulationis*, in: ASS 26, 1893–1894, 705–717.

95   Leo XIII, *Orientalium dignitas*, in: ASS 27, 1894–1895, 257–264.

96   Leo XIII, *Satis cognitum*, June 29, 1896; the text can be found at <https://www.papalencyclicals.net/leo13/l13satis.htm> (accessed July 8, 2020). See also the analysis of the encyclical in Esposito, *Leone XIII e l'Oriente cristiano*, 420–456.

97   Leo XIII, *Apostolicae curae*, in: ASS 29, 1896–1897, 193–203. On the Anglican orders, see Paul Avis's contribution in this volume.

98   The text can be found in Auffret-Pignot & Dallas, eds., *Encycliques des patriarches*, 51–73; Job Getcha, "La lettre encyclique patriarcale et synodale du Siège de Constantinople de 1895 en réponse au Concile Vatican I et au pape Léon XIII," *Istina* 54, 2009, 361–385. Catholic apologists issued many responses to the patriarch, such as that of the Italian Jesuit Salvatore Maria Brandi, *De l'Union des Églises: Réponse à la Lettre encyclique du Patriarche grec de Constantinople*, Rome, Imprimerie du Vatican, 1896, or also that of an anonymous Catholic priest, *Réponse à la lettre patriarcale et synodale de l'Église de Constantinople sur les divergences qui divisent les deux Églises*, Constantinople, A. Zellich, 1896.

99   Victor Petrovich Gajduk, "Russia e Vaticano tra XIX e XX secolo: Il dialogo secondo materiali d'archivio inediti," in: Massimiliano Valente, ed., *Santa Sede e Russia da Leone XIII a Pio XI: Atti del Simposio organizzato dal Pontificio Comitato di scienze storiche e dall'Istituto di storia universale dell'Accademia delle scienze di Mosca: Mosca, 23–25 giugno 1998*, Vatican City, Libreria Editrice Vaticana, 2002, 43–61, here 46.

100   Alexander Dmitrievich Belyaev, *O soedinenii cerkvej: Razbor èncikliki papy L'va XIII ot 20ì junja 1894 goda* [On church reunion: Analysis of Pope Leo XIII's encyclical of 20 June 1894], Sergiyev Posad, Snegireva, 1897, 63.

for their Latin faith."[101] These very negative reactions may explain that Leo XIII, at the end of his pontificate, and his successor Pius X published no more comprehensive texts on Christian unity.

Pius X's silence on the issue of unity is well known. However, this silence was not complete: his address to Eastern Catholics on Feb 13, 1908 returned to all the usual themes of unionism.[102] And, furthermore, the Modernist crisis had a great impact on his pontificate in this regard. Although unionism was never identified with Modernism, some of its aspects aroused the suspicion of the ecclesiastical authorities. For instance, the ordination of married men was an exception to ecclesial celibacy that might provoke a discussion of the rules in force in Latin Catholicism,[103] and historical study into the separation of the churches raised the question of the historical development of dogma. However, it was the crisis that erupted concerning Fr. Maximilian of Saxony, known for his *Praelectiones de liturgiis Orientalibus*,[104] that effectively associated unionism with Modernism.

In November 1910, Fr. Maximilian was invited to submit an article for the first issue of the unionist journal of Grottaferrata, *Roma e l'Oriente*. His article, entitled "Pensées sur la question de l'union des Églises," revisited the usual unionist doctrines but also proposed that the Eastern Churches maintain their dogma and encouraged the Western Church to acknowledge its faults in the birth and perpetuation of the schism. On Dec 26, the article was condemned in the letter *Ex quo*, and the pope asked pontifical representatives in the

East to reassert official doctrine on the reunion of the churches.[105] This crisis, which formed part of the context of anti-Modernist repression,[106] was widely publicized, particularly in Orthodox countries.[107] Despite these tensions, Pius X, following in the footsteps of his predecessors, contributed to the development of prayer for unity.

3.2   *The Popes and Prayer for Unity*

While prayer for church unity, rooted in specific liturgical moments (such as the Eucharistic Prayer and Good Friday prayers) has a long history, it has evolved since the second half of the 19th century. During Pius IX's pontificate, Rome acted mainly encouraging local initiatives through indulgences. Leo XIII's pontificate clearly amplified the magisterium's involvement and brought prayer for unity under Roman auspices. Promulgated on Sept 30, 1880, the encyclical *Grande munus* included the feasts of Sts. Cyril and Methodius in the calendar of the universal church so that those saints "might intercede with God and watch over Christianity in the East. May there be constancy in all Catholic men and the will to reconcile all dissidents to the true Church."[108]

In 1893, the Eucharistic Congress in Jerusalem – considered by the pope "a quiet but eloquent invitation to come and join with [the Catholic pilgrims] in a single and shared sense of faith, hope, and charity"[109] – was the occasion for many celebrations in the various Eastern Catholic rites. At the

---

101   Belyaev, *O soedinenìi cerkvej*, 36. More in general on the Russian reception, see Cesare Tondini de' Quarenghi, *La Russie et l'Union des Églises*, Paris, P. Lethielleux, 1897.

102   Pius X, *Allocutio ad Orientales*, in: ASS 41, 1908, 130–134.

103   Moreover, the objections raised by the "Modernists" to the "ecclesiastical celibacy" was harshly criticized by Pius X in September 1907 as an influence of the "Protestant masters"; *Pascendi dominici gregis*, in: ASS 40, 1907, 593–650.

104   Prince Maximilian of Saxony, *Praelectiones de liturgiis orientalibus: Habitae in Universitate Friburgensi Helvetiae*, 2 vols., Freiburg i.Br., Herder, 1908–1913.

105   Prince Maximilian of Saxony, "Pensées sur la question de l'union des Églises," *Roma e l'Oriente* 1, 1910, 13–29; Pius X, *Ex quo*, in: AAS 3, 1911, 117–121.

106   Croce, *La Badia Greca*, vol. 2, 158–170; Giorgio Del Zanna, "L'incontro con il cristianesimo orientale: 'Roma e l'Oriente,'" in: Marina Benedetti & Daniela Saresella, eds., *La riforma della Chiesa nelle riviste religiose di inizio Novecento*, Milan, Biblioteca francescana, 2010, 263–281, here 270–271.

107   Croce, *La Badia Greca*, vol. 2, 146–158.

108   Leo XIII, *Grande munus*, in: ASS 13, 1880, 145–153.

109   Audience of Leo XIII with pilgrims from the congress, Apr 15, 1893, cited in: *Congrès des œuvres eucharistiques tenu à Jérusalem les 28, 29 et 30 juin 1893*, Paris, P. Féron-Vrau, 1906, xxxi.

end of the congress, many of the conclusive wishes concerned the prayer for the East and the spreading of Eastern prayers in the West.[110] On Apr 15, 1895, Leo XIII's letter to the English, *Amantissimae voluntatis*, included an indulgenced prayer to the Virgin in which he implored that she "intercede for our dissident brothers so that they might be united with us in the only true flock of the supreme pastor, the vicar of your Son on earth."[111]

A few days later, on May 5, 1895, his brief *Provida matris* specified that the novena in preparation for the feast of Pentecost was to be performed with the particular intention of "reconciling our dissident brothers."[112] Finally, on May 9, 1897, the encyclical *Divinum illud munus* on the Holy Spirit[113] prescribed the novena to all parish churches. Prayer for unity was associated with an important feast, placing it therefore within the liturgical cycle. Imposed by Roman authority, it was relayed by the bishops[114] and encouraged by publications that mentioned the issue of union, although not necessarily highlighting this dimension.[115]

In turn, Pius X encouraged prayer for unity, as we have seen with the impulse given in 1909 to the octave of prayer for Christian unity launched from the United States by Fr. Paul Wattson. Pius X, above all, pioneered the integration of the Eastern rite into the ceremonies of pontifical Rome.[116] In the occasion of the fifteenth centenary of the death of St. John Chrysostom in 1907, Pius X wanted to celebrate Eastern rite ceremonies "in St. Peter's Basilica at the Vatican itself," which preserved relics of the saint, in order that "the Easterners separated from us may see and understand in what great and profound esteem We equally hold all the rites and that they may draw the conclusion ... to return to the saving embrace of their mother of old."[117]

Finally, on Feb 12, 1908, the ceremony took place in the Hall of Beatifications. The pope was not one of the celebrants, but the liturgy attributed him an important role: he entered on the *sedia gestatoria* wearing the papal crown, blessed the incense in Greek, which he pronounced "in the Eastern way," and invoked peace on the assembly in Greek before reading the Gospel.[118] The pope also enriched with indulgences the recitation of prayers in honor of St. John Chrysostom, "or any other prayer for the union of the churches," as well as three hymns to the Trinity used in the Greek liturgy.[119] This Catholic celebration of the anniversary of Chrysostom's death incited fiercely hostile reactions. The Greek Patriarchate decided not to organize anything, while the Russian Church tried to "compete with Catholicism in exalting the Holy Doctor."[120] Beyond the structuration of a theological corpus and the regulation of the liturgical norms, Rome was also an administrative center, whose concrete management of Christian diversity needs to be considered.

3.3 The Management of Eastern Catholics and Non-Catholics: An Evolution in Curial Administrative Practices

Curial management of Christian diversity is a vast issue that could only be studied with a thorough knowledge of the Roman archives of the various dicasteries. In the lack of a general survey, we will

110 Esposito, *Leone XIII e l'Oriente cristiano*, 377–378.

111 Leo XIII, *Amantissimae voluntatis*, in: ASS 27, 1894–1895, 583–593.

112 Leo XIII, *Provida matris*, in: ASS 27, 1894–1895.

113 Leo XIII, *Divinum illud munus*, in: ASS 29, 1896–1897, 644–658.

114 *Instruction pastorale de Son Eminence le Cardinal Langénieux*.

115 Bernard-Marie Maréchaux, *Neuvaine au Saint-Esprit, d'après l'encyclique "Divinum illud munus" de N.S.P. le pape Léon XIII*, Paris, X. Rondelet, 1898.

116 These ceremonies would often be repeated under Pius XI; see Gabriel Acacius Coussa, "Le bienheureux Pie X et les Églises d'orient," *Apollinaris* 25, 1952, 143–149.

117 Pius X, *Prope est*, in: ASS 40, 1907, 453–455, here 454.

118 ASS 41, 1908, 404; Cyrille Charon, *Le quinzième centenaire de S. Jean Chrysostome (407–1907) et ses conséquences pour l'action catholique dans l'Orient gréco-slave*, Rome, Collège pontifical grec, 1909, 72–107.

119 The texts of these indulgences from 1907 and 1908 have been published in Korolevsky, *Le quinzième centenaire*, 362–365.

120 "Cronaca contemporanea: Cose straniere," *CivCatt* 58/4, 1907, 740–762, here 750–751.

only mention a few milestones, distinguishing the treatment of Eastern Catholics from that of non-Catholics.

3.3.1 Fostering Union through a Good Curial Management

Since the 17th century, Rome regularly manifested its estimation for the Eastern rites and, especially beginning with Benedict XIV's pontificate, emphasized on the preserving of their ancient traditions.[121] From around the middle of the 19th century, the Eastern rites received renewed attention. This was evidenced, first of all, in the creation of a section for Eastern rite affairs within the Propaganda Fide congregation on Jan 6, 1862,[122] that aimed to "deal with and resolve all issues of the Eastern Churches according to a single principle."[123] Alongside this search for coherence was a concern to develop a Roman expertise regarding the different rites. The cardinals who were members of the section were attached to a specific rite, and the new institution's first task was to collect concrete up-to-date information.

Despite the significant difficulties in the 1880s in recruiting Eastern language specialists,[124] the congregation successfully coordinated certain operations such as the publication of theological works on the procession of the Holy Spirit based on the patristic tradition[125] as well as the ordinary supervision of the liturgical practices.[126] Leo XIII's pontificate also enhanced Roman seminaries, which specialized in the training of priests in the Eastern rites. New resources were granted to the Armenian (1885) and Maronite (1894) colleges, the Greek College was reorganized (1897), and a Ruthenian College was founded (1897).[127] In 1881, near Rome, the "pure" Greek rite was restored at Grottaferrata Abbey.[128] Such efforts, however, were not enough to ease tensions between Eastern and Latin rites within the Catholic Church.[129] This was reflected in regular proposals for an institutional reform, to separate Eastern-rite Catholics from Propaganda Fide, a dicastery which initially targeted "infidels" to be evangelized. The Eucharistic Congress in Jerusalem brought this claim, which was supported by Cardinal Langénieux, out into the open.[130]

---

121   Aurélien Girard, "*Nihil esse innovandum*?: Maintien des rites orientaux et négociation de l'Union des Églises orientales avec Rome (fin XVIᵉ–mi-XVIIIᵉ s.)," in: Marie-Hélène Blanchet & Frédéric Gabriel, eds., *Réduire le schisme?: Ecclésiologies et politiques de l'Union entre Orient et Occident (XIIIᵉ–XVIIIᵉ siècle)*, Paris, ACHCByz, 2013, 337–352.

122   Pius IX, *Romani Pontifices*, in: Pius IX, *Pii IX: Pontificis Maximi Acta*, part I, vol. 3, Rome, Typographia bonarum artium, 1864, 402–416. On the context of the creation of the Congregatio de Propaganda Fide pro negotiis ritus orientalis, see Giacomo Martina, *Pio IX (1851–1866)*, Rome, Pontificia Università Gregoriana, 1986, 359–371.

123   Pius IX, *Amantissimus humani*, Apr 8, 1862; the text can be found at <https://www.papalencyclicals.net/pius09/p9amant2.htm> (accessed July 8, 2020). This text ordered a vast survey from the Eastern bishops who, significantly, were to deliver a report on their diocese, in particular verifying that its liturgical books were free of "error."

124   Several of the congregation's meetings were devoted to these questions around 1880, such as *Orientali:*

125   Johann Baptist Franzelin, *Examen doctrinae Macarii Bulgakow episcopi russi schismatici et Iosephi Langen neoprotestantis bonnensis de processione Spiritus Sancti: Paralipomenon Tractatus de SS. Trinitate*, Rome, Typographia Polyglotta, 1876.

126   Giuseppe Mojoli, *Attività liturgica della S. Congregazione "De Propaganda Fide" per gli Affari di Rito Orientale nel periodo 1862–1892*, Vicenza, Esca, 1977.

127   Umberto Benigni, "Roman Colleges," *OCE* 13, 131–136.

128   Sacra Congregatio de Propaganda Fide, ed., "Orientalium Ecclesiarum ritus," Apr 12, 1881, the document is cited in Croce, *La Badia Greca*, vol. 1, 199ff.

129   See Joseph Hajjar, *Le christianisme en Orient: Études d'histoire contemporaine (1684–1968)*, Beirut, Librairie du Liban, 1971, 114–133.

130   Congregatio pro Ecclesiis Orientalibus, ed., *Verbali delle conferenze patriarcali sullo stato delle chiese orientali e delle adunanze della commissione cardinalizia per promuovere la riunione delle chiese dissidenti tenute alla presenza del S.P. Leone XIII (1894–1902), con note illustrative e appendice di documenti*, Vatican City, Tipografia Poliglotta Vaticana, 1945, doc. 2, 340–342.

Sulla necessità di promuovere maggiormente e di consolidare lo studio delle lingue orientali: E sulla erezione di un collegio d'Interpreti Orientali a servizio della S. Congregazione, in: ACO, ponenza, Sept 26, 1877 (9).

At the time, Leo XIII gathered the Eastern hierarchs to Rome for "patriarchal conferences." Dissident bishops were also invited but they all declined the offer and only Catholic leaders participated in the five meetings held between Oct 24 and Nov 8, 1894.[131] Among the demands made were the creation of a commission for Eastern Catholics independent of Propaganda Fide and the development of the Eastern Churches without the intervention of Latin missionaries.[132] The publication of the apostolic letter *Orientalium dignitas* was a direct result of these meetings as well as the creation of a new curial institution. The motu proprio *Optatissimae* on Mar 19, 1895 created a "permanent ... commission responsible in particular for applying its zeal to the reconciliation of dissidents." In 1895, it included eight cardinals chosen by the pope, besides a "certain number of consultors" and "delegates" of the Eastern patriarchs.[133]

This institution thus expressed the concerns for integrating Easterners and for increasing expertise. It bridged the lack of legitimacy (commissions being less prestigious than congregations) through the personal support of the pope and cardinals. The reports of the commission's 22 meetings, held from 1894 to 1902, reveal its fields of interest, straddling the affairs of Eastern Catholics and those of the dissidents: the Eastern colleges in Rome, the publication of medieval documents on union, the ongoing massacres of Armenians in the Ottoman Empire, the Anglican question, etc.[134] This commission, however, did not last long. It was convened for the last time on July 20, 1902, and its independence and pontifical character were

abolished in 1908 with the constitution *Sapienti consilio*, which reattached it to Propaganda Fide.[135] In the pontifical yearbooks of 1909 and 1910, Pius X was still indicated as its president, but the commission definitively disappeared from the curial structure in 1911.[136]

3.3.2   Dealing with Christian Diversity: Designations and Sacraments

The way in which Vatican institutions handled relationships with non-Catholic Christians is an area of research that is attracting increasing numbers of studies, especially with regard to concrete contacts concerning the sacraments (participation in liturgical worship,[137] mixed marriages, and conversions requiring a profession of faith),[138] but the way the other Christians are named also merits further study.

The archives of the Congregation for the Doctrine of the Faith, in particular the "doubts" (*dubia*) regarding the sacraments that were submitted to Rome, allow us to study concretely how the curial institutions dealt with non-Catholic Christians. While the baptism of "schismatics" was generally recognized as valid,[139] the practice

---

131   Leo XIII would have especially desired the presence of "official representatives of the Greek-Russian Church, with the mission of expressing their desires and complaints"; Tondini de' Quarenghi, *La Russie et l'Union des Églises*, 119. Serbian Orthodox bishops were invited through Archbishop Josip Stadler; Esposito, *Leone XIII e l'Oriente cristiano*, 392.

132   Esposito, *Leone XIII e l'Oriente cristiano*, 394–395.

133   Leo XIII, *Optatissimae*, in: ASS 28, 1895–1896, 323–324.

134   Congregatio pro Ecclesiis Orientalibus, ed., *Verbali delle conferenze patriarcali*.

135   Pius X, *Sapienti consilio*, in: ASS 41, 1908, 462–490, here § 8.

136   In GC, 1909, 73, among the titles and attributions of Pius X is the presidency of the "Pontifical Commission for the Reunion of the Dissident Churches," but the commission no longer appears in the index and its composition is not indicated. The same appears in GC, 1910, 75. In GC, 1911, the presidency of the commission disappears from Pius X's titles.

137   *Communicatio in sacris* (or *in divinis*) was called "positive" when a Catholic participates in a non-Catholic service and "negative" when the inverse occurs. See Raoul Naz, "Communicatio in sacris," DDC 3, 1091–1095; Cesare Santus, "La *communicatio in sacris* con gli 'scismatici' orientali in età moderna," MEFRIM 126, 2014, 325–340.

138   Marie-Hélène Blanchet & Frédéric Gabriel, *L'Union à l'épreuve du formulaire: Professions de foi entre Églises d'Orient et d'Occident (XIIIᵉ–XVIIIᵉ siècle)*, Leuven, Peeters, 2016.

139   Baptism conferred in the Russian Orthodox Church was "generally considered valid" except for particular

of "conditional Baptism" (i.e. on the condition that it had not been validly conferred before) was very common. At the beginning of the 20th century, the Diocese of Paris' forms of abjuration foresaw the possibility of "conditional Baptism" in the case of a renunciation of "schism" or "heresy."[140] The same ambivalence existed for Confirmation: it was generally recognized as valid but, in practice, things were more complex. In 1907, Pius X granted Jesuits travelling to Russia the power to confer the sacrament of Confirmation on converts from Orthodoxy because "this sacrament, administered by schismatic priests, is often invalid or somewhat dubious."[141]

The sacrament of marriage was undoubtedly the one about which Roman authorities were most frequently asked in both Central Europe and North America during the 19th century. Its regulation articulated a great firmness on principles (the rejection of mixed marriages) with a flexible adaptation to the local balance of interconfessional relations. The issue was not so much concerning marriage (for which dispensations could be granted) as for the faith and education of future children.[142]

With regard to the sacrament of Holy Orders, conversions of members of the Orthodox clergy

raised fewer questions about their validity than practical problems (integration into an equivalent rank, status of the possible wife).[143] During the 1890s, the magisterium reexamined the validity of Anglican orders, especially as several Catholic scholars (such as Fr. Fernand Portal, who was in contact with Lord Halifax, an Anglican viscount, and the historian Msgr. Louis Duchesne) pronounced themselves in favor of their validity in 1893/1894.[144] In 1896, Leo XIII convened a commission of theologians and canonists and gathered opinions from the cardinals. Although the conclusion was negative ("ordinations carried out according to the Anglican rite have been, and are, absolutely null and utterly void"),[145] the question was treated with true intellectual openness (including access to archives), that also allowed its reopening in the postconciliar context.[146]

reasons, which could be assessed by the Holy Office if there was a doubt; response of the cardinals of the Holy Office of Apr 5, 1916; confirmed by Benedict XV on Apr 6; at the request of the ordinary of Trani (Apulia) in March of 1916, in: ACDF, SO, DB 312/16, 1916, n. 2.

140 The text states that, after receiving the "profession of the Catholic Religion," the priest gave "absolution," and "then ... he [administered] Baptism." The form specifies here "write according to what was done, most often: conditionally"; HAAP, 9K2, 9 a'.

141 W. Ledóchowski to "Illustrissime ac R^me Domine," May 22, 1907, in: ASRS, AAEESS, III, Russia, pos. 915, fasc. 299, fol. 60.

142 Several decisions were taken for the Protestant countries between 1830 and 1840; see Gian Biagio Furiozzi, "Gregorio XVI e i protestanti," in: Romano Ugolini, ed., Gregorio XVI tra oscurantismo e innovazione: Stato degli studi e percorsi di ricerche, Pisa, Serra, 2012, 181–187. In general, see Raoul Naz, "Mariage en droit occidental," DDC 6, 740–787, here 784–787.

143 During this period, among the Russian married priests who joined the Catholic Church, Serge Werighine was ordained in 1889, abjured in 1907, and separated from his wife on that occasion; see Cyril Korolevsky, Kniga bytija moego: Le livre de ma vie: Mémoires autobiographiques, ed. Giuseppe Maria Croce, vol. 2, Vatican City, Archives secrètes vaticanes, 2007, 148; "Formula brevior Professionis Fidei pro Haereticis seu schismaticis orientalibus," S. Werighine, Aug 28, 1907, in: ACDF, SO, RV, 1907, n. 66, fol. 2.

144 Charles Morerod, "La questione della validità delle Ordinazioni Anglicane," in: Accademia nazionale dei Lincei & Congregazione per la Dottrina della fede, eds., Giornata di studio: L'apertura degli archivi del Sant'Uffizio romano (Roma, 22 gennaio 1998), Rome, Accademia Nazionale dei Lincei, 1998, 103–127; Régis Ladous, Monsieur Portal et les siens (1855–1926), Paris, Cerf, 1985, esp. 91–127; Albert Gratieux, L'Amitié au service de l'union: Lord Halifax et l'abbé Portal, Paris, Bonne Presse, 1951; Bruno Neveu, "Mgr Duchesne et son Mémoire sur les ordinations anglicanes (1895 ou 1896)," JTS n.s. 29, 1978, 443–457.

145 Leo XIII, Apostolicae curae. See also, Salvatore Maria Brandi, Rome et Cantorbéry: Commentaire de la bulle "Apostolicae curae" déclarant nulles les ordinations anglicanes: Examen de la réponse des archevêques anglicans, Paris, P. Lethielleux, 1898.

146 William Franklin, ed., Anglican Orders: Essays on the Centenary of "Apostolicae Curae" (1896–1996), Harrisburg PA, Morehouse Publishing, 1996.

If, from a theoretical point of view, the boundaries between Christian denominations seemed clearly defined, we can also highlight some examples that demonstrate how those boundaries could, at times, be permeable.

The first example concerns the Catholic profession of faith in the case of conversion. The formula of the profession of faith for Eastern Christians, written in the 16th century and then clarified under Urban VIII in 1632, was reworked by the Eastern rite section of Propaganda Fide between 1878 and 1881, in order to incorporate the changes made during Vatican I.[147] This text was, however, put to the test in the occasion of the conversion of the Russian Orthodox priest Nicholas Tolstoy.[148] Ordained a (married) priest in 1893, Tolstoy made his profession of Catholic faith on July 28, 1894 in Moscow in the Church of Saint-Louis-des-Français, writing a rather personal declaration in which he simply stated "to disavow everything in the teaching of the Russian Orthodox Church and its doctrines and practices that is opposed to the doctrine of the Holy Roman and Apostolic Catholic Church."[149] This document, examined by the Holy Office in November 1894, was considered by the consultor as a "kind of amorphous abjuration" and declared inadmissible.[150] The cardinals, joined by Leo XIII, then insisted that Tolstoy pronounce "the profession of faith for Ruthenians who convert."[151] The Russian priest then went to Rome to make his abjuration on Apr 30, 1895.[152] This case highlights

the Roman firmness, but also that local negotiations were possible. Some of them seem to have been accepted by the Roman authorities, such as "secret conversions."

Praised by missionaries in some Orthodox countries such as Russia, secret conversions allowed converts to remain in their own countries and milieus to develop a pro-Catholic influence. In 1910, the Apostolic Penitentiary thus validated the action of a missionary who, in the context of the sacrament of Confession, had given absolution to a young "Greek-schismatic" woman who was adhering to Catholic positions but was unable to convert because of her parents' opposition.[153] Similarly, a certain secrecy was maintained after some conversions. When Fr. Serge Werighine abjured in 1906, the Benedictine Hugo Gaisser, rector of the Greek College, asked Pius X to allow him to remain "exteriorly, for a certain time – due to serious reasons – in his previous situation as a (schismatic) priest," specifying that "in several cases in the past, His Holiness Leo XIII had permitted persons of the clergy and Russians in high positions to be secretly received in the Catholic Church but allowing them to remain exteriorly in the schism."[154] Pius X then addressed the Holy Office, stating: "I am surprised, as if by something incredible, that my venerable predecessors including Leo XIII of h[oly] m[emory] would have granted [this] exemption."[155] The issue of secret conversions was then debated and resolved negatively in June 1906.[156] This example shows the flexibility of the criteria of decisions in Rome, even at the highest level.

It is important however not to contrast the pontificates of Leo XIII and Pius X. It was Cardinal Mariano Rampolla, Leo XIII's former secretary of state, who recalled, in a meeting of cardinals of

---

147 "Profession de Foi pour les Orientaux," in: HAAP, 9K2, 9 a', fols. 26–27. Several *ponenze* of Propaganda Fide, Eastern Affairs Section, between 1878 and 1881 were devoted to drafting this document.

148 ACDF, SO, RV 119/11, 1911, n. 14. On Tolstoy, see Constantin Simon, *Pro Russia: The Russicum and Catholic Work for Russia*, Rome, PIO, 2009, 126–129.

149 ACDF, SO, RV 119/11, 1911, n. 14, fol. 2.

150 *Voto* of Luigi Avella, Dec 2, 1894, in: ACDF, SO, RV 119/11, 1911, n. 14, fols. 5–9.

151 Decision sheet, Feria IV Apr 24, 1895 and Feria V Apr 25, 1895, in: ACDF, SO, RV 119/11, 1911, n. 14, fol. 14v.

152 Arsenio Pellegrini to "Most Eminent Prince," Grottaferrata, May 15, 1895, in: ACDF, SO, RV 119/11, 1911, n. 14, fols. 19–20.

153 Joseph Bousquet, *L'unité de l'Église et le schisme grec*, Paris, G. Beauchesne, 1913, 397.

154 Fr. H. Gaisser to Pius X, June 6, 1906, in: ACDF, SO, RV, 1907, n. 66, fols. 6, 8.

155 Pius X to G.B. Lugari, June 7, 1906, in: ACDF, SO, RV, 1907, n. 66, fol. 7.

156 ACDF, SO, RV, 1907, n. 66, fol. 26.

the Congregation for Extraordinary Ecclesiastical Affairs in 1913, that the term "orthodoxy" should be excluded from pontifical documents and used only to designate the Catholic Church.[157] Besides, Pius X himself, in 1908, used the term orthodox to refer to the studies in Rome of "young indigenous priests" trained "according to the orthodox traditions of their countries."[158]

Moreover, again during Pius X's pontificate, there was a certain flexibility, especially in the case of *communicatio in sacris*. If a Catholic had to attend an Orthodox service for social convenience (and not to honor God), the rules were traditionally flexible. In 1910, the Holy Office authorized the apostolic administrator of Tiflis (Tbilisi), in the Russian Empire, to attend schismatic services, such as funerals,[159] provided avoiding any scandal.[160] Concerning "negative" participation, attendance at Catholic worship was generally considered a benefit for non-Catholics, but the context determined curia's decision with a gradient of tolerance inversely proportional to its proximity to Rome. In 1915, therefore, the Holy Office opposed that in Bari, in an "entirely Catholic country," Orthodox pilgrims might celebrate their worship in the Catholic basilica[161] on the grounds that their presence constituted "a strong and continuous incentive to religious indifferentism."[162] There

was greater tolerance in the missionary context, where "borderline" practices were more easily experienced. Despite an investigation by the Congregation for Extraordinary Ecclesiastical Affairs, in 1914, the Holy See allowed a small group of Greek-Russian-rite Catholics from St. Petersburg to publish a calendar that included both Catholic and Russian saints such as St. Seraphim of Sarov, who was canonized by the Holy Synod in 1903.[163]

Concrete relations with Orthodoxy thus demonstrate, without any discontinuity between the pontificates, the constant firmness of the Roman Curia as well as a pragmatism that combined missionary objectives, political considerations, and a theology capable of a certain flexibility.

4 Conclusions

The appearance of pontifical unionism, manifested through great magisterial texts and new curial practices in the second half of the 19th century, would remain incomprehensible if we were to ignore the ferment that, from the beginning of the century, shook many European Catholic groups that appealed to Roman authority and influenced it. Between the 1830s and the eve of World War I, Rome's position concerning the issue of church unity changed considerably. The words used were considered carefully and attenuated, the corpus of texts increased and was disseminated, and the apostolic experiences were enriched and diversified in very different cultural contexts. Although the ambiguity of unionism (the search for individual conversions, the desire for a proximity that did not assume equality) was obvious, it also opened the way to new encounters and to overcoming theoretical obstacles. This moment of transition in the Catholic relationship to Christian diversity surely deserves a renewed attention from historians as well as a critical reappraisal from the churches.

---

157   ASRS, AAEESS, Rapporti delle Sessioni, n. 1181, 1913, Minutes of the session, 1.

158   Pius X, *Allocutio Quam die 13 Februarii 1908 Pius X habuit ad Orientales*, in: *ASS* 41, 1908, 130–134.

159   Letter from Archbishop Sergio Der Abrahamian, Tiflis, Dec 30, 1910, in: ACDF, SO, DV 313/11, 1911, n. 16.

160   *Voto* of the consultor, the Franciscan David Fleming, Mar 30, 1911, in: ACDF, SO, DV 313/11, 1911, n. 16, ponenza. This advice was followed by the consultors (June 19, 1911), the cardinals (June 28), and the pope (June 29).

161   Ponenza: Suprema S. Congregatio S. Officii (mense Ianuario 1915), "Bari: Sopra alcune funzioni religiose che sogliono arbitrariamente celebrarsi da un pope russo scismatico nella Basilica di S. Nicola," in: ACDF, SO, RV 190/13, 1915, n. 10, fols. 1–3, pp. 1–6.

162   The consultor's negative advice on Jan 7, 1915 (in: ACDF, SO, RV 190/13, 1915, n. 10, fols. 1–3, ponenza, 5) was followed by the cardinals and the pope (see ACDF, SO, RV 190/13, 1915, n. 10, fol. 37).

---

163   "Kalendar," *Slovo istiny* 1, 1913, 16; ASRS, AAEESS, Rapporti delle Sessioni, 1185, 1914, ponenza, 13.

Translated from French to English by Susan Dawson Vásquez and David Dawson Vásquez.

The author wishes to thank the following for their advice: Paul Chopelin, Aurélien Girard, Luc Forestier, Sylvain Milbach, and Claude Prudhomme.

Bibliography

Boisson, Didier & Elisabeth Pinto-Mathieu, eds., *La conversion: Textes et réalités*, Rennes, Presses Universitaires de Rennes, 2014.

Brown, Stewart J. & Peter B. Nockles, eds., *The Oxford Movement: Europe and the Wider World (1830–1930)*, Cambridge, Cambridge University Press, 2012.

Chapman, Mark D., *The Fantasy of Reunion: Anglicans, Catholics, and Ecumenism (1833–1882)*, Oxford, Oxford University Press, 2014.

Croce, Giuseppe Maria, *La Badia Greca di Grottaferrata e la rivista "Roma e l'Oriente": Cattolicesimo e ortodossia fra unionismo ed ecumenismo (1799–1923)*, 2 vols., Vatican City, Libreria Editrice Vaticana, 1990.

Fouilloux, Étienne, *Les catholiques et l'unité chrétienne du XIXe au XXe siècle: Itinéraires européens d'expression française*, Paris, Le Centurion, 1982.

Franklin, William, ed., *Anglican Orders: Essays on the Centenary of "Apostolicae Curae" (1896–1996)*, Harrisburg PA, Morehouse Publishing, 1996.

Legrand, Hervé & Giuseppe Maria Croce, eds., *L'Œuvre d'Orient: Solidarités anciennes et nouveaux défis*, Paris, Cerf, 2010.

Santa Sede e Russia da Leone XIII a Pio XI: Atti del Simposio organizzato dal Pontificio Comitato di scienze storiche e dall'Istituto di storia universale dell'Accademia delle scienze di Mosca: Mosca, 23–25 giugno 1998, Vatican City, Libreria Editrice Vaticana, 2002.

Simon, Constantin, *Pro Russia: The Russicum and Catholic Work for Russia*, Rome, PIO, 2009.

CHAPTER 12

The Origins of Anglican Ecumenical Theology, the Chicago-Lambeth Quadrilateral, and the Question of Anglican Orders

Paul Avis

1 Introduction

We tend to think of the ecumenical movement – the main modern expression of the desire for Christian unity – as a purely 20th-century phenomenon, stemming, in its institutional form, from the WMC held in Edinburgh, Scotland, in 1910.[1] The standard ecumenical narrative portrays ecumenism as then gradually gathering strength with the founding of the Faith and Order and Life and Work conferences, from the 1920s, making a breakthrough with the birth of the Church of South India in 1947, achieving critical mass with the formation of the WCC in 1948, and then receiving a massive boost from the decree on ecumenism (*Unitatis redintegratio*) of Vatican II (1962–1965) and the raft of international bilateral dialogues that flowed from it throughout the second half of the 20th century. Cumulatively, these ecumenical developments produced a measurable qualitative difference in the relations between churches, world communions, and local Christian communities in many places. Incomprehension, suspicion, fear, hatred and mutual condemnation began to give way – not totally of course, but to a significant extent – to deeper mutual understanding, increased trust, greater cooperation, and occasions of shared worship, even though structural unions of churches remained rare events. The early 21st century has seen talk of "an ecumenical winter" and has witnessed a slow decline in ecumenical

energy and aspiration and in an intentional commitment to work for visible Christian unity.

2 Proto-Ecumenical Initiatives

However, it would be a serious historical error to assume that a desire and longing for unity in the hearts of Christians was negligible until the 20th century, not strong enough to make itself felt politically and to motivate constructive collective action. As far back as the violently disruptive events of the 16th century – to look no further back into church history – there were sporadic but concerted attempts to bring about reconciliation between the Reformers (including Martin Luther himself) and the Roman Church in order to avoid a permanent schism.[2] Some of the most eminent of the Reformers (particularly John Calvin, Thomas Cranmer and Philipp Melanchthon) worked for some kind of pan-Protestant council or alliance – in order to create a common front against Rome (which was unity of a sort).[3] In the 18th century,

---

1 Brian Stanley, *The World Missionary Conference, Edinburgh 1910*, Grand Rapids MI, Eerdmans, 2009. Of the same author see the contribution in this volume.

2 Martin Luther, *On the Councils and the Church* (1539), in: Martin Luther, *Luther's Works*, ed. Jaroslav Pelikan & Helmut T. Lehmann, vol. 41, Philadelphia PA, Fortress Press, 1966; Jaroslav Pelikan, *Obedient Rebels: Catholic Substance and Protestant Principle in Luther's Reformation*, London, SCM Press, 1964, 56–76; Paul Avis, *Beyond the Reformation?: Authority, Primacy and Unity in the Conciliar Tradition*, London, T&T Clark, 2006, ch. 10, esp. 113–118. See also next note.

3 John T. McNeill, *Unitive Protestantism: A Study in Our Religious Resources*, New York NY, Abingdon Press, 1930; John T. McNeill, "The Ecumenical Idea and Efforts to Realize It (1517–1618)," in: *A History of the Ecumenical Movement*, vol. 1, Ruth Rouse & Stephen C. Neill, eds.,

William Wake, the archbishop of Canterbury, made unity overtures to Reformed churches and especially to the Gallican Church (the independently-minded Roman Catholic Church in France).[4] We know, with the benefit of hindsight, that all these noble initiatives ultimately failed, but they still stand in the history of the Christian church as estimable manifestations of the drive to unity that is inherent in its very being. Some of these initiatives can also be seen as authentic expressions of the church's conciliar nature, a conciliarity that also belongs to its very essence.[5]

It is in the mid-19th century that we begin to see an actual coming together of Christian bodies – not necessarily churches as such – into some form of structured unity or at least a relationship of fellowship, cooperation and collaboration. The formation of the EA in Britain in 1846 is a prime example of a convergence which was achieved on the basis of evangelical faith and a common (stereotyped) conversion experience. The EA stood for unity in the spirit and in sound doctrine; considerations of sacramental communion and church order were absent. Originally conceived as an international organization, the EA designated itself as "ecumenical." It bridged the divide between Anglicans and Nonconformists who were united by their fear and detestation of Roman Catholicism (though they were not the most extreme anti-Catholics: the

Protestant Alliance was formed in 1851). The EA also brought its supporters together in opposition to secularism and unbelief.[6]

The origins of the Anglican Lambeth Conference of bishops in 1867 (now seen as the first in a series of meetings of the Anglican Communion's Lambeth Conference) also bear witness to an emerging international desire for unity, solidarity and conference among Anglicans.[7]

There was, however, an even earlier and often overlooked episode of the pre-history of ecumenism – albeit ecumenism in a private and unofficial form – and it began, as far as the Church of England is concerned, as early as the 1830s with the Tractarian or Oxford Movement – led by a breed of radicalized, campaigning High Churchmen. But, contrary to a widespread misconception of this movement as representing a Romeward tendency within the Church of England, we should note that, as Mark Chapman puts it, the "Tractarians were very far from being ecumenically minded."[8] With a few exceptions, the Tractarians were not attracted to Roman Catholicism: most were

1517–1948, London, SPCK, 1954, 25–69. Many other examples of early modern ecumenical aspirations and initiatives are given in *A History of the Ecumenical Movement*, vol. 1.

4   Norman Sykes, *William Wake, Archbishop of Canterbury (1657–1737)*, 2 vols., Cambridge, Cambridge University Press, 1957; Paul Avis, *Anglicanism and the Christian Church: Theological Resources in Historical Perspective*, London, T&T Clark, ²2002, 121–129.

5   Paul Avis, *Beyond the Reformation?*; Paul Avis, "Conciliarity in the Anglican Communion: History, Theology and Polemic," *CrSt* 32/3, 2011, 1085–1104; Paul Avis, "The Conciliar Tradition and the Anglican Communion," in: Paul Avis & others, eds., *Incarnating Authority: A Critical Account of Structures of Authority in the Church*, Munich, Utz, 2019, 15–52; Francis Oakley, *The Conciliarist Tradition: Constitutionalism in the Catholic Church (1300–1870)*, Oxford, Oxford University Press, 2003.

6   Ian M. Randall & David Hilborn, *One Body in Christ: The History and Significance of the Evangelical Alliance*, Carlisle, Paternoster Press, 2001; John Wolffe, "The Evangelical Alliance in the 1840s: An Attempt to Institutionalise Christian Unity," *SCH* 23, 1986, 333–346; *A History of the Ecumenical Movement*, vol. 1, 318–323. On anti-Catholicism see Edward Robert Norman, *Anti-Catholicism in Victorian England*, London, Allen & Unwin, 1968, and John Wolffe, *The Protestant Crusade in Great Britain (1829–1860)*, Oxford, Clarendon Press, 1991. On the broader evangelical background see David W. Bebbington, *Evangelicalism in Modern Britain: A History from the 1730s to the 1980s*, London, Unwin Hyman, 1989 (and subsequent editions).

7   Paul Avis & Benjamin M. Guyer, eds., *The Lambeth Conference: Theology, History, Polity and Purpose*, London, T&T Clark, 2017.

8   Mark D. Chapman, "The Oxford Movement and Ecumenism," in: Stewart J. Brown, Peter B. Nockles & James Pereiro, eds., *The Oxford Handbook of the Oxford Movement*, Oxford, Oxford University Press, 2017, 500–513, here 500, and Peter B. Nockles's contribution in this volume. On the views of the Tractarians on other Christian churches, especially the Roman Catholic Church, English Nonconformity and the German Lutheran Churches, see also Avis, *Anglicanism and the Christian Church*, chs. 9–12.

militantly hostile to Rome. They basically stood with the English Reformers of the 16th century and with the succession of Anglican divines through the succeeding centuries in rejecting what they regarded as the abuses, doctrinal errors and baseless claims of the Roman Catholic Church – while still regarding Rome as a Christian church, albeit in dire need of reform. For the mainstream of the Oxford Movement, any rapprochement with Rome could be premised only on the internal reform of that church in the direction of Reformation principles, principally the public availability and supreme authority of the Bible, a liturgy in the vernacular, the administration of Holy Communion in both kinds to the laity, and a priesthood that was allowed to marry. But the developments that transpired within the Roman Church in the second half of the 19th century seemed retrograde to Anglicans and to point in the opposite direction, not towards but away from Reformation principles: the dogma of the Immaculate Conception of the Blessed Virgin Mary in 1854, the papal decrees of universal jurisdiction and infallibility in 1869–1870 and, crushingly, the condemnation of Anglican orders in 1896.

The events of the middle decades of the 19th century cannot be understood without some knowledge of the Oxford Movement and its aftermath in the Anglo-Catholic movement within the Church of England, which was mirrored in other churches of the Anglican Communion, as well as in other traditions.[9] So now we turn to certain

bold, brave and sometimes misguided initiatives, mainly involving Anglicans and Roman Catholics, that were attempted roughly between the conversion (defection, from the Anglican point of view) to Rome in 1845 of John Henry Newman, the most notable Anglican theologian of his day and the leading light of Tractarianism, at one end of the time frame, and the turbulent aftermath of Vatican I at the other end.[10]

The authors of this first phase of the early overtures to modern ecumenism were fired by a romantic vision of the European Middle Ages, as an antidote to the rationalism and empiricism of certain aspects of the European Enlightenment and a reaction to the "dark Satanic Mills" of the industrialization of "Englands green & pleasant Land [sic]" (in the words of William Blake).[11] The entrancing vision of an idyllic, harmonious, hierarchical society, with the church at its heart and a benevolent paternalism ruling the rustic world from the safety of the ancient castle, began to be crudely outlined in "Gothic" novels, such as Ann Radcliffe's The Mysteries of Udolpho (1794) and Matthew Gregory Lewis' The Monk (1796), that were designed to make the flesh creep and were satirized by Jane Austen in Northanger Abbey (1817). The imaginative vision of an eerie but alluring medieval world was taken up by the early Romantic poets (e.g. Samuel Taylor Coleridge and John Keats), but was inspired chiefly and most widely by the poetry and novels of Sir Walter Scott, which had a massive influence on the Tractarians. In his narrative poems such as The Lady of the Lake (1810) and such novels as Ivanhoe (1819) and The Fair Maid of Perth (1828), Scott gave tantalizing glimpses of the then banned and condemned beliefs and practices of the medieval church in England and Scotland: masses for the dead, the veneration of saints, holy wells, candlelit altars, abbeys, monastic cells, holy hermits, the

---

9   R. William Franklin, *Nineteenth-Century Churches: The History of a New Catholicism in Württemberg, England, and France*, New York NY, Garland, 1987; Stewart J. Brown & Peter B. Nockles, eds., *The Oxford Movement: Europe and the Wider World (1830–1930)*, Cambridge, Cambridge University Press, 2012; Albrecht Geck, "The Oxford Movement in Europe," in: Brown, Nockles & Pereiro, eds., *The Oxford Handbook of the Oxford Movement*, 457–468; Jeremy N. Morris, *The High Church Revival in the Church of England: Arguments and Identities*, Leiden, Brill, 2016, chs. 4–5. There is also useful material in Norman Powell Williams & Charles Harris, eds., *Northern Catholicism: Centenary Studies in the Oxford and Parallel Movements*, London, SPCK, 1933.

10   See especially Mark D. Chapman, *The Fantasy of Reunion: Anglicans, Catholics, and Ecumenism (1833–1882)*, Oxford, Oxford University Press, 2014.

11   William Blake, *The Complete Poems*, ed. Alicia Ostriker, Harmondsworth, Penguin, 1977, 514 ("And did those feet in ancient time").

distant papacy and the rule of potent prelates. The Romantic poets and novelists generated fantasies of a restored feudal Europe and a united Western Church. It was an anachronistic vision of medieval Christendom imported wholesale into the rapidly industrializing and urbanizing context of Regency England.[12]

The first key figures, on the Church of England's side, of these doomed ecumenical endeavors were the architects of the Gothic Revival in church building, Augustus W.N. Pugin, and "the lord of the manor," medieval style, Ambrose Phillipps de Lisle, both converts to Roman Catholicism. Their initiative, fanciful and unrealistic though it was, was torpedoed behind the scenes by Henry Edward Manning, another convert from the Church of England who later rose to become cardinal archbishop of Westminster. For Manning no epithet was too harsh or too hurtful for his former church, and he had no wish to see it brought into the Roman fold.[13]

In mid-century, however, the prime Anglican protagonist *vis-à-vis* Rome was Edward Bouverie Pusey, Regius Professor of Hebrew at the University of Oxford and the *de facto* leader of the Oxford Movement after the loss of Newman. Pusey emerges as the heroic, embattled, but indefatigable exponent of "classical" (that is, post-Reformation, mainly 17th-century) Anglicanism against what Anglicans regarded as the innovations of Rome, but also with striking affinities to the Anglican Reformers and apologists of the 16th century, especially John Jewel and Richard Hooker. Pusey issued a threefold *Eirenicon* between 1865 and 1870, in which he set out the mainstream Anglican platform of the Scriptures and the Fathers (i.e. the teaching of the "primitive church"). Scandalized by excessive popular Latin devotions, especially to the Blessed Virgin Mary, Pusey called repeatedly for the Vatican to define what was *de fide* (necessary to be believed for salvation) so that Anglicans might know what they would be required to accept in belief and practice if the two churches were to become reconciled. Do we need to take on a raft of superstitious popular cults in order to enter into communion with the Roman Catholic Church?, he wanted to know.

Pusey's method, like that of other Tractarians (i.e. the authors of *Tracts for the Times*, 1833–1841), was to pile up evidence from the early church, citing father after father of the church in *catenae* of quotations, without much regard for the original context. Pusey was on a mission to explain and was all too prone to tell Roman Catholics what their church actually taught! Newman, now a Roman Catholic, retorted that Catholicism was not merely an intellectual matter, but was found in the hearts and lives of simple, uneducated folk. He accused Pusey, his former comrade in arms, of "discharging his olive branch as if from a catapult."[14] In Newman's view, Catholicism (the Roman version) was a complete package, including superstitions and excesses, and was to be embraced wholesale and without repining. Pusey's theology, by contrast, was a theology of the word, textual, historical, logical, rigorous, in the best Anglo-Saxon manner. Newman's theology was born of the heart's devotion, was guided primarily by intuition, and was felt, as with all his fellow Romantics, on the emotional pulse of the whole thinking, feeling, acting person. For Newman, history could yield no ultimate answers and logic was subordinate to the thinking-feeling capacity of the whole person for truth-seeking that he later designated "the illative sense."[15]

---

12   See also Stephen Prickett, "Tractarianism and the Lake Poets," in: Brown, Nockles & Pereiro, eds., *The Oxford Handbook of the Oxford Movement*, 67–78.

13   Alison Milbank, *God & the Gothic: Religion, Romance, and Reality in the English Literary Tradition*, Oxford, Oxford University Press, 2018.

14   "A Letter Addressed to the Rev. E.B. Pusey, D.D. on Occasion of his Eirenicon," 1; the text can be found at <http://www.newmanreader.org/works/anglicans/volume2/pusey/section1.html> (accessed Oct 12, 2020).

15   See John Henry Newman, *Newman's University Sermons: Fifteen Sermons Preached before the University of Oxford (1826–1843)*, London, SPCK, 1970, an Anglican work; and John Henry Newman, *An Essay in Aid of a Grammar of Assent*, ed. Ian T. Ker, Oxford, Oxford University Press, 1985, written as a Roman Catholic.

Pusey and his disciple in the Scottish Episcopal Church, Bishop Alexander Forbes of Brechin (1817–1875, the first Tractarian bishop), fought to avert the declaration of papal infallibility that eventually came at Vatican I in 1870. Such a declaration, Pusey and his supporters correctly believed, would be the end of any hopes of theological convergence between Anglicanism and the Roman Catholic Church. They proposed to send a set of theses, summarizing the Anglican position, to Rome. Newman (who was also opposed to a formal declaration of papal infallibility, at least at that time) showed them that you do not negotiate with the Vatican: the more you explain, the more material there will be available to condemn. The dogma of papal infallibility of 1870 was seen as a catastrophe by Pusey, killing off all hope of rapprochement. It was the second "ecumenical" catastrophe for Pusey – the first being Newman's defection in 1845. He did not live to see the third catastrophe, the condemnation of Anglican orders in 1896. The saintly, pastoral John Keble, the father-figure of Tractarianism, had given up hope of reconciliation with Rome after the promulgation of the dogma of the Immaculate Conception of the Blessed Virgin Mary in 1854. Pusey and Forbes – the scholarly recluse of immense erudition and the High Church bishop – regarded the declaration of papal infallibility as an ideological attempt to trump the facts of history and as the victory of an Ultramontane ideology that had betrayed the patristic heritage of the "undivided" church.

Vatican I was not the end of Anglican ecumenical hopes. They were deflected from Rome to the emerging national Catholic churches that rejected papal infallibility and papal universal jurisdiction and which later became the Old Catholic Churches of the Union of Utrecht (1889).[16] At this stage the main protagonists were: William Ewart Gladstone, High Churchman, public intellectual, redoubtable ecclesiologist and four times prime minister, whose booklet *The Vatican Decrees*

sold 150,000 copies; Henry Parry Liddon, protégé and biographer of Pusey, residentiary canon of St. Paul's Cathedral and Oxford professor; Ignaz von Döllinger, professor in Munich, widely regarded as the most learned man in Christendom, who could teach not only Roman Catholics but also Eastern Orthodox what their church actually believed (Döllinger never joined the Old Catholics, but was excommunicated by Rome nevertheless); and Eduard Herzog, first bishop of the Swiss "Christian Catholics," who toured England and America praising the Catholicity of what he called "the Anglo-American Church." As far as Herzog was concerned, Anglicans and Old Catholics were to have "one altar" and to share in episcopal consecrations, for was not the Church of England both "Old" and "Catholic," just like themselves?

The initial fervour of Anglican churchmen towards those who became the Old Catholics subsided when it became clear that the reform movement among episcopal churches on the mainland of Europe, born of reaction to the papal decrees of Vatican I, was not going to spread across Europe like wildfire and had in fact stalled. Anglican lovers of unity turned their attention to the developing Anglican Communion (the "first" Lambeth Conference was held in 1867 and the second in 1878, so those conferences were positioned on either side of Vatican I, the approach to which and the consequences of which overshadowed those Lambeth Conferences).

What was at stake for Anglicans and Roman Catholics (and, later, Old Catholics) in these passionate encounters of proto-ecumenism was the Catholicity of the one Church of Christ and consequently and deductively the Catholicity of particular churches that claimed it, and how that Catholicity was to be tested and known. Was it to be tried by the touchstone of Scripture, by the evidence of history and by well-founded theological principles ("reason"), according to the classical Anglican methodology? Or was it to be decided, in the last analysis, by an infallible living voice, that of the pope, that could, as it seemed, overrule the tradition of the "undivided" church? Among Anglicans who were ecumenists *avant la*

---

16   See Peter-Ben Smit's contribution in the third volume of this work.

lettre, Keble, Pusey and Gladstone reaffirmed and burnished the former, Anglican, method; while Newman (with reservations) and Manning (without reservations) opted for the latter, the Roman, papal and Ultramontane, route. These mid-19th-century tentative essays in ecumenism, driven by a desire and longing for Christian unity, but naive in their approach and generally counterproductive in their outcome, set the context for a key Anglican initiative in the 1880s that would provide the backbone of Anglican ecumenical policy up to the present day. That initiative was the Chicago-Lambeth Quadrilateral, a basic formula to guide and inform a process of rapprochement between Anglican and other churches. But one person more than any other had the making of the Quadrilateral, and that was the American episcopal rector William Reed Huntington, who set forth a quadrilateral of his own – four points essential to reunion between (in his case) the Protestant Episcopal Church of the United States and other Protestant Churches in America. So we must say something about Huntington's contribution next.

3   William Reed Huntington and the Origins of Anglican Ecumenical Theology

The strategy or method of modern Anglican ecumenical engagement, especially its connection with the Chicago-Lambeth Quadrilateral, begins with the work of a remarkable priest of the Protestant Episcopal Church of the United States, William Reed Huntington.[17] Born in Massachusetts

in 1838, Huntington graduated from Harvard University in 1859. Ordained in the Protestant Episcopal Church of the United States, he served as the rector of All Saints Church, Worcester MA, from 1862 to 1883, and of Grace Church, New York, from 1883 until 1909, when he died in harness. Huntington was prominent in ecclesiastical affairs, a leading light of the Episcopal Church. He was involved in liturgical renewal, serving as secretary of the Prayer-Book Revisions Committee of his church, and as joint editor of the *Standard Prayer-Book* of the Protestant Episcopal Church of the United States, published in 1892.[18]

Widely influential and respected, Huntington was hailed as the "first presbyter" of his church. Neither a bishop (though he turned down bishoprics) nor a professor (though he was well-qualified to be an academic in those times), Huntington was, as Mark Chapman puts it, "one of the most formative influences on modern Anglican identity."[19] The word "identity" is significant: Huntington's theological – and specifically ecclesiological – influence goes well beyond strict questions of ecumenical method to the broader principles of ecclesiology (the theological account of the nature and purpose of the church). In particular, Huntington sought to penetrate to the heart of what he believed Anglicanism stood for within the spectrum of Christian traditions and what it meant to any informed and reflective Anglican to stand within that tradition. He was on the track of "the essential, the absolutely essential features of the Anglican position ... Anglicanism pure and simple."[20] He did all this while explicitly resisting any identification of Anglicanism as such with the

---

17   J. Robert Wright, ed., *Quadrilateral at One Hundred: Essays on the Centenary of the Chicago-Lambeth Quadrilateral (1886/88–1986/88)* (= *AThR* supplementary series no. 10), Cincinnati OH, Forward Movement Publications, 1988; John F. Woolverton, "The Chicago-Lambeth Quadrilateral and the Lambeth Conferences," *Historical Magazine of the Protestant Episcopal Church* 53/2, 1984, 95–109; Mark D. Chapman, "William Reed Huntington, American Catholicity and the Chicago-Lambeth Quadrilateral," in: Avis & Guyer, eds., *The Lambeth Conference*, 84–106; John Wallace

Suter, *Life and Letters of William Reed Huntington*, New York NY, Century, 1925.

18   For the history of prayer book revision in the Episcopal Church, with special reference to the rites of Holy Week, see Laura E. Moore, *From Easter to Holy Week: The Paschal Mystery and Liturgical Renewal in the Twentieth Century*, Leiden, Brill, 2019.

19   Chapman, "William Reed Huntington," 86.

20   William Reed Huntington, *The Church-Idea: An Essay Towards Unity*, New York NY, Scribner's, ⁴1899, 124.

Church of England; in fact he pointedly distanced Anglicanism from its English expression.

For the purposes of this chapter we must confine our focus to Huntington's concept of church unity and the conditions that were necessary, in his view, for such unity to be realized. The desire for Christian unity, combined with the integrity and harmony of the church, were the dominant, motivating ideals of Huntington's life and thought. The unity of the Christian churches in America – the possibility of a comprehensive national church – was what exercised him, and he saw a critical role for a reformed and refined version of Anglicanism in both contexts. He envisaged Anglicanism as "the basis of a Church of the Reconciliation."[21] Writing soon after the end of the American Civil War of 1861–1865, Huntington was haunted by the need for reconciliation. Nearly thirty years after the publication in 1870 of *The Church-Idea*, in his preface to the fourth edition in 1899, he commented that what now held the United States together was not force but "a common understanding" and he implied a parallel in the spiritual or ecclesial order.[22] In his theology, Huntington was inclined to identify the Church and the Kingdom of God, but in a less subtle and dialectical way than Frederick Denison Maurice did when he set out his ecclesiology under the title *The Kingdom of Christ*.[23]

3.1 *Huntington and the Church of England*

Huntington was shaped, both positively (by assimilation) and negatively (by reaction) by the Tractarian movement in the Church of England. As a young man he travelled to England and visited John Keble at his parish of Hursley, Hampshire, from where Keble exerted a sustained and decisive influence – by example, writing and conference – on the Church of England for thirty-one years, until his death.[24] Keble was priest, pastor, poet and professor. He was the self-appointed guardian of the received Anglican tradition – he saw it as merely his duty as a priest in the Church of England. He stood for a return to "the old paths," to the sober, steady and generally unexciting High Churchmanship of the late 18th century – sometimes dubbed "High and Dry," but in Keble's case infused with inward spiritual fervor and outward devotion to parochial duties.[25] His poems to accompany the *Book of Common Prayer* (1662), *The Christian Year*, was the best-selling book of poems in the 19th century and has given us several still well-loved hymns. *The Christian Year* is probably the most eloquent tribute ever paid to the *Book of Common Prayer*. Keble's method was a kind

---

21   Huntington, *The Church-Idea*, 124. In an article of 1908 – therefore, strictly outside our period – Huntington argued that the church parties within Anglicanism corresponded to the structure of the human psyche. The High Church, with its emphasis on governance, corresponded to the will; the Low Church, with its affinity to evangelical Nonconformity, matched the affections; and the Broad Church, with its openness to scholarly research, fitted the intellect. Because the Episcopal Church contained all three schools of thought, it was eminently suited to play a mediatorial role between Christian churches and to be a catalyst for unity; William Reed Huntington, "The Anglican Communion: Our Ideals," in: *Pan-Anglican Papers: Being Problems for Consideration at the Pan-Anglican Congress (1908)*, London, SPCK, 1908. A bibliography of Huntington's works, as of 1988, is given in Edyth McKitrick, "William Reed Huntington: The Grace Church Collection of His Printed Works, Annotated with Particular Reference to Church Unity," in: Wright, ed., *Quadrilateral at One Hundred*, 213–223.

22   Huntington, *The Church-Idea*, xiii.

23   Huntington, *The Church-Idea*, 8. For Frederick Denison Maurice see below.

24   Georgina Battiscombe, *John Keble: A Study in Limitations*, London, Constable, 1963.

25   Peter B. Nockles, *The Oxford Movement in Context: Anglican High Churchmanship (1760–1857)*, Cambridge, Cambridge University Press, 1994; Frederick Clare Mather, *High Church Prophet: Bishop Samuel Horsley (1733–1806) and the Caroline Tradition in the Later Georgian Church*, Oxford, Clarendon Press, 1992; Richard Sharp, "New Perspectives on the High Church Tradition: Historical Background (1730–1780)," in: Geoffrey Rowell, ed., *Tradition Renewed: The Oxford Movement Conference Papers*, London, Darton, Lomngman & Todd, 1986, 4–23; Robert D. Cornwall, *Visible and Apostolic: The Constitution of the Church in High Church Anglican and Non-Juror Thought*, London, Associated University Presses, 1993; George Every, *The High Church Party (1688–1718)*, London, SPCK, 1956.

of *ressourcement*, a fresh mining of the *Book of Common Prayer* and of the classical Anglican divines, beginning with Richard Hooker. Keble was the first modern editor of Hooker's *Of the Lawes of Ecclesiasticall Politie* and his other works.[26]

For Keble, the past was the gold standard. The prayer book was inviolable. Change was to be deplored. Modernization was apostasy. Steadiness, sobriety, humility, self-denial, heart-felt devotion, unfailing observance of the ordinances of the church, combined with passionate loyalty to what had been received from the Fathers, saints and bishops of past centuries – these were Keble's recipe for a healthy, pastorally effective, doctrinally sound church, accompanying the suffering and sorrowful in their pilgrimage, but already tasting the joys of heaven. In the "Advertisement" that prefaced *The Christian Year* in 1827, Keble wrote:

> Next to a sound rule of faith [broadly the ecumenical creeds], there is nothing of so much consequence as a sober standard of feeling in matters of practical religion: and it is the peculiar happiness of the Church of England to possess, in her authorized formularies [here mainly The *Book of Common Prayer*, 1662], an ample and secure provision for both.

In conclusion, Keble singled out, as the principal effect of the prayer book, its "soothing tendency," which, he said, "it is the chief purpose of these pages to exhibit."[27] The epigraph or motto, that he placed on the title page of *The Christian Year*, was also typical of the ethos that Keble sought to evoke: "In quietness and confidence shall be your strength" (Isa 30:15, KJB).

John Keble's far-shining aura may be summed up in the phrase from the King James Bible, "the beauty of holiness" (Ps 96:9). It was, however, as with Newman, a tough beauty and an uncompromising holiness, conservative and even reactionary in its tendency. Keble was adamantly opposed (for example) to the extension of the democratic franchise, to civil and political rights for Roman Catholics and Protestant Dissenters, and to the first intimations of the historico-critical method in biblical scholarship. Modernity was antipathetic to him. Considered overall, Keble represented the ideological antithesis of the reforming, entrepreneurial and progressive spirit of early Victorian England (which was also the spirit of America). Furthermore, Keble was no ecumenist. He deplored the errors and excesses of Roman Catholicism, abhorred Protestant Dissent and the fanatical aspects of Methodism. He moved gradually to a jaundiced view of the Reformers and the Reformation and was prejudiced towards the Lutheran and Reformed traditions.[28] Yet, through the witness of his holy life, dedicated priesthood, poetic inspiration, careful scholarship and love of the church and its liturgy, Keble gave a significant impetus to the revival of ecclesiology in the High Church (Catholic, liturgical, sacramental, episcopalian) movement within Anglicanism. And with the birth of ecclesiological awareness comes – necessarily, even if eventually – a bad conscience about the church's divisions and a desire and longing for her restored unity. Encountering the spiritual and theological phenomenon that was John Keble was enough to make Huntington's head spin and his heart flutter. But it would also induce misgivings and resistance in the mind of a young American.

Huntington was clearly awestruck on this visit by Keble and all that he stood for, including the portentous phenomenon of the Church of England "as by law established," with its history going back through the centuries. The constitutional axis of church, monarch and parliament seemed so solid – and yet so alien – to Huntington,

---

26   Richard Hooker, *The Works of that Learned and Judicious Divine Mr. Richard Hooker: With an Account of his Life and Death by Isaac Walton*, ed. John Keble, 3 vols., Oxford, Oxford University Press, ³1845.

27   John Keble, *The Christian Year: Thoughts in Verse for the Sundays and Holydays throughout the Year*, London, Longmans, Green & Co., 1898, "Advertisement."

28   See Avis, *Anglicanism and the Christian Church*, 221–224.

though in fact it was fragile and insecure, as events were soon to show, as a reforming parliament laid its hands on the church's assets in Ireland and England and King William IV failed to prevent this as some supposed his Coronation Oath to uphold the rights of the church bound him to do. Whig reforming legislation (in this case the suppression of some Irish sees) called forth Keble's condemnation in his famous Assize Sermon of 1833, *National Apostasy*, which triggered the Tractarian campaign in defense of the church: its dignity, rights, assets, theology, and authority.

It seems probable that Huntington took Keble as a role model – a model of a parish priest and a scholar who had the integrity of the church deeply and passionately at heart. But, like most role models, this one was unattainable. It was a model that could not be replicated, for Keble was at heart a late-18th-century, dyed-in-the-wool English churchman, wedded to tradition and precedent, though with a Romantic sensibility which actually reinforced an atavistic attitude, while Huntington was a modern activistic, pragmatic American. There was also ambiguity in Huntington's attitude to what Keble represented and perhaps something of a reaction against it. Like many Episcopalians, then and now, Huntington entertained an ambivalent attitude to the Church of England. He could not help admiring it as the "mother church" of Anglicanism and could not deny how much he owed to the teaching and example of its great bishops, priests and scholars (as we shall see in a moment). But, at the same time, Huntington felt a compulsion to poke fun at its crusty old institutions and to mock its quaint customs, which he did very effectively. The word "Anglicanism," he said, "brings up before the eyes of some a flutter of surplices, a vision of village spires and cathedral towers, a somewhat stiff and stately company of deans, prebendaries, and choristers, and that is about all." But, he continued, "we greatly mistake if we imagine that the Anglican principle has no substantial existence apart from these accessories." We need to strip away the picturesque costume of English church life in order to discover the "Anglican

principle" underlying it. The Anglican *principle* was opposed to the Anglican *system* (Huntington's idiosyncratic term for the lived ecology of the Church of England, but also a distinct echo of Maurice's trademark antipathy to "systems").[29] Huntington was particularly allergic to the 16th-century Thirty-Nine Articles of Religion, to which Church of England clergy were, at that time, required to assent *ex animo*. The articles, he insisted, should be relegated to the historical archive.[30] He looked askance at the Church of England, not only for the quaintness and inefficiency of its way of doing things, but also because it had "muffled these first principles in a cloud of [such] non-essentials," with the result that "she mourns today the loss of half her children."[31] While the established church in England had ceased to be a truly comprehensive, national church, Huntington envisioned just such an ideal for America.[32]

Huntington now applied his critique of the Church of England to his own church, the Protestant Episcopal Church of the United States. If, he asked, the ambition of American Anglicans was merely to continue as an eminently respectable body, wrapping "the robe of dignity" around themselves and providing a refuge from rougher forms of Christianity for people of refinement and cultivation, that would be to "renounce any and all claim to Catholicity." But if, on the other hand, they sought to "bring the Church of Christ into the closest possible sympathy with the throbbing, sorrowing, sinning, repenting, aspiring heart of this great people," then they should press their "reasonable claims to be the reconciler of a divided household."[33] Their distinction as a church did not lie in a "preference for pointed architecture, and stained glass, and chanted music, and ministerial

29   Huntington, *The Church-Idea*, 124–125.
30   Huntington, *The Church-Idea*, 139.
31   Huntington, *The Church-Idea*, 126.
32   Huntington's last major exposition of his vision was *A National Church*, New York NY, Scribner's, 1897. Here he entered more into the mechanics of interdenominational unity in America.
33   Huntington, *The Church-Idea*, 169–170.

vestments," but in faithful "adherence to the primitive and Catholic standards of unity."[34]

In place of quaint English customs (which were irrelevant), antiquated formularies (which did nothing for a living faith), and uniformity of worship (which alienated many potential adherents), Huntington proposed what he dubbed "the Quadrilateral of pure Anglicanism": "The Holy Scriptures as the Word of God"; "The Primitive Creeds as the Rule of Faith"; "The Two Sacraments Ordained by Christ Himself"; and "The Episcopate as the Key-Stone of Governmental Unity."[35] Here we have the origin of the Chicago Quadrilateral of 1886 and the Lambeth Quadrilateral of 1888 and 1920. Clearly, Huntington is following the well-worn theological trajectory of the search for "the fundamentals of Christianity" and the quest for "the essence of Christianity." He insists that doctrines should be characterized by "brevity, definiteness, and antiquity," but also evinces a certain impatience with the elaborations of theology.[36] "Big guns and few" was his formula. Huntington had bracketed out the constitution, formularies and customs of the Church of England – but not its latest theology, as we shall shortly see.

Two decades after the publication of *The Church-Idea*, and at the height of his reputation in the Protestant Episcopal Church, Huntington returned to his chosen theme in *The Peace of the Church*.[37] Here we find both modification and refinement of some earlier positions.

(1) There can be no absolute separation between church and state because the state is involved in certain aspects of the church's life, especially the laws concerning property, contract, marriage and charities; and both institutions have an interest in education. Church and state are therefore to be conceived as overlapping circles. The church should emulate the state in its achievement of unity. But while the state bears "the sword," the church is "a union of hearts" and works by persuasion and an appeal to conscience.[38]

(2) While denominationalism is condemned for its "flagrant" practical evils, neither submission to the Church of Rome nor a mere federation of cooperating but autonomous churches would realize the ideal of Christian unity which was to be conceived as "a union under one self-consistent and well-understood system of polity and doctrine, with ample constitutional guarantees for a permitted diversity in the methods of worship and of work." This would bring about "the Catholic Church of America."[39]

(3) The route that Huntington proposes to achieve this goal is a frankly pragmatic one: each church in America should consider what would be "the most generous platform of union it can conscientiously offer to the rest" (that is to say, what is non-negotiable and what can be sacrificed). For Anglicans, this basis would be the "Chicago-Lambeth platform" (which had been endorsed by the 1888 Lambeth Conference three years' before).[40] The remainder of Huntington's book is an exposition and defense of the Quadrilateral.

(4) In expounding the fourth point of the Quadrilateral, Huntington drives an opposition between "Apostolic Succession" and the "Historic Episcopate." The former demands a particular philosophy of the ministry and would prevent non-Episcopal churches from accepting episcopacy; the latter simply expresses a fact – that episcopacy has been the prevailing form of church government in the history of the church – without insisting on any theory to support it.[41]

(5) In the last chapter (rather pointedly entitled "A Church by Love Established") Huntington

34   Huntington, *The Church-Idea*, 170.

35   Huntington, *The Church-Idea*, 125–126. He first adumbrated the quadrilateral concept in a sermon on Jan 30, 1870 in his parish of Worcester MA; Suter, *Life and Letters*, 162–163.

36   Huntington, *The Church-Idea*, 126.

37   William Reed Huntington, *The Peace of the Church*, New York NY, Scribner's, 1891.

38   Huntington, *The Peace of the Church*, 15–16.

39   Huntington, *The Peace of the Church*, 21, 41–43.

40   Huntington, *The Peace of the Church*, 45–47.

41   Huntington, *The Peace of the Church*, 204–205.

returns to his lifelong detestation of the Thirty-Nine Articles of Religion, arguing that they should have no place in the American prayer book, which was then undergoing revision and would be published the following year. He proposes that the Quadrilateral be inserted in the Constitution of the Protestant Episcopal Church to serve as its doctrinal standard in place of the articles. Huntington did not get his way: in the 1892 *Book of Common Prayer* the articles were retained, though relegated to the end of the book.

3.2 *Theological Influences on Huntington's Thought*

The key to Huntington's powerful impact on his own church and, more widely, on Anglican ecumenical method lies in the conjunction of diverse, but not necessarily opposed, streams of thought, that were united in his mind and ministry. He was a High Churchman, but not an Anglo-Catholic. He was theologically broad, but not a rationalist or reductionist. He stood in the tradition of such representatives of the "Broad Church" tendency as Samuel Taylor Coleridge, Thomas Arnold, Frederick Denison Maurice and (the later) William Ewart Gladstone, all of whom were impelled by a burning desire for Christian unity and put it into effect by setting out a vision of a comprehensive national church for England. But Huntington was not a philosophical Coleridgean (not very philosophically inclined at all, it seems); nor was he a Romantic, as Thomas Arnold was – Arnold was close in heart, mind and (even his) home to the early 19th-century Romantic poets, especially Coleridge and Wordsworth. And, although Huntington seems to have been influenced by Maurice, he did not adopt Maurice's theology wholesale (it was in any case obscure, idiosyncratic, and in fact unique).[42]

Huntington may be described as a principled, ethical but progressive pragmatist. He was, in English terms, Broad Church, but not ideologically liberal. He not only declined to identify himself as Broad Church, but also repudiated "Liberalism" as "the Distortion of the Divine Idea." Huntington deprecated "Liberalism" as impatient of authority in doctrine or discipline and definitely not the same as "liberality."[43] Huntington might be seen as most obviously a theological descendant of Richard Hooker, whose thought also fed into the work of Coleridge, Arnold, Maurice, Keble, Newman (for a time) and Gladstone.[44]

Huntington's four points (Scripture, creeds, sacraments and episcopate) belong within a long trajectory within Protestant and Anglican theology of enquiry into "the fundamentals" or "the fundamental articles" of the Christian faith and into "the essence of Christianity."[45] The intellectual genealogy of "fundamental articles" and the essence

---

42   In *The Church-Idea* Huntington mentions – of the authors referred to in this chapter – Hooker, Gladstone, Newman, Pusey and Church, but not always to the main purpose of his argument. Interestingly, he does not appear to discuss Coleridge or Maurice. I do not quite agree with Mark D. Chapman when he plays down the influence of the Coleridgeans on Huntington. According to Chapman, Huntington's method was "quite different" to theirs. "He was far less philosophical and far more a historicist in his understanding of the church. His Anglican principle was clearly located in the past rather than in the Platonist ether" (Chapman, "William Reed Huntington," 93). Agreed, Huntington was no Platonist, but neither was he particularly historically minded. His ecclesiology is rather two-dimensional. I find Huntington's continuity with the Broad Church Coleridgeans (a differentiated school in any case) in four connected strands: (1) his concept of a united national church as the paradigm for Christian unity; (2) his resistance to uniformity of doctrine and worship in such a national church; (3) his quest for a few fundamental articles of faith as a basis for unity; and (4) his appeal to an inner essence, idea or principle of Anglicanism, detached from any particular historical instantiation.

43   Huntington, *The Church-Idea*, 14–15, 75.

44   For summaries of most of these writers' views on church and state, together with those of Edmund Burke and Mandell Creighton, see Paul Avis, *Church, State, and Establishment*, London, SPCK, 2001, ch. 6, 45–62.

45   See Stephen W. Sykes, "The Fundamentals of Christianity," in: Stephen W. Sykes, John E. Booty & Jonathan Knight, eds., *The Study of Anglicanism*, London, SPCK, ²1998, 262–276.

quest connects with the humanist, Erasmian, moderate and somewhat doctrinally minimizing tendency that was at work in the Latitudinarians of the 17th century and the later Broad Church movement within Anglicanism. This tradition is represented principally by Lord Falkland (Lucius Cary), William Chillingworth, John Hales, John Locke and Bishop Gilbert Burnet in the 17th century. But it also appears in the moderate Catholic strand of Anglicanism, represented by such divines as John Bramhall (archbishop of Armagh), Bishops Jeremy Taylor and Edward Stillingfleet, and (moving now into the 18th century) William Wake (archbishop of Canterbury).[46] Richard Hooker's position in relation to this broad or moderate strand in Anglican thought is ambivalent because he also relates to the Reformed or Calvinist tradition.[47]

3.3 *Richard Hooker*

Huntington probably owed at least two major planks of his argument to his reading of Richard Hooker and probably also to the discussions of Hooker by Coleridge and Gladstone, to look no further: (1) Hooker's ideal of a united, comprehensive, national church; and (2) Hooker's concept of the handful of essential ingredients of unity.

(1) Hooker both assumed and advocated a concept of a national church that was both organically united and inclusively comprehensive. In the struggle for the political unity and theological integrity of the post-Reformation English Church, Hooker reaffirmed, for the English context, the inherited medieval concept of the one body of Christendom, the *Corpus Christianorum*, the Christian commonwealth, which the magisterial Reformers, both continental and English, had continued to uphold. In Hooker's day, the kingdom faced the internal threats of radical Protestant sectarianism (the Separatists), Puritan Presbyterianism within the Church of England, and Roman Catholic insurrection encouraged by the pope (the Rising of the Northern Earls, 1569), exacerbated by the external threat of Roman Catholic invasion, also promoted by the pope (the Spanish Armada, 1588). In *Of the Lawes of Ecclesiasticall Politie*[48] Hooker provided a theological legitimation of the regime of Queen Elizabeth I and her constitutional settlement of the church, both of which had been vulnerable from their inception in 1558–1559. Hooker restated the standard medieval doctrine that there existed one Christian commonwealth in which the pope and bishops, on the one hand, and the Holy Roman Emperor and national monarchies, on the other, respectively wielded two aspects of Christ's power: the spiritual and the temporal swords. In the reign of Elizabeth's father, Henry VIII, the roles of pope and emperor had been rolled into one and explicitly and blatantly assumed by the sovereign (Henry and his successors), with the church, its archbishops and bishops made subservient to the demands of Tudor statecraft. The Christian civil (not "secular" in the modern sense) power held the upper hand. But Hooker boldly cut back any claims or pretensions of the monarch to dictate doctrinal and sacramental aspects of the church's life.[49] In

---

46 See Avis, *Anglicanism and the Christian Church*, chs. 4–5. For the "Broad Church" in the 19th century, see Charles Richard Sanders, *Coleridge and the Broad Church Movement*, Durham NC, Duke University Press, 1942; Tod E. Jones, *The Broad Church: A Biography of a Movement*, Lanham MD, Lexington Books, 2003; Stewart J. Brown, "The Broad Church Movement, National Culture, and the Established Churches of Great Britain (c. 1850–c. 1900)," in: Hilary M. Carey & John Gascoigne, eds., *Church and State in Old and New Worlds*, Leiden, Brill, 2011, 99–128 (Brown casts his net widely within the Broad Church and Liberal Anglican tendencies; he emphasizes their concern for a comprehensive national church, but he does not elaborate on the philosophical and theological ideas of unity that were held by the Broad Churchmen).

47 See Avis, *Anglicanism and the Christian Church*, ch. 2.

---

48 Richard Hooker, *Of the Lawes of Ecclesiasticall Politie* = Richard Hooker, *The Folger Library Edition of the Works of Richard Hooker*, ed. William Speed Hill, vol. 3, Cambridge MA, The Belknap Press of Harvard University Press, 1981.

49 Malcolm B. Yarnell III, *Royal Priesthood in the English Reformation*, Oxford, Oxford University Press, 2013, is a useful guide to the territory and literature, though I do not accept the author's contention that King Henry VIII claimed to exercise sacramental functions and that Archbishop Thomas Cranmer acquiesced in this.

any power struggle between church and state, the integrity of the church was Hooker's overriding imperative. He was seeking to restore a better balance or equilibrium between church and state in the interests of a unified Christian and ecclesial commonwealth. So Hooker insisted: "There is not any man of the *Church of England* but the same man is also a member of the *Commonwealth*; nor any man a member of the *Commonwealth* which is not also of the *Church of England*."[50] Again Hooker insists: "One and the self same people are the *Church* and the *Commonwealth*."[51] Only heathens (Muslims) and heretics (Roman Catholics who refused to attend their parish church – "recusants" – together with militant Protestant Separatists) were outside the visible church. Church and nation were essentially coterminous.

(2) Huntington's four points serving to encapsulate the essentials of unity were possibly, even probably, influenced by Richard Hooker's historic statement about "the essence of Christianity." Speaking of the outward unity of the visible church (rather than, at this point, of the spiritual unity of the mystical Body of Christ, which for Hooker is to be conceived christologically and sacramentally), Hooker echoes Eph 4:4–5: "The unity of which visible body and Church of Christ consisteth in that uniformity which all several persons thereunto belonging have, by reason of that *one Lord* whose servants they all profess themselves, that *one faith* which they all acknowledge, that *one baptism* wherewith they are all initiated." He continues: "The visible Church of Jesus Christ is therefore one in outward profession of those things which supernaturally appertain to the very essence of Christianitie [*sic*] and are necessarily required in

every particular christian [*sic*] man."[52] In Hooker, the theological quest for "the foundation of faith" is intertwined with "fundamental articles of faith" and "the essence of Christianity." Here the disciplines of ecclesiology (the presenting issue of the unity of the church) and of fundamental theology (theological methods and norms) converge. The tendency here in Hooker is not towards minimalism in the substance of the faith, for what could be more momentous or more inexhaustible than "one Lord, one faith, one baptism"? The tendency of his argument is towards identifying those articles, few in number but great in import, that comprise the very core and heart of Christian faith and life.[53] So, when William Reed Huntington proposed his four points of unity, he was working, no doubt consciously, in an estimable tradition, which was given added luster by the contribution of Richard Hooker, who is generally acknowledged to be the greatest, most magisterial and most seminal Anglican theologian of all time.

3.4   *Samuel Taylor Coleridge*

Samuel Taylor Coleridge is famous as one of the early Romantic English poets, but he is also justly celebrated as probably the most brilliant and most seminal of lay Anglican philosopher-theologians. It is highly probable – even virtually certain – that Huntington's notion of a national, united church for America was informed by a reading of Coleridge's highly influential work *On the Constitution of the Church and State According to the Idea of Each* (1829).[54] In a moment, Coleridge's

---

50   Richard Hooker, *Of the Lawes of Ecclesiasticall Politie*, book VIII, ch. i, section 2 = Richard Hooker, *The Folger Library Edition*, vol. 3, 319 (italics original). For a summary of the medieval ideal, see Avis, *Beyond the Reformation?*, chs. 2–3.

51   Hooker, *Of the Lawes of Ecclesiasticall Politie*, book VIII, ch. iii, section 5 = Hooker, *The Folger Library Edition*, vol. 3, 355–356 (italics original).

52   Richard Hooker, *Of the Lawes of Ecclesiasticall Politie*, book III, ch. i, sections 3–4 = Hooker, *The Folger Library Edition*, vol. 1, Cambridge MA, The Belknap Press of Harvard University Press, 1977, 396.

53   On the essence of Christianity quest, see Stephen W. Sykes, *The Identity of Christianity: Theologians and the Essence of Christianity from Schleiermacher to Barth*, London, SPCK, 1984, and Paul Avis, "Stephen Sykes and the Essence of Christianity," *Ecclesiology* 15, 2019, 34–45.

54   Samuel Taylor Coleridge, *On the Constitution of the Church and State According to the Idea of Each* (1829), in: Samuel Taylor Coleridge, *The Collected Works of*

convoluted and opaque argument will be outlined, but first we should register both the influence of Hooker on Coleridge and Coleridge's admiration of Hooker. Coleridge cannot speak too highly of Hooker's thought, though he identifies Hooker as – unlike himself – an Aristotelian, that is a thinker attending to facts or empirical truths, rather than a Platonist, moved by visions, ideas and ideals, as Coleridge was. Being limited by his Aristotelian philosophical framework, Hooker's achievement was to have created, according to Coleridge, "a consummate Synthesis of Understanding and Sense," though "to the tranquil Empyrean of *Ideas* he had not ascended."[55] Coleridge himself was working at the level of "Ideas"; thus his work *On the Constitution of the Church and State* was not intended as an empirical description of the prevailing state of affairs, but as the ideal constitutional situation, as the rest of the title indicates: *According to the Idea of Each*. The book's function is teleological, stating an immanent aim and purpose. While this work is Coleridge's most complete statement of his ecclesiology, we are interested in it here from the point of view of his "idea" of Christian unity; therefore much in his account is omitted.[56]

In *On the Constitution of the Church and State*, Coleridge (like Hooker before him) was reaffirming and restating the ideal of a single, national, comprehensive and established church against what he perceived as a serious threat to its integrity. The threat, for both Hooker and Coleridge came, directly or indirectly, from the Roman Catholic Church. For Coleridge, the ostensible or presenting issue was Roman Catholic Emancipation (1829), the legislation to give Roman Catholic subjects civil and political rights in the United Kingdom of (almost entirely Protestant) Great Britain and (almost entirely Roman Catholic) Ireland for the first time since the Reformation. (However, internal evidence suggests that Coleridge had already drafted much of a book on the ancient English constitution before the period of constitutional crisis in 1828–1829).[57] Coleridge and Keble were of one mind in their fear of the ultimate effect of Lord Grey's Whig government's program of legislative reform.

The Test and Corporation Acts, which discriminated against Dissenters (Nonconformists), had been repealed in 1828 by the previous (Tory) government which also had enacted Roman Catholic Emancipation in the following year. Extension of the electoral franchise, by the succeeding Whig administration in the Great Reform Act of 1832, was followed by the rationalizing of episcopal and archiepiscopal sees in the Irish Church in 1833. This was the immediate trigger for Keble's Assize Sermon which launched the Tractarian movement for the defense of the rights, privileges and assets of the established church on the old High Church and Tory ideological platform. Coleridge's idiosyncratic defense of the ancient constitution of church and state was ultimately directed at the perceived ultimate threat of the disestablishment of the Church of England, a threat that rumbled on through much of the 19th century and into the 20th.

Coleridge's method of defending the integrity of the English Christendom was the highly

---

Samuel Taylor Coleridge, ed. Kathleen Coburn, vol. 10, *On the Constitution of the Church and State*, ed. John Colmer, London, Routledge & Kegan Paul, 1976. See further John Colmer, *Coleridge: Critic of Society*, Oxford, Clarendon Press, 1959; Pamela Edwards, *The Statesman's Science: History, Nature, and Law in the Political Thought of Samuel Taylor Coleridge*, New York NY, Columbia University Press, 2004; Luke Savin Herrick Wright, *Samuel Taylor Coleridge and the Anglican Church*, Notre Dame IN, University of Notre Dame Press, 2010, ch. 9. Among the voluminous literature on Coleridge, I would single out Frederick Burwick, ed., *The Oxford Handbook of Samuel Taylor Coleridge*, Oxford, Oxford University Press, 2009, and esp. ch. 12 by Pamela Edwards, "Coleridge on Politics and Religion: *The Statesman's Manual, Aids to Reflection, On the Constitution of Church and State*," 235–253.

55   Roberta Florence Brinkley, ed., *Coleridge on the Seventeenth Century*, Durham NC, Duke University Press, 1955, 162, 146–147.

56   For other aspects of Coleridge's ecclesiology, see Avis, *Anglicanism and the Christian Church*, 265–271.

57   Coleridge, On the *Constitution of the Church and State*, passim.

paradoxical one of making a distinction between the Church of Christ (the one holy Catholic and apostolic Church; broadly comparable to Hooker's "mystical" church) and the "Nationality" (sometimes misspelt "Nationality" in modern discussions) or "National Church," which was wider and more inclusive than the Church of England itself.[58] This strange entity, which Coleridge sometimes, but not always, calls a *Church*, is actually both more and less than a church: more than a church, because it has research and educative functions in the realms of the liberal arts and sciences laid upon it; but also less than a church because it lacks the dimension of sacramental communion with and through the Holy Trinity that the presence of "the Church of Christ" imparts to the Church of England. The established Church of England is conceived by Coleridge as an amalgam or union of the Church of Christ and the Nationalty, a conjunction that had come about by a "blessed accident"[59] of history, "a providential boon, a grace of God."[60] As an instantiation of the constitution, the national church is the guarantee of liberty of conscience for all. Coleridge's Nationalty contains (and in his argument is actually assimilated to) the "Clerisy" (which Coleridge derives from "clerk," a literate or basically educated person).[61] The "National Clerisy" is a body of educators and moral exemplars and guardians of the constitution (they were not necessarily ordained; the Clerisy included "schoolmasters"). The role and function of the Clerisy is to uphold the historic way of life of the English people, including their constitution, and to inculcate in the general population received Christian principles and values and to promote moral, literary and aesthetic "cultivation." Just as Coleridge's "Church of Christ"

is not identical with the Church of England, so the "Clerisy" is not identical with the Anglican clergy, but is interdenominational and thus comprehensive (or as we would say today, ecumenical) – but only up to a point! It did not include Roman Catholics, because Coleridge specified "only two absolute disqualifications" from membership of the Clerisy: "allegiance to a Foreign Power" and "the Acknowledgment of any visible HEAD OF THE CHURCH," other than the sovereign (i.e. the pope on both counts). (Coleridge coupled together with these two caveats compulsory celibacy "in connection with, and dependence on, a foreign and extra-national head.")[62] Amid the fears of Roman Catholic resurgence and possible eventual disestablishment of the Church of England, this was as far as Coleridge's highly distinctive "idea" of a united national church could go. It is inconceivable that Huntington was not influenced by Coleridge's ideal and ideas.

In this treatise, Coleridge, like Huntington after him, lists four marks or "characteristics" of the Church of Christ and its unity.[63]

(1)   The church is not a temporal kingdom or state, but stands over against all states and kingdoms: "The Christian Church is not a KINGDOM, REALM (*royaume*), or STATE ... of the WORLD ... but it is the appointed Opposite to them all *collectively* – the *sustaining, correcting, befriending* Opposite of the world! the compensating counterforce to the inherent and inevitable evils and defects of the STATE."

(2)   The church is neither invisible nor hidden, but has the nature of a public institution: "The Christian Church is not a secret community ... it is objective in its nature and purpose, not mystic or subjective ... existing only in and for the individual. Consequently the Church here spoken of is not the kingdom

58   Coleridge, *On the Constitution of the Church and State*, 125.

59   Coleridge, *On the Constitution of the Church and State*, 54.

60   Coleridge, *On the Constitution of the Church and State*, 54.

61   Ben Knights, *The Idea of the Clerisy in the Nineteenth Century*, Cambridge, Cambridge University Press, 1978.

62   Coleridge, *On the Constitution of the Church and State*, 81.

63   Coleridge, *On the Constitution of the Church and State*, 114–115.

of God which is within, and which Cometh not with observation but is most observable – a city built on a hill, and not to be hid – an institution consisting of visible and public communities ... it is the Church visible and militant under Christ."

(3) The church has no earthly head or center of authority, such as the papacy. It is definitively characterized by "[t]he absence of any visible head or sovereign, and by the non-existence, nay the utter preclusion, of any local or personal center of unity, of any single source of universal power."

(4) The church is universal and neither ethnically nor geographically defined; neither English nor Roman, neither Latin nor Greek. It does not belong to any nation. We should, therefore, speak of "the Church of Christ in England," rather than "the Church of England."

The unity of the Church of Christ for Coleridge is, therefore: (1) spiritually or supernaturally, not temporally or politically, defined or awarded; (2) not invisible, but visible, public and institutional; (3) not secured by an earthly human head or a single center of authority; (4) Catholic, as present in all nations and peoples.

3.5   *Thomas Arnold*

Thomas Arnold's *Principles of Church Reform* was published in the critical year for the Church of England of Keble's Assize Sermon and the first batch of the *Tracts for the Times*: 1833.[64] It unquestionably belongs within the genealogy of theological visions of unity, specifically the unity of a national church. Arnold's ruling intellectual passion was for the unity and integrity of the Christian nation or state, conceived as an organic whole and as having a moral and spiritual personality (and thus a profound affinity to the church). The components of such a Christian state would

be bound together, not by a uniformity of doctrine or a uniformity of liturgical texts and rites, but by a common basic religious practice and moral intentionality. Thus the ethical state would actually be coterminous with the church. The unifying bond of both church and society was moral purpose expressed in action, not belief expressed in creeds and confessions. In Arnold's ecclesiology, just as in Richard Hooker's, church and nation (or state) were correlative entities and identical in their membership. In his ecclesiological vision, Arnold was a successor not only of Hooker, but also of Burke and Coleridge, and was a precursor of Huntington – especially of the latter's minimalist formula for Christian unity – and thus exerted a long-term influence on the Chicago-Lambeth Quadrilateral.[65]

Thomas Arnold was a son of pre-Tractarian Oxford – specifically Oriel College – and was the famous reforming and innovating headmaster of Rugby School. He was also the father of the poet, literary and social critic and school inspector, Matthew Arnold, a great Victorian public intellectual.[66] Thomas Arnold was profoundly moved by the early Romantic poetry of Coleridge and William Wordsworth and later enjoyed a friendship with Wordsworth in the Lake District. But Arnold was no Romantic and deplored the Romantic idealization and mystification of the Middle Ages, as it was depicted, for example, in Coleridge's "Christabel," Keats' "La Belle Dame sans Merci," the Gothic tendency in popular literature, and certain of the *Waverley Novels* of Sir Walter Scott. Nor did Arnold, as an Aristotelian (like Hooker), see himself as a disciple of Coleridge the Platonist (though he was profoundly indebted to Coleridge's *On the Constitution of the Church*

---

64   Thomas Arnold, *Principles of Church Reform* (1833), in: Thomas Arnold, *The Miscellaneous Works of Thomas Arnold, D.D.*, London, B. Fellowes, 1845.

65   On Thomas Arnold, see Eugene L. Williamson, *The Liberalism of Thomas Arnold: A Study of His Religious and Political Writings*, Tuscaloosa AL, University of Alabama Press, 1964.

66   Nicholas Murray, *A Life of Matthew Arnold*, London, Hodder & Stoughton, 1996.

and State).[67] Arnold was a Broad Churchman, a Liberal Anglican, who believed in religious, moral and political progress.[68] He was a robustly practical social and religious reformer, preacher and prophet. He was influenced by the philosophy – and indeed theology – of history of the Neapolitan Giambattista Vico,[69] was versed in German historiography and theology, but averse to the cloudy speculations of German philosophy.[70] Arnold was an implacable foe of Tractarianism (the Oxford Movement), which was the antithesis of the Liberal Anglican movement and its reforming agenda. He regarded Tractarianism as backward looking and anachronistic, because (he believed) it promoted episcopacy as a panacea for the ills of the church and elevated the priesthood above the laity (which Arnold pilloried as "sacerdotalism," though that trend came with later generations of the Catholic and ritualistic movement in Anglicanism).[71] Arnold was a progressive thinker and doer. The significance of his thought for the trajectory of the desire for unity and the emergence of Anglican ecumenical method can be summarized in the following arguments.

Like Hooker, Coleridge, Maurice and Huntington, Arnold was concerned primarily with the concept of a national church and the means of its unity.

Also, like Huntington, Arnold did not believe that unity could be achieved on the basis of doctrinal uniformity and the enforcement of doctrinal credenda (such as the Thirty-Nine Articles). Uniformity had been tried; Parliamentary Acts to that effect had been attached to almost all of the various recensions of the *Book of Common Prayer* between 1549 and 1662. Arnold argued – rather speciously, I think – that doctrinal uniformity could only be imposed on the basis of an infallible ecclesial authority – which the Reformers had rejected in their theology and disclaimed for themselves, though they attributed a practical infallibility to the Bible.[72] However, Arnold perceived that there was an alternative model of unity to defined doctrinal unity, namely a voluntary unity of practice. "We may consent to act together, but we cannot consent to believe together ... action being a thing in our own power. But no motives can persuade us to believe together."[73] Arnold discerned a deep source of unity in a common tradition and a shared moral purpose, and in this approach he was following in the wake of Hooker, Butler, Burke and Coleridge.[74]

Whereas Huntington located the essentials of unity in four fundamental points (Scripture, creeds, sacraments and episcopate), Arnold placed unity in the realm of practice, in particular the practice of worship, of common prayer rather loosely understood, of Christians doing basically

---

67   David Newsome, *Two Classes of Men: Platonism and English Romantic Thought*, London, Murray, 1974.

68   See his essay, "On the Social Progress of States," appended to the first volume of his edition of Thucydides (1830) and republished in Arnold, *The Miscellaneous Works of Thomas Arnold*, 81–111, esp. 81; also his "Preface to the Third Volume of the Edition of Thucydides," in: Arnold, *The Miscellaneous Works of Thomas Arnold*, 383–399, esp. 399. For background, Duncan Forbes, *The Liberal Anglican Idea of History*, Cambridge, Cambridge University Press, 1952.

69   See Arnold's comments on Vico in "On the Social Progress of States" (Arnold, *The Miscellaneous Works of Thomas Arnold*, 82).

70   For Arnold's discussion of the great German historian Barthold Georg Niebuhr, his attack on Romantic history and the idealization of the European Middle Ages, see *Quarterly Review* 32, 1825, 67–92.

71   For Arnold's attacks on the Oxford Movement and its alleged sacerdotalism, see "The Oxford Malignants," *Edinburgh Review* 63, 1836, 225–239; the title of the article was not devised by Arnold. Also his *Fragment on the Church* (1844), ed. Mary Arnold, London, B. Fellowes, ²1845.

72   Arnold, *The Miscellaneous Works of Thomas Arnold*, 273.

73   Thomas Arnold, *Introductory Lectures on Modern History, Delivered in Lent Term, MDCCCXLII: With the Inaugural Lecture Delivered in December, MDCCCXLI*, London, B. Fellowes, ⁶1874, 39.

74   On the theological method of Bishop Joseph Butler and of Edmund Burke, see Paul Avis, *In Search of Authority: Anglican Theological Method from the Reformation to the Enlightenment*, London, T&T Clark, 2014, 326–339. Arnold acknowledged Butler's formative influence on his thought.

the same things, albeit for slightly different reasons. Such a national church could, he said, include within it "persons using a different ritual and
subscribing different articles."[75] The liturgy could
be devised to provide the boundaries of diversity –
and (Arnold suggested provocatively) even Unitarians, who denied the divinity of Christ, could be
accommodated.[76] Arnold and Huntington shared
a certain pragmatic approach to questions of doctrine and worship in the interests of Christian
unity.

Finally, Arnold aimed to include or comprehend
various tribes of Christian profession – the Anglican
and several Nonconformist churches – within a
single united national church. English church life
since the Reformation had been marked by a tension or (theologically speaking) a dialectic of toleration and comprehension, see-sawing between
the two poles of policy. Queen Elizabeth I had
managed a policy of intentional general comprehension, based on outward conformity and largely
turning a blind eye to harmless, low-profile deviations from the norm.[77] With the rise of Protestant

Dissent in the mid-17th century, after the English
Civil War, toleration became the urgent issue. But
toleration failed, bringing reciprocal persecution,
between the 1630s (the build-up to the Civil War)
and 1689 when the Toleration Act marked the beginning of a series of concessions to those who
would not conform to the established church.
As John Spurr has written, "The Toleration Act of
1689 marked the end of the Church of England's
claim to be the national church, the single all-
inclusive church of the English people."[78] The 1828
and 1829 acts in favor of Dissenters and Roman
Catholics respectively were further milestones
along the road of widening toleration. The ecumenical movement in England, signaled by the
Appeal to All Christian People, with its restatement
and reframing of the Lambeth Quadrilateral, put
out by the 1920 Lambeth Conference, revived the
vision of a comprehensive national church – the
Quadrilateral was intended to aid "home reunion."
But, as we look back on a century of theological
dialogue and interconfessional rapprochement,
the institutional results of that movement, in
terms of denominational unions, seem meagre,
while its fruits in changed attitudes and aspects of
practice have been momentous. Thomas Arnold
was emphatically campaigning for the comprehension, rather than the toleration, of Dissenters
(though not Roman Catholics) within a national
church. Recognizing that proposals for a liturgy
of comprehension had been abandoned in 1662,
Arnold believed that it could be accomplished, albeit with much looser parameters, in the different
circumstances of the mid-19th century.[79] In setting

---

75   Arthur Penrhyn Stanley, *The Life and Correspondence
      of Thomas Arnold, D.D.*, London, Ward Lock, ⁴1891, 431.
      Julius Charles Hare (1795–1855) deserves to be men-
      tioned along with Thomas Arnold as an advocate for
      a comprehensive national church that did not rely
      on uniformity of beliefs, rites or ecclesiastical polity.
      See Hare's preface to his archidiaconal charge "The
      Unity of the Church" (1845) in: Julius Charles Hare,
      Miscellaneous Pamphlets, Cambridge, 1855; also in
      Julius Charles Hare, *The Duty of the Church in Times
      of Trial*, London, J.W. Parker, 1848. On Hare's life and
      thought see N. Merrill Distad, *Guessing at Truth: The
      Life of Julius Charles Hare (1795–1855)*, Shepherdstown
      WV, Patmos Press, 1979. On Hare's ecclesiology, with
      special reference to his views on Luther and the
      Reformation and his hostile assessment of Newman
      and Tractarianism, see Avis, *Anglicanism and the
      Christian Church*, 280–287.

76   Arnold, *The Miscellaneous Works of Thomas Arnold*,
      285, 325–326.

77   "[T]he settlement itself was administered in a distinct-
      ly Nicodemite spirit. Scarcely draconian in its dictates,
      the law turned out to be even laxer in its application,
      requiring nothing more even of the queen's Catholic
      subjects than a certain attendance at, and an even

      more minimal conformity to, the rites and ordinances
      of the national Church"; Peter Lake, "'Puritans' and
      'Anglicans' in the Post-Reformation English Church,"
      OHA 1, 352–379, here 354–355.

78   John Spurr, *The Restoration Church of England
      (1646–1689)*, New Haven CT, Yale University Press,
      1991, 105. See further Norman Sykes, *From Sheldon to
      Secker: Aspects of English Church History (1660–1768)*,
      Cambridge, Cambridge University Press, 1959, ch. 3.

79   Arnold, *Introductory Lectures on Modern History*, 248;
      Timothy J. Fawcett, *The Liturgy of Comprehension,
      1689: An Abortive Attempt to Revise the Book of Common*

his face in this direction, he was swimming against the tide of 19th-century religious controversy in England, controversy that was entrenched, vitriolic and intractable – one example being the bitter animosity between Arnold himself and the Tractarians.

3.6   Frederick Denison Maurice

In a comprehensive research project devoted to "the desire for Christian unity," the Anglican theologian Frederick Denison Maurice deserves a secure place for he has much to teach us about the unity of the church.[80] Maurice confessed: "The desire for *Unity* has haunted me all my life through; I have never been able to substitute any desire for that" – but Maurice added: "Or to accept any of the different schemes for satisfying it which men have devised."[81] Growing up in a household simmering with religious tensions (his father was a Unitarian minister, albeit of moderate views; his mother converted from Unitarianism to Calvinistic evangelicalism), the young Maurice was filled with

longing for harmony, reconciliation, and unity. A hunger and thirst for unity was the guiding thread of his life, work, and writings. He eventually found the key to true unity, both in the church and in the world, in the orthodox Christian doctrine (and reality) of the Holy Trinity, the tri-une God.[82] He followed his mentor Coleridge in a theological and spiritual journey from rationalistic Unitarianism to the Church of England, where he wholeheartedly embraced its official formularies: the Thirty-Nine Articles of Religion, the *Book of Common Prayer* (1662) and the Ordinal of 1662 (which provided exclusively for episcopal ordination).

Maurice echoes the title and content of Coleridge's great but obscure work on ecclesiology by the constant deployment of the terms "idea," "constitution" and "church and state" in his writings on the church (along with "institution," "ordinance" and "sign"). As Jeremy Morris explains, "From Coleridge, Maurice learnt the merit of appreciating the complex nature of truth and its many-sidedness. No one opinion could claim to capture truth completely. The task of the theologian was to explore the complementary truthful insights embedded in apparently conflicting schools of thought within Christianity."[83] Maurice, like Coleridge, believed that individuals were often right in what they positively affirmed, but often wrong in what they denied, especially when they defined themselves and their views over against others.[84] This conviction led Maurice to shun ecclesiastical partisan positions ("church parties") and to oppose all forms of system-making in theology; to pursue system was to adopt a method of exclusion.

Prayer, Southend-on-Sea, Mayhew-McCrimmon for the Alcuin Club, 1973.

80   Frederick Denison Maurice, *The Kingdom of Christ*, ed. Alec R. Vidler, 2 vols., London, SCM Press, 1958; Frederick Denison Maurice, *Theological Essays*, London, James Clarke, 1957. On Maurice, see Alec R. Vidler, *The Theology of F.D. Maurice*, London, SCM Press, 1947; Alec R. Vidler, *F.D. Maurice and Company: Nineteenth Century Studies*, London, SCM Press, 1966; Michael Ramsey, *F.D. Maurice and the Conflicts of Modern Theology*, Cambridge, Cambridge University Press, 1951; Jeremy N. Morris, *F.D. Maurice and the Crisis of Christian Authority*, Oxford, Oxford University Press, 2005; Frederick Denison Maurice, *To Build Christ's Kingdom: F.D. Maurice and His Writings*, ed. Jeremy N. Morris, London, Canterbury Press, 2007; Olive J. Brose, *Frederick Denison Maurice: Rebellious Conformist*, Athens OH, Ohio University Press, 1971; Frank Mauldin McClain, *Maurice: Man and Moralist*, London, SPCK, 1971; Torben Christensen, *The Divine Order: A Study in F.D. Maurice's Theology*, Leiden, Brill, 1973.

81   Frederick Denison Maurice, *The Life of Frederick Denison Maurice: Chiefly Told in His Own Letters*, ed. John Frederick Maurice, vol. 1, London, Macmillan, 1884, 41.

82   The culmination of the argument in Maurice, *Theological Essays*, is essay 16, "On the Trinity in Unity."

83   Maurice, *To Build Christ's Kingdom*, 6. See Maurice's "Dedication" of the 2nd edition of *The Kingdom of Christ* (vol. 2, appendix) to Derwent Coleridge, the second son of Samuel Taylor Coleridge. On the problem of the extent of Maurice's intellectual debt to Coleridge, see Morris, *F.D. Maurice and the Crisis of Christian Authority*, 37–43.

84   E.g. Maurice, *The Life of Frederick Denison Maurice: Chiefly Told in His Own Letters*, vol. 1, 203.

Maurice is – at one and the same time – one of the most seminal and influential of all modern Anglican theologians and one of the most difficult to understand. His writing style verges on the opaque; his meaning is often obscure; his arguments are characterized by violent paradoxes. But Anglican ecclesiology and ecumenical theology have been decisively shaped by Maurice's thought, with regard to the driving vision of unity, the methodology of complementary truths, and the notion of certain essential components or elements in the construction of unity (see the Quadrilateral). Maurice's influence on the ecumenical enterprise extends much wider than Anglicanism (actually, wider *via* Anglicanism). Jeremy Morris points out that, in *The Kingdom of Christ*, "the genesis of modern ecumenical method can be discerned."[85] Maurice even uses the now ecumenically-favored term "communion" (or "law of communion") for the essence of human fellowship.[86] The famous *Appeal to All Christian People* of the 1920 Lambeth Conference not only faithfully reflects Maurice's ecumenical method, but also sometimes deploys his language verbatim.

It has often been noted that "there are striking similarities in structure, content, and vocabulary" between the thought of Maurice and that of William Reed Huntington.[87] Both evince a longing for unity; both look for deeply embedded principles, but are allergic to "systems"; both identify a number of marks or signs of a united church; both rather self-consciously stand aside (and stand aloof) from the generally recognized "parties" or schools of thought in the church; and both have a sense of Catholicity that goes beyond any purely domestic agenda.

A particular aspect of the relationship between the ideas of Maurice and Huntington that needs exploring is the correspondence between Maurice's six signs of the Kingdom of Christ and Huntington's four points of unity (his quadrilateral). There are also intriguing threads of influence and resistance, continuity and discontinuity, between Maurice, on the one hand, and Coleridge, Arnold, Newman and Gladstone, on the other. There is indeed, as John Coulson brought out, a "common tradition" at work here. Coulson develops the theological connections (and tensions) between Coleridge, Newman and Maurice. But I am intrigued by the indications of a much longer common tradition of theological method, extending from Hooker, through Burke, to Coleridge, Maurice and Gladstone and beyond, even to Charles Gore and William Temple.[88]

In terms of theological influences on Huntington, and therefore on the concept of the Quadrilateral, there are strong, though elusive, resonances between Maurice's *The Kingdom of Christ* (1838) and *Theological Essays* (1853), on the one hand, and Huntington's *The Church-Idea: An Essay Towards Unity* (1870), on the other. Given his American situation – not least the First Amendment to the Constitution (1791) which he quotes ("Congress shall make no law respecting an establishment of religion, or prohibiting the free exercise thereof") – Huntington could not for a moment entertain Maurice's doctrine of the union of church and state. Following principally Hooker and Coleridge, Maurice postulated a union between church and state that was instantiated in every one of the queen's subjects, for they were members of both. For Maurice, the state was just as much a divine

85   Maurice, *To Build Christ's Kingdom*, 12.
86   Maurice, *The Kingdom of Christ*, vol. 1, 166.
87   Michelle Woodhouse-Hawkins, "Maurice, Huntington, and the Quadrilateral: An Exploration in Historical Theology," in: Wright, ed., *Quadrilateral at One Hundred*, 61–78, here 61.

88   John Coulson, *Newman and the Common Tradition: A Study in the Language of Church and Society*, Oxford, Clarendon Press, 1970; Stephen Prickett, "Coleridge, Newman, and F.D. Maurice: Development of Doctrine and Growth of the Mind," *Theology* 76/637, 1973, 340–349; Stephen Prickett, *Romanticism and Religion: The Tradition of Coleridge and Wordsworth in the Victorian Church*, Cambridge, Cambridge University Press, 1976. See also Jeremy Morris, "Newman and Maurice on the Via Media of the Anglican Church: Contrasts and Affinities," *AThR* 85/4, 2003, 623–640. Morris here suggests that Newman and Maurice were "perhaps the two greatest Victorian theologians" (623).

creation as the church was, and the connection between the two was "a union which has cemented itself by no human contrivances, and which exists in the very nature of things."[89]

For Maurice, as quoted just above, human inventions and schemes could never deliver unity. But there existed a God-given provision that, in principle, already united the human race and only needed to be believed in, embraced and lived by, in order to be fully realized. That provision, that principle, was what Maurice called "the divine order." To Maurice the Platonist, as for Coleridge, an *idea* was the most real thing in existence. Reality subsisted in the idea, which was both foundational and teleological: foundational of all salutary human institutions and teleological with respect to their purpose, aim, and aspiration ("Become what you are" was Maurice's great imperative for both institutions and individuals). For him, the divine order permeated and upheld the creation and the organized human world. It was chiefly embodied in three institutions: the church, the family, and the nation (or state). The first of these institutions, the church, underpinned the second and third: family and nation.[90] "The Church was human society in its normal state; the World, that same society irregular and abnormal."[91] There was, therefore, an intimate, internal connection between the unity of the church and the unity of society. The path of well-being for all humankind was to become awakened to the fact of the divine order and one's place in it; to claim it as one's true home and then to conform one's life and faith to what was already a given reality.[92]

The divine order was, for Maurice, no ethereal or invisible entity; it was physically embodied in institutions and their structuring ordinances. The church was structured by the social forms that it found already existing in any given society or nation.[93] Maurice has a very robust doctrine of the ordinances of the church – they are what sustain it as an institution that serves the divine order in tangible ways. Maurice has six "signs" of the presence of the divine order: baptism, the creeds, liturgical forms, the Eucharist, the ordained ministry, and the Scriptures. These are human, social artifacts, as well as divine institutions. Remarkably, Maurice's signs are identical with those of William Reed Huntington and of the Chicago-Lambeth Quadrilateral, with the exception of liturgical forms, which could perhaps be regarded as included in the celebration of the sacraments. In the great work of his early years *The Kingdom of Christ* Maurice argues that sects (exemplified for him by the Society of Friends, the Quakers), by dispensing with ordinances such as the ministry, the sacraments, and the liturgy, have repudiated the appointed signs and so ceased to be vehicles or expressions of the divine order.

On the other hand, the Roman Catholic Church, according to Maurice, had made the divinely ordained structures of the church into instruments of control and repression, creating a rigid division between laity and clergy. The signs had been taken into captivity. The Church of England, however, unlike the Quakers, had retained the ordinances or signs and, unlike the Roman Catholic Church, had done so without alienating the signs from the divine order to which they belong as its expression and embodiment. In spite of all its shortcomings, therefore, the Church of England, as the established church with intimate ties to the nation and a cooperative relationship to the state, continued to serve the divine order. The Church of England could and did say, particularly in its liturgy and catechism, to every individual: "You have been made a child of God in your baptism. Claim your place in Christ's kingdom. Become what you are." For Maurice, the ordinances or signs were what made the Church of England a Catholic church

---

89   Maurice, *The Kingdom of Christ*, vol. 2, 212; see also 240–245, 305–312.
90   Maurice, *The Life of Frederick Denison Maurice: Chiefly Told in His Own Letters*, vol. 1, 306.
91   Maurice, *Theological Essays*, 276 (from the key essay 15, "The Unity of the Church").
92   Maurice, *The Kingdom of Christ*, vol. 1, 273 (Luther's sacramental theology as exemplifying this principle).
93   Coulson, *Newman and the Common Tradition*, 194.

(having the signs that belong to the one church of Christ), while its national extension, national involvement and national commitment were what made it a Protestant church (because the Reformers reclaimed the particular, national character and allegiance of churches in opposition to the universal, absolute claims of the papacy). Perhaps this is partly why Maurice could claim, in a typical extreme paradox, that a church was most Catholic when it was most Protestant.[94] In sum, Maurice's lifelong endeavor was to connect the unity of the church to the unity of all humankind and to ground this unity in the life of the Holy Trinity.

3.7 *William Ewart Gladstone*

As well as dominating British politics for half a century, serving as chancellor of the Exchequer four times and as prime minister four times, William Ewart Gladstone was also probably the most influential Anglican lay theologian of the 19th century after Samuel Taylor Coleridge.[95]

Deeply shaped in early life by evangelicalism, the young Gladstone embraced the High Church tradition that ran from Hooker, through the Caroline and Jacobean divines on either side of the Civil War years, through the High Churchmen of the 18th century, right up to his own day; the great contemporary exponent, to whom Gladstone was much indebted, being William Palmer of Worcester College, Oxford.[96] Gladstone then took the further step of aligning himself – not uncritically – for a time with the Tractarian movement, and subsequently moved beyond it into a more liberal Catholic position with affinities to the Broad Church. So Gladstone combined the evangelical emphases on conversion, justification by faith, individual piety and the doctrinal authority of Scripture, with the High Church platform of the sacraments, tradition and episcopacy (in the strong form of the doctrine of apostolic succession). But on principle (like Maurice) the mature Gladstone did not adhere to any ecclesiastical party and was critical of both prevailing forms of conservative Anglicanism: evangelicalism and Tractarianism. Gladstone found them wanting, mainly because, in their repudiation of developments in the growth of knowledge – in science, biblical criticism and social thought – they tried to withstand the intellectual currents of modernity, just as Ultramontanism, Gladstone's avowed foe, did.

---

94 Frederick Denison Maurice, *Subscription No Bondage: or The Practical Advantages Afforded by the Thirty-Nine Articles as Guides in All the Branches of Academical Education*, Oxford, J.H. Parker, 1835, 110; Frederick Denison Maurice, *Three Letters to the Rev. W. Palmer*, London, J. & G. Rivington, 1842, 13.

95 The following titles are a selection of the voluminous literature on William Ewart Gladstone. Biographical: Henry Colin Gray Matthew, *Gladstone (1809–1898)*, Oxford, Oxford University Press, 1997; Richard Shannon, *Gladstone*, vol. 1, *1809–1865*, London, Hamish Hamilton, 1982, and vol. 2, *1865–1898*, Chapel Hill NC, University of North Carolina Press, 1999; David W. Bebbington, *The Mind of Gladstone: Religion, Homer, and Politics*, Oxford, Oxford University Press, 2004; Perry Butler, *Gladstone: Church, State, and Tractarianism: A Study of His Religious Ideas and Attitudes (1809–1859)*, Oxford, Clarendon Press, 1982. Key relevant works by Gladstone: *The State in Its Relations with the Church*, 2 vols., London, J. Murray, ⁴1841; *Church Principles Considered in Their Results*, London, J. Murray, 1840; *The Vatican Decrees in their Bearing on Civil Allegiance*, ed. Philip Schaff, New York NY, Harper & Bros., 1875; *Vaticanism: An Answer to Reproofs and Replies*, London, J. Murray, 1875; *Correspondence on Church and Religion of William Ewart Gladstone*, ed. Daniel

Conner Lathbury, 2 vols., London, J. Murray, 1910; *Later Gleanings: A New Series of Gleanings of Past Years: Theological and Ecclesiastical*, London, J. Murray, ²1898. Discussion: Sheridan Gilley, "Gladstone on State and Church," in: Peter Francis, ed., *The Gladstone Umbrella: Papers Delivered at the Gladstone Centenary Conference 1998*, Harwarden, Monad Press, 2001, 1–13; Avis, *Church, State, and Establishment*, 52–54; Avis, *Anglicanism and the Christian Church*, 196–204; Richard Shannon, *Gladstone: God and Politics*, London, Hambledon Continuum, 2008.

96 William Palmer of Worcester, *A Treatise on the Church of Christ*, 2 vols., London, J.G. & F. Rivington, ³1842. Gladstone read the first edition of 1838; Bebbington, *The Mind of Gladstone*, 67–69. On Palmer's ecclesiology, see Avis, *Anglicanism and the Christian Church*, 188–195.

Gladstone was deeply distrustful of the logic of the Anglican Newman's theology, especially in his work on the development of doctrine (1845).[97] Gladstone held, rather startlingly, that Newman's way of arguing a theological case was nothing less than an attack on reason (Gladstone was far from alone in this).[98] But he also believed that, if Newman had ever acquired a through grounding in Anglican ecclesiology, it would have saved him from the disastrous defection to Rome. In spite of his staunch High Church views, Gladstone was cordial towards Nonconformists and took a positive stance towards continental Lutherans. Unlike the Nonjurors and the stricter Tractarians, he did not unchurch Lutherans for their lack of the episcopal succession. These attitudes separated Gladstone from the Tractarians and their immediate successors, the Anglo-Catholics, but they aligned him with such giants of the earlier High Church tradition as Bishop Lancelot Andrewes, Archbishops John Bramhall and William Laud, together with Herbert Thorndike (canon of Westminster). These notable divines tended to excuse the continental Lutherans for their lack of bishops, generously attributing this deficiency in apostolic order to the disruptive circumstances of the 16th century, and took the line that Lutheran "superintendents" were bishops in all but name.[99] A visit to Rome as a young man had given Gladstone a vision of the reunion of Christendom – indeed the cause of unity began to dominate his life at this time.[100] What Gladstone said much later, about the English Reformation, could stand for a principle that guided him in all his endeavors: "The instinct of national unity was throughout more powerful than the disintegrating tendencies of religious controversy."[101]

While Gladstone was significantly influenced by Roman Catholic theologians, especially Johann Adam Möhler, he was implacably hostile to the Ultramontane movement within the Roman Catholic Church, which became dominant during the second half of the 19th century. Gladstone's wrath was aroused by three actions of the Roman Church: first, the re-imposition in England of the Roman Catholic sees and episcopal hierarchy in 1850; second, the decrees of Vatican I in 1869–1870 which asserted the supreme, full, immediate and universal ordinary jurisdiction of the pope over the universal church, together with papal infallibility in faith and morals (under certain conditions); and third, the papal condemnation of Anglican orders in 1896.[102] At the deepest level, Gladstone deplored the Roman Catholic retreat into the citadel of unchallengeable dogma, with its hierarchical authoritarianism, unscholarly obscurantism and general repudiation of the advance of knowledge. Bebbington states that Gladstone, in a life of ceaseless controversy, saw the Roman Catholic Church as "his greatest antagonist."[103] Gladstone corresponded sympathetically with the most eminent and learned of Roman Catholic critics of the Vatican I decrees, Ignaz von Döllinger in Germany and Lord Acton at home, both of whom he felt to be kindred spirits. Apart from these three particular crises for relations between the Church of England (and the Anglican Communion after the first Lambeth Conference, 1867) and the Roman Catholic Church, Gladstone was deeply offended by Rome's inveterate unchurching of all churches

---

97   John Henry Newman, *An Essay on the Development of Christian Doctrine*, ed. James Munro Cameron, Harmondsworth, Penguin, 1974.

98   Bebbington, *The Mind of Gladstone*, 113.

99   Avis, *Anglicanism and the Christian Church*, ch. 6; Every, *The High Church Party*, esp. 145.

100   Butler, *Gladstone*, 32.

101   William Ewart Gladstone, "The Elizabethan Settlement of Religion" (1888), in: Gladstone, *Later Gleanings*, 159–180, here 159.

102   Gladstone referred to *Apostolicae curae* as "this damnatory Bull against English [*sic*] orders"; Gladstone, *Later Gleanings*, 405. For him it sealed the reputation of Rome as the enemy of Christian unity.

103   Bebbington, *The Mind of Gladstone*, 114. Gladstone dubbed claims for papal infallibility "preposterous" (Bebbington, *The Mind of Gladstone*, 117).

that were not in a relationship of communion and obedience to the Holy See. While he insisted that he knew of no "essential points" on which the Church of England differed from the Church of Rome, Gladstone nevertheless judged (as he wrote in 1850 to Henry Manning, the future archbishop of Westminster, but at that time still an archdeacon in the Church of England) that "[t]he rejection from the fellowship of the Christian covenant of all who do not receive the authority of the See of Rome is to me an awful innovation on the faith, and a dark sign of the future for the large part of Christendom which is in communion with that see, and with which we have so deep a common interest in the maintenance of the Faith."[104]

Although Aristotle was one of Gladstone's four "Doctors" (i.e. teachers or mentors, the others being St. Augustine of Hippo, Dante and Bishop Joseph Butler), Gladstone was also, in some respects, a profoundly Platonic thinker. In his work *The State in its Relation to the Church* (published in 1838 and expanded in 1842) he followed Coleridge in taking as his starting point one controlling idea, arrived at deductively, and uncontaminated in itself by any empirical expressions. Gladstone was also influenced by Coleridge's concept of the Clerisy and follows Coleridge's view that one function of the state broadly conceived is to develop "cultivation" among the population. Gladstone shared with Thomas Arnold and Frederick D. Maurice a commitment to the notion of providential national expressions of the church. He annotated Coleridge's *On the Constitution of the Church and State*, finding it "beautiful and profound." The title of Gladstone's own work *The State in its Relation to the Church* reverses the order of the substantives in Coleridge's title. It was intended primarily as a work of political philosophy and was complemented almost immediately by a work of ecclesiology: *Church Principles Considered in Their Results* (1840).

Underlying Gladstone's case for what is sometimes called "a confessional state" is the Aristotelian-

Augustinian – thus both classical and biblical – concept of the social and political constitution of human life, orientated to the common good and infused with the notion of *koinonia* (communion, fellowship).[105] For Gladstone, as well as for Coleridge, Arnold and Maurice, this common life finds its necessary expression in national identity, national destiny.[106] It followed for Gladstone, as well as for his predecessors, just mentioned, that the national church should be as comprehensive and inclusive as possible. The threshold of membership (communion) should be kept low. The conditions of eternal salvation and the conditions of participation in the national church were to be the same. As Gladstone put it in an unpublished memorandum, probably dating from as early as 1834, when the ideas that he would set forth in his great work on state and church were crystallizing, "Community is the very essence of the Church of Christ."[107] Gladstone's work for unity was grounded in a communitarian philosophy that was, at the same time, political, ethical, and theological.

With Edmund Burke, Gladstone affirmed that the state was a moral agent; it had corporate moral personality and was compelled to take moral decisions. It therefore had an affinity to the church, an affinity so close that the two bodies in England were actually coterminous. Gladstone's *The State in its Relation to the Church* was the last major vindication of the medieval and Hookerian ideal of the unity (though not complete identity) of church and state.[108] It was quixotic to launch it in 1838, only a few years after parliamentary legislation had removed some major civil and political disabilities for Nonconformists and Roman Catholics and had laid the legal foundations for the modern pluralistic state. Gladstone quickly recognized

---

104   Gladstone, *Correspondence on Church and Religion*, vol. 2, 26.

105   Bebbington, *The Mind of Gladstone*, cit., pp. 64–67.

106   Bebbington, *The Mind of Gladstone*, 64–67.

107   Bebbington, *The Mind of Gladstone*, 76.

108   In his work on the relations between state and church, Gladstone engaged closely with Hooker's and Coleridge's ideas on the subject, though finding a closer affinity with Coleridge than with Hooker, in Bebbington's view, Bebbington, *The Mind of Gladstone*, 57.

that his scheme was already anachronistic and he dropped it from his political and ecclesiastical agenda. But it is important to note that Gladstone abandoned his cherished idea not because he had ceased to believe in it as an ideal or thought it fundamentally misconceived, but because he accepted that his vision of unity – ecclesiastical and civil – was no longer viable or practicable in the decisively changed circumstances of mid-19th-century Britain. Gladstone's later reaffirmed (in his *A Chapter of Autobiography*) the view that some kind of alliance between church and state was desirable in principle (a statement to which Huntington took exception).[109]

Gladstone's vision of the confessional state (or, looked at from a different angle, a state church) was theology thinly disguised as political philosophy. It is important for the trajectory of Christian unity because it carries forward towards the ecumenical movement, which began to be embodied in institutional form at the Edinburgh WMC in 1910, a decade after Gladstone's death, the Hookerian, Burkean, and Coleridgean vision of the organic unity of society. The key ecclesiological point is that the unity of society or nation in these thinkers is premised on the organic unity of the church, precisely because the nation or society is the outward form of the church and the vehicle of its realization in the world. The sacramental conception of the church – the church as a divinely instituted visible society – was scarcely thought of in early 19th-century England, dominated as it was by the individualistic piety of the Evangelical revival.[110] But such a sacramental idea of the church, as given by God to reveal God and to mediate God, was rediscovered by Coleridge with the help of Hooker and the Caroline divines and carried forward by the Tractarians, Newman, Maurice, Gladstone (and then – though this is beyond the scope of this contribution – by Charles Gore and his colleagues in the Holy Party and *Lux Mundi*).

The sacramentality of the church needs the given contours of human sociality to give it form in the world.[111] The idea of the church becomes incarnated in national cultures and societies. This vision of unity was grounded in orthodox theological principles and embodied in ecclesiastical institutions with their structures and ordinances (principally the ministry in historical continuity, the liturgy and the sacraments). As an essentially organic and sacramental concept of the church, its ministry and its unity, this transatlantic Anglican tradition has made a major contribution to the theological underpinning of the ecumenical movement.

4   The Chicago-Lambeth Quadrilateral (1886–1920): Chicago 1886

In 1886, the House of Bishops of the Protestant Episcopal Church adopted what has become known as the Chicago Quadrilateral. The House of Deputies did not endorse it at the time but referred it for study and action to a newly created Joint Commission on Christian Reunion. The House of Deputies formally accepted the Quadrilateral in 1892, that is after the Lambeth Conference of 1888 had made it its own, with some changes. The Chicago Quadrilateral is notable for (1) being particularly addressed to other churches in America; (2) accepting all baptized persons as members of Christ's Church; (3) treating all "human" ordering of the church as *adiaphora* and negotiable; (4) repudiating any ecumenism premised on

---

109   William Ewart Gladstone, *A Chapter of Autobiography*, London, J. Murray, 1868.
110   Coulson, *Newman and the Common Tradition*, 188.

111   Coulson, *Newman and the Common Tradition*, esp. 38–48. See Richard William Church, *The Oxford Movement: Twelve Years (1833–1845)*, London, Macmillan, 1891, 129: "Coleridge ... had taken the simple but all-important step of viewing the Church in its spiritual character as first and foremost and above all things essentially a religious society of divine institution, not dependent on the creation or will of man, or on the privileges and honours which man might think fit to assign to it; and he had undoubtedly familiarized the minds of many with this way of regarding it, however imperfect, or cloudy, or unpractical they might find the development of his ideas, and his deductions from them."

"return" or "absorption"; (5) appealing to primitive simplicity as the basis for unity – with a naive, rather romantic invocation of "the undivided Catholic Church" – and the faith of that Church as non-negotiable ("the substantial deposit of Christian Faith and Order committed by Christ and his Apostles to the Church unto the end of the world"); (6) envisaging not some kind of "reconciled diversity," but "organic" unity.

The wording of the Chicago Quadrilateral differs from Huntington's original formulation in half a dozen ways: (a) it specifies that the Holy Scriptures consist of the Old and New Testaments (thus the Apocrypha is excluded); (b) Huntington's "The Primitive Creeds" is reduced to the Nicene Creed, and "the Rule of Faith," a technical term in early Christian doctrine, becomes "the sufficient statement of the Christian Faith" (presumably "sufficient" for unity or ecclesial communion); (c) "The Two Sacraments" of Huntington are specified, as are the elements to be used; (d) "The Episcopate" becomes "The Historic Episcopate" (other churches in America, notably the Methodist churches, had bishops, but they were not in historical succession); but the phrase "Apostolic Succession" is not deployed; (e) Huntington's emphasis on episcopal governance is dropped, presumably as a one-sided definition of episcopal ministry and as such unattractive to ecumenical partners; (f) flexibility in the form of the historic episcopate is introduced with the expression "locally adapted" and there is a strong hint of an inculturation of episcopacy in the words "in the methods of its administration to the varying needs of the nations and peoples called of God into the unity of His Church."[112] Here

the Chicago Quadrilateral appears to broaden its horizons to embrace the universal church.

4.1   *The Lambeth Quadrilateral* (1888)

The Lambeth Conference of 1888 took up the Chicago Quadrilateral of two years' before and enriched its content. In the context of several more specific resolutions that encouraged ecumenical conversations, resolution 11 stated:

> That, in the opinion of this Conference, the following Articles supply a basis on which approach may be by God's blessing made towards Home Reunion:
>
> (a)   The Holy Scriptures of the Old and New Testaments, as "containing all things necessary to salvation," and as being the rule and ultimate standard of faith.
>
> (b)   The Apostles' Creed, as the Baptismal Symbol; and the Nicene Creed, as the sufficient statement of the Christian faith.
>
> (c)   The two Sacraments ordained by Christ Himself – Baptism and the Supper of the Lord – ministered with unfailing use of Christ's words of Institution, and of the elements ordained by Him.
>
> (d)   The Historic Episcopate, locally adapted in the methods of its administration to the varying needs of the nations and

---

112   The last part of the Chicago Quadrilateral says: "As inherent parts of this sacred deposit, and therefore as essential to the restoration of unity among the divided branches of Christendom, we account the following, to wit: (1) The Holy Scriptures of the Old and New Testaments as the revealed Word of God; (2) The Nicene Creed as the sufficient statement of the Christian Faith; (3) The two Sacraments – Baptism and the Supper of the Lord – ministered with unfailing use of Christ's words of institution and of the elements ordained by Him; (4) The Historic Episcopate, locally adapted in

the methods of its administration to the varying needs of the nations and peoples called of God into the unity of His Church. Furthermore, deeply grieved by the sad divisions which affect the Christian Church in our own land, we hereby declare our desire and readiness, so soon as there shall be any authorized response to this Declaration, to enter into brotherly conference with all or any Christian Bodies seeking the restoration of the organic unity of the Church, with a view to the earnest study of the conditions under which so priceless a blessing might happily be brought to pass"; Joint Commission on Approaches to Unity, ed., *Documents on Church Unity*, Greenwich CT, Seabury Press, 1962, 7–8.

peoples called of God into the Unity of His Church.[113]

Several features of the 1888 text deserve attention.

(1)   The phrase "Home Reunion" reflects the fact that the Quadrilateral was embedded in the report of the Committee on Home Reunion. But it also suggests that its target was unity initiatives between Anglican churches and churches not episcopally ordered, rather than any overtures towards Rome or the Orthodox (though the Church of Sweden and the Old Catholic Churches are mentioned in subsequent resolutions of the conference).

(2)   The only one of the four points that remained unaltered from the 1886 Chicago version was the last, concerning the historic episcopate.

(3)   The first point reintroduces Huntington's word "rule," but supplements it with a quotation from article 6 of the Thirty-Nine Articles.

(4)   The second point adds to the Nicene Creed the Apostles' Creed in the context of baptism – looking towards a mutually accepted baptism in the future.

(5)   The third point, on the sacraments, nuances what Chicago had said: in place of "The two sacraments" (as though there could be only ever two sacraments in the church), it has "The two Sacraments ordained by Christ Himself," which is a slightly different matter.

4.2   The Lambeth Quadrilateral (1920 Version)

The Lambeth Conference of 1920, with its historic *Appeal to All Christian People*, lies beyond the time-frame of this contribution and this is not the place to attempt an overall assessment of the Quadrilateral in terms of ecumenical theology.[114]

But we may briefly note the elements of continuity and discontinuity with what has been surveyed here hitherto.

(1)   In the 1920 version of the Quadrilateral, the scope of unity is broadened from the national to the universal level, from "Home Reunion" to all-round ecumenism.

(2)   The idea of inclusion and comprehension that we find being developed in Hooker, Coleridge, Arnold, Maurice and Gladstone is reaffirmed: "We acknowledge all those who believe in our Lord Jesus Christ, and have been baptized into the name of the Holy Trinity, as sharing with us membership in the universal Church of Christ which is his Body."

(3)   The 1920 version of the Quadrilateral is rather scrambled together; it is a less rigorous text than that of 1888, more open to ambiguity, its terms less well-defined. There are now three articles, Scripture and the creeds being combined into the first. It might be said that the 1920 articulation of the Quadrilateral is inept, but its deficiencies are more than compensated for by the high tone of the *Appeal* as a whole.

(4)   What is said about the Bible appears to reflect for the first time: (a) the effect of modern critical biblical study and its implications for the theology of divine revelation (it is

---

113   Roger Coleman, ed., *Resolutions of the Twelve Lambeth Conferences (1867–1988)*, Toronto ON, Anglican Book Centre, 1992, 13. See also Alan M.G. Stephenson, *Anglicanism and the Lambeth Conferences*, London, SPCK, 1978, 64–67.

114   For the text of the *Appeal*, including the Quadrilateral and commentary, see Coleman, ed., *Resolutions*,

45–48; Michael Kinnamon & Brian E. Cope, eds., *The Ecumenical Movement: An Anthology of Key Texts and Voices*, Geneva, WCC Publications, 1997, 81–83. For background see Stephenson, *Anglicanism and the Lambeth Conferences*, ch. 9; Paul Avis, "Anglicanism and Christian Unity in the Twentieth Century," OHA 4, 186–213, here 193–196. For details of the making of the text of the *Appeal*, see Charlotte Methuen, "Lambeth 1920: The Appeal to All Christian People, an Account by G.K.A. Bell and the Redactions of the Appeal," in: Melanie Barber, Gabriel Sewell & Stephen Taylor, eds., *From the Reformation to the Permissive Society: A Miscellany in Celebration of the 400th Anniversary of Lambeth Palace Library*, Martlesham, Boydell & Brewer, 2010, 521–564; Charlotte Methuen, "The Making of 'An Appeal to All Christian People' at the 1920 Lambeth Conference," in: Avis & Guyer, eds., *The Lambeth Conference*, 107–131.

described as "the *record* of God's revelation"); (b) a personalist turn in philosophy and then theology (God's revelation is "*of Himself* to man").[115]

(5) The quotation from article VI ("containing all things necessary for salvation") is dropped, though the possible reasons for that are uncertain.

(6) In the point on the sacraments, nothing is now said about a requirement to use only the elements ordained by Christ.

(7) The episcopate is not explicitly mentioned. The fourth point simply refers to "A ministry acknowledged by every part of the Church as possessing not only the inward call of the Spirit, but also the commission of Christ and the authority of the whole body." Thus the "historic" aspect of episcopacy is downplayed, but episcopacy (not "the Historic Episcopate" as such) is introduced in gentle and irenic terms, in the commentary that follows, as serving the continuity and unity of the church:

> VII. May we not reasonably claim that the Episcopate is the one means of providing such a ministry? It is not that we call in question for a moment the spiritual reality of the ministries of those Communions which do not possess the Episcopate. On the contrary, we thankfully acknowledge that these ministries have been manifestly blessed and owned by the Holy Spirit as effective means of grace. But we submit that considerations of history and of present experience justify the claim which we make on behalf of the Episcopate. Moreover, we would urge that it is now and will prove to be in the future the best

instrument for maintaining the unity and continuity of the Church.

(8) There are remarkable resonances and echoes of language with the evolving Anglican ecumenical theology of the 19th century (especially the theology of Maurice). In addition to the explicit themes of inclusion and comprehension, referred to in (2) above, these resonances include: the idea of "fellowship" which is the leitmotif of the *Appeal*; the warm acknowledgment of the positive principles embodied in the non-episcopal churches; the key ecclesiological role accorded to baptism and baptismal unity. Even the statement "The vision which rises before us is that of a Church, genuinely Catholic, loyal to all truth, and gathering into its fellowship all 'who profess and call themselves Christians'" seems to be direct echo of Maurice when he wrote in *The Kingdom of Christ*, "... there rose up before me the idea [*sic*] of a Church Universal, not built upon human inventions or human faith, but upon the very nature of God himself, and upon the union which He has formed with his creatures ... that harmony which God has created, and of which He Himself is the centre."[116]

5   Lord Halifax, the Abbé Portal and the Question of Anglican Orders

Considering that the papal condemnation of Anglican holy orders by Leo XIII in the bull *Apostolicae curae* of 1896 constituted the greatest crisis in Anglican/Roman Catholic relations since the Reformation, it is surprising how little attention this episode has received in standard accounts of the church history of the period. In fact, general histories tend to skate over it so that the general reader would not know that *Apostolicae curae* provoked a major crisis in relations between Canterbury

---

115   Italics mine. See generally Balázs M. Mezei, Francesca A. Murphy & Kenneth Oakes, eds., *The Oxford Handbook of Divine Revelation*, Oxford, Oxford University Press, forthcoming, and in particular Paul Avis, "Revelation, Epistemology, and Authority."

116   Maurice, *The Kingdom of Christ*, vol. 2, 363.

and Rome and much heart-searching in both communions.[117]

117 In *A History of the Popes (1830–1914)*, Owen Chadwick has only this to say: "[T]he pope [Leo XIII] who set out to be friendly with the Anglicans achieved a condemnation which hurt relations between Rome and Canterbury more than any act of the pope since Dr. Wiseman's letter about the new hierarchy. The Bull was a supreme example of a self-contradictory policy in Rome"; Owen Chadwick, *A History of the Popes (1830–1914)*, Oxford, Clarendon Press, 1998, 541. In his earlier work, *The Victorian Church*, Chadwick refers in passing to Lord Halifax's visit to Leo XIII and makes a glancing reference to the condemnation of Anglican orders; Owen Chadwick, *The Victorian Church*, vol. 2, London, SCM Press, ²1987, 354–355, 407. *The Wiley-Blackwell Companion to the Anglican Communion* is concerned mainly with the life of the Communion today and on that topic it contains a wealth of information. As far as I can see in its 753 pages, the only discussion of Anglican orders is J. Robert Wright's authoritative but brief summary of the history of the Ordinal from 1550 to 1662. There is a section in this reference work on "Structures of the Communion" and I would have thought that there was a case for regarding the common, interchangeable ordained ministry as one of the structures – it is certainly at least a pillar – and mentioning the bitter controversy of 1896 and the vindication of Anglican orders by the two English archbishops; Ian S. Markham & others, eds., *The Wiley-Blackwell Companion to the Anglican Communion*, Chichester, Wiley-Blackwell, 2013, 88. Considering that continual defections by Church of England clergy to the Church of Rome, especially in the mid-19th century, was a running sore and the angst that the papal condemnation brought to the sense of priestly calling of many Anglo-Catholic clergy, we might expect it to be discussed in *The Oxford Handbook of Anglican Studies*, but it is impossible to find any reference to the issue of Anglican orders in it, not even under the section headed "Crises and Controversies"; Mark D. Chapman, Sathianathan Clarke & Martyn Percy, eds., *The Oxford Handbook of Anglican Studies*, Oxford, Oxford University Press, 2015. Just as extraordinary is the fact that the index of the relevant volume (vol. 3) of the generally highly impressive *The Oxford History of Anglicanism* contains no reference to Leo XIII or "pope," or to Halifax, Portal and *Apostolicae curae*. The only reference to "Orders, Anglican" in the index to this volume of *The Oxford History of Anglicanism* does not refer to this episode; *OHA* 3, 205–206.

5.1   *Halifax and Portal*

Charles Lindley Wood, 2nd Viscount Halifax (from 1885), was the aristocratic pillar of early Anglican ecumenical aspirations and the prime instigator of unofficial Anglican overtures to Rome in the late 19th and early 20th centuries.[118] The long-time president of the English Church Union, Halifax was the leading Anglo-Catholic layman in England (after Gladstone had moved away somewhat from Tractarianism to a broader position) and the most prominent Anglican papalist. Deeply influenced by Pusey and his series of *Eirenicons*, and by Pusey's disciple and biographer Henry Parry Liddon, Halifax took a rose-tinted view of the Roman Catholic Church and of the prospects for reunion. Although he firmly drew the line at certain points, he was willing at times to make greater concessions to Rome than most – even his fellow Anglo-Catholics – were able to stomach, let alone the rest of the Church of England. Deeply conservative in his amateur theological stances (such as his revulsion at the progressive symposium *Lux Mundi* that Charles Gore edited in 1889), Halifax was tireless in the quest for unity, consumed by a lifelong vision of the reunion of the Western Church.

Following their chance meeting in Madeira in 1890, a deep understanding and friendship was formed between Halifax and the Abbé Étienne Fernand Portal, a Lazarist priest, an intellectual and a disciple of the moderate, reforming bishop of Orléans, Félix Dupanloup. Halifax's biographer, John Gilbert Lockhart, comments that both Halifax and Portal "had a mind which minimized practical difficulties by comparison with ultimate ends, a characteristic which was the strength, as well as the weakness, of both men."[119] Halifax and Portal worked together on two fronts for the reconciliation of their respective churches. The first initiative was for the formal recognition of Anglicanism (represented, however

118   John Gilbert Lockhart, *Charles Lindley Viscount Halifax*, 2 vols., London, Geoffrey Bles, 1935.

119   Lockhart, *Charles Lindley Viscount Halifax*, vol. 2, 42.

inappropriately, by the Church of England alone) by the Roman authorities. This initiative eventually spread out in two phases over a 30-year period, only the first of which concerns us here.[120] It was prosecuted in the teeth of opposition by the English Roman Catholic hierarchy; Halifax tried in vain to cultivate the cardinal archbishop of Westminster, Herbert Vaughan, but the latter feared the consequences to the English hierarchy of steps to institutional reunion and professed to be concerned that the flow of individual conversions to Rome should not dry up. The second, allied, initiative was the founding of the *Revue Anglo-Romaine*, a journal dedicated to reunion, which was later suppressed by Archbishop Richard of Paris at the command of the pope.

Halifax introduced Portal to the archbishops of Canterbury (Edward White Benson) and York (William Maclagan) and to the great historian Mandell Creighton (at the time bishop of Peterborough, later of London). While Benson was more reluctant to be involved Maclagan was more supportive; Creighton would later play a major role in the Anglican response to *Apostolicae curae*. Halifax himself called on both Archbishop Benson and Pope Leo XIII, as well as on (now Cardinal) Newman and Gladstone. Halifax also brought in Father Puller of Cowley (Anglo-Catholic and an ally) and Wilfrid Ward (Roman Catholic, son of William George Ward, and later the biographer of Newman, who remained rather inscrutable but solidly loyal to the official Roman line). Portal produced a pamphlet in support of Anglican orders, but under the pseudonym Fernand Dalbus, which cunningly raised doubts about their validity on only an irrelevant point. He won the support of the Abbé Louis Duchesne, the most eminent patristic scholar of his church, and of Msgr. (later Cardinal) Pietro Gasparri, the professor of canon law in Paris, as well as of Baron Friedrich von Hügel, the most powerful Roman Catholic lay

thinker in England and beyond. Halifax and Portal persuaded the Holy See to set up a commission in 1896 to investigate the status of Anglican holy orders. Little did they realize that some within the Roman Church – notably the secretary to the commission, Msgr. Merry del Val, described by Halifax as "an influence altogether hostile to our action" – would use this as an opportunity to dash all hopes of reconciliation between the two communions.[121]

At this point, Gladstone, the most powerful Anglican voice of all, intervened in print. Aged 86 and retired from politics, Gladstone produced a pamphlet, *Soliloquium*, almost his swan-song, in praise of Leo XIII's initiative and in an attempt to forestall any disastrous outcome. It was addressed to Archbishop Maclagan, for transmission by him to Rome for the attention of the pope, and was also published in *The Times* of London.[122] For the tens of thousands of Anglican clergy throughout the Communion, Gladstone began, the question of their orders was one of "settled solidity." He was optimistic that the result of the Commission's work would be constructive; it was, he averred, "to the last degree improbable that a ruler of known wisdom would at this time put in motion the machinery of the Curia for the purpose of widening the breach" between Rome and Canterbury, thus making the divisions of Christendom more conspicuous to the world. If, Gladstone speculated, the Curia were not able to arrive at a positive assessment of Anglican orders, "wisdom and charity" alike would hold the Roman authorities back from any step that would lead to further "embittering

---

120 The second episode was the Malines Conversations of the early 1920s; see Bernard Barlow & Martin Browne's contribution in this volume.

121 On Portal see Fernand Portal, *Une vie sur la route de l'Unité*, Paris, Unité des chrétiens, 1976; Hippolyte Marie Hemmer, *Fernand Portal (1855–1926): Apostle of Unity*, ed. Arthur T. Macmillan, London, Macmillan, 1961; Régis Ladous, *L'abbé Portal et la compagne anglo-romaine (1890–1912)*, Lyon, Centre d'histoire du catholicisme, 1973; Régis Ladous, *Monsieur Portal et les siens (1855–1926)*, Paris, Cerf, 1985; Albert Gratieux, *L'Amitié au service de l'union: Lord Halifax et l'Abbé Portal*, Paris, Bonne Presse, 1950.

122 William Ewart Gladstone, "Soliloquium [1896] and Postscript [1897]," in: Gladstone, *Later Gleanings*, 384–406.

religious controversy." Gladstone paid tribute to the "paternal" attitude of Leo XIII, addressing him with a flattering "first bishop of Christendom."[123] They were both in the twilight of their long lives.

5.2 The Papal Condemnation of Anglican Orders

The commission's findings were submitted in the same year to the cardinals of the Holy Office who were unanimous in rejecting the validity of Anglican orders. On Sept 13, 1896, Pope Leo XIII issued the bull *Apostolicae curae*.[124] The main grounds of the papal condemnation were supposed doctrinal inadequacies in the historic

Anglican Ordinal of 1550/1662 regarding the Eucharistic sacrifice and the nature of priesthood (defects of "intention" and "form"), not, as is sometimes assumed, any supposed lack of "pedigree" in the historical succession of episcopal ordinations at the Reformation. In spite of the fact that the expert scholarly opinions that the pope had consulted were not of one mind and brought out various subtleties that needed to be considered, the papal verdict was unequivocal. The pope argued that the Anglican Ordinal lacked any clear reference to the priestly power to consecrate the Eucharistic elements and to offer sacramental sacrifice. Moreover, the bull claimed that, at the Reformation, all such references in the medieval rite had been deliberately removed. The "native character and spirit" of the Ordinal were (allegedly) unmasked as blatantly uncatholic. Anglicans did not ordain with the objective intention of doing what the church does in making priests. Therefore, Leo was able to "pronounce and declare that ordinations carried out according to the Anglican rite have been, and are, absolutely null and utterly void" (§ 36).

The bull was a devastating setback for any further hopes of Anglican/Roman Catholic rapprochement. Without valid holy orders, Anglican priests were not priests and Anglican bishops were not bishops; the archbishop of Canterbury was a layman masquerading as a prelate; the Anglican liturgical rites of ordination were a charade; the Eucharistic celebrations presided at by Anglican priests and bishops were a mockery. In attacking Anglican orders, Leo XIII's bull undermined the sacramental means of grace provided in the Church of England and in its sister churches within the Anglican Communion and thereby negated their claim to be regarded as Christian churches. Without a real ordained priesthood, Anglicans could have no real sacraments and so could not provide the way of salvation. The bull completely evacuated the *raison d'être* of Anglicanism. At the time, it was seen as a gratuitous insult to Anglicans and it still rankles, well over a century later. The great ecumenist Bishop George Bell later described the bull as "one of the sharpest and

---

123   *Mr. Gladstone's Memorandum*, in Thomas A. Lacey, *A Roman diary and other documents relating to the papal inquiry into English ordinations*, MDCCCXCVI, London, Longmans, Green and Co., 1910, 141, 149 and 142.

124   *Anglican Orders (English): The Bull of His Holiness Leo XIII, September 13, 1896, and the Answer of the Archbishops of England, March 29, 1897*, London, SPCK, 1957. For the Latin text, as well as the English, of the Anglican reply, see *Responsio archiepiscoporum Angliae ad litteras apostolicas Leonis Papae XIII: De ordinationibus Anglicanis*, London, Longmans, Green & Co., 1897, <http://anglicanhistory.org/orders/saepius .pdf> (accessed July 4, 2019). For an accessible text of *Apostolicae curae*, see Christopher Hill & Edward Yarnold, eds., *Anglican Orders: The Documents in the Debate*, Norwich, Canterbury Press, 1997; <http://www .papalencyclicals.net/leo13/l13curae.htm> (accessed July 4, 2019). The background is given in John Jay Hughes, *Absolutely Null and Utterly Void: The Papal Condemnation of Anglican Orders (1896)*, Washington DC, Corpus Books, 1968. See also his *Stewards of the Lord: A Reappraisal of Anglican Orders*, London, Sheed & Ward, 1970. More recent discussions include R. William Franklin & George H. Tavard, "Commentary on ARC/USA Statement on Anglican Orders," *JES* 27/2, 1990, 261–287; Mary C. Boulding & others, "Apostolicae Curae: A Hundred Years On," *OiC* 32, 1996, 295–309; R. William Franklin, ed., *Anglican Orders: Essays on the Centenary of "Apostolicae curae" (1896–1996)*, London, Mowbray, 1996, also published in *AThR* 78, 1996, 1–149; Simon Francis Gaine, "Defect of Sacramental Intention: The Background of *Apostolicae curae*," *NBf* 82, 2001, 4–23. Related matters are discussed in Stephen W. Sykes, "'To the Intent that These Orders May Be Continued': An Anglican Theology of Holy Orders," in: Franklin, ed., *Anglican Orders*, 48–63.

most public rebuffs that the Church of Rome can ever have administered to a peaceable Christian communion."[125] *Apostolicae curae* was a defining moment in Anglican/Roman Catholic relations and a point of disjunction that remains unresolved and unhealed. Halifax's blind zeal had provoked a gratuitous insult.

However, the fact that *Apostolicae curae* elicited a devastating rejoinder from the archbishops of Canterbury (by now Frederick Temple) and York (Maclagan), in which major weaknesses and flaws were exposed, means that its original promulgation was a signally unfortunate and regrettable step, not only for the Anglican churches, but also for the Roman Catholic Church, for Leo had been manoeuvred into an authoritative utterance that went against his best intentions and could hardly hold water theologically.

5.3 *The Anglican Response: Unofficial: Gladstone and Official:* Saepius Officio

Very different in tone was the *Postscript* (apparently penned before publication of the official Anglican response, which is mentioned with approbation in a footnote) that Gladstone now appended to his *Soliloquium*.[126] The language of his previous paper had been, he confessed, "entirely dislocated" by events. The commission had not undertaken a free enquiry, but had allowed itself to be hidebound by precedent – namely Rome's insistence in the reign of Queen Mary (Tudor) that certain Church of England clergy be (re)ordained. Now, Gladstone lamented, the case was closed and no Roman theologian could propose a contrary view. While a great battle loomed in Western civilization between the forces of belief and those of unbelief, Rome had gratuitously widened the divisions between those who held the same fundamental creedal faith. If the Roman Church claimed a "universal maternity," it was not unreasonable for other churches to look for "some

tokens of a mother's love." Throughout Gladstone's span of life (virtually the entire 19th century), he recalled, not one word of appreciation of other Christian traditions, not one small admission of deficiency on her own part, not one tiny attempt to diminish the differences between Christians, had been forthcoming from Rome. Leo had now added to the pile of obstacles that his predecessor, Pius IX, swayed by "flattery," had created: the dogma of the Immaculate Conception in 1854, the Vatican I (1869–1870) decrees of universal papal jurisdiction and *ex cathedra* infallibility; and now "this damnatory bull against English orders." The pontificate of Leo XIII now took its place with that of Pius IX "in the list of reactionary pontificates." Almost the last of Gladstone's public utterances was filled with disappointment and bitterness.

The papal argument was and still is vulnerable to criticism, particularly to accusations of inconsistency, illogicality and inaccuracy. The formal Anglican response set out to exploit these flaws. Roman Catholic scholars have tended to decline to defend the more specific claims of *Apostolicae curae*, but have regarded its general indictment of the "native character and spirit" of the Anglican Ordinal as the bull's strongest suit.[127] The papal decree, which dashed all hopes of rapprochement between the Anglican and Roman Catholic communions for three-quarters of a century, is notorious, but the remarkable reply (*Saepius officio*), issued by the archbishops of Canterbury and York on the advice of the most learned bishops of the Church of England of the time, is little known. It was pointedly addressed, like the original bull, to "the whole body of bishops of the catholic Church [cases original]," meaning the bishops of the universal church, not simply the Roman Catholic episcopate.

The text of the Anglican reply was drafted by John Wordsworth, bishop of Salisbury, a consummate Latinist and previously an Oxford professor, who had researched the matter of Anglican orders

---

125 George K.A. Bell, *Christian Unity: The Anglican Position*, London, Hodder & Stoughton, 1948, 68.

126 Gladstone, "Soliloquium and Postscript."

127 See Francis Clark, *Anglican Orders and Defect of Intention*, London, Longmans, 1956.

with a view to vindicating them in ecumenical overtures to the Swedish Lutherans and the Dutch Old Catholics (who had both needed to be convinced that the Church of England maintained "the Apostolic Succession").[128] Wordsworth consulted William Stubbs, bishop of Oxford, the most erudite and prolific British medieval historian of his time and formerly Regius Professor of Modern History at the University of Oxford. Stubbs was now within five years of the end of his life and, though he felt deeply indignant about the bull, replied to Wordsworth that he was reluctant to engage in controversy and so break the habit of a lifetime. But his comments reveal a sharp insight into the weaknesses of the bull.[129] Stubbs had been aware that a judgment on Anglican orders was being prepared in Rome. Before the bull was published he had pointed out to the clergy of his diocese that the Church of England had not submitted the question of the validity of its orders to Rome and, in any case, did "not regard her as qualified to speak for the Church universal." "We take our stand," Stubbs went on, "so far as our mission and position in the Church Catholic and in the National Church are concerned, on the fact that our Master sent them that sent us, that we have a mission, a succession, and a solemn historical title to our Orders." It was, he insisted, "an absurdity, as well as a profanation, for the Roman Church or any other Church to determine, or to pretend to, a right to determine, whether He in whom we have believed accepts our ordinations, hears our prayers, is present in our sacraments, or turns away from the cry of His people who call upon Him."[130]

A more central role in the preparation of the response was played by Mandell Creighton, who was renowned for having written the first huge volumes of a multi-volume history of the Renaissance papacy while serving as parish priest of Embleton in the North East of England, and on the strength of which had been elected the first Dixie Professor of Ecclesiastical History at the University of Cambridge. It was Creighton who had initiated the idea of a refutation and (as he modestly put it) had been acting "as the archbishop's secretary for this matter." His translation to the See of London prevented him from playing a larger part. Creighton believed that the Anglican response should "expose the ignorance" and deflate the "pretentiousness" of the Roman protagonists. He found the arguments of *Apostolicae curae* "creaking and lumbering."[131]

The draft text of the *Responsio* reached the archbishop of Canterbury, Edward Benson, on the day before he died (he was the guest of Gladstone at Hawarden Castle in North Wales). Benson was an extremely learned, astute and perceptive archbishop. Like most English churchmen of his time, he was a vehement critic of the papacy and held a one-sided, rose-tinted view of the English Reformation. His longing for the reunion of Christendom took as much account of the Eastern Churches and of the non-episcopal Protestant Churches of Europe as it did of the Roman Catholic Church. Before the *débâcle* of 1896, Benson wrote to Halifax: "If they did acknowledge our Orders, it would not alter *our* view of our position ... *their* coming to a sensible and historical standpoint ... would not settle the Roman controversy." The Church of England, Benson pointed out, would be no nearer to reunion with Rome than the Orthodox Churches

128   See Edward William Watson, *Life of Bishop John Wordsworth*, London, Longmans, Green & Co., 1915, esp. 327–333. Wordsworth's own account of the episode is given in a memorandum that he contributed to Ernest Grey Sandford, ed., *Memoirs of Archbishop Temple by Seven Friends*, vol. 2, London, Macmillan & Co., 1906, 388–397.

129   William Stubbs, *Letters of William Stubbs, Bishop of Oxford (1825–1901)*, ed. William Holden Hutton, London, A. Constable, 1904, 346–348.

130   William Stubbs, *A Charge Delivered to the Clergy and Churchwardens of the Diocese*, Oxford, Oxford University Press, 1896, 21–22.

131   Mandell Creighton, *The Life and Letters of Mandell Creighton*, ed. Louise Creighton, vol. 2, London, Longmans, Green, & Co., 1904, 180–183. Further on Creighton, see James Covert, *A Victorian Marriage: Mandell and Louise Creighton*, London, Hambledon & London, 2000; William Gordon Fallows, *Mandell, Creighton and the English Church*, London, Oxford University Press, 1964.

were (whose orders were recognized by Rome).[132] Benson was highly suspicious of Rome's motives in initiating the review of Anglican orders. If he had not been prevented by death from taking a further hand in revising the Anglican reply, it would have been even more devastating than it was. Benson had earlier privately expressed the view that "the pope's business was to eat dust and ashes".[133] Benson's initial response, left in draft at his death, insisted that the Church of England took a much more scholarly approach to the matter of orders than Rome did. Anglican researches, he insisted, had shown that "our Holy Orders are identical with those of the whole Catholic Church. They are in origin, continuity, matter, form, intention, and all that belongs to them, identical accordingly with those of the Church of Rome, except in the one modern point of subjection to the pope, on which point at the Reformation we deliberately resumed our ancient concurrence with the whole Catholic world besides."[134]

Benson's successor as archbishop of Canterbury, Frederick Temple, took it upon himself (in John Wordsworth's words) to "eradicate every trace of bitterness,"[135] or (as Temple put it himself) "cut out all the thunder."[136] Temple himself had not been unduly perturbed by the bull, being entirely "convinced that the Church of England was unquestionably preferable to any other manifestation of Christianity."[137] In his ecclesiology Temple stood in the old pre-Tractarian mainstream High Church

tradition.[138] He personally contributed material on the controversial areas of Eucharistic sacrifice and the "form" of a sacrament to the official response. Under Temple's supervision, the Church of England's reply to this lethal challenge to its ecclesial integrity was robust, dignified and cool, while nevertheless addressing the pope in fraternal, irenic and charitable terms.[139] The reply accurately pointed out that the bull "aimed at overthrowing our whole position as a Church." Significantly, the reply agreed with the pope that matter, form and intention were vital in sacramental actions, but it went on to claim that the Anglican Ordinal met these requirements in every respect. The archbishops stated the Anglican doctrine of priesthood and of Eucharistic sacrifice in a biblical and evangelical spirit, and in accord with the *Book of Common Prayer*. It forms the heart of the *Responsio*:

> We truly teach the doctrine of Eucharistic sacrifice and do not believe it to be a "nude commemoration of the Sacrifice of the Cross." ... But we think it sufficient in the Liturgy which we use in celebrating the holy Eucharist – while lifting up our hearts to the Lord, and when now consecrating the gifts already offered that they may become to us the Body and Blood of our Lord Jesus Christ – to signify the sacrifice which is offered at that point of the service in such terms as these. We continue a perpetual memory of the precious death of Christ, who is our Advocate with the Father and the propitiation for our sins, according to His precept, until His coming again. For first we offer the sacrifice of praise and thanksgiving; then next we plead and represent before the Father the sacrifice of the cross, and by it we confidently entreat remission of sins and all other benefits of the Lord's Passion for all the whole Church; and lastly we offer the sacrifice of ourselves to the

132 Arthur Christopher Benson, *The Life of Edward White Benson*, vol. 2, London, Macmillan, 1900, 611, 614. For background, see Geoffrey Palmer & Noel Lloyd, *Father of the Bensons: The Life of Edward White Benson, Sometime Archbishop of Canterbury*, Harpenden, Lennard, 1998; David Williams, *Genesis and Exodus: A Portrait of the Benson Family*, London, Hamish Hamilton, 1979.

133 Benson, *The Life of Edward White Benson*, vol. 2, 586.

134 Benson, *The Life of Edward White Benson*, vol. 2, 624.

135 Sandford, ed., *Memoirs of Archbishop Temple*, vol. 2, 393.

136 Sandford, ed., *Memoirs of Archbishop Temple*, vol. 2, 261.

137 Peter Bingham Hinchliff, *Frederick Temple Archbishop of Canterbury: A Life*, Oxford, Clarendon Press, 1998, 265.

138 Peter B. Nockles, *The Oxford Movement in Context: Anglican High Churchmanship (1760–1857)*, Cambridge, Cambridge University Press, 1994.

139 *Responsio archiepiscoporum Angliae*.

Creator of all things which we have already signified by the oblations of His creatures. This whole action, in which the people has necessarily to take its part with the Priest, we are accustomed to call the Eucharistic sacrifice.[140]

The archbishops claimed that the Anglican Ordinal was actually superior to the Roman ordination rite because it more clearly reflected Christ's intentions and the practice of the universal church. The archbishops showed with crushing effect that the papal doctrine of what was required in holy order was an innovation. They also argued, in an *ad hominem* manner, that "in overthrowing our orders, he overthrows all his own, and pronounces sentence on his own Church."[141] They forthrightly defended the Reformation and the right and duty of particular churches to reform themselves:

> [H]e who interprets the articles of our Church by mere conjecture and takes it upon himself to issue a new decree as to what is necessary in the form of Order, condemning our lawful bishops in their government of the Church in the XVIth century by a standard which they never knew, is entering on a slippery and dangerous path. The liberty of national Churches to reform their own rites may not thus be removed at the pleasure of Rome.[142]

6   Conclusions

The Roman Catholic Church still officially maintains the position set out in *Apostolicae curae* (notwithstanding a number of friendly gestures towards successive archbishops of Canterbury, by various popes, that point in a different direction). Nothing that has happened since, as part of ecumenical rapprochement, has led the Roman Catholic Church to revise its judgment: not the agreements achieved in theological dialogue between the two communions by the ARCIC, especially on the doctrinal questions concerning ordination and ministry and the nature of the Eucharist;[143] not the introduction of modern Eucharistic texts and revised Ordinals of the Church of England and other churches of the Anglican Communion, based more closely on patristic models, whose emphases should be more acceptable to Rome; not the involvement in Anglican episcopal ordinations of bishops of the Old Catholic Churches of the Union of Utrecht, whose orders are recognized by Rome.

Thankfully, however, the tone of ecumenical discourse today is now very different. Courtesy, charity and genuine respect and friendship between Anglican and Roman Catholic Church leaders and ordinary faithful alike has replaced the hostile, defensive and admonitory style of more than a century ago. The work of the ARCIC has achieved a genuine consensus on key ecclesiological issues. As Henry Chadwick has pointed out, ARCIC has had "the unintended side-effect of destroying the central argument of *Apostolicae curae*, viz. that Roman Catholics and Anglicans are committed to essentially different beliefs about the Eucharistic presence and sacrifice and consequently about the nature and office of ministerial priesthood."[144]

---

140   Hill & Yarnold, eds., *Anglican Orders*, 292–293 (*Saepius officio* § 23). Contrary to what is often assumed, Archbishop Thomas Cranmer, the author-compiler of the 1549 and 1552 prayer books of the Church of England, held a doctrine of Eucharistic sacrifice, one of sacramental commemoration, thanksgiving and self-dedication (not propitiatory); see Paul Avis, *The Identity of Anglicanism: Essentials of Anglican Ecclesiology*, London, T&T Clark, 2007, ch. V, esp. 92.

141   Hill & Yarnold, eds., *Anglican Orders*, 316.

142   Hill & Yarnold, eds., *Anglican Orders*, 305.

---

143   ARCIC, ed., *The Final Report: Windsor, September 1981*, London, CTS/SPCK, 1982. On the ARCIC process see Adelbert Denaux & Christopher Hill's contribution in the third volume of this work.

144   Henry Chadwick, *Tradition and Exploration: Collected Papers on Theology and the Church*, Norwich, Canterbury Press, 1994, 92.

Yet some of the issues that were at stake then remain unresolved. *Apostolicae curae* has not been retracted. It still has its full force and effect. The fact that the Roman Catholic Church has condemned the decision of the Church of England and of other churches of the Anglican Communion to ordain women to the priesthood, and warned of the dire consequences for relations between the two communions if the Church of England proceeded to ordain women as bishops (as it has now done), has highlighted the reality that Rome does not accept the orders of Anglican male priests either. The fact remains that Anglican clergy desiring to exercise a priestly ministry within the Roman Catholic Church are required to be (re-)ordained and that Roman Catholics are not permitted, under any circumstances, to receive Holy Communion at an Anglican celebration of the Eucharist. By contrast, the Church of England invites (as do other Anglican Churches similarly) all who are (1) baptized (2) communicants in a Trinitarian church and (3) in good standing within it – as well as any baptized person in immediate danger of death – to receive the sacrament at the celebration of the Eucharist in its churches.[145]

Bibliography

Avis, Paul, *Anglicanism and the Christian Church: Theological Resources in Historical Perspective*, London, T&T Clark, ²2002.

Avis, Paul, *The Identity of Anglicanism: Essentials of Anglican Ecclesiology*, London, T&T Clark, 2007.

Avis, Paul, "Anglicanism and Christian Unity in the Twentieth Century," *OHA* 4, 186–213.

Bebbington, David W., *The Mind of Gladstone: Religion, Homer, and Politics*, Oxford, Oxford University Press, 2004.

Chapman, Mark D., *The Fantasy of Reunion: Anglicans, Catholics, and Ecumenism (1833–1882)*, Oxford, Oxford University Press, 2014.

Chapman, Mark D., "The Oxford Movement and Ecumenism," in: Stewart J. Brown, Peter B. Nockles & James Pereiro, eds., *The Oxford Handbook of the Oxford Movement*, Oxford, Oxford University Press, 2017, 500–513.

Chapman, Mark D., "William Reed Huntington, American Catholicity and the Chicago-Lambeth Quadrilateral," in: Paul Avis & Benjamin M. Guyer, eds., *The Lambeth Conference: Theology, History, Polity and Purpose*, London, T&T Clark, 2017, 84–106.

Edwards, Pamela, "Coleridge on Politics and Religion: *The Statesman's Manual, Aids to Reflection, On the Constitution of Church and State*," in: Frederick Burwick, ed., *The Oxford Handbook of Samuel Taylor Coleridge*, Oxford, Oxford University Press, 2009, 235–253.

Franklin, R. William, ed., *Anglican Orders: Essays on the Centenary of "Apostolicae curae" (1896–1996)*, London, Mowbray, 1996; also published in *AThR* 78, 1996, 1–149.

Hill, Christopher & Edward Yarnold, eds., *Anglican Orders: The Documents in the Debate*, Norwich, Canterbury Press, 1997.

Morris, Jeremy N., *F.D. Maurice and the Crisis of Christian Authority*, Oxford, Oxford University Press, 2005.

Wright, J. Robert, ed., *Quadrilateral at One Hundred: Essays on the Centenary of the Chicago-Lambeth Quadrilateral (1886/88–1986/88)* (= *AThR* supplementary series no. 10), Cincinnati OH, Forward Movement Publications, 1988.

---

145   See Canon B 15A 1, in: *The Canons of the Church of England*, London, Church House Publishing, ⁶2000, 34.

CHAPTER 13

Scholarship and Unity in the 19th and 20th Century: Johann Adam Möhler and Adolf von Harnack Compared

Michel Fédou, S.J.

1   Introduction

It may seem surprising to bring the figures of Johann Adam Möhler and Adolf von Harnack together in the same chapter. The question is not that they lived in different eras, although Möhler lived in the first half of the 19th century and von Harnack in the second half of the 19th century and the first decades of the following one. Nor is it the difference in their ecclesial affiliation (a difference in type, one a Roman Catholic and the other a Lutheran) because they were both equally concerned with unity. It is rather the impression that is immediately evoked by the mention of the two names: Möhler is primarily known as the theologian who inspired Yves Congar and the other theologians engaged in the ecumenical movement; Harnack, on the other hand, is famous for his *History of Dogma* and *What Is Christianity?*, each of which contains highly critical assessments of both Catholicism and Orthodoxy.

However, one element in common can be noted: Möhler and Harnack were historians of the early church and they were both interested in drawing insights for their own time from the past. More in-depth investigation reveals the complexity of the positions defended by the two authors. The question can already be asked in regard to Möhler: however innovative and promising his thinking may have been (and we shall see that it was in many ways), was it also "ecumenical," as one would expect it to be at first sight? Or, if it really was, to what extent was it so, or within which limits? Inversely, must Harnack's position be assessed simply on the basis of his judgments of the

Roman Catholic Church and "Greek Catholicism"? At least heuristically, I should like to formulate this paradoxical question here: is Möhler's thought not less "ecumenical" than it has been presented to be (even if it is unarguably so on a certain number of points), and is Harnack's thought, on the other hand, not more open than the reading of only certain passages suggests? Whether or not this hypothesis will be confirmed, I shall in any case try to be favorably biased towards their writings, without hiding whatever does not correspond to our current understanding of ecumenism; but I shall also emphasize what (not only in Möhler but also in Harnack) shows a significant openness to the quality of ecclesial relations and to the promotion of Christian unity.

The difference between these authors and their orientations requires that we treat them separately. Following a chronological order, we shall first examine Möhler and then consider Harnack.

2   Johann Adam Möhler (1796–1838)

Born on May 6, 1796 in Igersheim, Württemberg, Johann Adam Möhler went to high school first in Mergentheim and then in Ellwangen. It was in the latter city that he also began his theological studies, which he continued from 1817 in the city of Tübingen, where notably he studied under Johann Sebastian von Drey. He was ordained a priest in 1819 and was principally (apart from stays in Berlin and other German cities) a professor of church history in Tübingen and (from 1835) in Munich. He knew the fathers of the church very well (writing several works on them). He wrote two works that are of great importance for our subject: *Unity in the Church*, published in 1825, and *Symbolism*, published in 1832.[1]

Möhler's name is linked to what is called the Tübingen School. This primarily refers to a current of exegesis and theology that originated in the Faculty of Protestant Theology of the University of Tübingen, which was influenced in particular by thinkers like Hegel, Schelling, and Hölderlin. But in 1817, for political reasons, the Faculty of Catholic Theology of Ellwangen was transferred to Tübingen, and it underwent an important development there. It was located in the "Wilhelmsstift," which was separated from the rest of the university (one should remember that at that time there was no communication between Protestants and Catholics: on the Protestant side, the tenet was *catholica non leguntur*, while on the Catholic side works judged to be "heretical" were prohibited). However, the principal lecturers at the Catholic faculty were characterized by orientations that, at least in one respect, were similar to those of the professors of the other faculty, and for this they were recognized as belonging to the Tübingen School. Walter Kasper has identified some of these orientations, which were expressed in particular through the *Tübinger Theologische Quartalschrift* (founded in 1819). The lecturers in Tübingen were theologians who "[thought] for themselves"; their reflections attested to a great concern for ecclesiality; it was, in one respect at least, a "practical" theology.[2] The spirit of Tübingen was also characterized by a willingness to be open to the thought of the time and, more broadly, to the contemporary culture (an openness that certainly did not prevent criticism). Drey, Möhler and other theologians of the faculty readily engaged with the positions of philosophers such as Schleiermacher, Schelling, and Hegel. They were marked, more generally, by debates with the Enlightenment, Idealist philosophy and literary Romanticism. Two features in particular deserve to be highlighted here: the vision of the church as a living organism and the concern to rediscover the great tradition, which, particularly for Möhler, meant direct contact with the writings of the fathers of the church. It is within this general framework that one must understand this theologian's reflections on unity and on the differences or contradictions among the different churches and Christian confessions. I provide an overview of these reflections based on the two books mentioned above.

2.1 Unity in the Church

The very title, *Unity in the Church*, might suggest that the work is governed entirely by an "ecumenical" design, in the sense in which we currently use the word. The subtitle, however, already announces

---

1 Johann Adam Möhler, *Die Einheit in der Kirche oder das Prinzip des Katholizismus: Dargestellt im Geiste der Kirchenväter der drei ersten Jahrhunderte*, Tübingen, Laupp, 1825; new edition ed. Josef Rupert Geiselmann, Cologne, Hegner, 1957; ET: *Unity in the Church, or, the Principle of Catholicism: Presented in the Spirit of the Church Fathers of the First Three Centuries*, trans. Peter C. Erb, Washington DC, Catholic University of America Press, 1996; Johann Adam Möhler, *Symbolik oder Darstellung der dogmatischen Gegensätze der Katholiken und Protestanten nach ihren öffentlichen Bekenntnisschriften*, Mainz, F. Kupferberg, 1832; new edition ed. Josef Rupert Geiselmann, Cologne, Hegner, 1958 (Geiselmann published a detailed commentary on *Symbolik*, with the same publisher, in 1960); ET: *Symbolism: Exposition of the Doctrinal Differences between Catholics and Protestants as Evidenced by Their Symbolic Writings*, trans. James Burton Robertson, London, C. Dolman 1843; trans. James Burton Robertson, intro. Michael J. Himes, New York NY, Crossroad, 1997. On Möhler's life and work, see, among others: Pierre Chaillet, ed., *L'Église est une: Hommage à Möhler*, Paris, Bloud & Gay, 1939 (several authors contributed, including Yves Congar); Josef Rupert Geiselmann, *Die theologische Anthropologie Johann Adam Möhlers: Ihr geschichtlicher Wandel*, Freiburg i.Br., Herder, 1955; Harald Wagner, *Die eine Kirche und die vielen Kirchen: Ekklesiologie und Symbolik beim jungen Möhler*, Munich, Schöningh, 1977; Michel Deneken, *Johann Adam Möhler*, Paris, Cerf, 2007 (with bibliography, 337–341).

2 See Walter Kasper, "Verständnis der Theologie damals und heute," in: *Theologie im Wandel: Festschrift zum 150 jährigen Bestehen der Katholisch-Theologischen Fakultät an der Universität Tübingen (1817–1967)*, Munich, Wewel, 1967, 90–115; Deneken, *Johann Adam Möhler*, 51–52.

the precise purpose of the book: *The Principles of Catholicism Presented in the Spirit of the Church Fathers of the First Three Centuries*. One realizes, first of all, that the study will be based on patristic studies; in fact, it benefits from the decisive engagement that the author had with the fathers of the church. More precisely, Möhler will give priority to the "first three centuries," that is to say, to the period when the "principle of Catholicism" was developed. The work is based throughout on references to Clement of Rome, Ignatius of Antioch, Irenaeus of Lyons and other fathers in the early centuries. However, the first words of the subtitle should especially be noted: Möhler will focus on what constitutes the "principles of Catholicism." The perspective of unity is clearly present, even central, yet it is immediately clear that the book will not only, nor principally, be about unity among Christians. Rather, or more exactly, the latter point of view will be part of a fundamental reflection on what constitutes the church, on what gives it its profound coherence, and on what assures its eternity. The two parts of the book are entitled, significantly, "Unity of the Spirit of the Church" and "Unity of the Body of the Church". The second part, in particular, best summarizes Möhler's primary intention:

> The concept of the Church is defined in a one-sided manner if she is designated as a construction or an association, founded for the preservation of the Christian faith. Rather, she is much more an offspring of this faith, an action of love living in believers through the Holy Spirit.[3]

It is clear that the perspective thus defined must have an impact on the relationships among Christians, and I shall have the opportunity to clarify this in due course. However, it is not this ecumenical question that takes first place here, but rather the question of what makes up the "principle of Catholicism." This question is itself addressed within the context of a primarily pneumatological problem, as Möhler points out in the foreword. If it is true that Jesus Christ is the center of the Christian faith, then it is truly the Holy Spirit who arouses the "whole development of the Church." Möhler thus "began with what is temporally first in our becoming Christians."[4] The originality of this choice cannot be overemphasized. Möhler expresses here his distance from the Enlightenment and, on the other hand, warmly welcomes Romanticism's concept of "life." The Spirit makes it possible for the human to participate mystically in the life of God, and this participation is "grounded in the essence of Catholicism."[5]

The work, constructed in a highly dialectical way, is composed of two perfectly balanced parts. It is important to examine them here, not to identify the multiple themes of the book but to capture what, in Möhler's reflection, has a (direct or implicit) bearing on the unity of Christians. The first part, "Unity of the Spirit of the Church," consists in four chapters: "Mystical Unity," "Intellectual Unity," "Diversity without Unity," and "Unity in Diversity." The first chapter is very important from a theological perspective, because here Möhler develops his foundational reflection on the Spirit as the source of communion. Unity, he writes, "*exists through a life directly and continually moved by the divine Spirit, and is maintained and continued by the loving mutual exchange of believers.*"[6]

The action of the Spirit is equally emphasized in the second chapter, which is principally devoted to Christian doctrine. This, Möhler writes, is the Christian Spirit expressing itself in concepts.[7] One finds, in the same section, pages of great importance for the relationship between Scripture and tradition. Möhler certainly sees Scripture as "the oldest embodiment of the Gospel" and emphasizes that, without it, "Christian doctrine would

---

3 Möhler, *Unity in the Church*, 209 (§ 49).

4 Möhler, *Unity in the Church*, 77.

5 Möhler, *Unity in the Church*, 82 (§ 1).

6 Möhler, *Unity in the Church*, 93 (§ 7, italics original).

7 Möhler, *Unity in the Church*, 102 (§ 10).

not have been kept in its purity and simplicity," but he also holds that tradition is itself "the expression of the Holy Spirit giving life to the totality of believers."[8] These pages will attract the full attention of some 20th-century theologians, such as Henri de Lubac and Yves Congar, who, in the same vein, will seek to clarify the relationship between Scripture and tradition, thus paving the way for the constitution *Dei Verbum* of Vatican II, which would contribute so much to overcoming the traditional dispute between Protestantism and Catholicism on the subject. Möhler's pages significantly prepared this remarkable evolution of Christian theology, thanks to his consideration of the oldest patristic texts.

Finally, the third and fourth chapters are particularly important for our subject as Möhler deals with the relationship between unity and plurality in the church. First, the negative aspect of the question is treated. In his chapter on "Diversity without Unity," he explains in what "heresy" fundamentally consisted for the early church: "Doctrine calling itself Christian, but separated from the continuing common life of believers. It is in opposition to the unity that forms believers. ... This unity is called 'Catholic.'"[9] Thus, "self-seeking" ultimately appears as the "source of all heresy."[10] But Möhler also points out that, correlatively, "the return to the unity of believers" is a "conversion to the unity of God." He continues, "Paul had already demanded unity of faith because we have *one* God and *one* Jesus Christ."[11] This is a rather remarkable statement: the accent is not *primarily* on the return of "heretics" to the Catholic Church (even though, for Möhler, progress towards unity had to necessarily take that form), but on "a return to the unity of Christ, indeed, a return to the unity of God."[12] Other statements are worth noting: thus Möhler states that if the primitive church

considered "heresy" to be evil, it was not the "the individual heretic" that was at issue. "The one who condemns heresy does not condemn heretics."[13] Moreover, adds Möhler, it is not a question of suggesting that "heresy" itself "does not have anything Christian in it."[14] It fights against particular truths by means of its own principles, but, insofar as they are not applied to the "rest" of its doctrine, this rest "forms within itself what is Christian and what still binds it to the Church."[15]

Finally, there is an important allusion to the current state of affairs (even though Möhler refers mainly to "ancient heresies"). Indeed, he makes the following statement:

> After Christianity is once more brought to a place of honor and Christ is acknowledged in his characteristic majesty once again, the desire for union raises itself again and does so *most among the most profound Protestant theologians*.[16]

Chapter 4, "Unity in Diversity," takes up the positive aspect of the question. Here Möhler affirms the existence of a legitimate plurality, as long as the faithful truly constitute a unity. He clearly states this in regard to the early church and, from there, makes a more general statement:

> Since the Church can have in it members of differing individualities, the needs of all can be satisfied. ... All together form a great organic whole enlivened by one Spirit. Single individuals grow and the whole flourishes. No constraint of individuality comes from *the Spirit* of the Catholic Church. Rather, she forms individualities in virtue and power. This can be seen in the character of Catholic writers. No Church has brought forth so

---

8   Möhler, *Unity in the Church*, 119, 117 (§ 16).
9   Möhler, *Unity in the Church*, 124 (§ 18).
10 Möhler, *Unity in the Church*, 149 (§ 29).
11 Möhler, *Unity in the Church*, 152 (§ 30; italics original).
12 Möhler, *Unity in the Church*, 156 (§ 31).

13 Möhler, *Unity in the Church*, 157 (§ 32).
14 Möhler, *Unity in the Church*, 162 (§ 34).
15 Möhler, *Unity in the Church*, 162 (§ 34).
16 Möhler, *Unity in the Church*, 152–153 (§ 30; italics original).

many great and influential persons as the Catholic [Church] has throughout the years of her existence.[17]

There is, therefore, room for a true diversity in the church, provided that this does not undermine unity but is rather included within it. Möhler always maintains a balance between the two affirmations: on the one hand, he says that unity is in truth and, on the other, that the infinity of differences equally requires unity in order to allow these to exist as such.[18] It is once again the concept of life that serves as a reference. True life, in fact, exists solely through the "penetration of that which opposes it."[19] Möhler observes in passing that the differences between East and West already existed in the first centuries but that, precisely, they both were "bound closely together by something other and higher."[20] He uses particular examples, including some from Irenaeus who, during the controversy over the date of Easter, had stressed the full compatibility between diversity of practice and communion in faith.[21] Möhler certainly did not mean to confuse this legitimate diversity with differences between "heresy" and "catholic" doctrine. However, his reflection on "unity in diversity" is nevertheless of great importance for later ecumenism for it will seek to discern what, in the other Christian confessions, could be recognized as "legitimate diversity" (thus compatible with unity). The book of Yves Congar *Diversity and Communion* is exemplary in this respect. Here one finds, among other things, the evocation of the controversy over the date of Easter at the time of Irenaeus but placed in a perspective that, this time, will be overtly ecumenical.[22]

The second part of the work, "Unity of the Body of the Church," clearly shows Möhler's concern not to identify ecclesial communion with a merely spiritual communion, or, to be more exact, he wants to show that the church is only truly spiritual when it is embodied. The first chapter ("Unity in the Bishop") theologically grounds this, affirming that the visible church realizes itself in a place, precisely in a diocese governed by a bishop. Chapter 2 specifically treats the "Unity in the Metropolitan" (the latter word does not refer here to Orthodox or Eastern ecclesiology but designates the metropolitan bishop according to the Western use of the term). It concludes with a development that emphasizes the importance of synods. Chapter 3 reflects on the "Unity of the Total Episcopate." At the end of this chapter, one finds Möhler's insistence on the necessary connection between unity and diversity. Indeed, in the face of the objection that union with the episcopate would be detrimental to particular members, the Tübingen theologian writes these words:

> Only because the Church is placed in time and place is there a multitude of bishops. If these are removed, there is no longer a Church. Thus the many individual bishops are there as a result of the particular needs and characteristics that have arisen through the aforementioned finite and limited forms. ... The spirit of unity is in each individual church, but the unity is not that which forms the special character of the individual part. ... So also finally each diocese and the embodiment of a number of those who constitute a metropolitan union by legislation and particular occurrences is directed for itself as long as it suffices for itself.[23]

Here again we see that Möhler is a pioneer. Not only does he retrieve the importance of the

---

17   Möhler, *Unity in the Church*, 186 (§ 42; italics original; the word was added by Möhler's English translator).

18   See Möhler, *Unity in the Church*, 196 (§ 46).

19   Möhler, *Unity in the Church*, 196 (§ 46).

20   Möhler, *Unity in the Church*, 203 (§ 48).

21   Found in Eusebius, *Hist. eccl.*, 5.24.16–17; see Möhler, *Unity in the Church*, 203–204 (§ 48).

22   See Yves Congar, *Diversité et communion: Dossier historique et conclusion théologique*, Paris, Cerf, 1982; ET: *Diversity and Communion*, trans. John Bowden, London, SCM, 1984, 15–17.

23   Möhler, *Unity in the Church*, 253–254 (§ 66).

episcopacy (which points towards chapter 3 of the constitution *Lumen gentium*), but he speaks in a way that strives to uphold the two poles of unity and diversity, according to what is required by his conception of ecclesial life. The fourth and last chapter completes these views with a reflection on "Unity in the Primate." Möhler admits, at the very beginning, that he had long "doubted if the primacy of a church belonged to the characteristic of the Catholic Church," and that he "had decided to deny it,"[24] on the one hand, because the idea of this church seemed to him sufficiently honored by the unity of the episcopate and, on the other hand, because the history of the first three centuries provided him with little evidence on the subject. Yet he explains that his reading of the patristic sources made him recognize the need for the primacy. Certainly, he writes, the earliest texts do not permit "definite conclusions ... for a primacy consciously established by Peter," but it is nonetheless evident that "to the extent that the unity of the church developed ever more fully as an external association, individuals felt drawn with partially conscious necessity to *one* point."[25] The task incumbent on the bishop of Rome, as the "center of unity," is to preserve or save each ecclesial entity from the "egoism" that threatens it, such that all may live in true communion. The last lines of the chapter, which are particularly noteworthy, broaden the scope by reiterating the essential connection between unity and diversity against extreme positions which, in one way or another, always risk calling such a bond into question.

> Two extremes are possible in ecclesiastical life, and both are called egoism. They arise if *each as an individual* or *one individual* wishes to be all. In the latter case, the bond of unity is so narrow and love so warm that one cannot free oneself of its strangling hold. In the first case everything falls apart, and love grows so cold that one freezes. One egoism begets the other. Neither one nor another must wish to be all. Only all can be all and the unity of all can only be a whole. This is the idea of the Catholic Church.[26]

The conclusion of the work summarizes the preceding chapters, then retraces some stages in the history of the church up until the reform movements of the Middle Ages and the beginning of the modern era. On this last point, Möhler recalls that certain 15th-century Reformers sought changes to the inner life of the church but that those attempts were "ridiculed." New attempts at reform then arose, but this time "externally."[27] Such a diagnosis was, in fact, inspired by the fundamental argument that Möhler developed in the first two parts of his book.

This work, considered as a whole, therefore addresses all the essential themes of a fundamental ecclesiology (even if it does so through the, seemingly very limited, investigation of a historical theology of the first three centuries). Admittedly, one must be careful not to give an anachronistic reading in the light of later ecumenism. In particular, Möhler's views on unity and diversity must not be understood as an initial formulation of what is called today a "reconciled diversity." Nevertheless, the German theologian's reflection on the connection between unity and diversity will inspire, in later times, the ecclesiologists of the 20th century. We also see other reflections which will equally be very fruitful for later theology, such as the reflections on Scripture and tradition, those on the necessary realization of the church in a particular place, besides those on the episcopate and synodality.

In its time, *Unity in the Church* was hailed as a book of great importance and although it also met with objections, it earned its author the reputation of being a first-class theologian.[28]

---

24   Möhler, *Unity in the Church*, 255 (§ 67).

25   Möhler, *Unity in the Church*, 260–261 (§ 69; italics original).

26   Möhler, *Unity in the Church*, 262 (§ 70).

27   Möhler, *Unity in the Church*, 266 (§ 71).

28   See Deneken, *Johann Adam Möhler*, 27–28.

2.2   Symbolism

This second work, *Symbolism: Exposition of the Doctrinal Differences between Catholics and Protestants as Evidenced by Their Symbolic Writings*, first needs to be located within its specific context. The city of Tübingen (where the Faculty of Theology of Ellwangen had been transferred in 1817, as noted above) was strongly influenced by Protestantism. However, the authorities of Württemberg had some hope that the transfer would allow for an "amalgamation" of the Catholic and Protestant faculties, "in a sort of theological place in which the confessional differences would only be differentiated instances of the same essential Christianity."[29] They were certain that this could pave the way towards a kind of merger, which naturally would be advantageous from a political point of view. However, the reality was very different: the Faculty of Catholic Theology, thanks precisely to the dialogue with the Faculty of Protestant Theology, underwent new developments. The confessional difference thus acted as a stimulus for research. It is in this context that Möhler, influenced by his teacher Johann Sebastian von Drey, became interested in the question of confessional doctrines and began to study the writings of the Reformers.

The work is also illuminated, more profoundly, by Möhler's own course and by the evolution of his thought on the church as well as of the relationship between "heresy" and doctrinal truth.[30] In 1827, he began to offer a course on the theology of symbolic texts, which he then reworked for publication. During the same period, two trips to the Rhineland (in 1827 and in 1828) allowed him to meet important figures of German Romanticism, and he increased his understanding of the Reformation through contact with them. He continued to take up the subject of *Symbolism* in his teaching and reworked the first edition, producing five editions before his death.

The initial motivations were, in fact, quite the opposite of an "ecumenical" attitude, if this is to be determined by these lines addressed by Möhler to his friend Gengler:

> I am trying, with the greatest sweetness and the most moderate judgment, to strike one of these blows to Protestantism that we have not seen the likes of for some time. The writings of the Reformers make up my inexhaustible arsenal that provides me with rifles, cannons, bullets, powder, and fire to battle it. I have used these munitions extensively. I also think that I have succeeded in restoring the original Protestantism in its authentic form, so that I believe I can teach it accurately to Protestants who, thus, will get to know it. They do not know it themselves and may have never known it; the Catholic must help them do so. If only I may succeed![31]

If we limited ourselves to the beginning of this passage, which is very offensive (despite the concern for "sweetness" and being "moderate"), we would obviously no longer be inclined to include Möhler among the precursors of ecumenism! The end of the passage, however, introduces a new element: Möhler intended to introduce Protestants to their true tradition. Although the passage cited above does not reveal it, it was a matter, on the contrary, of making some contribution to doctrinal unity, at least indirectly, by this very means. On the one hand, in effect, Protestants themselves would be able to correct some of their views by realizing that they are deviating from the original thinking of the Reformers. On the other hand, the Reform movements within Catholicism could benefit from a more accurate knowledge of Protestantism. Thus Michel Deneken does not hesitate to write: "The concern for Reform shapes *Symbolism* from the first to the last line. The presentation of

---

29   Deneken, *Johann Adam Möhler*, 93.
30   See Deneken, *Johann Adam Möhler*, 87–88.

31   Deneken, *Johann Adam Möhler*, 88.

confessional differences serves the theological and spiritual aim of reconciling the confessions."[32]

Certainly, such a vision does not eliminate the apologetic concern of the work, which, as Möhler himself stated, is not without controversy.[33] In his view, Protestantism has the same problem as the erroneous doctrines of the early church: it is a question of "heresy." However, since the publication of *Unity in the Church*, Möhler had acquired a deeper knowledge of Protestant doctrines and, on the other hand, his understanding of "heresy" had evolved. He recognized its positive function for Catholic theology itself. He emphasized, in particular and far more clearly, that the differences between Catholics and Protestants are not all of the same order. At times, it is only a matter of "opposition" ("Gegensatz"); at others, it is "contradiction" ("Widerspruch").

As far as the literary worth is concerned, *Symbolism* is at first glance less original than *Unity in the Church*. It seems to be connected to the polemical writings that were very widespread in modern Catholicism. However, it is much more innovative than it first seems. Indeed, apart from great authors like Bellarmine, polemical literature often offered a more or less deformed presentation of the opposing doctrines, while Möhler, on the contrary, tried to render them accurately. On the other hand, Möhler "does not seek the surrender of the adversary, even less his destruction."[34] He uses this significant formula: "Even the combat of one against another is nothing other than an aspiration to unity."[35] However, it is true that, for him, this unity implies that the opponent should acknowledge his error.

Like *Unity in the Church*, the work is tightly constructed, in a manner which, according to Josef Rupert Geiselmann, even bears the imprint of the author's contact with the Hegelian world.[36] It consists of two parts. The first concerns the disputes between Catholic and Lutheran-Reformed doctrine. These controversies are themselves presented in a thematic way in six successive chapters: the primitive state of man and the origin of evil, original sin, justification, the sacraments, ecclesiology and, finally, the relationship between the heavenly church and the earthly church. The second book concerns disputes between Catholic doctrines and those of other communities within Protestantism. It also has six chapters: Anabaptists and Mennonites, Quakers, Moravian Brothers, Pietists and Methodists, the doctrine of Swedenborg, the doctrine of the Socinians and the doctrine of the Arminians.

A few remarks will further help to clarify the object of *Symbolism*. First, it is important to recall the very definition of the word as given at the beginning of the work:

> By Symbolism we understand the scientific exposition of the doctrinal differences among the various religious parties opposed to each other, in consequence of the ecclesiastical revolution of the sixteenth century, as these doctrinal differences are evidenced by the public confessions or symbolical books of those parties.[37]

The disputes are obviously of a different nature, depending on the Protestant confession under consideration. Möhler's work intended to show that Catholic doctrine stands between two extreme positions of Protestantism: that of a

---

32 Deneken, *Johann Adam Möhler*, 89.

33 See Deneken, *Johann Adam Möhler*, 91.

34 Deneken, *Johann Adam Möhler*, 92.

35 Johann Adam Möhler, review of Johann Nepomuk Locherer's *Geschichte der christlichen Religion und Kirche*, ThQ 7, 1825, 99–108, here 101; see Deneken, *Johann Adam Möhler*, 92.

36 See Geiselmann "Introduction," in: Möhler, *Symbolism*, 1.

37 Geiselmann "Introduction," 1. The word "revolution" is to be noted in passing: during a trip that he took in 1828, Möhler met Romantics such as Clemens Brentano, Peter Alois Gratz and Georg Hermes, and he shared their understanding of the Reformation as a revolutionary movement. For his part, Novalis saw in the French Revolution a kind of temporal Protestantism; Deneken, *Johann Adam Möhler*, 93.

Rationalism that excludes the supernatural and that of a Pietism that does not recognize the rights of reason. It is also to be noted that he places a unique importance on disagreements in the field of anthropology. He recalls that the controversies with the East primarily concerned Christology. On the contrary, he says, the rupture of the 16th century concerned the question of man. However, it must be stated again that in the way in which he treats his subject, Möhler intended to present Protestantism in the fairest way possible. The distinction that we have seen between the concepts of "dispute" and of "contradiction" is crucial in this respect. On the one hand, there are between Catholicism and Protestantism not only points in common but also differences or oppositions that must be respected. On the other hand, there are contradictions, that is, elements that are in no way reconcilable with Catholicism. Discernment must thus be used when examining Protestantism, and the Catholic Church could itself benefit from this discernment in order to understand its own doctrines. In this way, Möhler's work is truly inspired by a concern that can be called "ecumenical" before its time.

We can see from this very fact the journey that has been made since *Unity in the Church*. In the latter, Möhler historically and theologically justified the vocation of the church to be fundamentally one (and this unity itself implied a real diversity, which, however, had to be carefully distinguished from the diversity that arose from the existence of "heretical" currents). In *Symbolism*, on the contrary, "he develops a historical and dogmatic method by which the church could be one."[38] The second work was not meant to correct the first, but it does testify to a significant evolution in Möhler's intellectual development, an evolution that, as we shall see below, was already anticipated in the early 1820s.

Like *Unity in the Church*, *Symbolism* provoked enthusiastic reactions; however, this work also met with strong opposition in Protestant academic

circles, particularly on the part of Ferdinand Christian Baur. Möhler published a response,[39] but the controversy made him very weary, even exhausted, which helps explain his departure from Tübingen for Munich.[40]

2.3 *Möhler, Precursor of Ecumenism*

I should now like to look at Möhler's thought as a whole: to what degree does it represent a contribution to ecumenism, and what are its limitations?

The fact that Möhler dedicated an entire book to the question of the unity of the church is already in itself very revealing, and one should also consider that his contribution to ecumenism consists first and foremost in his "theological definition of the concept of unity."[41] This expression must be taken in its most radical sense. For Möhler, who is fully in line with his teacher Johann Sebastian von Drey, the notion of unity is not simply an important one for a specifically ecclesiological doctrine. It has a central significance for the whole of theology. Unity was desired in creation itself; it has been broken by sin; it is the object of the economy of salvation, in the sense that Christ wanted to unite the human race; it is the gift of the Spirit at Pentecost. Möhler's intention, therefore, is not limited to the perspective of the unity between ecclesial communities. Far from it: he sees more extensively and more profoundly that unity that is (or should be) at work in the life of the church, that unity which itself is to be understood on the basis of the design of God, who wishes to gather humanity around himself, giving it a share in his own life. Möhler particularly emphasizes that such unity is made possible by Christ: "in Jesus … separation came to unity."[42]

---

38   Deneken, *Johann Adam Möhler*, 98.

39   Johann Adam Möhler, *Neue Untersuchungen der Lehrgegensätze zwischen den Katholiken und Protestanten: Eine Verteidigung meiner Symbolik gegen die Kritik des Herrn Professors Dr. Baur in Tübingen*, Mainz, F. Kupferberg, 1834.

40   See Deneken, *Johann Adam Möhler*, 35–38.

41   Deneken, *Johann Adam Möhler*, 207.

42   Möhler, *Unity in the Church*, 171 (§ 37).

As far as the church itself is concerned, Möhler holds it to have originally been one, even though it has been manifested from the beginning in the form of particular churches. This unity comes from the Holy Spirit, breathed forth by Christ resurrected, and it is guaranteed by apostolic succession and the transmission of true doctrine. It is the foundation of the communion of believers through the centuries, a communion of fraternal love. All this again bears the mark of the influence exercised by Drey. However, Möhler also takes into account (while distinguishing himself from) the reflections of a Protestant philosopher and theologian, Friedrich Schleiermacher. In the early years of the 19th century, Schleiermacher had recommended the union of the Lutheran and Reformed Churches. He held that even if a diversity of doctrines and practices had to be maintained, this could only be gained by the unification of the two churches. On the one hand, the church would appear as one within the Prussian state and, on the other hand, the ecclesial structures of each confession would benefit from such unification. Yet this required that the differences that separated the two churches be overcome. To this end, Schleiermacher proposed a minimal accord on the "first principles of Christianity" and, above all, on the recognition of a fundamental affinity of spirit, proper to Protestantism (the unity, thus, should not be extended to Catholicism).[43] Now, Möhler was certainly influenced by this thinker but he differs from him on a number of points. In particular, while Schleiermacher had in mind the union between different confessions thanks to the fact of their existence in a given place, Möhler proposed "the inner principle of a dynamic of unity present in every Christian sincerely committed to conversion to the Gospel." It is also especially clear that, for him, "the question of unity is understood as the unity of the Catholic Church."[44]

This unity itself grounds a totality ("Allheit" or "Ganzheit") but does not signify creating a uniformity that does not respect legitimate particularities. It must be repeated that, for Möhler, the unity of the church is a unity in diversity, which does not mean that it represents a combination of individuals or communities. In Möhler's perspective, which is profoundly organic, the unity is achieved rather in each individual and in each community, the exception being groups of "heretics" who, precisely, have broken the bond of communion.

However, how can we conceive of the relationship between the Catholic Church and the different confessions within Protestantism? This is (in connection with the fundamental reflection on unity), the other subject that attracted Möhler's attention. In a letter in 1822, thus after the publication of *Unity in the Church*, he had already developed three far-reaching considerations. On the one hand, he said, confessional differences are not only doctrinal but also have existential, cultural and especially anthropological aspects. On the other hand, it does not seem utopian to envisage a rapprochement or even reconciliation among the Christian confessions. Certainly, this might involve confrontations, even polemics, but the goal arising from the words of Christ "that all may be one" (John 17:21) must be kept in sight. Finally, the Christian confessions which are examined must be treated on the same level (at least in the sense of being able to acknowledge the deformations that have occurred in each of the traditions concerned).

As for *Unity in the Church*, at first it does not seem to challenge Protestant confessions. Certainly, Möhler's argument intends to highlight the fundamental correctness of the Catholic standpoint, which thus clearly implies a challenge to the positions held by Protestants (a challenge that becomes explicit towards the end of the conclusion). Yet the subtitle of the book (*The Principle of Catholicism*) suggests that "it is less a question of unity within the Catholic Church as Roman than that of the principle of Catholicity confessed by the apostolic creeds in the third *notae ecclesiae*."[45] In any case, the book bears witness to a fine

---

43   See Deneken, *Johann Adam Möhler*, 212–213.
44   Deneken, *Johann Adam Möhler*, 213.
45   Deneken, *Johann Adam Möhler*, 223.

attempt to understand what a factor of unity or division is and to present as honestly as possible the historical and theological justifications for the Catholic position on the subjects addressed.

It is clearly in *Symbolism*, however, that Möhler employs a new way of directly addressing confessional differences. The underlying conviction is that it is no longer possible to confine oneself to approximate presentations of Protestant doctrines, which would be caricatures, but that academic work must be carried out through a precise comparison of doctrines, and that this work must also be able to show that the doctrines held by the Catholic Church are well-founded. This is not an irenic attitude, for Möhler is undoubtedly aware that reconciliation among churches can only be achieved at the end of a long journey, but it is a doctrine that, at the very least, reflects a confidence in the resources of serious academic work, while at the same time appealing to the good faith of Protestant readers.

Admittedly, the approach taken is by no means one of neutral comparison. As Möhler wrote in an outline of a preface to *Unity in the Church*:

> An historian must be unbiased, I agree, but one can be unbiased only if one has religion, and this must be a specific religion since there are no unspecific ones. A Catholic will thus write history as a Catholic and a Protestant as a Protestant.[46]

There is more. By virtue of his very membership of the Catholic Church, Möhler thought that the doctrines of Protestantism themselves (even if they have their share of truth) have a share, as erroneous doctrines, in "heresy" properly thus termed, and even when he deals with ancient "heresies," he often has Protestant doctrines in mind (hence, it has been observed that he uses the same vocabulary for the Arians of the 4th century and for certain Protestants who, in his time, were tempted

to reduce Christ to an ideal of humanity).[47] It is a fact, in any case, that many readers criticized him for writing an anti-Protestant work (such as Baur, and many others following him).

Nevertheless, Möhler takes care to avoid any distorted representation of Protestantism. On the contrary, he wants to restore, as accurately as possible, the doctrines really held by the Protestants, thus allowing them to make an informed decision. This applies first and foremost to Luther himself. If Möhler is severe in his attitude towards Luther since he renounced the legitimate authority of the church, he also recognizes that the Reformer had "an incredible power of mind by which he could have built the church in a way that is not found in any of his contemporaries, if only he had acted with the idea in mind that he was standing before God." He equally perceived in Luther "a treasury of pious thoughts," he points out the quality of his work as translator of the Bible and he reveals his way of presenting the church as a "communion of hearts."[48]

In this way, Möhler is already on the path of future attempts to understand Luther better, beyond the distortions to which his work has given rise. On the other hand, he also expects Catholicism not to become closed in on itself but to accept the challenge of confronting the doctrines professed by other Christians. Apart from these issues, he is undeniably inspired by a concern for unity. This preoccupation with unity can be found from the very outset, as this passage written in 1838 attests:

> It appears increasingly doubtful that the peaceful coexistence of confessions in one and the same state will be able to bring about their future unity. On the other hand, unity must be achieved in the realm of the Spirit, in an open and loyal way, in freedom and in conscience, with eyes wide open, so that it may be accomplished based on intangible

---

46   Outline of a preface for *Unity in the Church*, printed as an alternative preface in: Möhler, *Unity in the Church*, 376–377. See Deneken, *Johann Adam Möhler*, 226.

47   See Wagner, *Die eine Kirche*, 194ff.

48   See Johann Adam Möhler, *Kirchengeschichte*, vol. 3, ed. Pius Bonifacius Gams, Regensburg, G.J. Manz, 1868, 105ff.

and ancient foundations, and by a superior motion.[49]

For these reasons, despite the limitations of his work in relation to contemporary dialogues between Catholics and Protestants, Möhler is certainly one of the thinkers who, from a distance, prepared for the birth of the ecumenical movement. Moreover, this interpretation is shared by several theologians of the 20th century, including Yves Congar, who at the end of a study on the Tübingen theologian quoted this very revealing passage from *Unity in the Church*: "Christians did not rejoice in and because of division; division caused pains. But when unity embraced hearts and spirits again, joy resounded throughout the whole Church."[50]

We now turn to another theologian, from within Protestantism this time, who requires our attention: Adolf von Harnack.

3   Adolf von Harnack (1851–1930)

Adolf von Harnack was born into a German family in Dorpat – now Tartu, in Estonia, then part of the Russian Empire. This birthplace is not without significance since it helps to shed light on the attention the theologian will later pay to the Russians, and more broadly to the situation of the Orthodox Church. Harnack's father was a professor of theology who taught at the University of Erlangen in Bavaria from 1853 to 1866. It was there that the young Harnack spent a large part of his childhood and youth. He carried out his theology studies in

Dorpat and, in 1870, received a prize for a work on Marcion. He then worked on a doctoral dissertation in Leipzig and, in 1879, was appointed professor in Giessen. During his years of teaching in that city, and then at Marburg, he devoted himself to writing his *History of Dogma* and his *Outlines of the History of Dogma*.[51] Influenced by Albrecht Ritschl (whom he had met in Göttingen), he developed the thesis that dogma could not be understood as the simple expression of the contents of the Gospel but rather should be seen as a form of explanation which had by now been surpassed. He presented post-Tridentine Catholicism, Socinianism and the Lutheran Reform as the "triple issue" of this history of dogma. Appointed to Berlin, he published in the area of Greek patrology, but, above all, in 1900 he published his famous work *What Is Christianity?*, which was a kind of manual for a "post-dogmatic" theology. In 1902, he then published a new book on historical theology: *The Mission and Expansion of Christianity in the First Three Centuries*.[52] Still later, Harnack returned to his earlier work on Marcion, dedicating a volume to him.[53]

---

49   Johann Adam Möhler, "Über die neueste Bekämpfung der katholischen Kirche," *Münchener politische Zeitung*, Jan 29–30 and Feb 14–17, 1838; reprinted in: Johann Adam Möhler, *Gesammelte Schriften und Aufsätze*, vol. 2, ed. Johann Josef Ignaz von Döllinger, Regensburg, G.J. Manz, 1840, 226–243, and Möhler, *Kirchengeschichte*, vol. 3, 436–482.

50   Yves Congar, "L'hérésie, déchirement de l'unité," in: Chaillet, ed., *L'Église est une*, 255–269. Congar here cites a translation slightly different from the original: see Möhler, *Unity in the Church*, 248 (§ 64).

51   Adolf von Harnack, *Lehrbuch der Dogmengeschichte*, 3 vols., Tübingen, J.C.B. Mohr, 1886–1890; ET (based on the 1893 3rd edition): *History of Dogma*, trans. Neil Buchanan, 7 vols., Boston MA, Little, Brown & Co., 1901 and Adolf von Harnack, *Grundriss der Dogmengeschichte*, Freiburg i.Br., J.C.B. Mohr, 1889; ET: *Outlines of the History of Dogma*, trans. Edwin Knox Mitchell, New York NY, Funk & Wagnalls, 1893.

52   Adolf von Harnack, *Die Mission und Ausbreitung des Christentums in den drei ersten Jahrhunderten*, Leipzig, J.C. Hinrichs, 1902; ET: *The Mission and Expansion of Christianity in the First Three Centuries*, trans. James Moffatt, London, Williams & Norgate, 1908.

53   Adolf von Harnack, *Marcion: Das Evangelium vom fremden Gott. Eine Monographie zur Geschichte der Grundlegung der katholischen Kirche*, Leipzig, J.C. Hinrichs, 1924; ET: *Marcion: Gospel of the Alien God*, trans. John E. Steely & Lyle D. Bierma, Eugene OR, Wipf & Stock, 2007. Among Harnack's other works, it is worth mentioning *Geschichte der altchristlichen Litteratur bis Eusebius*, Leipzig, J.C. Hinrichs, 1893, 1897, and 1904; *Entstehung und Entwicklung der Kirchenverfassung und des Kirchenrechts in den zwei ersten Jahrhunderten*, Leipzig, J.C. Hinrichs, 1910. On Harnack's life, work, and thought, see particularly Karl Heinz Neufeld, *Adolf von*

Harnack's life and work should in part be placed, from a political, cultural, and ecclesial point of view, within the context of the *Kulturkampf* and its aftermath. This was a major conflict, gaining particular intensity in 1871, which set the Prussian state against the Roman Catholic Church and its representative political party (the Zentrum). Bismarck initially used legislative means to fight Catholicism (notably in the institution of civil marriage), but Catholics had given proof of a great unity. The election of Pope Leo XIII in 1878 helped to ease the situation, and Bismarck relaxed his policies towards the end of the 1880s.

The reference to the *Kulturkampf* undoubtedly explains, on the one hand, the negative attitude that Harnack manifested in his works towards Catholicism, but, on the other hand, in this very context, Harnack studied the history of Catholicism and showed a keen interest in it (even if the judgment itself permitted no concessions). For him, Catholicism was in fact an indispensable step in the history of Christianity, but a step that had now been surpassed. Later, however, Harnack would develop positions that would demonstrate a true openness towards the Catholic Church, which could be seen in particular in his lectures and articles from the 1920s.

3.1   *The* History of Dogma *and* What Is Christianity?

It is important to focus first on two works that are among Harnack's most famous, *History of Dogma* and *What Is Christianity?*, since they reveal Harnack's views on Catholicism and Orthodoxy (and, at the same time, those on Protestantism).

First, what can be said about *History of Dogma* and *Outlines of the History of Dogma*? If we consider the second work (which is more synthetic than the first), we find, among other things, some

pages on the "orthodox system." This "system," according to Harnack, "lacks an inward, vital unity. ... The dogmas have become the sacred legacy of the classical antiquity of the Church; but they have sunk, so to speak, into the ground"; what now dominates are "*image-worship*, *mysticism* and *scholasticism*."[54] Above all, the last section devotes itself to the "triple issuing" mentioned above:

> Post-Tridentine Catholicism finally completed the neutralizing of the old dogma in an arbitrary papal legal organization; Socinianism appreciably disintegrated and came to an end; the Reformation, in that it both set the dogma aside and preserved them outright, looked away from them, backwards to the Gospel, forwards to a new formulation of the Gospel confession which shall be free from dogma and be reconciled with truthfulness and truth. In this sense the history of dogma should set forth the issues of dogma.[55]

The following pages develop each of these three "issues." As far as Catholicism is concerned, Harnack argues that the medieval doctrines were codified "in opposition to Protestantism"[56] (and represent the work of the council in this perspective); he gives an equally critical presentation of post-Tridentine Catholicism through Vatican I, where, he says, "the Romish Church has revealed itself as the autocratic dominion of the *pontifex maximus*."[57] The judgment on Socinianism is clearly more favorable: Socinian Christianity, despite its limits, "had the courage to simplify the questions concerning the reality and content of religion and to discard the burden of the ecclesiastical past," and "it tried to free the study of the Holy Scriptures from bondage to the old dogmas."[58]

Harnack: *Theologie als Suche nach der Kirche*, Paderborn, Bonifacius, 1977 (with bibliography, 360–369); Karl Heinz Neufeld, *Adolf Harnacks Konflikt mit der Kirche: Weg-Stationen zum "Wesen des Christentums"*, Innsbruck, Tyrolia, 1979 (with bibliography, 204–216).

54   Harnack, *Outlines of the History of Dogma*, 325 (italics original).
55   Harnack, *Outlines of the History of Dogma*, 509.
56   Harnack, *Outlines of the History of Dogma*, 510 (from the section title).
57   Harnack, *Outlines of the History of Dogma*, 528.
58   Harnack, *Outlines of the History of Dogma*, 540–541.

As for Protestantism, it is presented here through Luther's doctrine alone. Harnack points out that Luther criticized "the dominating ecclesiastical tradition" and "dogma."[59] However, he adds, there were "Catholic elements retained with and within Luther's Christianity" that led him into a certain number of "confusions" between the Gospel and the *doctrina evangelii*, between evangelical faith and ancient dogma, between the Word of God and holy Scripture, between grace and the means of grace or the sacraments.[60] According to Harnack, the subsequent history of Protestantism is marked by these various confusions; they have to be unraveled in the very name of Luther's profoundest intuition:

> The form which the churches of the Reformation took in the 16th century was not homogeneous or definite: This the history of Protestantism indicates even to this day. Luther once more lifted the Gospel, placed it upon the lamp-stand and subordinated dogma to it. It now remains to hold fast to and carry forward that which he began.[61]

It is to the latter task that the book *What Is Christianity?* aimed to contribute.[62] It was originally a set of lectures held during the years 1899–1900 and open to all the faculties. A student, Walther Becker, made a transcription and gave it to Harnack, who then decided to publish it.[63]

The first part, entitled "The Gospel," describes "the leading features of Jesus' message," then treats "the Gospel in relation to certain problems"[64] (the question of asceticism, the social question and other matters). The second part, entitled "The Gospel in History," begins with the birth of the Catholic Church, then proposes a comparative study of "Greek Catholicism," "Roman Catholicism," and "Protestantism."

It is the last study that should be noted, particularly in the perspective of our study. First of all, it states that "Greek Catholicism" is characterized by "traditionalism," "intellectualism" and "ritualism." The final diagnosis is harsh: "as a whole and in its structure the system of the Oriental Churches is foreign to the Gospel." Harnack only concedes that the "ecclesiastical apparatus" is relativized by monasticism, and that "the Gospel exercises its own influence on individuals."[65] He sees "Roman Catholicism" as being characterized by three elements: "catholicism," "the Latin spirit and the Roman World-Empire" and "Augustinianism." On the two first points, the diagnosis is also severe (Harnack notably emphasizes that "as an outward and visible Church and a State founded on law and on force, Roman Catholicism has nothing to do with the Gospel").[66] In monasticism, on the other hand, and especially thanks to Augustinianism, the Catholic Church has conserved "a deep element of life," and "ecclesiasticism has not availed to suppress the power of the Gospel."[67]

Finally, "Protestantism" is presented as a "reformation" and a "revolution." With it, "the Gospel was in reality re-won."[68] However (and this is

---

59   Harnack, *Outlines of the History of Dogma*, 551 (from the section title).

60   Harnack, *Outlines of the History of Dogma*, 557–567 (from the section title).

61   Harnack, *Outlines of the History of Dogma*, 567.

62   Aldof von Harnack, *Das Wesen des Christentums*, Leipzig, J.C. Hinrichs, 1902; ET: *What Is Christianity?*, trans. Thomas Bailey Saunders, New York NY, G.P. Putnam's Sons, ²1903.

63   See Jean-Marc Tétaz in his introduction to the French translation: Adolf von Harnack, *L'Essence du christianisme*, ed. Jean-Marc Tétaz, Geneva, Labor et Fides, 2015, 9–10. The notes of another student were published in 1994. All the information on the genesis of the book and its different editions (with their variants) can be found

in: Thomas Hübner, *Adolf von Harnacks Vorlesungen über das Wesen des Christentums unter besonderer Berücksichtigung der Methodenfragen als sachgemässer Zugang zu ihrer Christologie und Wirkungsgeschichte*, Bern, Peter Lang, 1994; see also Tétaz in: Harnack, *L'Essence du christianisme*, 73–77.

64   Harnack, *What Is Christianity?*

65   Harnack, *What Is Christianity?*, the quoted material is first from the table of contents and 244.

66   Harnack, *What Is Christianity?*, 264.

67   Harnack, *What Is Christianity?*, 266.

68   Harnack, *What Is Christianity?*, 284.

important for the rest of our discussion), Harnack also notes the "dark side" that has accompanied or followed this renewal of the Gospel: the institution of national churches, the unilateral insistence on the inner dimension of religion (in opposition to Catholicism, of course, but "to formulate one doctrine in sharp opposition to another is always a dangerous process"),[69] the complete disappearance of monasticism, and the failure of the Reformation to implement all the consequences of what it had nevertheless recognized as essential. Harnack repeats here what he had said in his *Outlines of the History of Dogma* on the "confusions" in Luther's own teaching. He adds that the churches emerging from the Reformation have been insidiously tempted to consider themselves "the true Church."[70]

The book had a notable response, and many editions of it were published; it aroused enthusiastic reactions in some quarters but also triggered fierce controversy (centered especially on the Christological question, which is not part of this study).[71] What must be remembered here is above all the vigor with which Harnack opposed Protestantism to "Greek Catholicism" as well as to "Roman Catholicism," a vigor such that, as stated

above, would lead one initially to deny that his writings had any interest from the perspective of ecumenism or even to find positions radically contrary to it.

However, in addition to the fact that Harnack, as we have seen, does not fail to recognize some positive elements in "Greek Catholicism" and "Roman Catholicism," we have noted that he is also aware of the limits inherent in Luther's work and, above all, in the developments of Protestantism. He even goes so far as to write that its state observed from the outside, particularly in Germany, seems at first sight "miserable."[72] It would, therefore, be wrong to confine ourselves to the works I have presented here, even if they are among Harnack's most famous writings, and we shall now turn to other texts that are far less famous but which, on the one hand, will correct our first impressions and present us, albeit undoubtedly not with an "ecumenical" Harnack ahead of his time, at least with a Harnack aware of the issues raised by the relations among churches and Christian confessions, which will contribute in some way to the progress of those relations for the benefit of ecclesial communion.

3.2   *A More Open Attitude*

Generally, one sees first of all that Harnack did not intend simply to discuss issues with Luther, Calvin or other theologians of the past but also wanted to engage with the thinkers of his time. It would be possible to consider first his reviews of the books by Nikolaus Nilles on the liturgical calendars of the Eastern Churches and Western Orthodox Churches. They bear the mark of his interest in works that afford a better knowledge of the traditions in question.[73] However, it is more important to focus on a few lectures or articles that reveal more profoundly the theologian's stance in relation to Catholicism or Orthodoxy.

---

69   Harnack, *What Is Christianity?*, 287.

70   Harnack, *What Is Christianity?*, 293.

71   Harnack took this up in the first part of *What Is Christianity?*. One formula, in particular, evoked strong opposition: *"The Gospel, as Jesus proclaimed it, has to do with the Father only and not with the Son"* (144; italics original). In fact, Harnack especially emphasized the form of the preaching of Jesus, who preached "with authority," and he saw the principle of this "authority" in the fact that "no one had ever yet known the Father in the way in which Jesus knew Him, and to this knowledge of Him he draws other men's attention" (144). In no way does he deny that Jesus was the Son of God but he sets in opposition the Gospel as a message announcing the closeness of the Kingdom, on the one hand, and the preaching that the Son of God has descended from heaven, on the other, and he states that this "second Gospel" could only be expressed in the Chalcedonian doctrine of the two natures. See Tétaz in: Harnack, *L'Essence du christianisme*, 35–46. On the reception of the work, see more broadly pages 57–72 of Tétaz' introduction.

---

72   Harnack, *What Is Christianity?*, 268.

73   See the reviews published in *ThLZ* 5, 1880, 635–636; 7, 1882, 213; 21, 1986, 350–352; 23, 1896, 112–113. I am grateful to Karl Heinz Neufeld for kindly referring me to these writings, as well as to the other writings presented in the following pages.

This particularly concerns a lecture held in 1891 on the theme "What Should We Learn from the Romish Church and What Should We Not Learn?"[74] The first part of the title shows a true open mind, and, in fact, in the body of the article, Harnack enumerates several teachings that Protestants should glean from the Catholic Church. The first teaching is that of "patience." If this church seems to offer a "pure and unified form," it took it "more than fifteen hundred years" to reach its present form, and Protestantism (which, perhaps, "still finds itself in the time of childhood illnesses"), should find a precious lesson there.[75] Secondly, the history of the Roman Church teaches that "reform and progress was never brought about by organizational reforms but only ever by people with a living and active faith." Harnack here refers to the "great monks" who "have brought about new steps in the development of the church" and adds that "a Franciscan became more powerful than many princes of the church."[76] The third teaching to learn from is the "idea of Catholicity, the path towards any communal and effective fellowship of men through the Gospel." One finds here a passage that, against all expectations, bears witness to a spirit that is truly "ecumenical":

> We [Protestants] have the feeling that this task, to join all people interiorly as children of God and brothers of Jesus Christ, is a rule only weakly developed. There are among us many who not only take the separation between Catholicism and Protestantism to be normal but also the division of the latter into numerous national and free churches which often even refuse fellowship with each other. But the major idea of the general unity of peoples to be brought about by Christianity is not replaced by other ideals. … We must thus aspire with all our energy for the unity of humanity in Christ, to be open-minded in our little circles and open-hearted so that we become capable of believing that the fraternal unity of humanity is not a dream of dreamers but a goal inseparable from the Gospel.[77]

Harnack adds that Protestantism still has other teachings to receive from Catholicism. Protestants, he writes, can well learn from the importance the Catholic Church attributes to inner life. Furthermore, although the Catholic conception of the Mass was to be criticized, Protestants unfortunately rejected the very idea of sacrifice. Moreover, under the pretext that they had to challenge the Catholic practice of the sacrament of penance, personal confession had been abandoned. Protestantism had also abolished monasticism. On all these points and others, Protestantism must allow itself to be instructed by Catholicism.

It is true that Harnack, as he announced in the second part of the title, also intended to highlight what Protestantism should not learn from Catholicism, and the last part of the lecture developed precisely this point. Protestants should not bind their Christianity to "a particular phase in [the development of] knowledge," nor must they "content [them]selves with submission to the church, to mere obedience." They must equally refuse "fanaticism."[78] It is not surprising that Harnack developed these points given the arguments that he presented at about the same time in his *History of Dogma* and which he would complete later in *What Is Christianity?*. Nevertheless, his 1891 lecture largely corrects the impression left by these other

---

74   Adolf von Harnack, "Was wir von der römischen Kirche lernen und nicht lernen sollen," in: Adolf von Harnack, *Reden und Aufsätzen*, vol. 2, Giessen, A. Töpelmann, 1904, 247–264. Harnack originally gave the lecture in January 1891 in Berlin; it was later published in *ChW* 18, 1891, 401–408.

75   Harnack, "Was wir von der römischen Kirche lernen," 251.

76   Harnack, "Was wir von der römischen Kirche lernen," 251–252.

77   Harnack, "Was wir von der römischen Kirche lernen," 252–253.

78   Harnack, "Was wir von der römischen Kirche lernen," 259–263.

works. The two parts give a far more balanced image of the position held by Harnack (the first, on the lessons to be received from Catholicism, is even a little more developed than the second!). Far from being satisfied with the situation that characterized Protestantism in his time, he invites it to let itself be instructed by the Catholic Church on a number of points, and, as we have seen, he strongly affirms the need to work for unity in Christ.

Furthermore, another text needs to be mentioned: "The Testament of Leo XIII: The Pontifical Encyclical to the Princes and Peoples of the Earth of June 20, 1984,"[79] which discusses the apostolic letter *Praeclara gratulationis*. After recalling Jesus' prayer for unity (in John 17:21), which is revealing in itself, Harnack essentially follows the development of the text on which he comments, first addressing the statements concerning the Greeks and the Slavic peoples, then those which concern the Reformation, and finally those concerning the Catholic Church. He highlights some of the characteristics of this recent encyclical.

Needless to say, there are scattered criticisms. For example, even though he does not doubt that the pope places real hope in a "return" of the Greeks and the Orientals, he nevertheless questions the validity of these hopes. He recalls, among other things, the traditional antipathy between Byzantium and Rome and, above all, he stresses that the recent dogma on papal infallibility represents "the most serious obstacle" to the achievement of Roman hopes.[80] However, in the opening pages of the text in particular, he notes the tone of hope that emerges from the pontifical text. He then emphasizes its concern for unity. The pope, he writes, strives to express only "ecumenical

Christian thoughts" ("ökumenisch-christlichen Gedanken"), ignoring controversial doctrines and Roman Catholic particularities.[81] Harnack also emphasizes the pope's "friendly" tone towards "heretics."[82]

Another important text is his address "Protestantism and Catholicism in Germany," presented for the Kaiser's birthday on Jan 27, 1907, at the University of Berlin.[83] Here Harnack raises the question: to what extent is a rapprochement between Catholics and Protestants possible? It must be considered neither an external unity nor a mixture. Harnack points out, in particular, that as far as the power of the church and the pope is concerned, it is not possible for the two to draw any closer. On the other hand, he evokes the perspective of an "interior community in which the Christian religion will once again be felt as the bond of unity":[84]

No one should wait for the German Catholics to become Lutherans, but it is to be hoped that they will appropriate the best of the evolution that began with the Reformation and conceive it in their own way. Conversely, no one should wait for the German Protestants to become Catholics again – how could they forget the fight against priestly domination! – but it is to be hoped that, in and alongside this struggle, they will learn more and more to understand their task in the history of the world in regard to freedom and fraternity. The churches will not disappear because religion is never without churches, but their future rests in this, that they themselves become more and more communities of spirit and fraternal help, and that their members

79   Adolf von Harnack, "Das Testament Leos XIII: Das päpstliche Rundschreiben an die Fürsten und Völker des Erdkreisens vom 20. Juin 1894," in: Harnack, *Reden und Aufsätzen*, vol. 2, 265–293; originally published in *Preußischen Jahrbüchern* 77/2, 1894.

80   Harnack, "Das Testament Leos XIII," 281; He returns to this point later, in the section on Protestantism, see Harnack, "Das Testament Leos XIII," 285–288.

81   Harnack, "Das Testament Leos XIII," 269.

82   Harnack, "Das Testament Leos XIII," 270.

83   Adolf von Harnack, "Protestantismus und Katholizismus in Deutschland," in: Adolf von Harnack, *Aus Wissenschaft und Leben*, vol. 1, *Wissenschaft, Schule und Leben*, Gießen, Töpelmann, 1911, 225–250.

84   Harnack, "Protestantismus und Katholizismus in Deutschland," 249–250.

cultivate a unity of spirit so that their religion may become pure and that their country may become strong and peaceful.[85]

We should also consider a brief article that Harnack published the following year under the title "Die päpstliche Enzyklika von 1907 nebst zwei Nachworten."[86] It concerns the encyclical *Pascendi*, directed against the errors of modernism. Certainly, in regard to the very context of this text, Harnack was very harsh (while recognizing with satisfaction that the question of the papacy did not here hold a central place). Yet above all it is worth noting that Harnack, in the crisis that the Catholic Church was then undergoing, highlighted the attitude shown by the majority of the bishops of Prussia, eager "to repel the worst and protect the Catholic faculties as well as they could."[87] He further saw hope in the response of those in Germany who had previously wanted to keep Catholic faculties outside universities: they did not exploit the situation to their own benefit.

In another context, Harnack also took a stand in the 1920s in regard to the beginnings of ecumenism in the Protestant world. Thus, in 1925, he wrote a letter to the archbishop of Uppsala, Nathan Söderblom, on the occasion of a conference in Stockholm planned to bring together representatives of various churches.[88] Unable to take part himself in the conference, he sent his best wishes for the project. In the same year, he discussed at length the *consensus quinque-saecularis*, a summary of the doctrines (principally trinitarian and Christological) articulated by the church from the beginning of Christianity to the middle of the 16th

century. There was then an attempt, on the basis of this *Consensus*, to bring separated Protestant Churches back to unity. Harnack formulated four theses on this subject:

I. The expression "consensus quinque-saecularis," whatever its significance may be, is either too narrow or completely indeterminate, and is thus useless in both cases.

II. A "consensus" encompassing all Christianity did not exist in the third, fourth, fifth or sixth century.

III. Even if it had existed, it would today be a totally unsuitable basis for the reunification of Christian confessions.

IV. The reunification of confessions is impracticable, but the study of the early church is, in any case, important for the comprehension and appreciation of confessions, and joint interconfessional work of the churches in the field of practical Christianity is possible and deserves to be pursued – it might perhaps lead to a confederation.[89]

If the first three theses offer a negative judgment, the fourth, by contrast, shows true "ecumenical" openness. The commentary that Harnack provides also states that, in itself, the prospect of reunification should first be based on the study of Sacred Scripture,[90] but since the latter's "exclusive sovereignty" has been lost, one can at least rely on the study of the early church. In any case, Harnack envisages, if not the unity of Christian confessions, at least a "confederation" among them. At the end of the text, he straightforwardly adds that it is not the *consensus quinque-saecularis* that will permit churches to come together but only "the Word of God and the love of Christ."[91]

I conclude by mentioning two texts which, despite their brevity, reveal Harnack's state of mind during the same period. The first was written in

---

85   Harnack, "Protestantismus und Katholizismus in Deutschland," 250.

86   Adolf von Harnack, "Die päpstliche Enzyklika von 1907 nebst zwei Nachworten," in: Harnack, *Aus Wissenschaft*, vol. 1, 251–265.

87   Harnack, "Die päpstliche Enzyklika von 1907," 256.

88   Adolf von Harnack, "Die Weltkirchenkonferenz in Stockholm" [Aug 20, 1925], in: Adolf von Harnack, *Aus der Werkstatt des Vollendeten*, Giessen, A. Töpelmann, 1930, 84–85. On Nathan Söderblom's ecumenical legacy see Dietz Lange's contribution in this volume.

89   Harnack, "Die Weltkirchenkonferenz in Stockholm," 66–67.

90   Harnack, "Die Weltkirchenkonferenz in Stockholm," 80.

91   Harnack, "Die Weltkirchenkonferenz in Stockholm," 83.

1926 for the sixtieth birthday of Nathan Söderblom. Here Harnack declares that the Protestant Churches have been, and remain, threatened by a danger of "inertia" ("Trägheit") and that they risk forgetting their obligations to the whole of Christianity and humanity itself. Yet, he adds, they have been sent people who have acted to fulfil these obligations, among whom the figure of Nathan Söderblom, "the ecumenical Lutheran."[92]

The second text was written in 1927 concerning a work by Fritz Vigener on "three figures of modern Catholicism: Möhler, Diepenbrock, Döllinger."[93] Harnack approved of the author's choice in bringing together three men who represented German Catholicism in the period prior to Vatican I (the first two died before it, the third was opposed to the dogma of papal infallibility and then broke away from the Catholic Church). First of all, let us consider his judgment: it is "right" for Möhler and Diepenbrock to be distinctly recalled by their church because "there were no better Catholics" (but "they will find no successors in the strict sense of the term," and, Harnack adds, "they would not have followed Döllinger's path if they had known the year 1870").[94] On the other hand, there is also this more specific praise:

> Among the presentations [that Vigener gives of these three theologians], I would like to praise that of Möhler, not because Möhler was the most important of the three in every respect – Döllinger is superior to him in the scholarly sense – but because the author grasped him and understood him thoroughly. Those who have already known him will know him better through the description and evaluation [that he gives], and those for

whom he is still unknown will be enriched by the knowledge of a theologian who in his time represents both the type and the summit of German Catholic theology – with the inevitable tension that always ends up being resolved in favor of the church.[95]

This last text can be retained for its symbolic value. It is pleasing to see Harnack presenting, in such a positive way, the figure of Möhler, whom we treated in the first part of this study. It further contributes to justifying our bringing the two authors together, a choice which, at first sight, did not seem obvious given that Möhler's and Harnack's thoughts seemed to develop in divergent directions.

The path that we have followed, however, confirms the initial hypothesis. On the one hand, it is clear that Möhler recognized the question of unity as a central issue, that he wanted to clarify its foundations and criteria, that he encouraged a more accurate knowledge of Protestantism in its various currents and that he bore within himself a deep desire for ecclesial communion. It is also clear that, for his part, Harnack did not restrain his criticisms of Catholicism and Orthodoxy, that he showed himself to be very severe towards them and that he did not envisage any true union among the divided churches because such a union would necessarily imply, in his eyes, Protestantism's compromise with the errors or abuses that had rightly led to the Reformation.

On the other hand, however, even if contemporary theology has legitimately perceived the novelty of Möhler's work and the promises that it bore, one must also be careful of projecting onto this work the more recent accomplishments of ecumenical theology. In particular, if the Tübingen theologian dedicated such effort to the most accurate presentation possible of the positions held by Protestants, this was not only to make use of historical truth beyond the distorted representations of the various positions but also, and even more so, because the accomplishment of such work

---

92   Adolf von Harnack, "Nathan Söderblom" (1926), in: Harnack, *Aus der Werkstatt*, 257.

93   Fritz Vigener, *Drei Gestalten aus dem modernen Katholizismus: Möhler, Diepenbrock, Döllinger*, Berlin, Oldenbourg, 1926; Harnack's article, entitled "Möhler, Diepenbrock, Döllinger," can be found in: Harnack, *Aus der Werkstatt*, 113–117.

94   Harnack, "Möhler, Diepenbrock, Döllinger," 113.

95   Harnack, "Möhler, Diepenbrock, Döllinger," 114.

would (at least he hoped) promote the "return" of Protestants to the Catholic Church. Moreover, Harnack's frequently severe judgments did not prevent him from displaying, particularly in the 1920s, far more open attitudes towards Catholicism and Orthodoxy, and we have seen that, in the context of Protestantism, he expressed the wish for a true "confederation" which might at least overcome the confessional divisions inherited from the past, if not achieve communion in the fullest sense of the term. Less than Möhler undoubtedly, but significantly, Harnack also had a desire, even yearning, for unity.

Translated from French to English by Susan Dawson Vásquez and David Dawson Vásquez.

Bibliography

Chaillet, Pierre, ed., *L'Église est une: Hommage à Möhler*, Paris, Bloud & Gay, 1939.

Deneken, Michel, *Johann Adam Möhler*, Paris, Cerf, 2007.

Geiselmann, Josef Rupert, *Die theologische Anthropologie Johann Adam Möhlers: Ihr geschichtlicher Wandel*, Freiburg i.Br., Herder, 1955.

Harnack, Adolf von, *Lehrbuch der Dogmengeschichte*, 3 vols., Tübingen, J.C.B. Mohr, 1886–1890; ET (based on the 1893 3rd edition): *History of Dogma*, trans. Neil Buchanan, 7 vols., Boston MA, Little, Brown & Co., 1901.

Harnack, Adolf von, *Grundriss der Dogmengeschichte*, Freiburg i.Br., J.C.B. Mohr, 1889; ET: *Outlines of the History of Dogma*, trans. Edwin Knox Mitchell, New York NY, Funk & Wagnalls, 1893.

Harnack, Adolf von, "Was wir von der römischen Kirche lernen und nicht lernen sollen," in: Adolf von Harnack, *Reden und Aufsätzen*, vol. 2, Giessen, A. Töpelmann, 1904, 247–264.

Harnack, Adolf von, "Das Testament Leos XIII: Das päpstliche Rundschreiben an die Fürsten und Völker des Erdkreisens vom 20. Juin 1894," in: Harnack, *Reden und Aufsätzen*, vol. 2, 265–293.

Harnack, Adolf von, "Protestantismus und Katholizismus in Deutschland," in: Adolf von Harnack, *Aus Wissenschaft und Leben*, vol. 1, *Wissenschaft, Schule und Leben*, Gießen, Töpelmann, 1911, 225–250.

Möhler, Johann Adam, *Die Einheit in der Kirche: oder Das Prinzip des Katholizismus dargestellt im Geiste der Kirchenväter der drei ersten Jahrhunderte*, Tübingen, Laupp, 1825; ed. Josef Rupert Geiselmann, Cologne, Hegner, 1957; ET: *Unity in the Church: or The Principle of Catholicism Presented in the Spirit of the Church Fathers of the First Three Centuries*, ed. and trans. Peter C. Erb, Washington DC, Catholic University of America Press, 1996.

Möhler, Johann Adam, *Symbolik: oder Darstellung der dogmatischen Gegensätze der Katholiken und Protestanten nach ihren öffentlichen Bekenntnisschriften*, Mainz, F. Kupferberg, 1832; ed. Josef Rupert Geiselmann, Cologne, Hegner, 1958; ET: *Symbolism: Exposition of the Doctrinal Differences between Catholics and Protestants as Evidenced by Their Symbolic Writings*, trans. James Burton Robertson, London, C. Dolman 1843; trans. James Burton Robertson, intro. Michael J. Himes, New York NY, Crossroad, 1997.

Möhler, Johann Adam, *Neue Untersuchungen der Lehrgegensätze zwischen den Katholiken und Protestanten: Eine Verteidigung meiner Symbolik gegen die Kritik des Herrn Professors Dr. Baur in Tübingen*, Mainz, F. Kupferberg, 1834.

Möhler, Johann Adam, *Kirchengeschichte*, vol. 3, Regensburg, G.J. Manz, 1868.

Neufeld, Karl Heinz, *Adolf von Harnack: Theologie als Suche nach der Kirche*, Paderborn, Bonifacius, 1977.

Neufeld, Karl Heinz, *Adolf Harnacks Konflikt mit der Kirche: Weg-Stationen zum "Wesen des Christentums"*, Innsbruck, Tyrolia, 1979.

Wagner, Harald, *Die eine Kirche und die vielen Kirchen: Ekklesiologie und Symbolik beim jungen Möhler*, Munich, Schöningh, 1977.

CHAPTER 14

The World Student Christian Federation and John R. Mott

Sarah Scholl

1 Introduction

In the seventh chapter of her 1954 history of the ecumenical movement, Ruth Rouse noted two starting points to what she called "the modern ecumenical movement": the Grindelwald Conferences and the SCM.[1] According to Rouse, this interdenominational Protestant movement, in which she herself worked, produced the main leaders of the ecumenical movement of the 20th century. She also showed that the American Methodist John Raleigh Mott was a perfect representative of it, saying of him, "the [World Student Christian] Federation was born in his heart and brain." This attitude was summarized in the words exclaimed to Mott: "You are the history of the Federation."[2]

The purpose of this contribution is to show how this historiographical thesis was constructed and what its relevance may be by analyzing the relationship between the SCM and ecumenical issues as they arose in the last third of the long 19th century. After describing the formation of the WSCF, I shall trace Mott's biography, deciphering his motives and the variations in his involvement. A final concluding section will return to the ecumenical issues of the student movement before World War I, addressing two problematics: its

relations with Catholicism and its relationship to the churches.[3]

2 From the YMCA to the WSCF

In August 1895, the WSCF was founded at a meeting of Scandinavian students in Vadstena Castle, Sweden. John R. Mott was one of its main architects. It was not only the beginning of a global movement but also the culmination of a long process of maturation that had its roots in the first student groups born in the middle of the 19th century.

2.1 The Birth and Aims of Youth Associations
The YMCA was established in England in 1844.[4] Founded by George Williams, it was designed from the outset to bring together young Protestants, regardless of their ecclesial affiliations. The first members, whose average age was then 22,[5] therefore belonged to different Protestant

---

1 *A History of the Ecumenical Movement*, vol. 1, Ruth Rouse & Stephen C. Neill, eds., *1517–1948*, Geneva, WCC Publications, ⁴1993, 338ff.; Christopher Oldstone-Moore, "The Forgotten Origins of the Ecumenical Movement in England: The Grindelwald Conferences (1892–95)," *CH* 70, 2001, 73–97.

2 Cited in: Suzanne de Dietrich, *Cinquante ans d'histoire: La Fédération universelle des associations chrétiennes d'étudiants (1895–1945)*, Paris, Éditions du Semeur, 1946, 27; ET: *Fifty Years of History: The World Student Christian Federation (1895–1945)*, Geneva, WSCF, 1993, 22.

3 This article is based on research conducted in the following archives: YDSL, RG 45, Personal papers of John R. Mott; YDSL, RG 46, World Student Christian Federation Records; and John Raleigh Mott, *Addresses and Papers of John R. Mott*, 6 vols., New York NY, Association Press, 1946–1947.

4 Régis Ladous, "Les unions chrétiennes de jeunes gens de 1844 à 1878: Les étapes et les causes de la construction d'un mouvement international," in: Gérard Cholvy, ed., *Mouvements de jeunesse chrétiens et juifs: Sociabilité juvénile dans un cadre européen (1799–1968)*, Paris, Cerf, 1985, 125–139; Gabrielle Cadier-Rey, ed., *Sur les Mouvements de Jeunesse* (= *BSHPF* 143/3, 1997); Clarence Prouty Shedd, *History of the World's Alliance of Young Men's Christian Associations*, London, SPCK, 1955; Charles Howard Hopkins, *History of the Y.M.C.A. in North America*, New York NY, Association Press, 1951.

5 Héctor Caselli, "The Objectives of the World Alliance of Y.M.C.A. Today as Compared to Those of the Founding Members," in: Roger Durand, ed., *De l'utopie à la réalité: Actes*

denominations. These young people's objective was to organize themselves around a meeting place and a religious program. The general principle that had been adopted could be summarized in the formula: "The evangelization of lay people by the laity, of young people by youth: our first field of action should be our work place."[6] The idea, therefore, was to use places of socialization linked to the age and specific interests of this or that population in order to instill a new evangelical dynamic within different Christian countries. This was a major shift in regard to religious affiliation, which, from the beginning of modern times, had been thought of in terms of geographical space, with each family's almost automatic attachment to their parish.

The spiritual dimension was absolutely central in the movement's early days, with an exaggerated focus on salvation and responsibility and even the need for Christians not only to convert individually but also to work to save souls. The purpose of the meetings was mutual edification through Bible study and prayer. The process also had a very important moral aspect from the beginning, with the pursuit of chastity (no sexual relations until marriage, rejection of a double standard, and the renunciation of alcohol). It was a question of setting up an everyday religion and not a theoretical one, a faith consisting of practices rather than beliefs.[7] In short, the YMCAs were intended to allow young men to come together around common values.

In particular, this choice made it possible to steer clear of dogmatic and especially ecclesiological quarrels within Protestantism without renouncing evangelization and the work of revival. From its beginning, then, the YMCA adopted a strict evangelical orthodoxy around the Trinitarian confession of faith. In a brochure from 1853, Henry Dunant, co-initiator of the YMCA's first

world conference and future cofounder of the Red Cross, summarized its substance:

> With God's assistance, we want to proclaim ever more strongly and resolutely the great evangelical truths, namely: the divine authority of all of the Word of God; the mystery of the Trinity; the eternal divinity and the humanity of our Lord Jesus Christ, the only and perfect Savior; the obligation for Christians, with the help of the Holy Spirit, to work in humility, prayer, and self-denial to make known everywhere the only name that has been given to men by which they can be saved.[8]

In its early decades, supporters of Rationalist Protestantism were explicitly rejected by the YMCA.[9] The movement, therefore, was intended to be a combative response to theological liberalism, religious indifference, and, in some places, to Catholicism.

These same principles were applied in the world of universities and colleges. In the United States, associations were set up in 1858 in some schools. The dual struggle against liberal theological thinking and against obligatory or habitual Christianity was at the heart of these new student groups. The setting was indeed conducive to new forms of religiosity. During the 19th century, the specialization and professionalization of education and teachers had led to a secularization of course content and the supervision and management of students.[10] The university was no longer conceived, above all, as a place of moral and religious learning but as a place for the transmission of secular knowledge.

---

du Colloque Henry Dunant, Geneva, Société Henry Dunant, 1988, 153–168, here 153.

6   De Dietrich, *Fifty Years of History*, 15.

7   "Viewing faith as practical rather than creedal"; David P. Setran, *The College "Y": Student Religion in the Era of Secularization*, Basingstoke, Palgrave Macmillan, 2007, 8.

8   Henry Dunant, *Deuxième circulaire, 23 février 1853: Correspondance étrangère de l'Union de Paris*, vol. 1, cited in: Gabriel Mützenberg, "Henry Dunant héritier de Calvin et critique de 'calvinistes,'" in: Durand, ed., *De l'utopie à la réalité*, 169–181, here 171.

9   Setran, *The College "Y"*, 28–58. In some universities, there was competition between the YMCA and liberal Protestant groups; Setran, *The College "Y"*, 31.

10   Setran, *The College "Y"*, 66.

Curricula then became secularized. David Setran showed that American public educational institutions finally stopped imposing religious practices on students in the 1890s.[11] One of the reasons given for this phenomenon was the mixing of Protestant denominations on campuses, as recruitment was no longer, in the second half of the 19th century, based on denominational criteria. These places of formation, therefore, gradually came to reflect the diversity of Protestant denominations present in the United States. Additionally, a sectarian or clannish atmosphere had become less and less acceptable in the context of developing academic freedom. A form of secularization, or at least deinstitutionalization, of the religious within schools had thus made way for private associations dedicated to evangelization. Religious activities then were relocated to the YMCA.

In 1877, students in the United States formed a branch of the YMCA specific to the university context, the Intercollegiate Young Men's Christian Association, at the instigation of Luther Deloraine Wishard, a 23-year-old Princeton student.[12] He became its "traveling secretary," with the objective of increasing the number of the YMCA's university branches. The organizational model was extremely flexible and efficient: students could freely structure themselves into associations on their campuses, and the various associations were then affiliated and adopted common functions and objectives. In 1884, this federation had 181 associations and 10,000 members in the United States.[13] It benefitted from the enormous growth in the number of students in higher education between

1870 and 1910. At the beginning of the 20th century, between 25 and 30% of American students were members.[14]

Established for mutual edification and to ensure proselytism within educational institutions, from the outset student associations also had an important missionary dimension. In those same years, 1882–1884, a group of volunteers for the mission – which grew and became institutionalized in the following years – was created at Princeton.

The same phenomenon occurred in Europe. In Great Britain, the first student associations were founded in the mid-19th century, for example in Cambridge. In Edinburgh, Professor Henry Drummond's actions were decisive. He was directly inspired by the American evangelist then touring Great Britain, Dwight Lyman Moody. As early as the 1880s, Bible circles were also organized in Germany.

2.2   Development on a "Universal" Scale: Global Alliances

One of the strengths of the Christian youth movement was its ability to bring together individuals from different Protestant Churches as well as from different countries. Networks were organized very quickly, building on the intensive work carried out within the YMCA since the 1850s. The YMCA was itself supported by the EA, a movement founded in London in 1846. The World Alliance of YMCAs was formed in Paris in 1855 to unite the national and local associations.[15] Impetus then came from the United States with William Landon as well as from France and Switzerland with Henry Dunant.[16] 99 delegates from Europe, the United States, and Canada gathered in the French capital for the World Expo. These alliances were explicitly intended to unite Protestant forces on a global scale to defend the Christian message.

---

11   This marked the end of "compulsory religious activities"; Setran, *The College "Y"*, 68.

12   Luther Wishard, *The Beginning of the Student's Era in Christian History: A Reminiscence of a Life*, New York NY, Association Press, 1890.

13   De Dietrich, *Cinquante ans d'histoire*, 17. See also, Ruth Rouse, *The World's Student Christian Federation: A History of the First Thirty Years*, London, SCM Press, 1948, and Philip Potter & Thomas Wieser, *Seeking and Serving the Truth: The First Hundred Years of the World Student Christian Federation*, Geneva, WCC Publications, 1997.

---

14   For a summary of the figures, see Setran, *The College "Y"*, 4.

15   Clarence Prouty Shedd, *Déjà cent ans!: Aperçu historique de 100 années de l'alliance universelle des U.C.J.G. (1855–1955)*, Geneva, n. pub., 1955.

16   Caselli, "The Objectives," 154.

In student associations, the movement's internationalization was achieved through exchanges between Europe and the United States and through missionary work. On the one hand, foreign delegates were invited, for example, to the Mount Hermon summer conferences that took place as early as 1886, and American delegates visited European countries. On the other hand, both American and European evangelists met themselves in mission territories, especially in Asia.[17] For example, the American Dwight L. Moody, during a tour of England, brought about the conversion of Edward Studd who in turn convinced three of his sons, all famous cricketers, to adopt the evangelical cause. Charles Thomas Studd was one of the Cambridge Seven who went on a mission to China. John Edward Kynaston Studd, a future lord mayor of London, was invited to the United States for an evangelization tour. He in turn helped stimulate vocations, notably that of John R. Mott. Another example of these exchanges was Luther D. Wishard, who spent nine months in Japan in 1889. He brought together some 500 students from both state institutions and missionary colleges. They sent a telegram to their colleagues in the United States entitled "Make Jesus King," which gave the movement its slogan.[18] Wishard continued his tour for more than two years, traveling to China, India, and Asia Minor. He thus inaugurated a methodology that would be at the federation's heart. Through travels and meetings, the main protagonists of student movements consolidated interdenominational relations. For instance, it is known that, in 1891, the American Methodist John R. Mott, the Swede Karl Fries, and the French Protestant Raoul Allier met at a YMCA conference in Amsterdam.

A twofold movement was at work: first, the establishment in each country of student associations, themselves based on the logic and spiritual methods of the YMCA and, second, the emergence of a desire to join these associations together in an international group. In his history of the federation, John R. Mott gives an account of its beginnings:

> In the early part of the year 1894, the writer was seized with the conviction that the time had at last arrived when a world-wide union of Christian students might be achieved, and he began to work toward this goal. During his visit to Great Britain and the Continent in the spring and summer of that year he had many conversations on the subject with Christian leaders, both students and professors. Before he left Europe, he received invitations from several countries to return the following year. In the subsequent months, similar invitations came from widely separated fields of Asia, and indirectly he was urged to visit Australasia. As a result of these requests he arranged to devote two years to a journey around the world with special reference to bringing about, if possible, a union of the Christian students of all lands. He decided to adopt a different plan from that which had been followed hitherto. Previous efforts had been confined largely to trying to effect such a union in the name and through the agency of the Young Men's Christian Association. The thought occurred to him that instead of attempting to organize the Christian students under any one name and according to any one plan of organization, it would be better to encourage the Christian students in each country to develop national Christian student movements of their own, adapted in name, organization and activities to their particular genius and character, and then to link these together in some simple yet effective federation. Before leaving America on his long journey, he secured the acceptance of his plan on the part of the supervisory committee of the North American Student

---

17   De Dietrich, *Cinquante ans d'histoire*, 22. For a presentation on the mainly American-centric aspect of these exchanges, see Ian Tyrrell, *Reforming the World: The Creation of America's Moral Empire*, Princeton NJ, Princeton University Press, 2010, 59–67.

18   De Dietrich, *Fifty Years of History*, 19.

Movement. The Foreign Department of the International Committee of the Young Men's Christian Associations, which fostered Young Men's Christian Associations among students in mission lands, also approved the proposed federation plan and appointed Mr. Wishard to accompany the writer to Europe in the interest of the undertaking.[19]

John R. Mott managed to convince all the partners involved, and, in 1895, the WSCF was created at a student meeting in Vadstena. The six men presiding over its foundation were: Karl Fries and Martin Eckhoff (Scandinavia), Johannes Siemens (Germany), John Rutter Williamson (Great Britain), John R. Mott (United States), and Luther D. Wishard (United States and mission lands). Initially, therefore, the grouping concerned the major historical regions of the Protestant tradition: North America, Great Britain, Germany, and Scandinavia. John R. Mott referred to them as the "great Protestant powers."[20]

Karl Fries was appointed president, and John R. Mott was appointed secretary general. Continuing his journey for two years, he made the function of secretary general a fully-fledged itinerant ministry. Mott's first world tour allowed the federation to have national associations on all five continents and in countries where Protestants were the minority. In France, for example, the Fédération française des associations chrétiennes d'étudiants, the "Fédé," was founded in 1897 (adopting its statutes in 1898). It brought together Reformed Christians and Lutherans. Raoul Allier, who was strongly influenced by Christian socialism, became its first president in 1899. The Fédé had 350 members in

1906 and 1,100 members in 1914 (the Women's Fédé had 300 members).[21]

The federation's first general committee meeting was held in 1897 in Williamstown, and a constitution was adopted. Its spirit was to organize an alliance of autonomous national movements. The aim, therefore, was to establish an organization that ensured respect for the specificities of each member association. It was also intended to maintain power in the hands of students and to ensure respect for the various faiths involved. Each movement had two representatives on the general committee in order to avoid any overrepresentation (given the hegemony) of Anglo-Saxons. In reality, however, the European territory became crucial only after the war, at the time of attempts at reconciliation. In 1930, the Frenchman Pierre Maury was appointed secretary general of the federation.

From the beginning, the idea was not only to unite existing associations but also to create new ones. The project, therefore, had an intrinsically missionary dimension. In 1897, the federation's goals were defined as follows:

> (1) to unite student Christian movements or organizations throughout the world; (2) to collect information regarding the religious conditions of the students of all lands; (3) to promote the following lines of activity: (a) to lead students to become disciples of Jesus Christ as the only Savior and as God; (b) to deepen the spiritual life of students; (c) to enlist students in the work of extending the kingdom of Christ throughout the whole world.[22]

Theologically speaking, therefore, the recognition of Jesus Christ, his work and salvation, was

---

19   John Raleigh Mott, *The World's Student Christian Federation: Origin, Achievements, Forecast: Achievements of the First Quarter-Century of the World's Student Christian Federation and Forecast of Unfinished Tasks*, London, WSCF, 1920, 3–4.

20   John Raleigh Mott, *Strategic Points in the World's Conquest: The Universities and Colleges as Related to the Progress of Christianity*, New York NY, F.H. Revell, 1897, 17.

21   Gérard Cholvy, *Histoire des organisations et mouvements chrétiens de jeunesse en France (19e–20e siècle)*, Paris, Cerf, 1999, 135.

22   Clarence Prouty Shedd, *Two Centuries of Student Christian Movements: Their Origin and Intercollegiate Life*, New York NY, Association Press, 1934, 361.

the rallying point, with the divine inspiration of the scriptures,[23] as had been the case both with the EA and with the young people's Christian associations. John R. Mott sought to keep evangelical convictions alive against liberal theology by developing a faith compatible with university studies. From an ideological point of view, the organization said it was explicitly nonpolitical, but tensions remained throughout its history, particularly regarding responsibility in social matters and in regard to justice. In the United States, these disagreements referred, in particular, to all analyses and actions concerning the situation of black Americans.

In 1905, women became full members of the federation. Several coed associations existed as early as the 19th century, particularly in Great Britain, and quickly requested recognition, but it took time to come to agreement on the issue among all local organizations. The English Anglican Ruth Rouse, already mentioned above, became involved in the student movement in the 1890s, undertook her first travel tour in 1897, and then began work at an international level. In 1905, she was appointed the federation's traveling secretary. Her activities and work style were comparable to those of John R. Mott.[24] They both made an impact on the early stages of the federation's life, on which this contribution focuses.

Suzanne de Dietrich, a specialist on, and leading player in, the federation's history, spoke of a first stage of consolidation and expansion that goes from its foundation in 1895, until 1920 when John R. Mott resigned as general secretary. For her, the period from 1920 to 1928 was one of a "regression in the missionary spirit" accompanied by doctrinal and theological doubts as well as by divergences among national groups. The next period, starting

when Dutch Calvinist Willem Visser 't Hooft became secretary in 1931, approached missionary and ecumenical issues from new perspectives.[25]

3 Theological and Ideological Background in John R. Mott's Life and Addresses (Pre-1910)

Born in New York in 1865, John R. Mott grew up in Iowa, on a farm in Postville, where his family had settled shortly after his birth. His father, an entrepreneur, was actively involved in the community, serving as its first mayor.[26] His family was Methodist. Church activities, such as Sunday school and the respect due to the pastor, were important in young Mott's upbringing. He grew up in an atmosphere imbued with a practical religiosity, as he himself said about his mother:

> The truly Christlike life she lived created in me, even in the tender years of childhood, the longing and inclination and purpose to go to Christ's way. Her religion was not simply thought out, it was not talked out, it was lived out. In the deepest sense it was contagious.[27]

As a teenager, he was moved by the preaching of itinerant pastors, both those from the YMCA as well as those of the Methodist circuit-riding pastors, such as the Reverend Horace E. Warner. From 1881, he studied at Upper Iowa University, a Methodist

---

23 De Dietrich, *Fifty Years of History*, 25, citing Mott: "The recognition of the supremacy of the Lord Jesus Christ and of His work as the only sufficient Saviour."

24 Ruth Franzén, *Ruth Rouse among Students: Global, Missiological, and Ecumenical Perspectives*, Uppsala, Swedish Institute of Mission Research, 2008; Ruth Franzén, "The Legacy of Ruth Rouse," *IBMR* 17, 1993, 154–158.

25 De Dietrich, *Cinquante ans d'histoire*, 48; Potter & Wieser, *Seeking and Serving the Truth*, table of contents, v–vi.

26 Charles Howard Hopkins, *John R. Mott (1865–1955): A Biography*, Grand Rapids MI, Eerdmans, 1979; Basil Mathews, *John R. Mott: World Citizen*, New York NY, Harper, 1934; Galen Merriam Fisher, *John R. Mott: Architect of Cooperation and Unity*, New York NY, Association Press, 1953; Robert C. Mackie, *Layman Extraordinary: John R. Mott (1865–1955)*, London, Hodder & Stoughton, 1965; Benjamin Vallotton, *Un homme: John R. Mott*, Lausanne, Éditions La Concorde, 1951.

27 Hopkins, *John R. Mott*, 8–9.

preparatory school, then, from 1885, at Cornell University. At Cornell, he was a member of the Cornell University Christian Association (CUCA), the local YMCA chapter. He became its president and significantly increased its memberships while raising the funds needed to erect a building. In 1888, he graduated with a degree in philosophy and history. Many career possibilities were open to him but, following a series of circumstances and especially encounters that he considered to be divinely orchestrated, he chose to devote himself to evangelization.

In recounting John R. Mott's spiritual journey, Charles Howard Hopkins' monumental biography of over 800 pages highlights in particular the visit to Cornell in January of 1886 of the famous English cricket player John Edward Kynaston Studd, then on an American evangelism tour. There were already transatlantic evangelical networks here which remained important for Mott.

Hopkins based his work on the life story that Mott himself gave to his biographers.[28] Mott spoke of successive conversions based not only on encounters but also on self-reflection and meditative practice, including study of the New Testament and a personal relationship with Christ. These concerns are indeed strongly present in his personal correspondence.[29] From this perspective, it was a question of going to the sources of Christianity with a "total commitment of the will."[30] Mott conceived of his life as one with the duty to be regulated and disciplined.[31] Matters of purity and abstinence were central for him. He joined the White Cross Army, which emerged from the vast temperance movement in those same years.

In 1886, he had the opportunity to attend the first College Student's Summer School in Mount Hermon MA as a delegate from his university. This meeting, whose model would have a long

history, brought together 251 student delegates from YMCAs across the United States, besides international representatives. It was organized by Dwight L. Moody himself. In the spring of 1886, Mott wrote to his parents to ask permission to go there using strong evangelical language. He said it was his destiny "to be *soul saving*." From then on, and the rest of his life, everything was clear to him: "While life lasts I am an evangelist".[32]

During this summer conference, his vocation as a missionary emerged and solidified. He was part of the Mount Hermon Hundred, the one hundred young persons who had committed themselves to going on foreign missions. John R. Mott was the twenty-third to sign up. These were the foundations of the SVM.[33] Mott would be part of it for more than thirty years. That summer at Mount Hermon, according to conclusions drawn by Hopkins, several decisive ideas had already emerged: the importance of interdenominational encounters and the subordination of abstract doctrines to central Christian truths and to action.[34] However, there was also a feeling of urgency and crisis, tinged with the millenarian effervescence also felt in the assembly. The idea of the urgent need for world evangelization was present from that period.

From the beginning, Mott's commitment went far beyond a personal spiritual and moral quest. He had the taste for, and skill to lead movements, find funding, and to trail blaze new organizing structures, institutions, and forms of evangelizing.[35] After graduating in 1888, Mott chose to become the national secretary of the Intercollegiate YMCA (United States and Canada). This position involved frequent travel and aimed at networking

---

28   Hopkins, *John R. Mott*, 19, who cites Clarence Prouty Shedd and Basil Mathews.

29   YDSL, RG 45, Personal papers of John R. Mott, box 104–106.

30   De Dietrich, *Fifty Years of History*, 23.

31   Vallotton, *Un homme*, 34.

32   Cited in: Hopkins, *John R. Mott*, 23.

33   John Raleigh Mott, "History of the Student Volunteer Movement for Foreign Missions," 1892, in: YDSL, RG 45, Personal papers of John R. Mott, box 142.

34   Hopkins, *John R. Mott*, 28–29.

35   Mott was supported economically by Nettie Fowler McCormick, a businesswoman and philanthropist from Chicago; Potter & Wieser, *Seeking and Serving the Truth*, 20.

the protagonists of youth and student associations at the North American level.

In 1891, he undertook his first intercontinental journey. In particular, he participated in the meeting of the Universal Alliance of the YMCA in Amsterdam,[36] which allowed him to meet the leaders of various student movements and to see for himself the scope and diversity of the movement. That year, Mott married Leila Ada White, a native of Wooster. They had four children.

In 1893, Mott spoke at the World's Parliament of Religions in Chicago. Hopkins comments:

> John Mott made his first speech to an international audience at one of these sessions. It was a description, in his best oratorical style, of the North American Intercollegiate Association Movement, an unashamed proclamation of its evangelical motivation and its ethical, social, and ecumenical aims.[37]

Events then quickly followed, leading to the formation of the WSCF in 1895, as described above. Mott was its general secretary for twenty-five years and then assumed its presidency from 1920 to 1928. He was the president of the YMCA's World Alliance from 1926 to 1937. He held several positions and headed the SVM from 1915 to 1928 and the IMC of the YMCA from 1921 to 1942.

From a formally missionary concern, his career led him to be at the heart of the structuring of the ecumenical movement: from his presidency of the 1910 Edinburgh WMC to his position as honorary president of the WCC in 1948. He was very active during the two world wars in organizing various forms of assistance, particularly to prisoners. He was awarded the Nobel Peace Prize in 1946 along with the American Emily Greene Balch. He died in 1955 in Orlando.

Mott's biographers all recognize his abilities as a lecturer (a preacher), a leader (from 1886),

an administrator, businessman, and ambassador (a position the White House offered him several times). Any career could have been open to him, such as in law or politics. "But someone else had laid his hand upon him: the goal of this leader is to lead to the Christ. Mott is his ambassador." Suzanne de Dietrich wrote in 1946.[38]

On the one hand, Mott was driven by the evangelical model of Anglo-Saxon Protestantism, defined as "optimist," "rooted in the individual religious experience and the idea that humanity collaborates in the coming of the Kingdom."[39] Mott was a fervent follower of the *Morning Watch*: thirty minutes of prayer every morning.[40] He also wrote guides to reading and studying the Bible with devotion ("devotional Bible study") for "personal spiritual growth."[41] He issued and published an impressive number of appeals to fight against temptation, against impurity, and for a healthy and religious life.[42] Spirituality and discipline were an integral part of his youth project within the YMCA. He spoke to young people about a Christianity that would profoundly change their life:

> When he speaks to great gatherings of students in all parts of the world, he seeks to bring them to Jesus Christ ... His message is simple and direct: he witnesses to the power of Christ to overcome temptation, to transform life.[43]

On the other hand, he thought of his commitment in a technical, even technocratic way, like an administrator. For example, he counted the number of meetings given and the number of converts in

---

36   It was attended by 500 delegates from 17 countries; Hopkins, *John R. Mott*, 91.

37   Hopkins, *John R. Mott*, 107–108.

38   De Dietrich, *Fifty Years of History*, 22.

39   Cholvy, *Histoire des organisations*, 137.

40   John Raleigh Mott, *The Morning Watch*, New York NY, The International Committee of the Young Men's Christian Association, 1893.

41   John Raleigh Mott, *Bible Study for Personal Growth*, New York NY, Association Press, [13]1920.

42   For example, those collected in YDSL, RG 45, Personal papers of John R. Mott, box 137, as well as Mott, *Addresses and Papers*.

43   De Dietrich, *Fifty Years of History*, 27.

each evangelism campaign with precision. He was in charge of raising funds and erecting buildings. His personal archives testify to this constant concern with administration, to the point that almost nothing distinguishes the notes he produced from those of a business administrator.[44] It is therefore necessary to understand his theological motivations and strategic choices. Why would he invest body and soul in the creation and operation of the WSCF?

3.1   Youth: Vocation and Mobilization

The first key aspect specific to the work that John R. Mott chose for himself concerns his prospective audience. He worked mainly with young people. He made this choice while he was himself a student but maintained it for the rest of his life. Such a choice is in line with the logic of the YMCAs themselves, whose aim was to supervise both rural migrants to the cities and students in residence far from home and therefore detached, if only temporarily, from their ecclesial roots. Those working for the YMCA based their actions on the fact that the period of life from 16 to 25 years old is a significant moment of personal choice and self-edification where the individual needs evangelical motivation and guidance as well as places and projects in which to become involved.

The YMCAs offered a Christian, but not dogmatic, socialization focused on Bible study, but also largely on the idea of a healthy life and sports. The objective was largely moral: to keep students away from music halls and brothels by offering them, with the associations' venues, places to meet and gather. As Arnaud Baubérot does, the argument can be made that one of the YMCA's "elemental" functions "consisted in taking over for traditional bodies of religious and social control that these young people were now escaping."[45]

To this was added the idea that youth, and especially university students, were the key to advancing Christianity and constructing a Christian society because they would hold important positions in the different professional environments. It was about working "among the upper classes of different nations and denominations," to use Mott's words.[46] Quoting Charles Simeon of Cambridge, Mott stated outright that one student was equivalent to 600 people: "Without question in many respects the most important field which the Church of Christ has entered is the field of students, because that field furnishes a vastly disproportionate number of the leaders in the various realms of thought and action."[47]

Moreover, student organizations provided a space for learning how an institution works and for creating connections and networks. Mott himself was a product of the YMCA program. He sought strong personal piety and lived a form of holiness[48] while at the same time constantly seeking to realize his faith through a concrete institutional commitment.

The mission of the YMCA was to design and propose a Christian way of life that spoke to young persons and motivated their commitment. This approach required a renewal of the forms of Christianity and removing religion from the liturgical and ecclesial context. This form of evangelization and unity among Christians led to the development of "techniques" – to repeat a term used by Suzanne de Dietrich – specifically targeted at young persons.[49] For example, "campaigns of speeches" led by Mott and others involved mastering both the art of speech and of preaching. The federation's evangelists formed a new clergy especially dedicated to the young. Historical research

---

44   See, for example, the journal and travel reports in YDSL, RG 45, Personal papers of John R. Mott, box 117.

45   Arnaud Baubérot, "De la vie sainte à la vie saine: Hygiène et sport dans les mouvements de jeunesse protestants (1890–1914)," ETR 87, 2012, 279–291, here 291.

46   Fédération universelle des étudiants chrétiens, ed., Compte-rendu du Congrès international de Constantinople, Robert College, 24–28 avril 1911, Paris, n. pub., 1912, 201.

47   Address delivered in December 1903; YDSL, RG 45, Personal papers of John R. Mott, box 143.

48   Setran, The College "Y", 63.

49   De Dietrich, Fifty Years of History, 16.

also highlights the function of "itinerant ministry," which was adopted by Mott.[50] Bible study meetings and summer camps were also other ways of forming "parishes," Christian communities specifically composed of young people or students. All together these techniques formed not only an expertise but a life knowledge that allowed for local life at a campus level as well as networking, first over vast national areas and then on a global scale. They created a common culture that, although not strictly speaking an ecclesial culture, offered solid common references and clear structures. The introduction of a universal day of prayer for students in 1897/1898 was a step in this direction.

Thus, by focusing on university youth, the Christian associations formed the future elites of society into a militant Christianity that was detached from ecclesial practices and could accommodate – and even accompany – disaffiliation, as will be described below. This aspect was crucial in the development of an ecumenical spirit among young people. It was strongly linked to the propagation of a missionary state of mind that also united young persons across ecclesial divisions, giving them a common purpose. The organization of student associations went hand in hand with that of the SVM, as Shedd says: "For Mott and other Student Movement leaders, the missionary spirit was so central to all Christian activity that building a strong national student movement always meant organizing as a part of it a Student Volunteer Movement."[51]

3.2   Evangelization: The Urgency of Action

In the summer of 1886, at the first meeting in Mount Hermon, John R. Mott made the commitment to embark on a distant mission; from that moment his activity was directed towards spreading Christianity. Mott's speech and practices used the channels of a Christianity that sought to be "virile," using words such as "superhuman" or "Christian heroism"[52] to signify a religiosity that preferred discourse on self-control, action and conquest to one of contemplation or theological reflection. In this sense, Mott was an archetypal representative of what historians call "muscular Christianity": a "faith ... rooted self-consciously in action rather than theology, and behavior rather than belief."[53] This new form of Christianization, as conceived by Mott, was based above all on a common project: to evangelize. Mott's speeches, therefore, called not only for young people to convert, but also for their missionary commitment, even in distant countries. To this end, he adopted a quasi-military strategy, focused precisely on evangelizing students. One of his first major texts, published in 1887, was entitled *Strategic Points in the World's Conquest*, the strategic points being universities. The book was a report of his world tour with analyses by region or country. In the preface, Mott summarized his program:

> It is hoped that this record will lead to a wider recognition of the great strategic importance of the universities and colleges in the spiritual conquest of the world, and awaken larger interest in the movement to make all institutions of higher learning strongholds and propagating centers of the Christian faith.[54]

In the same vein, Mott adopted the slogan "Evangelization of the World in This Generation," which was used by the SVM, as the title of his 1900 book. The idea was that the current generation's most urgent responsibility was to ensure the proclamation of the Gospel to the entire world. It can be noted that the motto was discussed at the Liverpool missionary conference, held by the BSVMU in January of 1896, in these terms:

---

50   De Dietrich, *Cinquante ans d'histoire*, 56; *Fifty Years of History*, 36.

51   Shedd, *Two Centuries*, 365.

52   John Raleigh Mott, *The Watchword of the Student Volunteer Movement as a Spiritual Force: An Address Delivered before the Third International Conference of the Student Volunteer Missionary Union: Edinburgh, January 4, 1904*, New York NY, SVM, 1904, 5, 11.

53   Setran, *The College "Y"*, 5.

54   Mott, *Strategic Points*, 11.

By evangelization we do not mean conversion, nor do we mean to disparage, but to emphasize the value of educational missions. What it meant is simply this: "The presenting of the Gospel in such a manner to every soul in this world that the responsibility for what is done shall no longer rest upon the Christian Church or on any individual Christian, but rest on each man's head himself."[55]

Mott embraced this perspective.[56] Suzanne de Dietrich commented on this mission in her 1946 book:

> Mott's vocation has always led him to those to whom the gospel has not yet been preached. His missionary campaigns have attracted thousands of students belonging to other religions – Muslims, Jews, Hindus, Shintoists – as well as those with no faith at all. He has, of course, come up against strong opposition: wherever the gospel really touches souls, there is bound to be a struggle. The most difficult skepticism to overcome seems to have been that of the intellectually blasé students of continental Europe; they received with amiable irony this American with his slightly simplistic faith, who was quite unimpressed by their rationality.[57]

The imperialist dimension inherent in this conception of mission has not escaped historians.[58] The issue, which goes beyond the scope of this chapter, was widely discussed after the publication of Ian Tyrrell's book in 2010 concerning the question of creating an American moral empire

using the evangelist niche.[59] Having said that, the figures that were conscientiously published in the federation's material did not, strictly speaking, show a world conquest. The movement had a phenomenal expansion, especially during the first period of Mott's travels, between 1895 and 1900.[60] However, while the figures were impressive for the federation itself and its international life, they were anecdotal when compared to the demographics of the various countries concerned, whether India or China or even France. The main impact of these international developments has undoubtedly been the diffusion of the perception that Protestants, leaders of youth movements, have contributed to the unity of Christianity and even, to some extent, that of humanity.

3.3   Unity and Globalization: The "Sense of the Unity of Christendom"

For Mott's generation, humanity was divided between the Protestant powers and all the rest. In his 1897 book, *Strategic Points in the World's Conquest*, Mott conceived of the world as geographical spaces to be conquered. He thus spoke of "Student Movements of the Occident" and "Students of Papal Europe," then divided the rest of the world as follows: Turkey, the Balkans, and Greece; Syria and Palestine; the Nile Valley; Ceylon; India; Australia; China; Japan; and the Hawaiian Islands. Each area was recognized to have its own specificities and difficulties. For example, in the "West," Germany was considered the most problematic country because it had to be saved from the danger of Rationalist universities and their academics spreading the same ideas in all places of knowledge. Catholic countries, in addition to being subjected to superstition (see below), were considered threatened by materialism.

---

55   Report of the Liverpool Conference, 71, cited in: Shedd, *Two Centuries*, 366.

56   John Raleigh Mott, *The Evangelization of the World in This Generation*, New York NY, SVM, 1900, 7.

57   De Dietrich, *Fifty Years of History*, 28.

58   Potter & Wieser, *Seeking and Serving the Truth*, 18–19; Andrew Porter, "Missions and Empire (c. 1873–1914)," *CHC* 8, 560–575.

59   Tyrrell, *Reforming the World*. For the debates generated by the book, see Rebekka Habermas & others, "Débat: *Reforming the World: The Creation of America's Moral Empire*, de Ian Tyrrell," *Monde(s)* 6, 2014, 148–168.

60   See the figures in Shedd, *Two Centuries*, 371.

As we have seen above, Mott explicitly envisioned his mission as global. For Tyrrell, the use of the word "world" was significant in this global and transnational vision underpinned by the WSCF: "The aspirations were global and reflected American evangelicalism's mission to take the Protestant Gospel to the whole world."[61] In the Romance languages, this aspiration was encompassed by the word "universal."

The fact of envisioning, and, in a certain way, acting upon, humanity as a whole, as a unity, was one of the key and innovative elements of this way of thinking, which was also steeped in paternalism and colonialism. Mott was fully aware of the novelty of this ideological globalization. From the beginning of the federation in 1897, he stated:

> The chief significance of the Federation is its unifying power. It is doing much to unify the plans and methods of Christian work among students in different countries. Moreover, it is uniting in effort and in spirit as never before the students of the world. It is helping to unite the nations by stronger and more enduring bonds than arbitration treaties, because it is fusing together by the omnipotent Spirit of Christ the students who are to be the leaders of the nations.[62]

His approach produced forms of union and networking that aimed to bring different cultures and peoples together in the name of a new Christianity, in addition to overcoming internal denominational barriers in the Protestant world. Again in 1897, he claimed that the federation had representatives from seventy different branches of the "Church of Christ."[63]

The birth of this Christian-Protestant globalism was directly linked to the operational manner of Mott and the WSCF. It is therefore worth outlining two of its main features here: travel, with the use of technological progress, and the establishment of international conferences.

At the end of the 19th century, various technological advances clearly brought the continents closer together, particularly in the field of transportation (with the train and steamboat in particular). A significant portion of Mott's correspondence could be used for a history of global transportation, since he described the hours spent on ships and trains! Telecommunications were also at the heart of this new way of looking at the world. In this atmosphere of scientific innovation, Mott stated: "This Federation has established a telegraph in things spiritual."[64] He used Gladstone's metaphor describing the importance of universities in the Middle Ages.[65]

Mott thought of his task as secretary general as a work in motion. Some have calculated that Mott traveled two million miles during his lifetime, or about seventy times around the world. The evangelist operated in successive rounds, organizing student associations wherever he stopped in collaboration with the people of each place. He has sometimes been compared to the Apostle Paul by his colleagues and biographers. Mott meticulously prepared his travels, made contact with important personalities from the various national movements, and galvanized the forces of the students who hosted him. During a stop, he would give both public lectures and private interviews. He was a counselor, confessor, and spiritual guide, but also an organizer and management consultant. His technique consisted in identifying "the most capable elements"[66] within the local groups and connecting them with more experienced people as well as helping them to travel and participate in international meetings. It was, therefore, a true work of weaving an international network, mainly carried out by the itinerant secretaries.

61 Tyrrell, *Reforming the World*, 25.
62 Mott, *Strategic Points*, 21.
63 Mott, *Strategic Points*, 22.

64 Mott, *Strategic Points*, 20.
65 Archibald Stodart-Walker, ed., *Rectorial addresses delivered before the University of Edinburgh (1859–1899)*, London, Richards, 1900, 10.
66 De Dietrich, *Cinquante ans d'histoire*, 54.

In order to understand Mott's approach, it is interesting to look at his travel accounts, which in fact form the bulk of his written work. In particular, his first intercontinental voyage from 1895 to 1897, which set the federation in motion, was the subject of his *Strategic Points in the World's Conquest.* The text took the form of a balance sheet, intended for both donors and future missionaries. He put his results into figures: for 20 months, he covered 60,000 miles, visited 22 countries and 144 universities, colleges, or schools; he attended 21 conferences or conventions that brought together 5,500 delegates representing 308 university institutions; he met about 1,300 missionaries; 70 student associations and unions were organized; 505 young men were "led to accept Jesus Christ as their personal Savior."[67] Like other "itinerant" personalities, Mott thus became the link connecting the movement on a global scale. This would not have been enough to build a common identity, however, without the international gatherings that were the world conferences.

WSCF's world conferences and general committees were held every two to three years, bringing together dozens of delegates from different countries (between one and two hundred people from 30 to 40 countries). As those present recounted, the locations of the meetings were chosen in order to support the logic of globalization. They were designed as a "concentration of resources."[68] Depending on the case, it could be a matter of consolidating an emerging movement or regrouping on known and friendly territory to reflect on what to do next. The first assemblies, therefore, took place in different parts of the world: Williamstown, in the United States in 1897, Eisenach, Thuringia, in Germany in 1898, Versailles in France in 1900, Sorø, Sjælland, in Denmark in 1902, Zeist in the Netherlands in 1905, Tokyo, Japan, in 1907, Oxford,

England, in 1909, Constantinople, Turkey, in 1911, and Lake Mohonk, in the United States in 1913. The federation seems to have been the first global organization to hold its meetings in the Far East.[69] It was explicitly stated that this allowed local associations to assume ownership of the federation. From meeting to meeting, the organization was refined to ensure networking and interpersonal relationship building objectives, specific measures were taken such as seating charts for meals.[70] The purpose of these meetings was to create unity. In 1900, at the Versailles conference, the results were in line with this sense:

> Now we have the World's Student Christian Federation, which unites all the Christian student movements of the world, which has set these movements to acting and reacting upon one another most helpfully, and which not only has made the students of each land intelligent concerning those of other nations and races and brought them into sympathy with one another, but also has developed among them a world consciousness.[71]

This beautiful formula of "world consciousness" well expresses the birth of a feeling of unity that was taking root among Protestant leaders on a world scale. Mott conceived of the federation's role mainly at this level: "By uniting ... those who are to be the leaders in the various branches of the Church of Christ, the federation has been instrumental in greatly hastening the realization of the prayer of our Lord 'that they may all be one.'"[72] This prayer was also the credo of the youth

---

67   Mott, *Strategic Points*, 208–212.

68   De Dietrich, *Fifty Years of History*, 29; Rouse, *The World's Student Christian Federation*; Potter & Wieser, *Seeking and Serving the Truth*, 20–45. The latter presents WSCF's history through its international meetings.

69   De Dietrich, *Cinquante ans d'histoire*, 56.

70   Potter & Wieser, *Seeking and Serving the Truth*, 41.

71   WSCF, ed., *Report of the Conference of the World's Student Christian Federation: Held at Versailles, France, August 3–8, 1900*, New York NY, WSCF, 1900, 86–87; cited in Shedd, *Two Centuries*, 372.

72   WSCF, ed., *Report of the Conference of the World's Student Christian Federation: Held at Sorø, Denmark, August 11–15, 1902*, New York NY, WSCF, 1902, 72; cited in Potter & Wieser, *Seeking and Serving the Truth*, 25.

movements. In 1911, Mott spoke of a "spirit" that started during the international conferences:

> Their benefit [of the national or international conferences] does not come from legislation. I have noticed that the conferences organized for this purpose are not the ones that do the most for unity. The benefit of the conferences, moreover, is not so much that which comes from education or even inspiration. The main service they render is to create an atmosphere, a spirit, and a disposition that influence Christians to come to see things more as Christ sees them. They also bring Christians closer to each other through a true common regard and friendship.[73]

The idea of universality that was being put in place under Mott's pen and through his work as secretary general was the awareness of the possible union of humanity on a planetary scale around an evangelical faith. The "ecumenism" resulting from the federation and Mott's work, therefore, was the result of several types of rapprochement: between individuals and between youth organizations; between members of different Protestant denominations, with a gradual expansion towards other confessions; and between representatives of different nations and continents. This ecumenism, however, remained extremely focused on the "Protestant powers" and their geopolitics. This approach was one of the variants of the new ways of seeing and understanding the world that emerged at the end of the 19th century, amidst colonialist efforts. In the last part of this chapter, it is also worthwhile identifying its limits.

4 Youth Organizations as Ecumenical Movements: Theory and Practice before World War I

Two elements have to be revisited here in conclusion in order to grasp the place of student youth movements in the history of ecumenism: first, the student federation's relationship with Catholicism and, second, the question of the relationship between the WSCF and the churches as institutions.

4.1 Protestant Unity, Anti-Catholicism, and Other Christian Traditions

Mott inherited the anti-Catholic discourse typical of Protestants, especially Americans.[74] He also perpetuated it to a considerable degree. In an article that the very young Mott published in 1884 in the *Fayette Collegian*, he revisited the classical themes of Reformed historical analysis based on the idea of the "abuses" of the church at the end of the Middle Ages, for which Luther called an end to, while affirming:

> "Never make fun of the bridge that has carried you over the stream," is a saying which should be kept in mind when commenting on the Church of Rome; for true it is that the Catholic Church has been the bridge spanning the abyss of the Dark Ages, over which has been safely carried the torch of civilization, lighted at the fires of ancient Hellas, the country of the Caesars, and the sacred shrines of the Holy Land.[75]

---

73   Fédération universelle des étudiants chrétiens, ed., *Compte-rendu*, 200.

74   Maura Jane Farrelly, *Anti-Catholicism in America (1620–1860)*, Cambridge, Cambridge University Press, 2018; Yvonne Maria Werner, ed., *European Anti-Catholicism in a Comparative and Transnational Perspective*, Amsterdam, Rodopi, 2013; John Wolffe, "A Comparative Historical Categorisation of Anti-Catholicism," *JRH* 39, 2015, 182–202; Timothy Verhoeven, *Transatlantic Anti-Catholicism: France and the United States in the Nineteenth Century*, New York NY, Palgrave Macmillan, 2010.

75   YDSL, RG 45, Personal papers of John R. Mott, box 137.

Even if viewed with respect, from his perspective the Church of Rome remained a historical object, clearly outdated from the 16th century. In Mott's writings, it is clear that he considered Catholicism to be a superstition. He concluded his 1884 text, writing:

> As we meditate upon these great abuses which were casting their blighting influences over all northern and western Europe, can we wonder that, when Luther's trumpet pealed forth from the banks of the Elbe, its echo was taken up and resounded through sunny France, across the lowlands of Holland and Denmark, and away up into the "Land of the Midnight Sun," reverberated up the passes of Switzerland, and wafted over the Isle of Britain, arousing and inspiring men to stand even against the giant power of Romanism – to suffer obloquy, torture, death?[76]

In Mott's perspective, Catholic territories were therefore considered mission lands in the same way as India or Japan. Protestant territories were, too, although to a lesser extent, since it was a question of converting, awakening individuals who had been raised in Christianity but who had never made that choice. In 1897, his diagnosis of students of what he called Papal Europe was definitive:

> Trustworthy testimony seems to indicate that in all these countries [Italy, France, Austria, Hungary, Spain, Portugal, Belgium] the Church of Rome has lost its hold on a strikingly large proportion both of students and professors. They have drifted into skepticism and agnosticism. The materialistic bent is becoming more and more pronounced. Impurity is the chief evil and is more prevalent than among the students of any other countries of Europe. Spiritual fires have been kindled among the students in France, Italy, and Hungary. May they prove to be foregleams of the coming day for the universities of all these lands, which have been so long enshrouded in the double darkness of superstition and skepticism.[77]

In Europe, Protestant unions were conceived from the outset as instruments in the struggle against both disbelief and Catholicism. The Catholic Church is a much older international and transnational organization than the evangelical Protestant federations and alliances, and it increased its centralization considerably in the 19th century, particularly under Pope Pius IX. Moreover, it had established its own youth and student organizations to deal with the same type of spiritual needs and social problems as the Protestants had.[78] The Protestant organizations and alliances, therefore, set themselves the objective of uniting the movements that had emerged from the Reformation in order to face Rome's institutional power.[79]

At first, the YMCAs only admitted students "attached" to a Protestant Church as their active and voting members. But this issue, which is discussed in detail below, provoked controversy. It was part of a broader issue, which was the relationship with the Christian churches present in the areas where missions were carried out, especially in traditionally Orthodox countries. For this reason,

---

76   YDSL, RG 45, Personal papers of John R. Mott, box 137.

77   Mott, *Strategic Points*, 43.

78   Cholvy, ed., *Mouvements de jeunesse chrétiens et juifs*, esp. 13–65.

79   This perspective was present at the movement's birth: "Many Christians in Geneva, in the canton of Vaud, in France, and probably in other parts of Protestant Christianity, considering the current state of the Church of Jesus Christ, feel the need to manifest more fully the great and beautiful unity that exists between those who, through the blood of Christ, were 'purchased for God … from every tribe and tongue, people, and nation' (Rev 5:9). They believe that, in the presence of the combined efforts of Rome and all the anti-Christian opinions, evangelical Christians had to rally around their Head and to join together by the confession of faith that was common to them"; Jean-Henri Merle d'Aubigné, *L'Eglise appelée à confesser Jésus-Christ: Discours prononcé à Genève le 27 septembre 1840*, Geneva, Libraire Béroud, 1841, iii.

John R. Mott and Ruth Rouse had both been to Russia between 1907 and 1909.[80]

In 1911, the federation held its world assembly in Constantinople, in the Ottoman Empire then ruled by the Young Turks, with the aim of establishing contact with the Greek Orthodox. The conference was not supported by a local student movement but was hosted by the American College of Constantinople. Mott and Rouse toured universities and patriarchates to prepare the ground: "The patriarch of Constantinople gave his blessing to the undertaking. Dr. Mott was able to declare at the opening of the conference that never since the great councils of the church had there been such an ecumenical meeting."[81]

From the preparatory meetings, the question had been raised as to how to make it possible for Orthodox and Catholics to join. Several delegates asked that the federation adopt a more interdenominational position. A resolution was passed by the general committee that granted access to the federation to all students who made a personal confession of faith, regardless of their ecclesial affiliation.[82] In other words, it was enough for the student to adhere to the evangelical message without necessarily changing their church.

In his history of the federation, Mott explained that this transformation was designed to allow the movement to expand into countries of Greek and Catholic traditions.[83] Openness to Catholicism, therefore, made its way into a broader reflection on the relationship between student associations and churches as well as on the criteria for admission of their members.

4.2   *Associations vs. Church*

How were the relationships between Protestant denominations perceived within the youth associations? The question of confessional, theological, and ecclesiological differences was not considered important by the movement's early leaders. For example, it was not included in the table of contents of Mott's 1920 balance sheet book.[84] It appears only in the section "The Guiding Principles of the Federation."[85] Mott explained: "The cornerstone principle is the recognition of the supremacy and the universality of the Lord Jesus Christ and of His work as the only sufficient Savior." This principle was formulated in both the local constitutions and that of the federation. He added: "Some of the most intense, prolonged, and memorable controversies in student fields have been the basis discussions. In almost every case they have finally ended in a larger appreciation of Christ and a fuller obedience to Him."[86]

Concretely speaking, in the constitution of the WSCF, the first subdivision of the third object of the federation (article 3.a see above), which concerns Christology, was the subject of the most successive revisions. "To lead students to become disciples of Jesus Christ as the only Savior and as God" became: "To lead students to accept the Christian faith in God – Father, Son, and Holy

---

80   The Mott archives contain many notes on the Orthodox question, which are very difficult to decipher: YDSL, RG 45, Personal papers of John R. Mott, box 122.

81   De Dietrich, *Fifty Years of History*, 38.

82   I.e. personally adhere to the Federation's declaration of faith; de Dietrich, *Fifty Years of History*, 38. The resolution read as follows: "The general committee puts on record its opinion that no student, to whatever branch of the Christian church he may belong, should be excluded from full membership in any national movement within the Federation if he is prepared to accept the basis of the Federation, or whatever equivalent is approved by the Federation"; cited in: Potter & Wieser, *Seeking and Serving the Truth*, 35. See the *Minutes of the Meeting of General Committee of the World's Student Christian Federation, held in Prinkipo and Bebek, Constantinople, Turkey, April 20–27, 1911*, especially in: YDSL, RG 46, World Student Christian Federation Records, box 265.

83   Mott, *The World's Student Christian Federation*, 10.

84   Mott, *The World's Student Christian Federation*.

85   Mott, *The World's Student Christian Federation*, 9. An extensive report from 1912 devoted to the question of "the basis of the Federation" is maintained at YDSL, RG 46, World Student Christian Federation Records, box 7.

86   Mott, *The World's Student Christian Federation*, 9.

Spirit, according to the Scriptures – and to live as true disciples of Jesus Christ."[87]

Apart from this debate, Mott was probably not wrong to say that the federation had left theological debates outside its area of concern. Firm in its relationship to the Bible and the centrality of the confession of faith, but flexible on the most divisive ecclesiological questions in Protestantism, student associations' constitutions permitted a large gathering of Protestants, excluding only the most liberal and Unitarians. As we have seen, it was above all a question of living the Christianity in universities and of bringing students from all churches back to the faith and of incarnating this faith in a form of healthy living.

On campuses, these organizations owed their existence to the very fact that they originated from, and were mainly organized by, students and that they denied being churches. They did not seek to replace the ministry of pastors. To express the concept as handed down in historical research, let us use Ruth Rouse's words: "In essence it was the idea of a movement in which the Churches would give their riches, not give them up; would share their heritage, not surrender it."[88] In the same way, WSCF leaders placed great emphasis on the fact that the organization was "interdenominational" and not "undenominational."[89] In this way, they tried to repel their detractors. The latter accused the organization of being the vehicle for a Protestantism of the "lowest common denominator faith."[90]

That is why, initially, the statutes provided that only individuals belonging to a Protestant Church could become full members. However,

that conception evolved, as Setran shows very precisely in regard to the United States. The links between the YMCA and evangelism grew weaker, especially within the student movement, and this from the beginning of the 20th century. At the 1907 International YMCA Convention in Washington, it was decided that active members could be those who were members of an evangelical church or those who accepted Jesus Christ and the association's statutes. The exact wording was:

> [The students who were] either members of evangelical churches or accept Jesus Christ as He is offered in the Holy Scripture as their God and Savior and approve of the objects of the Association, which are as follows: to lead students to become disciples of Jesus Christ as their divine Lord and Savior, to lead them to join the church, to promote growth in Christian faith and character, and to enlist them in Christian service.[91]

The growing importance of the question of service to the community and of work on oneself (a pure lifestyle, moralizing – "service and character") can be seen here. Mott supported this change. Setran, who highlights this new paradigm, noted that it was concomitant with a significant increase in the number of student associations. Bible groups, for example, became first and foremost spaces for solving moral and existential problems. In that context they gradually opened up to non-Protestants, especially Jews and Catholics.[92] Setran gives the example of the University of Louisiana (according to a 1909 report)[93] where a priest asked 25 Catholic students to leave the Bible study group. They refused, replying "that the studies did not address issues of a theological nature, focusing instead on

---

87   Mott, *The World's Student Christian Federation*, 89. The two other points were similarly rewritten to emphasize the centrality of the Bible and the importance of mission: "(b) to deepen the spiritual life of students and to promote earnest study of the Scriptures among them; (c) to influence students to devote themselves to the extension of the Kingdom of God in their own nation and throughout the world"; see Potter & Wieser, *Seeking and Serving the Truth*, 40.

88   *A History of the Ecumenical Movement*, vol. 1, 343.

89   *A History of the Ecumenical Movement*, vol. 1.

90   Setran, *The College "Y"*, 29.

91   Setran, *The College "Y"*, 125.

92   Setran, *The College "Y"*, 124.

93   Setran, *The College "Y"*, 124 and its source W.D. Weatherford, "Report to the Student Committee of the International Committee of the Young Men's Christian Associations for the Year Ending August 31, 1909," in: YDSL, Archives of the YMCA, Box 41, Folder 601.

practical living and social service." From then on, in the years that followed, some student groups came to eliminate a confession of faith from the conditions of membership (Brown University, the University of Chicago). Metaphysical conceptions of the nature of Christ were no longer considered criteria for admission.[94]

That choice was supported by some of the YMCA leaders. For example, David R. Porter, Mott's successor for the American students YMCAs, stated that "membership should be broad enough to include Catholics and Unitarians." Setran comments that "the shift from a creedal to a purpose basis signified not only a separation from churches and opening to non-evangelical religious groups but also a more generalized transformation in the very meaning of the 'Christian' focus of the organization."[95]

As we have seen, from 1911 the federation was officially opened to those who adopted its confession of faith without imposing the criterion of an ecclesial membership. These developments reinforced the problem of relations between the WSCF and the churches that had been recurring since the first YMCAs.

That same year, 1911, in Constantinople, the French theology professor Raoul Allier gave a report entitled "Comment intégrer dans l'œuvre essentielle de l'Eglise les membres de la Fédération" ("How to Integrate Members of the Federation into the Essential Work of the Church"). He recalled that the federation's "purpose does not lie in itself. It is neither a church nor the particular organ of any church." He wondered: "What will the members of the federation be and what will they do for the church ... when they leave our groups?"[96] He called for vocations to pastoral ministry among students as well as for the ecclesial commitment of all lay persons. At Lake Mohonk in 1913, the federation reaffirmed that it did not want to be

a substitute for the church. The movement then called itself a "place of passage."

Nevertheless, elements that could be fully part of the life of a church or a community of believers, with a lasting character, can be recognized in the social and religious practices of the federation. In other words, were not the students forming the flock of an informal ecumenical church, with its rites and liturgy? Moreover, WSCF's effects on church reunification were real, especially in mission areas.

5   Mission and Unity

The federation's institutional model and ideology had a direct impact on the representation that Protestants had of themselves and on their relationships with each other, with direct repercussions on the relations among churches. In addition to the interdenominational habits developed in Western universities, the missionary aspect played a key role. The ecumenism of the student associations was played out, above all, on the grounds of a Christianity that, while profoundly evangelical at the beginning, within a generation had transformed its theological ideal into an ideal of action, for personal asceticism but also towards a social mission and missionary work in non-Christian lands. In this process, the importance of the different elements of the evangelical (Trinitarian) confession of faith, as well as the specificities of each Protestant family, were overshadowed by the question of Christian commitment and activism. For Mott, "working together breaks down divisions among Christians."[97] Unity was conceived of as both the result of, and the condition for, the manifestation of the Holy Spirit in missionary outreach.

The Protestant concept of missionary work, by reducing religious differences to a Christian or non-Christian dichotomy (convert or to be converted), changed the traditional boundaries that divided

94   Setran, *The College "Y"*, 127.
95   Setran, *The College "Y"*, 128.
96   Fédération universelle des étudiants chrétiens, ed., *Compte-rendu*, 137.
97   Fédération universelle des étudiants chrétiens, ed., *Compte-rendu*, 201.

the Reformed world into competing chapels.[98] This intra-Protestant ecumenism, led by young students, was one of the main fruits of Mott's missionary work. According to him, it was a worthy model. He explicitly stated, several times:

> The Young Men's Christian Association, although it has been at work on the mission field less than a generation, by its interdenominational conferences, by actually uniting Christian young men of different branches of the Church in common efforts at metropolitan centers, and by fusing together through its student Associations the future leaders of all Christian bodies, has become one of the principal factors making for Christian unity.[99]

For him, it was quite clear that divisions among Protestant Churches had to disappear in mission lands. He welcomed the interdenominational conferences of missionaries that took place at the local and national level. He used the example of Japan, for its unification effort, but also of China and India:

> Moreover, it is of large importance that the native Christians on each field be united so far as possible – those of the same denominational family joining their forces and even those of different denominations, so far as practicable, uniting in one great Church, adapted to the conditions obtaining on that field – thus avoiding the reproduction on the mission fields of all accidental and unnecessary or unessential differences which bulk so largely in the sectarianism of Western lands.

This plan of uniting into one organic body the various branches of each denominational family – e.g. Presbyterians, Lutherans, Episcopalians, Methodists, Baptists – is the first stage in the union of the Christian forces, and encouraging progress has been made in the direction of its realization in each of the three great mission fields of Asia.[100]

To which he added: "Without doubt, the Church in non-Christian lands has important lessons to teach the Church in Christian countries, both in the theory and in the practice of Christian unity and co-operation."[101] It was therefore understandable that Mott had a front row seat at the Edinburgh Conference in 1910.[102]

6   Conclusions

With the WSCF, a new idea of the church emerged that was superimposed on that of the historical churches. In 1945, Robert C. Mackie summed it up in the formula: "Evangelization conducted within the framework of the universal church."[103] The leaders of the movement constantly spoke of the Christian church in the singular. In practice, there was no real question of merging the existing, traditional churches together. The WSCF leaders' speeches always insisted on the idea of federation, at all levels of the organization, as the bringing together of different, sovereign entities whose particularity was respected. This "church," therefore, corresponded to a form of "imaginary community," deeply Protestant and evangelical in its conception.[104] The beginnings of the federation

---

98 Fédération universelle des étudiants chrétiens, ed., *Compte-rendu*, 201: "This movement [the SVM] considers the Christian world in the face of the non-Christian world; the greater the task to be done grows, the more imperative the call becomes, the more unity there must be to achieve the goal."

99 John Raleigh Mott, *The Pastor and Modern Missions: A Plea for Leadership in World Evangelization*, New York NY, SVM, 1904, 30.

100 Mott, *The Pastor and Modern Missions*, 31, 34–35.

101 Mott, *The Pastor and Modern Missions*, 35.

102 It should be noted that the issue of the unity of the churches was not, strictly speaking, a priority of the conference; Brian Stanley, "The World Missionary Conference, Edinburgh 1910: Sifting History from Myth," *ExpTim* 121, 2010, 325–331; Brian Stanley's contribution in this volume.

103 De Dietrich, *Cinquante ans d'histoire*, 6.

104 Habermas & others, "Débat: *Reforming the World*," 159.

corresponded to a particular period concerning geopolitics within the Protestant world, which allowed it to be drawn into hegemonic utopias. For Mott and his contemporaries, the evangelical conquest of the world seemed within reach, but that was not the case a generation later. Professor Shedd of Yale University put it in interesting terms in 1934, describing what he thought of Mott's 19th century world:

> Protestant Christianity, in spite of its denominational and theological differences, had its blueprints for religion. The implications of religion were generally accepted as upright personal conduct; philanthropic benevolence toward the less privileged; service for better community, state, and nation; and world-wide sharing of the Christian evangel through evangelism at home and missions abroad. There were no questions about the social order or war so fundamental in character that the Christian must face them and deal with them if his evangelism were to have meaning. It was, indeed, a world in which there seemed to be security for individual and social values. In such a world crusading for world-wide expansion of Christianity was a fascinating adventure – there were enough obstacles to make it exciting, but they were not of a sort that shook confidence in fundamental assumptions.[105]

This Protestant Christianity literally exploded during World War I, whose front lines pitted historically Protestant territories against each other. Another ecumenical movement had to be built. But it was able to use the formidable "laboratory" (to use a term from Rouse) constituted by the WSCF and by the interpersonal links created within its associations.[106]

Translated from French to English by Susan Dawson Vásquez and David Dawson Vásquez.

Bibliography

Baubérot, Arnaud, "De la vie sainte à la vie saine: Hygiène et sport dans les mouvements de jeunesse protestants (1890–1914)," *ETR* 87, 2012, 279–291.

Cholvy, Gérard, ed., *Mouvements de jeunesse chrétiens et juifs: Sociabilité juvénile dans un cadre européen (1799–1968)*, Paris, Cerf, 1985.

Dietrich, Suzanne de, *Cinquante ans d'histoire: La Fédération universelle des associations chrétiennes d'étudiants (1895–1945)*, Paris, Éditions du Semeur, 1946; ET: *Fifty Years of History: The World Student Christian Federation (1895–1945)*, Geneva, WSCF, 1993.

Farrelly, Maura Jane, *Anti-Catholicism in America (1620–1860)*, Cambridge, Cambridge University Press, 2018.

Franzén, Ruth, *Ruth Rouse among Students: Global, Missiological, and Ecumenical Perspectives*, Uppsala, Swedish Institute of Mission Research, 2008.

Hopkins, Charles Howard, *History of the Y.M.C.A. in North America*, New York NY, Association Press, 1951.

Hopkins, Charles Howard, *John R. Mott (1865–1955): A Biography*, Grand Rapids MI, Eerdmans, 1979.

Porter, Andrew, "Missions and Empire (c. 1873–1914)," *CHC* 8, 560–575.

Potter, Philip & Thomas Wieser, *Seeking and Serving the Truth: The First Hundred Years of the World Student Christian Federation*, Geneva, WCC Publications, 1997.

Rouse, Ruth, *The World's Student Christian Federation: A History of the First Thirty Years*, London, SCM Press, 1948.

Setran, David P., *The College "Y": Student Religion in the Era of Secularization*, Basingstoke, Palgrave Macmillan, 2007.

Shedd, Clarence Prouty, *History of the World's Alliance of Young Men's Christian Associations*, London, SPCK, 1955.

Shedd, Clarence Prouty, *Two Centuries of Student Christian Movements: Their Origin and Intercollegiate Life*, New York NY, Association Press, 1934.

Tyrrell, Ian, *Reforming the World: The Creation of America's Moral Empire*, Princeton NJ, Princeton University Press, 2010.

---

105 Shedd, *Two Centuries*, 376–377.
106 *A History of the Ecumenical Movement*, vol. 1, 344.

CHAPTER 15

The Origins of Kimbanguism: Charismatic Autonomy and Narrative Unity in the Congo Sources

Silvia Cristofori

1 Inspiration

Simon Kimbangu was a thaumaturgic prophet of Baptist upbringing who began healing the sick and raising the dead in March 1921 in Nkamba, his home village in the district of Bas-Congo in what was then the Belgian Congo. From this small settlement, about 50 kilometers from Thysville, a vast religious movement radiated out into the entire Congo region, spreading over an area fragmented by Belgian, French, and Portuguese colonial domination. The dynamic of its propagation was the dispensation of charisms and the multiplication of prophets: shaken by strong spasms, they began to speak in a heavenly tongue and to heal, just as the apostles did after the descent of the Holy Spirit at Pentecost.

By virtue of the direct relationship between God and the prophet, this charismatic vector of diffusion encouraged the presence of differentiations and centrifugal tendencies. It was therefore a movement that was neither homogenous nor centralized but which, nevertheless, had a common source of inspiration in Kimbangu's prophetic work. In this sense, the literature uses the term "Ngunzism" to highlight both the incomplete traceability of the greater movement to the teachings of the Nkamba prophet and the intentional connection of the other prophets to him.[1] Those who manifested the charism of healing were proclaimed to be, like Kimbangu, *ngunza* (prophet). This Kongo term was in use in the translations and preaching of the Baptist Church (BMS) of which Kimbangu was a member,[2] and came to identify in the movement those prophets who exercised the power of healing in the collective interest, without personal gain.[3]

As early as May 1921, the Belgian colonial authorities took an interest in what was happening in Nkamba, observing the mass pilgrimages that went there. At first, the main cause for concern was the fact that the natives even traveled from remote areas, abandoning their working activities. When, beginning in the month of June, there was a decisive repressive intervention against Kimbangu and the other prophets, a part of the Ngunzist movement became radicalized: in fact, the number of those *ngunza* who preached the rejection of any form of collaboration with the Europeans multiplied, inciting their listeners not to pay their taxes and to abandon both their work for the whites and the missionary churches.

The charismatic figure of Simon Kimbangu and the wider movement he inspired has played a fundamental role in the history of religious studies in the 20th century. In the climate of political independence, the Congolese prophetic movement

---

1   See the unparalleled account of the history of Christianity in Africa: Adrian Hastings, *The Church in Africa (1450–1950)*, Oxford, Clarendon Press, 1994, 508–513.

2   For a reconstruction of the different lexical choices adopted by different missions as a translation for the Kongo term for prophet, see Jean-Luc Vellut, ed., *Simon Kimbangu: 1921: De la prédication à la déportation: Les sources*, vol. 1, *Fonds missionnaires protestants (2): Missions baptistes et autres traditions évangéliques: Le pays kongo entre prophétismes et projets de société*, Brussels, Académie Royale des Sciences d'Outre-Mer, 2010, 68.

3   Wyatt MacGaffey, *Modern Kongo Prophets: Religions in a Plural Society*, Bloomington IN, Indiana University Press, 1983, 181; Wyatt MacGaffey, "Cultural Roots of Kongo Prophetism," *HR* 17/2, 1977, 177–193, here 179.

of the 1920s assumed, in effect, the sense of a "revelatory"[4] event, not only of the colonial situation in equatorial Africa but, more generally, of the intercultural balance of power inherent to the process of violent modernization.[5] In this perspective, Kimbanguism and the more extensive Ngunzism appeared not as residual phenomena but as exemplary cases for the study of popular religiosity, always aimed, in its search for earthly salvation, at the solution to existential and cultural crises generated by historical changes. The crisis, in regard to the Congolese prophetic movement, derived from the "clash between [the] hegemonic, oppressive, and predatory minority" of the Europeans and the oppressed indigenous population.[6]

In this sense it was a question of seeing it as a "total reaction" to the unequal nature of the colonial relationship, which was expressed both on the sociopolitical and economic level and on the religious level in the missionary church.[7] The prophetic movement as a whole was therefore interpreted as a foreshadowing of political irredentism in the way in which it affirmed a religious autonomy, laying the foundation for a schismatic native church.

Such a church would come into existence over thirty years after Kimbangu's preaching. In the mid-1950s, just as scholars began to take an interest in the political scope of Congolese prophetism, the EJCSK took shape under the leadership of Joseph Diangienda, Kimbangu's son. Formally recognized by the colonial government in 1959, the EJCSK had as its symbolic founding event the return to Nkamba of the body of the prophet on Apr 3, 1960, two months before the declaration of Congo independence.

However, from the time of the prophet's arrest in September 1921, the term Kimbanguism, which was never used in the brief period of Kimbangu's preaching, came to indicate different realities over time.[8] In a first phase, marked by the expectation of the return of the prophet, it was a movement of dissent within the Protestant Churches, but it also indicated those prayer gatherings constituted of the faithful who chose to desert the missions polemically. In the 1940s, the noun Kimbanguism also included the openly anticolonial and antimissionary preaching of Simon-Pierre Mpadi, previously a member of the Salvation Army who, with his Mission des Noirs, proclaimed himself the spiritual successor to Kimbangu. Moreover, the foundation of the EJCSK did not succeed in bringing all those who saw themselves as followers of the Nkamba prophet together into one church; in this sense, therefore, when it was admitted to membership in the WCC in 1969, it did not bring with it a unified Kimbanguism.

The historical evolution of Kimbanguism did not follow the pattern of the antagonisms between the missionary churches, divided as it was into denominations and confessional rivalries. From its beginning, the movement crossed not only colonial borders but also denominational and confessional ones, pervading the Protestant communities and then involving the Catholics, even the mission of the Spiritans, who had no Protestant competition in the French Congo.

As we have already seen, the dynamics of diffusion did not follow a denominational vector but rather a charismatic one, which Kimbangu tried to control through the charism of discernment, recognizing the appearance of new prophets and disowning others as false prophets. In a profoundly changed context, marked by the decline of the colonial regime, the EJCSK also set itself against the

4 Georges Balandier, *Sociologie actuelle de l'Afrique noir: Dinamique sociale en Afrique centrale* , Paris, Presses Universitaires de France, 1982 [¹1955], 417–421.

5 Vittorio Lanternari, *Movimenti religiosi di libertà e salvezza*, Rome, Editori Riuniti, 2003 [¹1960].

6 Lanternari, *Movimenti religiosi*, 49.

7 Balandier, *Sociologie actuelle*, 417–418, 427.

8 Jean-Luc Vellut, "Introduction générale," in: Vellut, ed., *Simon Kimbangu*, vol. 1, *Fonds missionnaires protestants (1): Alliance missionnaire suédoise (Svenska Missionförbundet, SMF)*, Brussels, Académie Royale des Sciences d'Outre-Mer, 2005, xxi–xxv. See also Hastings, *The Church in Africa*, 512–513, 525–527.

prophets of Satan. The attempt was then, however, to construct a Kimbanguist tradition in opposition to the other branches of the movement begun by the Nkamba prophet. With the demonization of those who did not recognize the EJCSK, the movement crystalized in a Kimbanguist church under the stable leadership of the prophet's family.

The establishment of a centralized church was accompanied by the recognition of the primacy of Nkamba as a holy city which, with the return of Kimbangu's body, was named the "new Jerusalem." In particular, a 1961 text in Kikongo by the Kimbanguist church entitled *Zolanga Yelusalemi dia Mpa* (Faithfulness to the New Jerusalem) is significant in this sense.[9] In it, Nkamba was connected to biblical history since it was the place in which "the work of the Lord God [was] revealed by the hand of the Prophet"[10] and, therefore, in it the promise of a new Jerusalem was fulfilled. "But now many have bestowed prophethood upon themselves, ... and set themselves up as the equals of Simon Kimbangu; and they dissuade others from going to Jerusalem, for they also have their holy cities."[11] This situation was not, however, a novelty. In fact, in a previous passage, it was remembered how:

> With the work of the Lord God revealed by the hand of the Prophet, and the Heavenly Father made known to his people through his Prophet Simon Kimbangu, the hills of Satan[12] also were revealed, their eyes fired with jealousy and envy. What kind of hills were these? The prophets of Satan, missionaries, the Belgian government. These hills stood up strongly to fight against the Church

of our Lord Jesus Christ on the earth by his Prophet Simon Kimbangu.[13]

In this text a series of identifications were made. The last part identified Kimbangu's work with the Kimbanguist church, cancelling out the decades that had passed between the work of the former and the establishment of the latter. In its first part, instead, the missionaries appeared as false prophets; they and the colonial state were satanic enemies who, jealous of the divine power of Kimbangu, opposed the prophet and thus his church as well. It can therefore be seen here how, in the construction of a tradition of fidelity to the teachings of Kimbangu, the EJCSK identified itself with the origins of the movement, configuring it as schismatic. The appearance of the prophet, in fact, was said to have solicited the immediate (satanic) opposition of the missionaries, giving rise to the birth of a schismatic native church.

In Nkamba, during the first phase of the movement, Kimbangu's preaching had opened up an innovative ritual space, taking advantage of the wide autonomy already gained by Kongo deacons and catechists in the Baptist Church. It was an original charismatic configuration that consciously articulated a complex relationship with the missionary church. This articulation did not give rise to compromises of convenience; on the contrary, the European religious leaders were faced with the choice of whether or not to admit that the healings of the prophet in Nkamba were a continuation of the gospel message, verifying this with their own eyes.

In virtue of its charismatic nature, the movement therefore posed the question in terms of the recognition of the manifestation of God's power in the contemporary world. However, the relationship with the missionary church could not simply be reduced to a clear alternative between a schism or the integration of the movement into the missionary church, nor did the movement seek missionary recognition in order to be legitimated. In

---

9   The text was originally published under the name of Kimbangu's second son, Dialungana K. Salomon; an English translation is published in: Wyatt MacGaffey, "The Beloved City: Commentary on a Kimbanguist Text," *Journal of Religion in Africa* 2/1, 1969, 129–147.

10   MacGaffey, "The Beloved City," 139.

11   MacGaffey, "The Beloved City," 141.

12   Referring to Isaiah 14:13.

---

13   MacGaffey, "The Beloved City," 139.

the original Kimbanguism there was a need to affirm a deeper unity with the missionary work that was to be independent of the reactions of the European religious leaders to the prophetic movement. At this deeper level, the relationship with the missionaries took shape as a historical dynamic of continuity and advancement: the appearance of the prophet fulfilled the salvific announcement of the European missionaries and marked a continuation of "God's work" in human history.

This advance was not interpreted as a discontinuous opening of a new phase but rather as a return[14] of the manifestation of God's power in the present day. In other words, it was a continuation of the history that had begun with the biblical narrative. The work of the prophet thus continued the history of salvation in which the evangelical proclamation of the missionaries had constituted a fundamental moment. In this sense, Kimbanguism articulated not only a ritual space but also, from its outset, a narrative of itself anchored in a universal history. In this way, it configured, in addition to a ritual space, an autonomous ideological space at the very moment when it affirmed its own continuity with the missionary work.

To reconstruct this charismatic configuration in its ritual and ideological articulation, I shall use here primarily Kongo sources, which present an internal point of view of the movement that arose in Nkamba. These sources belong above all to the genre *nsamu angunza* (history of the prophet) or *nsamu miangunza* (history of the prophets). Their presence in itself already revealed the relationship of continuity and difference between the missionary church and the prophetic movement: the colonial mission, in fact, produced a written culture that evidently also belonged to the original Kimbanguism. However, while the mission wrote its own history in terms of a chronicle of relevant events, the movement wrote a history of itself that was intended to make the gospel message alive in the present.

2 The Railroad and the Typewriter

Kimbangu's prophetic and thaumaturgical activity, which began in March 1921, was, therefore, of short duration, marked by three months in hiding, and was definitively interrupted on Sept 12, when the prophet returned to Nkamba to surrender himself of his own accord to the Belgian territorial agent Laurent Snoeck. Taken to Thysville and tried before a military tribunal, he was sentenced, after a four-day trial, to hang for having threatened the security of the state. Then, on Nov 15, 1921, the death sentence was reduced to life imprisonment, which Kimbangu served until his death in Elisabethville prison, on the extreme southern outskirts of the Belgian Congo.

In the Nkamba prophet, the military tribunal had seen a political agitator at the head of a subversive organization that, according to the grounds for the death sentence, would have instigated a visceral hatred towards whites "resulting in an unsuccessful strike and the abstention from work of a large number of workers."[15] Such a plan manifested itself, for the time being, only "through seditious songs, outrage, and isolated episodes of rebellion" which might, however, have "led to the great revolt."[16]

This conspiracy theory had taken shape during the months of military occupation, introduced following the failure to capture Kimbangu. While the prophet was in hiding, perhaps more than ever, the administration felt insecure. The inquisitional and judiciary emergency powers introduced by

---

14   MacGaffey, "Cultural Roots"; Donald J. Mackay, "Simon Kimbangu and the BMS Tradition," *Journal of Religion in Africa* 17/2, 1987, 113–171.

15   The full text giving the grounds for the sentence pronounced by Captain Amédée de Rossi who presided over the military tribunal was published by the lawyer Jules Chomé, in: Jules Chomé, *La Passion de Simon Kimbangu (1921–1951)*, Brussels, Les Amis de Présence Africaine, 1959, 68–70. The book was intended to rehabilitate Kimbangu in the eyes of the Belgian public.

16   Chomé, *La Passion*, 68–70.

the military regime had in fact, brought to light widespread forms of resistance and insubordination. In rural areas, moreover, the prophetic charisms seemed to spread like a contagion, with the multiplication of *ngunza* who, in reaction to the repression, preached the refusal of any collaboration with the Europeans. These events seemed to be part of a single plot, skillfully woven by the fugitive prophet and his companions.

Among the evidence in support of this reconstruction, the grounds for the sentence cited written works, mentioning in particular a biography dictated by the prophet himself, in which he was said to have expressed the xenophobic and subversive intentions of his organization, camouflaging them in religious language:

> Through acts, intentions, behavior, writings, songs, and the biography that he himself dictated, Simon Kimbangu proclaimed himself the redeemer and savior of the black race by designating the white race as his enemy and calling it an abominable enemy. The sect of the prophet must be considered an organization created to harm the security of the state, a sect hidden under the veil of a new religion, aimed at demolishing the current regime.[17]

The works mentioned had been seized by the administrator of the Cataracts Territory, Léon Morel, on June 17, 1921, following the failed attempt to capture Kimbangu. It was material that had caused astonishment and concern among the Belgians, especially because it was typewritten. The presence of typed writings in the village of Nkamba suggested, in effect, connections between the rural religious movement and the urban environment of the "educated blacks."

The incriminating biography was actually a history of the prophet (*nsamu angunza*) in Kikongo which mentioned two writers, Nfinangani and Nzungu. We know very little about them: the French translation requested by the colonial administration added a brief note that mentioned them as "secretaries of the prophet."[18] While this is all that we have that mentions Nzungu, the name Nfinangani also appears in an undated letter from the territorial administration in Thysville, which reported that Simon Kimbangu's secretary, Nfinangani, had been arrested while teaching Kisolokela, the prophet's oldest child.[19]

The connection with the urban environment, however, was principally confirmed by a third person related to the prophet's history, Thomas Nduma, who had typed the text. For his service, which had been carried out in Nkamba, probably in May 1921, Nduma was arrested and, in August of that year, condemned by the civil tribunal of Thysville to six months' prison and confinement in Haut-Congo, from which he would not return until 1963.[20] Nduma was a deacon in the Baptist Church and worked near Inkisi Station, along the railway line between Thysville and Léopoldville, as an agent for the merchant and entrepreneur André Yengo, who lived in Léopoldville. Not only was Yengo a Kongo Baptist deacon and from the same region as Kimbangu, but he had also founded the proto-nationalist association Congomen.[21]

Even more alarming was the fact, as would emerge in the months of the military regime, that a few months before his preaching began, Kimbangu had left his village to work in Léopoldville in the oil mills of the Huileries du Congo Belge (HCB). The mills belonged to the British company Lever Brothers, and many of its workers came from

---

17   Chomé, *La Passion*, 68–70.

18   This introductory note can be found in Paul Raymaekers, "Histoire de Simon Kimbangu, prophète, d'après les écrivains Nfinangani and Nzungu (1921)," *Archives de Sociologie des Religions* 31, 1971, 15–42, here 19.

19   Raymaekers, "Histoire de Simon Kimbangu," 16.

20   Thomas Nduma was still alive in 1981 when Donald J. Mackay interviewed him in Kinshasa: Mackay, *Simon Kimbangu*, 113–71.

21   In November 1921, André Yengo was arrested in Thysville and condemned for having promoted an organization in Léopoldville in support of Kimbangu. His name appears on a list of deportees in 1941: Vellut, ed., *Simon Kimbangu*, vol. 1, *Fonds missionnaires protestants* (2), 352–353.

British colonies in West Africa. Kimbangu's brief working-class experience, which lasted only three months, suggested foreign influence on, or even foreign direction of, the movement. This was above all due to the fact that the HBC factories were considered the center of the spread of the pan-Africanist ideology and black nationalism of Marcus Garvey in the Congo. Indeed, stacks of the Garveyist newspaper *Negro World* were discovered there, destined for an African American Baptist, a certain Wilson, who was later expelled from the Belgian Congo.[22]

On July 17, 1921, the newspaper *L'Avenir Colonial Belge* supported the plausibility of a secret agreement between Marcus Garvey, Kimbangu, and Paul Panda Farnana.[23] The latter was a Congolese intellectual resident in Belgium who had participated, from its first meeting in Paris in 1919, in the pan-African congresses as a representative of the Union Congolaise, which he himself had founded. Moreover, before the Kimbangu case broke out, *L'Avenir Colonial Belge* had already published an intercepted letter in March 1921 in which Emmanuel John, a collaborator of Farnana's, had written to him observing how the Congo needed black representatives, police commissioners, and missionaries.[24]

In the summer of 1921, therefore, the typewritten documents were a lead for the Belgian administration and public opinion that arrived at the industrial zone and the educated Congolese living in the black district of Kinshasa. The evidence of the threatening combination of religious demands and political claims led them to believe that a foreign hand was at work, either that of Marcus Garvey or of Great Britain. In the climate of confessional rivalry between Catholic and Protestant missionaries, Kimbangu's religious formation in the BMS was a strong indication against the Protestant missionaries themselves, suspected of being agitators in the service of British power.

The assumption of foreign interference (Garveyist, British, and/or Protestant), however, was inconsistent and was not presented against Kimbangu at his trial. There still remained, however, the suspicion that the movement led by Kimbangu had a political origin and that, in particular, he had planned a strike by railway workers in July 1921; this suspicion eventually led to his condemnation.

The incriminating typed documents did, in fact, travel along the Matadi-Léopoldville route (a fundamental artery for the predatory colonial economy), seeming to win over its workers to the prophet's cause. The governor general's report to the Minister of the Colonies dated July 12, stated that the railway workers were singing seditious, typewritten songs and that they threatened to go on strike when Kimbangu was arrested.[25] On June 17, the chief of operations at the Matadi Station was arrested, having received "heavenly inspiration" to abandon his work, his possessions, and all his wives except the first, declaring that he could heal his sick brothers and sisters and that the world was about to change because the first would be made the last.[26]

While it seems unlikely that Kimbangu, in hiding, could have planned a strike, these reports certainly signal a receptivity towards the prophetic movement on the part of the railway workers, ready to undertake it in forms of disobedience against the whites' exploitation. In this sense, they

---

22 On the connections between the religious movement inspired by Kimbangu and Garveyism see: Damaso Feci, "Vie cachée et vie publique de Simon Kimbangu selon la littérature coloniale et missionnaire belge," *Cahiers du CEDAF* 9–10, 1972, 2–84.

23 "L'Affaire de Gombe-Lutete: L'état-major de Kibango arrêté," *L'Avenir colonial belge*, July 17, 1921, 3, cited in: Anne Mélice, "La désobéissance civile des kimbanguistes et la violence coloniale au congo belge (1921–1959)," *Les Temps Modernes* 658–659, 2010, 218–250, here 228.

24 Efraim Andersson, *Messianic Popular Movements in the Lower Congo*, Uppsala, Almqvist & Wiksells, 1958, 256.

25 Stefano Picciaredda, *Le Chiese indipendenti africane: Una storia religiosa e politica del Novecento*, Rome, Carocci, 2013, 172.

26 News of this arrest was communicated to the adjunct district commissioner of the Bas-Congo by Matadi's territorial administration on June 17: Picciaredda, *Le Chiese indipendenti africane*, 172–173.

are an indication of the movement's diffusion and its radicalization, beyond the intentions of its inspirer, in the repressive climate established by the military occupation.

As Jean-Luc Vellut notes, at this time the connection between urban demands and rural propheticism was rather tenuous.[27] Nevertheless, the interest of André Yengo in the prophetic movement in Nkamba was not incidental. The relationship between Kimbangu and Yengo, leader of the Congolese *évolués* in Kinshasa, preceded the beginning of the former's prophetic mission. Yengo, in fact, was a Ngombe *bisi*, thus a Kongo originally from the same region as Kimbangu. As Baptists, they were both members of the Ngombe Lutete (Wathen) Church,[28] where the BMS missionary station had had its headquarters since 1884.

Kimbangu therefore knew Yengo because he was one of the *bambuta*, that is, one of the church elders, a deacon, in Kinshasa, and when Kimbangu migrated to the city in 1920, he was able to rely on the solidarity of the church's network from Ngombe. So, it was the *bambuta*, and Yengo in particular, who took charge of Kimbangu when his plans to settle down in Kinshasa quickly fell through.

The unfortunate story of Kimbangu's attempt to migrate shows that, before the beginning of his prophetic movement, the deacons of the Baptist Church, independently of the missionaries, were able to mobilize social, and to a certain extent, economic resources along a Kongo network that united city and countryside. This agency of the church's indigenous component was even more evident in the relationship between Yengo and Kimbangu following the latter's vocation. In particular, among the papers seized in Nkamba Morel found no missives from the Kinshasa businessman that presented any element of proof of the supposed attempt by the urbanized Kongo to politicize the rural religious movement. In the letters in

question, on the contrary, Yengo wrote about the funding raised by the Kinshasa *bambuta* in support of the prophet and the intention to build a church in Nkamba.[29]

After his prophetic calling, the relationship between the church elders and Kimbangu was supportive, as it had been in Kinshasa, albeit in a profoundly changed context. Inspired by the young man from Nkamba, the movement had opened up a space into which to channel the Kongo resources, relationships, and skills of the Baptist Church. Yengo understood it to be a space for planning, which required neither the approval nor the involvement of the Ngombe Lutete mission in order to express itself. The offerings, which until then had been donated to the mission, were then diverted to Nkamba,[30] where the Kinshasa *bambuta* were hoping to build a church. In fact, Yengo was not only a wholesale trader but also the owner of a brick factory that had the BMS missionaries among its customers.[31]

The church in Nkamba, however, was an initiative achievable not only thanks to the economic and entrepreneurial skills of the deacons of Kinshasa, but it was also and above all conceivable because that village had become the heart of the spread of a prophetic movement. Different actors saw a variety of things in it: the military court saw in it the specter of the "great revolt"; the railway workers saw it as a place of possible disobedience; the deacons of Kinshasa saw it as the project of building a church without requesting the permission of Ngombe Lutete.

All these horizons, of threat or hope, of action and autonomy, had been aroused by a charismatic configuration that, above all, had been structured by Kimbangu himself and by his closest followers. In April 1921, as will be seen, the prophet's healing

27   Vellut, "Introduction générale," xv.
28   The Ngombe Lutete missionary station was named after its English benefactor Charles Wathen.
29   Mackay, "Simon Kimbangu," 169.
30   Picciaredda, *Le Chiese indipendenti africane*, 135.
31   This information is reported by the Baptist missionary David C. Davies in a letter of Sept 1, 1921, to the British Consul of Boma, published in Vellut, ed., *Simon Kimbangu*, vol. 1, *Fonds missionnaires protestants* (2), 121–122.

power was organized into a precise ritual action. Shortly afterwards, in May, the story of the prophet written by Nfinangani and Nzungu began to be composed in Nkamba. These two events appear to be closely connected: the new ritual arrangement was followed by the need to produce an ideological reading, controlled by Kimbangu's inner circle, of the prophet and his healing power in order that he might become the movement's point of reference.

3 "First of All, I Kinzembo …": The Prophet's Mother's Account

The story told by Nfinangani and Nzungu, therefore, is a source from within the movement that is of extraordinary importance; the original Kikongo language version, unfortunately, has been lost. The "Histoire de Simon Kimbangu, prophète, d'apres les ecrivains Nfinangani and Nzungu (1921)" was published in 1971 by Paul Raymaekers,[32] who found it among papers filed at the colonial offices of the AIMO in Kinshasa. The document, consisting in 15 typewritten pages, was presented as an appendix to a "Synthèse" that, drawn up by the administration for use by its officials, covered the main developments of the Kimbanguist movement between 1921 and 1927.[33] A brief introductory note to the appendix warned that the original text was incomplete and that a "very loose" French version was given.[34] As far as its reliability is concerned, Jeremy

Pemberton, who edited the English edition,[35] noted that the administration's translation often seemed to maintain the syntactic structure of the Kikongo, without attempting further French adaptations.[36] A certain fidelity to the original structure can thus be assumed.[37]

The story is told through a succession of short episodes in an order that is, for the most part, chronological.[38] The narrative, which is interspersed with short dialogues, is manly in the third person, although Kimbangu and his mother speak in the first person. The text's opening is entrusted to the latter: "First of all I, Kinzembo, am the mother of Simon Kimbangu."[39] After introducing herself in this way, Kinzembo begins the story of the prophet's childhood: "One day, a white man, Comber, came to the market. Everybody ran away. I alone stayed behind. The white man said to me, 'Peace be with you. Those who ran away will not have peace. You will no longer lose anything at all nor be hurt come what may. Go in peace'" (History, 202).

This first scene established a privileged bond between Kimbangu's mother and the first missionaries in the region. The white man she met in the market was, in fact, one of the Comber family missionaries, probably Thomas,[40] one of the founders in 1878 of the Congolese mission of the BMS. Thomas Comber had arrived from San Salvador to join his brother Sydney as soon as he had started

---

32   Raymaekers, "Histoire de Simon Kimbangu." Before Raymaekers's text, the *Storia del profeta di Nfinangani e Nzungu* was one of the principal sources of Marie-Louise Martin in a text favorable to Kimbanguism, which constituted a kind of official history prior to the work written by Joseph Diangienda, son of Kimbangu. See Marie-Louise Martin, *Kirche Ohne Weisse: Simon Kimbangu und seine Millionenkirche im Kongo*, Basel, F. Reinhardt, 1971; Joseph Diangienda (Kuntima), *Histoire du kimbanguisme*, Kinshasa, Edition Kimbanguiste, 2003 [¹1986].

33   The "Synthèse" is not found in Raymaekers, "Histoire de Simon Kimbangu."

34   Unlike the "Synthèse," this note is found in Raymaekers (Raymaekers, "Histoire de Simon Kimbangu," 19).

35   Jeremy Pemberton, "The History of Simon Kimbangu, Prophet, by the Writers Nfinangani and Nzungu, 1921: An Introduction and Annotated Translation," *Journal of Religion in Africa* 23/3, 1993, 194–231. Further quotations from this work will be referenced in the text as History.

36   History, 195.

37   The exception, as we shall see, is a story about the prophet's childhood which is presented in summary.

38   History, 197.

39   History, 202. According to the matrilineal custom in the Congo, Kimbangu was entrusted at an early age to Kinzembo, who was his maternal aunt, when his mother, Leuzi, died. Kinzembo was confined in October 1921 and died in 1929 in the hospital in Boma where she had been admitted for psychiatric reasons.

40   Raymaekers, "Histoire de Simon Kimbangu," 19.

construction of the Ngombe Lutete mission in 1884; Kinzembo was among the first baptized there.

The connection between the future prophet's mother and the beginning of the mission was strengthened by the story's subsequent development, this time directly involving Kimbangu, who was still a child at the time. Kinzembo continued, narrating how, on three different occasions, she met and helped the Reverend Ronald Cameron, quenching his thirst and feeding him when no one in Nkamba wanted to welcome him. During their third meeting, after eating and drinking, Cameron proposed that he and Kinzembo pray together: "After the prayers [Cameron] said to me, 'Peace be with you and your child. Your faith has saved you'" (History, 202).

Threatened by an armed gang, Cameron escaped, followed by Kinzembo, who was wounded. "They [the assailants] said, 'It would be better if you were dead, for you are related to the white man.' 'I will not die,' I replied, 'but you certainly will' ... Those who assaulted me died the same day. Everywhere [Cameron] went people died, until there remained very few" (History, 203).

Cameron's itinerant preaching, initially rejected everywhere, seemed to leave behind a trail of death. These were the years of the sleeping sickness that severely struck Central Africa; its spread was attributed to the whites.[41] Recalling the hostile rejection of the missionaries' message of salvation, Kinzembo had an interpretation of the epidemic's causes that contradicted that of those who wished her dead for being "related" to the whites.

The first missionaries' preaching was represented in the words that Comber and Cameron addressed to Kinzembo. In reporting them, Kinzembo configured the first of the complex associations with which the prophet's story was interwoven. In the first place, in fact, their words were not limited to simple biblical reminiscences. Certainly, "peace be with you" is a greeting that, for example, recalls Matthew 10:12 while with "your faith has saved you" Cameron echoed several passages from

the Gospels, such as Mark 10:52. However, besides being biblical references, these words of the missionaries, like those of Jesus and his apostles in the New Testament, had real effects: Kinzembo could not be hurt (by death) and was saved.

Secondly, Comber and Cameron's words took on a prophetic meaning. Kinzembo was saved because of her faith. Not only was she the only one who welcomed the missionaries and prayed with Cameron, but she also, because she believed in their message, proclaimed in front of her attackers that she would not be the one to die. In this sense, her meetings with the missionaries took on a deeper anticipatory function, seen in the light of Kimbangu's future healings. As the story unfolded, those healed or resurrected by Kimbangu were only those who had faith. Those who did not believe, however, were doomed to die.

The first episodes of the story, therefore, through a series of implicit parallels and analogies, wove a connection of continuity from the recounting of miracles in the Gospels and the preaching of the first missionaries, to the faith healings worked by the son of Kinzembo.[42]

The narration of these events is followed by a summary of Kinzembo's story interpolated by the translator:

> Here follows a story about how her child, having gone to a neighboring village, fell ill. At night she went to look for him, found some people seated round a fire, asked for some fire from them, and then left. When she had gone, someone called her back; she returned with the fire, but those seated round it had not called her. She found her child sick in a dirty house: he had dysentery. She strapped him to her back and left. The child asked to go a little away from her, he got lost and fell into a hole. In the end, someone found him, and she said that she had been helped by God [She put the child back on her back]. (History, 203)

---

41   Raymaekers, "Histoire de Simon Kimbangu," 21.

42   Mackay, "Simon Kimbangu," 139; History, 198.

After that summary, the text returns to a translation of the original, which moves into the third person: "[Kinzembo] met a man who told her that her son would be a healer" (History, 203).

As Comber had told her, Kinzembo could not lose anything and thus found her son who had fallen into a ditch. Cameron's words, which included Kimbangu in the blessing, also affected him through healing. Compared to previous ones, however, the episode seems to add new elements that contribute to outlining Kimbangu's future and, at the same time, his power as a healer. In fact, it was a third man who predicted healing in the child. There is some ambiguity in the French "son enfant guérira," which can either mean that the child was destined to heal (recover) or that he was destined (as a healer) to heal (others). Unlike the English version, "her son would be a healer," the French one left the possibility of reading the passage as the beginning of a cult of affliction. As we shall see, Kimbangu was, in effect, possessed and afflicted by a spirit that would give him the power to heal and that would also bring him a Bible.[43]

4 An Affliction Cult: Budimbu's Testimony

The above interpretation is supported by comparison with other stories that show some similarities with that of the prophet's mother. In this regard, the 1922 testimony by Aloni Budimbu,[44] a Kongo Christian of the ABFMS who became a pastor at the Lukunga station, is particularly significant.[45]

Budimbu was an extremely skeptical witness to the movement that had arisen in Nkamba.[46] His testimony in 1922, however, was accepted as a reliable source in a short biography of the prophet that was published by EJCSK in 1961.[47]

In effect, Budimbu said that he had heard the account of the visions that had preceded the healer's mission directly from Kimbangu himself. It is difficult to pinpoint the exact period of the biographical events that the prophet narrated to him. However, they seem to have occurred at a later date than the childhood episodes recounted by Kinzembo.

The first scene in this second story takes place in a village where Kimbangu and his parents had gone to attend the funeral of a friend. During the ceremonies, the prophet said:

> I fell in a fit and was unconscious. My father and mother took me home. On the way we met a man who was neither black nor white, nor was he a mulatto. He was very finely dressed. "Where are you taking the young man?" he asked. "We are taking him home; he is ill," my father replied. "No," said the stranger, "he is not ill. He will be right soon."[48]

Continuing his journey home, Kimbangu and his parents stopped for the night, during which Kimbangu went out to find water but fell into a deep hole. He continued, "I found that mother had fallen into the hole beside me. But suddenly we were lifted out of the pit without any effort upon our part."[49] In the first part of the story, retold by Budimbu, we find many elements in common with the one narrated by Kinzembo: Kimbangu's real or presumed illness, the nighttime fall, his mother's

---

43 MacGaffey, *Modern Kongo Prophets*, 187–188; Mackay, "Simon Kimbangu," 126–127; Vellut, "Introduction générale," xii.

44 This was published by Peter H.J. Lerrigo, a missionary doctor who was at that time secretary of the Foreign Administration of the ABFMS: Peter H.J. Lerrigo, "'The Prophet Movement' in Congo," *IRM* 11/42, 1922, 270–277, here 270–273.

45 Aloni Budimbu traveled in Europe and stayed in England between 1885 and 1887. In 1888 he founded a catechetical school in Lukunga. Thanks to the linguistic competence he acquired in England, he collaborated with Karl Laman on the translation of the Bible into Kikongo, which was adopted in 1907 by the ABFMS. See

Vellut, ed., *Simon Kimbangu*, vol. 1, *Fonds missionnaires protestants (2)*, 324–325.

46 See his story in Kikongo published with a parallel French translation in Vellut, ed., *Simon Kimbangu*, vol. 1, *Fonds missionnaires protestants (1)*, 207–208.

47 This biography was then published as an appendix in Raymaekers, "Histoire de Simon Kimbangu," 41–42.

48 Lerrigo, "'The Prophet Movement,'" 271.

49 Lerrigo, "'The Prophet Movement,'" 271.

presence near him in the pit, the mysterious rescue, and the encounter with a stranger who foretold the story of Kimbangu's healing or recovery.

In Budimbu's account, however, it was much clearer that the encounter with the stranger had been a supernatural event. The color of his skin, which did not fit into any kind of racial classification, indicated that the unknown interlocutor was a spiritual being. In this sense, the colonial hierarchies seemed to not belong to the spiritual realm. Indeed, the spirit neither subverted them ("not black"), nor reflected them ("nor white"), nor confused them by mixing them ("nor mulatto"). The encounter with this spiritual being was also connected to the world of the dead, since in Budimbu's story Kimbangu suffered a crisis during a funeral.

The connection to the world of the dead is also present, even if less explicitly, in Kinzembo's story of the episode of falling into the ditch. The popular legends collected by Wyatt MacGaffey speak of how, as a child, Kimbangu had fallen into a ravine and was lifted to safety by "an angel."[50] Once he reemerged, only the appearance of the original child remained, under which hid a powerful spirit. According to MacGaffey, in the Kongo context that he was studying, falling into a deep ravine or pit is the oneiric image that signifies contact with the world of the dead because in those places (just as in streams and waterfalls) reside *simbi*, spirits that, while different from those of ancestors (*bakulu*), belong to the more general category of the dead. Among these are included all the forces of the invisible world that mediate between the living and God (*Nzambi*).[51]

Simbi spirits can afflict with a disease those individuals they want to provide with spiritual powers. In such cases, the spirit would indicate that healing would only be possible through initiation into a *simbi* possesion cult, associated with maternal lineage. Kimbangu, with his mother, thus fell into the pit and reemerged transformed into a spirit.

None of MacGaffey's interlocutors, however, believed that Kimbangu was possessed by a *simbi* spirit, because that would have signified disavowing the profound novelty of his prophetic power.[52]

Kimbangu, therefore, was afflicted and possessed by a spirit that was different and new with respect to similar spirits, appearing in Budimbu's story in the guise of the unknown, neither black, white, nor mulatto. Moreover, of her own accord, Kinzembo had made this association between her son and the foreigners Comber and Cameron. Drawing a subtle parallelism between Scripture, the message of the first missionaries, and Kimbangu, she indicated that the healing power narrated in the Gospels brought by the missionaries was acting in Kimbangu.

The second and final part of Budimbu's story seems to support this sense of the connection and analogies drawn by Kinzembo. Kimbangu continued his narration thus:

> After we arrived home, I fell sick with *makwanza* (scabies) and had sores all over my body. There came to the house a man dressed in nothing but a meager rag, and he also was full of sores. He asked for water and my mother, who was a good Christian, took our cup and gave him water to drink. He turned to go and I said to mother: "Why did you give him to drink from our cup? He is full of sores." The stranger overheard me and came back. "Why do you speak thus?" he asked. "You also are full of sores. If you will rub yourself with palm oil, you will be cured."[53]

The spirit demanded Kimbangu's initiation, striking him with the disease of scabies and presenting himself dressed in rags with his body covered in the same sores that afflicted the future prophet. The spirit, therefore, was the sickness itself. Nevertheless, by advising him to apply palm oil,

---

50   MacGaffey, "Cultural Roots," 189.
51   MacGaffey, "Cultural Roots," 184–187.

52   MacGaffey, "Cultural Roots," 190.
53   Lerrigo, "'The Prophet Movement,'" 271.

he led Kimbangu to understand that if he himself were the cause, he would instruct Kimbangu on how to recover.[54] In fact, that same night, the stranger returned in Kimbangu's dreams, bringing him a Bible. He said to Kimbangu: "This is a good book; you must study it and preach." Kimbangu refused: "I am no preacher or teacher. I cannot do it."[55] The first indication, therefore, was of a Christian initiation: Kimbangu had to enter the church's organization actively.

When Kimbangu refused, the stranger's requests become more demanding. The spirit began insisting that Kimbangu exercise the power of healing that he had been given: "Then the stranger told me of a sick child in a neighboring village, saying that I must go there and preach for her recovery."[56] The Christian bedrock of this cult of affliction derived from a variety of elements. First the Bible was not primarily present as an object of power, but as a text to study for preaching. The initiation that was required as a teacher and preacher was also present in the Baptist hierarchies. Finally, the rite of healing had Christian characteristics, consisting of prayer and placing hands on a person. This charismatic manner was found in the definitive request for healing that the spirit demanded, laying claim to Kimbangu's soul: "Finally he came to me and said: 'There is a sick child in a certain village. You must go there, pray, lay your hands on the child and heal her. If you do not go, I shall require your soul of you.'"[57]

As in Kinzembo's story, in the initiation to the affliction cult narrated by Budimbu, the mother/son pairing is present. According to the latter, not only did they both fall into the deep hole, but the stranger also communicated his wishes to both the mother and the son. When the future prophet refused to study and preach, the spirit suggested that Kimbangu take the Bible to Kinzembo so that she would become a preacher: "Then take the book to your mother and tell her that she must preach." To which Kimbangu responded: "Why do you not speak to her yourself?,"[58] which is what the spirit did, appearing in a dream to tell her that her son refused to preach and heal.

Moreover, the spirit had asked his mother for water to quench his thirst and Kinzembo, "who was a good Christian," had let him drink from the container that the family drank from, not fearing contagion. In both stories, Kinzembo, as a convert, was the link between her son and a stranger considered to be the bearer of disease and the bearer of the Word of God (in one case, in the form of blessing and, in the other, of the text). In both stories, in fact, the strangers were God's emissaries, mediators of his word, which has the power to heal.[59]

5   "Kimbangu Finds the Way of Faith": His Vocation

After recounting the prodigious events that had studded the prophet's childhood, Nfinangani and Nzungu's story then tells of his vocation:

---

54   In fact, Mackay sees in this account a clear trace of the Congo possesion cults in which the spirit "behind" the illness indicates what the afflicted person has to do if he wants to get better (Mackay, "Simon Kimbangu," 126).

55   Lerrigo, "'The Prophet Movement,'" 271.

56   Lerrigo, "'The Prophet Movement,'" 271.

57   Lerrigo, "'The Prophet Movement,'" 271.

58   Lerrigo, "'The Prophet Movement,'" 271.

59   According to Mackay, there is not only an analogy between Cameron and the spirit that appeared to Kimbagu in a dream. In 1981, he had the opportunity to hear the same story of Aloni Budimbu from Thomas Nduma. He told him how, after the apparition of the spirit in a dream, Kimbangu asked the members of the church to become an evangelist. Kinzembo, then, remembered the protection offered to Cameron, understanding, in light of Kimbangu's request, that the missionary's blessing was the cause of his son's vocation. This association between the spirit and Cameron, according to Mackay, indicated that the blessing of God transmitted by the missionary had opened a channel between Kimbangu and the power of the spiritual world (Mackay, "Simon Kimbangu," 126–127).

"Kimbangu found the path of faith. To become a believer, he put himself under instruction, was baptized, and underwent a religious marriage ceremony" (History, 203). On July 4, 1915, Kimbangu, together with his wife Marie Muilu Kiawanga, were baptized in the Tombe River near the missionary station of Ngombe Lutete. On that very same day, the two were joined religiously in marriage. "Simon," the text continued, "wanted to teach but he didn't know enough." He therefore asked to be assigned to a catechist "but they didn't want to give him one. After many entreaties, he received one; the man took lodgings with him" (History, 203).

At this point, the text hints at the church's initial resistance to Kimbangu's vocation, who for his part was instead intent on respecting the hierarchical order, asking for formation (as was the custom) by a deacon or expert catechist in order to be able, in his turn, to teach others. The result of this orthodox path of formation was expressed by the teacher's opinion, reported by Kimbangu himself who, for the first time, takes the stage in the first person. "He [the teacher] said, 'I [Kimbangu] don't have a gift for reading, but I have a real understanding of religion'" (History, 203).[60]

It is difficult to understand in what terms Kimbangu considered this judgment, which, on the one hand, saw the student's reading ability to be inadequate and, on the other, seemed to recognize, if not an excess, an incomplete adaptability of his skills to the established formational standards. Whatever the state of his relationship with the church, at this point, Kimbangu decided to leave for Kinshasa, thus going against the church elders' wishes, who were against the move. Kimbangu, therefore, left against the deacons' judgment, but after having asked and obtained the authorization of the missionaries of Ngombe Lutete. His experience in the city was, as we have already seen, a failure. He accounted for that lack of success with his transgression of the prohibition of the

bambuta because, being on bad terms with the church (History, 204), nothing turned out for the best. He was ready to admit so when he returned to Nkamba. "I have come back because nothing of mine has succeeded because I left without your permission" (History, 204).

In the following episode, the latent tension between Kimbangu and the church developed into the crisis that led to his prophetic vocation: "Make me a catechist" (History, 204). Here too, Kimbangu turned to the elders, who consented, but the faithful of Nkamba contested his nomination: "At home they said I lacked the spirit for the task" (History, 204). The mistrust was, perhaps, due to his earlier decision to go to Kinshasa, thus shirking his obligations to the church and the congregation.

> I hid myself at home, threw myself face-down on the ground and prayed. Then I had a dream and God said to me, "I have heard your prayer; people think that you need the spirit to do my work, but I will give you something even greater." I took no notice of this. But from day to day I heard a voice that told me I would do the work of Peter and of John. I would be an apostle: "People don't want to give you the right to teach? But I will make you an apostle" (History, 204).

Feeling afraid, Kimbangu objected that the role of an apostle is a role unknown to all. He himself admitted that he did not understand "this work" (History, 205). The voice, however, reassured him: "Fear not, I will be your teacher" (History, 205).

Kimbangu was called to carry out a role that was still unknown, even though it was the same work as that of the apostles Peter and John. The Acts of the Apostles, in particular chapter 3:1–10, provided the reference that would define the vocation and the prophetic work that Kimbangu began from that moment on. It was a reference that also indicated that the events that were to occur in Nkamba had already taken place and that John 14:12 had anticipated them: "Verily, verily, I

---

60   In the French: "Il dit: Je n'ai pas esprit pour lire mais j'ai beaucoup intelligence de la religion."

say unto you, He that believeth on me, the works that I do shall he do also."[61]

If it was unknown work, therefore, it was so because it was an unknown to the church. Here the church was primarily that of the deacons, catechists, and Kongo faithful in a not strictly local dimension. A crisis developed between village and city along a trajectory that ran through the chain of the *bambuta*. Kimbangu left Nkamba on bad terms with the church, that is, with the deacons. As we have seen, it was again the deacons, this time in Kinshasa, who helped, or forced, him to go back. What remains distant in this narrative was not the urban context, but rather that of Ngombe Lutete: if the missionaries had once been central to the prodigious childhood narrated by Kinzembo, they were now only called upon for the permission that would allow Kimbangu to ignore the directives of the church elders. It was a choice, however, that would jeopardize the outcome of his plan.

The circumstances of his crisis and vocation thus highlighted the areas of power and autonomy that the Kongo component of the Baptist Church had acquired. The deacons' leading role, along with the catechists' fundamental contribution to evangelization, were the outcome of the specific dynamic that developed within the mission, particularly at the beginning of the century. While the few missionaries constituted the upper level of the church, Ngombe Lutete had jurisdiction over the vast region of the Bas-Congo, and was organized into districts and local centers where the deacons were those making the decisions concerning evangelization. The elders not only celebrated the monthly Lord's Supper and funerals but also raised money to finance the local catechists. It was always the *bambuta* who suspended or re-integrated a member into the Baptist Christian community. The missionary church, therefore, was governed by an iron-clad hierarchy that, due to its expansion, however, had to grant the indigenous component a wide margin of autonomy.[62]

It was within the tapestry of this hierarchy, therefore, that the work that Kimbangu was called to burst forth as a novelty. God would be his teacher, opening a direct channel with his disciple. Kimbangu's authority thus did not derive from the chain of transmission of knowledge, as was necessary in training a Baptist catechist. Instead, the Scriptures were the parameter and source of the legitimation of his prophetic activity.

From that moment on, Kimbangu was an apostle and messenger of God just as, according to Kinzembo, the European missionaries had been in the prophet's childhood, anticipating his mission through the parallels and associations that the narrative had woven with the Gospels.

This novelty *sui generis* of the role of an apostle, therefore, upset the church's hierarchical order, not in order to delegitimize its work, but rather to establish a complex and tight relationship consisting in differences, rejections, and continuity. It was not only the missionaries' blessing, reported by Kinzembo, that established this relationship: the episodes preceding that of his vocation, in which the divine voice promised something beyond the spirit needed to carry out the work of a catechist, were also centered around the notion of work. In particular, the work carried out in Kinshasa had proved unproductive; the money earned from it had been lost (History, 204). Just as illness was a sign that an afflicted person belonged to the spirit, so his loss of earnings showed that Kimbangu's work belonged to God. Kimbangu, therefore, had to return to Nkamba and make peace with the deacons who had advised him not to shirk the church's work.

His vocation now changed the terms of this relationship: if previously it was Kimbangu who had to admit his transgression, now it was the *bambuta* who had to recognize the work of Peter and John in

---

61 Quotation from the *King James Version*, which is used in the following biblical quotations. It is the version from which the Kikongo translation that Kimbangu knew was made. That translation is *Nkand'a Nzambi*, ed. William H. Bentley & Nzao Nlemvo, London, BMS, 1926.

62 Mackay, "Simon Kimbangu," 113–114; Vellut, "Introduction générale," xi.

the prophet's actions. This recognition was neither immediate nor can be taken for granted, since, even before his vocation, the church (deacons, catechists, and faithful) had, at various times, shown signs of resistance to Kimbangu's integration into their ranks. However, it was precisely this recognition that marked the beginning of the prophetic movement.

6　Samuel Mowala's Dream

Kimbangu carried out his first faith healing on Mar 13, 1921. Laying his hand upon Kintondo, a seriously sick woman, he healed her, speaking the following words: "You are blessed in the name of Jesus Christ. Be healed" (History, 205). Shortly afterward, Kimbangu turned to the catechist of the woman's village and said: "Go and see the miracle that has happened in the village you teach in. People who lack the Spirit say that I am mad, but you know what Kintondo was suffering from; now she is healed" (History, 205).

The next episode took place in the village of Lukengo, home to the Baptist center to which the Nkamba community belonged. A child from Lukengo had died in Ngombe Lutete. Kimbangu planned to resurrect him and was ready to perform the miracle at the missionary station. Before doing so, however, he had decided to meet Samuel Mowala, a catechist from Lukengo who had given Kimbangu the religious instruction required for baptism. The prophet, therefore, submitted his actions to the judgement of the men of the church, respecting their hierarchical, territorial organization. Mowala, however, greeted him with irony and mistrust: "When he arrived, he greeted me thus, 'Good day, blesser of men.' So I said, 'Isn't this good, are you not happy with it?' He then replied, 'Yes, it is good, but have you had a meeting with God?' I said, 'No, there is no one who can see God'" (History, 206–207).

Owing to Mowala's contentious attitude, God diverted the prophet from the purpose of resurrecting the child in Lukengo. The confrontation

with Kimbangu, however returned in the catechist's dreams.

He turned his eyes towards the place where he had had the dispute and this is what he saw: Two men carrying flags, a black and a white one. A great crowd followed, made up entirely of children. But [Mowala], terrified by the sight of these men, left his house and went to sleep at Samuel Nkunku's. Then, as he slept, he saw that tomorrow when you came to pray you should read Matthew chapter 25, verse 1. Then, take a clean bowl and put it on your right hand, and again, a dirty one and put it on your left hand (History, 207–208).

On the following day, Kimbangu heard Mowala tell of the dream and interpret Matthew 25, but he saw that the catechist had not understood what God intended to say to him, and what he had explained to Kimbangu "You, Mowala, who are a believer and a catechist, why are you denying the light of God in the thing that he has brought about?" (History, 208). The reproach addressed to Mowala was that he had not recognized God's work in Kimbangu's miracles or the beginning of a new order of which the inspired dream was an allegory, namely, a church united in following the dual guidance of the missionaries, represented by the man with the white flag, and of Kimbangu, embodied by the man who carried the black flag. The work of Peter and John, its revival in the present, placed Kimbangu, a black member of the church, alongside European missionaries. The event that "God produced" in this way was the light that shows the kingdom of heaven, just as in Matthew 25:1 it is said that "the kingdom of heaven [shall] be likened unto ten virgins, which took their lamps, and went forth to meet the bridegroom."

If in the dream the missionaries and the prophet had been placed on equal footing at the head of a single church, the key to interpreting it was supplied by Matthew 25, which showed that Kimbangu's miracles took place in order to distinguish the wise virgins from the foolish ones, just as the clean vase must be held in the right hand, separate from the dirty one, held in the left.

The dispute between Mowala and Kimbangu revealed that biblical exegesis was both a key to decoding the inspired dream and a source of interpreting the present events. The indication of Matthew 25:1 was intended to make Mowala repent, directing him toward recognizing God's light in the prophet's healing.

This hermeneutical relationship between Scripture and the present also acted on an underlying level in the narrative, configuring a series of implicit parallels between the gospel account and the story of the prophet. In the episodes of healings and resurrections, Kimbangu in fact operated by directing his actions within this interpretative framework aimed at making his deeds recognizable in the light of the Gospels. The evils that were cured, like the prophet's gestures and words, replicated and thus rendered present the miracles of Jesus and the apostles,[63] as if to verify the directives contained in Matthew 10:8: "Heal the sick, cleanse the lepers, raise the dead, cast out devils."

Kimbangu, therefore, literally did the same work as Peter and John in their following Christ, thereby tracing a clear continuity between himself and the apostolic church, and also between the gospel message and the present. It was thus a matter not only of seeing, through biblical exegesis, "God's light in the work that he has produced," but also of recognizing in the Bible itself a contemporary narrative.

The episode of the dispute had a subsequent development in the unfolding of the prophet's story when, in Kinzinga, the village from which Mowala came, a man proclaimed himself a prophet. This was Ninkunda, a relative of the catechist serving in Lukengo. Kimbangu recounted the judgment he had drawn from it: "But God defended me from believing this, because his brother[64] had argued with me, asking me if I had had a meeting with God.

This was the reason his relative was possessed by a devil" (History, 209). When asked about it, Kimbangu answered with a revision of Acts 5:38 and 1 John 4:1–6, explaining how to discern the spirit that possessed Ninkunda: "If this work is from God, let it carry on; if the work is not from God, it will collapse by itself" (History, 209).

A devil had thus taken possession of Mowala's family member because Mowala had argued with Kimbangu, denying that his work came from God. Later, observing Ninkunda's healing, Kimbangu would remark: "The devil made a way to enter your heart because of the sin of your nephew, Samuel Mowala" (History, 223). Whoever did not recognize the revival of the gospel narrative in the present was not only excluded from the kingdom of heaven but was also its enemy because his work did not come from God but from a devil.

In the confrontation with the catechist of Lukengo, therefore, the line of conflict destined to divide the Baptist community was drawn. The prophet's appearance questioned the exclusivity of the missionary leadership and the racial hierarchy of the church. Primarily, however, the conflict polarized along the question of how the truth of the Bible should be understood: whether or not its narrative continued in the present day and whether or not it was true in Nkamba.

7   Nkamba: The Thaumaturgic Center of a Conversion Movement

As with Samuel Mowala, the story of Nfinangani and Nzungu recounts, the other Baptist catechists and deacons "did not at first believe that Simon Kimbangu was healing in the name of Christ and stayed in their villages" (History, 210). The prophet's work, however, began to attract increasing numbers of sick people in search of healing, companions and relatives carrying the body of a deceased person to Nkamba to be brought back to life. In the absence of the men of the church, "the local people, who had been followers in the past but who had fallen into the hands of the evil one,

---

63   For an apocalyptic interpretation of this phenomenon, see Mackay, "Simon Kimbangu," 143–145.

64   Later, the text qualifies Ninkunda as Mowala's nephew.

began to bring people to the prophet" (History, 210). At first, therefore, Kimbangu's work counted on those who were expelled from the church and were attracted to the concrete possibility of a new form of integration into the religious community and participation in Christian life.

Soon, however, the History continued, the members of the church "came to see that it was not the work of man, but of God. Because of this, they arrived to organize prayer of all kinds and to administrate the work" (History, 210). "The followers were not happy that the lost children had begun to bring along the sick" and they asked one another: "Is it right before God that unbelievers should do this work?" (History, 211). This question was put to a council held in Kibula; after the council, Kimbangu left the organization of the work in the hands of the faithful.

There was, therefore, a conscious structural continuity between the movement and the church.[65] In order to truly be an apostle, the prophet felt the need for and sought, as his first attempt with Mowala shows, the cooperation of the church and the elders. With the deacons' recognition at the beginning of April 1921, the prophetic movement and the church structures merged. From that moment on, *bambuta* and catechists organized God's work and literally surrounded the prophet, intent on carrying out his charisms.[66]

Nfinangani and Nzungu's story is rather scanty concerning elements that might help to reconstruct the ritual process that, from that moment on, would take shape by channeling the prophet's power. Later sources that describe Nkamba as an authentic thaumaturgical center are, on the contrary, helpful to that end. The first of such sources, appearing after 1934, is the story of Jacques

Bahelele Nidimisina,[67] a pastor of the SMF, who was 10 years old in 1921.[68]

The pastor described how, at the sound of a bell, the sick would gather to pray and sing, after which the teacher read and explained the Scriptures. "When the teachings touched the prophet's heart deeply, his feelings awoke: then he would go into a trance."[69] The prophet would then enter a structure composed of three distinct courtyards. As the chants began to resound, the afflicted entered one at a time, passing through the first courtyard then reaching the one where Kimbangu stood, flanked on both sides by a choir. Kneeling before the prophet, the sick person would recount his/her sufferings or, if unable to do so due to illness, a companion would explain the case. Then the prophet would raise his eyes to heaven and, entering a "violent trance," would lay his hand on the sick person's head saying, "In the name of Jesus Christ I want to heal you, be healed."[70] Later, Bahelele Nidimisina continued, if the person was still afflicted, they entered the third courtyard where there was a teacher who asked them if they were saved, meaning "Have you changed paths and become a child of God?"[71] If the answer was affirmative, the teacher would urge them to persevere in God; otherwise he would advise them: "Change, put your hope in Jesus Christ. He is the one who will save you."[72] As for those who had been healed, they remained

---

65   Mackay, "Simon Kimbangu," 113, 132–133.

66   Mackay, "Simon Kimbangu," 132–133. According to Mackay, this is confirmed by the fact that the Kimbanguist church considers the date of the beginning of the movement to be Apr 6, 1921, the day on which Kimbangu's first faith healing took place.

67   This source is provided in Kikongo with a parallel French translation in Vellut, ed., *Simon Kimbangu*, vol. 1, *Fonds missionnaires protestants* (1), 58–67.

68   As Vellut shows, the memory of Bahelele Nidimisina reflects the memory of the preaching of Kimbangu in the early 1930s (Vellut, ed., *Simon Kimbangu*, vol. 1, *Fonds missionnaires protestants* (1), 59).

69   Vellut, ed., *Simon Kimbangu*, vol. 1, *Fonds missionnaires protestants* (1), 61.

70   Vellut, ed., *Simon Kimbangu*, vol. 1, *Fonds missionnaires protestants* (1), 61.

71   Vellut, ed., *Simon Kimbangu*, vol. 1, *Fonds missionnaires protestants* (1), 61.

72   Vellut, ed., *Simon Kimbangu*, vol. 1, *Fonds missionnaires protestants* (1), 61.

before the prophet and left through a door that led to the river in order for them to wash there.

The second source providing a description of the ritual structure that the prophetic work assumed is the 1961 EJCSK text, mentioned above, *Zolanga Yelusalemi dia Mpa*. This source confirms some of the characteristics seen in Bahelele Nidimisina's story.

> When the prophet was revealed, the dead in stretchers and the sick of all kinds were brought to the Prophet of God. But in everything, whether raising the dead, healing the sick, or giving a blessing in the name of Jesus, first there must be prayer, then hymns, and then a teacher must read the Bible and teach the doctrines that change hearts, in order that all men should leave their wickedness; for if that does not happen, then these blessings you have come to get become as fire to you. Believe in the Lord Jesus, he who saves you from your sins. For I am in obedience to him.[73]

When compared, the two sources insist upon a ritual process that articulated distinct places and moments around the prophet. The steps that preceded the faith healings alternated prayer and hymns and culminated in reading and teaching Bible doctrines. These "changed the hearts" of the afflicted before they were healed by faith. If a heart did not change, the EJCSK text warned, "the blessings you have received become like fire for you." Such backlash recalled the power that the spirit of a cult of affliction has over the possessed: the spirit has the power of healing, but also the power of death if the afflicted person transgresses its instructions and is not faithful to it.

Likewise, the two texts highlight that what arose in Nkamba was, primarily, a conversion movement that had emerged within the church. In this sense, the dialogue that according to Bahelele Nidimisina took place in the third and final courtyard between the teacher and the afflicted concerning the need to change in order to obtain salvation is particularly significant.

The prophet's charism had opened up a ritual space that could count on the deacons and catechists, who were already largely autonomous from the European missionaries in the field of evangelization, taking charge. The articulation of this charismatic area had strengthened that autonomy, permitting, on the one hand, the Kongo members of the church to express new forms of agency and, on the other hand, a vast population of those who had been expelled or did not belong to the Christian community to undergo ritually an experience of salvation and conversion, of healing and transformation of the self. It was a way of receiving the message of salvation that was very different from the methods of teaching and evangelization established by the mission.

> Now see how all the villages hastened to abandon their fetishes; see all the roads littered with fetishes of all kinds. People confessed their sins. Drums were broken, dancing forsaken. People struggled to seek out teachers. Churches were built overnight in all the villages. Those who had not cared to pray to God fought for places in church, and those who had had no use for schools fought to enter the classroom.[74]

In this way, the text, perhaps hyperbolically, describes the large-scale effects of Kimbangu's preaching in terms of a vast mass conversion. "Pagan" traditions were abandoned and people turned to the church and its teachings. The prophet's work had needed the recognition of the deacons as well as the church structures to reorganize them around itself in a novel charismatic space that, however, confirmed their role. It was the men of the church who read the Bible to illustrate its teachings, and they were still those who pointed to faith as the only path of salvation. These actions

---

73   MacGaffey, "The Beloved City," 138.

74   MacGaffey, "The Beloved City," 138.

were now included within a ritual process that had the prophet and healer at its center.

The ritual articulation of the charismatic space seemed to delineate the center of a schismatic church. The ecclesiastical hierarchies seemed to unite around a new pole: no longer the missionary buildings of Ngombe Lutete but the courtyards of the prophet of Nkamba. Nfinangani and Nzungu's story, written in those very courtyards, instead of telling of disputes and rejections, weaves a more complex relationship with the missionary church, a relationship that followed a narrative logic. The missionaries were, at the beginning of the prophet's story, introduced by the authoritative voice of his mother. Even before Kimbangu was born, Kinzembo had forged a bond between her son and Comber; therefore, at first the missionaries appeared as repudiated foreigners and emissaries of God's message, with their effective blessings charged with evangelical references, presentiments, and promises of salvation.

With Kimbangu's vocation, although he needed the church, he no longer needed the mediation of missionaries because God himself was his teacher in the work of an apostle. The missionaries and the prophet thus appeared in Mowala's dream as if they were jointly leading the same crowd of children. At the same time, however, through his work as a prophet and healer, Kimbangu brought the missionaries' blessings to completion, taking up the gestures, words, and actions of the Gospels in the present day. He fulfilled the promise contained in the missionaries' blessing/preaching. In the order of the narrative, the missionaries and the prophet were not aligned but were in a relationship of succession and surpassing. In this sense, the prophet's story was not, as the colonial administrators who seized it believed, a biography of the prophet, but rather a narrative of God's work.

8   "All Kinds of Stories"

Nfinangani and Nzungu were interrupted while writing the prophet's story on June 6, 1921, by Léon Morel who attempted to arrest them, resulting in the unfinished text being seized. There is, however, a second source that is helpful in retracing the subsequent course of events from a perspective internal to the movement. This source, which comes to us in an original Kikongo version,[75] consists in three texts that go by the title of *Nsamu Miagunza* (The history of the prophets).[76] They were written by Paul Nyuvudi[77] who at the time of the events was considered to be one of the most experienced catechists of the SMF in the French Congo. It was probably for this reason that he was sent by the Swedish missionaries to the village of Nkamba in 1921 in order to verify the news arriving from beyond the colonial borders concerning the activities of the prophet and healer. Nyuvudi's account is a later one that the author drew up in 1928, three years after his return to the Congo from Chad, where he had been deported in 1922 by the French colonial authorities for his involvement in the Kimbanguist movement.

The comparison between the story of Nfinangani and Nzungu and that of Nyuvudi is fruitful for more than merely reconstructing the epilogue to Kimbangu's preaching. In two of his texts, the SMF catechist took care to clarify the prophet's attitude towards those who had proclaimed themselves

---

75   The three manuscripts that go by this name are known thanks to Adrian Hastings who, at the end of the 1970s, sought the help of Efraim Andersson, realizing that the references to Nyuvudi's account in his *Messianic Popular Movements* suggested an unpublished written source.

76   The first is published with a parallel English translation in Donald Mackay & Daniel Ntoni-Nzinga, "Kimbangu's Interlocutor: Nyuvudi's 'Nsamu Miangunza' (The Story of the Prophets)," *Journal of Religion in Africa* 23/3, 1993, 232–265, while the other two appear, with parallel French translations by Stanislas Mfulani, in Vellut, ed., *Simon Kimbangu*, vol. 1, *Fonds missionnaires protestants (1)*, 67–91.

77   Born in about 1900 in Mukimbungu (Luozi) where he received his first religious instruction, Nyuvudi became a catechist in Musana in 1911 and was then ordained a pastor in 1942.

prophets in imitation of him.[78] The movement's growth, in fact, had followed the dynamics of the dispensation of charisms. New prophets and prophetesses had been recognized by Kimbangu, and he had appointed some of them as his helpers in God's work. For this reason, Nyuvudi's text was a story of prophets, in the plural. In the majority of cases, however, Kimbangu had disavowed the false prophets, chasing away the demons that possessed them or, if they persisted, denouncing them as enemies.

From Nfinangani and Nzungu's account, one learns that deacons retained the power to readmit those who had been expelled back into the church while Kimbangu, through the charism of discernment, recognized the origin of the power of those who proclaimed themselves to be prophets. In one of the episodes in which he confronted the false prophets, he asked them: "Is it out of jealousy that you want to do the work of God? ... Why did you not come and see me straight away?" (History, 223).

From these rhetorical questions, one may guess how Kimbangu, through discernment, endeavored to control the Ngunzist movement, bringing the centrifugal tendencies triggered by the spread of charisms and the multiplication of prophets back to himself.

The reasons why Nyuvudi was interested in this issue was his concern to clarify Kimbangu's attitude towards whites and, in particular, towards the missionary church. Indeed, Nyuvudi's story was intended to present an account based on his direct observation and the testimony of Kimbangu that he heard. The story he wrote, therefore, was intended to disprove and oppose the falsehoods circulating about the prophet, what he contemptuously called (contrary to his own) "all kinds of stories."[79] According to Nyuvudi, such stories were propagated by false prophets who were inciting people to abandon the mission and not to pay taxes.

Beyond the colonial borders, the Ngunzist movement had reached the mission of Musuna, where Nyuvudi was a catechist, creating tension in the church. When he wrote his account in 1928, he addressed it to the Christian community to which he had returned after serving his sentence. His intention was to defend the choice he had made to return to serve the missionary church as a catechist and therefore to make those who had abandoned it repent. In wanting to delegitimize all the mendacious news about the prophet, he also had another, personal reason: Nyuvudi himself had been the victim of those stories. His *Nsamu miangunza* included the history of the persecution that he had personally suffered as a consequence of the lies about the movement that had arisen in Nkamba, lies that the French colonial authorities had believed, thus leading to his condemnation and deportation.

Nyuvudi's texts, therefore, were studded with statements that, unlike hearsay, established the authoritativeness of his testimony by direct observation: "We went [to Nkamba] for the first time to see/watch what we heard about."[80] Or, on having listened to Kimbangu's words: "Look, that is exactly as it is. He himself told of it when we were sitting in that place."[81]

In his story, after the first attempt to arrest him, he decided to go back to the prophet who was then in hiding, with his colleague Biangana,[82] in order to question him:

18. "We have heard that you are no longer in community with the white missionaries; but the rest of us come[83] from the Musana station. Are we wrong?" He replied: "What

---

78   Mackay & Ntoni-Nzinga, "Kimbangu's Interlocutor," 243; Paul Nyuvudi, "Nsamu Miangunza/Nouvelle du prophète," in: Vellut, ed., *Simon Kimbangu*, vol. 1, *Fonds missionnaires protestants (1)*, 69, 75.

79   Vellut, ed., *Simon Kimbangu*, vol. 1, *Fonds missionnaires protestants (1)*, 69, 75.

80   Mackay & Ntoni-Nzinga, "Kimbangu's Interlocutor," 239.

81   Nyuvudi, "Nsamu Miangunza/Nouvelle du prophète," 73.

82   "Bengana" in Mackay & Ntoni-Nzinga's text.

83   What is meant here is that Nyuvudi and Musana were mission catechists and therefore worked with the white missionaries. In fact, in Mackay & Ntoni-Nzinga the question is posed in these terms: "How about us who still

have they done to you? Don't you know that if a woman divorces, that woman suffers. Continue with your whites because they are husbands, you are brides. You cannot leave them."

"In our region they have thought to take refuge in Ngombe [Lutete], I have encouraged them to go. They also planned not to pay taxes, but I myself went before them and paid the fees. So they all paid their taxes. ... Take back what you have seen and heard about me. Because I do not like the stories that others are circulating about me and which I did not say."[84]

Undoubtedly, Nyuvudi was a witness interested in presenting a conciliatory image of a prophet who, though persecuted, referred as much to an indissoluble and subordinate bond with the missionaries as to the duty to submit to state fiscal impositions. In Nyuvudi's memoirs, however, Kimbangu was more ambivalent than that passage leads one to believe.[85] In another version of the same episode, Kimbangu told his interlocutors: "Give them anything rulers ask you, give your heart to God."[86] This echoing of Jesus's indications regarding the taxes due to the empire suggested a superficial loyalty that, as will be seen, seemed to be granted to both administrators and missionaries.[87]

9   The Abominable Enemy

The first meeting between Kimbangu and Morel took place on May 12, 1921. The administrator had gone to Nkamba, not yet intending to arrest him, in order to investigate what was happening. Their dramatic confrontation was of particular weight in determining the death sentence pronounced

against Kimbangu. It was precisely this point in Nfinangani and Nzungu's narrative that was mentioned at the trial, where it was observed, with reference to Morel, that "the white man [was] in the prophet's eyes the abominable enemy" (History, 218).

In effect, Kimbangu and the deacons confronted him as an enemy, using the reading of the Bible against him. After reading from the book of Psalms, Kimbangu said to Morel: "We are all, in respect of your arrival, gathered here in God's hands. God is the living God; everything else in which men put their trust is absolutely meaningless" (History, 218). Later in the encounter, the prophet recited Psalm 3, in which God was invoked against enemies. Reading it, "the power of the Holy Spirit was manifested in him and he cried out in a loud voice, 'I have called to the Lord God with my [own] voice'" (History, 218). In a trance, Kimbangu and his assistants raised their eyes to the heavens and spoke a celestial language.

The book of Psalms also accompanied the prophet during the following month when he miraculously escaped arrest. Kimbangu told Nyuvudi that, during his escape, he fell into a pond and, when he reemerged, he realized that the book that he had had with him had remained completely dry.[88] This event recalled when he had fallen into the deep hole through which he had come into contact with the world of spirits and after which, according to Aloni Budimbu's testimony, a stranger had appeared to him in a dream bringing him the Bible and instructing him to study, preach, and heal.[89]

As we have seen, the prophet's preaching reactivated the gospel narrative in the present, working through the power of healing. It was now possible to see how the current relevance of the scriptures had a deeper meaning. God's power that was announced in these acts entered the prophet's body

---

go to work and mix ourselves with the whites?" (Mackay & Ntoni-Nzinga, "Kimbangu's Interlocutor," 243).

84   Nyuvudi, "Nsamu Miangunza/Nouvelle du prophète," 73.
85   Mackay & Ntoni-Nzinga, "Kimbangu's Interlocutor," 235.
86   Mackay & Ntoni-Nzinga, "Kimbangu's Interlocutor," 243.
87   Mackay & Ntoni-Nzinga, "Kimbangu's Interlocutor," 235.

88   Mackay & Ntoni-Nzinga, "Kimbangu's Interlocutor," 239–240; Nyuvudi, "Nsamu Miangunza/Nouvelle du prophète," 71–72.
89   Mackay, "Simon Kimbangu," 138.

and operated in the present. Indeed, Bahelele Nidimisina recalled how, in the first phase of the ritual process when the teacher was reading and explaining the Scriptures, "the teachings touched the prophet's heart deeply, his feelings awoke: then he would go into a trance."[90]

The trance he entered into in the colonial administrator's presence indicated that Kimbangu effected this (on that occasion just as during the healing ritual in Nkamba) through the working of the Holy Spirit. This time, however, the prophet's body was a means of spiritual war against the abominable enemy. As in the courtyards of Nkamba, the Scriptures acquired topicality through the rite of possession. It was, therefore, the ritual realization of the biblical narrative that was, in itself, of political significance. In this sense, the antagonism between the colonial order and the movement did not derive from an external source of interpretation or manipulation, but from the internal religious logic that animated the prophetic movement itself.

Kimbangu disavowed those prophets who preached the refusal to work for whites and who incited people to shirk their tax obligations to the colonial state. The wider Ngunzist movement had, however, drawn inspiration from the prophet of Nkamba because he had opened up a charismatic space in which the age of the apostolic church was ritually revived in the present. In this sense, the ritual space created the possibility of stepping out of the order of history.[91] It was the possibility, therefore, of escaping from the world's logic and the colonial situation.

10 On Jenning's Veranda

When Kimbangu decided to surrender to the colonial authorities, in an extraordinary parallel to the scene of the garden of Gethsemane, Nyuvudi reported:

> When his time came he said (so) to his disciples and they all went with him. "Let us go to my village. My time has come because Chief Mpiodi betrayed me to the white man." He stood up with all the crowd and they arrived at the village of Mpiodi. "Where is my betrayer?," but he saw nobody. He passed the mission at Ngombe and asked "If someone creates an enmity with you how do you call him?"[92]

This bitter farewell to the Ngombe Lutete mission was Kimbangu's last act of preaching, a farewell that, apparently, contradicted the directive, recalled by Nyuvudi himself, to respect the indissoluble bond of the church with the missionaries. It was, however, a directive that contained some uncertainty because the prophet had also recalled a higher fidelity, that owed to God.

That ambivalence, charged with tension, was also present during a previous visit Kimbangu made to the Ngombe Lutete station. In Nfinangani and Nzungu's narrative, the visit occurred after the deacons had acknowledged the prophet. The order of events suggests that once the movement was integrated into the church structures, Kimbangu sought a confrontation with the missionaries. The intention seemed to be to understand whether, like the deacons, the missionary church would also recognize God's light in his work or (there was no other alternative) if the missionaries, like Mowala, would be blind and would not see how the Bible story was unfolding before their eyes.

Kimbangu asked the parents of a little girl he had just resurrected to accompany him to the station the next day. Along the way, as the group

90   Vellut, ed., *Simon Kimbangu*, vol. 1, *Fonds missionnaires protestants* (1), 61.

91   Lanternari, *Movimenti religiosi*, 55. In this regard, on Lanternari, see Giuseppe D. Schirripa, "I 'Movimenti religiosi' di Vittorio Lanternari: L'autonomia del religioso all'interno di una concezione materialista della storia," in: Antonello Ricci, ed., *L'eredità rivisitata: Storia di un'antropologia in stile italiano*, Rome, CISU, 2019, 347–358.

92   Mackay & Ntoni-Nzinga, "Kimbangu's Interlocutor," 245.

approached their destination, the girl began to show signs of discomfort, and Kimbangu permitted the family to not follow him any further. Kimbangu finally reached Ngombe Lutete where he met Pastor Robert Jennings.

> When he got to Mr. Jennings's, he went on to the verandah, but as soon as he set foot on the stairs, he and the whole verandah began to shake. Then Mr. Jennings came to meet him, bid him good day, but Simon didn't reply. When he went into the room, they offered him a seat, but he didn't want to sit down. He never said so much as a word. After these forces had left him, he sat down on a chair. Then Mr. Jennings said to him, "Anger has no place in God's work, why didn't you reply when I greeted you?" He, in reply: "God is not mad; it is because of your intentions that I don't greet you" (History, 213–214).

Kinzembo's presence at the scene brings to mind the beginning of the story, marked by the meetings with the first generation of missionaries. The prophet's mother seemed to be a recollection of the consistent continuity of God's work that bound the first missionaries' preaching to her son's prophetic charism. If there was any discontinuity, therefore, it was between the two generations of missionaries.

As in the case of Mowala's family member, the devil seemed to have opened a path in Jenning's heart. A sign of this was the unease of the little girl whom Kimbangu had called back to life. God's power then was manifested to the missionary in the form of the tremors of the trance that pervaded Kimbangu's body and the area around it. It was a manifestation of anger, which did not escape Jennings, who nevertheless did not recognize God's work.

While the confrontation with the abominable enemy did not leave any room for doubt, the conclusion to the meeting, with shared prayer and farewell greetings between the missionary and the prophet, left the scenario open to possibilities

other than irremediable conflict. Paradoxically, it would be Nyuvudi himself who, after exile, would return to work with the Swedish mission and would recount that final farewell with which Kimbangu concluded the confrontation with Jennings.

11   The Reactions of the Protestant Missionaries

Without denying the hostility with which Kimbangu had ended his relationship with the European missionaries of Ngombe Lutete, Nyuvudi claimed the choice, as was consistent with the prophet's teaching, to return to his service as a catechist for the SMF. His position towards the mission seems more comprehensible in light of the differing attitudes which, at least initially, Protestant missionaries had had toward the prophetic movement.

The Swedish missionaries could be found on both sides of the colonial border between the Belgian and the French Congo, where they had arrived a few years after the SMF was established in 1878. It had emerged as the result of the evangelical wave of pietist inspiration that had led to a secession from the Lutheran Church during the 1870s. When the Congolese prophetic movement erupted in 1921, the memory of the Swedish evangelical awakening was, therefore, still alive, especially in the long-term missionaries who had welcomed the previous surge of mass conversions and religious enthusiasm. In particular, they interpreted these conversion movements – the one that had unfolded in 1886 within the American Baptist mission in Banza Manteke and that in 1895, which had led natives to deliver *nkisi* (fetishes) en masse to be destroyed at the SMF Kibunzi mission – as being similar to the North American and European awakenings.[93]

The attitude towards the unfolding Ngunzist movement, however, was more uncertain, as

---

93   The station, founded in 1887, was the site of the first Swedish mission school in the Belgian Congo.

demonstrated by the valuable text, edited by Vellut, of sources from the missionary archives in Stockholm.[94] It was more than the presence of younger missionaries, with less direct experience of the Swedish evangelical awakening, that motivated these hesitations. Indeed, Ngunzism aroused dual, interwoven concerns in the missionary generations. On the one hand, the Swedish missionaries saw the risk of not putting at the service of evangelization the spiritual energies that were liberated by the prophetic movement, and which they recognized as positive. On the other hand, there was a concern that Ngunzism, compared to the conversion movements of the turn of the century within the missions, would seriously jeopardize the unity among religious communities, whose autonomy, according to SMF, needed to develop within an organization that included the mother community.[95]

In the diary of the Kibunzi station on July 21, 1921, Sven August Flodén, one of Sweden's oldest missionaries in the Congo, reported: "I attended the *bangunza* [prophets] meeting. These encounters made me suffer. The Walders think that they are inspired by the devil or caused by a weakness of spirit. Some think they should not be allowed to continue. Jesus, help me, give me wisdom. I want my community to be united."[96] Despite his deep distress, Flodén himself observed that, during the morning prayer on Aug 13, "several people began to tremble. The manifestations of this movement are strange, but the spirit seems good."[97] On Aug 26, Carl Palmkvist, a missionary who had been in the Congo since 1904 reported in the diary of Kinkenge station that he insisted during the morning prayer that "religious fervor must always be governed by reason."[98] It was a recommendation imbued with paternalism and condescension towards the Kongo Christians, which nevertheless signaled the missionary's willingness to maintain their "religious fervor" within the framework of the church. He continued his reflection:

> There is need for indulgence, vigilance, and control so that this movement, with its good sides and its bad sides, does not lead the community of God to become lost. ... The thriving community of Wathen [Ngombe Lutete] has been annihilated. If the missionaries disassociate themselves from the movement or, worse still, oppose it, this movement will certainly end up in the service of evil.[99]

The ecclesiological vision of the SMF was different with respect to the British Baptist Missionaries of the BMS, who believed that the autonomy of Christian communities should be understood more radically. However, the missionaries in Ngombe Lutete were, from the outset, extremely skeptical about what they directly observed in Nkamba. Unlike the SMF missionaries, they were in no way inclined to recognize a positive potential for evangelization there.

Jennings, who found himself in Ngombe Lutete for a three-month replacement of the station's oldest missionaries, seems to have been reluctant to go to Nkamba. News of Kimbangu's miracles had already reached the station in early April and, on the 15th of that month, Jennings reported in his diary that Deacon Mbandila, speaking of Kimbangu, had told him of the assistance that the prophet's mother had given Cameron and of the blessing she had received, inferring that her son's miracles might be a consequence.[100] Perhaps referring to the same episode, another BMS

---

94   Vellut, ed., *Simon Kimbangu*, vol. 1, *Fonds missionnaires protestants (1)*.

95   Vellut, "Introduction générale," 4–6.

96   Vellut, ed., *Simon Kimbangu*, vol. 1, *Fonds missionnaires protestants (1)*, 11.

97   Vellut, ed., *Simon Kimbangu*, vol. 1, *Fonds missionnaires protestants (1)*, 12.

98   Vellut, ed., *Simon Kimbangu*, vol. 1, *Fonds missionnaires protestants (1)*, 17.

99   Vellut, ed., *Simon Kimbangu*, vol. 1, *Fonds missionnaires protestants (1)*, 17.

100 Vellut, ed., *Simon Kimbangu*, vol. 1, *Fonds missionnaires protestants (2)*, 50.

missionary, Joseph Sidney Bowskill, recalled that at the dawn of the movement Jennings was approached by deacons who asked him for an opinion on the truth of Kimbangu's divine call. Bowskill recalled that Jennings "told them that they would soon discover this for themselves if they looked, giving them scriptural advice, 'by their fruits ye shall know them.'"[101]

At the deacons' request, Jennings summoned Kimbangu to the station. The meeting, which is the same as that recounted by Nfinangani and Nzungu, was recorded in the diary of the English Baptist on Apr 19. In a 1936 account, he would remember the incendiary tone of the exchange and how he had understood that he was dealing "with a man who was obsessed with the idea that it was the will of God which he was doing."[102] The brief note in his diary concerning his visit to Nkamba a month later has the same skeptical tone: "Saw no miracles but folk who appeared demented." He returned to Ngombe Lutete convinced "of the falsity of it all."[103] The same pathologizing language can be observed in Bowskill, according to whom, based on the visit to Nkamba, the missionaries were forced to conclude that "Kimbangu preached in the name of Jesus and used that name in his attempts at cures, still he was – wittingly or unwittingly – under a delusion."[104]

Recalling that visit to Nkamba in his 1936 account, Jennings would more exhaustively remember that he was kindly invited to preach and introduced to the crowd "as their missionary who with others had brought to them the light of God's

word."[105] His memoir went on to report that he chose to preach from Romans 13:1–2 in order to remind them, with the words of the Apostle Paul, that all resistance to authority is rebellion against the order willed by God. It was an appeal to prudence in the English missionary's intentions, dictated by the perception of an impending conflict with the colonial authorities,[106] but which the Kongo deacons and faithful interpreted in other terms.

Quite different from the reaction of the Ngombe Lutete missionaries was that of the Danish Baptist Peter Herbert Frederickson and his wife Mathilda Reuter who, at the beginning of the movement, were serving in Bas-Congo at the Sona Bata station of the ABFMS. The couple interpreted the prophetic movement as a providential event. According to Mathilda Frederickson-Reuter: "We, with the Christians, had been praying for two years especially for a revival among us and in our field, we naturally felt that this spiritual awakening started with Simon Kibangu's [sic] preaching to thousands."[107] The missionaries of Sona Bata, therefore, welcomed the prophetic movement with gratitude to "God for His Spirit in the hearts of men," because they saw nothing wrong with it and were confident that "the bad effects of the 'false' prophets" could not "disturb the good and true movement."[108] It was a fully favorable attitude that, however, did not prevent them from observing how "in the African's interpretation of the scriptures and in the way of healing by faith, their mind is easily mixed up with their old inborn superstition."[109]

---

101   Vellut, ed., *Simon Kimbangu*, vol. 1, *Fonds missionnaires protestants* (2), 28.

102   These were typewritten notes composed by Jennings at the urging of a BMS missionary interested in a direct testimony concerning the Congolese prophetic movement; Vellut, ed., *Simon Kimbangu*, vol. 1, *Fonds missionnaires protestants* (2), 64.

103   The visit to Nkamba is recorded in the missionary's personal journal in the entries for May 18 and 19 (Vellut, ed., *Simon Kimbangu*, vol. 1, *Fonds missionnaires protestants* (2), 50).

104   Vellut, ed., *Simon Kimbangu*, vol. 1, *Fonds missionnaires protestants* (2), 28.

105   Vellut, ed., *Simon Kimbangu*, vol. 1, *Fonds missionnaires protestants* (2), 64.

106   Vellut, ed., *Simon Kimbangu*, vol. 1, *Fonds missionnaires protestants* (2), 64.

107   Vellut, ed., *Simon Kimbangu*, vol. 1, *Fonds missionnaires protestants* (2), 179.

108   Vellut, ed., *Simon Kimbangu*, vol. 1, *Fonds missionnaires protestants* (2), 179.

109   Vellut, ed., *Simon Kimbangu*, vol. 1, *Fonds missionnaires protestants* (2), 179–180.

Although some form of confusion with what was considered "innate superstition" was recognized, that mixture did not seem to prevent accepting the Congolese prophecy within a tradition of Christian revivalism.

The same complex positioning, far from the BMS Baptists' clear judgement, was observed with regard to the miraculous healings. The Baptist missionaries of Sona Bata were, in fact, willing to recognize divine intervention when they had the opportunity to see the improvements of the sick persons who had gone to Nkamba.[110] They did not fail to observe: "No doubt, as in all countries, most of sick prayed for, go home as they came. Neurotic patients seem to respond to prayers for healing, sooner than other sufferers."[111] The reaction of the Sona Bata missionaries had a tradition behind it. It was consistent with the history of the American Baptist mission in the Congo, which was marked by successive phases of awakening. This charismatic history began with Henry Richards[112] and the establishment of the Banza Manteke station in Bas-Congo. On that occasion, the missionary decided to rethink his preaching entirely, focusing exclusively on the Gospels and the life of Christ, his redemptive death, and his future return.[113] In a short time a mass conversion movement took place around the station that was still under construction, which took the name of the Congolese Pentecost.

In the founding of Banza Manteke we can recognize an exemplary moment in the history of those "mutual fascinations" that, according to Vellut, accompanied the relationship of "rejections and reconciliations" between the Africans and European missionaries.[114] On the one hand, there was a fascination for the mission world, sheltered from witchcraft and slavery. On the other hand, there was the missionary attraction to collective conversions as a possibility of witnessing the action of God's Spirit. Thus, mass conversions were both a new form of the anti-witchcraft movements developed in the bedrock of Congolese religiosity and one of the charismatic phases in Christian history.

When the Ngunzist movement emerged, however, the charismatic interpretation of the mission held by the Baptists of Sona Bata dwindled to a minority even in the ABFMS. The Banza Manteke missionaries interpreted the 1921 movement with skepticism, mainly seeing it as a dangerous pagan resurgence among the Kongo Christians or their disappointing propensity for credulity. One example of this was the severe theological indictment of Ngunzism, written in Kikongo in August of 1921 by the American pastor John E. Geil for the station's periodic publication, *Minsamu mia Mbanza Manteke*. Besides condemning the need to follow the prophets as a sign of spiritual poverty and worldly attachment, Geil stigmatized the pagan nature of the *ngunza*: "They proclaim themselves prophets of God but do the work of the *féticheur*. Their fetishes are not made by the hands of men but in the name of Jesus and through songs and prayer."[115]

In the same issue of the periodical there also appeared an investigation into a minor prophet aimed more generally at discrediting the Ngunzist movement, highlighting its pagan derivation and the falsehood of thaumaturgical claims.[116] It was conducted by Davidi Mbadi and Timoteo

---

110   See for example the case, reported by Mathilda Frederickson-Reuter, of a paralytic, a member of the church of Sona Bata whose condition improved significantly after a pilgrimage to Nkamba (Vellut, ed., *Simon Kimbangu*, vol. 1, *Fonds missionnaires protestants* (2), 181).

111   Vellut, ed., *Simon Kimbangu*, vol. 1, *Fonds missionnaires protestants* (2), 181.

112   Richards had arrived in the Congo in 1879 with the evangelical mission of the LIM. In 1884 he joined the ranks of the ABMU (later referred to as ABFMS) when it took over the LIM, which was in financial difficulty.

113   Vellut, ed., *Simon Kimbangu*, vol. 1, *Fonds missionnaires protestants* (2), 22–23.

114   Vellut, ed., *Simon Kimbangu*, vol. 1, *Fonds missionnaires protestants* (2), 22.

115   Vellut, ed., *Simon Kimbangu*, vol. 1, *Fonds missionnaires protestants* (2), 202.

116   The investigation is published with a parallel French translation in Vellut, ed., *Simon Kimbangu*, vol. 1, *Fonds missionnaires protestants* (2), 212–215.

Vingadio, Kongo members of the ABFMS community of Kimpese, where the Kongo Evangelical Training Institution (KETI) was based. Since 1909, it had been a professional and religious training center that adopted an ecumenical approach to the Protestant denominations and was inspired by a modern and pragmatic vision of social and Christian development.

In Bolenge in the Belgian Congo, where the eighth general conference of the Protestant missions of the Congo was held between Oct 29 and Nov 7, 1921, the interpretation of the prophetic movement held by Banza Manteke was the one that was represented, while the KETI imposed itself there as a missionary and pedagogical model.

12   The Protestant Ecumenical Alignment

Held just a few weeks after the death sentence passed on Kimbangu, the ecumenical conference was animated by the Protestant organizations' need to find a shared interpretation of the challenges posed by the prophetic movement to the Congolese missions, which were felt to be united despite differences in denomination. The concerns that were expressed thus concerned the relationship between the church and the movement and the tensions that the latter had generated, to varying degrees, in the Christian communities. In particular, during the session of Oct 30, the representatives of the missions that were present in Bas-Congo, who had found themselves close to the movement's epicenter, took the floor being able to offer first-hand testimony.

The addresses, of which we have a summary,[117] were held by the BMS (George Thomas for Ngombe Lutete, Robert Kirkland for Kinshasa) and ABFMS missionaries (John Geil, Judson King, and Thomas Hill for Banza Manteke, Seymour Moon for Kimpese, and Paul Metzger for Tshumbiri). The interwoven elements of these testimonies were then reflected in the conference resolutions, which indicated, as a common directive, the adoption of a clear separation from the prophetic movement. In particular, Bolenge's final decisions insisted on the practice of teaching natives to respect established political authorities and on the missions' incompatibility with a movement whose harmfulness "to the progress of Christianity and the normal development of the native population"[118] had been made apparent.

Yet Bolenge's resolutions also echoed the criticism of "judicial errors"[119] and the harshness of the military court's sentences, which both George Thomas and Jennings had witnessed in the trial that had just ended in Thysville with the death sentence pronounced on Kimbangu and the heavy prison sentences for his closest collaborators. This pronunciation gave explicit support to the attempts by Protestant missionaries to intercede with the Belgian authorities, which then led to the commutation of the death sentence to life imprisonment.

Nonetheless, the resolutions also declared firm support for the immediate and severe measures taken by the authorities to put a stop to a movement that might favor anticolonial propaganda, "endangering civilization itself."[120] In this sense, full support was expressed for the missionaries of the Bas-Congo, who had been strongly opposed to the movement since its inception.

Bolenge thus marked a decisive Protestant alignment with Belgian colonial policies. This alignment was part of a more general turning point effected by the Protestant ecumenical movement that, in those very same years, directed the missionary efforts to concentrate on progress in

---

117   This is the summary that Peter Lerrigo of the ABFMS kept in his diary, published in Vellut, ed., *Simon Kimbangu*, vol. 1, *Fonds missionnaires protestants* (2), 69–72, 203–206.

118   The final resolutions can be found in Vellut, ed., *Simon Kimbangu*, vol. 1, *Fonds missionnaires protestants* (2), 265–267.

119   Vellut, ed., *Simon Kimbangu*, vol. 1, *Fonds missionnaires protestants* (2), 266.

120   Vellut, ed., *Simon Kimbangu*, vol. 1, *Fonds missionnaires protestants* (2), 267.

the areas of education and health care as the basis for a more solid and profound evangelization. On the one hand, this less apostolic and more pragmatic vision favored the affirmation of those missionary attitudes of the rejection of a charismatic movement such as Kimbanguism and the broader Ngunzism. On the other hand, it showed the possibility of a convergence with colonial policies and an underlying solidarity with the ideology of civilization.

The decisive distancing of the missions from the prophetic movement was, in this sense, also a consequence of the attempt to overcome the historical tensions between the Protestants and the Belgian administration, which dated back to the time of the Leopoldian possession of the Congo and the related complaints by the British against the violence and systematic depredations suffered by the population. A Protestant policy of détente towards the administration had already made headway during the 1920s, when the *International Review of Missions*, published in Geneva, welcomed the reforms undertaken by Belgium in the Congolese colony.

In the second half of 1921, this policy of pacification had thus suffered a severe blow. With the establishment of the military occupation regime, the missionaries, especially those of Ngombe Lutete, found themselves once again denouncing the rights that were being trampled on in the Congo, this time defending their deacons, the majority of whom had been arrested and severely condemned by civil and military courts. This difficult position of the Protestant missions was aggravated by a heated rivalry with the Catholic missionaries. The protagonists of the anti-Protestant campaign were the Scheut missionaries, to whom the Apostolic Vicariate of the Belgian Congo was entrusted, and the Redemptorists, whose stations in the Bas-Congo were concerned with the prophetic movement. The Catholic missionaries in particular accused the Protestants of having consciously inspired an anticolonial movement and of having undertaken an anti-Belgian campaign with their defense of the natives who had been arrested.

The Kimbangu affair, amplified in the columns of *L'Avenir Colonial Belge* and *Le Progrès Colonial*, played a decisive role in consolidating the privileged link between the administration and the Catholic mission to which, from the first postwar period, the colony's educational and health care system was gradually entrusted.

Without any mention of the Catholic attacks, the resolutions of the Bolenge conference rejected as unjust defamation the heavy suspicions of disloyalty to Belgium advanced in the colonial press. The alignment of the Protestant missions on the Kimbangu case, developed by Bolenge, continued in the following months in the mediatory work with the Minister of the Colonies Henri Anet, as Secretary General of the Bureau des Missions du Congo, the Protestant interconfessional representative body in Brussels. The Protestants were thus able to avoid expulsion from the colony without having to deny BMS's attempts to stand beside their imprisoned deacons.

In the mission field of Bas-Congo, however, the sense of betrayal that the English Baptists and Kongo Christians had developed towards each other remained unresolved. The former felt betrayed by their spiritual children who had abandoned them to follow a false prophet with irrational enthusiasm. The latter, on the contrary, were convinced that, under the military occupation regime, it was their own missionaries who had denounced Kimbangu and their *bambuta* to the colonial authorities.

13 "To Our Old Teacher, Mr. G.R.R. Cameron"

The reports, letters, and personal diaries of the BMS missionaries are eloquent sources revealing the mutual sense of disappointment and betrayal felt by the European missionaries and Kongo Christians. For example, William Frame, who had served in Bas-Congo since 1896, in October 1921 observed in the interconfessional journal *Congo Mission News*:

the Christians were sorely disappointed in our attitude towards what they regarded as a religious revival. Were not our services better attended? Had not fetishes been cast away? Had not backsliders professed repentance? Had not more been accomplished in a few short weeks than in many years of our preaching? Such were the questions put to me. ... I think I may say for all our BMS folks in the affected area that we have been sadly disappointed and shocked by the credulity of our people.[121]

As mentioned above, many Kongo Christians of the BMS were also convinced that it was the missionaries of Ngombe Lutete, and Jennings in particular, who had requested military intervention. This unfounded accusation had begun to take shape following the seizure of the writings found in Nkamba by Morel in mid-June of 1921. According to Bowskill the missionary, among the writings were numerous letters that, reporting the names of the prophet's sympathizers and supporters, helped Morel to proceed with numerous arrests. "He captured almost all of our deacons – Mbandila, Kuyowa, Mafwata, Nkuba ... [The Christians] accused Mr. Jennings of bringing the soldiers."[122] Bowskill then recalled one of the most popular hymns of the movement at the time, which went: "Our leaders are in prison, and our Teachers (missionaries) put them there."[123]

Kimbangu, whose last appearance in Nkamba before being handed over was reconstructed by Bowskill, was also convinced of the missionary betrayal:

Sept 11, Sunday: Things were almost at their worst today. During morning service (only station children and a few workmen were

there) the Prophet himself came along with a vast crowd of people and made a demonstration outside the chapel. They came singing their songs: children dancing. They then formed up in a mass and the Prophet shouted out, "As the apostle Paul said, 'He that is not against us is on our part.' If you do not believe me, I shake off the dust of my feet to condemn you."[124]

According to Bowskill, Kimbangu bid farewell to the mission with those two references to the Gospel of Luke (9:50, 9:5). Although Kimbangu's farewell appeared to be definitive, there was an ideal continuation with the history of this relationship between the missionary church and the prophetic movement based on the Gospel as the undisputed common ground upon which misunderstandings and differences were grafted. It was a continuation in which Luke's verses (9:49 in particular) were once again among the New Testament references that nourished the mutual encounter as well as the shared sense of betrayal between the Baptist missionaries and the Kongo Christians.

This continuation was found in a letter that takes us back to the beginning of Nfinangani and Nzungu's history and Kinzembo's story. It was written by three deacons – Ntima, Kuyowa, and Mbandila – who wrote it on June 2, 1923, from Ponthierville Prison in response to a letter from the Reverend Ronald Cameron.[125] The arrests of Mbandila and Kuyowa were mentioned by Bowskill, who held them responsible for creating a native church that was separate from the mission.[126]

---

121 Vellut, ed., *Simon Kimbangu*, vol. 1, *Fonds missionnaires protestants* (2), 46.

122 Vellut, ed., *Simon Kimbangu*, vol. 1, *Fonds missionnaires protestants* (2), 29.

123 Vellut, ed., *Simon Kimbangu*, vol. 1, *Fonds missionnaires protestants* (2), 30.

124 Vellut, ed., *Simon Kimbangu*, vol. 1, *Fonds missionnaires protestants* (2), 30.

125 The letter was translated by Cameron from Kikongo into English and sent to the London office of the BMS. Cameron's translation was published as an appendix in Cecilia Irvine, "The Birth of the Kimbanguist Movement in the Bas-Zaire 1921," *Journal of Religion in Africa* 6/1, 1974, 23–76, here 73–76.

126 Vellut, ed., *Simon Kimbangu*, vol. 1, *Fonds missionnaires protestants* (2), 27.

From prison, the three *bambuta* resumed their dialogue with their former missionary, reminding him of when he was attacked on the road between Ntontani and Nkamba and was told that the woman who rescued him and whom he blessed was Kinzembo, the mother of the prophet. They urged him to rejoice because what he had asked of God, particularly in Kinzembo's blessing, had occurred in the prophet's teaching.

The letter from the three deacons was, in fact, intended to object to the observations of Cameron, who had reproached them in his letter for wanting to follow a "new teaching."

> This is not so, our Teacher; do not think that, it is just what you and Mr Bentley and our other teachers have taught us, it is not "new teaching." Only remember that whenever the word of God is made clearer to the eyes of men, others say this is "new teaching" ... Our Lord Jesus Christ was delivered up by the Chief Priests, who said that His teaching was new, but it was not new, and they killed Him because of His teaching. ... In the same way with Peter and John, their teaching and healing of the sick was not approved. Folks said it was a "new teaching," and they suffered much for it. Now today all their teaching is called good, in all lands it is approved.[127]

Ntima, Kuyowa, and Mbandila thus clarified in which sense the continuity between Kimbangu's teaching and that of their missionary teachers should be understood. Kimbangu had made the Word of God clearer, setting it before the eyes of men. The relationship between the mission and the prophetic movement was thus placed in a relationship of continuity and reactivation within a historical dynamic. It was a relationship that

makes sense in the unity of the history of God's work. There was an identity, not as a mere repetition, but because the one was the fulfilment of the other, just as Jesus's teaching fulfilled the Old Testament, verifying its promises, making them evident, and revealing their meaning.

However, there was also a consistency between Kimbangu's preaching and Cameron's teaching in the same sense in which the apostolate of Peter and John carried out what Jesus had taught. At every step of this history there was disavowal and martyrdom, but also growth: "They [Peter and John] suffered much for it. Now today all their teaching is called good, in all lands it is approved."[128]

When confronted with Kimbangu's teaching and the manifestations of his charismatic power of healing, the deacons opened the Bible and read Mark 16:16 and Luke 9:49. They thus recognized God's work, that is, the truth of the Gospels, for, as they observed later in the letter: "All that is written came to pass."[129] The gospel accounts were relevant today because they continued in the present. "Now, Mr Cameron, do you believe what Jesus said in Mark 16:16? and in Luke 9:49? Are they not true? Please remember what you prayed to God for."[130]

This exhortation was not only a reminder of his own personal coherence but the very construction of a unity within that same story. In Luke 9:49, Jesus explained to the disciples that those who heal in his name, even when they did not follow with the disciples, is not against but with them. In the verse from Mark that the deacons mentioned, Jesus instead said that those who believe will be saved but those who do not believe will be condemned. The letter, therefore, was not intended to point out a shortcut to an accommodating reconciliation with the missionary, but rather to present Cameron with the test that Kimbangu had already presented to the catechist Mowala and to the missionary Jennings in the story of Nfinangani and

---

127   "Ntima, Kuyowa, Mbandila, senior deacons of the Baptist Church, Ngombe Lutete, June 2, 1923, from The Prison, Ponthierville, Belgian Congo to: The Rev. George R.R. Cameron," published in: Irvine, "The Birth of the Kimbanguist Movement," 73–76.

128   Irvine, "The Birth of the Kimbanguist Movement," 73–76.

129   Irvine, "The Birth of the Kimbanguist Movement," 75.

130   Irvine, "The Birth of the Kimbanguist Movement," 75.

Nzungu. The point was whether Cameron would recognize his own teaching now that Kimbangu's healings had made it clearer to men's eyes. That is to say, whether he would believe the story of God's work that he himself had taught when it occurred.

Mark 16:16 and Luke 9:49, the deacons recalled, were the verses that Jennings himself had suggested to them when they asked for his advice about the miracles that were taking place in Nkamba. Jennings reportedly added: "These things are certainly in the Bible."[131] Taking this statement literally, the *bambuta* urged him to go to Nkamba and to "call together all the leaders of the Protestant Missions" so that they could see with their own eyes the unfolding of things that had happened in the Bible. Jennings, however, would decide to do otherwise, and sent in the army.[132]

Despite the belief that they had been denounced by the missionary, there was some agreement between the deacons' version and that of Jennings and Bowskill. The Ngombe Lutete missionaries themselves mentioned how the reference to the Gospels had been at the heart of the exchange with the deacons about the truth of Kibangu's miracles. Jennings also reported, in 1936, that he was presented to the crowd in Nkamba as one who, as a missionary, had brought the light of God's word. Although the *bambuta* had omitted this episode in their letter, they continued to refer to Cameron in the same sense, reminding him that he had given birth to a fundamental moment in the unifying history of the manifestation of the Word of God. For the deacons, the missionary's refusal to recognize Kimbangu's charismatic gifts was a disavowal of the truth of the Scriptures and thus a betrayal of the history that, in spite of everything, continued to unite the missionary church and the prophetic movement.

Translated from Italian to English by Susan Dawson Vásquez and David Dawson Vásquez.

Bibliography

Irvine, Cecilia, "The Birth of the Kimbanguist Movement in the Bas-Zaire 1921," *Journal of Religion in Africa* 6/1, 1974, 23–76.

MacGaffey, Wyatt, "The Beloved City: Commentary on a Kimbanguist Text," *Journal of Religion in Africa* 2/1, 1969, 129–147.

MacGaffey, Wyatt, *Modern Kongo Prophets: Religions in a Plural Society*, Bloomington IN, Indiana University Press, 1983.

Mackay, Donald J., "Simon Kimbangu and the BMS Tradition," *Journal of Religion in Africa* 17/2, 1987, 113–171.

Raymaekers, Paul, "Histoire de Simon Kimbangu, prophète, d'après les écrivains Nfinangani and Nzungu (1921)," *Archives de Sociologie des Religions* 31, 1971, 15–42.

Vellut, Jean-Luc, ed., *Simon Kimbangu. 1921, De la prédication à la déportation: Les sources*, vol. 1, *Fonds missionnaires protestants (1): Alliance missionnaire suédoise (Svenska Missionförbundet, SMF)*, Bruxelles, Académie Royale des Sciences d'Outre-Mer, 2005.

Vellut, Jean-Luc, ed., *Simon Kimbangu: 1921: De la prédication à la déportation: Les sources*, vol. 1, *Fonds missionnaires protestants (2): Missions baptistes et autres traditions évangéliques: Le pays kongo entre prophétismes et projets de société*, Bruxelles, Académie Royale des Sciences d'Outre-Mer, 2010.

---

131   Irvine, "The Birth of the Kimbanguist Movement," 73.
132   Irvine, "The Birth of the Kimbanguist Movement," 74.

CHAPTER 16

Liberal Theology and Its Aftermath

Mark D. Chapman

1 Introduction

On the evening of May 30, 1901, a public meeting was held at Westminster Town Hall in central London as part of the first Congress of the International Council of Unitarian and Other Liberal Religious Thinkers and Workers. There were several speakers, who included the Boston-based Charles William Wendté, general secretary of the International Council from 1900 to 1920 and mastermind behind the congress. He was well known in Unitarian circles and had earlier been one of the principal organizers of the World's Parliament of Religions in Chicago in 1893.[1] His unpublished lecture at the Westminster Town Hall meeting was entitled "The True Basis of Religious Unity," in which he is reported as having "graphically sketched the dissentions that had run through Christendom since the very days of the first Apostles."[2] The solution to such divisions, he held, could be achieved only by love: "Dogma could chain Christians together, but could never unite them."[3] No formulary could ever contain the great topics of religion. Indeed, he went on, "[e]ven when we united in saying 'I believe in God,' what a diversity there was, immediately we began to define what we meant by God." What mattered more than anything else, according to Wendté, was an "earnest heart."[4]

What Wendté's address amounts to is a simple statement of what might be referred to as "non-dogmatic ecumenism," or "ecumenism of humanity," which offered something quite different from other styles of nascent ecumenism in the early 20th century. It sought to move Christians away from their historic forms towards a more fundamental spiritual expression of unity resting in universal love. This was something promoted initially mainly by American and British Unitarians but it quickly drew support from other European liberals who frequently expressed their Christianity within the historic denominations, including the national churches of the German Empire. While such non-dogmatic ecumenism could appeal to universal concepts of humanity, it could at the same time be highly intolerant of forms of traditional religion that were considered dogmatic and superstitious. As will be shown, stripping away dogma and returning to the primitive message of Jesus could in part become a cipher for anti-Catholicism, particularly in Germany, which lacked a tradition of religious dissent, even if such attacks were usually more implicit than explicit. The liberal principle of freedom of religion could be highly intolerant of dogma.

2 The Problem of Definition

This example from the first Congress of the International Council of Unitarian and Other

---

1 On the World's Parliament of Religion see Arie L. Molendijk's contribution in this volume.

2 W. Copeland Bowie, ed., *Liberal Religious Thought at the Beginning of the Twentieth Century: Addresses and Papers at the International Council of Unitarian and Other Liberal Religious Thinkers and Workers, held in London, May, 1901*, London, P. Green, 1901, 334–354 ("Record of the Proceedings in London"), here 343.

3 Bowie, ed., *Liberal Religious Thought*, 343–344.

4 Bowie, ed., *Liberal Religious Thought*, 344.

Liberal Religious Thinkers and Workers reveals an approach to ecumenism that is based on the fundamental unity of all people. It is focused on a commonality, often intended as a longing for future fulfillment, rather than on the dogmatic certainties of the past, including those of the Protestantism that ultimately gave birth to such liberal movements. This highlights one of the most difficult aspects of liberal ecumenism: it proves extremely difficult to give a succinct and straightforward definition of precisely what constitutes liberal theology.[5] Whereas Catholic theology or Lutheran theology can be defined in terms of more or less agreed sources and structures of authority ranging from the teachings of the ecumenical councils to the Reformation confessions, there are no obvious agreed criteria for what is to be included within the phenomenon of liberal theology. Indeed, for many, it is precisely the absence of any dogmatic and confessional certainty that forms the principal characteristic of liberalism: in this it helps religion to come to terms with the modern world and to draw on its critical thought. This is what sometimes differentiates liberal theology (at times synonymous with liberal Protestantism) from other uses of the adjective "liberal" in religion, such as when it is added to Catholicism or Anglicanism, with their distinctive teachings.

Furthermore, liberal theology has complex relationships with the historical denominations.

While some liberal theologians, particularly in the English-speaking world, were members of distinct liberal denominations, and among them one might include Wendté, many others, who were equally resistant to dogma and creeds, were nevertheless content to remain within the historic denominations. Indeed in the conferences of the International Council that followed on from the initial London gathering, where there was only a handful of participants from the historic Protestant Churches, there were many more participants from mainline Protestant Churches. At the Berlin conference of 1910 of the International Council, for instance, two of the most prominent Protestant theologians of the time, Adolf von Harnack of Berlin, and Ernst Troeltsch of Heidelberg, were among the speakers, along with a host of lesser-known figures. Similarly, the Baptist Walter Rauschenbusch, pioneer of the Social Gospel in the United States,[6] as well as the Anglican Alfred Leslie Lilley,[7] interpreter of Catholic Modernists, were also present. What is clear is that trying to sift out the complexities of the term "liberal theology" is fraught with difficulties since it is a term that embraces a number of different themes and ideas both inside and outside the mainline churches.

In addition, and from a far more negative standpoint, there have been many caricatures of liberal theology that have come from its detractors. A critical and enlightened approach to theology was subject to vigorous attack for the perceived threat to the doctrinal truths of orthodoxy. Hans-Joachim Birkner has shown that the term, at least when applied to Germany, was frequently a construct of the anti-liberal theologians of the 1920s, including Karl Barth, Friedrich Gogarten, and Rudolf

---

5   For discussions of national expressions of liberalism, see Kenneth Cauthen, *The Impact of American Religious Liberalism*, New York NY, Harper & Row, 1962; Keith W. Clements, *Lovers of Discord: Twentieth-Century Theological Controversies in England*, London, SPCK, 1988; William R. Hutchison, ed., *American Protestant Thought: The Liberal Era*, New York NY, Harper & Row, 1968; Gangolf Hübinger, *Kulturprotestantismus und Politik: Zum Verhältnis von Liberalismus und Protestantismus im wilhelminischen Deutschland*, Tübingen, Mohr Siebeck, 1994; Bernard M.G. Reardon, *Liberal Protestantism*, London, Adam & Black, 1968; Alan M.G. Stephenson, *The Rise and Decline of English Modernism: The Hulsean Lectures (1979–80)*, London, SPCK, 1984; Friedrich Wilhelm Graf, ed., *Liberale Theologie: Eine Ortsbestimmung*, Gütersloh, Gerd Mohn, 1993.

6   Walter Rauschenbusch, "The Social Awakening in the Churches of America," in: Charles William Wendté, ed., *Fifth International Congress of Free Christianity and Religious Progress, Berlin, August 5–10, 1910: Proceedings and Papers*, Berlin-Schöneberg, Protestantischer Schriftenvertrieb, 1911, 563–567.

7   Alfred Leslie Lilley, "Modernism as a Basis of Religious Unity," in: Wendté, ed., *Fifth International Congress*, 354–364.

Bultmann. They needed some sort of homogeneous liberal theology to be able to attack with the quest for a new orthodox form of theology.[8] For instance, in his essay "Die liberale Theologie und die jüngste theologische Bewegung,"[9] Rudolf Bultmann attacks liberal theology on the basis of its reduction of theology to religious experience which detracted from the scandal at the heart of the Christian faith. What this indicates is that frequently "liberal theology" is a charge made by opponents: the sorts of self-conscious liberals such as those who gathered in London in 1901 were relatively few and far between. Several others who have shared many of the same ideas have refused the term as a self-designation: "liberal theology" is perhaps a somewhat artificial designation that can include many different types of thinkers, some of whom had very little in common.

Despite this, there are nevertheless certain characteristics that might usefully be included within the category of liberal theology. The first, and probably the most important, use of the term is to describe those theologians who adopt the principle of criticism as a method that can be used to evaluate tradition, authority, and ecclesiastical dogma: their basic presupposition was that theology should be open to the scientific methods of modernity. This sort of understanding entered into theology with Enlightenment. The dominant question that arises from this aspect of liberal theology is relatively straightforward, even if its application could be highly complex: how far and in what ways

has theology been able to open itself up to the traditions stemming from the Enlightenment, which in some parts of Europe, especially Germany and Britain, was strongly influenced by Christianity? In many places, particularly where there was an established church which was enmeshed in the structures of the state, liberal theology was often simply one aspect of a wider liberal approach to society and its structures. Indeed, at times theology could be threatening to the state. The Berlin biblical scholar, Wilhelm Martin Leberecht de Wette, for instance, was dismissed from his post in 1819 for espousing liberal political causes. Some others at much the same time who had used the term "liberal theology" included late Rationalists such as Heinrich Gottlieb Tzschirner, Wilhelm Traugott Krug, and Karl Gottlieb Bretschneider. Such men played a prominent part in the early political protests against Prussian authoritarianism in the name of democratic freedom: political progress and theological liberalism stood hand in hand. Protestantism was interpreted as a political principle to criticize the dominant hierarchies of the state as well as to promote freedom of conscience and constitutional freedoms including the right to vote: liberal theology was critical of all forms of authoritarianism. Liberal theology had consequently become one aspect of a wider constitutional change which saw the fundamental unity of all people in a humanity which shared constitutional rights and freedoms.

The term "liberal theology" itself originally developed out of the so-called Halle Neology of the late 18th century. It was used to describe a number of moderately enlightened theologians, who had become critical of the old dogmatic ways of doing theology. Famously, the Halle historian Johann Salomo Semler used the term *liberalis theologia* in 1774 to describe what he considered to be a purely historical investigation of the New Testament using an approach that tried to remove all theological presuppositions. Following in this direction, some theologians, especially those who were influenced by the great Prussian philosopher, Immanuel Kant, sought to challenge the grip of the

8   On the specific issues surrounding German liberal theology, see Hans-Joachim Birkner, "Liberale Theologie," in: Martin Schmidt & Georg Schwaiger, eds., *Kirchen und Liberalismus im 19. Jahrhundert*, Göttingen, Vandenhoeck & Ruprecht, 1976, 33–42; on the history of the term "liberal theology," see Friedrich Wilhelm Graf, "Liberale Theologie," EKL 3, 86–98.

9   Rudolf Bultmann, "Die liberale Theologie und die jüngste theologische Bewegung," in: Rudolf Bultmann, *Glauben und Verstehen*, vol. 1, Tübingen, Mohr Siebeck, [4]1964, 1–25; ET: "Liberal Theology and the Latest Theological Movement," in: Rudolf Bultmann, *Faith and Understanding*, vol. 1, ed. Robert W. Funk, trans. Louise Pettibone Smith, London, SCM Press, 1969, 28–52.

churches on the universities and questioned some
of the old doctrinal formulations of such subjects
as original sin or the atonement or eternal life. In
some senses, the description of the Enlightenment
project offered by Kant in his famous essay of 1784,
"What Is Enlightenment?," characterizes a method
that was shared by liberal theology:

> Enlightenment is the release of human beings
> from their self-incurred tutelage. Tutelage is
> the inability of human beings to make use of
> their understanding without direction from
> another. Self-incurred is this tutelage when
> its cause lies not in lack of reason but in lack
> of resolution and courage to use it without
> direction from another. *Sapere aude!* [Dare to
> know!]. "Have courage to use your own rea-
> son!" – that is the motto of enlightenment.[10]

Secondly, partly because it has been so closely
related to the political, ecclesiastical, and academic environment in which it developed, liberal
theology has always displayed strong national
characteristics: in Germany, for instance, it
emerged from the critical questioning of tradition from the late 18th century. Some, who
remained resolutely members of the traditional
churches, most famously Friedrich Daniel Ernst
Schleiermacher, drew on this critical understanding of theology, even though they resisted the
term liberal theology. While his theological system, as developed in *The Christian Faith*,[11] was in
many ways a form of proto-ecumenism in that he
sought to reconcile the different confessions of the
Lutherans and Reformed in the new Church of the
Prussian Union in terms ultimately of the common

experience of humankind,[12] it was nonetheless resolutely anti-Catholic and nationalist. For
Schleiermacher, Protestantism was the more modern form of Christianity. As with Schleiermacher
himself, many of his followers displayed a similar tendency to resist the term liberal theology,
preferring such terms as mediating theology. For
many liberals in this tradition the purpose of theology was in part to create cultural values for all
Germans: many liberals could use theological language to develop utopian visions that were often
deeply anti-pluralistic and illiberal. By the beginning of the 20th century, some other thinkers,
including the great patristics scholar and public
intellectual Adolf von Harnack, had moved away
from their Pietist upbringings towards an understanding of Christianity that tried to reduce it to
its purest essence, thereby removing the accretions of the past. His famous best-selling lectures
on *Das Wesen des Christentums* of 1899/1900[13] had
cemented his reputation as a religious liberal and
had helped make him a household name. They
focused on the barest minimum of dogmatic
content in the teaching of Jesus, which paved the
way for a far more sympathetic approach to like-
minded thinkers from outside Germany, including
the British and American liberals represented by
the International Council.

3   Liberal Ecumenism and the London Congress of 1901

The key liberal themes of autonomy and the
freedom to use critical reason to attack the dogmatic certainties of the past were undoubtedly
central to the project of many liberal theologians

10   Immanuel Kant, "What Is Enlightenment?," in:
Immanuel Kant, *On History*, ed. Lewis White Beck,
Indianapolis IN, Bobbs-Merrill, 1963, 3–10, here 3.
"*Sapere aude*" is a citation from Horace which had
become the motto of the Friends of Truth, a group
which had been important in the development of the
German Enlightenment.

11   Friedrich D.E. Schleiermacher, *The Christian Faith*, New
York Ny, Harper & Row, 1963.

12   Brian A. Gerrish, *Continuing the Reformation: Essays
on Modern Religious Thought*, Edinburgh, T&T Clark,
1982, 179–195 ("Schleiermacher and the Reformation:
A Question of Doctrinal Development").

13   Adolf von Harnack, *Das Wesen des Christentums:
Sechzehn Vorlesungen vor Studierenden aller Facultäten
im Wintersemester 1899/1900 an der Universität Berlin
gehalten*, Leipzig, Hinrichs, 1900.

whose heirs were to attend the conferences of the International Council at the beginning of the 20th century. In Britain and the United Sates, groups of religious freethinkers had developed out of the enlightened and deistic critique of traditional Christianity, as well as the Socinian and other non-Trinitarian groups that had formed Unitarianism. These groups provided the nucleus of the participants at the London Congress in May 1901. This congress, which lasted three days, was attended predominantly by British and American delegates with a modest number from France, Switzerland and the Netherlands, but only a handful from Germany. It was a large gathering, with some of the sessions attended by over 2,000 people. The idea of a universal religion for all people seemed to appeal to many for whom the petty denominationalism of the past seemed to have little relevance for the problems of the modern world. Over the course of the congress around 770 people from 21 different religious groups and 15 countries joined the International Council.[14]

The overwhelming characteristic of the lectures in 1901 was one of an overarching unity that would overcome the outmoded dogmatisms of the past: a form of anti-dogmatic ecumenism was on the agenda from the beginning. Typical of the published lectures was that of Samuel McChord Crothers, Unitarian minister at the First Parish in Cambridge MA. Speaking on "The Sympathy of Religions," he told his audience: "Away with our pettiness and our littleness!"[15] In an era of mass communication and unprecedented levels of progress, he boldly proclaimed that the "day of petty thought" is past.[16] Instead it needed to be replaced with something quite different that would serve to meet the demands of the newly globalized world.

The great word of religion to-day is the word not of Protestantism, it is the word of Catholicity, a world-wide thing, a mighty triumphant thing; and we as Liberals need to give up once for all the idea that we are standing for "the dissidence of dissent," and to take our place manfully as leaders in that Catholicism, vaster in its sweep and more practical than that which Hildebrand ever dreamt of. The great word of the ancient creed given to us Liberals, and given to us because we are Liberals, is: "We believe in the Holy Catholic Church." We believe in the Church universal, and we work for the Church universal.[17]

It was this new form of ecumenism, he held, that would work beyond the church, by serving the wider task of overcoming the rule of force with its selfishness and greed. There consequently needed to be a genuine sympathy with people from all religions and denominations in order for the problems of the modern world to be overcome. This would lead to a new understanding of religion, which was no "less vital" and was as equally "imbued with the primitive instincts and hope of men" than the religions of some far-off age.[18]

Many of the other speakers echoed similar sentiments. For instance, Joseph Estlin Carpenter, president of the congress and professor at Manchester College, the free Christian college that had recently been built in Oxford, claimed that no single religion would ever be able to absorb all the others, but, instead, all would aspire after unity:

> In divers ways it is already at work, drawing together churches that were once divided, creating larger groups with broader liberties, breaking down barriers of suspicion or

---

14   International Association for Religious Freedom, ed., *Centennial Reflections: International Association for Religious Freedom (1900–2000)*, Assen, Van Gorcum, 2001, 17.

15   Samuel McChord Crothers, "The Sympathy of Religions," in: Bowie, ed., *Liberal Religious Thought*, 29–37, here 31.

16   Crothers, "The Sympathy of Religions," 30.

17   Crothers, "The Sympathy of Religions," 31.

18   Crothers, "The Sympathy of Religions," 36.

reserve by the discovery of common sympathies and the hope of common ends.[19]

Like many others, he expressed a belief in "the boundless future" that would move beyond any sanctuary made with hands. He concludes by citing Tennyson's "In Memoriam." The whole creation would be moving towards:

> That God, which ever lives and loves,
> One God, one law, one element,
> And one far-off divine event,
> To which the whole creation moves.[20]

Liberation from the dogmatic religion of the past would thereby offer a freedom that allowed all of creation to move further into God.

The speakers at the London Congress adopted different approaches to presenting the topic of liberal religion: this was hardly surprising given that the ways in which the phenomenon had developed depended on the particular national context. Many of the papers were reports on the current state of liberal religion in various countries around the world which ranged from America,[21] to Belgium,[22] to Russia.[23] While in some countries, including Italy,[24] liberal religion was marginal to mainstream Christianity, in other countries, most importantly France and Germany, varieties of liberal Protestantism had been able to establish themselves as movements within the historic denominations. This made them rather different from Britain and America where Unitarianism maintained a distinct denominational identity, even if some mainline churches were increasingly open to liberal influences.

The French example was described by the Paris Protestant pastor, Ernest Fontanès, author of *Le christianisme libéral*,[25] and well known to English liberals,[26] who adopted a historical overview of religious progress in France in which the Revolution had an important role: the key theme was that of "non-subscription." Although implicitly anti-Catholic in its attacks on dogmatism, the lecture nonetheless advocates what might be called an ecumenism of humanity based on a stripping away of Christianity of "its dry dogmatic husk."[27] This would be likely to convince lapsed clergy and would work at "retaining the multitudes, and in substituting for the old quarrels and schisms the methods of peace and a unity based on liberty."[28] The watchwords were the removal of superstition along with a greater desire for "a deeper moral and spiritual life and a genuine sincerity."[29] Attacking the decision to base the confession of the Reformed French church on the Apostles' Creed after 1872,[30] he sought a nonsectarian Christianity based on a principle of universal love. Similarly, in a short paper on the Protestant divinity schools in France, Gaston Bonet-Maury praises the decision of the

---

19   Joseph Estlin Carpenter, "The President's Address," in: Bowie, ed., *Liberal Religious Thought*, 1–18, here 11.

20   Carpenter, "The President's Address," 18.

21   Charles William Wendté, "Church and State in America," in: Bowie, ed., *Liberal Religious Thought*, 79–89.

22   James Hocart, "The Struggle Against Catholicism in Belgium," in: Bowie, ed., *Liberal Religious Thought*, 126–134.

23   Vladimir Tchertkoff, "The Thoughts and Experiences of a Liberal Religious Thinker and Worker in Russia," in: Bowie, ed., *Liberal Religious Thought*, 242–255.

24   L.E. Tony André, "The Liberal Movement in Italy," in: Bowie, ed., *Liberal Religious Thought*, 154–196, esp. 161.

25   Ernest Fontanès, *Le christianisme liberal: Sermons*, Paris, Sandoz et Fischbacher, 1874. On French liberal theology, see André Encrevé, ed., *Actes du Colloque Protestantisme et libéralisme à la fin du XIXᵉ siècle: Charles Wagner et le libéralisme théologique*, Geneva, Droz, 2008.

26   He had contributed a lengthy article on Dean Stanley, England's most prominent liberal churchman within the Church of England: Ernest Fontanès, "Dean Stanley from Two Points of View: Le Doyen de Westminster," *Macmillan's Magazine* 44, 1881, 450–466.

27   Ernest Fontanès, "The Contribution of France to Religious Progress," in: Bowie, ed., *Liberal Religious Thought*, 90–114, here 106.

28   Fontanès, "The Contribution of France," 107.

29   Fontanès, "The Contribution of France," 107.

30   Fontanès, "The Contribution of France," 99.

Geneva and Paris theological schools to remain free of the "orthodox Creed" which allowed them liberty of thought.[31]

Such liberty was the mechanism by which Fontanès felt that Christianity would be able to strip away what he called (borrowing from Baron von Bunsen, the erstwhile Prussian minister in London) the dialect of Canaan and replace it with something that should "fit its garment to its growth and invest the eternal truths in ever new and fresh forms, lest, being stereotyped in the expressions of another age, they become obscure and meaningless."[32] This was to be achieved through a very straightforward principle that could be summarized as "Back to Jesus," that is, a return to the purity and simplicity of the original Gospel message.[33] This was not, he held, the same as the Christ-mysticism so beloved of the Catholic Church, neither was it the empty speculation of what Jesus might say about our modern problems, but rather it was a drawing out for the present of the teachings of the "Fatherhood of God and the Brotherhood of Man."[34] True religion, Fontanès concluded, is about "basing man's trust in a principle of Supreme Love, trust that is in the Heavenly Father."[35]

In similar vein, the most prominent French liberal Protestant of the period, Jean Réville, editor of the *Revue de l'histoire des religions*, lectured on "The Mission of Liberal Protestants among Catholic Peoples."[36] The best mechanism for ensuring that children were preserved from Catholic influences, he claimed, was for them to join a liberal Protestant Church. Expansion of liberal churches, however, was not the only goal:

We must also, and in Catholic countries I should say we must chiefly, be the leaven of the social paste, seeking to inspire ever new instructive, educative and reformative movements, so as to summon people who are not Protestants to a high moral level, to spiritual life, to a holy passion for justice and truth, to the untrammeled love of God and of their brethren – that is, as Jesus said himself, to all that is comprehended in the Law and the Prophets. The Liberal Protestant must not be a man of the chapel but a man of the Spirit. ... The Lord Almighty will allow the seed to grow and the harvest to ripen, for liberal Protestantism is the real religion of the modern age. There are already in the world many Unitarians who are not members of any Unitarian church, and there will be many more as the years pass by.[37]

Liberal religion could thus become the leaven for a wider religious revival.

In Germany too there were many within the mainline Protestant Churches who sought a non-dogmatic form of Christianity.[38] These were represented at the 1901 London Congress by Otto Pfleiderer, professor of systematic theology in Berlin, who had drawn on Hegel's philosophical system and sought a wider unity between all people rather than an alliance of dogmatic forms of Christianity. Pfleiderer's approach followed a tradition that could be traced back to the aftermath of the revolutions of 1848–1849, in the fallout of which a number of Ferdinand Christian Baur's Tübingen students and prominent theologians founded the Deutscher Protestantenverein in 1863. Its vision of liberal theology was in part used as a weapon against Lutheran confessionalism and the authoritarian state. After the founding of the German Empire, the theologians of the Protestantenverein were keen to develop a model of a national church

---

31 Gaston Bonet-Maury, "The Protestant Schools of Divinity in France," in: Bowie, ed., *Liberal Religious Thought*, 121–125, here 123.

32 Fontanès, "The Contribution of France," 111.

33 Fontanès, "The Contribution of France," 111.

34 Fontanès, "The Contribution of France," 114.

35 Fontanès, "The Contribution of France," 114.

36 Jean Réville, "The Mission of Liberal Protestants among Catholic Peoples," in: Bowie, ed., *Liberal Religious Thought*, 115–120.

37 Réville, "The Mission of Liberal Protestants," 120.

38 On this see the excellent account by Hübinger, *Kulturprotestantismus und Politik*.

appropriate to the new conditions of empire. This could easily lead to the promotion of illiberal forms of nationalism under the guise of liberal theology. The Protestantenverein had been influenced by moves towards what the freethinker Arthur Bonus in his book *Deutscher Glaube* had called in 1897 a "Germanization of Christianity." This form of purified Christianity, Bonus had claimed, would free Christianity from the elaborate dogmatic systems of the past. "The Christian God," he had written, "is a God of churches. Churches are his castles. There is a census every seventh day. ... Then they return to the emptiness of their everyday life."[39] What was needed to counter such a tendency was a new myth to clear out such problematic doctrines as that of original sin.[40] Much of the liberal Protestantism that developed in the German Empire was hostile to Roman Catholicism, which it regarded as non-German and superstitious. A return to the "simplicity" of Jesus' message as the point of unification for all Christians could easily become a means for intolerance of those who remained tied to the perceived dogmatism of the Latin Church. The subsequent course of German history reveals many examples of how Germanized understandings of the Gospel could be manipulated by radical nationalists such as Houston Stewart Chamberlain.

The Protestantenverein had sent greetings to the London Congress through Friedrich W.F. Nippold, professor of church history at Jena. In his strongly anti-Catholic message, he saw the key threat to "all Protestants without exception – orthodox as well as liberal" to rest in the "ever-increasing power of the Papacy in all countries."[41] In his paper at the London Congress, Otto Pfleiderer, who had been involved in the Protestantenverein, spoke of "The Religious Crisis of Our Age,"[42] which he saw as the product principally of materialism and Darwinism. To counter this crisis what was required was a form of Christianity "set free from ancient bonds."[43] Dogmatic Christianity had become so enmeshed with false science, he held, that it needed to be liberated from half-truths to reveal the "permanent truth."[44] Pfleiderer promoted an anti-dogmatic and distinctly modern version of Christianity: "Traditional doctrines may fall to the ground; but religion, thus disburdened of antiquated forms, will arise in greater unity and more vital energy."[45] What is consequently required for the future, he continued, is a form of Christianity

> relieved of its traditional dogmatic bonds, so as to enable its ethical leavening power to advance with greater freedom and might for the welfare not only of individual souls, but also of social life as a whole. The spirits of the age, which seem to threaten its very existence, science, politics social and international, must be brought into the service of the one end, the liberation of the religion of Christ, conceived as the worship of God in spirit and in truth, from its narrow ecclesiastical bounds, and its advance to new victories throughout the wide world. Another Pentecost is on its way.[46]

The first congress set the pattern for the subsequent congresses that tackled similar issues and continued to maintain a nondogmatic ecumenical

---

39   Arthur Bonus, *Deutscher Glaube: Träumereien aus der Einsamkeit*, Heilbronn, Salzer, 1897, 53; and Arthur Bonus, "Zur Germanisierung des Christentums," *Die Christliche Welt* 13, 1899, 57–59, 81–85, 101–103, 125–127, 147–150, 171–173, 195–197 and 219–222.

40   On this see Christopher Koenig, "Germanisation of Christianity: Early Medieval Conversion History and the Search for German National Identity (1890–1940)," in: Jan N. Bremmer, Wout J. van Bekkum & Arie L. Molendijk, eds., *Paradigms, Poetics and the Politics of Conversion*, Leuven, Peeters, 2006, 149–164, esp. 155–156; Friedrich Wilhelm Graf, "Germanisierung des Christentums," *RGG* 3, 754.

41   Bowie, ed., *Liberal Religious Thought*, 330–333 ("Extracts from Correspondence"), here 332.

42   Otto Pfleiderer, "The Religious Crisis of Our Age," in: Bowie, ed., *Liberal Religious Thought*, 38–56.

43   Pfleiderer, "The Religious Crisis," 38.

44   Pfleiderer, "The Religious Crisis," 41.

45   Pfleiderer, "The Religious Crisis," 42.

46   Pfleiderer, "The Religious Crisis," 56.

impulse that was almost inevitably anti-Catholic and anti-traditionalist in its ethos.

4   Amsterdam 1903

The congresses of the International Committee continued through the next decade with meetings in Amsterdam in 1903, Geneva in 1905, Boston in 1907, Berlin in 1910, and Paris in 1913. The first three in particular continued in much the same manner as had been initiated at the first congress in London in 1901: there were reports on the progress of liberal religion across the world, as well as lectures on specific questions and problems. In Amsterdam, the geographical spread of the 900 delegates ranged from the United States to India, but among the papers there was surprisingly little that was strikingly different from the first conference. Unlike in London, the proceedings were printed in the original languages, including Dutch, French, and German, rather than solely in English translation, which gives the volume more of an international flavor, even though the majority of international delegates were the same as in 1901.[47] Otto Pfleiderer was once again the leading German figure present, although it was also noted in the welcomes to foreign delegates that the founder of the Deutscher Monistenbund, Albert Kalthoff, was unable to attend (and whose views were certainly not mainstream in German Protestantism at the time).[48]

In his address as general secretary, Charles Wendté was to speak about some of the milestones that had recently been achieved in liberal theology. He singled out the founding of the non-denominational *Hibbert Journal* in Britain which was to serve as a vehicle to promote the free investigation of religion.[49] He also gave a lengthy account of the state of liberal theology in Germany, where he spoke of the *Druck von oben* which prevented the expression of free Christianity in the state churches. Nevertheless, he noted that there had been a flourishing of "accurate scholarship, the profound learning and the deep philosophic speculation without which all religious freedom and advance would be impossible." There were, he went on, 150,000 members of the liberal Protestantenverein. Once again he revealed his aversion to dogmatic forms of Christianity. Consequently, he claimed, despite the restrictions on the exercise of free Christianity, it was still highly likely that

> the great majority of educated Germans secretly sympathize with the liberal position. This fact, together with the liberalizing influence of the German Universities, cannot but in time win the victory over tradition and dogma. The land of Luther and Kant and Schleiermacher cannot forever continue to display an entire religious indifference on the one hand and a bigoted churchism on the other. Sooner or later there will be a rebirth of rational and spiritual Christianity.[50]

Wendté's hope was that the German state churches would move towards an anti-dogmatic position which would inject a strong dose of humanistic ecumenism into worldwide Christianity. In part,

---

47   The papers and proceedings of the Amsterdam Congress were published as Petrus H. Hugenholtz, ed., *Religion and Liberty: Addresses and Papers at the Second International Council of Unitarian and Other Liberal Religious Thinkers and Workers, held in Amsterdam, September, 1903*, Leiden, E.J. Brill, 1904. See Robert Traer, "A Short History of the IARF," in: International Association for Religious Freedom, ed., *Centennial Reflections*, 17–32, esp. 18.

48   Hugenholtz, ed., *Religion and Liberty*, 20–39 ("Welcome to foreign delegates"), here 28–29.

49   Charles William Wendté, "Report of the Executive Committee of the International Council of Unitarian and Other Liberal Religious Thinkers and Workers," in: Hugenholtz, ed., *Religion and Liberty*, 49–70, here 58. *The Hibbert Journal: A Quarterly Review of Religion, Theology and Philosophy* was published in London from 1902 to 1968.

50   Wendté, "Report of the Executive Committee of the International Council of Unitarian and Other Liberal Religious Thinkers and Workers," 62–63.

according to Wendté, this was due to the impact of German *Wissenschaft* with its enormous international reputation.

From within Germany, a pastor of the Free Religious Association, Dr. C. Schieler from Danzig, in his account of the state of religion in Germany, spoke of the difficulties facing free Christians and of the exclusiveness of the established churches, each of which claimed to be the one true church.[51] Schieler was deeply critical of the current expressions of Christianity, especially what he called "Jesuitism," which he saw as robbing it of its true freedom.[52] What was needed instead was "the main task of Jesus of Nazareth, who furthered religion and religiosity by reclaiming the law of freedom and responsibility in religion and the fundamental law of his Gospel."[53] Schieler's alternative was simple: the promotion of a version of free Christianity based on a "Back to Jesus" ideal. This became the basis upon which to attack traditional versions of dogmatic Christianity.

Otto Pfleiderer's lecture, "Das Christusbild des urchristlichen Glauben in religionsgeschichtlicher Beleuchtung,"[54] is a relatively dispassionate account of Christian origins, but once again his reading of the past led to strong criticisms of dogmatic Christianity. He begins by describing the ways in which the early Christians had clothed the original message of Christ in new myths drawn from the history of natural religion as Christianity had gradually cast itself off from the bonds of Judaism.[55] It was quite clear, on Pfleiderer's account, that the Jewish legal and apocalyptic framework that had shaped Jesus' own presuppositions could never be relevant to all

times and places: it was instead simply part of the contingent realm of history. Against such contingency, Pfleiderer concluded: "It was an absolutely necessity that the universally valid and eternal ideal content of the principle of salvation should be established as an eternal form, thereby freeing it from the particular historical confines of his personal appearance."[56] The goal of theology, he held, was consequently to find the eternal form from within the historical distortions of dogma. In this way, Pfleiderer sought to show that by using history we should be able to liberate ourselves from history in order to find the eternal God, who was, in biblical language, "the God of the living, not of the dead" (Mark 12:27).[57] On this basis, Pfleiderer concluded, we will be able to make the salvation myth present once again.[58] The version of ecumenism promoted by liberals was thus established on particular readings of history and dogma.

5　　Geneva 1903

Two years later, the congress met in Geneva.[59] Of the 568 persons registered, about 240 came from the United Kingdom (almost all Unitarians), 30 from the United States, and 80 from France. The latter came from a variety of churches and included an unnamed Roman Catholic priest, "Abbé X" as well as the well-known Modernist Albert Houtin, who would later attend the 1907 congress in Boston. There were also 170 from Switzerland including Emilie Loyson Meriman, American-born wife of the well-known French Gallican priest, Hyacinthe Loyson. She had shortly beforehand published an account of her travels, *To Jerusalem through the Lands of Islam among*

51　C. Schieler, "Befürchtungen und Hoffnungen bezüglich der religiösen Frage in Deutschland," in: Hugenholtz, ed., *Religion and Liberty*, 204–226, here 211. See also Paul Drews, "Die freien religiösen Gemeinden der Gegenwart," *ZThK* 11, 1901, 484–527.

52　Schieler, "Befürchtungen," 217.

53　Schieler, "Befürchtungen," 219.

54　Otto Pfleiderer, "Das Christusbild des urchristlichen Glaubens in religionsgeschichtlicher Beleuchtung," in: Hugenholtz, ed., *Religion and Liberty*, 251–271.

55　Pfleiderer, "Das Christusbild," 269.

56　Pfleiderer, "Das Christusbild," 269.

57　Pfleiderer, "Das Christusbild," 270–271.

58　Pfleiderer, "Das Christusbild," 270.

59　The papers and proceedings were published in: Edouard Montet, ed., *Actes du IIIme Congrès international du christianisme libéral et progressif, Genève 1905*, Geneva, Georg, 1906. On the congress, see Traer, "A Short History of the IARF," 18.

Jews, Christians, and Moslems.[60] She lectured on a related theme at the congress ("The Religious Condition of Oriental Women") in which she drew on her experiences and revealed a strong sympathy for the other religions of the Middle East.

There were other examples of a greater focus on other religions than had been the case at earlier congresses. A French Jewish delegate, for instance, Rabbi Louis-Germain Lévy, spoke on liberal Judaism.[61] Perhaps most interesting was the presence of members of the monotheistic Indian Brahmo Somaj movement. Benoyendra Nath Sen of Presidency College in Calcutta spoke of the importance of a universal spiritual religion as a sign of a greater unity between people of different religions.[62] In words that are almost identical to the majority of Western liberal Christians, he thought that all religion should find its focus in the teaching of Christ, liberated from dogma: "Liberal religion in India, therefore, looks up with the most eager yearning to Christ – not the Christ of dogma, but the living Christ as he is in the Christian consciousness of the West. It is this living contact with the living Christ that is necessary for our salvation."[63] This approach might indicate something of the success of missionary work in India in Christianizing Hinduism.[64]

Despite its relative proximity, the Geneva Congress attracted a mere nine Germans, including Pfleiderer, who had become a member of the organizing committee, as well as Adolf von Harnack, who had already become one of the most prominent figures in German theology after

the success of *Das Wesen des Christentums.* The Protestantenverein was represented by its president, the liberal politician, Karl Schrader, and Dr. Julius Websky its secretary. In his "Report of the Executive Committee," Wendté mentioned the visits of Harnack and Pfleiderer to the United States for the Congress of Arts and Sciences that accompanied the Louisiana Purchase Exhibition at St. Louis. This trip had helped establish the reputation of German scholarship across the Atlantic.[65] Pfleiderer's lecture in Geneva resembled that from two years' earlier in Amsterdam. It was summarized in a "Thesis on the Origin of the Christian Doctrine of Redemption," which was published in an appendix to the volume.[66] Once again, Pfleiderer clamored for the nondogmatic essence of Christianity: "We are authorized, by the example of the early Church, which renounced faith in the Millennium, to give up that which is temporal, as the mere fleeting form of the Christian doctrine of redemption. What remains as the indestructible essence of that belief, is the moral ideal of the personal redemption of humanity, by the solidarity created by love between its members, love which succours and educates."[67] The abiding essence of Christianity rested in the love expressed by human solidarity.

6 Boston 1907

The next congress was held two years later in Boston, which was a much more substantial affair with 2,391 participants.[68] Of the 172 non-Americans, 122

---

60 Emilie Loyson, *To Jerusalem through the Lands of Islam among Jews, Christians, and Moslems*, Chicago IL, Open Court Publishing Co., 1905.

61 Loyson, *To Jerusalem through the Lands of Islam*, 120–128.

62 Nath Sen, "The Problem of Religion in Modern India," in: Montet, ed., *Actes du IIIme Congrès international du christianisme libéral et progressif*, 102–109, here 103.

63 Sen, "The Problem of Religion," 107.

64 See Mark D. Chapman, "Exporting Godliness: The Church, Education and 'Higher Civilization' in the British Empire from the Late Nineteenth Century," *SCH* 55, 2019, 381–409.

65 Charles William Wendté, "Report of the Executive Committee," in: Montet, ed., *Actes du IIIme Congrès international du christianisme libéral et progressif*, 12–20, here 17.

66 Otto Pfleiderer, "Thesis on the Origin of the Christian Doctrine of Redemption," in: Montet, ed., *Actes du IIIme Congrès international du christianisme libéral et progressif*, appendix, 29–30.

67 Pfleiderer, "Thesis," 30.

68 Charles William Wendté, ed., *Freedom and Fellowship in Religion: Proceedings and Papers of the Fourth International Congress of Religious Liberals held at*

came from Great Britain with only a modest num-ber from other countries. As with the earlier con-gresses, the vast bulk were from free Christian and Unitarian churches. There were, however, some representatives from other religions, including the liberal Boston rabbi, Charles Fleischer. There were again a number of Indians present, including Gokura Suuba Rau and S.L. Joshi. There was also a lecture on "Liberal Mohammedanism" by Maulana Barkatullah of Bhopal.[69] As in Geneva, a number of Catholics attended, including Albert Houtin.[70] In his secretary's report Wendté again pointed to the importance of liberalism as a religious dispo-sition that was fundamentally opposed to dogma-tism and orthodoxy:

> Liberalism is to us a temper, an attitude of the mind, a disposition of the heart towards truth. Liberalism is the supremacy of the spirit over the letter in religion. It is the mind in a state of growth, and is thus differentiated from orthodoxy, which is the type of a mind that has stopped growing, which accepts finalities in religion and claims that its opin-ions are infallible. ... The true liberal not only speaks the truth but he speaks it in love ... He is not impatient with error if it be error held in the spirit of truth. The only unpardonable sin in his eyes is uncharity, – a loveless heart, an intolerant mind.[71]

He concluded with an ecumenical flourish: "Where the spirit of the Lord is, there is liberty," ending with an injunction to "build the Universal Church."[72]

Many others echoed Wendté's sentiments. For instance, Max Fischer, liberal pastor of St. Mark's Church in Berlin, speaking about "The Protestantenverein of Germany," noted the "Prot-estant conviction of the inwardness and freedom of all true religion."[73] Similarly, in his address, Samuel A. Eliot, president of the AUA, spoke of the importance of the reinterpretation of the Christian tradition that would lead to "certain positive and universal principles of thought and conduct. ... The great convictions we hold in common rest not on the authentication of any ancient book, not on any decree of Council or of Church, but on their appeal to the conscience, reason, and experience of men."[74]

There was some discussion of Roman Catholi-cism in the wake of the recently released sylla-bus *Lamentabili sane exitu* in which Pope Pius X had condemned a number of propositions drawn from Modernist writings. This had been followed by the encyclical *Pascendi dominici gregis* which condemned Modernism and was published in the same month as the congress. The leading French Protestant Jean Réville of the Sorbonne, for instance, responded to Modernism in the context of the 1905 law of separation between church and state in France:

> Some men of great sense, and amongst them my friend Paul Sabatier, with whose greeting for the Congress I am entrusted, think that a reaction will ensue from the exaggeration

Boston, U.S.A., September 22–27, 1907, Boston MA, International Council, 1907.

69 Mohammed Barakatullah, "The Liberal Mohammed-anism in India," in: Wendté, ed., *Freedom and Fellow-ship in Religion*, 542–545.

70 See C.J.T. Talar, "A Modernist among Liberals: Albert Houtin at the Fourth International Congress of Religious Liberals," *U.S. Catholic Historian* 20/3, 2002, 23–31.

71 Charles William Wendté, "Report of the Executive Committee of the International Council: Presented by Rev. Charles W. Wendté, of Boston, General Secretary," in: Wendté, ed., *Freedom and Fellowship in Religion*, 53–65, here 64.

72 Wendté, "Report of the Executive Committee of the International Council: Presented by Rev. Charles W. Wendté, of Boston, General Secretary," 64.

73 Max Fischer, "The Protestantenverein of Germany," in: Wendté, ed., *Freedom and Fellowship in Religion*, 76–88, here 83.

74 Samuel A. Eliot, "Opening Address of the President, Rev. Samuel A. Eliot, D.D.," in: Wendté, ed., *Freedom and Fellowship in Religion*, 48–52, here 50.

of this papal absolutism. They hope for a real Catholic regeneration, both democratic and scientific, wherein old dogmas shall be left to sleep in peace and all energies shall be consecrated to the social and moral work.[75]

Réville was aware that a liberal spirit had made considerable inroads among a group of scholars, including Alfred Loisy, Lucien Laberthonnière, and Albert Houtin. He nevertheless thought that it could never succeed in the face of absolutist dogma, which was exemplified by the papacy, which was "the real impediment for any Catholic reform."[76] "The pope," he continued, "carries to the utmost his intellectual absolutism as well as his ecclesiastical absolutism. The schism between the public mind and the Roman Catholic mind … thus grows worse every day."[77] What is clear from Réville's discussion is that the sort of ecumenism exemplified by the congress could make little progress with any form of religion which continued to maintain a strong dogmatic system. In much the same way, in his article on Modernism in Italy, Tony André praised the movement, but also felt that Modernists could never be contained within the Roman Catholic Church, but would have "to form a separate party, and create a new form of national and liberal Catholicism."[78]

While in the eyes of those who attended the congress, Roman Catholic Modernism was doomed to failure in the face of Catholic dogmatism, things were looking more positive for liberals in Germany where there had been significant progress in spreading the liberal message in the Protestant state churches. Although the location of the congress on the other side of the Atlantic meant that

there were only seven Germans able to attend, it is important to note that, along with Pfleiderer and Max Fischer, another German, Martin Rade, professor of theology at Marburg and one of the key figures in German liberal Protestantism, had joined the committee.[79] In his lecture, Rade spoke about "The Religious Situation in Germany and the Freunde der Christlichen Welt."[80] According to Rade, Germany was far behind Britain and the United States in the progress of liberal religion. Germans, he held, were "too inclined to go our own way in matters of church and religion."[81] This meant that there was unlikely to be any successful ecumenism except among conservative churchmen who adopted a dogmatic expression of Christianity. After describing the situation of the state church, Rade then went on to outline the complex theological situation[82] which made it very difficult for liberals, who were forced to organize themselves around newspapers and groups including the Protestantenverein along with Freunde der Christlichen Welt. *Die Christliche Welt* was a liberal Protestant newspaper that had been published since 1887 and which had been owned by Rade from 1899. From 1892 a group of friends of the journal met regularly to discuss important theological topics forming what became the Freunde der Christlichen Welt: the initial controversy had been over the use of the Apostles' Creed.[83] In his lecture, Rade summarized the aims of the movement:

75   Jean Réville, "The Situation of the Churches in France after the Separation of Church and State," in: Wendté, ed., *Freedom and Fellowship in Religion*, 89–97, here 95.

76   Réville, "The Situation of the Churches in France."

77   Réville, "The Situation of the Churches in France," 95.

78   L.E. Tony André, "Modernism and Modernists in Italy: A Study of the Present Situation of Catholicism," in: Wendté, ed., *Freedom and Fellowship in Religion*, 200–217, here 215.

79   Wendté, ed., *Freedom and Fellowship in Religion*, 4.

80   Martin Rade, "The Religious Situation in Germany and the Freunde der Christlichen Welt," in: Wendté, ed., *Freedom and Fellowship in Religion*, 100–114.

81   Rade, "The Religious Situation in Germany," 100.

82   Rade, "The Religious Situation in Germany," 107.

83   Rade, "The Religious Situation in Germany," 110. The group produced a private journal that has been published in facsimile: Vereinigung der Freunde der Christlichen Welt, ed., *An die Freunde: Vertrauliche d.i. nicht für die Öffentlichkeit bestimmte Mitteilungen (1903–1934)*, ed. Christoph Schwöbel, Berlin, De Gruyter, 1993. See also Hübinger, *Kulturprotestantismus und Politik*, and Johannes Rathje, *Die Welt des freien Protestantismus: Ein Beitrag zur deutsch-evangelischen*

We stand, before everything else, for the unconditional freedom of theological scholarship, and especially that of historical criticism. We know very well that no church and no religion can live on criticism and the negations which inevitably go with it. But we know also that the search for the truth must be completely unrestricted if it is to have any meaning at all, that the truth is a fact which reveals itself, and of itself compels recognition, while much in accepted tradition becomes untenable on careful examination.[84]

Although the Freunde understood themselves as a purely theological movement, rather than as one concerned with church politics, their agenda was clearly reformist.[85] Indeed the circle around *Die Christliche Welt* reacted against some of the earlier models of liberal theology, such as the statist model of the Heidelberg theologian Richard Rothe, and sought instead to find a form of cultural unity under the conditions of modernity against the various conservative and fanatical alternatives.[86] In his Boston lecture, Rade noted that about half of all German professors belonged to the Freunde der Christlichen Welt which was established to fight for free speech and doctrinal and church reform.[87] He concluded by pointing to the importance of international cooperation between German and English speakers in order to achieve

a more exact knowledge of the very different conditions which prevail, and a better understanding of the nature of each other's religion. If this is accomplished, then the result will surely be that each will have from the other some new gain for the inner life. And

thereby, too, our right of existence and the propagation of a truly religious Liberalism will have been furthered in the best possible manner.[88]

What is crucial here is the awareness on Rade's part both of German isolation from the wider liberal religious world, but also of the possibility of a liberal ecumenism that would eventually be dominated by the German professoriate that was unrivalled in its learning. Others, too, were beginning to take note of German scholarship in worldwide liberalism: many German professors who had been invited to the congress, but were unable to attend, sent messages of greeting, including the psychologist Rudolf Eucken, the New Testament scholars Hans Hinrich Wendt, Heinrich Weinel, and Wilhelm Bousset, and the most well-known liberal systematic theologian Ernst Troeltsch.[89] Three years later, the congress was held in Germany, which meant that the German voice would completely transform the nature of liberal ecumenism.

7   Berlin 1910

The openness towards liberal ecumenism that had been very tentatively displayed by Pfleiderer in the earlier congresses and by Rade in Boston was transformed in 1910 into something quite distinct as Germans came to dominate the congress, which had changed its name to the World Congress of Free Christianity and Religious Progress, a name change that served to distance it from Unitarian denominationalism.[90] The organizing body had

---

Geistesgeschichte dargestellt an Leben und Werk von Martin Rade, Stuttgart, Klotz, 1952.

84   Rade, "The Religious Situation in Germany," 111.
85   Hübinger, *Kulturprotestantismus und Politik*, 60.
86   Hübinger, *Kulturprotestantismus und Politik*, 142.
87   Rade, "The Religious Situation in Germany," 113.

88   Rade, "The Religious Situation in Germany," 114.
89   Wendté, ed., *Freedom and Fellowship in Religion*, 630–648.
90   The translations were published in: Wendté, ed., *Fifth International Congress*. The papers were also published in German: Max Fischer & Friedrich Michael Schiele, eds., *Fünfter Weltkongresses für Freies Christentum und Religiösen Fortschritt: Berlin, 5. bis 10. August 1910: Protokoll der Verhandlungen*, Berlin-Schoneberg, Protestantischer Schriftenvertrieb, 1910.

similarly changed its name to the International Congress of Free Christians and Other Religious Liberals: the ecumenical intentions are clear in the desire to avoid denominational labels.[91] The Berlin Congress provoked a great deal of discussion about the importance of international ecumenical cooperation among the members of the Freunde der Christlichen Welt in the pages of its private journal *An die Freunde*, even though only about 45 or so of its members came from outside the German-speaking world, most of whom were German expatriates:[92] there was a lengthy correspondence about the relationship between German Protestantism and what was called Anglo-Saxon free Christianity.[93]

The Berlin Congress was in many ways a showpiece for liberal German theology and church life. Around 150 pages of the proceedings and papers are devoted to this subject,[94] with many of the leading figures in liberal theology represented. These included Adolf von Harnack, who spoke on "The Double Gospel in the New Testament," and Ernst Troeltsch, the so-called "systematic theologian of the History of Religion School,"[95] who spoke "On the Possibility of a Free Christianity." Other members of the School were also represented, including Hermann Gunkel of Gießen, who spoke on "The History of Religion and Old Testament Criticism," and Wilhelm Bousset of Göttingen, who lectured on "The Significance of the Personality of Jesus for Belief." Others included Otto Baumgarten of Kiel, Friedrich Niebergall of Heidelberg, Hermann Freiherr von Soden of Berlin, and Arthur Titius of Göttingen. Many of

the participating Germans were associated with what Gangolf Hübinger has called the "spiritual emblem of the era," the first edition of *Die Religion in Geschichte und Gegenwart*, published by Paul and Oskar Siebeck at Jacob Christian Benjamin Mohr, along with more popular works, such as the *Religionsgeschichtliche Volksbücher*.[96] This was a form of culture-Protestantism that sought to embed liberal theology within the wider society rather than seeing religion simply as an act of free choice for the individual. Tellingly, the motto of the congress was "Einheit durch Freiheit."[97]

What is perhaps most significant about German theology in comparison to the other countries in which liberal theology had gained significant expression is the close connection between the professoriate and the German state: whereas free Christianity in most other parts of the world was characterized by its independence from the state, the development of the sort of liberalism represented by these German professors was closely entwined with the *Landeskirchen* and the state university system in which they were working. German liberalism was associated particularly with education, or *Bildung*, and the creation of what was often referred to as *Persönlichkeit*, which focused on the German idea of freedom whereby the individual found a social location in the wider society. In his lecture on "Religious Education in Germany," for instance, Baumgarten speaks of the importance of education in the home, which had been so frequently dropped in the "name of Protestant freedom, in confidence in the religious spirit which, left to itself and freed from the tyranny of the letter of the law, will create its own suitable forms." This, he felt, had robbed national and family life "of all educational power" and "must be changed" through a "religious attitude of mind." Consequently, he suggested, "the German Lutheran Church can receive important

91   Traer, "A Short History of the IARF," 20.

92   There are registers of members at the end of some editions of *An die Freunde*; see *An die Freunde* 32, 1910, cols. 353–364.

93   See for example the "Jahresbericht 1908/09," *An die Freunde* 30, 1909, cols. 301–305. See also Hübinger, *Kulturprotestantismus und Politik*, 251–262.

94   Wendté, ed., *Fifth International Congress*, 99–252 ("A Presentation of German Theology and German Church Life").

95   See Ernst Troeltsch, "The Dogmatics of the 'Religionsgeschichtlichen Schule,'" *AJT* 17, 1913, 1–21.

96   Hübinger, *Kulturprotestantismus und Politik*, 303.

97   Wendté, ed., *Fifth International Congress*, 11.

suggestions from the Protestant Anglican Church in England."[98]

The themes of the German presentations are familiar: a great deal of emphasis is placed on the presence of a universal nondogmatic humanistic Gospel of love beneath the dogmatic myths: Harnack, for instance, uses ideas he had earlier expounded in his lectures on *Das Wesen des Christentums*:

> The paramount issue today is not the miraculous or non-miraculous, but the question whether the soul of man has an eternal value which distinguishes it from all else; whether moral goodness is a conventional product, or a life-principle of the spirit; and whether there be a living and saving God or not.
>
> He who denies these questions, and they are denied in large circles at the present time, practically as well as in the name of Science, must reject Jesus' Gospel of the Kingdom of Heaven, and all the ideas, thoughts and prescriptions of the Sermon on the Mount. He must put in their place an entirely new ethic if indeed an ethic can be spoken of at all.[99]

Similarly, in his masterly account of the history of religion and the Old Testament, Gunkel writes that his aim is not to prove the absoluteness of Christianity but rather to show that "the historian in whose eyes the history of mankind is a Unity, cannot separate into two halves the evolution of what is Christian and what belongs to other religions."[100] The human universal was thus not simply a contemporary problem but characterized the study of the past, through the principle of

analogy. Crucially, Gunkel held, there was nothing to fear from such an account of religion. Instead "religion will shine forth all the more brightly in its marvellous greatness" and make "the treasures of the Bible dearer and more valuable than ever."[101]

In his extremely lengthy paper, Arthur Titius extends these themes in relation to the ethics of development and evolution. These issues again show that "in matters of faith and world-philosophy," we cannot "keep back the universal progress of mankind."[102] Evolution reveals that life is ever in development:

> Evolution is a Becoming, it is relativity, whereas according to [sic] old point of view, the moral laws and ideals are absolutely binding, absolutely unalterable. We have already been compelled to recognize that the moral ideals are indeed a Becoming and a Growing, becoming and growing in and with all spiritual life. History as well as Ethnology are unmistakable witnesses to the truth of this.[103]

Ultimately, he feels, this should lead to a form of Christian optimism

> to the hope that in spite of all opposition in small things, the power of development as a whole will still be triumphant, and that in spite of obstacles and retrogressions, mankind will never be forsaken by God but will keep on developing itself in an upward direction; and this belief fits in perfectly with our Christian optimism, our conviction that the influence of the saving love of God has not ceased even today.[104]

98   Otto Baumgarten, "Religious Education in Germany," in: Wendté, ed., *Fifth International Congress*, 201–207, here 207.

99   Adolf von Harnack, "The Double Gospel in the New Testament," in: Wendté, ed., *Fifth International Congress*, 99–107, here 105.

100   Hermann Gunkel, "The History of Religion and Old Testament Criticism," in: Wendté, ed., *Fifth International Congress*, 114–125, here 124.

101   Gunkel, "The History of Religion," 125.

102   Arthur Titius, "The Place and Limitations of the Theory of Evolution in Ethics," in: Wendté, ed., *Fifth International Congress*, 161–184, here 162.

103   Titius, "The Place and Limitations of the Theory of Evolution in Ethics," 166.

104   Titius, "The Place and Limitations of the Theory of Evolution in Ethics," 183.

A nondogmatic liberal religion would thus redirect Christianity towards the saving love of God and away from the pettiness of dogmatic religion.

From a different perspective, the New Testament scholar, Wilhelm Bousset, spoke of the difficulty of coming to an understanding of Jesus' life and his personality which could never be known in its true simplicity. This was because it was the dogma of the early communities that had distorted our "knowledge of the real facts of His life," about which we could know no more than "could be written on a slip of paper." He continued:

> The teaching or the Gospel of Jesus is a web often not to be disentangled, woven of the tradition of His community, and of possibly true words of the Master. What the Gospels tell us about the peculiar self-consciousness of Jesus, and its forms and therefore about His innermost life, is overshadowed by the dogma of His community.[105]

Despite this, history was nevertheless still important, since it

> is not merely a play and a succession of indifferent occurrences or even the corruption of original disposition, it is an act; for religion rests in the depths of human consciousness and to take possession consciously of these depths and affirm them is the weary toilsome labour which is effected in history.[106]

In the end, then, Jesus was understood as "the creative genius, who created the fundamental symbols of our belief and became Himself in His personality as represented to us in the Gospel entangled in an inextricable web of historical truth and fiction of His people the permanent

most efficacious symbol of our faith."[107] Once again, as with so much liberal theology, there was a fundamental animus against forms of dogmatic Christianity which had always served to distort the purity of the original Gospel.

In his discussion of the possibility of a free Christianity, which rounded off the contributions of the German theologians, Ernst Troeltsch spoke of two key themes as characterizing the phenomenon: first, he notes the way in which "it replaces the authority of the Church by an inward personal spirit born of the powerful communal mind which has evolved freely and unfettered in the individual." Secondly, he points to the transfiguration of "the ancient conception of a miraculous healing of mankind – sick unto death by reason of sin, into that of man's self elevated, liberated, saved, by winning a higher personal life from God."[108] Troeltsch's key question in discussing these twin themes, however, was whether free Christianity "contains in itself anything which is actually possible, anything which can live; or whether it is merely the last echo of a dying Christianity."[109] In trying to answer this question he suggests that no amount of the available alternatives of Rationalism or monism would ever be able to thwart the prophetic strand of Christianity which alone offered some basis for hope.[110] In addressing the second theme, Troeltsch emphasizes what he calls "Christ-mysticism" as central to the Christian religion, which helped to liberate it from its alternative, that is purely dogmatic forms. This sort of mysticism, he held, was something universal for all human beings. Consequently, Troeltsch writes:

---

105 Wilhelm Bousset, "The Significance of the Personality of Jesus for Belief," in: Wendté, ed., *Fifth International Congress*, 208–221, here 209.

106 Bousset, "The Significance of the Personality of Jesus for Belief," 215.

107 Bousset, "The Significance of the Personality of Jesus for Belief," 221.

108 Ernest Troeltsch, "On the Possibility of a Free Christianity," in: Wendté, ed., *Fifth International Congress*, 233–252, here 233.

109 Troeltsch, "On the Possibility of a Free Christianity," 234.

110 Troeltsch, "On the Possibility of a Free Christianity," 237.

Christian Theism, however, is not a decaying religion; it is the firm support of all that part of mankind which clings to the belief in Personality. In that case, our highest human powers and convictions, so far ahead as we can see, remain bound up with devotion to the historic communal life founded by Jesus.[111]

This leads Troeltsch on to a discussion of the importance of the community as the focus for the sociological expression of this mystical power of Christ in forming personality, which, he felt, was so often under threat in the modern world. Even though there is little to guarantee that such a sociological form would emerge, in the end what was important was that "whatever may become of our search after a free Christianity, God sits upon the throne and His Truth will be victorious. The vital thing is not that we should rescue Christianity, but that we trust in the victory of God."[112] In the end, according to Troeltsch, the whole edifice of Christianity might tumble down but God would still remain victorious.

8   Conclusions

Three years after the Berlin Congress, the next meeting took place in Paris where William Hamilton Drummond took over as conference secretary from Wendté. It continued in much the same vein as the earlier congresses, but with a significantly more modest representation from Germany. The international atmosphere in the years immediately before World War I did little to improve the ecumenical situation, which meant that the conference made little impact. The proceedings were published only in France, which means that their readership in the United States and Britain was limited.[113] Charles Wendté published a short book outlining the course of the congress, which reveals little that was new.[114] The Paris Congress certainly did not celebrate the achievements of German theology as had been done in 1910. Indeed, it was the Berlin Congress that marked the high point of what might be called "nondogmatic ecumenism" or the "ecumenism of humanity" as the liberal theology, which had grown within the German churches and which was represented by a significant proportion of Protestant professors of theology, began to shift away from the denominational basis which had characterized its expression in the Anglo-American world. The shift may not have lasted for long, and was soon cut off after German liberal theology was quickly associated with Prussian militarism, but it was important while it lasted in reshaping theology across the world.[115] Its association with the state churches, however, allowed Karl Barth and many others to dismiss liberal Protestantism as little more than an apology for German *Kultur*.[116]

In terms of the history of ecumenism, this survey of the congresses of religious liberals in the early years of the 20th century, which has inevitably been highly selective, has revealed a sense of unity that is based on a shared understanding of Christianity. What unites the contributors to the congresses is a perception that the essence of Christianity rests in a humanistic universalism that moves beyond any form of doctrinal Christianity, variously articulated as Christ-mysticism or as the

111   Troeltsch, "On the Possibility of a Free Christianity," 241.

112   Troeltsch, "On the Possibility of a Free Christianity," 249.

113   John Viénot, ed., *Travaux du 6e Congrès international du progrès religieux (chrétiens progressifs et libres-croyants), Paris, 1913*, Paris, Librairie Fischbacher, 1913.

114   Charles William Wendté, ed., *Religious Liberals in Council: An Appreciation of the Sixth International Congress of Religious Progress, Paris, France, July 16–22, 1913*, Boston MA, G.H. Ellis Co., 1913.

115   See Mark D. Chapman, *Theology at War and Peace: English Theology and Germany in the First World War*, London, Routledge, 2017, esp. 81–105.

116   See Mark D. Chapman, *Ernst Troeltsch and Liberal Theology: Religion and Cultural Synthesis in Wilhelmine Germany*, Oxford, Oxford University Press, 2001, esp. ch. 1.

expression of love. Perhaps ironically, however, the corollary of such an understanding makes nondogmatic ecumenism inevitably antagonistic to traditional expressions of Christianity, which are understood as stultifying the expression of the Gospel. Given the Protestant background to religious liberalism, it is hardly surprising that the obvious expression of animosity was towards Roman Catholicism. However, where liberal Christians began to gain ground within the mainline churches, especially in the German state churches, there were also frequent attacks on dogmatic Protestantism. What this reveals is an ecumenism of the like-minded which failed to move far from its own presuppositions by engaging with difference: here there is perhaps a similar sense of triumphalism which was expressed in other gatherings from the period, not least in Edinburgh in the same year as the Berlin Congress. A nondogmatic ecumenism based on a universalist understanding of humanity and its religion is as much a product of the wider circumstances of the period as the dogmatic Christianity expressed at such imperialist gatherings as the 1908 Pan-Anglican Congress in London.

Bibliography

Primary Sources

Bowie, W. Copeland, ed., *Liberal Religious Thought at the Beginning of the Twentieth Century: Addresses and Papers at the International Council of Unitarian and Other Liberal Religious Thinkers and Workers, held in London, May, 1901*, London, P. Green, 1901.

Fischer, Max & Friedrich Michael Schiele, eds., *Fünfter Weltkongresses für Freies Christentum und Religiösen Fortschritt: Berlin, 5. bis 10. August 1910: Protokoll der Verhandlungen*, Berlin-Schoneberg, Protestantischer Schriftenvertrieb, 1910.

Hugenholtz, Petrus H., ed., *Religion and Liberty: Addresses and Papers at the Second International Council of Unitarian and Other Liberal Religious Thinkers and Workers, held in Amsterdam, September, 1903*, Leiden, E.J. Brill, 1904.

Montet, Edouard, ed., *Actes du IIIᵐᵉ Congrès international du christianisme libéral et progressif, Genève 1905*, Geneva, Georg, 1906.

Viénot, John, ed., *Travaux du 6e Congrès international du progrès religieux (chrétiens progressifs et libres-croyants), Paris, 1913*, Paris, Librairie Fischbacher, 1913.

Wendté, Charles William, ed., *Fifth International Congress of Free Christianity and Religious Progress, Berlin, August 5–10, 1910: Proceedings and Papers*, Berlin-Schöneberg, Protestantischer Schriftenvertrieb, 1911.

Wendté, Charles William, ed., *Freedom and Fellowship in Religion: Proceedings and Papers of the Fourth International Congress of Religious Liberals held at Boston, U.S.A., September 22–27, 1907*, Boston MA, International Council, 1907.

Wendté, Charles William, ed., *Religious Liberals in Council: An Appreciation of the Sixth International Congress of Religious Progress, Paris, France, July 16–22, 1913*, Boston MA, G.H. Ellis Co., 1913.

Secondary Literature

Cauthen, Kenneth, *The Impact of American Religious Liberalism*, New York NY, Harper & Row, 1962.

Chapman, Mark D., *Ernst Troeltsch and Liberal Theology: Religion and Cultural Synthesis in Wilhelmine Germany*, Oxford, Oxford University Press, 2001.

Hübinger, Gangolf, *Kulturprotestantismus und Politik: Zum Verhältnis von Liberalismus und Protestantismus im wilhelminischen Deutschland*, Tübingen, Mohr Siebeck, 1994.

International Association for Religious Freedom, ed., *Centennial Reflections: International Association for Religious Freedom (1900–2000)*, Assen, Van Gorcum, 2001.

Rathje, Johannes, *Die Welt des freien Protestantismus: Ein Beitrag zur deutsch-evangelischen Geistesgeschichte dargestellt an Leben und Werk von Martin Rade*, Stuttgart, Klotz, 1952.

Vereinigung der Freunde der Christlichen Welt, ed., *An die Freunde: Vertrauliche d.i. nicht für die Öffentlichkeit bestimmte Mitteilungen (1903–1934)*, ed. Christoph Schwöbel, Berlin, De Gruyter, 1993.

CHAPTER 17

The American Social Gospel: Christian Socialism, Neo-Abolitionism, and Ecumenism

Gary Dorrien

1   Introduction

The American Social Gospel was one of the movements for Christian socialism and social Christianity that swept across England, continental Europe, and North America in the late 19th and early 20th centuries. However, even though it was an example of historic international trend, it was utterly distinct within this phenomenon for the American Social Gospel was a cultural earthquake that could be called the Third Great Awakening. It had an impact on US society that has no analogy anywhere else owing to America's Puritan heritage and its separation between church and state. The Social Gospel permanently redefined liberal theology in the United States, fusing almost completely with the liberal theology movement.[1] It created the field of social ethics, providing the field's only basis for 50 years. It not merely founded the ecumenical movement in the United States, but for many years *was* the ecumenical movement in the United States, as it influenced and groomed a generation of Christian actors, driving them and their churches beyond confessional borders on issues related to a common society. The Social Gospel had two major historic wellsprings: one Social Gospel came out of historic white Protestant Churches and was primarily about economic domination and ethical corruption; the other

came out of black Protestant Churches and was primarily about forging a new abolitionism.

The white Social Gospel, founded by Congregationalists, Episcopalians, and Baptists in the 1880s, was a response to the charge that churches did not care about exploited workers. This part of the Social Gospel story is broadly familiar because it emerged out of white middle-class churches that confronted a rising trade union movement and inspired a vast literature. Organizers for the Knights of Labor and other unions blasted the churches for doing nothing for poor and working-class people. The white middle-class ministers who founded Social Gospel organizations took this accusation personally and resolved to do something about it.

The black Social Gospel, founded by Methodists, Baptists, and Episcopalians in the 1880s, was an attempt to create a new abolitionism. It arose as a response to the abandonment of Reconstruction and an upsurge of racial terrorism. The founders of the black Social Gospel had no choice concerning what they should oppose, since it was forced upon them by oppression, exclusion, and a terrifying mania of racist lynching. The black Social Gospel had the same Progressive political concerns about economic domination and winning the support of the federal government that marked the white Social Gospel, but here the orienting question was horrifyingly specific: what would a new abolitionism require in a post-Reconstruction context of unleashed racist hatred? The black Social Gospel, especially in its Christian socialist stream that led to Martin Luther King Jr., was the wellspring of every form of liberation theology that privileges

---

1   Kenneth Cauthen, *The Impact of American Religious Liberalism*, Washington DC, University Press of America, 1962; William R. Hutchison, ed., *American Protestant Thought in the Liberal Era*, Lanham MD, University Press of America, 1968. See also Mark D. Chapman's contribution in this volume.

the experiences of oppressed and excluded peoples.

In the 1930s, theologian Reinhold Niebuhr ridiculed the Social Gospel for its ethical idealism, belief in cultural progress, and pacifist inclination, which branded the Social Gospel for two generations as a naïve failure, but the Social Gospel recovered the centrality of the Kingdom of God in the teaching of Jesus and the social justice emphasis of Hebrew and Christian scripture and was defined by social ethical convictions that Niebuhr could ridicule because he would took them for granted. It devised the theology of social salvation that undergirded the ecumenical movement and it put social justice on the agenda of those churches committed to ecumenism, creating the peace and justice organizations that still operate. Moreover, it paved the way to America's greatest liberation movement, led by King.

2   The White Social Gospel

The American Social Gospel was overwhelmingly Protestant. In fact, during the white Protestant movement heyday from 1875 to 1918 (the time frame of this chapter), there was only one Roman Catholic in it, social ethicist John Ryan, a lonely figure for 20 years who built the NCWC and its Department of Social Action into vital organizations after World War I. The Social Gospel had reformist and radical flanks just as its European counterparts did. There was a mainstream that was proudly middle-class, reformist, optimistic, and moralistic. It supported the Progressive movement and cooperatives, and sometimes it supported trade unions and municipal socialism. Episcopal political economist Richard T. Ely and Congregational pastor Washington Gladden were prominent figures in the reformist mainstream, as were Harvard Unitarian social ethicist Francis Greenwood Peabody, University of Chicago Baptist theologian Shailer Mathews, Congregational social ethicist Graham Taylor, AME bishop and

sociologist Richard R. Wright Jr., and black Baptist pastor Adam Clayton Powell Sr.

There was also a left flank that spoke the customary language of progressive idealism while advocating Christian socialism and radical economic democracy. The leading outright socialists were Episcopal cleric and sociologist William Dwight Porter Bliss, Congregational lecture circuit sensation George Herron, Baptist theologian Walter Rauschenbusch, AME bishop Reverdy Ransom, black Baptist orators George W. Woodbey and George Slater, Episcopal literature scholar Vida Scudder, Congregational cleric Herbert S. Bigelow, and Methodist social ethicist Harry Ward.

The reformers denied that the Social Gospel was socialist, while the socialists said it was important to replace capitalism, not merely reform it. Although this was the difference between the left wing of Social Gospel and its reformist majority, it was actually rather superficial. Nearly every Social Gospel leader supported producer cooperatives and public ownership of natural monopolies, and the explicitly socialist wing rejected the later Ely's identification of socialism with state socialism. In a broad sense of the term, all Social Gospel leaders were socialists, as Ely acknowledged.[2]

In political terms, all Social Gospel leaders were democratic progressives, seeking to achieve a cooperative commonwealth through liberal rights and democracy: power is an exchangeable thing that is attainable through good politics. Many Social Gospel socialists, however, absorbed Marxist theory better than they let on: power under capitalism is a commodity that is quantified, bought, owned, given, exchanged, or

---

2 See John F. Woolverton, *Robert H. Gardiner and the Reunification of Worldwide Christianity in the Progressive Era*, Columbia MO, University of Missouri Press, 2005, 47–49; Robert T. Handy, *Undermined Establishment: Church-State Relations in America (1800–1920)*, Princeton NJ, Princeton University Press, 1991; Robert T. Handy, *A Christian America: protestant Hopes and Historical Realities*, New York NY, Oxford University Press, 1971, 128–139.

stolen. Rauschenbusch, Ransom, Woodbey, Slater, Scudder, and Bliss espoused distinctly Marxist tropes in this area, and Herron was more Marxist than he realized.

The liberal and radical wings of the Social Gospel during its heyday both had numerous pacifists and non-pacifists. In the 1930s, debates over pacifism famously roiled the Social Gospel, but pacifism was not a field-dividing issue before that time. The two dividing issues were rather class struggle socialism and neoabolitionism. Liberal idealists spurned class analysis and did not want to talk about power, while radicals aimed precisely to democratize power. The latter group produced the strongest neoabolitionists, with notable exceptions, including Rauschenbusch.

Social Gospel socialists did not believe that middle-class idealism could transform society. Rauschenbusch said emphatically that idealists alone never won *any* social justice cause. In fact, the empowerment of the working classes and the organization of exploited people were necessary for the defense of their own class interests. Social justice is only achieved when classes fight for their rights. However, Rauschenbusch's American and German cultural background led him, until almost the end of his days, to be soft on issues of racism and imperialism.

Theologically, the Social Gospel was based on a novel doctrine of social salvation, which was based on the emerging sociological idea of social structure. The Social Gospel was defined by its novel claim that Christianity has a mission to transform the structures of society in the direction of freedom and equality. This does not mean that Christianity previously lacked a social consciousness or a social ethic. But only with the rise of Christian socialism did churches talk about transforming social structures in order to achieve social justice. This language had not existed before the 1880s. In the movements for Christian socialism and the Social Gospel, society became a subject of redemption. Social justice became intrinsic to salvation. If there was such a thing as social structure, redemption had to be re-conceptualized to

take account of it; salvation had to be personal *and* social to be saving.[3]

2.1   *Inventing the Social Gospel: Washington Gladden and Richard Ely*

Gladden and Ely came from humble backgrounds that left their mark on them long after they became national figures. Gladden grew up poor, and semi-orphaned in a rural area of Upstate New York. Ely's background was equally modest although he acquired an aristocratic temperament and a desire for academic respectability that put him in the conservative wing of the Social Gospel. The early Social Gospel owed its structural dimension mainly to his expertise in political economics. Gladden and Ely were prolific and industrious advocates of liberal rights, democracy, intellectual freedom, and almost everything else concerning modernity. They simply refused to believe that modern progress stopped with capitalism in the economic sphere; there had to be a stage beyond it.

As a youth, Gladden changed from being a Presbyterian to becoming a Congregationalist because the local Congregationalists were abolitionists. In 1860, after graduation, he began his first Congregational pastorate in Brooklyn, New York, where he lasted a few months. Brooklyn terrified him; the city felt like a buzzing, impersonal monster, and his congregation was debt-ridden and factional. Overwhelmed by the city, due to the outbreak of the Civil War and his own

---

3   This chapter contains highly condensed summaries of arguments and narratives in Gary Dorrien, *Soul in Society: The Making and Renewal of Social Christianity*, Minneapolis MN, Fortress Press, 1995; Gary Dorrien, *The Making of American Liberal Theology: Idealism, Realism, and Modernity (1900–1950)*, Louisville KY, Westminster John Knox, 2003, 73–150; Gary Dorrien, *Social Ethics in the Making: Interpreting an American Tradition*, Oxford, Wiley-Blackwell, 2011, 6–225; Gary Dorrien, *The New Abolition: W.E.B. Du Bois and the Black Social Gospel*, New Haven CT, Yale University Press, 2015; and Gary Dorrien, *Breaking White Supremacy: Martin Luther King Jr. and the Black Social Gospel*, New Haven CT, Yale University Press, 2018.

shortcomings, Gladden suffered a nervous break-down. He moved to the quiet climes of Morrisania, New York, where he found healing and converted to liberal theology, reading American theologian Horace Bushnell. Bushnell convinced him not to accept any doctrine that offended his sense of what is good or true. Gladden preached an early version of Social Gospel in New York and New England, and proceeded to become a journalist for a progressive national Congregational newspaper, the *Independent*. In both contexts he acquired new social ideas, contending that Christianity had to become relevant to a changing society. Gladden did not conceive liberal theology and social Christianity as different issues: to him they were complementary sides of one issue.

Gladden took his bearings from the golden rule: all are commanded to love their neighbors as themselves, so employers and employees should practice cooperation, disagreements should be negotiated in a spirit of other-regarding fellow-ship, and society should be organized to serve human welfare rather than profits. Nonetheless, the virtues of other-regarding cooperation are practicable only for individuals and small groups; thus, the early Gladden was against corporations and large unions.

Ely was born in 1854 and grew up in a farm near Fredonia, New York. His father was a self-taught engineer, impoverished farmer, and devout Presbyterian with a severely gloomy temperament. Calvinist predestination contributed mightily to his gloom and ended up driving Ely into the Episcopal Church during his college days at Columbia University. He later explained that Anglican humanism "offered a fuller and richer life." As a youth Ely devoured his father's library and enrolled at Dartmouth College. He earned a scholarship to Columbia and graduated in 1876, obtaining a fellowship to study abroad. Ely started these studies at the University of Halle, where he learned about the German historical school of economics led by Karl Knies, Adolf Wagner, and Gustav von Schmoller. He transferred to Heidelberg to study under Knies, embracing the

view that economics is a historical discipline, not a natural science.[4]

Ely earned his doctorate at Heidelberg in 1879 and began his teaching career two years later at Johns Hopkins University in Baltimore, Maryland, where he had to prove that students would enroll in his classes, as, at the time, American economists revered laissez-faire doctrine; Ely's approach was considered heresy. Many colleagues disliked Ely's enthusiasm for reform politics, which they considered an unseemly fixation for an academic, but he proved them right, and wrong, by writing a flurry of books and attracting students.[5]

His most controversial book was *The Labor Movement in America* (1886). While American newspapers condemned unions as coarse, violent, selfish, gangster-prone, and un-American, Ely reacted to this, contending that fear and prejudice prevailed in this area and were aggravated by the self-interests of newspaper owners. He surveyed the varieties of union that were being organized and argued that unions were mainly good for democracy; they were bulwarks of civilization because they helped many Americans feel themselves to be members of American society. Ely believed the Knights of Labor – a radical industrial

---

4 Richard T. Ely, *Ground Under Our Feet: An Autobiography*, New York NY, Macmillan & Co., 1938, 3–22, here 16.

5 These were the signature works of the early Social Gospel, and all were on political economics. His first book, in 1883, introduced American readers to French and German socialism, opining that Christian socialism offered a better basis for socialism than its "professorial" versions. His second book, in 1884, contended that all economic systems are shaped by cultural and political contingencies, as the German historical school said. Economics is not a science about an economic state of nature, it should not espouse unchangeable concepts, and a good society safeguards the common good by managing economic outcomes. His third book, in 1885, said that America was developing a social-ist tradition that had a constructive role to play in reform politics. See Richard T. Ely, *French and German Socialism in Modern Times*, New York NY, Harper, 1883, 245; Richard T. Ely, *The Past and the Present of Political Economy*, Baltimore MD, Johns Hopkins University Press, 1884; Richard T. Ely, *Recent American Socialism*, Baltimore MD, Johns Hopkins University Press, 1885.

union – was largely a positive force in American society, and, therefore, Americans should not believe what newspapers said about it.[6]

Ely and Gladden were diligent organizers, like the British Christian socialists they admired. In 1885 they joined the economists John Bates Clark and Henry C. Adams to found the AEA, which Ely served for seven years as founding secretary and later as president. In the same year, Ely and Gladden joined Congregational Social Gospel cleric Josiah Strong (leader of the American EA) in launching an activist ecumenical vehicle able to convene huge summer gatherings, the Interdenominational Congress. In 1890, Ely, Gladden, and Congregational cleric Lyman Abbott launched a summer program on social Christianity at the Chautauqua Society in upstate New York, which was later transformed into the American Institute of Christian Sociology, led by Ely. In 1891 Ely and Bliss founded an American branch of the CSU, a British Anglican organization led by upcoming luminaries Scott Holland and Charles Gore. Ely and Gladden organized it with a sense of urgency, insisting that Gilded Age capitalism was a crisis for American Christianity. Social Darwinism justified selfishness, bonded readily with economic orthodoxy, and justified cruel policies by appealing to academic dogmas. They warned that the growing popularity of Social Darwinism was morally toxic for American society, while struggling to say exactly where Darwinian science veered into something toxic.[7]

According to Darwinism, life is a continuous process of development from incoherent homogeneity to coherent heterogeneity, therefore Social Darwinism conceives human races as real and hierarchically ordered, with traits that can be measured. Any political intervention that impedes this "natural" process is harmful and all state-supported poor laws, education, sanitary supervision, and other measures that impede "natural weeding" out are repugnant, as are imperial ventures that waste resources and produce bloated, centralized governments.

Herbert Spencer's word on these topics settled the issue for many in the Gilded Age. The founders of the Social Gospel were informed, intimidated, attracted, and appalled by Spencer's system. They shared these opinions with upcoming American philosophers William James, Josiah Royce, and Borden Parker Bowne, and the founders of American sociology, notably Lester Ward, Charles Cooley, and Albion W. Small, and young William Edward Burghardt Du Bois, whose early writings on race were steeped in neo-Lamarckian Social Darwinism. The Social Gospel founders pored over Spencer's works for instruction and errors, by necessity. They took much of his system to be an authoritative scientific description of how the world works and played leading roles in persuading the churches that Darwinian biology had to be taken seriously and was compatible with Christianity. Meanwhile, they rejected or played down some aspects of Spencer's system, while coming to terms with Spencer's immense authority. An optimistic, vaguely religious version of Social Darwinism with a strong progress-motif became popular in American culture, and since American society was evolving in a good direction, Darwinism was not to be feared.[8]

The founders took help where they could find it, leaning on Darwin's leading American popularizer, John Fiske, to wring a spiritual worldview out of Darwinian theory. Fiske contended that

6   Richard T. Ely, *The Labor Movement in America*, New York NY, Thomas Y. Crowell, 1886, 121.

7   Herbert Spencer, *First Principles*, New York NY, Appleton, 1864; Herbert Spencer, *The Principles of Sociology*, 3 vols., New York NY, Appleton, 1876–1897; Richard Hofstadter, *Social Darwinism in American Thought*, Boston MA, Beacon Press, 1955, 31–50; Stephen Jay Gould, *Ontogeny and Phylogeny*, Cambridge MA, Harvard University Press, 1977; Charles Darwin, *The Descent of Man, and Selection in Relation to Sex*, London, J. Murray, 1874, 166–168.

8   William E.B. Du Bois, "The Conservation of Races," in: David Levering Lewis, ed., *W.E.B. Du Bois: A Reader*, New York NY, Henry Holt, 1995 [\u00b91897], 20–27; William E.B. Du Bois, *The Philadelphia Negro: A Social Study*, Philadelphia PA, University of Pennsylvania Press, 1996 [\u00b91899], 385–397.

Darwinism was compatible with a religious sensibility, even with the existence of God. Gladden and Ely welcomed the foundation of the nation's first sociology department at the University of Chicago in 1892, where Social Gospel progressives Small, Mathews, and Taylor said that sociology should be socio-historical, not biologically reductionist, and society should be shaped by progressive reforms, not erratic Darwinian weeding out.

To most of the Social Gospel founders, the moral issue cut the deepest and Social Darwinism was an overreach due to its denigration of the Gospel command to see Christ in the poor and vulnerable. Ely was less firm than other founders in this area, and in his later career, during World War I, he became extremely patriotic. The later Ely supported odious policies favoring white "Nordic" immigrants, very much in line with the trade unionists and Protestant gentility he sought to unite. In the early period, however, Ely's training in German historicism was a bulwark for the Social Gospel: it steeled him against laissez-faire economics and Spencer's anti-statism, undergirding the movement's signature arguments for unions, state taxation policies, public ownership of utilities, and industrial reforms.[9]

In 1885, Ely founded the AEA to oppose laissez-faire orthodoxy in politics and morality. He laid down four principles: (1) the positive work of the state is an indispensable condition of human progress; (2) political economics must avoid doctrinal dogmatism; (3) the clash between labor and capital must be mediated by the church, state, and academy; (4) progressive economic development and progressive legislation go together. Nearly 50 founders convened in Saratoga, New York to affirm these principles, where Ely stressed number three. The AEA founders included Social Gospel clerics

Gladden, Abbott, Leighton Williams, Amory H. Bradford, Newman Smyth, Richard Heber Newton, and Joseph H. Rylance.[10]

Ely continued to publish books, with two in 1888 on taxes and social problems and two in 1889 on political economy and social Christianity. In *Social Aspects of Christianity* (1889), Ely published his stump speeches, conveying the mood of an ascending movement. It was a bestselling landmark; for 20 years the book was assigned to every young minister participating in a conference of the Methodist Episcopal Church.[11]

Ely taught Social Gospel theologians that religion and science work together in the progressive unfolding of truth, since the divine indwells all things and theology is guided by the same truths discovered by social science. The same harmony, as Ely affirmed treasuring Anglican socialist Frederick Denison Maurice's teachings,[12] existed between church and state, rightly ordered, if harmoniously organized, as it were between religion and science, and even between labor and capital. Ely's was a comprehensively idealistic Social Christianity, calling for church, state, family, academy, and industry to work together to advance human progress.

---

9   John Fiske, *Through Nature to God*, Boston MA, Houghton Mifflin, 1899; John Fiske, *The Destiny of Man Viewed in the Light of His Origin*, Boston MA, Houghton Mifflin, 1884; Albion W. Small & George E. Vincent, *An Introduction to the Study of Society*, New York NY, American Book Company, 1894; Small founded the *American Journal of Sociology* in 1895.

10 Richard T. Ely, "The Founding and Early History of the American Economic Association," AER 26/1, 1936, 141–150.

11 Richard T. Ely, *Taxation in American States and Cities*, New York NY, Thomas Y. Crowell, 1888; Richard T. Ely, *Problems of Today: A Discussion of Protective Tariffs, Taxation, and Monopolies*, New York NY, Thomas Y. Crowell, 1888; Richard T. Ely, *An Introduction to Political Economy*, New York NY, Chautauqua Press, 1889.

12 Frederick Denison Maurice, *The Kingdom of Christ: Or, Hints to a Quaker Respecting the Principles, Constitution and Ordinances of the Catholic Church*, ed. Alec R. Vidler, 2 vols., London, SCM Press, 1958. On Maurice, see Jeremy Morris, *F.D. Maurice and the Crisis of Christian Authority*, Oxford, Oxford University Press, 2005; Jeremy Morris, ed., *To Build Christ's Kingdom: F.D. Maurice and His Writings*, Norwich, Canterbury Press, 2007 (this is a selection of Maurice's writings with an introduction). See also Paul Avis' contribution in this volume.

Ely was thus averse to radical rhetoric about the class struggle and, until 1889, he was convinced that society was evolving toward a cooperative commonwealth. He later began to say he was not like the young Social Gospel socialists, because they were radical. Gladden walked a similar tightrope, but his training as a preacher and journalist made him a less self-assured writer than Ely: he pressed for verdicts and followed the opposite trajectory to Ely's, drifting to the left as capitalism grew increasingly predatory.

In 1886, Gladden condemned the wage system as irredeemably immoral and anti-Christian. There were three fundamental choices in political economy, he said. Relations of labor and capital could be based on slavery, wages, or cooperation, and only the third was acceptable. The first stage in industrial progress featured the subjugation of labor by capital. The second stage was essentially a war between labor and capital. The third stage was the cooperative commonwealth in which labor and capital shared a common interest and spirit.[13]

For a while he tried to combine a structural criticism of the problem with an optimistic ethical solution. The solution was to persuade employers to set up profit-sharing enterprises, not to abolish capitalism from above or below. Gladden stressed that most employers were no less moral than the laborers they employed. Socialism was a poor alternative because it required an overreaching bureaucracy that placed important freedoms in jeopardy. Gladden said socialists were right to condemn capitalism, but wrong to suppose that humanity would flourish under a system that discards "self-regarding forces." What was needed was to channel self-interest to good ends, Christianizing the social order.[14]

Gladden appealed to the rationality and moral feelings of capitalist barons: in 1893 he was still calling for "industrial partnerships" based on profit sharing. However, cooperative ownership made little headway in America, and profit sharing would not occur without strong trade unions. The latter realization pulled him to the left, even as he deplored union violence and prized his capacity to mediate between labor and capital. The lopsided power of the capitalist class stymied any serious hope of achieving a nonsocialist, decentralized economic democracy, which is what Gladden stated from the pulpit.

His criticism of state socialism was sensible and prescient. Gladden warned that centralized state socialism denigrated the spirit of individual creativity and invention since it was too grandiose and bureaucratic to function well. It required great governmental power and virtually infinite bureaucratic wisdom. Gladden explained: "The theory that it proposes is too vast for human power. It requires the state to take possession of all the lands, the mines, the houses, the stores, the railroads, the furnaces, the factories, the ships – all the capital of the country of every description."[15] Under a socialist order, government bureaucrats would be vested with the power to set wages, prices, and production quotas for a sprawling continent of consumers and producers.[16]

Gladden and Ely developed a movement that radiated their ethical enthusiasm for cooperatives, democracy, Progressivism, and being peaceable. They were moralistic without being apologetic, allergic to Marxist rhetoric about destroying capitalism, and committed to Christianizing society. Society would be Christianized through progress, reforms, and evangelization. However, Gladden kept moving leftward, always with regret, protesting that the capitalist class destroyed better possibilities.

By 1909, when he wrote his memoirs, Gladden believed that America was heading into socialism. Two years later, in *The Labor Question*, he grieved

---

13   Washington Gladden, *Applied Christianity: Moral Aspects of Social Questions*, Boston MA, Houghton Mifflin, 1886, 25–33; Washington Gladden, *Working People and Their Employers*, New York NY, Funk & Wagnalls, 1894, 44–45.

14   Gladden, *Applied Christianity*, 98, 100.

15   Washington Gladden, *Christianity and Socialism*, New York NY, Eaton & Mains, 1905, 141.

16   Gladden, *Applied Christianity*, 264–265.

that corporations were more ruthless than ever, and labor organizing yielded harsh outfits like the anarchist IWW. Thus Gladden gave up his fantasy of a paternalistic economy based on sharing profits and cooperatives, taking his stand with a flawed labor movement. Unorganized labor, he lamented, was "steadily forced down toward starvation and misery,"[17] which left industrial unionism alone as a serious force of resistance against the corporate degradation of labor.

That was the "radical" position in American socialism and unionism Gladden was aligning to. Ordinary AFL unionism was not the answer, because it federated only the workers in skilled trades and was blatantly racist. Gladden ended up cheering for radical unionism that did not exclude anybody and did not regress into anarchism. It frightened him that he should end up so close to Rauschenbusch, the symbol of the turn toward socialism.

2.2 The Social Gospel Heyday: Walter Rauschenbusch

Walter Rauschenbusch grew up as the son of a German department professor and Baptist leader at Rochester Theological Seminary and began his ministerial career in 1886 at the Second German Baptist Church of New York City. There he served a poor, suffering, immigrant congregation on the northern edge of Hell's Kitchen and converted to the Social Gospel. Rauschenbusch's searing encounter with urban poverty, particularly the funerals he performed for children, drove him to social activism. Politics became unavoidable: in his opinion, if people suffered as a result of politics and economics, the church had to deal with politics and economics. He supported Henry George's campaign for mayor of New York, embracing George's call for a steep tax on urban land. He read Ely's books and converted to socialism, writing

impassioned articles on socialism, trade unions, and the Kingdom of God.

He said he had six books in his head. Five were scholarly and one was "dangerous." Three times he tried to write the dangerous one, but repeatedly started it again from the beginning. In 1891 Rauschenbusch decided, with deep sadness, that he had to resign from the ministry because he was going deaf. A surf-like roar in his ears made it difficult to do pastoral tasks; he called it "physical loneliness." Rochester offered him his father's former teaching position, but he doubted that teaching would work any better than ministry for a deaf person. Rauschenbusch decided to go abroad for a year, write the dangerous book, and launch a literary career. His congregation insisted, instead, on a paid sabbatical, which he took in Germany.

There he labored on a book, *Revolutionary Christianity*, in which he argued that Christianity should be essentially revolutionary, as Jesus had been. Contrary to the dramatic story he told, Rauschenbusch already fastened on to the Kingdom of God before he took his sabbatical, that is when he studied Ritschlian theology in Germany. At that time, he put a Ritschlian spin to kingdom theology: Christianity is a social-historical movement with a particular ethical character, rooted in the teaching of Jesus. Jesus proclaimed a postmillennial idea of the coming reign of God, and the church is assumed to be a new kind of community that transforms the world by the power of Christ's kingdom-bringing Spirit. The emphasis on radical transformation, however, came from Rauschenbusch, not Ritschl: "Here was a religious conception that embraced it all. Here was something so big that absolutely nothing that interested me was excluded from it ... wherever I touched, there was the kingdom of God. ... It carries God into everything that you do."[18]

---

17   Washington Gladden, *Recollections*, Boston MA, Houghton Mifflin, 1909, 305–308; Washington Gladden, *The Labor Question*, Boston MA, Pilgrim Press, 1911, 3–55, 98–110, here 55.

18   Walter Rauschenbusch, *The Kingdom of God*, YMCA lecture, Cleveland OH, 1913, cited in: Robert T. Handy, ed., *The Social Gospel in America (1870–1920): Gladden, Ely, Rauschenbusch*, New York NY, Oxford University Press, 1966, 264–267, here 267.

Yet he never finished *Revolutionary Christianity*. When Rochester Seminary called him, in 1897, Rauschenbusch agreed to carry on his father's work, teaching German language courses on a range of topics from literature, to zoology. This exhausting regimen, which lasted five years, left no time for his own work. Finally, in 1902, he was entrusted with the chair of church history (which is why his greatest works on the Social Gospel have a strong historical bent). Rauschenbusch made his living as a professor of church history, while going back to the "dangerous book."

He salvaged what he could from his sprawling outdated manuscript, in particular the starting point: Jesus and his kingdom. This was the basis for an almost completely new book, which he finished in 1907: *Christianity and the Social Crisis*.[19]

Rauschenbusch was aware that his book would make him lose his post. What most worried him was the chapter entitled "What to Do," a blazing manifesto for democratic socialism, and the part concerning church history, where he abundantly relied on Adolf von Harnack's work.

It is not by chance that Rauschenbusch asked the German historian for his assistance, as Harnack had founded in 1890 the German Evangelisch-Sozialer Kongress (itself inspired by the English Christian Social Union), and Rauschenbusch, who, due to its origins, knew more about German socialism than his books conveyed, always welcomed Bismarck's welfare state while embracing German Social Democracy. He blanched, though, at German militarism of the Wilhelmine era, and wrestled with his own blend of American and German nationalism.

Revolutionary Christianity's draft had patches of labored writing and clumsy connections, but all was smooth and sparkling when published in *Christianity and the Social Crisis*. The book enthralled a huge audience with its graceful flow of short, clear sentences, its charming metaphors, and its vigorous pace. It argued that prophetic

religion is the beating heart of scripture, that the prophetic spirit rose from the dead in Jesus and the early church, and that Christianity should be a prophetic Christ-following religion of the divine commonwealth.

For Rauschenbusch, the rise of corporate capitalism marked a crisis for American civilization and an opportunity to recover the lost kingdom ideal of Jesus. If production was organized on a cooperative basis, and distribution by principles of justice, and workers were treated as children of God, then it might be possible to live as Jesus taught.

Christianity and the Social Crisis was skillfully fashioned and perfectly timed. Instead of losing his post, Rauschenbusch returned from a sabbatical in Germany to find that his book provided a great stimulus to a burgeoning Social Gospel movement. It was reprinted thirteen times in five years and set a new standard for political theology. It pulled the Social Gospel to the left, until World War I erupted and the great destruction of progressive movements commenced. It drew Rauschenbusch into the campaign for an ecumenical organization, the FCCC, and its historic proclamation, the Social Creed of the Churches.

The FCCC fulfilled an American Protestant dream, one can say. 19th-century evangelicals, realizing that no denomination alone could possibly Christianize the entire expanding nation, had founded the ABCFM (1810), the ABS (1816), the ASSU (1824), and the AHMS (1826). Service oriented, youth-based forms of interdenominational cooperation were established in the 1850s and flourished after the Civil War, notably the YMCA and the YWCA.[20] Institutionally, the Social Gospel grew out of these evangelical organizations. The

---

19   Walter Rauschenbusch, *Christianity and the Social Crisis*, New York NY, Macmillan, 1907.

20   Clarence P. Shedd, *History of the World's Alliance of Young Men's Christian Associations*, London, SPCK, 1955; Charles H. Hopkins, *History of the Y.M.C.A. in North America*, New York NY, Association Press, 1951. See also Ruth Rouse, "Other Aspects of the Ecumenical Movement (1910–1948)," in: *A History of the Ecumenical Movement*, vol. 1, Ruth Rouse & Stephen C. Neill, eds., *1517–1948*, London, SPCK, [2]1967, 599–644.

YMCA and YWCA cultivated a generation of ecumenically minded church leaders leading to the founding of a major service organization in 1895, the WSCF, and to the FCCC in 1908, representing 33 denominations.[21] Social Gospel leaders dominated the FCCC, in particular Methodists Frank Mason North and Harry Ward; Baptists Samuel Z. Batten, Nannie H. Burroughs, Mathews, and Rauschenbusch; Congregationalists Gladden, Taylor, Strong, and Charles Macfarland; AME cleric Reverdy Ransom; AMEZ bishop Alexander Walters; disciple Charles Clayton Morrison; and Presbyterians William Adams Brown, Charles Stelzle, and Robert E. Speer. The council functioned as a laboratory for Social Gospel ideas that infiltrated the churches and seminaries. It sought to advance common social goals by excluding divisive doctrines.

Methodists were the heart of the early black Social Gospel, but white Methodists were Social Gospel latecomers until just before the FCCC was founded. Then North and Ward pulled the MEC into the Social Gospel. In 1907 Ward organized a national Methodist conference in Washington DC, that founded a new service organization, the Methodist Federation for Social Service. It included clerics Frank Mason North and Worth Tippy, labor economist John Commons, Indiana governor Frank Hanley, social worker Mary McDowell, and Denver judge Ben Lindsay. US Vice President Charles Fairbanks attended the conference, taking the group afterward to meet President Theodore Roosevelt. The Social Gospel Methodists, sensing the moment, struck for a role in the MEC General Conference of May 1908. Ward jotted the first draft of a Social Creed on a Western Union pad, listing eleven reforms, and the Methodist General Council endorsed it after a little editorial smoothening:

> We deem it the duty of all Christian people to concern themselves directly with certain practical industrial problems. To us it seems that the churches must stand:
>
> For equal rights and complete justice for all men in all stations of life.
> For the principles of conciliation and arbitration in industrial relations.
> For the protection of the workers from dangerous machinery, occupational diseases, injuries, and mortality.
> For the abolition of child labor.
> For such regulation of the conditions of labor for women as shall safeguard the physical and moral health of the community.
> For the suppression of the "sweating system."
> For the gradual and reasonable reduction of the hours of labor to the lowest practical point, with work for all; and for that degree of leisure for all which is the condition of the highest human life.
> For the release from employment one day in seven.
> For a living wage in every industry.
> For the highest wage that each industry can afford, and for the most equitable division of the products of industry that can ultimately be devised.
> For the recognition of the Golden Rule, and the mind of Christ as the supreme law of society and the sure remedy for all social ills.[22]

This original Social Creed did not mention racial justice, and its reference to the rights of women was restricted to the workplace, as working conditions were its focus.[23] Neither did any subsequent

---

21   See Sarah Scholl's contribution in this volume.

22   Charles H. Hopkins, *The Rise of the Social Gospel in American Protestantism (1865–1915)*, New Haven CT, Yale University Press, 1940, 289–301, here 291.

23   Since 1870 the condition of women in the workplace had extensively changed as they were newly and sensibly included in the production chain after a long absence due to the consequences of the industrialization of the

version of the Social Creed mention racial justice until the 1932 version by the FCCC. Consummating a 1905 plan of federation, the FCCC was founded in December 1908 in Philadelphia. North served as chair of the executive committee and chair of the committee on labor issues, composing an FCCC version of the Social Creed that added four reforms to Ward's creed. North was credited as the author, although in fact Ward wrote most of it.[24]

If the churches could not agree about doctrine, they could at least work together for social decency. In that spirit, the FCCC promulgated a Social Creed at its birth. Rauschenbusch had a hand in North's adaptation, celebrating the fact that Protestants finally had a major ecumenical fellowship. People repeatedly asked him for a sequel to *Christianity and the Social Crisis*. He recalled that for many years he shouted in a Baptist wilderness: "It was always a happy surprise when we found a new man who had seen the light. We used to form a kind of flying wedge to support a man who was preparing to attack a ministers' conference with the social Gospel."[25] But now the Social Gospel was sweeping ministerial conferences, and he rightly regarded this as a Third Great Awakening.[26]

Christianizing the Social Order (1912), the sequel, reworked familiar Rauschenbusch themes with heightened claims. The Reformation revived Pauline theology, but "the present-day Reformation is a revival of the spirit and aims of Jesus himself." Jesus naturally retained archaic thought-forms of his time, but what matters is the spirit and trajectory of his religion, not the dogmas he inherited. Instead of asking, "What did Jesus think?" the right question is, "In what direction were his thoughts working?"[27]

This time Rauschenbusch dwelt longer on the shortcomings of the Reformation. Luther and Calvin had little feeling for the kingdom, they recoiled at the book of Revelation, and they had little democratic spirit. The Reformation broke the Catholic imprisonment of the kingdom idea, but not to reclaim its true meaning. Modern social idealism and historical criticism were required in order to recover Jesus and his kingdom: "The eclipse of the Kingdom idea was an eclipse of Jesus. We had listened too much to voices talking about him, and not enough to his own voice. Now his own thoughts in their lifelike simplicity and open-air fragrance have become a fresh religious possession, and when we listen to Jesus, we cannot help thinking about the Kingdom of God."[28]

Christianizing the Social Order was a provocative title even at the high tide of the Social Gospel. Rauschenbusch appreciated the fact that rhetoric about Christianizing society was unsettling to many. He assured that he had no theocratic desires. To speak of Christianizing the social order was in no way an attempt to include Christ's name in the US Constitution or otherwise breach the American wall between church and state. He was a Baptist who treasured the wall. The Social Gospel was about social and cultural transformation, not state religion: "Christianizing the social order means bringing it into harmony with the ethical convictions which we identify with Christ."[29]

Rauschenbusch, in the end, used the words "Christianize," "moralize," "humanize," and "democratize" interchangeably, explaining, "Christianizing means humanizing in the highest sense."[30] Not even the Churches were excluded: for one thing, many of them took reactionary positions on "the public activities and the

---

food and textile sectors, which brought women out of the production process. See Claudia Goldin, "The work and wages of single women (1870–1920)," *Journal of Economic History* 40/1, 1980, 81–88.

24   Harry F. Ward, ed., *The Social Creed of the Churches*, New York NY, Eaton & Maine, 1912, 2–5.

25   Walter Rauschenbusch, *Christianizing the Social Order*, New York NY, Macmillan, 1912, 9.

26   Walter Rauschenbusch, *For God and the People: Prayers of the Social Awakening*, Boston MA, Pilgrim Press, 1910.

27   Rauschenbusch, *Christianizing the Social Order*, 49, 56.

28   Rauschenbusch, *Christianizing the Social Order*, 89–90.

29   Rauschenbusch, *Christianizing the Social Order*, 125.

30   Rauschenbusch, *Christianizing the Social Order*, 125.

emancipation of women."[31] A more up-to-date change of pace was then necessary.

Rauschenbusch was not, in any case, a paladin of women's rights. He was, in the end, a Victorian man, who even supporting equal social rights for women, wanted wives and mothers to stay at home and take care of their families, and grieved that most college-educated women remained unmarried. He urged his audiences not to undermine the middle-class ideal of family life in the name of capitalism, which was responsible of wives and mothers leaving their homes.[32]

In families, churches, schools, and politics, democracy was gaining, but in the economic system, depravity prevailed. Rauschenbusch said the problem was systemic, because capitalism is essentially predatory and corrupts. The only way to stop the autocratic power of landowners and bosses was, in fact, democracy. Democracy promotes freedom and equality, legitimates the necessary exercise of authority, and serves to restrain the will-to-power of privileged classes.[33]

Christianizing the Social Order did not repeat the admonition of *Christianity and the Social Crisis* that the class struggle is frighteningly real and unavoidable. Quite the contrary, as it seemed: the Social Gospel was soaring, the Socialist Party of Eugene V. Debs was popular and growing, and Progressives were fleeing the Republican Party. Rauschenbusch dared to hope that idealism might prevail without a class war. He counseled liberals and progressives to own up to the socialism in their creed: "Every reformer is charged with socialism, because no constructive reform is possible without taking a leaf from the book of socialism."[34] He said it was better to wear the label as a badge of honor than to cower from it. Sensitive to the charge that he fell away from "the high religious ground," Rauschenbusch claimed that all 476 pages of *Christianizing the Social Order* focused on the Kingdom of God and its salvation and that the Social Gospel was a call for a revival of religion and a Christian transformation of society:

> We do not want less religion; we want more; but it must be a religion that gets its orientation from the Kingdom of God. To concentrate our efforts on personal salvation, as orthodoxy has done, or on soul culture, as liberalism has done, comes close to refined selfishness. All of us who have been trained in egotistic religion need a conversion to Christian Christianity, even if we are bishops or theological professors. Seek ye first the Kingdom of God and God's righteousness, and the salvation of your souls will be added to you.[35]

For ten years Rauschenbusch fretted over Germany's military buildup and its antipathy

---

31 Rauschenbusch, *Christianizing the Social Order*, 135. When Rauschenbusch wrote this volume, in 1912, the cause of women's rights and the suffrage movement was at its political apex, as it became part of the platform presented by Theodore Roosevelt to the Progressive Party. Many were the women who took part in the suffrage movement and the Social Gospel. See: Wendy J. Deichmann Edwards & Carolyn De Swarte Gifford, eds., *Gender and the Social Gospel*, Urbana IL, University of Illinois Press, 2003; Mary Agnes Dougherty, "The Social Gospel According to Phoebe: Methodis Deaconess in the Metropolis (1855–1918)," in: Hilah F. Thomas & Rosemary Skinner Keller, eds., *Women in New Worlds: Historical Perspectives on the Wesleyan Tradition*, Nashville, Abingdon, 1981, 200–216; Mary D. Pellauer, *Toward a Tradition of Feminist Theology: The Religious Social Thought of Elizabeth Cady Stanton, Susan B. Anthony, and Anna Howard Shaw*, Brooklyn NY, Carlson, 1991.

32 The appropriation of the role of the "Republican mother" who held, in the post-war context, the role of mother and teacher, which had previously been played by fathers, was quite common, and it became both a means of justification for a public presence and an opportunity to self-recognize the appropriate language to fight against reactionary positions. Donald G. Mathews, "Women's History/Everyone's History," in: Thomas & Skinner Keller, eds., *Women in New Worlds*, 29–47, here 45.

33 Rauschenbusch, *Christianizing the Social Order*, 353.
34 Rauschenbusch, *Christianizing the Social Order*, 433.
35 Rauschenbusch, *Christianizing the Social Order*, 464–465.

toward Russia, France, and England, fearing a European bloodbath. Once it started, he plunged into depression, grieving that America public opinion favored England and pleaded against American intervention.[36] As he himself said, he loved Germany only a little less than he loved the United States. When in 1915 he publicly protested against the US's policy of selling armaments to the Allied powers, calling for a government prohibition that would enforce Washington line of neutrality, he provoked a firestorm of outrage.[37] To those who accused him of supporting German imperialism, he responded that his antimilitarism was a Christian conviction and his views were the result of a continuous inner evolution triggered by engaging, years before, with pacifist movements.[38] Incapable to defend his views, he withdrew from the public debate over the war, bruised from the attacks.[39]

His last two books fought off his deepening sorrow and depression caused by these last events. *The Social Principles of Jesus* (1916), a book for the Sunday School Council, summarized the teachings of Jesus on poverty, property, compassion, violence, justice, and the Kingdom of God, declaring that the kingdom "is a real thing, now in operation." The kingdom is within and among human beings, he explained. Sometimes it suffers terrible reversals – "we are in the midst of one now." But God wrings victory out of defeat: "The Kingdom of God is always coming; you can never lay your hand on it and say, 'It is here.' But such fragmentary realizations of it as we have, alone make life worth living."[40]

That was the tone of his last book, *A Theology for the Social Gospel*, which criticized the enthusiasm displayed by many Social Gospel leaders entering the war in 1917; he countered that the real Social Gospel teetered on extinction, surviving only on the hope of a resurrection after the war. *A Theology for the Social Gospel*, though, was mainly a chance to reflect upon sin and how its perception changed over time. Obsessed over men's personal foibles, the old theological orthodoxy had ignored for centuries that the poor suffered the ravages of exploitation and other social evils, and hallowed theologians never condemned "these magnificent manifestations of the wickedness of the human heart."[41]

Rauschenbusch said drug addiction, social cruelty, perversity, racism, and ethnic feuds are transmitted from one generation to the next by tradition. Human beings are bonded to each other by their bondage to sin, which is personal and social: "When negroes are hunted from a Northern city like beasts, or when a Southern city

---

36   He admitted to the magazine *The Congregationalist* that he felt overcome by "profound grief and depression of spirit"; Walter Rauschenbusch to *The Congregationalist*, Sept 24, 1914.

37   Walter Rauschenbusch, "The Contribution of Germany to the National Life of America," Box 92, in Rauschenbusch Family Collection, Colgate Rochester Seminary, Rochester NY; Rauschenbusch to "a Friend," Mar 7, 1917, Box 32, in: Rauschenbusch Family Collection. Walter Rauschenbusch, "Be Fair to Germany: A Plea for Openmindedness," *The Congregationalist*, Oct 15, 1914.

38   He said to a friend: "I have been a Christian supporter of the peace idea for some years. During the Spanish-American War I took the average attitude and voiced it effectively. But shortly afterward the peace movement got a strong grip on me"; Rauschenbusch to "a Friend," Mar 7, 1917, unmarked box, in: Rauschenbusch Family Collection. He also said that the spirits of Martin Luther and Oliver Cromwell were alien to him; as they despised the lower classes and "cheerfully" supported mass killing, but he could not combine Christianity and war without losing his faith: "Don't ask me to combine religion and the war spirit. I don't want to lose my religion; it's all I've got"; Rauschenbusch to John S. Phillips, May 16, 1917, Box 32, in: Rauschenbusch Family Collection.

39   In 1916, he joined the newly founded pacifist Fellowship of Reconciliation, telling a friend he was delighted to find people more radical than himself. See Walter Rauschenbusch to Washington Gladden, Jan 17, 1917,

Box 32, in: Rauschenbusch Family Collection; and also Walter Rauschenbusch to Algernon Crapsey, open letter published in *The Rochester Herald*, Aug 23, 1915.

40   Walter Rauschenbusch, *The Social Principles of Jesus*, New York NY, Association Press, 1916, 196–197.

41   Walter Rauschenbusch, *A Theology for the Social Gospel*, New York NY, Macmillan, 1917; new edition Louisville KY, Westminster John Knox Press, 1997, 34.

degrades the whole nation by turning the savage inhumanity of a mob into a public festivity, we are continuing to sin because our fathers created the conditions of sin by the African slave trade and by the unearned wealth they gathered from slave labor for generations."[42] He called the sum of these evils the "kingdom of evil," stressing that evil is real, powerful, organic, and solidaristic in modern life. All people are bound together in the condition of bearing the yoke of evil and suffering, which only the Social Gospel theologized.

He reasoned that if the Kingdom of God is democratizing in its ethical and spiritual character, so must be the God of that kingdom. God is a loving creator, not the feudal monarch of classical theology:

> A God who strives within our striving, who kindles his flame in our intellect, sends the impact of his energy to make our will restless for righteousness, floods our sub-conscious mind with dreams and longings, and always urges the race on toward a higher combination of freedom and solidarity – that would be a God with whom democratic and religious men could hold converse as their chief fellow-worker, the source of their energies, the ground of their hopes.[43]

Immediately after *A Theology for the Social Gospel* was published, Rauschenbusch began to feel desperately tired. He had no strength, he was unable to type, and his legs were stiff. Sensing that he was dying, he wrote several final statements. One of these accepted his early death as God's will: "Since 1914 the world is full of hate, and I cannot expect to be happy again in my lifetime."[44] Another said it would be a terrible calamity if Germany won the war – not quite what Rochester Seminary begged

him to say as reparation for what he said about the US' intervention, but as far as he could go.[45] He died of brain cancer on July 25, 1918, at the age of 56.

The cliché concerning Rauschenbusch is that he was hopelessly idealistic, and he certainly was at least in part. Rauschenbusch was too idealistic, but that was far from his worst failing. On crucial issues he failed to stand for mere decency. His feminism was tepid, late Victorian, and highly selective. He could never conceive his beloved American nation as an empire. He made special ideological concessions to German nationalism and came late to antimilitarism. Above all, he did not have a clear stance about racism until his last years.

On imperialism and cultural racism, though, Rauschenbusch had a clear idea as he knew the British Christian socialists, who were staunchly anti-imperialist and anti-racist. England had Fabian socialists who sang for nationalism, imperialism, and even eugenics, but Christian socialist leaders, such as Anglicans Charles Marson, Stewart Headlam, Thomas Hancock, Scott Holland, Charles Gore, and Maurice Reckett, Baptist John Clifford, and Quaker Samuel George Hobson, were adamantly opposed to them. In Rauschenbusch's early career he opposed racism and immigration restrictions, and welcomed the anti-imperialist reaction in England. Yet he made allowances for the two nations he loved: he believed that American imperialism was not imperialist, Germany needed to catch up with England, and America needed more Germans immigrants.[46]

In 1895, two years before he returned to Rochester, he wrote a racist fundraising letter for the German department: "Are the whites of

---

42   Rauschenbusch, *A Theology for the Social Gospel*, 79.
43   Rauschenbusch, *A Theology for the Social Gospel*, 179.
44   Walter Rauschenbusch, "Instructions in Case of My Death," Mar 31, 1918, Box 87, in: Rauschenbusch Family Collection.

45   Rauschenbusch to Cornelius Woelfkin, first draft, Apr 25, 1918; published version, May 1, 1918; Rochester Seminary press release version subtitled "ALWAYS AN AMERICAN," July 11, 1918, Box 91, in: Rauschenbusch Family Collection.
46   See Gary Dorrien, *Social Democracy in the Making: Political and Religious Roots of European Socialism*, New Haven CT, Yale University Press, 2019, 72–113.

this continent so sure of their possession against the blacks of the South and the seething yellow flocks beyond the Pacific that they need no reinforcement of men of their own blood while yet it is time?"[47] Two years later he wrote a similar letter, now as a faculty member, and in 1902 stood before a commencement assembly and said aggressively that Germans were first cousins of the British Anglo-Saxons, they helped to build modern democracy, and they deserved to be included in Manifest Destiny. It was short sighted to give British Anglo-Saxons exclusive credit for civilization. Modern democracy was created by a single Teutonic racial stock, an achievement imperiled by what he called "alien strains" arriving from places like France, Spain, the Slavic lands, Bohemia, Poland, and the Russian Jewish territories.[48]

Meanwhile, for many years, he failed to say anything about the racist violence before his very eyes. Conservative white Social Gospel leaders, such as Strong and Abbott, said that black Americans must assimilate to an Anglo-Saxon ideal. Left-leaning assimilationists, such as Gladden and Baptist Church leader Henry Morehouse, said the same thing with a stronger recognition of the rights of black Americans. Socialist neoabolitionists, such as Herron, Bigelow, and Crapsey, strongly defended the dignity and rights of African Americans, but they were too few in number.

Occasionally, someone made steps forward as far as this subject was concerned. Gladden was a patronizing left-assimilationist for most of his career, but in 1903 he read *The Souls of Black Folk*, by Du Bois, and changed his position. Gladden received an avalanche of hateful letters in reply.

Reading his mail, he said it frightened him to see with what black Americans had to contend. Meanwhile, Rauschenbusch said nothing. He knew only a few African Americans personally, had no moral authority on this subject, and everything he knew contradicted his claim that Christians were building the Kingdom of God. Rauschenbusch waited until his last years to break his silence. In *Christianizing the Social Order* he finally managed to say that the spirit of Jesus "smites race pride and prejudice in the face in the name of humanity."[49] In his last book he described lynching as the ultimate example of social evil.

These statements came from nowhere, raising a new subject for him. In 1914 he explained why it had taken him so long to write even a single sentence on the issue: "For years, the problem of the two races in the South has seemed to me so tragic, so insoluble, that I have never yet ventured to discuss it in public."[50] If he was to be an agent of hope in racist America, he could not mention racism, a hopelessly depressing topic. The black Social Gospel leaders that Rauschenbusch ignored knew all about the existential trauma of sustaining hope in a baneful situation. They dealt with it every day in ministering to people who suffered the tragedy. However, to them the response of mute hopelessness was an ethical impossibility. If Christianity had any moral meaning in the United States, it had to begin with the evils of racism and hatred that oppressed black Americans.

3   The Black Social Gospel

The black Social Gospel arose during the same period as the famous white one. It had its own identity and integrity, while sharing important aspects with white progressive Christianity. Martin Luther King Jr. was steeped in it. His role models were second-generation black Baptist Social

---

47   Walter Rauschenbusch, "What Shall We Do with the Germans?," *The Examiner*, Jan 10, 1895.
48   Walter Rauschenbusch (unsigned), "The German Seminary in Rochester," (pamphlet, 1897), Box 47, in Rauschenbusch Family Collection; Walter Rauschenbusch, "The Contribution of Germany to the National Life of America," Commencement address, Fiftieth Anniversary of the Rochester Theological Seminary German Department, Box 92, in: Rauschenbusch Family Collection, cited in: *The Democrat and Chronicle*, May 8, 1902.

49   Rauschenbusch, *Christianizing the Social Order*, 60.
50   Walter Rauschenbusch, "The Belated Races and the Social Problems," MR 40, 1914, 252–259, here 258.

Gospel leaders: Mordecai Johnson, Benjamin E. Mays, J. Pius Barbour, Adam Clayton Powell Jr., and Howard Thurman. Their role models, in turn, were black Social Gospel founders such as AME clerics Reverdy Ransom and Richard R. Wright Jr., Baptist clerics William Simmons and Adam Clayton Powell Sr., AME anti-lynching crusader Ida Wells-Barnett, Baptist educator Nannie Helen Burroughs, Episcopal cleric Alexander Crummell, and AMEZ bishop Alexander Walters. No tradition in American religious history has a greater legacy than this one. Yet the black Social Gospel tradition was ignored for decades and it lacked almost any literature until recently.

Numerous conventions have long prevented the black Social Gospel from being remembered. Supposedly, there was no black Social Gospel worth noting. It had only a few proponents, who had no impact. Black churches were too provincial and conservative to support social justice politics and Social Gospel theology. Booker T. Washington and Du Bois were not involved with the Social Gospel, and, in any case, religious intellectuals were no longer of any importance by the end of the 19th century. Niebuhr discredited the Social Gospel, and the white Social Gospel movement that did exist did not concern itself with racial justice.

All these conventions are wrong. The black Social Gospel had many proponents in its early years: they were an embattled minority in their denominations because the Social Gospel was divisive and it caused trouble to people. The founders and their successors fought hard for the right to advocate progressive theology and social justice politics. Washington and Du Bois represented the two poles of debate within the movement, until the Du Bois faction prevailed. The black Social Gospel helped to create a counter protest against public opinion and favored the public engagement of intellectuals that eventually led to the civil rights movement. Religious idealism kept it alive, notwithstanding what Niebuhr said against religious idealism, and much of the white Social Gospel did not shirk, like Rauschenbusch did, from addressing America's racial crisis.[51]

The founders of the black Social Gospel operated in repressed black spaces, counting for nothing in white society, but some prodded the FCCC to risk more for racial justice; Ransom, Burroughs, and Walters were especially active in FCCC ecumenism. They were succeeded by a generation of leaders that espoused Social Gospel theology from the beginning of their careers. Johnson, Mays, Barbour, Powell Jr., and Thurman showed King how to combine faith, protest activism, and intellectualism. Their legacy is immense, paving the way for the generation of King, James Lawson, Joseph Lowery, Andrew Young, Bernard Lafayette, James Bevel, Diane Nash, Pauli Murray, Cordy Tindell Vivian, John Lewis, and other civil rights leaders of the 1950s and 1960s – the heyday of the black Social Gospel. Niebuhr influenced some of them, but none believed that he invalidated the Social Gospel. King did not spring from nowhere, and neither did the embattled theology of social justice that he espoused.

Black social Christianity, like any tradition, can be defined broadly or narrowly. Broadly, there were four groups in the founding generation, plus a socialist flank. The first group identified with Booker T. Washington and his program of political accommodation and economic improvement. The second group contended that black Americans needed their own nation because white America was hopelessly hostile to blacks. Crummell and AME bishop Henry McNeal Turner were leading black nationalists. The third group advocated protest activism for racial justice, strongly opposing Washington. Ransom and Wright were leading figures in this group. The fourth group navigated between pro-Washington and anti-Washington forces, imploring against factional division. Powell Sr. and Burroughs were its leading figures.

---

51   Dorrien, *The New Abolition*, 1–33; Dorrien, *Breaking White Supremacy*, 1–23.

All four of these ideological factions existed before Du Bois emerged as the intellectual leader of the protest tradition. A fully-fledged black Social Gospel tradition emerged from them, mainly from the third and fourth groups. It stood for social justice religion and modern critical consciousness. This full-orbed black Social Gospel combined an emphasis on black dignity and personhood with protest activism for racial justice, a comprehensive social justice agenda, an insistence that authentic Christian faith is incompatible with racism, an emphasis on the social ethical teaching of Jesus, and an acceptance of modern scholarship and social consciousness.

Booker T. Washington was a figure of such colossal influence that for many years he compelled everyone in this story to take him into consideration. He was complex, wily, opaque, and extremely accomplished. He built Alabama's Tuskegee Institute in the face of Ku Klux Klan terrorism, a mania of lynching, a Southern civil religion of Lost Cause propaganda, and a suffocating plague of disenfranchisement and abuse. He cultivated an image of simple altruism while fighting in a sagacious, calculated fashion for as much power as he might obtain, fulfilling the American fantasy of ascending from poverty and disadvantage to greatness. He publicly accommodated disenfranchisement and segregation, while privately organizing legal efforts to thwart both. Washington denied that he made federal patronage appointments for blacks long after he had routinely made all of them. He attracted wealthy benefactors, became an advisor to four US presidents, launched hundreds of community schools, and amassed a powerful political machine.

Washington keenly understood that the white South did not want black Americans to succeed at anything besides picking cotton. Any black success at whatsoever else raised the frightening specter of "Negro rule." A black postmaster represented Negro rule. A black shopkeeper, black teacher, or black lawyer represented Negro rule. However, in order to give African Americans a glimmer of opportunity in a brutally hostile context, he

pretended not to know it. Washington bartered the civil and political rights of black Americans for a season of interracial peace and economic opportunity. On the few occasions when he explained his strategy, he wrote quintessential descriptions of political realism. Yet everything deteriorated for African Americans during this ostensible season, setting up Washington for the devastating objection that black Americans had not appointed him to be their leader. He was the first black leader to be selected by white Americans, an arrangement he lived to see unravel. For the "race problem" in America was white racism, and the antidote to it had no chance of originating in Alabama.

Washington epitomized an influential version of the Social Gospel. He was powerfully linked with the conservative assimilation wing of the white Social Gospel, led by Abbott, who serialized Washington's memoir *Up from Slavery* to his *Harper's Magazine* audience and lauded Washington as the answer to "the race problem." To Washington, religion nurtured the correct moral virtues and helped to build a good society – exactly as white Social Gospel leaders said.

The nationalist alternative to Washington called for national separation and/or African emigration. Then as now, there were different kinds of black nationalism – the idea that all people of African descent share something as a nation or people. In the 19th and 20th centuries, the posited basis for national belonging was sometimes biological, rendering the nation analogous to a biological organism, and/or ontological, making a claim about the distinct being of blackness, and/or cultural or socio-historical, making a claim about black cultural authenticity or distinctiveness. Having defined this broadly, however, there were nationalists in all four streams of black social Christianity. The more stringently nationalist group contended that blacks were a distinct people needing to create a sovereign nation-state and, even if the statehood project failed, a black civilization.

Some nationalists devoted themselves to colonizing West Africa, following Turner, or Haiti, following Episcopal Bishop James Holly, but many eventually renounced the idea of emigration, following Crummell. Much of the nationalist tradition shared the emphases of Crummell and Turner on moral uplift, authority, elite leadership, and the shortcomings of ordinary black Americans. Despite its rhetoric of separation, the nationalist tradition ironically played a major role in transmitting assimilationist values into African American culture. Most black nationalists were politically conservative and nearly all were culturally conservative. Black nationalism had an electrifying moment after World War I, with the rise of Marcus Garvey's back-to-Africa movement. A generation earlier, Crummell and Turner had clashed over the question as to whether nationalists should continue to strive for a separate nation-state. Turner became the dominant figure in this school of thought and activism by saying that they should.

The third group vehemently opposed Washington's strategy and his "Tuskegee Machine," calling for a new abolitionist politics of racial and social justice. The fully-fledged black Social Gospel emerged mainly from this group. In addition to Ransom, Wright, and Wells-Barnett, leading figures included Baptist clerics James Diggs, Peter James Bryant, and William Jefferson White, Congregational cleric Byron Gunner, and Episcopal socialist rectors Robert W. Bagnall and George Frazier Miller.

The fourth group helped to influence the way in which the argument over Bookerism turned out. In the early 1900s, the groups advocating protest and accommodation fought each other ferociously, with a great deal of offensive language. Both sides alienated people that disliked ideological bickering. Religious communities naturally brought together the rival camps and the nonaligned. Many clerics, having friends on both sides of the partisan divide, appealed to Christian fellowship and racial solidarity. The fourth group urged that Du Bois-style militancy and Washington-style realism were both indispensable. Its leading figures, besides Burroughs and Powell Sr., included sociologists Monroe Work and George Haynes, Methodist minister William Henry Brooks, and Baptist feminists Lucy Smith and Sarah Layten.

Meanwhile some figures in the third group added a socialist critique to civil rights militancy. Baptist ministers George Woodbey and George Slater were leading black Social Gospel socialists. Woodbey had a long career as a Socialist Party organizer and was also active in the IWW. Du Bois, Ransom, Bagnall, and Miller led the black socialist faction of the NAACP, but socialism had much to overcome in black communities: a fantasized solidarity with a racist white proletariat, the specter of appearing to be anti-American, and the desire of African Americans to own property and succeed in the existing system.

Two AME stalwarts with fiery temperaments, Wells and Ransom, played crucial roles in founding the black Social Gospel. In the 1890s, before and after she married Ferdinand Barnett, Wells conducted a brave personal crusade against the epidemic of lynching, telling her audiences that lynching was a matter of racial hatred of white communities, and not the alleged acts of sexual violence committed by black men on white women. These alleged crimes were, in fact, just an excuse to let furious racist lynching go unpunished.

Wells recoiled at exploring this subject in depth because her moralism ran very deep. She frequently attended three or four church services on Sundays, and she held preachers to a high standard of holiness. She hated the occurrence that "somebody" should turn out to be like her because writing about lynching was incendiary and dangerous, forcing her to flee from Memphis, and sometimes compelling her to write about salacious matters. Wells grieved that the salacious aspects of her reporting harmed her moral reputation. According to her, white men were the barbarians of the time, white women were more prone to sexuality than their husbands dared to imagine, black women were victimized by the predatory sexuality of white men, and black men were made to pay harshly for all of it.[52]

---

52   Ida B. Wells-Barnett, *Southern Horrors: Lynch Law in All its Phases*, New York NY, New York Age Print, 1892, 3–13; Ida. B. Wells-Barnett, *The Red Record: Tabulated Statistics and Alleged Causes of Lynching in the United*

Speaking on this topic anywhere in the Deep South was unthinkable. Wells tried, unsuccessfully, to lecture in border states. She often spoke to Social Gospel audiences in the North, but failed to build the organization she sought for lack of funds and moral support. At one point, she joined forces with the Afro-American Council, but Washington took control over it, and she resigned in disgust. She later tried to work with the NAACP, but did not like Du Bois or his enabler, Mary White Ovington, so she settled for a solitary activism. Wells was a catalyzing figure for what became the black Social Gospel, in particular for her pastor in Chicago, Ransom.

Ransom was the Du Bois figure among black church ministers. In his early career he served AME churches in Chicago and Boston, the two cities that seemed best suited to support a Social Gospel ministry. His fellow clergy drove him out of both cities for doing so. Ransom fought long and hard to legitimize Social Gospel theology in the AME Church. He gave highly stimulating speeches at protest meetings and abolitionist memorials, acquiring a national reputation. He emerged as a protest leader, anti-lynching activist, and socialist before Du Bois did, later joining Du Bois in the Niagara Movement. In 1912 Ransom made an ecclesiastical breakthrough by taking over the *A.M.E. Church Review*, which gave him a national audience and an independent basis as a general officer of the denomination. Ransom pushed hard for social justice theology, forming a tag team with Du Bois during the same period that Du Bois launched the NAACP's *The Crisis* magazine and had a spectacular period of success. Ransom and Du Bois conferred about topics, boosted each other, and offered a combined subscription to their magazines. Both aimed directly at the educated elite that Du Bois called "the Talented Tenth," and both

weathered constant complaints that they were too radical for the positions they held.

Ransom did not want to be a bishop, but he worked hard at establishing the Social Gospel in the AME Church, which carried him to a bishop's chair in 1924. In the 1930s, the nationalist strain in his thought grew stronger. It amazed Ransom that white Americans brutalized black Americans while mustering ample sympathy for persecuted Irish, Jews, and Armenians. Why were white Americans so fearful of blacks? Ransom puzzled constantly over this. He grieved that white Americans reserved a special loathing for blacks that defied American history. Black Americans had never been anything but loyal Americans and faithful Christians, but what did they gain from it? They went to church, achieved an education, learned a trade, and were still brutalized: "Their disillusionment is almost complete, since they find that Christ has not been able to break the American color line. If Jesus wept over Jerusalem, he should have for America an ocean of tears."[53]

Ransom held fast to the Social Gospel Jesus and the hope of the kingdom to come, preaching throughout his career that nothing compares to the figure of Jesus and his teaching. However, the later Ransom stopped saying that the kingdom was coming to America. It was hard to continue saying that black and white America would come together when white America clung to its racist supremacism. It seemed to Ransom that white America had lost its soul. In his later career, he taught that Asia, Europe, and the United States were heading downward, while the future belonged to the children of Africa. The Euro-American and Asian civilizations had no compelling spiritual vision for humanity. They stood for wealth, power, weapons, science, technology, and philosophy, all of which had failed, or were failing. The white world never created a great religion, and its substitutes were spiritually barren. The hope of the world was to be found in the last place where white Americans

---

States, 1895 pamphlet reprinted in: Ida B. Wells-Barnett, *On Lynchings*, Amherst NY, Humanity Books, 2002 [¹1895], 268–295; *Crusade for Justice: The Autobiography of Ida B. Wells-Barnett*, ed. Alfreda M. Duster, Chicago IL, University of Chicago Press, 1970.

---

53   Reverdy C. Ransom, *The Negro: The Hope or the Despair of Christianity*, Boston MA, Ruth Hill, 1935, 55.

thought to look: "The African and his descendants are the last spiritual reserves of humanity."[54]

The black Social Gospel founders refused to be denigrated. They rebelled against the regime of segregation and persecution imposed upon them. They applied the old abolitionist rhetoric to the new tyranny of Jim Crow, appealing always to the bedrock Christian doctrine that every human being bears the image and Spirit of God. They held fast to Jesus, especially Jesus on the cross, and the hope of the kingdom coming. And some lived to see their successors carry out the new abolition.

The black Social Gospel had all the standard tropes of the white Social Gospel, even the progress motif, and even a variation on Manifest Destiny. It preached about equality, democracy, peacemaking, and Jesus loving all the little children. It taught that God favors the oppressed and excluded. It taught that "Thy kingdom come" is the center of Jesus' teaching and Christians are called to build up the Kingdom of God. It puzzled that the church claimed the Christian name for centuries while ignoring the biblical ethic of justice. It proclaimed that the salvation of Christ offers deliverance from the bondage of selfishness and will-to-power. It affirmed that missionary zeal is a measure of one's devotion to Christ and the good. It employed "Christianizing" and "democratizing" as interchangeable terms and called for a new age of the Spirit that unleashed the spiritual power of Christ-following idealism.

Yet one thing was of greater importance than anything else in black Social Gospel testimony and worship, i.e. the cross of Jesus. Black Social Gospel ministers often preached the cross of Jesus in the manner of liberal theology, emphasizing moral and spiritual influence, where Jesus exemplified a religious ideal by suffering for others. At the same time, they inveighed against passivity and defeatism, inciting black Americans to rebel against the oppression and exclusion inflicted on them, usually avoiding any suggestion that the gospel inscribed an ethic of martyrdom. They constantly

upheld the notion that Jesus had nothing to do with accepting racial subjugation as God's will.

This was a slippery problem of theology and communication, for every atonement theory is shot through with the idea of redemptive suffering, and moral influence theory heightens the problem of sacrificial appropriation. Atonement doctrines turn the Gospel of Jesus into a rational concept that is explained by a theory of salvation-via-sacrifice. Moral influence theory perpetuates the logic of surrogate sacrifice and heightens its danger of masochistic appropriation. If Jesus exemplified a religious ideal by suffering and dying for others, the Gospel becomes a message of self-sacrifice and the perfectionism of love. Every black minister standing before a congregation had to feel the threat that these theories posed to the cross and to the well-being of every listener.

Yet nothing came as close to the cross of Jesus as a subject of black church preaching and worship. Black churches reverberated with hymns, gospel songs, spirituals, prayers, testimonies, and sermons about the crucifixion of Jesus and being with him at the cross. Jesus was a friend of oppressed people who knew about their suffering. Jesus achieved salvation for "the least of these" through his solidarity with them, even unto death. African American Christians, like Jesus, did not deserve to suffer. However, keeping faith in Jesus was the one thing that African American Christians possessed that white America could not control or take from them.

For black Christians, merely knowing that Jesus suffered as they did gave them faith that God was with them, even if they ended up, like Jesus, tortured to death on a tree. Liberation theologian James Cone, in *The Cross and the Lynching Tree*, luminously explains: "The more black people struggled against white supremacy, the more they found in the cross the spiritual power to resist the violence they so often suffered."[55] The crucifixion of Jesus placed God among a persecuted,

---

54   Ransom, *The Negro*, 6.

55   James Cone, *The Cross and the Lynching Tree*, Maryknoll NY, Orbis Books, 2011, 22.

tyrannized, tortured, and crucified people. White communities lynched black Americans in nearly every state of the United States. Lynching, as Cone remarks, was a "ritual celebration of white supremacy,"[56] suitable for family gatherings and sometimes drawing enormous crowds. Black Americans, like Jesus, were stripped, paraded, mocked, whipped, spat upon, and tortured to death. Just as Jesus was a victim of mob hysteria and imperial violence, black Americans were victims of mob hysteria and white supremacy. The cross and the lynching tree both struck terror into the heart of the subject community – terrorism being the point in both cases.

The black Social Gospel preachers, particularly Ransom, Powell Sr., and King, had the requisite imagination to see redemption in the cross without explaining it in a theory. They let the spiritual power of the cross do its work without enveloping it in a required doctrine. Powell took this tack even in his Revival sermons. Ransom acquired less company than he sought in struggling for the new abolition, and the black Social Gospel founders were soon forgotten. However, they helped to construct a counter-public and a civil rights movement. They planted the Social Gospel in the mainstream of the black Methodist and black Baptist Churches, and they inspired a stream of successors that carried out America's greatest liberation movement.

4 Conclusions: A Theology of Social Salvation for the Ecumenical Movement

As the account demonstrates, Ely and Gladden were the initiators of a movement which has its roots in the ironies and failures of the post-war socio-economic system, but finds the answers and reasons to react to it into a new form of Christianity which finds in that same society a source of salvation. Their social thought and action were not conceived based on theology, but by means of an approach which established

science and philosophy as a normative source for theology and biblical criticism, therefore bringing their progressivism into the very essence of the human relationship with God.[57]

Moreover, the account demonstrates that their lives and thoughts crossed, and were crossed by, the lives and thoughts of many of the men who became leaders of the ecumenical movement, both in the United States and abroad. Among them, there was Charles Henry Brent, father of Faith and Order and at that time serving at the Episcopalian St. Stephen's Church in Boston; William Reed Huntington, a prominent Episcopalian theologian who at the end of the 19th century promoted an organic union of American Churches; Robert H. Gardiner, Brent's right arm in the formation of Faith and Order, and Methodist John R. Mott, founder of the WSCF, chair of the 1910 World Missionary Conference of Edinburgh and honorary president of the WCC established in 1948.[58]

The Social Gospel was an interdenominational movement which set a precedent for the churches of a common theological reflection and social action, with a strong missionary background, exemplified by the YMCA, the YWCA, and the WSCF. Its debates and intellectual output nurtured somehow unexpectedly the less activist and more theology-centered Faith and Order movement and paved the way for the establishment of the FCCC.[59]

---

56 Cone, *The Cross and the Lynching Tree*, 9.

57 Gina A. Zurlo, "The Social Gospel, Ecumenical Movement, and Christian Sociology: The Institute of Social and Religious Research," *The American Sociologist* 46/2, 2015, 177–193.

58 Woolverton refers to this group as the "the conservatives." Woolverton, *Robert H. Gardiner*, 48. On the background and the legacy of Brent, Gardiner, Huntington, and Mott, see in this volume the chapters by Luca Ferracci, Paul Avis, and Sarah Scholl.

59 See Herbert Yoder, "Christian Unity in the Nineteenth-Century America," in: *A History of the Ecumenical Movement*, vol. 1, 221–259.

Bibliography

Cauthen, Kenneth, *The Impact of American Religious Liberalism*, Washington DC, University Press of America, 1983.

Cone, James, *The Cross and the Lynching Tree*, Maryknoll NY, Orbis Books, 2011.

Dorrien, Gary, *Soul in Society: The Making and Renewal of Social Christianity*, Minneapolis MN, Fortress Press, 1995.

Dorrien, Gary, *The Making of American Liberal Theology: Idealism, Realism, and Modernity (1900–1950)*, Louisville KY, Westminster John Knox, 2003.

Dorrien, Gary, *Social Ethics in the Making: Interpreting an American Tradition*, Oxford, Wiley-Blackwell, 2011.

Dorrien, Gary, *The New Abolition: W.E.B. Du Bois and the Black Social Gospel*, New Haven CT, Yale University Press, 2015.

Dorrien, Gary, *Breaking White Supremacy: Martin Luther King Jr. and the Black Social Gospel*, New Haven CT, Yale University Press, 2018.

Handy, Robert T., *A Christian America: protestant Hopes and Historical Realities*, New York NY, Oxford University Press, 1971.

Handy, Robert T., *Undermined Establishment: Church-State Relations in America (1800–1920)*, Princeton NJ, Princeton University Press, 1991.

Hutchison, William R., ed., *American Protestant Thought in the Liberal Era*, Lanham MD, University Press of America, 1968.

Woolverton, John F., *Robert H. Gardiner and the Reunification of Worldwide Christianity in the Progressive Era*, Columbia MO, University of Missouri Press, 2005.

CHAPTER 18

The World Missionary Conference at Edinburgh in 1910, and the Role of the Protestant Missionary Movement

Brian Stanley

1 The World Missionary Conference, Edinburgh 1910

The WMC[1] held in the Assembly Hall of the United Free Church of Scotland in Edinburgh from June 14 to 23, 1910, expressed the untroubled confidence and passionate enthusiasm of the Western Protestant missionary movement as it approached the zenith of its size and global influence in the age of high imperialism. Approximately 1,215 official delegates, 1,008 of them men, and 207 women, gathered in the Scottish capital to debate how the various Protestant mission agencies could collaborate more effectively to bring the Christian gospel to the non-European world. Only about twenty delegates came from the so-called younger churches planted by Western missions – it was an overwhelmingly white and entirely Anglophone occasion, with no attempt being made to offer translation of the addresses for the benefit of non-native speakers of English.

The conference was conceived as a great deliberative council of the Church Protestant. Participants or observers sometimes invoked memories of the medieval crusades, and of the Council of Clermont that launched the First Crusade in 1095. The WMC was intended to prepare its missionary armies to launch a concerted and final onslaught on the dark forces of heathendom that still ruled supreme beyond the frontiers of Western Christendom. Those who responded with quiet determination by committing themselves anew to this militant and intensely serious calling could, like the crusaders of the medieval age, be sure of the eternal blessing of God on their united endeavors.

Nevertheless, the intended appeal of the conference was not to the popular Christian imagination so much as to the concentrated attention of serious Christian minds. Almost from the outset, the conference was planned, as Rev. William H. Findlay, a former Methodist missionary in India and a member of the British executive committee, put it, "to be a Grand Council for the Advancement of Missionary Science."[2] Foreign missions, once so widely ridiculed, had come of age, and their most thoughtful advocates believed that the time had come for the application of the rigorous methods of modern social science to the challenges and problems that missionaries faced on the field. This conviction was held with peculiar force by the conference secretary, Joseph H. Oldham, a 34-year-old Scot who had served in India with the YMCA. Oldham was insistent that the call to urgent evangelistic action which would issue from Edinburgh must be based, not on emotional and stereotypical depictions of the plight of the "heathen world," but on the "ascertained and sifted facts" minutely analyzed in the weighty reports of the eight preparatory study commissions presented

---

1 This article draws upon my published monograph, *The World Missionary Conference, Edinburgh 1910*, Grand Rapids MI, Eerdmans, 2009. In addition to published primary sources, it is based on the following archival collections: WCCA, Minutes of the Third Ecumenical Missionary Conference (later World Missionary Conference); CUL, Bible Society Archives, BSA/F4, Letter-books of J.H. Ritson and Microfilm Minutes of London Secretaries' Association, 1893–1924; UTS, MRL 12, WMC papers; NCL, Oldham Papers; YDSL, Special Collections, RG32, George Sherwood Eddy Papers.

2 Cited in Stanley, *The World Missionary Conference*, 4.

to the conference. Oldham's hope was that the eight commission reports would become standard works of reference on world mission, distilling the best results of field experience and laying the foundations for the emergence of a new "science of missions" that would inform all future practice. Missions were becoming a matter of induction and experiment in which method was everything.[3] For nine days the delegates endured word-heavy sessions that began at 9:45 in the morning and did not conclude till 9:30 at night. They listened to some 300 consecutive speeches of 7 minutes each during the daytime, and 24 evening addresses of up to 40 minutes each.

Edinburgh 1910, as the WMC is commonly called, is one of a select number of events in the history of Christianity that have attained almost canonical status. It is sometimes seen as the first occasion on which Protestants convened something roughly corresponding to an "ecumenical council." The conference receives honorable mention in almost every textbook covering the ecclesiastical history of the 20th century. Among Protestants especially, it is frequently given a significance of epochal proportions, for the conference is widely seen as marking the inception of two major transitions in the modern history of Christianity: first, the transition from an age of denominational competition and rivalry to one of growing ecumenical cooperation and convergence; and second, the geographical transformation of Christianity from a predominantly European faith to one whose demographic composition and theological emphases have become increasingly reflective of the whole *oikumene*, that is, the entire global family of humanity. Neither of these perceptions is wholly false. The reality, however, is, as always, considerably more complex and ambiguous. This article will critically examine in turn these two common representations of the conference and its legacy for ecumenism. In so doing, it will form an assessment of the role played by the Protestant missionary movement in shaping these two

decisive reconfigurations of Christianity in the modern world.

2   Edinburgh 1910: The Evangelical Origins of Protestant Ecumenism

The spirit of pan-evangelical ecumenism did not suddenly appear in 1910. On the contrary, it had marked the Protestant missionary movement almost from the start, even though on occasion this high ideal was deeply compromised by tendencies to denominational rivalry in the mission fields. Although the first Protestant mission to Asia, the Danish-sponsored Halle mission to Tranquebar in South India initiated in 1706, was an exclusively Lutheran venture, it attracted widespread interest and some financial support from some other denominations, notably from the Church of England's SPCK. The full flowering of Protestant missions that followed at the end of the 18th century in the wake of the evangelical revivals was more explicitly ecumenical, both in ethos and frequently also in structure. William Carey, the founder of the English BMS, established in 1792, had appealed in his pamphlet, *An Enquiry into the Obligations of Christian to Use Means for the Conversion of the Heathens*, to "every one who loves our Lord Jesus Christ in sincerity" to respond to the missionary challenge. Yet Carey had conceded that "in the present divided state of Christendom," it would be more likely for good to be done by each denomination engaging separately in the work, then if they were to embark in it conjointly.[4]

Experience would eventually confirm Carey's sober realism, but the missionary awakening did nonetheless inspire some remarkable examples of interdenominational cooperation. The LMS, founded in 1795, eventually became almost exclusively identified with the Congregational (or Independent) denomination in Britain, but its

---

3   Stanley, *The World Missionary Conference*, 5.

4   William Carey, *An Enquiry into the Obligations of Christians to Use Means for the Conversion of the Heathens*, Leicester, 1792; new edition: London, Carey Kingsgate Press, 1961, 84.

original vision proclaimed pan-evangelical unity in the cause of spreading the gospel as a prophetic sign that the world was approaching the last days of human history: what one of its founders, the Scottish Independent David Bogue, applauded in a 1795 sermon as the "funeral of bigotry" was a prelude to the marriage-supper of the Lamb.[5] In its early years the Society drew significant support from Scottish Presbyterians. Its first directors included not simply Independents but also Presbyterians, Anglicans, and the occasional Wesleyan Methodist. Its missionaries included Anglicans, German and Swedish Lutherans, and Reformed Christians from France and the Netherlands.

Other societies followed the nondenominational pattern pioneered by the LMS. In Britain, the RTS (1799), the BFBS (1804), and the LSPCJ (1809) all bridged the ecclesiastical divide between the Church of England and Dissenters, though of these three only the BFBS succeeded in the long term in maintaining this ecumenical breadth. In the United States, the ABS was established in 1816, with a similarly nondenominational vision. The first American foreign missionary society, the ABCFM, originally drew support from Dutch Reformed and Presbyterians as well as Congregationalists, though, like the LMS, its constituency eventually narrowed to the Congregational denomination. On the European continent, the Basel Mission, established in 1815, although it drew its primary support from Lutheran Pietists in Württemberg, trained in its seminary many of the early missionaries of the evangelical Anglican CMS, founded in 1799.

Enthusiasm for foreign missions crossed not simply denominational boundaries but also national frontiers and even the Atlantic Ocean. The second foreign missionary agency established by American Protestants, the Baptist Triennial Convention (1814), had as its secretary William Staughton of Philadelphia, who had been one of

the founders of the BMS alongside William Carey in Kettering, Northamptonshire, in October 1792. The first missionary sent overseas by the Church of Scotland, Alexander Duff of Bengal, visited the United States and Canada in 1854 on behalf of the Foreign Missions Committee of the Free Church of Scotland (to which he had transferred his allegiance following the Scottish Disruption of 1843). His first address in the New World, to a crowd of 3–4,000 in Philadelphia, referred to America and Britain "shaking hands across the Atlantic as the two great props of evangelic Protestant Christianity in the world."[6] Duff's visit inspired a group of ministers in Philadelphia to organize at short notice a "General Missionary Conference" to take place in New York on May 4 and 5, 1854. The conference was modest in scale, attracting 156 participants, only eleven of whom were missionaries, but it marked the first missionary conference that transcended denominational and even geographical boundaries.[7]

Hence, contrary to what is often alleged, Edinburgh 1910 was not the first international missionary conference. The one held in New York in 1854 was followed by others in Liverpool in 1860, London in 1878, and then by two much larger conferences in London in 1888 and New York in 1900. The Centenary Missionary Conference in London in 1888, which rather loosely commemorated the beginnings of foreign missions from the Anglo-American world in the late 1780s, took obvious Protestant pleasure on at least two occasions in describing itself as an "oecumenical council" in what were surely calculated allusions to the use of that title by Vatican I (1869–1870). The chairman of one of its sessions, Sir S. Arthur Blackwood, proudly claimed that this was "an Oecumenical Council in the truest sense of the word" because its participants were "those engaged either in directing

---

5   Sermons Preached in London at the Formation of the London Missionary Society, London, Chapman, 1795, 425.

6   George Smith, The Life of Alexander Duff, D.D., LL.D., vol. 2, London, Hodder & Stoughton, 1879, 268.

7   William Richey Hogg, Ecumenical Foundations: A History of the International Missionary Council and Its Nineteenth-Century Background, New York NY, Harper, 1952, 37.

or carrying on Missionary enterprise throughout the world"; and the published conference volume noted in similarly hyperbolic vein that representatives hailed from an area "little short of the habitable globe, making the Council in the highest sense oecumenical."[8] The word "ecumenical" was then incorporated in the official title of the New York Conference in 1900, "not because all portions of the Christian Church are to be represented in it by delegates," as the New England Episcopalian, William Huntington, put it when addressing the assembly, but "because the plan of campaign which it proposes covers the whole area of the inhabited globe."[9] "Ecumenical" still implied global geographical reach, and not necessarily comprehensiveness of Christian affiliation or theological perspective.

2.1   The Edinburgh Conference: An Ecumenical Event?

It should be emphasized that the Edinburgh Conference was not an "ecumenical" conference in anything like the currently accepted sense of the word. Its original title was indeed the "Third Ecumenical Missionary Conference," since it was conceived as the sequel to the 1888 and 1900 gatherings. It is a nice irony that, when at a crucial conference planning meeting held at Wycliffe Hall in Oxford in July 1908 it was decided to abandon the title "Third Ecumenical Missionary Conference" in favor of "The World Missionary Conference," the reason given was that "the word 'Ecumenical' has acquired a technical meaning."[10] This was in fact its modern meaning, associated with the very movement for church unity with which Edinburgh has become widely associated in the collective Christian memory. As John H. Ritson, an English Wesleyan Methodist minister, secretary of the BFBS and member of the British executive committee, explained, the word "Ecumenical" had been dropped, "as it cannot be used truthfully while great sections of the Church are in no way connected with the Conference."[11] There were, of course, no representatives at Edinburgh of the Roman Catholic, Orthodox or Oriental Orthodox Churches. However, one Roman Catholic Modernist, Bishop Geremia Bonomelli of Cremona, did send a letter of greeting which was, eventually, read to the conference on June 21 by his friend, Silas McBee, an American Episcopal layman from New York, with the tacit and unofficial approval of the conference business committee.

The organizers of the Edinburgh Conference were thus humble enough to recognize that their overwhelmingly Protestant and broadly evangelical assembly could not justifiably claim the label of "ecumenical." The most that can be said is that it covered a slightly broader ecumenical range than its predecessors in that the oldest Anglican missionary society, founded in 1701, the SPG, to the chagrin of many of its High Church supporters, was for the first time represented in an avowedly Protestant missionary conference. However, the more distinctively Anglo-Catholic Anglican society, the UMCA, was not, since it refused to participate in such an overtly Protestant gathering. Despite the description of the conference in one recent academic study of 20th-century ecumenism as "the first modern assembly of world-wide churches,"[12] almost all the participating agencies in the Edinburgh Conference were voluntarist bodies with no ecclesial status. Some of the mission agencies were, as in the case of the Scottish Presbyterian missions, foreign mission committees of their respective churches rather than separate voluntary societies, but no Christian

---

8   James Johnston, ed., *Report of the Centenary Conference on the Protestant Missions of the World*, vol. 1, London, J. Nisbet, 1888, 467, XLIII.

9   *Ecumenical Missionary Conference New York, 1900*, vol. 1, New York NY, American Tract Society, 1900, 10.

10   WCCA, Third Ecumenical Missionary Conference (June 1910), Minutes of International Committee, July 14–20, 1908, 9.

11   J.H. Ritson to H. Smith, July 24, 1908, in: CUL, BSA/F4/3/1, fol. 69.

12   John Frederick Woolverton, *Robert H. Gardiner and the Reunification of Worldwide Christianity in the Progressive Era*, Columbia MO, University of Missouri Press, 2005, 113.

denomination as such had direct representation at Edinburgh. The delegates came from Western Protestant or Anglican missionary societies, with the addition of a few specially invited guests from Asia, who will be mentioned later.

Overseas mission experience, especially in Asia, supplied not simply the compelling dynamic but also the organizational template for the conference. Edinburgh 1910 represented a conscious departure from the more populist and exhortatory style of its immediate Western predecessors held in London in 1888 and New York in 1900. Unlike its two predecessors, it was conceived as a working conference based on discussion of weighty "scientific" reports prepared in advance by a series of eight study commissions composed of carefully selected experts. The precedents for such an approach came from Asia rather than the West even though the animating methodology was an emphatically Western "scientific" one. The models followed at Edinburgh were supplied by the fourth Indian Decennial Missionary Conference held in Madras in 1902 and, still more directly, by the Shanghai Missionary Conference of China missionaries held in 1907. The Madras Conference, which itself followed a pattern pioneered on a smaller scale by the regional South India Missionary Conference in 1900, had proceeded by allocating all delegates to eight subject committees, each with its own convener, who was charged to gather information and opinions well in advance from his apportioned delegates and more widely. Each committee then drafted a series of resolutions, usually preceded by preliminary remarks, for discussion and adoption by the conference in session. Five years later, the much larger Shanghai Conference adhered to a modified version of the same pattern, drawing a clear distinction between the members of the preparatory committees and the rest of the delegates: twelve program committees were established in advance, but in this instance with a limited membership of ten to thirteen persons; the chairman of each program committee was responsible for preparing a paper in consultation with his committee, which was to be printed in advance of the

conference, and for introducing the paper and its accompanying resolutions to the conference. It was this model that provided the basis for the eight study commissions appointed in 1908 to prepare for the Edinburgh Conference.

2.2   *The Ambiguous Place of Faith and Order at Edinburgh 1910*

The Edinburgh Conference continues to be regularly described as the starting point of the modern ecumenical movement. As early as 1961, Alec Vidler's volume in the *Pelican History of the Church* observed that "it is generally agreed that the movement, as it is now known, dates from the International Missionary Conference [*sic*] that was held at Edinburgh in 1910."[13] The English Methodist historian, John Kent, when passing an acerbic judgment on the ecumenical movement as "the great ecclesiastical failure of our time," referred to 1910 as the year "when the search for institutional unity was first systematically organized."[14] However, the potentially explosive questions relating to the differences in doctrine and ecclesiastical order between Christian churches were strictly prohibited from the discussions at Edinburgh. The exclusion was extracted from Oldham, the newly appointed conference secretary, in 1908 by Charles Gore, bishop of Birmingham, and Edward Talbot, bishop of Southwark, as the condition that would, they hoped, secure the participation in the conference of the SPG, many of whose supporters viewed the projected event as a lamentable gathering of Protestant evangelical sects with which no High Church Anglican could possibly be identified.

In point of fact, the terms of this imposed exclusion of faith and order were placed under some strain. The written reports presented to the conference by the eight study commissions had gathered

---

13   Alec R. Vidler, *The Church in an Age of Revolution: 1789 to the Present Day*, Harmondsworth, Penguin, 1961, 257.

14   John Kent, *The Unacceptable Face: The Modern Church in the Eyes of the Historian*, London, SCM Press, 1987, 203.

questionnaire replies received from samples of missionaries (and a few indigenous church leaders) from different parts of the globe. The weight of evidence submitted to Commission VIII on Co-operation and the Promotion of Unity clearly suggested that some Protestants in India, China, and Japan were already engaged in discussions, not merely about closer cooperation between mission agencies, but even about moves towards church union, the very subject that was formally excluded from the conference agenda. Taking note of existing moves towards the formation of united or federated churches in specific locations in India, China, and Japan was relatively uncontroversial, but if the conference had made any sustained venture into the forbidden territory of discussing the possible reunion of Western Christendom, its minority of Anglo-Catholic delegates would have promptly walked out, and disaster would have ensued.

As is well known, there is, nevertheless, good justification for tracing the genealogy of the WCC at least in part to the 1910 conference. John R. Mott, the American Methodist layman and student evangelist who took the chair at Edinburgh, was the first speaker at the inaugural assembly of the WCC at Amsterdam in 1948 and was made honorary president of the new World Council. The WCC was the offspring of the marriage in 1938 of the Faith and Order and Life and Work movements. The latter was, however, a response not to the WMC but to World War I. Its principal architect, Nathan Söderblom, Lutheran archbishop of Uppsala, was not a delegate at Edinburgh, though he was deeply influenced by the international student movement that was so formative for the collaborative and nondogmatic approach adopted by the conference.

The Faith and Order movement, by contrast, owed its genesis to Charles H. Brent, American missionary bishop of the Protestant Episcopal Church in the Philippines, who was present at Edinburgh, and spoke twice. His first address was a bold contribution to the debate on Co-operation and the Promotion of Unity, in which he urged

that "in any scheme, practical or theoretical, for unity, we must take into our reckoning the Roman Catholic Church, which is an integral part of the Church and of the Kingdom of God."[15] This was an emphasis that reflected his own experience in the Philippines, the most Catholic nation in Asia. His second address, made to the penultimate evening session on June 22, referred in general terms to the "new vision" that had been unfolded to the delegates.[16] According to Tissington Tatlow, general secretary of the SCM, "the new vision was the vision of a united Church,"[17] though there is no conclusive evidence that church unity rather than enhanced missionary cooperation was what Brent meant. In his old age, Oldham claimed that Brent had called at Edinburgh for another conference to tackle those questions of faith and order that had been excluded from the agenda. However, the evidence suggests that Oldham's memory was at fault. No such reference is recorded in the reports of either of Brent's conference addresses, and his diary records that the idea of a world conference on faith and order in fact came to him vividly at a morning Eucharist in Cincinnati on Oct 5, 1910 at the opening of the Convention of the Protestant Episcopal Church.[18]

If the Faith and Order movement owed its origins, at least indirectly, to the deep impression which attendance at Edinburgh made upon Charles Brent, as on many other delegates, the connection between the conference and the formation in October 1921 of the IMC at Lake

---

15   WMC, ed., *World Missionary Conference, 1910: To Consider Missionary Problems in Relation to the Non-Christian World*, vol. 8, *Report of Commission VIII: Co-Operation and the Promotion of Unity*, Edinburgh, Oliphant, Anderson & Ferrier, 1910, 199.

16   WMC, ed., *World Missionary Conference, 1910*, vol. 9, *The History and Records of the Conference: Together with Addresses Delivered at the Evening Meetings*, Edinburgh, Oliphant, Anderson & Ferrier, 1910, 330.

17   Tissington Tatlow, "The World Conference on Faith and Order," in: *A History of the Ecumenical Movement*, vol. 1, Ruth Rouse & Stephen C. Neill, eds., *1517–1948*, London, SPCK, 1954, 405–441, here 407.

18   Stanley, *The World Missionary Conference*, 297.

Mohonk, New York state, is self-evident and well known. The first major global ecumenical body was formed, with Oldham as its secretary, in direct succession to the Continuation Committee established at the close of the Edinburgh Conference.[19]

2.3   The Progression of Protestant Missionary Cooperation from National to International Level

What is rarely emphasized is that the formation of the IMC in 1921 as the first permanent international Protestant missionary body cannot be explained simply in terms of the legacy of the Edinburgh Conference, important though that undoubtedly was. Well before 1910, Protestant missions were forming national and even transnational bodies that gave institutional expression to their concern for cooperation in missions. This was notably the case in North America and continental Europe, where Protestant ecumenism was considerably further advanced than in Britain, which was ecclesiastically polarized between the Church of England and the Nonconformist denominations. In North America in January 1893, thirty-three Protestant foreign missionary societies of the United States and Canada had formed an annual conference.[20] By 1910, the Foreign Missions Conference of North America, as it became known, was a well-established feature of the North American Protestant landscape, representing over fifty missionary societies, and it was this body that took the initiative in suggesting that a sequel to the 1900 Ecumenical Missionary Conference in New York be held. Similarly, on the European continent, there were well-established regional or national ecumenical bodies representing Protestant missions in Scandinavia (from 1863), Germany (from 1885), and the Netherlands (from 1887).[21] A conference of representatives of mission boards from Germany, Denmark, Finland,

France, the Netherlands, Norway, Sweden, and Switzerland was formed as early as 1866, generally meeting every four years thereafter.[22]

With such embryonic national or regional structures in place, it was not surprising that some began to think in terms of coordination on an international plane. At the Centenary Missionary Conference held in London in 1888 a plan was submitted (*in absentia*) by the Lutheran founding father of the new missionary science of missiology, Professor Gustav Warneck of Halle, for the formation of a standing central committee, to be based in London, with representatives elected by national missionary conferences in "every Protestant nation."[23] It would promote cooperation, arbitrate in comity disputes and organize an international missionary conference every ten years. Warneck conceived of evangelical unity in mission as a necessary defense against the attacks on Protestant missions made by opponents, whether from Catholic sources or from within Protestant Churches. His proposal was not discussed though it was printed in the conference report.[24]

2.4   A Significant Ecumenical Milestone Rather than a Beginning

The breakthrough achieved in Edinburgh in 1910 was that the British finally, and not without considerable misgivings in some instances (almost all of them deriving from High Anglican quarters), fell into line behind the Americans, Germans, and others in accepting the necessity for a structured expression of international cooperation in mission. The way had been paved in December 1909, when the London Secretaries' Association, an informal gathering of English missionary society executives formed in 1819, first raised the idea of forming a conference of British missionary societies, prompted by Dr. Herbert Lankester, home

---

19   On this point, see Luca Ferracci's contribution in this volume.

20   *A History of the Ecumenical Movement*, vol. 1, 374.

21   Hogg, *Ecumenical Foundations*, 53–74.

22   Hogg, *Ecumenical Foundations*, 60–67; WMC, ed., *World Missionary Conference, 1910*, vol. 8, 121–122.

23   Johnston, ed., *Report of the Centenary Conference*, vol. 2, London, J. Nisbet, 1889, 437.

24   *A History of the Ecumenical Movement*, vol. 1, 329.

secretary of the CMS, who had visited the United States in 1906 and been impressed by the example of the Foreign Missions Conference of North America. The Association resolved to ask its secretary, John H. Ritson, to try to arrange a meeting of secretaries of British missionary societies during the Edinburgh Conference with a view to forming a conference of British missionary secretaries on the model pioneered in America.[25] No such meeting took place. The Conference of British Missionary Societies was, however, formed in June 1911, following a further meeting of the London Secretaries' Association in October 1910, at which Oldham was present and spoke about the recent Edinburgh conference, which clearly provided the decisive impetus for a step that was already under serious contemplation.[26]

The immediate fruits of the conference were far more limited in scope than the formation of the permanent international missionary body for which the Americans and Germans had pressed and which eventually came into being in 1921. The idea of proposing the establishment of a conference Continuation Committee, conceived by Father Walter H. Frere, the Anglo-Catholic liturgist from Mirfield in Yorkshire and later bishop of Truro, in personal consultation with Ritson during April–May 1910, was adopted as a minimalist measure calculated not to arouse Anglo-Catholic alarm at the prospect of a High Church mission agency being committed to a dubious course of action by a permanent representative body dominated by Protestants. Edinburgh 1910 was, thus, not the midwife of the ideal of Protestant missionary cooperation but rather the occasion on which leading Anglican figures hesitantly accepted a very modest expression of an ideal to which many Protestant mission leaders had been long committed in the spirit of pan-evangelical cooperation

nurtured by the 18th-century evangelical revival movements.

Edinburgh 1910, therefore, should be remembered, not as the moment at which Protestants began to move from competition to cooperation in their missionary task, but rather as an important milestone along the road that was leading Protestants towards finding more structured and comprehensive ways of expressing an existing cooperative missionary dynamic. It was a conference that significantly extended the existing boundaries of Protestant collaboration, across both theological and national frontiers. On the theological front, it included for the first time the missionaries and supporters of the SPG – Anglicans who in some cases accepted the label "Protestant" but who had always been decidedly guarded about any form of Christian fellowship with supposed "schismatics" such as English Nonconformists, German Lutherans or American Calvinists. Yet the conference organizers also found their overtures firmly rebuffed by the members of the UMCA – who as the most committed disciples of the Oxford Movement were quite emphatic that they were not Protestants but rather Catholic Anglicans.

Furthermore, other sections of the Christian family continued after 1910 to be excluded entirely from the scope of missionary cooperation as envisaged at Edinburgh. These included not simply the ancient communions of Roman Catholics, Orthodox and Oriental Orthodox but also the as yet small clusters of American or European Pentecostals – or "Apostolics" as they called themselves at this very early stage of the Pentecostal movement – who were already active in overseas missions in various locations but were not yet organized into the formal funded mission agencies that would have qualified them for representation at Edinburgh. Equally, the conference took little notice – other than a few dismissive references – of the emergence of the first "Ethiopian" churches in South Africa, independent expressions of African religious creativity and leadership that were destined to proliferate through much of the African continent over the next century into the massive

25   CUL, BSA/F4, Microfilm minutes of London Secretaries' Association, 1893–1924, Minutes of Oct 17, 1906 and Dec 15, 1909; J.H. Ritson to J.H. Oldham, Dec 16, 1909, in: CUL, BSA/F4/3/1, fol. 108.

26   CUL, BSA/F4, Microfilm minutes of London Secretaries' Association, 1893–1924, Minutes of Oct 19, 1910.

phenomenon of what later became known as African Independent, Initiated or Instituted Churches.

On the geographical front, the extension of the boundaries that took place in 1910 was more ambitious: for the first time since Warneck had raised the idea in 1888, Protestants from different continents had made tangible progress towards the creation of international forms of missionary cooperation that would have a degree of organizational permanence and solidity. Through the establishment of a Continuation Committee, Edinburgh 1910 brought Americans and Canadians, British and Australasians, Dutch and Swiss, Scandinavians and Germans together into an embryonic framework of structured international collaboration that had the potential to develop further and become permanent. The outbreak of world war in 1914 threatened to destroy that potential by placing the German Protestant missionary movement at bitter loggerheads with almost all its Edinburgh partners. The repercussions of that mutual alienation would continue throughout the inter-war period, although from 1921 the IMC made gradual progress in repairing the damage.

There can be little doubt that the vast majority of delegates arrived in Edinburgh in June 1910 with little thought of any movement towards the union of Christian churches in their minds. Rather, they had come on behalf of their mission agencies to discuss, and if possible resolve, the most pressing foreign missionary problems of the day. Of the eight commission reports that had been sent in advance, only the last one, on Co-operation and the Promotion of Unity, had an explicitly ecumenical focus. Nevertheless, it is clear that those most closely involved in the planning of the conference had developed a growing conviction that this was going to be more than just one more in the line of missionary conferences stretching back to 1854. Among some American mission leaders especially, there was a desire, as Silas McBee put it in a letter to Oldham in October 1908, that the conference should be given the freedom

to concentrate its attention and if possible, the attention of the whole Christian Church at home upon the mission field and upon Christ's purpose for the Church at home for that field, and thus to find a message from Him through the field to the home Church. There was to be no effort by resolution or otherwise to interfere with the autonomy and independence of the Churches, but the idea was to let the message bear its own inherent witness to the divided Churches of Christendom in the sure confidence that they would be drawn together in their witness for Christ.[27]

McBee's letter was in fact a protest against the British (and specifically Anglo-Catholic) insistence that the exclusion of questions of doctrine and church order was to apply not simply to any resolution that the conference might pass, but even to the commission reports. Oldham held his ground on a point on which Bishop Gore had given him no room for maneuver, yet at heart Oldham sympathized with McBee's impatience with any attempt to circumscribe the conference's freedom to pursue the logical imperative of a united Christian witness even so far as to trespass on the sensitive ground of Western Christendom. Oldham had a hunch that, however important it was to conciliate Anglo-Catholic sensitivities, the Edinburgh Conference might prove to be an occasion which transcended present ecclesiastical realities and unveiled a vision of a very different global Christian future. He told McBee in January 1910 of his conviction that

The necessity for closer cooperation seems to be so essential to the success of the work of the Church in the non-Christian world that I feel we ought not to be content to accept the present situation. I recognize that on all

27   S. McBee to J.H. Oldham, Oct 14, 1908, in: UTS, MRL 12, WMC papers, series 1, box 8, folder 1.

human calculations, the difficulties in the way of any important steps in advance are insuperable and decisive. But the issues are so great and the resources of God so incalculable, that I think we ought prayerfully to wait upon Him to know whether it is His will to bring us to something to which we cannot at present imagine a way.[28]

In retrospect we may conclude that Oldham's prayer was, in some measure at least, answered. Edinburgh 1910 transcended the constraints of contemporary ecclesiastical politics that had so strictly confined its terms of reference. Its delegates returned home fired by inchoate yet nonetheless exhilarating visions of what the world church might in the future look like, in which the Protestant desire for closer cooperation in the practice of mission could lead to some forms of institutional convergence that were as yet impossible to foresee.

3 Edinburgh 1910 and the Global Shift in the Center of Christian Gravity

We turn now to the second respect in which the WMC is often held to mark a significant ecumenical watershed, namely that it signaled the beginning of a momentous shift in the numerical, cultural and ultimately theological center of gravity of Christianity away from Europe and North America towards the so-called younger churches of Africa, Asia, Oceania, and Latin America. This shift in the geographical and ethnic composition of the global Christian community has continued and been strengthened down to the present day.

3.1 The Geographical Imbalance of the Edinburgh Conference

As is well known, only a tiny minority of the 1,215 official delegates at Edinburgh came from the non-Western world. None of them possessed the status of a delegate from their national churches: they were either selected by Western missionary agencies as symbolic fruit of their work or were specially invited guests of either the North American or the British conference executive committees. At the latest count, twenty such non-European visitors to the conference have been identified. There were nine Indians, including one Eurasian Methodist woman from Madras, Grace Stephens;[29] four Japanese; three Chinese; one Korean; one Burmese; one Anatolian, and a solitary and heavily Europeanized black African whose status as a last-minute addition to the delegate list remains rather unclear – Mark Christian Hayford, a Baptist from the Gold Coast (Ghana). At the level of indigenous representation, Africa was almost entirely neglected, apparently quite deliberately so, doubtless because its emerging Christian leaders were supposed still to be too educationally and spiritually immature to be able to flourish in such a Western "civilized" environment. More serious still, at the insistence of the Church of England, Latin America was excluded, not simply from the list of indigenous delegates, but even from the agenda of discussion, on the grounds that in large part it was deemed to form part of Catholic Christendom, and hence did not count as part of "the non-Christian world" that was supposed to be the sole object of Christian mission. Similar ecclesiastical judgments lay behind the covert exclusion from the conference agenda of the Caribbean (which was judged to have been substantially evangelized) and the ancient Christian heartlands of Western Asia (the Middle East). Hence, even if the term "ecumenical" is interpreted in its original and nonecclesiastical sense as meaning "representative of the entire global family of humanity," the WMC has only a very limited right to the title: it was, very largely, representative of the white Anglo-Saxon Protestant segment of humanity.

---

28 J.H. Oldham to S. McBee, Jan 12, 1910, in: UTS, MRL 12, WMC papers.

29 I owe the identification of Grace Stephens as a Eurasian to Professor Dana Robert of Boston University.

3.2   *Expectations of Conversion*

The Edinburgh Conference exuded pronounced optimism about the prospects for the conversion of substantial sections of the world's population to Christianity. It rejoiced at the enthusiastic reports of revival and rapid church growth coming from Korea. It expected the Western educated elites of Asia to lead their nations towards adoption of Christianity as the religion that had shaped Western civilization. It regarded even the nascent nationalism that was increasingly evident in China, Japan, and India as a phenomenon that, with sensitive missionary guidance, could be reoriented towards Christ. It was more guarded in its predictions of the religious future of Africa and the vast archipelago of the Dutch East Indies (Indonesia), where in both cases the rapid advance of Islam gave Christians cause for great concern. But even in sub-Saharan Africa, where Muslims and Christians were competing for the allegiance of indigenous "animists," the missionary consensus was that their conversion to a "higher" religion would be relatively easy and rapid. The only issue that preoccupied the minds of mission boards was a logistical one: whether Protestant missions could together deploy their spiritual troops with sufficient rapidity and efficiency of coordination to reach African peoples and reap the harvest of conversion before the forces of either Islam or the Roman Catholic Church did.

There is little doubt, therefore, that the WMC did anticipate that the Christian religion would make rapid progress throughout the globe over the coming years. Indeed, Archbishop Randall T. Davidson of Canterbury, in his opening address to the conference on June 14, went so far as to adapt the words of Christ as recorded in chapter 9 of Mark's Gospel to make the bold prediction that, if the churches devoted their united efforts to the evangelization of the world, "it may well be that 'there be some standing here tonight who shall not taste of death till they see,' – here on earth, in a way we know not now, – 'the Kingdom of God come with

power.'"[30] But this is not to say that the Edinburgh conference in itself presaged that shift in the global center of gravity of Christianity that is now so widely commented on in the scholarly literature. The great majority of the Edinburgh delegates still expected Western denominational mission agencies to set the agenda for future trends in Asia and Africa. Although they recognized that indigenous Christian agency would be crucial for the progress of conversion, they were distinctly limited in their capacity to anticipate that the cultural and theological styles of Christianity that would develop over the next century would be markedly different from those that characterized Western church life. Very few of them had any sense of the preeminent role that Africa was to play in the Christian growth of the next century. Nevertheless, there were some present at Edinburgh, notably the indigenous Asian delegates, who perceived with some clarity that Christianity must attempt to sever its centuries-old and paralyzing connection with European cultural identity. That perception was informed by their experience in their own national contexts of what was needed if Christianity were to appear to their compatriots as anything other than a Western religion. For some of them, an integral part of that experience was what they had already seen of the first attempts to transcend Western denominational divisions by experimenting with the idea of united churches. For others, attending the Edinburgh Conference in itself provided the crucial impetus and motivation to try such experiments.

3.3   *Edinburgh 1910 and Ecumenical Initiatives in China and India*

In the first of these two categories was a 28-year-old Manchu from Beijing, Cheng Jingyi. He was very possibly the youngest delegate at Edinburgh. Cheng had from 1906 to 1908 studied in Glasgow at the interdenominational Bible Training Institute,

---

30   WMC, ed., *World Missionary Conference, 1910*, vol. 9, 150.

an institution that owed its foundation to the third visit to the city in 1891 of the American evangelist Dwight L. Moody. In 1907 and/or 1908 Cheng had also visited the Keswick Convention in the English Lake District, a summer convention that brought together evangelical Christians from a variety of denominations to hear inspiring addresses on the theme of scriptural holiness and world missions. Cheng found deeply appealing the Keswick motto of "All One in Christ Jesus".[31] In February 1910, four months before the Edinburgh Conference, Cheng Jingyi contributed an article on "What Federation Can Accomplish for the Chinese Church," to the nondenominational missionary journal *The Chinese Recorder*, in which he wrote about the creation of a "union Chinese church where denominationalism will be out of the question." Chinese Christians, he wrote, took "little or no interest" in denominationalism.[32] When on June 16 in the debate on Cooperation and the Promotion of Unity he electrified the Edinburgh Conference with his striking assertion that "speaking plainly we hope to see, in the near future, a united Christian Church without any denominational distinctions,"[33] he was not speaking from impulse but expressing an already settled conviction that was already widely held and bearing fruit among Chinese Protestants.

The first moves towards a union of a federal kind of the Protestant Church in China were made as early as November 1902, when a meeting of the interdenominational Peking Missionary Association appointed a committee to consider progress towards church union in China, initially on a federal basis. It sent letters to all Protestant missionaries in China inviting their opinion on the desirability of federation: at least 90% responded in the affirmative. In April–May 1907 the Centenary Missionary Conference held in Shanghai to commemorate one hundred years of Protestant work in China recommended the formation of a federal union under the title "The Christian Federation of China."[34] Such moves were missionary rather than indigenous initiatives, but Chinese Christians were taking their own steps towards unity, inspired by more overtly patriotic ideals. In 1902 Yu Guozhen, a Shanghai pastor, formed a Chinese Christian Union that aimed to "connect Chinese Christians to be a union, to promote self-propagation in China, with the heart of loving the country and its people."[35] In 1906 Yu formed a federation of independent congregations in Shanghai bearing the title "The Chinese Jesus Independent Church." By 1909, the aggregate membership was over 10,000 and a general assembly was formed in 1910.[36] Hence the first attempts to form united Protestant Churches in China clearly preceded the Edinburgh Conference.

Notwithstanding his youth, Cheng Jingyi was the only Chinese to be selected as a member of the Continuation Committee at its formation on June 22, 1910, and was later appointed as joint secretary of its Chinese branch at its first meeting held in Canton from Jan 30 to Feb 4, 1913. Cheng ensured that in China also the consequences of Edinburgh would not be limited to the pursuit of cooperation between Western missions. The six conferences of the Continuation Committee held in China in early 1913 consistently stressed the goal of creating a self-supporting, self-governing and self-propagating church, and encouraged the idea of federation as a first step towards full union. The Continuation Committee in China led to the formation of the National Christian Council of China in 1922, of which Cheng was appointed secretary. He also served as the first moderator, and then

---

31   Marina Xiaojing Wang, *The Church Unity Movement in Early Twentieth-Century China: Cheng Jingyi and the Church of Christ in China*, Ph.D. thesis, University of Edinburgh, 2012, 70–71.

32   Cheng Jingyi, "What Federation Can Accomplish for the Chinese Church," *The Chinese Recorder* 41/2, 1910, 155–160, cited in: Wang, *The Church Unity Movement*, 88–89. The Bible Training Institute survived in Glasgow until 2015, latterly under the name of the International Christian College.

33   WMC, ed., *World Missionary Conference, 1910*, vol. 8, 196.

34   Kenneth Scott Latourette, *A History of Christian Missions in China*, London, SPCK, 1929, 667–669.

35   Wang, *The Church Unity Movement*, 81.

36   Wang, *The Church Unity Movement*, 82.

general secretary, of the Church of Christ in China, formed in 1927 from a union of some sixteen denominational groups, mainly of Presbyterian, Congregational or Baptist affiliation. Whilst the Church of Christ in China never succeeded in becoming fully self-supporting, it was indubitably self-governing and self-propagating. The vision of a single "three-self" nondenominational church, which the Communists forcibly imposed on the Chinese Protestant Churches after 1951, thus saw a partial realization over twenty years earlier, a fact which is often forgotten. The Edinburgh Conference had played an important part by giving Cheng Jingyi and other Chinese spokesmen the platform for the initial articulation of that vision. A parallel, but smaller, united Church of Christ was established in Siam (Thailand) in 1934.

In South India also, a degree of momentum towards church unity can be discerned even before 1910. The Congregational Churches planted by the LMS and the ABCFM united in 1908 with Presbyterian Churches planted by the Reformed Church in America and the Free Church of Scotland to form the South India United Church. In this case, however, the initiative in taking steps towards a limited expression of Protestant ecclesiastical convergence lay more among foreign missionaries than among Indian Christians. The Edinburgh Conference supplied additional impetus to an existing church union movement in South India, but significantly extended the scope of that movement beyond the existing fusion of two denominational traditions that shared a considerable theological affinity within the Reformed family.

One crucial aspect of the significance of the WMC was that it appears to have fired one Indian delegate in particular with enthusiasm for a more far-reaching and radical vision of a united expression of Protestant Christian faith. The Indian delegate concerned is the most widely remembered today of the twenty non-Western participants at Edinburgh. He was the South Indian Anglican clergyman, Vedanayagam Samuel Azariah. Azariah is remembered mainly on account of his

impassioned appeal to missionaries, made in one of the conference evening sessions, on June 20, to prove the reality of their Christian love by being prepared to form genuinely egalitarian friendships with Indian Christians. Western missionaries, he urged, had to accept that Indians could be full and equal partners in the construction, not simply of an Indian church, but even of an Indian theology and Christology:

> The exceeding riches of the glory of Christ can be fully realised not by the Englishman, the American, and the Continental alone, nor by the Japanese, the Chinese, and the Indians by themselves – but by all working together, worshipping together, and learning together the Perfect Image of our Lord and Christ. It is only "with all the Saints" that we can "comprehend the love of Christ which passeth knowledge, that we might be filled with all the fullness of God." This will be possible only from spiritual friendships between the two races. We ought to be willing to learn from one another and to help one another.
>
> Through all the ages to come the Indian Church will rise up in gratitude to attest the heroism and self-denying labours of the missionary body. You have given your goods to feed the poor. You have given your bodies to be burned. We also ask for *love*. Give us FRIENDS![37]

This forthright and highly controversial appeal aroused considerable embarrassment and some criticism among Azariah's Edinburgh audience and subsequent missionary commentators. There were as yet few Western Christians whose ecumenical vision stretched to the incorporation of distinctively Indian insights into theological thinking on a subject as fundamental as Christology. Azariah's first biographer, John Zimmerman Hodge, significantly describes this address as

---

37   The fullest record of the address is in WMC, ed., *World Missionary Conference, 1910*, vol. 9, 306–315.

perhaps "the first shot in the campaign against 'missionary imperialism.'"[38]

Despite his decidedly mixed reception at the conference, Azariah left Edinburgh with a determination to seek a pathway towards the creation of a church that would be both united and authentically Indian. On his voyage back to India, Azariah conferred with two American Congregationalist missionary delegates, George Sherwood Eddy and John Peter Jones, on what immediate steps could be taken towards church union in India. A three-day unofficial meeting followed at the residence of the bishop of Madras, Henry Whitehead, to discuss a possible basis for an ambitious union between the South India United Church (a union of Congregationalists and Presbyterians formed in 1908) and the Anglican Church. Although the firmest pressure for such a rapprochement came from the American Congregationalists, it seems that at this meeting Azariah played a crucial part in persuading the High Churchman Bishop Whitehead that the vision of church union was a goal that could and should be pursued.[39] As a result of the Madras meeting, the first regional conferences of the Edinburgh Continuation Committee, held in Ceylon (Sri Lanka) and India under John Mott's chairmanship in November and December 1912, ended up discussing not merely enhanced cooperation but also the issue of church union.[40]

The efforts to construct a united Protestant Church in South India in the years after the WMC sought to blend congregational, Presbyterian and episcopal elements in what was delightfully termed an "episcopresbygationalist" hybrid. In June 1919 George Sherwood Eddy, an important American missionary, met with Metropolitan Titus II Mar Thoma of the Mar Thoma Church – an evangelically reformed branch of the ancient East Syrian Church – and obtained his agreement to submit the proposal for a united Church of South India to his synod.[41] Eddy wrote home in ecstatic vein that there was now a prospect of uniting

> the three great divisions of the Christian Church, the Western Church, the Eastern Church, and the Free Protestant Churches. ... If this union is formed it will be the first time in four hundred years since the Reformation that the great division between the Episcopal and non-Episcopal Churches has been united. It will be the first time in nine centuries, since the division between the Eastern and the Western Church, that these two branches of the Church have ever come together.[42]

Eddy's heady rhetoric far outstripped reality. The Mar Thoma Church represented only one atypical branch of the Syrian Orthodox Church, and in the event did not participate in the protracted negotiations for a united Church of South India that followed. Similarly, representatives of the Lutheran tradition that had first brought Protestant Christianity to India in 1706 would take no part in the negotiations. Neither, of course, did the Roman Catholic Church. Even in a nation such as India where Christians are a small minority, the dream of a single Christian church has proved remarkably elusive. When the Church of South India was eventually formed in 1947, about half of its million communicants were former Anglicans, but most Anglo-Catholics stayed out, and their party leaders in England treated those who did not as apostates. By 1995, the Church of South India accounted for only 4.5% of the estimated Christian

---

38   John Z. Hodge, *Bishop Azariah of Dornakal*, Madras, Christian Literature Society for India, 1946, 6.

39   Susan Billington Harper, *In the Shadow of the Mahatma: Bishop V.S. Azariah and the Travails of Christianity in British India*, Grand Rapids MI, Eerdmans, 2000, 237.

40   Bengt Sundkler, *Church of South India: The Movement Towards Union (1900–1947)*, London, Lutterworth, 1965, 62–67.

41   Sundkler, *Church of South India*, 128–130. The Mar Thoma Church was formed in 1889 by a group within the Jacobite Church who had links with the CMS and wished to combine Syrian Orthodox tradition with evangelical faith.

42   Report letter dated Aug 15, 1919, in: YDSL, RG 32–3–66.

population of India.[43] Ecumenical progress in the 20th century does not correlate fully or neatly with the predominant trends in the growth of non-Western Christianity, where the sectors that have witnessed most rapid growth are very often the ones that have been largely independent of the formal ecumenical movement.

3.4 Church Union in Asia: Indigenous or Western Initiative?

While there is considerable truth in the suggestion that the long road that led eventually to the formation of the Church of South India in 1947, and later to the Church of North India in 1970, began at Edinburgh, this conclusion should not, therefore, be inflated in its significance. Much of the impetus in the first half of the 20th century for church union in Asia – and in China above all – undoubtedly came from indigenous church leaders who found the importation of Western denominational divisions preposterous and an obstacle to effective Christian witness. Nevertheless, in India the way in which Western missionaries went about the search for a united church could itself appear absurd to more astute indigenous church leaders, some of whom opposed church union schemes as alien cultural intrusions. In South India, for example, the Madras lawyer, Pandipeddi Chenchiah, playfully wrote in 1938:

> It appears to a convert indescribably funny that anybody should entertain the idea that by knocking together the Church of England, the Church of Scotland, Swedish and Lutheran and American churches, an Indian Church would be produced. But for the fact that the religious man rarely has any sense of humour, the scheme would never have

survived the mirth it provokes. It is a capital joke.[44]

Missionary logic was a powerful dynamic propelling Protestants in Asian contexts towards closer cooperation or even looser forms of union, but missionary and indigenous perspectives on what form Christian unity should take did not always coincide. Neither was the logic of evangelization the only force at play. In Japan similar trends towards the formation of federal or united Protestant Churches in the wake of the WMC can also be discerned. Here eight denominations, accounting for some 80% of all Protestant Christians in Japan, combined in late 1911 to form the Japanese Federation of Churches. But the decisive impetus to the foundation of the United Church of Christ (Nihon Kirisuto Kyōdan) in Japan in 1941 came from outside the Christian community altogether – namely, from the insistence of the Japanese imperial state that Protestants should form one body, and thereby be more amenable to political manipulation. Although the church survived the end of the Japanese empire, it did so only at the price of the secession of several large denominational families that wished to reassert their historic separate identities – among them Anglicans, Lutherans, Baptists, and Reformed. Asian Christians could be fiercely proud of their distinct denominational identities inherited from the West. A slightly different point can be made about the Protestant Church in China after 1949. The desire of the Communist Party to enfold all Protestant Christianity within one state-regulated Three-Self Patriotic Movement Church may have been rather more successful than the Japanese imperial state in weakening traditional denominational loyalties, but the continuing size of the non-registered or unofficial churches suggests that for Chinese Christians, as for many others, institutional unity is not necessarily the highest priority.

---

43   David B. Barrett, George T. Kurian & Todd M. Johnson, eds., *World Christian Encyclopaedia: A Comparative Survey of Churches and Religions in the Modern World*, New York NY, Oxford University Press, ²2001, 369, 371, gives adult membership of the Church of South India in 1995 as 1,471,000 and total adult membership of all churches in India in 1995 as 32,643,646.

44   G.V. Job & others, *Rethinking Christianity in India*, Madras, Sudarisanam, 1938, 188. The Lutheran Churches did not in fact join the Church of South India.

The last century has decisively given the lie to the fond, if initially plausible, supposition that denominationalism is a peculiarly Western religious disease. In Korea, for example, a single Presbyterian Church of Korea was established in 1907, served by four different missions (Northern Presbyterian, Southern Presbyterian, Canadian Presbyterian, and Australian Presbyterian); yet in the 1950s a process of continuous division started, which by the year 2011 had resulted in no less than 215 separate Presbyterian denominations in South Korea.[45] In India, despite the formation of the two united churches, the rapid multiplication of Pentecostal Churches since the late 1940s has made the face of Indian Protestantism far more, rather than less, diverse than it was in 1900. By 1994, there were an estimated one million Pentecostals in South India, about half as many as the membership of the Church of South India, and made up of a host of different groups and clusters of independent congregations.[46]

The decisive additional momentum that the Edinburgh Conference supplied to the pursuit of church unity in Asia is thus undeniable. The ultimate source of the momentum towards church union in Asia evident after 1910, however, was not the predominantly Western assembly of the WMC but the experience of often fragile and isolated Protestant Churches that found their Christian witness needlessly weakened by denominational divisions in contexts where Christianity was a small and vulnerable minority faith. It can plausibly be argued that it was the very weakness of Protestant Christianity in Asia in the early years of the century that supplied the dynamic which impelled missionary strategists and their educated indigenous elites to search for

closer relationships between Protestant missions and ultimately between indigenous Protestant Churches. Conversely, the more rapid expansion of multiple popular forms of Christianity in some parts of Asia (notably northeastern India, China, South Korea, and regions of Indonesia) later in the century undercut the compulsion for ecumenical rapprochement. Hence the observable shift in the center of gravity of Christianity away from the West – which is largely a post-1960s phenomenon – should probably be viewed as a quite distinct and indeed divergent trend from the older search for ecumenical convergence.

3.5   The General Failure of Institutional Ecumenism in Africa

African Christian experience largely reinforces this suggestion. In most of Africa church planting was still at too early a stage in the years immediately before or after 1910 for church union to be on the agenda. Nevertheless, there were some exceptions, notably in East Africa, where Protestant missions were acutely conscious of the fragility of their work in face of the expansion of Islam. Discussions about some form of inter-mission federation were initiated as early as 1907. In June 1909 – a full year before the Edinburgh Conference – a conference of Protestant missionaries assembled in Nairobi, in what was then the British East African Protectorate. The desirability of a Protestant church union of some kind was on the agenda. John Jamieson Willis, the Anglican archdeacon of Kavirondo, read a paper on "The Desirability of a Single Native Church in British East Africa." The conference resolved that "the orderly development, organization and establishment of a united, self-supporting, and self-propagating Native Church be a chief aim of all mission work."[47] A committee was appointed to take steps towards this goal, and drafted a constitution for a united church that was submitted to a second conference

45   Korean Ministry of Culture, Sports and Tourism, ed., *The Present Condition of Religions in Korea*, Seoul, 2011, 38–47. I owe this reference to Dr. Kyo-Seong Ahn of the Presbyterian University and Theological Seminary, Seoul.

46   Michael Bergunder, *The South Indian Pentecostal Movement in the Twentieth Century*, Grand Rapids MI, Eerdmans, 2008, 305–310.

47   Cited in Gordon H. Mungeam, ed., *Kenya: Selected Historical Documents (1884–1923)*, Nairobi, East African Publishing House, 1978, 148.

in Nairobi in January 1911. The conference failed to reach an agreement, and a further attempt was made at a third conference held at Kikuyu in June 1913. Representatives assembled of four Protestant missions – the CMS (evangelical Anglican), the Church of Scotland Mission (Presbyterian), the United Methodist Mission, and the nondenominational Africa Inland Mission. Although they proved unable to agree on organic unity, they did agree a proposed Scheme for a Federation of Missionary Societies, with the implication that it would lead to a federation of Protestant Churches. The conference ended with a united Anglican-rite Eucharist, celebrated by the bishop of Mombasa.[48]

The movement towards a federated Protestant Church in East Africa – which actually owed little or nothing to the Edinburgh conference[49] – came to a juddering halt following a bitter attack on the Kikuyu Conference by Frank Weston, the Anglo-Catholic bishop of Zanzibar. For Weston, the celebration of a united communion service was an abomination, and he formally indicted his fellow Anglican bishops of Mombasa and Uganda for heresy. Although he was unsuccessful in this, Archbishop Randall Davidson of Canterbury eventually ruled in 1915 that inter-communion was acceptable only in exceptional circumstances and that no such united communion service as was held at Kikuyu should be held in future in order to avoid "misunderstandings."[50]

After the Kikuyu Conference, no serious attempts at forming even a federated Protestant Church in Africa were made until the 1950s. The first united church in Africa was the United Church of Zambia, formed in 1965. In the Democratic Republic of Congo (formerly Belgian Congo, and later Zaire), a federal Église du Christ au Congo

was formed in 1970, but this was more of a federation than a union and was largely a response to pressures for national unification following national independence in 1960. Other attempts at Protestant church union, in Nigeria and Ghana, failed, in 1965 and 1983 respectively. Increasingly, Christianity in Africa in the 20th century gained its own independent momentum, expanding in size and multiplying in ecclesiastical form and allegiance. Church unity slipped down the scale of priorities. The fact that Africa is now the most Christian continent of the globe has rather little to do with the style of ecumenism represented by the WMC of 1910.

4 Conclusions

The WMC of 1910 was itself the product of a century-old tradition of Protestant ecumenical cooperation in the work of foreign missions. It took that existing tradition to a new level of structural organization. Furthermore, somewhat contrary to its own carefully elaborated terms of reference, it began to turn Christian minds to something deeper and more radical than mere collaboration in missionary action – that is, to the call coming from Asian mission fields for Western denominational divisions and identities to be transcended and even laid aside altogether. However, although the conference marked a turning point in the history of Western Protestantism, it should not be seen as more than a very incomplete anticipation of later 20th- and 21st-century trends in the relocation of Christianity from the heartlands of Western Christendom to the non-European world.

Bibliography

A *History of the Ecumenical Movement*, vol. 1, Ruth Rouse & Stephen C. Neill, eds., *1517–1948*, London, SPCK, 1954.

---

48 John J. Willis & others, *Towards a United Church 1913–1947*, London, Edinburgh House Press, 1947, 25–32.
49 Stuart P. Mews, "Kikuyu and Edinburgh: The Interaction of Attitudes to Two Conferences," in: Geoffrey J. Cuming & Derek Baker, eds., *Councils and Assemblies*, Cambridge, Cambridge University Press, 1971, 345–359.
50 Willis & others, *Towards a United Church*, 32–51.

A History of the Ecumenical Movement, vol. 2, Harold E. Fey, ed., *The Ecumenical Advance (1948–1968)*, Geneva, WCC Publications, ²1986.

Hogg, William Richey, *Ecumenical Foundations: A History of the International Missionary Council and Its Nineteenth-Century Background*, New York NY, Harper, 1952.

Stanley, Brian, "The Reshaping of Christian Tradition: Western Denominational Identity in a Non-Western Context," *Studies in Church History* 32, 1996, 399–426.

Stanley, Brian, *The World Missionary Conference, Edinburgh 1910*, Grand Rapids MI, Eerdmans, 2009.

Stanley, Brian, *Christianity in the Twentieth Century: A World History*, Princeton NJ, Princeton University Press, 2018.

Sundkler, Bengt, *Church of South India: The Movement Towards Union (1900–1947)*, London, Lutterworth, 1965.

WMC, ed., *World Missionary Conference, 1910: To Consider Missionary Problems in Relation to the Non-Christian World*, vol. 8, *Report of Commission VIII: Co-Operation and the Promotion of Unity*, Edinburgh, Oliphant, Anderson & Ferrier, 1910.

WMC, ed., *World Missionary Conference, 1910*, vol. 9, *The History and Records of the Conference: Together with Addresses Delivered at the Evening Meetings*, Edinburgh, Oliphant, Anderson & Ferrier, 1910.

CHAPTER 19

The Historical Turn: World War I

Frédéric Gugelot

1   Introduction

When war broke out, the editor of the Protestant journal *Christianisme au XXᵉ siècle*, Paul Doumergue, wrote in sorrow: "For twenty centuries now, in our so-called Christian civilization, the church has preached: love one another. This is certainly an hour of mourning for all Christians."[1] War, by its very nature, seemed to widen the gaps between confessions as it did between nations. The Christian ideals of fraternity, charity, and unity found no place for expression in the heart of a war that was on a path to total destruction.[2]

The outbreak of war proved that sharing a common faith did not prevent confrontation, even when all the warring nations subscribed to some form or another of Christianity or monotheism. If the Second International was not against entry into the war, neither were the Christian churches. Rare attempts, such as the Conference of Constance on Aug 1, 1914, were unable to reach a common position against the emerging conflict.

The very violence of the conflict, both real and ideological, seemed to present a major obstacle to any unification among Christians. The history of Christian unity is also the history of emotions split between the desire for unity and the despair of division. The image of Christian universalism was faced with the brutality and brutalization of the battles. Above all, war exposed not a religious basis but the strength of a nation's patriotism. On Oct 8, 1915, a Parisian priest noted: "Patriotism today is greater than religion."[3]

2   National Wars: The Nationalization of Churches

Between 1914 and 1915, the Christian faithful and clerics came together in a spirit of *union sacrée*, that is, in a suspension of political or spiritual preferences and internal strife that the Germans rightly called a "civil peace" (*Burgfrieden*). The social, religious, and political clashes are interrupted. This suspension of internal conflicts did not last for the duration of the war, and debate and expressions of hatred resurfaced during the conflict. But what differentiated one warring society from another was its ability to maintain a level of popular support for the war effort. Religious confessions played a role in this ability to maintain a level of the societies' engagement in the conflict. At its beginning, a war culture was crystallized in which the idea of waging a defensive battle and the hatred of one's enemies played an essential role.[4] The gradual entry into war of all European countries was accompanied everywhere by a cultural mobilization. The soldiers believed in the justice of their cause through the personal and collective value of their commitment, following the example of the United States in 1917. For some of them, therefore, it was the response to a call of faith. Although lassitude and disputes (and a

---

1 See Paul Doumergue's editorial in *Christianisme au XXᵉ siècle*, Aug 6, 1914, 297.

2 Roger Chickering & Stig Förster, eds., *Great War, Total War: Combat and Mobilization on the Western Front (1914–1918)*, Cambridge, Cambridge University Press, 2000; Annette Becker & Stéphane Audoin-Rouzeau, *14–18, retrouver la guerre*, Paris, Gallimard, 2000.

3 Arthur Mugnier, Marcel Billot & Jean d'Hendecourt, ed., *Journal de l'abbé Mugnier (1879–1939)*, Paris, Mercure de France, 1985, 293.

4 George L. Mosse, *Fallen Soldiers: Reshaping the Memory of the World Wars*, Oxford, Oxford University Press, 1990.

rising wave of strikes) appeared in 1916, civil peace persisted. In that very same year, the chief rabbi of Paris, Alfred Lévy, expressed the hope that, after the victory, "there will be no more religious disagreements …, that there will be nothing other than the French."[5] This showed that many clerics believed it possible to overcome religious division through patriotic unity.

In societies that were largely affected by religious expectations, it was first and foremost a matter of claiming God and mobilizing him: "Gott mit uns," "Dieu est de notre côté," and "God with us." While not everyone was a believer and even fewer practiced a religious faith, it was obvious that spiritual values (good, evil) and their vocabulary (mysticism of combat, *union sacrée*) nourished the perceptions of men and women who were convinced that they were participating in a veritable crusade. Throughout the 19th century, nations were sanctified as much as religions were nationalized. There was a clash between the "elected peoples," or those who considered themselves such. Thus, the court chaplain Ernst Dryander, during a sermon on the opening of a session of the Reichstag that he delivered in the Kaiser's presence in Berlin on Aug 4, 1914, could proclaim:

> We are going into battle for our culture against the uncultured, for German civilization against barbarism, for the free German personality bound to God against the instincts of the undisciplined masses. And God will be with our just weapons! For German faith and German piety are ultimately bound up with German faith and civilization.[6]

There was a superimposition of the struggle against barbarism, the war of law and civilization, and the holy war. The length of the war accentuated its eschatological aim. A "just peace" would be a revenge on the absolute evil of war and upon the enemy who had sought it. From the beginning of the war – and even more so at moments of discouragement along the Eastern Front in 1915 that culminated in the Russian Revolution in 1917, and along the Western Front from 1916, after the defeats at Verdun and the Somme – the belligerents believed in the mystical force of a conflict that could achieve the messianic promise of a new and radiant world free of war. The sense of waging a defensive, therefore just, war favored the nationalization of religions. Beyond a profane use of religious themes, the national churches assigned Christian objectives to the war with different levels of intensity according to the times, but in a recurrent fashion. It was termed a just war, that is, a war blessed by God, a holy war, an expiatory, regenerative, and redemptive war:[7]

> (1) individual purification that would benefit the country; (2) individual sacrifice for the souls in Purgatory and the rehabilitation of the country; (3) the patriotic defense of the country, … and (4) defense of the church in the person of its eldest daughter, France.[8]

Religious practice, vocabulary and imagination were then marshalled to lend meaning to the war experience. "Though different in many ways with regard to theology and practice, men and women, black and white, Protestant and Catholic saw the war in remarkably similar religious terms."[9]

5 ACIP, correspondence of 1916, cited in: Philippe-Efraïm Landau, "'Patrie et religion': Juifs et judaïsme dans la guerre totale," in: Xavier Boniface & François Cochet, eds., *Foi, religions et sacré dans la Grande Guerre*, Arras, Artois Presses Université, 2014, 163–182, here 166.

6 Cited in: Adrian Gregory & Annette Becker, "Religious Sites and Practices," in: Jay Winter & Jean-Louis Robert, eds., *Capital Cities at War: Paris, London, Berlin (1914–1919)*, vol. 2, Cambridge, Cambridge University Press, 2007, 383–427, here 390.

7 Wilhelm Achleitner, *Gott im Krieg: Die Theologie der österreichischen Bischöfe in den Hirtenbriefen zum Ersten Weltkrieg*, Vienna, Böhlau, 1997.

8 "La guerre et l'âme française," cited in: Richard Griffiths, *La Révolution à rebours: Le renouveau catholique dans la littérature en France de 1870 à 1914*, Paris, Desclée de Brouwer, 1971, 298.

9 Jonathan H. Ebel, *Faith in the Fight: Religion and the American Soldier in the Great War*, Princeton NJ, Princeton University Press, 2010, 18–19.

2.1   Expiation

The religious reading of the conflict interpreted it both as punishment for the country's sins as well as a salvation. A comparison of the French Jesuit and German Jesuit journals *Études* and *Stimmen der Zeit* reveals a common theological interpretation of the war (as a trial, with sorrow and resignation) and exactly inverse reproaches addressed to the enemy for noncompliance with the law and the rules of war.[10] During Lent in 1915, the archbishop of Paris pronounced the reminder that "France has sinned. As a nation, it believed it could do without God and distanced itself from him ... It is great sacrifice that will redeem the country."[11]

Christian thinkers, clerics and the faithful shared a common punitive and purgative interpretation of the war.[12] This interpretation of the war as divine punishment for sins committed before the conflict was not uniquely Catholic. Pastor Jules Pfender, president of the ERE permanent commission, in a pamphlet of Aug 4, 1914, wrote: "Let us humble ourselves in the pain of our transgressions, which have brought us the heavenly Father's just punishment."[13]

Such stances were based on the widely shared observation of a prewar decline. "Was the country's moral and religious standard rising in line with its economic prosperity? Sunday rest, attendance at Mass, respect for marriage and the laws of modesty ... what happened to them?"[14] The war's prolongation led to an abandonment of the sometimes triumphant tones of 1914, which all

the confessions mixed into their interpretation of the suffering and sacrifices being made. Expiation was not enough, however, as deaths amassed. The amount of sacrifice had to be given a meaning.

2.2   Messianism

Like the socialist movements, the major religions in France and Germany played the national unity card. They legitimized the struggle to safeguard the country and defend the highest spiritual values. In 1913, therefore, the Protestant Churches and Catholic dioceses jointly participated in a fundraising for the jubilee of William II, both identifying the aims of German culture with the Christian mission.[15] The national churches did not hesitate to affirm God's predilection for this or that country and tried to enlist worship in favor of national undertakings.[16] Sermons insisted on the idea that humanity's future was determined by the fate of France or Germany: "Other nations have their legitimate personalities ... but our particular mandate is to spread well here on earth these eternal principles of freedom, justice and fraternity that form the intangible Decalogue of modern times."[17]

This messianic view of the nations was accompanied by a negative portrayal of the opponent.

> Whatever they may say, our aggressors are certainly not the representatives of a principle, but of pride, ambition, lust, selfishness and hatred, even worse, of a spirit of

10   René Marlé, "La guerre de 1914 dans les *Études* et dans les *Stimmen der Zeit*," *Études* 321, 1964, 203–215.

11   Léon-Adolphe Amette, "Lettre pastorale de la carême 1915," *La semaine religieuse de Paris*, Feb 13, 1915, 237–248, here 242.

12   Hermann-Josef Scheidgen, *Deutsche Bischöfe im Ersten Weltkrieg: Die Mitglieder der Fuldaer Bischofskonferenz und ihre Ordinariate (1914–1918)*, Cologne, Böhlau, 1991.

13   Laurent Gambarotto, *Foi et patrie: La prédication du protestantisme français pendant la Première Guerre mondiale*, Geneva, Labor et Fides, 1996, 103.

14   Joseph Guérard, "Lettre pastorale de carême 1915," *La Semaine religieuse du diocèse de Coutances et d'Avranches* 10, 1915, 178.

15   Claus Arnold, "German Catholicism and National Integration (1870–1945)," in: Daniele Menozzi, ed., *Cattolicesimo, nazione e nazionalismo*, Pisa, Edizioni della Normale, 2015, 59–68, here 63.

16   Sante Lesti, "L'amore di predilezione' del Sacro Cuore nei confronti della Francia: Un topos fra conforto, apologia e nazionalizzazione del culto (1915–1919)," in: Menozzi, ed., *Cattolicesimo, nazione e nazionalismo*, 69–86.

17   Wilfred Monod, "Le Nom de l'Éternel," Paris, Aug 23, 1914, cited in: Laurent Gambarotto, "L'opposition radicalisée de deux nations, régimes politiques et visions du monde (français et allemand) dans la prédication de guerre du protestantisme réformé français," *BSHPF* 160, 2014, 35–55, here 39.

conquest, brutal aggression of force, that creates the law of injustice, of violence and of a contempt for human life. In short, of evil in all its horror.[18]

The homeland was a product of divine Providence and was presented as a quasi-divine entity, which used Christian language and symbols to express itself. Believers were spiritually enlisted. Among all the warring nations, a veritable national and bellicose recontextualization of practices of piety was expressed in adherence to the nation states' "religion of heroes." Religious and military values were merged into the figures of the hero, the saint and the martyr, which were adapted to the circumstances of war. Mass booklets, specifically written for soldiers, were proof of this mixing of genres. For instance, *La S. Messa ascoltata per i nostri caduti* (Mass for our fallen soldiers), published in Florence in 1915, suggested that those fallen in war, by virtue of the suffering endured in carrying out their "sacred duty," had gained paradise.[19] A war mentality was asserted, and the ritual sphere was marshalled to bless the conflict and to support the sacrifices. A national Christian imagination mixed faith, Christ-like sacrifice and patriotism. Such devotions reinforced an acceptance of the war, resignation to the sacrifices required and a habituation to the violence by ennobling it. Lawful war, just war: the belligerents were convinced of the tremendous truth of their cause. In Germany, history became God's judgment, *Gottes Gericht*: Erich von Falkenhayn calls *Gericht* (judgment) the attack of Verdun which would lead Germany to victory. Soldiers fought for their small homeland (region, village, city) and their greater homeland. Sensing danger, aggression, and encirclement, they sought to share the risks on a massive scale, out of loyalty to their companions and to their "culture,"

as well. Everywhere, engagement in the war was experienced as a struggle between life and death, between good and evil. Patriotism became a mysticism whose loyalties operated along absolute national lines in the fervent certainty of a defensive patriotism. This syncretism between religious and patriotic sentiment, far from being limited to the early months of the war, continued at different levels of intensity in the following years. On May 26, 1915, the papacy sent a pamphlet to the Italian bishops against displaying too ardent a patriotism during services. At the end of 1915 and the beginning of 1916, a movement of prayers for peace developed.[20] After the defeat at Caporetto, however, the remobilization reawakened its patriotic tones.

On a political level, the war accelerated the appeasement of the religious tensions of the *Kulturkampf*, Italian unification, the marginalization of English Catholicism and the 1905 French separation of church and state. The war blurred spiritual divisions within nations. In the context of war, the Catholic Church regained national functions, which was even acknowledged by a Protestant pastor at a ceremony in Vosges on Nov 1, 1918:

> This priest dressed in white, dominating the people, proclaiming the virtue of sacrifice and the sovereignty of the cross among tombs and these flags: this was an image of the power of Catholicism indissolubly associated with the life of the nation and capable, in decisive moments, of expressing what is deep within the national soul.[21]

This triumph of a national religion was endorsed by the Holy See after the war. Joan of Arc's canonization on May 16, 1920, two days before the

---

18 Louis Trial, "Motifs d'espérance," Nîmes, Aug 30, 1914, cited in: Gambarotto, "L'opposition radicalisée," 40.

19 Matteo Caponi, "Liturgies et dévotions de guerre: Le cas florentin (1914–1918)," in: Boniface & Cochet, eds., *Foi, religions et sacré*, 149–162, here 155.

20 Maria Paiano, *La preghiera e la Grande Guerra: Benedetto XV e la nazionalizzazione del culto in Italia*, Pisa, Pacini, 2017, 134–143.

21 André Encrevé, "Les *Notes de guerre* (*1915–1918*) du pasteur Henri Monnier, aumônier à la 66e division," BSHPF 161, 2015, 39–60, here 49.

appointment of an ambassador of France to the Holy See, proved that Rome was well aware of the process that had allowed Catholics to regain their place in France in the name of the nation's defense.

2.3   National Hatreds, Religious Hatreds, National Wars, Religious Wars?

Religion provided a vocabulary for interpreting war and its sacrifices; it played a role in the sacralization of the nation. The Great War was not a war of religions, even if it mobilized religions and churches, involving clerics and the faithful.[22] The American writer John Gardner affirmed:

> This is essentially a religious war. You feel it everywhere and these Allied armies are religious armies for the men of these armies are here to make the world better. It is a religious army even when it is a profane army.[23]

Religious representations of the war promoted a harmonization of Christian and military values while the churches insisted on the complementary nature of religious and patriotic duties. National defense was a civic and religious obligation. "In obeying men, you obey God,"[24] asserted French Pastor Henri Monnier in July 1916. The challenge was even more complex in countries where the rupture between Catholicism and the state was profound, such as Italy. While the Catholic soldier Pietro Ferrari stated that "the citizen's duty and obedience to God's holy law commands me to recognize any constituted authority as God's representative, which ensured my serenity,"[25] Fr. Gemelli called for passive obedience.

The just war became a crusade.[26] The Catholic writer René Bazin summed it up as follows: "It is the *chanson de geste* that continues; it is the unfinished crusade; it is God appearing through a purified France."[27] Not overly present at the beginning of the war, the theme developed as the fighting dragged on. There was an escalation in the rhetoric. The war became increasingly holy because it was increasingly devastating.[28] In this context of a "crusade" between Christian countries, preaching did not evoke questions of Christian unity.[29]

Affirming a convergence between faith and patriotism, between religion and homeland, however, was declined in various ways. A 1918 article in the Jesuit journal *Études* gave reasons for the fight, "Pourquoi se bat-on?": "On the lips of the soldiers of the Great War blossoms the same cry as on those of the crusaders of the Middle Ages: God wills it."[30] This crusade was not solely religious, but religion was all the more easily applied because it was also a crusade in defense of law, justice, and

22   Annette Becker, *La guerre et la foi: De la mort à la mémoire (1914–1930)*, Paris, Colin, 1994; Étienne Fouilloux, "Première guerre mondiale et changement religieux en Europe," in: Jean-Jacques Becker & Stéphane Audoin-Rouzeau, eds., *Les sociétés européennes et la guerre de 1914–1918: Actes du colloque organisé à Nanterre et à Amiens du 8 au 11 décembre 1988*, Nanterre, Publications de l'Université de Nanterre, 1990, 439–452; Roberto Morozzo della Rocca, *La fede e la guerra: Cappellani militari e preti-soldati (1915–1919)*, Rome, Studium, 1980; Nicolao Merker, *La guerra di Dio: Religione e nazionalismo nella Grande Guerra*, Rome, Carocci, 2015; Adrian Gregory, "Beliefs and Religion," in: Jay Winter, ed., *The Cambridge History of the First World War*, vol. 3, Cambridge, Cambridge University Press, 2014, 418–444.

23   John Gardner, *Letters to a Soldier on Religion*, New York NY, G.H. Doran, 1918, 73–74.

24   Encrevé, "Les *Notes de guerre*."

25   Xavier Boniface, *Histoire religieuse de la Grande Guerre*, Paris, Fayard, 2014, 248.

26   Philip Jenkins, *The Great and the Holy War: How World War I Became a Religious Crusade*, New York NY, Harper One, 2014.

27   René Bazin, *Récits du temps de la guerre*, Paris, Calmann-Lévy, 1915, 137.

28   Gerd Krumeich, "Gott mit uns?: Der Erste Weltkrieg als Religionskrieg," in: Gerd Krumeich & Hartmut Lehmann, eds., *"Gott mit uns": Nation, Religion und Gewalt im 19. und frühen 20. Jahrhundert*, Göttingen, Vandenhoeck & Ruprecht, 2000, 273–283.

29   Wilhelm Pressel, *Die Kriegspredigt 1914–1918 in der evangelischen Kirche Deutschlands*, Göttingen, Vandenhoeck & Ruprecht, 1967.

30   Benoît Emonet, "Pourquoi se bat-on?," *Études* 156, 1918, 257–276, here 275.

even civilization.[31] The defensive struggle was immediately seen as morally just. Jacques Rivière, a prisoner in Germany, expanded on the meaning of the conflict:

> We make war for almost nothing but here it is everything: a certain way of thinking, of feeling … we make war for a certain way of seeing the world. Every war is a war of religion … And indeed, who would not be ready to be killed rather than accept seeing good and evil, the beautiful and the ugly, the way our enemies see it?[32]

The war underway was a war of civilization. The American jurist Adrian Edwards, in his last letter to his mother, wrote that he was participating in the war "to save civilization and to prevent future wars," but also "to punish the Germans, who have disregarded every law of God and mankind, whose only God is the god of war and military force."[33] Saints Augustine and Thomas Aquinas were enlisted. On the other hand, Msgr. Luigi Taparelli d'Azeglio, a Catholic promoter of universal peace in his *Saggio teoretico di diritto naturale appoggiato sul fatto* (A theoretical treatise on natural law from an historical standpoint)[34] was not mentioned by either side.

The scale of the losses radicalized the struggle and reinforced the desire for a complete victory so that the people could enjoy a just and lasting peace. The crusade theme became a political argument that was brought in when circumstances required or made it possible. Events, such as when Edmund Allenby seized Jerusalem from Ottoman forces on Dec 11, 1917, fueled such representations. Russian nationalism also depended on Orthodoxy for its propaganda. Russia and the Holy See even dreamt of Hagia Sophia in Istanbul returning to the Christian rite.[35]

The destruction of places of worship reinforced religious divisions. The military advantage gained from the beginning of the conflict restricted this accusation to the troops of the Central Powers. When the Rheims Cathedral was bombed in September 1914, it was also interpreted as a crime against French culture and Catholicism. The cardinal of Rheims stated:

> In targeting the vulnerable building, the German has targeted a monument of our national origins for, while the Rheims Cathedral reminds us of the baptism of Clovis, converted by a victory obtained by invoking Christ, it reminds our neighbors across the Rhine of the defeat of their ancestors in the fields of Tolbiac. In targeting our cathedral, the Lutheran has targeted a monument of the Catholic faith, which our enemies' sovereign noted in indignation as a "monument of idolatry" … The Barbarian has targeted the ideal of a civilization that he dreams of replacing with his *Kultur*.[36]

The way in which the Germans waged war, in effect, burdened them with a collective embodiment of evil. The places of worship affected by the war symbolized both the enemy's barbarism as well as French resistance to invasion. The statue of Our Lady of Mt. Grappa, installed at that peak's summit in 1901 by then patriarch of Venice, Giuseppe Sarto, which was destroyed during a bombardment, became the object of pious images. Other

---

31   Alphonse Dupront, *Le mythe de croisade*, Paris, Gallimard, 1997, 1186.

32   Jacques Rivière, *À la trace de Dieu*, Paris, Gallimard, 1925, 37.

33   Cited in: Ebel, *Faith in the Fight*, 32.

34   Luigi Taparelli, *Saggio teoretico di diritto naturale appoggiato sul fatto*, Livorno, Mansi, 1845.

35   Cyrille Korolevskij, *Kniga bytija moego: Le livre de ma vie: Mémoires autobiographiques*, ed. Giuseppe Maria Croce, vol. 2, Vatican City, Archives secrètes vaticanes, 2007, 571–572. See also Giuseppe Maria Croce, "Le Saint-Siège, l'Église orthodoxe et la Russie soviétique: Entre mission et diplomatie," MEFRIM 105/1, 1993, 267–297, here 267.

36   Louis Luçon, "Discours a l'occasion de l'anniversaire de l'incendie de la cathédrale de Reims," *Revue rémo-ardennaise* 2, 1915, 19–24, here 22–23.

foreign places gained international importance. In 1915, the Germans battered the town of Albert in the Somme, including the basilica with its imposing 68-metre bell tower. On Jan 15, several shells shook the bell tower and the statue of the Virgin on top of it was struck. Her presence seemed to have been a particular target "of the Lutheran fury of our savage aggressors."[37] But the golden Madonna, leaning horizontally, remained fast on her support. That incredible image made its way around the world. British soldiers stationed in Albert sent postcards from "the basilica of the leaning Madonna" to their relatives. The Virgin seemed to protect soldiers and civilians. The periodical, *Prete al campo* portrayed "Our Lady of Brebières Struck by German Artillery" on Jan 16, 1918.[38]

Belgium's fate became emblematic of intraconfessional clashes around the theme of barbarism. Rome soon learnt the facts but could not commit itself on behalf of the country. On Sept 22, 1914, Msgr. Emanuele de Sarzana, the chargé d'affaires in Brussels, told Cardinal Gasparri of the Namur diocese's fate: "German troops have behaved very badly. Entire populations were mown down by enemy machine guns. It seems that twenty priests were killed out of Lutheran hatred."[39] The debate on the "truth" of the atrocities committed in 1914 reinforced the Catholic Churches' national orientation and made reconciliation between coreligionists impossible. The same was true for

Protestants. Hostility towards the enemy played an essential role in the fighters' tenacity. Only weapons would put an end to the war. The war's civilizational stakes made a negotiated peace impossible. The soldiers were waging a crusade and dying for the Gospel, in an *imitatio Christi* shared by both Protestants and Catholics. Condemning war as an absolute evil was the enemy's game. Hating the enemy became the strongest form of holy love for God and country mixed together.

In such a context there was no place for peace or unity. The failure of the pope's proposals and the impossibility of limiting patriotic expressions in the national churches' sermons and practices (such as the failure to remove the national flag from Italian Masses and pressure exerted on sermons) testified to the feeling that the scale of the sacrifices and the sacrificial interpretation of the conflict had led to a rejection of the idea of halting the war before complete victory was obtained.

3   The Suspension of Religious Struggles: "Union Sacrée," Religious Peace?

The same was not true of secular struggles. Although they paled in the context of war, many complaints remained, and many activities were imposed (such as religious symbols being forbidden in the French army and the tricolor national flag being removed from altars in Italy). In the crucible of the trenches, there was a decline in the prewar hatreds of anticlericalism, anti-Semitism and anti-Protestantism.

Nevertheless, the war reinforced the traditional sense of a social support for priests, pastors and rabbis both at the rear as well as at the front. The trenches were sometimes a boiling pot. War accelerated the decline in anticlericalism even if there were episodic recurrences. The papacy's neutrality was misunderstood. From the moment when the pope did not explicitly side with France or Belgium, which were seen as being under attack, he was considered pro-German. It was rumored that the clergy had wanted the war in order to take

37   Pierre Laboureyras, *La destruction d'une cité picarde et d'une basilique mariale: La ville d'Albert avant et pendant la guerre (1914–1915)*, Amiens, Grau, 1915, iv.

38   "Promotional advertisement: We have available nice, small images for the Marian month. On the front, a very sweet Madonna of the French and on the rear, a prayer written especially for our soldiers. They are on sale for 150 lire per hundred. Those who request it directly from our Administration, however, can have it for 125 lire per hundred"; ad published in *Il prete al campo*, May 16, 1918, 120, cited in: Mimmo Franzinelli, *Il volto religioso della guerra: Santini e immaginette per i soldati*, Faenza, Edit Faenza, 2003, 16.

39   E. de Sarzana to P. Gasparri, Oct 5, 1914, in: John Horne & Alan Kramer, *German Atrocities 1914: A History of Denial*, New Haven CT, Yale University Press, 2001.

revenge on Republican France and for the separation of church and state, which had supposedly received preferential treatment. Clerics seemed "swaddled," given assignments in the health services or in the rear. This "disgraceful rumor," as it was then called, was spread, for example, by anticlerical newspapers. The radical *La Dépêche de Toulouse* "challenges any *poilu* (but a real one!) to say they'd seen a priest or a millionaire standing guard in the trenches".[40] In response to this rumor, the clergy published lists of priests who had died in the war. *La Dépêche* was then forced to acknowledge that priests had lost their lives "like everyone else".[41] Nevertheless, in February 1917, a parliamentary amendment, named after the socialist deputy Anatole Sixte-Quenin, made it possible to assign clergymen to all the troop corps and thus largely in combat. The brotherhood of the trenches allowed the exiled religious to be reintegrated into the national community. The weight of the dead was also factored into this renewed acceptance.

On June 17, 1924, Prime Minister Édouard Herriot, president of the Chamber of Deputies and leader of the Cartel des Gauches, announced a break in diplomatic relations with the Holy See and called for the Separation Laws to be applied in the departments of Alsace and Moselle, which had become French again. In 1871, when Alsace-Moselle had been German, the concordat that Napoleon I signed with the papacy was applied, and those regions were not affected by the Separation Laws of 1905. Fr. Paul Doncoeur, head of the DRAC, proclaimed from the pulpit of Notre Dame: "We will not leave."[42] General Édouard de Castelnau, a veteran soldier of 1870 and 1914, father of three sons who died in the Great War, took over leadership of the FNC in 1925. The FNC was organized around a specific program: to defend, conquer, and restore. It faced the country's

secular forces: radical socialism, free thought and Freemasonry. Catholicism emerged victorious after the last great anticlerical thrust of the century. After the victory of the Cartel des Gauches in 1922, the government, led by radical socialist Édouard Herriot, announced its intention to apply secular legislation in Alsace-Lorraine and to close the French embassy to the Holy See. In the eyes of Catholics, it was a rupture of the *union sacrée* achieved during World War I. Thanks to massive demonstrations, the FNC managed to block the project. "The Vatican embassy is maintained, congregations remain in France, and the status of Alsace-Lorraine is respected."[43] The major demonstrations from October 1924 to September 1925 brought 2,200,000 people together. It had become impossible for men of religion who had come to fight in France to return to their country.

The war imposed encounters that would have been unlikely before. For instance, the Trappists of Westvleteren Abbey in Flanders welcomed soldiers:

> In the small room where Fr. Boniface had once lived, there is a Belgian, a sort of interpreter … This gentleman put the crucifix and the holy water font in the hallway … Images of girls and others replaced the crucifix. This is the first time such a thing has happened to us. We have given lodging to all sorts of people, even Jewish rabbis and Freemasons, and never has anyone removed statues or anything else.[44]

The indifferent were worse than those who believed differently, no matter what faith they professed.

---

40 *Poilu* is a term of endearment used during World War I to describe a French rustic infantryman [ed. note]; *La Dépêche de Toulouse*, Feb 13, 1916.

41 *La Dépêche de Toulouse*, July, 9, 1916.

42 Paul Doncoeur, *Correspondance (1924–1961)*, ed. Pierre Mayoux, vol. 1, Paris, Pierre Téqui, 1983, 38.

43 Second General Assembly of the FNC, cited in: Corinne Bonafoux-Verrax, *À la droite de Dieu: La Fédération nationale catholique (1924–1944)*, Paris, Fayard, 2004, 38.

44 Edmundus Joye, July 21, 1917, cited in: Dominiek Dendooven, "Face à leurs ouailles, aux infidèles, aux hérétiques: Les attitudes du clergé catholique de Flandre occidentale," in: Boniface & Cochet, eds., *Foi, religions et sacré*, 89–100, here 98.

The processes of national unity did not allow attempts at, or ideas of, Christian unity to become part of the national discourse. While the phenomena of national unity allowed for a religious peace, they did not eliminate divisions or hatreds. Differences in both patriotic and spiritual conceptions were also obstacles. The initiative of the Octave of Christian Unity was aimed at encouraging common prayer between Anglicans and Catholics. It was approved by Pope Pius X in 1909 following the conversion of its founder Fr. Paul Wattson to Catholicism.[45] An apostolic brief dated Feb 25, 1916, extended the practice to the universal church. In 1916, in the United Kingdom, the week of prayer was observed by several religious congregations[46] in an atmosphere of national tension that included, on Jan 5, the introduction in parliament of the first conscription law. The Catholic hierarchy, however, was cautious. Indeed, Cardinal Francis Alphonsus Bourne reasserted that the association of "church" and "unity" was not a renunciation on the part of the Catholic Church of its claim of being the sole bearer of truth.[47] Prayer for unity, therefore, remained restricted.

> Since the Armistice, many Bishops, priests, and Catholic journalists have laboured to make the Unity Octave known; and each year finds the tide of prayer rising higher. There are, however, too many Christians who have not yet grasped the fact that the Sovereign Pontiff would have them pray these prayers: indeed, they seem to think that the Octave is some hole-and-corner fad of a few self-accredited enthusiasts who may be left to look after it themselves.[48]

The manner in which Luther was interpreted illustrated the impossibility of unity. As early as 1915, in France, Jacques Maritain, christened a Protestant but a convert to Catholicism, denounced that "in the person of Luther and his doctrine, we are present – and that on the level of the spirit and religious life – at the Advent of the Self."[49] Maritain opposed Luther, "the German *par excellence*" to "that miracle of simplicity and uprightness, of candor and wisdom, of humility and magnanimity, of loss of self in God – Joan of Arc."[50] Maritain linked Lutheran Reform to German belligerence. In Germany, Luther was also enlisted in the war.[51] A committee consisting of Protestants (Adolf von Harnack) and Catholics (Sébastien Merkle) was formed to overcome religious stereotypes concerning the interpretation of the Reformation and to work on a patriotic German jubilee. Americans celebrated the reformer while the French decided to discretely celebrate the Reformation rather than Luther.[52] This disparity in commemorations reflected the cultural war being waged within the confessions. In 1915, French Protestants celebrated a major Reformation's anniversary, the bicentenary of the Synod of Montèzes:

> Although we celebrate Wittenberg, it is by refusing in the most explicit way to religiously link Luther's Germany to the Germany of today, which bears the responsibility for the

---

45   Charles V. LaFontaine, "Father Paul Wattson of Graymoor and Prayer for Christian Unity," *CHR* 67, 1981, 31–49.

46   "Church Unity Octave of Prayers," *The Tablet*, Jan 8, 1916.

47   *The Tablet*, Jan 15, 1925.

48   "Eam Coadunare Digneris," *The Tablet*, Jan 19, 1929.

49   Jacques Maritain, *Three Reformers: Luther, Descartes, Rousseau*, London, Sheed & Ward, 1929, 18.

50   Maritain, *Three Reformers*, 27–28.

51   Martin Greschat, "Reformationsjubiläum 1917: Exempel einer fragwürdigen Symbiose von Politik und Theologie," *WPKG* 61, 1972, 419–429; Martin Greschat, *Der Erste Weltkrieg und die Christenheit: Ein globaler Überblick*, Stuttgart, Kohlhammer, 2014; Hansjörg Buss, "Die Deutschen und Martin Luther, Reformationsjubiläen im 19. und 20. Jahrhundert," <http://www.luthermania .de/exhibits/show/hansjoerg-buss-die-deutschen -und-martin-luther> (accessed July 4, 2019).

52   Patrick Cabanel, "Charles Andler, Xavier Léon, Élie Halévy et le numéro spécial de la *Revue de Métaphysique et de Morale* pour le quatrième centenaire de la Réformation de Luther (1917–1918)," *Chrétiens et Sociétés XVIᵉ–XXIᵉ siècles* 23, 2016, 65–92.

most heinous and criminal of wars that has ever desolated the world.[53]

In his editorial in *La Fraternité* on Dec 7, 1918, Alfred Cadier wrote: "It is Calvin who has beaten Luther."[54]

The nation surpassed religious differences to the point that, after the war, American soldiers organized themselves outside spiritual classifications. The war favored a religiosity that mixed all forms of expressions: "The whole business shatters one's faith in religions."[55] In January 1919, Bishop Charles Brent, the chief of chaplains of the AEF, with the support of President Wilson and General John Pershing, founded Comrades in Service, the first veterans' organization, made up of Protestant and Catholic chaplains.[56] It was above all, however, the foundation of the American Legion that declared:

> Whereas the fundamental law of our country guarantees to all peoples equal rights and equal opportunities and the right to worship God as they see fit ... be it Resolved ... this 17th day of October 1923, that we consider any individual, group of individuals, or organizations, which creates or fosters racial, religious or class strife among our people, ... to be un-American.[57]

In order to preserve the unity of the trenches, the American Legion rejected everything that divided the country as "un-American," which implied, among other things, minimizing differences among religious denominations. At a time when the Ku Klux Klan was advancing and anti-Semitic and anti-Catholic campaigns were multiplying, the war experience led to a rejection of whatever was divisive.

On a religious level, the appeasement of rivalries was perceptible and sometimes went so far as discovering the other. The conditions of war also favored a limited but real ecumenism.

3.1 A "de facto *Ecumenism*"

Interstices of fraternity, a "*de facto* ecumenism,"[58] arose under the constraint of events but only in national contexts in the name of a solidarity of the front lines or in detention. This resulted in some points of interfaith convergence, particularly during funeral ceremonies. Marc Bloch, a French soldier of Jewish origin, wrote: "I always thought I was fulfilling a pious duty by commemorating the dead. What did the rites matter?"[59] In December 1915, within the space of a few days, Pastor Alfred Durrleman celebrated a funeral service with a Catholic priest and read psalms at the burial of a young Jew.[60] Pastor Timothée Roussiez testified that "twice for funerals, the priest has placed his church at our disposal. Twice I preached in the Catholic Church, and what is even more remarkable is that no-one in the village protested or grumbled."[61] These interstices of coexistence were part of the circumstances that generated them. War disrupted people's lives and forced them into unexpected proximities. Fernand Carrel, a chaplain with the 119 Infantry Regiment, reported finding one spring bed and one mattress with two chaplains of other faiths and an officer. "We quickly drew lots. The pastor sleeps beside the rabbi

---

53   Frank Puaux, "Discours de M. le Président," *BSHPF* 4, 1917, 275–281, here 276.

54   Cited in: Nicholas Champ, "Loin du front?: Les protestants de l'Ouest dans la Grande Guerre," *BSHPF* 160, 2014, 291–318, here 317.

55   Adrian Gregory, *The Last Great War: British Society and the First World War*, Cambridge, Cambridge University Press, 2008, 176.

56   Cited in: Ebel, *Faith in the Fight*, 171.

57   Minutes of the National Convention of the American Legion, 1923, cited in: Ebel, *Faith in the Fight*, 185.

58   Étienne Fouilloux, "Les voies incertaines de l'œcuménisme (1959–1999)," *Vingtième Siècle. Revue d'histoire* 66, 2000, 133–145, here 138.

59   Marc Bloch, *Souvenirs de guerre (1914–1915)*, in: Marc Bloch, *L'Histoire, la Guerre, la Résistance*, ed. Annette Becker & Étienne Bloch, Paris, Gallimard, 2006, 117–167.

60   Xavier Boniface, "'Nos pasteurs au feu': Les aumôniers protestants aux armées (1914–1918)," *BSHPF* 160, 2014, 105–122, here 119.

61   Timothée Roussiez, *Quelques églises du nord pendant l'occupation*, Caudry, C. Servin, 1919, 15.

(the Old and the New Testaments) and the dogma that I represent lies down beside free thought."[62]

Testimonials confirm this discovery of the other, in which a shared fervor, recognized identity and accepted proximity were mingled. The Protestant chaplain Henri Monnier reported a conversation that he had with a wounded soldier. "'The chaplain brings with him a little of the good Lord' ... And he willingly received it, even though a heretic. And then he perceived one who is so little!"[63] In 1914, after the Germans destroyed the church of Fond de Givonne in the arrondissement of Sedan, parishioners, including the Congar family, attended mass in the chapel of the École des Frères before Pastor Alfred Cosson offered them the one next to the Protestant orphanage. Patriotic ceremonies, such as "national prayers" were an occasion for copresence during the war and for the erection of war memorials to the dead afterwards. During a ceremony of the association Le souvenir français in the Rennes Cathedral, Pastor John-David Bost joined "his heart's prayers with those of the Roman Church to the extent that a common faith in God, in Jesus Christ and in eternal life, besides the common love for our earthy nation, permits it."[64]

In those times of violence, some believers continued to direct their lives and thoughts towards the Christian faith. One soldier testified:

> You have doubtless heard ... that I found a German New Testament on the banks of the Marne. You would not believe the attack of conscience, the dreary burden I felt for a few days. Was not this book proof that

those before me, fighting toe-to-toe, were Christians?[65]

The German exegete Adolf Deißmann studied to read the Bible in English during the war in order not to forget having Christianity in common with his prewar British friends.

These ecumenical endeavors were fortuitous, often individual encounters. They could temporarily erase distances but were too closely tied to circumstances to promote the advancement of Christian unity. In 1918, the French monk Dom Paul Chauvin, who had been conscripted in the CEO, encountered Deacon Athenagoras, then in the service of the metropolitan of Monastir, Stephanos. The two men met and discussed liturgical practices and the ordination of married men about ten times. Although the monk sometimes noted that "his theory of the Orthodox confession is very beautiful; it is so close to ours,"[66] he was also aware of what divided them.

> He is convinced that Constantinople has every right against Rome. Rome was always pretentious and eager to extend its hegemony everywhere ... I understand very well how jealous the Orthodox are of the pope's great prestige in claiming infallibility, such that the unity of the two churches has become even more difficult since the Vatican Council. Athenagoras admits that everything in the Greek-Latin division is a matter of pride, that political motives and rivalries between East and West have been the causes of division and schism much more than religious disputes. However, on the matter of dogmatic life, he says that we were wrong to want to introduce the *Filioque* into the Creed.

62   Nadine-Josette Chaline, "Les aumôniers catholiques dans l'armée française," in: Nadine-Josette Chaline, ed., *Chrétiens dans la première guerre mondiale: Actes des journées tenues à Amiens et à Péronne, les 16 mai et 22 juillet 1992*, Paris, Cerf, 1993, 95–120, here 107.

63   Encrevé, "Les *Notes de guerre*," 50.

64   Jean-Yves Carluer, "Les protestants bretons et la Première Guerre mondiale," *BSHPF* 160, 2014, 279–290, here 287.

65   Raoul Allier, *Avec nos fils sous la mitraille: Conférence donnée le 5 janvier 1915, dans le Temple de l'Étoile*, Paris, Librairie de Foi et Vie, 1915, 5–6.

66   Patrice Mahieu, "L'amitié d'un moine catholique et d'un jeune diacre orthodoxe nommé Athénagoras, Salonique 1918," *Istina* 63, 2018, 27–46, here 30.

Nothing should be added or subtracted from the Apostles' Symbol.[67]

Nevertheless, the two men shared the desire to understand each another. "I am pleased to hear Deacon Athenagoras enthusiastically say that he is delighted to see our mutual prejudices disappear as we come to know each other better."[68] The Frenchman regretted that contact between the Catholics of the expeditionary force and the Orthodox were limited.

> This leads me to express my regret to Deacon Athenagoras that there is no greater exchange during the war between the Latin and Orthodox clergy. ... Although there have been hundreds and thousands of Latin priests in Greece for three years, the question of the unity of the churches has not taken any step forward. The two clergy ignore each another.[69]

Despite the awareness that such encounters can generate, they could not create a groundswell of opinion capable of driving the ecclesial authorities towards unity.

3.2 Tracing Divisions

On the part of the faithful, the common struggles, while affording a new proximity, did not generate any movement of unity. Even within the same confessions, national differences prevented any closeness. Differences were expressed on many levels: both intellectually, as confrontation grounded in the theme of barbarism, and practically in the occupied areas, which had become the laboratory of an all-out war.

The accusation of barbarism was raised on all sides. It then became necessary to deny any affinity with coreligionists of the opposing side. For the Catholic part of the allies, there was an emphasis on the confessional aspect of combat.

> What they sought to destroy in Leuven was the center of Catholic culture in the northwest. It was the university that fought against the teachings of libidinous monks, instruments of princes' ambitions on church property. ... Rheims ..., the heart of nationality. Ceremonies were carried out there whose symbolic meaning was so closely tied to the nation's spirit and history that it formed a substantial part of it. That is why ... the German emperor burnt the Rheims Cathedral, the Saint-Remi Church, the basilica of the coronation.[70]

By attributing religious motivations to the German destruction of the Rheims Cathedral on Sept 19, 1914, by reducing Germany to Prussian Protestantism, Frédéric Masson turned the war into a religious one.

In as early as October 1914, the Manifesto of the Ninety-Three (Der Aufruf "An die Kulturwelt!"), signed by German intellectuals, rejected any accusation of barbarism:

> It is not true that our troops brutally destroyed Leuven. ... Every German would of course greatly regret if in the course of this terrible war any works of art should be destroyed. But although we cannot be surpassed by any other nation in our great love of art, to the same extent, we must decidedly refuse to buy a German defeat at the cost of saving a work of art.[71]

---

67 Mahieu, "L'amitié," 37.
68 Mahieu, "L'amitié," 32.
69 Mahieu, "L'amitié," 39.

70 Frédéric Masson, "Louvain, Reims, Koenisberg," L'Écho de Paris, Sept 23, 1914, 1–2, here 1.
71 Jürgen von Ungern-Sternberg & Wolfgang von Ungern-Sternberg, Der Aufruf "An die Kulturwelt!": Das Manifest der 93 und die Anfänge der Kriegspropaganda im Ersten Weltkrieg, Stuttgart, Franz Steiner, 1996, 233–234; Ulf Gerrit Meyer-Rewerts & Hagen Stöckmann, "Das 'Manifest der 93': Ausdruck oder Negation der Zivilgesellschaft?," in: Johanna Klatt & Robert Lorenz,

To combat the Allies' propaganda, Protestants (Adolf von Harnack)[72] and Catholics (Joseph Mausbach) cohabited, while clerics fought each other with manifestos, pamphlets, and articles, all the while without bringing about any unity, even within the various warring nations. The creation of the CCPFE in 1915, headed at the time by Fr. Alfred Baudrillart, led to an identical committee for French Protestantism, but without any possibility of the two merging.[73] In Germany, a committee founded by Matthias Erzberger and headed by Arthur J. Rosenberg and Mausbach responded to that of Baudrillart. When *La guerre allemande et le catholicisme*[74] was published in April 1915, which defined the war waged by the Germans as an anti-Catholic, Prussian aggression, the *Deutsche Kultur, Katholizismus, und Weltkrieg*[75] responded with a rejection of those accusations.

The French and English responded to the Manifesto of the Ninety-Three, the German intellectuals' rejection of the idea of German responsibility for the outbreak and savagery of the war. During the conflict, nation prevailed over confession. In his sermon of Jan 27, 1915, on the occasion of the Kaiser's birthday, Paul Grünberg commented on 1 Peter 2:17. Touching on "brotherly love," he clarified that Peter was thinking of

> the small Christian community that had to close ranks in a hostile pagan world. And it is not an arbitrary application of this text to say: the German people who are surrounded

by enemies must now firmly close ranks and faithfully hold fast.[76]

Likewise, in the debate on German atrocities committed during the invasion of Belgium, German Catholics were reluctant to defend the Belgian clergy out of fear of awakening anti-Catholic sentiment. On Sept 17, 1914, the army's deputy of General Staff sent instructions to maintain "the internal unity of the German people" by fighting against "unconfirmed rumors about the participation of Catholic clergy in atrocities committed in Belgium, rumors that were sometimes linked to hateful comments about the Catholic clergy in general."[77]

The war reinforced religious divisions. On July 21, 1918, Belgium's national day, Dean Capitular Léon Maubert of Soignies was unable to prevent the German army from using the church for a religious service. The conflict seemed exacerbated in the occupied areas. Priests whose parishes had been invaded were forced to share their places of worship with those of other confessions and other faiths.[78] Between 1915 and 1918, Catholic bishops, such as the bishop of Speyer at the time, Michael von Faulhaber, Cardinal Archbishop Franziskus von Bettinger of Munich and Cardinal Archbishop Felix von Hartmann of Cologne, visited the Western and Eastern Fronts to encourage and revive the Germans' faith. In April 1916, in Aisne, Hartmann declared: "Be and remain

eds., *Manifeste: Geschichte und Gegenwart des politischen Appells*, Bielefeld, Transcript, 2011, 113–134.

72   Julian Jenkins, "War Theology, 1914 and Germany's Sonderweg: Luther's heirs and patriotism," *JRH* 15/3, 1989, 292–310.

73   Denis Carbonnier, "Le Comité protestant de propagande française à l'étranger (1915–1927)," *BSHPF* 160, 2014, 185–217.

74   Alfred Baudrillart, *La guerre allemande et le catholicisme*, Paris, Bloud et Gay, 1915.

75   Georg Pfeilschifter, *Deutsche kultur, katholizismus und weltkrieg: Eine abwehr des buches "La guerre allemande et le catholicisme"*, Freiburg i.Br., Herder, 1915.

76   Paul Grünberg, "Festpredigt gehalten zur Kaisersgeburtstags Feier am 27. Januar 1915," cited in: Matthieu Arnold, "Les prédications de guerre protestantes prononcées en Alsace à l'occasion de l'anniversaire du Kaiser," *BSHPF* 160 2014, 57–76, here 60.

77   Cited in: Horne & Kramer, *German Atrocities*. At the time of the invasion, a rumor was spread accusing the Belgian clergy of attacking wounded Germans. "What if those who were believed to have ripped out soldiers' eyes were actually kneeling beside them to give them the last rites?" asked then Bishop Faulhaber on Oct 22, 1915; cited in: Horne & Kramer, *German Atrocities*.

78   With Protestant and Jewish chaplains, Dec 14, 1915; Fañch Postic, ed., *Moi, Louis-Joseph Le Port: Curé dans la France occupée (1914–1918)*, Rennes, Apogée, 1998, 60.

faithful and valiant soldiers of our emperor as you have also sworn to be valiant and faithful soldiers of Christ!"[79] These pastoral missions were also a means of reaffirming Catholics' fidelity to imperial power in the presence of the Kaiser himself for Cardinal Archbishop Hartmann on Apr 13, 1916 in Charleville. Cardinal Archbishop Luçon of Rheims wrote to Rome on Apr 22, 1916, to protest about these visits:

> Your Eminence will easily understand how painful and delicate the situation created by these visits is for the priests of the invaded countries … given the offence to patriotic sentiment that their presence causes with regard to their fellow citizens, who are not without prejudice towards the clergy and consequently, towards religion.[80]

Belonging to the same denomination did not even ensure assistance for urgent spiritual needs. On Jan 25, 1916, Archbishop Jean-Arthur Chollet of Cambrai wrote to Msgr. Johannes Arnold Middendorf, the delegate of the German military bishops in Brussels, to obtain a supply of olive oil for consecration during Holy Week. Middendorf refused him the 45 liters requested, referring him back to the American-assisted CANF.[81]

While the Frenchman Gustave Bardy offered a reminder that "these barbarians … are still children of the church," in February 1917, in *La Correspondance catholique mensuelle: Katholische Monastbriefe*, published by the Committee for the Defense of German and Catholic Interests during the War, Engelbert Krebs praised the German policy of pacification in Eastern Europe and the protection of Catholics against Russian Orthodoxy. In April 1917, he denounced the possible victory of Freemasonry in France and Italy, selfish British mercantilism and Russian intolerance. Although the journal continued to justify the validity of the German war, it nevertheless proposed calls for peace and Christian unity, albeit within the framework of a German peace. Then, in the article "Renouer les anciens fils rompus," published in October 1918, the vanquished lamented that the vanquishers had forgotten that they were Catholic.[82]

4 A Clandestine Circulation of Hope for Christian Unity

On the eve of war, two failures illustrated the impossibility of any rapprochement. In 1895, relations between Constantinople and Rome were strained after the outright rejection of papal offers included in the encyclical *Praeclara gratulationis* and, in 1896, the confirmation of the nullity of Anglican orders by Rome in the bull *Apostolicae curae*.[83]

4.1 Failure of the Christian Desire for Peace

In 1914, the universalism of the Christian message found no voice or means of expression. In that year, neither the red international of socialism nor the black one of Vatican succeeded in preventing the war. The only manifestation of a desire for peace of Christian origin was the meeting in Constance on

79   Yves Métivier & Raymond Verhaeghe, "Les visites pastorales de deux cardinaux allemands sur le front occidental en 1916: Félix von Hartmann et Franziskus von Bettinger," in: Xavier Boniface & Jean Heuclin, eds., *Diocèses en guerre (1914–1918): L'Église déchirée entre Gott mis uns et le Dieu des armées*, Villeneuve d'Ascq, Presses Universitaires du Septentrion, 2018, 105–136, here 113.

80   Letter from L. Luçon on Apr 22, 1916, accompanied by two articles from the *Kölnische Volkszeitung* (Apr 15, 1916) and *L'Humanité* (Apr 20, 1916) on the services held at Laon and d'Anizy-le-Château, in: AAR, Fonds Luçon, 7 J 60.

81   Caroline Biencourt & Olivier Georges, "Diriger une Église en territoire occupé, Mgr Chollet, archevêque de Cambrai," in: Boniface & Heuclin, eds., *Diocèses en guerre*, 35–52, here 41.

82   Jean Heuclin, "La *Correspondance Catholique Mensuelle – Katolische Monatsbriefe* ou l'impossible dialogue des frères ennemis," in: Boniface & Heuclin, eds., *Diocèses en guerre*, 267–288, here 273.

83   See Paul Avis's contribution in this volume.

Aug 1, 1914, which was dissolved on Aug 3. During those two days, the Austro-Serb declaration of war spread throughout Europe.[84] While the WA, which aimed at promoting arbitration between nations, grew out of this conference, the outbreak of war, and the national strife it occasioned, brought the meeting to a close. The president of the German committee of the WA, Friedrich Albert Spiecker, accused England of being solely responsible for the conflict.[85] From the Church of Rome's point of view, the project's Protestant inspiration impeded Catholic presence. The war had divided its flock, and the Holy See engaged in a policy of impartiality.[86]

Appealing to the spiritual brotherhood of Christians did nothing. As early as November 1914, in his encyclical on All Saints' Day, the pope wondered:

> Who would imagine as we see them thus filled with hatred of one another, that they are all of one common stock, all of the same nature, all members of the same human society? Who would recognize brothers, whose Father is in Heaven?[87]

On Aug 4, 1914, the French Pastor Charles Babut wrote to the German Pastor Ernst Dryander, whom he knew personally. He wished that, "despite the war, fraternal love, which must never cease to animate Christ's disciples, be upheld and proclaimed."

He proposed a common declaration of Christians in the countries at war, committing themselves "under the gaze and with the help of God, to banish all hatred from their hearts" and to "use all the influence at their disposal to ensure that the war is conducted with as much humanity as possible."[88] In his reply, Dryander stated that Germany did not need any "admonishment or effort to ensure that the war is conducted in accordance with Christian principles." He inverted the accusations, noting that the German was "a peaceful man set upon by three bloodthirsty hyenas at the same time" and that "when you are fighting for your life, you do not ask yourself if, during battle, you might be breaking down your neighbor's gate."[89]

The failure of Pastor Babut's appeal to Pastor Dryander is further proof. The repeated appeals of the pope and other clergy did not change anything. The humanitarian reorientation of Rome's commitment, however, marked a decisive development for the following century. When the pope received Jane Addams from the WILPF in 1915, she noted his powerlessness: "They [men of religious responsibility] are apparently powerless to do the one thing which might end it."[90]

In Italy, which was still neutral, the Protestant-inspired pacifism of the Turin publication *Il Savonarola* afforded a meeting with an American pastor, but such a minority could not oppose entry into war.[91] Benedict XV acquired a reputation as a pope in favor of unity among Christian churches. "Finally, he was pursuing ... this somewhat chimeric but grandiose idea of the union of all Christian

---

84 John S. Conway, "The Struggle for Peace Between the Wars: A Chapter from the History of the Western Churches," *EcRev* 35, 1983, 25–40, here 25–26. On the 1914 Conference in Constance and similar initiatives, see Gerhard Besier's contribution in this volume.

85 Kurt Nowak, "Les chrétiens à l'épreuve de la Première Guerre mondiale: Les protestants," in: Paul Colonge & Rudolf Lill, eds., *Histoire religieuse de l'Allemagne*, Paris, Cerf, 2000, 167–171, here 168.

86 Francis Latour, *La papauté et les problèmes de la paix pendant la Première Guerre mondiale*, Paris, L'Harmattan, 1996.

87 Benedict XV, *Ad beatissimi apostolorum principis*, in: *AAS* 6, 1914, 565–581, the text can be found at <http://w2.vatican.va/content/benedict-xv/en/encyclicals/documents/hf_ben-xv_enc_01111914_ad-beatissimi-apostolorum.html> (accessed July 4, 2019).

88 Gambarotto, *Foi et patrie*, 441.

89 Gambarotto, *Foi et patrie*, 443.

90 Cited in: Gearóid Barry, "Pope Benedict XV and Pacifism: 'An Invincible Phalanx for Peace?,'" in: Giovanni Cavagnini & Giulia Grossi, eds., *Benedict XV: A Pope in the World of the "Useless Slaughter" (1914–1918)*, dir. Alberto Melloni, vol. 1, Turnhout, Brepols, 2020, 319–335, here 319.

91 Alessandro Zussini, "I cattolici pacifisti torinesi de *Il Savonarola*: Una minoranza cattolica tra evangelici e socialisti negli anni della Prima guerra mondiale," *Quaderni del Centro Studi Carlo Trabucco*, Feb 4, 1984, 25–64, here 49.

churches."[92] At the end of the war, "none of the awaited harvests have occurred, but the workers are at work."[93]

4.2 Increasing Appeals: From Stockholm in 1917 to Lambeth in 1920

While the papacy called on the faithful to pray for peace on several occasions during the war, Rome also asked, on Apr 15, 1916, for prayers for the return of the Oriental Churches to the Chair of Peter. The tendency towards unity continued despite the war. Even religious initiatives, however, found it impossible for enemies of identical faiths to draw closer to one another. In 1916, a French Catholic, Mademoiselle de Rose worked on an Our Father for all Christian denominations and managed, with the help of a Protestant friend, Renée de Montmort, and her English correspondent, Francis H. Stead, to promote it among several religious authorities. Despite the support of several archbishops, she was unable to obtain any overall consensus. The council of the FPF even noted the risk of making use of a prayer which German Protestants were also called to pray for the sake of propaganda.[94]

Like the pontifical appeals for peace, churches called for unity during the war, which was widely perceived as a way of opposing it. The initiative came from the primate of the Swedish National Church, the Lutheran archbishop of Uppsala, Nathan Söderblom. He asserted that the war contradicted the Christian message and depreciated it. To warn Christians of the dangers that the war posed to their beliefs and values, he had the idea of bringing together clerics from the neutral countries in Stockholm in December 1917. This call from Stockholm for peace among Christians had no effect. Söderblom proposed a conference where representatives of the various Christian denominations would discuss their role in restoring

harmony among the warring nations. Scheduled for April 1918, the meeting was first postponed until September 1918 and then indefinitely. The conference never took place.[95]

Such initiatives seemed doomed to fail not only due to of war-related issues but also because, within the various confessions, war did not lead to any change in standpoint. Thus the twin meetings held in Geneva in August 1920 to prepare for the future Life and Work and Faith and Order conferences took place without any Catholic presence. Rome reiterated its refusal to participate, which had already been expressed before the war. Only the forms differed. Twice, on June 19, 1918, and Feb 20, 1921, Cardinal Gasparri, on behalf of the pope, politely declined the invitation to attend a Life and Work Conference. The American Episcopalian delegation that went to Europe in the spring of 1919 was received by Benedict XV, but left their audience of May 16 with the same refusal, accompanied by a copy of the decisions of 1864 and 1865 condemning the APUC, a result of the Oxford Movement in which English Catholics cooperated with Anglicans.[96]

While the Holy See indeed received, observed and was informed about ongoing projects, as soon as the move changed from informal to formal, Rome would reaffirm its position. For Rome, the Roman Church is the only Church of Jesus Christ on earth. Common activities are impossible since the only possibility for unity is to return to the bosom of true unity, that of the Catholic Church.

On the Orthodox side, the creation of a Commission for the Unity of the Churches on Aug 3, 1918, during the third session of the council of Moscow should not be misinterpreted. The commission adopted a resolution in which it considered "the reunion of the Christian churches to be especially desirable in the period of intense struggle with unbelief, crude materialism

92 Maurice Pernot, "Benoit XV," *Journal des débats*, Jan 23, 1922, 1.

93 Étienne Fouilloux, *Les catholiques et l'unité chrétienne du XIXᵉ au XXᵉ siècle: Itinéraires européens d'expression française*, Paris, Le Centurion, 1982, 96.

94 Fouilloux, *Les catholiques et l'unité chrétienne*, 78.

95 See in this volume the contributions by Gerhard Besier and Dietz Lange.

96 See Luca Ferracci's contribution in this volume.

and moral barbarism."[97] However, it addressed only Old Catholics and Anglicans and its "motivation is more ... defensive than theological."[98] Nevertheless, for the first time, the Orthodox Church stated that there was a possibility of approaching other Christian churches even though the council ended abruptly under pressure from the Soviet power.

4.3   The End to War

The end of the war rekindled community clashes that had existed before 1914. With the signing of the armistice, Alsace-Moselle once again became French. Religious tensions showed that, at times, confessional interpretations remained strong. In Oberbetschdorf, "the hostility between Protestants and Catholics ... is ... chronic and [has been so] for a very long time, ... the arrival of the French has nourished it. Catholics enthusiastically welcomed our troops. Protestants immediately took a reserved, almost hostile attitude, and there were skirmishes."[99]

Interpreting the peace varied considerably from one country to another and from one denomination to another. "From a religious point of view, Protestant contemporaries considered World War I to be the victory of Catholic nations over Protestant nations,"[100] whereas Aristide Briand asserted that Versailles was a "Protestant peace directed against Rome."[101]

The papacy, however, did not participate in the restructuring of Christian lands after the war. It was excluded from the peace conference negotiations and therefore was unable to influence the new borders of the continent, even if it attempted other means to count in the reconstruction.[102] It focused, instead, on resolving the Roman Question and protecting Catholics around the world, whose lives had been disrupted by the war. This was also because the Holy See felt closer to the conservative and authoritarian values of the Central Powers than to the French Republic, Anglo-Saxon Protestantism, or Russian Orthodoxy. The war led to the collapse of four empires: Germany, Austria-Hungary, Russia, and the Ottoman Empire. "From the East to Rome as from Rome to the East, the roads are freer. The spiritual police corps have disappeared."[103]

For the papacy, in addition to Catholicism's overall loss, such as that of Austria-Hungary, there was also a mistrust of the Anglo-Saxon advance, especially in the United States, which was then largely Protestant. While it did not change religious boundaries, the war profoundly disrupted national boundaries. The end of Austria-Hungary was a loss for the papacy as the church had relied on that Catholic empire. Since the German Empire had inherited Bismarck's anti-Catholic policy, its fall represented an opportunity for the papacy.[104] The increase in Christian parties after the war provides ample proof of this. Some of the new countries, such as Czechoslovakia and Turkey, pursued policies of severe secularization, which also affected Catholicism. Only the fall of the Romanov dynasty opened other perspectives.[105] The triumphant revolution was unfavorable for Orthodoxy, and an undeniable unionist revival continued after the war.[106] The papacy then launched a

---

97   Cited in: Hyacinthe Destivelle, *Le concile de Moscou (1917–1918): La création des institutions conciliaires de l'Église orthodoxe russe*, Paris, Cerf, 2006, 191.

98   Destivelle, *Le concile de Moscou*, 192.

99   Report of the military administrator of Wissembourg to the high commissioner of the Republic, Mar 3, 1919, cited in: Catherine Storne-Sengel, *Les protestants d'Alsace-Lorraine de 1919 à 1939: Entre les deux règnes*, Strasbourg, Société savante d'Alsace, 2003, 228.

100   Nowak, "Les chrétiens," 170.

101   Jacques Bariéty, ed., *Aristide Briand: La Société des Nations et l'Europe (1919–1932)*, Strasbourg, Presses Universitaires de Strasbourg, 2007.

102   Giuseppe Maria Croce, "Le Saint-Siège et la Conférence de la paix (1919): Diplomatie d'Église et diplomaties d'État," *MEFRIM* 109/2, 1997, 793–823.

103   Georges Goyau, "L'Église libre dans l'Europe libre II," *Revue des deux mondes* 52, 1919, 277–310, here 305.

104   Even if, for several years, the German Empire had abandoned that policy in favor of rapprochement; Stan M. Landry, *Ecumenism, Memory and German Nationalism (1817–1917)*, Syracuse NY, Syracuse University Press, 2013.

105   Croce, "Le Saint-Siège."

106   Étienne Fouilloux writes of "the second chance for unity" in the years 1914–1928.

"dynamic and innovative diplomacy."[107] In 1917, between the two revolutions of February and October, the papacy created the Congregation for the Oriental Churches and the PIO,[108] which were a sign of Rome's attention toward Russia and the Ukraine.[109] Prerogatives granted to the new curial congregation demonstrated the pope's willingness to pursue an active unionist policy. "All matters of any kind whatsoever relating either to persons, or disciplines, or rites of the Eastern Churches, even matters also concerning Latins, both in relation to things as well as persons" were placed under its authority.[110] A moment of religious freedom seemed favorable to conquering lands previously dominated by an Orthodox Caesaropapism.[111] The new power, however, was profoundly antireligious. Nevertheless, the Holy See attempted to develop relations by drafting concordat-like talks ("full freedom of conscience, full freedom of worship and religious instruction, and restitution of confiscated goods")[112] on the sidelines of the International Genoa Conference in the following year. It also played the humanitarian card, sending a mission to assist the hungry in Russia in 1921.

The disappearance of both the Ottoman and Russian Empires seemed to be an opportunity to establish a confederation of Orthodox and Anglican Churches around the patriarch of Constantinople. Those discussions were opposed both by the Holy See and by French and Italian diplomacy, which were not in favor of Greek influence in the eastern Mediterranean. Greece's military failure in Turkey in 1922 and the country's political weaknesses put an end to all attempts.[113]

The war also shifted the world's balance of power, as is shown by Africa, which was a battlefield as well as a territory providing soldiers and raw materials.[114] Doctor and theologian Albert Schweitzer concluded his book *The Primeval Forest* by identifying the impact of European domination on the world:

> Many natives are puzzling over the question how it can be possible that the whites, who brought them the Gospel of Love, are now murdering each other, and throwing to the winds the commands of the Lord Jesus. ... How far the ethical and religious authority of the white man among these children of nature is impaired by this war we shall only be able to measure later on. I fear that the damage done will be very considerable.[115]

At the end of the war, European domination was overthrown to the advantage of the United States. American involvement in the war had made a difference. Additionally, its entry into the war was proceeded by massive efforts of assistance, mainly of Protestant origin, to the occupied areas.[116]

107   Laura Pettinaroli, *La politique russe du Saint-Siège (1905–1939)*, Rome, École française de Rome, 2015, 255.

108   Giuseppe Maria Croce, "Benedetto XV e l'enciclica archiviata: Alle origini della Congregazione Orientale e del Pontificio Istituto Orientale," *OrChrAn* 284, 2009, 59–107.

109   Roberto Morozzo della Rocca, *Le nazioni non muoiono: Russia rivoluzionaria, Polonia indipendente e Santa Sede*, Bologna, Il Mulino, 1992.

110   Benedict XV, *Dei providentis*, in: *AAS* 9, 1917, 529–531, <https://w2.vatican.va/content/benedict-xv/it/motu_proprio/documents/hf_ben-xv_motu-proprio_19170501_dei-providentis.html> (accessed July 4, 2019).

111   Soviet Decree on Separation of Church from State, Jan 23, 1918.

112   Fouilloux, *Les catholiques et l'unité chrétienne*, 78.

113   Anastassios Anastassiadis, "Un 'Vatican anglicano-orthodoxe' à Constantinople?: Relations interconfessionnelles, rêves impériaux et enjeux de pouvoir en Méditerranée orientale à la fin de la Grande Guerre," in: Anastassios Anastassiadis, ed., *Voisinages fragiles: Les relations interconfessionnelles dans le Sud-Est européen et la Méditerranée orientale (1854–1923): Contraintes locales et enjeux internationaux*, Athens, École française d'Athènes, 2013, 283–302.

114   See Frieder Ludwig, "Das also ist Christentum?: Der Schock des europäischen Krieges 1914–18 und seine Auswirkungen auf Kirche und Mission in Afrika und Asien," in: Joachim Negel & Karl Pinggéra, eds., *Urkatastrophe: Die Erfahrung des Krieges 1914–1918 im Spiegel zeitgenössischer Theologie*, Freiburg i.Br., Herder, 2016, 484–512.

115   Albert Schweitzer, *The Primeval Forest*, Baltimore MD, Johns Hopkins University Press, 1998, 104–105.

116   Annette Becker, *Oubliés de la Grande Guerre: Humanitaire et culture de guerre (1914–1918)*, Paris, Hachette,

The papacy was also engaged in "assistance diplomacy,"[117] especially in the care of prisoners. These common commitments, however, remained largely defined by their denominational origin.

As early as 1915, a unit from the War Prisoners' Aid visited prisoner of war camps in Great Britain and Germany. After the war, the import of American Protestantism was felt in its strong presence during the reconstruction process, where it engaged in many philanthropic activities. With the thousands of its soldiers that had landed on the continent and its economic and financial power, the United States was mobilized in support of the war, but American assistance claimed to be partly Christian – a Christianity with shared values but different denominations.

From the Holy See's point of view, collaborating with such agencies was dangerous, or at least a source of confusion, even though the issues of promoting birth rates or defending morality could be shared. There was also a competition in offering assistance to soldiers. The YMCA, an "openly Christian organization,"[118] supervised soldiers and their leisure activities in Soldiers' Hostels.

French authorities imposed a strict religious neutrality, but disputes sometimes occurred. In October 1915, a center director stated: "We must be careful because of the military authorities ... but we are unafraid to assert ourselves every time the opportunity presents itself, and every soldier knows that he is among Protestants and that Protestants respect the conscience of others."[119] The Protestant Pastor Rodney "Gypsy" Smith, who was strongly opposed to Catholicism in Great Britain, nevertheless claimed to respect confessional affiliations at the front. "I limited myself to the essential and rejected everything that could appear as a source of division."[120]

The effects of war extended well beyond the war itself. In October 1919, the first postwar gathering of the WA was held near The Hague. The French delegates, Élie Gounelle and Wilfred Monod, did not attend the meeting because they had not received an acknowledgment that Germany had been to blame for the origin of the conflict from the German delegation. It took time for Germany to return to the international forums. Even in 1922, there were very few French people like Paul Doncoeur who agreed to write affirming the fraternity of all in a German journal.

> Then we realize that we are brothers, born of the same blood that flowed from the same heart on the one and the same Calvary. May this feeling of kinship of all the children of the church triumph over the obstacles that oppose the love and union that our Savior prayed for in his high priestly prayer: *Ut sint unum*.[121]

It is true that the defeated Germans were more interested in finding common ground than the victorious countries. This was especially true as a new threat which might unite Christians emerged: Bolshevism. Catholic philosopher Max Scheler published an article in the leading German

1998, and Irène Herrmann, *L'humanitaire en questions: Réflexions autour de l'histoire du Comité international de la Croix-Rouge*, Paris, Cerf, 2018.

117 Massimiliano Valente, "La nunziatura di Eugenio Pacelli a Monaco di Baviera e la 'diplomazia dell'assistenza' nella 'Grande Guerra' (1917–1918)," *QFIAB* 83, 2003, 264–287.

118 Hélène Trocmé, "Un modèle américain transposé: Les foyers du soldat de l'Union franco-américaine (1914–1922)," in: François Cochet, Marie-Claude Genet-Delacroix & Hélène Trocmé, eds., *Les Américains et la France (1917–1947): Engagements et représentations*, Paris, Maisonneuve & Larose, 1999, 5–23, here 16.

119 Recounted by Mme Arbousse-Bastide to Emmanuel Sautter, October 1915, cited in: Trocmé, "Un modèle américain transposé," 16.

120 *The Red Triangle*, Mar 23, 1917, 248, cited in: Michael Snape, "Le YMCA et le soldat britannique," in: Boniface & Cochet, eds., *Foi, religions et sacré*, 219–234, here 229.

121 Paul Doncoeur, "Die Gegenwartshoffnungen der Katholiken Frankreichs auf religiösem Gebiete," *StZ* 103, 1922, 183–200, here 200.

Catholic magazine, *Hochland*, calling for peace among confessions.

> Only then is it possible to avoid the bloodiest civil war and restrain the fall of the empire and the Bolshevization of Europe ... The question today is becoming clear to us, in order to avoid this, it means peace between the religious confessions in this fuller sense.[122]

Christian unity was never at the heart of what was at stake in the war or in its solution. Nevertheless, individual initiatives occurred. Bathed in the aura of his resistance to the German occupation of Belgium,[123] after a triumphant trip to the United States,[124] Cardinal Desiré-Joseph Mercier began to reach out to the Anglo-Saxons. He gave an address to the Episcopalian convention that brought about some concern from Rome and the pope himself owing to its evocative title: "Brothers in Christian Faith."

In December 1921, the cardinal agreed to meet in Malines the team that had made Anglican-Roman efforts before the war. Although Fernand Portal asserted that "religious understanding, the unity of the churches"[125] would be one of the essential elements of peace, this Belgian experience was only exploratory at the time of Benedict XV's death in January 1922.[126]

Christian unity also required an awareness of the need to share values and interpretations that were being challenged by modernity. Finding a common ground for Christians could only be achieved at the cost of a detachment from nationalism. While there were signs of a desire for unity, the continent's deep divisions, accentuated on an external level by war and on an internal level by differences in confession and conceptions of unity, forbad any establishment of common ground during the war.

The war among nations swept away the fragile glimpses of a desire to approach one another. A few chance encounters and personalities kept the flame alive. Within the nations, a closeness was created in the face of death, the great equalizer, in the face of victory or defeat, as well as in the face of time constraints. Such *de facto* ecumenism did not see any decisive development. The Great War was a lost chance for Christian unity, even if, at the end of the conflict, "the inter-confessional landscape was far less stable than it was in 1914."[127]

Obviously, "the awakening of French Catholics to the international dimension of their religious bearing seems to be one of the major, perhaps the most radical, changes that they experienced between the two world wars."[128] This, moreover, applied to other countries as well. Needless to say, within Protestantism, reflections on the churches' incapacity during the conflict were emerging. But there was no debate on their role during the war. No church acknowledged any responsibility

122 Max Scheler, "Der Friede unter den Konfessionen," *Hochland* 18, 1920–1921, cited in: Patrick J. Houlihan, *Catholicism and the Great War: Religion and Everyday Life in Germany and Austria-Hungary (1914–1922)*, Cambridge, Cambridge University Press, 2015, 237.

123 Ilse Meseberg-Haubold, *Der Widerstand Kardinal Merciers gegen die deutsche Besetzung Belgiens (1914–1918): Ein Beitrag zur politischen Rolle des Katholizismus im Ersten Weltkrieg*, Frankfurt a.M., Peter Lang, 1982.

124 Roger Aubert, "Cardinal Mercier's Visit to America in the Autumn of 1919," in: Roger Aubert, *Le cardinal Mercier (1851–1926): Un prélat d'avant-garde: Publications du professeur Roger Aubert rassemblées à l'occasion de ses 80 ans*, eds. Jean-Pierre Hendrickx, Jean Pirotte & Luc Courtois, Louvain-la-Neuve, Presses Universitaires de Louvain, 1994, 329–362.

125 Cited in: Régis Ladous, *Fernand Portal et les siens (1855–1926)*, Paris, Cerf, 1985, 418.

126 John A. Dick, *The Malines Conversations Revisited*, Leuven, Leuven University Press, 1989. On the Malines Conversation, see Bernard Barlow and Martin Browne's contribution in this volume.

127 Étienne Fouilloux, "An Indecisive Inter-Confessional Situation (1914–22)," in: Cavagnini & Grossi, eds., *Benedict XV*, vol. 1, 779–788, here 786.

128 Jacques Gadille, "Conscience internationale et conscience sociale dans les milieux catholiques d'expression française dans l'entre-deux-guerres," *Relations internationales* 27, 1981, 361–374.

or involvement in the massacre mourned by the continent or in the crimes committed during the battles.[129]

Translated from French to English by Susan Dawson Vásquez and David Dawson Vásquez.

Bibliography

Becker, Annette, *La guerre et la foi: De la mort à la mémoire (1914–1930)*, Paris, Colin, 1994.

Boniface, Xavier, *Histoire religieuse de la Grande Guerre*, Paris, Fayard, 2014.

Boniface, Xavier & François Cochet, eds., *Foi, religions et sacré dans la Grande Guerre*, Arras, Artois Presses Université, 2014.

Cavagnini, Giovanni & Giulia Grossi, eds., *Benedict XV: A Pope in the World of the "Useless Slaughter"* (1914–1918), dir. Alberto Melloni, vol.1, Turnhout, Brepols, 2020.

Fouilloux, Étienne, *Les catholiques et l'unité chrétienne du XIXᵉ au XXᵉ siècle: Itinéraires européens d'expression française*, Paris, Le Centurion, 1982.

Gambarotto, Laurent, *Foi et patrie: La prédication du protestantisme français pendant la Première Guerre mondiale*, Geneva, Labor et Fides.

Greschat, Martin, *Der Erste Weltkrieg und die Christenheit: Ein globaler Überblick*, Stuttgart, Kohlhammer, 2014.

Krumeich, Gerd & Hartmut Lehmann, eds., *"Gott mit uns": Nation, Religion und Gewalt im 19. und frühen 20. Jahrhundert*, Göttingen, Vandenhoeck & Ruprecht, 2000.

Merker, Nicolao, *La guerra di Dio: Religione e nazionalismo nella Grande Guerra*, Rome, Carocci, 2015.

Paiano, Maria, *La preghiera e la Grande Guerra: Benedetto XV e la nazionalizzazione del culto in Italia*, Pisa, Pacini, 2017.

---

129   Gerhard Sauter, "War Guilt," DEM, 1063–1064.

PART 3

Beginnings: Movements Become a Movement

∵

The Catholic Biblical Movement between Fear and Hope

Mathijs Lamberigts

1   Introduction

The different movements that played an active role in the preparation of Vatican II, that is, the biblical, patristic, liturgical, and ecumenical movements, probably cannot entirely be separated from each other. In fact, central players in one domain were often present in other domains, as was the case for Dom Bernard Botte, O.S.B., who became monk of Keizersberg[1] (Leuven) because of the inspiring example of Dom Lambert Beauduin, promoter of the liturgical and later the ecumenical movement.[2] Botte started his career dealing with the history of exegesis, then became a well-respected patristic scholar, editor of the *Apostolic Tradition* of Hippolytus, showed interest in the liturgies of the Eastern Churches, and was actively involved in the liturgical movement, offering study weeks at Keizersberg for priests and professors interested in liturgy for many years; he did similar things in Paris at Saint-Serge, where the focus was more on the great liturgical tradition of the church in the East.[3] It should be noted, however, that although the case of Botte shows how entwined the liturgical and ecumenical movements were from the beginning, it seems difficult to find a similar combination of biblical and ecumenical interest, at least before Vatican II.[4]

A second introductory observation has to do with the complex relation between science and faith. During the Enlightenment, scientists had already remarked that biblical ideas and insights were not confirmed by discoveries in the natural sciences. The positive approach developed in the natural sciences soon was taken over by historians who wanted to read and understand the Bible historically, thus not primarily taking into account its divine, inspirational character, an aspect, indeed, that could hardly be treated by a method focusing on historical data. Historical-critical Bible reading was born, a method which took into account insights as offered by rationalist philosophy, biblical archaeology, and comparative religious studies. This approach was very successful among the Protestant liberals, Adolf von Harnack being one of its great promoters. Harnack argued that, throughout its history, Christianity had been constantly characterized by development, change, diversity, and mutually incompatible theologies.[5] It goes without saying that such an interpretation was not well received in Catholic quarters. Vatican I had made clear that the books of the Bible were inspired and canonical because they had God as their author and were addressed to the church. The Roman Catholic Church was the authentic interpreter of the Bible, as had already been stated by the Council of Trent.[6] However, Vatican I did not explicitly address how such a position was compatible with the presence of inaccuracies in the Bible. As a result, Catholic scholars had to deal with the problem of how to

---

1   Also known as Mont César.

2   See André Haquin's contribution in this volume.

3   See Pierre-Marie Gy, "L'œuvre scientifique de Dom Bernard Botte," *QL* 54, 1973, 13–18.

4   I wish to thank Professor Gilbert Van Belle (KU Leuven) for the inspiring discussions in which he made clear to me that the biblical and ecumenical movements had less in common than often suggested in the post-Vatican II literature.

5   See John Kaufman, "Historical Relativism and the Essence of Christianity," *ST* 70, 2016, 4–21, here 4.

6   See Anthony C. Cotter, "The Antecedents of the Encyclical *Providentissimus Deus*," *CBQ* 5, 1943, 117–124, here 117–118.

reconcile "errors" in the Sacred Scripture with the claim of divine inspiration. Most of these scholars were of the opinion that it was impossible that errors were present in the Bible, thus defending its inerrancy. However, others such as August Rohling argued that one should distinguish between matters of faith and morals, both supported by historical facts, on the one hand, and profane matters, on the other.[7] Rohling's distinction was not approved of by the official Catholic voices.[8] The works of François Lenormant, an archaeologist, instead, were put on the Index in 1887 for having proposed a distinction between inspiration and revelation, responding to the fact that archaeological findings continued to call into question the inspirational character of Genesis.[9] Evidently time was not yet ripe for this distinction, and the hope of reconciling archaeological or historical evidence with a view of Scripture as composed of inviolable truths remained problematic.[10]

2   Papal Statements from Leo XIII to Benedict XV: Leo XIII's *Providentissimus Deus*

Historical research[11] seemed to call the historical truth of the Bible into question. Therefore, Leo XIII showed some hesitation with regard to the use of the historical-critical approach. Surely, Leo had encouraged the study of history and archaeology and promoted the diligent study of the natural sciences. He had opened the Vatican Observatory in 1891, but now he was confronted with disputes, if not open dissent, among Catholic scholars.[12] In 1893, he published the encyclical *Providentissimus Deus*, the first encyclical of a pope on biblical studies. In this encyclical, Leo described the need and value of the study of the Bible, the very soul of theology.[13] The pope criticized the so-called rationalistic approach which, making use of methods available in the natural sciences, read the Bible as a mere historical book, thus neglecting its inspirational character and divine authorship, a view in which human authors were reduced to that of instruments in God's hand. The pope condemned those positions that, attempting to give a place to insights from the natural sciences, in fact were reducing inspiration to the domain of faith and morals. Leo also emphasized the absolute inerrancy of the Bible,[14] thus obliging Catholic

---

7   For the details, see Cotter, "The Antecedents," 118–119.

8   Nevertheless, the idea that Scripture is inspired in matters of faith and morals, but not in "practical" matters such as Paul sending greetings at the end of his letters, was also held by John Henry Newman and well received on the European continent. However, books such as that of Salvatore Di Bartolo, *I criteri teologici*, 1888, going in the same direction, were put on the Index; see Cotter, "The Antecedents," 120–121. Even survey articles like the one of the rector of the ICP, Msgr. Maurice d'Hulst, suggesting that one could find three approaches with regard to biblical inerrancy (absolute acceptance, absolute rejection, and theoretical acceptance but practical hesitation, the so called *école large*) met with disapproval.

9   François Lenormant, *Les origines de l'histoire d'après la Bible et les traditions des peuples orientaux*, 3 vols., Paris, Maisonneuve, 1880–1884.

10   See Karim Schelkens, "From *Providentissimus Deus* to *Dei Verbum*: The Catholic Biblical Movement and the Council Reconsidered," in: Gilles Routhier, Philippe J. Roy & Karim Schelkens, eds., *La théologie catholique entre intransigeance et renouveau: La réception des mouvements préconciliaires à Vatican II*, Turnhout, Brepols, 2011, 49–67, here 50.

11   For a general survey of the issues under consideration, see Mathijs Lamberigts, "The Bible: A Book for *All* Faithful," *ASR* 10, 2017, 75–92.

12   See Richard T. Murphy, "The Teachings of the Encyclical *Providentissimus Deus*," *CBQ* 5, 1943, 125–140.

13   The encyclical inspired, in many ways, the study of the Eastern history and languages. Biblical introductions were published everywhere. The revision of the Vulgate was started. Bible translations appeared. An impressive number of journals and collections were founded; see Stephen Hartdegen, "The Influence of the Encyclical *Providentissimus Deus* on Subsequent Scripture Study," *CBQ* 5, 1943, 141–159.

14   On the Catholic background of the pope's concern, see Francesco Beretta, "De l'inerrance absolue à la vérité salvifique de l'Écriture: *Providentissimus Deus* entre Vatican I et Vatican II," *FZPhTh* 46, 1999, 461–501, here 461–463.

exegetes to opt for an approach that harmonized scriptural data and modern science.[15] Moreover, he wrote that even though Scripture was infallible, it was only part of supernatural revelation, which, "according to the belief of the universal Church, is contained both in unwritten Tradition, and in written Books" (*PD* 1).[16]

Distrust towards the historical-critical method was clearly an issue in the so-called Modernist crisis of the beginning of the 20th century, in a sense a clash between dogma and method. One of the protagonists was Alfred Loisy,[17] professor of exegesis at the ICP, who had already been under suspicion before the promulgation of *Providentissimus Deus*. In October 1892, the superior-general of the Sulpicians had already forbidden his religious to take classes with Loisy, stating that Loisy's lectures questioned the respect for and the attachment to Scripture. Soon, Loisy lost his chair of exegesis and was expected to limit his teaching to that of oriental languages, a position he would also lose after the publication of the article on "La question biblique et l'inspiration des Écritures" in his journal *L'enseignement biblique*. Further, Loisy was of the opinion that the Pentateuch was not the work of Moses,[18] and that Gen 1–5 could not be considered a literal account of historical events. He also believed that scriptural doctrine was characterized by development and evolution and that God revealed himself through human language, by definition situated in time and space. On this basis, Loisy called into question the absoluteness of the concept of divine inspiration. He held that our ideas about God continually change and evolve[19] and conceived of biblical truth as a reality in continual development, linked to changing historical circumstances. He read the works of Protestant authors such as Harnack and Auguste Sabatier – author of several books on the evolution of dogma[20] – but criticized both authors because they seemed to reduce religion to an individual relation of the person's conscience with God, while in Loisy's view religion shaped the true society and the true church. However, neither his defense of the church of Rome nor his attacks against Harnack for having broken, in his opinion, the link between church and gospel, prevented the ecclesiastical censure of his most famous work, *L'Évanglile et l'Église*,[21] in 1903, called for by the archbishop of Paris. Loisy's statement in that work, "Jesus proclaimed the kingdom, and what we got was the Church" came to stand for his heterodoxy, but he never had intended to deny the divine origins of the church nor to negate the fact that the church was the continuation of the gospel in history until the second coming of Christ.[22] In 1903, Loisy also published *Le quatrième Évangile*,[23] in which he denied the apostolic authorship of John, argued that the texts should be interpreted within a symbolic framework, and recommended that the gospel be read as a testimony of faith, not as history. Loisy also maintained that dogmas could not be considered divine truths; they are human constructions that

---

15   See Jean-Noël Aletti, "Conclusions," in: Claude Savart & Jean-Noël Aletti, eds., *Le monde contemporain et la Bible*, Paris, Beauchesne, 1985, 517–522, here 517.

16   See Christoph Theobald, "L'exégèse catholique au moment de la crise Moderniste," in: Savart & Aletti, eds., *Le monde contemporain et la Bible*, 387–439, here 389ff.

17   The literature on Loisy is abundant; see Maurilio Guasco, "Loisy (Alfred Firmin)," *DHGE* 32, cols. 1085–1100 (with bibliography).

18   It was indeed difficult to understand how Moses could describe his own death in Deut 34:5–7.

19   It is suggested that Loisy found his inspiration in John Henry Newman's view on the development of doctrine; see Guasco, "Loisy," col. 1088.

20   See e.g. Auguste Sabatier, *De la vie intime des dogmes et de leur puissance d'évolution*, Paris, Fischbacher, 1890, and Auguste Sabatier, *La doctrine de l'expiation et son évolution historique*, Paris, Fischbacher, 1903.

21   Alfred Loisy, *L'Évangile et l'Église*, Paris, Picard, 1902; ET: *The Gospel and the Church*, trans. Christopher Home, London, Ibister & Co., 1903.

22   See Jürgen Mettepenningen, "Malheur devenu bénédiction: Un siècle de modernisme," *RHE* 101, 2006, 1039–1070, here 1050–1051.

23   Alfred Loisy, *Le quatrième évangile*, Paris, Picard, 1903.

should be continually reinterpreted.[24] Loisy continued to defend the idea that the study of the Bible and early Christianity should follow the same criteria and methods used in other research. Catholic theologians blamed Loisy for espousing the theses of German Protestant writers such as Albert Schweitzer and Johannes Weiss. At the end of 1903, five books of Loisy were condemned by the Congregation of the Index. Needless to say, Loisy's positions had implications for the nature of Sacred Scripture, its inspiration, and the authorship of its books. Because of Loisy's condemnation, other scholars also fell under suspicion – such as the exegete Marie-Joseph Lagrange and the philosopher Maurice Blondel – or had to undergo censures and condemnations, like the historian Pierre Batiffol, the philosopher and mathematician Édouard Le Roy, and the historian, philosopher, and theologian Lucien Laberthonnière, to name a few. At the end of 1906, Loisy was forbidden to celebrate Mass. On July 3, 1907, the decree *Lamentabili sane exitu*, published by the Holy Office, condemned 65 propositions, mostly taken from Loisy's works. His excommunication followed in 1908.

2.1   *Pius X and* Pascendi dominici gregis

Pascendi dominici gregis, promulgated by Pius X on Sep 8, 1907, lumped these new approaches together under the label "Modernism," and called it "the synthesis of all heresies."[25] This encyclical was a major step in a process that began under Leo XIII and continued after its publication. In order to better control the developments in exegesis, Leo XIII had founded the PCB in 1902,[26] which was to promote study of the Bible in Catholic contexts and protect the Catholic faith against erroneous doctrinal positions. The commission was thus

expected to implement what was promulgated in *Providentissimus Deus*. However, it became a kind of magisterial control apparatus[27] and an institution that provided official answers to controversial questions.[28] During the pontificate of Pius X, it would contribute to a limitation of the freedom of research and the use of the historical critical method. Pius X founded the PIB (Biblicum) in 1909. In 1910, he introduced the anti-Modernist oath which all Catholic priests and religious had to swear.

It is useful to note how *Pascendi*[29] explicitly connected Modernist approaches with Protestantism. Pius X was of the opinion that the Modernists held that the divine reality, though truly existing, can be discovered only in the sentiment of the believer, a subjective relativizing of the truth of faith similar to the position of Protestants and pseudomystics (*Pdg* 14). Criticizing the "Modernist school" for the fact that it wanted to subordinate faith to science and wanted to subject the church to the state – the pope recognized that they did not say this in public but considered it as a logical conclusion of their argumentation –, Pius was of the opinion that it undermined ecclesiastical authority and put the church completely under the dominion of the state. It was for this reason, the pope continued, that liberal Protestants rejected external

24 Mettepenningen, "Malheur devenu bénédiction," 1051–1052.
25 Paragraph 39. The word Modernism, at the time, was a neologism; see Mettepenningen, "Malheur devenu bénédiction," 1039.
26 On the different names the commission received, see Albert Vanhoye, "Passé et présent de la Commission Biblique," *Greg* 74, 1993, 261–275, here 264–265.

27 Two Belgians, Laurent Janssens, O.S.B., and Alphonse Delattre, S.J., played an important role as uncompromising opponents of Modernism. The first served as secretary of the commission, beginning in 1905. According to Lagrange, "il n'avait sur l'Écriture ni connaissances, ni opinions personnelles"; see Marie-Joseph Lagrange, *Le Père Lagrange au service de la Bible: Souvenirs personnels*, ed. Pierre Benoit, Paris, Cerf, 1967, 152. The second, also member of the commission, was a tireless attacker of Americanism first, Lagrange thereafter; see Schelkens, "From *Providentissimus Deus* to *Dei Verbum*," 51–53. Schelkens stresses the anti-Protestant stance of Delattre.
28 See a survey of the answers in Vanhoye, "Passé et présent," 266–267. All these answers can be read as implicit critiques of Modernist positions.
29 Pius X, *Pascendi dominici gregis*, Sept 8, 1907; the text can be found at <www.vatican.va/content/pius-x/en/encyclicals/documents/hf_p-x_enc_19070908_pascendi-dominici-gregis.html> (accessed Nov 2, 2020).

worship and advocated individual religion. The pope suggested that Modernists had not yet reached this point but criticized their views on disciplinary authority (*Pdg* 25). Ridiculing the Modernist as a reformer of everything, the pope suggested that some of these Modernists, echoing the teaching of their Protestant masters, would promote the suppression of ecclesiastical celibacy (*Pdg* 39). The pope was convinced that Modernism would lead to the annihilation of all religions: the first step in this direction was taken by Protestantism, the second by Modernism, the next would lead to atheism (*Pdg* 39).

For Pius X, things were clear. Scripture had to be at the service of doctrine, and the only accepted and acceptable approach to Scripture was a suprahistorical one. Scripture was the reservoir used to defend neo-Thomistic doctrine as the official doctrine of the church.

The pope rejected what he considered to be a Modernist reduction of inspiration to a feeling, something like poetic inspiration (*Pdg* 22). Modernists took the Bible to be a human work, made for humanity's benefit, thus leaving no room for divine inspiration in what he saw as the Catholic sense (*Pdg* 22). The pope blamed the Modernists for affirming that especially the Pentateuch and the first three Gospels had been gradually formed by additions to a primitive brief narrative, thus admitting the evolution of the biblical books in correspondence with evolution of faith. The pope lamented the promotion of textual criticism, a method that aimed at showing that the scriptural style is defective, something which was, according to the pope, opposed to Catholic scholarship and immanentist and evolutionist. Those who embraced this method placed themselves in opposition to the Catholic faith (*Pdg* 34). The pope remarked bitterly that the chairs in seminaries and universities had become "chairs of pestilence." He criticized the use of pseudonyms,[30] people thus hiding their identity in order to spread their ideas and mislead their students. He deplored scholars' claims to liberty. He was sad because biblical questions were treated on the basis of Modernist principles, and curiosity was often the moving force in historical research, while historians were searching for anything that looked like a stain in the church's history, thus destroying the pious traditions of the people. For the pope it was clear that these people were offending both God and the church (*Pdg* 43).

Pius X explicitly prohibited all sympathizers of Modernism from holding teaching or governing functions in Catholic universities and seminaries. The same was to happen to those who dared to criticize scholasticism or refused to obey ecclesiastical authority. The exclusion was also meant for those who preferred "novelties" in history, archaeology, and biblical exegesis, as well as for those who promoted the "profane" sciences, preferring them over the sacred sciences (*Pdg* 48).

The results are well-known. Many professors had to relinquish their positions; some were excommunicated, all were stigmatized.[31] For decades, Catholic biblical exegesis would be characterized by defensive approaches, with the path barred to new developments, while Protestants had the academic freedom to continue their research.[32] This meant that no Catholic exegete would think of following these Protestant colleagues, who were explicitly criticized and denounced in the encyclical. The door to ecumenical dialogue on the basis of common biblical research was closed, to say the least.

---

30   Between 1898 and 1900, Loisy published eight articles in the *Revue du clergé français* under the pseudonym A. Firmin.

31   Gerard Loughlin, "Nouvelle Théologie: A Return to Modernism?," in: Gabriel Flynn & Paul D. Murray, eds., *Ressourcement: A Movement for Renewal in Twentieth-Century Catholic Theology*, Oxford, Oxford University Press, 2012, 36–50, here 39ff., offers an impressive list of non-French victims. Referring to Hans Boersma, *Nouvelle Théologie and Sacramental Ontology: A Return to Mystery*, Oxford, Oxford University Press, 2009, Loughlin makes clear that critics of George Tyrrell simply did not (want to) understand him; Loughlin, "Nouvelle Théologie," 42–47.

32   Mettepenningen, "Malheur devenu bénédiction," 1042.

2.2   Benedict XV: A Détente?

Under Benedict XV (pope from 1914 to 1922), often commemorated as the pope of peace,[33] the struggle against Modernism continued, albeit in a less offensive way.[34] As bishop of Bologna, Giacomo Della Chiesa had underlined the need to obey Pius X's decisions – like Pius X, he considered Modernism a danger[35] – but also argued that controversies in the field of religious studies should not be condemned *tout court*, for often they could lead to better insights in certain truths.[36] In Bologna, he also suffered from the anti-Modernist measures: he had to accept the removal of the rector of his diocesan seminary, and the work of one of his professors was put on the Index.[37] Della Chiesa knew what trauma such removals and condemnations meant for the victims. Once elected pope, he replaced Merry Del Val, one of the most tenacious opponents of modernism, as Secretary of State, giving him the presidency of the Fabbrica di San Pietro.[38] In his first encyclical, *Ad beatissimi apostolorum* (Nov 1, 1914), he reiterated Pius X's condemnation of Modernism[39] but also called for an end to the disputes and a search for concord.[40]

The pope was clearly opposed to the idea of maintaining an attitude suspicious of new opinions concerning matters on which the church itself had, often, not assumed a clear position. A new intellectual climate, more open to scholarly openness, was underway. Victims of the anti-Modernist persecution were rehabilitated. Bishops who wanted to put an end to anti-Modernist actions were supported.[41] Furthermore, in 1921, the Sodalitium Pianum, a society very active under Pius X in rooting out and collecting Modernist writings, ideas, and authors, was now abolished, once it became clear that it had functioned as a kind of secret society.[42] This is not to say that condemnations ceased, as witnessed in the case of an Italian introduction to the Bible that was put on the Index in 1916.[43] Finally, the publication of the encyclical *Spiritus Paraclitus* in 1920, on the occasion of the 1500th anniversary of Jerome's death, explicitly repeated the line of Leo XIII that there was no error in Scripture.[44] The pope lamented the fact that not only people outside the Catholic Church but even Catholic clerics and professors of sacred theology openly repudiated or in secret attacked the church's teaching on this point. The pope was not opposed to the use of critical methods, as long as Leo XIII's injunctions were respected. Whoever maintained that the historical parts of Scripture did not rest on the absolute truth of the facts was considered to be out of harmony with the church's

---

33   See e.g. John F. Pollard, *The Unknown Pope: Benedict XV (1914–1922) and the Pursuit of Peace*, London, Chapman, 1999; Yves Chiron, *Benoît XV: Le pape de la paix*, Paris, Perrin, 2014; Marcel Launay, *Benoît XV (1914–1922): Un pape pour la paix*, Paris, Cerf, 2014; Jörg Ernesti, *Benedikt XV: Papst zwischen den Fronten*, Freiburg i.Br., Herder, 2016.

34   For the reason why several authors have used the word "détente," see Étienne Fouilloux, *Une Église en quête de liberté: La pensée catholique française entre modernisme et Vatican II (1914–1962)*, Paris, Desclée de Brouwer, 1998, 16; Chiron, *Benoît XV*, 283–284, 288–289 (letter of Fr. Genocchi to his Protestant friend Paul Sabatier); Launay, *Benoît XV*, 83.

35   Chiron, *Benoît XV*, 283.

36   See Pollard, *The Unknown Pope*, 42.

37   See Pollard, *The Unknown Pope*, 43–45, who offers several examples where Della Chiesa tried to protect priests from the anti-Modernist attacks, sometimes successful, sometimes failing.

38   Pollard, *The Unknown Pope*, 68.

39   On the severe way in which the condemnation by Pius X was reiterated, see e.g. Chiron, *Benoît XV*, 284–285.

40   Pollard, *The Unknown Pope*, 68.

41   See the examples given in Chiron, *Benoît XV*, 288–290.

42   Chiron, *Benoît XV*, 287–288.

43   Luigi Salvatorelli & Eugen Hühn, *La Bibbia: Introduzione all'Antico e Nuovo Testamento*, Milan, Sandron, 1915, an adaptation of a work of Eugen Hühn, *Hilfsbuch zum Verständnis der Bibel*, 4 vols., Tübingen, Mohr, 1904–1905, was condemned on June 5, 1916; for the number of books condemned under Benedict XV's pontificate, see Chiron, *Benoît XV*, 291–292. A translation of the New Testament by the Austrian Cistercian Nivard Schlögl was also put on the Index. By a decree of the Holy Office, two studies of the Sulpician Jules Touzard, professor at the ICP, were condemned, without however mentioning his name.

44   Benedict XV, *Spiritus Paraclitus*, in: *AAS* 12, 1920, 385–422, here 393.

teaching. Indeed, the sacred narrative was held to be absolutely free from error.[45] The pope was speaking of modern innovators who even dared to claim Jerome as a patron of their views, something that evidently had to be rejected, and of other assailants of Holy Scripture who wanted to overturn the fundamental truth of the Bible, thus destroying Catholic teaching handed down by the Fathers. According to the pope, one had to avoid this insane freedom in putting forth such errors.[46] That one of the drafters of this encyclical was the rector of the Biblicum, Father Leopold Fonck, s.j., a convinced opponent of the historical critical method, did not help much.[47] Needless to say, after the publication of such an encyclical, Catholic exegetes had to remain prudent in their research. The fact that Rome was rather resistant to dialogue with other Christian denominations was also an inhibiting factor.[48]

3   Pius XI: Is the Wind Changing?

At the beginning of Pius XI's pontificate, people might have feared a return to the anti-Modernist era.[49] Some of its champions such as Cardinals

Gaetano De Lai, Rafael Merry del Val, and Willem M. van Rossum retained their functions as secretaries of the Consistorial Congregation (De Lai) and the Holy Office (Merry del Val), and as prefect of Propaganda Fide and president of the PCB (van Rossum). De Lai and Merry del Val were outspoken opponents of Modernism, while van Rossum was president of a commission that could not be suspected of promoting new approaches in Catholic exegesis. Moreover, Pius XI himself was seemingly not interested in biblical questions.[50]

On Dec 16, 1923, *L'Osservatore Romano* announced that the twelfth, thirteenth, fourteenth, and fifteenth editions of the *Manuel biblique: ou Cours d'écriture sainte à l'usage des séminaires* were put on the Index. This handbook, consisting of four volumes (two on the Old Testament, two on the New Testament), had for years been used in seminaries and universities, even at the Gregorian University in Rome. The handbook had been translated into Italian and English. The first edition had been published by the French exegete Fulcran Vigouroux, with the help of his confrère Louis Bacuez, between 1878 and 1880.[51] Vigouroux later became professor of exegesis at the ICP and was appointed as the first secretary of the PCB. He could hardly be described as a Modernist: on the contrary, he published books in which he tried to show that archeological discoveries supported the

---

45   Benedict XV, *Spiritus Paraclitus*, 393–395.

46   Benedict XV, *Spiritus Paraclitus*, 396–398.

47   Chiron, *Benoît XV*, 298–299.

48   It should be noted, however, that the so-called Malines Conversations (1921–1926) happened at this time. They were a series of private meetings between Catholic and Anglican theologians held under the patronage of the Belgian cardinal and archbishop Désiré Mercier. His death in 1926 signaled the end of this type of initiative. See, in this regard, the contribution of Bernard Barlow and Martin Browne in this volume.

49   The attitude of Pius XI towards the Protestants was not very positive; see Christophe-Jean Dumont, "L'œcuménisme," in: Gabriel-Marie Garrone & others, *La vie de l'Église sous Pie XII*, Paris, Fayard, 1959, 90–109, here 91–92. The encyclical *Mortalium animos* (1928) made clear why the Roman Catholic Church could not participate in the ecumenical movement, but it did not exclude "passive" participation in conferences such as that of Faith and Order in Edinburgh (1937). Official participation in the first meeting of the WCC in 1948 was forbidden to Catholics; see Dumont, "L'œcuménisme,"

99–100. Dumont offers an impressive list of "absences" of Catholics in ecumenical meetings during the pontificate of Pius XII. See also Josef Schmid, "Ökumenische Bewegung," *RGG* 4, cols. 1571–1586, making clear that in the Catholic hierarchical structure space is left for informal, individual dialogue, but that only official approval helps to make progress.

50   See Bernard Montagnes, "La question biblique au temps de Pie XI," in: École française de Rome, ed., *Achille Ratti: Pape Pie XI: Actes du colloque de Rome (15–18 mars 1989)*, Rome, École française de Rome, 1996, 255–276, here 255; see also Marcel Launay, *Pie XI: Le pape de l'Action Catholique*, Paris, Cerf, 2018, 88.

51   See Montagnes, "La question biblique," 264–266; Étienne Fouilloux, "Un regain d'anti-modernisme?," in: Pierre Colin, *Intellectuels chrétiens des années 1920: Actes du colloque, Institut catholique de Paris, 23–24 septembre 1993*, Paris, Cerf, 1997, 83–114.

historical reliability of the Bible. His *Dictionnaire de la Bible* defended the official Catholic positions with regard to the Bible. The condemnation was a surprise because none of the previous editions had been condemned under Pius X. The examination of their orthodoxy seemingly had already started under Benedict XV. The initiative for this condemnation was taken by bishops sympathetic to the work of Action Française.[52] The criticisms were what one might expect: minimization of the divine inspiration of the Bible and thus of its inerrancy. The fact that the handbook had highlighted contradictions in Scripture was also criticized. In sum, a handbook that for decades had been respected for its reliability was now reduced to an instrument that endangered the faith and the piety of seminarians.[53] However, not without reason, it has been suggested that the condemnation was indirectly aimed at Marie-Joseph Lagrange and the École Biblique in Jerusalem.[54]

In 1924, it was decided that all future professors of exegesis had to obtain degrees from the Biblicum; at that time it still functioned as protector of the anti-Modernist legacy and on this basis had ensured its position in the panorama of Catholic biblical studies.[55] That same year, the Holy Office asked superior generals to strictly respect the norms promulgated by popes Leo XIII, Pius X, and Benedict XV with regard to the study and the teaching of the Bible.[56]

However, since 1926, things had somewhat begun to change. The papal condemnation of Action Française, a shock for conservative Catholics such as the rector of the Séminaire Français in Rome – who stepped down in 1927 – and Pius XI's condemnation of totalitarian ideologies would create a breathing space for Catholic intellectuals. When Pius XI was alerted in

1927 to the plan of the University of Leuven to offer a doctorate *honoris causa* to Lagrange on the occasion of the 500th anniversary of the university, the pope simply mentioned that the warning was too late and that the doctorate had already been conferred to Lagrange.[57]

This apparent thawing in the papal approach, however, did not mean condemnations no longer happened, as the German scholar Friedrich Schmidtke, author of *Die Einwanderung Israels in Kanaan* (Breslau, 1933), would discover: his work was condemned by the Holy Office in 1934 and put on the Index. He lost his ecclesiastical mandate to teach exegesis, being expected to focus on oriental studies. The Holy Office felt the need to severely remind Catholic exegetes of their duties.[58]

Meanwhile, in 1930, a new rector was appointed for the Biblicum, the German Jesuit Augustin Bea, who initiated a prudent process of change. He was certainly not a man of wild ideas. Bea became member of the PCB in 1931, the Congregation for Seminaries and Universities in 1936, and the Holy Office in 1950. His active participation in the new translation of the Psalms from Hebrew into Latin, a task given to the Biblicum by Pope Pius XII in 1941,[59] contributed to his international fame. However, this translation did not sufficiently take into account the Hebrew context of the biblical texts and was not always well received by scholars, even Catholic ones.[60]

As professor and rector, Bea actively participated in study trips to the Near East, which included trips to Palestine. During archaeological excavations, he met non-Catholic colleagues, experts in archaeology, Eastern studies, and the Old

---

52   Fouilloux, "Un regain d'anti-modernisme?," 86–87.
53   Fouilloux, "Un regain d'anti-modernisme?," 88–90. Fouilloux speaks of a brutal attack and observes that the Sulpicians had to empty the cup to the bottom.
54   See, among others, Launay, *Pie XI*, 89–90.
55   Launay, *Pie XI*, 90–91.
56   Montagnes, "La question biblique," 268.

57   Montagnes, "La question biblique," 269.
58   *EnchBib*, 515–519. However, it should be said that exegetes seemingly suffered less from condemnations than other Catholic authors; see Fouilloux, *Une Église en quête de liberté*, 26–32.
59   It remains strange that the task was given secretly to the Biblicum, Tisserant not being informed about it; see Étienne Fouilloux, *Eugène, cardinal Tisserant (1884–1972): Une biographie*, Paris, Desclée de Brouwer, 2011, 267–268.
60   Fouilloux, *Eugène, cardinal Tisserant*, 267.

Testament.[61] In 1935, two Protestant colleagues, Paul Volz, professor of Old Testament at the University of Tübingen, and Johannes Hempel, professor of Old Testament at the University of Göttingen, invited the Biblicum to participate in the first International Congress for Old Testament Studies in Göttingen, an invitation Bea accepted after receiving the approval of Pius XI. Bea attended the conference and delivered a paper as well as the closing address. Bea himself considered this participation as a breakthrough in the relations between Catholics and non-Catholics, for it created the opportunity to overcome the attacks and polemics of the previous centuries and to initiate an open academic dialogue between colleagues. That same year, the Biblicum hosted an International Conference on the Ancient East.[62] Such contacts with other denominations, however, would not change Bea's attitude towards the genesis of the biblical books. In 1935, he still refused to accept that parts of the Pentateuch consisted of documents stemming from different origins and time periods.[63] Lagrange simply considered Bea his adversary.[64] Up until World War II, Catholics were allowed to make use of the same auxiliary instruments as Protestants but did not dare translate their insights into critical questions about the inerrancy of the Bible, the authors of the biblical books, and the like. When reading "technical" exegetical studies, one has the impression that the Catholic exegetes were more engaged in the refutation of Protestant authors such as von Harnack and Julius Wellhausen, philologist and historian, or the condemnation of Catholic authors such as

Loisy. These exegetical studies thus focused on the Mosaic origin of the Pentateuch, the chronology of the Pauline letters, the synoptic problem, or the exact itinerary of Paul's travels.[65]

In 1938, Pius XI appointed Cardinal Eugène Tisserant, a former student and friend of Lagrange, as president of the PCB. Tisserant, who meanwhile was also the secretary of the Congregation for the Oriental Churches, was well aware that not everyone applauded this appointment[66] but really wanted to improve the situation of biblical studies.[67] He intended to renew the PCB, looking for cardinals who had expertise in exegesis.[68] In 1939, the Belgian Dominican Jacques-Marie Vosté, first a student of the theology faculty of Leuven and later also a student as well as a great defender of Lagrange, was appointed as secretary.[69] Vosté, professor of exegesis at the Angelicum since 1911 and consultor of the PCB, was an expert in Syriac studies, and a good friend of Tisserant. Tisserant and Vosté would renew the PCB in such a way that the adherents of a return to the anti-Modernist era were reduced to a minority.[70]

In passing it should be said that, between the two world wars, within Catholic circles, the Bible became more and more important in the life of the faithful. The Catholic biblical movement started in Germany, and youth movements such as the JOC in France began to promote meditation on the Bible. Benedictine monks such as Dom Columba Marmion helped many priests and lay people rediscover the letters of Paul.[71]

---

61   For this period, the impact of biblical research on ecumenism is, in my view, not to be searched for in great statements but in the personal contacts between scholars during excavations and the like. Also, the focus on the study of oriental languages contributed to mutual respect.

62   See Stjepan Schmidt, *Augustin Bea: Der Kardinal der Einheit*, Graz, Styria, 1989, 108–109.

63   See the observations of Marie-Joseph Lagrange, "L'authenticité mosaïque de la Genèse et la théorie des documents," *RB* 47, 1938, 163–183.

64   Montagnes, "La question biblique," 261.

65   Roger Aubert, *La théologie catholique au milieu du XXᵉ siècle*, Tournai, Casterman, 1954, 20.

66   See Fouilloux, *Eugène, cardinal Tisserant*, 233.

67   Montagnes, "La question biblique," 259.

68   Fouilloux, *Eugène, cardinal Tisserant*.

69   Montagnes, "La question biblique," 267.

70   Joseph A. Fitzmyer, "The Interpretation of the Bible in the Church Today," *ITQ* 62, 1996, 84–100, here 88–89, observed that the commission's public image changed and that the commission gave up its watchdog role.

71   See Celia Kourie, "Understanding Paul: The Insights of Dom Columba Marmion and Elisabeth of the Trinity," *StSp* 14, 2004, 37–47.

By contrast, it should be said that Protestant exegetes in this period were not always very interested in Catholic biblical scholarship. They could not accept Roman Catholic claims for the authority of the church, for this would involve "not only giving up our freedom of thought and decision in favor of an authority of whose competence we are by no means convinced, but also accepting as true many things which we are bound to say we know to be false. If the authority of the Bible is inadequate, the authority of the Church is no more reliable."[72]

4   The Wind Changes, Slowly: Pius XII and the Promulgation of *Divino afflante Spiritu*

Catholic positions were sometimes met with amazement, as when they asserted that the use of exegetical methods was a kind of gateway to rationalism, Modernism, and the like.[73] The fact that the critique of the exegetical approach came from within the Roman Catholic Church obliged Pius XII to intervene, as he did with *Divino afflante Spiritu* (Sep 30, 1943),[74] published on the occasion

of the fiftieth anniversary of the promulgation of *Providentissimus Deus*. *Divino afflante Spiritu*, described as the charter of biblical renewal,[75] paved the way for the historical critical method to be positively received by and introduced into Catholic academic study of the Bible. The text was prepared by the PCB. Bea is sometimes considered to be one of the main drafters of the encyclical, but one should also not neglect the efforts made by Vosté.[76] In fact, decisive proof for Bea's sole authorship is missing, and Tisserant considered the encyclical a collective work.[77] In any case, up to this moment no serious Catholic scholarship was done on the book of Genesis, scholars thus avoiding any possible conflict with Rome.[78] Ironically, because of the rigid measures taken at the beginning of the century, later Catholic exegesis was still discussing the same problems, without making any progress.[79]

At that moment, Pius XII certainly wanted to promote biblical studies. Whether this promotion now was reconcilable with collaboration with Protestant colleagues cannot be derived from the encyclical. In any case, when he was nuncio in Germany (1917–1929), Pius XII had shared the common view that Catholic exegetes should not collaborate with their Protestant colleagues, since he considered exegesis a theological discipline

---

72   Millar Burrows, *An Outline of Biblical Theology*, Philadelphia PA, Westminster Press, 1946, 8–9. Burrows, a Presbyterian minister, was professor at Yale Divinity School, an expert with regard to the Dead Sea Scrolls, and several times director of the American School of Oriental Research in Jerusalem. As far as I can see, most of his bibliography (pp. 331–333) consists of Protestant literature.

73   See the work by Dolindo Ruotolo, *Un gravissimo pericolo per la Chiesa e per le anime: Il sistema critico-scientifico nello studio e nell'interpretazione della Sacra Scrittura, le sue deviazioni funeste e le sue aberrazioni*, 1940, criticized by the PCB in a letter sent to the bishops of Italy on Aug 20, 1941; see *AAS* 33, 1941, 465–472. See also Aubert, *La théologie catholique*, 23–24; Fouilloux, *Eugène, cardinal Tisserant*, 263–264.

74   It is quite revealing that Ruotolo's "spiritual" works were very much appreciated by many bishops, even though they were criticized by members of the PCB such as Alberto Vaccari, who could not be accused of being progressive. It is suggested that the attacks on Ruotolo were first and foremost directed against the Biblicum, which might explain the involvement of it

in the drafting of *Divino afflante Spiritu*; see Stanislas Lyonnet, "Pie XII et les études scripturaires," in: Garrone & others, *La vie de l'Église sous Pie XII*, 121–137, here 124–125.

75   See René Beaupère, "Notes sur le renouveau biblique dans le catholicisme," *Foi et Vie* 62, 1963, 329–337, here 332.

76   Fouilloux, *Eugène, cardinal Tisserant*, 265–267.

77   See Fouilloux, *Une Église en quête de liberté*, 268; Philippe Chenaux, *Pie XII: Diplomate et pasteur*, Paris, Cerf, 2003, 386.

78   Beaupère, "Notes sur le renouveau biblique," 331.

79   James Tunstead Burtchaell, *Catholic Theories of Biblical Inspiration since 1810: A Review and Critique*, Cambridge, Cambridge University Press, 1969, 281. Burtchaell speaks of the following weaknesses that block progress: an uncritical defense of official authority, an obsession with inerrancy, and a crude theology of divine-human collaboration.

and thus one that had to be guided by Catholic doctrine.[80]

In its introduction, *Divino afflante Spiritu* referred to the Council of Trent and praised both Vatican I (that explicitly stated that God was the author of the Bible)[81] and Leo XIII's *Providentissimus Deus* that defended the divine origin and the correct interpretation of the Bible. However, *Divino afflante Spiritu* was clearly in discontinuity with these previous documents.[82] The pope pointed out that excavations in Palestine had made significant progress since the time of *Providentissimus Deus*, offering more abundant and more accurate knowledge, and thus a more correct and better understanding of the sacred books. Also, the discovery of written documents that improved the knowledge of languages, letters, events, customs, and forms of worship of ancient times was praised, like the papyri that increased understanding of the time of Christ (*DaS* 11). He encouraged the study of ancient languages and happily observed that the study and knowledge of Greek and Hebrew and other oriental languages had found their way into exegetical research: it would be a shame, he wrote, to neglect such opportunities (*DaS* 14–15).[83] Pius emphasized the advantages of philological approaches and of literary criticism (*DaS* 16),[84] thus making clear that "profane" methods such as textual criticism, so successful in the study of profane writings, could be rightly used in biblical research, especially because this approach had made great progress since the time of Leo XIII (*DaS* 17–18). He further affirmed, with striking clarity, the fact that biblical texts

throughout the ages could be and were corrupted. Reverence for the sacred texts and exact observance of textual criticism rules go hand in hand (*DaS* 19). Discovering the literal sense of Scripture was a matter of philological, historical, and critical research.[85] These auxiliary sciences, together with archaeology, should, he said, contribute to a better understanding of the theological doctrine of the sacred books on the level of faith and morals. Furthermore, the work of exegetes was recommended as a help for priests proclaiming the Bible (*DaS* 23–24). The exegete was expected to search out and expound both the literal meaning of the words and their spiritual sense, provided it was clearly intended by God (*DaS* 26), thus warning against an exaggerated appeal to that spiritual sense (*DaS* 27). The pope was aware of the distinctive style of the ancient authors (*DaS* 30) and explicitly recognized that progress was made both on the level of the study of literary genres (*DaS* 33) and with regard to historical knowledge and thus the complexity of Scriptural texts (*DaS* 31–32). He even affirmed the unintelligibility of some passages in Scripture (*DaS* 31), stating that new questions and difficulties required new means and aids for exegesis. In such cases, the use of the historical-critical method was necessary to determine with relative certainty the peculiar context and historical circumstances in which each sacred writer worked and what sources (both written and oral) he had at his disposal (*DaS* 33). By the use of these methods (*DaS* 48), one could better understand the intention of the inspired writer (*DaS* 34). The pope recognized that the style of speaking and phrasing of the ancient authors of the East differed from that of the present time (*DaS* 35–36) and thus "the modes of expression which, among ancient peoples, and especially those of the East, human language used to express its thought" had

---

80   Chenaux, *Pie XII*, 385.

81   See *EnchBib*, 62.

82   See Fouilloux, *Une Église en quête de liberté*, 267 speaks of a rupture with thirty years of anti-Modernist reactions.

83   Without minimizing the importance of the Vulgate, the pope recognized that it only applied to the Latin Church (*DaS* 21).

84   In the Latin text it is described as "solida criticae artis peritia." In this paragraph, the pope underlined the enormous progress made since the time of Jerome and the Renaissance scholars of the 16th and 17th centuries.

85   The literal sense (*sensus litteralis*) was prioritized over spiritual readings, the literal sense being the object of both historical and philological approaches. This approach had been subject to critique, but was now defended by Pius XII; see Lyonnet, "Pie XII et les études scripturaires," 134.

to be reflected in the sacred books, "provided the way of speaking adopted in no wise contradicts the holiness and truth of God" (*DaS* 37).

Holding to the inerrancy of the Scripture did not mean that the exegete should not search for the correct and genuine interpretation of a biblical text (*DaS* 38), evaluating seeming errors of an author in the same way that figurative language is assessed in the "ordinary intercourse of daily life" (*DaS* 39). Discoveries in literature, ancient history, and archaeology should be integrated into the research of exegetes (*DaS* 40). A correct use of all these methods would not contradict Catholic doctrine (*DaS* 42–43)[86] but would lead to new insights and better understanding, then and in the future (*DaS* 45). Indeed, most of the Scriptural texts had never been the subject of definition by the church's authority and thus remained open for further discussion and research (*DaS* 47). The pope, clearly wanting to promote exegetical work, praised the work done by exegetes (especially at the Biblicum) in the beginning of his encyclical (*DaS* 10). He concluded the encyclical by encouraging exegetes to continue their work at the service of the faithful, defending Scripture against unbelievers and penetrating more and more deeply into its secrets (*DaS* 59–60).

The encyclical was published in the midst of World War II, and it took almost a decade for its influence and impact to be felt.[87] The encyclical nowhere used the term "historical critical method," but it clearly defended it and used the word "critical" several times in a positive sense. The encyclical invited Catholic exegetes to study the Bible in its original languages, taking into account the literary forms, in order to reach a better understanding. It made clear that exegesis should be more than philology and thus should have a theological focus, taking up again Lagrange's idea that

historical-critical exegesis did not exclude but included theological interests.[88] The document did not deny the divine character of the Bible but situated the biblical books in a historical context. Biblical texts were written by humans at different periods in history. As a result, concepts, vocabulary, and even style could be different. Not without reason, scholars judged the impact of this encyclical for biblical studies to be equal to that of *Rerum novarum* for Catholic social teaching.[89]

Across the span of centuries, people had attempted to harmonize the biblical stories, even apparently contradictory ones. Now, it was accepted that texts should be read in their contexts and that texts could contradict each other. As an example of the shift, during the Modernist crisis, many scholars were suspected if not condemned because they maintained that the Pentateuch was not written by Moses. In 1948, the PCB confirmed that Moses had not literally written those five books.[90]

4.1   *The Fruits of* Divino afflante Spiritu[91]

After World War II and probably as a result of *Divino afflante Spiritu*,[92] there was a growing interest in the doctrinal aspects of Scripture; what did God reveal in Scripture? What did he want to say through the biblical authors? What was needed now was the advent of biblical theology, with leading biblical scholars distinguishing clearly between exegesis and biblical theology, yet considering both

---

86   Several times the pope mentioned in a negative way that these approaches were misused by critics outside or hostile to the church; he speaks regularly of adversaries, although never explicitly mentioning Protestants; see e.g. *DaS* 42, 46.

87   See Fitzmyer, "The Interpretation of the Bible," 87.

88   Schelkens, "From *Providentissimus Deus* to *Dei Verbum*," 57.

89   See Jean Levie, *La Bible, parole humaine et message de Dieu*, Paris, Desclée de Brouwer, 1958, 156.

90   For the details, see Lyonnet, "Pie XII et les études scripturaires," 128–129. The leaders of the PCB were well aware of the fact that critical reactions were underway; see Fouilloux, *Eugène, cardinal Tisserant*, 272.

91   Lyonnet, "Pie XII et les études scripturaires," 132–133 makes clear that Pius XII throughout his pontificate stressed the importance of constant research by exegetes on the developments in their domain.

92   The encyclical indeed emphasized that exegetes should pay more attention to the religious content and theological importance of the Bible.

as needed and necessary.[93] Exegetes had always been interested in philology and archaeology but now also focused on the religious meaning of the biblical message, even though such an approach still could be the cause of conflicts.[94] Catholics started to do what Protestants had been doing for decades.[95]

The study and reading of the Bible gained momentum, with new Bible translations everywhere, study weeks, Bible groups, biblical pilgrimages, and the foundation of successful journals such as *Bible et vie chrétienne*. Collections such as *Témoins de Dieu* and *Lectio divina* reached many Catholics.[96] The success was visible in France, Spain, Italy, the Anglo-Saxon world, and in Latin America.[97] In the Netherlands, the ecumenical society of Saint Willibrord (Sint Willibrord Vereniging, SWV) was responsible for the spread of the so-called Petrus Canisius translation. The initiative was a huge success: 297,000 copies of the New Testament translation were distributed, 46,000 copies of the whole Bible.[98] Catholic scholars started to read the work of their Protestant

colleagues; in a sense they had no other option.[99] They developed a common biblical vocabulary, and mutual appreciation began to take root.[100] Gradually, insights developed by Protestant scholars such as the Lutheran Herman Gunkel, the founder of form criticism (*Formgeschichte*), who beginning in 1901 adapted this approach to the Old Testament (especially the book of Genesis and the Psalms), found their way into Catholic contexts.[101] The same occurred in New Testament studies, drawing from the approaches of Martin Dibelius and Rudolf Bultmann.[102] In Germany, from the 1950s onwards, important studies were also published in Catholic circles,[103] and sometimes works by Protestant authors such as the Lutheran Anders Nygren inspired Catholic

---

93 Ceslas Spicq, "L'avènement de la théologie biblique," *RSPT* 35, 1951, 561–574, here 561.

94 See Aubert, *La théologie catholique*, 16; Spicq, "L'avènement de la théologie biblique," 566–567.

95 This idea was clearly present in the Protestant world from the beginning of the 20th century; see Adolf Schlatter, *Die Theologie des Neuen Testaments*, Gütersloh, C. Bertelsmann, 1909; Maurice Goguel, "Le Jésus de l'histoire et le Christ de la foi," *RHPR* 2, 1929, 115–139. Burtchaell, *Catholic Theories*, 288–289, argues that Catholic exegesis up to the middle of the 20th century derived its premises from ecclesiastical doctrine, not taking the Bible as point of departure.

96 See Lyonnet, "Pie XII et les études scripturaires," 135 who observes that the success was such that the PCB had to publish a document that on the one hand encouraged these initiatives but on the other hand warned of possible dangers; for the success of local initiatives, see also Beaupère, "Notes sur le renouveau biblique," 335–336.

97 Beaupère, "Notes sur le renouveau biblique," 336.

98 See Jan Jacobs, *Nieuwe visies op een oud visioen: Een portret van de Sint Willibrord Vereniging (1948–1998)*, Nijmegen, Valkhof Pers, 1998, 87–88.

99 See Robert Bruce Robinson, *Roman Catholic Exegesis since "Divino afflante Spiritu": Hermeneutical Implications*, Atlanta, Scholars Press, 1988, 151–152. This is not to say that Catholics simply followed Protestant approaches, something the author makes clear on the basis of Lohfink's validation approach; see Robinson, *Roman Catholic Exegesis*, 159ff.

100 See Jeffrey Gros, "Ecumenism: From Isolation to a Vision of Christian Unity," in: John G. Deedy, ed., *The Catholic Church in the Twentieth Century: Renewing and Reimaging the City of God*, Collegeville MN, Liturgical Press, 2000, 131–147, here 136.

101 Because of the anti-Modernist reactions, Catholic exegetes did not significantly contribute to the research on Genesis; see Lyonnet, "Pie XII et les études scripturaires," 122–123.

102 For the reception of these approaches in Catholic scholarship, see e.g. Jean Steinmann, *Le prophète Isaïe: Sa vie, son œuvre et son temps*, Paris, Cerf, 1950; Raymond Jacques Tournay, *Les Psaumes*, Paris, Cerf, 1950. The Dominican Tournay studied at Le Saulchoir (Cain, Belgium) with Congar, Chenu, and Sertillanges. He continued in biblical studies at Leuven and became professor at the EBAF in Jerusalem in 1946. However, the use of the historical critical approach remained risky. Indeed, Steinmann's *La Vie de Jésus* (Paris, Denoël, 1959) was put on the Index in 1961. On Steinmann and his remarkable way of doing exegesis, see Paul Auvray, "Steinmann exégète," in: *Jean Steinmann* (*Revue Montalembert* 8–9, 1964), 17–31.

103 See e.g. Rudolf Schnackenburg, *Das Heilsgeschehen bei der Taufe nach dem Apostel Paulus*, Munich, Zink, 1950.

scholars.[104] In short, Catholic scholars began reading works written by their Protestant counterparts, even though this interest in Protestant scholarship was less present in German Catholic contexts than in France, in Belgium, or at the École Biblique in Jerusalem.[105] Scholars at the latter, since the time of its founder, Marie-Joseph Lagrange,[106] had paid much attention to archaeology and geography in order to better understand the historical context within which the books of the Bible came into existence. In Leuven, the tradition of historical-critical research, begun by Albinus Van Hoonacker and continued by his successors, resulted in well-received studies like the one of Lucien Cerfaux, *La théologie de l'Église suivant Saint Paul*, published in Paris in 1942.[107] Among Catholic scholars it had become clear that methods such as *Formgeschichte* did not destroy the historical value of biblical texts but could be used as instruments in order to better understand the milieu, the style, and the intentions of a biblical author. Authors like Cerfaux combined interest in form criticism with critical semantic research, thus better penetrating into the ideas of the biblical authors.[108] Together with Msgr. Joseph Coppens, Cerfaux

founded the Colloquium Biblicum Lovaniense (CBL) in 1948. In the beginning, the Colloquium was a meeting of local Catholic professors and students: professors of Sacred Scripture and related studies at the Catholic University of Leuven and those at the seminaries and theological training centers in Belgium as well as students who were enrolled in graduate schools of theology and biblical studies.[109] The CBL could be seen as a Catholic counterpart to the SNTS, which consisted mainly of Protestant exegetes. In fact, it was not until 1954 that a Catholic exegete of the Benelux was allowed to join the SNTS. For Catholics, the CBL was the only option, and it remained closed to scholars of other Christian confessions for a long time. In fact, when it did decide to open its membership to a broader audience, it was to Catholic scholars from the Netherlands and Luxemburg. Things changed only in 1954, when for the first time members of the Society for Old Testament Study were invited to participate in the CBL, thus giving the Colloquium a (modest) ecumenical dimension.[110] Before the opening of Vatican II, the presidency of the CBL was always in the hands of Catholic priests and religious.

During the World Exhibition of Brussels (1958), the Leuven exegetes organized the first International Catholic Congress for Biblical Studies in both Brussels and Leuven, thus making clear to the world who was responsible for the initiative.[111]

---

104   This was the case for Viktor Warnach, *Agape: Die Liebe als Grundmotiv der neutestamentlichen Theologie*, Düsseldorf, Patmos, 1951, who wrote this book partly inspired by Anders Nygren's *Agape and Eros*, first published in Swedish in 1930–1936 (two volumes), but then translated into many languages.

105   Aubert, *La théologie catholique*, 15.

106   Although he was not excommunicated, Fr. Lagrange was obliged to leave Jerusalem in 1912.

107   Lucien Cerfaux, *La théologie de l'Église suivant Saint Paul*, Paris, Cerf, 1942. Other important studies on Paul included his *Le Christ dans la théologie de Saint Paul*, Paris, Cerf, 1954; *Le chrétien dans la théologie pauli-nienne*, Paris, Cerf, 1962; *L'itinéraire spirituel de Saint Paul*, Paris, Cerf, 1968. Up to the publication of his book about Paul's theology of the church, Cerfaux had not published much in the area of exegesis. It is suggested that his nomination as member of the PCB gave him the confidence and free rein to publish on Sacred Scripture; see Joseph Coppens, "La carrière et l'œuvre scientifiques de Monseigneur Lucien Cerfaux," *ETL* 45, 1969, 8–44, here 15–16.

108   Aubert, *La théologie catholique*, 18–19.

---

109   See the circular letter of Cerfaux and Coppens in Frans Neirynck, ed., *Colloquium Biblicum Lovaniense: Journées Bibliques de Louvain: Bijbelse studiedagen te Leuven (1949–1989)*, Leuven, Peeters, 1989, 16.

110   See Neirynck, ed., *Colloquium Biblicum Lovaniense*, 17–18. Papers were read by Godfrey Rolles Driver, professor of Semitic philology at Oxford, and Harold Henry Rowley, professor of Semitic languages at Manchester University.

111   The list of contributions to this conference looks very impressive and international, but consists first and foremost of Catholic exegetes; see Joseph Coppens, Albert Deschamps & Édouard Massaux, eds., *Sacra pagina: Miscellanea biblica Congressus Internationalis Catholici de Re Biblica*, 2 vols., Gembloux, Duculot, 1959.

This shows that ecumenical openness in Catholic biblical circles was not absent in the immediate post-war years but only flourished after the mid-fifties. The initiative of the Leuven professors received the full support of Pius XII, who explicitly stated that the encyclical was meant to promote research in a climate of liberty and mutual trust, rather than condemn specific errors.[112]

In 1955, both the secretary and the sub-secretary of the PCB, commenting on a revised edition of the *Enchiridion Biblicum*, made a clear distinction between matters related to faith and morals and matters dealing with literary criticism, historical critical approaches, and the like. With regard to the second aspect, they explicitly stated that research should be done in all freedom, a statement that was quite evidently applauded by Catholic exegetes but even came to the attention of Protestant scholars.[113] The discrepancy between these statements and *Providentissimus Deus* was evident.

Thanks to these initiatives, one could gradually begin to speak of a Catholic biblical movement,[114] and soon Protestant scholars became aware that Catholics were now using the methods that they had been using for years. In other words, it could be said that in the course of the 1950s, Catholics and Protestants became aware that they had a common heritage and a common spiritual patrimony. They were well aware of the differences in confessions and thus in interpretations of biblical texts,[115] but gradually they began to grow closer and communicate with each another.[116] A good example here is the series of discussions, beginning in 1959, between the Catholic SWV and the Protestant NBG which were initiated in order to develop a common strategy for promoting the Word of God in the Netherlands. There was even talk of a common translation of the Bible, but it was still too early for such an enterprise, and the Catholics would soon find their own Katholieke Bijbelstichting Sint Willibrord (Saint Willibrord Catholic Bible Foundation). However, the two societies would continue their dialogues in the years to come.[117]

4.2   Control Remains

Catholic exegetes now could make use of the same methods as their Protestant colleagues; however, collaboration between the two remained problematic.[118] The case of Cerfaux, who had become well-known in Protestant circles for his studies on Paul, is interesting, for it shows the extremely arbitrary way this problem was often treated in Roman circles. In 1947, Cerfaux contributed to the Festschrift for Professor Fridrichsen of the University of Uppsala.[119] He had asked explicit permission to accept this invitation from Father Vosté, secretary of the PCB, and the latter had encouraged him to write an article and asked him to do his best to defend the Catholic point

---

112   See *L'Osservatore Romano*, Aug 25–26, 1958; *La Documentation catholique*, September 1958, 1253–1254.

113   For the details, see Joseph A. Fitzmyer, *A Christological Catechism: New Testament Answers*, New York, Paulist Press, ²1991, 121–123.

114   Fitzmyer, "The Interpretation of the Bible," 88, dates it rather late (1955), but I have the impression that one could even postpone the real beginning of the movement to Vatican II's decisions about the relation between Scripture and tradition.

115   A fine, critical, but respectful Protestant view on Roman Catholic exegesis was written by Jan Nicolaas Sevenster, professor of New Testament at the University of Amsterdam: Jan Nicolaas Sevenster, *Rome en de vrije Bijbel*, Amsterdam, Holland, 1956.

116   Beaupère, "Notes sur le renouveau biblique," 337.

117   Jacobs, *Nieuwe visies op een oud visioen*, 88–91.

118   See Fouilloux, *Eugène, cardinal Tisserant*, 267–270.

119   Lucien Cerfaux, "Le thème littéraire parabolique dans l'Évangile de saint Jean," in: Seminarium Neotestamenticum, ed., *Coniectanea Neotestamentica XI in honorem Antonii Fridrichsen sexagenarii*, Lund, Gleerup, 1947, 15–25. The otherwise critical colleague of Cerfaux, Msgr. Joseph Coppens had praised the high quality of the Festschrift, but had opined that the editors of the Festschrift could have shown more sensitivity towards the Catholic collaborators, Cerfaux, Spicq, Festugière, by rejecting an article of Kümmel, who argued against the virginal conception of Mary; see Joseph Coppens, "Review of *Coniectanea Neotestamentica XI*," RHE 44, 1949, 198–199.

of view.[120] In 1950, the dean of the Protestant Theological Faculty of Paris, Maurice Goguel, was honored on his seventieth birthday with a Festschrift entitled *Aux sources de la tradition chrétienne*. Goguel enjoyed a strong reputation in the exegetical world, having substantially contributed to the quest for the historical Jesus. For this reason, not only famous Protestant exegetes such as Rudolf Bultmann and Oscar Cullmann had been invited to contribute to this *Liber amicorum*, but also Catholic exegetes were asked, such as the Dominicans Pierre Benoit, François-Marie Braun, André-Jean Festugière, Ceslas Spicq, and Cerfaux. The latter, because of the permission given, three years before, to contribute to the Festschrift for Professor Fridrichsen, felt that he could accept the invitation. His (rather short) contribution dealt with Scriptural citations and the textual tradition in the book of Acts.[121] Great was Cerfaux's surprise when he received a letter from Cardinal Jozeph-Ernest van Roey in which the cardinal informed him that on Feb 17, 1950, the secretary of the Holy Office, Cardinal Francesco Marchetti Selvaggiani, had asked van Roey to urge Cerfaux to withdraw his contribution to the Festschrift for Goguel. According to Marchetti Selvaggiani, this was to be done because the article would contribute "to praising an exponent of non-Catholic and rationalist critical exegesis," and would cause scandal and surprise among the faithful.[122] Cerfaux was upset: "We did not expect that our contribution would be judged so severely."[123] Furthermore, the proofs of his contribution had already been corrected and sent back to the editors. He thus could

not withdraw his article at that point. Cerfaux's contribution was published, just like those of the other Catholic contributors to the Festschrift, even though all probably had received the request to revoke their contribution.[124] Rome wanted *all* Catholics to withdraw their contribution. Needless to say, this prohibition from Rome deeply hurt this man of the church and member of the PCB.[125] Stories like these make clear that "becoming ecumenical" as a biblical scholar was, even after *Divino afflante Spiritu*, absolutely not easy in the Catholic world, even though the president of the PCB had praised the Leuven professors for their research.[126]

At the same time, it should be said that Catholic faculties of theology were very prudent when non-Catholics wanted to obtain a theological degree at their institutions. In the 1950s, it was not common for non-Catholics to study at the Faculty of Theology in Leuven.[127] Before allowing such candidates, the faculty needed the permission of the bishops. Such students could never receive ecclesiastical degrees, only academic ones. In making the argument for the admission of non-Catholics, the faculty used arguments which did not always give evidence of ecumenical openness. Candidates mostly came from the Orthodox Churches, "desirous to be formed in a Catholic university rather than to enroll in a Protestant faculty where rationalist tendencies dominate."[128]

---

120   See L. Cerfaux to J.-E. van Roey, Mar 8, 1950, in: AAM, Papers van Roey, II, A1.

121   See Lucien Cerfaux, "Citations scripturaires et tradition textuelle dans le livre des Actes," in: *Aux sources de la tradition chrétienne: Mélanges offerts à Maurice Goguel à l'occasion de son soixante-dixième anniversaire*, Paris, Delachaux & Niestlé, 1950, 43–51.

122   "A glorificare un esponente della critica esegetica acattolica e razionalista"; F. Marchetti Selvaggiani to J.-E. van Roey, Feb 17, 1950, in: AAM, Papers van Roey, II, A1.

123   "Nous n'avons pas prévu que notre intervention serait jugée si sévèrement"; L. Cerfaux to J.-E. van Roey, Mar 8, 1950, in: AAM, Papers van Roey, II, A1.

124   See L. Cerfaux to J.-E. van Roey, Mar 21, 1950, in: AAM, Papers van Roey, II, A1: "Effectivement une lettre du Père Général m'a demandé de retirer ma collaboration aux mélanges Goguel, s'il en était encore temps, et de ne pas récidiver dans des cas analogues"; C. Spicq to L. Cerfaux, quoted by Cerfaux. In his letter, Spicq added that it was an honor for the Roman Catholic Church that its members were asked by Protestants to contribute to their publications.

125   J.-E. van Roey to F. Marchetti Selvaggiani, Mar 16, 1950, in: AAM, Papers van Roey, II, A1.

126   Fouilloux, *Eugène, cardinal Tisserant*, 275.

127   In fact, the same was also the case for the laity; see Dirk Claes, *Theologie in tijden van verandering: De theologische faculteit te Leuven in de twintigste eeuw (1900–1968)*, Ph.D. thesis, KU Leuven, 2004, 91–94.

128   "Désireux de se former dans une Université Catholique plutôt que de s'inscrire à une faculté Protestante où les tendances rationalistes dominent"; J. Coppens to H. Van Waeyenbergh, Nov 7, 1958, in: ASFT, 28bis.

In other words, the plea to allow Orthodox students was, still in 1958, based on an anti-Protestant argument.

Caution remained the key word. We can return to Augustin Bea for an example, often hailed as a leading figure in Catholic ecumenism after Vatican II. At the beginning of the 1950s, shortly after he had been named consultor for the Holy Office, Bea was contacted by the bishop of Paderborn, Lorenz Jaeger,[129] who needed a contact person in Rome to turn to with pressing ecumenical questions raised by the German bishops. Jaeger's concern was how to deal with increasing numbers of Protestant ministers who wanted to join the Catholic Church and meanwhile hoped to continue their service to the people of God.[130] Bea responded that his experience in ecumenical matters had only just begun.[131] In any case, the fact that the ordination of converted Protestant pastors became increasingly possible and encouraged shows that, throughout the 1950s, Catholic ecumenists saw no contradiction between a commitment to ecumenical dialogue and the welcoming of conversions.[132] It was through Jaeger that Bea was introduced to Johannes Willebrands, his future right hand in

the Secretariat for Christian Unity,[133] but some of Willebrands' ecumenical activities were not appreciated by Bea. In 1952, Willebrands had founded the CCEQ, whose relationship with the WCC worried Father Bea. In his opinion, the CCEQ risked not following Roman directives that had imposed a strict control by local ordinaries on activities that brought together Catholics and Protestants, particularly in the area of theological dialogue.[134] Bea in particular affirmed the instructions of the Holy Office that called for entrusting theological discussions to a group experts with episcopal oversight and prohibiting lay people – who were not held to be adequately prepared – from participation in ecumenical meetings.[135] As new consultor of the Holy Office, he made clear in meetings with the SWV that every ecumenical initiative that involved Catholics had to be always undertaken by the hierarchy and only by the hierarchy.[136] Furthermore, Bea recommended that Catholics should only engage in ecumenism in those regions where Protestantism was an important or majority factor in society.[137]

The fact that the efforts of Willebrands and the Sint Willibrord Society to establish contacts with the WCC were met with criticism in the Netherlands, especially in the Catholic southern

---

129   See Michael Quisinsky & Peter Walter, "Jaeger, Lorenz," in Michael Quisinsky & Peter Walter, eds., *Personenlexikon zum Zweiten Vatikanischen Konzil*, Freiburg i.Br., Herder, 2012, 141 (with further literature).

130   See the detailed description in Schmidt, *Augustin Bea*, 307ff.

131   See Saretta Marotta, "Augustin Bea auf dem Weg zum Ökumeniker (1949–1960)," *ZKG* 127, 2016, 373–393, here 376. Whether Bea before that moment had been involved in ecumenical issues, is a matter of discussion; see the positions of Dominik Burkard, "Augustin Bea und Alfredo Ottaviani: Thesen zu einer entscheidenden personellen Konstellation im Vorfeld des Zweiten Vatikanischen Konzils," in: Franz Xaver Bischof, ed., *Das Zweite Vatikanische Konzil (1962–1965): Stand und Perspektiven der kirchenhistorischen Forschung im deutschsprachigen Raum*, Stuttgart, Kohlhammer, 2012, 45–66, and Marotta, "Augustin Bea," 376.

132   This was clearly the case for Willebrands; see Leo Declerck, *Inventaire des archives personnelles du Cardinal J. Willebrands*, Leuven, Peeters, 2013, 242–254; see also Jacobs, *Nieuwe visies op een oud visioen*, 67–68.

133   On the importance of Willebrands in the ecumenical movement, see Adelbert Denaux & Peter De Mey, eds., *The Ecumenical Legacy of Johannes Cardinal Willebrands (1909–2006)*, Leuven, Peeters, 2012 (with an exhaustive bibliography of Willebrands); Karim Schelkens, *Johannes Willebrands: Een leven in gesprek (1909–2006)*, Amsterdam, Boom, 2020.

134   On the birth and the activities of the Catholic Conference for Ecumenical Questions, see the contribution of Peter De May and Saretta Marotta in volume II of this work.

135   Marotta, "Augustin Bea," 386–387.

136   All the steps taken by Willebrands and Thijssen were the result of prudent consultations, thus avoiding any friction with church leaders. In this regard, it is interesting to see that the Dutch Jesuit J. Witte, member of the daily management of the Sint-Willebrord Society, during a visit to Rome in 1951, first contacted three Jesuit confreres: Leiber, Bea, and Tromp.

137   Jacobs, *Nieuwe visies op een oud visioen*, 68–69.

part of the country, was again a proof that "doing" ecumenism was not an easy task in the 1950s.[138] For Bea, ecumenism was to be principally a matter of the study of the doctrinal differences between the churches, which is why he supported Jaeger's idea to found an Institut für Konfessions- und Diasporakunde (May 1, 1956) in Paderborn, today the Johann-Adam-Möhler-Institut für Ökumenik, an institute that, according to Bea, was preparing something unforeseen.[139] Bea held that ecumenical research should offer a clear idea of what the confessions had in common and what they did not,[140] which is why any initiative proposed by Jaeger or by the institute that deviated from this approach or included anyone not sufficiently qualified in theology met with Bea's disapproval.[141] Still in 1954, Bea did not have the courage to draw theological conclusions from his biblical research.[142] Discussions with the Protestant Hans Asmussen and his Sammlung,[143] a movement promoting a return to the earliest inspirations of the Reformation (the early church, the *Confessio Augustana*, etc.) and positive dialogue with the Catholics, ended immediately after the publication of the book *Katholische Reformation*, a collection of letters published by the Sammlung in previous years, that in fact brought about the end of that brief experience of dialogue.[144] Frictions such as the Rhodes incident, in the

summer of 1959,[145] increased Bea's distrust in the intentions of the WCC. On the eve of Vatican II, the relationship with both the Protestants and Orthodox was rather difficult, to say the least, and it goes without saying that incidents such as at Rhodes had their impact. When, finally, a Secretariat for Promoting Christian Unity was founded[146] – for a long time Bea focused on the Protestant denominations[147] –, Bea was very well aware that it needed to be composed of members coming from outside Rome with experience at the local level. The discussion that Bea and Willebrands had on June 2, 1960, makes abundantly clear that Bea was not naïve regarding the problems the Secretariat would confront in "the Roman Curia, Holy Office and the Congregation for the Oriental Churches."[148] He looked for consultors "who have carried the burden of work, but have little trust in Rome."[149] And indeed, most of the first members of the Secretariat

---

138   For a detailed description of the difficult journey of Willebrands, see Jacobs, *Nieuwe visies op een oud visioen*, 66–72.

139   Schmidt, *Augustin Bea*, 307.

140   On Bea's support, see Schmidt, *Augustin Bea*, 314–315.

141   Marotta, "Augustin Bea," 382.

142   On this issue, see Josef Höfer, "Das Geistliche Profil des Kardinal Bea," *Catholica* 26, 1972, 50–62.

143   Marotta, "Augustin Bea," 383; see also Schmidt, *Augustin Bea*, 307–309.

144   In fact, the Sammlung expressed demands that were unacceptable for Catholics at that time: Mary, the primacy of the pope, the rejection of the *sola scriptura* principle were all non-negotiable aspects in Rome; see Schmidt, *Augustin Bea*, 308.

145   See Karim Schelkens, "L'affaire de Rhodes' au jour le jour: La correspondance inédite entre J.G.M. Willebrands et Ch.-J. Dumont," *Istina* 54, 2009, 253–277.

146   Previous attempts had failed; see Mauro Velati, "'Un indirizzo a Roma': La nascita del Segretariato per l'unità dei cristiani (1959–1960)," in: Giuseppe Alberigo, ed., *Il Vaticano II fra attese e celebrazione*, Bologna, Il Mulino, 1995, 75–118.

147   This explains why it was mostly an affair among Germans. On the exchange of letters between Jaeger and Bea, see Saretta Marotta, "La genesi di un ecumenista: La corrispondenza tra Augustin Bea e il vescovo di Paderborn Lorenz Jaeger (1951–1960)," in: Luca Ferracci, ed., *Toward a History of the Desire for Christian Unity: Preliminary Research Papers: Proceedings of the International Conference at the Monastery of Bose (November 2014)*, Zürich, LIT, 2015, 159–191.

148   Most of the problems the Secretariat will be confronted with are listed in Willebrands' diary after his meeting with Bea, and it is the cardinal who highlighted these problems; see Johannes Willebrands, *"You Will Be Called Repairer of the Breach": The Diary of J.G.M. Willebrands (1958–1961)*, ed. Theo Salemink, Leuven, Peeters, 2009, 175–176, here 175.

149   Willebrands, *"You Will Be Called Repairer of the Breach"*, 163.

would come from abroad and would belong to the inner circle of either Jaeger or Willebrands. The list of consultors also makes clear that the ecumenical movement at the time was mostly oriented to the Protestant world; one looks in vain for experts familiar with the Orthodox world.

4.3 *The Ambiguous Role of* Humani generis

The publication of *Humani generis* in 1950[150] was experienced by many as an act aimed at reining in these new approaches.[151] It was published a couple of weeks after the publication by the PCB of the instruction *Sanctissimus Dominus* (May 13, 1950), an instruction that was rather ambivalent about the role of Catholic exegesis.[152] *Humani generis* was received with skepticism by exegetes for several reasons, including its defense of monogenism as a safeguard to the dogma of original sin, even though the book of Genesis did not speak in terms of an original sin. Moreover, while the encyclical preferred a literal reading of the Bible to a symbolic interpretation,[153] it did not do justice to texts such as Gen 4:16, which explicitly dealt with polygenism. But the encyclical also had its supporters. It was used by defenders of the anti-Modernist position to start criticizing colleagues who, in line with *Divino afflante Spiritu*, made use of the methods of historical criticism and literary criticism, considering them compatible with theological doctrine and the teaching of the church. While the latter were convinced that academic research would contribute to a better underpinning and understanding of a doctrine needing a reading

of the signs of the times in order time and again to adapt it to changing historical circumstances, the new champions of anti-Modernism were of the opinion that the Bible should function more as an instrument that supported the teachings of the church, and less as an inspiration for these teachings. Indeed, they reasoned, if the church's doctrine is immutable for supra-historical reasons, all approaches that suggest a genesis and growth of biblical insights are wrong, if not heretical. Both approaches could appeal to papal teaching, but at the end of the day, it would become clear that the second position was considered no longer tenable. However, the tension between the two approaches would continue to exist until Vatican II.[154]

In this tension, Holy Office played a role that should not be overlooked. Two examples will suffice. In 1958, the Holy Office asked the Congregation for the Seminaries and Universities and the Congregation for Religious to issue a warning against the first volume of André Robert's and André Feuillet's *Introduction à la Bible* (1957), an instrument for the formation of the clergy, published by these two professors of the ICP. The Holy Office suggested that this kind of "searching" exegesis was more destructive than constructive.[155] All this happened without consulting the PCB. Its president was furious, for this kind of examination destroyed its prestige and authority.[156] In any case, a second edition of their book was published in 1959, taking into account the suggestions as made by Bea and others.

The clash between the Lateran Seminary and the Biblicum at the end of the 1950s and the beginning of the 1960s is well known and is a good example of

---

150 Pius XII, *Humani generis*, Aug 12, 1950; the text is available at www.vatican.va/content/pius-xii/en/encyclicals/documents/hf_p-xii_enc_12081950_humani-generis.html (accessed Nov 2, 2020).

151 However, Lyonnet, "Pie XII et les études scripturaires," 130–131 offers a nuanced view on the impact of the encyclical. In a detailed way, Lyonnet shows that the encyclical did not close the door for exegetical research.

152 Schelkens, "From *Providentissimus Deus* to *Dei Verbum*," 60–61.

153 See *Humani generis* 23.

154 Joseph A. Komonchak, "The Struggle for the Council during the Preparation of Vatican II (1960–1962)," in: Giuseppe Alberigo, ed., *History of Vatican II*, vol. 1, *Announcing and Preparing Vatican Council II: Toward a New Era in Catholicism*, ed. Joseph A. Komonchak, Leuven, Peeters, 1995, 279.

155 For the details, see Fouilloux, *Une Église en quête de liberté*, 269–270.

156 Fouilloux, *Eugène, cardinal Tisserant*, 276–277.

"different" readings of *Humani generis*. Francesco Spadafora and Antonino Romeo, professors at the Lateran, openly criticized their colleagues of the Biblicum and related their teachings to those of the Modernists. As a result, two Jesuits, the German Maximilian Zerwick and the French Stanislas Lyonnet were, for a while, prohibited to teach.[157] This decision was reversed by John XXIII, who did not look favorably on criticisms of the Biblicum.[158] This shows that even though biblical studies had made much progress, a risk of being questioned, suspected, and eventually condemned, remained a reality until Vatican II. From 1963 onwards, in fact, the PCB would be filled with scholars (exegetes and cardinals) who were known for their openness to the modern interpretation of the Bible, and the results of this change were not long in coming.[159] While the *Monitum* of June 20, 1961, warning against positions that did not do justice to the historical and objective truth of the Scriptures, referred to the condemnation of such positions by *Humani generis*,[160] the PCB's *Instructio de historica Evangeliorum veritate* (Apr 21, 1964),[161] speaking about the historical truth of the gospels, preferred to not highlight the critique expressed by the Holy Office in the *Monitum* of three years prior. One could speak of a return to the climate following the publication of *Divino afflante Spiritu*. The fact that, in the time between the publication of these two documents, nineteen cardinals did not hesitate to accuse four theologians (one Frenchman, two Belgians, one German) for having criticized the schema *De fontibus Revelationis* during Vatican

II, makes clear that at the beginning of the Council some people still were opposed to developments in Catholic exegesis.[162]

5   Concluding Remarks

This survey of Catholic biblical studies has made clear that between *Providentissimus Deus* and *Divino afflante Spiritu* Catholic exegesis was constantly put on the defensive. Catholic exegetes could make use of archaeological, philological, and historical methods, as long as these methods contributed to proving the inerrancy of the Bible and supported the Roman Catholic doctrine as presented by the Council of Trent and Vatican I. Those who deviated from such approach, as was the case with Loisy, were condemned and excommunicated. For about forty years, Catholic exegetes did not dare or were not allowed to publish commentaries on books like Genesis. Between 1908 and World War II, no Catholic commentary was published on this book, and Lagrange was not allowed to publish his work on it, even though he was attempting to combine the historical critical approach with the theological meaning of the text. Catholic exegetes were controlled by the PCB and the Biblicum became the institute that gradually would become responsible for the exegetical training of future professors at universities and seminaries. As a result, Catholic exegetes, while sharing some technical methods with the Protestant colleagues, mostly were publicly writing against them, either out of conviction or because they had no other choice.

---

157   For the details, see e.g. Anthony Dupont & Karim Schelkens, "Scopuli vitandi: The Historical-Critical Exegesis Controversy between the Lateran and the Biblicum (1960–1961)," *Bijdragen* 69, 2008, 18–51.

158   See Sebastian Tromp, *Konzilstagebuch: Mit Erläuterungen und Akten aus der Arbeit der Kommission für Glauben und Sitten*, ed. Alexandra von Teuffenbach, vol. 1/1, Rome, Pontificia Università Gregoriana, 2006, 166–167.

159   Fitzmyer, *A Christological Catechism*, 124.

160   *AAS* 53, 1961, 507.

161   *AAS* 56, 1964, 712–718.

---

162   One of the accused exegetes, Frans Neirynck, professor at the Major Seminary of Bruges and later at KU Leuven's Faculty of Theology, published his personal dossier, which makes clear that some of the accusations came very near to backbiting; see Frans Neirynck, "Dagboeknotitie: Een preconciliair incident," in: Frans van Segbroeck & others, eds., *The Four Gospels: Festschrift Frans Neirynck*, vol. 1, Leuven, Peeters, 1992, 68–80.

Things changed with the appointments of Tisserant and Vosté to the head of the PCB. They stimulated Catholic exegetes to embrace methods such as the historical critical method and literary criticism. *Divino afflante Spiritu*, the charter for Catholic exegetes, not only resulted in a growing interest in the Bible among the faithful but also promoted Catholic research *in dialogue* with the Protestants.[163] The organization of conferences and study weeks contributed to a growing self-confidence among Catholic exegetes, and to a growing interest of Protestants in the work of Catholics, although free conversation and publications of Catholic authors in Protestant books still remained problematic. Even in the 1950s, discussions between Catholics and Protestants remained hesitant and cautious, as became clear in the attitude of Bea towards initiatives that wanted to accelerate ecumenical dialogue. Furthermore, the publication of *Humani generis* left space for the opponents of the historical critical method and literary criticism to attack the adherents of these approaches. Up to the eve of Vatican II, suspicion and temporary suspensions were still the fate of Catholic exegetes. The sometimes-tense relationships between the Holy Office and the PCB made clear that in the central offices of the Roman Catholic Church different ideas existed. It is not surprising that, in such contexts, biblical studies did not really get the opportunity to function as an efficient motor of ecumenical dialogue.

Bibliography

Aubert, Roger, *La théologie catholique au milieu du XXe siècle*, Tournai, Casterman, 1954.

Fouilloux, Étienne, *Eugène, cardinal Tisserant (1884–1972): Une biographie*, Paris, Desclée de Brouwer, 2011.

Fouilloux, Étienne, *Une Église en quête de liberté: La pensée catholique française entre modernisme et Vatican II (1914–1962)*, Paris, Desclée de Brouwer, 1998.

Lamberigts, Mathijs, "The Bible: A Book for *All* Faithful," *ASR* 10, 2017, 75–92.

Loughlin, Gerard, "Nouvelle Théologie: A Return to Modernism?," in: Gabriel Flynn & Paul D. Murray, eds., *Ressourcement: A Movement for Renewal in Twentieth-Century Catholic Theology*, Oxford, Oxford University Press, 2012, 36–50.

Robinson, Robert Bruce, *Roman Catholic Exegesis since "Divino afflante Spiritu": Hermeneutical Implications*, Atlanta, Scholars Press, 1988.

Schelkens, Karim, "From *Providentissimus Deus* to *Dei Verbum*: The Catholic Biblical Movement and the Council Reconsidered," in: Gilles Routhier, Philippe J. Roy & Karim Schelkens, eds., *La théologie catholique entre intransigeance et renouveau: La réception des mouvements préconciliaires à Vatican II*, Turnhout, Brepols, 2011.

Theobald, Christoph, "L'exégèse catholique au moment de la crise Moderniste," in: Claude Savart & Jean-Noël Aletti, eds., *Le monde contemporain et la Bible*, Paris, Beauchesne, 1985, 387–439.

---

163   In the literature consulted, I did not find substantial traces of a real exegetical interaction between Catholic and Orthodox scholars.

CHAPTER 21

The Role of Liturgical Movements in Developing an Ecumenical Awareness in Catholicism and Orthodoxy

Benedikt Kranemann and Adalberto Mainardi

1   Historical Overview

The Catholic liturgical movement, particularly in German-speaking areas, first arose in the 19th century and gradually developed during the following century along with the changes in the political, economic, and cultural context.[1] The years 1909 and 1947 may be considered indicative of this history, since it was in 1909 that a Roman Catholic congress was held in Malines, Belgium, at which Dom Lambert Beauduin,[2] a Benedictine monk of the Mont César Abbey at the time and future founder of the Amay-Chevetogne Monastery, asked the church for a fuller participation of all the faithful in liturgical celebration. The Benedictine suggested intervening in two ways: permission to celebrate the liturgy in the vernacular (requesting that a translation of the Mass and Sunday vespers be allowed) and that religious piety be oriented toward the liturgy.[3] This first phase, which could be defined as a preparatory stage, was followed by a "pastoral" phase, which lasted from 1918 to 1947. A third phase then began with that year's encyclical *Mediator Dei*, "which conceived of liturgical renewal in the sense of liturgical reform."[4]

A historical reconstruction of the liturgical movement is particularly complex today since it requires a critical examination of sources that also takes into account how, in the perception of many at the time, not least in relation to their own personal experience, the passage from the movement to Vatican II and then to the postconciliar liturgical reform occurred seamlessly. This conviction, however, does not seem to allow for how the social and ecclesial contexts of the 1920s and 1930s were totally different from those that marked the years after

---

1   We examine here the Roman Catholic liturgical movement; for the Protestant one, see Karl-Heinrich Bieritz, "Liturgische Bewegungen im deutschen Protestantismus im 20. Jahrhundert," in: Jürgen Bärsch & Benedikt Kranemann, eds., *Geschichte der Liturgie in den Kirchen des Westens: Rituelle Entwicklungen, theologische Konzepte und kulturelle Kontext*, vol. 2, *Moderne und Gegenwart*, Münster, Aschendorff, 2018, 125–163 and, the contribution by Martin C. Lenz in this volume. For an overview of the abundant literature on the Catholic liturgical movement, see Martin Klöckener, "Die katholische Liturgische Bewegung in Europa: 10 Thesen und Auswahlbibliographie," in: Bruno Bürki & Martin Klöckener, eds., *Liturgie in Bewegung: Beiträge zum Kolloquium Gottesdienstliche Erneuerung in den Schweizer Kirchen im 20. Jahrhundert, 1.–3. März 1999 an der Universität Freiburg, Schweiz / Liturgie en mouvement Actes du Colloque Renouveau liturgique des Églises en Suisse au XXe siècle, 1–3 mars 1999, Université de Fribourg, Suisse*, in collaboration with Arnaud Join-Lambert, Fribourg, Universitätsverlag, Geneva, Labor et Fides, 2000, 25–32; Theodor Maas-Ewerd & Klemens Richter, "Die Liturgische Bewegung in Deutschland," in: Martin Klöckener & Benedikt Kranemann, eds., *Liturgiereformen: Historische Studien zu einem bleibenden Grundzug des christlichen Gottesdienstes*, vol. 2, *Liturgiereformen seit der Mitte des 19. Jahrhunderts bis zur Gegenwart*, Münster, Aschendorff, 2002, 629–648; Jürgen Bärsch, *Kleine Geschichte des christlichen Gottesdienstes*, Regensburg, Pustet, ²2017, 157–170; Winfried Haunerland, "Liturgische Bewegung in der katholischen Kirche im 20. Jahrhundert," in: Bärsch & Kranemann, eds., *Geschichte der Liturgie*, vol. 2, 165–205. I should like to thank Dr. Lea Lerch of Vienna for her useful suggestions, especially in regard to bibliographical references.

2   See André Haquin's contribution in this volume.

3   See Lambert Beauduin, "Das eigentliche Gebet der Kirche," *LJ* 9, 1959, 198–202, here 202.

4   See Maas-Ewerd & Richter, "Die Liturgische Bewegung," 633. In the light of recent research, which underlines in particular the contextual character of the liturgical movement, it is doubtful that the post-conciliar liturgical reform truly carried out a transition "without interruptions" (647).

1968 and which alone are sufficient to demonstrate the need to consider some clear breaks within the history of the 20th century liturgical movement.[5]

It is from this perspective that experts in liturgical matters today seem to devote more attention to particularly delicate stages in the religious history of the 20th century, such as Modernism and anti-Modernism, in order to verify whether and to what extent it is possible to speak of this movement in terms of a unique and continuous historical phenomenon.[6] In the same way, they do not shrink from tackling the thorny question of which connections bound the liturgical movement of the early post-war period in Germany to the many movements of a political nature that were agitating Weimar Germany, including, needless to say, National Socialism.[7]

2   The Catholic Liturgical Movement in German-Speaking Countries: A Renewal of the Faith and of the Church

In the 19th century, the first steps towards a renewal of the liturgy were taken by the Abbey of Solesmes and, in particular, by Dom Prosper Guéranger. On the one hand, he succeeded in triggering a process of Romanization in the liturgy, in contrast to the particularism of the local rites that characterized French post-Tridentine diocesan liturgies. On the other, he sought to promote, through publishing works intended for a vast readership, greater access to the church's Eucharistic celebration.[8] Finally, a key role was played by the repopulation of some Benedictine abbeys in the German Reich, especially that of Maria Laach in 1892. Additionally, other centers that were important in spreading the liturgical movement in German-speaking areas were Klosterneuburg, near Vienna, the Leipzig Oratory, and Rothenfels Castle in northern Bavaria.

As is well known, the beginning of the 20th century, both in Germany and in Austria,[9] was characterized by several historical upsets announced by the winds of war that had already started blowing at the *fin de siècle*.[10] The end of World War I and the political upheavals that accompanied it (such as the fall of the monarchy and the great economic depression of the 1920s), along with the physical and psychological suffering experienced by veterans and those wounded in war, profoundly shaped the social reality and mentality of those two defeated nations, as of all those involved in the great European bloodbath. It was in this, to say the least, dramatic situation that the liturgical movement slowly began to appreciate its ability, through worship, to offer a spiritual program that might provide support and security and contribute to the respective nations' spiritual regeneration.[11]

---

5 See the forthcoming work Lea Lerch, *Modernisierung durch Kulturkritik: Historischer Kontext und theologische Heterogenität der Liturgischen Bewegung.*

6 See Benedikt Kranemann, "Die bekannte/unbekannte Liturgische Bewegung: Ein Ausblick," in: Andreas Redtenbacher, ed., *Liturgie lernen und leben – zwischen Tradition und Innovation: Pius Parsch Symposion 2014,* Freiburg i.Br., Herder, 2015, 219–222; in this sense, see also Maas-Ewerd & Richter, "Die Liturgische Bewegung," 638–642.

7 On the Protestant liturgical movement in regard to the *Völkische* movement see Alexander Deeg & Christian Lehnert, eds. *"Wir glauben das Neue": Liturgie und Liturgiewissenschaft unter dem Einfluss der völkischen Bewegung,* Leipzig, Evang. Verl.-Anst., 2014; on the Catholic Church, see Christiane Schäfer, "'Uns rufet die Stunde!' Die Sammlung 'Kirchenlied' von 1938 im Kontext ihrer Entstehungszeit," in: Deeg & Lehnert, eds., *"Wir glauben das Neue",* 223–235; for the bibliographical references on Catholicism, see Benedikt Kranemann, "'Wir glauben das Neue' – Forschungsperspektiven," in: Deeg & Lehnert, eds., *"Wir glauben das Neue",* 237–244.

8 See Hélène Bricout & Gilles Drouin, "Liturgie in Frankreich in der nachtridentinischen Epoche," in: Bärsch & Kranemann, eds., *Geschichte der Liturgie,* vol. 2, 7–50.

9 For the situation in Switzerland, see Guido Muff, "Inexistenz einer Schweizer Liturgischen Bewegung?," in: Bürki & Klöckener, eds., *Liturgie in Bewegung,* 130–139.

10 See Otto Weiß, *Kulturkatholizismus: Katholiken auf dem Weg in die deutsche Kultur (1900–1933),* Regensburg, Pustet, 2014, 19–27.

11 See Lea Herberg, "Hingabe und Heldentum: Liturgische Frömmigkeit und der Erste Weltkrieg bei Odo Casel," in: Lea Herberg & Sebastian Holzbrecher, eds., *Theologie im Kontext des Ersten Weltkriegs: Aufbrüche*

Paradoxically, it was precisely from the experience of war that lasting lessons were drawn, one of which imparted the rejection of individualism as modernity's most poisonous fruit. After 1918, trench warfare, also helped by propaganda, became an almost mystical, communal experience,[12] and, in many cases, served as the ideal basis for those engaged in the renewal of the church and society through liturgy.[13] It is no coincidence that one of the most incisive protagonists of the liturgical movement during those years was the canon regular of Klosterneuberg, Pius Parsch, who had been a military chaplain at the front during the war and who incorporated his experiences of that period into his liturgical and pastoral work.[14]

In the course of the same years, in a society exhausted by the conflict and political divisions, the many youth movements (*Jugendbewegung*) that had emerged at the beginning of the 20th century became the bearers of an ideal of national community animated by an ardent spirituality and cemented by the camaraderie experienced in the trenches in France.[15] On the Catholic side, the Quickborn youth movement, the students of the Jugendbund Neudeutschland (Youth Federation New Germany), and the Katholischer

Jungmännerbund (Young Men's Catholic Association) should be mentioned.

Besides Pius Parsch, the characters who indelibly marked this second phase of the liturgical movement were Odo Casel, Romano Guardini, Ildefons Herwegen, Kunibert Mohlberg, Heinrich von Meurers,[16] Josef Andreas Jungmann, and Johannes Pinsk.[17] They encouraged liturgical renewal both by fostering exchanges and contact among their supporters and by means of a fervid distribution of published materials of programmatic, theological, and pastoral interest. Indeed, it should be pointed out, that in addition to the numerous initiatives of liturgical formation that were being promoted in those years, a significant role in the dissemination of the movement's ideals was played not only by journals and magazines, but also by small format publications.

In the course of its existence, the liturgical movement did not fail to provoke critical reactions in the theological and ecclesiastical spheres. Neither was it immune from internal polarizations, which were often generated by certain positions being taken to extremes. This was particularly evident in the period we have considered so far, which has convinced historians to define the years between 1939 and 1944 as a phase of true crisis in the liturgical movement,[18] involving parish priests, bishops, and theologians, on both the German and the Roman side. This impasse was not overcome until, perhaps, 1947 when, at the conclusion of a lengthy process of discussion and study, Pope Pius XII promulgated the encyclical *Mediator Dei*,[19] which on

---

12   See Annette Becker, "Die Religionsgeschichte des Krieges (1914–1918): Eine Bilanz," in: Gottfried Korff, ed., *Alliierte im Himmel: Populäre Religiosität und Kriegserfahrung*, Tübingen, Tübinger Vereinigung für Volkskunde, 2006, 33–45.

13   See Lucia Scherzberg, "Liturgie als Erlebnis und Kirche als Gemeinschaft," in: Lucia Scherzberg, ed., *Gemeinschaftskonzepte im 20. Jahrhundert zwischen Wissenschaft und Ideologie*, Münster, Monsenstein und Vannerdat, 2010, 253–287, here 253–267.

14   See Rudolf Pacik, "Pius Parsch (1884–1954)," in: Benedikt Kranemann & Klaus Raschzok, eds., *Gottesdienst als Feld theologischer Wissenschaft im 20. Jahrhundert: Deutschsprachige Liturgiewissenschaft in Einzelporträts*, Münster, Aschendorff, 2011, 886–900 and 889. The publication of an edition of his diary at the front is forthcoming in the collection Pius-Parsch-Studien.

15   See Barbara Stambolis, ed., *Die Jugendbewegung und ihre Wirkungen: Prägungen, Vernetzungen, gesellschaftliche Einflussnahmen*, Göttingen, Vandenhoeck & Ruprecht, 2015.

und Gefährdungen, Würzburg, Echter, 2016, 205–230; see the further analysis at 205f.

---

16   See Guido Pasenow, *Heinrich von Meurers (1888–1953): Ein Förderer und Wegbereiter der liturgischen Erneuerung in Deutschland*, Trier, Paulinus, 2016.

17   For the biographies of the authors cited here and a summary description of their works, see Kranemann & Raschzok, eds., *Gottesdienst als Feld*.

18   See Theodor Maas-Ewerd, *Die Krise der Liturgischen Bewegung in Deutschland und Österreich: Zu den Auseinandersetzungen um die "liturgische Frage" in den Jahren 1939 bis 1944*, Regensburg, Pustet, 1981.

19   See Pius XII, *Mediator Dei*, Nov 20, 1947; the text can be found at <www.vatican.va/content/pius-xii/en/encyclicals/documents/hf_p-xii_enc_20111947_mediator-dei.html> (accessed July 15, 2020).

the whole conceded an approval of the liturgical movement's aims. The encyclical no longer considered the liturgical celebration from a juridical and rubrical viewpoint, but rather as a public worship that "our Redeemer as Head of the Church renders to the Father" (*MD* 20). The encyclical continued, speaking of such worship, "which the community of the faithful renders to its Founder, and through Him to the heavenly Father. It is, in short, the worship rendered by the Mystical Body of Christ in the entirety of its Head and members" (*MD* 20). The papal letter thus related the active participation of the faithful in the liturgical celebration to the theological precept of the common priesthood (*MD* 87), recommended communion within the Mass (*MD* 117), and encouraged an intensification of liturgical catechesis (*MD* 195–202).

3   Active Participation and Ecclesiology

The concept of active participation in the liturgy had already appeared in the 19th century with the Catholic Enlightenment and during the Restoration, but it only became established at the beginning of the 20th century: it can be found in Pius X's *motu proprio* of 1903, *Tra le sollecitudini*,[20] which, dealing with questions concerning music and liturgical chant, aimed at intensifying the Christian faith through the liturgy. As we read in the *motu proprio*'s preamble, the faithful draw their Christian spirit from "active participation in the most holy mysteries and in the public and solemn prayer of the Church."[21] However, the concept of "active participation" not only remained "evanescent"[22] but the context was also highly

clerical. Liturgical chants, in fact, were reserved for the celebrant and the *schola cantorum* consisting of clerics, while the other singers had the sole function of serving as substitutes.[23] Because singing in the *schola*, or choir, was a liturgical office, women were naturally excluded.[24]

In the course of the 20th century, we still find teachings of the Roman Magisterium on liturgical practice aimed at clarifying that, for example, priests and communities did not celebrate together, but rather that the priest alone "read" the Mass while, at the same time, the community was engaged in exercises of piety (saying the Rosary, reading a prayer, etc.). According to detractors of this practice, it not only prevented the liturgy from properly nourishing people's faith but also kept the church from experiencing itself as *ecclesia orans*, either as community or in the celebration of the Christian mystery itself. Indeed, it was only at this time that a new awareness of how participation in the liturgy and ecclesiology were closely related, and it was at that point that the liturgical movement entered the field to change the very conception and image of the church significantly. For example, Dom Beauduin maintained that the church was constituted in the Eucharist (an aspect that over the years led him to intensify his commitment to the faithful's active participation in worship)[25] even though his conception of the church and the liturgy remained strictly tied to a hierarchical image of ecclesial life. This apparent internal contradiction in Dom Beauduin's thought, in fact, represented the main problem that the Catholic liturgical movement had to solve in the years to come, that is, how to combine more

---

20   See Jakob Johannes Koch, "Das Motu proprio Pius X: 'Tra le sollecitudini dell'officio pastorale,'" in: Albert Gerhards & Matthias Schneider, eds., *Der Gottesdienst und seine Musik*, vol. 2, *Liturgik: Gottesdienstformen und ihre Handlungsträger*, Laaber, Laaber-Verl., 2014, 157–159.

21   Pius X, *Tra le sollecitudini*, ASS 36, 1903–1904, 387–395.

22   Stephan Schmid-Keiser, *Aktive Teilnahme: Kriterium gottesdienstlichen Handelns und Feierns: Zu den Elementen*

---

eines Schlüsselbegriffes in Geschichte und Gegenwart des 20. Jahrhunderts, vol. 1, Bern, Lang, 1985, 10.

23   Pius X, *Tra le sollecitudini*, § 12.

24   Pius X, *Tra le sollecitudini*, § 13.

25   On this point, Schmid-Keiser commented: "The celebration, even and properly of the Eucharist, appears to be excessively linked to the individual person called to represent Christ, while the representation of Christ in the assembled community, and therefore also in the individual believer, receives too little emphasis." see Schmid-Keiser, *Aktive Teilnahme*, vol. 1, 183.

fairly the vertical element of the representation of Christ, the minister, with the horizontal one, the praying community.[26]

The abbot of Maria Laach, Idelfons Herwegen, was of the opinion that the liturgy, "as a formal expression of the Christian spirit," should be a true and proper "lifestyle."[27] God, Herwegen continued, should be at the center of all Christian "existential inclinations," including "moral and societal aspirations."[28] The abbot of Maria Laach thus emphasized the importance of the liturgy at a time when the church found itself having to rethink its very structure fundamentally, mindful of the need of the faithful to participate in God's salvific work. For Herwegen, such participation meant an inclusion of individuals in the mystical presence of Christ and, at the same time, an inner change in the celebrating member of the faithful since the liturgy has no small capacity for directly influencing a person's character.[29]

Another leading protagonist in the liturgical movement during those years between the two world wars was undoubtedly Odo Casel. Reflecting on the New Testament and patristic sources, he developed a theology of the presence of the mystery of Christ in celebrating the liturgy that is well summarized in the following words:

> Christ's mystery in God's revelation in the saving action of his incarnate Son and the redemption and healing of the church. It continues after the glorified God-man has returned to his Father, until the full number of the church's members is complete; the mystery of Christ is carried on and made actual in the mystery of worship. Here Christ

performs his saving work, invisible, but present in Spirit and acting upon all men.[30]

Casel saw the past and future of salvation present here and now in the mystery of worship.[31] It was Christ himself, the true celebrant, who was present with his Pneuma, and the faithful, truly participating in the liturgy, not praying *during* it, therefore, but praying it, could live in the mystery of salvation.

> It is the Lord himself who acts this mystery; not as he did the primaeval mystery of the Cross, alone, but with his bride, which he won there, his church; to her he has now given all his treasures; she is to hand them on the children she has got of him.[32]

This salvific action necessarily has to be effected in order that the faithful might participate. In this sense, sacramentality took on new meaning, in contrast to the Scholasticism of the time. According to Casel, the objective event of the liturgy (the rite) and the subjective coexecution ("passive participation") had to be conceived of together as a union (in that the church is the Body of Christ and the priest acts in its name) while, however, maintaining the distinction between the action of the church (the priest who celebrates on behalf of all the faithful) and the assent of the congregation.

For theologians like Casel, however, the Old Testament remained foreign to this kind of argument, having been surpassed and removed by the mystery of Christ. This also applied to Judaism,

26   Schmid-Keiser, *Aktive Teilnahme*, vol. 1, 183.

27   Idelfons Herwegen, *Alte Quellen neuer Kraft: Gesammelte Aufsätze*, Düsseldorf, Schwann, ²1922, 77.

28   Herwegen, *Alte Quellen*, 78.

29   Herwegen, *Alte Quellen*, 144. On this topic, see Marc Breuer, *Religiöser Wandel als Säkularisierungsfolge: Differenzierungs- und Individualisierungsdiskurse im Katholizismus*, Wiesbaden, Springer VS, 2012, 379–388.

30   Odo Casel, *Das christliche Kultmysterium*, Regensburg, Pustet, ²1935; ET: *The Mystery of Christian Worship*, ed. Burkhard Neunheuser New York NY, Crossroad, 1999, 38.

31   See Arno Schilson, *Theologie als Sakramententheologie: Die Mysterientheologie Odo Casels*, Mainz, Matthias-Grünewald, 1987.

32   Casel, *They Mystery of Christian Worship*, 38.

which he considered provisional.[33] A similar approach is also found in Anton Baumstark, who considered Judaism a "phenomenon that has long since become marginal."[34] In the end, it can be said that both were followers of the theory of substitution and that, in comparison, Romano Guardini's approach, which was marked by a more systematic liturgical study, had, on the whole, proved to be "a solid basis for the study of Jewish-Christian commonalities and differences in their respective liturgical traditions."[35]

For Guardini, the liturgical community posed such a particular question that he reorganized the rooms of Rothenfels Castle, his operational headquarters for many years, on its basis. The principle that guided Guardini's work was that the individual should be able to participate in the liturgy, which had an existential significance. For him, the liturgy constituted a sacred "game" and was thus an event without purpose. The human person should take part in it as a body-spirit reality. His book, *Von heiligen Zeichen* clarified the weight he attached to the communication and participation in the liturgy by the human person in his/her bodily dimension.[36] Inner participation corresponded to external expression; the nonverbal component of the liturgy needed to be seriously reconsidered. Guardini wanted to contribute to the church's symbolic and communitarian attitude, directing its gaze to what is objective and keeping it focused on a liturgical exercise that was free of purpose. His short work *Vom Geist der Liturgie*,[37] which was first published in 1918 while World War I was still waging, offered an explanation of the liturgy based on the themes of prayer, fellowship, style, symbolism, playfulness, seriousness, and the primacy of Logos over ethos.

It is difficult to estimate today how widely Guardini's small volumes circulated. In the first four years of its appearance, for example, *Vom Geist der Liturgie* saw no less than 12 editions and 26,000 copies.[38] One must, however, bear in mind that his writings were also received in the circles of the then-nascent ecumenical movement.[39] Guardini wanted to educate participants toward a living concelebration of the Mass. He considered it necessary, "to study those actions that are still in present day use, those visible signs which believers have received and made their own and use to express the 'invisible grace.'" Guardini continued that this initially means a "liturgical education," not liturgical scholarship, "we need to be shown

---

33 See Peter Ebenbauer, *Mehr als ein Gespräch: Zur Dialogik von Gebet und Offenbarung in jüdischer und christlicher Liturgie*, Paderborn, Schöningh, 2010, 24f.; see also Peter Ebenbauer, "Jüdischer Gottesdienst im Urteil christlicher Theologie: Konstruktionen und Dekonstruktionen am Beginn und am Ende des 20. Jahrhunderts," in: Michael Konkel, Alexandra Pontzen & Henning Theißen, eds., *Die Konstruktion des Jüdischen in Vergangenheit und Gegenwart*, Paderborn, Schöningh, 2003, 223–239.

34 Ebenbauer, *Mehr als ein Gespräch*, 30.

35 Ebenbauer, *Mehr als ein Gespräch*, 32.

36 See Romano Guardini, *Von heiligen Zeichen*, 2 vols., Rothenfels a.M., Deutsches Quickbornhaus, 1922–1923; ET: *Sacred Signs*, trans. Peter Kwasniewski, Scotts Valley CA, CreateSpace, 2015.

37 See Romano Guardini, *Vom Geist der Liturgie*, Freiburg i.Br., Herder, 1918; ET: *The Spirit of the Liturgy*, trans. Ada Lane, New York NY, Crossroad, 1998.

38 See Stefan Waanders, "Zum Wesen der Liturgie: Anlässlich des 40. Todestages: Romano Guardinis Anstöße – Heutige Herausforderungen," 8; the text can be found at <https://fdokument.com/reader/full/zum-wesen-der-liturgie-anlaesslich-des-40-todestages-romano-> (accessed July 15, 2020); see also Stefan K. Langenbahn, ed., *Vom Geist der Liturgie: 100 Jahre Romano Guardinis "Kultbuch" der Liturgischen Bewegung, Begleitpublikation zur Ausstellung in Maria Laach, Heiligenkreuz Hochschule Benedikt XVI., Burg Rothenfels, Trier, Köln und München*, Cologne, Erzbischöfliche Diözesan- und Dombibliothek mit Bibliothek St. Albertus Magnus, 2017.

39 See Gunda Brüske, "Liturgische Bewegung und Ökumene: Ein Beitrag zur Vorgeschichte des Ökumenischen Arbeitskreises evangelischer und katholischer Theologen," in: Christoph Böttigheimer & Huber Filser, eds., *Kircheneinheit und Weltverantwortung: Festschrift für Peter Neuner*, Regensburg, Pustet, 2006, 555–575, here 557 and 558–563 for a consideration of the Catholic liturgy from the perspective of Lutheran theology.

how, or by some means incited, to see and feel and make the sacred signs ourselves."[40]

Casel and Guardini never came to an agreement either on what "popular devotion" meant or on what it was. For Guardini, the relationship between liturgy and popular devotion was certainly very important, but he wondered which role certain practices of piety, such as private prayer alongside the liturgy, should play. Guardini, and Jungmann with him, were firm in defending the preeminence of the liturgy over *pia exercitia*, without depriving them, however, of their meaning. This can be seen by the fact that, with his booklets on the Way of the Cross and the Rosary, Guardini, in a certain sense, nurtured these devotional forms,[41] which were categorically rejected by Casel and other exponents of the liturgical movement who believed they should recognize only the validity of the objectivity of the liturgy and not of piety, which was subjective in nature. In their opinion, the liturgy should instead nourish a new piety.[42]

Like Guardini, Pius Parsch was also able to reach an extensive audience in the German-speaking area through a Volksliturgisches Apostolat (Popular Liturgical Apostolate) that included intense publicity campaigns and numerous conferences. His works have been translated into many languages and also welcomed outside Europe. With his demand for active participation, which he thought of as true coparticipation, albeit linked to the idea of the laity's subordination to the clergy, Parsch

went far beyond the position of the theologians mentioned so far. In one of his most important works, he wrote: "We do not exhort ... passive participation but, plainly, the people's active participation in the liturgy. The liturgy is not a theatrical performance staged by the priest or the clergy, which the people are only called to hear or see."[43] Parsch expressed the people's actions within the liturgy with the verbs co-celebrate (*Mitfeiern*), co-sacrifice (*Mitopfern*), and co-pray (*Mitbeten*), concluding with the necessity, therefore, to be "co-participants in the liturgically acting church."[44] He warned against confusing the tasks and roles of the priest with those of the congregation, referring to the "Greek Mass"[45] in which the difference between the action of the priest and that of the community was prudently maintained, without limiting either one or the other in their proper acts.[46] On the basis of this conception, Parsch's idea differed from the traditional *Teilliturgie*, which, by accentuating the distinction of the roles of the celebrant and the faithful, made the active contribution of the congregation lessen.

It cannot be ignored, however, that, for Parsch, the priest was a mediator between God and humanity and therefore also between God and the community, a conception that had many repercussions on his very concept of the liturgy. For Parsch, the priest stands "in the middle and,

---

40   Guardini, *Sacred Signs*, 9.

41   See Arno Schilson, "Romano Guardini und die Liturgische Bewegung: Aspekte einer spannungsvollen Beziehung," in Klemens Richter & Arno Schilson, eds., *Den Glauben feiern: Wege liturgischer Erneuerung*, Mainz, Matthias-Grünewald, 1989, 49–77, here 67–69; Gunda Brüske, "Romano Guardini (1885–1968)," in: Kranemann & Raschzok, eds., *Gottesdienst als Feld*, 418–431, here 428f.

42   See Stephan Wahle, "Heimatlich und bodenständig: Zur Ästhetik der Volksfrömmigkeit," in: Guido Schlimbach & Stephan Wahle, eds., *Zeit – Kunst – Liturgie: Der Gottesdienst als privilegierter Ort der Ästhetik*, Aachen, Einhard, 2011, 27–36.

43   Pius Parsch, *Volksliturgie: Ihr Sinn und Umfang*, Klosterneuburg, Volksliturgischer Verlag, 1940, 102. The second edition, published in Vienna in 1952, has been recently reprinted: Pius Parsch, *Volksliturgie: Ihr Sinn und Umfang*, Würzburg, Echter, 2004. The following references the first edition.

44   Parsch, *Volksliturgie*, 102.

45   See Sabine Maurer, "Ökumenische Dimensionen im Denken und Wirken von Pius Parsch: Auf dem Weg zur una sancta ecclesia mit den 'Griechen,' in *Bibel und Liturgie* 1–21 (1926/27–1953/54)," in: Andreas Redtenbacher, ed., *Liturgie als Gnade und Rechtfertigung: Pius Parsch und die Liturgische Bewegung in ökumenischer Perspektive*, Freiburg i.Br., Herder, 2018, 106–130.

46   Parsch, *Volksliturgie*, 103.

reaching out one hand towards God and the other towards humanity, he reunites them. ... Therefore, he should be God and human at the same time, and he would then be the legitimate mediator."[47] Parsch thus considered the priest to be the representative of Christ and therefore head of the church, its Body. Despite all the inner tension in his theology, Parsch must still be credited with having clearly outlined, on the theological and practical levels and thanks to key concepts such as "popular liturgy," the need for the community's active participation in the liturgical act.

Parsch's consideration of the Sacred Scripture is of ecumenical relevance. Like other theologians of the time,[48] he also saw a connection between the liturgical movement and the biblical movement. He was hence in favor of a greater familiarity between believers and the Sacred Scripture, also committing to this on an ecumenical level,[49] attributing new meaning to homiletic preaching. Parsch called the first part of the celebration (what we call today the Liturgy of the Word) the rite of introduction, thus attributing to it a new meaning. For Parsch, who believed that with the private Mass the rite of introduction had become "fossilized,"[50] in so-called liturgical education[51] the "height of the Word of God" became particularly important. From this point of view, the rite of introduction was to be an "encounter with God in the Word."[52]

In Parsch, therefore, we can see, in contrast to a clerical image of church and liturgy, and despite all the aporias mentioned, the affirmation of a communal conception of the Mass that called traditional ecclesiology into question. In it, the church is constituted by the parish, where its belonging to the mystical Body of Christ becomes concretely manifest. In short, we could say with Parsch that a living parish community must be built from the baptistery and the altar.[53] Finally, even in the case of the Leipzig Oratory, the community of the faithful and their participation in worship were the pillars of the liturgical and pastoral program, with the addition of an unprecedented correlation between liturgical practice and social action, as could only be the case in a parish community largely consisting of workers.[54]

4   Implementing Liturgical Renewal: Liturgical Space and New Forms of Celebration

The reconfiguration of areas dedicated to the liturgy was carried out by influential architects of the time thanks to a continual dialogue with theologians of the liturgical movement, which was highly significant. Notable, once again in the German context, were the names of the architects

---

47   Parsch, *Volksliturgie*, 205.

48   See Benedikt Kranemann, "Bibel und Liturgie in Wechselbeziehung: Eine Perspektivensuche vor historischem Hintergrund," *BL* 80, 2007, 205–217, here 205f. with comparisons. See also Jörg Ernesti, *Ökumene im Dritten Reich*, Paderborn, Bonifatius, 2007, 38, 52f., 58, 62f., which also publishes as a source the transcription of the lecture delivered by Parsch at the ecumenical conference in Hermsdorf in 1943, 73f.; see also Brüske, "Liturgische Bewegung."

49   See Pacik, "Pius Parsch (1884–1954)," 895.

50   Parsch, *Volksliturgie*, 391.

51   See Parsch, *Volksliturgie*, 376–402.

52   Parsch, *Volksliturgie*, 391.

53   See Roman Stafin, *Eucharistie als Quelle der Gnade bei Pius Parsch: Ein neues Verhältnis zwischen Gott und dem Menschen*, Würzburg, Echter, 2004, 41–46; Boleslaw J. Krawczyk, *Der Laie in Liturgie und Theologie bei Pius Parsch*, Würzburg, Echter, 2007, 98–108.

54   See Andreas Poschmann, *Das Leipziger Oratorium: Liturgie als Mitte einer lebendigen Gemeinde*, Leipzig, Benno, 2001; Andreas Poschmann, "Klosterneuburg und Leipzig – zwei Zentren der liturgischen Bewegung," *HID* 58, 2004, 133–141. See also Klemens Richter, "Liturgie und Seelsorge in der katholischen Kirche seit Beginn des 20. Jahrhunderts," in: Klemens Richter, *Feiernde Gemeinde: Die Identität der Kirche und ihr Gottesdienst – eine Aufsatzsammlung*, eds. Benedikt Kranemann, Thomas Sternberg & Martin Stuflesser, Münster, Aschendorff, 2015 [¹1990], 35–56.

Dominikus Böhm,[55] Rudolf Schwarz,[56] and Martin Weber.[57] They were inspired by the seminal article "Christozentrische Kirchenkunst" by the priest Johannes van Acken, whose image of the ecclesial space started from the mystical Christ, therefore from the altar, and who saw the liturgical area as a place of community celebration. Consistent with this fundamental approach, the church's altar was to be located in the space intended for the community and, during the liturgy, the congregation's orientation was to correspond to the direction of prayer "per Christum ad Deum."[58] With these few but clear concepts in mind, in 1922, Böhm and Weber conceived an ideal plan that they called "Circumstantes,"[59] placing the altar at one of the building's focal points within an elliptical layout, preferably on an island, in order to permit the faithful to gather around it in a semicircle.[60]

Rudolf Schwarz, who created some of the important features of Rothenfels Castle, was one of the most incisive architects in redefining the liturgical area in harmony with the new guidelines emerging in the field. The Knights' Hall room (*Rittersaal*) in Rothenfels, which was used to host celebrations with a large number of participants, was left deliberately white and unadorned so that nothing distracted the faithful from the ongoing liturgical event. The seats consisted of black stools that could be arranged in different ways according to the needs and number of participants. Numerous sources of light also made variable lighting scenarios possible in order to infuse the environment with different shades depending on the type of gathering. In the chapel, the altar stood in a raised position near the wall, while a large, ring-shaped chandelier shed its light around forming a white circular space. In this chapel, the liturgical congregation was able to gather around the altar in the form of a semicircle and, in the Knights' Hall, in the form of a closed circle. Schwarz distanced himself from the concept of Christocentric church space, "stopping at the Christ symbolized on the altar,"[61] as he said, because for him ecclesial space was a "world on the threshold" and thus the present. Mass was to be understood in a theocentric sense, and space was to be thought of correspondingly.

There were also monasteries that, as we have seen, were the main centers from which liturgical reform was promoted, and which included its architectural variant. For example, the walls of the crypt of Maria Laach's abbey church (*Krypta-Messe*) were adorned with early Christian symbols, and Mass was celebrated around a table, as in the ancient Roman basilicas. Particular importance was also attached to the participation of all the celebrants in the offertory procession, as if to express a kind of collective participation in the Eucharistic sacrifice; in addition, the priest celebrated the community

---

55   See Ralf van Bühren, "Moderner Kirchenbau als Bedeutungsarchitektur: Die Lichtkonzeption Dominikus Böhms (1880–1955) als Ausdruck einer mystagogischen Raumidee," in: Hans Körner & Jürgen Wiener, eds., *"Liturgie als Bauherr"? Moderne Sakralarchitektur und ihre Ausstattung zwischen Funktion und Form*, Essen, Klartext, 2010, 241–256.

56   See Walter Zahner, *Rudolf Schwarz, Baumeister der neuen Gemeinde: Ein Beitrag zum Gespräch zwischen Liturgietheologie und Architektur in der Liturgischen Bewegung*, Altenberge, Oros, 1992.

57   See Adrian Seib, *Der Kirchenbaumeister Martin Weber (1890–1941): Leben und Werk eines Architekten für die liturgische Erneuerung*, Ph.D. thesis, Johann-Wolfgang-Goethe-Universität, 1996; Mainz, Selbstverlag der Gesellschaft für Mittelrheinische Kirchengeschichte, 1999.

58   See Herbert Muck, *Sakralbau heute*, Aschaffenburg, Pattloch, 1961, 54.

59   See Walter Zahner, "Raumkonzepte der Liturgischen Bewegung," in: Albert Gerhards, Thomas Sternberg & Walter Zahner, eds., *Communio-Räume: Auf der Suche nach der angemessenen Raumgestalt katholischer Liturgie*, Regensburg, Schnell & Steiner, 2003, 70–94, here 74f. with commentary.

60   Thus Zahner, "Raumkonzepte," 76f.

61   Albert Gerhards, "Bauen als 'Aussage religiöser Poesie': Ein theologischer Blick auf Rudolf Schwarz," in: Rudolf Schwarz, *Kirchenbau: Welt vor der Schwelle*, eds. Maria Schwarz, Albert Gerhards & Josef Rüenauver, Regensburg, Schnell & Steiner, 2007, xiii–xix, here xv.

Mass *versus populum*, which was a central aspect of the abbey's liturgical life.[62]

The place where Mass was held in the parish institute of youth assistance of the Leipzig Oratory was instead a renovated stable. Its celebrants sat in a semicircle with the ambo at its center and the altar on the outside. Tables covered with white cloth were set up for communion while the wall behind the altar was left bare as a sign of the coming of Christ.[63]

Architectural features of this kind were extraordinarily important for the Catholic Church in Germany and had a considerable impact on the liturgy, extending the possibilities for the community to participate in worship and, in many cases, influencing the very mentality of the clergy and the faithful. Indeed, it is no exaggeration to say that the redefinition and expansion of areas of worship established during this period, implicitly calling the traditional conceptions linked to the liturgy and the church into question, in a certain way anticipated the openings and progress in the liturgical and ecclesial field sanctioned decades later by Vatican II. Seeing the ecclesial and liturgical space as a symbol of collective identity,[64] it is normal that, by reshaping the former, the latter would be reflexively redefined. This process in many cases led to looking beyond confessional borders. It suffices to think of the importance, in Protestant buildings of worship, of cardinal concepts such as the renunciation of monumentality and the centrality of the congregation, concepts that could not fail to constitute a model for the pioneering innovations experienced in the German-speaking Catholic world long before the process of liturgical reform initiated by Vatican II.[65]

The aim of these new architectural conceptions was to give formal expression to a battle that had long been fought for suitable forms of liturgy, especially with regard to the celebration of the Mass. In the late 19th and early 20th centuries, this was limited to providing the faithful with translations of liturgical texts so that they could join the priest in reading the liturgy, as evidenced by the popular missals of the Benedictines Anselm Schott and Urbanus Bomm. The challenge then became the breaking down of any kind of barrier that would prevent the community's full involvement in the liturgy. Rothenfels Castle was invariably a site of experimentation, but the churches of St. Gertrude in Klosterneuburg, that of Leipzig-Lindenau, and the crypt of the abbey church of Maria Laach were all places where community participation was made concrete in the liturgy. Similar experiments also took place in various institutes dedicated to the spiritual care of young people and students.[66] Beyond celebrating the Liturgy of the Hours (including Compline for the youth), these experiments concerned especially the celebration of Mass, but also, for example, the Easter Vigil.

The guiding principle was, given the impossibility of changing the rites, that the focus should shift to concentrating on the forms of participation. For example, in the *missa recitata*, the priest might happen to recite all the texts, including the readings, in Latin, and then, if possible, he would also proclaim them again (in a low voice) in German while a reader transcribed them aloud into the language of Goethe. For its part, the congregation

---

62 See Martin Conrad, "Die 'Krypta-Messe' in der Abtei Maria Laach: Neue Untersuchungen zu Anfang, Gestaltungsformen und Wirkungsgeschichte," *ALw* 41, 1999, 1–40.

63 See Poschmann, *Das Leipziger Oratorium*, 133–139.

64 Klaus Raschzok, "'… geöffnet, für alle übrigens' (Heinrich Böll): Evangelische Kirchenbauten im Spannungsfeld von Religion und Gesellschaft," in: Hanns Kerner, ed, *Lebensraum Kirchenraum: Das Heilige und das Profane*, Leipzig, Evangelische Verlagsanstalt, 2008, 17–36, here 24. Extensively on this theme, see Klaus Raschzok, "Kirchenbau und Kirchenraum," in: Hans-Christoph Schmidt-Lauber, Michael Meyer-Blanck & Karl-Heinrich Bieritz, eds., *Handbuch der Liturgik: Liturgiewissenschaft in Theologie und Praxis der Kirche*, Göttingen, Vandenhoeck & Ruprecht, ³2003, 391–412, here 396–398.

65 See Raschzok, "'… geöffnet, für alle übrigens,'" 21f.

66 See Hans J. Limburg, "Zur Meßfeier in einer 'Erziehungsanstalt' 1921–1931: Missa recitata und ein heimeigenes Meßbüchlein im Jugendheim 'Johannesburg,'" *ALw* 43–44, 2001–2002, 72–96.

recited the chants of the *proprium* and the *ordinarium* in Latin. This was, in fact, the form that the German High Mass (*Deutsches Hochamt*) assumed in the course of time. In the *missa dialogata*, the faithful answered in Latin, but instead of the *ordinarium* and *proprium* the faithful sang hymns. The priest also celebrated the so-called *Betsingmesse* (prayed and sung Mass) in Latin, while a reader pronounced the texts in German. It should be recalled that these forms were experimented and practiced in open contradiction to liturgical law.[67] Rome only reappraised the practice of the spoken and sung Mass between 1943 and 1944, granting bishops the freedom to express their discretionary judgment on the matter.[68] In 1942, some guidelines for the liturgical structure of the parish Mass had already been published in Germany, and in 1947, a regulation for celebrating the Mass as a people's liturgy appeared in Austria.

The liturgical language was certainly not a secondary problem, even if Latin, while contested, was not yet generally rejected. Those who had declared themselves in favor of Latin did so in the name of the need to preserve the universal language of the church and, above all, to defend the unity of Catholics from nationalistic tendencies that were emerging in Germany; these were also feared since they might infiltrate the church through the liturgical movement's demands for the use of German. On the other hand, advocates of the national language used the criterion of comprehensibility and the demand for a liturgy that was upheld by the congregation.[69] In the new editions of diocesan

rituals or liturgical books, the vernacular was used to a greater extent, albeit unevenly.

This context concerns the many attempts made to renew sacred music, also aiming to involve the faithful in the congregation actively and consciously.[70]

All the attempts at liturgical renewal implemented up to this point, even in their experimental and pioneering aspect, had a very clear set of objectives. Essentially, they aimed to encourage a greater involvement, to varying degrees, of the congregation and, with it, of the faithful in their entirety in order to increase the intensity of the celebration and, through a better understanding of the texts, to establish clear symbolic acts. In all these cases, it was never mere liturgical practice that was at stake but always the faith of the people, which was to be strengthened through the liturgy, thus implying a renewal of ecclesiology.

5   A Liturgical Movement in Orthodoxy?

It may seem paradoxical that the Orthodox Churches of the Byzantine tradition, which accord primacy to liturgical life, have not experienced a liturgical movement similar to the Catholic one. To a certain extent, this impression arises from an error of perspective. In the eyes of Catholic

---

67   One important public event was the liturgical celebration during the Allgemeiner Deutscher Katholikentag held in Vienna, Sept 7–12, 1933. A *Betsingmesse* was held for about 200,000 faithful. On this point, see Lerch, *Modernisierung durch Kulturkritik*.

68   See Haunerland, "Liturgische Bewegung," 185; see also Rudolf Pacik, "Aktive Teilnahme des Volkes an der Messe: Die von Pius Parsch entwickelten Modelle," *HID* 58, 2004, 122–132. It is clear that among the various forms there were regional differences.

69   For an example of a journal's contribution to the discussion, see Annika Bender, "Programm und Rezeption

der Liturgischen Bewegung im Spiegel der 'Liturgischen Zeitschrift,'" *ALw* 51, 2009, 311–333, here 325–330.

70   See Theo Hamacher, "Der kirchliche Volksgesang," in: Karl G. Fellerer, ed., *Geschichte der Katholischen Kirchenmusik*, vol. 2, *Vom Tridentinum bis zur Gegenwart*, Kassel, Bärenreiter, 1976, 294–307; Philipp Harnoncourt, *Gesamtkirchliche und teilkirchliche Liturgie: Studien zum liturgischen Heiligenkalender und zum Gesang im Gottesdienst unter besonderer Berücksichtigung des deutschen Sprachgebiets*, Freiburg i.Br., Herder, 1974, 358–366; Andrea Neuhaus, *Das geistliche Lied in der Jugendbewegung: Zur literarischen Sakralität um 1900*, Tübingen, Francke, 2005; Rudolf Pacik, *Volksgesang im Gottesdienst: Der Gesang bei der Messe in der Liturgischen Bewegung von Klosterneuburg*, Klosterneuburg, Österreichisches Katholisches Bibelwerk, 1977; Thomas Labonté, *Die Sammlung "Kirchenlied" (1938): Entstehung, Corpusanalyse, Rezeption*, Tübingen, Francke, 2008.

observers, the Orthodox Church embodied "the liturgical spirit of the ancient church" and had no need of a liturgical movement since it would "never stray, in its piety, from its liturgical offices."[71] This conviction corresponded to a romantic vision of the Orthodox Church, in which the West saw "a mirror of its deepest desires."[72] In reality, the Orthodox liturgical tradition itself needed to be rediscovered and renewed.

In 1918, the year in which *Vom Geist der Liturgie* by Romano Guardini was published, Pavel Alexandrovich Florensky held a series of public lectures on the philosophy of worship in Moscow.[73] Although it is not possible to speak of a mutual influence, there is no lack of points of convergence, for example: the liturgy's symbolic structure and its "mysteric" character, the derivation of culture from worship (*cultus*), the social dimension of the liturgy, and the link between liturgy, mental prayer, and spirituality. Florensky's intention was clearly philosophical ("to express not worship in terms of philosophy but philosophy in terms of worship"),[74] but his reflection was part of the lively debate on the liturgy in the Russian Orthodox Church at the turn of the century, which found an outlet in the 1917–1918 Council of

Moscow. Alongside the developments in liturgical studies in theological institutes,[75] mention should be made of the popular and devotional movement initiated by the Presbyter Ivan Ilyich Sergiev (St. John of Kronstadt), the "prophet of Eucharistic rebirth."[76] The most visible features of that campaign were the frequent practice of communion, collective confession, and an intense diffusion of liturgical and Eucharistic piety. It should also be mentioned that liturgical experiences within fraternities of Christian life flourished at the beginning of the century.[77]

After the Bolshevik revolution, the establishment of a regime that was openly hostile to the Orthodox Church forcibly interrupted the council, and all plans for reform were suspended. Florensky's work on the liturgy, most of which was published posthumously,[78] could not be considered

---

71 Olivier Rousseau, *Histoire du mouvement liturgique: Esquisse historique depuis le début du XIXᵉ siècle jusqu'au pontificat de Pie X*, Paris, Cerf, 1945, 188.

72 Robert F. Taft, "L'apport des liturgies d'Orient à l'intelligence du culte chrétien," in: Paul De Clerck, *La liturgie, lieu théologique*, Paris, Beauchesne, 1999, 97–123, here 101.

73 He continued to work on his course text until 1922: Pavel A. Florensky, *Sobranie Sochinenij: Filosofiya kulta* [Collected works: Philosophy of the cult], ed. Andronik (Trubachev), Moscow, Mysl, 2004. There is an Italian translation: *La filosofia del culto*, ed. Natalino Valentini, Cinisello Balsamo, San Paolo, 2016, from which the quotations are drawn.

74 Florensky, *La filosofia del culto*, 179. Florensky saw in the liturgical action the coincidence of meaning and being, "the unity of transcendence and immanence, of the intellectual and the sensible, of the spiritual and the bodily," which the Kantian critiques had broken up. "The roots of the visible are in the invisible … and worship is the fixed point of the universe" (243).

75 Feodor (Pozdeevsky), rector of the Moscow Theological Academy held that liturgical theology "must be studied as the living and uninterrupted confession of the whole Orthodox church in its history"; cited in Hyacinthe Destivelle, *Les sciences théologiques en Russie: Réforme et renouveau des académies ecclésiastiques au début du XXᵉ siècle*, Paris, Cerf, 2010, 757; see also Hyacinthe Destivelle, "Prémisses d'une ecclésiologie eucharistique dans la théologie russe à la fin du XIXe siècle et au début du XXe Siècle," in: Jean-Marie Van Cangh, *L'ecclésiologie eucharistique*, Paris, Cerf, 2009, 115–136.

76 See Boris Sove, "Prorok evkharisticheskogo vozrozhdeniya" [The prophet of the Eucharistic rebirth], in: Aleksandr G. Kravetskij, "Tri stati B.I. Sove" [Three articles by B.I. Sove], *Tserkovno-Istoricheskij Vestnik* 6–7, 2000, 155–171, in particular 168–171. On John of Kronstadt, see Nadieszda Kizenko, *A Prodigal Saint: Father John of Kronstadt and the Russian People*, University Park PA, Pennsylvania State University Press, 2003.

77 See Natalija Ignatovič, "'Siamo operatori di pace e saremo riconosciuti tuoi figli': Nikolaj Nepljuev (1851–1908) e la sua Fraternità ortodossa di lavoro," in: Luigi d'Ayala Valva, Lisa Cremaschi & Adalberto Mainardi, eds., *Beati i pacifici: Atti del XXII convegno ecumenico internazionale di Spiritualità ortodossa, Bose, 3–6 settembre 2014*, Magnano, Qiqajon, 2015, 251–262.

78 Along with *Filosofiya kulta*, his essay on the icon should be mentioned, written between 1919 and 1922, it was first published in journals and then as a book: Pavel A. Florensky, "Ikona" [Icon], *Vestnik Russkogo*

at the time it was written. The issues raised at the Council of Moscow were nevertheless taken up by the theologians of the Russian Orthodox diaspora in the West, who helped develop them in fruitful association with Catholic and Protestant studies. The liturgy, as a field of study and as ecclesial experience, would be one of the prerequisites of some ecumenical initiatives involving the Orthodox, such as the Fellowship of St. Alban and St. Sergius[79] and the liturgical weeks of the Institute de thèologie orthodoxe Saint-Serge of Paris.

In the Greek context, the Zoe (life) movement, founded by the monk Eusebios Matthopoulos, brought the questions of participation in the Eucharist, frequent communion, and community practice of liturgical offices to the foreground. Even if the identitarian connotation and a distrust of the "West" that had been inherited from Apostolos Makrakis prevented the movement from being ecumenical, Zoe's experience was of great ecclesial and cultural importance.[80] John Meyendorff considered it "the most lively and active body of the entire modern Greek Church," appreciated

its effort to revive liturgical life, and saw in it an organic realization of the Orthodox "liturgical movement, of which many of us dream, entirely accomplished without fanfare or unhealthy emotions, in accord with the tradition of the Church."[81]

In the Romanian context, we can recall the rediscovery of the liturgy in the limited but intense experience of the Rugul Aprins (Burning Bush) movement from 1943 to 1958.[82] In 1930, the Inter-Orthodox Preparatory Committee, convened by the Ecumenical Patriarch Photius II to plan for the future pan-Orthodox council, included a series of liturgical themes in the list of topics to be discussed, from calendar reform to the unification of the *Typikon*.[83] At the beginning of the 1960s, Alexander Schmemann would take an initial stock of the relationship between Orthodoxy and the liturgical movement, identifying, "the uninterrupted liturgical tradition in the Orthodox Church, on the one hand, and the intense liturgical interest and research of the West, on the other" as "a twofold basis for the creative shaping of an Orthodox liturgical theology."[84]

Before examining the contours of liturgical awakening in Orthodoxy during the first half of the 20th century, it is important to mention the bi-ritual experiences within Benedictine monasticism that lie at the intersection between liturgical

---

Zapadno-Evropejskogo Patriarshego Ekzarkhata 65, 1968, 39–64; "Ikonostas" [Iconostasis], *Bogoslovskie trudy* 9, 1972, 82–148; *Ikonostas*, Moscow, 1994; ET: *Iconostasis*, trans. Donald Sheehan & Olga Andreijev, Crestwood NY, St. Vladimir's Seminary Press, 1996. See also the course held at the Moscow Theological Academy in 1921 on the Christian conception of the world: Pavel A. Florensky, "Kulturno-istoricheskoe mesto i predposylki khristianskogo miroponimaniya" [The historical-cultural dimension and presuppositions of the Christian view of the world], in: *Sochineniya v chetyrekh tomakh* [Works in four volumes], vol. 3/2, Moscow, Mysl, 2000, 386–488; and finally his articles "Khramovoe dejstvo, kak sintez iskusstv," *Makovets* 1, 1922, 28–32; ET: "The Church Ritual as a Synthesis of the Arts," in: Pavel Florensky, *Beyond Vision: Essays on the Perception of Art*, ed. Nicoletta Misler, trans. Wendy Salmond, London, Reakton Books, 2002, 95–112; and "Christianity and Culture," *The Pilgrim: A Review of Christian Politics and Religion* 4, 1924, 421–437.

79   See Dimitris Salapatas' contribution in the second volume of this work.

80   See Yannis Spiteris, *La teologia ortodossa neo-greca*, Bologna, EDB, 1992, 191–224.

---

81   John Meyendorff, "Zoi," *Vestnik RSChD* 43, 1956, 45–48, here 47.

82   See André Scrima, *Timpul Rugului Aprins: Maestrul spiritual în tradiția răsăriteană* [The era of the Burning Bush: the spiritual father in Eastern tradition], Bucharest, Humanitas, 1996.

83   At the meeting in Vatopedi (June 8–23, 1930), all the Orthodox Churches were present, except the Russian Orthodox Church, unable to participate for political reasons, and the Bulgarian and Albanian Orthodox Churches, who were not invited because they were then in schism with the Ecumenical Patriarchate. See Viorel Ioniță, *Towards the Holy and Great Synod of the Orthodox Church: The Decisions of the Pan-Orthodox Meetings since 1923 until 2009*, Fribourg, Institute for Ecumenical Studies, 2014, 16–21.

84   Alexander Schmemann, *Introduction to Liturgical Theology*, Crestwood NY, St. Vladimir's Seminary Press, 1975, 13.

renewal, rediscovery of the Christian East, and the awakening of an ecumenical awareness.

6 The Liturgical Movement and the Christian East

Lambert Beauduin's "monastic work for the unity of the churches" has already been treated elsewhere;[85] therefore, just a few comments on the complementarity between liturgical practice and ecumenical commitment will suffice here. For Beauduin, his encounter with *pietas anglicana* during his exile in World War I, his knowledge of the liturgies of the Eastern Catholic Churches and Russian exiles during his years of teaching at the Benedictine College of St. Anselm (1921–1925), and his contacts with the Metropolitan of Halych, Andrey Sheptytsky, signified not only the discovery of a rich liturgical heritage, but also the confidence to ask bold questions. Was it possible to deny full ecclesial reality to churches that celebrate in such a beautiful and traditional way? If participation in the heavenly liturgy was shared, what did the divisions in the pilgrim church mean?

Beauduin clearly saw the interdependence among liturgical formation, monastic life, and working for unity. The guidelines for a new foundation, "Une œuvre monastique pour l'Union des Églises,"[86] were presented as a "commentary" to a letter from Pius XI, who had given the project permission to continue (*Equidem verba*, Mar 21, 1924), but in fact extended its horizons. "I wonder if the Romans' intention, contrary to yours, is not to found a house of *missionaries*," Dom Maïeul Cappuyns had warned him.[87] Perhaps the

clarification between the formation of missionaries and the preparation of "workers for definitive reconciliation"[88] was precisely the way of understanding and living liturgical prayer. Was it not Leo XIII himself who referred to the Benedictines as "men of prayer and of the liturgy"?[89]

The monastic Liturgy of the Hours practiced by the same community in both the Latin and Byzantine-Slavic rites was not a missionary expedient but the very principle of "bringing the West and the East closer together in prayer."[90] "The great prayer of the church, the daily liturgy, ... will become an everlasting echo of the Master's priestly prayer: *ut unum sint*."[91] It will be one and the same community celebrating the complete *cursus* of the two main Christian liturgical traditions, practicing the asceticism of prayer as an exercise of knowing one another, of listening, and of a progressive removal of psychological reserves. The tension of unity implicit in the original intuition of monasticism thus discovered a different horizon in comparison to the unionist ideal that still animated Metropolitan Andrey Sheptytsky's monastic project.[92]

Lambert Beauduin was well aware of the difficulties. Monks who knew the Eastern languages and liturgy perfectly had great difficulty in finding

---

85 See the essay by André Haquin in this volume. Here we use the exhaustive monograph by Raymond Loonbeek & Jacques Mortiau, *Un pionnier: Dom Lambert Beauduin (1873–1960): Liturgie et unité des chrétiens*, 2 vols., Louvain-la-Neuve, Éditions de Chevetogne, 2001.

86 Lambert Beauduin, *Une œuvre monastique pour l'Union des Églises*, Leuven, Abbaye du Mont-César, 1925.

87 Maïeul Cappuyns to Lambert Beauduin, December 1923, draft, AMC, M. Cappunys, 1, cited in: Loonbeek

& Mortiau, *Un pionnier*, 382–383 (italics original).

88 Beauduin, *Une œuvre*, 12.

89 Beauduin, *Une œuvre*, 13. Dom Lambert refers to an account of Leo XIII's audience with the students of the new Sant'Anselmo's College sent by one of its auditors, Dom Urbain Baltus, a monk of Maredsous Abbey, to his father superior. Lambert Vos, "L'activité œcuménique du monastère de Chevetogne," in: Donato Giordano, ed., *Il ruolo del monachesimo nell'ecumenismo: Atti del Simposio Ecumenico Internazionale*, Siena, Abbazia di Monte Oliveto Maggiore, 2002, 175–191, here 176. This account was mentioned to Dom Lambert by Olivier Rousseau: Loonbeek & Mortiau, *Un pionnier*, 348–349.

90 Beauduin, *Une œuvre*, 22.

91 Beauduin, *Une œuvre*, 17.

92 See Andrey Sheptytsky, "La mission du monachisme dans la question de l'union des Églises," *Stoudion* 1, 1923, 9–12 e 33–40; Andrey Sheptytsky, "Le rôle des occidentaux dans l'œuvre de l'union des églises," *Stoudion* 6, 1926, 153–169.

a suitable way of practicing the Byzantine rite. The Latin monks themselves had not always been initiated into the authentic spirit of the liturgy, and even in their personal spiritual life were asked to put the church's fundamental worship before "many less theologically based devotions."[93] Beyond any external diffusion, such liturgical practice "would still be indispensable for the inner development of our ecumenical ideal."[94] The fulcrum of a Christian and monastic life is participating in the mysteries of Christ during the cycle of the liturgical year, centered around Easter. This led to the revaluation of Sunday, the "ideal ecumenical day" because "all divided Christians, Catholics, Orthodox, Lutherans, Calvinists, find themselves united in spite of everything to celebrate the weekly Easter."[95] "In Amay, the Lord's day must take on its ancient character."[96] In the *liturgia horarum*, lauds and vespers, "the two poles of the day," are brought back to the foreground; in them the Psalms, biblical prayers *par excellence*,[97] are sung in their entirety while the hymns are simply recited.

Despite Dom Beauduin's desire for the community as a whole to participate in the same celebrations in the two rites, the constitutions imposed by the Holy See in 1928 introduced the obligation to celebrate the office in its entirety in either the Byzantine or the Latin rite. Moreover, internal pressure went in the same direction. The monks were divided into two distinct deaneries: one according to the Latin rite, the other according to the Byzantine-Slavic one. Shared participation was reduced to the Eucharistic liturgy on Sundays and feast days.[98] In fear of a greater separation, Beauduin always opposed the "wild exclusivism of a rite" (for example, he refused to introduce a separate refectory as a complement to Eastern liturgical observances). "Our ecumenicality must dominate ritual specificity ... and the fact of being the Latin rite must in no way diminish the understanding, the love, or the competence of the Byzantine rite."[99] The two rites were to have been practiced in a "supra-ritual" spirit, without privileging one over the other. Every monk, however, would choose liturgical and cultural stability in one of the two rites: it was a profound initiation into a spirituality and a liturgical tradition that involved the monk's entire human and spiritual life with no amateur approaches and without passions dictated by an abstract idealism.[100]

Beauduin had also realized that the work of unity was incompatible with the charitable outreach towards Russian exiles promoted by the Holy See. Mixing the two plans would, in fact, have caused confusion and painful misunderstandings.[101] That is why the Byzantine liturgy in Amay was "celebrated only for Catholics of the West." If any Orthodox wished to attend, in order to

---

93 Lambert Beauduin, "Jubilé du Monastère de l'Union (1925–1950)," *Irén* 23, 1950, 369–376, here 372.

94 Lambert Beauduin, "Mémoire sur l'œuvre d'Amay," Rapport à dom Théodore Nève, [24 mars] 1940, Archives de Sint-Andriesabdij, Th. Nève, 11, in: Loonbeek & Mortiau, *Un pionnier*, 670.

95 Lambert Beauduin, "Notes sur les coutumes d'Amay-Chevetogne," manuscript (ca. 1955), AAC, Beauduin, Amay, 1, d. 12, in: Loonbeek & Mortiau, *Un pionnier*, 675.

96 Lambert Beauduin, "Mémoire," 8, in: Loonbeek & Mortiau, *Un pionnier*, 675.

97 "The Psalter! Our Lord recited the Psalter! ... When one is imbued with the mentality of the psalms, one becomes universal"; Lambert Beauduin, "Retraite à Cormeilles, 1944," in: Loonbeek & Mortiau, *Un pionnier*, 678.

98 Loonbeek & Mortiau, *Un pionnier*, 673.

99 Lambert Beauduin to Ildefonse Dirks, s.l., Feb 6, 1940, AAC, Ildefonse Dirks, in: Loonbeek & Mortiau, *Un pionnier*, 673–674.

100 Lambert Beauduin to Mechtilde de Volder, Chevetogne, Dec 24, 1951, AMT, in: Loonbeek & Mortiau, *Un pionnier*, 671.

101 "It is quite natural that, alongside a sincere gratitude to those who have benefited the Russian people, in the Russian soul ... there dwells an equally deep bitterness, distrust, and suspicion towards those Catholics who take advantage of the situation of the emigrants in order to 'capture' the Orthodox in every way"; Vasily V. Zenkovskij, "Russkoe studencheskoe khristianskoe dvizhenie: Istoriya, deyatelnost, zadachi" [The Russian Christian student movement: History, activities, duties], *Vestnik RSChD* 7/8, 1949, 3–19 and 9/10, 1949, 21–33, here 21.

eliminate any suspicion of proselytism, they had to present the permission of their parish priest.[102]

Equidem verba also bore consequences for the development of the bi-ritual experience of the Benedictine abbey of Niederaltaich, which had reopened in 1918 with the help of Metten Abbey after being secularized in 1803. Under the guidance of Prior Emmanuel Heufelder,[103] the monastery's ecumenical outreach began in the 1930s, developing contacts with the East (especially Romania) and with all churches in collaboration with the founder of the Una Sancta movement, Max Josef Metzger.[104] The general chapter of the Bavarian Benedictine congregation of July 21–22, 1936, declared Niederaltaich a "monastery of unity" in accordance with the intentions of the papal letter (the decision was approved on June 8, 1937, by the Congregation for the Oriental Churches). In 1949, Niederaltaich became completely independent of Metten Abbey, and Emmanuel Heufelder was unanimously elected its new abbot. A Byzantine rite deanery was established for the daily Liturgy of the Hours and the Eucharistic liturgy within the community, thanks also to the entry of new confreres, including two Russians. In 1955, its first Byzantine chapel was built.

The experiences of Amay-Chevetogne and Niederaltaich represented an ecumenical ministry that had never lost its roots in the liturgy. Another initiative, both liturgical and ecumenical, that continued over time were the liturgical weeks at Saint-Serge. At the beginning of 1953, Archimandrite Cyprian (Kern), at Lambert Beauduin's suggestion, enlisted Dom Bernard Botte along with Nicholas Nikolayevich Afanasev and Dom Olivier Rousseau in organizing a week of liturgical studies at the Institute de thèologie orthodoxe Saint-Serge in Paris in which Orthodox, Catholic, Anglican, and Protestant experts

participated. While ecumenical meetings inevitably wound up sidelined on points of disagreement, was there not room for a different type of meeting, where the tradition of the church could be studied together? A return to the liturgical sources would make people "aware of what brings Christians closer more than what separates them from one another."[105]

On July 6, 1953, Dom Beauduin pronounced the introduction to the first liturgical week,[106] and the initiative's exceptional success decreed its continuation. After an interruption in 1956 for incidental reasons, the meetings resumed in 1957 with a thematic program: the liturgical year (1957), Christian initiation (1958), ordination (1959), the Paschal mystery (1960), the prayer of the church (1961), and so on. Beginning in 1963, the papers of the liturgical weeks began to be published each year in edited volumes. In the preface to the new publication, Bishop Cassian (Bezobrazov), the rector of Saint-Serge, recalled Cyprian Kern and Lambert Beauduin as tireless pioneers of the liturgical weeks, "a new form of ecumenical activity that God has blessed with his grace." Applying an objective method to the study of liturgical events revealed "a unity that transcends the barriers that history has raised among us." It was a vision that would not be lost "on the eve of the Vatican Council."[107]

---

102   "Déclaration," *Irén* 3, 1927, 312.

103   See *Hören sein Wort: Festgabe für Abt Emmanuel M. Heufelder zum 70. Geburstag*, Niederaltaich, Dreiberg-Verlag, 1968.

104   On Metzger, see also Paul Metzlaff's contribution in this volume.

105   Bernard Botte, "Introduction," in: Monseigneur Cassien & Dom Bernard Botte, eds., *La prière des heures*, Paris, Cerf, 1963, 9–13, here 10.

106   Lambert Beauduin, "La messe en Oriente et en Occident" (typewritten manuscript), AAC, Lambert Beauduin 13/6. "Votre présence personnelle," writes Cyprian Kern on Dec 20, "a particulièrement contribué au succès de cette première rencontre liturgiques," in: Loonbeek & Mortiau, *Un pionnier*, 1439–1440. See also *Irén* 26, 1953, 308–310.

107   Cassien, "Preface," in: Cassien & Botte, eds., *La prière des heures*, 7–8.

7   Liturgical Reform at the Local Council of the Russian Orthodox Church of 1917–1918

The attention paid to liturgy by Russian diaspora theologians had its roots in the short but intense preparation of the council in prerevolutionary Russia. The Moscow Council of 1917–1918 represented the culmination of a long process of spiritual and ecclesial renewal that sought to respond to the revolutionary activity and the development of Russian society.[108] In the aftermath of the Revolution of 1905, Emperor Nicholas II authorized a convocation of the council, and the Holy Synod invited the episcopate to send their requests for the future council meeting.[109] A considerable number of the bishops' proposals touched upon liturgical problems of vital importance for the Russian Church: the use of Russian in the liturgy (Old Church Slavonic had become incomprehensible to the majority of the faithful), the revision of the Liturgy of the Hours (the *ordo* in force in the parishes, regulated by the *ustav* of 1682, was a monastic one and could not be celebrated in its entirety), the reform of the *ordo* of Eucharistic celebration and the lectionary, the correction of liturgical books, a more active liturgical participation of the people, and so on.[110]

On each of these issues, ecclesial public opinion, expressed by priests, bishops, and the laity, was divided into a wide range of positions, from more conservative ones, which defended the immutability of tradition (the use of Old Church Slavonic, strict respect for the *ordo*), to progressive ones, which asserted the goal of liturgical action, the sanctification of the people of God, and the need for wider participation and effective missionary outreach. Among the proposals were the "Russification" or the translation of the liturgy (especially biblical readings), a prudent reduction of the Liturgy of the Hours in parishes (to avoid arbitrariness and abuse), the reading of the Gospel *coram populo*, and the recitation of the Eucharistic prayer aloud. Some dioceses had ventured into partial solutions, but general expectations and hopes were placed in the future council, which was to increase the historical and theological understanding of the issues raised, formulating shared and viable pastoral solutions.

After the abdication of Tsar Nicholas II, when the council could finally be held, the growing hostility towards the Orthodox Church due to the revolutionary climate changed its agenda. Priority had to be given to the most urgent decrees that would ensure the church's survival in conditions of persecution. Liturgical issues, while attracting the greatest interest among the delegates, became secondary matters. The commission on the liturgy, preaching, and worship buildings, which was presided over by Metropolitan Evlogij (Georgievsky), continued to hold sessions, although its final report could not be discussed in the plenary assembly. Most of the experts' reports, minutes of the discussions, and drafts of the decrees still to be approved have, by now, been published.[111] The topics discussed included: (1) liturgical singing and music; (2) icon painting and liturgical art; (3) the problem of liturgical language; (4) calendar reform; (5) problems connected to the liturgical *ordo* (*typikon*) and the Eucharistic liturgy; and (6) the canonization of saints. The forced interruption of the council meant that only part of the relevant decrees was approved.

---

108   See Hyacinthe Destivelle, *La chiesa del concilio di Mosca (1917–1918)*, Magnano, Qiqajon, 2003; Hilarion Alfeev, ed., "Concilium Moscoviense – 1917–1918," in: COGD 4/2, 2016, 735–881.

109   *Otzyvy eparkhialnykh arkhiereev po voprosu o tserkovnoj reforme*, [Comments of the eparchal bishops on the question of liturgical reform] vol. 1–3, *Pribavleniya* [Supplement], St. Petersburg, Sinodalnaya tipografiya, 1906.

110   See Nikolay Balashov, *Na puti k liturgicheskomu vozrozhdeniyu* [Towards liturgical reform], Moscow, Kruglyj stol po religioznomu obrazovaniyu i diakonii, 2001.

---

111   Aleksandr G. Kravetskij, "Svyaschennyj Sobor Pravoslavnoj Rossijskoj Tserkvi: Iz Materialov otdela o bogosluzhenii, propovednichestve i khrame" [The Holy Synod of the Russian Orthodox Church: From the materials of the commission on the liturgy, preaching, and liturgical spaces], *Bogoslovskie trudy* 34, 1998, 200–388.

The conciliar constitution of Dec 1, 1917, insisted on the necessity that every Sunday celebration include a homily and admitted the possibility of entrusting this homily, "always with the blessing of the bishop and the authorization of the local priest," to "devout laymen capable of preaching" in addition to the clergy. These laymen would have to wear "the *stikhar* and would be called evangelizers (*blagovestniki*)."[112] The statute on parishes contained some clarifications of a liturgical nature, in particular on the importance of regular participation in the Sunday Eucharist and on the presence of all the faithful at the patronal celebration.[113] The council deliberated on a procedure for the canonization of saints,[114] while the important report on the "Language of the Liturgical Celebration" approved by the commission could not be promulgated but was sent by the assembly of bishops, chaired by Patriarch Tikhon (the council's "upper chamber"), to the higher ecclesiastical government. The document called for the translation of liturgical texts into Russian and Ukrainian on an experimental basis with the blessing of the ecclesiastical authorities in order to make the liturgical celebration more comprehensible to the faithful. Old Church Slavonic, in any case, remained the language of the liturgy. Patriarch Sergius (Stragorodsky) would appeal to this report in authorizing the celebration in Russian at a local level in 1935.[115] Several issues taken up at the council would be discussed within the Russian Orthodox diaspora in the 1920s and 1930s.

8   Reflection on the Liturgy in the Russian Diaspora and the Beginnings of Eucharistic Ecclesiology

Among the theologians of the Russian diaspora, the liturgy constituted an authentic laboratory of reflection on *Una Sancta* and a natural common ground with other Christians. Sergius Nikolaevich Bulgakov's participation in the World Conference on Faith and Order in Lausanne in 1927 was an experience of union with Christ in prayer, in the Word of God, in spiritual life, and in the recognition of a certain "sacramental communion" despite divisions.[116] In his address, he called the church a "worshipping fellowship," stating that unity in worship would be achieved "not so much through the common acceptance of liturgical forms as through the energy of love, drawn out by the irresistible attraction of spiritual beauty."[117] He then insisted on the veneration of the *Theotokos*, asking for a common doctrinal study on the issue. Bulgakov considered it "the central, though hidden, nerve of the entire movement towards reconciliation,"[118] and it was later included in the section on the "communion of saints" of the Edinburgh Conference in 1937 and mentioned in its final report.[119] Another Russian exile, present in Lausanne in the Bulgarian Orthodox Church's delegation, Nicholas Nikanorovitch Glubokovsky, did not hesitate to call the liturgy of the Word a "living

---

112   Alfeev, ed., "Concilium Moscoviense," 777, no. 2 (lines 1295–1305).

113   Alfeev, ed., "Concilium Moscoviense," 800, lines 2181–2184 and 2205–2210.

114   Constitution of 21 August (3 September) 1918: see Alfeev, ed., "Concilium Moscoviense," 860–861; see also Destivelle, *La chiesa del concilio*, 247 249.

115   See Adalberto Mainardi, "Il dibattito sulla lingua liturgica nella Chiesa ortodossa russa a cent'anni dal concilio di Mosca (1917–1918)," in: Slavia Barlieva & Marco Scarpa, eds., *Ezitsite na khristiyanskata molitva istoriya i savremennost – Lingue della preghiera cristiana: Storia e contemporaneità*, Sofia, Kirilo-Metodievski naučen centăr, 2018, 187–212.

116   Sergii Bulgakov, "U kladezya Iakovlya (In. 4,23): O realnom edinstve razdelennoj tserkvi v vere, molitve i tainstvakh" [At Jacob's Well: The real unity of the divided church, in faith, in prayer, and in the sacraments], in: *Khristianskoe vossoedinenie: Ekumenicheskaya problema v pravoslavnom soznanii* [Christian unity: The ecumenical problem in Orthodox conception], Paris, YMCA Press, 1933, 9–32.

117   Herbert Newell Bate, ed., *Faith and Order: Proceedings of the World Conference, Lausanne, August 3–21, 1927*, London, SCM Press, 1927, 208–209.

118   Sergius Bulgakov, "The Question of the Veneration of the Virgin Mary at the Edinburgh Conference," *Sobornost* 2, 1937, 28.

119   Leonard Hodgson, *The Second World Conference on Faith and Order Edinburgh, August 3–18, 1937*, New York NY, Macmillan, 1938.

communion with the Gospel," "a sacrifice of praise and thanks to God," whose frequency should not be less "than the daily breaking of bread among the first Christians."[120]

The evolution of the discussion on the liturgy can be traced through the journals of the Russian diaspora: *Put* (The Way), founded by Nicholas Berdyaev;[121] *Vestnik Russkogo Studencheskogo Khristianskogo Dvizheniya* (The Messenger of the RSCM);[122] and *Sobornost*, the bulletin of the Fellowship of St. Alban and St. Sergius.[123]

A new liturgical sensibility had developed within the RSCM.[124] In a conference held for the young people of the movement, Fr. Sergius Chetverikov, its spiritual leader, explained the Eucharist as "the center of Christian life." "The life of the church no longer has only a formal interest for us"; intellectual knowledge of the truth was not enough; the experience of ecclesial life in the shared liturgy, which revealed all the secret depths of the human heart, was necessary.[125] In early Christianity, in every Eucharistic celebration all those present received communion, testifying to the centrality of the Eucharist not only for individuals but for the entire Christian community. It was, however, a remote ideal, although "something similar" could be seen "with the Anglicans."[126]

In the debate over the Eucharistic celebration and frequent communion, alongside more traditional positions that emphasized the sacrificial aspect of the Eucharist,[127] others emerged that rediscovered the Eucharist as a sacrament of the church's "catholic" (*sobornoe*) unity (Nicholas Arsenev, Georges Florovsky, Boris Sove) and which began to question its ecclesiological implications (Nicolas Zernov, Nicholas Afanasev).

In his 1935 introduction to Orthodoxy, written for a Western audience, Sergius Bulgakov called the Orthodox liturgy "heaven on earth" (an expression from an ancient Russian chronicle), and "the manifestation of the beauty of the spiritual world"[128] (echoing Florensky's thought). The Orthodox liturgy "makes actual for us the mystery of the Incarnation." It recalls events that "are not simply commemorations, but they

---

120   Nicholas Glubokovsky, "The Church's Message," in: Herbert Newell Bate, ed., *Faith and Order: Proceedings of the World Conference, Lausanne, August 3–21, 1927*, Garden City NY, Doubleday, Doran & Co., 1928, 67–78, here 75–76.

121   See Antoine Arjakovsky, *La génération des penseurs religieux de l'émigration russe: La revue* La Voie (Put') *(1925–1940)*, Kiev-Paris, L'Esprit et la Lettre, 2002.

122   In 1927 the journal published an article on Amay by Andrej Lilienfeld, "Da budut vse edino" [That they may all be one], *Vestnik RSChD* 11, 1927, 17–20. An editorial note made it clear that the "'Monks of the Union of the Churches' had done so much to awaken the Catholic world to the beauty and the richness of Orthodoxy, their works are so filled with a spirit of loving understanding of the Orthodox Church, that we cannot refrain from praising this new movement in the Catholic Church" (17). The author, André de Lilienfeld, born Félix-Otto de Lilienfeld, from a noble Lutheran family, had converted to Catholicism in 1921 during a trip to France. In 1925, he entered the Benedictine abbey of Beuron and completed the novitiate at Amay, where he took his formal vows and was ordained a priest. From 1927 to 1928 he was the editor of *Irénikon*. He took care of Russian refugees in Brussels, and in 1933 obtained his exclaustration. In 1948 he became a Belgian citizen and was given the Croix de Guerre, the Médaille de la Résistance, and the Médaille Commémorative for his work in the resistance. He continued to write reviews for *Irénikon*, with the simple initial "A." (I would like to thank Lambert Vos, archivist of Chevetogne, for providing this information).

123   See Aidan Nichols, *Alban and Sergius: The Story of a Journal*, Leominster, Gracewing, 2018.

124   Zenkovskij, "Russkoe studencheskoe khristianskoe dvizhenie," 5.

125   Sergii Chetverikov, "Evkharistiya, kak sredotochie khristianskoj zhizni" [The Eucharist, center of Christian life], *Put* 22, 1930, 23–49.

126   Chetverikov, "Evkharistiya," 23.

127   Chetverikov defined the Eucharist as "the carrying out … of the expiatory sacrifice of Golgotha" ("Evkharistiya," 13); Florensky has a similar understanding (*La filosofia del culto*, 235–236).

128   Sergius Bulgakov, *The Orthodox Church*, trans. Lydia Kesich, Crestwood NY, St. Vladimir's Seminary Press, 1988, 129. Archimandrite Cyprian (Kern) defined the liturgy as "a peculiar world of unspeakable beauty"; see "Sobornaya molitva" [Common prayer], *Vestnik RSChD* 7, 1927, 7.

happen again in the Church."[129] The sacred building embodies the "Sophianicity" of the universe: not the Gothic striving toward the transcendent, but a "feeling of life in the house of the Father," the theanthropic union "between divine and human." It is the "transcendent that descends," concretely expressed in the architecture of the dome of the Hagia Sophia in Constantinople.[130] Bulgakov took up the traditional criticism of the Latin liturgy (the absence of the epiclesis in the anaphora, the exclusion of the laity from communion under the two species, Eucharistic adoration)[131] and justified the marginality of preaching in the Orthodox liturgy (an aspect criticized at the Council of Moscow), citing the abundance of teachings contained in the Orthodox liturgy with respect to the "liturgical poverty" of Protestant worship.[132]

A few years earlier, Bulgakov had spoken on frequent communion, commenting on a thesis promoted by a professor at the Saint Petersburg Theological Academy, Fr. Nicholas Nalimov.[133] The custom in the Russian Church not to take communion more than once or twice a year was linked to the severity of the penitential procedure for access to communion (John of Kronstadt remained an exception). Bulgakov looked favorably on the awakening of "a salvific thirst for frequent communion," of which Fr. Nalimov was "one of the most daring preachers," on the condition of "an incessant martyrdom for the faith."[134] However, Bulgakov considered it harmful to loosen Eucharistic discipline for the laity by admitting them to daily communion like the clergy.

Nalimov argued that subordinating access to communion to confession meant taking the Christian away from Christ.[135] Bulgakov objected that liberalizing the practice would weigh on the conscience of the believer with an unbearable burden, introducing an element of arbitrariness into the theology of confession.[136] He thus suggested resorting to "spiritual communion" and the "manducation of the (unconsecrated) Eucharistic bread, the prosphora, which has no correspondent in the Western Mass."[137] Despite the fact that Nalimov's proposal was justified by the specific historical conditions, according to Bulgakov, it could be criticized on theological grounds because he had forgotten that, between the laity and the Eucharistic sacrifice, "there is the priest," without whose mediation "the manducation of the sacrificial victim is not possible."[138]

Bulgakov would continue his reflections on the Eucharist in two other essays published in *Put'*.[139] To the Latin theology of transubstantiation, the Russian theologian opposed the Orthodox idea of participation in the glorious body of the Lord, which contained both the sacrifice of the cross and the mystery of glorification. "*Ascending* from the earthly condition of the body to the glorious and risen condition, the Lord does not annul that condition ... but includes it in His Divine Humanity."[140] "In this world and for the life of this world, bread and wine remain bread and wine. Their transposition [*perelozhenie*, μεταβολή] is not physical in

129 Bulgakov, *The Orthodox Church*, 130.

130 Bulgakov, *The Orthodox Church*, 130.

131 Bulgakov, *The Orthodox Church*, 134.

132 Bulgakov, *The Orthodox Church*, 135.

133 "Tezisy dokladov o sovremennoj pokayannoj distsipline professora petrogradskoj dukhovnoj akademii protoiereya o. Nalimova" [Theses from the lectures on the contemporary practice of confession by Archpriest Nalimov, professor of the Theological Academy of Petrograd], *Put'* 18, 1929, 79–87; the response of Bulgakov: "K voprosu o discipline pokayaniya i prichascheniya" [On the disciplinary issue of confession and communion], *Put'* 19, 1929, 70–78.

134 Bulgakov, "K voprosu o distsipline," 72.

135 "Tezisy dokladov," 84–85.

136 Bulgakov, "K voprosu o distsipline," 76.

137 Bulgakov, "K voprosu o distsipline," 73.

138 Bulgakov, "K voprosu o distsipline," 77.

139 Sergii N. Bulgakov, "Evkharisticheskiy dogmat" [The dogma of the Eucharist], *Put'* 20, 1930, 3–46, and 21, 1930, 3–33; Sergii Bulgakov, "Svyatoj Graal (Opyt dogmaticheskoj ekzegezy: In. 19,43)" [The Holy Grail – An experiment in dogmatic exegesis: Jn 19:43], *Put'* 32, 1932, 3–42.

140 Bulgakov, "Evkharisticheskij dogmat," *Put'* 20, 1930, 44.

nature, but metaphysical."[141] The authentic perspective for understanding Eucharistic dogma is a "sophianic" and kenotic one: the Lord, the new Adam, establishes "a perfect spiritual interpenetration of the body." Christ's humbling (*kenosis*) is the non-correspondence between divinity and human corporeality, while his glorification is "the re-establishment of the correspondence between divine and human nature."[142] To the younger generation of theologians, Bulgakov's sophiology, like Chetverikov's Eucharistic spirituality, could not be reconciled with what could be drawn from a study of the Eucharistic sources of the early church from an ecclesiological point of view.

In the representative collection of essays *Problemy russkogo religioznogo soznaniya* (Problems of the Russian religious mind) published by YMCA Press in 1924, Nicholas Arsenev submitted an article on the "Sacrament of the Eucharist in the Life of the Church."[143] His analysis of ancient anaphoras, drawing extensively on the work of Frank Edward Brightman,[144] James

Herbert Srawley,[145] Anton Baumstark,[146] Gillis Peterson Wetter,[147] Odo Casel,[148] Fernand Cabrol, and others highlighted the eschatological dimension, placing it in relation to the Slavophile ecclesiology of *sobornost*. The Eucharistic anaphora expresses the authentic "spirit of catholicity [*sobornost*], the natural bond of fraternity that, in a single act of prayer and thanksgiving to God, unites with one another all believers, living and dead, the whole church, triumphant and earthly, and even more, all of creation."[149] The Eucharist brings about the unity of the body of the church, embracing "the distant and the near, what is above and below, in a union of love through the God-Man" (with reference to Eph 2:14 and Col 1:20).[150]

Georges Florovsky also interpreted the Eucharist as the mystery of *sobornost*, the mystery of the church, but he sought its foundations in the church fathers (John Chrysostom, Symeon of Thessalonica, and Nicholas Cabasilas).[151] According to Chrysostom, the church is a kind of "fullness" (τὸ πλήρωμα, Eph 1:23) of Christ, who is the head of his body. "The Body of Christ, the church, becomes, is fulfilled, in time."[152] It is in the Eucharist that the faithful become the Body of Christ. It is "the sacrament of the Church, 'the sacrament of the congregation' [*sobranie*] (μυστήριον συνάξεως), 'the mystery of communion' (μυστέριον κοινωνίας)."[153] It is true ontological unity, the

141   Bulgakov, "Evkharisticheskij dogmat," *Put* 21, 1930, 6.

142   Bulgakov, "Evkharisticheskij dogmat," *Put* 21, 1930, 28–29.

143   Nikolay Arsenev, "Tainstvo evkharistii v zhizni tserkvi" [The Sacrament of the Eucharist in the Life of the Church], in: Nikolay Berdyaev, ed., *Problemy russkogo religioznogo soznaniya* [Problems of the Russian religious conscience], Berlin, YMCA Press, 1929. Arsenev devoted great attention to the liturgical movement in Germany (Guardini, Herwegen and the Maria Laach Abbey, Michels, Casel, and others), which he felt was close to Orthodoxy since it penetrated the "pathos of Christian realism" and the "recognition of the value of matter and body, sanctified by the incarnation of the God-Man." See Nikolay Arsenev, "Sovremennie techeniya v katolichestve i protestantizme v Germanii" [Contemporary Currents in Catholicism and Protestantism in Germany], *Put* 1, 1925, 161–68.

144   Frank Edward Brightman, *Liturgies: Eastern and Western*, vol. 1, *Eastern Liturgies*, Oxford, Clarendon Press, 1896.

145   James Herbert Srawley, *The Early History of the Liturgy*, Cambridge, Cambridge University Press, 1913.

146   Anton Baumstark, *Die Messe im Morgenland*, Kempten, Kösel, 1906; Anton Baumstark, *Vom geschichtlichen Werden der Liturgie*, Freiburg i.Br., Herder, 1923.

147   Gillis Peterson Wetter, *Altchristliche Liturgien*, 2 vols., Göttingen, Vandenhoeck & Ruprecht, 1921–1922.

148   Odo Casel, *Das Gedächtnis des Herrn in der altchristlichen Liturgie: Die Grundgedanken des Messkanons*, Freiburg i.Br., Herder, 1920.

149   Arsenev, "Tainstvo," 383–384.

150   Arsenev, "Tainstvo," 385.

151   Georges Florovsky, "Evkharistiya i sobornost," [Eucharist and sobornost] *Put* 19/11, 1929, 3–22.

152   Florovsky, "Evkharistiya i sobornost," 4.

153   Florovsky, "Evkharistiya i sobornost," 7.

realization of the one life in Christ. "The Eucharist is the catholic sacrament, the sacrament of peace and love, and therefore of unity. It is the *mysterium pacis et unitatis nostrae*, in the words of St. Augustine."[154]

Florovsky reread the patristic texts through the lens of the Slavophile ecclesiology of *sobornost*, but he "reoriented" it, centering it on the Eucharistic celebration. If Eucharistic communion is the "apex of ecclesial unity," then it is necessary that the whole congregation should participate in it, since "the Eucharistic celebration is, above all, communal and shared prayer [*sobornaya*], *publica et communis oratio*, as St. Cyprian of Carthage says."[155] The "we" of the praying congregation is not a grammatical plural, but expresses the spiritual unity of the church present, the indivisible *sobornost* of Eucharistic prayer. Florovsky drew a fruitful consequence from this for advancing Eucharistic ecclesiology: each "little church" was not only a part of, but also the concrete image of the whole Church, inseparable from its unity and fullness. That is why in every liturgy, in a mysterious but real way, the whole Church is present and shared.[156] The rediscovery of the Eucharist as a sacrament of church unity was not without consequences for rethinking the "separation of the Christian world, the division at the Eucharistic table," and the painful mystery of the laceration of the one, seamless robe of the Lord, his body: "Only love can overcome this division, the love of Christ who acts in us through the spirit of peace."[157]

The attention to patristic literature invited a comparison between liturgical practice as witnessed by ancient sources and contemporary practice, and posed new questions. Boris Sove, one of the first graduates of the Institute de thèologie orthodoxe Saint-Serge in Paris where he returned to teach after completing his studies at Oxford and the United States, linked the study of the early Christian tradition to the actual liturgical practice in the Russian Church from the 18th to the 20th centuries.[158] In addition to the problem of the correction of liturgical books,[159] Sove devoted his attention to the transformations in Eucharistic practice.[160] The study of the most ancient Eucharistic prayers revealed their fundamental ecclesial value. Ancient testimony, from Justin Martyr to John Chrysostom and Maximus the Confessor showed that the Eucharistic liturgy is the "shared work" (*sobornoe delo*) of the church. From the congregation, the presider receives the assent to share the work of prayer ("it is right and just") and "the whole community seals the Eucharistic prayer with the shared and solemn *Amen*."[161]

Sove was one of the first to emphasize the role of the laity (the people) in the Eucharistic celebration and refocused his theological reflection on the universal priesthood. The Eucharistic prayer "fulfilled the first communal action … one of the most important duties not only of the hierarchy, but also of all the members of the Church … 'a chosen race, a royal priesthood, a holy nation' (1 Pt 2:9, anaphora of St. Basil the Great) because, in the Church of Christ …

---

154 Florovsky, "Evkharistiya i sobornost," 8.

155 Florovsky, "Evkharistiya i sobornost," 9. See also Cyprian (Kern), "Sobornaya molitva," 7–9.

156 Florovsky, "Evkharistiya i sobornost," 14.

157 Florovsky, "Evkharistiya i sobornost," 22.

158 He dedicated his doctoral thesis to this problem: *Istoriya russkoj liturgiki* [History of Russian liturgical studies], defended in 1951 at Saint-Serge. The text has not been found: Kravetskij, "Tri stati B.I. Sove," 156.

159 Finished in 1940, it was published posthumously: Boris Sove, "Problema ispravleniya bogosluzhebnykh knig v Rossii v XIX–XX vekakh" [The problem of the correction of liturgical books in Russia in the 19th and 20th centuries], *Bogoslovskie trudy* 5, 1970, 25–68.

160 Boris Sove, "Evkharistiya v drevnej Tserkvi i sovremennaya praktika" [The Eucharist in the early church and modern practice], in: *Zhivoe predanie: Pravoslavie v sovremennosti* [Living tradition: Orthodoxy in modernity], Paris, YMCA Press, 1937 (reprinted in Moscow, Svyato filaretovskaya moskovskaya vysshaya pravoslavno-khritianskaya shkola, 1997, 194–222). It was also published in *Vestnik RSChD*, 1938, 2–3.

161 Boris Sove, "Sobornoe delo Tserkvi" [The common work of the church], *Tserkovno-Istoricheskij Vestnik* 6–7, 2000, 160. The article is not dated, but certain references suggest the end of the 1930s. See Sove, "Evkharistiya," 197.

the universal priesthood is made real."[162] The problem of frequent communion was thus gradually repositioned from a disciplinary and devotional terrain, as was still the case in Chetverikov and even Bulgakov, to an ecclesiological one. The communion of everyone at every liturgy was the norm in the ancient church, Sove recalled, tracing the evidence from the Council of Antioch in 341 to the Slavic *Kormchaya kniga* (canonical collection) of 1787 with the comments of Zonara and Aristenos (excommunication for those who are not "at Holy Communion until the end").[163] In the end, the introduction of reading the anaphora in a low voice eventually brought about the progressive weakening of liturgical life among God's people. The deplorable consequences for contemporary practice are the introduction of an element of community division (between the clergy and laymen), aggravated by the "sin of infrequent communion," which dissolves the *sobornost*, the shared work of the church, visible in the separate communion of ordained ministers and the people.[164] The Eucharistic liturgy thus takes second place to other parts of the liturgical cycle, and communion becomes rare. Making the preparation (*govenie*) and the sacrament of confession prerequisites for communion was a practice of monastic origin that replaced the insistence on frequent communion by church fathers from Cyril of Jerusalem to John Cassian, to Metropolitan of Kiev Ioann II and Symeon of Thessalonica.[165] Among the signs indicating a "revitalization of the communal dimension

[*sobornost*] in the church's Eucharistic life, similar to the powerful liturgical movement in the West,"[166] Sove noted the frequent communion practiced in Soviet Russia by Fr. Nalimov: the path of spiritual rebirth entailed a recognition of the "responsibility to participate communally [*soborno*] in the liturgy" in order to return a "catholic voice [*sobornym golosom*], ... to the characteristics of ancient liturgies, which had been obscured in Christians' minds ... but which were attested to in the liturgical books of the Holy Church."[167]

On the ecclesiological level, the consequences of the rediscovery of the Eucharistic practice of the early church would be brought to light by Nicholas Afanasev in a series of works that came together in his *Tserkov Dukha Svyatogo*.[168] Beyond the issue of Afanasev's ecclesiology and his sources,[169] we can distinguish three lines of reflection that have encouraged its development: the ecumenical problem and the meaning of church

---

162 Sove, "Evkharistiya," 197.

163 Sove, "Evkharistiya," 202.

164 Sove, "Evkharistiya," 214.

165 Sove, "Evkharistiya," 217. Sove had defended similar theses at the conference organized by the Anglican Walter Frere in April 1936 at the Community of the Resurrection in Mirfield, which was attended by Anglican theologians (including Gregory Dix, Lionel Thornton, Leonard Hodgson, John Albert Douglas) and Russian theologians (Bulgakov, Fedotov, Florovsky, Kartashev, Zernov, Zander): "Proceedings of the Conference at Mirfield between Anglican and Russian Orthodox Theologians: From the Community of the Resurrection," *Sobornost* 8, 1936, 44–48.

166 Sove, "Evkharistiya," 219.

167 Sove, "Evkharistiya," 221.

168 Nikolay Afanasev, *Tserkov Dukha Svyatogo*, Paris, YMCA Press, 1971; ET: *The Church of the Holy Spirit*, ed. Michael Plekon, trans. Vitaly Permiakov, Notre Dame IN, University of Notre Dame Press, 2007.

169 In particular Rudolph Sohm, *Kirchenrecht*, vol. 1, *Die geschichtlichen Grundlagen*, Munich, Duncker & Humblot, 1892: see the review by Louis Bouyer in *Istina* 21/1, 1976, 97–101; see also Élisabeth Behr-Sigel, "L'Église du Saint Esprit du Père Nicolas Afanassieff," *Contacts* 28/95, 1976, 263–269. More generally: André Joos, "Comunione universale o cattolicità dell'assemblea: Elementi di ecclesiologia negli scritti del P. N.N. Afanassiev," *Nicolaus* 1, 1973, 7–47 and 223–260; Peter Plank, *Die Eucharistieversammlung als Kirche: Zur Entstehung und Entfaltung der eucharistischen Ekklesiologie Nikolaj Afanas'evs (1893–1966)*, Würzburg, Augustinus-Verlag, 1980; Nicolas Koulomzine, "L'ecclésiologie eucharistique du Père Nicolas Afanassieff," in: *La liturgie: Son sens, son esprit, sa méthode, Liturgie et théologie, Conferences Saint-Serge, XXVIIIe semaine d'études liturgiques, Paris, 30 Juin–3 Juillet 1981*, Rome, Edizioni Liturgiche, 1982, 209–224; Aidan Nichols, *Theology in the Russian Diaspora: Church, Fathers, Eucharist in Nikolai Afanas'ev (1893–1966)*, Cambridge, Cambridge University Press, 1989.

unity, Eucharistic renewal, and the historic situation of the Orthodox Church.

The first outline of what would be Eucharistic ecclesiology appeared in a seminal article in 1934: "Dve idei vselenskoj tserkvi" (Two conceptions of the universal church).[170] It was Bulgakov who recommended its publication to Berdyaev, although he did not agree with its thesis. The coldness of the reception of Bulgakov, his spiritual father, led Afanasev to return to the history of the councils, broadening and increasing his understanding.[171] He believed that he had identified a gap in church tradition between the 3rd and 4th centuries when the juridical idea of the universal church, modeled on the notion of the *ecumene* (the boundaries of the empire) gradually replaced the ecclesiology

that was attested to in the New Testament and was based upon the intimate relationship between the sacramental body and the ecclesial body (1 Cor 10:16–17) such that the entire Catholic Church was present in the Eucharist celebrated by the entire community gathered around its bishop. The earliest ecclesiology, which Afanasev would define as "Eucharistic," found expression in the letters of Ignatius of Antioch, while the new paradigm was inaugurated by Cyprian of Carthage. The two ecclesiologies corresponded to two visions of church unity. While Cyprian, who witnessed the diffusion of Christianity throughout the empire, placed the unity of the church ("connexa et ubique conjucta unitas catholicae ecclesiae," *Epistle* 55.24) in the concord of bishops (*concors numerositas*), the concrete realization of the convergence (*compago*) of the ecclesial body, for Ignatius the fullness of the Catholic Church resided in the local community celebrating the Eucharist. "Just as the whole Christ is present in the Eucharistic sacrifice, so also in each ecclesial community resides the fullness of the Body of Christ. Hence the Ignatian idea that 'Where Jesus Christ is, there is the Catholic Church' (Ignatius, *Epistle to the Smyrnaeans*, 8.2)."[172] The local church is *one* because it has only *one* altar, that is, there is one Eucharistic congregation because there is only one bread and one cup. Conversely, Cyprian, transposing the Pauline doctrine of the Body of Christ composed of many members (1 Cor 12:12–13, 27) to the ecclesial level, made each individual ecclesial community a member (part of) the Body of Christ. The one church throughout the world is actually divided into many members ("una ecclesia per totum mundum in multa membra divisa est," *Epistle* 55) and its unity is represented by "the totality of these individual ecclesial communities,"[173] consisting in

---

170 Nikolay Afanasev, "Dve idei vselenskoj tserkvi," [Two conceptions of the universal church] *Put* 45, 1934, 16–29.

171 See Marianne Afanassieff, "La genèse de 'L'Église du Saint-Esprit,'" in: Nicholas Afanassieff, *L'Église du Saint-Esprit*, Paris, Cerf, 1975, 17–18. Afanasev worked on the councils from 1927 on (see Nikolay Afanasev, *Državna vlast na văseljienskim saborima* [Governmental power at the ecumenical councils], Skopje, 1927; Nikolay Afanasev, "Vselenskie sobory: Po povodu 'Obrascheniya k pravoslavnym bogoslovam'" [The ecumenical councils: Regarding "the call to Orthodox theologians"], *Put* 25, 1930, 81–92; Nikolay Afanasev, "Provintsialnye sobraniya Rimskoj imperii i vselenskie sobory: K voprosu ob uchastii gosudarstvennoj vlasti na vselenskikh soborakh" [The provincial assemblies of the Roman Empire and the ecumenical councils: On the question of the participation of the governmental power in the ecumenical councils], in: *Zapiski Russkogo Nauchnogo Instituta v Belgrade* 5, 1931, 25–46). His book on the councils, which he never finished, was recently published: Nikolay Afanasev, *Tserkovnye sobory i ikh proiskhozhdenie* [Church councils and their origins], Moscow, Svyato-Filaretovskij Pravoslavno-Khristianskij Institut, 2003. The title was given by his widow, Mariamna. Only the first part of the manuscript (251 pages), written in the years 1936–1939 and typed with commentary by Mariamna (106 typed pages), was ready for publication. The second part (chapters 5 and 6), also written in 1939–1940, on the 3rd century councils and the era of Cyprian of Carthage, remains in draft form (Afanasev, *Tserkovnye sobory* 179–180).

172 Afanasev, "Dve idei," 25. The quotations from the letters of Ignatius of Antioch here and below are taken from the translation in: Cyril C. Richardson, *Early Christian Fathers*, New York NY, Simon & Schuster, 1996.

173 Richardson, *Early Christian Fathers*, 17.

the episcopate, whose "concord" became a postulate. In this way, however, the Eucharist no longer represents the totality of the Catholic Church, but only an incomplete part of it.

Nicolas Zernov had already drawn attention to the ecumenical significance of Cyprian's turning point.[174] "Until Cyprian, the community and its life was considered the source of grace and the way to salvation. ... St. Cyprian turned the whole body of the church upside down, placing the hierarchy at the top."[175] Zernov located the limit of Cyprian's doctrine, never fully accepted by the church, not so much in the historical failure of the episcopate's unanimity, but in its desire to determine clearly the boundaries of the church with disciplinary criteria that left no room for the work of the Spirit.[176] For Afanasev, the change that occurred with Cyprian was more radical and involved the very idea of church. Roman doctrine would complete the model of Cyprian's universalistic ecclesiology, placing the bishop of Rome at the top of the episcopate. In order to do so, the incursion of law into the original experience of the Eucharistic congregation was necessary. This is what happened with the imperial church, where the notion of "ecumenical/universal" (within the *limes* of the empire) overlapped with that of "catholic." Along these lines although in different ways, both Rome and Constantinople pursued a "universal primacy over the universal ecumenical church."[177] Yet even Orthodoxy's fragmentation into the autocephalous churches of the modern era on the basis of nationality had not, after all, abandoned the juridical-universalistic conception of the church, which was reproposed in the "form of a national ecclesial imperialism."[178] Afanasev could see this effect in the Council of Moscow of

1917–1918, which defined the diocese (that is, the local church) as "a *part* of the Russian Orthodox Church, canonically administered by the diocesan bishop."[179]

This also explains the paradox that the Catholic Church, which attributes to itself a universal vocation, did not participate in the ecumenical movement: the reason lay precisely in its universalist conception. For Afanasev, the solution was not to oppose the papacy to the ecumenical council (the council itself, to be convened, presupposes the idea of primacy),[180] but to rethink the idea of the church's catholicity from its very roots, basing it not on the juridical principle of universality, nor even on the romantic ideal of *sobornost*, but on the reality of the Eucharist. Ignatius's formula, "where the bishop is present, there let the congregation gather" (*Epistle to the Smyrnaeans*, 8.2), approximately corresponded to Cyprian's "ecclesia in episcopo est et episcopus in ecclesia est." For Ignatius, however, this bond between the bishop and his community is effected through the Eucharist: "Be careful, then, to observe a single Eucharist. For there is one flesh of our Lord, Jesus Christ, and one cup of his blood that makes us one, and one altar, just as there is one bishop along with the presbytery and the deacons" (Ignatius, *Epistle to the Philadelphians*, 4).[181]

Rethinking the church in the light of the Eucharist meant rethinking it as a sacrament of communion with Christ. At the same time, it meant taking seriously the whole ecclesiological depth of Eucharistic renewal, without reducing it to a devotional act. This was Afanasev's central thesis, which

---

174   Nikolay Zernov, "Sv. Kiprian Karfagenskij i edinstvo vselenskoj tserkvi" [St. Cyprian of Carthage and the unity of the universal church], *Put* 39, 1933, 16–29.

175   Zernov, "Sv. Kiprian," 28.

176   Zernov, "Sv. Kiprian," 36.

177   Afanasev, "Dve idei," 23.

178   Afanasev, "Dve idei," 24.

179   Constitution of the Holy Synod of the Russian Orthodox Church on the eparchial administration (February 1918), ch. 1, §1: see Alfeev, ed., "Concilium Moscoviense," 756, lines 462–463 (italics mine); Afanasev, *Tserkovnye sobory*, 25. See also Nicholas Afanassieff, "L'Église qui préside dans l'amour," in: Nicholas Afanassieff & others, *La primauté de Pierre dans l'Église orthodoxe*, Neuchâtel, Delachaux et Niestlé, 1960, 7–64, here 11.

180   See Afanassieff, "L'Église qui préside," 20–21.

181   Afanasev, "Dve idei," 26.

he developed in 1952 in *Trapeza Gospodnya* (The Lord's Supper). The celebration of the Eucharist in the same place (επὶ τὸ αὐτὸ) lay at the origin of early ecclesiology. The celebration of the Eucharist in the community required that the faithful be "always everyone and always together."[182] The idea that, during the Eucharistic celebration, it might be possible for some to have spiritual communion (which Bulgakov still defended) was completely alien to authentic Orthodox theology. "There is no congregation in the church without concelebration but there is no concelebration without the congregation either. There is no banquet without participants and neither are there participants without the one who presides."[183] From this rediscovery of ancient practice also derived the persuasion that a possible liturgical reform should first of all distinguish "the immutable basis of our liturgical life from that which has penetrated it arbitrarily" in order to restore the "meaning of what the Church accomplishes" in its entirety.[184] In practice, the principle "always everyone and always together" had become its contrary, "not everyone and never together."[185]

In Afanasev's view, the historical situation of Orthodoxy, which had suffered the dissolution of the tsar's Orthodox empire and the chaotic canonical fragmentation of the diaspora, was paradoxically a favorable time to return to an authentic "catholic" understanding of the church, which despite the distortions of the Constantine era "had never been erased from Orthodox dogmatic consciousness." Even "Orthodoxy's historical weakness," the development of local churches, might prove its strength if the local church were founded on the true catholicity of the church.[186] Orthodoxy's growing role in the ecumenical

sphere, which revealed its authentic universal vocation, testified to this.[187]

9 Conclusions

It is possible to draw some conclusions. If until the 1960s, for contingent reasons (persecution in Russia, the dispersion of the diaspora and the political weakness of the ecumenical patriarchate), there was no liturgical movement in the Orthodox sphere comparable to the Catholic one, particularly the one that took place in the German-speaking countries, reflection on the liturgy by the Russian diaspora theologians was never lacking but entered into fruitful dialogue with the liturgical movement in the Protestant and Catholic spheres. It had the same objectives, with the Monastery of Amay-Chevetogne acting as a catalyst. Both the Catholic and Orthodox liturgical movements, in fact, aimed at responding to the need to renew the participation of the faithful in the liturgy, rediscovering their fundamental role at the ecclesiological level.

In this context, the rereading of ancient sources in Protestant and Catholic studies led to the Orthodox rediscovery of a "Eucharistic" ecclesiology as an answer to the question of the meaning of church "unity," which first flanked and then replaced the ecclesiology of *sobornost* inherited from Aleksey Stepanovich Khomyakov. There was a paradigm shift in what was beginning to take shape as Orthodox "liturgical theology." Liturgy was no longer read through a philosophical lens as a manifestation or incarnation of eternal "spiritual beauty" (an interpretation shared by Florensky and Bulgakov), but began to be studied in its historical development as the place where the sacrament of the church is fulfilled. The concept of *sobornost*, therefore, was progressively removed from an idealistic interpretation (which Bulgakov had borrowed from Khomyakov) and brought back to the original idea of "convocation" (*sobor*):

---

182   Nikolay Afanasev, *Trapeza Gospodnya*, Paris, YMCA Press, 1952; French translation: Nicolas Afanassieff, "Le repas du Seigneur," *Contacts* 68, 256, 2016, 445–571, here 450.

183   Afanassieff, "Le repas," 446.

184   Afanassieff, "Le repas," 447–448.

185   Afanassieff, "Le repas," 532–533.

186   Afanasev, "Dve idei," 29.

187   Afanasev, "Dve idei," 24.

the call of the faithful, those "called" (κλητοὶ) to the Eucharistic assembly, the *ekklesía*.

The Catholic liturgical movement not only gave life to new interpretations of the liturgy in a theological sense, in part already received by the papal Magisterium in the first half of the 20th century, but also stimulated experimentation with new forms of celebration that expressed, on the ritual level, the rediscovery of community participation in the liturgy.

The orientation of the Catholic liturgical movement would finally be taken up by the liturgical constitution of Vatican II and further developed, subsequently, both theologically and pastorally in the process of postconciliar reform.

In the same way, the Eucharistic ecclesiology that Afanasev developed in the 1950s and 1960s would be partly accepted by Vatican II,[188] in which Afanasev himself participated as an observer.[189] Theologians such as Alexander Schmemann and John Meyendorff, protagonists of the rebirth of Orthodox liturgical thought in the second half of the 20th century, would follow in his footsteps. The rereading of Afanasev's thought by a theologian such as John Zizioulas, who criticized his localism

without denying the intuition that the entire life of the church is shaped by the Eucharist, would open up new possibilities for ecumenical dialogue.

Translated from Italian to English by Susan Dawson Vásquez and David Dawson Vásquez.

Bibliography

Bärsch, Jürgen & Benedikt Kranemann, eds., *Geschichte der Liturgie in den Kirchen des Westens: Rituelle Entwicklungen, theologische Konzepte und kulturelle Kontext*, vol. 2, *Moderne und Gegenwart*, Münster, Aschendorff, 2018.

Bulgakov, Sergius, *The Orthodox Church*, trans. Lydia Kesich, Crestwood NY, St. Vladimir's Seminary Press, 1988.

Florensky, Pavel A., *Sobranie Sochinenij: Filosofiya kulta*, ed. Andronik (Trubachev), Moscow, Mysl, 2004.

Loonbeek, Raymond & Jacques Mortiau, *Un pionnier: Dom Lambert Beauduin (1873–1960): Liturgie et unité des chrétiens*, 2 vols., Louvain-la-Neuve, Éditions de Chevetogne, 2001.

Rousseau, Olivier, *Histoire du mouvement liturgique: Esquisse historique depuis le début du XIXᵉ siècle jusqu'au pontificat de Pie X*, Paris, Cerf, 1945.

Schmemann, Alexander, *Introduction to Liturgical Theology*, Crestwood NY, St. Vladimir's Seminary Press, 1975.

---

188   See Hervé Legrand, "L'ecclesiologie eucharistique dans le dialogue actuel entre l'Église Catholique et l'Église Orthodoxe: Convergences atteintes et progrès encore souhaitables," *Istina* 51, 2006, 354–374, esp. 356–361.

189   See Mauro Velati, *Separati ma fratelli: Gli osservatori non cattolici al Vaticano II (1962–1965)*, Bologna, Il Mulino, 2014, *ad indicem*.

CHAPTER 22

The Second Liturgical Movement in the German Protestant Churches: The "Catholicization" of the Liturgy and the Development of the Ecumenical Process

Martin Cyprian Lenz

1 Introduction

The aim of this contribution is to show the degree to which the second liturgical movement contributed to the birth of an ecumenical sensitivity and urgency in Germany's Protestant Churches. To that end, I will analyze two exemplary cases, two currents from the second liturgical movement, beginning with their origins: the Hochkirche and the Berneuchen movements.[1] As we will see, these can be seen as two paradigmatic poles whose tension fed the momentum of the liturgical movement. The observation of these two poles, which at first glance are extremely different, allows us to identify a common intention, expressed as a set of practical-theological principles that influenced the liturgical and ecumenical practice of German Protestantism in the early years of the 20th century.

2 The Individual Believer at the Center: Preliminary Stages

The fundamental characteristic of Protestantism is its plurality and pluriformity. This is a fact that cannot be ignored in studies of liturgical history. It would be presumptuous to assume that merely from a simple examination of the official liturgical formulae (*Leitagende*), or a local variant, we are in a position to draw conclusions about how Protestant worship in ecclesiastical province A at a given time may have differed from that of ecclesiastical province B. From its beginnings, Protestantism put particular stress on the value of individuality, and, consequently, it has had the difficult task of creating and preserving its own unique identity out of the multiple specificities. Thus, despite the presence of binding liturgical books and ecclesiastical ordinances, some of which date back to the work of the Reformers themselves, a *de facto* plurality of individual ritual forms must be assumed from one congregation to another. Precisely because of the value Protestantism places on individuality, liturgical forms depend at times on the personality of the pastor. For this reason, this contribution will inevitably be of a descriptive nature, and will be limited to outlining certain tendencies.

Like the centralized model of the Roman Catholic Church, which in response to the challenges raised by the Reformation had connected questions of liturgical structure in the *Missale Romanum* with the practice of the city of Rome and had significantly limited the variety of liturgical forms at the Council of Trent,[2] in the 19th century, each German principality, governed by a Protestant ruler, imposed a normative liturgical order. Depending on the principality's location, these orders belonged to different typologies,

---

1   The materials drawn upon in this study include those kept in the archives of the Hochkirchliche Vereinigung Augsburgischen Bekenntnisses e.V. and the Evangelische Michaelsbruderschaft e.V. I would like to express my thanks for their kind approval.

2   See Josef Andreas Jungmann, *Missarum Sollemnia: Eine genetische Erklärung der römischen Messe*, vol. 1, *Messe im Wandel der Jahrhunderte, Messe und kirchliche Gemeinschaft, Vormesse*, Vienna, Herder, ⁵1962, 186f.

which can be traced to the travels and the work of individual reformers, such as Martin Bucer or Johannes Bugenhagen.[3] In view of this, it is hardly surprising that these communities had a decisively ambivalent attitude toward the norms promulgated by the sovereigns. If Roman Catholicism concentrated its pastoral effort on integrating the faithful into "Catholic" unity – understood, in fact, as the affirmation of what has always and everywhere been believed, following the expression of Vincent of Lerins – the Protestant Churches wondered whether and how the teachings of the Christian tradition were still understandable in a changing world, with its increasing social problems. Therefore, the proposal of an adaptation of the traditional formal language was far more natural for them, than it was for the Roman Church which, at the beginning of the 20th century, still considered Modernism its enemy.

The mounting social crisis of the aristocracy during the 19th century and the consequent strengthening of the bourgeoisie and the birth of the working class, which in fact lead to the fall of many monarchies, resulted in a definitive reorganizing of the social world, with the dissolution of the traditional society divided into three orders. From a historical point of view, the *Agendenstreit* in Prussia is an important gauge for measuring the rejection in Protestantism of ruler-imposed forms. Although the ordo of 1821 was eventually used in an adapted form, this nonetheless marks among Protestants the start of a democratization of the process of liturgical reform. In a considerably expanded Prussia after 1815, the attempt to unite Lutheran and Reformed worship with the adoption of a single ritual failed when the possibility of adding elements from local traditions was introduced. With this unifying principle, criticized as an imposed liturgical normalization

(*Agendenzwang*), the way was prepared for the first liturgical movement. Characteristically, its inspiration came from the Rhine province, with the theologians Friedrich Spitta and Rudolf Smend, and the University of Bonn, where members of the Prussian civil service were educated. Beginning in 1887, the movement also took hold in Strasbourg, thanks to the renown that Spitta enjoyed as chair of New Testament and practical theology there.[4]

Following the same ideas condemned as modernist by Rome, the movement born in these areas aimed to find liturgical forms which put the person and his or her aesthetic, in their individual lived experience, at the center. It took as its model Friedrich Schleiermacher's liturgical theory, which saw the self-representation of the individual believer as the principle of any liturgical act. He was responding to the Enlightenment critique, which, denying the transcendental value of liturgical acts, had thereby questioned their very necessity. In response, Schleiermacher freed the phenomenon of "worship" from the Babylonian captivity of *ratio*. For him, any liturgy, by its very nature, can only be understood irrationally: it represents the individual's desire to give outward expression to the inner feeling of absolute dependence. This interpretation rescued liturgical doctrine from the threat of being eliminated in the name of reason. The reception of this thesis by the proponents of the first liturgical movement depended on a reinterpretation of Schleiermacher's liturgical theory. It was no longer a matter of assuming an apologetical stance against the predominance of an ultimately materialistic view of life; rather, the Schleiermacher's position could be understood in a thetic and thus liberating sense. Contrary to traditional conventions seen as imposed from above, each individual was encouraged to find the way to God according to what was best for them. The liturgical leaders in the movement therefore had a great variety of forms at their disposal, which,

---

3 See Rudolf Stählin, "Die Geschichte des christlichen Gottesdienstes von der Urkirche bis zur Gegenwart," in: Karl Ferdinand Müller & Walter Blankenburg, eds., *Leiturgia: Handbuch des evangelischen Gottesdienstes*, vol. 1, *Geschichte und Lehre des evangelischen Gottesdienstes*, Kassel, Stauda, 1954, 1–81, here 60–62.

4 See Konrad Klek, "Spitta Friedrich," *NDB* 24, 712–713, here 712.

as an expression of the theological climate of the time, were well suited to the society of the decaying German Empire and *Kulturprotestantismus*.

The first liturgical movement also sought to find new liturgical forms. Certain points are worth mentioning in this connection. First, its proponents often took traditional forms and filled them with modified content in order to render them newly accessible to the present reality. An example of this is the evening organ concert, which transposed the traditional evening vespers into a new form.[5] Thus vespers still had the psalms, readings, versicle or prayers, but the special emphasis of solo organ music as an independent liturgical element that accompanied the act of prayer of the assembly led to a new interpretation. What resulted, in fact, was a renewed liturgy of the hours. A second example is the use of individual cups during the celebration of the Supper, which symbolized the principles of the first liturgical movement in a particularly striking way. Whereas originally it was the one chalice of Jesus Christ that was offered in each celebration for participation in his blessed communion, there was now an individualistic concern for hygiene[6] among the communicants. For anti-Modernists, this was nothing less than a caricature of what was actually signified. However, these forms led to a new awareness for the celebration of the Lord's Supper that was taken up by the subsequent movement. Another key point, which to a certain extent is a consequence of the previous one, is the request by representatives of the first liturgical movement that churches be open every day and that there be daily worship services. In the Protestant tradition, the church building was not necessarily of central importance for everyday piety. Unlike Catholic churches, which offer a space for prayer in the bodily presence of the Lord, the Protestant Church was considered a place of assembly for the community, a functional conception not unlike that of a Jewish synagogue.[7] However, in the 19th century, industrialization and social problems led to an increase in the importance of places of retreat, especially in the cities. For this reason, the movement's proponents wanted to respond to this need by opening the doors of Protestant Churches – on the Roman Catholic model – for the individual believer's silent reflection.

Kulturprotestantismus and the first liturgical movement were above all interested in the individual believer. Therefore, unlike previous theologians, its representatives neither saw the liturgy as a place where theological trench warfare was waged nor did they attribute any special importance to the conservation of traditions. Indeed, their concentration on the individual enabled them to find a way out of the thicket of liturgical dogmatism. All of this was the product of a new conceptual framework that saw the strength of any individualism in the coexistence of individuals. Their presence in the same environment enables them to understand the manner of communication of each individual, offering a plethora of cultural forms of expression equally intelligible to all their contemporaries.

A movement primarily guided by immanence also faces many risks, however. First, it is more likely that the value of traditional content and one's own responsibility towards it may be neglected or even denied. Second, such a movement is in a constant state of decay: thanks to its immanent specialization on overcoming the contingency of a particular generation, the movement can only keep its identity for another generation at most, when it then has to adapt. Finally, such

---

5   See Christian Bunners, "Kirchenmusikalischer Gottesdienst," in: Hans-Christoph Schmidt-Lauber, Michael Meyer-Blanck & Karl-Heinrich Bieritz, eds., *Handbuch der Liturgik: Liturgiewissenschaft in Theologie und Praxis der Kirche*, Göttingen, Vandenhoeck & Ruprecht, [3]2003, 856–868, here 856f.

6   "Hygiene" as used here should be understood as a literal translation from the Greek signifying "health."

7   See Karl Bernhard Ritter, *Der Altar*, Schwerin, F. Bahn, 1930, 9, and Albert Hammenstede, *Die Liturgie als Erlebnis*, Freiburg i.Br., Herder, [4]1921, 76–78.

a movement is extremely susceptible to influence from the sociopolitical sphere.[8]

It can be seen that the first liturgical movement succumbed to all three dangers. As the transition to the next liturgical approach shows, its fundamental notion of describing the liturgy as the self-representation of the believing individual, following Schleiermacher, was also crucial for the subsequent movement even though in the meantime the social and political landscape had been radically transformed, and with it the expression of individual faith. Particular mention should be made here of the German crisis of 1918, preceded by the experience of the slaughter of human life in the trenches. The consequences of these were felt even by the ecclesiastical administration, creating such a degree of uncertainty as to make necessary a paradigm shift, and a move from immanence to transcendence: after the catastrophe, in fact, individuals found security in the cohesion of the collectivity. Thus, the dominance of immanent individual piety gave way to a piety of the collective that transcended the individual. That which followed the first liturgical movement was therefore no longer an expression of single subjects, who put their ideas into practice within their individual domains. The major figures in the second liturgical movement, in fact, joined together in groups distributed throughout the German-speaking areas. From these emerged, for the first time since the Reformation, the peculiar form of church order that would characterize Protestant spirituality from then on.

In reference to the early ecumenical movement in the Protestant Churches, some scholars interpret the first liturgical movement as its very early precursor. By transforming the traditional liturgical forms into creative instruments, even in a pedagogical sense, for the present day, the representatives of the first liturgical movement sparked a confrontation, often unintended, with the churches in which these forms were used every

day. Although without a doubt it is only with the second liturgical movement that one can speak of a more specific consciousness of the value of the Christian *oecumene*, the first liturgical movement nonetheless in its own way laid the foundations for the realization that Protestantism, too, could be seen as an element of the *una sancta catholica et apostolica ecclesia*.

3 Assumptions: Hansen's 95 Theses

"Protestantismus qui dicitur non habet causam iubilandi, sed poenitentiam agendi in cilicio et cinere."[9] Thus reads the second of the 95 theses of Lutheran pastor Heinrich Hansen. Protestantism would appear to have a certain weakness for this type of communication. One of the difficulties of the discipline of history is that it often must face the impossibility of identifying with precision the beginning and end of specific historical developments. Nonetheless, anyone researching the German offshoot of the Oxford Movement[10] will soon realize that the Hochkirche movement in Germany was inaugurated by this northern German pastor and his theses. He published them in 1917, when the Protestant Churches were commemorating the 400th anniversary of the posting of Luther's 95 theses in Wittenberg. Thus, his theses appeared exactly during the period in which the Protestant Churches were particularly absorbed with questions regarding their history and identity. Hansen called his theses *Stimuli et Clavi*, for they were to be "spurs and nails" in the flesh of his contemporaries who were celebrating the great jubilee with such pomp and

---

8   See Joachim Mehlhausen, "Nationalsozialismus und Kirchen," *TRE* 24, 43–78, here 47f.

9   "Protestantism has no reason to celebrate jubilees, but it certainly has reason to do penance in sackcloth and ashes"; thesis 2 from Heinrich Hansen, *Stimuli et clavi: Spieße und Nägel*, in: Theodor Hauf, ed., *Siebzig Jahre Hochkirchliche Bewegung (1918–1988): Hochkirchliche Arbeit: Woher? Wozu? Wohin?*, Bochum, HV, 1989, 33–52, here 33.

10 On this, see Peter B. Nockles's contribution in this volume.

circumstance. The theses provide a colorful negative print from which the ecclesiological and
liturgical situation of the Protestant Churches in
the period of the German Empire's decline can be
reconstructed. Was the legend of Protestant origins and the festive celebration of a schism truly
grounds for joy or, as Hansen recalled, were they
not in actual fact a reason for shame since they
reflected the human failure to live up to Christ's
own high priestly prayer (Jn 17)? Hansen's theses
are a particularly appropriate means of examining this situation because the desire for Christian
unity is their central, most forceful idea.

The language of the theses, which are cast
in modern Latin in order to mirror the style of
Luther's theses, must be described as often heavy
and provocative. Hansen wrote them on the North
Sea island of Pellworm. He criticized what he sees
as the widespread tendencies in his church that
he saw as expressions of subjectivism and individualism, which, to him, in the jubilee year of
1917, were being dramatically exaggerated. Hansen
warned that contemporary *Kulturprotestantismus*,
the dominant movement of the time, made the
individual member of the community its point
of reference. At the time, that largely immanently
oriented message celebrated the cultural achievements within the imperial state, in worship,
church music, and the daily life of the community. This was complemented by the fact that the
Protestant Churches had close connections with
the empire and with the state bureaucracy: "59.
Laudi sibi dent pastores pectora sua nuda ser-
vare omnibus insignisbus honoris civilibus, sed
implere amore Salvatoris et misericordia erga
miseros quoscumque."[11] The key to understanding Hansen's theses hence lies in his view that the
individual believer loses sight of God's objective
salvific act as a result of the subjective and individualistic action of his or her church. Levelling

his accusations against the Protestant Churches
in particular, Hansen came to the conclusion that
the Reformation must in point of fact be called
a deformation.[12]

Hansen's criticisms were principally aimed
at the widespread ecclesiology of the Protestant
Churches of the period. Their framework was first
the state, then the individual congregations, and
within them the individual members. Hansen contrasted this orientation, which derived specifically
from the Reformed tradition and was known and
promoted even by the Lutheranism of the period,
with the concept "catholicity," which he refers to
for the first time in the seventh thesis. "7. Surgat
et redeat nunc protestantismus, non ad ecclesiam
Romanam vel catholicismum, sed ad catholicitatem; non ad fratrem, sed ad patrem et ecclesiam
matrem."[13] This dictum that alludes to Cyprian
of Carthage shows how catholicity should be
understood.[14] With this concept Hansen denotes
an ecclesiological self-conception that can be
traced to the common origin of all Christianity
in antiquity. In an absolute antithesis to the celebrations of 1917, the new interpretation proposed
by Hansen was the following: the Protestant
Churches did not originate in 1517 with the simple and legendary posting of the theses, but they
emerged, just like all "catholic" churches, from the
Pentecostal baptism of fire of the Holy Spirit. They
are therefore part of the *una sancta*.

In the history of spiritual thought, we can
note a clear break in the new use of the concept
of catholicity in reference to Protestant theology. The predecessors to Hansen's theses can be
found in the 19th century restoration, which was
able to recognize the breadth of the Christian

---

11   "59. Pastors should seek their fame in keeping their
      breasts free of worldly medals and decorations of
      honor, while filling them with love of the savior and
      compassion for all suffering."

12   "4. Reformatio quae dicitur iure meritoque deformatio
      est dicenda, quia, quae enixe et bona fide expetebat,
      parum assecuta est" ("The Reformation can rightly
      be called a deformation, because most of its well-
      intentioned aims have gone wrong").

13   "7. Protestantism should return now, not to the Roman
      Church nor to Catholicism but to catholicity; not to the
      brother, but to the father and to the mother church."

14   See Cyprian, *De Ecclesiae cattholicae unitate*, 6.

tradition and offer to the Protestant world its first opportunity to emerge from the provincialism denounced by Hansen. His theses advance these efforts further, attributing to idea of catholicity a conceptual dimension that was made possible only with the development of the second liturgical movement in early 20th century Protestantism. He did this by abstracting from "catholic," which was claimed exclusively by each Christian confession, to arrive at "catholicity," which as an abstract idea includes all the confessions. The approach of Hochkirche theology takes is origins from precisely these concepts.

"38. Recte non sentiunt, qui verba symboli apostolici communionem sanctorum (ἀγίων κοινωνίαν) interpretantur: coetum sive populum sanctorum, i.e. hominum vere fidelium; interpretandum enim est: communionem sive participationem sanctarum rerum, i.e. Sacramentorum."[15] The objectivity of the sacrament, which when freed from its worldly relationships connects every age with the origins of everything Christian, appears as the logical consequence of Hansen's demands in the theses. The "communion in the holy things," as he translated it, should prevail over the usual translation "communion of the saints." In this way, on the one hand, he keeps the emphasis on the individual typical of Protestantism, on the other, he stresses the value of the objective. The new liturgics will develop precisely around this point.

Hansen's true innovation was to deduce from the ideas of catholicity and objectivity consequences for religious practice and pastoral discipline. From a historical perspective, his rejection of the bourgeois ideal of the Protestant Churches appears particularly evident at this juncture.

68. Abusus non tolit usum, ut est in proverbio. Multa quae ab antiqua ecclesia instituta erant, temporibus reformationis multis iisque magnis vitiis laborabant; quod autem a protestantibus, praecipue a Calvinianis, non solum abusus, sed ipsa instituta abrogata et explosa sunt, aequum et iustum non fuit.[16]

The individual practices of religious devotion and discipline reviled by the Protestant Churches as abuses, which were soon abolished during or after the Reformation period, are addressed by Hansen in the next theses. He cites the practices of fasting (thesis 69), monasticism (thesis 70), and priestly celibacy (thesis 71), which were recommended but not required either by the Apostle Paul or by Protestant pastors. Hansen clearly recommended their revival. It is notable that he wished to provoke the development of a specific mystical and spiritual quality in the Protestant Churches, which he saw already present in the other two major confessions. The *Kulturprotestantismus* of his time offered few inroads in this context.

It is not surprising that, although he does not openly criticize it, he questioned the central role that Protestantism traditionally attributed to the doctrine of justification *sola fide*. Because it suggests an automatic salvation, Hansen raised doubts about it in theses 76 to 79, calling it a dead faith. Against this, he vehemently affirmed the necessity that sanctification be a continuous "straining towards Christ." Together with the following theses (80 to 85), which were an apology for the objectivity of the sacraments, his argument concentrates on the reality of all of the sacraments. In regard to the function of the ministers, this means that Hansen saw in the sacramental action the only proven means to bring about the sanctification of

---

15   "38. They are in error who interpret the words of the Apostolic Symbol 'communion of saints' (ἀγίων κοινωνίαν) as the assembly or the people of the saints, that is those who are truly faithful; instead it should be understood as 'communion with' or 'participation in' holy things, that is, in the sacraments." Hansen, *Stimuli et clavi*, 40.

16   "68. Abuse does not eliminate use, says the proverb. At the time of the Reformation, many institutions of the old church were afflicted with many and great deficiencies; but it was not just and right for the Protestants, especially the Calvinists, to have eliminated and rejected not just the abuses but the institutions themselves." Hansen, *Stimuli et clavi*, 46.

the church members. For Hansen, it was beyond question that the central role given to preaching (theses 86 to 87) signified a subjective narrowing proper to *Kulturprotestantismus* that should not be encouraged in any way.

The final block comprises an interrelated set of theses (88 to 95) which call for repentance and humility. Within this group, three key points can be identified that are central to the whole work. In thesis 90, Hansen expressly stated the historical value of his propositions, which were intended to bring out the fruitfulness of the concept of catholicity: "90. Ubique ad veram catholicitatem redeundum est."[17] The demand for a return to catholicity leads to the central objective of the argument. The healing of divisions is to be prepared through the assumption of an attitude of humility: "93. Omnes ergo fideles ad demittendos animos commoveantur, ut, etsi non adsit potentia controversias tollendi, tamen discordia paulatim minuatur."[18] For Hansen, true reconciliation of the different confessions is no longer within the scope of human action: "95. Id ergo omnes ante omnia agant, ut quam concordissimi fiant et sint ante gloriosissimum adventum Domini."[19]

Hansen concluded his theses on this climactic note. It is noteworthy that, in a work that often adopts a combative tone, the structure of the argument leads to the return of Christ, and with this the end of all battles. Hansen does not blur the reality of the *una sancta* divided into various confessions. On the contrary, he sees it as the outcome of such gravely sinful behavior that Christ alone can overcome it. The humility he calls upon is the result of his acknowledgment of that sin. The return to catholicity, to follow Hansen's line of argument, is nothing other than the return to Christ as the *one* Lord of the *one* church.

3.1 The Birth of the Hochkirchliche Vereinigung in 1918 and Its Early Development

Today it is recognized that Hansen's theses have historical significance in that they inspired the Protestant Churches to reflect on their own identity and that they directly contributed to the foundation of the Hochkirchliche Vereinigung. From its beginnings in October, the union became an early laboratory for liturgical experimentation. It was the first institution that argued for the liberation of the *ius liturgicum*, regulated until then by the ecclesiastical administration, in order to put it in the hands of the those leading the liturgy. The 19th century restoration had already seen the spread of a large number of particular and unofficial formularies, which were the result of the liturgical effort of individuals not belonging to the ecclesiastical administration. It was, however, only with the foundation of the Hochkirchliche Vereinigung that a genuine interest group was formed that could become a place for liturgical experimentation. If in the beginning it did not manage to exercise direct influence on the life of Protestant communities, the value of its work lay in the reception of its ideas by groups of experts. The ideas proposed by the Hochkirche movement – and often even the hostile reactions to them – represent a critical moment in the evolution of liturgical thought, on the cusp of what will be called the second liturgical movement.

There is room here only to highlight a few stages[20] in the history of the Hochkirchliche Vereinigung des Augsburgischen Bekenntnisses

---

17   "90. Everywhere is to be returned to true catholicity."

18   "93. All believers should let themselves be stirred to humility so that, even if they are not able to overcome the existing divisions, at least the discord will be a bit diminished."

19   "95. Above all else, everyone should strive to become and be in perfect harmony before the glorious return of the Lord."

20   For a detailed account, see Helmut Martin Niepmann, *Chronik der Hochkirchlichen Vereinigung Augsburgischen Bekenntnisses e.V. über die ersten 50 Jahre ihres Bestehens (1918–1968)*, Bochum, Hochkirchliche Vereinigung Augsburgischen Bekenntnisses e.V., 1988.

e.V.[21] In first steps towards its foundation – the contact between Hansen and Pastor Heinrich Mosel, who would be the true initiator of the union – led to its rejection on the part of the Protestant press.[22] Its foundational meeting on Oct 9, 1918, in Berlin, was attended by ten people. By the middle of 1920, the number had risen to 192, and at the end of the same year there were already 235 members.[23] This rapid growth shows that the Hochkirche movement enjoyed a broad favor and probably also met with even wider interest. So, what was the reason for the reticence?

From the movement's beginning in the spring of 1918, the Protestant public took offense that the movement called itself "hochkirchlich." In choosing this adjective, the members of the union showed a strong affinity with the aims of Anglo-Catholicism, a point which was rather maliciously seized upon in the contemporary press. The widespread Anglophobia of the Germans becomes clear in this historical context and was further intensified at the time by the events of World War I. The problem, therefore, was not merely a matter of ecclesiology and theology but also reflected the international political situation. The actions of the most important Hochkirche figures transcended Protestant provincialism and were at heart animated by the same cosmopolitan attitude that would characterize vibrant climate of the 1920s, but which was quite new in the liturgical sphere.

Moreover, some were particularly incensed by the ecclesiological and liturgical program of the Hochkirchliche Vereinigung, which was universally regarded as catholicizing. It was thus vehemently criticized in virtue of the traditional reluctance of German Protestantism towards anything "catholic," a reticence which has given rise to many ecclesiastical forms that are specifically German. This attitude, softened today by a greater ecumenical sensibility, caused the early pioneers of the Hochkirche to be treated particularly harshly. The words of Friedrich Heiler in 1947, when the Hochkirchliche Vereinigung was refounded as the Evangelisch-ökumenische Vereinigung des Augsburgischen, are indicative of this:[24]

Indeed, the developments of the past 30 years teach that the fundamental ideas first advocated by the Hochkirchliche Vereinigung, and defended by the Evangelisch-ökumenische Vereinigung today, were disseminated in both German and non-German Protestantism to a previously unknown extent. What does it matter that those who pioneered these ideas, and not only fought but also suffered for them, are today mainly forgotten? It does not appear a truly Christian way of thinking if some of our friends are unhappy that others who have taken up and further developed our ideas have achieved greater fame and honor. We can do no better than repeat the words of the Psalmist: "Non nobis Domine, non nobis, sed nomini tuo da gloriam!"[25]

The expression of pathos found here, which probably derives from the place of the publication, should not disguise the fact that the efforts of the Hochkirche did indeed cause German Protestantism to engage with the (literally) "catholic," that is ecumenical, liturgy. This can be said in particular for all the proponents of the second liturgical movement because of the pioneering nature of their work. Today this is shown in the eponymous use of the expression High Church (hochkirchlich) to refer to worship of a traditional form.[26]

---

21 The full name will be shortened to Hochkirchliche Vereinigung or simply Hochkirche.

22 See Niepmann, *Chronik der Hochkirchlichen*, 9.

23 See Niepmann, *Chronik der Hochkirchlichen*, 15–17.

24 This was evidently the means of eliminating the attribute "hochkirchlich." This choice is symptomatic of the ecclesiastical policy that characterized the post-war situation (*lex Dibelii*, etc.).

25 Niepmann, *Chronik der Hochkirchlichen*, 8.

26 Even against the interpretation given it by the single liturgists.

3.2 *The Ecumenical Approach of Hochkirche Liturgical Renewal*

Among the principles of liturgical renewal promoted by the Hochkirche, in first place is the recognition given to all liturgical forms dating back to the time of undivided Christianity. From this is derived, secondly, a reticence towards all forms that were the fruit of later creative processes. These were deemed somehow deficient because were no longer connected to the purity of their origins. Lastly, Hochkirche liturgical studies owed a debt to Christian ecumenism, because it considered with an open mind the liturgical forms of the other churches and tried to render them useful for Protestant Churches. The latter point was a concrete response to Heiler's call for "evangelical catholicity." Heiler had already described his ideal church in 1919:

> A church that is both Protestant and Catholic at the same time, Christian and universal, a church whose soul is Protestant and whose body is Catholic: such a church is the ideal church, one which will never be completely realized but towards which we must strive, and to which we must gradually draw near.[27]

Shortly after its foundation in 1918, the Hochkirchliche Vereinigung started work on drawing up its own breviary. The commission in charge of this was to provide a Protestant version of the *Breviarium Romanum*. The liturgy of the hours had been identified as a treasure of spiritual modes of expression lacking in the Protestant Church. The simultaneous effort underway in the Berneuchen movement confirms the impression that the daily worship of the community as a whole was seen as a powerful form of expression by the proponents of the second liturgical movement. The

Breviarium Romanum was the perfect model since it provided a complete arrangement of psalms, prayers, and readings for the entire church year. Moreover, it was tested on a daily basis by the entire Roman Church. A distinctive element of the Hochkirche was a reluctance to accept even the creative processes from within the movement, since they were expressions of an individual contribution. Generally, in fact, *ad hoc* rituals, drawn up in a study and thus artificial, could only claim to be worthwhile if they were made up of already existing material that had already been proven by use.

For this reason, the Hochkirche liturgies, including the grand proposals of Heiler (discussed below), incorporated traditional formularies used by the regional churches. The elements that gave a new cast to the religious services were mainly the use of vestments and the celebration of Eucharist during the service. The latter was not common practice in many places. The Hochkirche movement, instead, saw in the Eucharist an important element, an emphasis that characterizes its theology and its approach to liturgy, which would also become influential to others.

With the merger in 1928 of the Hochkirchliche Vereinigung and the Hochkirchlich-ökumenischer Bund[28] (born in 1924 as a splinter of the Hochkirchliche Vereinigung), their common energy lent even greater impetus to ecumenism. If up until that point Hochkirche liturgical interests had been pursued in the name of Romanticism's *art pour l'art*, now the new combined movement concentrated on the form, with the goal of being recognizable and recognized in an ecumenical perspective.[29] For the Hochkirche, such an

---

27   Friedrich Heiler, "Evangelische Katholizität: Vortrag in Upplands Priestergesellschaft zu Uppsala Herbst 1919," in: Friedrich Heiler, *Evangelische Katholizität: Gesammelte Aufsätze und Vorträge*, vol. 1, Munich, Ernst Reinhardt, 1926, 150–179, here 179.

28   See also Paul Metzlaff's contribution in this volume.

29   On the distinction between *hochkirchlich* and *hochliturgisch*, see Martin Cyprian Lenz, "Viel Tradition, wenig Zukunft?: Zur Geschichte und Relevanz des hochkirchlichen Anliegens," in: Martin Cyprian Lenz, ed., *Ut omnes unum: Festschrift anlässlich des 100jährigen Bestehens der Hochkirchlichen Vereinigung Augsburgischen Bekenntnisses e. V.*, Norderstedt, Books on Demand, 2018, 42–57.

aspiration led to an intense work to recover the value of apostolic episcopal succession in the Protestant Churches. The aim was to bring about a sacramental renewal of German Protestantism. From this idea, which was not without controversy even within the Hochkirchliche Vereinigung, the practical approach of the entire movement emerged: the explicit goal was to bringing about a lived ecumenism. A significant influence on the Hochkirchliche Vereinigung was the Marburg historian of religion Friedrich Heiler. He belonged to the liberal wing of Catholicism before converting to Lutheranism after meeting Nathan Söderblom. From his book *Der Katholizismus*, Heiler drew the motto of the movement: from 1928 on, the task of Hochkirche members was to attain "evangelical catholicity." A firmly convinced idealist, with his work Heiler wanted to unify what he considered the best elements of the different confessions.[30]

In 1931, he drew up a liturgical formula, which he called the "Evangelisch-katholische Eucharistiefeier," for the l'Evangelisch-katholischen Eucharistischen Gemeinschaft, of which he had been the *apostolischer Vorsteher* since its foundation in 1929.[31] An analysis of his liturgy reveals a fusion of an extremely wide range of rites.[32]

Roughly speaking, the first noticeable aspect is the excessive length of the celebration, which conjures up the intensity of Orthodox liturgies. On the other hand, the rubrics show close links with those of the *Missale Romanum*. The performance is structured according to the logic of the Western Churches, as shown, for example, by the rite of incensing of the bread and wine during the recitation of the *Verba Testamenti*. In this ecumenical fusion of the different traditions, the aims of the Hochkirche find a concrete expression. At this juncture, the internal structure is particularly clear. The 1931 formulary does not aim to express the spiritual and liturgical needs of the individual, even though it was created by an individual, but to meet the needs of large collective in an ecumenical perspective.

The liturgy that was Heiler's own true work, known as the *Heiler-Messe*, is actually the *Deutsche Messe*, published in 1948 as a second revised and expanded version.[33] Heiler called it a liturgical "bridge between East and West."[34] In the Hochkirche movement it is to this day still the binding and unifying formulary.[35]

In regard to its composition, this rite, considerably pared down compared to its predecessor, is oriented for the most part towards the Western

---

30   See Lenz, "Viel Tradition, wenig Zukunft?," 43.

31   See the archives of the Hochkirchliche Vereinigung.

32   The Mass follows the following sequence: congregational hymn, Introit, entry of the clergy, incensing of the altar, prayers at the foot of the altar, Confiteor, versicle, Aufer a Nobis, intercessions from Chrysostom liturgy, Gloria, Collect, Epistle, Gradual chant, Tractus/Alleluia/possible sequence, Gospel, congregational hymn, sermon, congregational hymn, Creed (Nicene), Preparation of the Altar, offertory rite with collection, incense prayer and incensing of the altar, Lavabo, Prayer over the Offerings (Secreta), Preface, Epiclesis, Verba Testamenti, Anamnesis, Trisagion, Remembrance of the Saints, Intercessions, Our Father, Pax, Agnus Dei, Fraction Prayer (*Didache*), Preparation (Anglican liturgy), Sancta Sanctis (early church), communion of the pastor then the congregation (communion in the hand), Communion/Eucharistic hymn, versicle, thanksgiving, Postcommunion, Nunc Dimittis, Benedicamus, blessing, (prayer in the sacristy), Prologue of John, congregational hymn, exit of clergy.

33   Friedrich Heiler, *Deutsche Messe: Oder Feier des Herrenmahls nach altkirchlicher Ordnung*, Munich, Federmann, ²1948.

34   Friedrich Heiler, "Ein liturgischer Brückenschlag zwischen Ost und West," *EHK* 21, 1939, 249–256.

35   It follows this structure: congregational hymn, entry of the clergy, prayers at the foot of the altar, Confiteor, versicle, Aufer a Nobis, Introit with incensing of the altar, Kyrie, Gloria, Collect, Epistle, Gradual chant, Tractus/Alleluia (possible sequence), Gospel, congregational hymn, sermon, congregational hymn, Pax, intercessions from the Chrysostom liturgy, offertory with collection, incense prayer, Lavabo, Creed (Nicene), Preface, Sanctus, Postsanctus, Mysterium Fidei, Verba Testamenti, Anamnesis, Epiclesis, Our Father with embolism, Fraction Prayer, Communion Prayer, Sancta Sanctis, Agnus Dei, communion of pastor then the congregation (communion in the hand), Communion/Eucharistic Hymn, thanksgiving, Postcommunion, congregational hymn, Benedicamus, blessing.

Churches' liturgical tradition as expressed in the *Missale Romanum*, but it also embraces elements from different sources. The most distinctive feature of the *Heiler-Messe* is, in fact, the reception of the Christian tradition as a whole. In regard to geographical coverage, the sources range from the Celtic liturgy in the West (the fraction prayer *Sie erkannten den Herrn*)[36] to the liturgy of St. John Chrysostom (the Great Litany[37]) and the Syrian Jacobite liturgy in the East (prayer before the consecration *Ja, heilig bist Du*).[38] Heiler thus borrowed formularies from Syria, in the South, up to the Anglican Northeast (the communion prayer *Wir unterwinden uns*)[39] and the Latin rite of the Northwest (such as the incense hymn *Weihrauch und reines Opfer*).[40] The Heiler Mass is also historically wide-ranging: among the most recent formularies included is the *Ordnung der Deutschen Messe*, composed in 1936 by the Berneuchen movement. Heiler's aim in his *Deutsche Messe ... nach altkirchlicher Ordnung* was thus twofold. First, he wanted to create a form for the liturgy which would become a fundamental reference for all German-speaking areas, hence the name, just as the *Missale Romanum* was for the Latin Church in the West. Second, its quality was meant to be demonstrated through the broad range of interlocking sources.

The utopia of the *Heiler-Messe* nonetheless failed because the Hochkirche movement lacked a widespread influence. Its significance for the local church has mainly been indirect, insofar as it was accepted as the rite of the second liturgical movement after World War II. Further, it has also assumed an exemplary value because, in general, it demonstrated the possibility of pursuing a reform of the liturgy: for the Protestant Church in the early 20th century, which found it necessary to develop its own identity and liturgical language,

the *Heiler-Messe* and the Hochkirche movement as a whole represent the attempt to take the traditions of the oldest sister churches and examine their compatibility with their own theological tradition. "In the area of corporality, of the consideration of the person in his or her entirety, Heiler's observations find greater understanding today than during his own time."[41] Contrary to what can be deduced from the openness of this position, therefore, the Hochkirche attempt is not a naive copy of more ancient formularies but an adaption based on sound theological principles.

4   The Berneuchen Movement: Singing and Praying Youth

Originating just a little later than the Hochkirche movement is the current subsequently known as the Berneuchen movement. Its impetus sprang from the same historical circumstances already criticized by Hansen. Nonetheless, what was born in Berneuchen must be clearly distinguished from the Hochkirche approach. Today in Germany there is a tendency to see the representatives of the two movements as part of the same group of liturgical activists who advocated for Protestant liturgy based in tradition and having an ecumenical character, and sometimes even inaccurately lump them together under the name Hochkirche. However, this does not do justice to the distinctiveness and autonomy of either group.

While the Hochkirche movement was initiated by theologians in active ministry and from the beginning had very definite idea of the goals to be implemented (following the inspiration of Anglo-Catholicism, for example), the first steps of the Berneuchen movement were the fruit of an awakening of young people, and thus were freer

---

36   Heiler, *Deutsche Messe*, 33.
37   Heiler, *Deutsche Messe*, 13–16.
38   Heiler, *Deutsche Messe*, 25.
39   Heiler, *Deutsche Messe*, 34.
40   Heiler, *Deutsche Messe*, 19.

41   Karl-Heinrich Bieritz, "Liturgische Bewegungen im deutschen Protestantismus," in: Martin Klöckener & Benedikt Kranemann, eds., *Liturgiereformen: Historische Studien zu einem bleibenden Grundzug des christlichen Gottesdienstes*, Münster, Aschendorff, 2002, 711–748, here 731.

and less determined. The Jugendmusikbewegung, the youth music movement, which arose in a similar context and with the same motivations as the scouts, increasingly took issue with church practice in its different associations. The Berneuchen movement had as its objective the search for authentic principles for a generation of young people put off by the liberalism expressed by cultural Protestantism. The experience of Germany's defeat in 1918 and the subsequent constitutional restructuring of the former Reich led many of the movement's followers, who had originally been loyal to the Kaiser, to a profound reconsideration of their ideas. They now realized that the liberal rhetoric accompanying the theology of the long 19th century, which in fact had led an exultant German people to the carnage of Verdun, had proven to be false.

The path undertaken by those in the youth movement who joined the Berneuchen movement, led, as they sang, "from the gray city walls" into nature's midst. They, like the Romantics, held that in nature's vast expanse a very particular kind of encounter with God, his creation and revelation, awaited them. In nature, they found the direct path from sun to moon, day to night, light to darkness, which inspired them to find their own forms of the Liturgy of the Hours. There are clear parallels with the beginnings of monastic spirituality in early Christianity. First, there is the flight from the familiar diffused liberal social structure into solitude, and then the need to translate these natural conditions into specific forms of prayer. This is attained not only by developing original new liturgical structures but also by adapting already established ones to the new circumstances.[42] Both these aspects led this part of the youth movement to develop its own spirituality, a Berneuchen spirituality, which drew on the bitterness of the experience of war in order to flourish within the full spectrum of traditional Christian forms.

The archive of the Evangelische Michaelsbruderschaft indeed preserves a number of photographs from the early 1920s,[43] showing young adults doing physical exercise and taking part in liturgical celebrations in nature, but a detailed historical study of this period has not yet been carried out. While Hansen's Hochkirche theses were the work of a single individual, the *Berneuchener Buch* is a work of consensus that marks the end of the movement's first intensive phase of development, based exclusively on the diverse experiences of these early years. It was to be the first key work to influence the religious public. It not only gave the movement its name but also provided it with its basic orientation.

> It was the need shared by the youth and the church erupting during the tempestuous years of war and the successive upheavals that led the leaders from a number of youth groups to come together for their first meeting in Angern, near Magdeburg, in 1922.[44]

The profound concerns of this generation were points of departure for such meetings, which subsequently moved from Angern to the Viebahn family estate of Berneuchen in the Neumark. The participants "were part of a church they recognized and honored as the one called to proclaim the ultimate truth but which, however, was unable to speak the saving word."[45] After the great upheavals of the time, the church and its representatives had completely forfeited their credibility. The madness of war waged on an industrial scale and the madness of the efficiency with which those who took part were exterminated had contributed to the birth of a social climate very similar to that of the Baroque period. The art of this period

---

42   For the first monastic pioneers, this meant drawing on the ascetic currents in Judaism and on the "exploration" of the Psalter.

43   See the archive of the Evangelische Michaelsbruderschaft e.V.

44   Berneuchener Konferenz, ed., *Das Berneuchener Buch: Vom Anspruch des Evangeliums auf die Kirchen der Reformation*, Hamburg, Hanseatische Verl.-Anst., 1926, 9.

45   Berneuchener Konferenz, ed., *Das Berneuchener Buch.*

was coldly caught between the extremes of explosion and shock, while in its language and form the fleetingness of human structures and of life itself shown forth, like a *memento mori*. The value of an individual human life had been radically called into question by the rationalizing industrial order, and such value needed to be recuperated through religion. Although the national church of *Kulturprotestantismus* was still basing its message uncritically on the cultural achievements of previous generations, the post-war church was suddenly silenced during the night between Nov 9 and 10, 1918, after the abdication of Emperor William II and the proclamation of the Republic.

Various insights from systematic theology in this period, connected to the names of Paul Althaus, Karl Barth, Friedrich Brunstäd, and Paul Tillich, suggested a path out of Protestantism's greatest crisis and, in turn, influenced the authors of the *Berneuchener Buch*. A brief survey of the work of these great theologians of the early 20th century allows us to identify a climate of different political and systematic extremes, in which the Berneuchen movement operated. Neo-Lutheranism and the nationalist wing, which became the place of refuge for circles loyal to the Kaiser, were associated particularly with the names Brunstäd and Althaus, while Tillich and Barth represented religious socialism. These four systematic theologians, moved by the injustices of the age, raised the question of divine revelation and the human ability to express it. "The Protestant Church is fighting for its life and its essence."[46] Protestantism had always felt directly bound to the question of divine revelation. In this, they were very different from the Orthodox and Roman Catholicism who claimed for themselves – through a rigid traditional structure and through the person and succession of the bishops – the role of internal guarantors of unity beyond the institutions of state, in addition to[47] the revelation of God in Christ, which was

accessible to all. Following the collapse of church order bound to the sovereigns, which had conferred on Protestantism a stability similar to that of the Catholic episcopal hierarchy, it is hardly surprising that the systematic theology of this period now turned back to studying with greater intensity the theme of divine revelation as a theological *topos*.

In regard to its contents, the *Berneuchener Buch* is above all dedicated to the formulation of the problem. This was that the Protestant Church was not up to the task of responding to the call of the gospel (in the double sense of a call to action and a call to listening). The achievements of the Reformation era, with its liberating impetus, had become ossified, and in the process of the institutionalization of the Protestant Churches, God and his promise had been reduced to a mere function of ecclesiastical discourse.[48] The criticism has much in common with Hansen's analysis of the state of affairs in his theses. The current task of the Protestant Church, therefore, was to overcome its paralysis in three respects.[49] This task is of particular relevance for the question of ecumenism since the latter aims to bring about an opening of the Protestant Church towards its sister churches.

As a whole, the text marks a break with the church of the German Empire, shaped as it was by an optimism linked to progress and a historicist approach. First, it was necessary to expose the idea of human autonomy as hubris.[50] Any attempt to find the truth outside God was misguided (Jn 14). One should add for the sake of clarity: the task of theology is not to defend God, the church, and itself from the constant attacks of rationalism. The next step in the argument dealt with the limitations to be placed on objective thinking associated with rationalism. With all the positive aspects that historical criticism contributed to

---

46 Berneuchener Konferenz, ed., *Das Berneuchener Buch*, 15.

47 Note that this is not "against."

48 See Berneuchener Konferenz, ed., *Das Berneuchener Buch*, 17.

49 See Berneuchener Konferenz, ed., *Das Berneuchener Buch*, 75–88.

50 Berneuchener Konferenz, ed., *Das Berneuchener Buch*, 76.

theology, it is ultimately impossible for the church to deny the value of myth because divine revelation reaches depths so profound that they cannot be investigated by historical methodology.[51] Third, it affirmed that this methodology was an eternal relativism which restricted the validity of all statements of belief to a particular historical context. The Berneuchen movement countered this relativism with divine realism:[52] accordingly, the only positive call to action is the reference to the living Word, Christ himself. The church should focus on the eternal action of the Word.[53] In summary, we can conclude that the renewal of the church according to the principles of the *Berneuchener Buch* ultimately aimed at the rejection of Modernism. In this sense, it aligned with the majority positions of Roman Catholicism and Orthodoxy at the time.

It is no surprise that the book's publication provoked strong reactions. As with the Hochkirche theses, the Berneuchen aims were not literally put into practice but rather were part of the many contributions that influenced the internal Protestant debate. Therefore, it is incorrect to speak of the failure of the *Berneuchener Buch*, although its proponents quickly sought to relativize the harsh criticism.

4.1 The Theology of Revelation in Berneuchen Liturgical Renewal

It is possible that in a certain period the true, living link with the Fathers as regards liturgical form was broken to such an extent, indeed reduced to tatters, that this period must once again ask what is right, meaning what is appropriate in the circumstances, and that it must, in the radical seriousness of

this question, first turn away from the traditions with which it has grown up.[54]

The repercussions of the *Berneuchener Buch* can be seen most clearly in the liturgical decisions that were crucial for this current of the liturgical movement. At first it simply reacted to the new theology of revelation and to the contemporary historical developments. "The Berneuchener circle, formed (in 1923) around Wilhelm Stählin and Karl Bernhard Ritter, initially takes up the impulse of the youth movement in a highly original way but later moves increasingly closer to ecumenical forms."[55] In contrast to the Hochkirche movement, the Berneuchen circle was able to be extremely flexible because of the natural vagueness of forms appropriate to any new beginning. Its interest in the theory and practice of liturgy, which was quickly developed and exercised a decisive influence, took the often thematically arranged liturgical celebrations of *Kulturprotestantismus* as its point of departure. These were generally considered as a kind of negative model to be opposed. The Berneuchen movement applied to liturgical study the first formal criterion of theological discourse formulated by Paul Tillich: "The object of theology is what concerns us ultimately. Only those propositions are theological which deal with their object in so far as it can become a matter of ultimate concern for us."[56] In the Berneuchen liturgical language, the ultimate was the detachment from the usual subjective individualistic message, analogous to the Hochkirche position reflected by Hansen.[57] Yet compared to the latter, it is clear that Berneuchen succeeded in expressing its harsh criticism by starting from the current

---

51   Berneuchener Konferenz, ed., *Das Berneuchener Buch*, 90.

52   Berneuchener Konferenz, ed., *Das Berneuchener Buch*, 89.

53   Berneuchener Konferenz, ed., *Das Berneuchener Buch*, 89–91.

54   Wilhelm Stählin, *Berneuchen antwortet: Eine Erwiderung auf Gerhard Kunze's "Gespräch mit Berneuchen"*, Kassel, J. Stauda, 1939, 38.

55   Bieritz, "Liturgische Bewegungen," 717.

56   Paul Tillich, *Systematic Theology*, vol. 1, Chicago, University of Chicago Press, 1951, 12.

57   It is rather amusing that the solutions of both groups promoted the greatest individuality and subjectivity in the decisions of their members.

topoi of Protestant theology. Thus, Tillich's theory of symbol and Barth's dialectics, among others, became the starting points for their liturgical assessment.

The Protestant principle that Christ is the only mediator between humanity and God remains a fundamental element in Berneuchen liturgical renewal as well. However, its distinctiveness lies in achieving, under the influence of the pioneers of the theology of revelation, a "new"[58] self-awareness.

> Faith is the constant attack on mere subjectivity insofar as it shatters the illusion of a self-contained spiritual life. Yet this also breaks the spell of a skepticism that destroys any true seriousness, and the inner eye gains its sight. That is why faith must speak of what it sees; that is why its language is the language of believing realism. The believer does not talk about himself and his faith but testifies to God's reality.[59]

After the catastrophe of world war, the believers still found themselves in a sacramental world. For the Berneuchen movement, the sacramental renaissance of reality meant that the liturgy should introduce the effectiveness of God's salvific action for humanity. "Revelation, the Word of God is found only where the eternal transcendental You speaks to us 'with and within' a finite reality and calls for our decision in a concrete situation."[60] It is a distinctive feature of Berneuchen theology, due in particular to the influence of Karl Bernhard Ritter, to draw attention to a special proclamatory nature of the act of the Eucharist. Here, through reference to the Lutheran Formula of Concord, a link is created between God's call to his

congregation and the celebration of the Eucharist with the real presence of Christ. In this way, a new access to the liturgical tradition of the Western Church is opened up for Protestant theology.

The example of the *Ordnung der Deutschen Messe*,[61] one of the Berneuchen liturgical formularies of the mid-1930s, is a good illustration of this formal principle. Its second edition is particularly appropriate since it shows a number of characteristic Berneuchen features. The first edition, which like the *Berneuchener Buch* appeared in 1926, had contained some highly experimental pieces. Its authors make the following comments about these in the preface to the second edition:

> For a number of years now it has not been possible even for us to adhere to the order in its original form; but we have not presented the new order to the public until we tested it ourselves over the years and constantly reworked it based on the experience we have gained.[62]

These experimental pieces originated in Karl Bernhard Ritter's work as a pastor at the Deutscher Dom in Berlin in the 1920s and his contact with the youth movement there:

> Appointed by the Protestant High Church Council as the delegate for the *außerkirchlichen Jugendverbänden*, Ritter conducts "extremely radical liturgical experiments" with the youth movement and the university community in the rotunda of the Deutscher Dom, including Easter Vigil with candlelight processions and spiritual exercises. ... The resulting liturgical orders are published together with orders for confession and the Eucharist [beginning in] 1923 under the title *Der Deutsche Dom* by Karl Bernhard Ritter with the agreement of Count Lüttichau.

---

58   Perhaps, one should speak more precisely of a "renaissance," since this is actually a new version of late antique and early medieval theology.

59   Berneuchener Konferenz, ed., *Das Berneuchener Buch*, 89.

60   Berneuchener Konferenz, ed., *Das Berneuchener Buch*, 92.

---

61   *Die Ordnung der Deutschen Messe*, Kassel, J. Stauda, ²1936.

62   *Die Ordnung der Deutschen Messe*, i.

Significant in these orders is the omission of the sermon, for which Ritter offers his own religious service.[63]

It can be inferred from this that the second edition of *Die Ordnung der Deutschen Messe* developed over a longer period of time, and that the experimental pieces (inspired by the youth movement) found at the beginning had been erased, so that the work represented an example of Berneuchen liturgies which had been refined through practical experience. We can state, then, that: "The linking of natural and liturgical time, the interpenetration of traditional and novel liturgical elements, an expressive language oriented towards the Gospel of John, and the paradigm of community are its distinctive features."[64]

The order of the Mass mainly follows the liturgical tradition of the Western Church.[65] As was already the case with the two Hochkirche formularies, the *Ordnung der Deutschen Messe* was clearly constructed according to the model of the *Ordo Missae* of the *Missale Romanum*. The "Lord's Supper is the true and proper worship of the Christian church, the most important moment and the heart of all its liturgical acts."[66] This makes *Die Ordnung der Deutschen Messe* a formulary belonging to the second liturgical movement. Nonetheless, special mention may be made here of some Berneuchen peculiarities. For example, the Mass does not actually begin with the sacristy prayer but with meditative reflections and prayers by all the ministers, which are said in private as preparation. The meditative and mental involvement in the liturgical action, which is a typical formal feature of Berneuchen liturgies, starts the celebration of the Mass.[67]

In contrast to the other standard Protestant services, the *Ordnung der Deutschen Messe* feature three ministers, making a clear allusion to the Solemn Mass from the *Missale Romanum* in use at the time, one of whose distinctive characteristics was the fixed assignation of two deacons, called *Helfer* in the text, one on the epistle side and the other on the gospel side of the altar.[68] The fundamental aim of the Mass was to be the pedagogical formation of the community by the preacher and was to become the place in which the congregation responded to God's call with prayer and hymns.

The translation of specialist liturgical terms into German is another typical Berneuchen feature. Thus, *diaconus* becomes *Helfer* (helper), *Introitus* becomes *Eingangslied und Psalm*,[69] *Kyrie* becomes *Bittruf*,[70] *Gloria* becomes *Lobpreis und Lobgesang*.[71] This tendency of translating liturgical terms into German could certainly already be found in liturgical publications before *Die Ordnung der Deutschen Messe*,[72] but it henceforth

---

63   Wolfgang Fenske, *Innerung und Ahmung: Meditation und Liturgie in der hermetischen Theologie Karl Bernhard Ritters*, Leipzig, Edition Chrismon, 2011, 36f.

64   Wolfgang Fenske, "Karl Bernhard Ritter (1890–1968)," in: Benedikt Kranemann & Klaus Raschzok, eds., *Gottesdienst als Feld theologischer Wissenschaft im 20. Jahrhundert: Deutschsprachige Liturgiewissenschaft in Einzelporträts*, Münster, Aschendorff, 2011, 976–993, here 981.

65   Prayer in the sacristy, entrance, preparation, Confiteor (alternating), Introit, Kyrie, Gloria, Collect, Epistle, Alleluia, Wochenlied (instead of Gradual chant), Munda Cor, Gospel, hymn/choir, sermon, sermon hymn, Pax, Intercessions, offertory procession (with a procession around the altar), Preparation of the Gifts, Offertory Prayer, Creed (Nicene, with the *Filioque* and the standard Protestant translation of "catholicam" as "universal"/Luther's chorale/or similar), Preface, Sanctus, Verba Testamenti, Anamnesis, song of praise (according to church year, e.g. "Christ ist erstanden"), Epiclesis, Fractio Panis (Maranatha), Our Father, Sancta Sanctis, Agnus Dei, Communion, versicle of thanksgiving, prayer of thanksgiving, Last Gospel (Prologue of John), Postcommunion, Dismissal, final hymn, blessing, departure of clergy.

66   *Die Ordnung der Deutschen Messe*, i.

67   The influence of the Freemasons can be detected, as well as the central importance of meditation, which became a characteristic aspect of Berneuchen spirituality beginning in 1931 with the foundation of the Evangelische Michaelsbruderschaft. For further details, see Fenske, *Innerung und Ahmung*, 46f., 52f.

68   See *Die Ordnung der Deutschen Messe*, 17.

69   *Die Ordnung der Deutschen Messe*, 8.

70   *Die Ordnung der Deutschen Messe*, 8.

71   *Die Ordnung der Deutschen Messe*, 10.

72   For example, see Julius Smend, *Kirchenbuch für evangelische Gemeinden*, vol. 1, Gütersloh, Bertelsmann, ³1924.

became standard practice, even to the present day, thanks to the Berneuchen movement's influence.[73]

The substitution of the gradual chant with the *Wochenlied*, which today is part of the standard repertoire of a Protestant service, is an initiative of this period which was particularly appreciated by the members of the movement:

> The basic theory about how in the Mass proclamation to the congregation is ensured is thus the following: the *Wochenlied* must be there, the sermon may be there. It [the *Wochenlied*] is the true, proper, and guaranteed interpretation of the Sunday Gospel against any subjective contingencies due to the stupidity, laziness, indisposition, etc. of the pastor. That is why nothing is lost by foregoing a sermon but not the weekly hymn, and therefore this must be given the impressive rank between the two readings.[74]

As the Mass continues, of note is the rubric on the procession at the altar during the offertory: "According to ancient church custom, the congregation walks around the altar during the song and brings offerings which a helper, standing at the altar, collects."[75] The recovery of this practice of the early church may be a relic from the youth movement influences. It is not clear whether this rubric was ever put into practice. It should certainly be considered an unusual element, especially in view of the fact that *Die Ordnung der Deutschen Messe* offers an optional variant which foregoes the solemn procession at the altar. Further, an emphasis is placed on the idea of the Eucharist as a prayer of anamnesis rather than a sacrifice. This shift is evident in the expression "we 'proclaim' him as our pure, holy, unblemished sacrifice."[76] The offering to the Lord becomes a proclamation.

> Significant here is the expression "in memory of me." The word memory ("ἀνάμνησις") does not mean that the disciples should hold Christ in their memory (they do not need any exhortation for that), but that they should commemorate him before God. Hence, this passage means that the Eucharist is the validation of the crucifix and to his sacrifice before God.[77]

Even though normally innovations passed from the Hochkirche to the Berneuchen movements, especially at the beginning of the second liturgical movement, this particular formulation of the anamnesis was instead taken up by the *Heiler-Messe* of 1948.[78]

According to *Die Ordnung der Deutschen Messe*, communion is followed by the Johannine prologue, which paraphrases the sacramental action according to Tillich's theory of symbols.

> It [the Prologue of John] does not function as a reading but rather as a contemplative adoration, and therefore it makes sense not to deliver it as a reading to the congregation but, like the prayers and the Verba Testamenti (*Er-innerung* as remembrance-interiorization), facing the altar. This hymn of the Word of the Father who takes flesh impressively clarifies how much the sacrament proceeds from the incarnation.[79]

Precisely at this point it becomes clear how intensively Berneuchen drew on the Western liturgical tradition. The Last Gospel is also an example of how marked was the reception of the formularies of the Hochkirche, developed only a few years

---

73 See Vereinigten Evangelisch-Lutherischen Kirche Deutschlands & Evangelische Kirche der Union Kirchenkanzlei, eds., *Evangelisches Gottesdienstbuch: Agende für die Evangelische Kirche der Union und für die Vereinigte Evangelisch-Lutherische Kirche Deutschlands*, Berlin, Evang. Haupt-Bibelges. und von Cansteinsche Bibelanst, ³2003.

74 Gerhard Kunze, *Gespräch mit Berneuchen*, Göttingen, Vandenhoeck & Ruprecht, 1938, 21f.

75 *Die Ordnung der Deutschen Messe*, 16.

76 *Die Ordnung der Deutschen Messe*, 29.

77 Stählin, "Die Geschichte," 10.

78 See Heiler, *Deutsche Messe*, 29.

79 *Die Ordnung der Deutschen Messe*, ix.

earlier.[80] Numerous studies are dedicated to this phenomenon.[81] Still in regard to *Die Ordnung der Deutschen Messe*, the analysis of John 1 was to bring about subsequently an interpretation of the reception of the Eucharist as a meditative moment for the faithful.

In short, it can be argued that the theology of revelation inspired the *Berneuchener Buch*, such inspiration can also be traced in the liturgical theory based on it. God's revelation in the incarnation of the Logos is transmitted to the congregation objectively through the sacramental actions of the ministers. This is something on which all the figures of the second liturgical movement agree.

5 Catholicizing Tendencies as a Path Towards an Ecumenical Awareness

From the 1920s, the Hochkirche and the Berneuchen constantly interact with each other as different strands within the same movement born from similar needs. From two different approaches – the Hochkirche with a tendency towards exemplarity and the Berneuchen with one towards originality – the two currents produced similar results in the structuring of the liturgy. One reason for this is undoubtedly that their members knew one another personally. In regard to the initiator of the Berneuchen Conferences, Karl Bernhard Ritter, we can reconstruct that at the time of his term as pastor of the Deutscher Dom of Berlin he collaborated with the exponent of the Hochkirche Count Siegfried von Lüttichau, who occupied the role of second pastor there.[82] Soon afterwards, however, Marburg became the stronghold of the liturgical development in German Protestantism. At the University of

Marburg, Friedrich Heiler was ordinary professor of religious studies. From 1928 on, Heiler became one of the leading figures in the Hochkirche movement in Germany. From it, in 1929, he founded the Evangelisch-Katholisch Eucharistischen Gemeinschaft (today the Hochkirchliche St.-Johannes-Bruderschaft). It was in Marburg that the Evangelische Michaelsbruderschaft was established on the feast of Saint Michael in 1931 with Ritter, who was a pastor in the city at the time, as its first presbyter. Their connections to the University of Marburg occasioned numerous encounters between the two. Heiler celebrated a Mass according to his Hochkirche formulary for his students in a chapel opposite Saint Elisabeth's Church:

> Those attending the service included Karl Bernhard Ritter, pastor at the church of the University of Marburg, cofounder of the Berneuchen movement and subsequently the Evangelische Michaelsbruderschaft. When he left the chapel, he said vehemently (Heiler has told the story many times smiling): "No, it is not right!" Hardly a year later, Heiler then adds, he had changed his mind and become the initiator of a similarly Protestant-Catholic service by the Berneuchen movement.[83]

This turnaround in Ritter's thinking, recalled here in this vivid scene, determined the initial relationship between the movement's two strands: in 1926 the *Berneuchener Buch* made a number of indirect allusions to the Hochkirche endeavors taking place at the same time, although its authors were careful to distinguish themselves from their counterparts:

> But anyone who seeks simply to tear the forms of previous centuries from oblivion and revive them, who clings anxiously to tradition in the structuring of the liturgy, will never satisfy our generation's need for form by means of breviaries, hours, and

---

80   See the Protestant-Catholic Eucharist Celebration discussed above.

81   On this, see for example Bieritz, "Liturgische Bewegungen," 717f.; Hans Hartog, *Evangelische Katholizität: Weg und Vision Friedrich Heilers*, Mainz, Grünewald, 1995, 76; Stählin, "Die Geschichte," 78; Stählin, *Berneuchen antwortet*, 36.

82   See Fenske, *Innerung und Ahmung*, 36f.

83   Hartog, *Evangelische Katholizität*, 30.

ordinaries for the Mass. There are no immutable forms.[84]

The liturgical romanticism sharply criticized here, according to the Berneuchen movement, hence consisted in rendering the forms derived from long forgotten and yet (supposedly) better times absolute. These old forms would then be imposed on contemporary liturgical celebrations and, most importantly, on the people taking part in them. The Hochkirche undoubtedly trusted from the beginning in the performative effect of the liturgical act; yet they never claimed an immutability of form. Moreover, their historical approach to liturgy and the creation of new formularies clearly demonstrate this. On the contrary, in their view the liturgy was not *art pour l'art*, but must always be subordinate to the purpose: "To bring the heaven of the certainty of salvation into the poor hearts of men and through it give them the strength for a life of sacrifice in the service of their neighbor."[85]

In this respect, the Berneuchen circle saw itself as a movement of renewal of the Protestant Churches at a time when a new impulse in liturgical studies became necessary due to developments in theology. Almost by accident, this new impulse led to an opening towards the traditional forms of the Western Church. While the results from both movements reveal great similarities, the approaches taken by the two currents within the second liturgical movement continued to be seen as diametrically opposed. "It must be noted that the work of liturgical practice by the Hochkirche ... will have an indirect influence on the whole church, passing through the circuitous route of the Berneuchen ordinaries."[86] It is evident

that the pioneering value of their work should be recognized.

The subsequent period would be defined by the rise to power of the National Socialists and its battle against the churches. The climate of freedom that had made possible the numerous and varied liturgical experiments was lost: in the passage from a state system like that of the empire – which respected the freedom of the churches and ensured a space for them that still today is the basis for churches' freedom of action – to a totalitarian system which attempted to subordinate the churches to its own ideology, often with frightening success, the identity of the churches was subjected to an ordeal of many different challenges. The Berneuchen aspirations in particular were decisive for liturgical developments in Protestant Germany:

> Once again, the Berneuchen liturgical theory exercised a considerable influence on the liturgies that appear in the 1950s– communicated through the collaboration of its proponents in liturgical conferences, particularly the Lutherischen Liturgischen Konferenz Deutschlands.[87]

In this way, it was possible to transfer the findings of the second liturgical movement as a whole into regional church forms by the political developments after World War II.

5.1 Catholicizing Tendencies: A Controversial Concept Becomes Standard Policy

The criticism of the Protestant Churches in the 1910s and 1920s led to an internal debate over their own ecclesiastical identity. With the reception of the new approaches to the liturgy, the phrase "catholicizing tendencies" very soon began to be used to describe the different currents. After World War II, Wilhelm Stählin, a prominent figure within the second liturgical movement, attacked this concept in one of his works: "The

---

84 Berneuchener Konferenz, ed., *Das Berneuchener Buch*, 99. The exponents of the Hochkirche had decided to compose their own breviary as the first step in the renewal of the Protestant Church through daily prayer.

85 Friedrich Heiler, "Evangelisches Hochkirchentum," in: Heiler, *Evangelische Katholizität: Gesammelte Aufsätze und Vorträge*, vol. 1, 198–250, here 243.

86 Bieritz, "Liturgische Bewegungen," 718.

87 Bieritz, "Liturgische Bewegungen," 718.

expression 'catholicizing tendencies' is first of all – at least for many who use it with a pointed finger – an expression of a growing concern."[88] The term "catholicizing" could be understood in two ways. First, it could be seen as the perception of a threat to one's own identity: this point of view was the motive for many a doctrinal investigation. Second, however, it can be seen as contributing to the shaping of an identity: the limitations of Protestant provincialism can be surpassed, accentuating instead membership in the one church of the Christian ecumene.

The fear of "catholicizing," and therefore the fear of a loss of identity, appears to have its origins in the basic Protestant outlook. The concentration on the individual and preaching had resulted in a preference for verbal proclamation, which entailed a reluctance in recognizing the value of liturgical proclamation. The reverse could be said for the Roman Church. The renewal of the liturgy from predominantly Western Church sources, as was the case with the second liturgical movement, must have affected this rather emotional view of the liturgy.

> Thus, whoever warns of "Catholicizing tendencies" as soon as anyone declares his liking for dogma and wants to defend the binding doctrines of the church against all reasonable and unreasonable private opinions, must be told that he has a mistaken idea of the Reformation, that he takes the symptom of illness for the essential feature of Protestantism, and that he is not fighting with the Reformation against a "Catholic" threat but with the Enlightenment and the liberalistic dissolution against the true inheritance of the Reformation.[89]

However, if the term "catholicizing" is taken in its sense of shaping identity it can be seen to be at the

basis of the ecumenical ideal expressed by Heiler and by Hansen's theses (evangelical catholicity). Both wished to enrich the individual confessions with the strengths of the other churches. The aim of ecumenism, taken in an idealistic sense, was to be the perfecting of the individual confessions in the one church. This position was supported by the basic orientation of the fundamental works of Protestantism, as Wilhelm Stählin himself noted: "The confessional writings of our church knowingly wanted to be a *confessio catholica*, because they regarded themselves as members of the catholic, meaning universal, church."[90] A process of the formation of identity that is based on pointing the finger at the negligence of the other in matters of form and content necessarily leads instead to a closure, and thus a distancing from the "catholic" approach of *et-et*.

The intention to "catholicize" the Protestant Church also produced a paradigm shift: after a phase in which the individual was placed at the center, the emphasis on the importance of the collective element of the faithful becomes the concern. In this respect, the negative perception of the ecclesiastical principle of catholicity was determined by the fatal centralization around the figure of the Führer during the Third Reich. After 1945, unity and uniformity were tainted by their association with dehumanizing power structures. In this regard, shortly after the war, Stählin expressed the real threat of catholicizing tendencies, understood as the loss of identity, in these words:

> If we place in men the trust that is proper to God alone, if in an ecclesial setting we speak of political events with words appropriate only to the salvific work of God and the kingdom of heaven, if we speak of the political leader as the "foundation, cornerstone and jewel of the German nation," then these are "catholicizing tendencies" in the sense of the Reformation, because here earthly values

---

88   Wilhelm Stählin, *Katholisierende Neigungen in der evangelischen Kirche*, Stuttgart, Schwabenverlag, 1947, 7.

89   Stählin, *Katholisierende Neigungen*, 21.

---

90   Stählin, *Katholisierende Neigungen*, 33.

are placed next to Christ and adorned with names proper to him alone.[91]

The sociopolitical movement, which from the late 1960s on began to deal with Germany's own contemporary history, limited the scope of influence of the results of the second liturgical movement. By reemphasizing the importance of individuality, they brought about the second liturgical paradigm shift of the 20th century. The process of negotiation between the two paradigms, which shapes today's Protestant liturgical studies, now raises new questions, which in turn build on the achievements of the two movements and have their predecessors in the Berneuchen "aesthetics."[92]

The healthy criticism by the "catholicizers" of the provincialism of Protestant thinking after the fall of the German Empire led to a softening of positions. In fact, this "catholicizing" did not bring with it the loss of Protestant identity, but rather the honing of Protestantism's own profile. The second liturgical movement can therefore be described on the whole as a catholicizing tendency within the Protestant Church which, through its liturgical practice, smoothed the way for the subsequent ecumenical process.

> [Heiler] contributed in a consistent manner to opening up the Protestant Churches to pre-Reformation liturgical traditions and to those from other confessions. The enrichment of the liturgy from the other Christian confessions is today a common approach to drawing up liturgical formularies.[93]

The openness of Protestant liturgical studies is justified today by the idea of representing a liturgical form that regards itself as ecumenically open to the sister churches.[94] In addition to this, models are proposed in today's Protestant formularies which have a clear echo of the liturgical spirit of the pioneers. This does not regard only Heiler and the Hochkirche current but has its origins in the liturgical movements of the 20th century:

> Liturgical renewal is not a "catholicizing tendency" but a return to the fullness of liturgical life; it is not emigrating and settling in a foreign country but returning home to the house that our fathers built and left to us as a dwelling of the real and authentic presence of God in this world.[95]

Translated from German to English by Fiona Robb.

Bibliography

Hartog, Hans, *Evangelische Katholizität: Weg und Vision Friedrich Heilers*, Mainz, Grünewald, 1995.

Hauf, Theodor, ed., *Siebzig Jahre Hochkirchliche Bewegung (1918–1988): Hochkirchliche Arbeit: Woher? Wozu? Wohin?*, Bochum, HV, 1989.

Heiler, Friedrich, *Deutsche Messe: Oder Feier des Herrenmahls nach altkirchlicher Ordnung*, Munich, Federmann, ²1948.

Heiler, Friedrich, *Evangelische Katholizität: Gesammelte Aufsätze und Vorträge*, vol. 1, Munich, Ernst Reinhardt, 1926.

Klöckener, Martin & Benedikt Kranemann, eds., *Liturgiereformen: Historische Studien zu einem bleibenden Grundzug des christlichen Gottesdienstes*, Münster, Aschendorff, 2002.

Kranemann, Benedikt & Klaus Raschzok, eds., *Gottesdienst als Feld theologischer Wissenschaft im 20.*

---

91 Stählin, *Katholisierende Neigungen*, 10.

92 See Berneuchener Konferenz, ed., *Das Berneuchener Buch*, 99.

93 Hanns Kerner, "Friedrich Heiler (1892–1967)," in: Kranemann & Raschzok, eds., *Gottesdienst als Feld theologischer Wissenschaft im 20. Jahrhundert*, 449–460, here 459.

94 See Vereinigten Evangelisch-Lutherischen Kirche Deutschlands & Evangelische Kirche der Union Kirchenkanzlei, eds., *Evangelisches Gottesdienstbuch*, Bielefeld, Luther-Verlag, 5.13.18.

95 Stählin, *Katholisierende Neigungen*, 28f.

Jahrhundert: Deutschsprachige Liturgiewissenschaft in Einzelporträts, Münster, Aschendorff, 2011.

Lenz, Martin Cyprian, ed., *Ut omnes unum: Festschrift anlässlich des 100jährigen Bestehens der Hochkirchlichen Vereinigung Augsburgischen Bekenntnisses e. V.*, Norderstedt, Books on Demand, 2018.

Niepmann, Helmut Martin, *Chronik der Hochkirchlichen Vereinigung Augsburgischen Bekenntnisses e.V. über die ersten 50 Jahre ihres Bestehens (1918–1968)*, Bochum, Hochkirchliche Vereinigung Augsburgischen Bekenntnisses e.V., 1988.

CHAPTER 23

The Role of the Peace Movements in the Ecumenical Encounter (1907–1919)

Gerhard Besier

1 Christian Peace Initiatives between 1907 and 1914

Although it may seem surprising, the decade that preceded the outbreak of World War I was characterized not only by numerous crises but also by several Christian peace initiatives that originated, in particular, in Great Britain and Germany and were above all intended – in the face of the manifold political tensions between both countries (due to naval and colonial rivalry)[1] – to promote binational understanding.[2] The editor

of *The Peacemaker*, a Christian journal that may in some ways be described as the flagship of the movement, dated its beginnings to the year 1907.[3] The event that triggered the Christian initiative was the Second Hague Peace Convention in mid-October 1907.[4] By pure coincidence, two laymen – the liberal representative from London, Joseph Allen Baker,[5] a Quaker, and Baron Eduard de Neufville, from Frankfurt am Main – spoke

---

1   See Christopher Clark, *The Sleepwalkers: How Europe Went to War in 1914*, London, Allen Lane, 2012, esp. 413–417. Religiohistorical and religiocultural aspects lie beyond the scope of Clark's approach, as is also the case in Jörn Leonhard, *Die Büchse der Pandora: Geschichte des Ersten Weltkriegs*, Munich, Beck, 2014; only in his chapter "Kriegsdeutungen" does the latter take up those of the liberal theologian Ernst Troeltsch (Leonhard, *Die Büchse der Pandora*, 238–240). An entirely different approach is adopted in Herfried Münkler, *Der Große Krieg: Die Welt 1914 bis 1918*, Berlin, Rowohlt, 2013; for this, see his chapter "Der Sinn und die Ziele des Krieges," 215–288. See also Gerhard Hirschfeld & Gerd Krumeich, *Deutschland im Ersten Weltkrieg*, Frankfurt a.M., Fischer, 2013, and Oliver Janz, *Der Große Krieg*, Frankfurt a.M., Campus, 2013, ch. 5; Ernst Piper, *Nacht über Europa: Kulturgeschichte des Ersten Weltkriegs*, Berlin, Propyläen, 2013 (without mention of the Christian churches, but with a chapter on the situation of the Jews within the nations, "Zur Lage des Judentums inmitten der Völker," 315–367). See also Jay Winter, ed., *The Cambridge History of the First World War*, 3 vols., Cambridge, Cambridge University Press, 2014; vol. 3 includes a chapter on "Beliefs and Religion" by Adrian Gregory, 418–444.

2   See Gerald Deckart, *Deutsch-englische Verständigung: Eine Darstellung der nichtoffiziellen Bemühungen um eine Wiederannäherung der beiden Länder zwischen 1905 und 1914*, Ph.D. thesis, University of Munich, 1967, esp. 90–108;

Günter Hollenberg, *Englisches Interesse am Kaiserreich: Die Attraktivität Preußen-Deutschlands für konservative und liberale Kreise in Großbritannien (1860–1914)*, Wiesbaden, Steiner, 1974, 60–113, 132–146.

3   See John Henry Rushbrooke, "Die Bewegung unter den britischen christlichen Kirchen zur Pflege freundschaftlicher Beziehungen zwischen Deutschland und Großbritannien," *Die Eiche* 1, 1913, 9–11; see also Keith Clements, "100th Anniversary of the Anglo-German Churches' Exchange Visits," *Gemeindebrief: Christuskirche Oxford-Petersham, Pfarramtsbereich London-West*, April/May 2008, 4f., available at <http://www.ev-kirche-london-west.org.uk/downloads-links/downloads> (accessed Nov 6, 2020); Keith Clements, "A Notable Ecumenical Anniversary: The Anglo-German Churches' Exchange Visits of 1908–09," unpublished paper, 2008. The relevant archives are preserved at WCCA, Boxes 212.020 and 212.021, World Alliance for Promoting International Friendship through the Churches.

4   For this conference, see Jost Dülffer, *Regeln gegen den Krieg?: Die Haager Friedenskonferenzen 1899 und 1907 in der internationalen Politik*, Frankfurt a.M., Ullstein, 1981; Walther Schücking, *Der Staatenverband der Haager Konferenzen*, Munich, Duncker & Humblot, 1912.

5   See *The Times*, July 4, 1918, 3, and July 17, 1918, 6. See also Elizabeth B. Baker & Philip John Noel-Baker, *J. Allen Baker, Member of Parliament: A Memoir*, London, Swarthmore, 1927; Harmjan Dam, *Der Weltbund für Freundschaftsarbeit der Kirchen (1914–1948): Eine ökumenische Friedensorganisation*, Frankfurt a.M., Lembeck, 2001, 19ff.

about the possibility of mobilizing the religious communities of both countries in the cause of international understanding. Eduard de Neufville, like Baker a convinced pacifist[6] who had already endeavored to promote literary contacts between both nations, was consternated by the total absence of German church representatives at the second peace conference.[7] They both shared the conviction that religion, as the "soul" of their peoples, should no longer be marginalized, the more so as a broad "ecumenical" scope had been inherent in it from time immemorial. Baker and de Neufville contacted the British prime minister, Henry Campbell-Bannerman, and the German imperial chancellor, Prince Bernhard von Bülow, who both assured them of their support for the peace project. Thanks to the commitment of Joseph Allen Baker, who had in the meantime become president of the Metropolitan Free Churches Federation, an interdenominational committee was formed in Great Britain; under its auspices, 133 German ecclesiastics and theologians were invited to London and Cambridge in late May/ early June 1908. The speaker of the delegation was the general superintendent of Berlin, Ernst von Dryander;[8] and renowned theologians, such as Paul Althaus (Göttingen), Martin Rade (Marburg), and Hans von Soden (Berlin), gave the delegation an intellectual profile. The representative of the

Roman Catholic Church was the provost of St. Hedwig's Church in Berlin, Carl Kleineidam, who substituted the archbishop of Cologne. The guests were welcomed by the archbishop of Canterbury, Randall Davidson,[9] the cardinal archbishop of Westminster, Francis Bourne,[10] the president of the Free Churches, John Clifford,[11] himself a Baptist, and by the British chief rabbi. In addition to visiting church institutions and attending worship ceremonies, the German delegates had the opportunity to exchange views with representatives from all denominations and politicians of all political parties, including the prime minister, Herbert Henry Asquith. The reception hosted by King Edward VII at Buckingham Palace was seen as the highlight of the entire encounter.[12] A return visit in the following year afforded some 110 representatives of the Christian churches of Great Britain the opportunity to become acquainted with German cities and to gain a firsthand impression of the religious situation in Germany. Emperor William II invited the delegation to Potsdam, gave a warm speech, and entertained the British guests at Sanssouci.[13] Subsequently, the guests attended a speech on "International and National Christian Literature,"[14] delivered by the church

---

6 On the history of the Deutsche Friedensgesellschaft, founded in 1892 in Berlin by Bertha von Suttner and Alfred Hermann Fried, see Dieter Riesenberger, *Geschichte der Friedensbewegung in Deutschland: Von den Anfängen bis 1933*, Göttingen, Vandenhoeck & Ruprecht, 1985; Brigitte Hamann, *Bertha von Suttner: Kämpferin für den Frieden*, Vienna, Christian Brandstätter Verlag, 2013. On Great Britain, see Martin Ceadel, *Pacifism in Britain (1914–1945): The Defining of a Faith*, Oxford, Clarendon Press, 1980, esp. 20f., 34ff.

7 See Roger Philip Chickering, "The Peace Movement and the Religious Community in Germany (1900–1914)," *CH* 38/3, 1969, 300–311.

8 See Gerhard Besier, "Ernst Hermann von Dryander," in: Gerd Heinrich, ed., *Berlinische Lebensbilder*, vol. 5, *Theologen*, Berlin, Colloquium, 1990, 249–260; Bernd Andresen, *Ernst von Dryander: Eine biographische Studie*, Berlin, De Gruyter, 1995.

9 See Ernest Oldmeadow, *Francis Cardinal Bourne*, London, Burnes, Oates & Washbourne, 1940.

10 See James Marchant, *Dr. John Clifford, C.H.: Life Letters and Reminiscences*, London, Cassell, 1924.

11 See George K.A. Bell, *Randall Davidson, Archbishop of Canterbury*, 2 vols., London, Oxford University Press, 1935.

12 See Friedrich Siegmund-Schultze, *Der Friede und die Kirche: Peace and the Churches: Souvenir Volume of the Visit to England of Representatives of the German Christian Churches May 26 to June 3rd, 1908: Including the Visit to Scotland June 3rd to 7th, 1908*, London, Cassell, 1908.

13 Friedrich Siegmund-Schultze, ed., *Friendly Relations between Great Britain and Germany: Souvenir Volume of the Visit to Germany by Representatives of the British Christian Churches, June 7th to 20th 1909*, Berlin, H.S. Hermann, 1909.

14 See Adolf von Harnack, "Internationale und nationale christliche Literatur," in: Adolf von Harnack, *Reden und Aufsätze*, vol. 4, Giessen, A. Töpelmann, 1923, 23–40. See also Christian Nottmeier, *Adolf von Harnack und*

historian and renowned liberal theologian Adolf von Harnack in the auditorium of the University of Berlin. The theologian concluded his speech by stating that from the "perspective of science and religion, the cry of 'war' appears like madness, like a cry from the depths from which we have long since risen."[15] Von Harnack was one of the founders of the Verband für internationale Verständigung,[16] a pacifist association that he had joined on account of his preoccupation with the fundamental beliefs of early Christianity.[17] During both encounters, resolutions were approved that were intended to reassert the objective of mutual understanding and ultimately led to the establishment of the Associated Councils of the Churches in Britain and Germany for Fostering Friendlier Relations between the Peoples of the British and German Empires (Assoziierte Ausschüsse zur Pflege freundschaftlicher Beziehungen zwischen Großbritannien und Deutschland). The presidency of the British council was assumed by the archbishop of Canterbury; Joseph Allen Baker was assigned the function of executive president, while Sir Willoughby Hyett Dickinson, a parliamentarian from the Liberal Party, served

as the council's secretary. In Germany, the executive presidency was assumed by Friedrich Albert Spiecker, an industrialist,[18] while the secretarial duties were entrusted to the young pastor and educator Friedrich Siegmund-Schultze[19] from Berlin. A key foundation of the work conducted by both councils was the publication of the quarterly journals *The Peacemaker*, which addressed British readers, and *Die Eiche*, which was intended for the German public. The editor of the first issue of *The Peacemaker*, which was launched in July 1911 and soon reached a circulation of 67,000 copies, was John Henry Rushbrooke, a Baptist minister from Hampstead who had spent two years studying in Marburg and Berlin and whose wife was German;[20] *Die Eiche*, which was launched in January 1913, was edited by Siegmund-Schultze. The wider circle of the German council included 4,000 prominent personalities from all over Germany whose names were listed in the first issue. In many cases, the same essays and accounts of important church events were – after appropriate translation – printed in both publications in order to overcome the linguistic-cultural barrier.

Both sides were well aware that there was only limited room to ensure the success of this "ecumenical" endeavor: many of the movement's supporters were politically liberal-minded laypersons with a (free) church background and excellent connections to their respective levels

---

die deutsche Politik 1890–1930: Eine biographische Studie zum Verhältnis von Protestantismus, Wissenschaft und Politik, Tübingen, Mohr Siebeck, 2004, 367–377; Christian Nottmeier, "Religion, Krieg und Demokratie: Berliner Theologieprofessoren im Ersten Weltkrieg," *DtPfrBl* 8, 2005, 413–415; Jan Rohls, "Die deutsche protestantische Theologie und der Erste Weltkrieg," *Mitteilungen zur Kirchlichen Zeitgeschichte* 8, 2014, 11–58; here: 28ff.

15 Harnack, "Internationale und nationale christliche Literatur,"40.

16 See Chickering, "The Peace Movement," 309; Roger Philip Chickering, "A Voice of Moderation in Imperial Germany: The 'Verband für internationale Verständigung' (1911–1914)" *JCH* 8, 1973, 147–164. See also Karl Holl, *Pazifismus in Deutschland*, Frankfurt a.M., Suhrkamp, 1988, 94–97.

17 See Adolf von Harnack, *Das Wesen des Christentums*, Leipzig, J.C. Hinrichs, 1900; ed. Trutz Rendtorff, Gütersloh, Chr. Kaiser/Gütersloher Verlagshaus, 1999; Adolf von Harnack, *Militia Christi: Die christliche Religion und der Soldatenstand in den ersten drei Jahrhunderten*, Tübingen, Mohr, 1905.

18 See Jochen-Christoph Kaiser, "Friedrich Albert Spiecker (1854–1936): Eine Karriere zwischen Großindustrie und freiem Protestantismus," in: Theodor Strohm & Jörg Thierfelder, eds., *Diakonie im Deutschen Kaiserreich (1871–1918): Neuere Beiträge aus der diakoniegeschichtlichen Forschung*, Heidelberg, Heidelberger Verl.-Anst., 1995, 105–144.

19 See Stefan Grotefeld, *Friedrich Siegmund-Schultze: Ein deutscher Ökumeniker und christlicher Pazifist*, Gütersloh, Chr. Kaiser/Gütersloher Verlagshaus, 1998, esp. 82ff.

20 See Bernard Green, *Tomorrow's Man: A Biography of James Henry Rushbrooke*, Didcot, Baptist Historical Society, 1997. See also Keith Clements, "Baptists and the Outbreak of the First World War," *BQ* 26/2, 1975, 74–92, here 77–80.

of government. The interdenominational character restricted the scope of the undertaking to general peace concerns, without allowing for in-depth theological justifications or even alliances. In contrast to the situation in Great Britain, the German branch of the movement received little support from the mainstream churches because the rivalries among the other denominations and the misgivings towards them were still too great. Against the background of the German traditions, the initiative lacked the characteristic ecclesiastic-theological signature, whereas the postmillennialist Social Gospel movement in the Anglo-American world[21] had contributed to a leveling of theological differences in the interest of the common social concerns. Nevertheless, for the time being, the high-ranking "religious tourism" in the interest of peace seemed to be working very well on the practical level.

However, a careful examination of the lead article written by the editor of *Die Eiche* reveals yet another problem: Siegmund-Schultze used the old, nationalistically charged symbols without the slightest reservations and sought only to extend their meaning in a very limited way. *Die Eiche* was to remain the symbol of Germanity, of German strength, loyalty and patriotism, but was now also meant to stand for the ethnic kinship between Germany and Great Britain. "Truly a symbol of German strength, a guardian of the German coast; but at the same time an emblem of Germanic kinship, Old Saxon brotherhood, [and] German loyalty! A memorial to the imperial dictum: blood is thicker than water."[22] The attempt to harmonize decidedly conflicting elements under the banner of racial-cultural maxims could hardly succeed, all the more so as Siegmund-Schultze's already questionable constructions or

emulations of the traditional Romantic stereotypes of a British/German "collective character" might quite well be taken for a subordination of the British character to the German one. What the initiative lacked was a consequent ideological modernization that would have implied a rejection of outdated formulas of national reassurance. However, the consensus in the national councils does not seem to have gone that far. As a result, the attempt to revise the negative stereotype of the "perfidious Albion" and to reconcile it with the positive self-image of "Germanity"[23] threatened to fail as soon as serious crises began to loom on the horizon, thereby leading to a relapse into the barely overcome prejudices.[24]

Between 1909 and 1914, both national councils held further meetings that were attended, among others, by Adolf von Harnack, who travelled to London together with Spiecker in February 1911 and delivered an address that attracted considerable attention.[25] In the interest of maintaining good British-German relations, Joseph Allen Baker remained in permanent contact with the British Foreign Office and Lambeth Palace during the Second Moroccan Crisis, from July to November 1916,[26] in order to pour oil on the troubled waters of mutual indignation. Von Harnack's "politically pragmatic pacifism," on the other hand, did not permit him to place himself

21   See Martin E. Marty, *Modern American Religion*, vol. 1, *The Irony of It All* (*1893–1919*), Chicago IL, University of Chicago Press, 1986, 282ff.; Susan Curtis, *A Consuming Faith: The Social Gospel and Modern American Culture*, Baltimore MD, Johns Hopkins University Press, 1991. See also Gary Dorrien's contribution in this volume.

22   As stated in *Die Eiche* 1, 1913, 2.

23   See Gerhard Besier, *Weder Gut noch Böse: Warum sich Menschen wie verhalten*, Berlin, LIT, ²2013, 81ff.

24   It has recently been said that "so long as British Christians spoke of their Empire as God's chosen instrument, and Germans spoke of their *Kultur* in similar vein, this simply conceded the perilous dynamic of the situation till the collision occurred – and made it all the more bitter"; see Clements, "Baptists and the Outbreak," 85.

25   See Adolf von Harnack, "Der Friede und die Frucht des Geistes," in: Adolf von Harnack, *Aus Wissenschaft und Leben: Reden und Aufsätze: Neue Folge*, vol. 1, Giessen, A. Töpelmann, 1911, 203–209.

26   See Gerd Fesser, "Der Panthersprung nach Agadir: Mit dem deutschen Marineabenteuer vor Marokkos Küste begann am 1. Juli 1911 der Weg in den Ersten Weltkrieg," *Die Zeit*, June 30, 2011, 24 <https://www.zeit.de/2011/27/Panthersprung> (accessed July 4, 2019).

against the "German national consciousness"; he rejected a joint resolution of both councils that aimed to reaffirm their commitment to mutual understanding.[27] Afterwards, however, the mutual relations improved to such a point that the archbishop of Canterbury began to doubt whether the Associated Councils were still necessary. On the other hand, the British council was initially far more active in the public sphere than its German counterpart. In Berlin, attempts were made to remedy this shortcoming with a high-level conference that was held late in April 1914 in the Prussian House of Representatives, at which von Harnack, Superintendent Friedrich Lahusen and other prominent personalities spoke.[28]

The general sense of optimism was also a consequence of the fact that the British-German peace movement had by now aroused considerable interest in other parts of the world – not least in the United States.[29] In the summer of 1910, the British council was invited to New York City, where it was

to take part in a conference that since 1895 was held once a year in a hotel on Lake Mohonk and served as a kind of sociopolitical forum for academics, members of the clergy, judges, army officers, industrials, and others. The two British delegates, William Moore Ede and William Thomas, secretary of the Metropolitan Free Church Federation, sought to enlist support for the plan to organize an "ecumenical world conference" that would seek to influence both public opinion and that of the governments of Europe and of the United States in favor of amicable relations among peoples and to resolve dissensions between nations by means of an international court of justice, and no longer by military means. The United States were better suited to promote this cause than any other nation because the European antagonisms were foreign to them.[30] The participants in the conference at Lake Mohonk were so enthralled by the peace visions of their British guests that they immediately decided to consecrate a session of their next year's conference to this topic and to invite British as well as German delegates from the associated English-German councils. The opportunity proved favorable, as the only recently established union of Protestant Churches, the FCCC, was won over to the project. The British delegation at the 1911 conference of Lake Mohonk included Baker, Moore Ede, and Clifford, while the German side was represented by Siegmund-Schultze. The European delegates' idea of an ecumenical world conference was enthusiastically received by the participants in both conferences. In preparation for this conference, the secretary of the FCCC, Frederick Lynch, visited London and Berlin in the very same year amid renewed tensions between the two governments. Lynch was also secretary of the CPU,[31] which now took up the idea of a world conference and convened a preparatory conference

---

27 See Nottmeier, *Adolf von Harnack*, 371f. See also Rüdiger vom Bruch, "Deutschland und England: Heeres- oder Flottenverstärkung?: Politische Publizistik deutscher Hochschullehrer (1911/1912)," *Militärgeschichtliche Mitteilungen* 29, 1989, 1–35, here 17f.; Hartmut Lehmann, "'Es ist eine tiefernste, aber eine herrliche Zeit': Adolf von Harnack und die Kaiser-Wilhelm-Gesellschaft im Ersten Weltkrieg," in: Kurt Nowak & others, eds., *Adolf von Harnack: Christentum, Wissenschaft und Gesellschaft*, Göttingen, Vandenhoeck & Ruprecht, 2003, 189–206.

28 See *Die Eiche* 2, 1914, 214. Harnack's speech is printed in *The Peacemaker*, 1914, 20–22. Since Nottmeier (*Adolf von Harnack*, 375, footnote 714) writes that he had no access to the respective issues of *The Peacemaker*, the speech is reproduced in the appendix.

29 See Charles S. Macfarland, *International Christian Movements*, New York NY, F.H. Revell, 1924; Charles S. Macfarland, *Steps Toward the World Council: Origins of the Ecumenical Movement as Expressed in the Universal Christian Council for Life and Work*, New York NY, F.H. Revell, 1938, 27–37; *A History of the Ecumenical Movement*, vol. 1, Ruth Rouse & Stephen C. Neill, eds., *1517–1948*, London, SPCK, 1954, 511–515. See Karl Bornhausen, "Die Freundschaftsbeziehungen zwischen deutschem und amerikanischem Protestantismus," *Die Eiche* 1, 1913, 66–72. In the latter, the author deplores that only the scholarly results of German theology are noted in the United States, not their connection with

the German national spirit and the German culture of piety.

30 WCCA, Box 212.020, *The Churches and International Friendship: Movements Leading up to the Conferences at Constance and Liege, August 1914*, 9.

31 See *EIA* 27/1, 2013.

in Switzerland in May 1914, which was attended by leading personalities from the host nation as well as from Great Britain and Germany. At this event, the decision was made to hold the world conference in Constance in August 1914. Since the European states had already mobilized in late July 1914, only 85 of the 153 delegates from 10 countries were able to reach Constance. Those who did attend opened the conference on Aug 1, 1914 – when Germany and Russia had already declared war and France and Germany had started the mobilization of their armies. The participants had to leave Constance with all speed, but before doing so, they sent a telegram to the European heads of state and to the US president in which they implored them "to save the Christian civilization from the catastrophe."[32] A core group appointed a Continuation Committee in London and named it the World Alliance for Promoting International Friendship through the Churches.[33]

Against this background, it is all the more surprising that only a few days or weeks later, many of those who had participated in these Christian peace conferences went on to formulate and/ or sign manifestos of a decidedly belligerent nature.[34] The ecumenical spirit appeared to have suddenly disappeared, at least in the nations at war. Adolf von Harnack, who had been at the forefront of the peace initiative between Great Britain and Germany, now told students at Berlin University: "As the war now approaches with brazen steps, how do we receive it? We need only look to the street! Calmly, strongly, and eventually also cheering! We are now entering a time of eagerness for sacrifice."[35] Later, he sometimes even spoke out in favor of unrestricted submarine warfare.[36] Von Harnack was no exception but rather representative of the sudden reversal of opinion among German, but also British and French theologians, scientists,[37] artists,[38] and intellectuals.[39] Even the appeals for peace and neutrality voiced by Pope Benedict XV, who had been elected only in early September 1914, ultimately remained misunderstood,[40] with both sides suspecting the head of the Roman Catholic Church of secretly siding with the enemy.[41] This sudden shift from

---

32   On this event, see Jürgen Wandel, "Das vergessene Konzil von Konstanz," *Zeichen der Zeit* 8, 2004, 12–15.

33   See Harmjan Dam, *Der Weltbund für Freundschaftsarbeit der Kirchen (1914–1948): Eine ökumenische Friedensorganisation*, Frankfurt a.M., Lembeck, 2001; Karl Heinz Voigt, *Ökumene in Deutschland: Internationale Einflüsse und Netzwerkbildung: Anfänge 1848–1945*, Göttingen, Vandenhoeck & Ruprecht, 2014, 100ff.

34   See Gerhard Besier, *Die protestantischen Kirchen Europas im Ersten Weltkrieg: Ein Quellen- und Arbeitsbuch*, Göttingen, Vandenhoeck & Ruprecht, 1984; see also Gerhard Besier, *Krieg, Frieden, Abrüstung: Die Haltung der europäischen und amerikanischen Kirchen zur Frage der deutschen Kriegsschuld (1914–1933)*, Göttingen, Vandenhoeck & Ruprecht, 1982; Clements, "Baptists and the Outbreak."

35   Cited in: Klaus Schwabe, *Wissenschaft und Kriegsmoral: Die deutschen Hochschullehrer und die politischen Grundfragen des Ersten Weltkrieges*, Göttingen, Musterschmidt, 1969, 38. See also Thomas Kaufmann, "Die Harnacks und die Seebergs: 'Nationalprotestantische Mentalitäten' im Spiegel zweier Theologenfamilien," in: Manfred Gailus & Hartmut Lehmann, eds., *Nationalprotestantische Mentalitäten in Deutschland (1870–1970): Konturen, Entwicklungslinien und Umbrüche eines Weltbildes*, Göttingen, Vandenhoeck & Ruprecht, 2005, 165–122.

36   See Münkler, *Der Große Krieg*, 512. See also Adolf von Harnack, "Wilsons Botschaft und die deutsche Freiheit," in: Adolf von Harnack & others, eds., *Die deutsche Freiheit*, Gotha, F.A. Perthes, 1917, 1–13.

37   See Roy MacLeod, "The Scientists Go to War: Revisiting Precept and Practice (1914–1919)," *JWCS* 2, 2009, 37–51. See also Gerhard Besier, *Die Mittwochs-Gesellschaft im Kaiserreich: Protokolle aus dem geistigen Deutschland (1863–1919)*, Berlin, Siedler, 1990, 41ff., 291–295.

38   See Peter Harrington, "Religions and Spiritual Themes in British Academic Art during the Great War," *FWWS* 2, 2011, 145–164.

39   See Christophe Prochasson & Anne Rasmussen, *Au nom de la patrie: Les intellectuels et la première guerre mondiale (1910–1919)*, Paris, La Découverte, 1996.

40   See Arnold Struker, ed., *Die Kundgebungen Papst Benedikts XV. zum Weltfrieden: Im Urtext und in deutscher Übersetzung*, Freiburg i.Br., Herder, 1917.

41   See Wolfgang Steglich, ed., *Der Friedensappell Papst Benedikts XV. vom 1. August 1917 und die Mittelmächte diplomatische Aktenstücke des Deutschen Auswärtigen Amtes, des Bayerischen Staatsministeriums des Äussern, des Österreichisch-Ungarischen Ministeriums*

a moderate Christian-ecumenical pacifism to the religious affirmation of an enthusiastic culture of war requires some explanation.[42]

After only four months, however, the enthusiasm of many soldiers gave way to mounting disillusionment. Instead of returning home as victors,[43] the soldiers of all warring parties had to celebrate Christmas 1914 in the trenches. In the no man's land between the front lines, spontaneous scenes of fraternization took place – an event that was elevated to legend, especially on the British side –, a final reminder of the unifying power of the peace message of the Gospel.[44] Roughly 100,000 soldiers took part in the so-called 1914 Christmas truce, while military chaplains gave the feast its customary ritual splendor.

Even missionary ecumenism – the actual origin of the ecumenical movement[45] – was negatively impacted by the war events, the more so the longer it lasted. When the German missionary representatives declared in August 1917 that they could no longer accept the US-American John R. Mott[46] as president of the Edinburgh WMC's Continuation Committee[47] because the latter was working on an American commission in Russia, the leadership of the British and American missions established a new, provisional organ: the Emergency Committee of Co-operating Missions. Until the beginning of the world war, the fundamental principle of supranationalism had belonged to the generally accepted maxims of missionary work and had been explicitly confirmed by the colonial powers in the so-called Congo Act of 1885.[48] However, as a result of the armed conflict, this principle was no longer applied, thus leading to the internment or expulsion of roughly 1,800 German missionaries from the enemies countries' colonies. Joseph Houldsworth Oldham,[49] the secretary of both the Continuation Committee and the Emergency Committee, did his best to prevent the British authorities from confiscating the property of the German missions. Although he was successful in this (§ 438 of the Treaty of Versailles stipulated

---

des Äussern und des Britischen Auswärtigen Amtes aus den Jahren 1915–1922, Wiesbaden, F. Steiner, 1970; Wolfgang Steglich, ed., Die Verhandlungen des 2. Untersuchungsausschusses des Parlamentarischen Untersuchungsausschusses über die Päpstliche Friedensaktion von 1917, Wiesbaden, F. Steiner, 1974; René Schlott, Die Friedensnote Papst Benedikts XV vom 1. August 1917: Eine Untersuchung zur Berichterstattung und Kommentierung in der zeitgenössischen Berliner Tagespresse, Hamburg, Kovač, 2007. See also John F. Pollard, The Unknown Pope: Benedict XV (1914–1922) and the Pursuit of Peace, London, Chapman, 1999. For more recent studies on Pope Benedict XV, see Giovanni Cavagnini & Giulia Grossi, eds., Benedict XV: A Pope in the World of the "Useless Slaughter" (1914–1918), dir. Alberto Melloni, 2 vols., Turnhout, Brepols, 2020.

42   With regard to the signatories of the appeal to the cultural world from Oct 4, 1914, Oliver Janz also notes that: "Prior to 1914, quite a few of the signatories had been involved in organizations that promoted peace and international understanding"; Janz, Der Große Krieg, 206. See also Gerd Krumeich, Der Erste Weltkrieg: Die 101 wichtigsten Fragen, Munich, Beck, 2014, 99–103. On how this religious Kriegskultur inhibited ecumenical rapprochements during WWI, see Frédéric Gugelot's contribution in this volume.

43   See Stuart Hallifax, "'Over by Christmas': British Popular Opinion and the Short War in 1914," FWWS 1, 2010, 103–121.

44   See Michael Jürgs, Der kleine Frieden im Großen Krieg: Westfront 1914: Als Deutsche, Franzosen und Briten gemeinsam Weihnachten feierten, Munich, Goldmann, 2005. See also Tony Ashworth, Trench Warfare (1914–1918): The Live and Let Live System, London, Pan, 2000.

45   See William Richey Hogg, Ecumenical Foundations: A History of the International Missionary Council and Its Nineteenth-Century Background, New York NY, Harper and Brothers, 1952; Portland OR, Wipf & Stock, 2002; Jens Holger Schjørring, Norman A. Hjelm & Kevin Ward, eds., Geschichte des globalen Christentums, vol. 3, Stuttgart, Kohlhammer, 2018.

46   See Charles Howard Hopkins, John R. Mott (1865–1955): A Biography, Grand Rapids MI, Eerdmans, 1979. See also Sarah Scholl's contribution in this volume.

47   See Jutta Koslowski, Die Einheit der Kirche in der ökumenischen Diskussion: Zielvorstellungen kirchlicher Einheit im katholisch-evangelischen Dialog, Berlin, LIT, 2008, 46ff.

48   See Stig Förster, Wolfgang J. Mommsen & Ronald Robinson, eds., Bismarck, Europe, and Africa: The Berlin Africa Conference 1884–1885 and the Onset of Partition, Oxford, Oxford University Press, 1988.

49   See Keith Clements, Faith on the Frontier: A Life of J.H. Oldham, Edinburgh, T&T Clark, 1999, 164ff.

that the property of the missions was to be used for missionary purposes only), the German missionary societies still had to relinquish all claims to their former property. This is the reason why the German missionary leadership initially refused to be officially represented in the international cooperation of the missionary societies after 1918.

2   The Berlin-Uppsala Axis of Church Diplomacy during World War I

While the urgent peace note which Pope Benedict XV sent to the belligerent powers on Aug 1, 1917 is well known – as are his peace initiatives from 1914 onward[50] –, the initiatives of the Protestant Churches are still partly shrouded in darkness. In spite of all differences, however, there was one glaring parallel: both warring parties suspected that the churches were not interested in neutral mediation but themselves partisan to one or the other side. Both the Entente and the Central Powers believed that the pope's peace note from the summer of 1917 was a diplomatic maneuver in favor of the adversary and accused Pope Benedict XV of being the "pope of the enemy." In the French perspective, he was *le pape boche* ("the Kraut pope"), whereas Erich Ludendorff, the German general field marshal, always spoke of *Franzosenpapst* ("French pope"). In the main passage of his peace note, the pope had asked that Belgium should return to independence, thus displeasing the Germans, while he seemed to take for granted the Reich territorial integrity, thus disappointing French and British expectations. Benedict XV did not even receive an official response to his peace note, and neither was the Holy See invited to take part in the peace negotiations in Versailles in 1919 on Italy's explicit request.

The fact that both churches had lost so much trust on account of their national ties and patriotic involvement, and that they were even accused of not standing above the warring parties, was perhaps the most serious setback suffered by Christianity in this war. On the Protestant side, this was undoubtedly a consequence of the close ties between ecclesial and diplomatic officials, as illustrated in an exemplary fashion by the exchanges that took place between Stockholm and Berlin in the years 1917/1918 on a peace initiative of the archbishop of Uppsala and Lutheran primate of Sweden, Nathan Söderblom.[51]

In the summer of 1917, the Swedish committee of the WA, inspired by the socialist peace conference in Stockholm (June 2–19, 1917)[52] and assisted by the newly born British Council for Promoting an International Christian Meeting, asked Söderblom to convene a general assembly of all member churches in Uppsala, to be held in mid-December 1917 before the end of the war. Söderblom went further and offered to host a parallel meeting, concomitant with the conference of church representatives from neutral and belligerent countries. Supported immediately by German diplomatic circles, which saw the alleged Germanophilia of the primate of Sweden as a guarantee of reliability, Söderblom's proposal did not, however, seem to meet with the favor of authoritative ecclesiastical representatives of the Reich.

The chairman of the DEKA and president of the High Consistory, Bodo Voigts, was, as stated in a letter from the DEKA to the Foreign Ministry, "not really inclined to accept the offer"; however, he wished "to be informed about the opinion of the Foreign Ministry before taking further action."[53] The German Embassy in Stockholm, in

---

50   See Laura Anna Friedrichs, *Die Friedensinitiativen des Vatikans während des Ersten Weltkrieges*, Norderstedt, Books on Demand, 2015.

51   For a biographical portrait of Nathan Söderblom and his ecumenical legacy, see Dietz Lange's contribution in this volume.

52   See Ludger Heid, *Oskar Cohn: Ein Sozialist und Zionist im Kaiserreich und in der Weimarer Republik*, Frankfurt a.M., Campus, 2002, 172; Gerhard Hirschfeld & others, eds., *Enzyklopädie Erster Weltkrieg*, Paderborn, Schöningh, 2009, 511.

53   See J. Duske, Oberkonsistorialrat, to Auswärtige Amt, Nov 9, 1917, in: AAA R 20539-1, vol. 1, 12.

a communication to Imperial Chancellor Georg von Hertling, in office since Nov 1, 1917, drew his attention to the great political significance which the Lutheran faith has, as a connecting link, for German-Swedish relations. "It is of the utmost importance that these confessional ties be intensively cultivated, the more so as the English side is going to great lengths to remind the Swedes over and over again of how similar their church constitution and worship are to those of the Anglican High Church. ... As for Archbishop Söderblom's personality, his genuine sympathy for Germany is beyond doubt. It is well known that a son of the archbishop is serving in the German army."[54]

Söderblom's project aimed to "increase the reputation of the Swedish Church ... and to secure a leading role" among the European churches "for the latter." It was imperative to take this into account and to avoid offending the archbishop through a lack of responsiveness from the German side. For this reason, it was considered "politically highly advisable" to allow the German delegates to travel to Sweden. Unlike the diplomats, the president of the Parliament of all German Protestant State Churches, Bodo Voigts, voted against sending a German delegation. On Nov 13, 1917, he sent a letter to Söderblom in which he expressed concern over the fact that "a small number of German delegates [would] face a strong majority from other nations, chiefly those that are at war with us."[55] Voigts feared that the arrival of the Germans would be interpreted as a sign of weakness, something that is not compatible with "our Christian honor." In order to find a way out of this dilemma, it was suggested that the archbishop should invite "personalities whom you deem suitable directly and, because of the shortness of time, telegraphically" to take part in the conference among belligerent nations.[56] The personalities already

contacted by Söderblom – namely the general superintendent Lahusen, the New testament scholar Adolf Deißmann,[57] the mission directors Karl Axenfeld and August Wilhelm Schreiber, Friedrich Siegmund-Schultze, and the theologian Emil Ohly, whose wife was Swedish – were to travel to Uppsala as part of an unofficial delegation. Moreover, Emperor William II expressed the wish that General Superintendent Wilhelm Haendler be included in the German delegation.[58] This wish remained unfulfilled, while the now senior court chaplain Ernst von Dryander was also forced to cancel his trip for health reasons.[59]

The WA Conference eventually took place, as scheduled, on Dec 14, 1917, with the sole participation of neutral countries,[60] while the meeting extended to representatives of the churches of the belligerent nations was postponed for the first time until March of the following year, ceding to the perplexities of those who considered the date initially indicated too close to Christmas.[61]

In a letter to the Foreign Ministry, Axenfeld suspected that the warring countries of the Entente would refuse to issue passports to their citizens.[62] This assumption proved to be correct and the city chosen for the conference did not play a marginal role. The German ambassador in Stockholm, Hellmuth Lucius von Stoedten, wrote to the Foreign Ministry, stating that it would be in "our political interest" if the follow-up conference with the church delegates from the warring nations would also take place in Uppsala, "since

54 Stockholm Embassy to G. von Hertling, Nov 10, 1917, in: AAA R 20539-1, vol. 1, 26.

55 B. Voigts to N. Söderblom, Nov 13, 1917, in: AAA R 20539-1, vol. 1, 38–42.

56 K. Axenfeld & E. Ohly to N. Söderblom, Nov 13, 1917, in: AAA R 20539-1, vol. 1, 85–88.

57 See Christoph Markschies, "Adolf Deißmann: Ein Heidelberger Pionier der Ökumene," *JHMTH* 12, 2005, 47–89.

58 R. Valentini, secret civil cabinet, to the imperial chancellor, Nov 25, 1917, in: AAA R 20539-1, vol. 1, 111.

59 See E. von Dryander to the undersecretary of state, Nov 30, 1917, in: AAA R 20539-1, vol. 1, 144.

60 See Auswärtige Amt, Berlin, to Stockholm Embassy, Dec 2, 1917, in: AAA R 20539-1, vol. 1, 150.

61 See H. Lucius von Stoedten, Stockholm Embassy, to Auswärtige Amt, Dec 3, 1917, in: AAA R 20539-1, vol. 1, 146.

62 K. Axenfeld to Auswärtige Amt, Dec 3, 1917, in: AAA R 20539-1, vol. 1, 160.

Söderblöm's pro-German stance offers the best guarantee for desirable proceedings."[63]

In the letter of invitation to this ecumenical conference, Söderblom had already voiced an unmistakable preference for Uppsala.[64] In his support, German diplomatic investigations showed that public sentiments concerning other possible venues such as Bern or in Norwegian Christiania (Oslo) were by far not as Germanophile as Uppsala.[65]

In order to ensure that the Uppsala Conference, finally scheduled for mid-April 1918, could be held, an intense church-diplomatic activity also took place in Germany during the following weeks and months; in the end, the Germans were able to inform the Foreign Ministry that they had prevailed with regard to the conference venue,[66] but that it had proved necessary to postpone the conference itself until September 1918.[67] If indeed the bishop of Christiana, Jens Frølich Tandberg, had withdrawn his consent to the conference venue in Christiania, the British government had unofficially signified that it did not want such a "world peace conference" at that moment in time. As a consequence, following a first dilatory reply, the archbishop of Canterbury wrote to Söderblom that the Church of England could only send representatives to such a conference if the other mainstream churches, the Roman and the Eastern Churches, would also agree to do so. Since it was beyond doubt that the Roman Catholic Church would decline to send an official delegation, this response was tantamount to a refusal.[68]

On Mar 18, 1918, Lucius von Stoedten informed Imperial Chancellor von Hertling that the Protestant Church of France had declined the invitation to an ecumenical conference in September 1918.[69] "It is at your Excellency's gracious discretion to determine to what measure this refusal should be exploited for propagandistic purposes."[70] At the request of the Foreign Ministry, the negative reply of the French Protestants was discussed in the German church press.[71] Subsequently, the French side attempted to stir up opposition to the planned conference in the Nordic countries.[72] A low blow to the possibility of success of the conference, which was now scheduled for Sept 8, 1918, also came from Germany itself: the DEKA, in fact, informed the Foreign Ministry that Söderblom had not consulted the official German Church for the ecumenical conference but had turned to individual church personalities instead, so the DEKA had no obligation to issue a statement.[73]

The aforementioned Uppsala church conference of December 1917, with delegates from the neutral countries, had made the decision to launch an appeal to the American churches for the benefit of Finland, with the request "that these organizations employ themselves, either privately or publicly, so as to ensure that Finland is supplied with food during the famine that it currently endures."[74] Other than that, the participants passed various resolutions emphasizing the

---

63   H. Lucius von Stoedten to Auswärtige Amt, Dec 17, 1917, in: AAA R 20539-1, vol. 1, 174.

64   See the letter of invitation to the church conference in April 1918, in: AAA R 20539-1, vol. 1, 209–211.

65   See A.W. Schreiber to Auswärtige Amt, Feb 6, 1918, in: AAA R 20539-1, vol. 1, 228; Pastor Günther, Christiania, Jan 30, 1918, in: AAA R 20539-1, vol. 1, 237f.

66   See A.W. Schreiber to Auswärtige Amt, Jan 19, 1918, in: AAA R 20539-1, vol. 1, 207.

67   See A.W. Schreiber to Auswärtige Amt, Mar 5, 1918, in: AAA R 20539-1, vol. 1, 241.

68   See Besier, *Krieg, Frieden, Abrüstung*, 83ff.

69   See Norwegian newspaper *Aftenposten* 136, Mar 15, 1918.

70   H. Lucius von Stoedten to G. von Hertling, Mar 18, 1918, in: AAA R 20539-3, vol. 1, 243–245.

71   A.W. Schreiber to Auswärtige Amt, Apr 18, 1918, in: AAA R 20539-3, vol. 1, 251; K. Axenfeld to Auswärtige Amt, Apr 27, 1918, in: AAA R 20539-3, vol. 1, 259.

72   See German General Consulate of Geneva to G. von Hertling, Sept 6, 1918, in: AAA R 20539-3, vol. 1, 267. See also *Journal de Genève*, Sept 6, 1918.

73   R. Moeller, DEK, to Auswärtige Amt, July 24, 1918, in: AAA R 20539-3, vol. 1, 263f.

74   Ohly's report on the neutral church conference in Uppsala, Dec 14–16, 1917, in: AAA R 20539-3, vol. 1, 176–182, here 177.

THE ROLE OF THE PEACE MOVEMENTS IN THE ECUMENICAL ENCOUNTER

fact that Christianity stood above nationality and demanded that this be particularly respected in the field of missionary activities.[75]

Due to events of the war, Söderblom was again compelled to postpone sine die the other conference, the one planned for September 1918 with the belligerent countries.[76] As will be seen later, it was not until September 1919 – once peace had been reached – that the Christians from the warring nations would finally be able to meet again at the Dutch castle of Oud Wassenaar.

In the eyes of the Entente states, the fact that Söderblom's son had fought as a volunteer in the German army undermined his credibility as a neutral mediator. In the spring of 1918, the dean of St. Paul's in London, William Ralph Inge, wrote the following words to the archbishop of Canterbury: "I do not believe that Söderblom is really neutral in his feelings."[77] This stigma was not attached to Söderblom alone; the Entente states did not believe in the neutrality of Sweden that "in certain ecclesial circles of England and the United States, ... was seen as pro-German."[78]

3   The German Declaration of Guilt at Oud Wassenaar (1919)

French and British efforts to put an end to nationalistically motivated hatred by means of a joint appeal on the part of ecumenical Christianity, for example, the letter from Nîmes, which Charles Babut sent to Dryander on Aug 4, 1914, failed to achieve anything during the war, notably because German theologians also adopted the position that the war had been forced upon their homeland and that the German Empire was

therefore not to blame for the military conflict.[79] By September 1915, finally, the bilateral contacts between the churches of the warring nations had been entirely discontinued. News about ecclesial life on the other side only seeped through sporadically, so that one may indeed speak of a temporary end to ecumenical relations.

From December 1914, the representatives of the Protestant Churches of France proclaimed that the main objective of the French participation in the war was the "liberation of Alsace-Lorraine" and declared that as a consequence of the German aggression the relations between German and French Christians would remain disrupted for a long time.[80]

In the face of such attitudes, the appeal for peace which the archbishop of Uppsala, Nathan Söderblom, addressed to leading personalities of the belligerent countries in September 1914 went unheard. In it, he reminded "especially our Christian brethren of various nations that war cannot sunder the bond of internal union that Christ holds in us."[81]

More nuanced statements than those of the German and French pastors and theologians were made by representatives of the Church of England and of the Free Church Federation. Alfred Ernest Garvie, one of the prominent representatives of the British Free Churches, evoked their pacifist tradition and, at a joint conference of the Church of England and of the Free Church Federation in early February 1915, proposed a resolution that contained the following words:

---

75   See *Aftenbladet* 339, Dec 13, 1917; 341, Dec 15, 1917; 342, Dec 16, 1917.

76   See H. Lucius von Stoedten, Auswärtige Amt, to G. von Hertling, Aug 17, 1918, in: AAA R 20539-3, vol. 1, 268–270.

77   Cited in: Besier, *Krieg, Frieden, Abrüstung*, 86.

78   Bengt Sundkler, *Nathan Söderblom: His Life and Work*, London, Lutterworth, 1968, 210.

79   See Besier, *Krieg, Frieden, Abrüstung*, 28ff.

80   "We do not know when these relations can be resumed and how it may prove possible to organize a convention such as the missionary conference of Edinburgh [in the year 1910] in the future" said the representatives of the Fédération des Églises Protestantes de France, see "Déclaration de la Fédération des Églises Protestantes de France," in: Nils Karlström, *Kristna samförstandssträvanden under världskriget 1914–1918: Med särskild hänsyn till Nathan Söderbloms instats*, Stockholm, Akademisk avhandling, 1947, 614.

81   See Sundkler, *Nathan Söderblom*, 162ff.

We most urgently desire to assure our brothers in Christ in Germany and Austria that our hearts grieve over the current alienation of those who should be one in Christ, and that we long for a rapid reconciliation in order that the presently interrupted cooperation for the Kingdom of God might soon be fully restored for the glory of his hallowed name, to which it is your glory and ours to confess.[82]

The resolution failed to gain approval due to the opposition of the English state church. Personal initiatives, such as the correspondence between the archbishop of Canterbury, Randall Davidson, and the New Testament scholar Adolf Deißmann from Berlin, who was concerned about the mission in the German colonial territory of Cameroon, proved equally as fruitless[83] as Söderblom's letter to Davidson regarding another missionary matter. The archbishop of Uppsala's proposal to place the entire Evangelical-Lutheran mission in India under the supervision of the Swedish Church remained essentially unanswered.[84]

The year 1917 brought fundamental changes to the war and new initiatives for church unification. The United States' entry into the war, in particular, also changed the ecclesial landscape in the United States. The FCCC created a General War-Time Commission that represented the denominations within and outside the FCCC. In the opinion of Samuel McCrea Cavert, later secretary general of the FCCC, this step marked a high point in the cooperation among the Protestant denominations.[85] This newborn US ecumenical council of originally separately operating Protestant denominations – thus the testimony of the Swiss ecumenist Adolf Keller[86] – also sparked

a series of corresponding unification movements in Europe and was one of the post-war impulses in favor of the World Conference of Life and Work that convened in Stockholm in 1925 under Söderblom's presidency.

In the summer of 1917, even Adolf von Harnack revealed a complete change of mind in a memorandum to Imperial Chancellor Theobald von Bethmann-Hollweg. In this communication, he stated that Germany should issue a manifest in which it

> once again declare[d] that we are prepared to make every sacrifice to end this war, which we have waged as a defensive war, so long as it abides our *status quo ante*, and, furthermore, that we, as a Christian nation, are as deeply concerned about humanity as we are about our fatherland, because with our fatherland, we have a vocation for the former. ... Among the sacrifices, and I say this to avoid ambiguities, I count Belgium, Poland, and indeed even negotiations regarding border adjustments in Alsace-Lorraine.[87]

It was within this framework that Söderblom decided to organize, with the war still ongoing and in addition to the conference of neutral countries convened by the WA, the above-mentioned meeting in Uppsala between the ecclesial representatives of the belligerent nations. But just as the International Socialist Congress in Stockholm and the attempt promoted by the Scandinavian committees of the WA had failed, this personal initiative of Söderblom, as seen before, was destined to suffer continual postponements and ultimately result in a total fiasco.

The invitation only reached the FPF in mid-February 1918. The French response from

---

82   Cited in: Besier, *Krieg, Frieden, Abrüstung*, 72.

83   See Bell, *Randall Davidson*, 919–924.

84   Bell, *Randall Davidson*, 930.

85   William J. Schmidt, *Architect of Unity: A Biography of Samuel McCrea Cavert*, New York NY, Friendship Press, 1978, 47.

86   See Samuel McCrea Cavert, "Impressions of the Religious Situation in Europe," *Federal Council Bulletin*

6, September–October 1923, 11. See also Marianne Jehle-Wildberger, *Adolf Keller (1872–1963): Pionier der ökumenischen Bewegung*, Zurich, TVZ, 2008.

87   Cited in: Günter Brakelmann, *Der deutsche Protestantismus im Epochenjahr 1917*, Witten, Luther-Verlag, 1974, 41f.

Feb 26, 1918 already hinted at how difficult the new ecumenical beginning would be after the war. Indeed, the text of the French response states: "We cannot imagine entering into a dialogue with men – not even indirectly via well-intentioned and caring mediators – whose soldiers are shooting at our sons and brothers and still occupy portions of the sacred soil of our fatherland."[88] Unlike Söderblom, the French had no desire to keep the causes of the conflict and the political terms of its settlement out of the church debates; quite to the contrary, the responsibility for the catastrophe was an issue that they definitely wished to address.

In January and September 1918, the FPF sought to intensify its collaboration with the Church of England. As a first step, the French Protestants proposed holding a joint prayer day on Mar 17, 1918, which was to be devoted "to fervent and pious prayer for our peoples, our armies, our fleets, our rulers, and to the Kingdom of God on earth."[89] The archbishop of Canterbury, through the intermediary of the English chaplain in Paris, Stanley Blunt, replied that the Church of England had already held such a prayer day for the year 1918. However, the French brothers could rest assured that the faithful of the Church of England held them fast in their hearts and that their prayers would join those of their fellow brethren in France. The second attempt to initiate a closer cooperation between the two churches took place by way of an invitation to the Church of England for November 1918. A delegation of British clergymen was to go to France in order to demonstrate "the closer bonds of fraternal love that should now unite our peoples." A return visit was planned for January 1919. The archbishop of Canterbury was not very happy with this proposal, which the president of the FPF, Wilfred Monod, had already made a few months earlier during a visit to Great Britain. He wrote a letter to William Ralph Inge, stating that it was necessary to ensure that the English state church not be tied "to French Protestantism in the sense

of an opposition to French Catholicism."[90] He went on to say that it was difficult to make the French Protestants understand "that in Roman Catholic countries [as France], the English state church does not formally associate with the Protestants during official activities that are conducted independently of the national churches of these countries."[91]

Adolf Deißmann, who had entertained close ties to Sweden and repeatedly visited Stockholm and Uppsala during the war, addressed an appeal to Archbishop Söderblom on Nov 15, 1918, four days after the signing of the armistice. He wrote in it that Germany was not unwilling to make reparations; however, it was feared that peace would not bring about reconciliation but only worsen the misery.

> Having been involved in international-Christian understanding since the beginning of the war, I consider it my duty, at war's end, to appeal to the Christian leaders known to me in the countries that have since then been at war with us so that these may exercise their entire influence in such a way that the imminent world peace does not hold the seed of new world catastrophes but gives rise to all possible forces of reconciliation and constructiveness.[92]

He asked Söderblom to forward his letter to the archbishop of Canterbury, Randall Davidson.[93] However, Deißmann had been one of the signatories of the German Manifesto of the Ninety-Three in 1914, in which the war had been presented as an existential struggle that had been forced upon the Germans, and Prussian-German militarism was an integral part of German culture. The manifesto had even justified the violation of Belgian neutrality. Moreover, during the war, the New Testament

---

88   *Le Christianisme au XXᵉ siècle*, Mar 28, 1918, 98.

89   Cited in: Besier, *Krieg, Frieden, Abrüstung*, 82.

90   Besier, *Krieg, Frieden, Abrüstung*, 87.

91   Besier, *Krieg, Frieden, Abrüstung*, 87.

92   *Evangelischer Wochenbrief* 91/92, Nov 16, 1918, 5.

93   See Bell, *Randall Davidson*, 934.

scholar from Berlin had published several essays and speeches in which he defended the German position. He only began to revise his standpoint in his *Evangelischen Wochenbrief* from Nov 16, 1918, with an article on "Das belgische Unrecht und Wiedergutmachung" in which he described the invasion of Belgium as a morally "serious crime" and deemed it necessary to make reparations. He claimed that he had previously not been able to say this publicly due to the censorship that had been imposed in Germany.

It was clear that Deißmann intended to support the initiative of his friend Söderblom, who, after the war was over, was convinced that the general conference he had initially planned for Christmas 1917, but which he had failed to convene either in March, April or even September of the following year, would fall between the signing of the armistice (November 1918) and the beginning of peace negotiations, so that the churches could make their voices heard in favor of a reconciliation inspired by the Christian faith. Moreover, on Nov 17, 1918, Söderblom himself, as president of the Swedish section of the WA, addressed a message to the victors that in many places echoed the letter written to him by Deißmann two days earlier: it was essentially an appeal to the victorious powers "to conduct the upcoming peace negotiations with the intention of concluding an agreement that ... will prevent the rise of new hatred and lust for revenge and lay the foundations of a peace that leads to reconciliation and mutual trust between the peoples – of a peace that will pave the way for the rule of love and justice in the world."[94]

However, once again, Archbishop Davidson did not feel ready to adhere to Söderblom's new initiative: "When once peace terms have been decided upon and accepted by Germany," he wrote to a friend, "the situation will in my opinion change. But until that time I cannot confabulate with Germany on mere terms of Christian amity."[95] On Nov 25, after conferring with the conservative

politician Robert Cecil, who had served as undersecretary of state in the British Foreign Office and as minister of the blockade during the war, Davidson reminded Söderblom and Deißman of the dreadful events of the past:

> We cannot forget the terrible crime wrought against humanity and civilization when this stupendous war, with its irreparable agony and cruelty, was let loose in Europe. Nor can we possibly ignore the savagery which the German High Command has displayed in carrying on the war. The outrages in Belgium in the early months, and indeed ever since; the character of the devastation wrought in France, including the inhuman deportation of innocent citizens; the submarine warfare against passenger ships like the Lusitania and the rejoicings which ensued in Germany, the unspeakable cruelties exercised on defenseless prisoners down to the very end, including even the last few weeks; all these things compel the authorities of the Allied Powers to create security against the repetition of such a crime. The position would be different had there been on the part of Christian circles in Germany any public protest against these gross wrongs, or any repudiation of their perpetrators.[96]

On the same day, in a letter to Söderblom, Davidson also declined his invitation to take part in the international church conference in Uppsala. What did not completely convince the Archbishop of Canterbury was precisely the idea that the conference should be held before the conclusion of the peace treaty, a choice that in his opinion risked being interpreted by the states as an attempt to influence the ongoing negotiations.

After obtaining full knowledge of the peace terms late in May 1919, Davidson wrote a letter to Lloyd George in which he cautiously expressed reservations about the harsh terms of the treaty.

---

94   For the resolution, see AAA R 20539-3, vol. 1, 288.

95   Cited in: Bell, *Randall Davidson*, 935f.

96   Cited in: Bell, *Randall Davidson*, 937–938.

However, the prime minister replied that "it is always difficult in human affairs to adjust mercy and justice, and, if it is important that we should remember mercy, it is no less important that we should remember justice. No nation has ever committed such a crime against its neighbors as have the German people, under the instigation of Prussian *Kultur*."[97]

The British stance was of course still moderate in comparison to the reactions within French Protestantism. Justice must now be imposed, as the Protestant newspaper *Le Christianisme au XXe siècle* proclaimed on Dec 26, 1918,

> that is, rather severe material sanctions so that those who are guilty can assess from their own sufferings the full extent of the torments caused by them, so that the possibility of comparable horrors reoccurring may be banned forever from the face of the earth. For depending on how – in consequence of the punishment – the repentance and transformation of Germany takes place, the peace will either be permanent or followed by new wars.[98]

No other Protestant Church declined Söderblom's invitation to an ecumenical church conference quite as brusquely as the FPF did. For reasons of conscience and for the sake of the love of Christ, as the reply stated, they could not take part in such a conference until law and justice had been restored and truth brought to victory. Crimes needed to be branded as such if one did not wish to encourage the guilty to perpetrate further crimes against humanity. They strictly rejected the Nordic hypothesis of an equal responsibility of all nations for the catastrophe of the world war.[99]

After the failure of Söderblom's second personal attempt and once the peace in Versailles had been reached, the WA was at least able to gather its international committee in what was to all intents and purposes the first post-war Christian conference. The meeting was held in Oud Wassenaar, near The Hague, from Sept 30 to Oct 3, 1919 and, in order not to compromise its chances of success, the organizers carefully avoided mentioning in the invitation letter the problem of responsibility for the outbreak of war (the so-called *Schuldfrage*).

However, the French and Belgian representatives of the WA would not agree to such a meeting without preconditions. They demanded a unilateral admission of guilt on the part of the German delegates as a precondition for a first postwar meeting and for the justification of a future fellowship. After the secretary of the WA, the US-American George Nasmyth, had received a corresponding notice from the French national committee in July 1919, he advised Siegmund-Schultze to enter into correspondence with the president of the French section of the WA, Wilfred Monod, in order to clarify the situation. As a result of this correspondence, the German side came to express its regrets over the violation of Belgian neutrality and over the German share in the responsibility for unleashing the war. Monod, on the other hand, would express his regrets over the continuation of the blockade following the signing of the armistice and over the detainment of German war prisoners in France.

In his letter to Monod of Sept 15, 1919, Siegmund-Schultze limited himself to a personal condemnation of the violation of Belgian neutrality. The key sentence runs as follows: "As for me personally, I can also say that I will come to the WA Conference with a deep awareness of the guilt which Germany in particular has incurred."[100]

While Nasmyth appeared very pleased with the letter, Monod, who had expected a formal declaration of guilt, was in no way satisfied. The use of the word "also" in the sentence in particular had alarmed him, as it indicated that Siegmund-Schultze also assigned some of the

---

97 Cited in: Bell, *Randall Davidson*, 947–949.
98 *Le Christianisme au XXe siècle*, Dec 26, 1918, cols. 3–4.
99 *Le Christianisme au XXe siècle*, Apr 17, 1919, 166–168.

100 *Die Eiche* 8, 1920, 199f. Siegmund-Schultze's letter to Monod is dated Sept 15, 1919.

blame to the other belligerent powers. For this reason, the two leading French Protestants, Wilfred Monod and Élie Gounelle, editor of the official publication organ of the French section of the WA *Revue du christianisme social*, decided not to attend the conference in Oud Wassenaar. Instead, they sent letters to the conference's participants in which they insisted on a broad declaration of guilt on the part of the Germans as a fundamental requirement for a future participation in the conferences of the WA. The very few French delegates in Oud Wassenaar asked that Monod's letter be read out publicly. After a series of preliminary talks that were held in private, it was finally decided that the letter should be read aloud on the evening of the second conference day, after prayer, and that Siegmund-Schultze should respond to it in an informal manner.

In agreement with the other German delegates, Siegmund-Schultze began by publicly stating that they all shared the view that the violation of Belgian neutrality had been morally wrong. Although the British and the Americans had emphasized that a formal declaration of guilt was not necessary, Siegmund-Schultze nevertheless delivered a statement on the next morning, prior to the beginning of the agenda, in which he formally declared, in English, that: "We, the five delegates to this conference, personally consider the violation of the Belgian neutrality in 1914 as morally wrong." Rather skillfully, the declaration then mentioned Monod's absence at the meeting and ended with the account of the reconciliation ceremony among French, Belgian, Italian and German delegates on the evening of the first day of the proceedings: "We confess, we join hands, we condemn war, we condemn the idea of revenge."[101]

At first, the delegates appeared deeply impressed by the solemn statement, and the French, in particular, expressed this in their subsequent response.

However, various analyses and interpretations of the events in Oud Wassenaar, as well as

of the conference documents by those whose had stayed at home, led to a notable shift in mood – particularly in Germany and France. Numerous church journals in Germany strongly criticized the allegedly unpatriotic conduct of the German delegates; the tone of the debates in France was very similar. The confession of the German delegates was frequently seen as a national humiliation by their fellow countrymen. Many French, on the other hand, viewed the document as a shrewdly formulated testimony of a German lack of repentance that had succeeded in deceiving their unsuspecting delegates. Notwithstanding this, the German declaration and the subsequent reaction of the Belgian and French delegates can be seen as a breakthrough in the barrier of resentment that the war had raised among the Christian nations of Europe. After consultation with its two delegates who had attended the conference in Oud Wassenaar, the French committee of the WA, in a resolution passed on Oct 7, 1919 in Paris, decided to resume fraternal relations with *those* Christians in Germany who could endorse the German declaration of Oud Wassenaar.[102] Without the declaration of guilt of Oud Wassenaar, the ecumenical movements Life and Work and Faith and Order would have had little chance of success.[103]

In Oud Wassenaar, the question of the freedom and unity of the Christian mission had also been on the agenda. The German delegates continued to insist on the fundamental principle that the mission stood above nationality. They agreed with the other conference delegates that the situation of the German missions – hindered in many non-European countries – presented a serious obstacle to any progress towards an international Christian fellowship. In a corresponding resolution, the

---

101   *Die Eiche* 7, 1919, 245 f.

102   *Revue du christianisme social* 2, 1919, 156f.

103   As also concluded by Wolfram Weiße, *Praktisches Christentum und Reich Gottes: Die ökumenische Bewegung Life and Work (1919–1937)*, Göttingen, Vandenhoeck & Ruprecht, 1991, 43. See also Hanns Kerner, *Luthertum und ökumenische Bewegung für praktisches Christentum (1919–1926)*, Gütersloh, Mohn, 1983.

conference expressed the hope that the German missions might be allowed to resume their work as soon as possible in their former missionary fields. The property of the German missions should be restored to the German missionary societies as soon as these received permission to return to their old missionary fields. In the eyes of the missionaries, Oud Wassenaar was "a spiritual peace conference."[104]

Another two years would elapse before the IMC was finally constituted in October 1921 at the Lake Mohonk Conference.[105] However, representatives of the German missionary societies were still absent at the conference. Not until April 1922 did the commission of the German missionary societies appoint representatives for the IMC, who were once again able to attend the meeting of the council in Oxford in July 1923.

However, the Nordic and Western Churches were not the only ones to generate decisive impulses for reconciliation and for the union of the Christian denominations after World War I. Independently of Söderblom's plans and initiatives, the Holy Synod of the Church of Constantinople was the first to take the initiative. On Jan 10, 1919, the Ecumenical Patriarchate of Constantinople officially agreed on a resolution to invite all Christian churches to form a league of churches. During the session, the *locum tenens* of the Ecumenical See, the Metropolitan Dorotheos of Bursa, delivered a statement to the effect that the recommendation to unite the Christian churches in a league of churches should come "from the great Church of Constantinople in the East"[106] – just as the founding of the League of Nations had been initiated by the great state in the West, the United States. The Theological School of Halki,

in particular its dean Germanos Strenopoulos, the metropolitan of Seleukia, was commissioned to draft a corresponding report. On Nov 19, 1919, the Holy Synod approved this report and sent out the encyclical in January 1920. In this encyclical, it is stated that the individual churches "should no more consider one another as strangers and foreigners, but as relatives, and as being a part of the household of Christ and 'fellow heirs, members of the same body and partakers of the promise of God in Christ' (Eph 3:6)."[107] The encyclical was undoubtedly motivated by the collapse of the Ottoman and Russian Empires and by the resulting insecurity of the Ecumenical Patriarchate, but also by the proselytism of Western Churches and missions among Orthodox Christians. The text of the encyclical explicitly refers to this. Although it was not widely circulated, the Greek Orthodox delegates were able to present their encyclical at the preparatory conferences of Faith and Order and Life and Work in Geneva in the summer of 1920, where it met with a very positive response.[108] However, many years would pass before an official ecumenical league of churches – such as the one proposed in the 1920 patriarchal encyclical – was finally established.

Translated from German to English by Robert Meyer.

Bibliography

Besier, Gerhard, "The Intervention of the German Empire in the Finnish Civil War 1917/18: From Revolutionary State to Kingdom," in: Gerhard

---

104   Nils Karlström, "Movements for International Friendship and Life and Work (1910–1925): 'A Spiritual Peace Conference,'" in: *A History of the Ecumenical Movement*, vol. 1, 509–539.

105   See Kenneth R. Ross's contribution in this volume.

106   Vasil T. Istavridis, "The Work of Germanos Strenopoulos in the Field of Inter-Orthodox and Inter-Christian Relations," *EcRev* 11/3, 1958 1959, 292.

---

107   "Encyclical of the Ecumenical Patriarchate, 1920: *Unto the Churches of Christ Everywhere*," in: Gennadios Limouris, ed., *Orthodox Visions of Ecumenism: Statements, Messages, and Reports on the Ecumenical Movement (1902–1992)*, Geneva, WCC Publications, 1994, 9–11, here 9–10.

108   See "What the Members of the Conference Say," *The Christian Union Quarterly* 17, 1927, 242. See Stylianos Tsompanidis's contribution in this volume.

Besier & Katarzyna Stokłosa, eds., *1917 and the Consequences*, London, Routledge, 2020, 47–79.

Dam, Harmjan, *Der Weltbund für Freundschaftsarbeit der Kirchen (1914–1948): Eine ökumenische Friedensorganisation*, Frankfurt a.M., Lembeck, 2001.

Jehle-Wildberger, Marianne, *Adolf Keller (1872–1963): Pionier der ökumenischen Bewegung*, Zurich, TVZ, 2008.

Karlström, Nils, "Movements for International Friendship and Life and Work (1910–1925): 'A Spiritual Peace Conference,'" in: *A History of the Ecumenical Movement*, vol. 1, Ruth Rouse & Stephen C. Neill, eds., *1517–1948*, London, SPCK, 1954, 509–539.

Kerner, Hanns, *Luthertum und ökumenische Bewegung für praktisches Christentum (1919–1926)*, Gütersloh, Mohn, 1983.

MacLeod, Roy, "The Scientists Go to War: Revisiting Precept and Practice (1914–1919)," *JWCS* 2, 2009, 37–51.

Schjørring, Jens Holger, Norman A. Hjelm & Kevin Ward, eds., *Geschichte des globalen Christentums*, vol. 3, Stuttgart, Kohlhammer, 2018.

Slotte, Pamela, "'Blessed Are the Peacemakers': Christian Internationalism, Ecumenical Voices and the Quest for Human Rights," in: Pamela Slotte & Miia Halme-Tuomisaari, eds., *Revisiting the Origins of Human Rights*, Cambridge, Cambridge University Press, 2015, 293–329.

Voigt, Karl Heinz, *Ökumene in Deutschland: Internationale Einflüsse und Netzwerkbildung: Anfänge 1848–1945*, Göttingen, Vandenhoeck & Ruprecht, 2014.

Weiße, Wolfram, *Praktisches Christentum und Reich Gottes: Die ökumenische Bewegung Life and Work (1919–1937)*, Göttingen, Vandenhoeck & Ruprecht, 1991.

Winter, Jay, ed., *The Cambridge History of the First World War*, 3 vols., Cambridge, Cambridge University Press, 2014.

CHAPTER 24

Latin American Rebound Effect: The Panama Congress on Christian Work

Juan Sepúlveda

1   Introduction

Just as the WMC in Edinburgh in 1910 had been for the rest of the world,[1] the CCWLA (Panama, 1916) is regarded as the birthplace of the Latin American ecumenical movement[2] in its first intra-Protestant phase, by then termed "movement of missionary cooperation." The literature available makes it sufficiently clear that the Panama Congress was largely an effect of what had happened in Edinburgh, but it is a little more complex to distinguish what is a myth from what really happened, in the generally accepted interpretation of the kind of causal relationship that existed between both events.

According to the generally accepted interpretation, the Panama Congress was organized by North American missionary societies, which were dissatisfied not only with the exclusion of Latin America from the deliberations of the Edinburgh conference but especially with the supposed rejection of Protestant missionary work in this territory that had already been "occupied" by the Roman Catholic Church. According to the official report of the Panama Congress,

some German societies objected to the introduction of Latin America among the mission countries to be discussed at Edinburgh, on the grounds of its being, nominally at least, Christian, and because a proper use of current terminology and a truly scientific method of survey would exclude Latin America from consideration along with non-Christian lands, because of the essential difference of the problems to be considered. A similar exclusion was the price of the complete cooperation of all elements of the established Church of England.[3]

The purpose of this contribution[4] is to demonstrate that the question regarding the legitimacy of Protestant missionary work in Latin America was, especially since the Spanish-American War (1898), primarily a matter of internal debate among North American missionary boards. In that context, some of the promoters of Protestant work in Latin America, chiefly Robert Elliott Speer, saw the decision to delimit the deliberations of the Edinburgh Conference to missionary work among non-Christian peoples as an opportunity to generate in North America a current of opinion more favorable to the recognition of Latin America as

---

1 Kenneth Scott Latourette, "Ecumenical Bearings of the Missionary Movement and the International Missionary Council," in: *A History of the Ecumenical Movement*, vol. 1, Ruth Rouse & Stephen C. Neill, eds., *1517–1948*, London, SPCK, 1954, 351–401, here 362. On the same argument see Kenneth R. Ross's and Brian Stanley's contributions in this volume.

2 Dafne Sabanes Plou, *Caminos de unidad: Itinerario del diálogo ecuménico en América Latina (1916–1991)*, Quito, Consejo Latinoamericano de Iglesias, 1994.

3 CCLA, ed., "The Inception and History of the Congress," in: CCLA, ed., *Christian Work in Latin America*, vol. 1, New York NY, Missionary Education Movement, 1917, 3–37, here 6.

4 The contribution is the result of the updating and rearranging of materials of chs. 8 and 9 of my Ph.D. unpublished thesis: Juan Sepúlveda, *Gospel and Culture in Latin American Protestantism: Toward a New Theological Appreciation of Syncretism*, Ph.D. thesis, University of Birmingham, 1996.

a legitimate mission field. Consequently, they designed a thorough strategy to use the purely methodological exclusion of Latin America from the Edinburgh agenda as a battle cry to awaken, mainly in North America, a great movement in favor of missions within the "neglected continent."

From the outset, this strategy included the idea of organizing a gathering which could do for Latin America what the planned Edinburgh conference was about to do for the non-Christian world, by developing a sound justification for Latin American missions. That the myth about the rejection of missions in Latin America by the Edinburgh Conference is still held as the standard interpretation on the relation between both events may be seen as the best demonstration of the success of such a strategy.

2   Non-Catholic Missions to Latin America before Edinburgh 1910

Although recent scholarship shows that the relationship of missions to colonialism has been rather complex and dynamic,[5] it is a worldwide fact that the opening of new missionary fields has historically followed the paths of trade and colonial conquests. This is what happened with the first evangelization of Latin America by Spanish and Portuguese Catholicism. Moreover, such had also been the case with the early non-Catholic missions to Latin America and the Caribbean.

Throughout the 17th and 18th centuries, the English, the Dutch and the French were struggling against the Spanish and Portuguese monopoly on trade with the New World, or trying to seize some of the less occupied territories, particularly in North America and the Caribbean.[6] It is claimed that the early attempt to establish a colony

of French Huguenots in an island in the harbor of Rio de Janeiro (1555–1560) was supported by Calvin himself when a few pastors were sent from Geneva.[7] After Admiral Nicolas Durand de Villegagnon, the leader of the colony, denounced Protestants coming from Europe as heretics, three pastors, Jean du Bordel, Matthieu Vermeil and Pierre Bourdon, were killed on Feb 9, 1558, and the rest of Huguenots had to flee,[8] the whole venture ending in failure.

During the years 1624–1655, the Dutch succeeded in occupying northern Brazil. Under the government of Maurice de Nassau, based in Pernanbuco, two classes and a synod of the Reformed Church were established, and religious freedom was respected so that Catholics and Jews were allowed to worship alongside Protestants.[9] Since the English seizure of Jamaica in 1655,[10] every English possession, island or part of the mainland, besides the Dutch and Danish possessions, were soon recognized as areas for missions. Therefore, the 18th century saw the beginning and development of the Quaker, Moravian, Methodist, Baptist and Church of England missions in the Caribbean.[11]

In 1797, the English seized Trinidad and instructed its governor to investigate the possibilities of helping local rebellions against the Spanish crown on the mainland. The same year, after blockading the Channel of Gibraltar to prevent the Spanish ships from leaving the Mediterranean heading towards the American colonies, the English forced the Spanish government to decree

---

5   Lamin Sanneh, *Translating the Message: The Missionary Impact on Culture*, Maryknoll NY, Orbis Books, 2009; Norman Etherington, ed., *Mission and Empire*, Oxford, Oxford University Press, 2005.

6   John H. Parry, *The Spanish Seaborne Empire*, Berkeley CA, University of California Press, 1990, 251–271.

7   Francis E. Clark & Harriet E. Clark, *The Gospel in Latin Lands: Outline Studies of Protestant Work in the Latin Countries of Europe and America*, New York NY, The Macmillan Company, 1909, 288.

8   Erasmo Braga & Kenneth George Grubb, *The Republic of Brazil: A Survey of the Religious Situation*, London, World Dominion Press, 1932, 18.

9   Braga & Grubb, *The Republic of Brazil*, 18.

10   Parry, *The Spanish Seaborne Empire*, 263.

11   Kenneth Scott Latourette, *A History of the Expansion of Christianity*, vol. 3, *Three Centuries of Advance*, New York NY, Harper & Brothers, 1939, 232–239.

the opening of the ports of the Indies.[12] Although the opening was meant only for neutral ships, in fact it marked the end of Spanish control over the Indies trade. Thus, both English and North American trading increased rapidly, and small English speaking colonies started to grow in the main ports, for instance, in Rio de Janeiro, Buenos Aires, Valparaiso, and Callao. Perhaps this development encouraged Commodore Home Riggs Popham's short-lived invasion of Buenos Aires in 1806.[13]

The Spanish-American wars of independence took place between the years 1808–1814 and 1816–1825.[14] By 1825, the hitherto Spanish provinces of the New World, except for Puerto Rico and Cuba, had become independent nations. Although the English government did not provide the help some of the revolutionary leaders had expected, most of the new governments welcomed trade with the English. The size of the English colonies grew and they started to explore new areas of economic interest, such as mining and railway building.

The presence of those groups of immigrants was the point of departure for a new missionary interest for some circles in the Church of England. On the one hand, those circles wanted to provide spiritual care for the English and other Protestant immigrants living in South America, which they did by sending chaplains to different places. On the other hand, the information they received from the immigrants themselves, or from the chaplains already at work, about the religious situation of Indians, *mestizos* (half-breeds) and *criollos* (those born in Latin America from Spanish or Portuguese parents) began to awaken the desire to extend their efforts toward those groups. An outstanding representative of these circles was Allen Francis Gardiner,[15] who left the Royal Navy, of which he was a commander, to devote himself to missionary

work. Between the years 1838 and 1851, he explored on three different journeys many areas of Argentina, Chile, Bolivia and in particular Tierra del Fuego in order to establish some missionary stations. Although he was mainly interested in the non-Christian Indians, he always thought that missionary stations had a threefold purpose, namely: to work with the non-Christian and "uncivilized" Indians; to care for the Protestant immigrants; and to preach the Gospel to the so-called nominal Catholics, *criollos* and *mestizos*.

Having failed to convince the existing missionary societies to enter that field, Gardiner, with the support from some Low Church friends, organized in 1844 the Patagonian Missionary Society, later to become the SAMS.[16] In 1851, Gardiner, along with his party of six fellow workers, died of starvation in Puerto Español, Tierra del Fuego. However, this very tragedy helped to raise in England the interest in missionary work in South America. In 1869, Waite Hockin Stirling, the former secretary of the SAMS, was consecrated bishop of the Church of England to South America, based in the Falklands. Following the SAMS's steps, in 1897 the RBMU, which had originated in 1873 and was based in London, started working in Peru.[17]

Another form of British missionary work in Latin America was the distribution of the Scriptures in Spanish and Portuguese promoted by the BFBS, which, taking advantage of the opening of the South American ports, started its work very early in the 19th century. James Thomson, a Scottish Baptist pastor, served both as educator (on behalf of the BFSS) and agent of the BFBS from 1818, staying in Argentina, Chile, and most of the capital cities on the Pacific Coast, even going as far north as Mexico. He expected the diffusion of the Scriptures to arouse a spontaneous reformation within the

---

12   Parry, *The Spanish Seaborne Empire*, 346.

13   Parry, *The Spanish Seaborne Empire*, 346.

14   Parry, *The Spanish Seaborne Empire*, 344–360.

15   John W. Marsh, *A Memoir of Allen F. Gardiner*, London, J. Nisbet, 1857.

16   Wendy Mann, *An Unquenched Flame: A Short History of the South American Missionary Society*, London, South American Missionary Society, 1968.

17   Arturo Piedra, *Evangelización protestante en América Latina: Análisis de las razones que justificaron y promovieron la expansión protestante (1830–1960)*, vol. 1, Quito, Consejo Latinoamericano de Iglesias, 2000, 2–49.

Catholic population and therefore welcomed the cooperation of liberal Catholic priests.[18] Another BFBS agent in Central America was Frederick Crowe, a naturalized Englishman born in Belgium, who arrived at Guatemala in 1843, becoming the pioneer of Guatemalan Protestantism.[19]

It was these circles of mainly Low Church and Nonconformist British Christians that started to speak of South or Latin America as "the neglected continent" regarding missionary work. It appears that the expression was used for the first time as the title of the written account of the missionary tour of Rev. George C. Grubb and his party in 1893, carried out on behalf of the SAMS.[20]

The earlier North American initiatives followed James Thomson's steps. In the years 1823–1824, John C. Brigham toured Argentina and Chile, sent by the ABCFM to explore the possibilities of starting missionary work in South America. After travelling overland from Buenos Aires to Valparaiso, Brigham recommended opening in Valparaiso a store for the dissemination of the Bible on the west coast of South America. Following this recommendation, in 1834 Isaac Wheelwright arrived in Valparaiso, sent by the ABS as its first agent in South America. The store opened by Wheelwright was short-lived since he was forced to close it in 1837 due to pressure from the Roman Catholic hierarchy.[21]

In 1845 some US American residents in Valparaiso requested from the FES (New York) "a minister to preach in English, and also to carry the

Gospel to the Chileans."[22] Towards the end of that year, the Congregational minister David Trumbull, who eventually became the founder of the national Presbyterian Church, was sent by the FES in cooperation with the SFS. In 1896, the Mennonite Henry L. Weiss, a naturalized US American born in Germany, presented himself to the CMA as a volunteer to go to Chile as a missionary, but his appointment was denied on the grounds that Latin America was not a priority missionary area for the CMA. Together with the Methodist Albert Dawson, Weiss set out to carry out missionary work in Chile on their own. They settled in Concepción, and later, invited by German colonists, Weiss went further south to Victoria. The following year, the CMA board in New York received news of Weiss and Dawson's work and decided to give them official support.[23]

Both the examples in the last paragraph illustrate the policy of most denominational and interdenominational North American missionary boards concerning missions to Latin America during the 19th century. They would send missionaries or support missionaries already in the field in response to specific appeals but not on their own initiative. Those who were of a different opinion had to devise their own missionary structures. Such was the case of the Methodist holiness preacher of the Holiness Movement, William Taylor. After some years establishing "self-supporting churches" in South India, Taylor, recalling a short visit to Valparaiso in 1849, chose the west coast of South America as a field for the experimentation of his method of "self-supporting missions." Owing to old differences regarding missionary policies, Taylor started his South American enterprise, carrying out a surveying trip in 1877,

18   Jean Baptiste August Kessler, *A Study of the Older Protestant Missions and Churches in Peru and Chile*, Goes, Oosterbaan & Le Cointre, 1967, 19–23.

19   Virginia Garrard-Burnett, *Protestantism in Guatemala: Living in the New Jerusalem*, Austin TX, University of Texas Press, 1998, 8.

20   Edward C. Millard & Lucy E. Guinness, *South America: The Neglected Continent*, New York NY, F.H. Revell Company, 1894.

21   Tomás S. Goslin, *Los evangélicos en la América Latina: Siglo XIX, los comienzos*, Buenos Aires, La Aurora, 1956, 29–30.

22   Florence E. Smith, "Some Significant Aspects of the History of the Chile Mission," in: W. Reginald Wheeler, ed., *Modern Missions in Chile and Brazil*, Philadelphia PA, Westminster Press, 1926, 112–151, here 121.

23   Kessler, *A Study of the Older Protestant Missions*, 243–255.

with no official backing from the MEMB.[24] Thus Taylor became the pioneer of the Methodist work in Chile and Peru, which was taken over by the MEMB after his death.[25]

Another relevant example of an independent Latin American missionary enterprise was the creation of the nondenominational faith mission based in Dallas, the CAM. It was founded in 1890 by Cyrus Scofield, the same biblical scholar who popularized dispensationalism through his Scofield Reference Bible.[26] During the 20th century, CAM became notorious due to its linguistic projects among the indigenous peoples of Central America.

1898 witnessed the brief war between the United States and Spain. The United States had started the war claiming that it was for humanitarian reasons, namely, to protect the Cubans from the bloody Spanish repression of their movement for independence. However, it ended with the great nation's seizure of Puerto Rico, the Philippine Islands and Guam, leaving Cuba in a situation of nominal independence (the Platt Amendment), and obtaining naval control of the Caribbean, which was of strategic importance for the construction of the Panama Canal. Thus the Spanish-American War marked the birth of US imperialism.[27]

The outcome of this war awakened a new interest in the life of their southern neighbors among US Americans, and revived the Monroe Doctrine inaugurated by President James Monroe (1817–1825) in his message of Dec 2, 1823. According to that doctrine, the United States would consider any new colonial adventure of any European power against any of the new American independent

nations to be an attack on its own territory.[28] It was in that context than some leading missionary thinkers, among whom Robert Elliott Speer, secretary of the PBFM and John Raleigh Mott, the long-serving Methodist leader of the YMCA and the WSCF, started to see Latin America as a suitable field for North American missions.

In his lectures at Beloit College in Wisconsin, at the Theological Seminary in Hartford CT, at the Union Theological Seminary, New York City, and on the Graves Foundation at the Theological Seminary in New Brunswick NJ, later expanded and published as a book in 1904, Speer denounced the fact that some North Americans, who were favorably impressed by the Roman Catholic Church in the United States and assumed that this church was the same everywhere, were vigorously opposed to missionary work in Latin America:

> It is said that it is an intrusion upon territory already occupied and fully covered by another branch of the Christian Church; that this other branch of the Church is a true Church, exerting a beneficial influence and much better adapted than the Protestant Churches to meeting the needs of romantic and emotional people like the Latin Americans, who are deeply devoted to their Church, and who can only be either perplexed or angered by Protestant invasion.[29]

Speer felt that such a view acted as a hindrance to the support of Latin American missions, and particularly to the attraction of monetary donations to them. In order to counter that position, he offered a six-point justification for Protestant missions in Latin America, based in other authors'

24 William Taylor, *Ten Years of Self-Supporting Missions in India*, New York NY, Phillips & Hunt, 1882, 92–116.

25 Goodsil Filley Arms, *History of the William Taylor Self-Supporting Missions in South America*, Cincinnati OH, Methodist Book Concern, 1921.

26 Garrard-Burnett, *Protestantism in Guatemala*, 24–26.

27 Philip S. Foner, *The Spanish-Cuban-American War and the Birth of American Imperialism (1895–1902)*, New York NY, Monthly Review Press, 1972.

28 Hubert Herring, *A History of Latin America from the Beginnings to the Present*, New York NY, Knopf, 1956, 745–766; John Edwin Fagg, *Latin America: A General History*, New York NY, Macmillan, 1969, 758–778.

29 Robert Elliott Speer, *Missions and Modern History: A Study of the Missionary Aspects of Some Great Movements of the Nineteenth Century*, vol. 1, New York NY, F.H. Revell Company, 1904, 219.

observations. To support his conviction that North Americans "should share with these people [the Latin Americans] our Christian inheritance to which they are strangers," quoted a letter sent by William Thorp to the *New York Sun* (Oct 6, 1903):

> From a study of the question on the spot, one is forced to the conclusion that the only way permanently to safeguard the Monroe Doctrine is for America to come boldly forward and guarantee to Europe the preservation of law and order throughout Latin America. ... For example, it should be possible to secure the cooperation of the Latin-American Powers which have manifested a desire for orderly civilization and commercial expansion. I refer particularly to Mexico, Chili and Argentina. Could they not be induced to assist America in keeping their ill-behaved sisters in order?[30]

The background to these preoccupations about the "misbehavior" of some Latin American nations may have been the Venezuelan incident of 1902–1903. The government of Venezuela's defiant attitude of not paying its external debt caused as a reaction the blockading of its coastline by German and British warships. The warships removed the blockade only after the United States protested in the name of the Monroe Doctrine. A similar "misbehavior" of the Dominican Republic led in 1905 to the formulation of the so-called Roosevelt Corollary of the Monroe Doctrine. President Roosevelt stated to the Senate of the United States:

> Under the Monroe Doctrine [the United States] cannot see any European power seize and permanently occupy the territory of one of these republics; and yet such seizure of territory, disguised or undisguised, may eventually offer the only way in which the power in question can collect any debt,

unless there is interference on the part of the United States.[31]

With this corollary, the Monroe Doctrine, which was originally intended to protect the Latin American nations from foreign intervention, evolved toward a justification for the United States' intervention. Speer thought that the sharing of their "[Protestant] Christian inheritance" was the best way to discipline their "ill-behaved" South American neighbors,[32] thus developing a missionary counterpart to the Monroe Doctrine.

John R. Mott is considered the author, or at least as one of its main promoters, of the famous watchword "The Evangelization of the World in this Generation."[33] The sense of urgency manifested in the expression was another reason that some North American missionary boards maintained for not considering Latin America a priority mission field. All efforts were to be directed to places where no kind of Christianity had been established, according to the initial policy of CMA, which we have already mentioned with regard to Chile. John R. Mott himself had omitted Latin America from his appeals launched during his 1895 tour attending national student conferences in Great Britain, Germany, Scandinavia, and Switzerland; he collected these messages in his book *Strategic Points in the World's Conquest*.[34] He revealed his change of mind after the Spanish-American War in a new book, *The Home Ministry and Modern Missions: A Plea for Leadership in World Evangelization*,[35] by consistently mentioning Latin America, alongside Asia and Africa, as an equally significant area for missions.

31   Cited in: Herring, *A History of Latin America*, 759.

32   Speer, *Missions and Modern History*, vol. 1, 225.

33   John Raleigh Mott, *The Evangelization of the World in this Generation*, New York NY, SVM, 1900.

34   John Raleigh Mott, *Strategic Points in the World's Conquest*, New York NY, F.H. Revell Company, 1897.

35   John Raleigh Mott, *The Home Ministry and Modern Missions: A Plea for Leadership in World Evangelization*, London, Hodder & Stoughton, 1905.

30   Speer, *Missions and Modern History*, vol. 1, 225.

Both Speer and Mott were members of the international committee responsible for the organization of the 1910 WMC, which leads us to the question about their role in the decision of excluding Latin America from the oncoming deliberations in Edinburgh. However, before coming to that, it will be useful to examine what was the situation before 1910.

3 Latin America and Missionary Cooperation before Edinburgh 1910

It is claimed that William Carey, the Baptist pioneer of modern Protestant missions, had himself called for a world missionary conference exactly a century before Edinburgh 1910.[36] The earlier international missionary conferences were held in New York (lasting one day) and London (two days) in 1854. The one held in Liverpool in 1860 was the first to be organized more "for the Directors, Secretaries, and Missionaries of all Societies and Churches, to obtain an opportunity of meeting together and conferring together about their common work."[37] The Rev. Waite H. Stirling, who had by then become secretary of the SAMS, had the opportunity to present a short report of their work among indigenous peoples of Tierra del Fuego belonging to "the most degraded of the human race."[38]

At the Centenary Conference on Protestant Missions of the World, held in London in 1888, two reports on missionary work in South America were presented, one by Alfred Pite, of the SAMS, and other by Emanuel Van Orden, a missionary in Brazil and corresponding member of the Anti-Slavery Society of London. Pite recalled as an inspiration for their work the dying words of Gardiner, found in his diary: "Fuegia and South America will not be abandoned. Missionary seed had been sown here, and the Gospel message ought to follow." The purpose of the work was also described in the words of Gardiner's diary: "Missionary to the heathen, and ministerial to our own people, with evangelistic work among the varied nationalities of South America."[39] Van Orden claimed that the very recent abolition of slavery in Brazil had been the result of the distribution of "millions of copies of God's Word" by the ABS and the BFBS, because the Church of Rome in three hundred years had done nothing to end slavery. In his view, this black population, now living in freedom, was a missionary priority.[40]

At the EMC in New York, April 1900, Francisco de Castells, Agent of the BFBS in Costa Rica, sought to rectify two prevalent erroneous ideas concerning the countries to the South of the United States. The first was that they were all Spanish-speaking countries, when the reality was one of a use of an enormous diversity of indigenous languages, besides a significant number of European languages (Spanish, Portuguese, English, Dutch, and French). The second was the fallacy of classifying the peoples of South America as "Christians," as the handbooks of geography did:

> South America is a priest-ridden continent, without family life, given up to domestic anarchy, to religious bacchanals, to the worship of grotesque images, to the practice of pagan or semi-pagan rites, and to the control of a most profligate priesthood whose main business seems to be the shameful traffic in souls for which they have attained worldwide notoriety. ... Outside of the 750,000 Protestants which there may be, most of whom are foreigners, not only are the words

---

36 Keith Clements, *Faith on the Frontier: A Life of J.H. Oldham*, Edinburgh, T&T Clark, 1999, 90.

37 The Secretaries of the Conference, eds., *Conference on Missions held in 1860 at Liverpool*, London, J. Nisbet, 1860, 1.

38 The Secretaries of the Conference, eds., *Conference on Missions*, 40–41.

39 James Johnston, ed., *Report of the Centenary Conference on the Protestant Missions of the World*, vol. 1, London, J. Nisbet, 1888, 352–356.

40 Johnston, ed., *Report of the Centenary Conference*, 356–358.

of the Gospel not known, but, I venture to say without fear of contradiction, that for most of the people in those parts, the death of Christ is still a meaningless tragedy.[41]

Hubert W. Brown, doing missionary work in Mexico, was the first US American missionary to speak in favor of Latin America as a legitimate mission field at an international missionary gathering, sharing his view about the failure of the missionary methods the Roman Catholic Church used there:

> Now, why do we say that the Roman Catholic missions failed? Why do we claim it is necessary to send men and spend money to establish missions in those countries? In the first place, because of the corrupting influence that entered into the priesthood and into the monasteries, owing to increase of wealth and power. The wealth amassed was not always employed for the conversion of the people. For many of the missionaries of the first centuries of Roman Catholicism; for their heroic sacrifices; for their wonderful efforts, we have nothing but admiration. But they were representatives of a system radically defective.[42]

It is clear that this negative evaluation of Catholic missions tended to blur any priority of missions to the "heathen" Indians over the missions to the "nominal Christians." Castells recognized that most of their efforts had "hitherto been directed to the Spanish-speaking Mestizos and Creoles, and the poor aborigines have remained uninfluenced by our work."[43] Charles Dreese, a Methodist missionary in Buenos Aires, also a US American, had no problem in insisting on yet another Christian group as a missionary target: the thousands of southern European immigrants arriving in Argentina. "These people, uprooted from the old home in Spain or Italy, removed from the surveillance of the priest, become wonderfully susceptible to the influence of the Gospel of Christ."[44]

It has to be said, however, that for the SAMS, despite agreeing to work with "nominal" Catholics, the practical priority was the difficult work with the "savages." William B. Grubb, perhaps the most outstanding representative of this society's work with indigenous peoples, was also present at the EMC. There he described some aspects of his nine years' working among the Indians of the Paraguayan Chaco, starting with the basic task of learning their language by means of signs, and reproducing it in writing. In his testimony, Grubb revealed a rare appreciative approach to indigenous culture.[45]

The New York conference was defined as "ecumenical," in the words of William Huntington, "not because all portions of the Christian Church [were] represented in it by delegates, but because the plan of campaign which it proposes covers the whole area of the inhabited globe."[46] The conference was, in fact, an Anglo-American Protestant event and it resembled to a large extent the previous ones. As far as the Church of England was concerned, only some societies linked to the so-called Evangelical or Low Church sector had hitherto fully participated. However, the international committee for the organization of the Edinburgh conference had decided to bring the continental or European missionary societies, and the Catholic or High Church tradition of Anglicanism, into the missionary movement for cooperation in order to make it more widely representative.[47] In view of

41   Edwin M. Bliss & others, eds., *Ecumenical Missionary Conference: New York, 1900*, vol. 1, London, Religious Tract Society, 1900, 476–477.

42   Bliss & others, eds., *Ecumenical Missionary Conference*, vol. 1, 480.

43   Bliss & others, eds., *Ecumenical Missionary Conference*, vol. 1, 479.

44   Bliss & others, eds., *Ecumenical Missionary Conference*, vol. 1, 482.

45   Bliss & others, eds., *Ecumenical Missionary Conference*, vol. 1, 480–482.

46   Bliss & others, eds., *Ecumenical Missionary Conference*, vol. 1, 10.

47   Clements, *Faith on the Frontier*, 73–99; Tissington Tatlow, "The World Conference of Faith and Order," in: *A History of the Ecumenical Movement*, vol. 1, 403–441.

this purpose, some differences and sources of tension had to be resolved.

There is no evidence that the inclusion of Latin America in the deliberations of the previous international conferences had been one of these sources of tension. On the contrary, Bishop Henry Montgomery, secretary of the SPG, the official missionary body of the Church of England, wrote on the missionary implications of the Monroe Doctrine even before Robert E. Speer:

> This continent [South America] ought to be watched over by the missionary statesman. It bids fair to rival Africa as the future home of a huge population. At present there are 30,000,000, chiefly half-bloods, 6,000,000 however being Indians. It must be confessed that the continent is in a debased condition. Rome is in possession, and is at its worst. Few documents contain such plain speaking as one of Leo XIII, addressed to the clergy of one of the American republics, to be read in "From Cape Horn to Panama."[48] Fresh populations when immigration sets in with vigour ought to have purer teaching. ... It is worth asking whether, if the Monroe Doctrine holds in politics, the claims of South America are not one of the first duties of our brethren in the States, not to the exclusion of others, but as a very direct call of God.[49]

But there were other causes of irritation. A small continental delegation had indeed been present at the 1888 Centenary Conference in London. There, Gustav Warneck, the leading thinker of the continental European missiology at the time, delivered a paper basically intended to support the

ideas of "comity" (cooperation) and unity among Protestant missionary societies and the practice of decennial international mission conferences. But, in Warneck's view, serious obstacles had to be overcome if that goal was to be achieved. One of them was the ignorance of Anglo-American missions concerning German missions and the religious situation in Germany:

> I will make no mention of names; but up to the present time Missionary reports have passed through my hands, in which Africa, Central America, South America, China, Germany, India, Turkey, and Japan are being mentioned in one sentence as Missionary fields. Suppose a Hindu or a negro were to read such reports, he would necessarily be led to believe that Germany was a heathen country, standing on the same footing with India or the Congo. And what are you to say when a Methodist preacher writes from Berlin: "Here is a field for work with over one million souls, with *only one worker*"?[50]

What was at stake in this discussion were differences about the accurate definition of a "mission field" among European and North American mission scholars, as seen in the following quotations:

> I understand by Missions the whole operations of Christendom directed towards the planting and organisation of the Christian Church among non-Christians, that is, their Christianisation; Dennis understands by it also the proselytising of non-Protestants. I hold even such non-Christians as dwell in a Christian land – the Indians as well as the negroes of North America – to be proper objects of Missions; Dennis excludes them from Missions to the heathen, or, as

---

48   Robert Young, *From Cape Horn to Panama: A Narrative of Missionary Enterprise Among the Neglected Races of South America, by the South American Missionary Society*, London, Simpkin, Marshall, Hamilton, Kent and Co. Ltd, ²1905, 94–95.

49   Henry H. Montgomery, *Foreign Missions*, London, Longmans, Green & Co., 1902, 117, 121.

50   Gustav Warneck, "The Mutual Relations of Evangelical Missionary Societies to One Another," in: Johnston, ed., *Report of the Centenary Conference*, vol. 2, 431–437, here 434f. (italics original).

they are called in England and America, Foreign Missions, and relegates them to Home Missions.[51]

The reader will ... note that, unlike writers of the Continental school, the author includes missionary operations among the Catholic populations of Latin America. In Volume II, statistics of Protestant missionary societies laboring in the Papal countries of Europe are likewise included, for the reason that an account of these societies would be incomplete without statistical reference, at least, to missions among communities that are not deemed proper mission fields by some distinguished writers. On the other hand, no reference is here made to labors for the colored population of the United States, though both Dr. Grundemann and Professor Warneck consider them as falling within the province of the "Heidenmission." While admitting the inconsistency which Dr. Warneck points out of including the colored population of the West Indies and omitting the negroes of the United States, it may still be said that when the Protestant colored churches of only six denominations have a membership of 3,314,581, thirty-eight per cent. of the entire colored population according to the census of 1900, – a far larger proportion of church members than prevails among the whites, – they can hardly be considered as included in the list of heathen, notwithstanding their African ancestry.[52]

Harlan Beach indeed included missionary work among Catholic populations in Latin America, but the following quotation shows that such an inclusion was not the main reason for Warneck's uneasiness:

The great South America, with its population of about 38 millions, made up of whites, half-breeds, and Indians, is nominally Catholicised, with the exception of a heathen Indian remnant of some hundreds of thousands. The Catholicism, indeed, is of a kind that, according to even Catholic testimonies, is more heathen than Christian, and its morality is on a sadly low level. There are many crosses, but no word of the Cross; many saints, but no followers of Christ.[53]

What worried Warneck was the inclusion of Europe, particularly Germany, as a "proper mission field" by some North American missionary boards. Another problem was the uneasiness of the continentals at the growing enthusiasm of the Anglo-Americans about the possibility of covering the whole inhabited world in just one generation, as the famous watchword of the WSCF put it. For them, that attitude meant to privilege urgency over thoroughness, expansion over concentration. At the 1897 meeting of the Continental Mission Conference in Bremen, the decision was taken not to send a delegation to the New York EMC, but only a single observer. Warneck decided to send a polemical paper containing his criticism to counter the overenthusiasm of the Anglo-American missions.[54]

The official participation of the Church of England was prevented additionally because of its internal tensions. According to Bishop Montgomery, the SPG, the authoritative voice of the Church of England in missionary affairs, became High Church only because, after the founding of

---

51   Gustav Warneck, *Outline of a History of Protestant Missions from the Reformation to the Present Time: A Contribution to Modern Church History*, Edinburgh, Oliphant, Anderson & Ferrier, 1901, xi.

52   Harlan P. Beach, *A Geography and Atlas of Protestant Missions*, vol. 1, New York, SVM, 1901, vii.

53   Warneck, *Outline of a History*, 181.

54   Werner Ustorf, *Christianized Africa, De-Christianized Europe?*, Seoul, Tyrannus Press, 1992, 75–93. The paper sent by Warneck was published in a condensed form with the title "Thoughts on the Missionary Century," *The Missionary Review of the World* 13/6, June 1900, 413–417.

the CMS, Evangelicals left it.[55] Therefore, it was not easy for Montgomery and other High Church bishops to think of the SPG's participation in the movement of missionary cooperation as being on the same footing as the CMS or the SAMS.

4   Latin America in the Preparatory Work and the Proceedings of Edinburgh 1910

The first meeting of the international committee responsible for the organization of the WMC was held at Oxford from June 14 to 18, 1908, with John R. Mott and Robert E. Speer among the five members from North America. To ensure the participation of continentals, as well as the official participation of the Church of England, the following resolution was taken:

> In view of the fact that the Missionary Societies to be represented were organised for the work of varying scope and purpose, it was necessary to confine the purview of the Conference to work of the kind in which all were united; and accordingly the subject of the deliberations of the Conference was defined as missionary work among non-Christian peoples.[56]

This decision meant the exclusion of Latin America from the agenda of the conference, except for those groups belonging to the category of "non-Christians of the Western Hemisphere" (the Indians not yet evangelized and non-Western immigrants). The introduction to the report of the Panama Congress states that "the representatives of Latin-American missions agreed to their omission at the Edinburgh Conference, reserving at

the same time the privilege of identifying themselves at some future time with a movement for a Latin-American conference."[57] There is little doubt that the British and continentals effectively granted such recognition as none of them was truly opposed to the work among "nominal" Catholics in Latin America. It was perhaps at this point that Speer realized that, because "the regulations adopted for the conference did not declare missionary work in South America illegitimate …, probably this exclusion will do far more to draw attention to work in South America than its inclusion could have done,"[58] and he therefore started to develop a strategy to convert such an exclusion into the leitmotiv of a new movement in favor of Latin American missions.

The regulations of the conference had indeed excluded from participation those societies working exclusively in the so-called Christian lands, but the societies working both in "non-Christian" and "Christian" lands were free to choose their delegates within the number conceded to them. Making use of that freedom, the North American boards, along with the British "Evangelical" societies, were able to designate about sixty missionaries from Latin America, working either with "pagan" Indians or with "nominal" Catholics, all of whom as official delegates. This kind of undercover delegation was not meant to push the "Latin American issue" onto the official agenda, but provision was made for the parallel assembly of this delegation on two occasions with the purpose of debating the idea of a future gathering on Latin American missions.

The PBFM decided that one of its secretaries should devote six months to a survey trip through South America before the Edinburgh Conference with the purpose of producing a more elaborate justification for Latin American missions, based both on personal experience and on first-hand

---

55   Clements, *Faith on the Frontier*, 87.

56   WMC, ed., *World Missionary Conference, 1910: To Consider Missionary Problems in Relation to the Non-Christian World*, vol. 9, *The History and Records of the Conference: Together with Addresses Delivered at the Evening Meetings*, Edinburgh, Oliphant, Anderson, & Ferrier, 1910, 8.

57   CCLA, ed., "The Inception and History of the Congress," 6.

58   Robert Elliott Speer, *Missions in South America*, New York NY, Board of Foreign Missions of the Presbyterian Church, 1909, 148.

testimonies collected in the field. This responsibility obviously fell to Robert E. Speer, but before he started his tour, in Great Britain Joseph H. Oldham, secretary of the international committee, had to face extremely difficult tests during the preparations for the conference.

Oldham had been designated for such a crucial role precisely because, as secretary of the SCM, he had succeeded in involving representatives of the Anglo-Catholic tradition of Anglicanism in conferences of that movement. He had also spent some time in 1905 in Halle, Germany, where Gustav Warneck taught, so that he was better acquainted with the views and sensitivities of the continentals.[59]

The Church of England and the SPG agreed to participate in the preparatory commissions after being assured that the conference would be "inter" rather than "undenominational" in character, and that matters of doctrine and church policy would not be discussed.[60] However, in February 1909 three bishops reacted against the statistical work being carried out in North America for Commission I, "Carrying the Gospel to the Non-Christian World," whose chairman was John R. Mott and vice chairman George Robson, president of the Mission Study Council of the United Free Church of Scotland and translator of Warneck's *Outline of a History of Protestant Missions*. On Feb 20, Edward S. Talbot, bishop of Southwark, writing also on behalf of Bishop Montgomery, alerted Oldham that the North American counterpart of Commission I was violating the regulations of the conference by including in their statistical work "missions or enterprises directed towards other Christian communions."[61] The letter also gave notice that they might suspend their involvement in the preparatory commissions if such violation continued.

In his reply (Feb 23), Oldham sought to reassure the bishops that the regulations would be respected, while at the same time he recognized that some practical difficulties might arise particularly regarding South America and the Near East. He mentioned that in South America "there is ... a very large and neglected half-Christianized community, nominally Roman Catholic," but even so he reaffirmed that "any mission work which is immediately and predominantly directed towards Christian communities will be excluded from the returns."[62]

The apparent ambiguity of Oldham's answer provoked a stronger letter, this time from Charles Gore, bishop of Birmingham (Feb 25), announcing the suspension of his membership of Commission III, at least until he was sure than no mention would be made of South American missions aimed at converting Roman Catholics. "I do not suppose that Roman Catholics would consent to join our Conference in any case. But I cannot write in the principles or methods of a Conference, if there is anything that would exclude them, supposing they were willing to join."[63]

There followed an intense correspondence involving mainly Oldham and Robson on the British side, and Mott (who was half-way through a missionary tour in Russia), Arthur J. Brown, secretary of the American Executive Committee, and James Dennis, who was working on missionary statistics along with Harlan Beach, on the North American side. In a letter to Oldham (Mar 13), Brown explained that some members of the North American committee, while agreeing with the decision to confine the conference to working among non-Christian people, suggested that the statistical survey "should be as comprehensive as possible for purposes of information, and that it should therefore include all forms of foreign

---

59   Clements, *Faith on the Frontier*, 58–63, 79–80.

60   Clements, *Faith on the Frontier*, 79, 87–88; Tatlow, "The World Conference of Faith and Order," 406.

61   Cited in: Clements, *Faith on the Frontier*, 81.

62   Clements, *Faith on the Frontier*, 81.

63   Clements, *Faith on the Frontier*, 82. Clements dates this letter on Feb 24, while Arturo Piedra, who did extend archival work on this issue, dates it on Feb 25; Piedra, *Evangelización protestante*, vol. 1, 129.

missionary work wherever conducted." Even so, some days later (Mar 25) Brown cabled Oldham: "New York members Executive and Statistical Committee personally willing to conform to judgment of British Executive on Statistics. Confer Mott."[64]

The negotiations effected in order to reach a final agreement for Oldham involved meeting some of the Anglican bishops personally, as well as a visit to the North American Executive Committee in New York, where he received the suggestion of a slight change to the name of Commission I: "Carrying the Gospel to *All* the Non-Christian World."[65] The British executive's final decision on statistics set out rules concerning particular regions (Turkey, Persia and Egypt; South Eastern Europe; South America and the West Indies). It also stated that the "main objective to be borne in mind was that of showing how much more work *still needed to be done* throughout the world, rather than a league-table of achievements by missionary agencies."[66] The North American suggestion of changing the name of Commission I was accepted.[67]

One may conclude that this very difficult episode in the preparation for the conference occurred because Dennis and Beach, despite the agreement to confine the deliberations to work among non-Christian peoples, started their statistical work having in mind their own understanding of a mission, which included "work ... wherever conducted," as Arthur Brown put it. The particular reference to South America occurred because Oldham, even before consulting the North American side, mentioned it as the example of a place where "hard lines were difficult to draw."[68] However, the incident became the perfect unforeseen proof required to sustain the strategy designed by Robert E. Speer for promoting among North American missionary boards the idea of a special conference on Latin American missions. Therefore, although the decision to confine the scope of the conference to work among non-Christian people had already been taken in 1908, most historians of missions assert that the "exclusion" of Latin America was the outcome of this incident, and that Montgomery, Walter Frere and Gore were determinant in such an exclusion.[69]

Soon after Speer made his long Latin American tour accompanied by his cousin Joseph Cook, who was studying with the prospect of being sent as a medical missionary, from May 5 to Oct 27, 1909. Throughout his visit, he found the local missionaries worried about the implications of the decision of the organizers of the WMC. "[They] feared that the home Churches were abandoning them and consenting to view their work as of inferior missionary warrant. We pointed out to them that the regulations adopted for the conference did not declare missionary work in South America illegitimate."[70] In the last chapter of the extended report that he published in the same year, whose heading was the question "Should Evangelical Churches Be Excluded from South America?," Speer develops nine reasons for missionary work in the "neglected continent":

(1) The moral condition of the South American countries warrants and demands the presence of the form of evangelical religion which will war against sin and bring men the power of a righteous life. ... (2) The Protestant missionary enterprise with its stimulus to education and its appeal to the rational nature of man is required by the intellectual needs of South America. ... (3) Protestant Missions are justified in South America in order to give the Bible to the

---

64   Clements, *Faith on the Frontier*, 82.

65   Piedra, *Evangelización protestante*, vol. 1, 139.

66   Cited in: Clements, *Faith on the Frontier*, 85 (italics original).

67   Piedra, *Evangelización protestante*, vol. 1, 139.

68   Clements, *Faith on the Frontier*, 81.

69   So does Arturo Piedra, who considers that Latin America was "the apple of discord" during the preparations of the Edinburgh Conference (Piedra, *Evangelización protestante*, vol. 1, 113); and so also does Timothy Yates, *Christian Mission in the Twentieth Century*, Cambridge, Cambridge University Press, 1994, 29.

70   Speer, *Missions in South America*, 148.

people. ... (4) Protestant missions are justified and demanded in South America by the character of the Roman Catholic priesthood. ... (5) Protestant missions in South America are justified because the Roman Catholic Church has not given the people Christianity. ... (6) Protestant missions are justified in South America because the Catholic Church is at the same time so strong and so weak there. ... (7) The South American countries must not be left to the South American religious system, because it is opposed to political liberty and popular institutions. ... (8) The Roman Catholic Church in South America needs the Protestant missionary movement. ... (9) And lastly, Evangelical Christianity is warranted in going to South America because it alone can meet the needs of the Latin American nations.[71]

It is very likely that when the Latin America delegation met in their unofficial gathering in Edinburgh, many of them had already read Speer's report. The secretaries of missions boards already working in Latin America were present at the second meeting. The main issues discussed were the need to call attention to the "fundamental spiritual rights of the Latin-American nations," the lack of adequate Christian literature in Spanish and Portuguese, and the need for cooperation among Latin American missionary agencies. The participants in both meetings were "convinced that these great needs could be met only as some gathering might be held which would do for Latin-American peoples what the Edinburgh Conference was seeking to do for all the mission work among non-Christian nations."[72] A specifically appointed committee drafted a statement not to be presented to the conference itself but to be sent to the North American churches and missionary boards:

> The undersigned delegates to the World Missionary Conference, rejoicing over the success of that great gathering and the impulse it must give to the evangelization of the non-Christian world, feel constrained to say a word for those missions in countries nominally Christian that were not embraced in the scope of the Edinburgh Conference. We do not stop to inquire whether the dominant Churches in these lands are or are not Christian Churches, or whether they are or are not faithful to their duty; we only affirm that millions and millions of people are practically without the Word of God and do not really know what the Gospel is.[73]

The full statement was published in the leading church papers of the United States as the starting point for the movement towards a Latin American missionary conference. On Mar 12–13, 1913, a conference on Latin America was held in New York as part of a series of conferences on the different regions in the world organized by the Committee of Reference and Counsel of the FMCNA, the most representative body of North American missions at the time. The main resolution of this conference, in which thirty boards took part, was the appointment of a special committee to deal with the Latin American missionary problems, the CCLA, under the chairmanship of Robert E. Speer.

To return to the official conference of 1910, the report of Commission I repeated the slogan so dear to the advocates of South American Protestant missions: compared to other fields, South America is a "neglected Continent." However, loyal to the conference's regulations, the report indeed pronounced a critical word about North American missions:

---

71   Speer, *Missions in South America*, 148–178.

72   Harlan P. Beach, *Renaissant Latin America: An Outline and Interpretation of the Congress on Christian Work in Latin America, Held at Panama, February 10–19, 1916*, New York NY, Missionary Education Movement, 1916, 8. Beach follows an account of Speer.

73   Cited in: CCLA, ed., "The Inception and History of the Congress," 7.

The missionaries sent to this continent by the Churches of North America have occupied themselves chiefly in work on behalf of the nominally Roman Catholic white and coloured population. A heavy obligation rests upon these Churches to do more to reach the non-Christian population. ... It should be reiterated that the North American societies already at work in South America might most advantageously enlarge their work to reach the Indians scattered through the vast forests of the interior of this great continent. It is to be hoped that the South American Christians will also co-operate increasingly in meeting this great need.[74]

It should be noted that this statement represents very well the policy of the SAMS, the oldest missionary society fully devoted to work in South America, and that it was carefully worded in order to emphasize the "heavy obligation" to reach the non-Christian Indians without making the work with the "nominally Roman Catholic" population illegitimate.

Robert E. Speer himself mentioned Latin America neither in his opening address at the conference,[75] nor in his intervention in the discussion of the report of Commission I.[76] However, he did not lose the opportunity to put forward the "Latin American issue" in his Duff Lectures, delivered in January and February 1910, only a few months before the conference, in Edinburgh, Glasgow, and Aberdeen. The lectures were written on steamships while traveling along the coast of South America, and published under the title *Christianity and the Nations*.[77]

5   Context and Preparation of the Panama Congress on Christian Work

Soon after its appointment, the CCLA set to work to put into practice the ideas discussed in Edinburgh.[78] A letter was sent to the missionaries in Latin America informing them about the purpose and program of the committee, as well as raising questions about the nature, right time and place for the expected conference on missions in Latin America. The matter was also personally discussed with many missionaries in the field by Samuel G. Inman, a missionary of the CWBM in Mexico and later executive secretary of the CCLA, who was then visiting Puerto Rico, Jamaica, Panama, Peru, Chile, Argentina, Uruguay, and Brazil.

The opinions gathered in the field were analyzed in a meeting of the CCLA held in New York, on Sept 22, 1914, this time extended to include a representative of each missionary board working in Latin America. As most of the opinions favored one inclusive and deliberative gathering, the decision was taken to call a general conference on missions in Latin America. The next issue was to decide the place. From the very start, it was agreed that the conference should take place in a Latin American city, because a North American location would misrepresent its purpose, as if it were forcing North American ideas onto the Latin Americans. Buenos Aires and Rio de Janeiro, the largest Latin American cities, were suggested. However, the obvious advantage of a more equidistant place led to the election of Panama.

Yet there were more than practical reasons for choosing Panama. This location was seen as symbolic of the context and the mood underlying the preparations for the conference. The Panama Canal, recently opened in 1914, was interpreted as a kind of bridge that was to overcome old prejudices, suspicions and enmities between South and North America, and to increase the interchanges

---

74   WMC, ed., *World Missionary Conference, 1910*, vol. 1, *Report of Commission I: Carrying the Gospel to All the Non-Christian World*, 249–250.

75   WMC, ed., *World Missionary Conference, 1910*, vol. 9, 115–155.

76   WMC, ed., *World Missionary Conference, 1910*, vol. 1, 425f.

77   Robert Elliott Speer, *Christianity and the Nations*, New York NY, F.H. Revell Company, 1910, 44, 360–361.

78   CCLA, ed., "The Inception and History of the Congress," 7ff.

and cooperation between the Americas in trade, industry, science and, why not, religion. Moreover, the opening of the Canal was seen as a major technological achievement that came to confirm the leading role of the United States in the path of progress of a united Western hemisphere.[79] The context was, thus, one of growing North American enthusiasm for the viability of Pan-Americanism.

As early as June 1826, Panama had hosted representatives of Colombia, Guatemala, Mexico, Peru and the United States, who had been invited by the Venezuelan leader Simón Bolívar, to discuss the idea of a league of American nations to resist Spain, as well as any attempt of intervention by other European powers.[80] Bolívar's project failed, but it was revived in 1881 by the US Secretary of State James Blaine, who sought to draw the American nations together, this time to promote commercial exchanges. Once again, the initiative was deferred by domestic political developments, but the rapid and threatening evolution of European imperialist expansion and colonialism in the 1880s led US President Stephen G. Cleveland to reactivate the project in 1888. Between October 1889 and April 1890 delegates from all the American nations, except Canada and the Dominican Republic, gathered in Washington, marking the beginning of the Pan-American movement, the predecessor of the Organization of American States.[81]

Although further Pan-American meetings had been celebrated at Mexico City in 1901–1902, Rio de Janeiro in 1906 and Buenos Aires in 1910, the practical results were poor, and the suspicion with which the Spanish-speaking republics regarded the United States was still very much alive. However, some new developments were sources of hope and enthusiasm for the North American promoters of the Panama Congress. President Woodrow Wilson had succeeded in involving the so called ABC States, Argentina, Brazil, and Chile,[82] in a diplomatic effort to mediate in the Mexican conflict, a mediation which resulted in the resignation of Victoriano Huerta in July 1914, and the installation of the provisional government of Venustiano Carranza. A Pan-American Scientific Congress held in Washington only a few weeks before the Panama Congress had also raised hopes of scientific and technological cooperation among the American nations.[83]

At a time when most US citizens innocently believed in the unselfishness of their nation's policies toward Latin America, the organizers of the Panama Congress saw it, and the movement of cooperation on Latin American missions that it was meant to promote, as a necessary religious complement to Pan-Americanism. They expected the congress to help overcome the unfounded "long established barriers of reserve, misunderstanding and dislike which have, in the past, so deeply affected the intercourse of Latin America and other parts of the civilized world."[84] Their enthusiasm prevented them from realizing that the "ideal" location chosen for the congress had precisely the sort of ambiguous connotations they wanted to avoid. Panama had come into being as an independent nation in 1903 because, as John Fagg put it, "President Theodore Roosevelt grew impatient with the rulers of Colombia in negotiations for an isthmian canal route."[85] As the exact location of the congress was within the Canal Zone, it was actually held, contrary to the initial intention of its organizers, in a US controlled territory.

The mutual prejudices dividing South and North Americans had as their background the long-lasting conflicts between the British Protestants (accused by enemies of being "heretics") and Catholic Spain (accused in turn of "Romanism") both in Europe and in the New World. Thus, the questions of the policy and attitude of the congress

79   Fagg, *Latin America*, 611.
80   Fagg, *Latin America*, 384, 758.
81   Fagg, *Latin America*, 760–762.
82   Fagg, *Latin America*, 445–505.

83   Beach, *Renaissant Latin America*, 5–6.
84   CCLA, ed., "The Inception and History of the Congress," 3.
85   Fagg, *Latin America*, 610.

toward the Latin American culture and religion were carefully discussed in the various preparatory meetings. In a meeting held in Caldwell, June 9–10, 1915, the name Congress on Christian Work in Latin America replaced an initial designation as Latin-American Missionary Conference, in order to avoid undesirable interpretations of the word "missionary."[86] In the same meeting, the following resolution concerning the approach toward the religious situation of Latin America was adopted:

> This Conference strongly recommends that those who are making arrangements for the Panama Conference, as well as all writers and speakers at the Conference, bear in mind that, if the best and most lasting results are to be obtained, while frankly facing moral and spiritual conditions which call for missionary work in Latin America, and while presenting the gospel which we hold as the only adequate solution of the problems which those conditions present, it shall be the purpose of the Panama Conference to recognize all the elements of truth and goodness in any form of religious faith.[87]

A new statement of purpose to clarify better the nature of the congress as a cooperative effort was adopted at a meeting of the Committee on Arrangements in New York, on Aug 6, 1915:

> Realizing the ever-increasing interdependence of the civilizations of the world, and especially those of North and Latin America, as well as those of both with that of the continent of Europe, the Congress at Panama has been called in order: First – To obtain a more accurate mutual knowledge of the history, resources, achievements and ideals

of the peoples so closely associated in their business and social life. Second – To reveal the fact that these countries may mutually serve one another by contributing the best in their civilizations to each other's life. Third – To discover and devise means to correct such defects and weaknesses in character as may be hindering the growth of those nations. Fourth – To unite in a common purpose to strengthen the moral, social and religious forces that are now working for the betterment of these countries, and to create the desire for these things where absent. Fifth – To discover the underlying principles upon which true national prosperity and stability depend, and to consider ways and means by which these principles may be put into action and made effective.[88]

It appears that the subscribers to this statement of purpose were quite certain that they had already discovered these principles. However, one cannot fail to recognize that this was a brilliant piece of strategic policy: the whole purpose was to strengthen, not to compete with, the religious forces already at work in Latin America! A further proof of sincerity was the invitation issued in the same meeting, after discussing the advisability of inviting representatives of the Roman Catholic Church to the congress:

> All communions or organizations which accept Jesus Christ as Divine Savior and Lord, and the Holy Scriptures of the Old and New Testament as the revealed Word of God, and whose purpose is to make the will of Christ prevail in Latin America, are cordially invited to participate in the Panama Congress, and will be heartily welcomed.[89]

---

86 CCLA, ed., "The Inception and History of the Congress," 17.

87 CCLA, ed., "The Inception and History of the Congress," 16.

88 CCLA, ed., "The Inception and History of the Congress," 18–19.

89 CCLA, ed., "The Inception and History of the Congress," 19.

The statement of purpose put the Panama Congress closer to the purposes and agenda of the Pan-American movement than to the purposes and agenda of the missionary movement, as they were understood by the Edinburgh WMC. The passion for evangelizing the non-Christian peoples is noticeable by its absence. Here, the missionary purpose looks more like the big nation helping its little southern neighbors to develop themselves.

What was indeed modeled on the experience of Edinburgh, was the methodology of the process of preparation and the proceedings of the congress itself. Eight commissions were appointed: I. On Survey and Occupation; II. On Message and Method; III. On Education; IV. On Literature; V. On Women's Work; VI. On the Church in the Field; VII. On the Home Base; and VIII. On Cooperation and Promotion of Unity. By December 1914, these commissions had been organized, and the scope of their investigations determined. Most of these commissions prepared questionnaires and sent them to a large number of people, including missionaries, church leaders, and open minded intellectuals "in the field," and specialists and experienced people "at home" (in the United States and Europe). An editorial committee, with Frank K. Sanders, the director of the Board of Missionary Preparation, as chairman, and Charles H. Fahs of the New York Missionary Research Library, as secretary, was appointed to coordinate and unify the style of the reports.

During July and August 1915 all the reports were completed, and sent in proof sheets to the hundreds of correspondents already appointed plus additional experts for further comments. The criticism gathered in this way was processed at a meeting at Garden City, on Nov 16, and all the reports turned over to the editorial committee for their final revision and publication. A large majority of the delegates received most of the reports before starting their long journey to Panama, and not a few groups of discussion were organized aboard the steamers that transported the delegations.

On the planned date, Feb 10–20, 1916, according to the official statistics, 304 delegates gathered at the US government's Hotel Tivoli, in the Canal Zone, 149 from Latin America, and 155 from United States, Canada, Great Britain, Spain, and Italy. Adding local visitors, the total attendance reached 481 participants, representing 29 denominational boards and 15 interdenominational societies from the United States; 1 denominational board from Canada; 2 interdenominational and 1 denominational societies from Great Britain. Therefore, the theological spectrum within Protestantism was widely represented. Harlan Beach candidly comments that the

> statistics of the Congress may suggest the preponderance of outside elements, ... yet that slight disparity in numbers does not indicate that there was a corresponding difference in viewpoint, as delegates from outside Latin America were all deeply sympathetic with the objectives and desires of the Latin American group.[90]

However, these statistics are in point of fact misleading. As the missionaries working in Latin America were counted as Latin American representatives, along with the official visitors from the Canal Zone (22), the so-called Latin American group was overwhelmingly Anglo-Saxon, the "Latin" names being a rather small minority (28). As far as the "outside elements" were concerned, the great majority of them came from the United States. All but one of the British delegates were counted among the Latin American group, there were three Canadians (one of them counted among the Latin Americans), one Spaniard, and one Italian.[91]

Professor Eduardo Monteverde, of the University of Uruguay and the YMCA of Montevideo, was elected president of the congress; Robert E. Speer, chairman of the day sessions, and John R. Mott, chairman of the Business Committee. Therefore,

---

90   Beach, *Renaissant Latin America*, 15.
91   CCLA, ed., *Christian Work in Latin America*, vol. 3, appendix A, 451–462.

the actual work of the congress was to be conducted by Speer and Mott, two old friends and outstanding leaders of the North American missionary movement at the time, while Monteverde's presidency ensured that the symbolic head of the congress would be a Latin American personality. If English dominated, particularly as the language of the congress' written documentation, Spanish and Portuguese were also recognized as the official languages of the gathering, and interpreters were provided whenever necessary.

6 The Latin American Claims: The Justification for Protestant Missions

It may rightly be said that the whole gathering concerned justifying Latin American missions. However, the issue was specifically tackled by Commission I On Survey and Occupation, and presented in chapter 3 of its report "The Claims of Present-Day Latin America on the Message and Service of Evangelical Christians and Churches."[92] In conformity with the recommendation issued at the Caldwell meeting, Commission I clearly avoided building its argument chiefly on the weaknesses of the Latin American "religious system," as Robert E. Speer had previously done. It argued instead that the justification for Protestant missions lies in a number of "claims" or problems arising from the contemporary situation of Latin America, and particularly from some rapid social and cultural changes occurring there.

In the first place, there were the claims arising from immigration and commerce. The thousands of immigrants per year pouring into various Latin American countries from Europe, as well as from the United States, were seen as a missionary problem owing to the disintegrating effects of migration on morals and religion. Furthermore, the purely commercial interest of some foreigners was causing, rather than solving, social problems,

as their complacency with industrial injustice and the diffusion of the vice of drunkenness indicated. Against this background, missionary work was seen as part of the duty that Europe, and the "Anglo-Saxon race [had] to discharge in respect to the moral welfare of Latin America."[93]

In the second place, there were the claims arising from the threat to any form of religious faith by the arrival of modern learning and thinking in Latin America. Religious faith was collapsing and giving way to unbelief, not because faith and modern thought are always and necessarily in conflict, but because "the dominant religious leaders [were] devoting their energies to impeding the irresistible currents of untrammeled learning instead of Christianizing them."[94] In every country, the educated classes were adopting different types of unbelief, from passive religious dissatisfaction to violent anticlericalism. The Evangelical approach was necessary, therefore, to check the spreading of unbelief by presenting "the modern Christian position," a faith whose fundamentals "have not been destroyed by scientific truth and knowledge."[95]

The third claim is connected to the traditional missionary motive, that is to say, the commitment to carrying the Gospel to nonevangelized populations. As the Edinburgh Conference had already insisted, large numbers of the native Indians and the descendants of former negro slaves were still in a pagan condition, without any contact with Christianity. Moreover, even many of the Indians that were thought to have been Christianized were still adhering to their old religion:

> They constitute a field of pure missionary endeavor as apostolically conceived, which no body of Christians can ignore who accept responsibility for the world's evangelization. Scarcely less appealing are the spiritual needs of even more numerous bodies of

---

92   CCLA, ed., *Christian Work in Latin America*, vol. 1, 72–122.

93   CCLA, ed., *Christian Work in Latin America*, vol. 1, 75.
94   CCLA, ed., *Christian Work in Latin America*, vol. 1, 77.
95   CCLA, ed., *Christian Work in Latin America*, vol. 1, 83.

people who are without any commensurate means for entrance upon Christian discipleship, instruction and growth.[96]

In the fourth place, there were the claims based on the effects of spiritual freedom on individual and national character. Here Commission I provides the most interesting argument, that is, the discovery that no Christian communion can truly claim that its doctrine exhausts the fullness of the Christian faith, and therefore, that the different communions need one another's contributions in order to approach that fullness.

> The progressive rapprochements of many of the great Christian Communions are teaching this generation that isolation and aloofness are inimical to spiritual fruitfulness; and also that each body has some God-given contribution to make in the discovery and appropriation by all of the Christian message and ideal in their fullness.[97]

What follows from this is that, just as the Roman Catholic Church was making, side by side with other communions, its legitimate contribution in northern Europe and North America, Evangelical Christians have not only the right, but also the obligation to make their contribution to the life of the Latin American peoples. Precisely, according to the report of Commission I, one of the specific contributions that Evangelical Christianity can share is its conviction that intellectual freedom is healthier for true religion than intolerance:

> Evangelical Christianity, though not yet without bigots, has sufficiently learned the lessons of history, many of them painful, to throw the preponderance of its strength into the scale for freedom of intellect and conscience. It seeks this boon for Latin America in good faith, believing that the acceptance

and observance of the principle by all Communions in those lands would serve there as elsewhere the cause of true religion and the related interests of humanity far better than do the voice of authority and the machinery of suppression.[98]

Another contribution of Evangelical Christians is their recognition of peoples' right to an "open Bible."[99] By "open," peoples' direct access to the Bible in the vernacular language was intended, according to the conviction that the Bible itself has the power to communicate the Word of God and to guide them to righteousness, notwithstanding the teaching ministry of the churches. That recognition is followed by a real passion for the diffusion of the Bible.

Without claiming to be exhaustive, Commission I pointed out a third contribution of Evangelical Christianity, that is to say, the right to a "democratic management" of the churches.[100] This rather formal formulation meant the respect and promotion of the participation of lay people both in the internal life of the churches and in its service and testimony to the world. The fact that the movements of Sunday schools and the YMCA were the fruits of lay initiative was presented to illustrate this kind of contribution.

Finally, there were the claims arising from the application of Christianity to social needs and problems. Since all Christian communions were called to share their God-given contributions to enrich the whole of Christianity, the different civilizations were called to share their knowledge and experience in order to improve Christian civilization morally and socially.

> The enlightened peoples of the world are sharing with one another acquired

---

96   CCLA, ed., *Christian Work in Latin America*, vol. 1, 84–85.
97   CCLA, ed., *Christian Work in Latin America*, vol. 1, 105.

98   CCLA, ed., *Christian Work in Latin America*, vol. 1, 105.
99   CCLA, ed., *Christian Work in Latin America*, vol. 1, 105–109.
100   CCLA, ed., *Christian Work in Latin America*, vol. 1, 109–110.

knowledge, experience, leadership and financial assistance in the advancement of health, education, character and other fruits of Christian civilization. Such interchange should increasingly characterize the relations between Latin America and the Anglo-Saxon-Teutonic nations.[101]

In the context of such necessary interchange, Evangelical Christianity was willing to cooperate in Latin America with the extension of popular education, the improvement of public health, support for Indians, war against intemperance, the campaign for social morality (sex education and anti-vice regulations), and the suppression of gambling.[102] It goes without saying that an evident presupposition was that North America was far more advanced in the solution to these problems than Latin America, and, therefore, that the former was in the position of the teacher while the latter in that of the pupil. This was the missionary version of Pan-Americanism.

The diagnosis of the Latin American religious situation underlying this justification of Protestant missions, basically follows the same lines as Robert E. Speer's interpretation of the South American problems after his 1909 tour. Its approach, however, is clearly more positive and dialogical. This difference of approach could be explained simply by noting that while the report of Speer's tour was addressed chiefly to North American Evangelical Christians, in order to awaken their interest in Latin American missions, the reports of the Panama Congress were to be seen as the official Protestant policy toward Latin American religion, and therefore, open to scrutiny by the interested Latin American public.

7   The Neglected Groups: The "Uncultured Masses" and the "Cultured Classes"

As far as the missionary work was concerned, it is clear that for the Panama Congress the most significant groups were the two poles of Latin American societies: on the one hand, the "uncultured" or "uneducated" masses, in Spanish America mostly Indian and *mestizo*, in Brazil mostly black and *mulato*. On the other hand, the "educated classes," mostly *criollo* and European.

In continuity with the view already presented in the New York EMC, the "uneducated" indigenous and mixed masses were described as living in a state of semi-paganism, that is to say, externally adhering to a basic form of Catholicism, but inwardly abiding by their old religions. "They [the Indians] have never been really converted to the religion of Spain; they rather have converted it to their own paganism."[103]

The so-called baptized paganism was seen as the result of the Spaniards' policy of crushing the civilization of the conquered peoples. The pre-Hispanic religious situation ranged from "the crude barbarian animism of the Amazonian and La Plata tribes to the more elaborate polytheism of the great confederacies like the Incas of Peru, the Muiscas or Chibchas of Colombia, the Mayas of Central America and the Aztecs of Mexico." The latter groups had developed societies which could be compared fairly well with the higher non-Christian civilizations, having, alongside "much that was primitive and horrible in their worship, ... exalted ethical conceptions symbolized in gorgeous ritual and embodied in systematic teaching."[104] But rather than assimilating or elevating to higher standards the more valuable aspects of the old religions and cultures, those elements were systematically destroyed.

While these higher tendencies of the native religions, which might have been converted

---

101   CCLA, ed., *Christian Work in Latin America*, vol. 1, 111.

102   CCLA, ed., *Christian Work in Latin America*, vol. 1, 111–122.

103   CCLA, ed., *Christian Work in Latin America*, vol. 1, 92.

104   CCLA, ed., *Christian Work in Latin America*, vol. 1, 253.

into moral and spiritual capital, were broken down, the more vulgar superstitions and practices of paganism survived, being perpetuated to this day. ... For example, at Guadalupe, the most holy shrine in Mexico, and at Copacabana, on Lake Titicaca, the Indians still dance before the church, perform other religious rites exactly as their pre-Christian ancestors did, and the Church permits these practices as part of their religious pilgrimages. ... All that can be truthfully said is that the higher native religions were swept away, that the popular beliefs and practices of the lower cults – blind gropings, superstitious fears, and crude ritual – have become mixed with the prevailing religion of to-day.[105]

The above quotation suggests that, at least in theory, the Protestant critique was not addressed against a supposed policy of adaptation of the Roman Catholic Church. Quite the contrary: it was the lack of a wise policy of adaptation that led to the destruction of the "higher" forms of worship, while permitting the mingling of "lower" religious practices with Christian worship. As an example of a "higher form of worship" which was unhappily destroyed, Commission II mentions the "gleams of light as flashed out in the ethicized and spiritualized sun-worship of the Incas, illuminating the way to a pure monotheism centered about Pachacamac, the Quichuan creator of the world."[106] Curiously enough, the natural conclusion of this assessment of the Iberian missions was that the field was ready for a fresh start from nothing. Since everything that survived was "lower" – blind gropings, superstitious fears, and crude ritual – nothing was left to be assimilated or converted into moral and spiritual capital by the new messengers of true religion.

Turning now to the opposite pole of Latin American society, the "cultured" or "educated" classes, these sectors were described as living in a growing climate of unbelief and skepticism resulting from the diffusion of modern science and knowledge. This was an area where the "Latin American problems" were much closer to the challenges faced by Christianity "at home" (in the United States and northern Europe) and elsewhere.[107] The difference was that in Latin America there was little presence of a "vital" form of Christianity that could be recognized by the educated classes as compatible with true democracy, science, and reason. Such was the "crux of Latin-American life," as Commission II put it.[108]

Although the problems affecting the "uncultured" and "educated classes" were of a different nature, they were somehow interconnected. A chief cause of the rejection of any sort of religion by the educated and forward-looking sections of the Latin American population was, in the interpretation of the Panama Congress, a reaction to the effect of the traditional religious system upon the "uncultured" masses. Rather than uplifting them, traditional religion would keep them in their backwardness. Superstition and half-paganism among the uneducated population was deemed an obstacle to progress, and therefore, one of the reasons for the growth of unbelief among the progressive educated minorities. The presentation of the pure and simple Gospel was an urgent task if Christianity was to have any future in Latin America.

In theory, this evangelistic endeavor was meant to win over both "the scholarly Saul of Tarsus" (the educated classes) and "the slave Onesimus" (the uncultured masses) to the Gospel,[109] but the reports of the Panama Congress taken as a whole reveal a kind of "preferential option" for the scholarly Saul of Tarsus. Indeed, there were words of appreciation for the few agencies that had turned to the indigenous population, as well as words of invitation for others to enter "into the Christ-less

---

105   CCLA, ed., *Christian Work in Latin America*, vol. 1, 253–254.

106   CCLA, ed., *Christian Work in Latin America*, vol. 1, 253.

107   CCLA, ed., *Christian Work in Latin America*, vol. 1, 232ff.

108   CCLA, ed., *Christian Work in Latin America*, vol. 1, 247.

109   CCLA, ed., *Christian Work in Latin America*, vol. 1, 194.

wildernesses."[110] But much of the energies of the congress itself were spent reflecting on how to present the Christian message to the educated classes. Commission II devoted a full chapter of its report to this issue,[111] and the point was highlighted in the findings of almost every commission.[112]

A very practical reason for this preference was the presupposition that it would be easier to secure an adequate local leadership if some members of the student class were attracted to Evangelical Christianity and recruited to the ministry. There was also the conviction that the sectors of the Latin American societies that were more sympathetic toward Protestant missionary work in Latin America were precisely the educated classes. Although the missionaries would soon realize that such a welcoming attitude toward missions had a sociopolitical rather than a religious motivation, by the time of the Panama Congress it was expected that a closer acquaintance with "the modern Christian position" would lead the Latin American educated classes to embrace Evangelical Christianity.

However, underlying this preference there was a deeper theoretical or ideological presupposition: the quasi social Darwinist view that while the educated classes represented the future of Latin America, the "backward" peoples were no more than "survivals" of bygone times. The following statement, although referring specifically to the "more savage" peoples, reveals this evolutionist outlook:

> The future of these peoples must see either their civilization or their destruction; they cannot long exist as they are, for if not exterminated by the rifle, they will disappear under the influence of vice and disease, and with their disappearance will also vanish a potential source of useful and profitable

labor suitable to climate and country. ... The proximity of savagery does not encourage immigration. The opinion of the civilized world and of the cultured leaders in South American states is averse to extermination. Herein lies one of the great claims for missionary occupation and conquest by Christianity, the saving from destruction of a people who, under proper Christian training and development, are capable of becoming quiet and orderly citizens, and of being trained in moral rectitude, a healthy and honest people.[113]

In other words, the only way to prevent the physical destruction of the more "savage" people was paradoxically deemed to be the destruction of their traditional way of life and its replacement by the basics of Christian civilization. The reason for working with these "neglected" peoples was, therefore, basically humanitarian and civilizing. However, as the future of Christianity in Latin America rested less upon the indigenous problem than upon the reversing of the tendency towards unbelief, the educated classes were the chief missionary priority for Evangelical Christianity.

There was a single voice that dissented with this preferential option for the "educated classes," that is to say, Samuel H. Chester, a Presbyterian pastor, who remembered that Jesus' emphasis was "on preaching the gospel to the poor," and feared that such a priority would encourage class distinctions within the Christian Church.[114] Yet the report of Commission VI, on "The Church in the Field," had a ready-made answer to Chester's preoccupations: "The feeling is increasing ... that whatever may be the risk of producing class distinctions in the churches through specialized effort, the hazard is still greater if men of high social standing and influence are not won to the open confession of Christ."[115]

---

110   CCLA, ed., *Christian Work in Latin America*, vol. 1, 194.

111   CCLA, ed., *Christian Work in Latin America*, vol. 1, 301–315.

112   CCLA, ed., *Christian Work in Latin America*, vol. 3, 102–103.

113   CCLA, ed., *Christian Work in Latin America*, vol. 1, 95–96.

114   CCLA, ed., *Christian Work in Latin America*, vol. 2, 331.

115   CCLA, ed., *Christian Work in Latin America*, vol. 2, 238.

8   Conclusions

The only official resolution of the Panama
Congress was the decision to extend and accord a
more permanent mandate to the CCLA, and it is
because of such a decision that this gathering may
rightly be seen as the birth place of the ecumenical movement in Latin America. The CCLA was
understood as a consultative and advisory organ
dedicated to following up the findings of the congress and to monitoring the process of missionary
cooperation that those findings had urged.[116]

However, the great significance of this congress
lies in its proposal for a highly elaborate *rationale*
for Protestant missions in Latin America. In this
sense, the findings of the congress are the evidence
that the strategy, designed mainly by Robert Elliott
Speer, to take advantage of the Edinburgh conference's exclusion of Latin America from its agenda
for involving most of North American missionary
boards in missions in that area, was truly successful. Moreover, the fact that such findings were later
embraced by the international missionary movement that followed the 1910 WMC confirms the
assertion that there was no real European opposition to missionary work in Latin America.[117]

The Panama Congress took place before the
theological debate between liberals and funda-
mentalists had fully divided the North American
missionary movement into two conflicting
fronts,[118] and the boards present in it represented

the wider North American theological spectrum.[119]
Thus, the ensemble of these elements may safely
be regarded as the common ground for every
Protestant missionary adventure in Latin America
for many years to come, whatever the problems
and failures that occurred in the attempts to put it
into a shared practice.

Bibliography

CCLA, ed., *Christian Work in Latin America*, 3 vols., New
York NY, Missionary Education Movement, 1917.

Clements, Keith, *Faith on the Frontier: A Life of
J.H. Oldham*, Edinburgh, T&T Clark, 1999.

Piedra, Arturo, *Evangelización protestante en América
Latina: Análisis de las razones que justificaron y pro-
movieron la expansión protestante (1830–1960)*, vol. 1,
Quito, Consejo Latinoamericano de Iglesias, 2000.

Sabanes, Dafne, *Caminos de unidad: Itinerario del
diálogo ecuménico en América Latina (1916–1991)*,
Quito, Consejo Latinoamericano de Iglesias, 1994

Speer, Robert Elliott, *Missions in South America*,
New York NY, Board of Foreign Missions of the
Presbyterian Church, 1909.

---

116   See Minutes of the Congress in: CCLA, ed., *Christian
Work in Latin America*, vol. 3, 448f.

117   At the Jerusalem meeting of the IMC (1928) the legitimacy of Latin America as a mission field was simply
taken for granted. The CCLA was accepted as member of
the IMC, and three seats were given for Latin American
representatives in the committee of the council; IMC,
ed., *Report of the Jerusalem Meeting of the International
Missionary Council, March 24th–April 8th, 1928*, vol. 7,
London, Oxford University Press, 1928, 24, 84, 87, 124.

118   William R. Hutchison, *Errand to the World: American
Protestant Thought and Foreign Missions*, Chicago IL,
University of Chicago Press, 1993, 138ff.

119   Still by 1989 two evangelical writers claimed the legacy
of the Panama Congress as part of a common Latin
American Evangelical-Protestant memory: Emilio
Antonio Núñez & William David Taylor, *Crisis in
Latin America: An Evangelical Perspective*, Chicago IL,
Moody Press, 1989, 152. However, another Presbyterian
delegate, John Fox, soon after the Panama Congress
protested against the predominantly liberal outlook
of its leading thinkers, in his article "Christian Unity,
Church Unity, and the Panama Congress," *PTR* 14/4,
1916, 545–578.

Unto the Churches of Christ Everywhere: The Ecumenical Patriarchate's 1920 Encyclical

Stylianos Tsompanidis

1 The Ecumenical Movement: The Greatest and Most Valuable Effort

Since the mid-19th century, the birth and development of the ecumenical movement have been inextricably intertwined with the historical circumstances that marked the emergence of the contemporary age, particularly with its tensions and crises. Furthermore, it may be argued that the ecumenical movement became one of the ways in which the churches responded to the challenges of modernity, especially as it developed in the 20th century: industrialization, the fall of the great empires, internationalism, secularization, colonialism, global economic crises, the rise of fascism, and the two world wars. The hope connected to the birth of the ecumenical movement was one of a renewal of the church, attained after finally overcoming the boundaries between ecclesial traditions, confessions, and peoples. In short, in a certain sense the development of the ecumenical movement can be seen as an effort by the Christian churches, first and foremost by the Protestant and Orthodox ones, to face modernity and its consequences for society.[1]

The contacts and dialogue that developed among the churches in the 20th century differed from those attempted in previous historical periods, both in purpose as well as in form and content. Their characteristics were completely new

since historical circumstances presented new, revolutionary features. Indeed, in the ecumenical dialogue emerged themes that previously, in the ecclesiastical tradition, had not given rise to controversy or discussion, such as contemporary political and social issues besides ecclesiological problems. While dialogues in the past were characterized by an attitude of opposition, hostility and a lack of systematic organization, this new dialogue was peaceful, organized, and frictionless. Moreover, a new style of personal encounter and conversation replaced the older practice of dialogue through letters and formal papers. The ecumenical movement has had a multifaceted history in which many varied points of origin, perspectives, movements, facts, and trends intersect.

2 The Desire for Christian Collaboration and Unity

Orthodoxy not only shared the desire for collaboration and unity but was also involved in writing the introduction and content of the most splendid chapter of ecclesiastical history in recent years.[2] The history of the ecumenical movement and of the WCC, along with their backgrounds, is

---

1 For a summary of the connection between the evolution of the historical events in the 19th century and the birth of the ecumenical movement, see Konrad Raiser, "Die Ökumene in einer schweren Bewährungsprobe," *Der Überblick* 34, 1998, 4–8.

2 See Alexandros Papaderos, "Oikoumenika kektīmena kai opheilomena," [Ecumenical facts and debts] in: Ioannis Petrou, Stylianos Tsompanidis & Moschos Goutzioudis, eds., *O oikoumenikos dialogos ston 21° aiōna: Pragmatikotītes, proklīseis, prooptikes, Timītiko aphierōma ston omotimo kathīgītī Petro Vasileiadī* [Ecumenical dialogue in the 21st century: realities, challenges, perspectives, a tribute to emeritus professor Petros Vasileiadis], Thessaloniki, Vanias, 2013, 93–114, esp. 97.

interwoven with Orthodoxy. From the beginning of the 20th century, amid rapid crises and sociopolitical changes, in a world seeking a new direction, the Orthodox Churches – under the leadership of the Ecumenical Patriarchate – felt the urgency for a union of churches and a common witness for them. As has been shown by both historians and theologians,[3] the Orthodox Churches' contribution to the birth of the ecumenical movement was decisive – first in the creation of the Life and Work and the Faith and Order movements, then in the subsequent foundation of the WCC.[4]

It is an established historical fact that one of the first, most serious, and specific exhortations to create a *"koinonia of churches"* came from an Orthodox Church, with the famous 1920 encyclical of the Ecumenical Patriarchate of Constantinople, *Unto the Churches of Christ Everywhere*.[5] In his speech on Nov 8, 1967, on the occasion of Patriarch Athenagoras I's visit to the Geneva headquarters of the WCC, Willem Visser 't Hooft recognized that the Church of Constantinople had been the first in modern history to remind Christians that they could not remain disobedient to the will of Christ, who desired the unity of the people of God and of his body. Thus, "with its 1920 encyclical, Constantinople rang the bell for our assembly."[6]

Thanks to the encyclical, a landmark in the history of the ecumenical movement and a "definite expression of Orthodox ecumenism,"[7] the Ecumenical Patriarchate laid the foundations for the collective responsibility for the future of the church, at both the pan-Orthodox and the interconfessional levels. This future would be assured only by the encounter, consensus, and constructive collaboration between Christians. Furthermore, the encyclical helped emphasize the importance of strengthening ties between Orthodox Churches and their ecumenical relations with other Christian churches. At the same time, it served to awaken its synodal conscience, thus providing an impetus to the process of convoking a pan-Orthodox synod.

At the dawn of the 20th century, therefore, Orthodoxy – whose liturgy continually repeats prayers "for the union of all" and "for the peace of the whole world" – undertook an initiative that aimed at the birth of what would later be called the "ecumenical movement." The factor that made it impossible to ignore the vital force of Christianity outside Orthodoxy and not to imitate the *non possumus* of the Roman Catholic Church was the spirit of freedom and pure catholicity of the Orthodox Church as highlighted by Professor Hamilcar Alivisatos, the wise Nestor of the modern ecumenical movement.[8]

The 1920 text is the direct successor to, and direct result of, two previous letters from the Ecumenical Patriarch Joachim III. It is therefore opportune, before entering into the details of the encyclical, to analyze briefly these two documents. They were the first Orthodox manifestation in the

---

3 Besides the other studies cited, it is necessary to refer to Nicolas Zernov's important contribution "The Eastern Churches and the Ecumenical Movement in the Twentieth Century," in: *A History of the Ecumenical Movement*, vol. 1, Ruth Rouse & Stephen C. Neill, eds., *1517–1948*, Geneva, WCC Publications, ³1986, 643–674.

4 The most specialized and original study of this question is Georges Tsetsis's dissertation, *Ī symbolī tou oikoumenikou patriarcheiou stīn idrysī toī paukosmiou symbouliou ekklīsiōn* [The contribution of the Ecumenical Patriarchate to the foundation of the World Council of Churches], Ph.D. thesis, Aristotle University of Thessaloniki, 1988.

5 "Encyclical of the Ecumenical Patriarchate, 1920: *Unto the Churches of Christ Everywhere*," in: Gennadios Limouris, ed., *Orthodox Visions of Ecumenism: Statements, Messages, and Reports on the Ecumenical Movement (1902–1992)*, Geneva, WCC Publications, 1994, 9–11.

6 See Willem Adolf Visser 't Hooft, "O mī synagōn met' emou skorpizei," [Whoever does not gather with me, scatters] *Stachys* 16–17, 1969, 18–21, esp. 19. See Georges Tsetsis, "The

Meaning of the Orthodox Presence in the Ecumenical Movement," in: Limouris, ed., *Orthodox Visions*, 272–277, here 272.

7 Tsetsis, *Ī symbolī tou oikoumenikou patriarcheiou*, 194.

8 See Hamilcar Alivisatos, "To Synedrion tīs Lozannīs" [The Lausanne Conference], *Ekklīsia* 5, 1927, 185–186, 193–195, 201–204, esp. 201, 203. See also his opening speech at the first conference of Orthodox theology, published in: Hamilcar Alivisatos, ed., *Procès-verbaux du premier Congrès de théologie orthodoxe à Athènes, 29 nov.–6 déc. 1936*, Athens, Pyrsos, 1939, 44ff., esp. 45, 48.

20th century of support for a rapprochement with other churches and, broadly speaking, are considered the foundation of the Orthodox Church's presence within the wider field of Christianity.

3 Prelude: The Patriarchal and Synodal Encyclicals of 1902 and 1904

Renouncing the centuries-old theoretical support of intolerance and prejudice, Joachim III's two famous letters – addressed to the leaders of the autocephalous churches in 1902 and 1904 – represented a true leap forward. They symbolized a completely new spirit that would, for the Eastern Churches, clear the air of the fog of past disagreement and militant theology.

3.1 The 1902 Encyclical

The first of these letters was addressed to "their Beatitudes and Holinesses, the Patriarchs of Alexandria and Jerusalem, and to the most holy autocephalous sister-Churches in Christ, in Cyprus, Russia, Greece, Romania, Serbia and Montenegro."[9] It called for the necessary steps to be taken in order for the Orthodox people to be able to come together in Christian love and harmony to strengthen the Orthodox faith and face the challenges of the century more effectively. Moreover, the letter also focused on the subject of future relations with the other "two great growths of Christianity," that is to say, of course, the Western Churches, understood as the Catholic and Protestant Churches, including the Old Catholic ones.

It is absolutely fundamental to note that, in the encyclical, the term by which the other two "churches" or "growths" of Christianity are explicitly defined is consistent, in a way that is completely simple and natural, with the premises of Orthodox ecclesiology. It emphasized that it is "pleasing to God, and in accordance with the

Gospel, to seek the mind of the most holy autocephalous churches on the subject of our present and future relations with the two great growths of Christianity, viz. the Western Church and the Church of the Protestants."[10] The phrase "great growths of Christianity" with which the encyclical referred to Western Catholics and Protestants had been chosen with great care for its neutrality "so that an equivalence might be maintained while, at the same time, the benevolent attitude would not veil the difficulties."[11]

The clause thus implied a positive evaluation of the Protestant and Catholic Churches as growths of Christianity but was still very prudent. On the one hand, it remained firmly attached to Orthodox ecclesiology while, on the other, it recognized a concrete ecclesial form in Western ecclesiastical entities that were separate from the Orthodox Church. This ecclesiological approach did not diminish or relativize Orthodox self-awareness of its authentic continuity with the one, holy, Catholic, and apostolic Church. Moreover, it also defined, in a figurative sense, the character of ecclesial entities existing outside the Orthodox Church, in order not only to highlight the scandal of the division of the church, but also, indeed, to emphasize the need for sincere theological dialogue aimed at its reparation.[12]

---

9   "Patriarchal and Synodical Encyclical of 1902," in: Limouris, ed., *Orthodox Visions*, 1–8, here 1.

10   "Patriarchal and Synodical Encyclical of 1902," 2–3.

11   Evangelia Varella, *Diorthodoxoi kai oikoumenikai scheseis tou Patriarcheiou Kōnstantinopoleōs kata ton 20. aiōna* [Inter-Orthodox and ecumenical relations of the Patriarchate of Constantinople during the 20th century], Thessaloniki, Patriarchikon Idryma Paterikōn Meletōn, 1994, 160.

12   See Vlassios Pheidas, "Ai egkyklioi tou 1902 kai tou 1904 ōs prodromoi tīs egkykliou tou 1920 en tī eurytera oikoumenistikī prooptikī tīs Mītros Ekklīsias" [The encyclicals of 1902 and 1904 as precursors of the encyclical of 1920 in the broader ecumenical perspective of the Mother Church], *Orthodoxia* 10, 2003, 129–139, esp. 135–136. See also Konstantinos Skouteris, "Ī egkyklios tou 1902 kai oi diorthodokses scheseis kata tīn epochī tīs ekdoseōs tīs, idiōs sta Balkania kai tī Mesī Anatolī, kai ī sīmasia tīs gia tin tote kai gia tīn enestōsa pragmatikotīta" [The encyclical of 1902 and inter-Orthodox relations at the time of its publication, especially in Balkans and the Middle East and

The late Metropolitan of Myra Chrysostomos (Constantinidis) considered the term "growths" highly expressive and effective because, from an Orthodox point of view, it coincided ecclesiologically with the terms *vestigia veritatis*, or more generally, *vestigia ecclesiae*, widely used in the ecumenical movement. He wondered whether

> could, therefore, these growths, which might have and maintain their *vestigia ecclesia*, also have and maintain equivalent *vestigia sacramenti*, from a mysteriological point of view? Today, could this concept, which is always open to theological discussion, perhaps facilitate the beginning of theological discussion on mysteriological problems, in particular, discussion on the recognition of heterodox sacraments in a spirit of *oikonomia*?[13]

Moreover, in a very interesting passage, this decisive question was asked: How do we establish points of contact and encounter, or even determine issues on both sides, that might be legitimately passed over (turning "a blind eye to certain irregularities")?[14] The encyclical proposed considering the opportunity of holding a "pre-conference" in order to help the autocephalous churches understand the desire for unity and to prepare the grounds for its achievement.[15] The letter also defined the unity of Christians, with pious and fraternal words "hoped-for and longed-for."[16] Besides the fact that what is cited here already contained the idea of a pan-Orthodox synodal process, it is important to highlight not only this last expression, which illustrates the concrete

responsibility for unity and its heartfelt expectation, but also the importance of the phrase "to turn a blind eye to certain irregularities." In his excellent article "Die Grenzen der Kirche," Theodor Nikolaou correctly observes that "turning a blind eye" is something more than factual overcoming the insurmountable barriers that impede encounter between the Orthodox and other churches. The move to meet and welcome the other is rather a dutiful and necessary concession on the part of the Orthodox Church.[17]

Finally, the Ecumenical Patriarchate's 1902 initiative was not only received unanimously, despite the legitimate doubts of some local churches, but also served, as has been pointed out, to cement a pan-Orthodox consensus regarding the Patriarchate of Constantinople's further initiatives, since support for this proposal created a precedent for future initiatives promoting ecumenical dialogue.[18]

3.2 *The 1904 Encyclical*

Two years later, in 1904, Joachim III wrote another encyclical in response to letters sent to Constantinople by the other sister churches in reaction to the 1902 encyclical.[19] The new encyclical also expressed, even more intensely, the desire that the churches draw nearer, that they work together, and even, if possible, that there be unity between the holy churches of God, a unity for which the Orthodox Church had never ceased to pray. On this occasion, the Anglican Church was also one of the Western Churches mentioned. After having first and foremost warned the leaders of the Orthodox Churches of the threat of their adversaries, the patriarch also stressed that

> we ought also to look to the concerns of others and pray with all our soul for the union

---

its importance for the reality of the time and today], *Orthodoxia* 10, 2003, 229–241, esp. 236–237, 239–240.

13   Chrysostomos S. Constantinidis, *Ī anagōrisī tōn mystīriōn tōn eterodoksōn stis diachronikes scheseis Orthodoksias kai Rōmaiokatholikismou* [The recognition of the sacraments of the heterodox in the timeless relations of Orthodox and Roman Catholics], Katerini, Epektasi, 1995, 192–194.

14   "Patriarchal and Synodical Encyclical of 1902," 3.

15   "Patriarchal and Synodical Encyclical of 1902," 3.

16   "Patriarchal and Synodical Encyclical of 1902," 4.

---

17   Theodor Nikolaou, "Die Grenzen der Kirche in der Sicht der Orthodoxen Katholischen Kirche," *ÖR* 21, 1972, 316–332, here 326.

18   See Pheidas, "Ai egkyklioi tou 1902 kai tou 1904," 138.

19   See the Encyclical of 1904 in: "Response to the Reactions of the Local Orthodox Churches," in: Limouris, ed., *Orthodox Visions*, 5–8.

of all, not adding to the difficulties nor holding that the matter does not bear discussion or is quite impossible, but considering the possible ways of progress in the good work of the union of all: walking in wisdom and in the spirit of gentleness towards those who disagree with us, and remembering that they too believe in the All-Holy Trinity and glory in the name of our Lord Jesus Christ and hope to be saved by the grace of God.[20]

This quotation is extremely important: in addition to showing the desire to work for unity – which is pleasing to God – Patriarch Joachim III emphasized the importance for the Orthodox not to wait for others to come to them, but to work themselves toward welcoming "separated brethren" with wisdom and a gentle spirit. This would be fundamental in order to create "space" for others. It demonstrated an open attitude toward non-Orthodox Christians and other ecclesial entities besides the recognition of the presence in them of an authentic hope and true Christian faith. Belief in the most holy Trinity created an unbreakable bond among Christians. This was a basic element in every declaration of the Orthodox Churches in the journey toward ecumenism, especially after the establishment of the WCC.

It should be mentioned here that, according to Georges Florovsky, one of the most important representatives of Orthodoxy in the ecumenical movement, belief in Christ the Savior and God unites those who maintain and profess it, even if this unity cannot yet be expressed in a single logical formula. The simple fact of unity exists beyond any doubt or dispute.[21] Florovsky thus expressed the position of the Orthodox Churches before and after the WCC was founded, determining it at the same time.

Indeed, it is well known that he had a profound influence on Orthodox positions on ecumenism, particularly in regard to the specific statements issued, from those at the first assembly of Faith and Order in Lausanne in 1927 to those at the third assembly of the WCC in New Delhi in 1961.

What most concerned Patriarch Joachim III in his second letter was the lack of unanimity among the Orthodox Churches regarding the recognition of the baptism and ministry of the non-Orthodox, which condemned out of hand any attempt toward rapprochement or dialogue. That is why he emphasized the need to determine a common faith and plan of action. In order to achieve this result, it was proposed that, every three years, a meeting of representative theologians from the individual Orthodox Churches be organized and that "their carefully considered opinions were to be notified to the other churches by the first in order, the archbishop of Constantinople, for their final decision."[22] This particular proposal was abandoned due to the historical events of the period. Nevertheless, it became the precedent upon which all bilateral dialogues inaugurated by the Orthodox Church were based during the second half of the 20th century.

What has been noted regarding the 1904 encyclical, particularly regarding the paragraph cited here, cannot be denied:

> This evaluation of the positions of the entirety of the faithful with regard to the plan of salvation would become the heart of the Orthodox ecclesial evaluation, particularly for the World Council of Churches, because it accepted the existence and work of the structured ecclesial entities of all the rest of Christianity without renouncing the singleness of the one, holy, Catholic, and apostolic Church … Milestones of pan-Orthodox consensus, Joachim III's letters, therefore, became the precursors of coordinates that

20   "Response to the Reactions of the Local Orthodox Churches," 7.
21   Georges Florovsky, "The Orthodox Contribution to the Ecumenical Movement," in: Richard S. Haugh, ed., *The Collected Works of Georges Florovsky*, vol. 13, Georges Florovsky, *Ecumenism I: A Doctrinal Approach*, Vaduz, Büchervertriebsanstalt, 1989, 160–164, here 162.

22   "Response to the Reactions of the Local Orthodox Churches," 7.

defined the Orthodox Church's position in the wider area of Christianity, defining the canonical limits and the conditions for establishing interconfessional contacts.[23]

It should be added that the conditions, both in the Orthodox Church and in other confessions, for the synodal encyclical of 1920 to indicate a true and proper common Christian path that could clearly and amply delimit ecumenical relations were prepared precisely by the patriarchal and synodal encyclicals of 1902 and 1904,[24] which were written in a completely new spirit, replete with Christian meekness and love.

4   The 1920 Synodal Encyclical

The 1920 encyclical stood in full continuity with the experiences of the Church of Constantinople – which, fully aware of its ecumenical mission, has always been dedicated, through its ministry, to the entire body of the Church – besides being direct consequence of them. This extremely important document appeared at a time when the Ecumenical Patriarchate had already begun to establish contacts with Western representatives, particularly those of the American Episcopal Church and the Lutheran Church of Sweden. Unlike the two letters preceding it, which were addressed solely to the primates of the Orthodox Churches, this encyclical was addressed *Unto the Churches of Christ Everywhere*. Its promulgation arose out of the conviction that the Church of Constantinople had to define its position and its attitude through a process of dialogue and collaboration. Through the encyclical, it sought to fulfill an essential function in the life of the church, that is, to bear witness to the content of the faith within the context of historical events, which are constantly evolving. Without a witness of faith in the world – which means not only preaching and

teaching but also a true love of the world, practice, outreach, and hard work – it cannot be truly called a living church.[25] The question that all Christians engaged in ecumenical efforts, almost contemporaneously, posed themselves was therefore: how does the church express its faith within the dramatic context of history and in the face of the challenges that it poses?

4.1   *Motivations and Context of the Church of Constantinople's Proposal*

What drove the Ecumenical Patriarchate to promulgate the encyclical was, above all, the awareness of the need to bear witness to the faith, a love for the world, and the pastoral concern for the many needs of the faithful, together with the conviction that only through collaboration among the churches on a global scale could the challenges of the century be faced.[26]

In describing the background to the 1920 encyclical, Metropolitan Germanos (Strenopoulos) of Thyateira – who played an essential role in the ecumenical ferment during the first part of the 20th century – stated that the fundamental question of the time was whether the churches of Christ, the Prince of Peace, would be surpassed by political institutions. There was thus the intention to render the churches, once more, a powerful moral and spiritual force for renewal in the world after World War I.

---

23   Varella, *Diorthodoxoi kai oikoumenikai scheseis*, 161.

24   See Pheidas, "Ai egkyklioi tou 1902 kai tou 1904," 138.

25   Nikos Matsoukas, "Oligai apopseis peri tou oikoumenikou dialogou" [Some views concerning ecumenical dialogue], *Grīgorios Palamas* 55, 1972, 38–43, here 39.

26   See Tsetsis, *Ī symbolī tou oikoumenikou patriarcheiou*, 33, 194. Moreover, Orthodox theology has always considered that problems of injustice, violence, illiberality, hunger, the oppression of human rights, and, ultimately, dehumanization are not merely secondary problems pertaining to the century, but are real theological problems that "belong to the absolute – though not exclusive – jurisdiction of theology"; Marios Mpegzos, *Phainomenologia tīs thrīskeias* [Phenomenology of religion], Athens, Ellīnika Grammata, 1995, 339. This concern was examined explicitly by the WCC, especially during the last quarter of the 20th century.

Immediately after the end of World War I and the Russian Revolution, with the immense problems faced by the faithful in Asia Minor, the Ecumenical Patriarchate stood firm in its intention to promote relations between the churches, keeping them alive and active. Taking the recent formation of the LN in Geneva as a model, Metropolitan Dorotheos of Bursa, *locum tenens* of the ecumenical see, then stated before the Holy Synod assembled on Jan 10, 1919 that:

I think the time has already come for the Orthodox Church to consider seriously the matter of union of the different Christian Churches, especially that with the Anglican, the Old Catholic and the Armenian Churches. As the most significant announcement and command for union of the different nations in a League of Nations have come from the great Republic of the United States of America in the Western World, so also the most significant announcement and command for the study on the approach and the union of the different Christian denominations in a League of Churches ought to come from the Great Church of Constantinople in the East. Our Church therefore should take the initiative and after a thorough study on this subject give the impetus for the union of all churches in Christian love.[27]

After having discussed the proposal, the formation of a special committee was approved to study the matter and present a report to the synod. The committee was composed of metropolitans and of the first secretary of the Holy Synod, and members of the Theological School of Halki took part in the committee. Among them, Germanos (Strenopoulos), then dean and metropolitan

of Seleukia (later metropolitan of Thyateira), and Professors Ioannis Ephstratiou, Vasileios Stephanidis, Vasileios Antoniadis, and Pantoleon Komninos.

In the meantime, on Apr 10, 1919, the Ecumenical Patriarchate officially responded to the invitation from a delegation of the newly established Faith and Order movement to promote the "holy mission" of Christian unity through the creation of a *koinonia* of churches. In its response, the synod declared that, despite the difficult situation in which the Church of Constantinople had found itself in the past five centuries, it would make every effort. It therefore expressed joy since "the desired occasion is now presented to us in better circumstances and according to God's good will ... to continue his work until that moment expressed only in general terms." The Church of Constantinople gave assurances that its delegates would participate in the planned preparatory conference in the spirit of assisting those who worked, as they did, in the vineyard of the Lord.[28]

This synodal letter was the first to mention officially the establishment of a *koinonia* of churches, a term that essentially came from the work of the commission that had been established in January. The report that it had prepared provided the basis for drafting the encyclical, which was edited and finally approved by the synod on Oct 19, 1919. Its promulgation in Greek, French, English, and Russian, however, took place only in January 1920.

Metropolitan Germanos's role was undeniable and fundamental,[29] not only during the drafting of

---

27 Cited in Vasil T. Istavridis, "The Work of Germanos Strenopoulos in the Field of Inter-Orthodox and Inter-Christian Relations," *EcRev* 11, 1959, 291–299, here 292. The information in the next paragraph also comes from this page.

28 See the text of the letter "Apantīsis tou oikoumenikou patriarcheiou eis to gramma tīs antiprosōpeias tīs kinīseōs 'Pistis kai Taksis'" [Reply of the ecumenical patriarchate to the letter of the delegation of the movement "Faith and Order"], in: Tsetsis, *Ī symbolī tou oikoumenikou patriarcheiou*, 249–250.

29 Some historians of the ecumenical movement consider Metropolitan Germanos to be the sole author of the encyclical: see, for example, Stephen C. Neill, *Men of Unity*, London, SCM Press, 1960, 68. In his review of Neill's book (*Theologia* 32, 1961, 651–654, here 653), Vasilios T. Stavridis stressed that Germanos collaborated with the rest of the professors of Halki, but that

the encyclical, but also during the phase when it was received by the non-Orthodox churches and by the ecumenical movement.[30] The metropolitan embodied the genuine and mature ecumenical awareness of the Church of Constantinople. An astute and cultured man, he was one of the pioneers of the ecumenical movement. His commitment in the area had begun as early as 1911 when he took part in the conference of the WSCF. It was an occasion that allowed him to come into contact with the avant-garde of the ecumenical movement, such as John R. Mott and Nathan Söderblom, and which gave, in a final analysis, a fundamental impulse to the rapprochement between the Orthodox and the federation.

Before the official formation of the two organizations that founded the ecumenical movement, Faith and Order and Life and Work, the encyclical of 1920 provided all the Christian churches with a complete and precise model upon which to build a network of relationships and collaboration.[31]

4.2   *The Encyclical's Content*

The encyclical opens with the observation that – despite the differences that exist at a dogmatic level – it is possible for the churches to achieve a rapprochement and a fellowship, especially in regard to social and ethical issues, and that

such a rapprochement is highly desirable and necessary. It would be useful in many ways for the real interest of each particular church and of the whole Christian body, and also for the preparation and advancement of that blessed union ... in accordance with the will of God.[32]

It therefore emphasized that it was precisely the right time for rapprochement and a *koinonia* of the churches, especially after the founding of the LN. For this mission to succeed, it was necessary to affirm two fundamental principles: an overcoming of mutual distrust and the full expression of the power of Christian love.

> First, we consider as necessary and indispensable the removal and abolition of all the mutual mistrust and bitterness between the different churches which arise from the tendency of some of them to entice and proselytize adherents of other confessions ... After this essential re-establishment of sincerity and confidence between the churches, we consider, [s]econdly, that above all, love should be rekindled and strengthened among the churches, so that they should no more consider one another as strangers and foreigners, but as relatives, and as being a part of the household of Christ and "fellow heirs, members of the same body and partakers of the promise of God in Christ" (Eph 3:6).[33]

The encyclical then proceeded with a series of concrete proposals for the application of these principles in order to improve relations between the Christian churches. Some of the proposals were inspired by practices of the ancient church that expressed the unity of the church, such as the exchange of fraternal letters for important religious celebrations. Others were decidedly new for the time and totally innovative when observed by

---

his contribution was important. Georges Tsetsis seems to share the same opinion (*Oikoumenikos thronos kai oikoumenī: Episīma patriarchika keimena* [Ecumenical throne and oikumene: official patriarchal texts], Katerini, Tertios, 1989, 57). Willem Adolf Visser 't Hooft expressed the opinion that Germanos composed the major part of the encyclical (see *The Genesis and Formation of the World Council of Churches*, Geneva, WCC Publications, 1982, 6; as well as his *Memoirs*, Philadelphia PA, Westminster Press, 1973, 255).

30   Istavridis, "The Work of Germanos Strenopoulos," 293.

31   Vasilios T. Stavridis & Evangelia Varella, *Istoria tīs oikoumenikīs kinīseōs* [History of the ecumenical movement], Thessaloniki, Patriarchikon Idryma Paterikōn Meletōn, 1996, 56. See ch. 4 for the *"Koinonia of Churches"* proposed by the Ecumenical Patriarchate in: Tsetsis, *Ī symbolī tou oikoumenikou patriarcheiou*, 169ff.

32   "Encyclical of the Ecumenical Patriarchate, 1920," 9.

33   "Encyclical of the Ecumenical Patriarchate, 1920," 9–10.

modern eyes, such as the establishment of contact between various theological faculties or student exchange programs.

The encyclical thus continued by affirming that:

Such a friendship and kindly disposition towards each other can be shown and demonstrated particularly in the following ways: (a) By the acceptance of a uniform calendar for the celebration of the great Christian feasts at the same time by all the churches. (b) By the exchange of brotherly letters on the occasion of the great feasts of the churches' year as is customary, and on other exceptional occasions. (c) By close relationships between the representatives of all churches wherever they may be. (d) By relationships between the theological schools and the professors of theology; by the exchange of theological and ecclesiastical reviews, and of other works published in each church. (e) By exchanging students for further training among the seminaries of the different churches. (f) By convoking pan-Christian conferences in order to examine questions of common interest to all the churches. (g) By impartial and deeper historical study of doctrinal differences both by the seminaries and in books. (h) By mutual respect for the customs and practices in different churches. (i) By allowing each other the use of chapels and cemeteries for the funerals and burials of believers of other confessions dying in foreign lands. (j) By the settlement of the question of mixed marriages between the confessions. (k) Lastly, by wholehearted mutual assistance for the churches in their endeavors for religious advancement, charity and so on.[34]

The final passages of the encyclical summarize the text's main points in a brief commentary underlining that the patriarchate had been moved to promulgate the encyclical within the context of

its struggles against the secularism manifest in contempt for the "higher ideals," in the emergent consumerism, in the divinization of wealth, and in the existential demoralization following the end of World War I. After the founding of the LN, therefore, in order to achieve the abovementioned objectives, the patriarchate proposed the creation of a *koinonia* among the churches.[35]

It should be noted that, between 1919 and 1920, there were two other proposals for a *koinonia* of the churches. The second chronologically was contained in a memorandum by Joseph H. Oldham delivered to the international missionary conference in Crans in June 1920, while the first was made in 1919 at the WA Conference by Nathan Söderblom, the Lutheran archbishop of Uppsala. In it, the archbishop hoped for the creation of an international "ecumenical council" that would be the voice of a "Christian conscience" and promote peace and a new world order based on justice.[36] Nikos Matsoukas is right to highlight that, in the context of the ecumenical relations of the time, the initiative and the Patriarchate of Constantinople's proposal had the effect of "stirring up all the Protestant movements of the time, in which many eminent representatives had planned and imagined an ecclesial organization at work in the reality of social upheaval. Orthodoxy, once again, had – at least provisionally – taken the pulse of the situation."[37]

4.3   The Encyclical's Theological and Ecclesiological Foundation

According to a former secretary general of the WCC, Konrad Raiser, the truly notable aspect of

---

34   "Encyclical of the Ecumenical Patriarchate, 1920," 10.

35   "Encyclical of the Ecumenical Patriarchate, 1920," 10–11.

36   See Willem Adolf Visser 't Hooft, "The Genesis of the World Council of Churches," in: *A History of the Ecumenical Movement*, vol. 1, 695–724, esp. 697, and, in the same work, Willem Adolf Visser 't Hooft, "The Word 'Ecumenical': Its History and Use," 735–740.

37   Nikos Matsoukas, *Oikoumenikī theologia: Ekthesī tīs christianikīs pistīs – proypotheseis enos oikoumenikou dialogou* [Ecumenical theology: an account of the Christian faith – conditions for unity, ecumenical dialogue], Thessaloniki, Pournaras, 2005, 219–220.

the encyclical was the biblical and ecclesiological foundation to the proposed *koinonia* of churches, which was rooted particularly in Paul's teachings on the Body of Christ in Eph 3:6, 4:15, and following.[38]

In modern Greek, the term *koinonia* carries the meaning of "association" or "league" or even "communication" or "encounter." Naturally, however, the encyclical does not exclude the evangelical sense of the term, which is of fraternal communion. Metropolitan Germanos himself – who, as we have seen, played a key role in drafting the encyclical – affirmed:

> How wide the conception is which the Encyclical teaches at this point, becomes clear in that it widens the notion of the relationships between the members of every single church – as members of one and the same body according to St. Paul's wonderful teaching – so as to apply it to the relationships between the several churches.[39]

In the context of interecclesial relations during the 20th century, the term *koinonia* was used as a key concept in the ecumenical discussion taking place concerning the church and its unity. The proposal and description of the *koinonia* contained in the 1920 encyclical, together with its evangelical origin, also contributed to giving shape to the first words of the WCC's basis: "The WCC is a fellowship of member churches." Even if the term "fellowship" does not have the same ecclesial meaning as expressed by a *"koinonia* in the sacraments," it explicitly shows that the relationship between the churches of the WCC is not a merely utilitarian agreement. The WCC was meant to be a council of the Churches of Christ and not just a federation of religious organizations.

The great Greek theologian Ioannis Karmiris, working from Paul's teaching in Eph 3:6, which was cited in the encyclical, commented on the text in ecclesiological terms, stating that:

> Of course, compared to the Western Churches, the Eastern Churches have always more vigorously emphasized the universality of the salvation of those who accept it, whether heterodox or even gentile, who therefore have the possibility of being called, through the faith and a virtuous life, "to participate in the same inheritance, to form the same body, and to be copartners in the promise through the Gospel" (see Eph 3:6). This Pauline teaching was precisely the basis for the Ecumenical Patriarchate's promulgation of the authoritative 1920 encyclical, *Unto the Churches of Christ Everywhere*, in which other Christians were not considered as unknown or strangers, but as familiar and family members in Christ who are called "to participate in the same inheritance, to form the same body, and to be copartners in the promise through the Gospel." It is clear that heterodox confessions and communities were thus recognized by the Orthodox Church as "churches of Christ" and the Christians belonging to them were seen as "Christians beyond the walls and boundaries" of the Orthodox Church who formed "churches beyond the church" that Christ's saving grace works upon and through which the heterodox Christians belonging to them – if believers and baptized – are saved.[40]

Karmiris continued:

> It is therefore possible to affirm that, in Orthodoxy, the maxim "no salvation outside

---

38 See Konrad Raiser, *Schritte auf dem Weg der Ökumene*, Frankfurt a.M., Lembeck, 2005, 116.

39 Cited in "Report of the General Secretary to the Central Committee 1959," *EcRev* 12, 1959, 70–77, here 73.

40 Ioannis Karmiris, "Ī sōtīria tōn ektos tīs Ekklīsias anthrōpōn tou Theou" [The salvation of the people of God outside the Church], *Praktika tīs Akadīmias Athīnon* 56, 1981, 391–434, esp. 401–402.

of the church" (*extra ecclesiam nulla salus*) has lost its relevance and that salvation is not out of the question for those who do not believe in the true church ... for which Christ died ... and through which Christ is proclaimed.[41]

Consequently, Karmiris concluded that

> the Orthodox Church admits the existence of a church in the broad sense, or rather, of various churches beyond the true Orthodox Church (*ecclesia extra ecclesiam*) as well as of Christians beyond its boundaries (*extra muros*), where God's saving grace is freely extended to all.[42]

It cannot be ignored, therefore, that, from the beginning of the ecumenical movement, Orthodoxy has defined its position on the basis of the indisputable existence of ecclesial realities parallel to the Orthodox Church, as the three patriarchal and synodal encyclicals from the beginning of the 20th century prove.

It was the 1920 encyclical in particular that defined the patriarchate's position with regard to the division among Christians, in an attempt to address the problem and find shared spaces for witness in practical matters such as justice and peace. In short, it constituted one of the foundations of the entire ecumenical movement and, thanks to its extraordinary influence, it is still an integral part of the definition of the WCC. Metropolitan Chrysostomos (Costantinidis) of Ephesus – who served for four years as the president of both the inter-Orthodox preparatory commission for the Great and Holy Synod as well as the pre-conciliar conferences and who made an essential contribution to the development of ecumenical dialogue – had this to say about the encyclical:

Was this initiative, this attempt, however, an unacceptable extension of the traditional ecclesiological foundation of Orthodoxy? Certainly not. It was rather a request, imposed for many reasons, to deal in a Christian way with the scandal of the Church's division, the fragmentation of the one Body of Christ. Why did the Ecumenical Patriarchate have the courage to take such an initiative? Because once again, but with more conviction and more decisively, it was called upon to define its position with regard to the divided Christian world, a position informed by its divine origin as church, by its Magisterium centered in the Spirit, by its experience in the field of interecclesial and interconfessional relations, and, above all, by its self-awareness as an institution that must proceed in an innovative way and that must define its attitude towards the atrocious and unacceptable reality of division.[43]

4.4 *The Encyclical's Importance*

The impetus that the encyclical gave to the Orthodox Church was comparable to that which the 1910 WMC in Edinburgh gave to the Protestant world.[44] Today, this episode is recognized as "the charter of Orthodox participation in the ecumenical movement," as historian Vasilios T. Stavridis defines it.[45] Besides this, it was very important for the entire ecumenical movement. In fact, Stavridis continues, the encyclical gave all the churches a theoretically perfect and practical model to follow

---

41 Karmiris, "Ī sōtīria," 401.

42 Karmiris, "Ī sōtīria," 402.

43 Chrysostomos S. Constantinidis, "Ī thesī tīs orthodoxias sto sygchrono christianiko kosmo," [The position of Orthodoxy in the Christian world today], in: Chrysostomos S. Constantinidis, *Orthodoxoi katopseis*, vol. 1: *Theologia*, Katerini, Tertios, 1991, 317–330, here 327.

44 See Johannes Oeldemann, *Orthodoxe Kirchen im ökumenischen Dialog: Positionen, Probleme, Perspektiven*, Paderborn, Bonifatius, 2004, 19.

45 Stavridis & Varella, *Istoria tīs oikoumenikīs kinīseōs*, 54. See also Christos Yiannaras's "provisional" considerations in regard to the encyclical in his interesting work, *Alītheia kai enotīta tīs ekklīsias* [The truth and the unity of the Church], Athens, Grigoris, 1977, 196ff.

in matters of interecclesial relations and collaborations. Many points of this model were successfully implemented.[46]

Praising the Ecumenical Patriarchate's initiative, Visser 't Hooft noted the encyclical's triple importance: (a) The Church of Constantinople was the first to decide to propose the formation of a fellowship or permanent council to the other churches; (b) he stressed that "its significance is above all in the fact that it called upon 'all churches of Christ of different confessions throughout the world' not to look upon each other as strangers and foreigners, but as relatives and as being part of the household of Christ and 'fellow heirs, members of the same body and partakers of the promise of God in Christ.'"(see Eph 3:6); (c) moreover, in stating that collaboration between churches in practical matters should not be postponed until after the conclusion of a doctrinal agreement but should rather prepare the way for reunification, the patriarchate established a fundamental principle. This principle, concluded Visser 't Hooft, would later become one of the ecumenical movement's pivotal points.[47]

This did not mean that the Orthodox Church had renounced discussing doctrinal problems. Theological discussion, in fact, was at the center of the first world conference on Faith and Order held in 1927 in Lausanne. It was, however, unrealistic at the time to think that an agreement could be reached on these issues. Indeed, the most widespread idea, and the most pragmatic strategy, was that of abandoning the matter in order not to drag the churches – at such a delicate historical moment – into endless and divisive discussions about unity when instead the world's concrete problems required an immediate, direct, and common response on the part of all Christians. Continuing his commentary on the encyclical,

Visser 't Hooft correctly interpreted the objective of ecumenical commitment, as it has been understood by the Orthodox Churches from 1920 to today, affirming that:

> Thus we are reminded of the fact that while active collaboration between the churches is an important part of the common calling of the churches, it is by no means the whole of that calling. Cooperation in service and witness has its own specific value, but it must not become a substitute for the realisation of that fuller *Koinonia* and unity which is meant in John 17 and Ephesians 4.[48]

Certainly, the whole ecumenical vocation, especially in its expression in the WCC, includes John's vision "that they may all be one" (John 17:21) and connects it to Paul's vision in the Letter to the Ephesians, where the apostle refers to the supreme objective of a holy *oikonomia* and the divine will "to sum up all things in Christ" (Eph 1:10). Obviously, as we know, the effort to connect these two biblical visions is weakened by the dichotomy, at times even rivalry, between those who emphasize the social dimension of the ecumenical movement and those who instead emphasize its theological and ecclesiastical dimension.[49]

Overcoming this polarization and balancing these two aspects of the movement is one of the Orthodox Church's desires that still awaits a

---

46   Stavridis & Varella, *Istoria tīs oikoumenikīs kinīseōs*, 56. See ch. 4 concerning the "*Koinonia* of Churches" proposed by the Ecumenical Patriarchate in: Tsetsis, *Ī symbolī tou oikoumenikou patriarcheiou*, 169ff. See "Report of the General Secretary," 71.

47   See "Report of the General Secretary," 73.

48   "Report of the General Secretary," 73.

49   See *Common Understanding and Vision of the World Council of Churches*, §§ 2.1–2.5, <www.oikoumene. org/en/resources/documents/assembly/2006-porto-alegre/3-preparatory-and-background-documents/common-understanding-and-vision-of-the-wcc-cuv> (accessed July 4, 2019). This particular tension contributes to maintaining the fragility of the ecumenical movement, as already noted in the sixth general assembly in Vancouver. Several attempts have been made to overcome it. I examined this issue in Stylianos Tsompanidis, *Orthodoxie und Ökumene: Gemeinsam auf dem Weg zu Gerechtigkeit, Frieden und Bewahrung der Schöpfung*, Münster, LIT, 1999, 62ff.

solution on the part of the WCC.[50] Throughout the various stages of the WCC's history, the Orthodox Church has developed a comprehensive perception of ecumenism that embraces both the commitment to Christian unity and the common witness to justice, peace, the protection of human rights, and the integrity of creation.[51] Within this worldview, unity and witness, Church and world, social, spiritual and missionary dimensions, history and eschatology, and liturgy and ministry are inextricably linked. This connection was summed up after the 1960s in the motto "the liturgy after the Liturgy" and is rooted in the cosmic Eucharistic vision of unity and life.

The importance of the 1920 encyclical was not understood immediately, and it took a long time before it found its well-deserved place in the Christian world – about forty years, until the meeting of the WCC's central committee in Rhodes in 1959. This was for many reasons: the inability of some churches to overcome their complex of self-sufficiency; the reluctance of others to cease their proselytizing activities; the fact that the encyclical was not well distributed due to the inexistence of any real channels of preexisting communication between the churches;[52] and the inadequacy of the English and French translations, which did not express the content of the original text properly. The main difficulty encountered by translators was the text's use of the concept of a *koinonia* between the churches because it could have two meanings: it could imply a communion in a spiritual and mystical sense or it could refer to a league or covenant in the sense of a permanent

organization. Finally, the encyclical did not have the impact it might have had because, at the same time, the Lutheran Archbishop of Uppsala Nathan Söderblom was promoting a similar proposal for the establishment of an international ecumenical council. His project began to spread in German and English-speaking circles and, towards the end of 1919, was submitted to the congress of the WA.

When the encyclical began to circulate in ecumenical circles in January 1920, therefore, the idea of a *koinonia* of churches was already familiar to many church leaders. The fact that the Patriarchate of Constantinople's proposal was the first to come through official channels from a church did not arouse due attention at the time. The encyclical's genesis, however, was completely separate from Söderblom's proposal.[53] The archbishop himself recognized this in a speech in 1929, leaving no further doubt as to the patriarchate's spontaneity in proposing a *koinonia* of churches.[54] Obviously, as it is true that the two initiatives were made at the same time and covered the same ground, scholars do not exclude the possibility that contacts and exchanges of ideas and proposals had previously been made between Uppsala and Constantinople.[55]

4.5 An Explicitly Ecumenical Vision: Hamilcar Alivisatos and Metropolitan Germanos Explain the Orthodox Proposal for a "koinonia of Churches"

As Visser 't Hooft explained, during this pre-ecumenical phase in 1920, "the Orthodox delegates had a much clearer vision of the ecumenical calling of the Church than the delegates of other

---

50   See for instance the "Declaration of the Ecumenical Patriarchate on the Occasion of the 25th Anniversary of the World Council of Churches, 1973," in: Limouris, ed., *Orthodox Visions*, 50–54, here 52, §§ 12, 13, 14.

51   See Tsompanidis, *Orthodoxie und Ökumene*, where this position is examined. See also Alexandros K. Papaderos, "Aspekte Orthodoxer Sozialethik," in: Ingeborg Gabriel, Alexandros K. Papaderos & Ulrich H.J. Körtner, eds., *Perspektiven ökumenischer Sozialethik: Der Auftrag der Kirchen im größeren Europa*, Mainz, Grünewald, 2006, 23–126, esp. 30–37, 67–69, 92–96.

52   Varella, *Diorthodoxoi kai oikoumenikai scheseis*, 165.

53   "Report of the General Secretary," 71–73.

54   "Report of the General Secretary," 73.

55   It is well known that Ioannis Kolmodin, a young diplomat stationed at the Swedish embassy in Constantinople, had a friendly relationship with Metropolitan Germanos, with whom he often exchanged opinions on current issues in the ecclesiastical field. Kolmodin corresponded regularly with Archbishop Söderblom through letters and reports; see Tsetsis, *Ī symbolī tou oikoumenikou patriarcheiou*, 90–91.

churches" and "sought to convince the other churches of the need for an ongoing ecumenical organization of the churches."[56] At the time, the ecumenical movement was still under construction and, with the exception of some individual and collective initiatives, it was manifested in three forms: the world conference on Faith and Order, the WA, and the world conference on Life and Work. According to various historians of the ecumenical movement, 1920 is considered the year of its birth.[57]

During the summer of that year, the Orthodox Church had the opportunity, at the two ecumenical conferences, to present its program based on the synodal encyclical.

From Aug 9 to 12, a preliminary conference was held in Geneva that was to lay the foundations for the birth of the Life and Work movement. Metropolitan Germanos, responding to Söderblom's invitation, participated in the conference accompanied by the Metropolitan of Nubia Nikolaos and Archimandrite Chrysostomos Papadopoulos (later archbishop of Athens). During this preliminary meeting, the encyclical received the attention that the patriarchate expected. Metropolitan Germanos declared that the Orthodox hierarchy welcomed the convocation of the world council and added that his objectives were in harmony with those of the patriarchate's encyclical. As he himself recalled:

> The well-known leader of the ecumenical movement, the late Archbishop of Uppsala, Dr. Söderblom, studied and understood the spirit of the above Encyclical ... Holding the Encyclical in his hand, he addressed the representatives of the Orthodox Church, emphasizing the existing similarities between the Encyclical and the new plan, and proposed that the Orthodox Church be invited to participate in the preparation.[58]

A preliminary conference on Faith and Order took place in 1920, from Aug 12 to 20. It was the moment in which the possibility of presenting in detail the project of a *koinonia* concretely presented itself. The occasion was particularly favorable since all the Orthodox Churches present at the conference had declared their support for the encyclical's proposal. A total of 18 hierarchs, ministers, and theologians, representatives of 10 local churches, took part in the meeting. According to Zernov, the large number of Orthodox delegates present at the conference was the precise result of the promulgation of the Ecumenical Patriarchate's encyclical in the previous months. The encyclical indicated "a departure from the usual cautious attitude of the Orthodox towards the West, and showed the desire of some at least among their hierarchs to take the lead in the movement towards closer fellowship."[59]

On behalf of the entire Orthodox delegation, Metropolitan Germanos addressed a greeting to the assembly that highlighted the churches' common purpose and the Ecumenical Patriarchate's invitation to collaborate in a "*koinonia* of churches." Explaining the core of the encyclical, and expressing the Orthodox desire for unity, he made some interesting points:

> Great praise is due to those who took the initiative in convening this great conference. The invitation from the sister American Episcopal Church came to the Orthodox Church as it was entertaining similar ideas as to the unity of the Churches. The Orthodox Church, and in particular the Ecumenical Patriarchate of that Church, resolved to send brotherly greetings to all the Churches of Christ throughout the world and to invite them to cooperate in a League of Churches; and while the Church of Constantinople was being asked to accept this invitation there came to the Patriarchate an invitation

---

56   See "Report of the General Secretary," 73.

57   Istavridis, "The Work of Germanos Strenopoulos," 293.

58   Cited in: Visser 't Hooft, *The Genesis and Formation*, 6.

59   Zernov, "The Eastern Churches," 654. See Tsetsis, *Ī symbolī tou oikoumenikou patriarcheiou*, 96ff.

to attend the World Conference which was accepted with great joy.[60]

Professor Hamilcar Alivisatos's contribution, rooted in the encyclical's content and in the proposal of a *koinonia* of the churches, was very important for the success of the preparatory conference in Geneva. His speech illustrated and integrated the encyclical's content in a way that proved fundamental. After a brief presentation of Orthodox teaching on the nature of the church, in which he emphasized that all the Eastern Orthodox Churches constituted the "one, holy, catholic, and apostolic Church," Alivisatos presented the Orthodox plan for ecumenism:

> The program's ... basic idea is the establishment of a truly friendly communication among the various Christian groups on the basis of the supreme law, given to us by our Lord, the law of love. The submitted program aims at ... the formation of a *koinonia* of churches [*koinōnias tōn ekklīsiōn*] in the way of the League of Nations [*koinōnias tōn ethnōn*], which will prepare its final objective, which is a unity in faith and administration. For this, it is first necessary to eliminate all ignorance, hostility, and selfishness. Therefore, the first point of our program is the cessation of proselytism among the various Christian churches and the extension of mutual communication regarding the mission to non-Christians ... The second point of our program is a solidarity among Christian churches. The third point is the communication and collaboration of churches to support Christian principles, mainly against any system opposing them ... The fourth point is the mutual knowledge and study of the churches ... The fifth point is the union of the small churches that are related to one another ... The sixth point is

the examination of doctrinal differences in a spirit of peace,[61] and the seventh point is the abstention of the churches from political questions, which should be left to political authorities. If we apply all of the above, we can definitely hope that we will reach the eighth point of our program, which is also the objective of the congress, that is, the unity of faith and administration.[62]

Referring to the question "How do we believe that these points can be achieved?," he continued:

> This is precisely the goal of the *koinōnias tōn ekklīsiōn*, which we believe should be structured as follows: (a) to designate a permanent central committee of the *koinōnias tōn ekklīsiōn* in order to achieve the goal mentioned above, (b) to designate various committees in every church represented in the *koinōnias tōn ekklīsiōn*, which will communicate and collaborate with the central committee, (c) to form a special media body of the *koinōnias tōn ekklīsiōn*, (d) to establish, in regard to the above goals, different conferences, the time and the place of which will be decided by the central committee of the *koinōnias tōn ekklīsiōn*, and (e) to decide now the place and the time of the first pan-Christian congress.[63]

A month later, in September, Metropolitan Germanos paid a visit to Sweden, invited by Archbishop Söderblom. During two of his lectures on "The Ecumenical Patriarchate and Church

---

60   Cited in: Istavridis, "The Work of Germanos Strenopoulos," 295.

61   In a certain sense, the sixth point integrated the encyclical's content more substantially. It proposed that the objective of a *koinonia* of churches should be not only collaboration in matters of a practical nature, but also the study of doctrinal differences. Naturally, as already discussed above, in no way did the encyclical ignore the importance of theological-doctrinal dialogue within the context of the ecumenical movement.

62   Stavridis & Varella, *Istoria tīs oikoumenikīs kinīseōs*, 93–94.

63   Stavridis & Varella, *Istoria tīs oikoumenikīs kinīseōs*, 94.

Unity," he had the opportunity to return to the proposals made in Geneva and to show, once again, how the Orthodox Church had a clear and precise idea of the form that the proposed intereclesial permanent organization should take. He was extremely satisfied with the support expressed by the Church of Sweden through Primate Archbishop Nathan Söderblom, both for the patriarchate's proposals and for the idea of a necessary unity in doctrinal and practical matters.[64]

4.6 Orthodox Participation in the Preliminary Phase of the Ecumenical Movement in the Spirit of the Encyclical

The ardent Orthodox desire to fulfill Christ's will concerning unity and, in general, his ecumenical vision, was expressed two years after the encyclical's publication by the Patriarch of Constantinople Meletios IV (Metaxakis). In continuity with his predecessors, the patriarch, in one of his encyclicals on the subject of "the divine objective of unity," emphasized that:

> The Most Holy Church of Constantinople, kindled from the beginning with zeal for universal union, and always keeping in mind the Lord's prayer to his Heavenly Father just before his saving passion, has always followed with interest every movement in the separated churches, and has examined with care and study their any and every expression of faith which might point towards a rapprochement with Orthodoxy ... in the hope that the Heavenly Ruler of the Church will supply that which is lacking through His all-inspiring Grace, and will guide all who believe in Him to a full knowledge of the truth and to full union, in order that there may be one flock under one chief shepherd,

the true shepherd of the sheep, Our Lord Jesus Christ.[65]

The spirit of the 1920 encyclical can also be found in the separate statements that the Orthodox Churches were compelled to submit within the context of the Faith and Order movement, in which they did not hesitate to recognize the non-Orthodox churches as limbs of the one Body of Christ and to decisively declare that they would help remove the obstacles blocking the path to unity. The contributions made by the Life and Work movement will not be discussed here, as it is obvious that their practical character was fully consonant with the positions of Constantinople.

It is, however, interesting to note that during the first Faith and Order world conference held in Lausanne in 1927, although the Eastern delegates emphatically declared[66] their inability to agree with the assembly's conclusions because they were incompatible with the Orthodox Churches' faith,[67] they were also convinced that they had entered into true dialogue with the other churches. They therefore expressed their positive attitude by declaring:

> We beg to assure the Conference that we have derived much comfort here from the experience that, although divided by dogmatic differences, we are one with our brethren here in faith in our Lord and Savior Jesus Christ. Declaring that in the future we shall not cease to devote ourselves to labor for the closer approach of the Churches.[68]

---

64   Visser 't Hooft, *The Genesis and Formation*, 7. See also Istavridis, "The Work of Germanos Strenopoulos," 298.

65   See the article by Francis House, "The Ecumenical Significance of the Patriarchate of Constantinople," *EcRev* 9, 1956, 310–320, here 311. The text of the encyclical was also published in *Ekklīsiastiki Alīthia* 42, 1922, 343–344.

66   See "First World Conference on Faith and Order, Lausanne, Switzerland, 1927," in: Limouris, ed., *Orthodox Visions*, 12–14.

67   "First World Conference," 12.

68   "First World Conference," 14.

Metropolitan Germanos also played a fundamental role in the 1927 conference. His speech began with a reference to the first ecumenical steps taken in 1920 and to the role of Orthodoxy in responding to the call of its Western brothers and sisters to participate in the conference. In accordance with the spirit of the encyclical, it was said that all those who believe in Christ and consider him their guide should undoubtedly be one body. His statement that Orthodoxy rejects the exclusive theory (in the German text, the term *engherzige Lehre*, "narrow-minded doctrine," is used) of churches that consider themselves the only true Church of Christ and hold that all those seeking unity should find it only by entering into their fold, is noteworthy. Such an idea of reunification, which would mean the absorption of all other churches into one, was totally contrary to the principles of the Orthodox Church, which has always been aware of the difference between unity and uniformity. As Germanos mentioned, it indeed follows the precepts of St. Augustine: *in dubiis libertas* and *in necessariis unitas*.[69]

In the Orthodox delegation's declaration at the second Faith and Order world conference held in Edinburgh in 1937, it was noted that the discussion in the assembly was in complete harmony with the theological and ecclesiological premises of the 1920 encyclical:

> We are constrained and rejoice to utter a few words by which to emphasize the great spiritual profit which we have drawn from our daily intercourse with you, the representatives of other Christian Churches. With you we bewail the rending asunder of the seamless robe of Christ. We desire, as you, that the members of the one body of Christ may again be reunited ... For, in spite of all our differences, our common Master and Lord is One – Jesus Christ, who will lead us to a more and more close collaboration for the edifying of the body of Christ.[70]

These words assume even greater importance if one takes into account the numerous doubts that the Orthodox Churches still had concerning dialogue and the ecumenical movement.

4.7 The Proposal for a "koinonia of Churches" and the Creation of the World Council

The birth of the WCC took place at the Utrecht conference in 1938 and, officially, at the general assembly in Amsterdam in 1948, when the two movements, Faith and Order and Life and Work, merged into a single organization. The newborn council was a completely new reality in comparison to the previous ecumenical entities, being, in name and fact, a council of churches. For the first time in history, churches, confessions, and groups of different kinds came together and founded an ecclesiastical organization on a global scale with a precise purpose and well-defined principles.

The WCC was immediately faced with the immense task of creating a statute, rules, and regulations for itself. In addition to the definition of its statute, according to which the "World Council of Churches is a fellowship of churches which confess the Lord Jesus Christ as God and Savior," it is important to recall its objectives, defined by the assembly as follows:

> The functions of the World Council of Churches will be to: (1) continue the work of the world movements Faith and Order and Life and Work; (2) facilitate joint activities

---

69 See the address by Metropolitan Germanos, which can be found in: Herbert Newell Bate, ed., *Faith and Order: Proceedings of the World Conference, Lausanne, August 3–21, 1927*, New York NY, George H. Doran Company, 1927, 18–23. See the German text in: Hermann Sasse, ed., *Die Weltkonferenz für Glauben und Kirchenverfassung: Deutscher amtlicher Bericht über die Weltkirchenkonferenz zu Lausanne 3–21 August 1927*, Berlin, Im Furche, 1929, 105–109, 107ff.

70 "Second World Conference on Faith and Order, Edinburgh, Scotland, 1937," in: Limouris, ed., *Orthodox Visions*, 15–17, here 17.

of the Churches; (3) promote joint study; (4) cultivate an ecumenical conscience in the members of all Churches; (5) establish relations with world confessional organizations and other movements of ecumenical character; (6) convene world conferences to discuss questions dictated by the circumstances. The conferences will be authorized to publish their own conclusions; (7) support the churches in their evangelical work. In matters that affect all churches and that are the responsibility of Faith and Order, the Council will always act in agreement to the principles of the conferences of Lausanne (1927) and Edinburgh (1937).[71]

Concerning the council's organization and structure, the statutes provided that it would carry out its activities through three branches: a general assembly; a central committee that would meet once a year and appoint an executive committee; and various committees for the supervision and implementation of the council's work, which would answer to the central committee.[72]

Comparing the points of the 1920 encyclical with the WCC's objectives as described in its statutes, one realizes how the Orthodox delegates to the assembly in Amsterdam, led by Metropolitan Germanos, Hamilcar Avilisatos, and Georges Florovsky, were able to infuse the encyclical's spirit into the conclusions of the assembly's work. The WCC was founded following the guidelines of a structure that was substantially no different from that articulated and proposed at the time of

the encyclical's promulgation by Germanos and Alivisatos.[73]

The seven points of the WCC's list of functions have many basic similarities with the eleven proposals for interecclesial collaboration in the "*koinonia* of churches" formulated in the encyclical. According to the encyclical, overcoming the spirit of mutual distrust and resentment between the different churches and strengthening the relations of Christian love could be witnessed, among other things, by the exchange of fraternal letters on the occasion of the great Christian holiday, by a rapprochement between the representatives of different churches, by communication between different schools and students of theology, by a convocation of pan-Christian conferences to study the questions of interest to all the churches, by impartial and in-depth study of doctrinal differences, by the mutual respect of the different customs and practices of the different churches, and finally, by a mutual assistance in the areas of religious progress, charity, and others. All these points were also part of the newborn council's objectives.[74]

Of equal importance was also the very proposal and description of the *koinonia* contained in the 1920 encyclical, as well as its origins in the New Testament, which helped to shape the concept of the council as a fellowship, as described in its basis. Even if the term does not have the same precise ecclesiological charge as a "*koinonia* of sacraments*," it is also clear that it does not describe a purely utilitarian association. The council was to be a true council of the Churches of Christ, not simply a federation of religious organizations. It was no coincidence, therefore, that the very man who had played such an important role in drafting

---

71   Cited in: Stavridis & Varella, *Istoria tīs oikoumenikīs kinīseōs*, 115; and Tsetsis, *Ī symbolī tou oikoumenikou patriarcheiou*, 170. See also, *Die Unordnung der Welt und Gottes Heilsplan*, vol. 5, Willem Adolf Visser 't Hooft, ed., *Die erste Vollversammlung des Ökumenischen Rates der Kirchen in Amsterdam vom 22. August bis 4. September 1948*, Zürich, Gotthelf, 1948, 266–267.

72   Stavridis & Varella, *Istoria tīs oikoumenikīs kinīseōs*, 116. See *Die Unordnung der Welt*, vol. 5, 268ff.

73   Tsetsis, *Ī symbolī tou oikoumenikou patriarcheiou*, 172. Alivisatos's words at the 1920 preliminary conference in Geneva in regard to its proposed structure should be noted. Metropolitan Germanos repeated the same points one month later during his visit to Sweden; see "Report of the General Secretary," 72.

74   Tsetsis, *Ī symbolī tou oikoumenikou patriarcheiou*, 175–176.

the encyclical and who had then promoted the activities of the Ecumenical Patriarchate in collaborating with other churches, Metropolitan Germanos, would express great satisfaction on behalf of the Orthodox for the foundation of the WCC. In particular, he said that he was delighted to have had the opportunity to meet and discuss common issues concerning the nature, mission, and ministry of the church in the modern world. He also stated that he wished for "God to support and strengthen our common efforts for unity in the one, holy, catholic, and apostolic church, according to His will."[75]

5 One Hundred Years Later

The importance of the 1920 encyclical is even more evident today, one hundred years later. Since its promulgation, its basic principles as well as its corollaries have become the parameters within which the activities and functions of the major intereccesial organizations are constituted and decided. In addition to providing the impetus for the entire Christian community to move toward establishing new ecumenical relations in a spirit of Christian love, the encyclical gave all the churches a clear vision and precise plan for their establishment. It challenged them to go beyond their institutional limits, to change their traditional forms of expression, and to break down doctrinal, moral, theological, national, and confessional walls. In short, it encouraged them to go beyond the boundaries behind which they had protected themselves for centuries. The encyclical favored a dynamic and decisive transition from ecclesiastical egocentricity to interaction through dialogue, from excessive concern for one's self to ecumenical commitment, from controversial to creative commitment, and from a self-defense to movement towards the other.

The encyclical was also a milestone for the Orthodox Church. It is considered "the foundation of Orthodox participation in the ecumenical

movement" and defined the boundaries of rules and consensus regarding contact with other churches, thus giving a precise profile to future initiatives taken to promote ecumenical dialogue for Christian unity. Since then, the common denominator of all of the Orthodox Church's official positions, up to the most recent declaration of the pan-Orthodox Council of Crete in 2016,[76] has been precisely the conviction that the Orthodox Church – despite considering herself the one, holy, catholic, and apostolic church – does not deny the existence of different elements of ecclesial reality (or ecclesiality) in other churches or ecclesiastical communities.

The recognition of the reality of the other churches is, therefore, the foundation of Orthodox participation in the ecumenical movement.[77] At the same time, this participation gave the Orthodox Churches the opportunity to meet not only non-Orthodox believers, but also one another, thus helping them to escape the isolation

---

[76] For the synod's resolutions see *COGD*, 4/3, 2016.

[77] From the third pre-synodal conference in Chambésy in 1986, the text "Relations of the Orthodox Church with the Rest of the Christian World" stated: "As it is the one, holy, catholic and apostolic Church, the Orthodox Church is fully aware of its responsibility for the unity of the Christian world, it recognizes the existence *de facto* of the Christian Churches and Confessions, but it believes at the same time that its relations with them should lead to the clarification of their ecclesiology" (§ 2); see Viorel Ioniță, *Towards the Holy and Great Synod of the Orthodox Church: The Decisions of the Pan-Orthodox Meetings since 923 until 2009*, Basel, Reinhardt, 2014, 171. Using slightly different expressions, the Pan-Orthodox Council of Crete, in its corresponding report, stated: "The Orthodox Church, as the One, Holy, Catholic, and Apostolic Church, in her profound ecclesiastical self-consciousness, believes unflinchingly that she occupies a central place in the matter of the promotion of Christian unity in the world today ... the Orthodox Church accepts the historical name of other non-Orthodox Christian Churches and Confessions that are not in communion with her, and believes that her relations with them should be based on the most speedy and objective clarification possible of the whole ecclesiological question"; <www.holy-council.org/-/rest-of-christian-world> (accessed July 4, 2019).

---

[75] Tsetsis, *Ī symbolī tou oikoumenikou patriarcheiou*, 159ff.

imposed by both sociopolitical circumstances and internal divisions, along with erroneous behavior. In this way, they were able to strengthen the *koinonia* and fraternal relations that should have existed from the beginning, and they also learned of the existence of profound differences that until then had been ignored. Above all, through the new contacts and dialogue, the Orthodox were able to see Orthodoxy and their self-awareness in a completely new light and thus take new steps towards its expression in the *ecumene*.[78]

Translated from Italian to English by Susan Dawson Vásquez and David Dawson Vásquez.

Bibliography

Bate, Herbert N., ed., *Faith and Order: Proceedings of the World Conference, Lausanne, August 3–21, 1927*, New York NY, George H. Doran Company, 1927.

"Encyclical of the Ecumenical Patriarchate, 1920: *Unto the Churches of Christ Everywhere*," in: Gennadios Limouris, ed., *Orthodox Visions of Ecumenism: Statements, Messages, and Reports on the Ecumenical Movement (1902–1992)*, Geneva, WCC Publications, 1994, 9–11.

Florovsky, Georges, "The Orthodox Contribution to the Ecumenical Movement," in: Richard S. Haugh, ed., *The Collected Works of Georges Florovsky*, vol. 13, Georges Florovsky, *Ecumenism I: A Doctrinal Approach*, Vaduz, Büchervertriebsanstalt, 1989, 160–164.

House, Francis, "The Ecumenical Significance of the Patriarchate of Constantinople," *EcRev* 9, 1956, 310–320.

"Patriarchal and Synodical Encyclical of 1902," in: Gennadios Limouris, ed., *Orthodox Visions of Ecumenism: Statements, Messages, and Reports on*

the Ecumenical Movement (1902–1992)*, Geneva, WCC Publications, 1994, 1–8.

Pheidas, Vlassios, "Ai egkyklioi tou 1902 kai tou 1904 ōs prodromoi tīs egkykliou tou 1920 en tī eurytera oikoumenikī prooptikī tīs Mītros Ekklīsias," *Orthodoxia* 10, 2003, 129–139.

"Report of the General Secretary to the Central Committee 1959," *EcRev* 12, 1959, 70–77.

"Response to the Reactions of the Local Orthodox Churches," in: Gennadios Limouris, ed., *Orthodox Visions of Ecumenism: Statements, Messages, and Reports on the Ecumenical Movement (1902–1992)*, Geneva, WCC Publications, 1994, 5–8.

Skouteris, Konstantinos, "Ī egkyklios tou 1902 kai oi diorthodokses scheseis kata tīn epochī tīs ekdoseōs tīs, idiōs sta Balkania kai tī Mesī Anatolī, kai ī sīmasia tīs gia tin tote kai gia tīn enestōsa pragmatikotīta," *Orthodoxia* 10, 2003, 229–241.

Stavridis, Vasilios T. & Varella, Evangelia, *Istoria tīs oikoumenikīs kinīseōs*, Thessaloniki, Patriarchikon Idryma Paterikōn Meletōn, 1996.

Stavridis, Vasilios T., "The Work of Germanos Strenopoulos in the Field of Inter-Orthodox and Inter-Christian Relations," *EcRev* 11, 1959, 291–299.

Tsetsis, Georges, *Ī symbolī tou oikoumenikou patriarcheiou stīn idrysī toī paukosmiou symbouliou ekklīsiōn*, Ph.D. thesis, Aristotle University of Thessaloniki, 1988.

Tsompanidis, Stylianos, *Yper tīs tōn pantōn Enōseōs. Ī Symbolī tīs Orthodoxīs Ekklīsias kai Theologias sto Pankosmio Symboulio Ekklīsion*, Thessaloniki, Pournaras, 2008.

Varella, Evangelia, *Diorthodoxoi kai oikoumenikai scheseis tou Patriarcheiou Kōnstantinopoleōs kata ton 20. aiōna*, Thessaloniki, Patriarchikon Idryma Paterikōn Meletōn, 1994.

Visser 't Hooft, Willem Adolf, *The Genesis and Formation of the World Council of Churches*, Geneva, WCC Publications, 1982.

Zernov, Nicolas, "The Eastern Churches and the Ecumenical Movement in the Twentieth Century," in: *A History of the Ecumenical Movement*, vol. 1, Ruth Rouse & Stephen C. Neill, eds., *1517–1948*, Geneva, WCC Publications, [3]1986, 643–674.

78　For a more in-depth analysis see Stylianos Tsompanidis, *Yper tīs tōn pantōn Enōseōs. Ī Symbolī tīs Orthodoxīs Ekklīsias kai Theologias sto Pankosmio Symboulio Ekklīsion* ["For the Union of All": The Contribution of the Orthodox Church and Theology to the World Council of Churches], Thessaloniki, Pournaras, 2008.

CHAPTER 26

The Life and Work of Nathan Söderblom

Dietz Lange

1 The Early Years

Lauritz (Lars) Olof Jonathan Söderblom, called Nathan from his boyhood, was born in the small village of Trönö, province of Hälsingland, Northern Sweden, on Jan 15, 1866. He was the second of seven children, two of whom had died in infancy. His father Jonas, an adherent of Carl Olof Rosenius's new-evangelical revival movement, was the Lutheran pastor there. This movement was strongly indebted to Anglo-Saxon Congregational and Methodist influences, in particular to the Scottish preacher George Scott. Jonas Söderblom was well versed in theology, with a particular interest in foreign missions, and extremely conservative. A workaholic with a somewhat ascetic bent, he was a tireless servant of his congregation and an effective preacher. In the family, he was a loving father but very strict as far as his children's upbringing was concerned. His extremely conscientious sense of duty recurred in his son Nathan, who coped with an incredibly heavy workload throughout his life, being able to concentrate on several different things simultaneously. Jonas' wife, Sophia, was the daughter of a Danish physician. She shared with her husband his revivalist piety, but was otherwise quite different from him. A gentle woman of great empathy, she was capable of compensating for her husband's harshness towards the children. She was interested in poetry and had a good sense of humor, which her son inherited. Nathan later called her his best teacher.[1] The children's upbringing was strictly pietistic, with daily evening prayer, participation in the Sunday service with its hour-long sermons, no alcohol and no party games.

Helping on the small farm, which Swedish country pastors used to have as a side-activity at that time, was a matter of course for them from an early age.

Nathan received his first schooling at home. His father, having recognized his son's high intellectual capabilities early on, taught him Latin from the age of five. The young boy went to grammar school in nearby Hudiksvall and graduated from high school at the age of 17. Being an outgoing person, he was on very good terms with his classmates, took part in all kinds of mischief (such as climbing the steep church steeple one day), but also became involved in his share of fights with less privileged boys. In the end, he had received a solid classical education, with German and French as foreign languages, developed his musical talents (he played the cornet), and showed a strong interest in Scripture and history. In 1883, he enrolled at Uppsala University for the 3-year liberal arts course, which he completed with flying colors, especially in the classical languages and Arabic.

To the great joy of his father, Nathan decided to continue by studying theology. The Uppsala faculty was not very attractive at the time since it adhered to a rather sterile orthodoxy, anxiously excluding all modern criticism of the Bible and dogma from abroad, particularly that from Germany. There were two exceptions to this: one was the church historian Robert Sundelin, and the other the pious and mildly conservative professor of biblical exegesis Waldemar Rudin, whose specialty was the thought of Søren Kierkegaard.[2] Söderblom's own focus was on church history, notably the works of Adolf von Harnack. For a time, he considered making it his lifelong profession. However, he also studied the works of Kierkegaard with great

---

1 Jonas Jonson, *Nathan Söderblom: Called to Serve*, Grand Rapids MI, Eerdmans, 2016, 12.

2 Jonson, *Nathan Söderblom*, 27–29.

intensity, as is evident from the extent of underlinings in the edition of his works he owned.

Söderblom became acquainted with the broad stream of critical theology more extensively on a private basis. A fellow student had brought with him from Germany a copy of Julius Wellhausen's *Prolegomena zur Geschichte Israels*, which was unavailable in Uppsala's libraries at the time and which he eagerly read. Likewise, he read the works of the Göttingen-based Religionsgeschichtliche Schule. This satisfied his scholarly curiosity but cast a severe doubt on his conservative religious convictions.

He also took a strong interest in foreign missions, leading him to become a founding member of the Student Missionary Association in 1884. This group organized lectures and discussions on the missions throughout the world. Söderblom rose to be the redactor of its journal and published his first scholarly article there, with the first medieval missionary to Scandinavia, Ansgar, as its subject.[3] These activities were still in good tune with the religious tradition of his home.

During his university years, Söderblom took part in a host of student activities, of which I may mention in particular his regular Sunday meetings with two friends, Nils Johan Göransson, later professor of theology, and Samuel Andreas Fries, an Old Testament scholar, later minister in Stockholm. They discussed recent theological books, philosophy, and international belles-lettres. At this time, Söderblom was especially enthusiastic about the great Swedish historian and philosopher Erik Gustaf Geijer and his philosophy of personality.[4]

Cheerful student life could not prevent the clash of modern critical theology with the revivalist piety of his parental home from causing a prolonged religious crisis, which lasted from the spring of 1888 until early 1890. Radical historical criticism seems to have shaken the very foundation of his faith. It took him two different steps to overcome his insecurity. The first was his

discovery, thanks to Albrecht Ritschl, that God does not reveal something *about* himself in a book or a doctrine, but *himself*, through creative action in the person of Jesus Christ. However, the crisis went much deeper than intellectual doubt. On the existential or religious level, Söderblom felt that he lacked the consciousness of sin so essential to revivalist piety. This is reminiscent of Luther's view that having no tribulation is itself the worst tribulation of all.[5] Things became even more intricate than that. Under the influence of Kierkegaard's radical interpretation of sin in his *Sickness unto Death*,[6] Söderblom considered even his yearning for certitude of faith as selfish and sinful. Liberation from this entanglement came through the small famous devotional book *"Grace and Truth" under Twelve Different Aspects* by the Scottish revivalist preacher William Paton Mackay, an associate of the American evangelist Dwight L. Moody.[7] Mackay's point was that you have to turn away from destructive self-analysis toward the crucified Christ.

The dissolution of his religious crisis liberated Söderblom – not from the revivalist type of piety as such, to which he remained true throughout his life, but from its narrowness. It enabled him to become independent of theological partisanship, reconciling historical criticism of the Bible, dogma, and progressive social ethics with his basic Lutheranism.

Shortly after this episode, Söderblom had the opportunity of traveling to the United States of America for two months. He was a delegate to an international and interdenominational student conference in Northfield MA organized by Moody in 1890. Prior to the conference, he had attended a lecture at Yale University on US church life by the

---

3 Jonson, *Nathan Söderblom*, 24–25.

4 Jonson, *Nathan Söderblom*, 21.

5 See Martin Luther, WA 3, 424.11: "Nulla tentatio omnis tentatio."

6 Søren Kierkegaard, *Sygdommen til Døden*, Kjøbenhavn, C.A. Reitzel, 1849; ET: *The Sickness unto Death*, trans. Alastair Hannay, London, Penguin, 1989.

7 See William Paton Mackay, *"Grace and Truth" under Twelve Different Aspects*, Chicago IL, F.H. Revell, 1872, followed by no less than 72 editions.

Congregationalist Newman Smyth. Its basic thesis was that denominations are as important for the Kingdom of God as the states for the United States, but they must take care of good mutual relations, making them transparent for the One Church in them all. Deeply impressed, Söderblom noted in his diary, "Oh Lord, grant me the humility and the wisdom to serve the great cause of free unity of Thy Church."[8]

The conference itself was the first occasion for him to meet people from churches other than his native Lutheran one. The free discussions and common worship, without anyone's renunciation of his/her respective religious identity, fascinated him as much as did Moody's leadership. He made friends with some of the delegates, who were to become important ecumenical collaborators in later years: John Mott, later general secretary of both YMCA and WSCF, Wilfred Monod, later professor of practical theology at the Faculté libre in Paris and from 1912 president of the ERF.

Söderblom graduated in 1892, after his return to Uppsala. In the same year, he published a lengthy paper on Ritschl,[9] acknowledging what he had learned from him but criticizing him on two counts. One was Ritschl's polemics against mysticism and pietism. For Söderblom, mysticism is part of every religion because religion concerns the inner life of a person. Disparaging that aspect makes divine revelation an "objective" fact of ordinary history, depriving it of its supernatural quality. The other point concerned the relationship between faith and moral action. Ritschl had described it as elliptic, with two foci, attributing to them relative independence of each other. The Kingdom of God is hence both the highest good and the aim towards which human endeavors strive. Söderblom insisted, with Luther, that the Kingdom is God himself coming into the world.

This evokes faith, which in turn becomes the source of "good works."[10]

This essay was important because Ritschl was thought to be somewhat of a "liberal" bogeyman by theological conservatives in Sweden at the time (most of whom had probably never even taken the trouble of ploughing through his difficult German). Söderblom, who was considered to be a disciple of his, felt he had to change the general opinion about this. However, even today some people still consider Söderblom a "Ritschlian," probably thinking of his book on Luther, published one year later.[11] He seems indeed to be following Ritschl's footsteps here, for instance by criticizing Luther for not sufficiently proclaiming the "positive work for the Kingdom of God" in his early years[12] or by asserting that, according to Luther, God's judgment no longer concerns Christians.[13]

However, this state of affairs may equally have reflected his feeling of great relief at having solved his religious crisis.

Be that as it may, his interpretation of Luther was to change drastically later, based both on his improved knowledge and on another incisive religious experience (Mar 11, 1894). In a dramatic inner turmoil, Söderblom discovered the severity of God's judgment in spite of his being the God of love. His diary reveals little about this event. "It is a fearful thing to fall into the hands of the living God" (Heb 10:31) is the only comment.[14] However, its importance cannot be underestimated. From that time on, his view of God became bipolar. Grace remained the last word, but never without the dark background of judgment. This is the personal background to his later discovery of the idea of "holiness" as being constitutive of all religion.

---

8 N. Söderblom, note of June 20, 1890, in: UUB, NSS B, *Dag- och anteckningsböcker*, vol. 2, 1890, *Amerikaresan*, part 2, 64.

9 Nathan Söderblom, "Kristendomen och den moderna tidsandan: En blick på den Ritschlska teologien," *Svensk tidskrift* 2, 1892, 105–111, 157–192.

10 Jonson, *Nathan Söderblom*, 52.

11 See Nathan Söderblom, *Den Lutherska reformationens grundtankar*, 2 vols., Stockholm, L. Hökerberg, 1893; Jonson, *Nathan Söderblom*, 49ff.

12 Söderblom, *Den Lutherska reformationens grundtankar*, vol. 2, 86

13 Söderblom, *Den Lutherska reformationens grundtankar*, vol. 2, 11.

14 See UUB, NSS B, *Dag- och anteckningsböcker 1894*.

2   Pastor in Paris

In the meantime, Söderblom had decided to extend his studies by taking up the history of religions. He very soon found a subject for a doctoral thesis, the eschatology of the ancient Persian religion of Mazdeism. However, for several reasons, progress on this project was slow, in spite of his extraordinary working capacity. The most important of these was his engagement, immediately after his graduation, to Anna Forsell, daughter of a sea captain and a student of history. Moreover, he now had to pay his own living expenses. Following ordination in 1893, he became chaplain at the psychiatric ward in Ulleråker, a small town just outside Uppsala. His salary was scanty and he therefore still needed his father's financial support. Only a year later, after hearing by chance that the pastorate for the Scandinavian congregation in Paris had become vacant, he applied for the post and obtained it. Shortly after this, he married Anna, after which he hastily tried to finish his thesis in the little time he had at his disposal before his departure. He submitted it to the faculty, but it was not accepted. He therefore had to revise it in Paris.[15]

Söderblom served his new congregation from 1894 to 1901. Its members were mainly poor people, such as servants and manual workers, together with a few artists and diplomats, all living in different quarters of the huge city. In the summertime, he was obliged to work with Scandinavian sailors in Calais. In both places, he became thoroughly acquainted with the social misery of the time and personally supported needy parishioners whenever he could: thanks to his affable personality, he had no difficulties with these relationships. His participation in the meeting of the ESK in Erfurt in 1896, financed by a wealthy Norwegian merchant, introduced him to the international dimension of the social problems, and its chairman Friedrich Naumann made a lasting impression on him.

Two publications reflect both his own experience and that conference. One of these, *Jesu bergspredikan och vår tid*, was an interpretation of the Sermon on the Mount. It juxtaposed Tolstoy's pacifism and Luther's doctrine of the two governances, praising Tolstoy's religious seriousness but preferring Luther's realism, although he chided him for describing the role of government in overly negative terms and merely suggested preventing evil rather than more actively improving social justice. The other, *Religionen och den sociala utvecklingen*, was a treatise on religion and social development, which developed the basic elements of a general social theory. Turning against both capitalism of the Manchester School and Marxism, Söderblom pleaded for a peaceful contest between labor and management, presaging the more complete form his theory later attained, that is to say, a dialectical relationship of contest and cooperation.[16] Politically, to a certain extent he began to resemble the left-wing Social Democrats during these years. He greatly admired the French Socialist leader Jean Jaurès. At the same time, the infamous Dreyfus affair overshadowed his Paris years and reinforced his abhorrence of anti-Semitism.[17]

Beside his professional work as a pastor, Söderblom engaged in an ambitious program of studies at the Sorbonne. Not only did he attend lectures of historians of religion, such as Antoine Meillet and Albert Réville, who were important for his dissertation project, but also of the eminent philosophers Émile Boutroux and Henri Bergson, along with the systematic theologian

---

15   Jonson, *Nathan Söderblom*, 64ff.

16   See Nathan Söderblom, *Jesu bergspredikan och vår tid*, Stockholm, Åhlén & Söners Förlag, 1898 (second edition in: Nathan Söderblom, *Tal och skrifter*, vol. 6, Malmö, Världslitteraturens Förlag, 1930); Nathan Söderblom, *Religionen och den sociala utvecklingen*, in: Samuel Andreas Fries, ed., *Religionsvetenskapliga kongressen i Stockholm 1897: En fullständig framställning af kongressens uppkomst och förhandlingar jämte porträtt af dess president, bestyrelse och samtlige talare*, Stockholm, Bohlin, 1898, 76–143; GT: *Die Religion und die soziale Entwicklung*, SgV 10, Freiburg i.Br., J.C.B. Mohr, 1898.

17   Jonson, *Nathan Söderblom*, 84ff.

Auguste Sabatier, who was to become his doctoral supervisor. Sabatier's view that all religious statements are symbolic became part of his own philosophy of religion and theology. As a matter of course, he contacted many French churchmen, both Protestant and Catholic. Most importantly, he became friends with the eminent Catholic Modernist scholar Alfred Loisy, who was later excommunicated by Rome.

As far as his private life is concerned, the most obvious development was the rapidly growing family. Their first five children (of a total of twelve) were born in Paris, one of whom died in infancy. Neither their lively family nor the limited space in their small apartment prevented the couple from extending generous hospitality to colleagues from Paris and abroad, to Scandinavian artists, and others. They also took advantage of the rich cultural life of the metropolis, attending concerts and going to exhibitions of modern (i.e. impressionistic) art, of which they even were able to purchase some pieces to take home.

Furthermore, there remained the task of revising his doctoral thesis. Söderblom decided to enlarge it from a specialist study on ancient Iranian religion into a comparative treatment of eschatology in the major world religions. It turned out to be the first significant study in the new field of the phenomenology of religion.[18] He passed his doctoral exam with honors in 1901.

In June of that year, Söderblom's father died. Nathan had hurried home in time to see his father while he was still alive, and the two were able to achieve reconciliation. Before he closed his eyes, the old man impressed his lifetime leitmotif on his son: "Not that we lord it over your faith; we work with you for your joy" (2 Cor 1:24 RSV). Only weeks later, after his return to Paris, Söderblom received a telegram informing him of his appointment to the chair of the history of religions at the University of Uppsala for which he had applied.

3   Professor of the History of Religions

Söderblom's reception at his arrival in Uppsala was mixed. The conservative faculty eyed him with suspicion because of his liberal views, and the tensions did not abate in the course of the years, on the contrary. They increased when Söderblom's friend Samuel Fries, a widely acknowledged Old Testament scholar, was denied a professorship in 1902 in favor of a decidedly less qualified candidate. The situation became even worse in 1903 when they did not permit Torgny Segerstedt, a highly competent student of Söderblom's, to pass his doctoral exam, in spite of favorable judgment on the part of renowned members of the philosophical faculty. The reason given was an alleged "lack of Christian substance." For a while, Söderblom even considered resigning from his post.[19]

The students, on the other hand, were enthusiastic about him. They already knew him from the two lectures he had held, in connection with his application, on Schleiermacher's *On Religion: Speeches to Its Cultured Despisers*[20] and a comparative study on temptation in Buddha, Zoroaster, and Jesus. Now, as their new professor, they greatly appreciated his inauguration lecture, which became a milestone in the history of the faculty.[21] Söderblom congratulated his students for having chosen a fascinating subject, theology

---

18   See Nathan Söderblom, *La vie future d'après le Mazdéisme à la lumière des croyances parallèles dans les autres religions: Étude d'eschatologie comparée*, trans. Jacques de Coussange, Paris, E. Leroux, 1901.

19   Jonson, *Nathan Söderblom*, 103–104.

20   Friedrich Schleiermacher, *Über die Religion: Reden an die Gebildeten unter ihren Verächtern*, Berlin, Unger, 1799; ET: *On Religion: Speeches to Its Cultured Despisers*, trans. John Oman, New York NY, Harper & Brothers, 1958.

21   See Nathan Söderblom, *Den allmänna religionshistorien och den kyrkliga teologien*, Uppsala, W. Schultz, 1914, reprinted in: Nathan Söderblom, *Om studiet av religionen*, ed. Erland Ehnmark, Lund, Gleerup, 1951, 13–48; GT: "Die allgemeine Religionsgeschichte und die kirchliche Theologie," in: Nathan Söderblom, *Ausgewählte Werke*, ed., Dietz Lange, vol. 1, Offenbarung

not generally being a very attractive field of study in Sweden at the time. He passionately pleaded that Christian piety and free scientific research should be united by means of a common respect for reality. In particular, he inculcated the importance of his own field of the history of religions for theology, in that it could open one's eyes to both Christianity's kinship with, and specific difference from, other religions. He insisted that for such studies some sort of religious experience was necessary, although one had to do justice to every religion's self-understanding rather than judge it from a preconceived Christian perspective.[22]

The title of Söderblom's chair was clad in the rather unusual terms of "encyclopedic preconceptions of theology." It referred primarily to the history of religions but left ample room for a whole range of other subjects. He concentrated on the former but also included philosophy of religion, besides such theological subjects as Roman Catholic Modernism, Luther, and Swedish Church history.

The field of history of religions was in the process of rapid expansion during the latter half of the 19th century, due to progressing colonialism, improvements in global traffic, and to foreign missionaries' increasing efforts to inquire about indigenous religions. Towards the turn of the century, many of them began to become aware of the fact that authoritarian methods of conversion, imposing Western standards of social life and entanglement with exploitation by the colonial powers were bound to jeopardize the missionary efforts themselves. We see Söderblom at the forefront of a corresponding attempt to revise established practice.[23] He was well aware of the fact

that this involved walking a tightrope. Measures such as raising natives' working morale, improving agricultural techniques and medical care did seem desirable, yet all these fields were related to religious convictions. When a Christian mission encounters indigenous religion, it must therefore do so with respect. In this sense, Söderblom energetically pleaded that the new churches should carefully become acculturated and work for independence from their mother churches in Europe or America as soon as possible. The dialectic of peaceful contest and cooperation thus also applies to the relationship among religions.[24]

Söderblom's reflections on missions are inseparable from his research on the world of religions. At his time, the relation between the two fields was in any case very close since scholarly and empathetic missionaries were providing a large amount of knowledge about non-Christian religions. In line with contemporary tendencies, Söderblom took a special interest in the so-called primitive religions. Scholars in general were hoping to come closer to the essence of religion by exploring its earliest manifestations. As we shall see shortly, Söderblom viewed things somewhat differently but felt obliged to take part in the ongoing discussions.

Söderblom's first important publication in his new position was an article dealing with revelation as a basic phenomenon in all religions.[25] Occasion for it was provided by a series of lectures by the German orientalist Friedrich Delitzsch, who claimed that the Jewish religion was morally inferior to its Babylonian counterpart and, therefore, could not have originated in divine revelation.

---

und religionen, Göttingen, Vandenhoeck & Ruprecht, 2011, 23–50.

22   Jonson, *Nathan Söderblom*, 100–101

23   See Gustav Warneck, *Abriß einer Geschichte der protestantischen Missionen von der Reformation bis auf die Gegenwart*, Berlin, M. Warneck, 9 1910, 512f.; Nathan Söderblom, "Missionens dårskap," in: Nathan Söderblom, *Tal och skrifter*, vol. 3, *Tal (1892–1927)*, Stockholm, Åhlén & Söners Förlag, 1933, 117–122.

24   See Nathan Söderblom, "Missionens motiv och kulturvärde," in: Nathan Söderblom, *Ur religionens historia*, Stockholm, P.A. Norstedt, 1915, 170–199, here 193–199.

25   See Nathan Söderblom, *Uppenbarelsereligion*, Stockholm, Svenska kyrkans diakonistyrelses bokförlag, 2 1930; ET: *The Nature of Revelation*, trans. Frederic Ernest Pamp, Oxford, Oxford University Press, 1933; see Friedrich Delitzsch, *Babel und Bibel*, Stuttgart, Deutsche Verlags-Anstalt, 1903.

Söderblom dismissed that argument, maintaining that the essence of religion is not identical to its outward cultural appearances, including morals, because divine revelation is supernatural. He then proceeds to differentiate between revelation in a wider and a stricter sense. There are religions of nature and culture, on the one hand, that reflect a general revelation, and personal religions such as Judaism, Christianity, Mazdeism, and Islam, that refer to a special revelation in history. In either case, religion is not part of culture but *sui generis*, although it does avail itself of cultural means of expression. The two types of religion also differ intrinsically. They both correspond to a kind of "mysticism" or inner life, but religions of nature or culture tend to cultivate a "mysticism of infinity," with a dissolution of the individual as its goal, as in Neo-Platonism or Buddhism, whereas personal religion, which is a "mysticism of conscience," hopes for personal salvation. Söderblom does not declare that this distinction presents alternatives, however. Elements of both types occur in every religion; it all depends on which one is dominant. This modification serves to do justice to the philosophical criticism of anthropomorphism.[26]

The next step in Söderblom's deliberations referred to the relationship between Christianity and other religions. The best exposition of this issue is the brilliant booklet *Studiet av religionen*, which for a long time did not encounter the attention it deserved. Standing in the tradition of Schleiermacher's *Brief Outline for the Study of Theology*, this is nonetheless an independent study. It treats Christianity as a special case in the general history of religions, which does not imply relativizing Christianity as merely one of many religions. Rather, the author wishes to remind the reader that any claim to superiority requires a fair comparison with the merits of the other religions.[27]

The book begins with the "special science of religion," i.e. Christian theology. The first chapter in this part deals with the New Testament, followed by the Old Testament as its background and church history as its continuation. The author stresses, in particular, that the New Testament is not a blueprint for present day theological teaching but a collection of quite different witnesses to the faith, unique in its historical closeness to the person of Christ.[28] Systematic theology, therefore, constantly refers to these sources, but also to expressions of faith in the intervening ages, since God has never ceased to reveal himself. Its specific purpose is working out an ideal of Christian piety based on the present-day experience of God's revelation.[29]

The general history of religions, the subject of the next part, must analyze the individual characteristics of every single religion, not force them into some sort of preconceived scheme of unity, such as evolutionism does. As no religion – not even Christianity – can lay claim to objective truth in the sense of rational proof, the future of the history of religions remains open from a scientific point of view. This does not preclude their evaluation by means of comparison, although that contains an inevitable element of subjectivity. Comparative history of religions as a science ends by exposing two basic types of religion, one with a negative and one with a positive attitude towards the world, exemplified by Buddhism and Christianity as its classic representatives. This is as far as scientific discourse

26   Jonson, *Nathan Söderblom*, 105–116
27   Nathan Söderblom, *Studiet av religionen*, Stockholm, Ljus, 1908, ²1916, reprinted in: Söderblom, *Om studiet av religionen*, 49–152; GT: "Das Studium der Religion,"

in: Söderblom, *Ausgewählte Werke*, vol. 1, 165–252. Friedrich Schleiermacher, *Kurze Darstellung des theologischen Studiums*, Berlin, Realschulbuchhandlung, 1811; ET: *Brief Outline of the Study of Theology*, trans. William Farrer, Edinburgh, T&T Clark, 1850. For a more detailed analysis, see Dietz Lange, "Von Schleiermachers 'Kurzer Darstellung des theologischen Studiums' zu Söderbloms 'Studiet av religionen,'" in: Michael Pietsch & Dirk Schmid, eds., *Geist und Buchstabe: Interpretations- und Transformationsprozesse innerhalb des Christentums: Festschrift für Günter Meckenstock zum 65. Geburtstag*, Berlin, De Gruyter, 2013, 383–406.
28   Söderblom, *Studiet av religionen*, 78 (190).
29   Söderblom, *Studiet av religionen*, 88f. (200).

can go. Eventual religious unity remains an open question: no kind of synthesis will be able to attain it, even less any search for the smallest common denominator. Peaceful contest remains the only option. Söderblom does not thereby eschew the question of truth but leaves it until the end of the treatise, because it is a matter of personal conviction alone. This does not render it arbitrary, as that conviction refers to divine revelation, i.e. to being subject to the grip of Holiness (resp. God). Personally, Söderblom is convinced that the "universal significance of Christ" will prevail in the end.[30]

Apart from his literary feats, Söderblom's academic activity also involved his establishing the Olaus Petri Foundation (named after the prominent Sweden's Reformer), which had been made possible by the donation in 1907 of a wealthy Stockholm lady who wished to see in Sweden something analogous to the famous Hibbert and Gifford Lectures in the United Kingdom. The foundation was formally set up in 1909 and stipulated that it should be left to Söderblom's discretion to decide during his lifetime whom to invite. The foundation obviously lived up to expectations. In the course of the first years, renowned scholars such as Wilhelm Herrmann, Franz Cumont, Ignaz Goldziher, Adolf von Harnack and others held their lectures. Outstanding churchmen later came in support of Söderblom's ecumenical endeavors. The foundation is still in existence today.

4   Church and Ecumenical Activities

Besides his work at the university, Söderblom served as a prebendary at nearby Trinity Church (Trefaldighetskyrka). When he preached, the pews were always crowded especially with educated people. This was reminiscent of Schleiermacher preaching in the church of the Charité hospital in Berlin. Axel Hambræus in his autobiographical novel provides a moving testimony to this.[31]

Beyond this local assignment, Söderblom reached out to the entire Swedish Lutheran Church. For some time, a reform movement had been unfolding with a particular emphasis on active lay participation in church life. This movement gained momentum with the rise of Swedish nationalism in the wake of the dissolution of the union with Norway in 1905. A leading figure was Johan Alfred Eklund, bishop of Karlstad. His particular strength lay in his winning young people over to the church. His view of the Lutheran Swedish nation as the elected people of God found an enthusiastic echo among many. Somewhat less nationalistic were two other leaders of the Ungkyrkorörelsen (Young Church Movement), as it came to be called: Einar Billing, professor in Uppsala, and Manfred Björkquist, its chief organizer. The movement sent students into villages and towns, two by two, to talk to people on the street. It was the most significant reform effort of the Swedish Church in the early 20th century. Söderblom supported it with some reservations. He was totally in favor of its missionary efforts but unequivocally critical of its nationalism.[32] This bent diminished after the outbreak of the war, not least thanks to his influence.

During his tenure as professor, Söderblom took his first step towards ecumenism. One day in 1908, he paid a visit to Johann August Ekman, archbishop of Uppsala. On his desk, he noticed a letter from the Anglican Archbishop Randall Davidson and asked for permission to read it. The letter was inquiring about the conditions for closer communion with the Swedish Church. Ekman had been hesitant to react to previous advances, bearing in mind the affiliation of the Swedish Lutheran Church with its US "daughter church," the Evangelical Lutheran Augustana Synod in North America, which did not have an episcopal

---

30   Söderblom, *Studiet av religionen*, 103 (213).

31   See Axel Hambræus, *Annelis son*, Stockholm, Diakonistyrelsen, [3]1961, 123f.

32   Jonson, *Nathan Söderblom*, 123ff.

structure and therefore could have been an obstacle in relations with the Church of England.
Söderblom, however, succeeded in persuading the
archbishop to give a positive reply. He arranged an
invitation to the Lambeth Conference for Henry
William Tottie, bishop of Kalmar, a High Church
man with Scottish roots who proved to be a skillful
negotiator.[33] The leaders of the two churches met
for the first time in Uppsala in September 1909.
The Swedish party included Uppsala professors
Söderblom, Billing, and Lundström.[34]

The central subject of this meeting was the
ministry, with special reference to the apostolic
succession of bishops. The Swedes claimed that
they respected this criterion, since all bishops
(except one) had agreed to the Reformation decree
of the Diet of Västerås in 1527, thus preserving the
apostolic continuity of his own episcopal line.
However, Söderblom clearly stated that his church
considered the succession a "blessing from the
God of history" but not essential for a church to be
a true one. The church as an institution is human,
no more than a "vessel for … Divine revelation."[35]
This would hardly have pleased the Anglican High
Church wing. Moreover, Davidson also had some
misgivings concerning the validity of the Swedish
ministry because it lacked a diaconate. The conference did not produce a final communiqué,
although the overall reaction was favorable and
the bishops did celebrate communion together.

Further negotiations stalled owing to the war of
1914–1918. In the meantime, Söderblom wrote two
articles in English that were meant to let Anglicans
become better acquainted with the Swedish
Church.[36] The first of these, "On the Character
of the Swedish Church," dealt with its history,

stressing the fact that in their meeting of 1593 the
Swedish bishops had succeeded in rejecting the
efforts of Sigismund, the king at the time, to revert
the country to Catholicism, thereby securing a
significant measure of freedom from the state for
the future. The other article, "On the Soul of the
Church of Sweden," concerned the Reformation
idea of freedom of personal religion being superior to all institutionalism.

At the very end, the second article contains
the nucleus of Söderblom's theory of ecumenism.
He considered the talks with the Church of
England the first step towards a united *corpus
evangelicorum*. This was not a plea for a single
church body, history having refuted that Roman
Catholic ideal, but for a combination of peaceful contest and cooperation, including dialogue,
between churches of Protestant persuasion. He
thus applied his earlier idea concerning the relationship between labor and management to the
relationship among churches. He would later also
use it for the world of religions, making it the basis
for his social theory as a whole.

In the year after negotiations with the Church
of England had begun, Söderblom wrote another
important work concerning ecumenism. It was
a treatment of Roman Catholic Modernism,
occasioned by the excommunication of leading
Modernists by Pope Pius X in 1907.[37] Its aim was
to show, first, that Catholicism is not the monolithic unity it often claims to be, and, second, that
Modernism is not a halfway Protestantism but
represents the more genuine form of Catholicism
compared to its political version in the official
church. Proof of the former proposition is the
presentation of such different thinkers as John
Henry Newman, Alfred Loisy, George Tyrrell, and
Friedrich von Hügel, and likewise equally different popes. Söderblom likened Modernist piety to
that of St. Francis of Assisi, which he held in high

---

33   Jonson, *Nathan Söderblom*, 135.

34   Jonson, *Nathan Söderblom*, 138.

35   See his handwritten note *Statement as to the Doctrine of
      our Church about the Holy Ministry and the Ecclesiastical
      Constitution*, Sept 22, 1909, in: UUB, NSS C, kapsel 54,
      Intercommunion.

36   See "On the Character of the Swedish Church" and "On
      the Soul of the Church of Sweden," *The Constructive
      Quarterly* 3, 1915, 281–310 and 506–545.

37   See Nathan Söderblom, *Religionsproblemet inom katoli-
      cism och protestantism*, Stockholm, H. Geber, 1910. See
      also the encyclical letter by Pius X, *Pascendi dominici
      gregis*, AAS 40, 1907, 593–650.

esteem. However, Modernism is definitely Catholic because it maintains that obeisance to the infallible teachings of the church is indispensable for salvation, however minimalistic its interpretation of infallibility may be. That is why the admirable freedom of Modernist exegesis in the final analysis is in reality something that closely resembles the medieval type of intellectual freedom.[38]

In short, according to Söderblom there is a difference in kind between Catholicism, including its Modernist version, and Protestantism, which he would later define as the difference between institutional and personal religion.[39] This hails back to Schleiermacher's famous distinction between Catholicism that makes salvation by Christ dependent on membership of the Church, and Protestantism that views the church as resulting from the common faith in Christ.[40]

5   The Culmination of a Scholarly Career

In 1909, Berlin University included Söderblom on its list for the succession to Otto Pfleiderer's chair, which it had converted from systematic theology to the history of religions. Söderblom was hesitant about accepting such a post. He felt deeply rooted in his Swedish environment, thinking of his many children (eight at the time). He therefore did not mind when the call went to his Danish friend Edvard Lehmann. His reaction was different when he received a call to the professorship in the history

of religions at Leipzig University three years later. He accepted on condition that it was for a limited number of years, and that he could maintain his chair in Uppsala (which was possible thanks to a different division of the academic year).[41]

Leipzig was a wealthy industrial city of 600,000 inhabitants with a lively cultural life. The theological faculty included such well-known scholars as Albert Hauck, one of the foremost church historians of the time, the Old Testament professor Rudolf Kittel, the practical theologian Franz Rendtorff, who was involved in an organization attempting to improve relations with the United Kingdom, and the systematic theologian Ludwig Ihmels. Söderblom was also in contact with the philosophical faculty, especially with the historian Karl Lamprecht.

Leipzig saw the height of Söderblom's academic career. Separated from his church duties and his large circle of friends in Sweden, and obliged to teach in a foreign language (although he already knew it very well), he was able to concentrate more exclusively on his lectures and publications. Among the latter, the book on the genesis of the belief in God stands out.[42]

The title of the Swedish original *Gudstrons uppkomst*, the origin of belief in God, seems to suggest that the book would limit itself to primitive religions. In point of fact, it is far more than that. The title of the German translation, a considerably enlarged version of the original, states it more accurately: *Das Werden des Gottesglaubens*, the genesis of belief in God. It actually covers the whole history of religion, albeit not as a single evolutionary process as conceived by the great systems of philosophy of religion such as Hegel's. Söderblom also broke away from the assumption to which so many of his contemporaries adhered, i.e. that primitive religions of today represent the

---

38   Jonson, *Nathan Söderblom*, 154–160.

39   See Nathan Söderblom, "Evangelisk katolicitet," in: Edvard Lehmann, Nathan Söderblom & Knut Bernhard Westman, *Enig kristendom*, Stockholm, Svenska kyrkans diakonistyrelses bokförlag, 1919, 65–126; GT: "Evangelische Katholizität," in: Söderblom, *Ausgewählte Werke*, vol. 2, *Christliche Frömmigkeit und Konfessionen*, Göttingen, Vandenhoeck & Ruprecht, 2012, 165–208..

40   See Friedrich Schleiermacher, *Der christliche Glaube* ([2]1830/1831), ed. Rolf Schäfer, vol. 1, Berlin, De Gruyter, 2008, § 24; ET: *The Christian Faith in Outline*, trans. Donald Macpherson Baillie, Edinburgh, W.F. Henderson, [2]1922, § 24.

---

41   Jonson, *Nathan Söderblom*, 176–177.

42   See Nathan Söderblom, *Gudstrons uppkomst*, Stockholm, H. Geber, 1914; GT: *Das Werden des Gottesglaubens*, Leipzig, Hinrichs 1916; not available in English.

origin of all religion and thereby provide the key to the essence of religion itself. For one thing, these religions are the result of a lengthy, undocumented evolution. Secondly, it is the fundamental error of the prevailing theories of his time to derive the multifarious world of religions from a single historic root, be it animism, totemism, fetishism, early belief in High-Gods, or ancient monotheism. "No key opens all doors," as Söderblom was fond of saying.[43]

Söderblom postulated several different lines in the history of religions. He thereby transformed his previous distinction between personal mysticism and mysticism of infinity into a threefold division: animism resp. animatism, the numinous powers of mana and taboo, and the ancient High-Gods. Needless to say, he was availing himself of existing ideas. What was new is that he did not incorporate them into a single evolutionary theory. Moreover, he warned against constructing genealogical ties within any one such type as they occur in very different parts of the world.

Insistence upon irreducible variety does not render superfluous the quest for something that all these different phenomena have in common since he was convinced that it must be possible to determine what the concept of religion really means. A first approximation gleaned from his earlier writings would be the reference to revelation on the part of "someone" or from "something" supernatural, as opposed to both subjectivist (Ludwig Feuerbach) and social (Émile Durkheim) theories, i.e. explanations of religion either as projections of

ideal humanity into an imagined transcendence or as society's authorization of its moral code, its self-deification as it were.

In *Gudstrons uppkomst* Söderblom goes a step beyond that by describing what he considers to be a common characteristic of all such revelations: the dialectic of mana and taboo, creative power and annihilation. This implies that the divine or supernatural is inaccessible and at the same time inescapable.[44] Both mana and taboo evoke awe, even fear, as well as fascination and relief. Söderblom combines these aspects in one single term, holiness.[45] He thereby preceded Rudolf Otto's famous book, which characterized holiness by the terms *mysterium tremendum* and *fascinans*.[46] Söderblom was the first to use holiness in a specifically religious sense for the whole world of religions.[47] Apart from that, Söderblom had overcome two shortcomings in his own earlier discussions of the matter. First, in the earliest version published in 1909, he had interpreted holiness

43   See Nathan Söderblom, "Über den Zusammenhang höherer Gottesideen mit primitiven Vorstellungen," *AR* 17, 1914, 1–14, here 2. Recent research suggests that the idea of the most archaic examples of religion betraying its very essence is but an expression of a Romantic yearning for an "innocent" antiquity that was less technical and materialistic, less complicated and less evil. Such an attitude was widespread in the late 19th century, fueled by an aversion to the belief in relentless progress and its perceived heartlessness; see Hans G. Kippenberg, *Die Entdeckung der Religionsgeschichte: Religionswissenschaft und Moderne*, Munich, C.H. Beck, 1997, 96.

44   See Nathan Söderblom, *Natürliche Theologie und allgemeine Religionsgeschichte*, Stockholm, A. Bonnier, 1913, 109.

45   In the philosophy of religion, holiness is a more specific concept than transcendence or supernatural. In the religious realm, it is more basic than God or the Divine, since neither is there a God in original Buddhism, nor are spirits or fetishes in primitive religions actual Gods. See Nathan Söderblom, "Holiness (General and Primitive)," *ERE* 6, 731–741; Nathan Söderblom, *Heiligkeit, einschließlich Tabu, unrein, rein etc.*, Leipzig, summer term 1913, in: UUB, NSS C, MS 1913, kapsel 42.

46   See Rudolf Otto, *Das Heilige: Über das Irrationale in der Idee des Göttlichen und sein Verhältnis zum Rationalen*, Breslau, Trewendt & Granier, 1917 (many later editions); ET: *The Idea of the Holy: An inquiry into the Non-Rational Factor in the Idea of the Divine and its Relation to the Rational*, trans. John W. Harvey, London, H. Milford, 1923.

47   Predecessors were William Robertson Smith, *Lectures on the Religion of the Semites: The Fundamental Institutions*, London, A. & C. Black, ³1927, who used it only for Semitic religions, and Wilhelm Windelband, "Das Heilige: Skizze zur Religionsphilosophie," in: Wilhelm Windelband, ed., *Präludien*, vol. 2, Tübingen, Mohr, 1911, 295–332, who called it a *norm* for theoretical, practical and esthetic reason, thereby in the final analysis making it a meta-ethical category.

largely as the ultimate foundation of morals.[48] Second, as late as in his lecture on the concept, one can find a certain imbalance between the creative power of mana and the destructive power of taboo, in favor of the latter.

6   The Archbishop-to-Be and World War I

Söderblom experienced the extreme nationalism rampant in pre-war Germany, and he found it totally abhorrent. Sweden had its own brand of nationalism, too; the great explorer Sven Anders Hedin, and the aforementioned Bishop Eklund were perfect examples of it. However, the German atmosphere was far more poisonous. It shocked both Söderblom and his wife and was also the main reason why they never felt entirely at home in Leipzig, in spite of all the cultural amenities the city had to offer, the friendly faculty and his own teaching success at the university.

On May 20, 1914, Sweden's king appointed Söderblom archbishop. This event caught everyone by surprise, even the candidate himself. For a while, he had been planning to found an institute for teaching history of religions at Leipzig University. Therefore, he had arranged with the university chancellor for an extension of his tenure until at least the summer of 1915. Needless to say, he had heard about the rumors concerning the upcoming election, which started soon after Archbishop Ekman had died in 1913. However, knowing only too well that his liberal theological position was abhorrent to many in his church, he considered his chances for nomination to be extremely slim, to say the least. In fact, the list the church had submitted to the king, who had to make the final decision, did include his name but in a hopeless third place.[49] However, the advice of

the secretary of church affairs prevailed ultimately in Söderblom's favor.

Why, at the age of 48, did he decide to renounce a successful academic career in favor of the episcopacy? First, the opportunity to shape church life actively and to work for "regular people" must have seemed enticing to him. Although he had never held a high office in the church, he could build upon his experience as a pastor in Paris, and he would have a chance to expand and in part put his ecumenical ideas into effect. Furthermore, he was probably convinced that he would be able to lead the church into a new era better than his conservative contenders could.

Only a few weeks after his appointment, the Great War broke out. Söderblom sensed almost immediately that this was an incipient catastrophe of global dimensions, since he spoke of a world conflagration in a postcard home on Aug 5.[50] A couple of days before, the WA had conducted its founding conference in Constance, Germany. Söderblom could not attend, but certainly heard about it. Later, in 1917, he even became chairman of its Swedish committee. The WA turned out to be one of the formative forces of the nascent ecumenical movement.

The war obliged Söderblom to leave Germany as soon as possible. It was a hectic return, made even more difficult by the fact that his wife had become seriously ill after the birth of their twelfth child.

Söderblom used the time until his installation, on Nov 8, establishing a network for his future activities. He also began working on a declaration calling for peace. It had been his hope that leading churchmen from the warring nations would also sign it, but this was in vain. On Oct 4, a memorandum – the Manifesto of the Ninety-Three – by leading German Protestant churchmen and professors was made public claiming that Germany was the victim of the

---

48   See Nathan Söderblom, "Helig, Helighet," in: *Nordisk familjebok*, vol. 11, Stockholm, Nordisk familjeboks förlag, [2]1909, 310–314.

49   See Staffan Runestam, "Det dramatiska ärkebiskopsvalet 1914," *Svensk Kyrkotidning* 106, 2010, 447–451.

50   See Nathan Söderblom, *Brev, Lettres, Briefe, Letters: A Selection from his Correspondence*, ed. Dietz Lange, Göttingen, Vandenhoeck & Ruprecht, 2006, no. 70.

Allies who had forced this war on it.[51] Söderblom was profoundly disappointed to discover among the signatories several luminaries, such as Adolf von Harnack. He countered it by a peace appeal, *For Peace and Christian Fellowship*, published in several languages on Nov 27 and signed by churchmen from neutral countries.[52]

Prior to that, on Sept 6, Söderblom had preached an impressive sermon in Trinity Church, where he had previously served as prebendary. Its subject was *De två gudarne* (The Two Gods, 1914),[53] referring to the god of nation (actually a plurality of gods), on the one hand, and the Father of Jesus Christ, on the other. He was critical of all warring nations but with particular severity accused Germany of violating Belgian neutrality and committing war crimes in that country. Churchmen in all the warring countries had turned the religion of peace into a religion of war. Söderblom was equally critical of nationalism in Sweden and the self-righteousness inherent in its neutrality, explicitly devoting a later sermon to that aspect.[54] In both cases, he combined his expertise as a historian of religion with a critical prophetic voice. In a positive key, he pleaded for peacefulness of contest and cooperation of the nations for the common good, a basic tenet of his social theory even in this context.

7   Primate of Sweden's Church

Nov 8, 1914 (his deceased father's birthday) was the day of Söderblom's installation as archbishop in Uppsala Cathedral, in the presence of King Gustaf V, conducted by the old bishop of Lund, Gottfrid Billing, who had once ordained him. Söderblom would dearly have liked to see an Anglican participation in the ceremony. The war prevented that, but his former Leipzig colleague, Franz Rendtorff, and Theodor Kaftan, a German church leader, did attend.

Two days later, on Luther's birthday (once again a symbolic date), he published his voluminous pastoral letter, as is customary for Swedish archbishops.[55] By way of introduction, he took up his father's maxim from 2 Cor 1:24, precluding any kind of clericalism for his time in office and stressing the joy at the freedom of faith. This freedom of the spirit granted by God's grace included independent theological research, the purpose of which is to penetrate dogma for the simple faith behind it, which is common to all Christians. It was a plea for cooperation with the strong conservative forces in the church. He then turned to social problems, calling for thoroughgoing reforms and more justice for the working class. A chapter on the inner life of the church pleaded for the reforms the Ungkyrkorörelsen had initiated and for an opening to the Free Churches. The longest part of the letter by far addressed the new world situation caused by the war. The neutral countries should do everything in their power to bring the warring nations to the negotiating table and to work for the establishment of an international legal order. The letter concluded with a guideline for the daily life of the Christian, built upon the Lutheran conception of a mundane profession, "Pray, work, believe."

True to the special interest in foreign missions he had cherished since his revivalist upbringing,

---

51   See *Aufruf deutscher Kirchenmänner und Professoren: An die evangelischen Christen im Ausland* (1914), in: Gerhard Besier, ed., *Die protestantischen Kirchen Europas im Ersten Weltkrieg: Ein Quellen- und Arbeitsbuch*, Göttingen, Vandenhoeck & Ruprecht, 1984, 40, 42–45.

52   Bengt Sundkler presents the English version of this appeal in his biography: Bengt Sundkler, *Nathan Söderblom: His Life and Work*, Lund, Gleerup, 1968, 163.

53   See Nathan Söderblom, *De två gudarne*, in: Nathan Söderblom, *När stunderna växla och skrida*, vol. 2, Stockholm, Geber, ³1935, 103–112; GT: "Die beiden Götter," in: Söderblom, *Ausgewählte Werke*, vol. 2, 127–137.

54   See Nathan Söderblom, "Neutral egenrättfärdighet: Botdagspredikan," *Kristendomen och vår tid* 12, 1916, 116–122; ET: "Our Spiritual Peril as Neutrals," *The Constructive Quarterly* 5, 1917, 91–96.

55   See Nathan Söderblom, *Herdabref till prästerskapet och församlingarna i Uppsala ärkestift*, Uppsala, F.C. Askerberg, 1914.

his first official act was the ordination of missionary Paul Sandegren.[56] During his tenure, the number of Swedish missionaries nearly doubled, not least owing to the fact that the Germans had to abandon many a foreign post because of the war.

Central to his professional work were the visitations. They were the key to his popularity, given his extremely good rapport with people from all walks of life, his memory of single persons and events, and his sense of humor. During his 17 years in office, he visited every one of the 240 congregations in his diocese at least once. In the course of the years, he often asked ecumenical guests to accompany him, in order to reinforce the gradual opening up of the isolated Swedish Church on the grassroots level. Equally important for him was pastoral care, to which some of his personal letters bear witness.[57]

Another crucial aspect was church social work. In the dire need caused by the war and its aftermath, this often went far beyond the usual scope of church activities, comprising humanitarian initiatives in the broadest sense of the term. Söderblom collected money in the countryside to help city dwellers who were hard-hit by food rationing during the war. He organized aid for prisoners of war on both sides, in close collaboration with the Swedish Red Cross. When the war was finally over, he invited scores of starving children from Saxony, Germany, for a stay in Sweden. One outstanding personal example is his support for Albert Schweitzer, who was ill, highly indebted and feared that he would have to give up his hospital in Lambaréné (in the French Equatorial Africa, today Gabon). Söderblom invited him to Sweden to recover and organized organ concerts for him in order for him to be able to repay his debts and continue his work in Africa. There are, moreover, countless instances in which Söderblom supported

individual poor persons with money from his own purse or in some other practical way.[58]

One particular type of conference, of the many he attended after his election, is worth mentioning. In 1920 he began to promote regular meetings of Scandinavian bishops in order to discuss common problems of church policy and ecumenism, with the aim of furthering cooperation across national borders.

One serious political conflict occurred during Söderblom's tenure, which concerned the relationship between the church and the state.[59] The Swedish Social Democratic Party (Sveriges socialdemokratiska Arbetareparti, SAP) convention issued a decree in 1920 calling for an end to the state church system. The party won the election in the same year and formed the first Social Democratic government in Swedish history. Shortly thereafter, Arthur Engberg, who belonged to the party's radical anti-Christian wing, followed up on the decree and proposed to the Riksdag (Diet) the abolition of the church's right to veto any changes in state church law. His motion did not pass but was a cause for alarm. Söderblom therefore convened the general synod and held a major speech there, pointing out that this initiative aimed at stifling the church, ultimately leading to its demise.[60] It is worth noting that otherwise Söderblom very much agreed with the party's social politics. Evidence of this is his invitation and cordial welcome to the new prime minister, Hjalmar Branting, at the synod meeting. This shrewd move helped to defuse the relationship between church and Social Democrats in the future. Söderblom was well aware of the problems the state church

---

56   Jonson, *Nathan Söderblom*, 301.

57   Jonson, *Nathan Söderblom*, 226ff.

58   See Staffan Runestam, *I kärlekens tjänst: Från Nathan och Anna Söderbloms humanitära verksamhet*, Uppsala, Vulkan, 2013.

59   See Staffan Runestam, *Söderblomsstudier*, Uppsala, Svenska institutet för missionsforskning, 2004, 25–70.

60   See Nathan Söderblom, "Kyrkans frihetskrav," in: Nathan Söderblom, *Samtal om kyrkan: Föredrag vid tionde allmänna kyrkliga mötet i Stockholm 1920*, Stockholm, Svenska kyrkans diakonistyrelses bokförlag, 1920, 58–79.

system posed and might even have been ready for change, had the circumstances not been so hostile.

However, it is a fact that Söderblom was a conservative as far as church organization was concerned. He was never a church reformer in the usual sense of the word, apart from his support for the Ungkyrkorörelsen. There were complaints about the undue delay of some changes in this field under his leadership. He was not a believer in reviving genuine Christian life by means of organizational measures. He did provide a host of practical resources, such as writing textbooks for teaching religion and the history of religions in schools or providing support for practicing music, but what his leadership really built on was personal relationships – and ultimately prayer. He remained a genuinely pious person throughout his life.

8 The Goal of Church Unity

In addition to his duties as archbishop, Söderblom gradually became one of the driving forces of the ecumenical movement. Considering the vast number of letters written for this purpose to church leaders, politicians and critics, journeys to international church conferences, meetings with individual persons, and the countless speeches held, one must realize that this turned out to be a second full-time job, comparable to a modern general secretary of the WCC. Above all, when Söderblom began his ecumenical activities, there was no generally acknowledged concept of church unity. Most pronounced was the traditional Roman Catholic claim to represent the true church into whose fold it expected all others to return. Another idea was the so-called branch theory, first developed by William Palmer of the Church of England in 1833, which promoted a closer relationship among the old episcopal churches, Roman Catholicism, Eastern Orthodoxy, and Anglicanism. Starting from 1888, official Anglicanism was considering an institutional unity based on a common episcopate in its Lambeth conferences. The liberal

Protestant theologian, Adolf von Harnack, suggested a friendly relationship between the Roman Catholic and Protestant Churches, each keeping its own identity but cooperating in worldly matters.[61] The Edinburgh WMC in 1910 proclaimed the necessity for the churches to speak with one voice in the mission field, but leaving open the question of implementation and only marginally considering the implications for the home base of foreign missions. Finally, there were those who resisted any change whatsoever.

How did Söderblom place himself in this confusing scene? He began by connecting to his earlier work on social problems and on the relationship of religions. The history of Christian churches, like that of religions and of society in general, is full of antagonism and violence. Therefore, it is imperative to transform this pattern into peaceful contest and cooperation if human life is to attain its destination. This calls for dialogue rather than hegemony or monopoly. Furthermore, religion, including Christianity, is a relationship with an inescapable, yet inaccessible, holiness and must therefore generate an awareness of its own limitations together with its failures. The war experience made this way of thinking even more urgent. That is what led Söderblom to extend his earlier idea of a new corpus evangelicorum to Christendom as a whole.

Cooperation in this context was for him a term primarily referring to the field of ethics and most frequently concerns alleviating social misery, such as that resulting from the Great War. However, it has an analogy with the spiritual realm. Although religion has its seat primarily in individuals, these share their faith in the communion of believers. They interpret their faith differently, it is true, but this should not prevent them from coming together for common worship and more specifically common celebration of the Lord's Supper, as

---

61   See Adolf von Harnack, *Protestantismus und Katholizismus in Deutschland*, in: Adolf von Harnack, *Aus Wissenschaft und Leben*, vol. 1, Gießen, A. Töpelmann, 1911, 225–250.

agreed by the Churches of England and Sweden. The importance Söderblom assigned to this issue is evident from a passage in the lecture he held at the Faith and Oder Conference in Lausanne in 1927: "There is little use speculating about the forms of a United Church before we have attained the condition sine qua non for such unity, I mean fellowship at the Lord's Table."[62]

For his concept of contest and cooperation among the churches, Söderblom coined the term "evangelic catholicity."[63] This expression has frequently met with misunderstandings, most notably by the great German historian of religion, Friedrich Heiler. He construed it to be a synthesis of personal Protestant freedom of faith and Roman Catholic esteem for the ecclesiastical institution. He found this ideal realized in the Church of Sweden with its preservation of the episcopate and many rites from medieval times.[64] This interpretation of Söderblom's stance, while frequently reiterated, particularly by High Church representatives of the Church of Sweden, is erroneous. It simply reflects Heiler's own position, who had converted to Protestantism but was still yearning for his old religious home in the Catholic Church. What Söderblom really means is that there are three kinds of "catholicity," i.e. three main forms of Christianity claiming universal validity, Roman, Eastern Orthodox, and Protestant catholicity. They all have equal rights, while each preserves its own identity. They are one in their faith in Christ; however, that unity will never spell uniformity but will remain a unity in variety.[65] In organizational terms, this spells federative unity. Söderblom in fact promoted the idea of a WCC as early as

1919, almost 30 years before it actually came into being.[66] In religious terms, this implies that none of the Christian churches as a historical entity is *in possession* of absolute truth; the same is true of Christianity as a whole – the individual's personal certitude notwithstanding.

These ideas have sometimes been associated with the branch theory mentioned above. This is due to the fact that Söderblom himself occasionally used the term "branch" for the Christian denominations.[67] However, this is completely different from the Oxford Movement's theory. By branches, Söderblom intends the three forms of catholicity, including Protestantism, whereas the Oxford branch theory excludes Protestantism as it did not belong to the ancient episcopal churches.

The concept of unity in variety stood in stark opposition to the 1870 Catholic dogma in particular, which held that church unity must also be a unity of doctrine and jurisdiction, a unity that existed only in the Roman Church, to which all Christians that have gone astray must eventually return. In a series of lectures delivered to a Munich audience in 1923, Söderblom responded to this standard position. As he had pointed out in 1910 in his book on Catholicism and Protestantism, in the Protestant type of piety church unity is constituted by personal faith, as opposed to the Roman institutional type, and it is for him the sole type true to the original spirit of Christianity. This, in its turn, is the basis for his concept of unity in variety. Therefore, all the churches, including Roman Catholicism, must in the end convert to this Protestant view. If one considers all the aspects of this, not all divisions among churches are detrimental; on the contrary, some of them, like the Reformation, have proved necessary.[68]

---

62   See Nathan Söderblom, "The Unity of Christendom and the Relation thereto of Existing Churches," in: Herbert Newell Bate, ed., *Faith and Order: Proceedings of the World Conference, Lausanne, August 3–21, 1927*, London, SCM Press, ²1928, 321–331.

63   See Söderblom, "Evangelisk katolicitet."

64   F. Heiler to N. Söderblom, June 26, 1919, in: Söderblom, *Brev, Lettres, Briefe, Letters*, 235 (no. 138).

65   See Nathan Söderblom, *Christian Fellowship: or The United Life and Work of Christendom*, New York NY, F.H. Revell, 1923, 21.

---

66   See Söderblom, "Evangelisk katolicitet," 119–122 (203–205).

67   See Nathan Söderblom, "Evangelische Katholizität," in: *Festgabe für Adolf Deissmann: Zum 60. Geburtstag, 7. November 1926.*, Tübingen, Mohr, 1927, 327–334, here 329f.

68   See Nathan Söderblom, "Religionsgeschichtliche Betrachtung der christlichen Frömmigkeitstypen:

Just as Söderblom's ecumenical activities were closely tied to his peace efforts during the war, so they remained after the war. His wholehearted support for the League of Nations proves this. The latter organization was for him a prime example of contest and cooperation in the realm of politics since it attempted to settle differences at the negotiating table. Nonetheless, he was never blind to its weaknesses, its very limited power and its internal squabbles. It merely lacked common moral norms, which in turn ultimately had to rest on a religious basis of conviction. Continuing to think in terms of a "Christian world," he demanded that this basis or "soul" of the League be the Christian faith, analogous to the needs of the state.[69] However, this does not refer to the Christian church as an institution, as one High Church Swede has suggested.[70] That would spell theocracy, something Söderblom abhorred. Even so, one may legitimately question a Christian soul of the League of Nations, which even then was not composed exclusively of (nominally) Christian nations. However, there is an explanation for this standpoint: the world catastrophe of the war had elicited in his deeply religious mind an almost eschatological interpretation of the upheaval of Western civilization it had brought about. He was hoping that it would mean the demise of the bland materialism and belief in progress characterizing the previous age, and that the immense amount of suffering incurred in the war would provide the opportunity for a revival of the religion of the Cross.[71]

9   On the Way to the World Conference

The peace appeal of 1914 having failed to obtain the desired attention and the war meanwhile relentlessly taking its course, for some time Söderblom did not launch any new action in this regard but concentrated on work for his home church. Then a glimmer of new hope for peace appeared for an instant in 1917 with the February Revolution in Russia and increasing news about a growing tiredness of war on the Western Front. That hope proved short-lived, however, when the United States joined the war in April. Söderblom reacted by issuing a new peace appeal the following month, again signed by church leaders from neutral countries, whose heading recalled the Reformation anniversary in that very same year.[72] In September, in an article, the Anglican William Temple urged the churches to arrange for a peace conference.[73] Others joined the appeal. Söderblom acted quickly and suggested that the Scandinavian bishops should convene such a conference in November. It did meet a couple of weeks later together with the WA. They discussed the plan for a more comprehensive conference to convene in the following year. After several delays due to the war, the tide

Volesungen in München 7.–9.5.1923," in: Söderblom, *Ausgewählte Werke*, vol. 2, 209–304, here 278, 297–299.

69   See Söderblom, "Evangelisk katolicitet," 105–107, 113f. (194f., 199f.); concerning the state, see Nathan Söderblom, *Religionen och staten*, Stockholm, P.A Norstedt & Söner, 1918, 96–100, 183, 185, 189, 200.

70   See Sven-Erik Brodd, "The Church as the Soul of European Civilization: Archbishop Nathan Söderblom on Church and Society," *Kirchliche Zeitgeschichte* 4/1, 1991, 128–138, here 135–138.

71   See Nathan Söderblom, *Gå vi mot religionens förnyelse?*, Stockholm, Sveriges kristliga studentrörelses förlag, 1919; GT: "Gehen wir der Erneuerung der Religion entgegen?," in: Söderblom, *Ausgewählte Werke*, vol. 2, 139–163; Dietz Lange, "Sollen wir eine Erneuerung der Religion erwarten?," *ZThK* 112, 2015, 490–506.

72   He called it *Appeal for Peace and Remembrance of the Reformation* and published it in several languages; see Nathan Söderblom & others, *Appeal for Peace and Remembrance of the Reformation*, in: Nils Karlström, *Kristna samförståndssträvanden under världskriget 1914–1918: Med särskild hänsyn till Nathan Söderbloms insats*, Uppsala, Almqvist & Wiksell, 1947, 626–631.

73   See William Temple, "Notes of the Week," *The Challenge* 7, 1917, 301.

turned at a WA meeting in Oud Wassenaar, in the Netherlands, in October 1919. The delegates were unanimous in placing the responsibility for the "great" conference on the churches, which started preparations in earnest in Geneva in 1920.

The Geneva conference took place immediately after the Faith and Order Conference in the same location. In the same place and days, the parallel Life and Work movement came into being. Söderblom was a vice president of Faith and Order but believed that negotiations on doctrine and church order were a long-term issue, while the practical needs arising from the destruction, both physical and spiritual, caused by the war demanded immediate action on the part of the churches, which is why he always gave priority to the Life and Work movement. Moreover, he was of the opinion that debates on doctrine were necessary for facilitating better mutual understanding among the churches but in all likelihood would never lead to complete agreement and doctrinal unity. His work on the history of religions had convinced him that differentiation among them was not necessarily a result of failure, or even sin, but a natural consequence for any religion that extends across different cultural environments.

After the Geneva Conference, it still required several more meetings and much insistence by Söderblom and his collaborators until the first universal conference on Life and Work could finally meet in Stockholm in 1925.

Why did it take so long even after the main obstacle, the ongoing war, had vanished? The main reason was the debate on German responsibility for the outbreak of the war (*Schuldfrage*), which was not only highly controversial but continuously fueled by fierce nationalism on both sides and the harsh conditions of the peace Treaty of Versailles.[74] Through tenacious negotiations, Söderblom succeeded in preventing the question of guilt, being political in nature, from becoming part of the Stockholm agenda. In addition, a more personal issue jeopardized the whole plan. In 1919,

The Saturday Review discovered that Söderblom's son, Sven, had fought in the war on the German side (against his father's will). In the heated atmosphere of the time, it took him considerable efforts to dispel the allegations of partisanship with the Germans.

During the preparation of the conference, the visits of Sadhu Sundar Singh, from India, to England and the United States in 1920 and to several European countries, including Sweden, in 1922, were subject to much publicity throughout the Western world. Söderblom received him in Uppsala. Singh was a Hindu turned Christian mystic through a vision of Christ. He had toured his home country as an evangelist and purportedly also wrought several miracles. These aroused a heated debate in Europe later in the 1920s. A flood of pamphlets for and against him appeared, the latter accusing Singh of being a quack and impostor.[75] Söderblom was probably skeptical in this regard but did not join in that part of the discussion. He was more interested in the genuinely religious aspect, about which he wrote a long essay in a booklet on mysticism, faith, and science.[76] Here he pictures Singh as a true Christian, albeit with obvious traces of his former Hinduism. He maintains that Singh's piety focused entirely on God's forgiveness in Christ and that his asceticism was not motivated by the desire for merit but by service to one's neighbor. He does not deny certain shortcomings, such as a lack of sensitivity concerning the depth of sin and a correspondingly weak sense of social responsibility, as he indirectly points out in the second chapter of the book (which is dedicated to Luther). Furthermore, he chides (again, indirectly, in the third chapter) Singh's skepticism of modern science as being incompatible with Christian freedom and the respect for reality. Overall, however, he attributes to Singh a

---

74   On this subject see Gerhard Besier's contribution in this volume.

75   See Michael Biehl, *Der Fall Sadhu Sundar Singh: Theologie zwischen den Kulturen*, Frankfurt a.M., Lang, 1990, especially 49–86.

76   See Nathan Söderblom, *Tre livsformer: Mystik* (*Sundar Singh*), *förtröstan, vetenskap*, Stockholm, H. Geber, ²1922, 11–52.

true biblical faith in an Indian guise.[77] Hoping for a Christianized world, he probably saw the Sadhu as a living rebuke of Ernst Troeltsch's skepticism concerning Christianity's ability to transcend the realm of Western culture.

Another seeming distraction, in view of the rapidly approaching deadline for the Stockholm conference, was Söderblom's 3-month journey to the United States in the fall of 1923. He had received invitations for such a visit several times before, but had always had to decline. On this occasion, he accepted after some initial hesitation. The Evangelical Lutheran Augustana Synod in North America and the CPU organized and financed the trip. Three things seem to have persuaded Söderblom to overcome his scruples. One was the chance to contact the Evangelical Lutheran Augustana Synod (which, as already mentioned, was affiliated with the Swedish Church) in person; another the opportunity to propagate his ecumenical plans; and finally the opportunity to hold the planned lectures at American universities on peace and European reconstruction, along with those on Lutheran theology and the history of religions. All this turned out to be an extremely tiring schedule even for a healthy person, and even more so for Söderblom, who had suffered a heart attack the year before. His hosts received his lectures and sermons enthusiastically everywhere. The journey proved a resounding success, also providing him with the chance of reunion with some people he had met on his previous visit in 1890.

10   Life and Work in Stockholm 1925

After his long absence, Söderblom had to catch up on preparations for the great conference. He did so with fervor. Although he had a very efficient staff as well as very efficient collaborators abroad, such as Charles McFarland of the FCCC, he seems to have taken care of every important detail:

recruiting sponsors, arranging for accommodation for all foreign delegates, compiling a special hymnbook, organizing gala receptions by the king, the Stockholm mayor, Uppsala University, and foreign embassies. Even more astounding, amid this bustle, is the fact that he never for once neglected his duties towards his own church. Thus, he conducted a well planned visit during the heated phase of preparations for the conference. It was his principle throughout that his home church always took precedence.

As far as the conference itself is concerned, it was clear from the outset that it would require the utmost diplomatic skills and tactful leadership. Söderblom had therefore decided not to deliver a major speech, apart from welcoming the delegates and from a concluding sermon, and to concentrate on his role as moderator and on personal contacts in the background, in order to defuse any tensions that might arise. He did all he could to create as friendly an atmosphere as possible, for instance by providing private accommodation and by giving voice to Swedish cultural life one evening, with the contribution of Elsa Brändström, the "angel of Siberia" who had been working with prisoners of war, the famous writer Selma Lagerlöf, and the renowned opera singer John Forsell (his brother-in-law).

The number of delegates, about 600, was truly impressive, and highly varied. Söderblom had taken pains to have as many Christian communities represented as possible. For this purpose, he had advised his preparation committee to use a complex mathematical code to guarantee participation even to small communions. As a result, the delegates who actually arrived represented virtually all the churches, with two great exceptions: the Roman Catholic and the Russian Orthodox Churches, the former having declined participation, the latter not being able to obtain permission to travel from the Soviet government. Some ultra-conservative groups, such as the Southern Baptists and the Lutheran Missouri Synod of the United States, did not attend, either. Furthermore, the

---

77   See also Jonson, *Nathan Söderblom*, 325–329.

committee had asked all the churches to ensure that the different lines of thought and types of piety within each denomination (liberal, conservative, etc.) were represented. The Americans complied best with this requirement. The Germans did not, but sent a predominantly conservative group. The overall representation consisted overwhelmingly of church officials and professors of theology, whose average age was, of course, quite advanced. There were few lay people, few women, few non-white persons, and few delegates from outside the Western world. From a modern day perspective, this was a major drawback. However, in its time and under the circumstances, it was quite a remarkable enterprise.[78]

Therefore, finally, having overcome countless obstacles both at home and abroad, Söderblom's perseverance paid off. On Aug 19, 1925, he was able to open the ecumenical conference on Life and Work in Stockholm, along with dignitaries from the major participating churches and in the presence of the king and the mayor of Stockholm. It was in point of fact the first global church conference on issues of social ethics ever to be held.

The working agenda of the conference was as extensive as the number of pressing problems raised by the war and its aftermath. There had been so many requests for issues to be included in the program that it is impossible to list them here. Regrettably, however, the actual preparation by the delegations turned out rather uneven. The British had been the most thorough, having conducted a special Conference on Christian Politics, Economics, and Citizenship (COPEC) explicitly for this purpose, under the leadership of Archbishop Temple, the year before.

Critics have said that the sheer multitude of social issues discussed had the effect of excluding, or suffocating, the Christian spirit at this meeting. Nothing could be farther from the truth. Even though its subject was not Christian doctrine, there are clear indications that Christian faith permeated the whole course of events. This is evident, for example, from the daily worship services, beginning before the official opening on the first day. Söderblom called them the backbone of the conference.[79] A highly symbolic act, in this sense, was the celebration of intercommunion on Aug 23. The same is true of the final service in Uppsala Cathedral on Aug 30, with the patriarch of Alexandria reading the Nicene Creed in the original Greek.

Moreover, the one subject determining the whole conference, despite its not having been assigned a preparatory commission, was explicitly theological, namely the Kingdom of God. The major contention here was between Anglo-Saxons and European Lutherans. The former were mainly adherents to, or sympathizers of, the American Social Gospel. One prominent speaker in this group was Frank Theodore Woods, bishop of Winchester, who preached the sermon in the opening service. For him, Christians are to be "conspirators for its [i.e. the Kingdom's] establishment," which includes turning away from the atrocities of the war in repentance and promoting the progress of human civilization and international law.[80] Such activities require empowerment by God, he added; but the emphasis was on human endeavor. The bishop of Saxony and former Leipzig professor of theology, Ludwig Ihmels, represented the opposing Lutherans. He insisted that the Kingdom of God as such is not a human project but God's own reign introduced by Christ. The church is to bear witness, not to establish it. This witness does include social responsibility, but within the given framework of the "orders of creation" such as family, nation, state.[81]

Söderblom, who as moderator refrained from delivering a speech of his own, expressed his opinion on the matter in the voluminous report that he

78 See also Jonson, *Nathan Söderblom*, 336–374.

79 See Nathan Söderblom, *Kristenhetens möte i Stockholm, augusti 1925: Historik, aktstycken, grundtankar, personligheter, eftermäle*, Stockholm, Svenska kyrkans diakonistyrelses bokförlag, 1926, 151f.

80 See George K.A. Bell, ed., *The Stockholm Conference 1925: The Official Report of the Universal Christian Conference on Life and Work held in Stockholm, 19–30 August 1925*, Oxford, Oxford University Press, 1926, 38–45, here 38.

81 See Bell, ed., *The Stockholm Conference 1925*, 72–79.

published on the proceedings. According to him, both those views contain elements of truth but also are problematic. The Anglo-Saxons tend to equate the Kingdom of God with certain historical developments, thereby depriving it of its essential transcendent dimension. However, active commitment in favor of a better world is preferable to a passive, conventional church mentality. On the other hand, Lutheranism is right in maintaining that the kingdom is solely God's own work. It is wrong, however, in upholding the neo-romantic concept of fixed orders of creation. Human social order is a mixture of God's creation and human sin. In short, one must not sanctify either a future worldly goal or a present day worldly state of affairs.[82] The conference did not solve this controversy; it has been determining ecumenical meetings ever since, with the Anglo-Saxon view increasingly gaining the upper hand.

The second major topic, intertwined with but not identical to the first, was the relationship of nations to one another. On the surface, this concerned the evaluation of the role of the League of Nations. The delegates from the Western democracies viewed it as providing the chance for peace, in spite of its obvious flaws. The Germans thought it was subservient to the Treaty of Versailles, which they felt undeservedly humiliated them. Söderblom clearly sided with the Western Europeans and Americans on this matter.[83]

Was this conference a success? At first sight, one is inclined to give a negative answer to this question, pointing to the "Message," instead of a final communiqué, that was issued. It was full of pale generalities. Even the condemnation of war in number 8 varied in tone in the three languages from resolute (English) or forceful (French) to lame (German), mirroring the vastly different opinions expressed in the debates, which ranged from radical pacifism to the view that war was in

fact inevitable.[84] Nonetheless, public opinion as expressed in the media was overwhelmingly positive, if you ignore a couple of wildly nationalistic tirades in Germany and one-sided polemics in Roman Catholic and orthodox Protestant quarters complaining of a lack of Christian substance.[85] The favorable comments acknowledged the fact that a meeting of this kind, in its attempt to bridge such deep animosities such as that between Germans and French, had been possible at all and had been carried out in an atmosphere that was on the whole amiable. This was indeed quite astounding, and credit is due primarily to Söderblom's preparatory work and to his constant encouragement and mediation behind the scenes.

The criticism launched by Roman Catholics and Protestant conservatives is mainly secondhand and easy to refute. However, there are two points of criticism that will remain valid. First and foremost, the preparatory committee had put up too little resistance to the incessant flood of suggestions for yet more items on the program. Söderblom himself admitted as much. Probably nobody listened to all of the 134 speeches. Skipping many of them was the only way to have sufficient time for personal conversations, which are so important for any large conference. Second, the conference failed to recognize the importance of the problem of racial discrimination and allotted far too little time to considering it.

---

82 See Söderblom, *Kristenhetens möte i Stockholm*, 252f., 257–259, 262f., 265.

83 See Söderblom's criticism; Söderblom, *Kristenhetens möte i Stockholm*, 522.

84 See Friedrich Heiler, *Die Weltkonferenz für praktisches Christentum in Stockholm*, in: Friedrich Heiler, *Evangelische Katholizität*, Munich, Reinhardt, 1926, 56–150, here 126.

85 For the Roman Catholic side see *L'Osservatore Romano*, Sept 14–15, 1925; Pierre Batiffol, "L'évolution du mouvement pour l'union des églises," in: Comité catholique des amitiés françaises à l'étranger, ed., *Almanach catholique français pour 1927*, Paris, Bloud & Gay, 1927, 85–88. For the conservative Protestants see the Finnish Archbishop Gustaf Johansson, "Die Stockholmer Weltkonferenz und das Luthertum," *AELKZ* 57, 1924, 821–824; for the nationalists see the German pastor Wilhelm Laible, "Der Weltkongress für praktisches Christentum in Stockholm vom 19. bis 30. August 1925," *AELKZ* 58, 1925, 663–666, 685–689, 707–714, 724–727.

This legitimate criticism notwithstanding, the fact that this historic meeting could have taken place at all was a great success under the circumstances. The atmospheric changes among the churches that it wrought somehow survived even the fierce backlash by fascism and World War II. This is an undiminished tribute to Söderblom's patience and perseverance. The Stockholm meeting was undoubtedly the culmination of his church career, although in his modesty, he clearly recognized its limitations. In his concluding sermon on Mark 7:31–37, "Eph'phatha" ("Be Opened"), he stressed that work on ecumenism had only just begun and that everything depended on obeying the guidance of the Holy Spirit in the years to come.[86]

The bold enterprise did take its toll, on Söderblom personally. He was quite simply exhausted, and his health, always fragile, soon deteriorated. He increasingly had to leave key responsibilities to others. Work on continuation turned out to be difficult and often ineffective, due both to planning errors and to lack of resources, but even more to waning interest towards the ecumenical effort in many quarters as well as to the resurgence of nationalism in various European countries. Furthermore, Söderblom had to endure unfair personal attacks, for instance from his former disciple Torgny Segerstedt, who accused him of having betrayed essential Christian values for the glamor of a world conference.[87] Söderblom continued his exacting schedule of work and even produced one of his best books, *Kristi pinas historia*, in the years to come; but in many ways his last years turned out to be somewhat of an anticlimax.

11   Faith and Order in Lausanne 1927

As one of the vice presidents of Faith and Order, Söderblom was one of the leading figures at the conference in Lausanne, although he was decidedly less prominent than in Stockholm. The field of the Faith and Order movement concerned the longer-term problems of doctrine and church organization. Thus the theological issue of church unity, which had remained in the background in Stockholm, inevitably came to the fore. The controversies that would erupt here were not those fueled by nationalist resentment but such as arose from different religious convictions. This did not make them any less potentially explosive, and Bishop Charles Brent, as president of the conference, was well aware of it. Hence his repeated admonitions to be patient and not to aim for a definitive solution.[88]

Söderblom's role at the conference was twofold. First, he delivered an introductory statement, and then led the most important commission on "The Unity of Christendom and the Relation thereto of Existing Churches." In his speech, he enumerated three options with regard to church unity.[89] They were "institutionalism," adhered to by Roman Catholicism and conservative Lutheranism (in that it adhered to a legalistic interpretation of its confessional writings), "spiritualism," and "incarnationalism." Personally, he would prefer the second of these, were it not for its failure to provide the necessary institutional coherence. His real choice would, therefore, be the third concept. This sounds like a concession to the Anglican view that the church is the continuation of God's incarnation in Christ. In fact, however, he had in mind the image of soul and body used in his book on the body and soul of the Swedish Church.[90] In his interpretation of this image, the "soul," i.e. the communion of believers, creates the institutional "body," which is thus the work of human ingenuity. As such, it is subject to variation, transitoriness and fallibility. Its unity is therefore not a "visible" one of doctrine or jurisdiction but consists in each

86   English translation in: Bell, ed., *The Stockholm Conference 1925*, 739–745.

87   See Torgny Segerstedt, *Händelser och människor*, Stockholm, Geber, 1926, 112.

88   See his opening address, Charles Henry Brent, "The Call to Unity," *EcRev* 29, 1977, 162–166.

89   See Söderblom, "The Unity of Christendom."

90   See Söderblom, "On the Character of the Swedish Church" and "On the Soul of the Church of Sweden."

individual's personal relationship to Christ. For this reason, unity cannot be monolithic but only a "unity in diversity." In his commission report, he demanded that every church organization leave room for "diverse types of doctrinal statement and of the administration of church ordinances."[91]

The last sentence, in particular, provoked a sharp rebuke on the part of the old episcopal churches, voiced most succinctly by the former Anglo-Catholic Bishop Charles Gore, who even threatened to terminate Anglican participation in Faith and Order. For him, "organic" unity did permit of a certain range of difference in matters of doctrine, but its basis in the Bible and the ancient creeds, as well as the apostolic succession of bishops, were indispensable. His reaction provoked a vote for the revision of the report. The second version came to the floor on the day before adjournment, with the basic ideas intact. Söderblom had already left by that time, purportedly because of inescapable duties at home but possibly because of his profound disappointment with the discussions. One might be tempted to attribute this course of events to a clash between two strong personalities or to the fact that due to his frail health Söderblom had not been able to prepare his part in the conference adequately. While there is a measure of truth to both of these assumptions, this is by no means the whole story, since the two men represented the views of large church bodies. In the final analysis, it was these views that had proved to be irreconcilable.

In the year following the Lausanne Conference, Pope Pius XI launched a passionate and highly official attack on the ecumenical movement in his encyclical letter *Mortalium animos* of 1928. It may have been a reaction to the debacle of Lausanne but was aimed even more at the Stockholm meeting. In particular, the pope obviously had Söderblom and his concept of church unity in mind – without ever mentioning his name. In an apparent allusion to Söderblom's work as a historian of religion, the pope asserted that the various conferences on religions had assembled all kinds of Christians, non-Christians and downright heathens and thereby rejected true religion, or even degraded it to naturalism and atheism. Analogously, the ecumenical movement, called "pan-Christian," was a chaotic hodgepodge of all kinds of Christians striving for some sort of flimsy federative union, thereby ignoring the one and only true church represented by the Vatican, which essentially made them guilty of the same sin.[92]

The German Jesuit, Max Pribilla, seconded the encyclical with an article published in 1929 and Söderblom wrote a lengthy refutation to each of them.[93] He vehemently denied any anti-Catholic prejudice, pointing to his life-long esteem for genuine Catholic piety, such as the Franciscan tradition, as well as to the fact that he had invited the Vatican to his Stockholm Conference. However, the Roman Church was wrong, he says, to claim to be the one and only Christian church. Essential unity of the church exists exclusively in Christ and is, therefore, not subject to church authority. That is why visible unity can only be a unity in diversity. It is true even for the Roman Catholic Church itself, which harbors an enormous wealth of different expressions of faith within its communion. He sees the principal fault of official Catholic doctrine to be its interpretation of faith as the acknowledgment of prescribed doctrinal propositions, instead of simple trust in God. In this way, the church *de facto* subordinates faith to human legislative authority, contradicting such witnesses as St. Paul, who wrote, "not that we lord it over your faith" (2 Cor 1:24). Söderblom agrees with Schleiermacher that this is the basic difference between Roman Catholicism and Protestantism, the roots of which

---

91 See Söderblom, "The Unity of Christendom," 398 (first draft), 436 (second draft).

92 See Pius XI, *Mortalium animos*, AAS 20, 1928, 5–16. See also Marie Levant's contribution in this volume.

93 See Max Pribilla, *Um kirchliche Einheit: Stockholm, Lausanne, Rom: Geschichtlich-theologische Darstellung der neueren Einigungsbestrebungen*, Freiburg i.Br., Herder, 1929; Nathan Söderblom, *Christliche Einheit!*, Berlin-Steglitz, Evangelischer Preßverband für Deutschland, 1928; Nathan Söderblom, "Pater Max Pribilla und die ökumenische Erweckung: Einige Randbemerkungen," *Kyrkohistorisk Årsskrift* 31, 1931, 1–99.

go far deeper than the level of theological theory; they represent two different types of piety, as he had elaborated in his Munich lectures of 1923.

12   The Archbishop as Writer

It is a cause for marvel how much Söderblom was able to publish during his twofold commitment as archbishop and ecumenical leader. Most of it consists in sermons, articles, and the like. However, there are also real books constituting important contributions to both theology and the history of religions.

The first of the books is *Humor och melankoli och andra lutherstudier* (Humor and Melancholy and other studies in Luther), published in 1919.[94] It contains twelve lectures for the most part delivered on the occasion of the Reformation anniversary in 1917. As the title indicates, this is neither a biography nor a doctrinal treatise. Instead, Söderblom starts out from Luther's piety and illustrates it with characteristic moments in his life, making extensive use primarily of the correspondence and the *Table Talk*. This was quite an original approach at the time, the approach of a historian of religion. His intent is not to explain Luther's distinction of law and gospel psychologically, as a modern reader might suspect, nor does he simply attach humor to the gospel and melancholy to the law. Rather, they are two basic reflections of the bipolar relationship of faith to the holy God who is both a terrifying judge and a merciful redeemer. Luther's famous sense of humor represents both the critical distance from the self, caused by God's radical demand, and the joyful sense of liberation and grateful certitude thanks to salvation. It also means mockery of religious superficiality and hypocrisy, sometimes in a very boisterous form. Humor is off

limits, however, in the encounter with holiness itself. Cynical jokes about the Eucharist, as Luther had experienced them as a monk, are nothing other than blasphemy.

Melancholy, on the other hand, is not identical with the clinical term depression but refers to tribulations and despair over one's sin as well as over suffering from natural causes. It implies a criticism of hubris, including any attempt to "justify" God's actions by some kind of theodicy. Söderblom then discusses the various remedies for tribulation that Luther recommended, such as humor, music, and above all prayer and the Gospel, proclaiming salvation through Christ's vicarious suffering. Contemplation of Christ's own tribulation is a special source of comfort.

The second part of the book deals with the certitude of faith. This certitude is, according to Söderblom, the central theme of Luther's theology (as well as of his own). Only from this vantage point is it possible to understand what the theological formula *sola fide* really means. His prime biographical example is Luther's appearance before the Diet of Worms in 1521. Certitude is the dialectical unity of humility and courage, freedom and obedience of faith. The author contrasts this with the religiously non-committal attitude of the great scholar Erasmus of Rotterdam. Contemporary Roman Catholic criticism of Luther considered Luther's certitude of faith as pure hubris, since it snubs the authority of the church, which alone can guarantee that certitude. Söderblom holds that it is the very point in Luther's idea of certitude that Christianity is a personal, not an institutionalist religion. He views such Catholic criticism as a recurrence of the ancient fear that human hubris provokes the envy and the vengeance of the gods – a fear Christ had laid to rest once and for all.

Finally, the lecture on Luther and the Peasants' War is of interest here. Söderblom emphasizes that Luther was critical of both the princes and the peasants in the name of the holy order of law. The German research of his time was primarily interested in defending the right of the authorities to restore order, even if it be by coercion and

---

94   See Nathan Söderblom, *Humor och melankoli och andra Lutherstudier*, Stockholm, Sveriges kristliga studentrörelses förlag, 1919; GT: *Humor und Melancholie und andere Lutherstudien*, in: Söderblom, *Ausgewählte Werke*, vol. 4, *"Der Prophet" Martin Luther*, Göttingen, Vandenhoeck & Ruprecht, 2015, 23–318.

force, and maintained that political action did not have to follow the injunctions of the Sermon on the Mount. Söderblom disagreed. He was very critical of Luther's second brochure, which was written after the peasants had launched their uprising and urged the authorities to crush it by any means. This is medieval dualism, he says. The Gospel does not promise justice in the world, nor indeed the fulfillment of any political desires. It does have social consequences, however, insofar as love must be the ultimate measure even in the political realm. It has to provide justice, as Luther himself had demanded in his first brochure. One must distinguish, but not separate, the so-called two Realms (i.e. the relationship to God vs. the relationship to humans). This point concerns not only the historical evaluation of Luther but also was of contemporary relevance, since conservative Lutheranism had been one of the main supporters of the authoritarian government in Germany.

In the years following the book on Luther, Söderblom wrote several smaller works on his ecumenical ideas, the contents of which we discussed earlier in this essay. Then came the disappointment with the Lausanne Conference. His enthusiasm for the unity of the church was undiminished, but he was now convinced that for the time being not much progress was likely to be made. He therefore deemed it necessary to take a fresh look at the essentials of the Christian faith, to which any ecumenical endeavor ultimately has to refer. That is to say, to his mind, the vicarious suffering of Christ. The result of such deliberations is his book on the Passion of Christ (1928), arguably one of his best.[95]

Kristi pinas historia (The story of Christ's Passion) is a devotional book – on the face of it. Doubtless, it serves that purpose very well, but it has far more to offer. It is actually no less than a well thought-out Christology in narrative form. It roughly follows the course of the biblical story. The rationale for this approach is not that it is *only* a devotional book; a tongue-in-cheek attitude was always something he detested. Rather, his reasoning is the following. The traditional speculative approach of dogmatics deriving Christology from the doctrine of the Trinity does not do justice to the fact that God's revelation occurred in the historical person of Christ. Revelation addresses the heart and does not promulgate a metaphysical doctrine appealing to the intellect. Dogma is not superfluous but is clearly secondary to the event of revelation itself, besides being subject to correction since it is a fallible human attempt at intellectual clarification.

Söderblom lets the story develop like a drama. His model is the story of the Passion in the second part of the Swedish hymnbook, which is also divided into "acts" and "scenes." Apart from this, the recollection of a Passion play that he attended in Athens in 1911 plays a role, since it had reminded him of classical Greek tragedy.[96] This reminiscence led him to introduce a "choir" announcing each new step in the action, by placing Gospel texts at the head of each act or respective scene. He conceived them as a harmonization of all four Gospels. This might otherwise seem surprising, as Söderblom, being an astute exegete, was well aware of the significant differences between the various accounts; but a choir is necessarily a unity of many voices.

Diverging from classical tragedy, Söderblom does not let the *dramatis personae* play their roles directly on the "stage" but acts as the narrator. In this way, he tries to do justice to the exegetically established fact that the biblical narratives do not relate the results of historical research but proclaim the Gospel in narrative form.

---

95   See Nathan Söderblom, *Kristi pinas historia: Vår Herres Jesu Kristi lidande: En passionsbok för stilla veckan och andra veckor*, Stockholm, Svenska kyrkans diakonistyrelses bokförlag, 1928; GT: *Geschichte des Leidens Christi*, in: Söderblom, *Ausgewählte Werke*, vol. 3, *Jesus in Geschichte und Gegenwart*, Göttingen, Vandenhoeck & Ruprecht, 2014, 49–410.

96   See Nathan Söderblom, "Frälsaretypen i religionshistorien" (1911), and "Antikens frälsaregestalter och frälsaren i evangeliet" (1914), in: Söderblom, *Ur religionens historia*, 57–64 and 217–252.

In his overall conception, Söderblom is particularly interested in two things. One is to impress on the reader that the story of Christ's Passion is not merely something that occurred in the distant past but concerns the reader's own life: *tua res agitur*. Therefore, the passage on the Lord's Supper is of particular importance. Not only is it the longest of all, but it also includes a chapter on the faithful participation in the Eucharist. The same purpose is served by the stanzas from the hymnbook he inserted at the end of many scenes: they bring the "congregation" onto the "stage."

The second is the emphasis on the universality of salvation. One can discern two literary means for opening up such a wide outlook. One is the introduction of saviors in other religions, who appear to be many preparatory "Old Testaments," as it were; the other is the presentation of views on the Passion in the history of devotional life, art, and literature. They are meant to demonstrate that divine revelation in Christ has not ceased but continues and takes place in the present time.

As for Jesus' vicarious suffering itself, Söderblom takes care not to isolate it from the life of the historical Jesus, as Christological dogma tends to do. He achieves this by emphasizing the connection of the Eucharist with the meals Jesus had with publicans and sinners. Salvific communion is the point in both cases. Moreover, this bond connects the Eucharist to creation, as its elements parallel the food enjoyed in those earlier meals. Söderblom had been interested in the unity of the Jesus of history and the Christ of faith, from his earliest articles on Christology. He had always been critical of Adolf von Harnack's famous thesis that only God the Father, not the Son, belongs to the Gospel. Likewise he contradicted Johannes Weiss's contention that Jesus had been disparaging the world because he expected its imminent demise, and therefore Christians today must affirm the progress of civilization instead. Jesus did expect the near end, Söderblom replies; however, the essence of his eschatology is not to be located in the temporal element but in the utter seriousness of an immediate encounter with God. He was therefore able to combine his expectation of the *eschaton* with a high esteem of natural life and the created world in general, as well as with deep respect for the rule of law in worldly affairs. This was one of his most original contributions to the history of religions.[97] In this way, he rejects both a liberal Christology of Jesus as teacher and moral role model and the lifeless dogmatic construct of many an orthodox conception.

What this means in a positive sense becomes clear when we look at the interpretation of the crucifixion itself. If Jesus was a real human being, his suffering must also be real, and his final cry on the cross, "My God, my God, why hast thou forsaken me?" (Mark 15:34 RSV) must have expressed real despair. None of the many apologetic attempts at explaining that away deserves credence. However, skipping from here to the blasphemous conclusion that God cynically let Jesus down is equally unacceptable. If the vicarious suffering of Christ is an expression of God's love, then "God's heart really broke on the cross."[98] Söderblom holds with Luther that this paradoxical thought, despite its bordering on the ancient heresy of patripassionism, is the only way of doing justice to the love of God.

The story ends with an "annex" concerning the resurrection. The word annex does not imply marginality. On the contrary, Söderblom calls the resurrection of Christ a historic fact. However, it is historic with regard to its bearing, not as something verifiable by scientific research. In other words, it is a fact of faith, namely the firm belief in Jesus' continuing communion with God and

---

97   See Nathan Söderblom, "Jesus eller Kristus?: Den snara väntan i evangeliet," in: Söderblom, *När stunderna växla och skrida*, vol. 2, 275–301 (enlarged ed. 1921); GT: *Jesus oder Christus? Die Naherwartung im Evangelium*, in Söderblom, *Ausgewählte Werke*, vol. 3, 23–47; Adolf von Harnack, *Das Wesen des Christentums: Sechzehn Vorlesungen vor Studierenden aller Fakultäten im Wintersemester 1899/1900 an der Universität Berlin*, ed. Claus-Dieter Osthövener, Tübingen, Mohr Siebeck, 2005, 91; Johannes Weiss, *Die Predigt Jesu vom Reiche Gottes*, Göttingen, Vandenhoeck & Ruprecht, 1892, 67.

98   Söderblom, *Geschichte des Leidens Christi*, 383.

our participation in it. This makes any fixation, on the part of both believers and nonbelievers, about the question as to whether the tomb was empty or not, pointless.

Söderblom corroborates his standpoint by referring to modern exegetical insights. The most ancient tradition, 1 Cor 15:3–8, equates the resurrection experience of the first disciples with that of Paul himself, which was clearly a vision. Paul underlined this view by emphasizing that "it is sown a physical body, it is raised a spiritual body" (1 Cor 15:44), and that "flesh and blood cannot inherit the kingdom of God" (1 Cor 15:50).[99] In other words, it is not the outward appearance that is crucial but the essential simultaneity with Christ (Kierkegaard), the presence of eternity in the hearts of the believers. This presence transcends the limits of the original mission of Jesus and potentially spans the whole world. The crucifixion ceases to be a conclusion and becomes a new beginning.

The book combines deep personal piety with critical exegesis, a wide perspective on the world of religions and culture, and high quality literary art. It is equally as far from dishonest apologetics as it is from cynicism. Söderblom always attributed a religious quality to the "respect for reality," which includes acknowledgment of the limits of human knowledge.

The honorable invitation to deliver the Gifford Lectures in 1931 provided Söderblom with the opportunity to return to his field of scholarly research, the history of religions. His presentation is an impressive résumé of his life work. He called it *The Living God*.[100] The first – and only – part of the lectures took place from May 19 until June 8,

1931. The foundation had scheduled the second part for the following year. However, death prevented that plan, and only a table of contents, a collection of materials, and a few notes are extant.

The basis of the first part is Söderblom's old distinction between the mysticism of infinity (or ascetic exercise) and personal mysticism, exemplified in particular in Buddhism, on the one hand, and in the Jewish-Christian tradition, on the other. He does not aim at a complete overview of all religions but concentrates on those with which he is most familiar, often returning to earlier works of his, albeit giving them a new form. Moreover, most of the material he had previously published was only in Swedish, so it was new for his Edinburgh audience. The overall tendency of the texts compared to earlier versions is a certain attenuation of sharp contrasts. This is true even of the most basic distinction between personal and institutional religion; as indicated by the subtitle, he now claims the prevalence of the personal even for primitive religions. His intention with this is to extol more than previously the overwhelming power of holiness over the inner life in its being the essence of all religion. On the other hand, he claims that personal religion has an affinity to the mysticism of infinity in the creative potency of the ingenious artist or in the speculative vision of the theoretical thinker. These phenomena bear witness to the continuing divine creation to which all human activity owes its vigor.

The same tendency is evident in the description of the polarity between Indian religions and the Judeo-Christian tradition. It is noteworthy that two of the four chapters dedicated to Indian religions deal with their Bhakti version, the belief in a merciful deity. In this respect, they offer an analogy to biblical religion, although Hinduism's unlimited tolerance for all kinds of deities in the final analysis makes it incompatible with its Western counterparts. Similarly, the role mercy plays in Mahayana Buddhism constitutes an analogy to Christianity, even though the Buddhist emphasis on doctrine contrasts with faith in divine redemptive activity in the Passion of Christ.

---

99   See Söderblom, *Jesu bergspredikan och vår tid*, 267; N. Söderblom, note of May 10, 1929, *Om Kristi lekamliga uppståndelse*, in: UUB, NSS C, MS 1/3/1929, *Tron på Kristi uppståndelse: Svar på Åbo underrättelser*.

100   See Nathan Söderblom, *Den levande guden: Grundformer av personlig religion*, Stockholm, Svenska kyrkans diakonistyrelses bokförlag, 1932; ET: *The Living God: Basal Forms of Personal Religion*, London, Oxford University Press, 1933.

Of particular interest is the chapter dealing with Socrates. It contains the preliminary results of a monograph Söderblom had planned but not been able to complete. Perhaps inspired by Kierkegaard's book *On the Concept of Irony*,[101] it compares Socrates' religion to that of Jesus. Both share the certitude of a belief in the deity. However, the certitude of Socrates is the religion of the clear conscience relying on an eternal, anonymous world order, Söderblom maintains, whereas the certitude of Jesus is that of belief in a personal God. Being equally as firm as Socrates, he had to endure the tribulation of God's apparently forsaking him.

This last monograph by Söderblom is indeed a very impressive achievement, as vivid and captivating as ever, and perhaps even somewhat "wiser," even though it does not convey the same freshness of originality as *Gudstrons uppkomst*.

13   Peace Endeavors and the Nobel Prize

In the years following the Stockholm Conference, Söderblom relentlessly continued to work for world peace. He had never been a radical pacifist, inasmuch as he always deemed a truly defensive war to be legitimate. However, the personal letters of his son and the famous anti-war novel by Erich Maria Remarque, *All Quiet on the Western Front*,[102] had made him more directly aware of the reality of war. Given the harsh regulations of the Treaty of Versailles and the concomitant nationalist resentment among all parties concerned, he soon feared, along with the English economist John Maynard Keynes, that a new war might occur in the not

too-distant future.[103] Consequently, the tone of his calls for peace gradually became more urgent.

One example is the sermon on Mark 9:49–50. that he preached in Geneva on the occasion of Germany's becoming a member of the League of Nations in 1926.[104] Its theme is "Salt and Peace." Söderblom interprets the analogy of the taste of salt with the heat of fire as the need for repentance. First, the church must repent, and then *la Société* (society) and *la Société des Nations* (League of Nations) must do likewise because the basis for world peace is personal peace with God. The preacher then extends the social relevance of the text beyond international relations to society in general and includes the rivalry of classes and economic competition. Just as peace between nations will not come about by merely maintaining a balance of power without actively combating nationalism, the economy will not thrive just by giving a free hand to cutthroat competition (written three years before the great Wall Street stock market crash!). In this context, Söderblom criticizes the bickering within the League of Nations and calls for peaceful and effective cooperation. His Burge Memorial Lectures at King's College in London in May 1929 strike a similar vein. They add the need for the unity of the church as the basis for its preaching peace among the nations.[105]

Yet more radical is the tone of Söderblom's peace appeal in his exposition concerning the so-called Eisenach resolution of the Life and Work Conference in 1929, which Bishop George Bell had introduced there. The fourth paragraph stipulates that churches must not support a war

101   Søren Kierkegaard, *Om Begrebet Ironi med stadigt Hensyn til Socrates*, Copenhagen, P.G. Philipsen, 1841; ET: *On the Concept of Irony: With Constant Reference to Socrates*, trans. Lee M. Capel, New York NY, Octagon Books, 1983.

102   Erich Maria Remarque, *Im Westen nichts Neues*, Berlin, Propyläen, 1929; ET: *All Quiet on the Western Front*, trans. Arthur W. Wheen, New York NY, Little, Brown and company, 1929.

103   See Nathan Söderblom, *Tidens tecken*, in: Oscar Ekman, ed., *För tanke och tro: Skrifter tillägnade Oscar Ekman på hans 50-årsdag den 17 mars 1923*, Stockholm, Sveriges kristliga studentrörelses förlag, 1923, 1–43, here 6–9; John Maynard Keynes, *The Economic Consequences of the Peace*, London, Macmillan, 1919.

104   See Nathan Söderblom, "Sermon pour l'ouverture de la VIIme Assemblée de la Société des nations," *La semaine littéraire* 34, 1926, 433–435.

105   See Nathan Söderblom, *The Church and Peace: Being the Burge Memorial Lecture for the Year 1929*, Oxford, Clarendon Press, 1929.

if the government has declined arbitration. The Germans vetoed the resolution and thus prevented its acceptance. Söderblom, who had not been able to participate in the meeting, presented an even more pointed version to the general synod of the Church of Sweden: churches should condemn such a war. The proposal was passed, but, as a result, Söderblom became increasingly isolated in this debate both at home and abroad.[106] Even in ecumenism in general, his influence declined after the Stockholm Conference, not least because of his failing health and because of the unsolved conflict at the Faith and Order Conference in Lausanne.

Nevertheless, he still enjoyed an excellent reputation throughout the world. The most notable recognition was the Nobel Peace Prize that he received in 1930 for his ecumenical work. In his short address following the award, he mentioned the fact that he probably was the only laureate who had known Alfred Nobel personally. Nobel had in fact consulted him about his intended foundation in Paris in the 1890s, and he had even pondered the idea of an international Court of Appeals and sanctions against war. Söderblom ended with praise for Norway, something that, coming from a Swede only a quarter of a century after the dissolution of the union between the two countries, was much appreciated. In his main speech on the following day, Söderblom talked about the church's duty to preserve peace. The church is obliged to engage in the interplay between Christian love and international legal order, and the activities of the ecumenical movement are located where the two intersect.

14   The End and the Legacy

Söderblom had prepared a speech for the conference of the IMC in Jerusalem in 1928. He could not deliver it there because he had to revoke his acceptance of the invitation at the last minute, but he did have it printed. The Swedish version appeared only three years later, shortly before his death.[107] It is a summary of his most important ideas. On the one hand, he pleads for careful acculturation in the missionary field instead of any kind of cultural colonialism. On the other hand, he corroborates his view of the uniqueness of Christ by means of comparisons with other religions as a justification for Christian missions, although respect is due to those religions as manifestations of natural revelation. The church should act as a unity in variety even in the missionary field and not try to form an *ad hoc* monolithic organization, as this would betray dishonesty or shabby compromise. At all events, it must be remembered that the Christian faith is neither an intellectual acknowledgment of certain propositions nor an execution of some prescribed rites but a personal trust in God. The church's function is that of a news agency proclaiming the Gospel, not self-promotion. Its motto is "Thy Kingdom come."

On July 5, 1931, Söderblom preached his last sermon. On the following day, he wrote a short circular letter to the ministers in his diocese, exhorting them to missionary activity at home. He suggested that they proceed to some village or town in the coming year, two by two like the first disciples and like the Ungkyrkorörelsen, publicly preaching the Gospel and talking to the people. Obviously, the increasing secularization of Swedish society worried him. Taken together, these two examples read like Söderblom's testament for posterity.

On July 8, a sudden bout of extreme pain struck him. The diagnosis was ileus. His doctors had to perform surgery immediately as his life was in danger, despite concern about his heart condition. The operation was successful, but two massive heart attacks on July 12 presaged the end. In the remaining hours, Söderblom thanked everyone,

---

106 See Staffan Runestam, "Nathan Söderblom: Perspektiv på krig och fred," in: Runestam, *Söderblomsstudier*, 199–219.

107 See Nathan Söderblom, "The Historic Christian Fellowship," in: International Missionary Council, ed., *Report of the Jerusalem Meeting of the International Missionary Council, March 24th–April 8th, 1928*, vol. 3, *The Relations between the Younger and the Older Churches*, London, Oxford University Press, 1928, 133–154.

including doctors and nurses, and gave instructions for his funeral (no eulogies, only biblical contemplations). He reminded his family of his life's maxim, "Not that we lord it over your faith; we work with you for your joy" (2 Cor 1:24 RSV), said the Lord's Prayer with them, and died.

He was buried in Uppsala Cathedral, the king and many notables from Sweden and abroad attending his funeral. The whole country was in mourning. Stores closed, and traffic came to a standstill; flags were flown at half-mast, a proof of how much veneration and love he had enjoyed in his lifetime.

Bibliography

Primary Sources

Söderblom, Nathan, *Religionen och den sociala utvecklingen*, in: Samuel Andreas Fries, ed., *Religionsvetenskapliga kongressen i Stockholm 1897: En fullständig framställning af kongressens uppkomst och förhandlingar jämte porträtt af dess president, bestyrelse och samtlige talare*, Stockholm, Bohlin, 1898, 76–143; GT: *Die Religion und die soziale Entwicklung*, SgV 10, Freiburg i.Br., J.C.B. Mohr, 1898.

Söderblom, Nathan, "Holiness," *ERE* 6, 731–741.

Söderblom, Nathan, *Gudstrons uppkomst*, Stockholm, H. Geber, 1914; GT: *Das Werden des Gottesglaubens*, Leipzig, Hinrichs 1916.

Söderblom, Nathan, *Christian Fellowship: or The United Life and Work of Christendom*, New York NY, F.H. Revell, 1923.

Söderblom, Nathan, *Kristenhetens möte i Stockholm, augusti 1925: Historik, aktstycken, grundtankar, personligheter, eftermäle*, Stockholm, Svenska kyrkans diakonistyrelses bokförlag, 1926.

Söderblom, Nathan, *Den levande guden: Grundformer av personlig religion*, Stockholm, Svenska kyrkans diakonistyrelses bokförlag, 1932; ET: *The Living God:* *Basal Forms of Personal Religion*, London, Oxford University Press, 1933.

Söderblom, Nathan, *Brev, Lettres, Briefe, Letters: A Selection from his Correspondence*, ed. Dietz Lange, Göttingen, Vandenhoeck & Ruprecht, 2006.

Söderblom, Nathan, *Ausgewählte Werke*, ed. Dietz Lange, 4 vols., Göttingen, Vandenhoeck & Ruprecht, 2011–2015.

Secondary Sources

Andræ, Tor, *Nathan Söderblom*, Uppsala, Lindblad, 1931; GT: *Nathan Söderblom*, trans. Emmy Groening & Albrecht Völklein, Berlin, A. Töpelmann, [2]1957.

Bell, George K.A., ed., *The Stockholm Conference 1925: The Official Report of the Universal Christian Conference on Life and Work held in Stockholm, 19–30 August 1925*, Oxford, Oxford University Press, 1926.

Jonson, Jonas, *Jag är bara Nathan Söderblom satt till tjänst: En biografi*, Stockholm, Verbum, 2014; ET: *Nathan Söderblom: Called to Serve*, trans. Norman A. Hjelm, Grand Rapids MI, Eerdmans, 2016.

Karlström, Nils, ed., *Nathan Söderblom in memoriam*, Stockholm, Svenska kyrkans diakonistyrelses bokförlag, 1931.

Lange, Dietz, *Nathan Söderblom und seine Zeit*, Göttingen, Vandenhoeck & Ruprecht, 2011.

Runestam, Staffan, *Söderblomsstudier*, Uppsala, Svenska institutet för missionsforskning, 2004.

Runestam, Staffan, *I kärlekens tjänst: Från Nathan och Anna Söderbloms humanitära verksamhet*, Uppsala, Vulkan, 2013.

Sundkler, Bengt, *Nathan Söderblom: His Life and Work*, Lund, Gleerup, 1968.

CHAPTER 27

Charles Brent and the Faith and Order Project: From Its Origins to the Lausanne Conference of 1927

Luca Ferracci

1   Brent: Missionary Bishop

When, on June 14, 1910, at the age of 48, Charles Henry Brent set foot in the meeting room of the United Free Church of Scotland, where the WMC of Edinburgh was to take place, he already boasted of moderate international fame, nine years of experience as missionary bishop in the Philippines, and several articles in *The New York Times* recounting his successes in converting the peoples of Southeast Asia along with the war he was waging against the trafficking and illegal consumption of opium that was flourishing in the western Pacific and that was shaping up to be a genuine social scourge on those islands. He was born in 1862 in Newcastle, Ontario, the third of ten children of Henry Brent, rector of St. George's Church. The young Charles spent a peaceful childhood fishing and attending Sunday services, with a tender and caring mother to compensate for the severity of a father whose pastoral duties often kept him away from the family.[1] His religious vocation, Brent's biographies say, emerged rather early and quite naturally. After earning his Bachelor of Arts degree in 1887 at Trinity College, University of Toronto, at the age of 25, he was ordained priest of the Episcopalian Church and assigned to the parish of St. Andrew in Buffalo, New York; he would not return to Canada except for the occasional, sporadic family visits. In 1891, after a stay of a few months in England where, by chance, during a missionary service, he heard an Indian Quaker speak of problems related to the trafficking of opium, the time came for Brent to move to Boston, where he was called by Bishop Phillips Brooks to serve in St. Stephen's parish, the new location of the general headquarters of the city mission. It would be for Brent a true baptism by fire: the almost 30-year-old country pastor, who had recently left the Cowley Fathers, one of the most successful Protestant attempts at the coenobitic life imported directly from England in mid-century, would be catapulted into the heart of a metropolis where the economic development was leaving a heavy trail of inequality and social injustices. In Boston, for ten years Brent would personally experience the poverty of a proletariat reduced to misery and ghettoized, a situation that the first mass immigrations from Europe only served to intensify. There were problems tied to integration, political disorder, union disputes, and confessional tensions, which in Boston, as in any other large city on the East Coast, were accompanying the slow conquest of the public square by a Catholicism no longer in the minority, thanks to the contribution of the Irish and Italian immigrant communities.

The years in Boston were, in short, crucial ones in Brent's life. He was the apostle of a church still almost exclusively directed at a colonial elite who lived a gentrified life distant and isolated from the industrial peripheries. He found himself immersed in a wounded and suffering world where an entire

---

1   The unpublished documentation cited in this chapter all come from the Robert Gardiner Collection (series 23.0.003–23.0.014) conserved in the WCCA. In regard to Charles Brent, there is no more recent biography than that written in 1948 by Alexander Zabriskie, a close collaborator with Brent in the years of the development of Faith and Order. His profile of Brent is almost an epic: Alexander C. Zabriskie, *Bishop Brent: Crusader for Christian Unity*, Philadelphia PA, Westminster Press, 1948.

generation of Christians was beginning to recognize in the missionary impulse that united it the possibility of opening spaces for dialogue and cooperation among the churches. His reading of Frederick Denison Maurice introduced him to the problem of Christian division as a fracture that historically manifests itself in the social body of a given national community, and his friendship with the two Christian socialists William Dwight Bliss and Vida Scudder put him on the same wavelength as the turbulent panorama of the Social Gospel in which Brent found many of the friends that would help him in his lifelong ecumenical undertaking.[2]

It was a time of action, therefore, but also a time of great personal ascetic rigor, where being in close contact with the lowliest became a way for him to face the Christian vocation itself. In fact, two collections of writings and thoughts destined to make Brent's fortune among the general American public date back to his time in the Boston suburbs. These are *With God in the World*, printed in 1899, and *The Consolations of the Cross*, which, although published in 1904 when Brent was already in Manila, was a collection of Good Friday sermons delivered by the then pastor of St. Stephen's. His most mature and in some respects best-known work, *The Mount of Vision*, would be published in 1917 and be an appeal, less erudite but more spontaneous in its contrition, to experience the current war as an ordeal of expiation and conversion.[3]

---

2   He was also a member of the Christian Social Union, an interdenominational organization that collected field data to be provided to experts in economic and social matters, and a personal friend of Robert Woods, a leading man in the Settlement Movement that battled for housing and decent lodging for the migrants who crowded the outskirts of the country's large industrial cities; Mark D. Norbeck, "The Legacy of Charles Henry Brent," *IBMR* 20/4, 1996, 163. On the phenomenon of the Social Gospel and its impact on the ecumenical movement, see the contribution by Gary Dorrien in this volume.

3   Charles H. Brent, *With God in the World*, New York NY, Longmans, Green & Co., 1899; Charles H. Brent, *The Consolation of the Cross*, New York NY, Longmans, Green & Co., 1904; Charles H. Brent, *The Mount of Vision*, New York NY, Longmans, Green & Co., 1918.

The telegram in October 1901 informing him that the House of Bishops had chosen him to be bishop of the Philippines – a territory recently annexed to the United States after the Blitzkrieg against Spain in 1898 – caught the almost 40-year-old Brent completely unprepared. He had been a US citizen for ten years by then, and the news caused a good deal of confusion in the life of a man who considered himself lacking the preparation and the temperament needed to carry out such a task in a situation so far removed from the way in which he had imagined he would serve out the rest of his missionary ministry. The difference in the landscape in respect to his native Ontario, not to mention the climate, and the fact that at the time many Americans had become aware of the existence of these islands only thanks to the naval victory over the Spaniards in Manila Bay that was promptly flaunted by national propaganda, explain why Brent did not exult at the news of his appointment. If it is added, then, that the church entrusted to his care was a young and minute church in one of the most Catholic Asian nations, one can also understand why Brent took a month to communicate his formal acceptance of the assignment.

In any case, whether in a spirit of obedience or adventure, after being consecrated bishop on Dec 15, 1901, in May 1902 Brent was on his way to Southeast Asia in the company of the future president of the United States William Howard Taft, also newly appointed as governor of the Philippines. Before reaching their destination, the two stopped in Rome to allow Taft to negotiate with the Holy See about the fate of some missionary friars of whom the Philippine authorities wanted to free themselves at all cost because they saw in them the last reminder of the long Spanish domination. This was the first direct contact Brent had with the heart of Roman Catholicism and its rites, after which he was on his way to the Pacific, having before him all the time necessary to set down on paper the first draft of his pastoral program. As a first point, he listed the desire to cooperate with the American colonial government and to support its every effort. Secondly, he wanted to avoid any kind of collision with the Philippine Catholic Church and renounced any proselytism among the people. Third, Brent intended to open a fraternal dialogue with the Protestant communities already present on the islands, but not to endorse the proposal of dividing up the mission areas on a denominational basis. The fourth point was the commitment to take the Gospel to the non-Christians in those lands.[4]

From the moment he set foot in the Philippines, until January 1917, when he was recalled to New York to replace the recently deceased Bishop William Walker, it cannot be denied that Brent remained faithful to the brief program that he had written aboard the ship that was taking him to Manila. In those fifteen years he built his missionary church from almost nothing; he concerned himself with the religious and academic education of the children of diplomats sent from the United States; he travelled far and wide throughout the Philippines to establish new missions (such as those to the Muslims of the Sulu islands and the Igorots of Luzon); he travelled relentlessly by land and by sea in search of financial and political support for his war on opium trafficking – a battle that without the help of his friend Taft would never have reached the desk of President Theodore Roosevelt – or more simply to attend the annual general assemblies of the American Episcopal Church.[5]

It is not surprising, then, to find him in Edinburgh that summer of 1910 with, as an exceptional witness like the elderly Joseph Oldham always said,[6] a proposal in his pocket that would change the face of modern ecumenism; that is, the idea of launching a movement that would call upon the churches to discuss the points of doctrine that separated them.[7] In between there was a world

---

4 Zabriskie, *Bishop Brent*, 51–52.

5 There is no lack of studies on the episcopate of Brent in the Philippines and its legacy, however: Michael C. Reilly, "Charles Henry Brent: Philippine Missionary and Ecumenist," *Philippine Studies* 24/3, 1976, 303–325; Mark D. Norbeck, *The Protestant Episcopal Church in the City of Manila, Philippine Islands, from 1898 to 1918: An Institutional History*, M.A. thesis, University of Texas at El Paso, 1992; Emma J. Portuondo, *The Impact of Bishop Charles Henry Brent upon American Colonial and Foreign Policy (1901–1917)*, Ph.D. thesis, Catholic University of America, 1969, and Leon G. Rosenthal, *Christian Statesmanship in the First Missionary-Ecumenical Generation*, Ph.D. thesis, University of Chicago, 1989.

6 Charged with drafting the chapter on the IMC for the first edition of the *History of the Ecumenical Movement* and not finding any written testimony to the fact that, as many were claiming, it was Brent himself who proposed to the Edinburgh Assembly the calling of a new world conference on the themes of faith and order, Kenneth Latourette turned to the almost 80-year-old Oldman who had been secretary of the Edinburgh Assembly in 1910, when he was just over 30. Explaining that "stenographic resources in those days were very meagre," Oldham assured him in any case that he had no doubts that Brent personally made that proposal in one of those speeches that are hard to forget. Knowing well "the kind of man Bishop Brent was," Oldham added that he was immediately confident that "sooner or later something would happen." "Edinburgh 1910 and the International Missionary Council: Comments on the Chapter by Professor Latourette by Dr. J.H. Oldham," May 1950, in: WCCA, 23.4.031. Oldham's testimony, as will be seen below, would prove to be completely fallacious.

7 To reconstruct the origins of Faith and Order, one cannot of course ignore Tissington Tatlow, "The World Conference on Faith and Order," in: *A History of the Ecumenical Movement*, vol. 1, Ruth Rouse & Stephen C. Neill, eds., *1517–1948*, London, SPCK, 1954, 405–444. In reality, already in 1929, Lutheran pastor and theologian Hermann Sasse, the future comrade of Martin Niemöller and Dietrich Bonhoeffer, had edited the German edition of the acts of the Lausanne conference of 1927, writing a long introduction that reconstructed in detail the path followed by the movement from that point on. See Hermann Sasse, *Die Weltkonferenz für Glauben und Kirchenverfassung: Deutscher amtlicher Bericht über die Weltkirchenkonferenz zu Lausanne, 3.–21. August 1927*, Berlin, Furche-Verlag, 1929. To remain in Germany, Reinhard Frieling wrote the first significant monograph on the history of Faith and Order, even though this strictly focused on the contribution of evangelical German theology to the birth of the movement. See his *Die Bewegung für Glauben und Kirchenverfassung (1910–1937): Unter besonderer Berücksichtigung des Beitrages der deutschen evangelischen Theologie und der evangelischen Kirchen in Deutschland*, Göttingen, Vandenhoeck & Ruprecht, 1970. Two years later, but again in German, the first history of the origins of Faith and Order based on archival sources was published: Karl-Christoph Epting, *Ein*

war, which Brent experienced on the battlefields of France following the American expeditionary corps; however, unlike other noble fathers of the ecumenical movement, and many Christians in general, this experience does not seem to have marked in Brent's life a clear break, or produced a discernible sense of guilt for a tragedy that no one had been able to stop. In both his diaries and his war sermons, the theme of violence remained just beneath the surface of a pronounced sense of duty in regard to his country that never gave in either to a "painful" rhetoric or to truculent language against the enemy. The man that had left for the Philippines fifteen years earlier, convinced that he was doing his part in the "civilizing mission" that history had assigned to his country,[8] on June 28, 1917, addressed, from the turret of a canon, eleven thousand sailors of the Grand Fleet gathered at the Scapa Flow base without uttering a single word of hate and without abdicating for a second his task of speaking to the heart and souls of those soldiers. Perfectly at ease in his military uniform (and the numerous photographs from those years seem to prove this), he never let the man of the church be buried under ranks and insignia, either for his own part or in regard to his subordinates. During the months spent at the front, he served as a link between the YMCA active at the rear and the officials of the American army, but in his memoirs there is no evidence of that shock that assailed Nathan Söderblom when he was faced with the bloodshed by an entire generation of Christians thrown into the massacre.[9]

Brent's biography is without a doubt out of the ordinary, or perhaps it is similar in some ways to that of other Protestant saints of ecumenism, such as John Mott, Nathan Söderblom, George Bell, and Willem Visser 't Hooft. However, notwithstanding

the possible judgment concerning the need to trace forms, motives, and stylistic features of a certain ecumenical hagiography, the task of recounting the origins of Faith and Order now requires a few words dedicated to the biography of Brent's church, shared by the costar in this story: the indefatigable and at the same time less known Boston lawyer, Robert Hallowell Gardiner.

2 The Episcopal Church in America: High Church Concerns and the Ecumenical Movement

As a blossoming of the branch that the American Revolution cut off from England, the Protestant Episcopal Church in America, had, in the course of the 19th century, succeeded in rescuing itself from the weakened and marginal condition to which it had been relegated during the colonial period. Supported by an elite increasingly detached from strong religious visions, the Anglican component of North American Christianity had in fact grown with difficulty in the shadow of the more numerous and better organized Presbyterian and Congregationalist churches that, mindful of the conflicts with the bishops back in England, invoked every means of opposition to the institution of episcopates on Yankee soil. Things had been no better during the period of the Great Awakening in 1730–1740 that shifted the compass of religious life in the colonies towards a form of Christianity far removed from the traditional institutional structure. In the course of the 19th century, however, making inroads into the prejudices of the Puritans (who considered Episcopalians the unwanted remnants of Anglicanism) and taking advantage of the slow extinction of the second and significantly more radical awakening with the exhaustion of the expansionist drive westward, the Episcopal Church managed to maintain and increase its own strongholds in New England.[10] It was this very rediscovered missionary impetus

---

Gespräch beginnt: Die Anfänge der Bewegung für Glauben und Kirchenverfassung in den Jahren 1910–1920, Zürich, TVZ, 1972.

8   See Kenton J. Clymer, Protestant Missionaries in the Philippines (1898–1916): An Inquiry into the American Colonial Mentality, Urbana IL, University of Illinois Press, 1986.

9   Zabriskie, Bishop Brent, 131–132.

10   Raymond W. Albright, A History of the Protestant Episcopal Church, New York NY, Macmillan, 1964.

within the heart of a reality into which Europe had transplanted all its schisms intact that forced the Episcopal Church to face the problem of Christian unity.

There are at least three salient figures worth recalling here. The first is Reverend Thomas Hubbard Vail of Hartford, Connecticut, who in 1841 proposed a model of union that was far more advanced than the interdenominational approach that characterized the initiatives brought into play by the waves of evangelical revival. It was based, however, on a preestablished ecclesiastical structure, naturally that of the Protestant Episcopal Church, the only one to retain the *forma ecclesiae* suitable as a basis for unity because it included all three hierarchical levels of the clergy, the sole criterion for an authentic, visible unity.

The other prominent figure is William Augustus Muhlenberg, who, at the general meeting of the Episcopal Church in 1853, became the spokesperson of a group of priests who delivered to the assembly of bishops what history recalls as the Muhlenberg Memorial. The divisions of American Christians and a dangerous reflux of Roman Catholicism due to the first waves of migration from Europe led the petitioners to express the desire that the Episcopal Church become the lodestone of the attention of American Protestant Christianity. The Memorial thus asked the assembled bishops to prepare

> some ecclesiastical system, broader and more comprehensive than that which you now administer, surrounding and including the Protestant Episcopal Church as it now is, leaving that Church untouched, identical with that Church in all its great principles, yet providing for as much freedom in opinion, discipline, and worship as is compatible with the essential faith and order of the Gospel.[11]

One of the practical proposals put forward by the Memorial was the suggestion to extend the

authority of the bishops, who would be entrusted with ordaining ministers belonging to other churches besides their own.

However, it was above all after the Civil War that the question of Christian unity returned to the center of public discourse since it represented an alternative means of mending the fabric of American society. The first book by William Reed Huntington, entitled *The Church Idea: An Essay toward Unity*,[12] dates back to 1870. Here he assigned to the Protestant Episcopal Church the burden of gathering all Christians around itself to form what he called "the Catholic Church of America." The boundary of this church, from its strongly nationalistic connotation, would be set by four pillars: (1) Sacred Scripture; (2) the Nicene-Constantinopolitan symbol of faith; (3) the sacraments of Baptism and Eucharist; and (4) the episcopate as cornerstone of ecclesial governance.[13]

This was what the general convention of the Episcopal Church held in Chicago in 1886 distilled into a conception inspired by military strategy, the "quadrilateral," an expression that derives directly from the Italian Risorgimento and alludes to the complex of fortresses near Lake Garda with which the Austrians defended the Kingdom of Lombardy-Venetia.[14] Two years later, the Lambeth

---

11   Albright, *A History of the Protestant Episcopal Church*, 270–294.

12   William R. Huntington, *The Church Idea: An Essay toward Unity*, New York NY, Dutton, 1870.

13   Mark D. Chapman, "William Reed Huntington, American Catholicity and the Chicago-Lambeth Quadrilateral," in: Paul Avis & Benjamin M. Guyer, eds., *The Lambeth Conference: Theology, History, Polity and Purpose*, London, T&T Clark, 2017, 84–106. For a broader and more exhaustive treatment of Huntington, 19th century Anglican theology, and the problem of Christian unity, see the contribution by Paul Avis in this volume.

14   This use of military terminology to express religious concepts is not surprising: Huntington himself, after all, fond of the language that had become familiar after the American Civil War, had compared the confessions to old battleships and the creeds to cannons. This detail is related in Don Herbert Yoder, "Christian Unity in Nineteenth-Century America," in: *A History of the Ecumenical Movement*, vol. 1, 221–262, in particular 250–251.

Conference of 1888, which had by then already become the Anglican Communion, adopted the Chicago schema and decided to test it by discussing the suitability of opening its doors to the Swedish Lutheran Church precisely because it also boasted of an episcopal hierarchy and an uninterrupted apostolic succession.[15]

With the Chicago-Lambeth Quadrilateral, the Anglican Churches on both continents had therefore condensed their proposal for union into what could be called a kind of High Church manifesto based on the need to share an episcopal structure of apostolic succession and a sacramental life conforming to the Nicene-Constantinopolitan creed. It was a kind of suspension bridge over the Atlantic that allowed the Episcopalians to play on the same chessboard the ecumenical games that British Anglicanism was playing with Catholics, Old Catholics, and Orthodox.[16]

The special relationship that existed between the Anglicans of the Old and New World was not only a question of genetic makeup but of very precise historical processes. The core of the Episcopal Church inspired by the Oxford Movement that in the second half of the 19th century had borne overseas those very demands that had shaken the foundations of the Church of England: the claim of the Catholic continuity of the Anglican Churches,

the rediscovery of the authority of the Fathers, a return to the idea of revelation as the supreme source of religious knowledge, and, on the level of religious life, the defense of the sacred character of the episcopal office.[17]

It was, in short, an authentic High Church revival, or low papism, as its detractors called it, that affected the Episcopal dioceses of the East Coast and which ended up involving every aspect of ecclesial life, from theology, which rediscovered a strong interest in ecclesiology, to religious architecture, distinguished no differently than in Europe by a marked taste for the neo-Gothic style and a greater attention to liturgical principles in the architectural design of churches. However, it was the liturgy that caused the tensions between the Catholic and evangelical wings of the Episcopal Church to reach breaking point, since appeals to the *Book of Common Prayer* were not enough to stem the ritualistic wave that looked to contemporary Roman usage as a model to be brought back into vogue. The result was a war between gangs of bishops, fought with removals and minor schisms, which ended up seriously undermining the internal integrity of the Episcopal Church.[18]

An exemplary episode in this ritualistic war occurred in the diocese of Boston, the diocese most affected by the Anglo-Catholic currents coming from England, and concerned the Church of the Advent, a parish founded by a group of important people of the city in 1844, just four years after the appearance of the first tract in England. It had the aim of putting into practice the principles of the Oxford Movement. The public recitation of morning and evening prayer was hence revived, and the Eucharist was returned to its place as

---

15   John Robert Wright, ed., *Quadrilateral at One Hundred: Essays on the Centenary of the Chicago-Lambeth Quadrilateral (1886/88–1986/88)*, Cincinnati OH, Forward Movement Publications, 1988. The opening to the Swedish church had, in reality, already been discussed at the 1867 Lambeth Conference, when the Anglican Communion was founded, provoking the angry reaction of Edward Pusey who doubted the apostolicity of the Swedish bishops, given that they were Lutheran. Discussed again at the 1888 conference, the initiative ran aground again and only regained support in 1908 thanks to the initiative of Söderblom, who at the time was professor of the history of religions at the University of Uppsala. This is also discussed in Dietz Lange, *Nathan Söderblom und seine Zeit*, Göttingen, Vandenhoeck & Ruprecht, 2011, 182–204.

16   See Mark D. Chapman, *The Fantasy of Reunion: Anglicans, Catholics, and Ecumenism (1833–1882)*, Oxford, Oxford University Press, 2013.

17   George E. DeMille, *The Catholic Movement in the American Episcopal Church*, Philadelphia PA, Church Historical Society, ²1950. On the Oxford Movement and the figure of John Henry Newman, see the contribution by Peter Nockles in this volume.

18   This is the ritualistic war that DeMille spoke about and which occurred in two waves: the first in the 40s and the second in the 70s of the 19th century. See DeMille, *The Catholic Movement*.

the central act of worship on Sunday. The experiment, however, had a brief, troubled life: without even a pastoral visit, the newly installed bishop of Boston, Manton Eastburn, a member of the most intransigent evangelical wing, publicly denounced the papist rites that were being celebrated in the Church of the Advent and adopted strict measures against the clergy and parishioners.[19]

It was to be a struggle with a long aftermath, since there were also echoes of it forty years later in an episode in Brent's life, if it is true that the reason why he left Buffalo for Boston was a dispute with his bishop concerning some candles that he had decided to place on the altar of his church.[20] It is no coincidence that the Cowley Fathers were also in Boston. They were one of the few Anglican monastic orders that managed to take root in North America and with whom the 27-year old Brent spent three years, from 1888 to 1891. This male monastic order was generated thanks to Charles Chapman Grafton and Reverend Richard Meux Benson, two of the most fervent supporters of the Tractarian Movement, both advocates of a piety centering on devotion to the Eucharist. Together with a few others, they founded a male order based on a combination of the Benedictine and Dominican rules at Cowley, not far from Oxford. The members were bound by the three vows of poverty, chastity, and obedience.[21] In 1870, Grafton moved to Boston, one of the most Catholic cities in the United States, to continue what he had begun in England and to found a monastic community that closely followed the example of Cowley: the Society of St. John the Evangelist. It

took its name from the church where Grafton was now pastor and where he established the cœnoby. The man who took up the baton in America was Arthur Crawshay Alliston Hall, the future bishop of Vermont, a good friend of Brent's during the years he spent in the monastery and his contact during the incubation of Faith and Order.

This is enough to demonstrate how even a small, elitist entity such as the Cowley Fathers, which was furthermore a strictly minority complement to a church dominated by an ever-strong evangelical component in regard to the institution, could manage to make its own imprint on some of the most appreciated bishops of the next generation. This is because it would in fact be precisely the gradual loss of institutional leadership that would progressively condemn the evangelical party to a condition of inferiority within the Episcopal Church, which by that time, at the end of the century, was led by a generation of leaders completely freed from a sectarian mentality and reconciled to its historical and spiritual roots.

In conclusion, to maintain the geometric theme, the catalyst for one of the most ambitious and long-lasting expressions of the modern ecumenical movement thus had the form of a triangle, a "High Church triangle" that united the London suburb of Lambeth, Söderblom's Uppsala, and Brent's Boston.

3 Cincinnati 1919: Brent Sets the Project in Motion

Contrary to what Oldham affirmed, in neither of the two speeches by Brent in Edinburgh is there an allusion to the idea of a world conference on the themes of faith and order, and this is enough to bet on the possibility that age and memory had played a bad trick on the elderly former leader of the IMC.[22] After all, in the eyes of those who do

---

19   In 1856, the case was brought by his successor before the General Convention of the Episcopal Church of American which, as a countermeasure, urged its bishops to make more frequent visits to the parishes of their dioceses: DeMille, *The Catholic Movement*.

20   The episode occurred in 1887 when the newly ordained Charles Brent was serving at St. Andrew's Mission Chapel in Buffalo. There is an identical account of the incident in both Eleanor Slater, *Charles Henry Brent: Everybody's Bishop*, Milwaukee WI, Morehouse Pub. Co., 1932, and in Zabriskie, *Bishop Brent*, 24.

21   DeMille, *The Catholic Movement*, 135–141.

22   To learn in brief what Brent really said during the two addresses, see Brian Stanley's contribution in this volume.

not feel bound by any official chronology, it is not a problem if the evidence of the facts demands that we postpone for a few months the moment when clear talk of a great ecumenical conference on Christian doctrine was heard. What Brent probably merely alluded to in Edinburgh he clarified once and for all less than four months later, at the general convention of the Episcopal Church held in Cincinnati in October of 1910. The way in which the idea emerged at the margins of this assembly, while three friends were out for an evening stroll, is narrated with a good dose of the anecdotal by the Philadelphia lawyer George Wharton Pepper, one of the first to be involved in Brent's plans:

> One evening walking back from the convention hall to the hotel we three were reviewing the change of name controversy and the whole problem of Christian unity. Said the Bishop [Brent], "There never can be an approach toward unity until we all discuss our differences as well as our agreements. We must drag our differences out of the shadow and bring them into the sunlight." We all three stood still. "Why not agitate for that very thing?" I asked. "Why not advocate a World Conference on questions of Faith and Order" suggested Gardiner. "We cannot begin too soon," said the Bishop, "there is no time like the present; but we must make it clear that our purpose is to exclude the promotion of any scheme of unity and merely to create a better understanding by a frank discussion of different points of view."[23]

Something very specific justified the human and intellectual harmony that united these three highly aristocratic New England WASPs, and it was the fact of having actively served in the Social Gospel movement, an experience that for all three had refined their sensibilities and ability to take action against these problems, which

might urge the churches to operate beyond confessional barriers.[24] And if there were someone whose life would change forever that evening, it was precisely Robert Gardiner, who saw his office in Boston become, as he later told a reporter, "the unlikely center of a global movement." The amount of correspondence that in the space of fourteen years passed across his desk reached such a size as to lead *The New York Times* to speak of him as "the wielder of the largest religious correspondence that one man has ever conducted in America," while myths arose regarding his alleged gift of tongue, and the US post office was forced to provide him personalized services.[25]

One should not be surprised at this apparently unusual professional partnership: the Vincentian Fernand Portal would have been able to do very little for the Anglican-Catholic friendship without the collaboration of Charles Wood, second Viscount of Halifax, and, to cite perhaps the most improbable and least known couple, it is quite likely that Paul Couturier would not have belatedly voted for spiritual ecumenism without the advice for interpretation offered by the Lyon-based industrialist Victor Carlhian.[26]

---

23   George Wharton Pepper, *Philadelphia Lawyer: An Autobiography*, Philadelphia PA, J.B. Lippincott, 1944, 305.

24   The life, mission, and legacy of Gardiner, together with his existential commonalities with Brent, Pepper, and a number of other protagonists of American religious life at the beginning of the 20th century, are reconstructed in John Frederick Woolverton, *Robert H. Gardiner and the Reunification of Worldwide Christianity in the Progressive Era*, Columbia MO, University of Missouri Press, 2005.

25   Woolverton, *Robert H. Gardiner*, 7–8. Woolverton notes that at a certain point it seems that all it took in order for mail from any part of the world to reach him, it was enough to write on the envelope simply "Gardiner, USA." Gardiner wrote about himself, "I stand ready to give every ounce of the strength God gives me and every moment of the time I can spare from my duties to this work, which I consider the greatest opportunity that has ever been offered to a man for many centuries"; R.H. Gardiner to B.T. Rogers, Dec 31, 1910, in: WCCA, 23.0.012.

26   On the role of Carlhian in Couturier's ecumenical "conversion," see Étienne Fouilloux's contribution on Paul Couturier and spiritual ecumenism in the second volume of this work.

In any case, whether it is plausible or not (the clarity with which Brent already had in mind the features and purpose of the conference can only arouse some suspicion), Pepper's reconstruction of the nighttime chat at least clarifies the incisiveness with which the three friends decided to act before the conclusion of the Cincinnati meeting. Thus, on Oct 12, the then pastor of Trinity Church in New York, William Thomas Manning, offered to present to the assembly a draft resolution for the creation of a joint committee composed of seven bishops, seven presbyters, and seven lay people to promote and organize a conference that would bring together "all Christian bodies throughout the world which accept our Lord Jesus Christ as God and Savior, for the consideration of questions pertaining to the Faith and Order of the Church of Christ."[27] The first report was scheduled for 1913, but Brent wasted no time in showing the rest of the delegates that the newly formed preparatory commission already had a clear idea of what was to be done. The opportunity to illustrate better the proposal made the week before was given to him on Oct 19. For the commission to succeed in its intentions, Brent explained, this conference would have no legislative power, nor would its decisions be binding for the churches. For the moment, Brent clarified, with a phrase destined to make history in regard to Faith and Order, that the roots of unity are found "in the clear statement and full consideration of those things in which we differ, as well as of those things in which we are as one,"[28] which was all that was needed to keep the project going.

The resolution passed unanimously, and the new commission was able to meet for the first time the following day. It was made up of bishops Brent, Boyd Vincent (South Ohio), Thomas Gailor (Tennessee), Reginald Heber Weller (Fond du Lac), David Hummell Greer (Western New York), Frederick Joseph Kinsman (Delaware); of pastors Benjamin Talbot Rogers (Fond du Lac), Edward Lambe Parsons (Berkeley); and of the lay people Pepper, Samuel Mather (businessman from Cleveland), and Francis Lynde Stetson, attorney for the banker John Pierpont Morgan, who in his role as patron of the new ecumenical course taken by the Episcopal Church had already donated to the commission the sum of 100,000 dollars.[29] Since it was impossible for Brent to assume the leadership of the commission given his imminent return to the Philippines, George Zabriskie, a lawyer from New York, was elected president *ad interim*, and chose his colleague Gardiner as secretary.

Two decisions were made immediately: the first was the formation of a Committee on Plan and Scope under the chairmanship of Manning with Gardiner as secretary;[30] the second concerned the way in which the commission would spread the news to the other churches. One aspect, that of communication, which fell under the direct responsibility of Gardiner, soon became the most delicate point of the entire project. In fact, within a few weeks a press office was created, and in a short time the news of the conference began circulating in the principal religious newsletters of the United States. However, it was not until the end of 1910 that the decision was made to send a circular letter to all the bishops of North America to ask for their help in spreading the news, along with a special prayer for the success of the new enterprise.[31]

---

27   *Journal of the General Convention of the Protestant Episcopal Church in the United States of America: Held in the City of Cincinnati from October Fifth to October Twenty-First, Inclusive, in the Year of our Lord 1910*, New York NY, Winthrop Press, 1910, 310.

28   *Journal of the General Convention of the Protestant Episcopal Church*, 377.

29   The news and amount of the donation is also given in Tatlow, "The World Conference on Faith and Order," 382.

30   From this first subcommittee, one "on literature" emerged, concerned with promoting *ad hoc* publishing on the problems of ecumenism, and another on finances entrusted to Francis Lynde Stetson, a lawyer for J.P. Morgan, which would manage the accounts of the commission. See Tatlow, "The World Conference on Faith and Order," 377.

31   The circular letter, sent on Jan 11, 1911, turned out to be a total failure: of the 110 bishops addressed, only 12 replied. Gardiner blamed this failure on the scant

4   First Theological Problems

It was obvious that sooner or later the members
of the commission would begin to ask what kind
of unity they intended to build. In a letter to the
bishop of Chicago, Charles Palmerston Anderson,
Gardiner restricted himself to stating that the
motto of Faith and Order was the same as that
of Lambeth, "not compromise but understanding, not uniformity but unity," and that the scope
of the conference would be that of creating a
space for discussion and mutual comprehension
between the different churches and Christian
denominations.[32] Fortunately or unfortunately,
however, the theological issues were not left in the
hands of the lawyers.

The first to speak on this were Francis Joseph
Hall, professor at Western Theological Seminary,
and Newman Smyth, a prolific Episcopal theologian particularly sensitive to the theme of
intra-Protestant unity. The fuse that ignited a continual long-distance contrast in the early months
of 1911 was a meeting organized by Gardiner in
Boston in November 1910 on the theme "Value and
Limits of Federation." The title, however, must not
be misleading: the question of the model of unity
was in reality the pretext to tackle, in an exchange
of views wholly within the Episcopal theological milieu, the nucleus that was understandably
at the heart of a church with a long High Church
tradition: whether and to what degree to tie the
encounter with the nonepiscopal churches to
the preservation of a hierarchical order based on
the apostolic succession of bishops. Between the
two, the one that seemed to hold more intransigent standpoints seemed to be Hall, for whom the
hypothesis of a federation of churches would be
admissible only if it implied "a parity of ministries in all the bodies that accepted the scheme."[33]

However, after seeing and considering the weak
plausibility of such a concord, at least in the short
term, the federation was confirmed to be a model
of unity capable of operating only and exclusively
among churches with similar governmental structures. This was a solution that would certainly not
have made considerable progress in the ecumenical cause and would have, to the contrary, widened
to a greater extent the gap between Protestant
Churches and those of a Catholic tradition. For
Hall, finally, "the only unity that has real vitality is
one that is in some sense organic; because no other
unity brings its participants into the relations that
preserve intimate mutual understanding."[34] One
could define Hall as a representative of the more
markedly Catholic wing of the Episcopal Church:
he stated, in fact, that regardless of the model of
unity, "the Catholics" – as he called those who were
more commonly designated Anglo-Catholics –
would have the duty to preserve at all costs the
institution of the episcopal ministry.[35] Attracting
the Roman Catholic Church into the orbit of this
movement thus became in the eyes of Hall a natural and at the same time indispensable need, even
at the cost of isolating the Episcopalians from
the rest of the Protestant world. However costly,
Hall concluded, it was still the price to pay for
remaining faithful to a doctrine of the ministry
corroborated "by a truer and juster appreciation
of the real significance and value for humanity of
sacerdotal principles."[36]

Although he belonged to the same current as
Hall, Smyth took a far more pragmatic approach
to the issue. First of all, he rejected his colleague's
assertion that the *Prayer Book* contained a clear
reference to "the priestly doctrine of ministry," in
the sense that Hall intended it, or implied that
Anglican bishops could not ordain ministers
that did not share a specific conception of the
priesthood. What Hall took for a fact of Anglican
doctrinal heritage was perhaps nothing more than

publicizing commitment by the rest of the commission. Epting, *Ein Gespräch beginnt*, 58.

32   R.H. Gardiner to C.P. Anderson, Nov 15, 1910, in: WCCA, 23.0.03.

33   F.J. Hall to N. Smyth, Jan 9, 1911, in: WCCA, 23.0.007.

34   F.J. Hall to N. Smyth, Jan 9, 1911.

35   F.J. Hall to N. Smyth, Feb 18, 1911, in: WCCA, 23.0.007.

36   F.J. Hall to N. Smyth, Feb 18, 1911.

the historical product of a precise cultural influence, that which had come from the other side of the Atlantic along with the Tracts. To deny one's own belonging to Protestantism and to harden one's positions that in reality had never constituted the original doctrinal legacy of the Episcopal Church would mean closing a door in the face of all the other Protestant denominations, "and I must prefer to think that no man can close that door,"[37] Smyth concluded.

The final hope was that any form of unity, even one which included the Roman Catholic Church, would not take place on the basis of an abstract theory of priesthood and episcopal ministry, "but rather [would be realized] in the restoration of the more primitive Episcopate, in its universal recognition as expedient among other Christian communions, and ultimately ... in the protestant Episcopate, standing for the liberty of us all, [which would] have voice and power before the ... Episcopate of the Roman Church."[38]

Thus ended the first significant theological contest in the history of Faith and Order, and it is no wonder that it did not know how to go beyond a reexamination of the historical roots and the Protestant identity of North American Anglicanism. The news of this movement that was born in Cincinnati had not yet crossed the borders of the Episcopal dioceses on the East Coast, and the process of inclusion that in the space of twenty years would define the structure of Faith and Order, together with its agenda of themes, had just begun.

5   The Inclusion of the Other Churches (from Rome Down)

The balance of the confessional composition of Faith and Order was in the end a concern that arose from the outset, together with the awareness that the purpose and nature of the movement would depend largely on the specific weight given it by each confessional family.

The involvement of Rome immediately became an urgent issue with many implications: it would enable the conference to avoid taking on a pan-Protestant connotation, but at the same time it would risk alienating the sympathies of a great number of the churches born of the Reformation. The commission was certainly not short of plans: for Brent and Francis Hall, everything rested on having "the Anglican Communion at the back."[39] While Bishop Anderson wagered on the importance of predicting their opponent's moves, certain of the fact that if the Protestant churches managed to present themselves as a united front, perhaps even gaining the support of the Orthodox world, "the Roman Church [would] see that they must deal with the movement."[40]

What was missing perhaps was a real awareness of what the papacy in the meantime had become and of how, beyond the stereotypes, the Catholic Church approached the problem of Christian unity. It was thought that the pope's weakness was his fear of being isolated, when in reality the definitions of papal primacy and infallibility, the anti-Gallican obsession, and the ultramontane currents that circulated in the general climate of restoration at the end of the 19th century had by then crystallized the idea that the only possible unity was that of a single flock and a single supreme shepherd. Some mistakenly believed they could lure Rome with the purple of Anglican cassocks, but they forgot perhaps that the rejection of the writings of a Tractarian of the caliber of Edward Pusey in 1864, and the final word on the question

---

37   N. Smyth to F.J. Hall, Feb 21, 1911, in: WCCA, 23.0.007.

38   N. Smyth to F.J. Hall, Feb 21, 1911.

39   J. Hall to R.H. Gardiner, Oct 14, 1912, in: WCCA, 23.0.007. The attitude of the Anglicans, Brent claimed, "will tend to influence both the Roman and the Orthodox Greek Churches"; C.H. Brent to R.H. Gardiner, Aug 31, 1911, in: WCCA, 23.0.02.

40   C.P. Anderson to R.H. Gardiner, Aug 7, 1911 in: WCCA, 23.0.003. This was a strategy with which Peter Ainslie of the Disciples of Christ was also in full agreement: see P. Ainslie to R.H. Gardiner, Apr 11, 1914, in: WCCA, 23.0.003.

of Anglican orders spoken by *Apostolicae curae* in 1896, revealed the suspicion with which the Holy See regarded the attempts at reconciliation that derived from the Anglican world.[41] Only with difficulty, therefore, would the strategy to present itself as a compact block of Protestant Churches be successful in the game with the Church of Rome, since the latter was far from agreeing with the idea of playing an active role in the issue of unity and thus also of being only one of the parties taking part.

In any case, the first contact with the Roman Catholic Church was by means through the channel that Rev. Manning opened in April 1911 with the archbishop of Baltimore and primate of the United States, Cardinal James Gibbons. The cardinal was presented with the salient points in the project and, according to Manning, the relationship immediately proved to be "non-committal, but distinctly interested and friendly."[42]

At first, no one doubted the feelings of Cardinal Gibbons, but few were convinced that these were enough to ensure the direct involvement of Rome in the conference. Gardiner was certainly one of these; having always considered the involvement of the Catholics a priority, he decided to become involved personally. On Dec 3, 1913, he managed to extract from Gibbons the commitment to present the case to Rome with the promise that the confession of apostolic faith would be inserted among the discussion points of the conference.[43] Gardiner's move seemed to suddenly reopen the contest: six months later, Manning obtained from John Farley, the cardinal of New York, the promise that, during a trip to Europe scheduled for the end of 1914, a delegation of the commission could visit

the apostolic palace and meet certain members of the curia in order to present their project.[44]

Not everyone, however, was in a hurry to rejoice. Reverend Smyth, for example, felt obliged to warn Gardiner of the dangers of a "useless courtship of Rome" that would only end up irritating the great majority of Protestants in exchange for nothing as far as relations with the Catholic Church were concerned. In relations with Rome, one could never be too prudent, particularly if you did not want to find yourself regretting, when all was said and done, having taken for certainties what in reality were only the vague promises of some Roman cardinal.[45]

Meanwhile, against all odds, the support of the Anglican Communion was proving to be anything but predictable. There was, in fact, the need to dispel the doubts and prejudices of the English in regard to the advisability of putting themselves on an equal footing with Protestant Churches that lacked an episcopal structure and apostolic succession. On the other hand, there were those who had not forgotten the harassment suffered in the past "at the hands of the established church," and who considered "any theory of apostolic succession" little more than superstition.[46] This forced the

---

41   On this, see Paul Avis's contribution in this volume.

42   W.T. Manning to R.H. Gardiner, May 31, 1911, in: WCCA, 23.0.011. It was also Manning who maintained a relationship also with the Archbishop of New York John Farley, who interviewed him on the subject in May 1914 (see W.T. Manning to R.H. Gardiner, May 5, 1914, in: WCCA, 23.0.011). Manning also dealt with the distribution in Catholic circles of the first printed material from the preparatory commission.

43   R.H. Gardiner to G.W. Pepper, Dec 3, 1913, in: WCCA, 23.0.015.

44   Among the conditions dictated to Manning by Farley, the possibility of an audience with Pius X was not even contemplated. The delegates would simply inform the ecclesiastical authorities of the initiative "without asking any definite expression from them but simply leaving the matter before them for their consideration"; W.T. Manning to R.H. Gardiner, May 18, 1914, in: WCCA, 23.0.011. The prohibition of presenting to the Holy See a formal invitation to the conference did not bother Gardiner too much because it permitted the commission not to lose face before a certain refusal on the part of the pope: R.H. Gardiner to P. Ainslie, Apr 15, 1914, in: WCCA, 23.0.003.

45   N. Smyth to R.H. Gardiner, Feb 17, 1914, in: WCCA, 23.0.007.

46   The Methodist Edwin H. Hughes wrote again in 1918, commenting on the proposals for Faith and Order with a mixture of skepticism and irony: "Now how in the name of High Heaven, can we get together at all with a barrier like this standing between us? I know that the suggestion is made that the question of order must not now be discussed. In other words, we are asked not to

commission to intensify contact with the British Isles: a number of meetings between Episcopalians and members of the Anglican Communion took place in the summer of 1912 and only ended when, in October, the archbishop of Canterbury was talked into forming a special commission with the task of coordinating the participation of the Anglican Churches in the American project.

However, this was not enough for the commission to consider its work in the kingdom of George V over. No contact was yet established, in fact, with the Puritan and nonconformist communities, i.e. with all the forms of Low Church Protestantism in the British Isles. Consequently, the first decision of the Inter Commission Conference on May 8, 1913, in New York was to organize a mission to the non-Anglican churches in Great Britain "to secure their co-operation in the movement."[47] The delegation set sail from the United States on New Year's Eve of 1913 and set foot in England on Jan 7 of the new year. The first appointment was with the press; then, on Jan 9, American delegates met, in London, a delegation of the National Council of the Evangelical Free Churches, and, on the 16th, in Edinburgh, they had a meeting with 150 representatives of the Scottish and Irish Presbyterian Church. In regard to personal contacts, Peter Ainslie, of the Disciples of Christ, met representatives of the English Quakers and of the Moravian Church, while Rev. Smyth found time for courtesy visits to the bishop of Oxford and the archbishop of Canterbury.

They did not encounter any great resistance; rather, the American delegates were surprised to see how their visit had in some way facilitated an easing of tensions in the relationship between the Church of England and the non-Anglicans. These are the words that Ainslie sent to Gardiner upon his return from his mission in the United Kingdom:

The non-Anglicans have expressed themselves cordially relative to their desire for cooperation with the Church of England, and in no non-Anglican conference have we heard any remarks other than those of courtesy toward and fraternity for the Church of England. On the other hand, the Church of England, in its expression to us, has been quite as gracious relative to the non-Anglicans. We have been glad to bear these messages from one to another, and this is a far more delicate matter than anything that exists in America.[48]

Contacts with the German evangelical churches turned out, on the contrary, to be slower and more difficult, due also to the intensification of the preludes to war. The best ally that Gardiner had in Germany at that time was undoubtedly Friedrich Siegmund-Schultze, whom he met in August 1914 at Constance during the meeting of the WA. This was when all 85 delegates, after what could not exactly be called a leisure trip among deployed armies and border checkpoints, had to hurriedly pack their bags as soon as the telegraphs began to transmit the rebound of declarations of war by one European chancellery after the other.[49] However, it was one thing to assure the support of a Lutheran theologian of proven pacifist spirit and quite another to win the hearts of the leaders of the German churches.[50]

---

discuss at all the most dreadful line of cleavage. Can we make progress by silence that is far more adroit than it is religious?"; E.H. Hughes to R.H. Gardiner, Apr 6, 1918, in: WCCA, 23.0.07.

47   Epting, *Ein Gespräch beginnt*, 116.

48   P. Ainslie to R.H. Gardiner, Apr 4, 1914, in: WCCA, 23.0.003.

49   On the meeting at Constance and on the Christian-inspired pacifist movements prior to and after World War I, see Gerhard Besier's contribution in this work. The contribution of Siegmund-Schultz to the birth of Faith and Order has been reconstructed in Frieling, *Die Bewegung*.

50   Siegmund-Schultze himself had in any case alerted Gardiner to the possibility that his project would struggle to make headway among the German ecclesiastical leaders. He wrote the following, commenting on the chance that the leading figures of the evangelical churches in the Reich would gather in Berlin to meet Gardiner: "I do not hope that people of other

In spite of the intense correspondence in 1911 between Gardiner and Bodo Voigts, president of the DEKA, on Mar 12, 1912, the evangelical churches of the Reich only expressed a vague interest in what was being prepared across the Atlantic, demonstrating that they saw it as a project with markedly Anglo-American traits and interests. This impression was confirmed at the meeting of the DEKA two years later when Hermann von Zeller, the president of the assembly, expressed unequivocally that the Faith and Order project was not applicable to the religious situation in Germany: "The idea of a world conference on faith and order is the result of the attitude that the Americans usually have towards their ecclesial divisions," he said. Further, showing that he had, perhaps, not completely understood that the objective of the conference was to go beyond a simple interdenominational repacification, he specified that "in Germany there are already fraternal relationships among the various *Landeskirchen*."[51] Von Zeller in any case considered the desire to solve doctrinal questions as if they were simple diplomatic quarrels an illusion: "The problems regarding doctrine and the church cannot be imposed through union negotiations." He treated the idea of modifying the confessions of faith as if it were offensive. In the end, the Kirchenauschusse supported von Zeller's position and adopted an attitude in regard to Faith and Order that the assembly protocol defined as "a wait-and-see position."[52] Seven months later, the outbreak of war would put on ice what a combination of theological reasons and political prejudices had already cooled.

To establish ties to the Orthodox world, on the other hand, the commission availed itself again of Manning's personal contacts with the metropolitan of New York, Platon, who for his part was responsible for contact with the Holy Russian Synod. Although the Archbishop's Eastern Churches Committee in Canterbury guaranteed an institutional channel of communication with the complex Orthodox world, for the Americans, there was still no better approach than a direct one: in May 1913, therefore, the formal desire was expressed for a special delegation to go to Russia as soon as possible, and that then, with a list of churches and important Orthodox people to meet in hand, it would travel far and wide throughout the Near East and Europe to visit all four patriarchates. The group was not to return before it had visited Rome where, according to the promises of Archbishops Gibbons and Farley, they would find some eminent cardinal in the curia ready to receive them.

The proposal was quickly accepted by the Executive Committee, a recently instituted body with the task of putting into effect the decisions of the preparatory commission, which, on Mar 10, 1914, named Anderson, Rhinelander, Brent, and Rev. Manning as members of the delegation to be sent to Europe.[53] The hopes and expectations of the commission placed on this first official voyage to the most ancient Christian churches are contained in this message by Gardiner to one of his English collaborators:

> In the unanimous judgment of our Commission, the time has now come when, in accordance with the instructions laid upon us, the Catholic World must be definitely and formally notified of the movement or these Communions will have the right to feel that they have not been shown due consideration and they have not been given opportunity

---

      places as D. Dibelius, President von Zeller, D. Hartwig or D. Kaftan would come also to such a meeting here in Berlin. The interest for the union work is not yet strong enough in Germany"; F. Siegmund-Schultze to R.H. Gardiner, July 23, 1914, in: WCCA, 23.0.007.

51   Frieling, *Die Bewegung*, 29–30.
52   Frieling, *Die Bewegung*, 29–30.

53   Rev. Chauncy Brewster, Gardiner, and Mott were added to these four in April because of their vast and consolidated relationships with Europe. R.H. Gardiner to W.T. Manning, Mar 30, 1914, in: WCCA, 23.0.011. Like Brent, Mott also preferred to not join the group because of prior commitments.

to participate in the movement from its beginning.[54]

According to the plans, the delegation was to leave at the end of the summer. However, on Aug 5, 1914, with Europe having already been immersed in war for forty-eight hours, Gardiner sent a telegram from Konstanz with the three words: "Deputation trip impossible."[55]

6 Waiting for Peace

The outbreak of a war of unpredictable duration and outcome would usually be enough to discourage anyone from undertaking any long-term project, that is, anyone not called Robert Gardiner. On Aug 14, the Boston lawyer wrote: "I think the suspension may be good for our project if we will now take time for the careful thought and efficient planning, which we have hitherto neglected, and this dreadful war will make men eager for every kind of peace and make us see that only Christ can rule the world."[56]

One of the aspects to which the commission paid more attention during the war was surely the relationship with Rome. The first official contact with the Holy See was, in fact, on Nov 2, 1914, and was established by means of a letter that Gardiner sent to the Cardinal Secretary of State Pietro Gasparri.[57] For the next three years, the two men, in point of fact, were restricted to a correspondence of generic content and formal tones; Gardiner updated the secretary of state on the progress of the commission, asking each time for the pope to pray "pro Congressu totius orbis de Fide et Constitutione Ecclesiae,"[58] and Gasparri never tired of ensuring "exhortationem, suffragium, fervidasque precem Romani Pontificis"[59] for the work underway. For three years, they discussed the expected return of peace and the urgency of reinstating unity in the church of Christ, without either of them raising any controversial issue or Gardiner finding the words to ask the most important thing, i.e. that the Holy See endorse the participation of Catholics in the movement. For the time being, Gardiner's aim was to keep Rome's interest in Faith and Order alive and to give his colleagues on the preparatory commission the impression that he was only waiting for the right moment to take an official step.[60]

Things took on a faster pace only on June 14, 1917, when, prompted by Brent, the commission discussed the possibility of rescheduling the mission to Rome, Russia, and the Eastern patriarchates after the end of the war. However, if the road to Rome seemed to be clear of obstacles, thanks to the confidence vaunted by Gardiner concerning the reassurances of his Vatican contacts,[61] Russia's difficult political and military situation soon forced the commission to consider matters with greater caution: with the Kerensky government in its death throes, and with the rout

54 R.H. Gardiner to T. Tatlow, May 21, 1914, in: WCCA, 23.0.013.

55 On Aug 7, Manning notified Ralph Brown of the telegram received by Gardiner, in: WCCA, 23.0.011.

56 R.H. Gardiner to C.B. Brewster, Aug 13, 1914, in: WCCA, 23.0.009. Gardiner found a supporter in Roberts, who wrote on Sept 18: "I regard the war as a reason for continuance of the work of preparation. We should go forward with the work, without reference to difficulties and obstacles, with increasing faith in God"; W.H. Roberts to R.H. Gardiner, Sept 18, 1914, in: WCCA, 23.0.006.

57 The correspondence between Gardiner and Gasparri from 1914 to 1917 amounted to ten letters, all scrupulously written in Latin and then translated into English.

58 R.H. Gardiner to P. Gasparri, June 9, 1917, in: WCCA, 23.0.010.

59 P. Gasparri to R.H. Gardiner, Apr 7, 1915, in: WCCA, 23.0.010.

60 "The iron is pretty hot and if we don't strike it now, we may lose our chance," Gardiner wrote at a certain point; R.H. Gardiner to C.P. Anderson, June 1, 1917, in: WCCA, 23.0.003.

61 Gardiner wrote in July to a member of the commission: "There are very many indications that we shall have a favorable reception in Rome. Even if we should fail entirely, the fact that the effort was made would have immense value"; R.H. Gardiner to B. Vincent, July 5, 1917, in: WCCA, 23.0.013.

of the Russian army expected at any time, it was President Woodrow Wilson himself who ordered a postponement of the mission until the political picture in Petersburg became clearer and more reassuring.[62]

In England, meanwhile, a special team under the supervision of the archbishop of Canterbury met regularly certain representatives of the free churches of the United Kingdom. In March 1916, the first *Ad Interim Report* was issued, which clearly spoke of the need to construct a visible unity of the churches and which established some firm points in regard to questions of a doctrinal and institutional nature.[63] Having never hidden the fact that he considered the Church of England a valid presence in Europe and a natural bridge with Rome and the Eastern Orthodox, Gardiner made every effort to ensure that the experience gained by the Anglicans in bilateral dialogues would be taken up by Faith and Order. Capitalizing on what the Anglican Church had accomplished in the past towards Rome had very likely been Gardiner's greatest concern if, in 1917, he already hoped that the question of ordinations would be at the top of the agenda of the conference.[64] With his ear straining to capture the slightest movement between the two sides of the English Channel, Gardiner certainly did not have any difficulty intercepting the network of contacts that was forming around Portal and Lord Halifax, even though he never managed to break through the Roman blockade by other means, or take credit for the start of the Malines Conversations.[65]

While awaiting peace to return to Europe, the movement was also making progress in its internal organization. In the meantime, an Advisory Committee had been set up, and in 1916 unanimously passed a proposal to organize a preparatory conference, a kind of general rehearsal, as soon as the war ended. The purpose of this meeting was to be the examination of "what steps should be undertaken so that the movement for the World Conference could take full advantage of the situation present at the end of the war."[66]

Zabriskie, on the other hand, proposed setting up a North American Preparation Committee to assist the commission in the preparation of the conference and lighten its workload. Zabriskie had to work hard in order for the rest of the group to set aside their fear of an "Americanization of the movement," but in the end his motion passed.[67]

In short, there was a widespread awareness that peace would open up new scenarios for the churches and that they should be ready for its return. Less than a week after the Compiègne armistice, Gardiner wrote to Bishop Boyd Vincent: "This is a crucial time for the World Conference movement and for the Christian religion. If the differing Christian churches can only manifest their unity, the voice of the Church will be efficient in establishing the new order of things; but if the churches remain divided and therefore voiceless, nothing permanent can be hoped for."[68]

---

62   See Epting, *Ein Gespräch beginnt*, 237–238.

63   The text of the document is provided by Epting, *Ein Gespräch beginnt*, 355–357.

64   These were Gardiner's hopes: "The whole question of Orders must be discussed at the World Conference, and it would seem much more probable that permanent results would be reached if that discussion begins at the beginning and is carried on by representatives of the Roman, Eastern, and Anglican Churches and the various Protestant churches"; R.H. Gardinert to C.H. Brent, Jan 15, 1917, in: WCCA, 23.0.003.

65   There is consistent evidence of his correspondence with Portal and Halifax, with Cardinal Desiré-Joseph

Mercier and with Pierre Batiffol. Especially with Mercier and Portal, however, the correspondence does not seem to go beyond a simple exchange of opinions and news on each other's initiatives.

66   Epting, *Ein Gespräch beginnt*, 217.

67   Almost one hundred people were asked to take part in the North American Preparation Committee by a commission established for this purpose that met on Dec 13, 1915. See Epting, *Ein Gespräch beginnt*, 314–315 and R.H. Gardiner to G. Zabriskie, Nov 21, 1916, in: WCCA, 23.0.013.

68   R.H. Gardiner to B. Vincent, Nov 16, 1918, in: WCCA, 23.0.013.

7 "Like Babes into the Woods": Five Pilgrims on a European Trip

With the return of peace, the commission wasted no time. At the meeting on Dec 5, 1918, it was decided that a delegation would leave for Europe as soon as possible, already at the beginning of the new year.[69] The group was to include Bishops Charles Anderson, Boyd Vincent, and Reginald Weller, and the Pastors Edward Parsons and Benjamin Rogers, but not Manning or Gardiner, the latter fearing that he would be out of place in a delegation of ecclesiastics. He therefore limited himself to entrusting to God the fate of those who – in his eyes – were setting out "like babes into the woods."[70]

The transatlantic liner Aquitania, with the five aboard, set sail from New York on Mar 6, 1919, and, after a little over a week's crossing, anchored in Liverpool. From England, the group proceeded to Paris and then to Athens, where they were to meet the metropolitan of the Greek Orthodox Church at the beginning of April, inviting him to participate in the conference. From Athens, the group went to Constantinople to speak to the Holy Synod, thus securing the support of the Ecumenical Patriarchate. From there, they headed for Rome, first making stops in Sofia, Bucharest, and Belgrade. Finally, on May 16, the delegation had an audience with the pope. Needless to say, Gardiner had laid the groundwork in the best possible way: all the major Italian newspapers had been informed of the visit, and the delegates took a letter to the pope that had been carefully prepared in the preceding months.[71]

The meeting held no surprises, however. Benedict XV cordially and respectfully welcomed the delegates and expressed his best wishes for the initiative's success, but the written request to send "prestantissimos Romanae Ecclesiae legatos" to the conference was soundly rejected. The only official record of that visit is the statement that the group issued to the Associated Press on leaving the Apostolic Palace:

> The deputation had an audience with the Pope and Cardinal Gasparri. The Pope stated that it would not be possible for the Roman Catholic Church to take part in the World Conference. The deputation regrets that the Roman Catholic Church will not be represented, as substantially all the rest of Christendom has promised to cooperate. Preparations for the Conference will proceed and the deputation will continue its work until invitations have been presented to those Communions which it has hitherto not been possible to reach.[72]

The outcome of that long-awaited and carefully prepared audience did not really surprise anyone. "It was perfectly clear that the answer was ready long before we got to Rome,"[73] Anderson declared, updating Gardiner on the papal visit. Brent offered the following comment to the Episcopal Church's newspaper: "Rome had the opportunity to present the best aspect of papism to the Christianity

---

69 See "Minutes Com," Dec 5, 1918, and R.H. Gardiner to W.T. Manning, Nov 11, 1918 in: WCCA, 23.0.011. The text of the pamphlet sent in this regard by Gardiner and Manning to the rest of the Executive Committee can be found in Epting, *Ein Gespräch beginnt*, 320.

70 Gardiner's reasons are explained better in his letter to B. Rogers of Dec 19, 1918, and the latter's reply dated Dec 30, 1918, (WCCA, 23.0.012). "I feel as the Deputation were going off like babes into the woods but perhaps the Lord will take care of them," Gardiner had confessed to Zabriskie a few days before the group's departure; R.H. Gardiner to G. Zabriskie, Feb 13, 1919, in: WCCA, 23.0.013.

71 R.H. Gardiner to B.T. Rogers, Apr 1, 1919, in: WCCA, 23.0.012. The text of the letter in Latin that was intended for Benedict XV and its relative drafts are preserved together with the correspondence exchanged by Gardiner with Cardinal Gasparri; WCCA, 23.0.010.

72 The text of the declaration is also in Epting, *Ein Gespräch beginnt*, 263.

73 C.P. Anderson to R.H. Gardiner, May 27, 1919, in: WCCA, 23.3.003.

gathered there. Instead, it decided beforehand to present its worst aspect."[74]

In Rome, the delegation split up. Anderson, Vincent, and Parsons went north while Bishop Weller and Pastor Rogers went east.

The first three returned to Paris where they met with Wilfried Monod for the final agreements on the participation of French Protestants. They then went to London and set off for Scandinavia. In Oslo, they obtained the Norwegian Lutheran Church's agreement to participate and then, in Sweden, they met Söderblom in Uppsala. Germany remained inaccessible due to its diplomatic isolation, and there was not enough time to visit Denmark, Finland, or the Netherlands. In June, having arrived back in England, the three returned to the United States.

Meanwhile, at the end of May, Weller and Rogers had set off from Naples for Alexandria where they were received by Patriarch Photius. From here, they continued their journey to Cairo, where the patriarch of the Copts awaited them; then they went to Jerusalem, escorted by General Edmund Allenby's occupying troops. On June 4, heading back to Cairo, the two stopped in Damascus to meet the patriarch of Antioch, Gregory.[75] Back in England, they found time for a brief visit to the archbishop of Canterbury, and then the pair retook to the sea for their journey back to New York, where they landed on July 22.

Great fervor and enthusiasm awaited the two delegations on their return. The commission was convinced of having achieved an unimaginable success, reaching the whole of Christianity and gathering praise and support almost everywhere. Gardiner said it was further confirmation of the fact that the conference "must be supported by the whole body of the Christian world, and not simply

by a number of ecclesiastics, however saintly and distinguished they may be."[76]

8   The Preparatory Conference of Geneva in 1920

The dress rehearsal of what would be Faith and Order's inaugural conference was held in Geneva from Aug 10 to 20, 1920,[77] the ecumenical movement's *annus mirabilis*. In January of that year, the great multinational empires having disappeared from the world's maps, the Ecumenical Patriarchate of Constantinople had, in fact, taken the stage, issuing the encyclical *Unto the Churches of Christ Everywhere*.[78] Also in 1920, from June 21 to 28, near Geneva, John Mott had convened a meeting of the Continuation Committee – the body established ten years earlier to carry out the work initiated in Edinburgh in 1910.[79] Then, between July and August, the decennial Lambeth Conference took place, and the world heard its *Appeal to All Christian People*, which called upon the churches to make efforts toward unity that might atone for the sins of the war. Finally, still in the summer of 1920 and near Geneva, Söderblom presided over what Samuel McFarland, Secretary General of the FCCC in America, defined as "the most important of all meetings" in the history of Life and Work.[80] It was, in fact, at the closing of that meeting on

---

74   Charles Henry Brent, "The Imperative of Unity," *The Living Church*, June 21, 1919, 264–269, here 267.

75   *Report of the Deputation from the World Conference Commission to Egypt, Palestine and Syria*, 16–17, cited in: Epting, *Ein Gespräch beginnt*, 265.

76   R.H. Gardiner to S. Mather, May 19, 1919, in: WCCA, 3.0.005.

77   For details regarding the convocation, see the letters: R.H. Gardiner to C.P. Anderson, Oct 27, 1919, and Nov 15, 1919, in: WCCA, 23.0.003.

78   Theodoros A. Meimaris, *The Holy and Great Council of the Orthodox Church and the Ecumenical Movement*, Thessaloniki, Stamoulis, 2013 (an English translation of the encyclical is given in the appendix, 248–252). See Stylianos Tsompanidis's contribution in this volume.

79   See the contribution by Kenneth Ross in this volume.

80   Charles Stedman Macfarland, *Steps Toward the World Council: Origins of the Ecumenical Movement as Expressed in the Universal Christian Council for Life and Work*, New York NY, F.H. Revell, 1938.

Aug 12, that the decision was made to inaugurate within five years the first "Universal Christian Conference."[81]

Two days earlier, as mentioned above, Faith and Order's preparatory conference had begun at the Athénée in Geneva. Directorship of the works was entrusted to Brent who, in the meantime, had returned from the Philippines to take up the position of bishop of the Diocese of Western New York.[82]

Gardiner's efforts to remedy the absence of an official delegation from Germany, which had been punished by the peace Treaty of Versailles, were of little use. There were only a few members of the German Lutheran Churches who attended the conference, and, moreover, they were there in an unofficial capacity.[83]

From the point of view of the content and tendency of the discussions, the decisive factor was once again the predominance of the Anglican component, which by far dominated the Lutheran, Reformed, and Orthodox contingents. Ecclesiological matters monopolized the debate and, when the time came to discuss the issue of "The Church and the Nature of the United Church," a taut contrast took place between the former Anglican Bishop of Oxford Charles Gore, a strong supporter of the Tractarian principles, and the Historian James Bartlet of the English Congregationalist Church. The former, from an Anglo-Catholic position, did not allow exceptions to the principle that unity requires "certain conditions of validity with regard to sacraments and ministry,"[84] while the latter invited the churches of Catholic tradition to consider "whether a new and different attitude to the ancient formulations may not be allowable, as at present in churches which emphasize the experimental aspects of faith, professed in terms of a direct personal relation established between the soul and God in Christ."[85]

Fortunately, under Brent's guidance, the conference also managed to make some practical decisions. Following the example of what Life and Work had effected a few days earlier, a Continuation Committee was also created for Faith and Order "with the duty of carrying on the work of preparation for the World Conference or Conferences on Faith and Order, correspondence and cooperation with the Commissions of the various communions, fixing the time and place of a Conference, and performing all such other duties as may be necessary to arrange for the Conference."[86]

It was the first truly plural body in the history of Faith and Order. Indeed, 51 people of Anglican, Baptist, and Congregationalist extract were invited to participate along with representatives from the Moravian Church, the Disciples of Christ, Eastern Orthodox, the Society of Friends, the German Evangelical Churches, Lutherans, Methodists, Old Catholics, Presbyterians, and the Reformed Churches. Brent was elected president and Gardiner secretary.[87] Thus the passing of the torch that the commission appointed in Cincinnati had hoped and prepared for since 1910 finally took place. The conference's organization was now in the hands of a truly international and metaecclesial committee.

81 This topic is widely dealt with in Dietz Lange's contribution in this volume.

82 World Conference on Faith and Order, ed., *Report of the Preliminary Meeting at Geneva, Switzerland, August 12–20, 1920: A Pilgrimage toward Unity*, Continuation Committee, 1920.

83 Besides Siegmund-Schultze, the delegation was made up of August W. Schreiber, Heinrich G.W. Mosel, Otto-Reinhard Roth, Walter Schmidt, and Hans Fliedner; see Frieling, *Die Bewegung*, 35–36.

84 World Conference on Faith and Order, ed., *Report of the Preliminary Meeting*, 41.

85 World Conference on Faith and Order, ed., *Report of the Preliminary Meeting*, 47–48.

86 World Conference on Faith and Order, ed., *Report of the Preliminary Meeting*, 73.

87 The complete list of those elected is reported in World Conference on Faith and Order, ed., *Report of the Preliminary Meeting*, 83–87.

9   Notes on the Agenda

The Continuation Committee's first meeting was held on the day after the Geneva meeting. Its purpose was to establish a possible agenda for the first Faith and Order conference, and it was decided to do so with the assistance and involvement of the churches. A Subjects Committee – appointed at that time and entrusted to the leadership of Edwin James Palmer, the Anglican bishop of Bombay – sent the churches various questionnaires in order to identify an order of issues to be discussed. These were a series of questions mainly focusing on matters of an ecclesial nature (issues of ministry and the historical episcopate were the themes that received the most attention), which ended up disappointing both the expectations of those who had written them and of those who, from every corner of the world, found themselves having to answer them. Heading into a new meeting that the Subjects Committee was to hold in Oxford in September 1923, it was Gardiner himself who communicated to Palmer the not entirely satisfactory outcome of this first round of consultations.

> One of the criticisms of the questions is that they are dry and unimaginative. There is no mention of that which is the centre of life and the foundation of the movement – the Incarnation of the Son of God. ... The criticism has been made, which we think entirely unjustified, that the questions presuppose Anglican answers. That comes from the presupposition, which we have had to encounter from the beginning, that the whole movement is intended to make converts to Anglicanism.[88]

Once again, the movement was urged to overcome its Anglican bias and to fall in line with the plurality of churches and confessional traditions that it now encompassed.

No one can deny the commitment with which, in the following four years, the Faith and Order offices focused on discussing a working agenda under the pressure of the countdown that had been started in Stockholm in 1925, when the Continuation Committee slated the conference that was to launch the movement to take place in Lausanne in the summer of 1927.[89]

Between 1923 and 1925, the Subjects Committee had already invited the churches to express themselves on three other series of questions regarding the themes of the ministry, the church, the sacraments, and Christian morality, gathering a fair number of responses. On the basis of these, in July 1925, the Subjects Committee drew up a detailed report of the consultation along with a possible agenda for Lausanne and some practical recommendations in order that the conference would run smoothly. Given the ever-strong differences on issues such as ministry and the episcopacy, the team advised, for example, avoiding the expectation that the conference approve documents "by majority vote." Rather, it was hoped, the 1925 report continued:

> That it will register its agreement upon subjects on which it is able to reach unanimity,

---

88   R.H. Gardiner to E.J. Palmer, Mar 6, 1923, in: WCCA, 23.0.007.

89   At Gardiner's proposal, having Faith and Order's baptism in Stockholm – the same city where Life and Work's launch was to be held – was taken into consideration. It was necessary to relinquish such plans, however, in the face of Söderblom's clear opposition. He was convinced of the profound difference between the two movements and thus felt the need to keep them as distinct as possible. The archbishop of Uppsala, therefore – also speaking on behalf of Life and Work's Executive Committee – responded to Gardiner, rejecting his proposal to celebrate the two events in the Swedish capital. "The realization of the ideal of the Faith and Order movement must be comparatively remote ... Life and Work confines itself in the main to the cooperation of the Churches in the application of the Spirit and teaching of Christ to social, national, and international relationship while Faith and Order devotes its attention to the ultimate but more remote goal of unity in Doctrine and Church Order"; N. Söderblom to R.H. Gardiner, Aug 14, 1922, in: WCCA, 23.0.007.

and, where unanimity is not reached, that it will record the fact that it is unable at present to attain a unanimous decision; and further, that in some cases it will be able to say that, although not unanimously agreed, it concurs in thinking that the absence of agreement is not a fundamental obstacle to unity, while in others it might be compelled to say that such an absence of agreement is an obstacle which cannot at present be surmounted, and is, therefore, a matter for further consideration.[90]

There was never a more useful opinion in the history of Faith and Order. Assuming that, at the time, Brent and Gardiner were looking for a good working method for the next sixty years of the movement, there is a good chance that the few abovementioned lines caught their attention. In fact, they contained at least three of the movement's future *Grundprinzipien*: a constant listening to the churches and their involvement in decisional procedures, a dynamic acceptance of consensus according to a progressive view of ecumenical dialogue, and the unshakeable certainty that there was no theological impasse or knot that could not be untangled by a specially appointed commission of scholars.

The facts immediately showed the truth of the first point. In Bern, in December 1926, the Subjects Committee approved an agenda that essentially covered the seven points that the churches had studied during the previous three years: (1) the call for unity; (2) the Gospel – the church's message to the world; (3) the nature of church; (4) the common confession of faith for the church; (5) the ecclesiastical ministry; (6) the sacraments; and (7) Christian unity and the place of the various churches within it.

In the months preceding Lausanne, however, the churches' dissatisfaction concerning the *a priori* established agenda and its apparent inflexibility became so strong that the "themes committee" was forced to make the statement that not only did the official program merely indicate the topics proposed for discussion, but also that "no declaration would be adopted unless it was unanimously – or *nemine contradicente* – accepted."[91]

10   The 1927 Lausanne Conference

The days of the Lausanne Conference finally came, but Gardiner was not fortunate enough to see them. Dying in 1924, he was not granted the three years required to see the fruits of all his efforts. On the morning of Aug 3, 1927, after gathering in the cathedral for a worship service, 394 delegates hailing from Europe, the Americas, Africa, and Asia and representing 108 Lutheran, Reformed, Old Catholic, Anglican, Orthodox, Methodist, Congregationalist, and Baptist Churches poured onto the streets leading from the cathedral to the University of Lausanne.[92]

Two Catholic priests, both German, Hermann Hoffmann and Max Josef Metzger,[93] were among

---

90   World Conference on Faith and Order, ed., *A Report from the Subjects Committee to the Continuation Committee, July 1925, to which is Appended a Suggested Agenda for the World Conference, together with Statements on the Church, the Ministry, and the Christian Moral Ideal*, Edinburgh, Neill & Co., 1925, 6–7.

91   It concluded: "In case a statement does not gain this measure of acceptance, the Conference shall determine what further steps if any shall be taken on that subject." These words come from the report of a meeting of the commission appointed in Bern to choose the speakers for the Lausanne Conference (WCCA, 23.0.005). It seems that the decisive factor in the easing of the commission's positions was the pressure from the German group headed by Siegmund-Schultze which had thus returned, in the run-up to Lausanne, and played a fully respectable role in the preparation of the conference; see Sasse, *Die Weltkonferenz*, 53–58, and Frieling, *Die Bewegung*, 58–87.

92   The conference proceedings, including the documents approved, decisions made, and list of delegates with their respective affiliation churches are found in Herbert Newell Bate, ed., *Faith and Order: Proceedings of the World Conference, Lausanne, August 3–21, 1927*, Garden City NY, Gerger H. Doran Company, 1927.

93   On Metzger, a pioneer in ecumenism in Germany in the 1930s, see the contribution by Peter Zimmerling in the second volume of this work.

the crowd. They had arrived in Switzerland on the precise orders of the nuncio in Freiburg who, in turn, had been charged by Gasparri to report in detail on what was taking place in Lausanne since Rome continued to keep its distance from the ecumenical ferment that seemed to be affecting half the world's churches. Repeated attempts to involve it, however, and the publicity campaign surrounding the conference, had convinced the pope and his secretary of state to monitor the situation constantly, if only to add another file to those accumulating on the desk of the editor of *Mortalium animos*.[94]

Under the watch of the two Catholic guests, the assembly elected Brent as its president, who, despite ill-health, agreed to oversee the work for the duration of the conference. This was fortunate because, as in Geneva seven years earlier, Brent's presence ensured the pragmatism necessary to prevent Lausanne from being transformed into a battleground for theologians. The conditions for that to happen were all there, Brent himself emphasizing in his introductory address theology's place in the new scenario unfolding on that August morning.

> We try to get together in matters of practical import, but as often as not we find ourselves thrown back on our conception of Christ, the nature of the Church, God's mode of governing His Church, the substance of the Gospel message. Christology may not be slighted. The value of theology must be admitted.[95]

However, seventeen years of preparation had sufficed to teach Brent, who was not a theologian,

that the only viable path to unity ran along that thin line separating a capacity to overcome doctrinal differences from an obstinacy that would lead almost any theological controversy to its breaking point. That is why, a little further down, Brent urged those present not to struggle in the search for "clear conclusions" since they had been called to hold a conference, not a theological disputation. To those unclear as to the difference between the two, he addressed these words:

> Conference is a measure of peace; controversy, a weapon of war. Conference is self-abasing; controversy, exalts self. Conference in all lowliness strives to understand the viewpoint of others; controversy, to impose its views on all comers. Conference looks for unities; controversy exaggerates differences. Conference is a co-operative method for conflict; controversy, a divisive method. I do not say that there may not be occasions where controversy may be necessary. This is not one of them. This is a Conference on Faith and Order.[96]

Yet, it is easy to imagine the disappointment that Brent, at times, had to face during the thirteen days of debate that followed, when the favorable winds that had accompanied the first four days seemed to suddenly abandon them and the conference entered difficult waters. Once the introductory and ceremonious welcoming speeches were over, it was time to tackle the heart of matter, and no sore spot was as sensitive as that of the episcopal ministry, which was a fault line along which the assembly was split in a way that Brent would have preferred to avoid. Of all the discussions preceding the vote on the seven final documents, the one on the text produced by Söderblom's group – "The Unity of Christendom and the Relation thereto of Existing Churches" – proved particularly heated and problematic. In fact, the Anglican Bishop of Gloucester, Arthur Headlam breathed a storm over the already

---

94   Philippe Chenaux, "Le Saint-Siège et les débuts du Mouvement œcuménique: La Conférence de Lausanne (1927)," in: Andreas Gottsmann, Pierantonio Piatti & Andreas E. Rehberg, eds., *Incorrupta monumenta ecclesiam defendunt: Studi offerti a mons. Sergio Pagano, prefetto dell'Archivio Segreto Vaticano*, vol. 1, *La Chiesa nella storia: Religione, cultura, costume*, Vatican City, Archivio Segreto Vaticano, 2018, 213–226.

95   Bate, ed., *Faith and Order: Proceedings of the World Conference*, 8.

96   Bate, ed., *Faith and Order: Proceedings of the World Conference*, 4–5.

restless sea. To those who held that a hierarchical principle was not the sole one to express the church's essence and to Söderblom's conciliatory attempts in proposing an "incarnationalist" ecclesiological model capable of pleasing even the Anglicans,[97] Headlam held up the certainty of the fact that any unity spoken of would have to be "a unity of faith, a unity in the sacraments, and a unity in the ministry" and that "union in the ministry must mean the acceptance of the traditional form of Christian ministry, the acceptance of episcopacy and of episcopal ordination."[98] Rather than question the episcopal ministry, Bishop Gore added, it should be discussed how to adapt it to those churches without any hierarchical order. He specified that no other type of unity should be spoken of other than an organic one, that is, a complete unity from a doctrinal and institutional point of view. He even declared himself ready to reconsider Anglican participation in the movement if such conditions were not met.[99]

Having had to leave the conference before it ended, Söderblom probably did not witness the deepest thrust that the Anglo-Catholic faction had in store for the text written under his responsibility. A decisive consideration in the decision to refer the report to the Continuation Committee was that, by accepting the report as it was, that is with the father of Life and Work's still too evident stamp, the conference would have adopted a conception of ecumenical relations that privileged practical collaboration among the various churches at the expense of a unity in faith and order.

Support for alternative solutions could certainly not come from the delegates of the handful of Orthodox Churches present in Lausanne.[100] Divided amongst themselves and incapable of taking a unanimous stand on the documents proposed in the assembly, they communicated through Archbishop Germanos their decision to vote in favor of the report of the second section, "The Church's Message to the World: The Gospel," but to abstain from all others – having judged them completely "inconsistent with the principles of the Orthodox Church."[101]

While speaking of a result that fell short of expectations does not do justice to the work of Faith and Order's first conference – with the exception of the report on section VIII, the other six were eventually approved *nemine contradicente* – the regret at having to leave Lausanne without finding a way to celebrate the Eucharist together, as the Life and Work Conference had managed to do two years earlier, certainly weighed on the delegates making their way home.

11   **Conclusions**

After a new Continuation Committee[102] had been appointed to lead the movement towards the celebration of a second conference and the assembly had dissolved, a reporter present in Lausanne commented: "We now know, almost as

---

97   The reference is to the German Lutheran Werner Elert, who recalled that what was essential for the unity of the Protestant Churches was already expressed in Article VII of the *Confessio Augustana* (therein, pp. 13–17) and to the Swiss Calvinist Eugène Choisy, who instead recalled the intimate Christological nature of the church (therein, pp. 28–31). The address by which Söderblom – in presenting the document produced by his section – attempted to mediate between the opposing factions is given in: Bate, ed., *Faith and Order: Proceedings of the World Conference*, 321–331.

98   Bate, ed., *Faith and Order: Proceedings of the World Conference*, 331–342, here 333.

99   Bate, ed., *Faith and Order: Proceedings of the World Conference*, 161–165; for the amendments proposed by Gore to Söderblom's text, 402–402.

100   In addition to the patriarchates of Constantinople, Alexandria, Jerusalem, and Antioch, delegates from the Orthodox Churches of Greece, Cyprus, Romania, Serbia, Bulgaria, Russia, Poland, Georgia, and Armenia were present in Lausanne; Bate, ed., *Faith and Order: Proceedings of the World Conference*, 528.

101   Bate, ed., *Faith and Order: Proceedings of the World Conference*, 383.

102   The new Continuation Committee was headed by Brent, who remained in the office until his death in 1929. The secretary of the new body was Ralph W. Brown, who had replaced Gardiner as Faith and Order secretary since 1924; Bate, ed., *Faith and Order: Proceedings of the World Conference*, 534.

well as they can be known, the points of agreement and difference in the various branches of
the Christian Church. What could another similar
conference, in five years or ten years or even in
fifty years, do unless there has been in the meantime a significant change in attitude which ought
to be registered? Very little, I am inclined to say."[103]
Although, like most predictions, this was stated
blindly, it seems to touch on the three issues at the
heart of every historical phenomenon such as the
one unfolding before their eyes: nature, purpose,
and method.

Born of the initiative of churches that shared
a strong High Church connection, the project
established by Brent and Gardiner found it difficult to become a credible interlocutor for all the
churches that hardly considered an episcopal
hierarchy and the apostolic succession of bishops
as the two indispensable ways in which to bear
testimony to the gospel in history. In any case, no
member of the preparatory commission had said
or thought it would be an easy task. If the goal was
to bring ecumenical dialogue to the heart of theological issues in order to heal historical factures
and to translate into intellectual terms a unity
experienced as yet only practically, it would have
been very unlikely that they would give up navi-
gating problems as great as continents without
having first scoured the coastline, searching each
bay that might prove to be an isthmus between
two oceans. It is true that, for most of the 1950s,
more typically Protestant themes such as the relationship between scripture and the Word of God
managed to keep Faith and Order out of the shal-
lows of ecclesiology. However, with the large-scale
entry of Orthodox Churches into the WCC and the
beginning of Catholic interest in the ecumenical
movement, the tide quickly turned and eventually
led the theological commission in Geneva back
onto routes that may have been less safe but which
were more in keeping with its design.

With the early globalization of the modern era
having resulted in a bloodbath, Faith and Order
probably saw the choice to borrow from multilateral diplomacy – which had, at the dawn of the
1930s, already seemed to have exhausted its cards –
as obligatory. It was a practice consisting in two
rules: to circumscribe conflicts and orchestrate
solutions. In short, whether it was the Eucharist or
the ministry, for a long time the method of investigation remained that adopted in Lausanne: to
purge the atmosphere of misunderstandings of a
historical nature in order to bring the specificity of
each doctrinal tradition to a common denominator of universal value in time and space. It would
appear to be an impeccable *modus operandi*, if
not for the fact that, put to the test by resistance,
stumbling, and natural lags in enthusiasm – not to
mention the progressive replacement of the ecclesiastical component with an elite team of highly
specialized theologians – it wound up turning into
a flight towards an exhausting search for theological consensus that sometimes put Faith and Order
out of step with the times and expectations of the
churches. But no one in Lausanne could have fore-
seen all that.

*Translated from Italian to English by Susan
Dawson Vásquez and David Dawson Vásquez.*

Bibliography

Bate, Herbert Newell, ed., *Faith and Order: Proceedings
of the World Conference, Lausanne, August 3–21, 1927*,
Garden City NY, Doubleday, Doran & Co., 1928.
Epting, Karl-Christoph, *Ein Gespräch beginnt: Die
Anfänge der Bewegung für Glauben und Kirchen-
verfassung in den Jahren 1910–1920*, Zürich, TVZ, 1972.
Frieling, Reinhard, *Die Bewegung für Glauben und
Kirchenverfassung (1910–1937): Unter besonderer
Berücksichtigung des Beitrages der deutschen*

---

103   Edmund Davison Soper, *Lausanne: The Will to
Understand*, Garden City NY, Doubleday, Doran & Co.,
1928, 142, cited in: Karl-Christoph Epting, "Lausanne
1927: The First World Conference on Faith and Order,"
EcRev 29/2, 1977, 167–181, here 180.

evangelischen Theologie und der evangelischen Kirchen in Deutschland, Göttingen, Vandenhoeck & Ruprecht, 1970.

Tatlow, Tissington, "The World Conference on Faith and Order," in: *A History of the Ecumenical Movement*, vol. 1, Ruth Rouse & Stephen C. Neill, eds., *1517–1948*, London, SPCK, 1954, 405–444.

Woolverton, John Frederick, *Robert H. Gardiner and the Reunification of Worldwide Christianity in the Progressive Era*, Columbia MO, University of Missouri Press, 2005.

Zabriskie, Alexander C., *Bishop Brent: Crusader for Christian Unity*, Philadelphia PA, Westminster Press, 1948.

CHAPTER 28

The Malines Conversations

Bernard Barlow and Martin Browne

1 **Lord Halifax and Abbé Portal: Between *Apostolicae curae* and New Paths in the Anglican-Roman Catholic Dialogue**

The two moving spirits behind the conversations at Malines (1921–1925)[1] were Charles Lindley Wood, viscount of Halifax, an Anglican layman who was for many years president of the English Church Union and a man who had dedicated most of his life to the reconciliation of the Church of England and the Church of Rome, and Fr. Fernand Portal, a French Lazarist priest who was similarly dedicated to the cause of reunion of the churches. They had succeeded in interesting Pope Leo XIII in the idea of studying the various problems which would be involved in any eventual reunion.[2] The commission that they established in Malines did not give the expected results, and when on Sept 13, 1896, the apostolic letter *Apostolicae curae* of Pope Leo XIII was published, its conclusion was uncompromising: "We pronounce and declare that ordinations carried out according to the Anglican rite have been, and are, absolutely null and utterly void."[3]

The document cited four main reasons for its negative judgment regarding Anglican ordinations.[4] Firstly, that the rejection had been the consistent position of the Catholic Church since the

reign of Mary Tudor, and that "Custom is the best interpreter of law."[5] Secondly, that the Elizabethan Ordinal suffered from a "defect of form," in that the words of the bald formula "'Receive the Holy Ghost,' certainly do not in the least definitely express the sacred Order of Priesthood."[6] Thirdly, that the addition in 1662 of "for the office and work of a priest," was a recognition by the Church of England – too late – that its previous formula was insufficient.[7] Fourthly, that the Anglican Ordinal also suffered from a "defect of intention," in that the new rite had the "manifest intention ... of rejecting what the Church does," regarding the making of priests to offer the Eucharistic sacrifice.[8] The apostolic letter judged the Anglican Ordinal's *nativa indoles ac spiritus* – its "native character or spirit" – as defective. "Hence, if, vitiated in its origin, it was wholly insufficient to confer Orders, it was impossible that, in the course of time, it would become sufficient, since no change had taken place."[9]

For both Halifax and Portal, the publication of *Apostolicae curae* had been a great disappointment, but both accepted the failure of their effort in a Christian spirit. Halifax, in a letter to Portal shortly after the promulgation of the apostolic letter, wrote: "We have failed for the moment but, if God wishes it, His Will be done, and if he allows

---

1 For the full story of the Malines Conversations, see Bernard Barlow, *"A Brother Knocking at the Door": The Malines Conversations (1921–1925)*, Norwich, Canterbury Press, 1996. See also John A. Dick, *The Malines Conversations Revisited*, Leuven, Leuven University Press, 1989.

2 See Paul Avis's contribution in this volume.

3 Leo XIII, *Apostolicae curae*, AAS 29, 1896–1897, 193–203, § 36; the text can be found at: < https://www.papalencyclicals.net/leo13/l13curae.htm> (accessed Sept 2, 2020).

4 Mary C. Boulding & others, "*Apostolicae Curae*: A Hundred Years On," *OiC* 32/4, 1996, 295–309, here 297–298.

5 Cited in: *Apostolicae curae*, § 16.

6 Council of Trent, sess. XXIII, *de sacr. Ord.*, can. 1, cited in: *Apostolicae curae*, § 25.

7 *Apostolicae curae*, § 26.

8 *Apostolicae curae*, § 33. See Francis Clark, *Anglican Orders and Defect of Intention*, London, Longmans, Green & Co., 1956, 11–25.

9 *Apostolicae curae*, § 31.

us to be disappointed, it is because He wishes to accomplish it (union) Himself."[10]

Almost 25 years later, another opportunity to continue their ecumenical effort was unexpectedly presented to them. At the Sixth Lambeth Conference, held at the Archbishop's palace in London from July 5 to Aug 7, 1920, the 252 bishops assembled there announced that they were willing, in the cause of reunion of the Christian churches, to accept a form of commission from the authorities of other churches in order that the ministry of the Anglican clergy might be recognized by others.[11] In fact, this statement was aimed principally at nonepiscopal churches, but its formulation was so wide that it was capable of being applied also to the Church of Rome.

This appeal issued by the Church of England was the fruit of a wider impetus among Christian churches and denominational bodies of the early 20th century, and in some ways the Anglicans were latecomers to the movement.[12]

Following the publication of the Lambeth Conference appeal of 1920, Abbé Portal, who in the intervening years had continued to work actively in affairs of reunion through a new publication, *Revue catholique des Églises*, was struck immediately by the possibility of the Lambeth Appeal (as it came to be known) being applied in the case of reunion with Rome. On Jan 24, 1921, he wrote to Cardinal Désiré-Joseph Mercier, recalling his original idea of a series of conferences which he had first broached to Leo XIII. He mentioned also how the pope had been in favor of such conferences, and indeed had suggested Brussels as a suitable place for holding them.

Before Belgium, several places were suggested as possibilities, including the United States, but both Portal and Halifax were reluctant to leave Europe. Since the peace Treaty of Versailles, and the vindictive treatment of Germany by France, political relations between France and England were not too friendly, and so Paris was not thought suitable. England itself was a possibility, although this would mean inviting the English Roman Catholic bishops, but Halifax liked the idea and began to plan for the "conversations at Hickleton," Hickleton being his family home in Yorkshire. Geneva was also another consideration, as Switzerland was a small neutral country, but it was also the base of the recent Faith and Order and Life and Work meetings, and as the Holy See had forbidden Catholics from participating in these movements, too close a proximity might lead to suspicion of influence by these bodies.[13] The process of elimination led them to Belgium, that small country which had been established by the Treaty of London in 1830 as a buffer state between France and Germany, and whose destiny was to be a mediating one between the Great Powers. Brussels had also been one of the places mentioned by pope Leo XIII as a suitable place for such discussions at the preliminary stage of the Anglican orders debate, before that got bogged down in the diplomatic tussle with Westminster.[14]

Another fact in Portal's mind would have been the international reputation of the primate, Cardinal Mercier, both for his scholarship[15] and

---

10   Charles Lindley Wood Halifax, *Leo XIII and Anglican Orders*, London, Longmans & Green, 1912, 358.

11   "An Appeal to All Christian People," in: *Conference of Bishops of the Anglican Communion: Holden at Lambeth Palace July 5 to August 7, 1920: Encyclical Letter from the Bishops, with the Resolutions and Reports*, London, SPCK, 1920, 133–161.

12   See Dietz Lange's contribution in the second volume of this work.

13   See Dietz Lange's contribution, and Luca Ferracci's contribution in this volume.

14   Pope Leo XIII presumably thought Belgium a sort of theological halfway house between England and France, but more probably his favor was due to the fact that he had been papal nuncio in Belgium before his elevation to the pontificate, and he knew the country well.

15   Cardinal Mercier was the founder and first president of the neo-Thomistic philosophy school ISP at the Catholic University of Leuven, and the initiator in 1894 of the *Revue néo-scolastique de philosophie*. See Édouard Beauduin, *Le Cardinal Mercier*, Tournai, Casterman, 1966, 45–54.

for his actions during the Great War. Mercier's continued defense of the rights of the Belgian people against the German forces of occupation, through his numerous pastoral letters in particular, had accrued enormous respect for the primate throughout the whole world.

What Portal was unaware of was that Mercier himself had been thinking along somewhat similar lines, namely, of holding a series of conversations with non-Catholics of various denominations, with a view to dissipating the prejudices which impeded the progress of reunion. To this end, he had already written to Pope Benedict XV on Dec 21, 1921, that is, fully one month prior to receiving the letter from Portal, but there was no reply to the cardinal's letter.

On the other side of the Channel, Lord Halifax was encountering a similar reticence on the part of the Anglican authorities in giving any sort of official blessing to the idea of a meeting with the Catholics. The archbishop of Canterbury, Randall Davidson, declined to give him a letter of presentation or delegation, but did agree to write a letter of introduction to Cardinal Mercier on behalf of Halifax, praising him as one who was dedicated to the idea of a reunited Christendom. At the same time, he made it quite clear that Lord Halifax was in no way an official representative of the Church of England and that the opinions that he expressed would be his own personal opinions and not the authorized opinions of the corpus of the Anglican Church.

On Oct 17, 1921, Lord Halifax left England for Calais, where his friend Fr. Portal was waiting for him. Together they paid a brief visit to the battlefield of Flanders, and then on Oct 19 they arrived at the episcopal palace at Malines. Cardinal Mercier made them very welcome and invited them to stay for lunch. It was during this visit that Lord Halifax asked the cardinal if he would be willing to host a meeting between Anglicans and Catholics. Mercier then asked the obvious question, namely, for such a meeting between Anglicans and Catholics surely the persons to approach would be the authorities of the Catholic Church in England. Halifax and Portal, doubtless recalling the opposition they had encountered from England in their

first attempt at Anglo-Catholic rapprochement, replied that the attitude of mind was not yet favorable in England. In Halifax's opinion: "The English Catholics are anxious only for individual conversions and reject any attempt at reunion. Any such attempt is impossible except outside England."[16] The cardinal therefore agreed to participate in such a meeting as Halifax and Portal had suggested, making clear that it would be simply private conversations. Mercier's motives for joining the conversations were later explained in a pastoral letter to his diocese by the following phrase: "Nothing in the world would permit me to allow one of our separated brothers to say that he had knocked on the door of a Roman Catholic bishop and that the bishop had refused to open the door for him."[17]

This, then, was the immediate background to the beginnings of the Malines Conversations. From the very beginning the meetings were regarded as simple "conversations," private meetings between individuals, and in no way as "negotiations." In order to negotiate one must have a mandate, and neither Cardinal Mercier nor Lord Halifax had mandates to negotiate on behalf of their respective churches. The goal of the conversations was later described by the cardinal as a work of rapprochement which consisted of clarifying the atmosphere "to rid ourselves of misunderstandings and prejudices and to reestablish the historical truth."[18] The immediate goal of the conversations was not reunion, but to clear the path for its realization.

After their meeting with Cardinal Mercier, the two friends continued their journey, and on Oct 29 Lord Halifax returned to England. There was much to be done in the way of preparation for

---

16   Charles A. Bolton, *A Catholic Memorial of Lord Halifax and Cardinal Mercier*, London, Williams & Norgate, 1935, 116.

17   Désiré-Joseph Mercier, *Oeuvres Pastorales, actes, allocutions, lettres*, vol. 7, Brussels, A. Dewit, 1929, 297 (Jan 18, 1924).

18   Jacques Bivort de la Saudée, *Anglicans et catholiques: Le problème de l'union anglo-romaine (1833–1933)*, Paris, Plon, 1949, 30.

the conversations: the choice of other members of the group, an agenda of points for discussion, etc. One most important item was dealt with personally by Lord Halifax. On Nov 29, Halifax went to see Cardinal Bourne, the archbishop of Westminster, and he reported on this meeting in a letter to Portal written the same day:

> I told him that we had seen Cardinal Mercier and talked with him on the subject of reunion of the churches, etc. etc. "Ah! Cardinal Mercier," he said, "I know him well and have great regard for him: we were at Louvain together. He is a great man, a most distinguished personality with strong influence. I am *very glad* you have seen him." My visit was a complete success.[19]

2   The First Malines Conversation, Dec 6–8, 1921

The members of the Anglican group for the first conversation were Lord Halifax, Walter H. Frere (superior of the Community of the Resurrection), and Dr. Joseph Armitage Robinson (dean of Wells). As regards the agenda of points for discussion, Lord Halifax prepared a memorandum, based on those elements which were in common to both the Anglicans and Roman Catholics and which were considered essential by both the Thirty-Nine Articles and the decrees of the Council of Trent. The memorandum could be divided roughly into two distinct parts, the first dealing with the constitution of the church and the nature of the sacraments – baptism, Eucharist, and the necessity of episcopal ordination – and the second dealing with the Lambeth Appeal. In posing a topic such as the constitution of the church, Halifax was trying to avoid walking immediately into the thorny issue of the nature of the church, in

which both sides had clear and often opposing views. In many ways this first conversation was to have an exploratory perspective and, as Bishop George K.A. Bell (at that time chaplain to the archbishop of Canterbury) noted, was "to see whether there was a case for the holding of conferences between Romans and Anglicans, with some real, though at first informal, encouragement from the highest authorities on both sides."[20]

After a certain amount of discussion and correction, this memorandum was accepted by the three to serve as a basis for discussion, was translated into French and copies sent to Malines in advance of the first conversation. Thus, on the evening of Sunday Dec 4, the members of the Anglican group met at the London house of Lord Halifax, and the following day set out for Malines.

The first of the conversations began on Tuesday Dec 6, 1921.[21] The Catholic group consisted of Cardinal Mercier himself, Fr. Portal, and Msgr. Joseph-Ernest van Roey, a doctor of theology of the University of Leuven and vicar general to Cardinal Mercier (he would eventually succeed Mercier as cardinal archbishop of Malines-Brussels). At 10:00 AM the cardinal invoked the Holy Spirit for guidance, and the conversations opened with Lord Halifax presenting his memorandum as a proposed basis for discussion. The whole of the first day was spent in the reading and discussion of the memorandum, which included such points as the necessity of baptism for membership of the church, the relationship of the Thirty-Nine Articles to the Council of Trent, and the conditions under

---

19   John Gilbert Lockhart, *Charles Lindley – Viscount Halifax*, vol. 2, *1885–1934*, London, The Centenary Press, 1935, 275 (italics original).

20   George K.A. Bell, *Randall Davidson, Archbishop of Canterbury*, vol. 2, London, Oxford University Press, 1935, 275.

21   The nature of this contribution does not allow us to enter into a detailed description of each of the five conversations held at Malines, but we shall try to draw out some of the salient points of the discussions while of necessity passing over many of the details. The texts of the papers presented at Malines, together with the *compte rendu* of the actual meetings, can be found in the little volume edited by Charles Lindley Wood Halifax, *The Conversations at Malines (1921–1925): Original Documents*, London, P. Allan, 1930.

which a truth becomes an article of faith in the Catholic Church. In the course of the afternoon session, the participants discussed the sacraments of the Eucharist, Extreme Unction and Penance, and also the role of a dogma and the exercise of jurisdiction. Two outstanding points in this session concerned the Eucharist and the role of a dogma. Concerning the Eucharist, as the minutes of the discussion report, "on the doctrine of transubstantiation, the Anglicans said they admitted the changing of the bread and wine into the body and blood of Christ by the consecration. To the eyes of the Catholics, the word transubstantiation did not mean other than this."[22] Concerning dogmas, everyone recognized that there were truths of faith which imposed themselves. The Anglicans, however, wished to know by what criterion the Catholics could discern *defined* truths of faith from those which were not. The Catholic participants replied that when authority wished to define a truth of faith, certain formulas were used, such as *si quis dixerit ... anathema sit*, or in the case of the definition of the Immaculate Conception, *definimus auctoritate*.

The following day, Dec 7, the conversations continued with a reading and discussion of the Lambeth Appeal. Concerning chapter 4 of the appeal, the Anglicans noted that a certain diversity in unity was necessary, especially concerning disciplinary matters, adding that the Church of England was very desirous of retaining its own usages. One point of considerable divergence appeared when the participants came to discuss chapter 6 of the appeal. The bishops had proposed "that the visible unity of the church will be found to involve the wholehearted acceptance of Holy Scriptures, as the record of God's revelation of himself to man, and as being the rule and ultimate standard of faith." The Catholics objected to

the use of the term "ultimate standard," because Holy Scripture has to be interpreted, and it was the church alone who had the right to interpret.

But the lengthiest discussion took place on chapter 7 of the appeal, that concerning the episcopacy. The bishops at Lambeth had been proposing the episcopacy as a means of maintaining the unity and continuity of the church (obviously directing at nonepiscopalian churches). Cardinal Mercier, on being asked for a rigorous evaluation of this particular chapter, replied that the episcopacy, in itself, could be an agent of unification, but even the bishops needed a visible head, a sign of their unity. Every society needs a head, continued the cardinal, even the bishops.

Another part of the discussion centered on that part of the Lambeth Appeal which had brought about the very conversations themselves, namely, the chapter dealing with ordinations. The actual wording of this session is important enough to be quoted in full:

> We believe that, for all, the truly equitable approach to union is by the way of mutual deference to one another's consciences. To this end, we who send forth this appeal would say that if the authorities of other Communions should so desire, we are persuaded that, terms of union having been otherwise satisfactorily adjusted, bishops and clergy of our Communion would willingly accept from these authorities a form of commission or recognition which would commend our ministry to their congregations, as having its place in the one family life. It is not in our power to know how far this suggestion may be acceptable to those to whom we offer it. We can only say that we offer it in all sincerity as a token of our longing that all ministries of grace, theirs and ours, shall be available for the service of Our Lord in a united church.[23]

---

22   Halifax, *The Conversations at Malines*, 11. For the commented text of the appeal see Roger Coleman, *Resolutions of the Twelve Lambeth Conferences (1867–1988)*, Toronto, Anglican Book Centre, 1992, 45–48, see also Alan M.G. Stephenson, *Anglicanism and the Lambeth Conferences*, London, SPCK, 1978, 128–154.

23   "An Appeal to All Christian People," 135 (§ 8).

Concerning this section of the appeal, dean Robinson and Dr. Frere noted firstly that the formulation of this chapter had in mind principally the nonepiscopal Protestant Churches such as the Presbyterian Church of Scotland, which claimed a presbyterial ministry coming from the apostles. But with regard to those churches which already have an episcopacy, they were certain that the Anglican bishops would accept whatever was necessary to regularize their position in the eyes of other churches. This, of course, would have been an admirable answer to the difficulties posed by Leo XIII's apostolic letter, *Apostolicae curae*, concerning the question of Anglican orders, but, surprisingly enough, Cardinal Mercier showed himself to be somewhat reticent on this question, remarking that ordination *sub conditione* might be a necessary and satisfactory requisite.

The following day, Dec 9, saw the close of the first conversation. The participants decided not to publicize their discussions for the time being, and Lord Halifax thanked the cardinal for his hospitality in receiving them in his palace.

Though not then conceived of as a distinctive ecumenical method, the suggestion from the bishops at Lambeth that their clergy might accept from other churches "a form of commission or recognition which would commend our ministry to their congregations" was theologically significant in that it gave priority to ecclesial reality over sacramental "validity." Such an attitude suggested that recognizing one another as true churches comes first, with recognition or reconciliation of ministries coming second. The bishops gathered at Lambeth were effectively affirming the apostolicity of churches like the Church of Scotland, thus opening a pathway towards the mutual recognition of ministry. Such a starting point was to be used in various unity schemes in the century since the Lambeth Appeal, most notably in the Church of South India and the Church of North India and in agreements between Anglicans and Lutherans in North America and Anglicans and

Methodists in Ireland.[24] Notwithstanding Frere's contention that Anglican bishops would accept "whatever was necessary to regularize their position," it is extremely doubtful that the authors of the Lambeth Appeal would have countenanced anything that amounted to admitting that *Apostolicae curae* was correct in denying the validity of their orders. It would have been absurd of them to do so. To describe an ordination rite as invalid is to say that the rite is incapable of producing its proper effects and that ordination has therefore not truly happened, whereas the Lambeth bishops' appeal was made with confidence that they were true bishops in a true church.

3   Mercier's Request to Rome for Support and the Beginnings of Adverse Reactions to the Conversations

More than fifteen months were to elapse before the second of the conversations. Within this period of time, several events occurred which had a direct bearing on the conversations. On Jan 22, 1922, Pope Benedict XV died, and his successor, Cardinal Ratti (who took the name Pius XI) was a personal friend of Cardinal Mercier. The Belgian primate took the opportunity of writing a pastoral letter to his diocese on the subject of the papacy and the rights of the successor of Saint Peter, a subject which he considered so important that he asked Lord Halifax to publish an English translation of the letter. The viscount was not at all enthusiastic about so doing, for the pastoral letter contained certain phrases and expressions which would fall harshly on English ears. His misgivings are reflected in a letter to a friend on July 7, 1922: "I am afraid it won't do us much good. Let us only hope that it won't do harm. Foreigners can never understand the English mind. Of course, this was written for

---

24   See Will Adam, "Squaring the Circle: Anglicans and the Recognition of Holy Orders," *OiC* 49/2 (2015), 254–269.

Belgians, but the translation is for us, and even I could demur to it."[25]

However, once started on the project, the viscount began to so expand the scope of the intended publication that the final document not only included the pastoral letter and a foreword but also an account of the first conversation and the text of the memorandum which Halifax himself had presented as a basis for the initial discussions. Because of the agreement reached by the participants at the first conversation not to publicize their meeting and discussions, Halifax had to obtain the consent of the others before he could publish. Not all were in total agreement with the contents of the proposed booklet, but Halifax went ahead, and in September 1922 the booklet appeared under the title *A Call to Reunion*.[26] The publication had a mixed reception in England, but it provided Cardinal Mercier with another opportunity to seek approval from Rome.

On Nov 14, 1922, Mercier wrote to Pope Pius XI, mentioning his pastoral letter and the remarkable introduction by Lord Halifax. He continued by saying that,

> the Anglicans, notably the Archbishop of Canterbury, desire, as we ourselves desire, that the conversations continue. But the Anglicans expect that their first gesture towards Rome should be reciprocated by some sign from Rome. Could the Holy Father authorize me to tell them that the Holy See approves and encourages our conversations?[27]

A reply to this letter was received by Cardinal Mercier from the secretary of state to the Holy See, Cardinal Gasparri. In this letter, dated Nov 25, 1922, Cardinal Gasparri said that the pope had not yet received a copy of Lord Halifax's publication, but that he would very much like to read it. The letter, however, continued, "he [the pope] authorizes Your Eminence to tell the Anglicans that the Holy See approves and encourages your conversations and prays with all his heart that God will bless them."[28]

This message was all that Cardinal Mercier had been waiting for, and he communicated the news to Lord Halifax, asking him to be most discreet about it. At Halifax's prompting, the cardinal wrote to Archbishop Davidson on Jan 10, 1923, communicating the news of the Holy See's encouragement. But not all the news was in the same encouraging vein. Cardinal Francis Bourne, the archbishop of Westminster, was beginning to show displeasure. During a meeting in London, Davidson had confided to other Anglican bishops what had taken place at Malines, and had encountered from them expressions of considerable doubt and misgivings. The problem of the revision of the *Prayer Book* was another element which caused him anxiety, as he had to ensure that it passed through the church's Convocation, the General Assembly of the Church of England, and the British Parliament. One success on the horizon was the recognition of the validity of Anglican orders by the patriarch of Constantinople,[29] so much so that Portal thought that Davidson was paying too much attention to the Orthodox and not enough to the Roman Catholics, but in truth the archbishop felt much uneasiness about the forthcoming Roman encounter.

Fr. Portal, in the meantime, was also growing uneasy at the obstacles and negative portents which seemed to be reappearing from the Anglican orders affair. In a letter to Lord Halifax, he recalled the Jesuits' strong opposition at the

---

25   Lockhart, *Charles Lindley*, vol. 2, 280.

26   Charles Lindley Wood Halifax, *A Call to Reunion, by Viscount Halifax, Arising out of Discussions with Cardinal Mercier to Which is Appended a Translation of the Cardinal's Pastoral Letter to His Diocese*, London, A.R. Mowbray, 1922.

27   Roger Aubert, "Les conversations de Malines: Le cardinal Mercier et le Saint-Siège," *Bull. Cl. lett. sci. morales polit.* (*Acad. r. Belg.*) 53, 1967, 87–159, annex XIII, 139–140.

28   Aubert, "Les conversations de Malines," annex XIV, 140–141.

29   George K.A. Bell, *Documents on Christian Unity* (1920–1930), London, Oxford University Press, 1930, 93–99.

time and said that similar forces were assembling again. The fight for influence at Rome was about to begin once more.[30]

The situation on the eve of the second conversation at Malines was consequently a rather tense one, with many tender and even sore points skirted round but not resolved. The enthusiasm of Mercier, Halifax, and Portal for the continuation and even development of these meetings was undoubtedly the force that carried them through to the next stage, where the participants went to Malines with at least a degree of official backing and authorization from their respective authorities. But this would be the last conversation at which their participation as simple "friends" would predominate. After this second conversation, the "experts," whether historians or theologians, would increasingly take over the agenda and discussions in an attempt to allay the fears of the leaders of their respective churches.

4   The Second Round: Malines, Mar 13–14, 1923

The second conversation was held on Mar 13–14, 1923. The participants were the same six persons as on the previous occasion (Mercier, Portal, and van Roey on the Roman Catholic side; Robinson, Frere, and Halifax as the Anglican group), despite several suggestions that their number be augmented. It was again the Anglicans who prepared the memorandum for discussion, although a suggestion that the Catholics prepare a similar document never seems to have been followed through.[31] Consequently, towards the end of February 1923, Robinson, Frere, and Halifax spent two days drawing up a memorandum for discussion at Malines. This memorandum turned out to be restricted principally to practical issues concerning the Church of England which would have to be solved

were doctrinal agreements ever reached between the two churches.

A copy of the proposed memorandum was sent to Cardinal Mercier prior to the meeting. The practical nature of the contents of this draft was a surprise to Mercier, who was expecting a more doctrinally-centered discussion, but he nevertheless accepted the proposed agenda.[32]

Two particular aspects of this agenda can be noted immediately. First, the fact of reunion as the objective of the conversations is taken almost for granted. This was in sharp contrast to the preparatory work for the conference on Faith and Order of Lausanne of 1927, that instead proposed as methodology to reach unity a process of gradual growth resulting from the sharing of differences. The second aspect to note is that the practical nature of the agenda for this second conversation evidently reflects more the membership and experiences of the individual Anglican participants than it did the wider Anglican Communion. As John G. Lockhart points out in his biography of Lord Halifax, this emphasis on practical issues seems out of place at this particular point in the conversations, as there were many much more serious points of dogma and doctrine to be settled before even the smallest practical issue could be dealt with. On the other hand, by taking some of the practical issues now and seeing if there were indeed possible solutions to them, then the real implications of reunion would be made clearer, and it would be possible to revert once again to the doctrinal differences. If, however, it were obvious that there were no practical solutions to the question of reunion, then to have held detailed doctrinal discussions would have been a waste of time.[33]

---

30   Bivort de la Saudée, *Anglicans et catholiques*, 69.
31   Lockhart, *Charles Lindley*, vol. 2, 287.

32   The memorandum did conclude with the following phrase, indicating the purpose of a "practical" agenda: "The topics of a practical nature which we have outlined appear to us to call for preliminary consideration. If an understanding could be reached as to the solution of the question thus raised, it would pave the way to further conferences of a yet more authoritative kind"; Halifax, *The Conversations at Malines*, annex III, 82.
33   Lockhart, *Charles Lindley*, vol. 2, 287–288.

Nevertheless, the lack of doctrinal content at this second conversation is still more surprising from the instructions that the archbishop of Canterbury had written out for inclusion by the Anglicans in the discussion:

> Don't detract from the importance of the XXXIX Articles. Don't budge an inch as to the necessity of carrying the East with us in ultimate Reunion steps. Bear constantly in mind that in any admission made as to what Roman leadership or 'primacy' may mean, we have to make it quite clear too that which it must not mean – i.e. some of the very things which the Cardinal's Pastoral claims for it.[34]

In the end, the four principal points in this memorandum were as follows:

(1) A highlighting of the difference of conditions, both numerically and geographically, between the present Anglican Communion and the Church of England of the Reformation period. In the 16th century there were only 21 bishops charged with responsibilities in England alone. Now there were 268 bishops with worldwide responsibility, looking to Canterbury as their center.

(2) Concerning the jurisdiction of the pope should the Anglican Communion eventually be reconciled to Rome, it was suggested that this jurisdiction should be conceived not as interfering with the jurisdiction of the archbishops and bishops, but rather as pre-eminence for him before others in matters concerning the whole church. A further suggestion on this point was that, in the event of reunion, the present English hierarchy need not come under the jurisdiction of Canterbury but could be directly dependent on the Holy See.

(3) A suggestion made here was directly related to the Lambeth Appeal. If any rectification be thought necessary in the matter of Anglican orders, one method of dealing with this would be the granting of the pallium by the pope to the archbishop of Canterbury. Regularization of the Anglican bishops and clergy could then be dealt with through the intermediary of the archbishop of Canterbury, as he would then have a position similar to one of the ancient patriarchs.

(4) The last point dealt with the necessity of the recognition and retention of Anglican usages and traditions. Three are specifically mentioned: the use of the vernacular and the English rite, communion in both kinds, and authorization of marriage of the clergy.

Several interesting points of discussion were raised on the basis of the Anglican memorandum. On the subject of papal jurisdiction, Msgr. van Roey remarked that it was necessary to distinguish between *the fact* and *the right*: the pope could not renounce his right of ordinary and immediate jurisdiction, but he could, in fact, restrain his exercise of this right to exceptional cases. To this, Dean Robinson replied that he recognized that the pope could not renounce his right, and he thought that the practical difficulty would be overcome if papal interventions were restricted to exceptional cases.

The discussions ranged over the kind of "rectification" that would be required for the consecration of the archbishop of Canterbury and of the other bishops in the Church of England. Msgr. van Roey gave as his opinion that the archbishop of Canterbury could be conditionally reordained by the imposition of hands by the pope or the pope's delegate, and that the archbishop himself would then do likewise for his suffragans. Lord Halifax, on the contrary, thought that perhaps the "rectification" could be confined to the porrection, accompanied by some suitable formula which would clarify totally the "intention" of the Church of England. Van Roey did not think this would be

---

34   Bell, *Randall Davidson*, vol. 2, 1260–1261. The reference here to the "Cardinal's Pastoral" is to Cardinal Mercier's 1922 pastoral letter to his clergy on the occasion of the election of Pope Pius XI, which Halifax had translated and published in English in his pamphlet *A Call to Reunion*, London, Mowbray, 1922.

sufficient as Anglican orders were considered by the Roman Church as at least doubtful, objectively speaking, and hence the imposition of hands, even if it was *sub conditione*, would probably be judged necessary. On being asked by the cardinal whether the archbishop of Canterbury would accept such a "rectification," Dean Robinson replied that, if the dogmatic issues had been resolved, then he thought that the archbishop "would resign himself to such condition."[35]

Abbé Portal's next intervention was an obvious attempt to pour soothing oil on this very sensitive issue. He pointed out that there appeared to be two aspects to the problem: the Catholics could not ask the Anglicans to deny over three centuries of their history; on the other hand, the Anglicans could not ask the Catholics to reverse the nullity judgment on their orders which had been in force for the same three centuries. This was now a matter for theologians. They should try to find an acceptable means of arriving at the desired goal, always keeping in mind the sensitivities of both parties, just as diplomats do analogously in civil and political matters. The Lambeth Conference seemed to have opened the door to one possibility. Dean Robinson added to this his wish that the question of orders be reopened, because, he continued, it was felt in England that a great injustice had been done by the mother church, Rome, to her daughter, and it would be important to find a means of making reparation for this hurt in order to smooth the path for any eventual "rectification."

Another interesting discussion followed on the fourth point of the memorandum. Cardinal Mercier was of the opinion that the use of the vernacular and the English rite and communion in both kinds would present little difficulty. However, there would be some difficulty on the matter of married clergy. He thought it probable that, in the event of reunion, those of the clergy who were already married could continue to exercise their ministry. But he found it difficult to see how the church could permit the marriage of

newly ordained priests. Fr. Portal added that they should not project too much on the example of the Catholic Uniates, because Rome would certainly fear that the discipline of celibacy would be compromised in certain countries if priests in England were allowed to marry. He reminded the group that the marriage of bishops was contrary to the traditions of both East and West.

It was at this second conversation that both groups drew up summaries of points which might serve for further discussion and submission to church authorities. The Catholic statement was drawn up in French and the Anglican one in English, with all six participants signing both statements. The question of Anglican orders was dealt with somewhat obliquely. The "French statement" posed the question as to whether the Holy See might recognize the archbishop of Canterbury as primate of the Anglican Church, if the archbishop accepted both the spiritual supremacy of the pope "and the ceremonial judged by him necessary for the validity of the consecration of the archbishop."[36] This recognition would be symbolized by the concession to the archbishop of the pallium. Several open and complex questions lay behind this seemingly tidy solution. While the Lambeth Appeal had indicated Anglican willingness, in the interests of Christian unity, to accept "a form of commission or recognition" from other church authorities, the conversations were not able to reach a clear view as to what form the "ceremonial" judged necessary by the pope would have to take.

The corresponding "English statement" did not pose the question as to how far an archbishop of Canterbury would be willing to go in order to be reconciled with Rome in this way. Unless Rome repudiated or otherwise altered the core judgment of *Apostolicae curae*, the "form of commission or recognition" necessary for the archbishop of Canterbury might have to be reordination and reconsecration, with the archbishop, in turn, reordaining and reconsecrating other bishops,

35   Halifax, *The Conversations at Malines*, 33.

36   Halifax, *The Conversations at Malines*, 83–88.

until the whole Anglican episcopate had undergone the same "validation rite accepted by the archbishop."[37] It certainly could not be taken for granted that any archbishop of Canterbury would agree either to acknowledge the spiritual "supremacy" of the pope or to submit to reordination. The former bishop of Oxford and theologian Charles Gore wrote to the archbishop of Canterbury: "The concessiveness of our delegation to Malines, apparently at the first conference and certainly at the second, seems to me more disastrous and perilous the more I think of it."[38] Other issues about discipline and the internal polity of the Church of England would be moot if this most sensitive issue could not be resolved satisfactorily.

5   From the Third Conversation to the Death of Cardinal Mercier

The period between the second and third conversation was a rather tense one, and at one point there was even a question as to whether the conversations would resume again. Archbishop Davidson, having read and studied the minutes of the second meeting and both summaries, felt bound to make clear his own feelings. This he did in a long letter to Armitage Robinson, dated Mar 19, 1923.[39] In his letter, the archbishop said he was somewhat disappointed that the second conversation had dealt with questions which were administrative rather than doctrinal. Important though these questions may have been, they presupposed that doctrinal accord had already been reached, and he feared that this distinction might not be clear in the minds of some who would read the minutes if and when they were made public.

Eventually, however, it was decided that the conversations should continue, but by augmenting the members by two on each side. On the Anglican side, the archbishop of Canterbury invited Charles Gore, and Dr. Beresford James Kidd, warden of Keble College, Oxford.

With Gore's nomination to the Anglican group, it was almost a foregone conclusion that one of the new Roman Catholic members would be Msgr. Pierre Batiffol, canon of Notre-Dame de Paris, with whom Bishop Gore had been in dispute. Batiffol was acknowledged as perhaps the leading French church historian of the times, a disciple of Msgr. Louis Duchesne of the ICP. As second member of the Roman Catholic delegation the choice was another French historian at the ICP, Père Hippolyte Hemmer, parish priest of La Sainte-Trinité in Paris.

As concerned the agenda for the forthcoming conversation, the archbishop urged that questions of an administrative kind should be put aside for the present until the essential doctrinal problems had been tackled. He then quoted from a private memorandum which he had drawn up some two months previously, outlining the type of questions he hoped would be dealt with: "The position and authority of Holy Scripture, the meaning and authority of Tradition, the existence or non-existence of a Supreme Authority upon earth, a Vicariate of Christ, and what it means as regards both doctrine and administration."[40]

The cardinal, for his part, was fearful that the next conversation would dissolve into a controversial exchange between Bishop Gore and Msgr. Batiffol, and he did not see his place, a cardinal of the church, charged with the office of peacemaker, as being a party to such an exchange. He suggested that there be a preliminary discussion between these two without him being present, but Archbishop Davidson would not hear of this.[41] The key to the solution as seen by Halifax and Portal was that Bishop Gore should be exposed to the cardinal's personality, to be able to witness at close hand the holiness and charity of the cardinal.

---

37   Bivort de la Saudée, *Anglicans et catholiques*, 81–86.
38   Cited in: Bell, *Randall Davidson*, 1267.
39   Cited in: Bivort de la Saudée, *Anglicans et catholiques*, 81–86.

40   BIA, Halifax, Malines Conversations, correspondence and papers, file A4 271, box 3, Memorandum of Archbishop Davidson, Aug 19, 1923.
41   Dick, *The Malines Conversation Revisited*, 113.

The third of the Malines Conversations took place on Nov 7–8, 1923. In preparation for the third meeting, Robinson prepared a paper entitled "The Position of St Peter in the Primitive Church: A Summary of the New Testament Evidence,"[42] and Kidd prepared two papers, the first entitled "The Petrine Texts, as Employed to A.D. 461"[43] and the second entitled "To What Extent Was the Papal Authority Repudiated at the Reformation."[44] A further two papers[45] were composed by Msgr. Batiffol in reply to the first two Anglican papers.

As the titles of the papers noted above would suggest, this encounter was predominantly a scholarly one, and the discussions were all of a historical-doctrinal nature. There was a new formality in this meeting because of the increased number of participants and because of the nature of the subjects being discussed. Frere struck a very human note when he remarked that "the new members took a very prominent part in it: Lord Halifax less than before, for he found increasing difficulty on hearing what went on since we had enlarged numbers and the table around which we sat."[46]

The *compte rendu* for this third conversation is fairly brief. Only the chief points of the topics touched upon during that first day (Nov 8) are mentioned, and the largest part is taken up with the text of two summaries which the groups produced at the end of the first day's discussions.[47] A heated debate was held during the afternoon session of Nov 9, when Kidd read the second of his prepared papers, this one dealing with the measures which were taken at the time of the Reformation to reject the pope's authority. In an exchange on the meaning of "jurisdiction," Robinson stated that the Anglican Church could not accept the

term "universal jurisdiction," either as claimed for St. Peter or for the Roman Church. A more acceptable expression would be "spiritual leadership" or "a general superintendence" understood as the duty "to care for the wellbeing of the church as a whole." Robinson thought that this interpretation would be easier to accept and was better than a primacy of honor. Gore, however, disagreed, stating that he would find it difficult to accept "general superintendence" and would prefer "spiritual leadership." This difference of opinion even among the Anglicans is indicative of the tenor of the whole discussion. Walter Frere noted that the biblical arguments that Robinson had proposed were not really faced by the Romans, and that the two sides gradually slid into an impasse.[48]

In terms of achievement, besides the extremely positive impression that Gore had of Cardinal Mercier, suffice it to say that these discussions revealed the width of the chasm.

It was during the interval between the third and fourth conversations that news of the conversations became public. Although no official reports had been published concerning the meetings at Malines, nevertheless unofficial news of the conversations had spread in both Catholic and Anglican circles. This situation was disturbing to Archbishop Davidson, and so he decided to publish a letter to the bishops of the Anglican Communion, presenting the conversations as emanating from the general movement towards reunion with the various churches as an effect of the Lambeth Appeal.[49] To the archbishop's surprise, his letter was well received. The Roman Catholics in England, however, seemed to take the matter more seriously, and many were greatly upset to find out what was going on. The final effect, however, was not the outrage one might have expected from a situation in which the

---

42   Halifax, *The Conversations at Malines*, 89–102.
43   Halifax, *The Conversations at Malines*, 123–133.
44   Halifax, *The Conversations at Malines*, 151–158.
45   Halifax, *The Conversations at Malines*, 103 and 135–149.
46   Walter Howard Frere, *Recollections of Malines*, London, The Centenary Press, 1935, 42.
47   Again, for a full account of the discussions we must refer the reader to the original documents published in Halifax, *The Conversations at Malines*.

---

48   Frere, *Recollection of Malines*, 42–44.
49   Randall Davidson, "Letter from the Archbishop of Canterbury to the Archbishops and Metropolitans of the Anglican Communion," Christmas 1923, in: Bell, *Documents on Christian Unity*, 130–140.

majority of Catholics regarded "reunion" very much in terms of the complete submission of the other churches to Rome. The fact also that the Anglicans were meeting with "continental" bishops rather than with their own English hierarchy certainly irritated some, and the Rome correspondent of *The Times* remarked scathingly on the French and Belgians mixing in English affairs, suggesting that the pope should not allow himself to be influenced by such goings-on.

However, despite the publicity now surrounding it and the mixture of praise and criticism directed towards it, the fourth of the conversations got under way. On May 19, 1925, the ten participants once again met at the episcopal palace at Malines. There were no new members of the groups, and so the representatives were the same as those of the third meeting, namely, Cardinal Mercier, Walter Frere, Charles Gore, Armitage Robinson, Beresford Kidd, Msgr. van Roey, Fernand Portal, Msgr. Pierre Batiffol, Hippolyte Hemmer.

Once again, the main topic for discussion was the papacy, but this time the two papers on the topic were presented by the Catholic members. Msgr. van Roey presented a paper entitled "L'Épiscopat et la Papauté au point de vue théologique,"[50] and Fr. Hemmer read a paper entitled "Rapports du Pape et des évêques considérés du point de vue historique."[51] One other paper was due to be read, that of Bishop Gore, entitled "On Unity with Diversity," and Msgr. Batiffol was to reply to the bishop's paper.

It was during the course of the second day that Cardinal Mercier surprised the other participants by reading the famous paper on *L'Église anglicane unie, non absorbée* that he personally asked Dom Lambert Beauduin, O.S.B., a monk of the Abbey of Mont César in Leuven, to prepare for the occasion.[52] One of the people present described the situation as follows:

He [the cardinal] had long since come to the conclusion that the Roman Church could not hope to absorb the Anglicans into its own Latin and Western church organization. At the same time it could not give up its own ways and tenets. Therefore some middle term seemed to be needed, if possible, which would bring an end to the separation of Anglicanism from Rome, whilst at the same time not absorbing it. He had therefore put the question to a canonist, "is it possible that the English Church could be reunited without being absorbed in the Roman Church?" and he had elicited from him a paper which he submitted to us for our consideration.[53]

Participants were surprised in two ways, firstly because the paper had not been previously circulated as had been the practice and therefore they knew nothing about it, and secondly, they were surprised by the scope of the paper and the concessions which it seemed to offer to the Anglicans. As Frere recalled, "all this took our breath away, especially as it seemed to lead up to a proposal for a Canterbury patriarchate."[54] In a sense it was an answer to the implicit question which is always present at meetings of this genre, namely, how far is the other side prepared to go in order to meet us?

This was a question the cardinal had obviously posed himself some time beforehand. He was obviously aware of the benefits which such a reunion with the Church of England would bring to the Catholic Church, their experiences, the Anglo-Saxon spirit, and also the tremendous capacity for spreading the faith that the British Empire would bring. But the big danger was that Anglicanism would be merely absorbed into the Latin framework of the Church of Rome. Roger Aubert offers another possible explanation when he points out that the cardinal had been greatly

---

50   Halifax, *The Conversations at Malines*, 159–174.
51   Halifax, *The Conversations at Malines*, 187–240.
52   Lambert Beauduin, *L'Église anglicane unie, non absorbée*, Mechelen, Archevêché de Malines-Bruxelles, 1977.

On Lambert Beauduin see André Haquin's contribution in this volume.
53   Frere, *Recollections of Malines*, 55–56.
54   Frere, *Recollections of Malines*, 56.

surprised at the position the Anglicans had taken over the issue of the pallium, which had arisen at the second conversation, and he had begun to realize the importance of the historical aspects which would present themselves in the practical matters of an eventual reunion.[55]

However, although these are presented as possible explanations of the cardinal's motives, there is no doubt regarding the facts. In October 1924, Mercier had asked Dom Beauduin to write a paper from a historical point of view, on a possible reunion between the Anglican Church and the Roman Church. Dom Beauduin worked on this project while he was teaching at the College of Sant' Anselmo in Rome during the winter of 1924–1925, and he sent the finished article to Mercier on Jan 31, 1925. Cardinal Mercier was very pleased with the *mémoire*. He told Beauduin, in a letter of Feb 15, 1925, that it was a real revelation to him. Although he had never lost hope in the conversations, he had nevertheless thought that reunion would be impossible except perhaps in the distant future. Now he had great hope in the present.

In fact, it would seem that the cardinal was taking a tremendous responsibility on his shoulders by offering this *mémoire* for consideration by the Anglicans, for its contents went further than anything which had ever been proposed before, particularly from a personage with as high an office and of such weighty authority as Cardinal Mercier. However, there is no doubt that Mercier was recalling the letter of Mar 30, 1923, in which the pope, via Cardinal Gasparri, had said that the Anglicans can be completely reassured that the Holy See will make all the concessions possible in order to facilitate the reunion so desired.[56] So perhaps Mercier was confident that he was expressing views which would be more or less acceptable at Rome. In any case, when the cardinal presented the *mémoire*, he introduced it as coming from a Roman canonist, but he made it quite clear that he was speaking

privately and was in no way implicating the Holy See in these opinions.

The first part of the paper contains Beauduin's attempt to show that in the pre-Reformation Church of England ever since the time of St. Augustine, the archbishop of Canterbury had enjoyed a patriarchal jurisdiction, conferred on him by the pope by the sign of the pallium. He compares this situation with the Uniate churches of the East and finds a parallel. This, therefore, suggested Beauduin, would be a means of reunion without absorption: the Church of England could come into communion with the Church of Rome and still retain its rite, language, customs, etc. by the recognition by Rome of its Uniate status, and by the acceptance of the pallium from the hand of the pope by the archbishop of Canterbury.

It will be instructive to take a closer look at the principal conclusions arrived at by Beauduin: (a) that there does exist a method or formula of reunion of the two churches which avoids the absorption of the Church of England and which safeguards and respects the internal autonomy of that church while at the same time maintaining the unity of the universal church; (b) that if ever there was a church which, by its origins, its history, and customs, has the right to concessions regarding autonomy it is the Church of England; (c) that the archbishop of Canterbury would be reestablished in his traditional right as patriarch of the Anglican Church after having received the pallium from the pope. This would give him complete power over the interior organization of the church in England, such as enjoyed by the patriarchs of the Uniate churches; (d) that the Latin Code of Canon Law would not be imposed on the Anglican Church, just as it even now does not apply to the Oriental rites. Therefore, if it were judged opportune by the Anglican Church, there would be no obligation to adopt clerical celibacy; (e) that the English Church would have its own proper liturgy, which, Beauduin asserted, was the old Roman liturgy of the 7th and 8th centuries; (f) that the old traditional sees of the English Church be preserved, and the new Catholic ones, created

---

55   Aubert, "Les conversations de Malines," 119.
56   Aubert, "Les conversations de Malines," annex XVII, 142–143.

since 1851 (such as Westminster, Southwark, Portsmouth, etc.) be suppressed – obviously, remarked Beauduin, this would be a serious measure, but no more serious than when Pius VII demanded the resignation of over a hundred French bishops and suppressed their dioceses when he was negotiating the concordat with Napoleon; (g) the major problem which Beauduin foresaw was the question of whether the patriarch would have the same standing or status as a cardinal. He proposed the resolution of this problem, however, by suggesting the creation of a new order of cardinals, namely cardinal-patriarchs. Beauduin pointed out that the order of cardinal-bishops was only created in the 8th century, several hundred years after the creation of cardinal-priests and cardinal-deacons.

The main reaction of the participants to the reading of the *mémoire* was one of surprise, as it had not been circulated beforehand. Even after the conversations were finished, the proposals made by Mercier did not make anything like the impact that one might expect such a document to make. There was no substantial discussion of the proposals in the paper either during the conversations or afterwards. In all, there came only two critiques of value within a reasonable period which touched the subject matter of the *mémoire*. The first was by Fr. Francis Woodlock, a Jesuit from Farm Street in London, and a most consistent opponent of the theory of "corporate reunion," and the second by Outram Evennett, a historian from Cambridge.

Fr. Woodlock pointed out firstly that there was no parallel between the Church of England and the Eastern Catholic Churches, as the Uniates had always guarded the validity of their orders. Indeed, the question of orders was not treated at all in the paper read by Cardinal Mercier. Woodlock noted also that the Anglicans should have no fear of interventions from Rome when, in fact, the English bishops are named by the British prime minister, who is often not even a member of their church. He added that even Anglicans complain that politics are too much involved in the nomination of bishops. Yet another objection by Woodlock concerned the retention of the Anglican liturgy after

reunion. He pointed out that the so-called national liturgy had been composed by the Reformers to replace the Roman missal and to exclude the idea of propitiatory sacrifice from the Mass, and therefore it could not be possible for the two rites to coexist. Woodlock's most serious criticism was directed at the idea of "reunion and not absorption," pointing out that High Church Anglicans, by holding onto the "branch theory," believed that they were already "catholic" and that reconciliation with Rome would not imply any abdication of the historical pretentions of Canterbury, but simply a union of two churches under the primacy of Peter.

The criticism of Outram Evennett begins by pointing out that there is a great difference between individual concessions such as married clergy or communion under both species, and the transformation of the Church of England into a Uniate body. It is true, he states, that the Uniate liturgies and disciplines have an inherent right to a place within the Catholic Church. They grew up concurrently with their Latin counterparts, but outside the Latin Patriarchate, and some of these churches have never at any period been out of communion with Rome. Their rites, their customs, their discipline, their autonomy, represent things ancient and catholic; their orders are unquestioned. No parallel can be drawn between such bodies and the Church of England, whose latter-day liturgy was composed in direct antagonism to the Catholic conception of the Eucharistic sacrifice, whose discipline embraces not only the ordination of married men but the free, unfettered marriage of bishops as well as priests: whose orders have been so solemnly condemned as invalid: and whose Catholic predecessors never enjoyed the patriarchal self-governance of the great patriarchs of the East.[57]

Evennett accused Dom Beauduin of falling into the most elementary trap of historians, that of searching for those facts of history which accord

---

57   H. Outram Evennett, "An Historian looks at Malines," *DubRev* 186, 1930, 246.

with the historian's preconceived plan. He notes that Dom Beauduin is an acknowledged expert on Oriental churches, and he suggests that Beauduin had already conceived the idea of the Church of England as a Uniate church before he began his research and that this preconceived notion influenced his objectivity.

Evennett's criticism, though harsh, has merit. The *mémoire*'s assertion of historical evidence for the patriarchal status of the Church of England is deeply flawed. The document cites various letters, bulls, and histories in Latin in support of Canterbury being a patriarchate. However, in each of these cases the document in question refers to the office of "primate" rather than "patriarch." The terms are not interchangeable, and neither were they interchangeable at the time of Pope Gregory I and St. Augustine of Canterbury. While it is true that Canterbury exercised jurisdiction over other English sees from earliest times, it is also true that other primatial sees exercised similar jurisdiction in their territories. None of these claimed to be or was described as a patriarchate. In fact, the archbishops of Lisbon, who have held the title of patriarch since the 18th century, do not exercise primacy over the bishops of Portugal; the archbishop of Braga is primate of Portugal. The *mémoire* goes to great lengths to suggest how an Anglican patriarchate might function in practice, modelling this on the author's evident familiarity with the Melkite Greek Catholic Church.[58] No matter how attractive this model might be, the asserted parallels between the Melkite Church and the Church of England were not valid.

Beauduin's *mémoire* asked the question: "What will Rome think of this project?" The question also needed to be posed as to what Canterbury would think of it, and, more importantly, what the Anglican Churches outside England would think of it. The document uses the terms "Church of England" and "Anglican Church" almost interchangeably and seems to presume that the level of patriarchal authority it envisages for the

archbishop of Canterbury would be found congenial by other Anglican Churches. Even before the 21st century divisions in the Anglican Communion, certain churches of the communion, most notably those of Scotland and America, have been fiercely proud of their independence and distinctive identity. They would be most unlikely to be willing to be "absorbed" by Canterbury in such a way.

Furthermore, the significance of the granting of the pallium to archbishops of Canterbury is exaggerated in the document. While the wearing of the pallium was originally the prerogative of the pope alone, popes soon began to confer it on other bishops, Pope Gregory the Great, who gave the pallium to St. Augustine of Canterbury, similarly honored Syagrius of Autun, Donus of Messina, and John of Syracuse,[59] none of whom was even a metropolitan, let alone a primate. It is therefore not reasonable to infer that Gregory intended to confer patriarchal status on Augustine by the bestowal of the pallium. Furthermore, since the 8th century, the pallium was worn by all metropolitans, including, until the Reformation, the archbishop of York. Ironically, in the high medieval period, the pallium, though nominally a sign of sharing in the pope's dignity and authority, became a centralizing mechanism by which popes exercised control over local churches, rather than one which signified the autonomy of these local churches.[60]

In the absence of serious discussion of the assertions made in Mercier's surprising paper, the fourth conversation ended on a note of hopefulness for an early resumption. Only Gore did not feel happy about the prospects for the future discussions. In the course of this last meeting an intensive discussion had developed between Gore and Msgr. Batiffol on the subject of *de fide* truths, and the Anglican felt that the Catholics would not

58   Beauduin, *L'Église anglicane unie*, 2.1, 2.11.

59   Joseph Braun, *Die Liturgische Gewandung im Occident und Orient: Nach Ursprung und Entwicklung, Verwendung und Symbolik*, Freiburg i.Br., Herder, 1907, 629.

60   See Steven Schoenig, *Bonds of Wool: The Pallium and Papal Power in the Middle Ages*, Washington DC, Catholic University of America Press, 2016.

budge on questions of dogma even though they were most pliable on questions of organization. The archbishop of Canterbury, however, thought that there should be one more meeting, and then both sides could pause to survey the terrain.

The fifth conversation was provisionally arranged for January 1926, but in December 1925 Cardinal Mercier fell ill. The cardinal had been unwell for some time, but his doctors thought that a surgical operation and rest should allow him to resume work. The operation (for cancer) was not successful, and Mercier died on Jan 23, 1926. The conversations had been postponed till June, but yet another misfortune was to befall the participants. In April, just as Fr. Portal was about to celebrate Mass, he suffered a seizure which incapacitated him. Two months later he suffered another seizure, and this one killed him. Thus, within a very short period of time, two of the central figures of the conversations were gone. When the fifth meeting finally took place on Oct 11–12, it was a meeting only to discuss a memorandum which was to be published.

6   Conclusions

It is difficult to speak of the conversations in terms of success or failure, and in some ways, it is irrelevant to speak of them in such terms. The importance of the conversations lies in the vision which they leave, a vision of Christian spirits yearning after reconciliation among the churches, and a willingness to give all and to suffer all in the service of reunion.

In terms of the immediate reaction of the authorities of the two churches, there was an immediate cooling towards any resumption of discussions on the subject of reunion. Both the Anglican and Roman authorities were opposed to the publication of the papers from Malines, and it was only the determination of Lord Halifax which eventually led to their printing. There was a distinct change in attitude from Rome after Mercier's death, with the Holy See's attention now directed

to dealing with the blowback of Modernism and in particular with any activity motivated by the desire for restoring Christian unity that was suspected to not be orthodox, loyal, and completely intransigent and uncompromising in the matter of the dogmatic requirements for union with the Catholic Church. On July 8, 1927, just before the Faith and Order Conference at Lausanne, Cardinal Merry del Val's Holy Office issued a reminder of Benedict XV's regulations about Roman Catholic participation in ecumenical assemblies: that Catholics must not take part in "congresses, meetings, lectures, or societies which have the scope of uniting into a religious confederation all who in any sense whatever call themselves Christians."[61] The spirit of the 1928 encyclical *Mortalium animos*, in which Pope Pius XI condemned certain unnamed movements involved in the efforts for Christian unity and seemed to close the door on ecumenical engagement by Catholics, was already in the air.[62]

What was decisive, indeed, in both the Anglican orders debate and in bringing the Malines Conversations to an inconclusive end was that because of his position in Rome, Merry del Val was taken as an expert and consultant in things concerning England and English Church affairs. His experience as secretary of state to Pope Pius X and his involvement in the anti-Modernist campaign, left him with an abiding suspicion of any signs of Modernism, something which he considered clearly evident in the Church of England. He was also the inside advisor at the Vatican for those ecclesiastics and lay people in England who were opposed to corporate reunion with Rome. Finding himself in such a pivotal position, the English-born cardinal used it to the fullest in advancing his own conservative convictions.

In England, Archbishop Davidson was occupied by the controversy involving the revised *Prayer Book* and its passage through parliament.

---

61   J. Derek Holmes, *The Papacy in the Modern World (1914–1978)*, London, Burns & Oates, 1981, 29.

62   See Marie Levant's contribution in this volume.

Discussions were in progress since 1915, when a Joint Committee of the Convocation of Canterbury presented its initial proposals for some changes to the *Prayer Book*, including a rearrangement of the Communion service, that caused much alarm among evangelical churchmen. Although entirely unconnected with the happenings at Malines, many of the more Protestant-inclined members of the Church of England were linking these attempts to revise the *Prayer Book* with the conversations.

Despite that, a further, little-known set of discussions about reunion took place in London in 1931 and 1932.[63] The driving force behind the meetings, Sir James Marchant, was, curiously, neither Anglican nor Catholic, but a ritualist nonconformist minister, who combined passionate activism on the subject of public morals with an almost obsessive interest in establishing and maintaining correspondence with the leaders of church, state, and society. The Anglican participants were altogether less part of the mainstream establishment than the Malines participants. They were "Anglo-Papalist" by conviction and had been spurred to explore going over to Rome by developments in the Anglican Communion such as the approval of artificial contraception by the Lambeth Conference of 1930. The Catholic participants included the former Archbishop of Bombay Alban Goodier, the Benedictine abbot of Downside Cuthbert Butler, and the provincial of the English Dominicans Bede Jarret. These "Thackeray Hotel Conversations" failed to attract the support or interest of the Church of England authorities, and little was achieved by the meetings.

As the first direct discussions between Anglicans and Catholics in three hundred years, the conversations at Malines stand out as a historical moment in reunion efforts, and the fact that they took place at all probably produced their most enduring success. This can be clearly seen in three distinct areas. First of all, the conversations allowed the Roman Catholic Church to "test the waters" of ecumenical discussion without being totally or officially involved in their organization. Through the efforts of Cardinal Mercier, acting in his own name but with semiofficial blessing from the Holy See, the Roman Church, while officially banning the participation of Roman Catholics in any joint or collaborative ventures with other churches or communions such as the Life and Work or Faith and Order meetings, was able tentatively to involve itself in a similar venture. This tiny move was a real opening of doors in terms of future ecumenical relations.

Secondly, the method and process of discussion employed at Malines laid, in a very real sense, the groundwork for an acceptable methodology in ecumenical discussion which was to become the norm of future meetings. The objectives of *unity by convergence*, an acceptable *unity in diversity*, and the *emphasis on common beliefs*, as well as the concept of *unity without absorption*, have all since become the basis of ecumenical discussions between the Church of England and the Roman Catholic Church.[64]

Finally, the influence which the person and writings both of Cardinal Mercier and Lord Halifax and their ecumenical efforts had, long after their deaths, on Cardinal Angelo Roncalli, the future pope of Vatican II, is testified both by Jean Guitton,[65] a student and disciple of Abbé Portal, and Msgr. Loris Capovilla, private secretary to Pope John XXIII.[66]

In conclusion, it is surely more than conjecture to say that the Malines Conversations could have

---

63   See Mark Vickers, *Reunion Revisited: 1930s Ecumenism Exposed*, Leominster, Gracewing, 2017.

64   In his address on the occasion of the visit to Rome of Archbishop Donald Coggan in April 1977, Pope Paul VI, in speaking of the flowering of ecumenical activity in the preceding years, concluded that "these words of hope 'the Anglican Church united not absorbed' are no longer a mere dream"; Paul VI, "Address to Frederick Donald Coggan, Archbishop of Canterbury," AAS 69, 1977, 284–285.

65   Jean Guitton, *Dialogue avec les précurseurs: Journal œcuménique (1922–1962)*, Paris, Aubier, 1962, 61ff.

66   Cited in: John J. Hughes, *Absolutely Null and Utterly Void: An Account of the Papal Condemnation of Anglican Orders (1896)*, London, Sheed & Ward, 1968, 209.

BARLOW AND BROWNE

been instrumental in enabling the Roman Catholic ecumenical engagement that Vatican II enabled to come out of the shadows of church life from the mid-1960s onwards, or the event of Pope Paul VI's personal reception in Rome of the archbishop of Canterbury, Michael Ramsey, in March 1966, culminating in Pope Paul spontaneously removing his episcopal ring and placing it on Ramsey's finger. The Joint Declaration signed by the two leaders on the occasion initiated talks that led eventually to the setting-up of the ARCIC in 1970, thereby marking a new era in Anglican-Roman Catholic relations.

Bibliography

Aubert, Roger, "L'Histoire des Conversations de Malines," *ColMechl* 52/1, 1967, 43–54.

Barlow, Bernard, *"A Brother Knocking at the Door": The Malines Conversations (1921–1925)*, Norwich, Canterbury Press, 1996.

Bell, George K.A., *Randall Davidson, Archbishop of Canterbury*, 2 vols., London, Oxford University Press, 1935.

Bivort de la Saudée, Jacques, *Anglicans et catholiques: Le problème de l'union anglo-romaine (1833–1933)*, Paris, Plon, 1949.

Bolton, Charles A., *A Catholic Memorial of Lord Halifax and Cardinal Mercier*, London, Williams & Norgate, 1935.

Dick, John A., *The Malines Conversations Revisited*, Leuven, Leuven University Press, 1989.

Frere, Walter Howard, *Recollections of Malines*, London, The Centenary Press, 1935.

Halifax, Charles Lindley Wood, *The Conversations at Malines (1921–1925): Original Documents*, London, P. Allan, 1930.

Ladous, Régis, *Monsieur Portal et les siens (1855–1926)*, Paris, Cerf, 1985.

Lockhart, John Gilbert, *Charles Lindley – Viscount Halifax (1885–1934)*, 2 vols., London, The Centenary Press, 1935.

CHAPTER 29

The Beginnings of Ecumenism in Germany: From the Hochkirche Movement to the Development of the Una Sancta Groups

Paul Metzlaff

1 Introduction

The religious landscape in Germany in the 1920s and 1930s was a vibrant one characterized by a desire for spiritual renewal and authenticity. From the Catholic tradition emerged the Bible movement in which Catholics sought to find a new vigorous relationship to Holy Scripture. This current helped bring about a rapprochement with Protestantism and contributed to the foundation of the Katholisches Bibelwerk in 1933. Drawing on 19th-century explorations of the liturgy, the liturgical movement highlighted the importance of everyday practice and participation of the Catholic faithful in religious life. In the largely Protestant Jugendbewegung, the German youth movement, young people sought to translate their experience of nature to a new vision of faith and society. Many figures active in these movements from both the Protestant and Catholic confessions would later be decisive in the origins of the ecumenical movement. These include such key thinkers as Pius Parsch, Romano Guardini, Lambert Beauduin, Friedrich Heiler, and Karl Bernhard Ritter.[1]

These movements for renewal each formed their own links with the emerging ecumenical movement. This chapter will look at one of these relationships by studying the transition from the Hochkirche movement, whose influence was reaching a peak at the time, to the Una Sancta

movement. A pivotal role in this transition is held by the Berlin-Hermsdorf Conference, the first ever ecumenical conference to take place in Germany. It laid the foundations for the Una Sancta movement, which soon followed. An in-depth treatment of this movement is justified in view of its importance in these wider developments.

I shall use the example of the Munich group to illustrate the origins, working method, and influence of the Una Sancta in the 1930 and 1940s. This affords a more detailed view of local pioneering ecumenical work based on the available archive material. The constant unifying thread in the origins of ecumenism in Germany is the enormous dedication of individuals whose parrhesia would come to form the basis for the subsequent ecumenical understanding among the churches. In some cases, these are well-known figures such as Romano Guardini or Friedrich Heiler. However, they also include countless ordinary people who were not theologians, but the very "People of God," to use the terminology of Vatican II, who gave expression to an unmistakable clamor for unity and in so doing acted as pioneers.

2 The Hochkirche Movement: The Roots of Ecumenism in Germany

In 1917, the Lutheran pastor Heinrich Hansen published his own 95 theses, entitled *Stimuli et clavi*, to mark the 400th anniversary of the Reformation.[2] This may be regarded as providing

---

1 For the liturgical movement in the Catholic Church see Benedikt Kranemann and Adalberto Mainardi's contribution in this volume; for German Protestantism and liturgical renovation in the same period, see Martin C. Lenz's contribution in this volume.

2 Heinrich Hansen, *Stimuli et clavi i.e. theses adversus huius temporis errores et abusus, quas publice sive disputando*

the decisive momentum for the foundation of the Hochkirchliche Vereinigung.[3]

Hansen had already spent much of his life studying the Roman Catholic Church and inter-confessional relations and had published an article on the subject in 1909 "On the Divisions in the Church,"[4] in which he refers for the first time to "a holy Catholic Church." His grand idea of Catholicity would later reappear in greater detail in his theses.

At the same time as the 95 theses, Hansen published the essay *Open Letter to the Divided Brethren*,[5] significantly shortened from its original conception as a major work on ecumenism. Here he suggests the foundation of a league of peace, which would take place shortly afterwards. He was joined by Pastor Heinrich Mosel, who spoke for the first time in this context of Hochkirche in the *Deutsches Pfarrerblatt* in June 1918. This expression eventually prevailed over Hansen's own suggestion of a *Gralsbund* (grail union) at the foundation meeting held in Berlin on Oct 9, 1918. Meanwhile, Hansen himself was elected president of the union, a post which in the end he occupied for barely a year.[6]

The principles set forth at the Hochkirche assembly of October 1918 clearly bear the hall-marks of Hansen's influence. As an example, the Hochkirche sought to raise awareness among Protestants of their "membership of the whole church of Christ," i.e. Catholicity. They also wanted to institute an episcopal constitution, as Hansen had recommended in thesis 40, lend "greater weight to the significance of the holy sacraments and their objective nature" (thesis 80), and saw it as one of their tasks to draw up a breviary for Christians from the Protestant tradition, a project which Friedrich Heiler would subsequently bring to fruition.[7] These principles laid the foundations for a rapprochement with other confessions on which ecumenical ideas in Germany could be built.

2.1 Friedrich Heiler and the Development of the Hochkirchliche Vereinigung

Friedrich Heiler was born in Munich in 1892. He was awarded his doctorate in 1918 for an investigation into prayer in philosophy from the perspective of the history of religion.[8] As part of his research, he studied the compendium on religious history written by the Swedish archbishop, Nathan Söderblom,[9] which he read to great effect. This led to the start of a rich correspondence between the two.[10] Heiler had originally planned to train as a Catholic priest but his scholarly work in the religious field caused so much offense in ecclesiastical circles that he moved away from Catholic theology. On May 15, 1918, Heiler wrote to Söderblom describing his state of mind:

> I am basically a Christian in the Protestant tradition; ... However, the outward structure of my personal Christianity is the mystical,

    sive scribendo defendet, in: Theodor Hauf & Ursula Kisker, eds., *Siebzig Jahre Hochkirchliche Bewegung (1918–1988): Hochkirchliche Arbeit: Woher? Wozu? Wohin?*, Bochum, HV, 1989, 33–52. For an insight into Hansen's theses, see in this volume Martun C. Lenz's contribution.

3   A short biography with a particular focus on the existential roots of the theses can be found in Heinrich Kröger, "Zur Vorgeschichte der 95 Thesen von Heinrich Hansen," in: Hauf & Kisker, eds., *Siebzig Jahre Hochkirchliche Bewegung*, 22–29.

4   Heinrich Hansen, "Über Spaltungen in der Kirche," *Kirchen- und Schulblatt*, 1909.

5   Heinrich Hansen, *Offener Brief an die getrennten Brüder*, Altona, 1918.

6   Kröger, "Zur Vorgeschichte der 95 Thesen von Heinrich Hansen," 28.

7   On this, see "Grundsätze der Hochkirchlichen Vereinigung: Angenommen in der begründeten Mitglieder-Versammlung zu Berlin am 9. Oktober 1918," in: Hauf & Kisker, eds., *Siebzig Jahre Hochkirchliche Bewegung*, 53f.

8   Friedrich Heiler, *Das Gebet: Eine religionsgeschichtliche und religionspsychologische Untersuchung*, Munich, E. Reinhardt, 1918.

9   Nathan Söderblom, *Tiele-Söderbloms Kompendium der Religionsgeschichte*, Berlin-Schöneberg, T. Biller, [5]1920.

10 Friedrich von Hügel, Nathan Söderblom & Friedrich Heiler, *Briefwechsel (1909–1931)*, ed. Paul Misner, Paderborn, Bonifatius, 1981.

sacramental experience of worship of the Catholic Church. I have completely broken with the rigid dogmatism and hierarchical political organization of the Catholic Church. But the Eucharistic mystery, the very center of its worship, binds me to this church.[11]

In 1919, he traveled to Sweden at Söderblom's invitation. There he received Holy Communion, which in Sweden at the time was regarded as a confessional act and binding expression of conversion. One of the lectures he gave already contains his subsequent program for "Evangelical Catholicity." He does not consider the differences between Protestant and Catholic piety as unassailable but rather argues that they complement each other, particularly in terms of individual and communal devotion.

The mystery of the Eucharist was the culmination of the divine service as far as he was concerned. The possibility of restoring this mystery to the Evangelical divine service was not a remote fantasy. Heiler also mentions here for the first time the Hochkirche movement as an example of how strong the desire in Germany was for Evangelical-Catholic church services.[12] This shows that he must already have known of the Hochkirchliche Vereinigung in his time.

In 1920, through the mediation of Rudolf Otto, he became professor for religious history at the Protestant theological faculty of the University of Marburg. There he attended the cold and sobering Protestant church services that almost led him to renounce his path of Evangelical Catholicity. His desire for devout worship was assuaged by the new student church services in Marburg, in which he took part and also led. They were characterized by Bible readings and sermons, psalm recitals, guided and free prayer, and silent worship. Heiler was also invited by Söderblom to the two major ecumenical

congresses held in Stockholm (1925) and Lausanne (1927), which he then brought to the attention of the German-speaking public through a number of publications.

The principles of the Hochkirchliche Vereinigung were shared by Heiler. Inversely, his work *The Essence of Catholicism*[13] and the concept of Evangelical Catholicity it represented was in turn drawn upon by the union in its early days. Not surprisingly, therefore, he was invited to speak at the *Hochkirchentag* in 1921, although for unknown reasons he did not accept the invitation.

In 1924, there was a split in the Hochkirchliche Vereinigung between the wing more focused on the identities of the various regional state churches and the more ecumenical one. The union's president, Pastor Mosel, hoped that Heiler would be able to help heal the division. This time he did accept the invitation and gave the main lecture on the Evangelical Hochkirche at the *Hochkirchentag* in December 1925.

In his lecture, Heiler makes it clear that only someone who, as a Christian from the Protestant tradition, embraces the common paths of all churches until the 9th century and believes in the continuing connection among all churches in Jesus Christ can be a Hochkirche member. He also stresses the importance of the Apostolic succession and the office of bishop, together with the reverence in which the sacrament of the Eucharist was held in the early church. This was fully consonant with the idea of *sola gratia*. For "nowhere else does man experience the miracle of grace, forgiveness, justification and sanctification as deeply as at the Communion table."[14]

Heiler's talk did indeed contribute to overcoming the division: on Jan 18 and 19, 1927, the

---

11   F. Heiler to N. Söderblom, May 15, 1918, cited in: Hans Hartog, *Evangelische Katholizität: Weg und Vision Friedrich Heilers*, Mainz, Matthias Grünewald, 1995, 15.

12   Hartog, *Evangelische Katholizität: Weg und Vision*, 17.

13   Friedrich Heiler, *Das Wesen des Katholizismus*, Munich, Ernst Reinhardt, 1920.

14   Friedrich Heiler, "Evangelisches Hochkirchentum: Vortrag auf dem 7. Hochkirchentag," in: Friedrich Heiler, *Evangelische Katholizität: Gesammelte Aufsätze und Vorträge*, vol. 1, Munich, E. Reinhardt, 1926, 198–250, here 228, cited in: Hartog, *Evangelische Katholizität: Weg und Vision*, 27.

organization decided to embark on a collaborative working relationship among the different groups, which resulted in more activities than ever before in the years leading up to 1930. This included working more intensively on the Evangelical breviary, publishing a community parish leaflet in addition to the existing *Die Hochkirche* publication, and the appearance in September 1927 of the first version of an Eucharist celebration of the Hochkirchlichen Vereinigung.

In 1927, Heiler was ordained according to the Hochkirche rite by Pastor Gustav Adolf Glinz, president of the Schweizer Diakonievereins. In the same year he celebrated a "Evangelical Mass" in the Marburg university chapel, in which Karl Bernhard Ritter, minister at the Marburg university church and cofounder of the Berneuchener Movement, took part. He still maintained at this time that a celebration in this Evangelical-Catholic form was not possible, a view which he later changed. The university's Protestant congregation consequently forbade Heiler and the group of students around him from using the chapel owing to the offence caused by this form of service, after which they worshipped in a private chapel.

Heiler was elected president of the Hochkirchliche Vereinigung at its assembly held on Oct 3 and 4, 1929. In an article published shortly afterwards, entitled "High Church Duties", he writes: "Evangelical Catholicity as the true Catholicity is the shining ideal guiding the Hochkirche movement."[15]

Heiler considered having himself ordained priest by an Old Catholic bishop according to the Hochkirche episcopal ideal in order to become part of the line of the Apostolic succession. He stood firm nonetheless in rejecting conversion to the Old Catholic Church, since this would "destroy all our work so far and cut us off from any chance of influencing Protestant circles."[16] He also upheld

this principle of rejecting conversion with respect to the Catholic Church, since this would otherwise make true ecumenism impossible.

Having decided against being ordained by the Old Catholic Church, Heiler sought an alternative. On Aug 28, 1930, he was consecrated bishop by the Gallican bishop, Pierre-Gaston Vigué, bishop Aloys Stumpfl, and Pastor Glinz, who himself had been ordained bishop only the day before. From this time onwards, confirmations were celebrated by the Hochkirchliche Vereinigung and deaconesses consecrated in the Old Church tradition. The main criticism of the consecration of bishops came from the *Landeskirchen* wing, but Heiler still managed to hold the movement together.

Other important projects of the movement were put into practice over the next few years. Thus, in May 1931, a new church service formula called the "Eucharistic Celebration of the Protestant-Catholic Eucharistic Community" was published in *Die Hochkirche* magazine.[17] It is heavily influenced by the *Missale Romanum* but also contains passages from the Eastern Church tradition. In December 1932, the long-desired "Evangelical-Catholic breviary," first announced in the foundation program of 1918, finally appeared.[18] Both these publications demonstrate that the Hochkirche movement aimed to add objective forms to supplement Protestant subjective experience:

> By means of this truly comprehensive "draft" of an Evangelical-Catholic breviary, in an extremely short period of time Heiler placed the Hochkirche movement on all three of the pillars on which Evangelical Catholicity is founded: the church ministry reintegrated

15   Friedrich Heiler, "Hochkirchliche Aufgaben," *HKi* 11, 1929, 328, cited in: Hartog, *Evangelische Katholizität: Weg und Vision*, 33.

16   Friedrich Heiler, unpublished letter to the Old Catholic bishops' conference, Aug 10, 1928, cited in: Hartog,

Evangelische Katholizität: Weg und Vision, 36–38, here 36.

17   "Eucharistiefeier der Evangelisch-katholischen Eucharistischen Gemeinschaft," *HKi* 13, 1931, 145–162.

18   "Evangelisch-katholisches Brevier: Erster Teil: Sonderheft der Hochkirche: Im Auftrag der Brevierkommission der Hochkirchlichen Vereinigung," ed. Friedrich Heiler, *HKi* 14, 1932.

into the *successio apostolica*, the celebration of the Eucharist, and the Old Church Liturgy of the Hours.[19]

2.2 The Hochkirche Movement and National Socialism

In two articles published on Mar 7 and 14, 1932, Heiler attacked the seizure of power by the National Socialists: "What German Christianity needs right now is a Protestant-Catholic front of unity against all the forces threatening the core of Christianity, regardless of whether they emanate from the right or the left."[20]

This is the founding idea behind the Berlin-Hermsdorf Conference and the later Una Sancta movement, namely that of the confessions coming together out of equal necessity, and it is consequently decisive for the development of ecumenism in Germany. However, many members of the Hochkirche movement placed their hopes in the German church and particularly in the Reich's bishop, which seemed to satisfy their idea of an episcopal guide. They therefore asked Heiler to bring the Hochkirchliche Vereinigung into line with the Deutsche Christen. Heiler's profound theological convictions would not permit him to do so. He also regarded such operation as a threat to the individual identity and independence of the union. This made internal conflict within the Hochkirche inevitable.

Heiler resigned as first president of the Hochkirchliche Vereinigung and was supposed to be replaced by a pastor sympathetic to the National Socialists. His successor was Pastor Walter Drobnitzky from Lipny in Upper Silesia. However, for Drobnitzky, too, bringing the two churches into line was out of the question, and he advised the members of the union to follow him in leaving the Deutsche Christen. At the *Hochkirchentag* held from Mar 6 to 8, 1934, the diametrically opposed views regarding National

Socialism clashed once again.[21] New elections were held in which Drobnitzky was confirmed as first president and Heiler elected second president, against all expectations.

The events at the *Hochkirchentag* show that the National Socialist rulers were manipulating the Deutsche Christen for their own propaganda purposes. It was already known that the Confessing Church would meet in Barmen to draw up a theological declaration. Heiler himself could foresee that not only Protestants, but Christianity as a whole, were under threat. The looming conflict with National Socialism was not a matter for one sole confession. Joint action was required, and there was also a chance for ecumenical rapprochement. Heiler had learned of the great desire for dialogue on the part of the Catholics when he and Karl Bernhard Ritter had sat together after a lecture by Romano Guardini in Marburg and found that their ideas were surprisingly similar. This led Heiler to wonder whether it might not be possible to hold such talks officially.

No sooner had the *Hochkirchentag* decided against incorporation into the Deutsche Christen than Heiler and Drobnitzky were authorized by the assembled to embark upon interconfessional talks with Catholics and Anglicans.[22] The foundation stone for the first ecumenical conference in Germany in Berlin-Hermsdorf had been laid.

3 The 1934 Berlin-Hermsdorf Conference

The conference held at the seminary in Hermsdorf, near Berlin, during Pentecost (May 22–25) in 1934 can be seen as the first significant expression of the growing interest in interconfessional rapprochement, mutual understanding, and the hoped-for unanimous resistance to religious repression that would result from this.[23] The conference minutes

19   Hartog, *Evangelische Katholizität: Weg und Vision*, 55.
20   Hartog, *Evangelische Katholizität: Weg und Vision*, 57.
21   Hartog, *Evangelische Katholizität: Weg und Vision*, 61f.
22   Hartog, *Evangelische Katholizität: Weg und Vision*, 64.
23   See Jörg Ernesti, *Ökumene im Dritten Reich*, Paderborn, Bonifatius, 2007, 42–123; Leonard J. Swidler, *The*

show that its origins date back to a lecture held by Romano Guardini in Marburg and a conversation that took place afterwards between Guardini, Heiler, and Ritter.[24] Ritter provides a vivid description of the impulse given by the Berlin professor of the philosophy of religion:

> It was in Marburg. We were sitting together after a lecture by Guardini, and began conversing into the night and early hours of the morning. It became clear to me that night that my previous view of the other side's position was untenable. I realized that the weapons I had been equipped with by my theological teachers were aimed against opponents that did not even exist. The questions raised by the theological controversies of the 16th and 17th centuries turned out to be redundant.[25]

The result of this conversation with Guardini and Heiler not only had a long-lasting influence on Ritter, but was to be reaffirmed in numerous subsequent interconfessional discussions, particularly "the inspiring week of interconfessional discussions that met in May 1934 ... in the seminary in Berlin-Hermsdorf."[26] It appears that the idea of "dogmatic discussions between Protestant and Catholic theologians"[27] came from Guardini but was executed by Heiler.

Heiler approached the bishop of Berlin, Nikolaus Bares, "because he had shown a particularly sympathetic attitude to the separated Protestant brethren,"[28] as can be seen from his speech to Protestants in the Berlin Sportpalast on Feb 11, 1934, held two months before the conference's preparatory meeting on Apr 22, 1934. Bishop Bares stressed the need for Christians to work together to resist the National Socialist regime, which he did not mention by name, referring to it instead by using the common ecclesiastical codename of "Neopaganism."[29] Thus, the first theological conference between Protestants and Catholics on German soil should be understood within the context of the harsh reprisals taken by the Nazi regime. In his speech, Bishop Bares proceeded to demand a joint commitment on the part of both denominations, thereby signaling his willingness for a rapprochement. It was now Heiler's task to start detailed planning of the conference. He was entrusted with this by the 15th Hochkirchliche Vereinigung assembly and, together with Drobnitzky, proceeded to act on the resolution passed there to make contact with Anglican and Roman Catholic circles.

The resolution authorized him to make contact with Bishop Bares since the latter had already shown his openness to dialogue.[30] In a letter dated Mar 28, 1934, Canon Georg Banasch informed Heiler of Bishop Bares' offer to hold the conference in his own diocese of Berlin. The bishop would provide the seminary of Hermsdorf as the location, thus clearly showing that he was assuming patronage of an event that would bring together 24 high-ranking Protestant and Catholic theologians.[31]

Ecumenical Vanguard: The History of the Una Sancta Movement, Pittsburgh PA, Duquesne University Press, 1966, 135–137.

24   See the minutes of the Berlin-Hermsdorf Konferenz, which were prepared by the Vicar Renate Ludwig from her own shorthand notes and reviewed by Friedrich Heiler, "Protokoll der Berlin-Hermsdorfer Konferenz: Erstellt zwischen 25. und 27.7.1934," in: Ernesti, *Ökumene*, 72–100, here 72.

25   Karl Bernhard Ritter, "Begegnungen mit dem römischen Katholizismus (1956)," in: Karl Bernhard Ritter, *Kirche und Wirklichkeit: Gesammelte Aufsätze*, ed. Christian Zippert, Kassel, Stauda, 1971, 196–213, here 198.

26   Ritter, "Begegnungen mit dem römischen Katholizismus," 198.

27   Minutes of the preparatory meeting dated May 4, 1934, cited in: Ernesti, *Ökumene*, 42.

28   Ernesti, *Ökumene*, 42.

29   Ernesti, *Ökumene*, 42f.

30   Ernesti, *Ökumene*, 43, note 119.

31   See Friedrich Heiler, "Utopie oder Wirklichkeit der *Una-Sancta*-Arbeit?," *Ökumenische Einheit* 1, 1948, 6–31, here 10.

3.1 Preparatory Meeting in April 1934

Banasch's letter was followed by a well-documented preparatory meeting that took place in his home on Apr 22, 1934. Its purpose was to decide who else should take part in the conference, the subjects to be discussed, and the method of debate.[32] According to the SD Intelligence Report on "Reunification Attempts between Catholicism and Protestantism," this meeting was attended by "Prelate Dr. *Banasch*, Berlin, Jesuit priest Max *Pribilla*, Munich, Cathedral Dean *Simon*, Paderborn, Professor Pius *Parsch*, Klosterneuburg Abbey on the Catholic side, and Professor *Heiler*, Marburg, Professor *Stählin*, Münster, Professor Anders *Nygren*, Lund, and Legation Priest Birger *Forell*, Berlin, on the Protestant side."[33] Missing from the SD Report is a note of the attendance of the vicar of Berlin Cathedral, Max Prange, and it also gives the dates of the conference as from May 22 to 26,[34] whereas the minutes cited by Jörg Ernesti refer to the week of the Pentecost (May 22–25).[35] The long distances traveled by many of the participants and the detailed planning of subjects and invitees show that the organizers intended the conference to be much more than a brief exchange of views; they aimed at a true Protestant-Catholic theological conference. It was to include a wide range of ecclesiastical representatives to facilitate collaboration between Protestant and Catholic theology, which was attributed with great significance within the ecumenical rapprochement.[36] "Georg Schulz (priest from Barmen), Heinz Dietrich Wendland (university lecturer from Heidelberg), Walter Drobnitzky (priest from Upper Silesia), then the first president of the Hochkirchliche Vereinigung, and 'a Protestant layman' were to be invited" from the Protestant side.[37]

By inviting a representative of the bishop of Chichester, George Bell, president of the ecumenical council Life and Work, the preparatory meeting attempted to forge links with both the Anglicans and the official ecumenical movement. In a letter to Heiler's wife, Anne Marie, on May 16, 1934, the bishop agreed to send his cathedral deacon,[38] but for unknown reasons he appears not to have taken part in the conference.

Besides the Anglican Church, the Swedish Church was also to be invited,[39] namely Birger Forell and Anders Nygren. The Hochkirchliche Vereinigung had long felt close liturgical and theological ties to the tradition of this church, not to mention the fact that the conference was a way for Heiler to fulfill the wish of his former, now deceased, mentor, Nathan Söderblom.[40] His desire not only to create a dialogue between Lutherans and Catholics but to achieve the greatest possible ecclesiastical representation led Heiler to contact the Protestant theologian Adolf Keller, who, however, turned down the invitation in a letter dated May 16, 1934.[41] Heinrich Kahlefeld and Karl Adam were also unable to attend. Nonetheless, the final participants still accounted for a wide spectrum of ecclesiastical and academic life.[42]

3.2 The Conference

Although Bishop Bares did not take part in person in the preparatory meeting or in the theological discussions, he still performed a special role. He

---

32   See Ernesti, *Ökumene*, 58.

33   "Lagebericht des SD: 'Wiedervereinigungsbestrebungen zwischen Katholizismus und Protestantismus': Zwischen dem 9.8. und 6.11.1940 (erschlossen)," cited in: Ernesti, *Ökumene*, 248–300, here 249.

34   "Lagebericht des SD," 249.

35   Ernesti, *Ökumene*, 58.

36   See Adolf Deißmann, *Una Sancta: Zum Geleit in das ökumenische Jahr 1937*, Gütersloh, C. Bertelsmann, 1936, 56.

37   Ernesti, *Ökumene*, 58.

38   Ernesti, *Ökumene*, 59, esp. note 187.

39   See Heiler, "Utopie oder Wirklichkeit," 10.

40   See Ernesti, *Ökumene*, 59f., and furthermore: "Prof. Heiler: A doctrinal irenic dialogue between Protestants and Catholics is the longing of the Germans and represents fulfillment of the wish of the deceased Archbishop Söderblom"; "Protokoll der Berlin-Hermsdorfer Konferenz," 72.

41   Ernesti, *Ökumene*, 60 with note 193. A short biography of Adolf Keller can also be found there.

42   Ernesti, *Ökumene*, 60f.

was constantly informed about the status of the talks and represented the official Catholic side of the dialogue, together with the dean of Paderborn Cathedral, Paul Simon, and the canon of Berlin Cathedral, Georg Banasch. While Bares was the patron and Banasch in charge of the official minutes, the brilliant Simon was the chairman of the ecumenical symposium on theological controversies.[43] The conference itself could not have the status of official talks of union as the 1928 encyclical, *Mortalium animos*, had forbidden Catholics from participating in any such meetings.[44] Heiler had to find a way of keeping this tension in delicate balance when making the preparations.

Heiler was able to find a way of including the official church hierarchies – he even sent a memorandum of the conference to Rome – while also stressing the unofficial nature of the discussions. The initial uncertainty about the nature of the event is shown by the fact that in the minutes of the preparatory meeting and of the conference itself it was sometimes described as a "meeting" or "discussion," and on other occasions referred to as "theological conference," "religious discussion" and "discussion about controversial dogmatic teachings."[45] It is extremely interesting to note the distinction, if only in terms of different terminology, between an unofficial encounter suggested by the expressions "meeting" and "discussion," and a serious at least semi-official dogmatic debate indicated by the other phrases used.

While the meeting was dedicated to dogmatic discussions, as Guardini had termed it, it

was also bound to address the aim expressed by Bishop Bares of forming a joint resistance to the Nazi outlook. This meant maintaining the utmost secrecy. Despite this, a significant amount of information about the conference is found in the SD Report, including knowledge of one of its aims, namely "for Protestantism and Catholicism to join together in a united front against National Socialism."[46] In addition to the preparatory meeting of Apr 22, 1934, held in Banasch's home, the SD Report also reflects the conference's underlying purpose – for 400 years the churches had talked only about separation and now it was time to look at what they had in common[47] – along with the topics and the participants, even though it does contain some inaccuracies.

The list of participants was not compiled centrally, for example by Bishop Bares, but rather each confession drew up its own. This procedure was also adopted after the war by the Jaeger-Stählin circle.[48]

The following figures took part in this meeting in Hermsdorf: 1) Cathedral Dean Dr. Simon ..., 2) Dr. Damasus Winzen ..., 3) Priest Grosche ..., 4) Priest Dr. [Karl Bernard] Ritter ..., 5) Prof. DDr. Stählin ..., 6) Dean Beta ..., 7) Choir Master Dr. Pius Parsch ..., 8) Canon Monsignor Dr. Banasch ..., 9) Legation Priest Birger Forell from the Swedish Church ..., 10) Priest Georg Schulz ..., 11) Prof. Dr. Anders [Nygren] ..., 12) Vicar Ludwig ..., 13) Prof. Dr. Bernhard Rosenmöller ..., 14) Max Pribilla ..., 15) Univ. Prof. DDr. Jos. Koch ..., 16) University Pastor

---

43   See Heiler, "Utopie oder Wirklichkeit," 10.

44   Ernesti, *Ökumene*, 43. Given that there is only one Christian church, namely the Catholic Church, according to Pope Pius XI, it does not suffer under the wrongly assumed deficiencies of division, but is already one, which is why he points out: "In this state of affairs, it is evident that the Apostolic See cannot take part in their symposia under any circumstances and that on no account may Catholics support or encourage such undertakings [relating to unification]"; cited in: Pius XI, *Rundschreiben über die Förderung der wahren Einheit der Religion*, Freiburg i.Br., Herder, 1928, 19.

45   Ernesti, *Ökumene*, 44.

46   "Lagebericht des SD," 249.

47   On this, see also Pribilla's remarks looking back on the beginnings of the ecumenical movement in Germany: "It has come about from a combination of adversity and faith that the issue of unity for all Christian churches has once again become a question of conscience, which they cannot ignore without grave violation of their duty"; Max Pribilla, *Die Una Sancta-Bewegung: Eine erste Einführung*, Meitingen, Kyrios Verlag, 1948, 4.

48   Ernesti, *Ökumene*, 44.

Dr. Joh. Pinsk ..., 17) Dr. phil. Paula Schäfer ..., 18) Prof. Friedrich Heiler ..., 19) Priest Friedrich Schöfer ..., 20) Professor Romano Guardini ..., 21) Privatdozent, Dr. Walter [Künneth] ..., 22) Cragg, Chaplain of the British mission in Berlin, 23) Dr. Bate, Deacon of York, England, 24) Cathedral Vicar Dr. Max Prange.[49]

Friedrich Heiler and Paul Simon were the conference coordinators. Simon had been invited by Banasch with Bishop Bares' agreement, and as its highest-ranking Catholic provided the link to the Catholic hierarchy.[50] Short biographies of the most important participants can be found in the work of Jörg Ernesti, although his evaluation is, needless to say, subjective.[51]

On Tuesday, May 22, 1934, Paul Simon opened the four-day conference at the Berlin-Hermsdorf seminary with the welcome speech, and Friedrich Heiler spoke of the (personal) "motivation" given to the ecumenical encounter through Archbishop Söderblom and Guardini's lecture in Marburg as its immediate catalyst. He also mentioned the subject of "grace" as one of the conference's central questions and stressed that the *Confessio Augustana* aimed "to be a confession for the unity of the church."[52]

After these opening words, the first introductory lecture was given by Pius Parsch on the "Essence of Catholic Piety".[53] This was not followed by the scheduled talk by Friedrich Schulz even though he was present. Instead, Dean Beta spoke on the subject of "The Essence of Protestant Piety".[54] Consistent with the methodological program, these introductions were followed by a discussion.

On May 23, Nygren spoke on "Grace and Justification" from a Protestant point of view, while the talk scheduled to be held by Karl Adam,

who could not attend due to illness, was presented by Professor Josef Koch from Breslau, who dealt with the subject from a Catholic position.[55] The absence of the minute-taker the following morning means that only the discussion for the afternoon is recorded.[56] Lectures by Wilhelm Stählin and Romano Guardini on the question of "Grace and Church" were intended to be held in the morning. A lecture by Guardini held at the conference called "On the Position of Protestantism to Catholicism" is preserved as indicated by the handwritten date on the manuscript ("22.–25.5.34").[57]

The talk scheduled to be given on May 25 by Paul Simon was instead presented by Damasus Winzen, who spoke on the "Sacrament" from a Catholic perspective, which was followed by a lecture on the same subject, this time from the Protestant point of view, by Heiler. This concluded the series of conference lecturers. The SD Report confirms that the plan drawn up at the preparatory meeting regarding the order of subjects and the method of dual confessional presentations was adhered to, but does not provide further information about whether the Protestant lecture on "grace and church" was in fact given by Wilhelm Stählin or whether this had had to be changed: "At this meeting, the following questions were each dealt with by Catholic and Protestant theologians: 'Essence and Piety,'[58] 'Grace and Justification,' 'Grace and Church,' 'Grace and Sacrament'".[59]

3.3 *Final Impressions*

Heiler, Ritter, and Stählin expressed their delight and gratitude for the successful outcome of the first interfaith dialogue between Catholic and Protestant theologians held in Germany. The

---

49 "Lagebericht des SD," 250f. The text is integrated with the annotations of Ernesti.

50 Ernesti, *Ökumene*, 51.

51 Ernesti, *Ökumene*, 46–58.

52 "Protokoll der Berlin-Hermsdorfer Konferenz," 72.

53 "Protokoll der Berlin-Hermsdorfer Konferenz," 73.

54 "Protokoll der Berlin-Hermsdorfer Konferenz," 74.

55 "Protokoll der Berlin-Hermsdorfer Konferenz," 77–86.

56 "Protokoll der Berlin-Hermsdorfer Konferenz," 86–90.

57 See "Romano Guardinis Referat auf der Berlin-Hermsdorfer Konferenz: *Über die Stellungnahme des Protestanten zum Katholizismus*: [ohne Ortsangabe] 1934 Mai 22.–25.," in: Ernesti, *Ökumene*, 100–121.

58 According to Ernesti, *Ökumene*, 250, note 768, change to "essence *of* piety" ("Wesen *der* Frommigkeit").

59 "Lagebericht des SD," 250.

heartfelt and open encounter of brotherly communion had moved them deeply and opened up previously unimagined perspectives on a shared future.[60] However, although the appraisal by the three Protestant theologians of this inspiring breakthrough and the experience of coming together was similar, their summary of the content of the discussions was quite different.

Ritter considered that the theological issues which had been discussed did not lead to the kind of contradictions that would justify division of the church and held that "the doctrine of justification by faith alone no longer separates us from the living representatives of Catholic theology."[61]

Practically the opposite appraisal of the situation at the conference was given by Stählin when he referred to both what had been discussed and what had been left unsaid as a "dividing wall."[62] However, perhaps above all for him, precisely this discrepancy which he felt between the sense of togetherness on the one hand and the theological debate on the other played a key role in his desire to continue the theological interconfessional dialogue that had begun in 1934 and to revive it, together with Paul Simon, in the Jaeger-Stählin circle from 1946 onwards.[63]

Whereas for Stählin the theological work had just begun, for Heiler there no longer appeared to be any major doctrinal differences, an impression which cannot be confirmed from the minutes of the recorded discussion when we read them today. In fact, a curious event involving Heiler took place shortly after the Berlin-Hermsdorf conference when several newspapers reported

his conversion to the Catholic Church, which he vigorously denied.[64]

Heiler had indeed stated that the repression by the National Socialists made the time ripe for a return and that he had also been in Rome for talks on the interconfessional issue, but he stopped short of a unilateral conversion since that would undermine his efforts to achieve the rapprochement of larger groups with the Catholic Church. In a letter to Bishop Bares,[65] it becomes clear that the ecumenical dialogue, particularly the conference in Berlin, had taken on a deeply spiritual almost mystical dimension for Heiler. He stresses that his friend Drobnitzky had persuaded him to change his mind about converting on his own because this would prevent the possibility of a wholesale institutional union.[66] Heiler hoped that his postponement of his personal goal would ultimately serve attainment of the greater aim, that of institutional union, and he continued to work relentlessly towards this. According to Ernesti, he gave Bishop Bares a memorandum containing a report on the Berlin-Hermsdorf Conference and a possible union, which Bares was to take to Rome.

In his work on the Una Sancta movement, Leonard Swidler cites a typewritten document in his possession entitled "Memorandum regarding the Reunification of German Protestants with the Roman Catholic Church"[67] and everything leads to think that this is the same memo cited by Ernesti. Swidler quotes from a statement by a conference participant in whose opinion it

> clearly showed that there existed between the representatives of the Hochkirchliche Vereinigung and the Catholic theologians no points of dispute, and that there was

60   Ernesti, *Ökumene*, 67f.

61   Ritter, "Begegnungen mit dem römischen Katholizismus," 198.

62   Ernesti, *Ökumene*, 68.

63   For the discussions in the Jäger-Stählin circle, see: Hermann Volk & Edmund Schlink, eds., *Pro veritate: Ein theologischer Dialog, Festgabe für Erzbischof Dr. h.c. Lorenz Jaeger und Bischof Prof. D. Dr. Wilhelm Stählin D.D.*, Münster, Aschendorffsche Verlagsbuchhandlung, 1963.

64   Ernesti, *Ökumene*, 68f.

65   See "Friedrich Heiler an Bischof Nikolaus Bares: 1934 (3. November?)," in: Ernesti, *Ökumene*, 121–123.

66   "Friedrich Heiler an Bischof Nikolaus Bares," 122.

67   "Denkschrift betreffend die Wiedervereinigung deutscher Evangelischer mit der römisch-katholischen Kirche," in: Swidler, *The Ecumenical Vanguard*, 136, note 112.

a surprisingly far-reaching agreement even between the representatives of other Protestant schools of theology and the Catholic theologians; therefore a continuation of this discussion should take place in smaller circles so as gradually to attain complete agreement with Catholic dogma.[68]

Three points become clear from this. The author of the text in question must have been Heiler. Not only was he the sole representative of the Hochkirchliche Vereinigung at the conference, but he also took it for granted that there were no longer any doctrinal disputes between Protestants and Catholics,[69] holding the view that interconfessional discussions should be continued in smaller regional groups.[70] These circumstances point to Heiler's authorship, a hypothesis reinforced by Swidler himself. First, he dates it to 1934 based on the note on the document indicating that the Berlin conference took place "this year," and second, he concludes that it was written by a Hochkirchliche Vereinigung conference participant.[71]

The second point to which attention must be drawn, in addition to these remarks about Heiler's possible authorship (which is, in my opinion, very likely), is that it is clear from the quotation that the theological debate to be initiated in smaller groups – the later Una Sancta groups – was intended to be continued in its own way.

According to Swidler, a third element becomes clear in the cited document, namely that what mattered to the members of the Hochkirchliche Vereinigung were not so much dogmatic questions as those relating to liturgy and discipline. Thus, the author asks whether the Catholic Church could not concede five requests of importance to the union. These concerned the use of the vernacular language in the celebration of Mass; the

basic retention of the centuries-old Lutheran form of the liturgy with adjustments and enlargements being made to correspond to the Catholic dogma; the use of a simplified ceremonial for at least a transitional period; the reception of Communion under both forms; the retention of a married clergy at least for converted Protestant clergy.[72] The memorandum was delivered by Bishop Bares to Cardinal Secretary of State Eugenio Pacelli and Pope Pius XI in Rome and was received "with much understanding and sincere goodwill."[73]

Heiler hoped that through the concession of these five requests the current tradition would be maintained and complemented, thus showing other Protestants the way to achieve unity with the Catholic Church without betraying their own religious legacy. His rejection of the idea of converting on his own as expressed in his letter to Bishop Bares suggests that the bishop's attempt to persuade him to do so after his return from Rome was doomed from the start. Heiler remained convinced that any individual move on his part would destroy his previous work and the rapprochement between the confessions already underway, and for this reason he devoted himself to continuing the dialogue.

4 The Una Sancta Movement

Heiler began to correspond with the co-organizer of the Berlin-Hermsdorf Conference, the Paderborn dean, Paul Simon. Simon asked Heiler about his plans for continuing the process of theological rapprochement after the death of Bishop Bares, bearing in mind that it would be unlikely that additional conferences could be held at the Berlin seminary.[74] The two met in Paderborn early in 1935, almost a year after the conference, to talk about further possible ecumenical meetings. "In 1935, a discussion group of Protestants and

---

68   Cited in: Swidler, *The Ecumenical Vanguard*, 136.

69   Ernesti, *Ökumene*, 67. According to note 223, this view was expressed by Heiler in *Mitteilungsblatt der Hochkirchlichen Vereinigung* 4, June 11, 1934.

70   Ernesti, *Ökumene*, 7of.

71   Swidler, *The Ecumenical Vanguard*, 136, note 112.

72   Swidler, *The Ecumenical Vanguard*, 137.

73   Ernesti, *Ökumene*, 70.

74   Ernesti, *Ökumene*, 7of.

Catholics was formed in Kassel, with more than 200 members, theologians and laity, belonging to the Catholic Church, the regional state churches, and the free churches."[75]

4.1   The Foundation of Ecumenical Discussion Groups

After his visit to Paderborn, Heiler reported that there was also a unification discussion group in Bielefeld with members from the laity. This is unlikely to have been exactly what Heiler had in mind since he was primarily interested in groups consisting of theologians.[76] By October 1937, ecumenical discussion groups had already been set up, or were in the course of being formed, in Berlin, Hamburg, Frankfurt, and Cologne, to name a few.[77] In the document "Ecumenical Work within the Catholic Church,"[78] the Berlin discussion group is listed first, suggesting that this was already the most important or largest group. It is apparent that the conference in Hermsdorf was acting as a direct stimulus to the foundation of smaller ecumenical circles which would carry on the rapprochement at a local level. They would soon be known as Una Sancta groups and would be brought together in a loose structure in the Una Sancta movement. I shall now consider one of these in detail, the Una Sancta group in Munich. There are two main reasons for this: first, the description of the origin and activities of a single group provides direct insight into local pioneering ecumenical work and thus the particular features of Una Sancta and, second, there is simply a lack of archive material for probably the most important group, that in Berlin, which makes an account of that group nearly impossible.

4.2   Una Sancta Group in Munich: A Case Study of Ecumenical Development in Germany

While the Berlin-Hermsdorf Conference in 1934 marks the start of what would evolve into an ongoing ecumenical dialogue in Germany, Friedrich Heiler in particular immediately sought to create discussion groups to harness this momentum and continue what the conference had begun. He decided to travel to the South of the Weimar Republic in 1935, to Munich, to found an ecumenical discussion group in the city.[79]

By Aug 16, 1936, at the latest, Heiler was in Munich with the Jesuit Max Pribilla, the only participant from Munich to have attended the Berlin-Hermsdorf Conference. There they were joined by Anna Söderblom, widow of the Swedish archbishop Nathan Söderblom, who was friend of Pribilla.[80] It is conceivable that Heiler and Pribilla started an initial discussion group unbeknownst to the church authorities. Although there is no evidence of correspondence between Pribilla and Heiler, this meeting could have been the decisive event marking the beginnings of ecumenism in Munich.

Contacts with the Hanover professor, Otto Urbach, also came about through Heiler. Urbach travelled to hold a lecture on ecumenism in Munich in 1937, and it was here that he met the Munich spiritual leader, Cardinal Michael Faulhaber. Faulhaber may possibly already have known of a Munich discussion group when Michael Höck, the editor of the *Münchener Kirchenzeitung*, sent him a document on ecumenism. Höck may then have been instructed by Faulhaber to make contact with the movement, representing the start of his ecumenical role as Faulhaber's Catholic go-between during the early years. Emerging from the contacts between Pribilla and Heiler, the Munich

---

75   Michael Buchberger, *Aufbruch zur Einheit und Einigkeit im Glauben*, Freiburg i.Br., Herder, 1948, 18.

76   Ernesti, *Ökumene*, 71.

77   M. Höck to M. von Faulhaber, Oct 13, 1937, in: EAM, NL Faulhaber 3713, 1.

78   "Oekumenische Arbeit innerhalb der katholischen Kirche," in: EAM, NL Faulhaber 3713, 3–5 (4 pages).

79   Ernesti, *Ökumene*, 71. The source is cited in note 236 on the same page as a letter from F. Heiler to P. Simon dated July 4, 1935.

80   See "Das Tagebuch des Jesuiten Max Pribilla (1933–1940), thematisch relevante Auszüge, für die Jahre 1934 und 1935 kein Eintrag," in: ADPSJ, no. 47/646/2.

group developed steadily from 1935/36 until the foundation year of 1938 inaugurated by Fr. Hugo Lang, O.S.B.[81] However, I think it would be more accurate to describe this as the year in which the group became publicly known to the Catholic hierarchy and began to grow rapidly.

4.3 The Overwhelming Success of Una Sancta: Description of the Munich Group and Their Activities

A brief description of the Una Sancta group in Munich under National Socialism should precede any detailed account of its organization and practices. Paula Linhart, one of the group's founding members, said that in the secret meetings of common prayer and celebration of the Eucharist the ecumenical movement experienced a truth "that would not ever again separate them from one another and their common task."[82] Although these words testify to the sheer boundless explosive power of the ecumenical idea at this early stage, there was also room for frustration over the inner conflict, which influenced the participants of these first ecumenical meetings. This was crystallized when the Protestant, Alo Münch, cried out during a celebration of the Eucharist at which only the Catholics received the sacrament: "Oh my Lord, I beg you to end this intolerable situation where we stand at the same altar and do not eat at the same table!"[83] Both these statements reveal a rift between hope and disappointment, zeal and pessimism, high spirits and despondency, contrasting emotions that seem to have been experienced

as even more unbearable than the potential threat of National Socialist reprisals.

The pressure from National Socialism, which suspected that the real purpose of the gatherings was to organize resistance to the regime, represented precisely the kind of emergency situation created by the presence of a common enemy. This impelled the Munich Christians to dare to seek an ecumenical rapprochement[84] and also forced them underground in order to keep their actions secret. This predicament was rendered even more critical by the ban on assembly of 1939, under which the gathering of merely three people constituted a meeting subject to authorization. The incipient movement, therefore, met in people's homes or in church buildings, which for the first time opened for interconfessional worship and collective Bible work – noteworthy in this context was the joint Bible group of Gottfried Simmerding and the Protestant minister, Kurt Frör. Cardinal Faulhaber, who was a great ally of the group, gave them permission to use the cathedral sacristy for discussions and collective readings of Scripture.[85]

Various Bible study groups, prayers, and talks were held in halls, apartments, and church buildings, and were both well-attended and edifying.[86] The 500 members who gathered over the years had extremely diverse religious and professional backgrounds; Protestant laity would come together with the members of religious orders, Protestant ministers with Catholic students.

The organization on the Catholic side was led by Michael Höck, who reported to Faulhaber on the activities, and on the Protestant side by Baron Wilhelm von Pechmann, who was not only a confidant of Faulhaber but also the main agitator of the Munich group and supported the Una Sancta in

---

81   See "Bericht des Münchener Diözesanvertreters für Una-Sancta-Fragen, Pater Hugo Lang O.S.B., erstattet auf der Tagung zu Limburg, 15. Februar 1951," in: EAM, NL Faulhaber 3712–2, 234: "Since about 1938, meetings of mutual understanding between Catholics and non-Catholics have been held in Gauting outside Munich at the house of Frau von Bornstädt and other private homes."

82   Norbert Stahl, *Eins in Ihm: Der Una-Sancta-Kreis München (1938–1998)*, Munich, Katholische Akademie in Bayern, 1998, 10.

83   Stahl, *Eins in Ihm*, 9.

84   See M. von Faulhaber to Fr. Alfred Rothe, Nov 9, 1945, in: EAM, NL Faulhaber 3712/1, 33. Decisive here is the phrase "that the Una Sancta was more strongly forged precisely because of the shared adversity here and there."

85   Stahl, *Eins in Ihm*, 9.

86   See "Bericht des Münchener Diözesanvertreters für Una-Sancta-Fragen," 234–236.

times of need through several important written pronouncements. Otto Urbach gave another talk in 1938, probably also in Munich, and in 1939 at the first Meitingen religious discussion. Max Joseph Metzger, August Rehbach, Max Pribilla, and Hugo Lang were invited to this from Munich and undoubtedly other members of the Una Sancta group were also present.[87]

In those lectures, it is likely that Urbach expounded his fundamental position of anti-Nazi ecumenism before meeting personally with Cardinal Faulhaber. Urbach's lectures in Munich are not the only evidence of the Munich group's activities. Its student members also met on Tuesday May 3, 1938 for a talk in Munich by Max Pribilla on the "Religious and Spiritual Situation."[88] The Jesuit gave another talk to scholars later that year (on Friday Nov 25) about the "Dialogue between the Confessions."[89]

Although Faulhaber had chosen another Jesuit, Erich Przywara, to develop the Christian ethical position during this period, in those early years it was above all Pribilla who stands out through his lecturing activity. In February 1940, the expression "Una Sancta" is used for the first time in Pribilla's diary, from which it can be inferred that an established group with this name had been formed by this time to pursue the movement's ecumenical aims. This name may have arisen during the course of the foundation of the Bruderschaft der Una Sancta by Max Josef Metzger at Pentecost 1939.[90] His intention was to leave the existing groups unchanged and merely link them together in a very minimal organization through the brotherhood.[91]

In addition to the talks given by Pribilla, Cardinal Faulhaber also actively set out to shape the conscience of the Munich group by inviting its members, signifying at least one hundred Protestants, through the auspices of Michael Höck, to a talk by Erich Przywara in December 1940. However, not only was the talk regarded as abstract and aloof, but there was not enough common prayer at the event. This was not to the group's liking given than it saw itself as a "praying community."

By no means did the ecumenical group in Munich meet for these lectures alone. It saw itself as a community of fraternal exchange, mutual cooperation, amicable connectedness, and above all communal prayer. The life shared in a spirit of fraternity and personal contact was always more important than the subjects discussed at lectures or evening talks. On Thursday, Oct 12, 1939, the group organized a collective prayer hour based on John 17 and Ephesians 4, significant Bible passages for ecumenism.[92] In November 1939, the two confessions came together in Munich to celebrate the Holy Mass.[93] In a letter at the beginning of 1940, the Berlin priest Paul Pietryga wrote: "There is so much desire for faith and zeal for prayer in Munich, which to my great joy I never fail to find in both Catholics and Protestants."[94] Pietryga also wrote that there was a common prayer week from Jan 18 to 25, 1940, and another from the Ascension to Pentecost. Although he mentions this specifically in relation to Berlin alone, he also writes that what he experienced in Berlin also applied to Munich by

---

87   See "Max Josef Metzger an Friedrich Heiler: Meitingen bei Augsburg, 1939 Januar 26," in: Ernesti, *Ökumene*, 199–201, here 201.

88   "Das Tagebuch des Jesuiten Max Pribilla."

89   "Das Tagebuch des Jesuiten Max Pribilla."

90   Ernesti, *Ökumene*, 183.

91   "Max Josef Metzger an Friedrich Heiler: Meitingen bei Augsburg, 1938 November 23, 1938," in: Ernesti, *Ökumene*, 195–196.

92   See P. Pietryga to the Munich Una Sancta, Sept 20, 1939, in: EAM, NL Faulhaber 3711, 234f.: "Next Monday, September 25, at 4 PM, our autumn work will begin with Romans 8 at the Protestant site. For Thursday October 12, I shall start at the same time as Munich a joint prayer hour *here* (from John 17 and Eph 4) at the Catholic site. It will happen elsewhere *at the same time*. I am working hard on this."

93   See P. Pietryga to the Munich Una Sancta, end of 1939, in: EAM, NL Faulhaber 3711, 238.

94   P. Pietryga to the Munich Una Sancta, Berlin, Jan 11, 1940, in: EAM, NL Faulhaber 3711, 250.

extension.[95] In December 1940, worship took place at Rochusstrasse and the Church of the Trinity for the joint celebration of Advent. Przywara considered this a mistake since, like the joint Bible study, it would only blur matters. He held, on the contrary, that the clear differences should be emphasized, something which Faulhaber also urged in his preaching to the group.[96]

While the Munich group was inspired by a particularly strong zeal in organizing talks and the experience of praying together,[97] a number of members became active in spreading ecumenical ideas among different social classes. The group's Catholic head, Michael Höck, sought out sympathetic minds among the reactionary Catholic aristocracy, and Fr. Josef Kornreiter taught ecumenical philosophy to a ladies' circle. The Una Sancta in Munich thus also increasingly came to the attention of the Gestapo, and an SD report on it was compiled between Aug 9 and Nov 6, 1940.

The Nazi authorities regarded the ecumenical movement as opposition to the regime from the start, not least owing to Otto Urbach and Freiherr Wilhelm von Pechmann, the main agitator of the Munich Una Sancta. They attempted to prohibit ecumenical ideas through increased surveillance and repression. Since the Gestapo considered it an illegal organization, the Munich ecumenical movement increasingly suffered from reprisals. The shared pain and agony, and later the martyrs, became ever more important for the *Christian* engagement of both Catholics and Protestants.

4.4 The Archbishop Cardinal Michael Faulhaber and Ecumenism

Many Una Sancta members who took up opposition to the regime found a sponsor and defender in the Munich spiritual leader, Cardinal Michael

Faulhaber, who was able to save some of them from attacks by the Gestapo. In his papal homily on May 3, 1940, and New Year's sermon on Dec 31, 1941, Faulhaber praised his city's ecumenical group for having succeeded in removing prejudice and building a psychological bridge to make ecumenical dialogue possible in the first place. He expressed his joy at the existence of the group and proved a great sympathizer but he also criticized the attempts towards unity on the grounds that this could not be built on feelings of joy alone; the doctrinal differences also had to be brought to the fore and discussed. The aim should not be a kind of identity based on compromise but a clear and truthful rapprochement. To use the terminology of later ecumenism, it can be said that Faulhaber insisted not just on a dialogue of love but also on one of truth.

This idea of "mutual coming together" was defended by the Cardinal in his letter to the papal nuncio to Germany, Cesare Orsenigo, in 1941,[98] who had asked him for an appraisal of the situation. Faulhaber explains that the aim of the Una Sancta is neither to prepare the way for a return to Rome and nor should mass conversions be expected. At the same time, the mutual rapprochement and removal of prejudice about the Catholic Church should be welcomed by Rome and the discussions not forbidden. He mentions the endeavors in Munich, although he once again raised the criticism that Catholic truths must be afforded clear expression. He had entrusted the Jesuit Przywara with this task, who was discharging this responsibility at a very high level. In praising the actions of the Munich Una Sancta in harnessing all their powers against the regime, he proved himself a spiritual leader who also sought to follow the path of ecumenism in his dealings with Rome. Ultimately, Faulhaber must be seen as the most

---

95 P. Pietryga to the Munich Una Sancta, Berlin, Jan 11, 1940, 256.

96 See Dr. Knoch to E. Przywara, Dec 21, 1940, in: ADPSJ, no. 47/646/3.

97 P. Pietryga to the Munich Una Sancta, Berlin, Jan 11, 1940, 256. Pietryga writes that he wants to highlight strongly that Munich zeal at a talk in Berlin on Jan 17, 1940.

98 Card. M. von Faulhaber to C. Orsenigo, Munich, Aug 5, 1941, in: Michael von Faulhaber, *Akten Kardinal Michael von Faulhabers (1917–1945)*, vol. 2, *1935–1945*, ed. Ludwig Volk, Mainz, Matthias Grünewald, 1978, 775–780, no. 822.

important sponsor of the Una Sancta in Munich as he defended it against the Nazi authorities and against Rome, and also supported its individual members through his extensive correspondence.

As can be seen from his wide-ranging correspondence from 1939 and 1940 or indeed the numerous diary entries of Max Pribilla from this period, the idea of unification and its representation by the Munich group was able to make significant progress until 1941. However, it became clear from 1942 that the Una Sancta movement would face harsh reprisals.

4.5 Period of Adversity: Unity through Common Martyrs

The profound mutual appreciation that prevailed among Una Sancta members in Munich could not prevent the growing pressure from the Nazi regime from obliging the large ecumenical group to meet in secret, mainly in private homes. These were usually provided by Rudolf and Emmy Miller couple and Paula Linhart. The young ecumenical movement had been renamed Una Sancta during the first Meitingen gathering at Pentecost (1939), which reflected the greater self-assurance and growth of the ecumenical group in Munich. However, the second meeting at Pentecost in 1941 officially heralded the period of adversity for the movement.

On May 21, 1941, Michael Höck was arrested by the Gestapo in Meitingen, where he was taking part in the second Una Sancta meeting there. He had publicly supported Martin Niemöller and Rupert Mayer after their arrests. The Catholic leader was taken into custody in Dachau, while the head of the Protestants, von Pechmann, was spared this fate. He continued to promote the ecumenical cause in Munich, as can be seen from his work "Why Una Sancta?" dated Sept 17, 1942.[99] Here Pechmann describes opposition to National Socialist ideology as an imperative. He also shows how ecumenical work in the Una Sancta was

practiced. First, each religion's own historical, dogmatic and indeed emotional wrongdoings had to be specified before criticizing other confessions. This allowed prejudices to be broken down and paths of rapprochement to be created. At a time that all denominations recognized as critical, doctrinal disputes could not be allowed to overshadow the current situation and the missionary task of Christianity as a whole. At least within Una Sancta, at a time of extensive surveillance, he clearly attacked the Nazi rulers. Through his fruitful relationships with Cardinal Faulhaber and the local Protestant bishop, besides through his writings – such as the works "Why Una Sancta?" of 1942 and "On the Question of the Una Sancta" of 1944[100] – the Protestant aristocrat thus proved a great advocate of ecumenism in Munich in that time of adversity, along with, without doubt, the Jesuit Pribilla.[101]

4.6 Theological Profile of Ecumenism in Germany

Pribilla takes the meetings of Faith and Order in Lausanne and Life and Work in Stockholm as his starting point. He states that the "impotence of a divided Christianity in public life"[102] and the material hardship of many churches during and after World War I led them to come together. The same could be said for the ecumenical movement that arose in Germany in response to pressure from the Nazi dictatorship. It is clear that Pribilla's aim is to rouse his audience to renew and strengthen their ecumenical engagement even in the face of the adversity brought about by repression, and he appeals to the responsibility they bear

---

99   See Wilhelm Freiherr von Pechmann, "Warum Una Sancta?," Sept 17, 1942, in: EAM, NL Faulhaber 3711, 335f.

100   See Freiherr von Pechmann, "Zur Frage der Una-Sancta," in: Friedrich Wilhelm Kantzenbach, *Widerstand und Solidarität der Christen in Deutschland (1933–1945): Eine Dokumentation um Kirchenkampf aus den Papieren des D. Wilhelm Freiherrn von Pechmann*, Neustadt/Aisch, Degener, 1971, 25–27.

101   See "Das Tagebuch des Jesuiten Max Pribilla."

102   Max Pribilla, "Der Wille zur christlichen Einheit," lecture (slightly expanded) given on May 19, 1942 at the Munich Bürgersaal, in: EAM, NL Faulhaber 3711, 186.

not for history but for one another at the present time. Finally, Pribilla testifies to the fact that Una Sancta work was carried out by private individuals. These people did not see themselves as either a theological congress or a church council; they did not want to achieve unity but to prepare the way for it. Efforts had to continue to be made in order to overcome the previous antagonism and controversies while defending what the confessions had in common, which indeed had to exist since otherwise they would not both be persecuted together. The cause of the shared adversity is used by Pribilla as the point of departure for positions acceptable to both sides, an approach which could also be considered in ecumenism today.

He goes on to say that both confessions have the sacred duty of taking care of the sick and weak, an area of work that opens the way to practical collaboration through the Christian idea of loving one's neighbor. Nevertheless, Christians should show not just a common commitment but also a worldview aimed against Nazi ideology and which points the way to a shared spiritual conduct and way of life. What matters for Christians is not succeeding in life and holding on to this fleeting world. They must not stir up racial hatred either, but are bound to defend the right of all peoples to their freedom, culture, language, and religion. Here Pribilla stresses the bonds of righteousness and thus takes aim at a regime that has devoted itself to violence.

He also stresses the role of Holy Scripture as the common heritage of both confessions – a legacy of the Bible movement – and that there are similarities in prayer, too, deriving from the common biblical source. Pribilla mentions the liturgy as another link between the confessions. The liturgy had found momentum both in the Protestant Church in the Berneuchener Movement and in the Catholic Church in the liturgical movement, making mutual rapprochement possible. This shows the unifying element first inherited by the Hochkirche movement.

Precisely this rapprochement could not be destroyed at that time by religious arrogance. Each

Christian had to be conscious of his own lack of significance. Furthermore, theological controversies should not stand in the way of rapprochement but should be swept away by the desire for Christian unity, so that the patience needed to listen to the other position is attained and no lazy compromises are reached. Theological debates of this kind would require experienced theologians capable of contributing to unity, foregoing both hasty criticism and impossible fantasies.

According to Pribilla, every Christian is called upon to contribute to unity through individual or collective prayer, through acts of love, the correction of a prejudice or error, dispelling a false rumor, peaceful and brotherly discussion, or through a good book.[103] In addition to these various activities, some of which are drawn no doubt from the practice of the Munich group, Pribilla observes that the effort to achieve unity in actual fact fosters an understanding of one's own religion. The purpose of these practices is not to be successful but derives from God's will to strive for unity. This motivation may at first seem strange. However, it should not be forgotten that the central biblical passage of the ecumenical movement was John 17:21, which expresses God's desire for unity. Pribilla saw himself in the tradition of the ecumenical movement – he was, after all, a friend of Söderblom – and raises the Una Sancta movement to the same level through his references to Stockholm and Lausanne at the outset. This afforded the group's members, facing extreme repression at that time, much needed support. They could see that the movement spread worldwide beyond their own efforts at early ecumenical activity while also rooting their own actions as individuals in the motivation to fulfill God's direct wishes.

4.7 Discussion about the Mystici Corporis Encyclical

Pribilla's lecture shows that in the period between 1942 and 1945 the history and words of Holy

---

103   Max Pribilla, "Der Wille zur christlichen Einheit," 206f.

Scripture represented the movement's foundation. In addition to this broader context, the immediacy of the experience of martyrdom and personal adversity should not be overlooked.

The ecumenical dedication of the Munich group once again sought expression in February 1944 in a planned joint rally of the Una Sancta with the Catholic hierarchy. However, this attempt was vetoed by Cardinal Faulhaber since a public meeting could not take place between the Una Sancta and the Catholic Church but only between the Catholic Church and the Protestant regional state church.[104]

Although we have no further lectures by Pribilla or writings by Pechmann from 1944 and 1945 pointing to communal religious services or worship, the Una Sancta was nonetheless far from inactive. For example, the *Mystici corporis* encyclical published in 1943 was the subject of lively debate, albeit in secret. Faulhaber wrote to Pastor Venghaus on Feb 17, 1944: "Particularly the most recent utterances of the Catholic magisterium regarding the concept of the church have once again stirred rich and peaceful debate."[105] He had previously written to Pope Pius XII on Dec 5, 1943: "The demand [for the encyclical] is high, there is particularly strong interest in the Una Sancta."[106] The Pope replied, on Feb 22, 1944, that a well-known figure from the Una Sancta, without being properly informed of the encyclical's content, had attacked the Catholic Church because it upheld its claim to being the sole true church. For his part, the pope was certain that if Catholics in those circles had previously held a different concept of the church, then the clarity of text was even more justified in order to

demonstrate the truth.[107] This situation is given a similar appraisal by the archbishop of Paderborn Lorenz Jaeger in a letter to Faulhaber dated Feb 22, 1944,[108] in which he points out that the crucial question, that of the definition of the concept of church, "has now been unequivocally answered in the dialogue of the Catholics with their separated brethren."[109] The last extant correspondence of the Catholic hierarchy in Munich in the debate of the Una Sancta movement over the encyclical is a letter from the archbishop's secretary to Legation Councilor Otto Knoch on Aug 10, 1944, himself a strong supporter of the ecumenical movement:

> The clouds that gathered in some places on an initial reading of the *Mystici corporis* are bound to disperse gradually. It is only of benefit to the ecumenical movement that clearly defined doctrinal teachings are laid down for the study and understanding of the other side to prevent insubstantial populist apologetics from creeping in.[110]

While the doctrinal proclamation was particularly welcomed by the Catholic hierarchy in order to bring clarity to the ecumenical discussion, it is also likely to have disappointed some Protestants, who had moved towards the Catholic Church full of hope but without being able to see any reciprocation. This movement was driven into the private sphere of the family through war and repression, where it sought to survive the bombing of Munich. At the end of the war, the first priority was the

---

104   See H. Wagner to Prof. Seitz, Munich, Feb 5, 1944, in: Faulhaber, *Akten Kardinal Michael von Faulhabers*, vol. 2, 1012.

105   M. von Faulhaber to Pastor Venghaus, Feb 17, 1944, in: EAM, NL Faulhaber 3711, 275.

106   M. von Faulhaber to Pope Pius XII, Munich, Dec 5, 1943, in: Faulhaber, *Akten Kardinal Michael von Faulhabers*, vol. 2, 1008.

107   See "Aus einem Schreiben des Heiligen Vaters an Kardinal Faulhaber vom 22. Februar 1944 über Mystici Corporis," in: EAM, NL Faulhaber 3711.

108   Archbishop L. Jaeger to Card. M. von Faulhaber, Paderborn, May 26, 1944, in: EAM, NL Faulhaber 3712/1, 87.

109   Archbishop L. Jaeger to Card. M. von Faulhaber, Paderborn, May 26, 1944, in: EAM, NL Faulhaber 3712/1, 87.

110   Archbishop secretary Dr. Wagner to Legation Councilor Dr. Knoch, Munich, Aug 10, 1944, in: EAM, NL Faulhaber 3711, 324.

reestablishment of the necessities of life in the heavily destroyed city before further progress could be ventured in the Una Sancta or anything similar.

The movement inaugurated its post-war work with a memorial service for the murdered Max Metzger and Alfred Delp in the Church of the Trinity on Mar 8, 1946. The address was pronounced by Michael Höck, who had recently been released from the concentration camp of Dachau.[111] Thus, there was an attempt to build on the shared experience of adversity and the early personal structure in the form of Höck. However, both these factors soon ceased to apply because the National Socialists had been destroyed, and Höck had to withdraw from leadership of the Una Sancta as head of the Freising seminary.[112]

5   Conclusions

The first ecumenical conference held in Germany at Berlin-Hermsdorf served as a personal and thematic link between the various movements for renewal within the different religious denominations. The dedicated work of Friedrich Heiler, Karl Bernhard Ritter, and Romano Guardini built a bridge from the Hochkirche movement to the Una Sancta movement. The experience of shared adversity brought about by National Socialism acted as a catalyst for ecumenical endeavors. In this chapter, I have concentrated exclusively on a detailed account of the Munich group in order to show this pioneering ecumenical work at a local level. However, the same kind of commitment,

which always depended on the respective bishop's sponsorship or prevention of ecumenical activity, could equally be studied for the groups in Berlin, Kassel, Cologne, Stuttgart, and the Oratorians in Leipzig, among others.

It is clear that ecumenism in Germany rests on the pioneer work of committed individuals who paved the way for an ecumenical understanding between the churches at an institutional level. These beginnings were then built upon in the Jaeger-Stählin circle, for example, founded just after World War II in March 1946 by Dean Paul Simon and Archbishop Lorenz Jaeger.[113] On the first day, a meeting was held by Catholic theologians, including Bernhard Rosenmöller, who, like Simon, had taken part in the Berlin-Hermsdorf conference. On the second day, Catholic theologians met Protestant theologians and founded a theological group. Among these was the Lutheran bishop Wilhelm Stählin, another participant at Berlin. Given that some of the figures were the same, it is not surprising that some of the methods from the earlier gathering were put to use in the new one. For example, the list of participants was not compiled centrally but was drawn up by each church.[114] As in Berlin, the subjects were treated in two papers, one from each denomination. Thus, in 1946, a Catholic and a Protestant group were founded and always met in parallel. Not until 1968 were they brought together under the Ökumenischen Arbeitskreis katholischer und evangelischer Theologen. Just as the Una Sancta movement, this group made a significant contribution during its existence to the ecumenical rapprochement between both churches in Germany.

Translated from German to English by Fiona Robb.

---

111   See "Einladungskarte zur Gedenkfeier am 8. März 1946 in der Dreifaltigkeitskirche München," in: EAM, NL Faulhaber 3712–1, 34.

112   See "Besprechung: Beauftragter des Hochwürdigsten Herrn Erzbischof Dr. Lorenz Jaeger von Paderborn Professor Höfer mit Herrn Card. Faulhaber von München, ferner anwesend Sekretär J. Thalhammer – am Freitag 18. Juni 48 im Bischofshof in München: Una Sancta," in: EAM, NL Faulhaber 3712–2, 50.

---

113   For a history of the Jaeger-Stählin circle, see Barbara Schwahn, *Der Ökumenische Arbeitskreis evangelischer und katholischer Theologen von 1946 bis 1975*, Göttingen, Vandenhoeck & Ruprecht, 1996.

114   Ernesti, *Ökumene*, 44.

Bibliography

Buchberger, Michael, *Aufbruch zur Einheit und Einigkeit im Glauben*, Freiburg i.Br., Herder, 1948.

Ernesti, Jörg, ed., *Die Entdeckung der Ökumene: Zur Beteiligung der katholischen Kirche an der ökumenischen Bewegung*, Paderborn, Bonifatius, 2008.

Ernesti, Jörg, *Ökumene im Dritten Reich*, Paderborn, Bonifatius, 2007.

Faulhaber, Michael von, *Akten Kardinal Michael von Faulhabers (1917–1945)*, vol. 2, *1935–1945*, ed. Ludwig Volk, Mainz, Matthias-Grünewald-Verlag, 1978.

Günther, Johannes, *Gemeinsam unter dem Kreuz : Der Weg der Una Sancta Berlin*, Berlin, CZV Verlag, 1982.

Hermelink, Heinrich, *Katholizismus und Protestantismus im Gespräch zwischen den Konfessionen um die Una Sancta*, Stuttgart, Ehrenfried Klotz, 1949.

Heß, Christian, *"Ohne Christus, ohne tiefstes Christentum ist Krieg": Die Christkönigsthematik als Leitidee im kirchlich-gesellschaftlichen Engagement Max Josef Metzgers*, Paderborn, Bonifatius, 2016.

Kantzenbach, Friedrich Wilhelm, *Widerstand und Solidarität der Christen in Deutschland (1933–1945): Eine Dokumentation um Kirchenkampf aus den Papieren des D. Wilhelm Freiherrn von Pechmann*, Neustadt/Aisch, Degener, 1971.

Kuhlmann, Sebastian, *Martin Niemöller: Zur prophetischen Dimension der Predigt*, Leipzig, Evangelische Verlagsanstalt, 2008.

Laros, Matthias, *Schöpferischer Friede der Konfessionen: Die Una-Sancta-Bewegung, ihr Ziel und ihre Arbeit*, Recklinghausen, Paulus, 1950.

Linhart, Paula, "Der Una-Sancta-Kreis München," in: Heinrich Fries & Ulrich Valesko, eds., Versöhnung: Gestalten, Zeiten, Modelle, Frankfurt a.M., Knecht, 1975, 181–198.

Linhart, Paula, "Der Una-Sancta-Kreis München," *Una Sancta* 39, 1984, 12–22.

Pribilla, Max, *Die Una Sancta-Bewegung: Eine erste Einführung*, Meitingen, Kyrios-Verlag, 1948.

Pribilla, Max, *Um kirchliche Einheit: Stockholm, Lausanne, Rom: Geschichtlich-theologische Darstellung der neueren Einigungsbestrebungen*, Freiburg i.Br., Herder, 1929.

Stahl, Norbert, *Eins in Ihm: Der Una-Sancta-Kreis München (1938–1998)*, Munich, Katholische Akademie in Bayern, 1998.

Swidler, Leonard J., *The Ecumenical Vanguard: The History of the Una Sancta Movement*, Pittsburgh PA, Duquesne University Press, 1966.

Voderholzer, Rudolf, "Stimme des Gewissens im Kampf gegen das Böse: Wilhelm Freiherr von Pechmann (1859–1948)," *MThZ* 52, 2001, 245–259.

Volk, Hermann & Edmund Schlink, eds., *Pro veritate: Ein theologischer Dialog, Festgabe für Erzbischof Dr. h.c. Lorenz Jaeger und Bischof Prof. D. Dr. Wilhelm Stählin D.D.*, Münster, Aschendorffsche Verlagsbuchhandlung, 1963.

CHAPTER 30

Dom Lambert Beauduin, Founder of the Monastery of Amay-Chevetogne: A Prelude to Ecumenism in the Catholic Church

André Haquin

1 Introduction

When browsing through the impressive biography compiled by Raymond Loonbeek and Jacques Mortiau,[1] the reader may gain the impression that Fr. Lambert Beauduin lived several consecutive lives: first as a diocesan priest involved in education (1897–1899) and as a labor chaplain (1899–1906),

then as a Benedictine monk at Mont César Abbey in Leuven (1906) and as the initiator of the Belgian liturgical movement (1909–1914). After the interlude of World War I, he reappeared as professor at the Benedictine College of Sant'Anselmo in Rome (1921–1925) and, upon his return, as founder of the monastery of Amay-Chevetogne, known from its very beginning as the Union Monastery (1925). Then came the time of his trial and exile in France (1932–1951), and finally his return to Chevetogne, where he was to spend his final years. This apparent "discontinuity," as we shall presently see, actually conceals the "continuity of the vision of Dom Lambert Beauduin".[2] Indeed, he was quite fond of saying that he had been "social" with Pope Leo XIII, a "liturgist" with Pope Pius X, and an "ecumenist" with Pope Pius XI.[3]

---

1 Raymond Loonbeek & Jacques Mortiau, *Un pionnier, dom Lambert Beauduin (1873–1960): Liturgie et unité des chrétiens*, 2 vols., Louvain-la-Neuve, Collège Érasme, 2001. In this work, which remains the reference biography, there are many archival resources mentioned, including the public collections, in particular of the abbeys of Chevetogne, Leuven, Maredsous, Bruges and Sant'Anselmo in Rome (1565–1577), the private collections (1577–1578), the printed and handwritten works of Dom Lambert (1547–1558), the unpublished writings (1558–1565) including the numerous epistolaries used (1909–1960); moreover, an onomastic index (1579–1602) shows the network of his relations and the many texts that clarify his work. For a more concise account, see Jacques Mortiau & Raymond Loonbeek, *Dom Lambert Beauduin, visionnaire et précurseur (1873–1960): Un moine au cœur libre*, Paris, Cerf, 2005. See also Jean-Jacques von Allmen & others, *Veilleur avant l'aurore: Colloque Lambert Beauduin*, Chevetogne, Éditions de Chevetogne, 1978; "Dom Lambert Beauduin (1873–1960)," *Unité des Chrétiens* 29, 1978, 1–27; Claude Soetens, "Beauduin," in: *BNB* 44, 27–47; Sonya A. Quitslund, *Beauduin: A Prophet Vindicated*, New York NY, Newman, 1973; Louis Bouyer, *Dom Lambert Beauduin: Un homme d'Église*, Tournai, Casterman, 1964. Other studies focus on a particular period in Dom Lambert's life: André Haquin, *Dom Lambert Beauduin et le renouveau liturgique*, Gembloux, Duculot, 1970, and André Haquin, "L'exil de Dom Lambert Beauduin au monastère d'En-Calcat (1932–1934)," *RHE* 80, 1985, 51–99, 415–440; Maïeul Cappuyns, "Dom Lambert Beauduin (1873–1960): Quelques documents et souvenirs," *RHE* 61, 1966, 424–454, 761–807.

2 Emmanuel Lanne, "Liturgie et unité chrétienne: Continuité de la vision de Dom Lambert Beauduin," in: Allmen & others, *Veilleur*, 277–293, here 277. A monk from Amay-Chevetogne, Fr. Lanne served as an expert at Vatican II and was active in the Faith and Constitution Commission of the WCC from 1968 to 1998. See in particular Emmanuel Lanne, *Tradition et communion des Églises: Recueil d'études*, Leuven, Leuven University Press, 1997.

3 In a letter pertaining to Dom Lambert Beauduin's jubilee as a priest, we find the following reference: "My 50 years were inspired by the papal directives: social action under Leo XIII (it was, in fact, the encyclical *Rerum novarum* from 1891 that drew me into this movement) – liturgical action under Pius X: the appeal to the Benedictines, the sole fruit of which was Amay – not to mention the patriotic action of the period of World War I"; Dom L. Beauduin to Dom P. Dumont, Jan 29, 1947, in: AAC, fonds P. Dumont 1897–1947.

1.1   *Diocesan Priest and Labor Chaplain*

Born into a family of landowners from the region of Liège who engaged in trade and politics, Octave Beauduin entered the diocesan seminary of Liège,[4] where Fr. Antoine Pottier,[5] professor of moral theology, had taken up the cause of social Catholicism and defended the rights of laborers to organize themselves into unions. Those were the days when Leo XIII, in his encyclical *Rerum novarum* (1891),[6] called upon Christians to take action on behalf of the working class. Ordained as priest in 1897, Octave Beauduin joined the Société des Aumôniers du Travail in 1899, an organization established by his bishop, Msgr. Victor-Joseph Doutreloux. Having been placed at the head of a highly industrialized bishopric, the latter was anxious to ensure a Christian presence among young workers. To a certain extent, this project may be seen as a forerunner of the initiative launched by Joseph Cardijn, a young priest from Brussels who two decades later founded the JOC. Beauduin's move from a diocesan college to a pastoral ministry in a working-class environment is typical of his sensitivity to the problems of his time. After seven years, however, he left the Société in search of another path. Why did he choose to do so? Two factors, at least, appear to have been decisive. Following the appointment, in Liège, of the conservative bishop Msgr. Martin-Hubert Rutten, the chaplains had been compelled to shift the focus of their activities and to devote themselves to technical and vocational education. Moreover, Beauduin had retreated from the labor movement, which was making more and more demands. He felt that he was no longer able to fulfill his priestly

duties in this environment. Would he choose the life of a Carthusian monk as he had already considered doing before entering the seminary? Or rather that of a Dominican monk, as he did not possess the necessary disposition to become a "preaching friar"? On the advice of the canon regular Jacques Laminne, professor at the Faculty of Theology of Leuven, he knocked at the door of the young Abbey of Mont César (1906), which had been founded in 1899 by the Abbey of Maredsous. Must this be seen as a break or is there a continuity between the labor chaplaincy and the life of a Benedictine monk? The break, in any case, is far from being total, as Beauduin would always remember that the church consists not only of its clerical hierarchy but of all the baptized, including the humblest ones.

1.2   *At Mont César*

By taking part in the abbey's classic liturgy, the man who would henceforth call himself Dom Lambert came to realize that its celebration is not identifiable with rules and practices but is above all the "prayer of the church."[7] Thanks to the spiritual conferences of the prior, Dom Columba Marmion,[8] which were rooted in biblical revelation and liturgy, the 30-year-old novice discovered a new world. Having passed from "deprivation" to "liturgical richness," he deplored that this treasure remained inaccessible to most Christians: "We are the aristocrats of the liturgy," he said to the monks. "It is time to democratize it," that is, to restore it to all the baptized. Appointed since 1907 to lecture

---

4   See Loonbeek & Mortiau, *Un pionnier*, vol. 1, 5–37.

5   See Jean-Pierre Delville, "Réseaux démocrates chrétiens et appuis pontificaux: L'action de Mgr Antoine Pottier (1849–1923) à Rome sous Léon XIII et Pie X," in: Jean-Pierre Delville & Marko Jačov, eds., *La papauté contemporaine (XIXe–XXe siècles): Hommage au chanoine Roger Aubert, professeur émérite à l'Université Catholique de Louvain, pour ses 95 ans*, Leuven, Collège Érasme, 2009, 195–238.

6   See Philippe Levillain & Jean-Marc Ticchi, eds., *Le pontificat de Léon XIII: Renaissances du Saint-Siège?*, Rome, École française de Rome, 2006.

7   Haquin, *Dom Lambert Beauduin*, 66–244; André Haquin, "De Grégoire XVI (1831–1846) à Paul VI (1963–978): Les papes et le mouvement liturgique aux 19e et 20e siècles," in: Delville & Jačov, eds., *La papauté contemporaine*, 71–89. See also Loonbeek & Mortiau, *Un pionnier*, vol. 1, 55–250, and Honoré Vinck, *Pie X et les réformes liturgiques de 1911–1914: Psautier, bréviaire, calendrier, rubriques*, Münster, Aschendorff, 2014.

8   See Mark Tierney, *Dom Columba Marmion: A Biography*, Dublin, Columba Press, 1994. See also Columba Marmion, *Correspondance (1881–1923)*, ed. Mark Tierney & Réginald-Ferdinand Poswick, Paris, Francois-Xavier de Guibert, 2008.

on *De Ecclesia* to his young fellow brothers, he presented the church as a spiritual reality or, better still, as the "Mystical Body of Christ,"[9] though without deviating from the *koinè* of the day, according to which the Catholic Church was the "only true Church." "Si existit Ecclesia apostolica, est nostra," he wrote.[10]

The year 1909 would prove crucial to his development and pastoral action: at the Congrès des Œuvres Catholiques that was held in September of the same year in Malines, he spoke about the importance of liturgy in his lecture "La vraie prière de l'Église" through the following points: true prayer of the faithful; powerful bond of unity; comprehensive religious instruction.[11] This speech is widely recognized as the beginning of the Belgian liturgical movement. From then on, "church" and "liturgy" were inseparable for him. In June 1909, he had already approached the general chapter of the Benedictine Congregation of Beuron, to which the abbey of Mont César belonged, and submitted a report entitled "De promovenda sacra liturgia" in which he discussed the study of liturgy; the relationship between spiritual life and liturgy; and the liturgical apostolate,[12] which was intended to promote the celebration of liturgy in, and by, the Benedictine order. He then came to the realization that liturgical action could only have a future if it was supported by study. In July 1909, hoping to initiate a liturgical revival in the parishes, he formulated his wishes for a more participative form of liturgy in a 14-page letter addressed to Cardinal Désiré-Joseph Mercier,[13] the primate of Belgium.

The positive reception of his speech at the congress of Malines led Dom Beauduin to initiate various actions that were to prove highly successful: the publication of a monthly missal review entitled *La Vie liturgique*, which contained translations of the liturgical texts; the creation of the journal *Questions liturgiques* and of its Dutch counterpart *Liturgisch Tijdschrift* (1910), which was intended for the clergy; and various publications such as Latin-French and Latin-Dutch missals. Liturgical weeks and retreats were organized every year, in both languages, for the training of priests and lay apostles, the true "militants" of the liturgical cause. He also elaborated a *Projet d'école liturgique* (1910 and 1912)[14] for Benedictines but also for professors of liturgy at the seminaries (a two-year course with 18 hours of classes per week), which was to be launched at Mont César. Unfortunately, this project was never implemented.

Various tensions between the liturgical apostolate and modern spiritualities poisoned the atmosphere during the months that preceded the outbreak of World War I. In an effort to defuse these tensions with the advocates of private devotions, spiritual exercises, and prayer, Dom Beauduin published a booklet entitled *La piété de l'Église* in May 1914.[15] It may be seen as the charter of the Belgian liturgical movement, a movement of a pastoral, even parochial type. All kinds of issues are addressed in it, without resorting to polemics. The first part deals with the liturgical restoration (why and how to conceive the liturgical movement); the second part discusses the secondary functions of liturgy (liturgy does not constitute the totality of the church's life, but it is linked to all its aspects: ascesis, prayer, preaching, theological

9   At Vatican I, the church constitution proposal drafted by Fr. Clemens Schrader, s.j., which did not meet with approval, was entitled *Ecclesiam esse Corpus Christi Mysticum*. See also Emile Mersch, *Le corps mystique du Christ: Études de théologie historique*, 2 vols., Paris, Desclée de Brouwer, 1936.

10   Haquin, *Dom Lambert Beauduin et le renouveau liturgique*, 70–72.

11   French text in: Haquin, *Dom Lambert Beauduin*, 238–241.

12   Latin text in: Haquin, *Dom Lambert Beauduin*, 234–237.

13   Reproduced and commented in Haquin, *Dom Lambert Beauduin*, 81–88. See also Roger Aubert, *Le*

cardinal Mercier (1851–1926): Un prélat d'avant-garde: Publications du professeur Roger Aubert rassemblées à l'occasion de ses 80 ans, ed. Jean-Pierre Hendrickx, Jean Pirotte & Luc Courtois, Louvain-la-Neuve, Presses Universitaires de Louvain, 1994.

14   Commented text in: Haquin, *Dom Lambert Beauduin*, 136–148.

15   Lambert Beauduin, *La piété de l'Église: Principes et faits*, Leuven, Abbaye du Mont César, 1914.

scholarship). As indicated by the booklet's cover, the goal of true Catholic devotion is *ut unum sint* (John 17:23), or the "summing up of all things in the Father, through the Son, in the unity of the Spirit."[16] This goal is consistent with the motto chosen by Pope Pius X: *Instaurare omnia in Christo*. Indeed, did the latter not express the view that "active participation in the sacrosanct mysteries and in the public and solemn prayer of the church" was the precondition for the "renewed flourishing of the true Christian spirit"?[17] Vatican II would later take up this topic of the "active participation" of the baptized, not only in liturgy but in the entire life of the church.

A twofold continuity emerges between the activities of the diocesan priest and of the Benedictine monk of Leuven: the church is the grand project of God towards which the entire apostolate converges, that of the diocesan priest, of the labor chaplain in the bosom of the working class, and of the Benedictine through liturgical action. Moreover, does not the image of the Altar of Confession in Saint Peter's Basilica in Rome, printed on the cover of *La piété de l'Église* along with the quote *ut unum sint*, resemble the implicit "announcement" of the following period? This prayer of Christ, shortly before his Passion, symbolizes the intimate bond between the unity of the liturgical assembly and the unity of the church in the best possible, concise manner.

The Great War broke out in August 1914, interrupting the liturgical action of Mont César and of its principal inspirer. During the first months of the conflict, Cardinal Mercier decided to write a pastoral letter that was to be read out in the churches; entitled *Patriotisme et endurance*,[18] it provided a

few guidelines on how to conduct oneself in the face of the German occupier. Dom Beauduin was consulted on this occasion and suggested that the cardinal should use stronger language. The letter was read out at Sunday Mass in every church on Jan 1, 1915 and was well received by the population. After a period of activity in the resistance, Dom Lambert resided in the Benedictine house of study in Edermine (Ireland), where he served as subprior. He assumed numerous functions, notably as chaplain to Belgian soldiers hospitalized on the British coast and spiritual counselor to several Belgian seminarians. During these years in Great Britain, he discovered a less rigid monasticism that was more open to pastoral action and suited his own intuitions.

2   At the Benedictine College of Sant'Anselmo

Dom Lambert returned to Mont César in 1919, bearing the halo of his wartime feats but feeling rather uprooted. Classes and liturgical publications needed to be resumed. He was convinced that the young monks of Leuven did not understand the spirit of the 1909 movement. At this point, he was chosen to teach the theology of dogmas at the international Benedictine College of Sant'Anselmo in Rome, which had been reestablished by Pope Leo XIII in 1887 for the purpose of working towards a union of the churches.[19] The pope wanted to make it one of the priorities of his pontificate, as he was convinced that

---

16   Beauduin, *La piété de l'Église*, 16.

17   Excerpt from Pius X, "Tra le sollecitudini," in: *ASS* 36, 1903, 329–339, available at <http://w2.vatican.va/content/pius-x/it/motu_proprio/documents/hf_p-x_motu-proprio_19031122_sollecitudini.html> (accessed July 12, 2019). See also *La Maison-Dieu* 241, 2005.

18   See Henri Haag, "Les origines de la pastorale 'Patriotisme et endurance' du cardinal Mercier," *RHE*

94, 1999, 436–470, and Jan De Volder, *La résistance d'un cardinal: Le cardinal Mercier, l'Église et la Guerre (1914–1918)*, Namur, Fidélité, 2016. Regarding the letter *Patriotisme et endurance*, see Roger Aubert, *Les deux premiers grands conflits du cardinal Mercier avec les autorités allemandes d'occupation*, Leuven, Peeters, 1998, 15–73.

19   On the preliminary steps towards a union of the churches and the role of Leo XIII, see Lambert Vos, "L'activité œcuménique du Monastère de Chevetogne," *Les Amis des Monastères* 142, 2005, 14–28.

the Benedictine monks were destined to play an important role in the rapprochement with the East. He had had the brilliant insight that both Western and Eastern monasticism, thanks to the fact that it preceded the 11th-century schism, was best suited to working towards such a union. In an audience granted to the students of Sant'Anselmo in 1893, he said: "You know how dedicated I am to the reconciliation of the Eastern Churches. Well, then! I am counting on you to help me achieve this goal."[20] The reconciliation with the East was also one of the issues discussed at the International Eucharistic Congress of Jerusalem[21] (1893). In his encyclical *Orientalium dignitas* (1894), Leo XIII urged Catholics to respect the ritual and the discipline of the Eastern Churches united in Rome, thereby contradicting the Latinization policy practiced by certain missionaries. On the same line, his successor Benedict XV would later establish both the Congregation for the Oriental Churches and the PIO (1917) as a "house of studies open to Catholic and Orthodox Christians" for the purpose of providing "comparative instruction in the Catholic and the Orthodox doctrines."[22] Dom Ildephonso Schuster, the abbot of the Basilica of St. Paul Outside the Walls, was appointed rector of the institute in 1919.

In what state of mind did Dom Beauduin arrive in Rome? He admits that he had no clear conception of the union of churches at that time. His unfinished autobiographical *Mémoires* (1932) make room for a severe self-criticism:

> In October 1921, I arrived in Rome at the College of Sant'Anselmo, as professor for fundamental theology. Entirely unfamiliar

with the unionist issues until then, I was as exclusively Latin as one can be, or should I rather say: the issue simply did not exist for me. In my suitcases, the lecture notes that I had prepared during the holidays were carefully sorted: schismatics and heretics as well as Jews and infidels were all condemned therein; the four classic attributes of the true church, no more and no less, seemed marvelously evident and hardly left room for goodwill; and the axiom "out of the church, no salvation" suffered no exception; my orthodoxy was irreproachable.[23]

Such words reflect a widespread mentality within the Catholic Church of the time. Hence, the theology of Thomistic inspiration was characterized by legalism and apologetics; it was frequently a theology of controversies, and Dom Beauduin was indeed a child of his times, albeit not entirely since he had already developed new perspectives while lecturing on *De Ecclesia* at Mont César, and had discovered the soul of liturgy thanks to the liturgical movement. His beliefs were to assert themselves to an even stronger degree; at Laminne's suggestion, he put aside the manuals and delved into the sources of revelation: Holy Scripture, the Fathers, and the councils. It is not surprising that he awakened his students to fundamental realities and sparked their enthusiasm.

2.1   *The Encounter with Eastern Christians*

For Dom Lambert, the years in Rome were an opportunity to meet numerous people in the Benedictine world, but also various personalities with an interest in the East and in the former Russian Empire that had become the Soviet Union, which many believed might well disappear, thus opening up the country for the missionary activities of the Catholic Church. Dom Olivier Rousseau, a young monk from Maredsous, was a

---

20   See Lambert Beauduin, *Une Œuvre monastique pour l'union des églises*, Leuven, Abbaye de Mont César, 1925, 13.

21   Claude Soetens, *Le Congrès eucharistique international de Jérusalem* (1893): *Dans le cadre de la politique orientale du pape Léon XIII*, Leuven, Nauwelaerts, 1977.

22   Benedict XV, "Orientis catholici," in: AAS 9, 1917, 531–533.

23   Excerpt from Lambert Beauduin, *Mémoires de ma vie*, in: AAC, LB, Biographie I/7.

student at Sant'Anselmo's. He met Beauduin as professor at Mont César. Together, they attended the Greek College in Rome, which had been entrusted to the monks of Maredsous in 1919 and where the Byzantine rite was celebrated on a daily basis. Dom Placide de Meester,[24] a distinguished orientalist and future consultor to the Congregation for the Oriental Churches resided there. A few months later, another student arrived at Sant'Anselmo's, the young Louis (later known as Lev) Gillet, a monk from Farnborough who was fascinated by the Russian soul. Beauduin, the professor, and his two students Rousseau and Gillet[25] would come to form a famous "trio," a kind of think tank that would strive to give a concrete answer to the Holy See's wishes for a rapprochement with the churches of the East. They regularly kept in touch with another learned orientalist, Fr. Cyrille Korolevskij (born François Chiron),[26] a French citizen who, from 1909, stood under the jurisdiction

of the Ukrainian Greek Catholic Church headed by the metropolitan Andrey Sheptytsky of Lviv. Korolevskij would become an assistant to Cardinal Tisserant at the Vatican Library and then consultor to the Congregation for the Oriental Churches. In 1923, Msgr. Sheptytskij paid a visit to Rome in an attempt to raise the awareness in the West of the situation of his church, an Orthodox community that had been placed under the authority of the Holy See during the Union of Brest (1596) and which practiced the Byzantine rite. He sought the help of the Western Benedictines in order to bolster his efforts to restore monastic life, having already founded Univ Lavra (Lviv) as a monastery dedicated to the formation of Studite monks. His speech at the PIO moved Dom Beauduin through its insistence on liturgy as the educator of the Christian people and on account of the role which the Benedictines could play. Beauduin's wish was that Mont César should assume the responsibility for this East-West collaboration. The trio consisting of Beauduin, Rousseau, and Gillet planned a journey to Lviv in 1923, which was cancelled due to the refusal of the Benedictine authorities of Belgium to commit themselves to the path of cooperation. After concluding their studies, the two young monks returned to their monastery.

2.2   *For an* Institut monastique en vue de l'Apostolat de l'union des églises

The summer visit to Lviv having been cancelled, Dom Beauduin would henceforth reside in his abbey of Mont César. The Eastern contacts established in Rome and the encounter with the metropolitan inspired him to elaborate an unprecedented plan for the union of churches. He was not the first to entertain such a dream. Dom Gérard van Caloen, from Maredsous, had already expressed the wish to establish a Benedictine monastery of Eastern rite in Perugia around 1887; in 1901, at the Congrès des Œuvres Catholiques in Malines, he had submitted a project that aimed to effect a rapprochement with the Orthodox world and had specified the appropriate spirit in which

---

24   Daniel Misonne, "de Meester," *NBN* 5, 109–110. A specialist in Byzantine liturgy and professor at the Greek College, he was procurator of the Belgian Benedictine congregation from 1920 and became consultor of the Congregation for the Oriental Churches in 1923. The monks of Maredsous, Placide de Meester and Hugo Gaisser, would dwell on Mount Athos for a time in 1905; see Antoine Lambrechts, "Pèlerins bénédictins du Mont Athos," *Irén* 71/2–3, 1998, 281–289.

25   See Élisabeth Behr-Sigel, *Lev Gillet: "Un moine de l'Église d'Orient": Un libre croyant universaliste, évangélique et mystique*, Paris, Cerf, 1993. Having become a monk in Lviv, in the lavra established by Metropolitan Andrey Sheptytsky, Lev Gillet would publish several works of spiritual liturgy in the Éditions de Chevetogne, under the author's name "Un moine de l'Église d'Orient."

26   See Cyrille Korolevskij, *Kniga bytija moego: Le livre de ma vie: Mémoires autobiographiques*, ed. Giuseppe Maria Croce, 5 vols., Vatican City, Archives secrètes vaticanes, 2007, esp. the interesting foreword by Étienne Fouilloux at the beginning of vol. 1. See also Cyrille Charon, *Histoire des patriarcats melkites (Alexandrie, Antioche, Jérusalem) depuis le schisme monophysite du sixième siècle jusqu'à nos jours*, 3 vols., Rome, Imprimerie du Sénat, 1909–1911; Cyrille Korolevskij, *Le prophète ukrainien de l'unité: Métropolite André Szeptyckyj (1865–1944)*, Paris, Guibert, ²2005; Giuseppe Maria Croce, "Korolevskij (Cyrille)," *DHGE* 29, 671–672.

this goal was to be achieved: the renunciation of the "Uniatist" policy of individual conversions and of all proselytism.[27]

According to Dom Beauduin, the aim is to work towards "bringing the Eastern Churches closer to the center of the Catholic union and, thereby, to lay the groundwork for the return of the Eastern Christians to the ecumenical unity of the church."[28] How? By way of contacts with Eastern monasticism, by "creating an atmosphere of mutual trust that will pave the way for the union."

The guiding thoughts of the project is to establish a main monastery in Rome for the purpose of biblical and Eastern studies. "A very strong commitment of the union monks to the Roman Church" and to the Holy See is to be fostered, in conjunction with the promoting of knowledge, love, and admiration for the Eastern Churches. Monachism has a unique role to play in the apostolate for the union, since the monastic institution in both East and West predates the separation; there is thus a "common traditional heritage" between East and West to explore and upon which to draw. Since Leo XIII, the popes have repeatedly called for the "reconciliation of the Eastern Churches" with the Catholic Church. In order to emphasize their specific mission, the monks of the future institute are to be called "monks of the union" rather than Benedictine monks. They are to be directly subordinated to the Holy See. Their recruitment will be international and any form of nationalism that would run contrary to the pursued goal is to be avoided.

Secondary houses are to be established in various countries, whereas the main house is to be in Rome. The activities of the union monks will take place by way of an "indirect apostolate" with regard to Westerners and by a "direct apostolate" towards the East. Regarding the former, according to Dom Beauduin, it will be necessary to demonstrate "an enlightened zeal in the work for the union of churches," through prayer, the study of the history, liturgy, and theology of the Eastern Churches, and the dissemination of popularized works. As far as the direct apostolate was concerned, the Western monks will spend time in the East, and Eastern monks, priests, and laymen will be welcomed in Rome. "If an Orthodox Church or monastery desires to return to the Roman unity ... they will be assisted in this endeavor." A foundation will also be set up in the Near East, possibly in conjunction with an educational or training program, as is the case in certain Western monasteries, notably in the form of abbey schools.

Concerning the practical realization, this project requires the approval of the Holy See and the recommendation of the abbots and bishops. Each monastery could contribute one monk to this apostolate. The annual budget will be shouldered by the union monks, the maintenance of the Eastern students by the "Œuvres orientales," and the initial setup by the Holy See. The institute will be directly subordinated to the Holy Father and it will be assimilated to the confederated Benedictine congregations under the authority of the abbot primate. Pending the drafting of its own constitutions, the Benedictine constitutions approved by the Holy See will be adopted.

Regarding liturgy, in Rome, the official rite will be the Byzantine-Slavic rite; as in the Greek College, there will be a chapel for the Roman worship. In the houses located in other countries, the official liturgy will follow the Roman rite, with a separate chapel for the Byzantine-Slavic rite. In the houses of the Near East, the liturgy will follow the Byzantine-Slavic rite.

Such a project, which was meant to be read by the competent authorities, primarily by Pope Pius XI, is quite characteristic of Dom Beauduin. He begins

27   On Gérard van Caloen, see Nicolas Huyghebaert, "Caloen," BNB 31, 1962, 152–162, and Étienne Fouilloux, "De Gérard van Caloen à Lambert Beauduin: Réalité et limites d'une 'influence,'" in: Allmen & others, *Veilleur*, 135–165.

28   Here and following, *Projet d'érection d'un institut monastique en vue de l'Apostolat de l'union des églises* (Nov 24, 1923); AAC, Actes relatifs à la Fondation, no. 4, ten typewritten pages.

by outlining the essential points: the ultimate goal and the spirit that is to govern its realization as well as the guiding thoughts. As this project corresponded to the aspirations of the recent popes, how could Pope Pius XI not be interested in it? Among the guiding thoughts, he highlights the privileged role of the monks in East and West, on the basis of their common heritage and common vocation, which is rooted in the many centuries that preceded the fateful separation of the 11th century.

It should also be noted that the focus on the East does not entirely exclude any interest in the other Christian confessions: "The rapprochement between the Eastern Churches, Anglicanism, and Protestantism will be closely monitored." The formulation is a little vague but not without substance. It shows that from the very onset, the rapprochement with certain churches, as Beauduin conceived it, could not exclude any of them. Is this not the path that Amay-Chevetogne would follow over the years and in the face of many difficulties? The so-called psychological approach is also typical of the project: rapprochement by way of mutual understanding and mutual esteem in conjunction with study and prayer, such are the main ingredients of unionism and, even more clearly, those of ecumenism when it would begin to take shape within the Catholic Church. Finally, the project's international, or better yet "catholic" nature, in the full sense of the term, is also worthy of note. Nationalism would truly be a mortal sin in this respect! This international character is precisely why Beauduin wanted the endeavor to be sponsored by the pope himself and the Holy See, and, in second place, by the Benedictine order, as represented by the primate and the abbots, who showed little interest at this point in time.

The practical accomplishments appear in their turn, namely in the implementation. The financing and the legal status are far from negligible. They are not at the heart of the project but at its service. No institution will prove durable without sufficient economic support. No project will prove sustainable without institutional clarity. By addressing these two aspects, Dom Beauduin demonstrates a sense of realism. Money is a means, not an end, and the Beauduin family would always prove very knowledgeable in this field.

2.3 How to Bring the Project to the Pope's Attention?

Dom Lambert had two assets at his disposal: Cardinal Mercier, whom he knew well and who was anxious to promote the union of the churches, and Msgr. Michel d'Herbigny,[29] an influential Jesuit in Rome who was in favor of the apostolate for the union, albeit with a dual orientation: in his opinion, the project was to be limited to Russia alone, and this in a strictly unionist perspective of bringing about its return to the Catholic Church.

Roman circles, in particular the pope, showed great interest in the East, as is attested by the encyclicals *Ubi arcano Dei* (Dec 23, 1922), *Ecclesiam Dei* (Nov 12, 1923), and *Rerum omnium* (Jan 26, 1923). Pope Pius XI had a genuine compassion for the

---

29   For Msgr. Michel d'Herbigny, see Léon Tretjakewitsch, *Bishop Michel d'Herbigny SJ and Russia: A Pre-Ecumenical Approach to Christian Unity*, Würzburg, Augustinus-Verlag, 1990, and the book review by Emmanuel Lanne in *Irén* 64/2, 1991, 314–315. In 1922, d'Herbigny became director of the PIO, until then in the hands of the Benedictines. His dream was that the Catholic Church would experience a massive influx of Orthodox Russians who had been weakened by the Soviet regime. In 1924, he became consultor to the Congregation for the Oriental Churches, and in 1925 consultor, then head, of the papal commission Pro Russia, which had been established at his request by Pius XI. In 1926, in Berlin, he received the episcopal consecration from the hands of the Nuncio Eugenio Pacelli. During clandestine missions to the Soviet Union, he consecrated three Catholic bishops. His power in the Holy See's Eastern politics grew steadily and would be heavily felt in the work of the monks of Amay-Chevetogne. See Antoine Wenger, *Rome et Moscou (1900–1950)*, Paris, Desclée de Brouwer, 1987, and the critical book review by Emmanuel Lanne, "*Rome et Moscou (1900–1950)*: Une certaine manière de lire l'histoire," *Irén* 60, 1987, 218–228. The author of the book appears to view Russia as a land that must be evangelized and shows little sympathy for the Orthodox Church that had existed there for centuries.

numerous Russian refugees who had emigrated to the West, and Dom Beauduin believed that this was an opportune moment to approach the pope.

It is difficult to reconstruct the exact scenario of this diplomatic maneuver, which extended over a period of several months. The biographers Loonbeek and Mortiau[30] attempted to do so on the basis of the equally rich and fragmentary documentation which they were able to sort out together, but this reconstruction would require confirmation from the Roman sources. It involves four key players: Dom Beauduin, Cardinal Mercier, the Benedictine primate Dom Fidelis von Stotzingen, and Msgr. D'Herbigny. During the summer of 1923, Dom Lambert probably discussed his plans with Mercier. In October 1923, the cardinal wrote a private letter to the pope suggesting that a monastery be established for the union. Subsequently, Dom Beauduin submitted his *Projet d'érection* to the cardinal, since he feared that the Eastern mission might be entrusted to the Jesuits. Mercier may have written a second petition to the pope in which he warmly recommended Lambert Beauduin for this task.

Dom Lambert handed his report to d'Herbigny in December 1923, and the latter presented it to the pope, who expressed his readiness to entrust Beauduin with the proposed foundation. Then came the phase of deliberations, within a group that included the primate, Msgr. Michel d'Herbigny, Dom Beauduin, and a few others. On Dec 23, d'Herbigny presented the pope with a summary of the group's discussions. According to some of Beauduin's writings, it seems as though the pope had originally intended to address his papal letter directly to Beauduin. The latter is believed to have dissuaded the pope from doing so and asked him to send it to the primate instead, who would have the task of soliciting the support of the abbots for this apostolate. This letter, which bears the title *Equidem verba*, is dated Mar 21, 1924, the feast of St. Benedict; the letter bears the stamp of the primate and of Msgr. d'Herbigny.

2.4 Equidem verba

Addressed to the primate, the papal letter[31] is brief and it partly takes up the content of the *Projet d'érection*. However, it restricts it in two ways. Only Russia is mentioned in the papal text, which thus limits the scope of the endeavor to the Christian East, at most. Furthermore, the project was to be elaborated within the Benedictine order, which probably reflects the dual influence of Msgr. d'Herbigny and of von Stotzingen. The latter played his part by consulting the abbots of the order, but he was not enthused by the project. He was pleased that this document was not included in the pontifical *Acta*.

As the project would necessarily be developed in the context of the Benedictine order, Dom Beauduin envisaged the foundation of a new monastery devoted to prayer, study, and works, rather than attaching an "extraneous Eastern work"[32] to an already existing monastery. The pope's letter was to play an important role in the founding of Amay. Pope Pius XI begins with a reference to the *ut omnes unum sint* and asks the Benedictine monks to follow the primate's invitation to engage in prayer, study, and action and to "care for the Russian refugees with all possible compassion."[33] He expressed the wish that a monastic congregation of Slavic rite be established someday, with a central monastery in Rome.

---

30 Loonbeek & Mortiau, *Un pionnier*, vol. 1, 361–448.

31 This document has not been published in *ASS*. The Latin text and its translation can be found in: Beauduin, *Une œuvre monastique*, 3–6; but also in: *La Documentation catholique* 14, 1925, 734–755. A detailed description of the letter is given by Cyrille Korolevskij in *Studion* 1, 1924, 97–122. Concerning Pius XI (1857–1939), see Marcel Launay, *Pie XI: Le pape de l'Action catholique*, Paris, Cerf, 2018, (including a bibliography, 220–229), and Roger Aubert, "Pie XI pape," in: Gabriel Jacquemet, ed., *Catholicisme hier aujourd'hui demain*, vol. 11, Paris, Letouzey & Ané, 1986, 287–300.

32 Loonbeek & Mortiau, *Un pionnier*, vol. 1, 414.

33 Loonbeek & Mortiau, *Un pionnier*, vol. 1, 408.

2.5   A Monastic Work for the Union of the Churches

Written in February 1925 and constantly reedited, this booklet entitled *Une œuvre monastique pour l'union des églises* is described by Dom Beauduin as the "trustworthy commentary" to *Equidem verba*.[34] It is, in fact, a "maximalist" commentary. True to his habit, Dom Lambert builds on the papal text to enhance his project, even if he does emphasize certain points of his own or modifies others. Here are a few examples of the manner in which he does so.[35] The papal text restricts the future apostolate to Russia, whereas Dom Beauduin sees it within a much broader perspective. Dom Lambert, in fact, ascribing his thoughts to the pope, attributes to Pius XI the intention not to connect the apostolate for union with an already existing monastery. He advises the Catholics to seek out the truths that are held in common, whereas *Equidem verba* expresses the wish that Catholics be informed of what distinguishes them from the Orthodox: in short, as the biographers put it, "the model was unionist, but the commentary was ecumenical *avant la lettre*."[36] Moreover, Dom Beauduin considers that the pontifical document constitutes the "charter of the union of churches."[37] One cannot ignore the richness of this text. Indeed, the booklet *Une œuvre monastique*, in which Dom Beauduin comments on the papal text, is clearly ahead of its time. It accurately conveys the spirit of the future monastery of Amay.

Let us begin with the title. In response to the wishes of Pius XI, the monastery of Amay would be established "for the union of the churches"; this is its specific nature or, so to speak, its DNA. The configuration of the monastic life would be its illustration. The founding of Amay was "a monastic work," that is, the Benedictine monks' own service or contribution to the rapprochement with the Eastern Christians. The fact that the pope chose the Benedictine order to pilot this project is not without significance. The latter had not been affected by the "modern devotions," unlike other religious orders that emerged at a later date in the West. Moreover, even if they did witness the profound changes brought about by the Renaissance, the Reformation, and the French Revolution, they remained committed to the legacy of the early church.

The plan for the establishment of *Une œuvre monastique* was substantially the same as the one outlined in the *Projet d'érection*.[38] It was penned by the same author. As always, it is characterized by a careful argumentation, a great attention to pedagogy, and sufficient elaborations to lend credibility to the broad lines of the project. The most striking feature of the text is its "modernity," even if the vocabulary does alternate between "union of the churches" and their "return" or between "ecumenical union" and references to the rapprochement among all Christian churches. At the heart of the project, one discovers a true fraternity in which Eastern and Western monasticism will each put their own richness at the service of a cause that transcends them. A quote from Cardinal Mercier expresses this very thought: "The rapprochement of the hearts is not the unity of the faith

---

34   I have used here the second edition of 1926, published at the Prieuré de l'Union, Amay-sur-Meuse, Belgium. The text is identical to that of the first. However, each reedition was to grow through the addition of new, more recent official documents. The line of thought does not diverge from the *Projet d'érection d'un institut monastique en vue de l'Apostolat de l'union des églises*. Its structure is as follows: chapter 1: Goal and Guiding Principles (Roman spirit; Eastern soul; monastic regime; Catholic meaning); chapter 2: Means of Implementation (indirect apostolate: prayer, propaganda, studies; direct action: hospitality, short visits, foundations, statutes).

35   Loonbeek & Mortiau, *Un pionnier*, vol. 1, 421–425.

36   Loonbeek & Mortiau, *Un pionnier*, vol. 1, 424.

37   Loonbeek & Mortiau, *Un pionnier*, vol. 1, 421.

38   The *Projet d'érection* consisted of three chapters: 1) But; 2) Idées maîtresses; 3) Moyens d'action. Amay's programmatic booklet *Une œuvre monastique* opens with the translated text of the letter of Pius XI, *Equidem verba*. Subsequently, Dom Beauduin structures the content into two chapters, the second of which is the most voluminous.

but creates a disposition for it [but is favorable to it]."[39] Moreover, dialogue and collaborative work imply that the partners retain their own identity, as is underlined in the paragraph devoted to the "Roman spirit": "The monks of the union will above all need to distinguish themselves through their strong commitment to the Roman Church, [itself] drawn from an intensive and sound education in theology and patristics."[40] Other passages speak of "inculturation," albeit not in the current sense but as a way of saying: "Let us be Byzantine with the Byzantines and Latin with the Latins"![41] The approach is indeed quite subtle: objective study based on the same sources will bring everyone together and the "scholarly apostolate" (i.e. the rich corpus of Western works) will facilitate exchanges. Thus, a well conducted study will make it possible to overcome the prejudices and preconceived ideas stemming from geographical separation and ignorance of one another.

3   The Malines Conversations

As early as the 19th century, under the influence of the Oxford Movement, Lord Halifax[42] and Abbé Fernand Portal[43] were animated by the desire to achieve a rapprochement between the Catholic Church and the Anglican Communion. Lord Halifax entertained the hope that Rome would recognize the validity of Anglican ordinations. Leo XIII's rejection of this in *Apostolicae curae* (1896) was a great disappointment for the advocates of the union.[44] In 1920, the bishops of the Anglican Communion, who had convened in Lambeth, launched an "Appeal to All Christian People" to work towards a rapprochement among the churches, thereby rekindling the hope of the two pioneers. They proceeded to search for a compelling personality who could sponsor an initiative to bring Anglicans and Catholics together. Portal wrote to Mercier on Jan 24, 1921; on Oct 19, he and Halifax then paid a visit to the cardinal, who expressed his interest under the condition that the talks be of a private nature. This positive response had only been possible on account of an earlier meeting between Mercier and Benedict XV in December 1920; the Cardinal had asked for permission to "successively invite one or two theologians from each of the main dissident churches, Anglican and above all Orthodox, to Malines,"[45] where they were to engage in a *tête-à-tête* with a Catholic theologian. Benedict XV gave his consent, a decision which the Cardinal would later relay to Benedict's successor Pius XI.

The conversations were held at the primatial see of Malines from 1921 to 1925.[46] The informal designation "conversations" aptly conveys the atmosphere of the meetings; this was primarily an opportunity to speak and listen to one

---

39   "Paroles du Cardinal Mercier," *Irénikon-Collection* 3–4, 1927, 10.

40   Loonbeek & Mortiau, *Un pionnier*, vol. 1, 413.

41   Loonbeek & Mortiau, *Un pionnier*, vol. 1, 415.

42   For biographical details regarding Halifax, see Joseph Huby, "Lord Halifax (1839–1934): L'homme, sa formation, son caractère," *Les études*, Mar 5, 1937; Yves Congar, "Halifax," in: *Catholicisme* 5, 496–497; Denys Gorce, "Halifax (Charles Lindley Wood)," DSAM 7, 50–52; "Halifax (Charles Lindley Wood)," DHGE 23, 152.

43   See Régis Ladous, *L'abbé Portal et la campagne anglo-romaine (1890–1912)*, Lyon, Université de Lyon, 1973, and Régis Ladous, *Monsieur Portal et les siens (1855–1926)*, Paris, Cerf, 1985. See also Albert Gratieux, *L'amitié au service de l'union: Lord Halifax et l'abbé Portal*, Paris, Bonne Presse, 1951.

44   See Paul Avis' contribution in this volume.

45   Ladous, *L'abbé Portal*, 414.

46   On the Malines Conversations, see Aubert, *Le cardinal Mercier*, 393–452; Charles Lindley Wood Halifax, *The Conversations at Malines (1921–1925): Original Documents*, London, P. Allan, 1930. See also John A. Dick, *The Malines Conversations Revisited*, Leuven, Leuven University Press, 1989 (see 216–225 for the text "L'Église anglicane unie non absorbée"); Adalbert Denaux & John A. Dick, eds., *From Malines to ARCIC: The Malines Conversations Commemorated*, Leuven, Leuven University Press, 1997, especially the essay by Emmanuel Lanne, "'L'Église anglicane unie non absorbée' et le contexte œcuménique au moment des Conversations de Malines," 3–33; see also Bernard Barlow and Martin Browne's contribution in this volume.

another, in the greatest mutual respect. However, these conversations did not consist of desultory exchanges, as specific topics of the most delicate nature were addressed and became the subject of communications that were then read aloud and debated within the group. During the fourth conversation, on May 20, 1925, the Cardinal privately read a report entitled "L'Église anglicane unie non absorbée".[47] It later became known that this document had been drawn up by Dom Beauduin at the request of Mercier, who had asked him the question whether it was possible for the Anglican Church to be reunited without being absorbed into the Roman Church. Dom Lambert attempted to establish this possibility on the basis of the special ecclesial status that Canterbury had held since Gregory the Great, which, in his opinion, could in some way or other be viewed as the equivalent of a patriarchate. He argued on the basis of ancient history and of the current situation of the Uniate churches, that is the Eastern Churches united in Rome. Did the latter not have true "autonomy," notably in terms of liturgy? The first part consists of a long argumentation of a historical nature that concludes with the words: "Union, not absorption, this is thus, in our opinion, the formula of reconciliation."[48] The second part is of a canonical nature, inspired by the organization of the Eastern Uniate Churches.

Even though theologians and historians writing after the Malines Conversations responded critically to this argumentation, which they believed to be based on a historical error (can one really speak of Canterbury as a patriarchate in the traditional sense of the word?), the question was taken seriously. The formula, in any case, seemed promising for the future as it was characterized by a spirit of openness, not only for the Anglican Church but in one way or another for all Christian confessions. How would it be possible to achieve a union that would not be tantamount to absorption? Dom

Beauduin's work was that of an "ecumenist" rather than of a "historian" in the strictest sense of the word. The formula retains its appeal even today because it stands aloof from a narrowly conceived unionism ("return to the fold") that prevailed in the first half of the 20th century and leaves room for a more flexible formulation, the content and modalities of which remain to be specified.

4 The Founding of the Union Monastery at Amay-sur-Meuse

The years 1923–1926 were prolific on account of various achievements, notably the attempts at collaboration with the monks of Univ and the Dames de l'Union, a Parisian community fostered by Abbé Portal, as well as the installation of two Benedictine monks from Affligem Abbey (Dom Constantin Bosschaerts and Dom Franco de Wyels, both affiliated with Amay) in Schootenhof (Antwerp). Mention should also be made of the week for the union of churches of 1925 in Brussels, which was meant to raise public awareness on the eve of Amay's foundation, occurred in late 1925, and the creation of the journal *Irénikon* in 1926.

However, these signs of hope should not obscure the fact that the pioneers were soon confronted with all kinds of difficulties: in 1927, soon after the founding of Amay, a decree of the Congregation for the Oriental Churches reminded the monks of the multiple jurisdictions under which they stood, namely that of Mont César, the Belgian Benedictine Congregation, the Congregation for the Oriental Churches, and the papal commission Pro Russia, which had been established in 1925. In addition, there were also protests from the English Catholics and from the Catholic archbishop of Westminster, who deemed it intolerable that the monks of Amay should meddle in English affairs.

4.1 *A Common* Typikon *for East and West*
On Apr 9, 1925, Dom Beauduin paid a visit to the metropolitan Andrey Sheptytsky in Lviv in order to become acquainted with Eastern monasticism

---

47   See the edited text in Dick, *The Malines Conversations*, 216–225.
48   Dick, *The Malines Conversations*, 224.

and to negotiate an agreement for a monastic con-federation, of which Amay would constitute the Western and Lviv the Eastern pole. The underlying idea was that the metropolitan himself would be responsible for the foundation in Belgium and would entrust it to the Belgian monks. The fundamental principles granted the monasteries a large degree of autonomy with regard to monastic discipline and vested the new confederation with legislative and executive powers. A *Typikon* was drawn up and jointly signed by the Eastern and Western partners.[49] However, this agreement never came into force, as the differences with the metropolitan became more and more apparent.

4.2 The Week for the Union of Churches in Brussels

Dom Beauduin knew that a favorable public opinion was vital for the successful launching of a new movement.[50] On the eve of the founding of Amay, he looked for an opportunity to raise the awareness of Western Christians of the riches of the East. This was the year in which the 16th centenary of the Council of Nicaea was to be celebrated at the request of Pius XI. The initiative was organized in just a few months. Renowned speakers were sought and found, including the Metropolitan Sheptytsky as well as the two Western monks who resided in Lviv: Lev Gillet and André Stoelen. Cardinal

Mercier also agreed to speak, as did Abbé Portal, a major protagonist of the Malines Conversations. On each day of the conference, the participants listened to five or six lectures and were invited to take part in a liturgy of Byzantine rite accompanied by a specialized choir. The participants came in large numbers and appeared interested. However, the Benedictine abbots were conspicuously absent, with the exception of Dom Robert de Kerchove from Mont César. Here are some of the topics addressed during the week: *La psychologie de l'Union* (Metropolitan Sheptytsky); *L'union des églises et le concile du Vatican* (Beauduin); *L'église anglicane et l'union des églises au XIXe siècle* (Portal); *La répartition des églises chrétiennes considérées du point de vue de l'union* (Gillet); *L'union des églises* (Mercier); *Nos frères séparés et leur capacité à l'égard du fruit de la messe* (Maurice de La Taille, s.j.); *La Russie, centre de l'orthodoxie, and La Russie et les rites* (Auguste Maniglier). This week of reflection and exchanges was not without consequences. Similar events were organized in numerous Belgian cities, sometimes with the same speakers. Numerous study circles were also established, especially in university towns.

4.3 The Birth of the Monastery in Amay

While Dom Lambert was working on the plan for a temporary monastery, which was to be built in Tancrémont (Pepinster), the bishop of Liège informed him that the monastery of Amay-sur-Meuse was available.[51] The French Carmelites who had taken refuge there following the promulgation of the laws on the expulsion of religious orders were now able to return to their country. Thanks to the support of his family, Dom Beauduin was able to purchase this convent and settled there as prior in

---

49   *Typicon de la Confédération des monastères de l'Orient et de l'Occident pour l'Œuvre de l'Union des Églises*, April 1925, in: AAC, Actes relatifs à la Fondation, no. 15, six typewritten pages. Here, the term *typikon* is not employed in the sense of an *ordo* designed to regulate the liturgy of the monasteries but rather in the sense of a collaboration agreement pertaining to the rights and duties of each institution engaged in a common work. The document consists of five chapters: (1) But et principes fondamentaux; (2) Autonomie des monastères; (3) Points soumis directement à la juridiction de la Confédération; (4) Chapitre général; (5) Commission des épitropes et délégués de l'Epitaxie.

50   See Loonbeek & Mortiau, *Un pionnier*, vol. 1, 618–638, and Olivier Rousseau, "Après dix ans: La semaine unioniste de Bruxelles de 1925," *Irén* 12/6, 1935, 599–611 (for a list of the papers that were actually presented, see 604–605).

51   See Lambert Vos, "Amay-Chevetogne et le Proche-Orient: De la fondation (1925) au Concile Vatican II (1962)," in: Nagi Edelby & Pierre Masri, eds., *Mélanges en mémoire de Mgr Néophytos Edelby (1920–1995)*, Beirut, CEDRAC, 2005, 467–487; Lambert Vos, "Les 75 ans du monastère de chevetogne," *Lettre de Maredsous* 30, 2001, 171–178.

December 1925, together with the first two union monks, Dom Ildefons Dirks and Dom Lev Gillet. Living conditions were difficult and the furnishings only provisional. The financial resources were limited. In spite of this, Dom Lambert made sure that a few basic collections for the future library were acquired, for instance Mansi's study of the councils and Migne's patrology.

What are the main features of the monastic life of apostolic type that was practiced in Amay? Essentially those found in the booklet *Une œuvre monastique*, in particular prayer, study[52] (six hours a day), and manual labor, in accordance with the *Rule of Saint Benedict*. The community was to consist of priest monks and non-priest monks, as is the tradition in the East. All were to partake of the same liturgical and convent life and "would, in this perfect Christian fraternity, find the unity of heart and soul that is crucial for the success of their endeavor."[53] The ascesis was to be tempered, human, accessible to all,[54] as observances are not an end in themselves. Their significance is christological and ecclesiological. Through the Christian ascesis,[55] the monk becomes one with Christ in his Paschal mystery and in his Eucharistic sacrifice. Moreover, ascesis unites us with the church, the Body of Christ; it is common to all Christians, even if each of them, particularly the monk, lives it in accordance with his individual vocation. Finally, ascesis makes it possible to take part in the prayer of Christ *ut omnes unum sint*. These

few notes provide an insight into the originality of Beauduin's thoughts on monastic life.

4.4   Irénikon

During the week for the union of churches in Brussels, Abbé Portal suggested that the organizers should found a journal and call it *Irénikon*, that is, message of peace. This title hints at an entire agenda that would take a long time to accomplish: "Before envisaging the official and legal unification, it is necessary to achieve the spiritual reconciliation of the minds and hearts."[56] The leading article of the first issue, "De quoi s'agit-il?,"[57] attempts to clarify a few misunderstandings. On no account will Westerners be asked to "modify their liturgical and disciplinary customs and to adapt them to Eastern tradition." Nor should an "opportunistic arrangement" be sought in a manner that would ignore the unpleasant issues, such as certain dogmas. It would indeed be better to undertake an "irenic study of our dogmas." Equally, the intention is neither to create a "federation of churches that are essentially alien to each other, based on charitable and fraternal relations," nor to transform ourselves into diplomats, nor to encourage individual conversions or "collective reconciliations." "No line fishing in the neighbor's pond, that is agreed; but no fishing with nets either." The fundamental goal is the "spiritual rapprochement of the minds and hearts ... May every Christian soul ... strive to be a *unifying factor* in the Mystical Body of Christ."[58] Such a perspective implies a true work of conversion on the part of the different protagonists: to become the servant of the union that is the work of God.

The second issue takes up the same topic: "Dans quel esprit nous voudrions travailler."[59] Three warnings are issued, or three false paths denounced, in which one recognizes the style of

---

52   "It is my wish that our future constitutions impose on us every day one half hour of Holy Scripture *sub gravi* or equivalent private vow, in the absence of a prescription. Private vow. To ensure a collective and joint result," in: AAC, LB, note 2.21, "La Règle," one typewritten page.

53   Beauduin, *Une oeuvre monastique*, 33.

54   Loonbeek & Mortiau, *Un pionnier*, vol. 1, 655.

55   See Nicolas Egender, "Les principes monastiques de dom Lambert Beauduin," in: Allmen & others, *Veilleur*, 235–273; André Haquin, "L'activité spirituelle de dom Lambert Beauduin (1873–1960) d'après quelques documents inédits: Correspondances et notes de retraite," in: Allmen & others, *Veilleur*, 169–203; André Haquin, "Le prêtre selon Dom L. Beauduin," QL 48, 1977, 211–223.

56   "À nos Lecteurs," *Irén* 1/1, 1926, 2.

57   "De quoi s'agit-il?," *Irén* 1/1, 1926, 4–10.

58   "De quoi s'agit-il?," 4–9 (italics original).

59   "Dans quel esprit nous voudrions travailler," *Irén* 1/2, 1926, 117–119.

Dom Beauduin: no proselytism; no beneficence; no imperialist conception.

Any "proselytism" that would tend to "disaffect (i.e. alienate) our estranged Brothers from their church in order to bring them back to us" must be excluded. For every apostle of the union, the ultimate goal is without any doubt the "reconstitution of the ancient and undivided Christianity, but excluding any apologetic and polemic attitude, owing to closer contacts that are imbued *'with respect, charity, and mutual trust.'"*[60] In short, the twofold emphasis is placed on compassion and truthfulness.

The course of action of the monks of Amay is to work for the benefit of the union and, to this end, they are not to engage in charitable works, which are otherwise very useful and respectable, such as providing assistance to Russians. Without this resolve, "everything would be compromised and your charity would lose its halo of selflessness, and your apostolate would become suspicious."[61] It was thus necessary to choose, and the monks of Amay made their choice.

"No imperialist conception." The union of the churches cannot be conceived as "a dream of unification" or of centralization, as "a nostalgic longing for a universal empire." This "imperialist conception of religious unity" must be avoided at all cost.[62]

In April 1927, Dom Beauduin returned to the subject of the "Vrai travail pour l'Union"[63] by illustrating it with the example of the theological work on the dogmatic definitions that separate churches. Roman Catholics must engage in in-depth work that will make it possible to reset the established truths in their historical contexts. This method requires patience: the goal is to attain a better understanding of their specific meaning.

Moreover, who knows whether a future council might not even choose to revoke "previous dogmatic decisions by way of authentic clarification." Finally, the projected work has both an intellectual and a supernatural dimension. As shown by the Malines Conversations, it also includes psychological elements: becoming acquainted with one another, learning to talk to one another, to appreciate one another, and to love one another.

Subsequently, the journal addresses the topic of "Union et conversions".[64] The directive is clear: neither Uniatism nor Latinization.[65] Nor is there any reason to adopt Eastern ways in order to attract Easterners. Cardinal Mercier's "psychological method" would also be that of Amay: respect, trust, sympathy. Unity is to be achieved by way of study, conversation, intellectual labor, prayer, and spirituality. The strategy that needs to be adopted is that of peace (*irénikon*). Dom Beauduin's ecclesiology is of crucial importance here: the aim is to contemplate the church of God and not to focus on the institutional church. The work for the union is not a strategy that is to be implemented as if we were its main protagonists. Quite to the contrary, the union is the object of a prayer that is addressed to God in all sincerity.[66]

---

60 "Dans quel esprit nous voudrions travailler," 117 (italics original).

61 "Dans quel esprit nous voudrions travailler," 118.

62 "Dans quel esprit nous voudrions travailler," 119 (italics original).

63 Lambert Beauduin, "Le vrai travail pour l'Union," *Irén* 2/1, 1927, 5–10.

64 Lambert Beauduin, "Union et conversions," *Irén* 5/10–12, 1928, 481–492.

65 The journal *Irénikon* was very soon supplemented by special issues entitled *Irénikon-Collection*, which in particular included Cyrille Korolevskij's study *L'Uniatisme: Définition – causes – effets – étendue – dangers – remèdes* (*Irénikon-Collection* 2/5–6, 1927). See also André de Lilienfeld, *Pour l'Union* (*Irénikon-Collection* 2/10, 1927).

66 For the history of *Irénikon*, see Lambert Vos, "*Irénikon* dans tous ses états," in: Nagi Edelby & Souraya Bechealany, eds., *Le défi de l'Église Une: Mission de la revue œcuménique francophone: Actes du colloque de Beyrouth 12–14 novembre 2015*, Beirut, CERPOC, 2018, 33–44. The first issue of the journal was printed in 4,000 copies; in April 1927, the figure is 1,100; after *Mortalium animos*, the journal lost approximately 500 subscriptions.

## 5	The Difficult Years: 1926–1932

The biographers Loonbeek and Mortiau have given a detailed account of the difficulties encountered by Amay and its founder from 1926 onward, the year of Cardinal Mercier's death, in which the union of the churches lost its great protector. Subsequent events unfolded rapidly and were characterized by a high degree of complexity. The difficulties resulted from several factors, first of all from the differences of opinion between the Roman and the Benedictine authorities and the prior and the monastery of Amay, which welcomed monks with different views and expectations. Things became even more complicated in 1928, the year of the encyclical *Mortalium animos* but also of the canonical institution and of the approbation of the Constitutions of Amay. In the same year, following the conclusion of proceedings that aimed to restrict the work of Amay to Russia alone, Dom Beauduin decided to offer his resignation as prior of Amay in the hope of saving the union project.[67] His resignation was accepted in December 1928. Dom Beauduin was removed from the monastery that he himself had founded and spent the next year traveling to various destinations in Europe and the Middle East. Subsequently, the young institution was burdened by new difficulties. Dom Lambert was summoned to appear before the Pro Russia commission in Rome (1931), which disapproved of him. The fate of the founder and his house once again became a topic of debate. The house itself was saved, but its former prior was sentenced to a long exile in France, where he would spend almost twenty years (1932–1951).

### 5.1	Mortalium animos

This lengthy document issued by Pius XI, which was addressed to the episcopate, deals with the "means of achieving the true unity of religion."[68] It focuses on the great interfaith conferences such as those of Stockholm (1925) and Lausanne (1927). He begins with a long denunciation of the false conception of church unity that is frequently encountered at these meetings of non-Catholics. Some, whom he calls "pan-Christians," are said to entertain the idea of uniting the churches in a kind of "universal federation" or "Christian Federation" that will allow them to "oppose strongly and with success the progress of irreligion" by sacrificing the unity of faith and the unity of the Body of Christ. Among these, some are said to reject the divine nature of Christ and of his mission. If the differences in matters of faith are ignored, does this not amount to "indifferentism" and to what is commonly known as "modernism"? The pope urges the Catholics to abstain from attending conferences of this type; he wishes to give precedence to "the return to the one true Church of Christ of those who are separated from it." For the pope, this "return" of those who "left the home of their fathers," the Church of Rome, to their common father is the obligatory path that leads to true unity.

The text is surprising on account of its intransigency and it marks a turning point in the way Pius XI talks about the rapprochement with the estranged brothers. Placing it in its historical context, the encyclical may be seen as a concession from the pope to the conservative branch of the curia headed by Cardinal Rafael Merry del Val, leader of those who opposed any kind of resolution of the Roman Question.[69] What the pope emphasizes in *Mortalium animos* is the danger of

67	"I admit that I very reluctantly abandoned the broader ideals of the beginning, but I submitted my resignation myself in order not to jeopardize the project"; Dom Beauduin's project of a "Lettre à envoyer par Capelle au Primat," in: AAC, LB, note 1.11, En-Calcat, 7 ("Travail pour l'Union"). This quote refers to the apostolate for the union, which, according to the instructions of the Holy See, was to be limited to Russia alone.

68	Pius XI, *Mortalium animos*, in: AAS 20, 1928, 5–16. For Dom Beauduin's commentary, see "L'encyclique 'Mortalium animos' du 6 janvier 1928," *Irén* 5/2, 1928, 81–91. On *Mortalium animos* see Marie Levant's contribution in this volume.

69	The efforts of the Vatican's diplomacy led to the famous Lateran Accords, which were concluded with Mussolini in 1929. On this issue, see also Marc Agostino, *Le Pape*

a rapprochement between the churches that does not take into account doctrinal issues, as the ecumenical movements of Life and Work and Faith and Order had shown to do in those years, according to Rome.[70] But was this stance really only the result of pressure from the conservative wing of the curia or did it express the pope's own fears?

In any case, in the Catholic world, the encyclical was perceived as a serious setback to the efforts to achieve the union of Christians. It would freeze relations with the estranged brothers for years to come. In addition, the AAS successively published the decree[71] imposing tight restrictions on the activities of Amay.

5.2 Amay on Trial

It is hardly possible to enter into the details of the complex history of Amay during the years 1928–1932. The present study will merely provide references to available publications while mentioning a few events and dates.[72] In 1926, the novitiate of Amay was introduced, followed by the canonical foundation of the monastery itself in 1928. Faced with growing internal and external difficulties, the prior of Amay, Dom Beauduin, submitted his resignation. Would the journal Irénikon survive or would it be better to sacrifice it in order to preserve the cause of the union? This was what Dom Lambert asked himself. In the end, the

decision was made to retain the journal, although the number of subscribers would decline sharply in the wake of Mortalium animos.

Beauduin attempted to follow up on the Malines Conversations by engaging in a discrete exchange of letters with those who were committed to dialogue, notably Protestants and Anglicans. The communications of this circle are known as the "Postal Conversations of Malines" (1929). This endeavor was quickly banned by the authorities on the grounds that it contradicted the strict objectives that had been imposed on Amay.[73] Dom Lambert distanced himself and undertook various journeys to Rome, the East, and the Middle East (1929–1930). In 1931, a canonical visit to Amay ensued, notably on account of the monastery's financial situation following the malversations of Walthère Boland, Dom Lambert's business manager. In January 1931, Dom Beauduin appeared before the Pro Russia commission: his situation grew increasingly precarious and the fate of Amay seemed uncertain. He was compelled to leave Belgium and took up residence in Strasbourg. Hoping to remain in the country, he had himself assigned to the Royal Library of Belgium in order to develop a new section devoted to Oriental studies (1932); he would soon be forced to abandon this plan. The exile became more and more apparent. After a canonical visit of the abbots of Bruges and Maredsous to Mont César, which was to conduct

---

Pie XI et l'opinion (1922–1939), Rome, École française de Rome, 1991, 349–435.

70   On Lausanne, see de Lilienfeld's commentary, who appreciated the conference's emphasis on analyzing the historical and psychological factors at play in divisions between churches: André de Lilienfeld, "Lausanne," Irén 3/5, 1927, 267–273. Today, the theologian and historian of ecumenism Joseph Famerée takes a positive stand on the first world conference of Faith and Order, defining it an authentic spiritual "fellowship"; see Joseph Famerée, "Lausanne," DHGE 30, 1120–1122.

71   AAS 20, 1928, 26–27. The decree is printed after the encyclical Mortalium animos.

72   See Loonbeek & Mortiau, Un pionnier, vol. 2, 919–1080; Quitslund, Beauduin, 111–168; Cappuyns, "Dom Lambert Beauduin," 764–788; Haquin, "L'exil de Dom Lambert Beauduin."

73   "These Conversations did not go beyond the planning stage. This project was spontaneously abandoned after two weeks, by myself and without any intervention on the part of the authorities, when I was made to understand the criticism that it could provoke. This circular letter was sent out in March 1929; after this date, nothing more as sent out. However, my accusers maintained that such dealings took place until late March 1930. These facts have been recognized as inaccurate (Rome, in January 1931) by those who had accused me"; Dom Beauduin, "Lettre à envoyer par Capelle au Primat." One might gain the impression that further contacts between estranged Christians were discontinued in England. The recent book of an English Catholic priest who officiated as pastor in London shows that this was not the case; see Mark Vickers, Reunion Revisited: 1930s Ecumenism Exposed, Leominster, Gracewing, 2017.

an investigation into the ideas of Dom Lambert and his influence on the young monks, his banishment became inevitable. The Cardinal Secretary of State Eugenio Pacelli, who would later become Pope Pius XII, sent a letter to the Abbé Bernard Capelle on Mar 30, 1932[74] in which he ordered him to send Dom Beauduin to the abbey of En-Calcat (Toulouse) for a period of two years.[75] The threat of exile had become a reality. The banishment would last for almost twenty years.

6   Dom Lambert's Exile in France (1932–1951)

Dom Lambert perceived this exile as a great injustice, but he decided not to appeal against the decision. In spite of the warm welcome he received in En-Calcat, the two years that he was obliged to spend in the austere abbey were very much a time of trial. What would become of him in 1934? It was as though he existed in a legal vacuum; nothing seemed planned for him. Convinced that his return to Belgium was neither desired nor possible, he chose to remain in France, not too far from Paris, and sought to be of service as a chaplain for nuns. He devoted himself in particular to preaching at religious retreats. From 1934 to 1939, he was first welcomed by the Olivetan Oblates of Mary in Cormeilles-en-Parisis, then by the sisters of the Good Shepherd of Caen in Chatou, from 1939 to 1951. Throughout this period, he was involved in countless aborted projects, notably in a liturgical initiative for France headed by the bishop of Chartres, Msgr. Raoul Harscouët, an appointment to teach liturgy at the Institute Catholique of Paris, an appointment as rector of the Melkite Greek Patriarchal College of Beirut, and so on.

This demonstrates how much the authorities mistrusted him.[76]

However, Dom Lambert's participation in the early days of the CPL in Paris was sought and appreciated; he presided over the inaugural session of May 20, 1943. Had he not been the founder of the Belgian liturgical movement before the Great War? The codirectors of the first years, the Dominicans Pie Duployé and Aimon-Marie Roguet, were only too glad to profit from his competence. From 1943 to 1951, he assisted in the center's work and collaborated in its various publications and conferences.

The years in France also gave Dom Beauduin the opportunity to renew his ties with Anglicanism and to associate with certain French pioneers of ecumenism in the Catholic context, especially with Fr. Yves Congar. He welcomed the activities of the Abbé Paul Couturier of Lyon, the initiator of spiritual ecumenism. He was consulted regarding the inception of the interconfessional liturgical weeks of the Institute de théologie orthodoxe Saint-Serge. Fr. Cyprian Kern (from St. Sergius) and Dom Bernard Botte (from Mont César) were the founders of this initiative, which was launched in 1953.[77] These gatherings still take place every year. They constitute a forum for dialogue and develop an ecumenism that is both spiritual and intellectual, allowing each participant to address the topic chosen every year.

7   The Final Years in Chevetogne

The Union Monastery was transferred from Amay to Chevetogne (diocese of Namur) in 1939. It is in this peaceful setting that the founder was reunited with his brothers in 1951, thanks to the initiative of

---

74   On the abbot of Mont César, see André Haquin, "Dom Bernard Capelle (1884–1961): De la science biblique au mouvement liturgique," in: André Lossky & Goran Sekulovski, eds., *Liturges et liturgistes: Fructification de leurs apports dans l'aujourd'hui des églises*, Münster, Aschendorff, 2015, 125–148.

75   Haquin, "L'exil de Dom Lambert Beauduin," 80–99.

76   Haquin, "L'exil de Dom Lambert Beauduin," 423–430.

77   See Nicolas Egender, "Aux origines des Semaines d'études liturgiques de Saint-Serge: L'archimandrite Cyprian Kern, dom Lambert Beauduin et les moines de Chevetogne," in: André Lossky & Goran Sekulovski, eds., *60 semaines liturgiques à Saint-Serge: Bilans et perspectives nouvelles*, Münster, Aschendorff, 2016, 241–267.

the prior, Dom Thomas Becquet. Here, he received many visitors who were captivated by his optimism and his faith, by his capacity for empathy and persuasion. He had the great joy of seeing his old friend Cardinal Roncalli[78] accede to the Chair of Saint Peter as John XXIII and announce, in January 1959, the convocation of an ecumenical council that would bear the name Vatican II. These sessions mark the official entry of the Catholic Church into ecumenism *per se*, as demonstrated by the dogmatic constitution *Lumen Gentium* and the decree on ecumenism entitled *Unitatis redintegratio*.[79] The first words of this decree set the tone: "Promoting the restoration of the unity of all Christians is one of the principal goals of the Holy Ecumenical Council of Vatican II." Dom Beauduin died on Jan 11, 1960, surrounded by his brothers. The founder's tomb bears the inscription *Vir Dei et Ecclesiae*. No words could better express his passion for the mystery of the Holy Trinity and for the church and its unity.

8   A Life "under the Banner of the Church of God"

Throughout his life, Dom Beauduin felt a passion for the church. Not for the ecclesiastical organization with its rules and customs but for the church according to God or, as he was fond of saying, the "Mystical Body of Christ."[80] He would often invite his listeners and readers to behold the world as God sees it; it was in this way that he looked upon the church, by seeing it as God did. He did not write any treatise on ecclesiology, but he did discover God's great plan to unite and even reconcile humanity in Christ.

During his monastic youth in Leuven, he experienced the richness of church liturgy, particularly through the spiritual conferences of Dom Columba Marmion (1907). He enabled him to discover the sacramental nature of the church as Body of Christ through his lectures, numerous retreats, spiritual conferences, and abundant correspondence. Finally, he devoted the greater part of his life to the church and to the cause of unity. How is it possible to explain this many-faceted discovery? Three complementary factors can be cited here: the revelation of a God who discloses himself, the profound faith of the monk and his *sensus fidei*, and finally the circumstances of his life, which one might call the "signs of the time," in which he discerned the God's calls.

Through the classic liturgy celebrated at Mont César, Dom Beauduin experiences the mystery of salvation that is celebrated both on earth by the Church Militant and in heaven by the Church Triumphant. This is the same sole Church of Christ and the same sole liturgy. Does not the *ut omnes unum sint* prayer of Christ to his Father find its first fulfilment when the Christians are united in one and the same liturgy? Moreover, Dom Beauduin discovers the diversity of the Christian liturgies, each of which expresses the wealth of God's gift in its own way.

His lectures at Sant'Anselmo and the encounter with Eastern Christians, both Catholic and Orthodox, afforded Dom Lambert an even deeper insight into the mystery of the church. Do the Christian churches, even if relatively separate, not

---

78   On this topic, see Lambert Vos, "Angelo Giuseppe Roncalli et les origines d'Amay-Chevetogne," *Irén* 87/1–2, 2014, 112–144.

79   Regarding the participation of Chevetogne in Vatican II, see Emmanuel Lanne, "Le rôle du Monastère de Chevetogne au deuxième concile du Vatican," in: Doris Donnelly & others, eds., *The Belgian Contribution to the Second Vatican Council: International Research Conference at Mechelen, Leuven and Louvain-la-Neuve (September 12–16 2005)*, Leuven, Peeters, 2008, 361–388. It involved Dom Thomas Becquet (1896–1985), Dom Pierre Dumont (1901–1970), Dom Olivier Rousseau (1898–1984), and Dom Emmanuel Lanne (1923–2010). See André Haquin, "In memoriam: Dom Emmanuel Lanne (1923–2010)," *RTL* 41/4, 2010, 613–614. See also Lambert Vos, "Le Monastère de Chevetogne et Vatican II," in: Nagi Edelby, ed., *Actes du colloque international: Vatican II et les Églises orientales (7 au 10 mai 2014)*, Beirut, CERPOC, 2016, 267–283.

80   See Lambert Beauduin, "L'encyclique *Mediator Dei*," *La Maison-Dieu* 3/13, 1948, 7–25.

attest to the unique plan of God, namely to unite the scattered children of God in one single family? Can it be that the one Body of Christ remain divided? The appeals of the popes, the favorable circumstances for a rapprochement with the Anglicans, and many other realities of the 20th century prompted Dom Lambert to follow this call. Casting off the dualism of "all or nothing," he learned to appreciate the individual riches of each church.

Rather than striving for a rapprochement based on a "conquering Catholicism," he proceeded to develop a methodology that respected the riches of each tradition, advocating union rather than absorption, encounter and joint progression rather than a simple return to the fold. This attitude was far from widespread in the early 20th-century Catholic Church. It was on these foundations that the plan to establish the monastery of Amay was elaborated; its numerous vicissitudes are well known. Rather than renouncing the ideals that he had discerned, Dom Beauduin chose to renounce his functions as prior of Amay. The twenty years of exile in France would be a time in which the seed that he had sown would bear fruit.

As early as the 1920s, Dom Beauduin expressed the wish that monastic life refocus on the essential aspects of Christian life and that it be simplified. Through his preaching activities at religious retreats, he testified to what he himself had discovered, particularly the fundamental truths of the faith that have been handed down through Scripture, especially in Saint Paul's Epistles and Saint John's Gospel. Christology and the centrality of the resurrection of Christ were among these discoveries. Free of all psychological concerns, his retreats opened new horizons; they allowed him to raise the awareness of an extensive public for the inestimable value of the work that aimed to achieve the union of the churches.

The ascesis of the monk and of every Christian is not an end in itself. This is one of the main beliefs of the founder of Amay. It has a Christological significance in that it enables us to become one with Christ in his Paschal mystery and in the Eucharistic sacrifice which the church offers as a memorial. Is not ascesis first and foremost to "Live God's today" (as Roger Schutz said),[81] to welcome the happy and unhappy events of life, and to face them in the spirit of the Gospel? Following the same line of thought, Dom Beauduin wished to promote a monastic way of life that was less attached to observances of Beuronian type, less individualistic, and less dominated by devotional practices. Dom Beauduin's dream was that the monastery should become an *ecclesiola*, a church in miniature. This was his wish for Amay, the monastery dedicated to the cause of Christian unity. A monastery where the unity of brothers of different origins and with different sensibilities would be able to grow, a sort of laboratory of ecumenism in which the Latin and Byzantine-Slavic liturgy would be celebrated alternately.

9   Union of Churches and Unionism, Union of Christians and Ecumenism

Each period has its own vocabulary to express the desire for unity and to describe the initiatives that strive for a rapprochement.[82] Moreover, each word conveys a certain vision. The term ecumenism, more recent than the term unionism, long viewed as a Protestant concept by the Catholic world, is in itself suggestive of universality. Since Vatican II, the word ecumenism has asserted itself along with the expression Christian unity.

Until the 1930s, the term unionism or union of the churches was dominant in the French-speaking Catholic world, even though this term had numerous nuances among those who employed it. In

---

81   Roger Schutz, *Vivre l'aujourd'hui de Dieu*, Paris, Le Club du livre chrétien, 1960.

82   Étienne Fouilloux, *Les catholiques et l'unité chrétienne du XIXe et XXe siècle: Itinéraires européens d'expression française*, Paris, Le Centurion, 1982; see esp. 7–17 and 925–932 for the attempt to periodize unionism and ecumenism within the Catholic Church. See also Étienne Fouilloux, "Histoires de l'œcuménisme," *RHE* 95/3, 2000, 489–503.

Roman circles, the union or reunion is conceived as a return to the fold, as the return of the "dissidents." This expression refers to a classic ecclesiology that would be reaffirmed in 1943 by Pius XII in the encyclical *Mystici corporis Christi*, which states that the Catholic Church is the only true church. In contrast, the monastery of Amay and Dom Beauduin, but also Cardinal Mercier and the pioneers of unity, assigned a far more open meaning to the word union.

In 1894, Leo XIII had spoken of a "reconciliation"[83] of the Eastern Churches and warned against "Uniatist" practices, a reference to the "Latinization" of the Easterners. Pius XI, in *Equidem verba*, spoke of an "apostolate for the union of the churches" and evoked the *ut unum sint*, inviting believers to prayer, study, and action. In *Mortalium animos*, the tone and the context have changed; it is now the false conception of church unity which the pope denounces: he used "pan-Christianism," "Christian Federation" in order to combat atheism and indifferentism, advocating the return to the paternal house, the Church of Rome.

The pioneers of ecumenism, such as Cardinal Mercier, intuitively knew that the work for the union of the churches could not remain limited to the East but should also include the Reformation churches. The cardinal advocated both union and reconciliation. He appeared to imply that there was a shared responsibility for the divisions. During the Malines Conversations, he called for dialogue and outlined a conception of the union that would not be tantamount to absorption, as he believed that the centuries of division could not be ignored. And how could the union depend on the Christians alone when prayer causes us to turn to God, the mastermind behind the plan?

From the very first years of his monastic life, Dom Lambert underwent a development that caused him to shift from a classic ecclesiology of a legalistic-dogmatic type to a biblical ecclesiology of the Body of Christ inspired by Saint Paul. This turning point would become a determining factor in all his activities. In the *Projet d'érection* and in *Une œuvre monastique*, it is the vocabulary of the union of churches and of the rapprochement that prevails, albeit without superseding the terminology of the return of the estranged brothers and even that of ecumenical unity. By occasionally employing the vocabulary of the return to "Roman" unity, is he simply trying not to collide with the prevailing opinion of his time or is he expressing his deep conviction? Union, at any rate, implies a certain measure of reciprocity; all must undergo a process of conversion, as the responsibility for the divisions is shared by all. In other words, the return applies not only to the "dissidents." And most importantly, the path to the union must be understood in relation to the Mystical Body of Christ, that is, in relation to the plan authored by God himself. The insistence on prayer, conversion, compassion, and patience is indicative of this approach.

The title of the journal *Irénikon* sets the tone. Peace and compassion among the churches must be promoted. There can be no union of the churches without the union of the heart and mind, without the "spiritual reconciliation of the minds and hearts."[84] The journal warns against false visions, against an "opportunistic arrangement" that would ignore the unpleasant issues, but also against the "creation of a federation of foreign churches," as if compassion could dispense with truth, and finally against the diplomatic attitude, as if the whole thing were no more than a legal union that concerns the ecclesiastical authorities alone. Neither the path of individual conversions nor that of "collective reconciliations"[85] are to be envisaged. Proselytism, works of beneficence for the sake of Russian emigrants, and finally centralization or unification into some sort of universal

---

83   See Leo XIII, *Orientalium dignitas*, Nov 30, 1894; the text can be found at < https://www.papalencyclicals.net/leo13/l13orient.htm> (accessed Mar 8, 2021).

84   "À nos lecteurs," 2.

85   "De quoi s'agit-il?"

empire must be excluded.[86] Curiously, some of these warnings would resurface two years later in *Mortalium animos*. It was already becoming clear that it would take a long time to achieve the union of the churches. First, because the union would be the work of God, and second, because the slow conversion of the hearts is the precondition of a true reconciliation.

In the context of the publication of his article "Union et conversions" in *Irénikon*,[87] Dom Beauduin proposed several visions of unity that were consistent with the concepts and with the interpretation thereof by certain people, although he does not mention anyone by name. He asks himself whether the designation union of the churches is in any way acceptable for Catholics. Moreover, what are we to make of the unity *within* the church or of the unity *of* the churches? The union of the churches is an expression that is not found in contemporary papal documents, probably because it could now be understood to have a "pan-Christian" meaning; however, it was once in use in other contexts (Council of Florence, 1439). The word church may refer to human, ritual, or institutional realities, or conversely the divine dimension, according to which there is only one true church, which rules out any prospect of a federation or of pan-Christianism. However, the one Church of Christ encompasses many legitimate variations with regard to worship and organization.

The expression unity within the church is not acceptable to a Catholic if it implies the branch theory, that is, a kind of partnership rather than an adherence to the one true Church of Christ. The author is evidently in favor of the expression "union of the churches," provided that it is not conceived as a mere federation. The restoration of the union or of the communion, in the singular, underlines the affiliation to the one Church of Christ, and more specifically to the Holy See, while the plural "churches" expresses the diversity within the unity. The author concludes his reflections by emphasizing that the "unionist action" raises hope for a rapprochement of the alienated churches in view of rediscovering true Christian unity. The goal is to reconcile the churches, and not only individual Christians. The pedagogy of individual conversions on the basis of narrowly conceived apologetics that disaffect or separate the believers from their churches is not desirable, nor are mass conversions. Moreover, true union must be achieved with the participation of the respective hierarchies, taking their mission and their own responsibilities into account. The final directive, which has already been voiced, is thus of a spiritual and theological nature: "May everyone strive to be a *uniting factor* in the Mystical Body of Christ."[88]

It may be argued that Christian unity is conceived in different ways, not only by the various alienated churches and by the Catholic Church but also within each Christian confession. Thus, the unionism that is officially advocated by the Roman Catholic Church may be thought of as a union without absorption, as Cardinal Mercier, Dom Lambert, and the monks of Amay understood it, or as a return to the fold, as Pius XI and Msgr. d'Herbigny preferred to see it. As far as metropolitan Andrey Sheptytsky was concerned, he was mostly preoccupied with the progress of his Uniate Christian communities, which explains why the paths followed by him and Dom Beauduin gradually went in different directions. Fr. Korolevskij, while opposed to Uniatism in the sense of a Latinization praxis, does not appear to have conceived of unionism other than as a return to Roman unity.

Between 1930[89] and 1950, the unionism of the monks of Chevetogne (among others), a minority within the French-speaking Catholic

---

86   "Dans quel esprit nous voudrions travailler."

87   Beauduin, "Union et conversions."

88   Regarding the Uniate churches, see also Emmanuel Lanne, "Églises unies ou Églises sœurs: Un choix inéluctable," *Irén* 48/3, 1975, 322–342 (italics original).

89   Mention should be made of the crucial role of the theologian Yves Congar in the theological evolution of the Catholic world, beginning with his first decisive publication *Chrétiens désunis: Principes d'un "œcuménisme" catholique*, Paris, Cerf, 1937.

world, progressively transformed the body of the church leading to the astounding declarations of Vatican II. Étienne Fouilloux emphasizes that Catholic ecumenism did not emerge by way of a spontaneous generation but grew out of unionism, because what "Rome fears more than anything else [are] breaks in continuity, changes that are difficult to justify."[90]

10   The Reconciliation of the Churches Will Take Time!

A handwritten text by Dom Beauduin, entitled "Le travail de rapprochement" (1929),[91] advocates a long-term perspective on the reconciliation of the churches. Here are a few excerpts from this text:

> We must imagine the union of the churches as the Jews of the Old Testament imagined the coming of the promised Messiah. Their religion was to hope and prepare for this coming, not to see and realize it. Generations of excellent Jews lived and worked for this promise: it was their providential mission, and the fact that they did not see [it] neither cooled their zeal nor weakened their faith and their hope, nor diminished their merits.[92]

The Christian people that pray for the union must be given "the hope of an imminent reconciliation" so that they may not abandon their dream of the union:

> But for a true and serious worker of the rapprochement, there can be no illusion: our generation and – alas! – probably many a generation after it will know only the current divisions: we must resign ourselves to this great trial, and recognize that we do not partake of the grace of reconciliation ... we are in the desert and will not see the promised land.[93]

Moreover, "a reunification in the shorter term is by no means desirable, quite to the contrary!" Why? Because the Christians of the various churches are not ready for it. Prejudices, uncompromising attitudes, and antipathies have not disappeared. It would thus be premature. In the meantime, it is required to work towards the true union.

The difficult times after the death of Cardinal Mercier did not give Dom Beauduin any reason to be optimistic, all the more so as he had no way of knowing that the Catholic Church would convoke a council in 1962, following the creation, in Rome, of the Secretariat for Promoting Christian Unity.

Translated from French to English by Robert Meyer.

Bibliography

Allmen, Jean-Jacques von & others, *Veilleur avant l'aurore: Colloque Lambert Beauduin*, Chevetogne, Éditions de Chevetogne, 1978.
Aubert, Roger, *Le cardinal Mercier (1851–1926): Un prélat d'avant-garde: Publications du professeur Roger Aubert rassemblées à l'occasion de ses 80 ans*, eds. Jean-Pierre Hendrickx, Jean Pirotte & Luc Courtois, Louvain-la-Neuve, Presses Universitaires de Louvain, 1994.

---

90 Fouilloux, *Les catholiques et l'unité chrétienne*, 929.
91 Lambert Beauduin "Le travail de rapprochement," in: AAC/LB/18.12, 8 pages. This typewritten, incomplete text addresses only the first of three problems that were to be the subject of three discussions: 1) Pourquoi travailler au rapprochement ? cur ?; 2) Que faire dans ce sens ? quid ?; 3) Comment le faire ? quomodo ? The indication "CMP, I/1, VI-29" provided at the footer seems to indicate that this is an early document of the Malines Postal Conversations, which were quickly banned by the authorities. See Beauduin, "Lettre à envoyer par Capelle au Primat," note 54.
92 Beauduin "Le travail de rapprochement," 1.

93 Beauduin "Le travail de rapprochement," 1–2.

Bouyer, Louis, *Dom Lambert Beauduin: Un homme d'Église*, Tournai, Casterman, 1964.

Cappuyns, Maïeul, "Dom Lambert Beauduin (1873–1960): Quelques documents et souvenirs," RHE 61, 1966, 424–454, 761–807.

De Volder, Jan, *La résistance d'un cardinal: Le cardinal Mercier, l'Église et la Guerre (1914–1918)*, Namur, Fidélité, 2016.

Denaux, Adalbert & John A. Dick, *From Malines to ARCIC: The Malines Conversations Commemorated*, Leuven, Leuven University Press, 1997.

Dick, John A., *The Malines Conversations Revisited*, Leuven, Leuven University Press, 1989.

Donnelly, Doris & others, eds., *The Belgian Contribution to the Second Vatican Council: International Research Conference at Mechelen, Leuven and Louvain-la-Neuve (September 12–16 2005)*, Leuven, Peeters, 2008.

Fouilloux, Étienne, *Les catholiques et l'unité chrétienne du XIXe et XXe siècle: Itinéraires européens d'expression française*, Paris, Le Centurion, 1982.

Haquin, André, "L'exil de Dom Lambert Beauduin au monastère d'En-Calcat (1932–1934)," RHE 80, 1985, 51–99, 415–440.

Haquin, André, *Dom Lambert Beauduin et le renouveau liturgique*, Gembloux, Duculot, 1970.

Korolevskij, Cyrille, *Kniga bytija moego: Le livre de ma vie: Mémoires autobiographiques*, ed. Giuseppe Maria Croce, 5 vols., Vatican City, Archives secrètes vaticanes, 2007.

Korolevskij, Cyrille, *Le prophète ukrainien de l'unité: Métropolite André Szeptyckyj (1865–1944)*, Paris, Guibert, ²2005.

Loonbeek, Raymond & Jacques Mortiau, *Un pionnier, dom Lambert Beauduin (1873–1960): Liturgie et unité des chrétiens*, 2 vols., Louvain-la-Neuve, Collège Erasme, 2001.

Mortiau, Jacques & Raymond Loonbeek, *Dom Lambert Beauduin, visionnaire et précurseur (1873–1960): Un moine au cœur libre*, Paris, Cerf, 2005.

Quitslund, Sonya A., *Beauduin: A Prophet Vindicated*, New York NY, Newman, 1973.

Soetens, Claude, *Le Congrès eucharistique international de Jérusalem (1893): Dans le cadre de la politique orientale du pape Léon XIII*, Leuven, Nauwelaerts, 1977.

Tretjakewitsch, Léon, *Bishop Michel d'Herbigny SJ and Russia: A Pre-Ecumenical Approach to Christian Unity*, Würzburg, Augustinus-Verlag, 1990.

Vinck, Honoré, *Pie X et les réformes liturgiques de 1911–1914: Psautier, bréviaire, calendrier, rubriques*, Münster, Aschendorff, 2014.

Wenger, Antoine, *Rome et Moscou (1900–1950)*, Paris, Desclée de Brouwer, 1987.

CHAPTER 31

The Positioning of the Roman Catholic Church in the Interwar Period: The Encyclical *Mortalium Animos*

Marie Levant

1 Introduction

It is beyond doubt that the ecumenical movement was relaunched after the Great War.[1] The conflict lent a sense of urgency to the desire for reconciliation and unity, while the fall of the German, Austro-Hungarian, Ottoman and Russian Empires had changed the religious balance in many countries of the European continent and opened new mission spaces in the East. The defensive outlook with which the intra-Christian cooperation groups had been imbued for some decades[2] may have been less visible but was nevertheless equally pregnant, regardless of whether they were concerned with finding remedies for civil disorders or with erecting a barrier to impede the advance of secularization, atheism, and Marxism. The intellectual, theological, and practical initiatives taken to overcome Christian divisions thus became more numerous, first among the Protestants (it was thanks to Anglican and Protestant efforts that, during the 1920s and 1930s, the Faith and Order and Life and Work movements were born, and, subsequently, the WCC was instituted in 1948),[3] but also, and this time more visibly than during

the preceding period, among the Catholics, on the side of both the laity and the clergy.

How did the Roman authorities react in the face of the new dynamics of ecumenism and of the renewed Catholic unionist effort? One can see initially a reaction characterized by a certain degree of openness, noticeable in a more subdued vocabulary and in Eastern policies founded on understanding and charity, in continuation of the pontificates of Pius IX and Leo XIII, in the support given to local unionist initiatives, but also in the tolerance shown towards reconciliation efforts as the Anglo-Catholic talks in Malines or the pre-ecumenical initiatives of Dom Beauduin in Amay-sur-Meuse.[4] From the mid-1920s, however, a stiffer stance began to emerge which was finally articulated in the encyclical *Mortalium animos*, published on Jan 6, 1928: it clarified the meaning of unionism and condemned ecumenism without appeal, thereby delaying the possibility of the Catholic Church's participation in the ecumenical dialogue for several decades.

This stance and this positioning of the Roman authorities *vis-à-vis* a certain number of intra-Christian undertakings is precisely what I intend to investigate, with a particular focus on the situation in Germany, where the "ecumenizing" Modernism in the postwar years, as Roman observers came to call it, played a triggering role in the elaboration process of *Mortalium animos*; thereafter, I

---

1 In this regard, see Frédéric Gugelot's contribution in this volume.

2 See Laura Pettinaroli's contribution in this volume.

3 See Étienne Fouilloux, *Les catholiques et l'unité chrétienne du XIXe au XXe siècle: Itinéraires européens d'expression française*, Paris, Le Centurion, 1982. On the origin of Life and Work and Faith and Order movements see Dietz Lange's and Luca Ferracci's contributions in this volume. For the creation of the WCC in 1948 see *A History of the Ecumenical Movement*, vol. 1, Ruth Rouse & Stephen C. Neill, eds., *1517–1948*, London, SPCK, 1954.

4 See recently Étienne Fouilloux, "An indecisive Inter-Confessional Situation (1914–22)," in: Giovanni Cavagnini & Giulia Grossi, eds., *Benedict XV: A Pope in the World of the "Useless Slaughter" (1914–1918)*, dir. Alberto Melloni, 2 vols., Turnhout, Brepols, 2020, 779–788.

shall attempt to arrive at a better understanding of the meaning and contents of this meaningful Roman-Catholic magisterial document.

2 The Holy See and the Desire for Christian Unity

In order to understand Rome's stance on the burgeoning of intra-Christian initiatives, it is useful to examine it in the light of the basic features that characterized the policies of the Holy See in Europe in the immediate postwar period, which were aimed at the Christian reconquest of society.[5] How then does this "intransigentism," as it is most frequently defined,[6] correlate with the longing for Christian unity which was also emerging from the base of Roman Catholicism itself?

2.1 The Burgeoning of Initiatives

After the first world conflict, the longing for Christian unity thus manifested itself in a new drive emanating from an ecumenism that had already been firmly implanted in Anglican and Protestant circles for half a century, in clearer rapprochements between Anglicans and Orthodox Christians as well as between Catholics and Orthodox, but also in a certain number of interconfessional undertakings. Mention should also be made of the pursuit of a Roman unionism, which sometimes wavered towards a nascent Catholic ecumenism. The aim of this chapter is not to provide a detailed analysis of all such phenomena but to examine a few noteworthy examples that will bring these new intra-Christian dynamics to light.

The Orthodox Churches and the Anglican Communion were the firsts to actually explore the ecumenical field. As early as in January 1920, the Holy Synod of the Phanar sent an encyclical *Unto the Churches of Christ Everywhere*, inviting them to renounce mutual suspicions and intra-Christian proselytism, to establish and develop contacts in view of a better mutual understanding, and to work towards the founding of a League of Churches inspired by the recent creation of the League of Nations.[7] While Rome evinced little reaction, the Anglicans invited the patriarchate to appoint observers to the Lambeth Conference in the following summer, an event that was going to become a milestone of the ecumenical movement.[8] At the end of the sixth Lambeth Conference, the delegates issued the famous "An Appeal to All Christian People." It established the principles that were to guide the Anglican Churches in their endeavor to move ahead towards a visible union with the churches of other traditions.[9] This distinctly ecumenical document (it read: "We acknowledge all those who believe in our Lord Jesus Christ, and have been baptized into the name of the Holy Trinity, as sharing with us membership in the universal Church of Christ which is his Body")[10] took shape in fact in the context of an ongoing effort to effect a rapprochement between Anglicans and Orthodox Christians, which had begun in the late 19th century, the condemnation of Anglican

---

5 Daniele Menozzi, *La Chiesa cattolica e la secolarizzazione*, Turin, Einaudi, 1993; Fabrice Bouthillon, *La naissance de la Mardité: Une théologie politique à l'âge totalitaire: Pie XI (1922–1939)*, Strasbourg, Presses universitaires de Strasbourg, 2001.

6 Émile Poulat, *Église contre bourgeoisie: Introduction au devenir du catholicisme actuel*, Casterman, Tournai, 1977; Giovanni Miccoli, *Fra mito della cristianità e secolarizzazione: Studi sul rapporto chiesa-società nell'età contemporanea*, Genova, Marietti, 1985.

7 N. Gvozdavo-Golenko, "Vers l'union des Églises: Deux documents orthodoxes," *Échos d'Orient* 20/124, 1921, 461–470. See also the chapter by Stylianos Tsompanidis in this volume.

8 The Lambeth Conference, which was held about every ten years under the chairmanship of the archbishop of Canterbury, brought together the bishops of the Anglican Communion. For an in-depth study of the theological orientations of Anglicanism at the turn of the two centuries see the chapter by Paul Avis in this volume.

9 Owen Chadwick, "The Lambeth Conference: An Historical Perspective," *AEH* 58/3, 1989, 259–277.

10 For the text of the *Appeal* see Roger Coleman, ed., *Resolutions of the Twelve Lambeth Conferences (1867–1988)*, Toronto ON, Anglican Book Centre, 1992, 45–48.

ordinations by Rome having led the Church of England to look on the Orthodox Churches more attentively, but had intensified since the end of the war, both on account of the persecutions suffered by Christians in Russia and Asia Minor, and on account of British imperialism in the Near East.[11] In this regard, in the following year, the archbishop of Canterbury, Randall Davidson, responded to the Patriarchate of Constantinople's encyclical that the recognition of the Anglican ordinations had to remain a precondition for any Anglo-Orthodox union. The patriarch took note of it and officially recognized them, followed rapidly by the patriarchs of Jerusalem and of the Church of Cyprus; the dialogue between the Christian East and the Anglican Communion would continue along these lines even after World War II.[12]

The movement for Christian unity also took root in the Middle East in the very same years: from 1924 a series of regional conferences laid the groundwork for the creation of a formal institution, the Near East Christian Council, which initially consisted of Anglicans and Protestants before gradually integrating Orthodox, and which became the NEEC in the 1960s. Today, however, relatively little is known about this institution, the history of which has yet to be written.[13]

At the same time, the movement Life and Work, born shortly before the conflict at the initiative of the Lutheran bishop Nathan Söderblom, began to gain momentum. Promoting unity through "practical Christianity," i.e. through practical collaborations between Christians of different confessions that were planned and implemented on the economic and social level, it convened a first international conference in Stockholm in 1925. The second major ecumenical movement, Faith and Order, founded in the aftermath of the Edinburgh Missionary Conference by the Anglican bishop Charles Brent, also organized itself on a global basis in view of holding another international conference, which convened in Lausanne in 1927.[14]

Alongside these Christian internationalisms, mention should also be made of the leagues and associations for the promotion of peace – such as Max Josef Metzger's Internationale Katholische Liga or the WA – or of the organizations for young people and for women (starting with the YMCA and the YWCA), which also flourished after the first world conflict.[15] These tended to take the form of interconfessional organizations, particularly when they appeared in Anglo-American contexts, whereas, as far as the Catholic side was concerned, the opposition from the church hierarchy often prevented similar association to grow. The collaborations between Catholics and Protestants in the fields of politics and labor unionism were viewed with greater tolerance by the hierarchy (as was the case, for instance, in German and Hungary), provided that they pursued nonreligious goals, did not involve doctrinal issues, and were occasional in nature.

On the side of the more directly Catholic initiatives, the postwar dynamics are above all embodied by the well-known Anglican-Catholic Conversations of Malines (1921–1925), initiated by Lord Halifax and the French priest Fernand Portal and presided over by Cardinal Désiré-Joseph Mercier, which aimed to renew the dialogue with the Anglicans and to restore church union with the Church of England,[16] but also by the founding, thanks to the initiative of the Benedictine

---

11 Léon Tretjakewitsch, *Bishop Michel d'Herbigny SJ and Russia: A Pre-Ecumenical Approach to Christian Unity*, Würzburg, Augustinus-Verlag, 1990.

12 Antoine Wenger, "L'Église orthodoxe et les ordinations anglicanes," *NRT* 76/1, 1954, 44–55.

13 Harry G. Dorman, "Churches and Mission in the Near East," *IRM* 51/201, 1962, 42–49; John Gordon Melton, "Middle East Council of Churches," in: John Gordon Melton & Martin Baumann, eds., *Religions of the World: A Comprehensive Encyclopedia of Beliefs and Practices*, vol. 4, Santa Barbara CA, ABC-CLIO, 2002, 1912–1913.

14 These meetings, in which several Orthodox Churches participated, would, as is well known, ultimately give birth to the WCC after World War II. See Jean Baubérot, "L'organisation internationale du protestantisme: Le Conseil œcuménique des Églises," *HC* 12, 56–65.

15 See Gerhard Besier' contribution in this volume.

16 See John A. Dick, *The Malines Conversations revisited*, Leuven, Leuven University Press, 1989.

friar Dom Lambert Beauduin, of the Union Monastery of Amay-sur-Meuse,[17] along with its journal *Irénikon*, not to mention the activities in the East of the apostolic visitor Angelo Roncalli (future Pope John XXIII) in Bulgaria between 1925 and 1934.[18] On the other hand, the action of the Greek-Catholic bishop Cyrille Korolevskij, committed to preserving the Byzantine liturgy of the Uniate churches, is more in keeping with the traditional Roman Uniatism;[19] this is even more so in the case of the Catholic welfare work in the contexts of Greek and Russian emigration, which did not fail to raise accusations of proselytism.[20]

2.2   *The Unity of Christians according to Rome*

In this time, Rome's activities concerning Christian unity were characterized by an ambitious Eastern policy. After the fall of the Ottoman and Russian Empires, the Catholic Church directed towards Eastern Christians a fresh unionistic impetus, "which works towards effecting the return of the Eastern Christians alone under pontifical authority by means of partial unions, but as a body, which distinguishes them from the individual missionary

proselytism."[21] In 1917, under Benedict XV, the Congregation for the Oriental Churches and the PIO were established. While the pope was concerned about the fate of the congregations that had been united with Rome after the collapse of the empires, he also took advantage of the weakening of Greek and Slavic Orthodoxy to reiterate both the call for union and the Uniate strategy, directed in particular towards the Bulgarians and Romanians.[22] The union with the East was one of the main objectives of the pontificate of Pius XI, who, in his inaugural encyclical, called upon the unbaptized and the alienated Christians to return to the fold of the Roman Catholic Church.[23] This was followed during the 1920s by a blossoming of new initiatives aimed towards the Christian East,[24] notably in terms of aid, for instance with the Papal Relief Mission to Russia and the CNEWA but also by way of institutional structures (for example, the creation of the commission Pro Russia in 1925). Familiarity with Eastern Christian traditions was encouraged: while several journals were launched, the collections of the Vatican library and of the library of the PIO were considerably enlarged thanks to the efforts of Msgr. Michel d'Herbigny and of the Korolevskij-Tisserant mission. Teaching activities were promoted through the establishment of various colleges and seminaries in Rome and elsewhere, particularly in the wake of the encyclical *Ecclesiam Dei* (1923).[25]

17   See, in this volume, André Haquin's contribution and Raymond Loonbeek & Jacques Mortiau, *Un pionnier, dom Lambert Beauduin (1873–1960): Liturgie et unité des chrétiens*, 2 vols., Louvain-la-Neuve, Éditions de Chevetogne, 2001.

18   Giuseppe Alberigo, *Papa Giovanni (1881–1963)*, Bologna, EDB, 2000; Angelo Giuseppe Roncalli-Giovanni XXIII, *Tener da conto: Agendine di Bulgaria (1925–1934)*, ed. Massimo Faggioli, Bologna, Istituto per le scienze religiose, 2008; Lorenzo Botrugno, *L'arte dell'incontro*, Venice, Marcianum Press, 2013.

19   Cyrille Korolevskij, *Kniga bytija moego: Le livre de ma vie: Mémoires autobiographiques*, ed. Giuseppe Maria Croce, 5 vols., Vatican City, Archives secrètes vaticanes, 2007.

20   Giuseppe M. Croce, "Le Saint-Siège, l'Église orthodoxe et la Russie soviétique: Entre mission et diplomatie (1917–1922)," *Mélanges de l'École française de Rome: Italie et Méditerranée* 105/1, 1993, 267–297, here 296–297; Laura Pettinaroli, *La politique russe du Saint-Siège (1905–1939)*, Rome, École française de Rome, 2015.

21   Étienne Fouilloux, "De l'unionisme à l'œcuménisme," in: Comité mixte catholique-orthodoxe en France, ed., *Catholiques et orthodoxes: Les enjeux de l'uniatisme: Dans le sillage de Balamand*, Paris, Bayard, 2004, 201–219, here 201–202.

22   Giuseppe M. Croce, "Catholiques et orthodoxes de Pie IX à Jean XXIII," in: Hervé Legrand & Giuseppe M. Croce, eds., *L'Œuvre d'Orient: Solidarités anciennes et nouveaux défis*, Paris, Cerf, 2010, 189–211.

23   Fouilloux, *Les catholiques et l'unité chrétienne*, 233–235.

24   Giovanni Coco, "Pio XI e l'unità dei cristiani: Le Chiese d'Oriente," in: Cosimo Semeraro, ed., *La sollecitudine ecclesiale di Pio XI*, Vatican City, Libreria editrice vaticana, 2010, 260–313.

25   Pettinaroli, *La politique russe du Saint-Siège*, 353–527.

This impetus towards the East went hand in hand with a resurgence of pontifical unionism. The Holy See did not restrict its activities to direct interventions but also supported and regulated the numerous local Catholic initiatives. At the same time, the priorities of the Catholic missions in Central and Eastern Europe and in the Near East were to work towards the reunification of churches and to combat Protestant influence. For instance, the CNEWA, which had been established to provide assistance to the Christians suffering from persecutions in Turkey, became an instrument of the Holy See's unionist strategy.[26] In reality, Pius XI had fallen victim to the Russian mirage, that is, to the hope of converting Orthodox Russia to Roman Catholicism as a result of the demise of the Tsarist Empire and of the persecution carried out by the communist regime,[27] this being the reason why his action was more strongly oriented towards the Russian and Slavic than to the Greco-Byzantine world.

This growing openness towards the Eastern Churches was accompanied by closing the doors to the churches born of the Reformation. If the Protestants and the Orthodox, from Rome's point of view, were called upon to return to the sole Church of Christ, under the authority of the pope, the end of the worldwide conflict was also marked by a new campaign against Protestant proselytism.[28] While the papal nuncio in Berlin Eugenio Pacelli (later Pope Pius XII) worried about the *furor protestanticus* in Germany, in 1915 Benedict XV warned Cardinal Basilio Pompili, president of the Opera per la preservazione della fede in Roma, against the treacheries of "these emissaries of Satan … who scatter with liberal hand falsehood and calumny against the Catholic religion and

its ministers."[29] Four years later, in his encyclical *In hac tanta*, the pope exhorted the Protestants to rejoin the fold of the Roman Church,[30] having with this standpoint the sole effect of deepening the divide between the Catholic Church and the ecumenical movement.

How, then, can the Catholic Church's point of view and this unprecedented unionist dynamism be justified? The fall of the empires certainly nourished hopes that those who had gone astray might return, possibly in the near future, to the Roman fold due to different reasons: in Germany, after the fall of the monarchy and the confessional state many Protestant Churches suddenly found themselves weaker, because of the loss of any privilege; in Russia and in the Near East Christians faced persecutions, and in Central and Eastern Europe were emerging forms of Catholic Revival. Behind the scenes of unionism, and equally so in the ecumenical movement, the idea still persisted that a "Christian front" could be formed against the modern threats of secularization and laicism, of liberalism and Marxism, of socialism and atheism. Moreover, while the Great War did raise awareness of the scandal of Christian disunity on both sides, it also raised concerns with regard to the durability of Western civilization. For the popes of the interwar period, the expected consequence of those historical upheavals was the return of humankind to the Church of Rome, bastion of eternity in an everchanging and troubled world, as had been the case at the fall of the Roman Empire. The restoration of Christian unity was thus inseparably linked to the reactivation of the uncompromising plan for the rebuilding, *mutatis mutandis*, of a Christian society as a response to the crisis of the Western world at the end of the global conflict. This was, in fact, what had already been expressed

26   Marie Levant, "A transnational relief effort in the Middle East after the Great War: the Catholic Near East Welfare Association," ENDS 6/1, 2022.

27   Pettinaroli, *La politique russe du Saint-Siège*, 489–527.

28   Raffaella Perin, *L'atteggiamento della Chiesa cattolica verso ebrei e protestanti da Pio X a Pio XI*, Ph.D. thesis, University of Padua, 2010.

29   The allocution is also published in Ugo Bellocchi, ed., *Tutte le encicliche e i principali documenti pontifici emanati dal 1740*, vol. 8, *Benedetto XV (1914–1922)*, Vatican City, Libreria Editrice Vaticana, 2000, 79–82, here 80.

30   Marie Levant, *Pacelli à Berlin: Le Vatican et l'Allemagne, de Weimar à Hitler (1919–1934)*, Rennes, Presses universitaires de Rennes, 2019, 76–77.

in *Divinum illud munus*, the encyclical of 1897: the return of the separated brothers is a fundamental step in the global reconquest of society. This specific idea of reunification thus explains what may, in the eyes of other Christians in the 1920s, have appeared to constitute an ambivalence in the magisterium's stance.

3   The Hesitation of Rome

In the aftermath of the war, a certain number of Christian initiatives for the reunification of Christians were viewed, if not positively, at least with relative tolerance in Rome. They were nevertheless under constant surveillance, and many of them ended up irritating the ecclesial authorities, mainly because they appeared to move gradually from unionism towards ecumenism. As a result, they were slowed down, suspended, or normalized in the years 1926–1927, in what had now become an atmosphere of general suspicion.

3.1   *The Anglican-Catholic Conversations of Malines: A Suffered Tolerance*

The history of the four meetings held in Malines, Belgium, between 1921 and 1925 is nowadays well documented and studied.[31] However, the Vatican's archives for the pontificate of Pius XI, which were made available to scholars in 2006, afford a better understanding of how Rome went from an initial openness to the clear and categorical rejection of 1927. The Roman papers document three phases.

Pope Benedict XV initially encouraged the initiative by addressing a few favorable words to

the organizers of the conversations before these began. Cardinal Mercier, the primate of Belgium, who presided over the talks, asked then for a more straightforward approval in order to conduct them. The latter reached him in the spring of 1922 when the secretary of state, Cardinal Pietro Gasparri, congratulated him in the name of the Holy Father: Pius XI fully endorsed the undertaking and encouraged its realization, albeit only on condition that it be conducted in a strictly private setting;[32] he also consented to the forwarding of these words of encouragement to the Anglican primate.

The first difficulties appeared afterwards. On one hand, the public was now informed that these conversations were being held, which sparked bitter polemics, notably on the part of the English Catholics and of the Holy Office. On the other hand, the continuation of the conversations was put at risk when the idea of a possible Anglican-Catholic reunion began to emerge in the course of the debates, one that was to be based on the model of the Eastern Christians' union with Rome via the patriarchates. In this sense, the specific Anglican-Catholic rapprochement followed at Malines risked to be integrated into the numerous more global project of Christian reunion: Rome, in fact, began to fear that while its scope was widened and the stakes were raised, the undertaking would slip from unionism into interconfessionalism. Thus, when Cardinal Mercier faced a series of accusations and asked the Roman authorities to lend their official support to the conversations, his request was denied, in 1923 and again in 1924.[33]

The chill set in 1925, following two reports that the British Catholics were dissatisfied with the conversations, which, moreover, were said to have reduced the rate of individual conversions. The death of Cardinal Mercier in January 1926 thus only precipitated a decision that had already been

---

31   See, in this volume, Bernard Barlow and Martin Browne's contribution. See also Dick, *The Malines Conversations revisited*; Régis Ladous, *Monsieur Portal et les siens (1855–1926)*, Paris, Cerf, 1985; Roger Aubert, "Les conversations de Malines: *Le cardinal Mercier et le Saint-Siège*," in: Roger Aubert, *Le cardinal Mercier (1851–1926): Un prélat d'avant-garde: Publications du professeur Roger Aubert rassemblées à l'occasion de ses 80 ans*, eds. Jean-Pierre Hendrickx, Jean Pirotte & Luc Courtois, Louvain-la-Neuve, Presses Universitaires de Louvain, 1994, 393–452.

32   ASRS, AAEESS, Stati Ecclesiastici, periodo IV, pos. 312, fasc. 66.

33   ASRS, AAEESS, Stati Ecclesiastici, periodo IV, pos. 312, fasc. 67–68.

taken. Following a stern warning in December of the same year, the secretary of state, Cardinal Gasparri, forwarded the orders of the Holy See to the nunciature in Brussels in March 1927, instructing the latter to pass them on to those concerned: the conversations were henceforth assimilated to the various Protestant movements for the union of confessions and accordingly suspended.[34]

Attempts to revive the conferences on the part of Lord Halifax, their sponsor on the Anglican side, failed to achieve anything: when *Mortalium animos* appeared, the initiative was already dead.

3.2 The Velehrad Congresses: Towards a Rigid Unionism

Unionism continued to be developed in Orientalist journals and congresses. The latter included the Congresses of Velehrad, in Moravia, which were inaugurated in 1907 to promote the union of Orthodox Christianity with the Church of Rome other than through mission or Latinization. The fourth congress, which convened from July 31 to Aug 3, 1924, was strongly encouraged by the pontiff. In reality, however, the spirit was not quite the same as it had been before the war: the congress was now less concerned with promoting mutual understanding than with finding methods to accelerate the conversion of individuals or groups to Roman Catholicism. This shift may be seen as the consequence of the death, in 1923, of the congresses' initiator, Archbishop Antonín Cyril Stojan, as well as of the greater role now played by Msgr. d'Herbigny, the Holy See's special counsel for Russian affairs, with his narrower views on unionism. However, since then the influence of the Holy See on the Congresses of Velehrad was undoubtedly more decisive. It toughened its stance towards the Orthodox participants, who were no longer invited to give conferences but only to participate in the discussions. The Orthodox presence, for that matter, diminished considerably, also because

the Russians were no longer able to attend because of the Soviet regime's restrictions: of 300 participants in 1924, only about ten were Orthodox intellectuals. For the fifth congress, which took place from July 20 to 24, 1927, the Congregation for the Oriental Churches tightened the rules even further, and the Orthodox were no longer allowed to participate in the public sessions but only in private gatherings that were restricted to a small group of experienced theologians.[35] Moreover, the secretary of state did not allow the archbishop of Gniezno and Poznań to attend.[36]

This Roman takeover of the Velehrad Congresses came as no surprise: in the late 1920s, the Holy Office prohibited Catholics from participating in ecumenical meetings and congresses when these had been organized by non-Catholics; from then on, the presence of the latter at events sponsored by the Catholics was also less and less desired.

3.3 The Work of Dom Beauduin in Amay: Normalization and Russification

Dom Lambert Beauduin was one of the Catholic pioneers of ecumenism. Influenced by the ideas of the Congress of Velehrad, he was animated by the same spirit as that which had once motivated Abbé Fernand Portal and Lord Halifax, even going as far as to sympathize with a number of ecumenical undertakings that had been initiated by Protestants. His attempts to enter into a frank and incisive dialogue with other Christians led to the founding, in 1925, of the Union Monastery at Amay-sur-Meuse, in Belgium, and to the launching of the affiliated journal *Irénikon* in the following year.[37] Here again, the Holy See initially supported the undertaking before expressing its

---

34 Manuela Barbolla, "La genesi della *Mortalium animos* attraverso lo spoglio degli archivi vaticani," RSCI 2, 2012, 495–538.

35 See Pettinaroli, *La politique russe du Saint-Siège*, 510–513; Léon Tretjakewitsch, *Bishop Michel d'Herbigny SJ and Russia: A Pre-Ecumenical Approach to Christian Unity*, Würzburg, Augustinus-Verlag, 1990.

36 Barbolla, "La genesi della *Mortalium animos*," 503.

37 See, in this volume, André Haquin's contribution. See also Jacques Mortiau & Raymond Loonbeek, *Dom Lambert Beauduin, visionnaire et précurseur (1873–1960): Un moine au cœur libre*, Paris, Cerf, 2005.

disagreement, or in this case even a growing hostility. Indeed, this union-minded monasticism did not fail to draw criticism. In June 1927, the nuncio in Brussels alerted the office of the secretary of state to the dangers posed by the "exaggerations" and "imprudent acts" committed by the monks of Amay under the influence of their spiritual lead, Dom Beauduin: by placing the Roman, Orthodox, and Protestant Churches on a more or less equal footing, Dom Beauduin manifested his desire to achieve the union of Christians on the basis of equality, whereas the Catholic Church refused to consider any form of union that was not based on subordination to Rome.[38] The Amay project had clearly moved away from unionism towards ecumenism.

What then ensued was a series of reprobation measures behind which the influence of Msgr. d'Herbigny can also be detected; the latter defended another conception of union, namely one that was founded on Catholic penetration into Eastern Christianity, whereas Dom Beauduin strove to find a meeting point for East and West within the context of monasticism.[39] By decree of the Congregation for the Oriental Churches (from July 1927), the monastery was placed under the direct supervision of the Pro Russia commission: all dealings with the Anglicans were suspended, and the monks of Amay were instructed to devote themselves exclusively to Russian Orthodoxy; thereafter, the apostolic visit carried out in the spring of 1928 confirmed the harm caused by the Benedictine monk, also accusing him of dubious modes of management and governance; he was accordingly forced to resign as prior at the end of the same year. From 1929 to 1931, the journal *Irénikon* was the object of redoubled vigilance, many initiatives were postponed and the work of Dom Constantin Bosschaerts, who supervised the mission's Flemish branch in Shotenhof (near Antwerp), was severely hampered. In 1932, Dom

Beauduin's influence being considered deleterious, he was removed and sent to the Toulouse region in France.[40] The monastery was relocated to Chevetogne in 1939.

4   The Question of Catholic Participation in the Ecumenical and Interconfessional Movements

The question as to whether or not Catholic Christians should be allowed to participate in interconfessional associations and gatherings was not new, particularly when one recalls the prohibitions that had been imposed on the Oxford Movement (starting with the condemnation of the APUC – which constituted an Anglo-Catholic movement born as a spin-off of the Oxford Movement – uttered by Rome in 1864), and as far as the Easterners are concerned, one could even go back to early modern times.[41] However, the question gained greater urgency in the interwar period, and focused primarily on the meetings promoted by Protestants and Anglicans, suspected of masking proselytizing activities among Catholics through their ecumenical initiatives, in Europe and America. The Holy See's answer was not consistent and depended on the nature of the collaboration (social, political, literary, etc.), the political context, the situation of Catholicism in the respective country, or the local status of the Catholic Church. Even in contexts that were more intimately linked to worship, such as in the *communicatio in sacris*, it is difficult to discern a clear-cut course valid on all occasions.[42] The general trend, however, remained

---

38   Micara to Gasparri, Bruxelles, Jun 8, 1927, in: AAV, Arch. Nunz. Belgio, b. 211, fasc. 1.

39   Coco, "Pio XI e l'unità dei cristiani," 271–274.

40   AAV, Arch. Nunz. Belgio, b. 211, fasc. 1, and ASRS, AAEESS, Belgio, period IV, pos. 191, fasc. 55.

41   See Cesare Santus, *Trasgressioni necessarie: Communicatio in sacris, coesistenza e conflitti tra le comunità cristiane orientali (Levante e Impero ottomano, XVII–XVIII secolo)*, Rome, École française de Rome, 2019.

42   As becomes clear, for example, when reading the Holy Office's indexes of gatherings – or *Ferie* – during the years 1920–1930; see ACDF, SO, Acta Congr. Generalis, 1922–1938.

one of firmness, which increased in the course of the 1920s, calling for a reduction in contacts with non-Catholics while limiting or prohibiting the participation of Catholics in Protestant or interdenominational organizations and gatherings promoted by Protestants.

4.1 The YMCA: A Protestant Threat to Be Countered

The YMCA is a Christian youth organization that was founded in Great Britain in the mid-19th century as a Protestant relief organization that was intended to provide assistance to the victims of the Industrial Revolution. When George Williams, a young Anglican who had converted to Congregationalism, arrived in London in the 1840s in order to work in a textile factory, he was struck by the dreadful conditions in which the city's young workers were forced to live. He therefore decided to create a safe environment that would provide dormitories, spiritual assistance, and a place for physical exercise: the YMCA. The latter spread rapidly across the country, then to France – where it was embedded in an international structure, the World Alliance of the YMCAS, that later moved to Geneva – and in particular to the United States and Canada. It was in North America that it assumed the form of a missionary and transnational movement that spread to Europe after World War I.[43] Indeed, the association gained wider recognition during the conflict on account of its humanitarian work among the soldiers and in areas that had been particularly ravaged by the warfare, above all in Catholic countries such as Italy, France, or Poland, where it presented itself as an interconfessional movement. As a result, it was closely monitored by the Roman authorities. Furthermore, and most importantly,

the YMCA became the first target in their struggle against Protestantism.

As a matter of fact, the postwar years witnessed the resurgence of the Vatican's anti-Protestant and anti-Modernist struggle,[44] waged primarily by the Holy Office. The issue, as is well known, played a central role in the relations with the Italian government, as evidenced by the proscription measures against the Modernist and anti-Fascist priest Ernesto Buonaiuti, although also famous names such as the French fathers Marie-Joseph Lagrange and Antonin-Dalmace Sertillanges, to name but a few, were not spared by condemnations and restrictions.

In this way, the activities of the Supreme Congregation's secretary, Cardinal Rafael Merry del Val, came to focus more on Germany, Great Britain, the United States, and Canada, countries that had been relatively spared by the anti-Modernist repression of the prewar period.[45] The fact that the ecumenical organizations had developed in these countries did not surprise the Roman censors, for whom the roots of these phenomena were to be sought in Modernism and Protestantism. Accordingly, they were convinced that a Protestant proselytism could be found behind nearly every ecumenical undertaking. And that is precisely how the YMCA was seen. This is well documented by a Roman dossier produced to study and oppose the association, in which one can identify three distinct phases.[46]

The first phase was Italian. In April 1920, the Holy Office prohibited Catholics from affiliating themselves with the Federazione italiana degli studenti per la cultura religiosa, which, along with the dependent journal *Fede e Vita*, had been identified as Modernist and Protestant. Moreover, the

---

43   Charles Howard Hopkins, *History of the YMCA in North America*, New York NY, Association Press, 1951; Thomas Winter, *Making Men, Making Class: The YMCA and Workingmen (1877–1920)*, Chicago IL, University of Chicago Press, 2002.

44   See Perin, *L'atteggiamento della Chiesa Cattolica*, 122–138. Giovanni Vian, "Modernism during the Pontificate of Benedict XV: Between Rehabilitation and Condemnation," in: Cavagnini & Grossi, eds., *Benedict XV*, vol. 1, 691–705.

45   AAV, Segr. Di Stato, Spogli di Cardinali e Officiali di Curia, Rafael Merry del Val, b. 5–7.

46   ACDF, SO, Rerum variarum, 1920, n.7, vols. 1 and 2.

decision was also made to conduct an in-depth investigation into the presence of the YMCA in Italy, to which the aforementioned association was believed to be linked. Although the investigators had difficulty ascertaining what exactly the responsibilities of this organization were and which were not, it was confirmed that the YMCA posed a threat to Catholicism in Italy.

In a second step, in the month of November of the same year the Holy Office issued a letter to the bishops that was more directly aimed at the YMCA: it described the latter as the parent organization of a certain number of Italian interconfessional associations, warned against the Protestant proselytism of which it was the instrument, and emphasized that ecumenical and interconfessional undertakings led to indifferentism and atheism.[47] While the condemnation targeted specifically Italian organizations and publications, the warning was of a more general nature. In fact, the Holy Office had received reports from several other countries that also stressed how dangerous the association was: the "YMCA threat" had evolved from an Italian threat into a global one.

The hostility towards the YMCA phenomenon on the global level grew steadily in the course of the 1920s. An inquiry conducted among European and non-European bishops, which contributed to foster Roman fears, underlined its importance, notably in Central Europe, Poland, and Bulgaria, but also among Russian emigrants. Such fears, in the context of the stern measures taken against several ecumenical initiatives in the second half of the 1920s, pushed Roman authorities to contemplate a new condemnation, this time on a global scale, of the YMCA. Instead, they simply reiterated the text of 1920, which would be extended to other national contexts in the 1950s, namely to Poland, South America, and the Philippines.

In the meantime, an inquiry conducted in the spring of 1927 broadened the scope of the investigation to the United States and to other associations that were suspected of Modernism and proselytism under the guise of interconfessionalism, in other words of a residual Americanism, especially the WA and the CPU.[48] Both the Catholic laity and the members of the clergy were prohibited from joining any of these organizations. At the same time, they were not allowed to participate in the International Good-Will Congress in the United States, which had been planned by these very same organizations in order to promote world peace. The apostolic delegate in Washington, who was assigned the task of supervising the implementation of these directives, was also informed that a stricter and more global statement regarding these different movements was being prepared in the Holy Office: it would be published as the encyclical *Mortalium animos*.

4.2   *The Ecumenical Conferences of the 1920s*

It is a well-known fact that the international conferences convened, during the interwar period, by the ecumenical organizations Life and Work and Faith and Order played an important role in the process that led to the establishment of the WCC in 1948. The Roman authorities' attitude towards these organizations is indicative of their relationship to other Christians in this period.

The more the practical Christianity promoted by the Lutheran archbishop of Uppsala Söderblom, his integral ecumenism of sorts, diminished the significance of doctrinal divisions, the more alien it became to the Roman perception of unity. Moreover, by seeking to attract Eastern Christians, it fueled the fear that anti-Catholic alliances might be formed. The resulting animosity on the part of the Vatican should, therefore, not come as a surprise. Notwithstanding this, the censors of the Holy Office and the diplomats of the curia showed relatively little interest in the conferences of Stockholm (1925) and Oxford (1937), since Catholics were hardly involved. The vicar apostolic in Sweden was merely asked to keep the Holy See

---

47   *AAS* 14, 1920, 595–597.

48   ACDF, SO, Rerum variarum, 1927, n. 29; Barbolla, "La genesi della *Mortalium animos*," 503.

informed about the conduct and the results of the first conference.[49]

This was not the case of the first conference held by Faith and Order in Aug 3–21, 1927, in Lausanne. The aim of this movement, which had arisen in an Anglican context, was quite different compared to Life and Work: dialogue and debate on doctrinal issues among the Christian confessions for the purpose of overcoming divisions and establishing an organic unity while maintaining a mutual respect for differences. The plan to organize an international conference was conceived even before the outbreak of the global conflict, when, in 1910, the proposal of the Episcopal Church of the United States led to the setting up of a commission that was presided over by a layman (and friend of the initiator Charles Brent), Robert Gardiner. In the following years, the latter established contacts with the Church of England and several British churches, but very soon turned to the Orthodox and the Catholics, as well. In doing so, he made every effort to ensure that the Catholic Church was represented at the conference, and for a time, the answers that he received raised hopes of a positive outcome. Indeed, the secretary of state informed him in December 1914 that the Holy Father was not formally opposed to the project, provided that the pope remain "the source and the cause" (*principium et causa*) of Christian unity.[50] The thus manifested goodwill did not preclude firmness, as is still apparent in the answers given in April 1919, when the request was renewed, then in the following month of August, after an audience with Benedict XV had been granted to the movement's representatives: in April, Cardinal Bonaventura Cerretti responded to Gardiner, who was asking for the Catholic Church to send its representatives to the future Faith and Order Conference: "His Holiness fully appreciates the loftiness of your

purpose, and He welcomes with a deep feeling of fatherly love the yearning of so many Christians for reunion and your eager wish for the complete restoration throughout the world of the one fold of Christ under one Shepherd."[51] However, the Catholic doctrine and praxis of Christian unity (the return to the Roman fold as the sole possibility of reconjunction) made it impossible for the Catholic Church to participate in the planned conference. A decree issued shortly before by the Holy Office confirmed this interdiction.[52]

This friendly refusal took on a harsher tone under Pius XI, in the weeks before the conference in Lausanne began. A decree dated July 8, 1927, reiterated the 1919 prohibition. The ordinary of Lausanne-Geneva-Freiburg, Msgr. Marius Besson, was assigned the task of communicating it to the clergy and the laity; moreover, the Secretary of State Gasparri, while criticizing him for his decision to allow two German priests to the conference, Hermann Hoffmann and Max Josef Metzger, required Msgr. Besson to provide full information on the progress of the conference.

The gathering in Lausanne and the hesitations of Msgr. Besson are indicative of a certain "dichotomy ... between the positions of the Roman magisterium on the one hand, and those of the local churches on the other."[53] As such, they confirmed the Holy See's opinion that a strong, clear, and unambiguous text was needed in order to

---

49 Telegrams of the Secretary of State Cardinal Gasparri to the apostolic vicar Mons. Müller, August–September 1925, in: ASRS, AAEESS., Stati Ecclesiastici, pos. 7, fasc. 2, fol. 83–85.

50 Letter of Dec 18, 1914; cited in Baubérot, "L'organisation internationale du protestantisme," 56–65.

51 Letter of the secretary of the Congregation for Extraordinary Ecclesiastical Affairs, Bonaventura Cerretti, to Robert Gardiner, Rome, Apr 4, 1919, and (non-dated) protocol of Benedict XV's answer to the members of the preparatory commission; in: ASRS, AAEESS, Stati Ecclesiastici, pos. 1433, fasc. 582, fol. 20 and 48–50.

52 Philippe Chenaux, "Le Saint-Siège et les débuts du mouvement œcuménique: La conférence de Lausanne (1927)," in: Andreas Gottsmann, Pierantonio Piatti & Andreas E. Rehberg, eds., *Incorrupta Monumenta Ecclesiam defendunt: Studi offerti a mons. Sergio Pagano, prefetto dell'Archivio Segreto Vaticano*, vol. 1/1, *La chiesa nella storia: Religione, cultura, costume*, Vatican City, Archivio Segreto Vaticano, 2018, 213–226, esp. 215–216.

53 Chenaux, "Le Saint-Siège et les débuts du mouvement œcuménique," 225–226.

compensate for the lack of firmness shown by the local hierarchies in the face of reunionist "pan-Christian" undertakings, as *Mortalium animos* will define them. All that said, the gathering in Lausanne made anyway little impact on the actual elaboration of the encyclical, which appeared five months later the Faith and Order gathering. In this summer of 1927, the text of the encyclical had in fact already been written and approved. Its publication was postponed in order to allow for possible adjustments in the light of the conference results, but above all to avoid narrowing the scope of the document and creating the impression that the danger would be limited to undertakings of this type.

5 Anti-Modernism, Anti-Protestantism, and Anti-Ecumenism: The German Focus of *Mortalium animos*

"The union of Christians can only be promoted by promoting the return to the one true Church of Christ of those who are separated from it, for in the past they have unhappily left it."[54] Thus remarked *Mortalium animos*, promulgated on Jan 6, 1928, the anti-ecumenical encyclical *par excellence*, the negative counterpart, so to speak, of the decree of 1964 entitled *Unitatis redintegratio*. It condemns the various initiatives for Christian reconciliation that had multiplied since the end of the war, as soon as these pursued goals other than the return of the dissidents to the Roman fold without any consideration for the integrity of doctrine. The document primarily targets the so-called pan-Christian conferences of Life and Work and Faith and Order, thereby following up on the decree of July 1927, which prohibited Catholics from collaborating with the gathering in Lausanne. The condemnation is also an extension of the one issued to APUC in 1864. This time to fall under the axe of Rome was a German organization with an objective very similar to the English one, the

Hochkirchlich-Ökumenische Bund and its journal *Una Sancta*.[55] In fact, this movement did play a role in the Roman authorities' decision to take a harder line against reunification initiatives in Germany, as it greatly intensified the general feeling of anxiety in the face of the threats posed by Protestant proselytism and, by consequence, of the perverse chain that held together Modernism, Protestantism, and ecumenism. It was, possibly, the spread of the Hochkirche movement in Germany that finally led to the realization that strong and resolute action was required on the part of the magisterium, and was thus a "triggering factor" in the process that led to the publication of *Mortalium animos*.[56]

5.1 The Encyclical's Course

The encyclical was entirely drawn up at the Holy Office, under the guidance of its secretary, Cardinal Merry del Val, although the pope supervised its redaction and made a number of emendations. The harsh tone of the document surprised its contemporaries but caused little stir in Germany, either at the time of its publication or afterwards. The country, as was often the case in those days, did not really feel concerned by this positioning of the magisterium, and indeed, every effort was made to avoid offending German feelings at a time when a concordat was about to be signed with Prussia. At the request of the Nuncio Pacelli in Berlin, care was taken to mask, if not the German thrust of the encyclical, then at least its triggering element: the "ecumenizing" Modernism on German soil.[57]

The confirmation of the causality bond existing between *Mortalium animos* and the German religious reality after World War I is shown by the explanatory text drawn up at the Holy Office some ten days after the publication of the encyclical. Intended for the members of the Congregation, Ernesto Ruffini's report of Jan 21, 1928, identifies

---

54   Pius XI, *Mortalium animos*, in: AAS 20, 1928, 5–16.

55   See also, in this volume, Paul Metzlaff's contribution.

56   Barbolla, "La genesi della *Mortalium animos*.", 513.

57   Levant, *Pacelli à Berlin*, 178–196.

the phases that led to the publication of the document:[58] after receiving an alarming diagnosis of intellectual and theological Germany in the aftermath of the Great War, the Holy See endeavored to reform theological studies and to renew the episcopate in the country; thereafter, the Holy Office focused on cleansing Catholic intellectual thinking by sanctioning the theologians who were suspected of Modernism, notably in its "ecumenizing" variant. This, in turn, drew its attention, almost accidentally, to a little known and recently created organization, the Hochkirchlich-ökumenischer Bund: the investigation of this organization cast suspicion on the various initiatives for Christian reunification and triggered the process that led to the more general condemnation of ecumenism beyond the borders of Germany alone.

5.2 The Starting Point: "The Cultural Crisis of German Catholicism"

In the 1920s, German Catholic thinking experienced a revival that differed from the cultural ghetto in which it had allowed itself to be somewhat confined in the times of the Wilhelmine Empire.[59] Under the Weimar Republic, just as the situation of Catholicism found itself reinforced in the political and social sphere, Catholic scholarship gained a new recognition on the German intellectual scene. The fame enjoyed by Carl Sonnenschein, Hermann Platz, Max Scheler, Carl Schmitt, or Hugo Bell, the circulation of the journals *Hochland* or *Stimmen der Zeit* beyond Catholic circles, and the growth of the Katholischer Akademikerverband (the association of thinkers and professors who took it upon themselves to spread the Catholic spirit in the world of culture) all reflect what has been called a

"return of German Catholicism from exile."[60] The diagnosis arrived at in Rome was entirely different: what was perceived was the crisis into which the German Catholic culture was sinking. And this crisis had a name: Modernism.

Even before the end of the war, and the phenomenon would only accelerate afterwards, a series of reports, investigations, and assessments reached Rome or were prepared in the city itself; they painted a picture of Germany as a country contaminated by the luminaries of error, or even as the land of the Modernist heresy.[61] The intellectuals were targeted for their excessive efforts to adapt Christian thinking to modern culture and society. They were accused of injecting the poison of Modernism into the souls of the German flock, souls which, by no longer listening to the priest, turned away from the Catholic moral teachings on sexuality and the family. What was most strongly condemned was an "ecumenizing" Modernism, that is, a scientific and literary approach that emancipated itself from ecclesiastic control, took up the core issues of the Lutheran undertaking, and was accompanied by a benevolent attitude towards Protestantism. This approach caused them to contemplate ecumenism and the establishment of a sole Christian Church united with Protestantism, but also led them to direct their criticism against Rome, its government, and its decrees, in short, to an anti-Romanism that raised the specter of a Protestantization of Catholicism. The latter touches upon a characteristic aspect of German Modernism in the postwar period, which was perhaps less marked by a renewal of exegesis than by a new openness to the enemies of the Catholic faith.

These fears were moreover fanned by the appearance of a sort of "practical interconfessionalism"

---

58 ACDF, SO, Rerum variarum, 1927, n. 30, fol. 30–31; text reproduced and published in unabridged form by Barbolla, "La genesi della *Mortalium animos*," 515–516.

59 The expression "the cultural crisis of German Catholicism" is cited in Alois Hudal, "Relazione sulla formazione dei professori cattolici per le università in Germania, Austria, Jugoslavia, Cecoslovacchia," Dec 17, 1927; ACDF, SO, Rerum variarum, n. 18, fol. 2–5.

60 Heinz Hürten, *Deutsche Katholiken: 1918 bis 1945*, Paderborn, F. Schöningh, 1992, 63–74.

61 See especially Eugenio Pacelli's final report before leaving the nunciature in Berlin, published in Hubert Wolf & Klaus Unterburger, *Eugenio Pacelli: Die Lage der Kirche in Deutschland 1929*, Paderborn, F. Schöningh, 2006.

arising from Catholic-Protestant friendships and collaborations in a certain number of journals and theological faculties, close contacts at schools and universities (the *raison d'être* of confessional schools having been questioned in the Weimar period), confessionally mixed labor unions, and a certain number of leagues and associations of various types, while the Zentrum party refused to assert its Catholic identity in a clear and unambiguous manner. This interconfessionalism was all the more frightening as it entertained political ties with the left, and raised the question as to what extent these modernizing and left-leaning thinkers were responsible for the fact that a part of the Catholic youth and some of the Catholic workers voted for socialist and communist parties. The case of an intellectual such as Ernst Michel, whose seminal work *Politik aus dem Glauben*[62] was put on the Index in 1929, illustrated this danger in the eyes of the curia. Modernistic and very critical of the Catholic Church's governance, a militant of ecumenism and a supporter of the social democrats, he confirmed the link between religious rebellion and political radicalism that had already been unveiled by Pius X.[63]

Those targeted by the Holy See were not so much the intellectuals but the clergymen, more precisely the theologians of the German faculties. The verdict was harsh: the theological education dispensed in Germany was flawed, yes, even dangerous. Rome deplored a spirit of independence and scientific freedom *vis-à-vis* the Roman authorities, the inadequacy of Thomistic instruction, and the proximity to Protestantism, notably in the disciplines in which the Catholics were weakly or poorly represented, such as in archeology or history, which led the Catholic students to attend classes that were taught by Protestants. The picture that arises from the study of the Roman archives

is well and truly that of a Germany in the grip of Modernism:[64] the country had not been purified of the Modernist poison, as France and Italy had been before the war; in the postwar years, the Roman authorities planned to remedy this situation.

5.3   *Reforming Ecclesiastical Studies*

In order to counter Modernism and Protestant infiltration into German thinking, the Holy See decided that the educational institutions at which future priests and future theologians received their training were to be dealt with first. Accordingly, a project for the restoration of ecclesiastical studies was conceived in the 1920s, based on the preferred strategy of the uniforming and "Romanizing" Christian thought, which was nothing other than Thomism at the time.[65] The Sacred Congregation of Seminaries and Universities issued instructions for the reform of ecclesiastical studies in Germany, which the Nuncio Pacelli relayed through constant and sustained interaction with the bishops. The reform aimed, among other things, to impose the strict adherence to the doctrine and method of Thomas Aquinas, in order to reorganize teachings in favor of dogmatic theology, to prolong the training by one or two additional years, and to enlist the services of the Jesuits as spiritual guides. In addition, the theologians of the "sound" doctrine were asked to publish more in the German scholarly journals. More or less the same principles are found in the apostolic letter of Aug 1, 1922, *Officiorum omnium*: undoubtedly addressed to Catholic Christianity as a whole, it nevertheless lent additional weight to the reform that was being attempted in Germany. This reform also had an institutional focus. Several decrees were intended to reinforce the control of the Roman authorities over public ecclesiastic education, particularly with regard to the choice

---

62   Ernst Michel, *Politik aus dem Glauben*, Jena, Diedrich, 1926.

63   Pacelli to Gasparri, July 14, 1928, in: ASRS, AAEESS, Germania IV, pos. 563, fasc. 80, fol. 46–49; ACDF, Censura librorum, 333/1927.

64   See especially AAV, Arch. Nunz. Berlino, busta 67–68.

65   See Klaus Unterburger, *Vom Lehramt der Theologen zum Lehramt der Päpste?: Pius XI., die Apostolische Konstitution "Deus scientiarum Dominus" und die Reform der Universitätstheologie*, Freiburg i.Br., Herder, 2010.

of teachers: the bishops, fundamental instruments of Roman control in Germany, had a say in the awarding of teaching appointments but they were still required to obtain the approval of Rome. Moreover, the Bavarian Concordat of 1925 granted extended powers to the local ordinaries in this matter. Nothing of the sort was agreed upon in the concordat signed with Prussia (1929), although the one signed with Hitler in 1933 explicitly recognized the validity of the Roman norms in the matter of ecclesiastical training, and more specifically the apostolic constitution *Deus scientiarum Dominus* (May 24, 1931).

The outcome of this ambitious reform project was, however, rather disappointing: although it succeeded in reinforcing the control of the ecclesiastical hierarchy over the training of clergy in seminaries and in modifying the curricula here and there in the country according to the wishes of the Roman congregations, on the whole the result of the efforts deployed by Rome remained decidedly below expectations.

5.4 Renewing the Episcopate

In the eyes of the nuncio, no reform of ecclesiastical studies was possible and no effective control of the theologians conceivable without good bishops. Thus, another prerequisite for a sound restoration of intellectual life in Catholic Germany, according to him, in the renewal of the episcopate in a more "Roman" fashion. There was a need for docile bishops who practiced preventive censorship, promptly implemented the instructions coming from Rome, and were fully committed to the reform of studies. It was imperative that seminarians and young clerics be sent to Rome. However, it was even more important that the vacant positions be filled with candidates who had received part of their training in Rome, or, failing that, in irreproachable institutions such as the Episcopal Seminary in Mainz or the Jesuit institutions. Both in Bavaria and in the rest of the country, the rights of the cathedral chapters in the election of bishops were curtailed, thereby increasing the Holy See's room for maneuver.

At least in this regard, Rome's reforms had been successful. Of the bishops who held office at the fall of William II's regime, in 1918 only one quarter had passed through Rome during their ecclesiastical training, and in most of these cases, it had only been during the years of specialization following their ordination. However, from the late 1920s to the early 1930s, the ratio was reversed: two thirds of the appointed bishops had pursued the major part of their studies under the Jesuits of Innsbruck or at a Roman institute, the Pontifical Gregorian University, the German Santa Maria dell'Anima college, or the Collegium Germanicum; by 1935, as many as half of the ordinaries in Germany now possessed this "certificate of Romanity."[66]

The reinforcement of the magisterium's authority over the Catholic milieu of Germany thus followed the institutional, reformist, and doctrinal path. However, it could not entirely dispense with more radical methods.

5.5 Suppressing Modernism

The Holy Office, in a certain manner, followed up on these measures by sanctioning all aspects of German thinking that could be likened to Modernism. By way of semiofficial censures or public condemnations, discrete suppression and proscription measures, it was at least able to create an inquisitorial atmosphere in Germany, similar to that which had reigned in France or Italy at the time of the Modernist crisis, under the pontificate of Pius X.

This suppression of German Modernism, in its ecumenical or its Protestantizing variant, found its place directly in the genesis of *Mortalium animos*. There are excellent examples. Indeed, the aforementioned Ruffini's text that outlines the process of how the encyclical was drawn up refers to a priest named Joseph Wittig, a theologian from Breslau who was condemned in 1925, then excommunicated in 1926, notably on account of his contacts with German associations of ecumenical orientation. The entire

---

66   ACDF, SO, Censura librorum, 1924, 829 and 829 bis; Levant, *Pacelli à Berlin*, 196–198.

affair had actually begun with another priest and theologian, Arnold Rademacher, a professor at the University of Bonn. His publications on the topic of grace were repeatedly denounced by Pacelli in 1922, whereupon the Holy Office, in 1925, asked the latter to conduct an in-depth investigation into the matter. Pacelli's investigation underlined three incriminating points: in the first place the author, arguing in the name of evolutionist theories, was accused to have attempted to circumvent the principle of the inerrancy of Scripture; in doing so, he began to praise Protestantism and to find points of convergence with the latter in the free interpretation of the Bible; he expressed a loud and strong desire to reconcile the facts of faith with those of science. Since the views expressed in these publications were dangerously close to both Modernism and ecumenism, the Holy Office considered setting these on the Index, before finally deciding to ban only his last work and to issue a call to order. In one of the reports on Rademacher, however, the Nuncio Pacelli had mentioned another censurable theologian, Joseph Wittig, a native of Silesia and a lecturer in history and Christian archeology at the faculty of Breslau. Throughout his works, the report says, Wittig displayed a certain anti-curialism by criticizing the functioning of the Roman institution that had falsified primitive Christianity; he professed a Protestant conception of the church, since he described the pope not as the authentic successor of Peter but as an exemplary teacher. Moreover, he collaborated with Protestant editorial projects. The ordinary of Breslau, Cardinal Bertram, was accordingly assigned the task of calling the theologian to order, forbidding him to publish, and revoking his teaching license. In the face of the cardinal's hesitations, the Holy Office decided to go even further, putting the works of Wittig on the Index and demanding his resignation from the faculty. Although Wittig agreed to resign, he refused to retract his writings: he was excommunicated and subsequently deposed as a priest.[67]

At the same time, various journals and organizations were put under pressure and sometimes called to order, without going any further: the Catholic journal *Hochland*, which entertained the wish to work towards reconciliation and hoped for the end of the confessionalization of Germany; the Jesuit journal *Stimmen der Zeit*, which was sometimes accused of being too benevolent towards the Modernists; more generally, Romano Guardini's liturgical movement and the youth movement Quickborn.[68]

5.6   *Condemning Ecumenism*

The investigation into the Hochkirchlich-ökumenische Bund had broader implications, as it led from the condemnation of the alliance to that of the entire ecumenical movement.

Indeed, after the Wittig affair, the other major case on which the dicastery focused its attention was that of the Hochkirche movement. Its name came up during the investigation of the theologian from Breslau: it was discovered that, like the latter, a certain number of Catholics who were already under surveillance – such as Rademacher or Ernst Michel – were more or less directly collaborating with the alliance and its journal, *Una Sancta*. The organization wished to unite Christians in one sole church, *una* and *sancta*, albeit without abandoning one's original confession, each of which was regarded as one of the many branches of the common house. Furthermore, interconfessional contact was to help enrich everyone's religion and to build up the common treasure: the Hochkirche would thus result from the fusion of the best that each branch of Christianity had to offer.[69] It was inevitable that these syncretic principles should collide with Roman unionism, which stated that the only possible union of Christians lay in the return of those who had gone astray to

---

67   Levant, *Pacelli à Berlin*, 180–192; and Unterburger, *Vom Lehramt der Theologen zum Lehramt der Päpste?*, 292–317.

68   ACDF, SO, Censura librorum: 1922, n. 217; 1927, n. 540; 1927, n. 617.

69   AAV, Arch. Nunz. Berlino, envelope 40. On the Hochkirche, see Leonard J. Swindler, *The Ecumenical Vanguard: The History of the Una Sancta Movement*, Pittsburgh PA, Duquesne University Press, 1966.

the one and true Church of Christ, the Church of Rome. Not to mention that the members of the Hochkirchlich-ökumenische Bund held in high regard elements of what Rome had condemned of Protestantism: intellectual freedom with regard to the Bible and the rejection of pontifical authority. Moreover, *Una Sancta* exploited the affair of Wittig, presented as a martyr, to denounce the Roman institution as such, which was said to have led original Christianity astray.

The Holy Office thus called for a thorough investigation, which was entrusted to the Nuncio Pacelli. His conclusions were the following: (1) the alliance was recent (1924), little known in Germany, and still in its embryonic stage, with no more than one hundred followers, of which, in the entire country, about fifteen were Catholic; (2) the founders were inspired by other authors who were suspected of Modernism, or had already been condemned on these grounds, and praised their works (among them older ones such as Ignaz von Döllinger, Hermann Schell, or George Tyrrell, and more recent ones such as Guardini, Wittig, and Rademacher); (3) thus, Protestants' attraction to this organization was not geared towards Roman orthodoxy but focused on those Catholics who deviated most from it.

The Holy Office decided then to take action by sending a first circular letter to the bishops in September 1926, in order to warn them of the threat posed by the association, and a second one in April 1927, in order to compel them to condemn the organization and to forbid Catholics to join it. However, in view of the negative impact which the latter might have on the negotiations for the concordat the Holy See was negotiating with Prussia, its publication was suspended.

In the meantime, another decision was made in Rome. The affair went beyond Germany alone and was to be linked to "a series of movements organized in other countries, in Europe and in America" – movements that manifested, once again, "Protestant infiltrations into the mentality of a large number of Catholics" and betrayed "the undeniable influence of the fallacies ... of dogmatic liberalism and of Modernism in all its forms."[70] Accordingly, the Roman authorities resolved to purely and simply condemn ecumenism and all that was attached to it, and to do so by means of an encyclical. *Mortalium animos*, which was published in the following January, thus belongs in the context of these German affairs.

6   Conclusions

The encyclical begins by acknowledging the increased desire for fraternal relationship between Christians, which was manifested in the proliferation of initiatives aimed at achieving Christian unity since the end of the world war, but also, correspondingly, in the spread of civil and social disorder. Christianity, which carries fraternity in its heart, is indeed capable of responding to the universal need for reconciliation. The desire for unity is in fact intrinsic to Christianity, and the movement to achieve it has something irresistible about it. Nevertheless, although the objective of Christian reunification is encouraged, Pius XI denounces the current modalities. He emphasizes the extent to which the undertaking is being undermined by initiatives such as the ecumenical congresses and conferences, and by the plan promoted by the latter, namely to establish a federated church constituted by several branches of the same Church of Christ. For there is only one, unique, true, and visible Church of Christ, the seat of which is in Rome and the guidance of which is entrusted to the Holy Father. The Catholic Church, as a *societas perfecta*, cannot negotiate this truth, nor can it seek compromises. The accusation is forceful: ecumenism is tantamount to "blasphemy" and "false religion," and constitutes a "pernicious" strategy. Accordingly, there is only one path to unity: that of the return to the fold of those who have gone astray, or in other words, that of unionism.

---

70   Report and *voto* of Merry del Val, in: ACDF, SO, Rerum variarum, 1927, n. 28, fol. 100–116; cited in Barbolla, "La genesi della *Mortalium animos*," 518–522, here 518.

The pontiff warns of the threat posed by these "pan-Christians" undertakings and these "propagators of fallacies," which are assimilated to a kind of reunionist imperialism operating at the expense of the Roman Church. The Catholic Church does not fundamentally reject the idea of establishing an intra-Christian solidarity in order to combat secularization and atheism, or even – as can be read between the lines – socialism and communism; however, the Modernism and ecumenism to which these misguided undertakings adhere lead to religious indifferentism and thus to atheism. Hence, while Catholic unionism is praised, the initiatives for reunion that deviate from it are condemned, and the Catholics are not authorized to participated in them: "This being so, it is clear that the Apostolic See cannot on any terms take part in their assemblies, nor is it anyway lawful for Catholics either to support or to work for such enterprises; for if they do so they will be giving countenance to a false Christianity, quite alien to the one Church of Christ."[71]

Mortalium animos thus aims to clarify the position of the Church of Rome *vis-à-vis* the various initiatives for Christian reunion, by underlining the fundamental differences between Catholic unionism and ecumenism – differences which, as the text emphasizes, bear on the very essence of the Christian faith, namely tradition, hierarchy, and the Eucharist. Consequently, the encyclical definitively condemns ecumenism, and casts suspicion on the ecumenical deviations of Catholic unionism in order to confine the latter within strict limits.

The sources of this encyclical must be sought in the anti-Modernist struggle waged by the Roman authorities in Germany during the Weimar period: a biconfessional Germany, the fatherland of Martin Luther, with a two-thirds Protestant majority; a Germany in which Modernism, more than anywhere else, looked back to the Lutheran Reformation and aroused the fear of a Protestantization of German Catholicism; a Germany in which the ecumenical praxis was also a well-established reality, be it

in the confessionally mixed labor unions, in the Zentrum party that refused to identify itself as Catholic, or in a multitude of associative and literary undertakings that brought together and sometimes promoted interconfessionalism. While the German context, and especially the case of the Hochkirchlich-ökumenische Bund, served as a triggering factor, the text of the encyclical did not concern Germany in particular. In other words: it gave Cardinal Merry del Val the opportunity to bring out the encyclical that he had been thinking about for many years, practically since the issue of Anglican ordinations, of which he had never lost sight ever since he was decisive in establishing their nullity in 1896.

Mortalium animos thus constitutes the major expression of a more global stiffening of the papacy in the face of ecumenical dynamics in the whole Christianity, from Great Britain to the United States, in Germany and in the whole of Central and Eastern Europe, extending even as far as the Christian communities in the Near East. Yet the anti-ecumenical struggle, like the anti-Modernist struggle, took shape within a more global, intransigent project that aimed to restore a Christian society in Europe, a project which the papacy had never ceased to pursue since the French Revolution (which aimed to destruct Christianity) and which sought to reestablish the political and social ascendancy of the Church of Rome. This brings us back to Germany, where this project assumed a particular meaning: the heart of Christianity had once pulsed in the lands of the Holy Roman Empire, and it was Germany that had made the first breach with the Reformation.

Translated from French to English by Robert Meyer.

Bibliography

Barbolla, Manuela, "La genesi della *Mortalium Animos* attraverso lo spoglio degli archivi vaticani," RSCI 2, 2012, 495–538.

---

71   Pius XI, *Mortalium animos.*

Coco, Giovanni, "Pio XI e l'unità dei cristiani: Le Chiese d'Oriente," in: Cosimo Semeraro, ed., *La sollecitudine ecclesiale di Pio XI*, Vatican City, Libreria editrice vaticana, 2010, 260–313.

Fouilloux, Étienne, *Les catholiques et l'unité chrétienne du XIXᵉ au XXᵉ siècle: Itinéraires européens d'expression française*, Paris, Le Centurion, 1982.

Levant, Marie, *Pacelli à Berlin: Le Vatican et l'Allemagne, de Weimar à Hitler (1919–1934)*, Rennes, Presses universitaires de Rennes, 2019.

Miccoli, Giovanni, *Fra mito della cristianità e secolarizzazione: Studi sul rapporto chiesa-società nell'età contemporanea*, Casale Monferrato, Marietti, 1985.

Pettinaroli, Laura, *La politique russe du Saint-Siège (1905–1939)*, Rome, École française de Rome, 2015.

Unterburger, Klaus, *Vom Lehramt der Theologen zum Lehramt der Päpste?: Pius XI, die Apostolische Konstitution "Deus scientiarum Dominus" und die Reform der Universitätstheologie*, Freiburg i.Br., Herder, 2010.

CHAPTER 32

The International Missionary Council between 1910 and 1961

Kenneth R. Ross

1 From Gestation to Birth

The emergence of the IMC from the Edinburgh 1910 WMC was like the birth that comes at the end of a long gestation period.[1] The subtitle of William Richey Hogg's classic history of the IMC is revealing: *A History of the International Missionary Council and Its Nineteenth-Century Background.*[2] After tentative beginnings in the 18th century, the Western Protestant missionary movement truly came into its own from 1800, leading Kenneth Scott Latourette to describe the 19th as the "great century" in the story of the expansion of Christianity.[3] The Industrial Revolution in the Western world had opened up possibilities to expand commercial and political influence globally and the Evangelical revival created a spiritual fervor that could exploit new possibilities of travel and communication for missionary purposes. In keeping with the free enterprise of the age, missionary societies sprang up wherever there was sufficient enthusiasm and launched their efforts with little thought of collaboration with others. Indeed, if anything, they approached their task in a competitive spirit, most

acutely in their rivalry with the Catholic missions but also at times with one another.

Both missionary organizations and individual missionaries tended to be fiercely independent. Nonetheless, there were certain unifying factors: a shared spirituality arising from the Evangelical revival, a post-Enlightenment confidence in Western civilization, and the experience of cross-cultural mission. There was therefore a sense of being part of the same movement even though geographically scattered and organizationally fragmented. Thus, from an early stage there was an awareness that it could be beneficial to come together for purposes of conference. At the beginning of the 19th century William Carey, the pioneer Baptist missionary in India, had proposed a decennial interdenominational world missionary conference and had suggested that the first should be held in Cape Town in 1810.[4] Another Bengal missionary, Alexander Duff, who later would become professor of Evangelistic Theology at New College in Edinburgh – the first chair of mission studies in the English-speaking world – retrieved and promoted the idea during his celebrated lecture tour of the United States in 1854.[5] In due course large-scale conferences were held in Liverpool in 1860, London in 1878, London again in 1888, and New York in 1900. In preliminary ways each of these strove to cultivate cooperation among Protestant missionary societies. The late 19th and early 20th centuries also saw missionaries from different churches and societies coming together for conference in the countries where they served. Such initiatives

---

1 The research on which this contribution is based benefitted from the hospitality and helpfulness of staff at New College Library, School of Divinity, University of Edinburgh, the Library of the Bossey Ecumenical Institute, Geneva, and The Burke Library at Union Theological Seminary, Columbia University Libraries, New York NY. The author's grateful acknowledgments are here recorded.

2 William Richey Hogg, *Ecumenical Foundations: A History of the International Missionary Council and Its Nineteenth-Century Background*, New York NY, Harper, 1952; Eugene OR, Wipf & Stock, 2002.

3 Kenneth Scott Latourette, *A History of the Expansion of Christianity*, vol. 4, *The Great Century*, New York NY, Harper, 1941.

4 Ruth Rouse, "William Carey's 'Pleasing Dream,'" *IRM* 38, 1949, 181–192.

5 Andrew Alexander Millar, *Alexander Duff of India*, Edinburgh, Canongate Press, 1992, 169–176.

at national level, as Richey Hogg remarks, "became a main current flowing into Edinburgh, 1910"[6] and also gained impetus from it. No less significant was the emergence of indigenous churches in the "mission fields." Commonly, they found that the denominational differences they inherited from their Western parent bodies were of limited importance, and they were motivated to think of cooperation and even church union between the different emerging movements.

Another major factor in the gestation that led to the birth of the IMC was the rise of the SCM in the late 19th century. Significant movements of Christian faith with a strong missionary orientation emerged in the universities and colleges of Great Britain and North America. Taking advantage of the rapidly improving communications of the time, they built a strong sense of association, both nationally and internationally. They also quickly developed a global outlook and a strong sense of the catholicity of the church. When John Raleigh Mott looked back on his long period of service as the chairman of the IMC, he recognized that the formation provided by the SVM and the WSCF had been highly significant in preparing the way: "Practice games in weaving together the nations and communions."[7] The student movement comprised a variety of national and international organizations with overlapping membership and leadership. Mott and other future leaders of the IMC drew inspiration particularly from the SVM, which sought to promote missionary service and, in 1888, adopted the watchword, "the evangelization of the world in this generation."[8] Both the inspirational missionary vision and the forms of association and collaboration that were developed within the student movement helped to shape the emergence of the IMC a generation later.

2   Edinburgh 1910: A Fountainhead

After this long gestation, the birth of the IMC took place at Edinburgh in 1910. Though it would not formally come into existence until 1921, the formality was a delayed outcome of what for all practical purposes was settled and begun at the WMC held at Edinburgh in 1910. On any reckoning, this was a highly significant occasion in the history of Protestantism and indeed of Christianity as a whole. John R. Mott, the conference chairman, called it "the most notable gathering in the interest of the worldwide expansion of Christianity ever held, not only in missionary annals, but in all Christian annals."[9] Over subsequent years many have recognized the significance of the 10-day event, perhaps none more eloquently than William Richey Hogg:

> Edinburgh, 1910, appears to be the non-Roman Christian world's ecumenical keystone. The keystone, specially cut, stands as the central stone at the crown of an arch. It holds together and strengthens all beneath that converges in it. The arch it crowns provides a foundation upon which a superstructure can be built. The keystone is neither arch nor wall, but it belongs to both. Remove it, and both will collapse. It is unique. Thus it is with Edinburgh, 1910. It belongs to the nineteenth and to the twentieth centuries. It is the keystone through which developments in mission and unity in the one century relate to those in the other and apart from which the full meaning of neither can be assayed.[10]

When compared with earlier international missionary conferences, Edinburgh was distinguished by the range of its participants, the breadth and

---

6   Hogg, *Ecumenical Foundations*, 17.

7   John R. Mott, cited in: Hogg, *Ecumenical Foundations*, 81.

8   Hogg, *Ecumenical Foundations*, 88.

9   John R. Mott, cited in: Charles Howard Hopkins, *John R. Mott (1865–1955): A Biography*, Grand Rapids MI, Eerdmans, 1979, 342.

10   William Richey Hogg, "Edinburgh, 1910: Ecumenical Keystone," *Religion in Life* 29/3, 1960, 339–351, here 339.

depth of its inquiry, the scale of its ambition, the sense of urgency and opportunity with which it was imbued, and the magnitude of its historical legacy in mission and ecumenism. Its leaders were united in the conviction that they stood at a moment of unprecedented opportunity in terms of fulfilling the church's task of taking the Christian message to the whole world. They were convinced that they had arrived at a moment when political, economic, and religious factors had combined to create opportunities for worldwide missionary advance which, if not now grasped, might never recur. The conference therefore convened with a strong sense that it had a role to play in world evangelization that would prove to be historic. It also had a sense that the time was ripe for structures to be created to strengthen united action and practical cooperation.

Already established was a common understanding among leaders of the missionary movement that they would hold a major international missionary conference on a roughly decennial basis. With this in mind Fairley Daly, the secretary of the Livingstonia Mission of the United Free Church of Scotland, wrote to Robert Speer of the PBFM in New York, in 1906, asking if there were plans to follow up the 1900 New York Conference.[11] The answer came back that the Americans would welcome such a conference in Britain. A group of Scottish mission secretaries met in Glasgow and issued a call for a larger consultation of Scottish missions to consider the possibility of convening a new conference. Twenty-seven missionary boards and societies met in Edinburgh in January of the following year, and decided to convene a WMC, in Edinburgh, in 1910.[12]

The process that was thus set in motion gathered momentum, initially under a UK General Committee and a US Committee on Reference and Council. These were quickly superseded by a full International Committee, comprising ten British, five North American and three continental representatives. It met for the first time in Oxford in June 1907 and achieved the extraordinary feat of organizing the first WMC in exactly three years.[13] In doing so, it set a pattern that would shape the life of the IMC in decades to come.

Two figures quickly established their leadership in the preparatory process and went on to play dominant roles in the conference and its sequel, the IMC. John R. Mott, the American Methodist layman, was a figure of growing international reputation among Protestant missions.[14] He first became involved by joining the SVM, committing himself "if God permit, to become a foreign missionary." He would later become the student secretary of the YMCA and general secretary of the WSCF, and use his influence in these positions to recruit large numbers of young people for mission. He was also one of the cofounders of the FMCNA. His first publication, entitled *The Evangelization of the World in this Generation* (1900), gave the North American missionary movement its watchword in the early 20th century.[15]

If Mott generated the grand vision and energy of the preparatory process for Edinburgh 1910, it was his Scottish counterpart, Joseph Houldsworth Oldham, who handled the immensely complex details of planning the conference. He did so with an administrative flair that brought luster to the event and established his own distinguished career in missionary and ecumenical circles. Nearly ten years Mott's junior, and still only in his mid-30s, Oldham was born of Scottish missionary parents in India. Following his graduation from Oxford he worked with the YMCA in India before returning to Europe for theological studies in Edinburgh and

---

11   WMC, ed., *World Missionary Conference, 1910: To Consider Missionary Problems in Relation to the Non-Christian World*, vol. 9, *The History and Records of the Conference: Together with Addresses Delivered at the Evening Meetings*, Edinburgh, Oliphant, Anderson, & Ferrier, 1910, 5–6.

12   WMC, ed., *World Missionary Conference, 1910*, vol. 9, 6.

---

13   WMC, ed., *World Missionary Conference, 1910*, vol. 9, 8–17.

14   See Hopkins, *John R. Mott*.

15   See John R. Mott, *The Evangelization of the World in This Generation*, London, SVM, 1900.

Germany. As the United Free Church of Scotland's secretary for mission studies, he attended the inaugural meeting of the International Committee in Oxford, where he was appointed secretary to the committee with fulltime responsibility for the preparation of the conference.[16] Combining administrative efficiency with breadth of vision and philosophical acumen, Oldham was being prepared for his role as the first secretary of the IMC.

3   The Shaping of Edinburgh 1910 and the Making of the IMC

The Committee swiftly decided the focus, nature, and process of the WMC. Mott's watchword – the evangelization of the whole world in this generation – expressed the vision to which most of the International Committee members could subscribe. But it was not, as sometimes supposed, adopted as an official motto of the conference. Some continental mission leaders were uneasy with it. Gustav Warneck, the German founder of the modern science of mission studies, made this clear in a letter to Mott. Warneck expressed anxiety that qualitative concerns for the consolidation of Christianity in Africa and Asia should not be subordinated to quantitative goals of expansion. "A predilection for the watchword 'the occupation of the whole world in this present generation'" – he wrote to Mott, slightly misquoting the watchword – "can easily miss the most hopeful opportunities ... The great lesson which the foreign missionary enterprise of our time has to learn from the history of the expansion of Christianity during the first three centuries is that the principal strength of missions lies in the native congregations ... We are at present in that stage of modern missions when the watchword

must be the self-propagation of Christianity."[17] Sensitive to such criticism, the International Committee settled for a judiciously sober title for the conference that signaled its reflective purpose: "World Missionary Conference: To Consider Missionary Problems."

Complex ecclesiastical diplomacy lay behind the composition of the conference and the framing of its inquiry. A major objective of the organizing committee was to secure the participation of the Anglo-Catholic or High Church Anglican missionary societies – the SPG and the UMCA.[18] In order to do so, they had to concede that territories where Eastern Orthodox or Roman Catholic Churches predominated should be regarded as already evangelized, not a view usually taken at that time by Evangelical Protestant missions. Hence Latin America, much of the Middle East, and Eastern Europe were effectively excluded from the consideration of the conference. Its discussion was framed around the "Christian world" of Western Europe and North America and the "non-Christian world" of Africa, Asia, and the Pacific. The question was how to take the gospel of Christ from the former to the latter. The full conference title thus emerged: "World Missionary Conference: To Consider Missionary Problems in Relation to the Non-Christian World." Oldham's diplomatic skills had been fully tested in formulating an approach that satisfied the Low-Church missionary movement while enabling the Anglo-Catholics also to participate. Looking back fifty years later, he commented: "This was the turning point of the ecumenical movement."[19]

To further allay apprehensions among the societies and boards invited to participate, the International Committee agreed, "to confine

---

16   Keith Clements, *Faith on the Frontier: A Life of J.H. Oldham*, Edinburgh, T&T Clark, 1999, 73–99.

17   Gustav Warneck, "Letter to Mr. Mott from Dr. Gustav Warneck, Ex-Professor of Missions in the University of Halle," in: WMC, ed., *World Missionary Conference, 1910*, vol. 1, *Report of Commission I: Carrying the Gospel to All the Non-Christian World*, 434–435.

18   See Clements, *Faith on the Frontier*, 81–88.

19   Joseph H. Oldham, "Reflections on Edinburgh 1910," *Religion in Life* 29/3, 1960, 329–338, here 333.

the purview of the Conference to work of the kind in which all were united. ... No expression of opinion should be sought from the Conference on any matter involving any ecclesiastical or doctrinal question on which those taking part in the Conference differed among themselves."[20] This meant that the conference was necessarily oriented to practical issues of method, administration and cooperation in missionary work, though in the event it was not able to exclude the aspiration toward greater church unity that would shape its legacy.

A distinctive feature of Edinburgh 1910 was that it did not aim to be a rallying of the faithful supporters of the missionary movement. Whereas earlier gatherings had concentrated on a demonstration of enthusiasm, Edinburgh aimed to be a working conference, as its subtitle showed. It was distinguished by its attempt to achieve a more unified strategy and greater coordination within the worldwide engagement of Christian mission. The aim of the organizing committee was that it should be "a united effort to subject the plans and methods of the whole missionary enterprise to searching investigation and to coordinate missionary experience from all parts of the world."[21] This was a novel methodology at the time and proved to be one that would shape the life and activity of the IMC in the years ahead.

It was the Edinburgh Conference that pioneered a process that would serve the IMC well in decades to come. The International Committee received recommendations from both Great Britain and the United States that an "earnest study of the missionary enterprise" was in order. Accordingly eight themes were selected, each being in the committee's judgement "of cardinal importance and special immediate urgency."[22] The preparation of each topic was assigned to a commission, or preparatory working group, mandated "to gather up, and

present in summary form, the results of the largest experience and best thoughts of missionaries in the field."[23] Eight commissions were thus created. Commission I was given the task of preparing, and presenting to the conference, the Report on Carrying the Gospel to all the Non-Christian World; Commission II was charged to report on The Church in the Mission Field; Commission III, Education in Relation to the Christianization of National Life; Commission IV, The Missionary Message in Relation to the Non-Christian Religions; Commission V, The Preparation of Missionaries; Commission VI, The Home Base of Missions; Commission VII, Relation of Missions to Government; and Commission VIII, Cooperation and the Promotion of Unity.

Each commission comprised twenty specialists from both sides of the Atlantic, five having British conveners, with American and European vice chairs, and three being chaired by Americans, with British and continental vice chairs. Among Oldham's chief tasks was to provide central support for the commissions, a challenge to which he brought the skills of scholar-cum-organizer that had distinguished him as study secretary for the United Free Church of Scotland. Under his leadership the International Committee constructed a questionnaire for each commission, and in February 1909 these were sent to missionaries in different parts of the world. Through a communication effort unprecedented in its scale and ambition, they gathered the accumulated wisdom of the missionary movement in relation to their assigned topics. About one thousand replies were received, many written at considerable length. This "raw material" provided the commissions with the data on which to construct the eight reports, each combining the views of missionaries, reflections of the commissioners, and recommendations of the commissions. Each commission was given a day to present its report, and delegates had the opportunity to respond with what were then considered very short speeches – maximum seven

20   WMC, ed., *World Missionary Conference, 1910*, vol. 9, 8.

21   Clements, *Faith on the Frontier*, 77.

22   William Henry Temple Gairdner, *"Edinburgh 1910": An Account and Interpretation of the World Missionary Conference*, Edinburgh, Oliphant, Anderson & Ferrier, 1910, 19.

23   WMC, ed., *World Missionary Conference, 1910*, vol. 9, 11.

minutes. The final published versions of the commission reports include the speeches made by way of response at the conference itself. It is these eight volumes that constitute the documentary outcome of Edinburgh 1910, which extended its reach and influence.

4 Edinburgh and the Desire for Unity

The Edinburgh Conference was driven by the belief that the missionary movement had arrived at a unique moment of opportunity. There was a great sense of urgency to the conference, prompted by a conviction that the opportunity could be lost if the right strategy were not formed and implemented. "Never before," stated its flagship text, "has there been such a conjunction of crises and of opening of doors in all parts of the world as that which characterizes the present decade."[24] In the words with which Mott titled the book he published soon after the conference, it appeared to be "the decisive hour of Christian missions."[25]

Its significance, however, went much further. Though its terms of reference explicitly excluded consideration of divisive doctrinal and ecclesiastical questions, the Edinburgh Conference spawned an epoch-making vision of church unity. The Asian delegates, though few in number, were particularly influential in voicing an aspiration for greater church unity, spurred by movements in this direction which were already underway in their contexts. These in turn took fresh impetus from the dynamic of the conference. A direct line of continuity runs from the Edinburgh Conference to the formation of the Church of South India (1947), the Church of North India (1970), a single nondenominational Protestant Church in China (1951) and the United Church of Christ in Japan (1941).[26] Though

the conference was an exclusively Protestant affair, there were moments when it looked to a wider church unity. Silas McBee, editor of the Anglican theological journal *The Churchman*, read a letter from Bishop Geremia Bonomelli, the Roman Catholic bishop of Cremona, in which the bishop wrote that he recognized amongst the Edinburgh delegates elements of faith "more than sufficient to constitute a common ground of agreement, and to afford a sound basis for further discussion, tending to promote the union of all believers in Christ."[27]

Ralph Wardlaw Thompson of the LMS told the conference: "I long for the time when we shall see another Conference, and when men of the Greek Church and the Roman Church shall talk things over with us in the service of Christ."[28] Thus the conference proved to be the widely acclaimed starting point of the 20th-century ecumenical movement, with a direct line of continuity running through to the formation of the WCC in 1948. "Edinburgh 1910," wrote Hugh Martin, "was in fact a fountain head of international and inter-Church cooperation on a depth and scale never before known."[29]

In his closing remarks Lord Balfour of Burleigh, church elder, former British cabinet minister and president of the conference, spoke strongly of the need for greater "intercommunication" among missionary societies in matters of political representation. This echoed the unanimous opinion of the chairmen of all the other commissions, cooperation being seen essential for the advance of every aspect of mission. Commission I raised the issue at the beginning of the conference, and the business committee scheduled an earlier hearing of the Commission VIII's report on Cooperation

---

24 WMC, ed., *World Missionary Conference, 1910*, vol. 1, 1.

25 John R. Mott, *The Decisive Hour of Christian Missions*, New York NY, SVM, 1912; see WMC, ed., *World Missionary Conference, 1910*, vol. 1, 363.

26 See Brian Stanley, *The World Missionary Conference, Edinburgh 1910*, Grand Rapids MI, Eerdmans, 2009,

310–312. By the same author see his contribution in this volume.

27 WMC, ed., *World Missionary Conference, 1910*, vol. 8, *Report of Commission VIII: Co-Operation and the Promotion of Unity*, 220–221.

28 WMC, ed., *World Missionary Conference, 1910*, vol. 8, 216.

29 Hugh Martin, *Beginning at Edinburgh: A Jubilee Assessment of the World Missionary Conference 1910*, London, Edinburgh House Press, 1960, 3.

and the Promotion of Unity – in anticipation of its central recommendation:

> That a Continuation Committee of the World Missionary Conference be appointed, international and representative in character ... to maintain in prominence the idea of the World Missionary Conference as a means of coordinating missionary work, of laying sound foundations for future development, and of evoking and claiming by corporate action fresh stores of spiritual force for the evangelization of the world.[30]

The idea of a Continuation Committee was not new or unheard of when it was brought to the floor of the conference by Commission VIII. The previous year, as continental European missionary societies looked forward to Edinburgh, they submitted a memorandum proposing the creation of an international missionary agency: "The missionary societies of the Continent of Europe take the liberty to propose ... the formation of a 'International Committee' dealing with international missionary questions."[31] They made reference to the numerous replies received by Commission I recommending the establishment of such a body. When the FMCNA held its meeting in January 1910, it responded favorably to this suggestion from Europe and indicated that American missionary leaders had already been thinking along the same lines. "John R. Mott grasped the situation at once," observed Richey Hogg, "and advocated that British societies be urged to form an organization similar to those in Germany and America and to unite with these other two bodies in an international missionary committee."[32] It thus became clear that there was a groundswell in favor of creating a permanent international instrument of missionary unity and cooperation.

The debate preceding the unanimous adoption of this motion demonstrated the delegates' ecumenical vision. If most contributions concentrated on the first element of the commission title – "cooperation" – the issue of "unity" was by no means ignored. Some urged that ecclesiological issues be suborned to the imperative demands of practical cooperation in mission fields; others cautioned of the need to resolve ecclesial differences in order that joint action could be a genuine expression of unity. Some European delegates were surprised to discover how both dimensions were being combined in Australia. Others spoke of the urgent need for discussions with both the Roman Catholic and Orthodox Churches. In what must rate as among the most impressive speeches of the entire conference – and a foundational contribution to the ecumenical movement – the Chinese delegate, Cheng Jingyi (LMS) explained the pioneering role of the Christian federation movement in China, that had developed inter-Christian cooperation in educational and evangelistic work to the point where it was possible "to see in the near future a united Christian Church without any denominational distinctions."[33]

The conference thus reached its high point with the decision to create a Continuation Committee with thirty-five members, ten from the UK, North America, and the Continent respectively, and one apiece from South Africa, Australasia, Japan, China, and India. It was a relatively conservative approach but included in the mandate of the Continuation Committee was the responsibility to work towards the formation of a "permanent International Missionary Committee."[34] The unanimity and enthusiasm with which the proposal was adopted by the conference left the delegates with the sense that something momentous had occurred. Spontaneously they stood and sang the

---

30   WMC, ed., *World Missionary Conference, 1910*, vol. 9, 95–96.

31   "Memorandum on Appointment of a Standing Committee, Submitted by the Missionary Societies on the Continent of Europe," Sept 15, 1909, cited in: Hogg, *Ecumenical Foundations*, 117.

32   Hogg, *Ecumenical Foundations*, 118.

---

33   WMC, ed., *World Missionary Conference, 1910*, vol. 8, 195–197.

34   WMC, ed., *World Missionary Conference, 1910*, vol. 8, 203.

doxology, "Praise God from Whom All Blessings Flow." As Hogg remarked, "Something new had happened. Those present knew that from within their midst something different was emerging. It was a desire for an inclusive togetherness unknown before."[35] It was this impetus that would bring the IMC into being. The new solidarity that had been discovered in Edinburgh called for institutional expression. The conference had also yielded the leadership that could fulfil its aspiration. The partnership of Mott and Oldham that had delivered the conference would become a constant factor at the heart of the IMC.

Edinburgh 1910 proved to be the first glimpse of what Archbishop of Canterbury William Temple would describe as "the great new fact of our time" – a truly worldwide Christian church.[36] The great drama of the coming century, in terms of church history, would be the growth of Christian faith in Asia, Africa, Oceania, and Latin America. Since this epoch-making vision of the church as a truly global missionary community found its first concentrated expression at Edinburgh in 1910, the unique place of the conference in the history of Christianity is assured. However imperfect its conceptual equipment, the Edinburgh Conference, like no other, anticipated the transformation through which Christianity would become a truly worldwide faith. As Andrew Walls has written:

> The World Missionary Conference, Edinburgh 1910, has passed into Christian legend. It was a landmark in the history of mission; the starting point of the modern theology of mission; the high point of the modern Western missionary movement and the point from which it declined; the launch-pad of the modern ecumenical movement; the point at which

Christians first began to glimpse something of what a world church would be like.[37]

If we describe Edinburgh 1910 as a "proto-ecumenical" conference, concerned with advancing "cooperation and unity" in the study and practice of mission, its most significant achievement was that it raised – arguably for the first time in European Christian history – the vision of the church as a global reality. The sense that Christianity was poised to transform itself by becoming truly global was evident in many of the conference debates. It would be the task of the IMC to keep this vision before the ecumenical movement as, in its interwar development, the latter focused its concerns mainly on cooperation among European churches – Protestant and Orthodox – with scant attention to the rest of the world. As Kenneth Scott Latourette insisted: "It cannot be said too often or too emphatically that the ecumenical movement arose from the missionary movement and continues to have at its heart worldwide evangelism."[38]

5   The Continuation Committee

The only formal outcome of Edinburgh 1910 was the unanimous decision to establish a Continuation Committee. It met briefly just after the close of the 1910 WMC and elected John Mott as chairman, Eugene Stock of the Anglican CMS and German missionary leader Julius Richter as vice chairmen, and Joseph H. Oldham as its full-time salaried secretary. Its responsibility was "to confer with the Societies and Boards as to the best method of working toward the formation

---

35   Hogg, *Ecumenical Foundations*, 130.
36   William Temple, *The Church Looks Forward*, London, Macmillan, 1944, 2–3.

37   Andrew F. Walls, *The Cross-Cultural Process in Christian History: Studies in the Transmission and Appropriation of Faith*, Maryknoll NY, Orbis Books, 2002, 53.
38   Kenneth Scott Latourette, "Ecumenical Bearings of the Missionary Movement and the International Missionary Council," in: *A History of the Ecumenical Movement*, vol. 1, Ruth Rouse & Stephen C. Neill, eds., *1517–1948*, London, SPCK, 1954, 351–402, here 362.

of such a permanent International Missionary Committee as is suggested by the Commissions of the Conference and by various missionary bodies apart from the Conference."[39] First, however, it set up nine commissions to continue work on the themes that had claimed the attention of the Edinburgh Conference. Oldham set to work, his first task was the editing and publication of the voluminous reports that the commissions had prepared for the 1910 conference.

Another highly significant step, taken by the Continuation Committee at its meeting at Bishop Auckland in May 1911, was the decision to launch a journal, the *International Review of Mission*. The journal, edited by Oldham, was dedicated to continuing Edinburgh 1910's emphasis on the disciplined study of mission, attempting to contribute to the "science of mission."[40] He brought out the first issue in January 1912. As Latourette commented:

> The *Review* immediately took its place as the outstanding supraconfessional international journal in the field of missions. Its wide range of contributors and reviewers, from many lands and differing ecclesiastical and theological traditions, its extensive bibliographies, and its annual surveys of world mission, covering as they did Roman Catholic as well as Protestant developments, contributed notably to the nourishment of the ecumenical spirit.[41]

In due course, the IRM became the house journal of the IMC. It has continued to appear regularly and is unsurpassed as a barometer of thinking about mission over the past century.[42]

When the committee met at Lake Mohonk in 1912, it remained highly motivated to continue what had been begun at Edinburgh but took the view that it was premature to take any action on the proposed International Committee. There was still work to be done to win the confidence of the missionary societies as regards the role of such a body. Meanwhile Mott set out on an extensive tour of Asia – from Colombo to Tokyo – to raise awareness of the work of the Continuation Committee and consult about future plans. He convened twenty-one conferences on the model of Edinburgh 1910. In China, a large conference determined to drive forward the cause of Christian unity and established its own China Continuation Committee, with a requirement that not less than one-third of its members would be Chinese. Similar developments occurred in other Asian countries also, laying the foundations for National Christian Councils that would emerge in the 1920s. Within two years the Continuation Committee helped form the Conference of British Missionary Societies with its membership of forty missionary societies. The two bodies shared single premises in London, suitably named Edinburgh House. This initiative pointed the way that would be followed in many other countries also.

Meanwhile in November 1913 the Continuation Committee met in The Hague, in the Netherlands. In order to address concerns that it was going to create structures that would dominate or control the life and work of mission boards and missionary societies, the committee formulated the so-called Hague Principle: "The only Bodies entitled to determine missionary policy are the Home Boards, the Missions, and the Churches concerned."[43] This aimed to make it clear that the work being developed by the Continuation Committee was not aiming to capture initiative and influence at the expense of the existing boards and societies but rather to give them the opportunity to confer and act together in relation to challenges that they commonly shared.

---

39   WMC, ed., *World Missionary Conference, 1910*, vol. 9, 96.

40   *IRM* 1/1, 1912, 1.

41   Latourette, "Ecumenical Bearings," 363–364.

42   See *A Century of Ecumenical Missiology* (*IRM* 100/2, 2011), particularly Brian Stanley, "Edinburgh 1910 and the Genesis of the IRM," *IRM* 100/2, 2011, 149–159.

43   Continuation Committee Minutes, The Hague, Nov 14–20, 1913, 55, Minute 153, cited in: Hogg, *Ecumenical Foundations*, 161.

The Continuation Committee had planned to meet at Oxford in September 1914 but, in fact, it was never to meet again. The outbreak of World War I brought to an end the pattern of annual conferences and international commissions through which the committee had done its work since Edinburgh 1910. In terms of organizational structure, it made limited progress during the four years of its lifespan, but it did much in terms of building mutual confidence among key leaders of the Western missionary movement and developing the Hague Principle as a basis for future collaboration. It also allowed Mott and Oldham to hone their complementary leadership skills. In all these ways, essential foundations were laid for the life and work of the IMC in the coming decades.

The happy collaboration that had been developing between British and German missionary leaders suffered an abrupt setback with the outbreak of the war. Indeed, the entire missionary enterprise worldwide suffered much disruption as the war took its toll. German missions were particularly severely affected, with many missionaries being interned or repatriated. Here, however, the international missionary cooperation developed through Edinburgh 1910 showed its value as support was provided to enable the German missions to continue in these difficult circumstances. National bodies played a generous role in this: the National Missionary Council of India, the China Continuation Committee, the Conference of British Missionary Societies and the FMCNA. Though the Continuation Committee as such was not meeting or functioning, the common cause and collaboration that it represented was growing in strength as it met the challenges of the war. As Richey Hogg concludes: "Thus during the war in a limited but real sense, what may be spoken of as the Continuation Committee became what the International Missionary Council was later to be – a body composed of and functioning through national councils."[44]

As the war drew towards a close, the Standing Committee of the Conference of British Missionary Societies took the initiative to form a new body to guide international collaboration on missionary matters during the transition from war to peace. It was called the Emergency Committee of Cooperating Missions and comprised eight American and six British representatives, along with one representative from any other country wishing to be involved. Relating to governments on behalf of missionary bodies in relation to the many issues raised by the war was an important part of the Emergency Committee's work. Hence it was agreed that it should move its offices from Edinburgh to London, initially to temporary quarters while plans were made to acquire permanent office premises to be named Edinburgh House. Deep mutual suspicion and misunderstanding had built up between the German missionary leadership on the one hand and the British and American leaders of international missionary cooperation on the other. Bridging this gulf was a major item on the agenda of the Emergency Committee.

Some progress had been made by the time an *ad hoc* international missionary conference was convened at Crans, near Geneva in Switzerland, in June 1920. This was a meeting neither of the Continuation Committee nor of the Emergency Committee but included many of the personnel who had become familiar in this sphere since Edinburgh 1910. The conference dealt with political issues of the postwar context, particularly the return of German missionaries to their former fields. It also addressed the question of what form of international missionary organization would be needed to meet the challenges of a new era. On the basis of a proposal from Oldham, it took up the Hague Principle of 1913 and envisaged a body based on the national councils that would concern itself with distinctively international issues. Already Oldham could see that this new body might be the stepping stone to "something that may represent the beginnings of a world league of churches."[45]

---

44   Hogg, *Ecumenical Foundations*, 169.

45   Joseph H. Oldham, "International Missionary Organization," cited in: Hogg, *Ecumenical Foundations*, 197.

Meanwhile it was agreed that the responsibilities of both the Continuation Committee and the Emergency Committee would be handed on to the new international committee when it was formed. Importantly, this included the *IRM*. During the tumultuous decade that followed Edinburgh 1910, the foundations had been laid on which the IMC would be built.

6   Foundation of the Council: Lake Mohonk 1921

After having existed in shadow form during the years since Edinburgh 1910, the IMC formally came into being at Lake Mohonk, in the autumn of 1921. By this time national agencies of missionary cooperation had been created in many countries, and it was these that sent their delegates to Lake Mohonk to found the IMC. It was mainly a North American and European affair with a small number of Asian delegates also included. Conspicuously absent were the Germans who had concluded that they could not participate in international conferences so long as they were placed under restrictions as a result of the war.

The preparatory meeting at Crans had proposed the title "International Missionary Committee" but at Lake Mohonk it was decided to change "Committee" to "Council" with a view to making it clear that it was not an executive body. The Hague Principle remained fundamental and it was spelled out that, "the only bodies entitled to determine missionary policy are the missionary societies and boards, or the churches which they represent, and the churches on the mission field."[46] Drawing on the protocol established at Edinburgh 1910, the new council also resolved that it would not act or speak "on any matter involving an ecclesiastical or doctrinal question, on which the members of the Council or bodies constituting the Council may differ among themselves."[47] The council was united on the basis of shared commitment to the missionary task of bearing witness to the gospel of Jesus Christ, and its members would agree to differ on points of doctrine and polity on which they held divergent positions.

The responsibilities that it accepted included stimulating thinking and investigation on missionary questions, coordinating the endeavors of the various national missionary agencies, bringing about united action when necessary, lobbying on behalf of religious freedom and issues of justice, publishing the *IRM*, and calling a world missionary conference as and when required.[48] It was agreed that there would be 70 members, all delegates of national missionary agencies, with 20 from the FMCNA, 14 from the Conference of British Missionary Societies, 6 from the German DEMA. The remaining places were allocated among smaller national bodies. Additionally, provision was made for the cooption of up to 10 members from areas not otherwise represented – Africa, the Near East, and Latin America. The inclusion of Latin America was particularly significant since its exclusion from Edinburgh 1910 still rankled. The constitution also provided for the appointment of a 12-person committee to guide the affairs of the council between meetings.

The Lake Mohonk meeting also addressed a question that would run right through the entire history of the IMC: the relation between foreign missions and indigenous churches. It put to missionary societies a series of questions that were far-reaching in their significance:

(1) whether the time had not come for missionaries to work under the authority of nationals and with the same ecclesiastical status as their national colleagues? (2) Whether matters affecting the program of a younger church ought not to be discussed

---

46   IMC Minutes, Lake Mohonk NY, Oct 1–6, 1921, 34, cited in: Hogg, *Ecumenical Foundations*, 204.

47   IMC Minutes, Lake Mohonk, 1921, 40, cited in: Hogg, *Ecumenical Foundations*, 204.

48   IMC Minutes, Lake Mohonk, 1921, 36, cited in: Latourette, "Ecumenical Bearings," 367.

by missionaries and nationals together as representatives of the church rather than by a predominantly missionary group? (3) Whether all funds from abroad ought not to be administered jointly by the national church and the contributing agency? (4) And how best to encourage and train indigenous leadership for the different kinds of work in each country?[49]

The council also took steps to champion the readmission of German missionaries to territories from which they had been excluded as a result of the war. Mott was elected as chairman; Oldham and Abbe Livingston Warnshuis, an American missionary to China, were elected secretaries. The officers were given wide-ranging remits to investigate current international conditions, particularly in regard to missionary freedom and social issues, as these bore on the work of the missions. Oldham was reappointed editor of the *IRM*.

The council met again in Oxford in July 1923 and wrestled once again with the question of how to accommodate theological differences. It concluded that, "our differences in doctrine, great though in some instances they are, have not hindered us from profitable cooperation in counsel. When we have gathered together, we have experienced a growing unity among ourselves, in which we recognize the influence of the Holy Spirit."[50] Within a framework of accepting doctrinal differences, missionary agencies had shown that they could cooperate effectively on such matters as Bible translation, production and distribution of Christian literature, the running of schools, colleges and medical facilities, and the training of missionaries.

During the 1920s German missions remained a major concern of the IMC, and extensive efforts were made to channel support, both in terms of finance and personnel, to missions that had been cut off from their original resource base in Germany. Related to this was responsibility for negotiations with government, in which securing permission for German missionaries to return to their former fields remained a central concern. Education was another major preoccupation – seeking to coordinate and provide direction to the vast educational enterprise of the missionary movement. Connected to this was the promotion of Christian literature as in many contexts publishing and dissemination of literature was in its infancy. A major focus on Africa found expression in an influential conference organized by the IMC at Le Zoute in Belgium in 1926. Social questions were also prominent on the agenda, particularly the opium trade, race, slavery, and industrialization. The wide extent of its program called for a strengthening of the core staff, and in 1927 William Paton, after extensive experience in India, joined Oldham and Warnshuis to begin his influential career in the secretariat. Together with Mott they formed an "extraordinarily able corps of officers," remarked Latourette, who "through their extensive travels and wide contacts ... helped to knit together in growing understanding and fellowship Christians of many lands and confessions."[51] By now it was time to bring to fruition the plans for another major conference to undertake a largescale examination of the most urgent issues facing the missionary movement.

7 Jerusalem 1928: Mission and the Kingdom of God

The first full meeting of the IMC took place in Jerusalem in 1928. This gathering saw the younger churches much more widely represented than they had been at Edinburgh, revealing the direction of travel for the coming century. Of the 250 participants, more than 50 were nationals from the mission field. "Among them," recalled Richey

49 IMC Minutes, Lake Mohonk, 1921, 46–48, cited in: Hogg, *Ecumenical Foundations*, 207.

50 IMC Minutes, Oxford, 1923, 37–38, cited in: Hogg, *Ecumenical Foundations*, 217.

51 Latourette, "Ecumenical Bearings," 368.

Hogg, "one saw a bright yellow Indian sari, the blue silk gown of a Chinese scholar, here a fez, there a turban ... here was gathered the first truly representative, global assembly of Christians in the long history of the church."[52] The voices of "national" leaders were influential and made it clear that the time had come for the indigenous churches to take responsibility for mission in their contexts. This would mean a change of role for the missions, involving handover of property and mission staff coming under the authority of the churches with which they served. From Jerusalem onwards it would be the indigenous churches rather than the Western missions that would become central to missionary thinking. Taking advantage of the Jerusalem venue, the IMC also seized the opportunity to establish fraternal relations with Orthodox Churches, another initiative that would have far-reaching effects.

It also meant that the division of the world into "Christian" and "non-Christian" on geographical, territorial terms had already become obsolete. The vitality and maturity of the churches on the mission field on the one hand, and the growing secularism of the so-called Christian world on the other, made it plain that a Christendom understanding of the world was no longer serviceable. The challenges involved in mission to a secularized Western world were registered for the first time at Jerusalem. "We go to Jerusalem," stated the Quaker Rufus Jones in an influential address, "not as members of a Christian nation to convert other nations which are not Christian, but as Christians within a nation far too largely non-Christian, who face within their own borders the competition of a rival movement as powerful, as dangerous, as insidious as any of the great historic religions."[53] Such conviction resonated with the conference, which identified secularism – variously described

as humanism, scientism, and materialism – as the most significant challenge to faith.

There was also a much sharper awareness of the dangers posed to the missionary enterprise by the risk of being complicit in colonialism. Far more than had been the case at Edinburgh, a hermeneutic of suspicion was applied to the relation between the missionary enterprise and the global domination of the West. This led to greater sensitivity to the pitfalls facing Western-based missions and a determination to ground mission on a theological and Christological basis. Rather than thinking of the advance of Christian mission simply in quantitative terms, there was new attention to the qualitative aspect. This would have far-reaching effects. As Jooseop Keum comments: "Since Jerusalem, the two different approaches, the quantitative and qualitative concept of mission, have become a missiological backbone of the division between ecumenical and evangelical perspectives in mission."[54]

The Jerusalem Conference followed the pattern of Edinburgh in commissioning comprehensive preparatory studies. These studies started already to deconstruct the terms on which the Edinburgh Conference had been held. Whereas Edinburgh 1910 worked on an assumption of agreement about the content of the Christian message, by the time of Jerusalem 1928 this was an issue that was very much at question. World War I had badly shaken confidence in Western civilization as the embodiment of the gospel, prompting critical reflection on the substance of the Christian message. Metaphors of warfare and conquest no longer seemed appropriate in relation to other faiths. In fact, delegates such as William Ernest Hocking were inclined to think much more in terms of mutual understanding and cooperation between the different faiths, a trend that would soon find

---

52   Hogg, *Ecumenical Foundations*, 244.

53   *The Christian Life and Message in Relation to Non-Christian Systems, Report of the Jerusalem Meeting of the International Missionary Council, March 24th–April 8th, 1928*, vol. 1, London, Oxford University Press, 1928, 273; Hogg, *Ecumenical Foundations*, 247.

54   Jooseop Keum, "Beyond Dichotomy: Towards a Convergence Between the Ecumenical and Evangelical Understanding of Mission in Changing Landscapes," in: Margunn Serigstad Dahle, Lars Dahle & Knud Jørgensen, eds., *The Lausanne Movement: A Range of Perspectives*, Oxford, Regnum, 2014, 383–398, here 386.

more extensive expression in the Laymen's Foreign Mission Inquiry of 1932–1933.[55]

Others were alarmed by this new direction of thought and feared that the missionary movement was moving towards syncretism. European continental delegates met with John Mott in Cairo two days before the conference to express such misgivings.[56] There was new sharpness to the challenge of how to be irenic towards people of other faiths without undermining confidence in the gospel of Christ. The Council Statement, drafted by William Temple, at that time archbishop designate of York and later archbishop of Canterbury, and Robert Elliott Speer, long-serving secretary of the American Presbyterian Mission, sought to reflect a new sensitivity to adherents of other faiths while strongly affirming the core of Christian belief.

Another major point of tension was the question of how far Christian mission should be concerned with effecting change in the social and economic order as opposed to an exclusive concentration on personal conversion and the growth of the church. Again, Anglo-Saxon perspectives on social witness contrasted with continental Europeans' insistence that the focus on eternal salvation must not be compromised. Jerusalem already attempted to offer a both-and rather than an either-or approach, arguing that the church's task is "both to carry the message of Christ to the individual soul, and to create a Christian civilization within which all human beings can grow to their full stature."[57]

The preparatory studies revealed a broadening scope of enquiry, including such topics as religious education, race conflict, industrialization, and rural problems. This widening of the understanding of mission was energizing for some, but others feared that this rethinking of Christian mission in terms of its engagement with the political and economic structures of society was moving in the direction of the Social Gospel and losing its evangelistic edge. Theologically, this found expression in an intense debate about the meaning of Kingdom of God between those who argued that it was essentially built by men, and others who disagreed with this position. This tension was recognized, though perhaps not resolved, in the reference in the council's statement to working "in preparation for the coming of the Kingdom of God in its fullness."[58]

The Jerusalem Conference also provided the opportunity for the council to renew its organization to take account of the increased presence and profile of indigenous churches from parts of the world that had once been regarded as the mission field. Membership of the committee responsible to guide the affairs of the IMC between conferences was increased to 37 to allow broader representation particularly from the younger churches. The council also elected three vice chairs: Cheng Jingyi, general secretary of the National Christian Council of China, St Clair George Alfred Donaldson, bishop of Salisbury in the UK and Baroness Willelmina Elisabeth van Boetzelaer van Dubbeldam from the Netherlands. After the Jerusalem Conference, Mott relinquished other responsibilities in order to be more fully committed to his work as chairman of the IMC. William Paton succeeded Oldham as editor of the *IRM*. During the troubled decade of the 1930s the IMC had a very active period, seeking to support the missionary cause in times of change. It also played an historic role in the development of worldwide Christian unity. As Hogg remarks, "for years no other body existed to knit the younger churches, through the National Christian Councils, into the organized fabric of world Christianity. In that particular

55 See William Ernest Hocking, ed., *Rethinking Missions: A Layman's Inquiry After One Hundred Years*, New York NY, Harper & Brothers, 1932; Orville Anderson Petty, ed., *Laymen's Foreign Missions Inquiry: Supplementary Series*, 7 vols., New York NY, Harper & Brothers, 1933.

56 Hogg, *Ecumenical Foundations*, 242.

57 *The Christian Life and Message*, vol. 5, 141–143; Hogg, *Ecumenical Foundations*, 250.

58 *The Christian Life and Message*, vol. 5, 481; see discussion of this phrase in Timothy Yates, *Christian Mission in the Twentieth Century*, Cambridge, Cambridge University Press, 1994, 68.

sense the International Missionary Council for a time *was* the Ecumenical Movement."[59]

8   Tambaram 1938: The Christian Message in a Non-Christian World

The IMC held its second major international conference at Tambaram, near Madras (now Chennai) in South India in 1938. By now representatives of the younger churches were clearly in a majority with almost half of the 471 delegates coming from Asia and significant delegations from Africa and Latin America. An important backdrop to the conference was the speed at which the relationship between Western missions and indigenous churches was changing. By now it was fully apparent that responsibility for mission was transferring to the indigenous churches whose leaders set the tone at Tambaram. This dynamic meant that the church was very much at the center of attention. As John Mott stated in his opening address: "It is the Church which is to be at the center of our thinking ... the Divine Society founded by Christ and His apostles to accomplish His will in the world. It is a worshipping Society, a witnessing Society, a transforming Society – the veritable Body of Christ."[60]

The Asian delegates in particular brought a passion for church unity, arguing powerfully that the divided state of the church was proving a grave impediment to mission in their contexts. "The real significance of Madras," in Richey Hogg's assessment, "lay in what it was rather than in what it did. It was a unifying event in the life of the whole church – an event that revealed to the churches the fellowship of the church universal. No other experience made so deep an impact on those at Madras as that of the church, of a worldwide community united in love."[61] Eloquent representatives of the younger churches argued that "passionate longing ... exists in all countries for visible unity of the churches," and pled with the missionary societies and boards of the "sending" countries to work with them toward the attainment of church unity.[62] At the same time, the conference was marked by a concern for indigenization of the faith – a theme that would preoccupy generations to come. Another significant contribution to the conference was the work led by Merle Davis on the economic basis of the church and the need for the younger churches to become self-supporting. Meanwhile a group convened by Bishop Stephen Neill highlighted the urgency and importance of the development of theological education with a view to the formation of the leaders required by the younger churches.

The question of the Christian understanding of other religions and its implications for missiology remained prominent. An important part of the preparation for Tambaram was a commission to the Dutch missiologist Hendrik Kraemer to "state the fundamental position of the Christian church as a witness-bearing body in the modern world, relating this to conflicting views of the attitude to be taken by Christians towards other faiths and dealing in detail with the evangelistic approach to the great non-Christian faiths."[63] The result was a book entitled *The Christian Message in a Non-Christian World*.[64] This volume represented a very different approach to that of the Laymen's Foreign Mission Enquiry of the early 1930s. The church, Kraemer argued, draws its true identity "from the apostolic urgency of gladly witnessing to

---

59   Hogg, *Ecumenical Foundations*, 283 (italics original).

60   John R. Mott, "The Possibilities of the Tambaram Meeting," in: IMC, ed., *Addresses and Other Records: International Missionary Council meeting at Tambaram, Madras, December 12th to 29th 1938*, Tambaram Series 7, London, Oxford University Press, 1939, 4.

61   Hogg, *Ecumenical Foundations*, 301.

62   IMC, ed., *The World Mission of the Church: Findings and Recommendations of the International Missionary Council, Tambaram, Madras, India, December 12th to 29th, 1938*, London, IMC, 130–131; Hogg, *Ecumenical Foundations*, 301–302.

63   IMC Ad Interim Committee Minutes, Old Jordans, 1936, cited in: Yates, *Christian Mission*, 108.

64   Hendrik Kraemer, *The Christian Message in a Non-Christian World*, London, Edinburgh House Press, 1938.

God and his saving and redeeming Power through Christ."[65] He expressed strong suspicion of any notion that the Kingdom of God would come through human effort, stressing instead the divine initiative.

Nor could Christianity, in Kraemer's view, be regarded as the fulfilment of other religions. Rather a dialectical approach was required in which the presence and action of God in other religious traditions could be affirmed but where this would always be seen in the light of the unexpectedness and "discontinuity" of God's decisive action in Jesus Christ. If missionaries lacked the confidence that Jesus was "the Way, the Truth, and the Life" how would they be able to call men and women to costly conversion? "Cast in one piece," observed Carl Hallencreutz, "his book was decisive for Tambaram 1938."[66] Kraemer's Barthian approach to some degree polarized the conference, which in the end had to acknowledge divergence as regards how to understand non-Christian religions: "As to whether the non-Christian religions as total systems of thought and life may be regarded as in some sense or to some degree manifesting God's revelation Christians are not agreed. This is a matter urgently demanding thought and study."[67] It also proved to be a matter that would remain high on the agenda of the ecumenical movement.

The rise of Nazism and the impending World War II formed an unmistakable background to the conference. China and Japan were already at war and, in this context, it was moving to see Chinese and Japanese delegates taking communion together. Kraemer's insistence on the centrality of the apostolic witness was driven, in part, by the need to counter the claims of such false absolutes as Fascism, National Socialism, and Communism. As Timothy Yates comments:

Neo-pagan darkness was indeed about to descend on Europe: it was a context of sharp polarities, when shades of grey were of little value to embattled Christians. Rather the need was for the ringing tones of the Barmen Declaration of 1934, for Barth's outright rejection of nationalist religion rooted in nature, and for Kraemer's concentration on Christ as the Light shining with absolute clarity in a world of darkness, darkness made all the more profound by way of the calls for total allegiance by fascist and communist to the state and its purposes, those pseudo-absolutes Kraemer had condemned with such great effect.[68]

9   Whitby 1947: Partnership in Obedience

The fear of war that had been so evident at Tambaram soon became a reality. The next year saw the outbreak of World War II, and the IMC was soon absorbed by practical considerations entailed in sustaining the missionary enterprise in wartime conditions, particularly the "orphaned" missions that were cut off from their normal sources of support by the war. This absorbed much of the council's energy, turning into practical effect the sense of being a world Christian communion that had been fostered by Tambaram and discovering what a postwar report to the IMC meeting at Whitby would describe as the "supranationality of missions."[69] The war years also saw major changes in the leadership of the IMC. Oldham had resigned at Madras, Mott and Warnshuis both retired in 1942, and Paton died the following year. Other leaders who had been prominent in the life of the IMC also died around this time, including Cheng Jingyi, Elisabeth van Boetzelaer, William Temple, and Vedanayagam Samuel Azariah. It was time for

65   Kraemer, *The Christian Message*, vi.

66   Carl F. Hallencreutz, *Kraemer Towards Tambaram: A Study in Hendrik Kraemer's Missionary Approach*, Uppsala, Gleerup, 1966, 307.

67   IMC, ed., *The World Mission of the Church*, 44; Hogg, *Ecumenical Foundations*, 296.

68   Yates, *Christian Mission*, 124.

69   IMC Minutes, Whitby, 1947, 40–45, cited in: Hogg, *Ecumenical Foundations*, 318.

a new generation of leadership: John W. Decker, in New York, and Norman Goodall, in London, were appointed secretaries, and the Whitby meeting appointed John A. Mackay as chairman and Charles W. Ranson to the newly created post of general secretary.

After all the disruptions of the war years, the IMC was eager to reconvene for an "enlarged meeting" of its committee. While not a full meeting of the council, like Jerusalem and Madras, the meeting at Whitby in Canada in 1947 took on something of the character of the WMCs that by tradition had been held on a decennial basis. Postwar austerity meant a smaller gathering than previously. "Expectant Evangelism" was its theme as it sought to return to core business after the disruptions of the war years. Having come through the chaotic environment of wartime, the delegates were determined to focus afresh on the centrality and urgency of the proclamation of the gospel. The small size of the gathering – just 112 delegates – perhaps fostered the intimacy between representatives of the older and younger churches which led to a sense of equality and mutuality such as had never been known before. As it was expressed by a Chinese delegate: "At Jerusalem and Madras the relationship between older and younger churches was like that between a father and his children. Here it is like that between an older brother and a younger brother."[70] The result was a new emphasis on "partnership in obedience" as the keynote of their working together. They understood themselves to be partners in obedience to the will of God in the fulfilment of a common task. Foreign missionary and indigenous pastor were called to work together, on an equal basis, in the task of evangelism. By this time Latin American leaders had become familiar figures in IMC gatherings, their exclusion from Edinburgh 1910 becoming a distant memory.[71] Despite its small size there was a compel-

ling sense that the gathering represented the worldwide unity of the Christian faith, now reassembled after the fragmentation of the war years.

10   Willingen 1952: *missio Dei*

The global landscape was changing rapidly when the IMC met at Willingen in Germany in 1952. Two world wars had fatally undermined the moral authority of the "Christian" West. The advent of the UN placed a premium on mutual understanding and cooperation among nations and implicitly questioned the role of the Christian missionary enterprise. Colonial rule had come to an end in south Asia and was increasingly under question in Africa. The Communist revolution in China had led to the expulsion of all missionaries from what had been regarded as a premier mission field. Meanwhile the continuing rise of secularism in the West eroded the strength of what had once been the "home base" of missions. It was a shattering and soul-searching time for missionary leaders. Familiar features were disappearing from the landscape. The outlook was unclear, confusing, and threatening. Mission, it appeared, was in crisis. As Max Warren, general secretary of the Anglican CMS put it: "We have to be ready to see the day of missions, as we have known them, as having already come to an end."[72]

The crisis prompted a quest for a deeper theological meaning and justification of mission. The far-reaching result was a new focus on an understanding of mission as the mission of God. Anthropocentric and ecclesiocentric conceptions of mission gave way to theocentric, Christocentric, and basileio-centric conceptions. Though the term *missio Dei* was not used at Willingen, it was coined soon afterwards by German missionary leader Karl Hartenstein to describe the main theological

---

70   Hogg, *Ecumenical Foundations*, 340–341.

71   See further J. Samuel Escobar, "The Missiological Significance of Latin American Protestantism," *IRM* 100/2, 2011, 232–243.

72   Lesslie Newbigin, "Mission to Six Continents," in: *A History of the Ecumenical Movement*, vol. 2, Harold E. Fey, ed., *The Ecumenical Advance (1948–1968)*, London, SPCK, 1970, 171–197, here 178.

emphasis of the conference. This was truly a new departure in the understanding of mission, one that rested on the pioneering theological work of Karl Barth. As David Bosch observed:

> In the new image mission is not primarily an activity of the church, but an attribute of God. God is a missionary God ... Mission is thereby seen as a movement from God to the world; the church is viewed as an instrument for that mission. There is church because there is mission, not vice versa. To participate in mission is to participate in the movement of God's love toward people, since God is a fountain of sending love.[73]

This new understanding has subsequently been recognized as a decisive paradigm shift for ecumenical missiology and has ever more widely commended itself as a key to understanding the meaning of mission. This led, in turn, to the emergence of consensus about the missionary character of the church. This conviction would soon find its most celebrated expression in the opening words of *Ad gentes*, the Vatican II's statement on mission: "The Church on earth is by its very nature missionary since, according to the plan of the Father, it has its origin in the mission of the Son and the Holy Spirit."[74] Such an understanding of mission was anticipated by the Willingen Conference.

This theological understanding of mission provided an anchor in changing times. However, it also provoked questions that would be unsettling in the missionary movement. *Missio Dei* was an inspiring but also an ambiguous conception. For some it represented a radically new conception of mission in which the world rather than the church was the primary locus of God's activity. The Dutch missiologist Johannes Christiaan Hoekendijk was an especially strong critic of the church-centric understanding of mission and urged that the Kingdom of God should be understood on the much broader basis of the totality of the action of God in the life of the world, particularly within political, cultural, and scientific movements of the time.[75] This proved to be a fertile line of thought that would have great influence in the ecumenical movement in the 1960s and 1970s. Yet it also provoked a reaction from those who feared that the distinct meaning of Christian mission was being dissolved and who continued to view the planting and growth of churches as the core of the missionary project. The Willingen Conference worked hard to hold these emphases in tension, particularly by grounding the missionary calling of the church in the Triune life of God and by its oft-quoted dictum that there is no participation in Christ without participation in his mission to the world.

Once again national Christian leaders from the younger churches spoke eloquently of the urgency and importance of church unity. They were acutely conscious that the integrity of mission depended on the unity of the church. The gospel of reconciliation would always sound hollow if it did not give rise to reconciled communities. A significant development at Willingen, in terms of participation, was the presence of Pentecostal leaders. Moreover, they prepared a statement that was submitted by David du Plessis and included in the official record:

> After nearly half a century of misunderstanding and ostracism, for which they recognize they have not been entirely without blame on their own part, the Pentecostal Churches offer their fellowship in Christ to the whole of the Church in this grave hour of her history. They believe they have something to gain by

---

73   David J. Bosch, *Transforming Mission: Paradigm Shifts in Theology of Mission*, Maryknoll NY, Orbis Books, 390.

74   *Ad gentes* § 2, in: Austin Flannery, ed., *Vatican Council II: The Conciliar and Post Conciliar Documents*, Northport NY, Costello, 1975, 814; see further Stephen B. Bevans, "Mission at the Second Vatican Council (1962–1965)," in: Stephen B. Bevans, ed., *A Century of Catholic Mission: Roman Catholic Missiology 1910 to the Present*, Oxford, Regnum, 2013, 101–111.

75   See Johannes Christiaan Hoekendijk, *The Church Inside Out*, Philadelphia PA, Westminster Press, 1966.

larger fellowship with all who truly belong to Christ. They are greatly encouraged by many worldwide tokens that old prejudices are melting and a new era of mutual appreciation dawning. Brethren, let us receive one another, as Christ also received us to the glory of God.[76]

11 Achimota 1957–1958: Church and Mission

When the WCC was formed in 1948, the IMC was formally "in association." The officers of the IMC had been very significant players in the inception of the WCC, with Mott and Paton serving on the provisional committee that laid the groundwork.[77] In 1948 a joint committee of the WCC and IMC was formed, and soon the question was raised as to whether the two global bodies should be integrated. With Tambaram having brought a clear understanding that responsibility for mission lies primarily with the church, there was a strong theological argument in favor of integration. A WCC meeting at Rolle in 1951 had adopted an influential statement on "The Calling of the Church to Mission and Unity," drafted by Lesslie Newbigin, which argued at a theological level for the integral connection of mission and unity.[78] It stated that "the obligation to take the Gospel to the whole world, and the obligation to draw all Christ's people together, both rest upon Christ's whole work and are indissolubly connected. Every attempt to separate these tasks violates the wholeness of Christ's ministry to the world."[79] Others, however, were concerned that a church-centric view of mission was inhibiting missionary initiative. Max Warren argued that "today the gravest embarrassment of the mission societies lies in the actual unwillingness of the younger churches to set them free to perform the tasks for which they properly exist – the pioneering of those new frontiers, not necessarily geographical, which have not yet been marked with a cross."[80] There were also fears among mission activists that the mission agenda would be swamped by the ecclesial and bureaucratic concerns of a body like the WCC. This debate came to a head when the IMC met at Achimota, Ghana, at the end of 1957.

As well as wrestling with the question of the best institutional framework in which to advance ecumenical commitment to mission, the Achimota Conference was concerned with the very definition of mission. As Mark Laing remarks:

> At one level the debate on integration was about organizational structures. But beyond structural obsessiveness lay more searching theological questions on the relationship between mission and church. By the middle of the twentieth century there was a realization that the Protestant missionary movement had reached a crisis. Factors within and outside the movement forced those engaged in missions to the realization that missions not only needed to be reorganized, the concept of mission itself required rehabilitation.[81]

76 Norman Goodall, ed., *Missions Under the Cross: Addresses Delivered at the Enlarged Meeting of the Committee of the International Missionary Council at Willingen, in Germany, 1952*, London, Edinburgh House Press, 1953, 250.

77 Latourette, "Ecumenical Bearings," 372.

78 See Lesslie Newbigin, *Unfinished Agenda: An Updated Autobiography*, Edinburgh, Saint Andrew Press, 1993, 133–134; Mark T.B. Laing, *From Crisis to Creation: Lesslie Newbigin and the Reinvention of Christian Mission*, Eugene OR, Pickwick, 2012, 61–69.

79 Lesslie Newbigin, "The Missionary Dimension of the Ecumenical Movement," *EcRev* 14/2, 1962, 2017–215, here 208; Michael Kinnamon & Brian E. Cope, eds., *The Ecumenical Movement: An Anthology of Key Texts and Voices*, Geneva, WCC Publications, 1997, 343.

80 Warren, cited in: Steven Cornelis graaf van Randwijck, "Some Reflections of a Mission Board Secretary," in: Ronald Kenneth Orchard, ed., *The Ghana Assembly of the International Missionary Council, 28th December, 1957, to 8th January, 1958*, London, Edinburgh House Press, 1958, 94.

81 Laing, *From Crisis to Creation*, 33.

The *missio Dei* thinking which had emerged at Willingen was again prominent. The German missiologist Walter Freytag spoke of how missions had lost their way and suggested that understanding mission broadly as God's reality in this world was the best basis on which to face the future. While some were ready to embrace this new understanding of mission, others espoused a more traditional evangelistic approach. It was a point of divergence that was to have far-reaching effects.

An influential initiative of the Achimota Conference was the establishment of the generously endowed Theological Education Fund, which would play a significant role in enabling the development of theological education in the younger churches. In the years to come it would foster and resource the training and formation of many of those who were to provide leadership to the ecumenical movement. Lesslie Newbigin, who had been an increasingly influential figure in the IMC during the postwar years, was elected chairman of the council at Achimota and soon afterwards was seconded by the Church of South India to serve fulltime as general secretary. To him fell the task of guiding the IMC through the process of integration with the WCC.[82]

12   New Delhi 1961: Integration of IMC and WCC

While there were structural and organizational arguments in favor of the integration of the IMC and the WCC, it was also driven by the theological conviction that church and mission belonged together. For Lesslie Newbigin, IMC general secretary, the unity of the church was essential to the integrity of mission just as much as its missionary nature was essential to the integrity of the church. As he looked to the New Delhi assembly where the two councils would be integrated, he emphasized the theological and evangelical rationale:

I have sought to remind you of the deep interconnection between our two councils from the very beginning of their histories, and of the source of this interconnection in the nature of the Gospel itself. Mission and unity are two sides of the same reality, or rather two ways of describing the same action of the living Lord who wills that all should be drawn to Himself. But it would be a false simplification to suggest that within the whole ecumenical movement, the IMC stands for mission and the WCC for unity. A moment's reflection on the history of the two councils is enough to dispel the idea. From the Edinburgh Conference onwards, the IMC has been profoundly concerned about unity. No stronger call for visible reunion has come from any meeting than those which were given by the IMC conferences at Tambaram in 1938 and at Willingen in 1952.[83]

There was thus a theological imperative driving the integration process, as well as practical and organizational considerations. This found expression in a change to the "basis" of the WCC at the New Delhi assembly where integration was formally enacted. Originally, the WCC had identified itself as "a fellowship of churches which accept our Lord Jesus Christ as God and Savior." At New Delhi the verb "accept" was replaced by "confess" and a new phrase was added: "and therefore seek to fulfill together their common calling to the glory of the one God, Father, Son, and Spirit." This gave the WCC a much more missionary orientation as integration with the IMC was recognized in fundamental constitutional terms.[84]

However, the resistance to integration that had found expression at Achimota had by no means abated. It was viewed with deep suspicion by a

82   Geoffrey Wainwright, *Lesslie Newbigin: A Theological Life*, Oxford, Oxford University Press, 2000, 9.

83   Newbigin, "The Missionary Dimension of the Ecumenical Movement," 208; Kinnamon & Cope, eds., *The Ecumenical Movement*, 343.

84   WCC, ed., *The New Delhi Report: The Third Assembly of the World Council of Churches, 1961*, London, SCM Press, 1962, 152–159; Laing, *From Crisis to Creation*, 120.

growing evangelical constituency. IMC General Secretary Norman Goodall estimated that, in 1957, 70% of foreign missionaries were American. Of these only 42% belonged to agencies that related to the National Christian Council of Churches. The other 58% worked with agencies that did not cooperate with the IMC or WCC.[85] This growing evangelical constituency was forming its own networks that were often defined by their opposition to the trends evident in the IMC and WCC. The Protestant missionary movement was increasingly marked by a sharp division between "Ecumenicals" and "Evangelicals." As Mark Laing observes: "The loose, broad-based association the IMC had maintained for decades was fractured, and the relationship between evangelicals and 'ecumenicals' became increasingly polarized and antagonistic."[86]

Though integration, ironically, was to lead to a fragmentation of the missionary movement, its historic significance cannot be underestimated. As Stephen Neill remarked:

> This was indeed a revolutionary moment in Church history. More than two hundred Church bodies in all parts of the world, assembled in the persons of their official representatives, had solemnly declared themselves in the presence of God to be responsible as Churches for the evangelization of the whole world. Such an event had never taken place in the history of the Church since Pentecost.[87]

The assembly gave the following mandate to the Department of World Mission and Evangelism:

> To assist churches, missions and other Christian bodies to recognize and draw the

practical conclusions from the fact that: (1) The Christian mission is one throughout the world, for the Gospel is the same and the need of salvation is the same for all men. (2) This world mission has a base which is worldwide and is not confined to the areas once regarded as constituting "Western Christendom." (3) The mission implies a reaching out both to one's own neighborhood and "to the ends of the earth."[88]

This latter point was emphasized in an influential paragraph of the New Delhi report which was drafted by Lesslie Newbigin:

> We believe that the unity which is both God's will and his gift to his Church is being made visible as all in each place who are ... reaching out in witness and service to all and who at the same time are united with the whole Christian fellowship in all places and all ages in such wise that ministry and members are accepted by all, and that all can act and speak together as occasion requires for the tasks to which God calls his people.[89]

The interrelation of the universal horizon and the local congregational expression of church life proved to be a constant preoccupation of ecumenical missiology in the years to come.

Another influential development at New Delhi was the admission of several Orthodox Churches to full membership of the WCC. From this point onwards their perspectives would exercise growing influence on the ecumenical understanding of mission, through such characteristic themes as the cosmic character of salvation, the eschatological nature of mission, and the duty to incarnate the gospel in every culture.[90] Soon Vatican II would

85   Laing, *From Crisis to Creation*, 49.
86   Mark Laing, "The Church Is the Mission: Integrating the IMC with the WCC," *IRM* 100/2, 2011, 216–231, here 218.
87   Stephen Neill, *The Church and Christian Union*, London, Oxford University Press, 1968, 108–109; Yates, *Christian Mission*, 157.
88   Newbigin, "Mission to Six Continents," 188.
89   WCC, ed., *The New Delhi Report*, 116; Laing, *From Crisis to Creation*, 202.
90   Anastasios Yannoulatos, "The Purpose and Motive of Mission," *IRM* 54, 1965, 281–297.

open the way for greatly increased involvement of the Roman Catholic Church in ecumenical missiology. Though it never became a member church of the WCC, from the 1960s the Roman Catholic Church became an influential collaborator in ecumenical missiological endeavor.

13 The IMC: A Retrospect

Though always a small operation in terms of staffing and budget, the IMC occupied a position of no little significance during the first half of the 20th century as it provided a common platform for thinking and action on the part of the various missionary societies and boards that had emerged during the preceding century. Perhaps even more significantly it proved to be the instrument through which the younger churches that were emerging in Asia, Africa, Latin America, and Oceania were drawn in to a worldwide Christian communion. It also contributed much to the developing understanding of the missionary dimension of Christianity – the "science of missions" – as is evident from the pages of its influential journal *IRM*. On such matters as the theology of mission, the nature of evangelism, theology of other religions, and a wide range of social questions, the IMC was an indispensable agency in creating shared understanding and common purpose on a global basis.

Its commitment to the Hague Principle of 1913, that decision making and action lay with each of its member bodies, and that it claimed no governing authority, limited the role of the IMC to one of coordination and recommendation of policy. Yet it also made possible the creation of a network of collaboration that spanned the globe, fostering and deepening the desire for unity that had driven its development since Edinburgh 1910. The IMC's integration with the WCC in 1961 ensured that its institutional memory would continue to inform the advance of the ecumenical movement as it moved to a new stage.

Bibliography

Clements, Keith, *Faith on the Frontier: A Life of J.H. Oldham*, Edinburgh, T&T Clark, 1999.

Hogg, William Richey, *Ecumenical Foundations: A History of the International Missionary Council and Its Nineteenth-Century Background*, New York NY, Harper, 1952; Eugene OR, Wipf & Stock, 2002.

Hopkins, Charles Howard, *John R. Mott (1865–1955): A Biography*, Grand Rapids MI, Eerdmans, 1979.

IRM 1–51, 1912–1962.

Kinnamon, Michael & Brian E. Cope, eds., *The Ecumenical Movement: An Anthology of Key Texts and Voices*, Geneva, WCC Publications, 1997.

Laing, Mark T.B., *From Crisis to Creation: Lesslie Newbigin and the Reinvention of Christian Mission*, Eugene OR, Pickwick, 2012.

Latourette, Kenneth Scott, "Ecumenical Bearings of the Missionary Movement and the International Missionary Council," in: *A History of the Ecumenical Movement*, vol. 1, Ruth Rouse & Stephen C. Neill, eds., *1517–1948*, London, SPCK, 1954, 351–402.

Newbigin, Lesslie, "Mission to Six Continents," in: *A History of the Ecumenical Movement*, vol. 2, Harold E. Fey, ed., *The Ecumenical Advance (1948–1968)*, London, SPCK, 1970, 171–197.

Ross, Kenneth R. & others, eds., *Ecumenical Missiology: Changing Landscapes and New Conceptions of Mission*, Oxford, Regnum, 2016.

Stanley, Brian, *The World Missionary Conference, Edinburgh 1910*, Grand Rapids MI, Eerdmans, 2009.

Wainwright, Geoffrey, *Lesslie Newbigin: A Theological Life*, Oxford, Oxford University Press, 2000.

Yates, Timothy, *Christian Mission in the Twentieth Century*, Cambridge, Cambridge University Press, 1994.

Index of Names

Abbot, George   136
Abbott, Lyman   394–395, 404, 406
Abraham, William J.   223
Achleitner, Wilhelm   431n
Acton, John E.E.D.   170n, 172n, 185n, 286
Adam, Karl   665, 667
Adam, Will   31n, 645n
Adams, Henry C.   394
Addams, Jane   444
Afanasev, Nicholas N.   24n, 34–35, 489, 492, 496–500
Afanasieff, Marianne   497n
Agostino, Marc   694n
Ahn, Kyo-Seong   427n
Ainslie, Peter   625n–627
Airhart, Phyllis D.   77
Aksakov, Ivan S.   189, 200–203, 205, 209
Aksakov, Konstantin S.   187, 189, 202
Aksakov, Sergey T.   189
Albanese, Catherine L.   48n, 65
Alberigo, Giuseppe   2n, 9n–11n, 15–17, 75n, 78, 470n–471n, 706n
Albright, Raymond W.   618n–619n
Aleksei I of Russia   205
Aleksov, Bojan   114n
Aletti, Jean-Noëlata   455n, 473
Alexander I, Tsar of Russia   245
Alexander II, Tsar of Russia   187, 204
Alexander III, Tsar of Russia   204
Alexander, Michael S.   152
Alexeev, Anatoly A.   8n
Alighieri, Dante   287
Alivisatos, Hamilcar   566, 577, 579, 582
Allchin, Arthur M.   163n
Allen, Louis   142n–143, 145n, 158n
Allenby, Edmund   435, 632
Allier, Raoul   323–324, 337, 440n
Allies, Thomas W.   145n, 148, 154, 159–160, 198
Allmen, Jean-Jacques von   31n, 74, 679n, 685n, 692n, 701
Altenstein, Karl vom Stein zum   214
Althaus, Paul   513, 524
Amanze, James   77n
Ambrose of Optina   188
Amette, Léon-Adolphe   432n
Amiet, Robert   249n
Ammann, Albert M.   249n
Anagnostopoulou, Sia   113n, 126n, 129n
Anastasiadis, Ioannis   181
Anastassiadis, Anastassios   72n, 447n
Anderson, Charles P.   624–625, 628–629n, 631–632
Anderson, Gerald H.   4n, 17

Andersson, Efraim   345n, 358n
Andræ, Tor   614
André, L.E. Tony   376n, 383
Andrea, Alfred J.   9n
Andreijev, Olga   486n
Andresen, Bernd   524n
Andrewes, Lancelot   286
Andronik (Trubachev)   625n, 485n
Anet, Henri   367
Angelini, Giuseppe   87n, 108
Anselm of Aosta   100n
Ansgar   586
Anthim I of Vidim   115
Anthimus VI of Constantinople   116
Antoniadis, Vasileios   571
Aquino, Frederick D.   141n, 147n, 154n, 161n
Arbousse-Bastide, *madame*   448n
Ariarajah, Seevaratham W.   7
Aristenos, Alexios   496
Aristotle   287
Arjakovsky, Antoine   492n
Arms, Goodsil F.   545n
Arnold, Claus   432n
Arnold, Mary   280n
Arnold, Matthew   279
Arnold, Matthieu   442n
Arnold, Thomas   274, 279–283, 287, 290
Arsenev, Nicholas S.   492, 494
Artières, Philippe   3n
Ashworth, Tony   529n
Askani, Hans-Christoph   83n
Asmussen, Hans   470
Asproulis, Nikolaos   104n
Asquith, Herbert H.   524
Astafieva, Elena   246n–247n
Aston, Nigel   138n
Atatürk, Mustafa Kemal   130
Athenagoras I of Constantinople   17n, 130, 440–441, 566
Aubert, Roger   2n, 42n, 46n–47n, 50n–51n, 54n–55n, 57n–63n, 65, 67, 69n–70, 72n, 77, 93n, 250n, 253, 449n, 461n–462n, 465n–466n, 473, 646n, 652–653n, 658, 681n–682n, 687n, 689n, 701, 708
Audoin-Rouzeau, Stéphane   430n, 434n
Auffret-Pignot, Hélène   254n–255n
Augustine of Canterbury   653, 655
Augustine of Hippo   30, 32, 147, 190, 287, 435, 495, 581
Aurelius, Erik   70n
Austen, Jane   266
Auvray, Paul   465n
Avella, Luigi   261n

Avis, Paul   134n, 136n, 153n, 161n, 178n, 220n, 237n, 248n,
        255n, 264–265n, 269n, 271n, 274n–277n, 280n–281n,
        285n–286n, 290n–291n, 298n–299, 395n, 410n, 443n,
        619n, 626n, 640n, 689n, 704n
Axenfeld, Karl   531–532n
Azariah, Vedanayagam S.   424–425, 737

Babut, Charles   444, 533
Bacuez, Louis   460
Baggs, Charles   148
Bagnall, Robert W.   407
Bahelele Nidimisina, Jacques   356–357, 361
Baillie, Donald M.   594n
Bailly, Vincent de Paul   251n
Baker, Derek   428n
Baker, Elizabeth B.   523n
Baker, Joseph A.   523–527
Balabin, Eugène (Yevgeny Petrovich)   247
Balandier, Georges   341n
Balashov, Nikolay   490n
Balch, Emily G.   327
Bale, John   142
Baltus, Urbain   487n
Banasch, Georg   664–667
Bancel, Nicolas   225n
Banks, F.E.   246n
Barakatullah, A.H. Mohammed (Maulana Barkatullah)   382
Barber, Melanie   290n
Barbolla, Manuela   71n, 709n, 712n–715n, 719n–720
Barbour, Josephus P.   405
Bardy, Gustave   443
Bares, Nikolaus   664–669
Bariéty, Jacques   446n
Barlieva, Slavia   491n
Barlow, Bernard   293n, 449n, 459n, 640, 658, 689n, 708n
Barnave, Antoine   54
Barnett, Ferdinand   407
Barnett, Stephen J.   8n
Barot, Madeleine   67
Barrett, David B.   426n
Barrington, Shute   138
Barrows, John H.   224n, 226–242
Barry, Gearóid   444n
Bärsch, Jürgen   474n–475n, 500
Barth, Karl   29n, 71, 95–100n, 108, 372, 388, 513, 515, 737, 739
Bartlet, James   633
Baruh, Lorans T.   122n
Basdekis, Athanasios   80n, 123n–124n, 127n, 130n–131
Basil the Great   495
Basil, John D.   254n
Bassett, Joshua   161n
Bate, Herbert N.   491n–492n, 581n, 584, 600, 635n–638, 667
Batiffol, Pierre   456, 605n, 630n, 650–652, 655
Batten, Samuel Z.   399
Battiscombe, Georgina   270n, 253n

Baubérot, Arnaud   328, 339
Baubérot, Jean   77n, 705n, 713n
Baudrillart, Alfred   442
Baum, Gregory   67, 253n
Baumann, Martin   705n
Baumgarten, Otto   385–386n
Baumstark, Anton   479, 494
Baur, Ferdinand C.   308, 310, 377
Bazin, René   434
Bea, Augustin   75, 78, 460–462, 469–471, 473
Beach, Harlan P.   550, 552–554n, 556n, 558
Beauduin, Édouard   641n
Beauduin, Lambert   75, 453, 474, 477, 487–489, 652–655,
        659, 679–688, 690–701, 703, 706, 709–710
Beaupère, René   462n, 465n, 467n
Bebbington, David W.   265n, 285n–287n, 299
Bechealany, Souraya   693n
Beck, Hans-Georg   176
Beck, Lewis W.   374n
Becker, Annette   430n–431n, 434n, 439n, 447n, 450, 476n
Becker, Jean-Jacques   434n
Becker, Walther   313
Becker, Werner   78
Beckx, Pierre J.   247n
Becquet, Thomas   697
Bedell, Gregory T.   181
Behr-Sigel, Élisabeth   74, 496, 684n
Bell, George K.A.   71, 290n, 294–295n, 524n, 534n–537n,
        604n, 606n, 612, 614, 618, 643, 646n, 648n–651n, 658,
        665
Bell, Hugo   715
Bellarmine, Robert   307
Bellenger, Dominic   137n
Belley, Pierre-Antoine   1n
Bellocchi, Ugo   707n
Beloeil, Dominique   74n
Belyaev, Alexander D.   255–256n
Bender, Annika   484n
Benedetti, Marina   256n
Benedict of Nursia   687
Benedict VIII (Theophylact of the counts of Tusculum), Pope
        176
Benedict XIV (Prospero Lorenzo Lambertini), Pope   52n,
        244, 258
Benedict XV (Giacomo Della Chiesa), Pope   69, 73, 127n,
        250, 260n, 444–445, 447n, 449, 454, 458–460, 528–530,
        631, 642, 645, 656, 683, 689, 706–708, 711n, 713
Benedict XVI (Joseph Ratzinger), Pope   9n, 11n, 14n, 34, 81
Benedict, Burton   225n
Benigni, Umberto   258n
Benjamin, Walter   1n
Bennett, William J.E.   155
Benoit, Pierre   456n, 468
Benrath, Gustav A.   212n–213n
Benson, Arthur C.   297n

Benson, Edward W.   293, 296–297
Benson, Richard M.   621
Bentley, William H.   353n, 369
Berdyaev, Nikolaj A.   492, 494n, 497
Beresford-Hope, Alexander   185n
Beretta, Francesco   454n
Berger, Peter   68
Berger, Teresa   7
Berggren, Ludvig   70n
Bergson, Henri   588
Bergunder, Michael   427n
Berkvens-Stevelinck, Christiane   12n
Berlis, Angela   146n
Berman, Harold J.   14, 15, 17
Berthe, Pierre-Marie   81n
Bertier de Sauvigny, Guillaume de   46n, 65
Bertram, Johannes A.   718
Bertrand, Guy M.   72n
Beshoner, Jeffrey B.   199n, 247n
Besier, Gerhard   71n, 75n, 444n–445n, 523–524n, 526n, 528n, 532n–535n, 539–540, 597n, 602n, 627n, 705n
Besson, Marius   713
Best, Geoffrey   152n
Best, Thomas F.   29n
Bestuzhev-Ryumin, Konstantin N.   203
Beta, Eduard B.F.   666–667
Bethmann-Hollweg, Theobald von   534
Bettinger, Franziskus von   442–443n
Bevans, Stephen B.   100n, 105n–106, 739
Bevel, James   405
Beyer, Michael   223
Biber, Edward G.   145
Biehl, Michael   602n
Biencourt, Caroline   443n
Bieritz, Karl-Heinrich   474n, 483n, 503n, 511n, 514n, 518n–519n
Bierma, Lyle D.   311n
Bigelow, Herbert S.   391, 404
Billing, Einar   592–593
Billing, Gottfrid   597
Billington Harper, Susan   425n
Billot, Marcel   430n
Bingham, Joseph   135n
Biot, François   67
Bird, Robert   187n–196n, 198n–200n, 209
Birkbeck, William J.   155n–156, 194n, 196n–198n
Birkner, Hans-Joachim   372–373n
Bischof, Franz X.   161n, 164, 166n–168n, 170n, 172n, 184n, 186, 469n
Bismarck, Otto von   312, 398, 446
Bivort de La Saudée, Jacques de   69–70, 642n, 647n, 650n, 658
Björkquist, Manfred   592
Blackwood, S. Arthur   414
Blaine, James G.   556

Blake, William   266
Blankenburg, Walter   502n
Blaschke, Olaf   165n
Blennerhassett, Charlotte J.   174n
Bliss, Edwin M.   548n
Bliss, William D.P.   391–392, 394, 616
Bloch, Étienne   439n
Bloch, Marc   6n, 439
Blomfield, C. James   142n, 145
Blondel, Maurice   456
Bloxam, John R.   142–143
Blûme, N. Sophie   585
Blunt, Stanley   535
Boegner, Marc   68
Boerneke, LeRoy A.   111n
Boersma, Hans   457n
Boetzelaer van Dubbeldam, Willelmina E. van   735, 737
Böger, Astrid   225n
Bogue, David   414
Böhm, Dominikus   482
Bois, Jean   249n
Boisson, Didier   246n, 263
Boland, Walthère   695
Boller, Paul F.   48n
Bolognesi, Pietro   99n
Bolotin, Norman   225n, 243
Bolshakoff, Serge   193n
Bolton, Charles A.   642n, 658
Bomm, Urbanus   483
Bonafoux-Verrax, Corinne   437n
Bonald, Louis-Gabriel-Ambroise de   245
Bonaparte, Napoleon   59–64, 138, 183, 245, 437, 654
Bonet-Maury, Gaston   376–377n
Bonhoeffer, Dietrich   10n, 17n, 71, 617n
Boniface, father   437
Boniface, Xavier   431n, 433n–434n, 437n, 439n, 443n, 448n, 450
Bonino, José M.   7
Bonney, Charles C.   224–226, 228–230, 234–235, 242
Bonomelli, Geremia   415, 727
Bonus, Arthur   378
Booty, John E.   134n, 274n
Borden, Morton   48n
Bori, Pier Cesare   8n, 17
Bornhausen, Karl   527n
Bornstedt, Maria von   671n
Bosch, David J.   100n, 106n, 739
Bosschaerts, Constantin   690, 710
Bost, John-David   440
Botrugno, Lorenzo   706n
Böttcher, Hartmut   212n
Botte, Bernard   453, 489, 696
Böttigheimer, Christoph   479n
Boudens, Robrecht   172n, 186
Bouillard, Henri   91n

Boulding, Mary C.   294n, 640n
Bourdon, Pierre   542
Bourgine, Benoît   79n, 81n, 83n
Bourne, Francis A.   438, 524, 643, 646
Bousquet, Joseph   261n
Bousset, Wilhelm   384–385, 387
Bouthillon, Fabrice   704n
Boutroux, Émile   588
Bouyer, Louis   74n, 142, 496n, 679n, 702
Bowden, John   304n
Bowie, W. Copeland   371n, 375n–378n, 389
Bowne, Borden P.   394
Bowskill, Joseph S.   364, 368, 370
Boyens, Armin   75
Boyer, Charles   395
Bradford, Amory H.   373
Braga, Erasmo   542n
Brakelmann, Günter   534n
Brambilla, Franco G.   87n, 93
Bramhall, John   275, 286
Brandi, Salvatore M.   255n, 260n
Brandreth, Henry R.T.   101n, 149n–150n, 157n, 163
Brändström, Elsa   603
Branting, Hjalmar   598
Braun, François-Marie   468
Braun, Joseph   655n
Braun, Reiner   213n
Braybrooke, Marcus   243
Bremer, Thomas   81n, 102n–104n, 106n–108
Bremmer, Jan N.   378n
Brent, Charles H.   410, 417, 439, 606, 615–618, 621–623, 625,
    628–633, 635–638, 705, 713
Brent, Henry   615
Brentano, Clemens   307n
Breton, Nicolas   82n
Bretschneider, Karl G.   215, 373
Breuer, Marc   748n
Breward, Ian   12n
Brewster, Chauncey B.   628n–629n
Bria, Ion   79n
Briand, Aristide   446
Bricout, Hélène   475n
Briggs, John H.Y.   5
Brigham, John C.   79n, 544
Brightman, Frank E.   494
Brinkley, Roberta F.   277n
Broade, George E.   174, 176, 183n
Brodd, Sven-Erik   601
Brooks, Phillips   615
Brooks, William H.   407
Brose, Olive J.   282n
Brown, Arthur J.   552–553
Brown, Hubert W.   548
Brown, Ralph W.   629n, 637n

Brown, Stewart J.   146n, 149n, 153n, 155n, 215n, 247n, 253n,
    263, 265n–267n, 275n, 299
Brown, William A.   399
Browne, Harold E.   172–173, 177, 181
Browne, Martin   293n, 449n, 459n, 640, 689n, 708n
Bruce, Alexander H. (Balfour of Burleigh)   727
Bruch, Rüdiger vom   127n
Brunstäd, Friedrich   513
Brüske, Gunda   479n–481n
Bryant, Peter J.   407
Bucer, Martin   135, 502
Buchanan, Colin   254n
Buchanan, Neil   311n, 319
Buchberger, Michael   670n, 678
Buddha   589
Budimbu, Aloni   349–351, 360
Buel, Samuel   175n
Bugenhagen, Johannes   502
Bulgakov, Sergius N.   491–494, 496–497, 499–500
Bullinger, Heinrich   135
Bülow, Bernhard H.K. von   524
Bultmann, Rudolf   373, 465, 468
Bunners, Christian   503n
Bunsen, Christian K.J. von   151–153, 377
Bunsen, Frances   153n
Buonaiuti, Ernesto   711
Burgess, Thomas   138–139
Burigana, Riccardo   76
Burkard, Dominik   469n
Burke, Edmund   274n, 279–280, 283, 287
Bürki, Bruno   474n–475n
Burnet, Gilbert   275
Burroughs, Nannie H.   399, 405, 407
Burrows, Millar   462n
Burtchaell, James T.   462n, 465n
Burwick, Frederick   277n, 299
Bushnell, Horace   393
Buss, Hansjörg   438n
Butler, Charles   139
Butler, Cuthbert   657
Butler, Joseph   280, 287
Butler, Perry   158n, 285n–286n
Byaruhanga, Christopher   93n
Byrnes, Joseph F.   60n, 65, 245n

Cabanel, Patrick   438n
Cabrol, Fernand   494
Cadier-Rey, Gabrielle   320n
Cadier, Alfred   439
Çağlayan, Murat   121
Calvert, George   46n
Calvin, John   153, 264, 314, 400, 439, 452
Cameron, G. Ronald R.   348–351n, 363, 367–370
Cameron, James M.   286n
Campbell-Bannerman, Henry   524

Canisius, Petrus 465
Cano, Melchor 94
Capel, Lee M. 612n
Capelle, Bernard 696
Capes, John M. 156n
Capitani, Ovidio 30n
Caponi, Matteo 433n
Capovilla, Loris 657
Cappuyns, Maïeul 487, 679n, 695n, 705
Carbonnier, Denis 442n
Cardijn, Joseph 680
Carey, Hilary M. 275n
Carey, William 413–414, 547, 722
Carlhian, Victor 622
Carluer, Jean-Yves 440n
Carmichael, Amy 5
Caron, Nathalie 48n
Caronello, Giancarlo 12n
Carosio, Maria 80n
Carpenter, Joseph E. 236–237, 239, 242, 375–376
Carranza, Venustiano 556
Carrel, Fernand 439
Carrichia, Marco 143
Carroll, Charles 46
Carroll, Daniel 46
Carroll, John 46–47, 411
Casalis, Georges 77n
Casel, Odo 476, 478, 480, 494
Caselli, Héctor 320n, 322n
Cassan, Stephen H. 139n
Cassian (Bezobrazov) 489
Cassian, John 11n, 496
Cassin, Matthieu 250n
Castells, Francisco de 547–548
Castelnau, Édouard de 437
Cauthen, Kenneth 372n, 389–390, 411
Cavagnini, Giovanni 127n, 444n, 449n–450, 529n, 703n, 711n
Cavazza, Antonella 10n, 17
Cavert, Samuel M. 534
Ceadel, Martin 524n
Celsus 39
Cereti, Giovanni 80n
Cerfaux, Lucien 466–468
Cerretti, Bonaventura 713
Certeau, Michel de 1n, 3n, 6, 17
Chaadayev, Petr Y. 106–107, 189
Chadwick, Henry 298
Chadwick, Owen 76n, 170n, 175n, 178n–179n, 184n–186, 292n, 704n
Chaillet, Pierre 301n, 311n, 319
Chaillot, Christine 80n
Chakravarti, Gyanendra N. 235–236
Chaline, Nadine-Josette 6n, 440n
Chalmers, Thomas 217
Chamberlain, Houston S. 378

Champ, Nicholas 439n
Chandler, Andrew 71n
Chant, Laura O. 236, 239
Chapman, Mark D. 69, 141n, 143n, 153n, 156n–159n, 161n, 163, 170n, 179n–180n, 184n, 186, 237n, 252n, 263, 265–266n, 269n, 274n, 292n, 299, 371, 381n, 388n–390n, 619n–620n
Charlemagne, Emperor 176n
Charles I, King of Great Britain and Ireland 137, 148
Charles II, King of Great Britain and Ireland 237
Charlot, John 21n, 41
Charon, Cyrille (Jean François Joseph) see Korolevskij, Cyrille
Chateaubriand, François-René 62
Chauvin, Paul 440
Chenaux, Philippe 71n, 81n, 462n–463n, 636n, 713n
Chenchiah, Pandipeddi 426
Cheng, Jingyi 728, 735, 737, 422–424
Chenu, Bruno 67n
Chenu, Marie-Dominique 2n, 465n
Cheong, Michael 108
Cherubini, Bruno 81n–82n
Chester, Samuel H. 173, 563
Chetverikov, Sergii S. 492, 494, 496
Chetwynd-Talbot, Charles H. 148
Cheza, Maurice 68n
Chickering, Roger P. 430n, 524n–525n
Chillingworth, William 275
Chilton, Bruce D. 9n
Chiron, Yves 458n–459n
Choisy, Eugène 637n
Chollet, Jean-Arthur 443
Cholvy, Gérard 320n, 324n, 327n, 334n, 339
Chomé, Jules 343n–344n
Chopelin, Paul 245n, 263
Christensen, Torben 282n
Chrysostomos (Constantinidis) 568, 575
Chrysostomos (Papadopoulos) I of Athens 578
Church, Richard W. 153
Churton, Ralph 138n
Cifres, Alejandro 70n
Cioffari, Gerardo 101n, 107n–108n
Claes, Dirk 468n
Clark, Christopher 523n
Clark, Francis E. 295n, 542n, 640n
Clark, Harriet E. 542n
Clark, John B. 394
Clarke, Sathianathan 292n
Claydon, Tony 136n
Clement I, Pope 302
Clement VIII (Ippolito Aldobrandini), Pope 244
Clements, Keith W. 70–71, 372n, 532n, 525n–526n, 528n–529n, 547n–548n, 551n–553n, 564, 725n–726n, 743
Cleveland, Stephen G. 556
Clifford, Catherine E. 27n, 75n

Clifford, John   403, 524, 527
Clovis I, King of the Franks   435
Clymer, Kenton J.   618n
Coburn, Kathleen   277n
Cochet, François   431n, 433n, 437n, 448n, 450
Cochrane, Eric   2n
Coco, Giovanni   706n, 710n, 721
Coggan, Donald   657n
Coleman, Roger   290n, 644n, 704n
Coleridge, Derwent   282n
Coleridge, Samuel T.   266, 274–280, 282–285, 287–288, 290
Colin, Pierre   459n
Colmer, John   277n
Colombo, Giuseppe   93n–94n, 108
Colombo, Paolo   88n, 90n–92n
Colonge, Paul   444n
Comber, Sydney   347
Comber, Thomas   347–350, 358
Commons, John   399
Cone, James   409–411
Congar, Yves-Marie-Joseph   6n, 9n, 31n, 34, 67–68, 74–75,
    78, 87n–88n, 90–92, 108, 194n, 300–301n, 303–304, 311,
    440, 465n, 689n, 696, 700n
Conley, Tom   3n, 17
Conord, Paul   67n
Conrad, Martin   483n
Consalvi, Ercole   60n
Constantine I, Roman Emperor   2n, 12n
Conway, John S.   444n
Conzemius, Victor   166n, 170n, 174n, 186
Cook, Joseph   553
Cooley, Charles H.   394
Cope, Brian E.   290n, 740n–741n, 743
Coppens, Joseph   466–467n, 469n
Corboli Bussi, Giovanni   253
Cornelius   195
Cornwall, Robert D.   270n
Cosin, John   136
Cosson, Alfred   440
Costermans, Monique   68n
Cotter, Anthony C.   453n–454n
Coulson, John   163n, 283–284n, 288n
Courtois, Luc   70n, 449n, 681n, 701, 708n
Coussa, G. Acacius   257n
Couturier, Paul   27, 74, 622, 696
Covert, James   296n
Cragg, Roland H.   667
Cranmer, Thomas   264, 275, 298
Cranny, Titus   249n–250n
Crapsey, Algernon S.   402n, 404
Creighton, Louise   296n
Creighton, Mandell   274n, 293, 296
Cremaschi, Lisa   485n
Cristofori, Silvia   340

Croce, Giuseppe M.   69, 74, 244n, 246n, 250n, 256n, 258n,
    260n, 263, 435n, 446n–447n, 684n, 702, 706n
Cromwell, Oliver   402n
Cross, Anthony R.   5n
Crowe, Frederick   544
Crummell, Alexander   405, 407
Cullen, Paul   139
Cullmann, Oscar   30, 33, 468
Cuming Geoffrey J.   428
Cumont, Franz   592
Currie, Robert   68
Curtis, Susan   526
Curzel, Emanuele   75n
Cuza, Alexandru I.   114
Cyprian (Kern)   489, 492n, 495n, 696
Cyprian of Carthage (Thascius Caecilius Cyprianus)   11n,
    26n, 35, 134, 495, 497–498, 505
Cyril   117, 199, 249, 251, 256
Cyril I Lucaris   136
Cyril of Jerusalem   496
Cyril VII of Constantinople   117

Daggers, Jenny   4n
Dahle, Lars   734n
Dahle, Margunn S.   734n
Dalbus, Fernand see Portal, É. Fernand
Dalferth, Ingolf   10n
Dalgairns, John D.   149n
Dallas, Démétrius   254n–255n
Daly, Fairley   724
Dam, Harm-Jan van   523n, 528n, 540
Damjanović Barišić, Darija   249n
D'Amore, Benedetto   93n
Daniel-Rops, Henri   67
Danieluk, Robert   247n
Danilevsky, Nikolay Yakovlevich   202
Dardavesis, Theodoros I.   122n
Darwin, Charles R.   394
Daskalov, Roumen   117n
Daubeny, Charles   134–135n, 138n, 142, 147
Daughrity, Dyron B.   4n
D'Avenia, Marco   1n
Davenport, Christopher (Franciscus Sancta Clara)   148, 161n
Davidson, Randall T.   422, 428, 524, 534–536, 592–593, 642,
    646, 650–651, 656, 705
Davies, David C.   346n
Davies, Noel A.   76n
Davis, Merle J.   736
Davis, Morris L.   221n
Davison, Roderic H.   119n
Dawson Vásquez, David   17, 41, 65, 83, 130, 263, 319, 339, 370,
    450, 500, 584, 638
Dawson Vásquez, Susan   17, 41, 65, 83, 130, 263, 319, 339, 370,
    450, 500, 584, 638

Dawson, Albert   544
Dawson, Christopher   146–147n
d'Ayala Valva, Luigi   485n
Debs, Eugene V.   401
de Buck, Victor   157n–158
De Chirico, Leonardo   99n
Deckart, Gerald   523n
Decker, John W.   738
De Clerck, Paul   485n
Declerck, Leo   469n
Dederen, Raoul   254n
De Dobbeleer, Michel   114n
Deedy, John G.   465n
Deeg, Alexander   475n
De Franceschi, Sylvio H.   247n, 250n
Deichmann Edwards, Wendy J.   401n
Deißmann, Adolf   440, 531, 534–536, 665
de Jonge, Christiaan   12n
de Kerchove d'Exaerde, Robert   691
Delacroix, Christian   3n
De Lai, Gaetano   459
Delattre, Alphonse   456n
Delgado, Mariano   166n
de Lisle, A.L.M. Phillipps   142–143, 149, 154, 156–158, 162, 247, 267
de Lisle, Edwin   142n
Delitzsch, Friedrich   590
Dell'Acqua, Stefano   71n
Delp, Alfred   677
de Lubac, Henri-Marie   34, 303
Delville, Jean-Pierre   680n
Del Zanna, Giorgio   69n, 254n, 256n
Demacopoulos, George E.   33n
De Maeyer, Jan   146n, 247n
De Mey, Peter   75, 78n–79n, 469n
DeMille, George E.   620n–621n
Denaux, Adelbert   78n, 80n, 298n, 469n, 689n, 702
Dendooven, Dominiek   437n
Deneken, Michel   301, 305n–310n, 319
Denison, George A.   155, 157
Dennis, James   549, 552–553
Der Abrahamian, Sergio   262n
Deringil, Selim   119n
Derré, Jean-René   245n
Derrida, Jacques   8n
Desan, Suzanne   57n–58n, 60n–62n
de Sarzana, Emanuele   436
Descartes, René   97n
Deschamps, Albert   466n
Dessain, Charles S.   156n, 162n
Destivelle, Hyacinthe   73n, 80, 446n, 485n, 490n–491n
Devlin, Judith   187n
de Volder, Jan   682n, 702
de Volder, Mechtilde   488n
de Wette, Wilhelm M.L.   97, 373

Dewey, John   200–201
de Wyels, Franco   690
d'Hendecourt, Jean   430n
d'Herbigny, Michel   73, 203n, 247n, 251, 686–687, 700, 706, 709–710
d'Hulst, Maurice   454n
Diamandouros, Nikiforos P.   129n
Diangienda, Joseph (Kuntima)   341, 347n
Di Bartolo, Salvatore   454n
Dibelius, Martin   465
Dibelius, Otto   628n
Dick, John A.   70–80n, 449n, 640n, 650n, 658, 689n, 690n, 702, 705n, 708n
Dickinson, Colby   141n
Dickinson, Willoughby H.   525
Didion, Joan   225n
Diepenbrock, Melchior von   318
Dietrich, Suzanne de   320n–323n, 325–332n, 335n, 338n–339
Diggs, James   407
Dimanopoulou Cohen, Pandora   72n, 111n
Dingel, Irene   164n
Dirks, Ildefons   488n, 692
Distad, N. Merrill   153n, 281n
Dix, Gregory   496n
Dmitrieva, Katia   247n
Dodd, Charles H.   30
Dodsworth, William   154n
Doll, Peter M.   136n
Döllinger, J.J. Ignaz von   146, 164, 166–186, 268, 286, 311n, 318, 719
Dombois, Hans   154n
Donaldson, St Clair G.A.   735
Doncoeur, Paul   437, 448
Donnelly, Doris   697n, 702
Donus of Messina   655
Dorman, Harry G.   705n
Dorotheos of Bursa   127, 539, 571
Dorrien, Gary   222n, 390, 392n, 403n, 405n, 411, 526n, 616n
Dosse, François   1n, 3n
Dostoevsky, Fyodor M.   105, 202, 204n
Dougherty, Mary A.   401n
Douglas, John A.   496n
Doumergue, Paul   430
Doutreloux, Victor-Joseph   680
Doyle, James   139–140n
Dragonas, Thalia   129n
Dreese, Charles   548
Drews, Paul   380n
Drey, Johann S. von   92n, 300–301, 306, 308–309
Dreyfus, Alfred   588
Driver, Godfrey R.   466n
Drobnitzky, Walter   663–665, 668
Drouin, Gilles   475n
Drummond, Henry   322
Drummond, William H.   388

Dryander, Ernst von   431, 444, 524, 531, 533
Du Bois, William E.B.   394, 404–408
du Bordel, Jean   542
Duchesne, Louis-Marie-Olivier   260, 293, 650
Duchhardt, Heinz   164n
Duff, Alexander   414, 722
du Jon, François the Elder (Franciscus Junius)   12n
Dülffer, Jost   523n
Dulles, Avery   163n
Dumont, Christophe-Jean   459n
Dumont, Pierre   679n, 697n
Dunant, Henry   219, 321–322
Dunn, James D.G.   21n, 41, 138n
Dupanloup, Félix-Antoine-Philibert   159, 292
du Pin, Louis E.   137, 139, 158
du Plessis, David J.   739
Duployé, Pie   696
Dupont, Anthony   472n
Dupont, Jacques   8n
Duprey, Pierre   7
Dupront, Alphonse   435n
Durand, Jean-Dominique   6n, 11n
Durand, Roger   320n–321n
Durkheim, Émile   595
Durrleman, Alfred   439
Duske, Johannes   530n
Duster, Alfreda M.   408n
Dvornik, Francis   8n, 33, 41

Eastburn, Manton   621n
Ebel, Jonathan H.   431n, 435n, 439n
Ebenbauer, Peter   479n
Eckhoff, Martin   324
Eddy, George S.   425
Edelby, Nagi   691n, 693n, 697n
Edward VII, King of Great Britain and Ireland   524
Edwards, Adrian   435
Edwards, Pamela   277n, 299
Egender, Nicolas   692n, 696n
Ehnmark, Erland   589
Eiland, Howard   1n
Eklund, Johan A.   592, 596
Ekman, Johann A.   592, 596
Ekman, Oscar   612n
Elert, Werner   637n
Eliot, Samuel A.   382
Elizabeth I, Queen of England   275, 281
Elliot, Elisabeth   5n
Elliott, Walter   236
Ellis, Ian M.   7on
Ellis, Steven G.   121n
Elton, Geoffrey R.   2n
Ely, Richard T.   391–397, 410
Emonet, Benoît   434n

Encrevé, André   94, 96n, 98n–99n, 108, 376n, 433n–434n,
     440n
Engberg, Arthur   598
Engelstein, Laura   187n
Ephstratiou, Ioannis   571
Epting, Karl-Christoph   70, 617n, 624n, 627n, 630n–632n,
     638
Erasmus of Rotterdam   12n, 608
Erb, Peter C.   301n, 319
Ernesti, Jörg   7, 10n, 67, 75, 166n, 458n, 481n, 663n–670n,
     672n, 677n–678
Erzberger, Matthias   442
Escobar, J. Samuel   738n
Esposito, Rosario F.   253n–255n, 257, 259n
Essen, Georg   167n
Esterka, Peter   250n
Etherington, Norman   542n
Eucken, Rudolf   384
Eusebios (Matthopoulos)   486
Eusebius of Caesarea   2n, 12, 21n, 304n
Evans, Craig A.   9n
Evans, Gillian R.   170n, 186
Evennett, H. Outram   654–655
Every, George   270n, 286n
Evlogij (Georgievsky)   490
Expilly, Louis-Alexandre   55
Ezekiel   235

Faber, Frederick W.   148, 155
Fabre, Pierre-Antoine   3n
Fagg, John E.   545n, 556
Faggioli, Massimo   706n
Fahs, Charles H.   558
Fairbanks, Charles W.   399
Falkenhayn, Erich von   433
Falkland, Lucius C.   275
Falloux, Alfred-Pierre   246
Fallows, William G.   296n
Famerée, Joseph   37n, 82n, 695n
Farley, John M.   626, 628
Farnana, P. Panda   345
Farrelly, Maura J.   333n, 339
Farrer, William   591n
Farrugia, Edward G.   73n, 101n, 249n
Fatti, Federico   9n
Faulhaber, Michael von   442, 670–674, 676–678
Fawcett, Timothy J.   281n
Feci, Damaso   345n
Fedotov, Georgy P.   512n
Fédou, Michel   89n, 166n, 300
Feiner, Johannes   78
Fellerer, Karl G.   484n
Felmy, Karl C.   102n, 109
Fenske, Wolfgang   516n, 518n

Feodor (Pozdeevsky)   485n
Ferguson, Robert A.   48n
Ferracci, Luca   14n, 28n, 66, 79, 82n, 129n, 410n, 418n, 445n, 470n, 615, 641n, 703n
Ferrari, Andrea   99n
Ferrari, Pietro   434
Fesser, Gerd   256n
Festugière, André-Jean   467n–468
Feuerbach, Ludwig   595
Feuillet, André   471
Fey, Harold E.   5, 66n, 429, 738n, 743
Ffoulkes, Edmund S.   157
Filser, Hubert   479n
Findlay, William H.   412
Finney, Charles   230
Finstuen, Andrew   48n
Firmin, A. *see* Loisy, Alfred
Fischer, Max   382–384n, 389
Fisher, Galen M.   325n
Fisichella, Rino   109
Fiske, John   394–395n
FitzGerald, Thomas E.   223
Fitzmyer, Joseph A.   461n, 464n, 467n, 472n
Flannery, Austin   739n
Fleckenstein, Gisela   76n
Fleischer, Charles   382
Fleischmann-Bisten, Walter   221n
Fleming, David   262n
Fliche, Augustin   77, 244n
Fliedner, Hans   633n
Flodén, Sven A.   363
Flogaus, Reinhard   80n
Florensky, Pavel Alexandrovich   105, 485–486n, 492, 499–500
Florovsky, Georges   24, 32, 35, 101n–109, 492, 494–496n, 569, 582, 584
Flynn, Gabriel   457n, 473
Fonck, Leopold   459
Foner, Philip S.   545n
Fontanès, Ernest   376–377
Forbes, Alexander P.   157–159, 172n–174n, 181, 268
Forbes, Duncan   280n
Forell, Birger   665–666
Forestier, Luc   263
Forsaith, Peter   212n
Forsell, Anna O.   588, 670
Forsell, John   603
Forster, Charles   138n
Förster, Stig   430n, 529n
Fortna, Benjamin C.   113n
Fouilloux, Étienne   3n, 6, 10n, 17, 27n, 66, 69n, 73n–75n, 77, 82, 244n, 250n, 263, 434n, 439n, 445n–447n, 449n–450, 458n–464n, 467n–468n, 471n, 473, 622n, 684n–685n, 698n, 701–703n, 706n, 721
Fox, John   564n

Foxe, John   142
Frame, William   367
Francis of Assisi   593
Francis, Peter   285n
Franco, Niccolò   246
Franklin, R. William   69n, 260n, 263, 266n, 294n, 299
Fransen, Piet F.   9n
Franzelin, Johann B.   258n
Franzén, Ruth   4n, 325n, 339
Franzinelli, Mimmo   436
Frederick I, King of Prussia   136
Frederick William III, King of Prussia   214
Frederick William IV, King of Prussia   151, 215, 218
Frederickson Reuter, Mathilda   364–365n
Frederickson, Peter H.   364
Frere, Walter H.   419, 496n, 553, 643, 645, 647, 651–652, 658
Freytag, Walter   741
Fridrichsen, Anton   467–468
Fried, Alfred H.   254n
Friedrich, Johann   172, 186n
Friedrich, Martin   211–216n, 223
Friedrichs, Laura A.   530n
Frieling, Reinhard   70n, 617n, 627n–628n, 633n, 635n, 638
Friemel, Franz G.   164n
Fries, Heinrich   678
Fries, Jakob F.   97
Fries, Karl   323–324
Fries, Samuel A.   586, 588n–589, 614
Frings, Josef   11n
Frör, Kurt   671
Frost, Francis   77
Froude, Richard H.   142, 146
Fuchs, Martin   117n
Fujinami, Nobuyoshi   126n
Funk, Robert W.   373n
Furiozzi, Gian Biagio   260n

Gabriel, Frédéric   258n–259n
Gabriel, Ingeborg   577n
Gadamer, Hans-Georg   31n
Gadille, Jacques   88n–89n, 92n, 109, 245n, 449n
Gagarin, Jean-Xavier (Ivan Sergeyevich)   199, 201, 244n, 247, 249, 251–252n
Gahbauer, Ferdinand R.   223
Gailor, Thomas   623
Gailus, Manfred   528n
Gaine, Simon F.   294n
Gaines, David P.   67n
Gairdner, William H.T.   726n
Gaisser, Ugo   261, 684n
Gajduk, Victor P.   255n
Galavotti, Enrico   36n
Gambarotto, Laurent   432n–433n, 444n, 450
Gams, Pius B.   167n, 310n
Gaquère, François   12n

Gardiner, Allen F.   543, 547

Gardiner, Robert H.   410, 618, 622–635, 637n–638, 713

Gardner, John   434

Garrard-Burnett, Virginia   544n–545n

Garrone, Gabriel-Marie   459n, 462n

Garvey, Marcus   345, 407

Garvie, Alfred E.   533

Gascoigne, John   275n

Gascoyne-Cecil, Robert   536

Gasparri, Pietro   293, 436, 445, 629, 631, 636, 646, 653,
       708–710n, 713, 716n

Gassmann, Günther   3n, 22n, 29n

Gavalda, Berthe   67

Geck, Albrecht   146n, 215n, 266n

Geffert, Bryn   72n, 111n

Geijer, Erik G.   586

Geil, John E.   365–366

Geiselmann, Josef R.   89n, 165n, 301n, 307, 319

Gemelli, Agostino   434

Genet-Delacroix, Marie-Claude   448n

Genet, Jean-Philippe   1n

Gengler, Adam   165n, 306

Gennadios (Limouris)   13n, 80n, 123n–124n, 127n, 130n–131,
       539n, 566n, 584

Genocchi, Giovanni   458n

George v, King of the United Kingdom   627

George, Henry   397

Georges, Olivier   443n

Gerd, Lora   112n, 121n, 130

Gerdes, Uta   75n

Gerhards, Albert   477n, 482n

Germanos (Strenopoulos)   13, 539, 570–572n, 574, 577–579,
       581–583, 637

Gerrish, Brian A.   374n

Getcha, Job   255n

Giampiccoli, Franco   71n

Gianotto, Claudio   9n

Gibbons, James   229, 626, 628

Gibson, William   221n

Gifford, Carolyn De Swarte   401n

Gill, Jill K.   77n

Gill, Joseph   9n

Gillet, Lev (Louis)   74, 684, 691–692

Gilley, Sheridan   136n, 285n

Gilyarov-Platonov, Nikita Petrovich   202

Giordano, Donato   487n

Giordano, Filippo M.   71n

Girard, Aurélien   250n, 258n, 263n

Girardot, Norman J.   230n

Giraud, frére   247n

Gladden, Washington   391–397, 399, 402n, 404, 410

Gladstone, William E.   158n, 166–168, 171–172n, 181, 183,
       268–269, 274–275, 283, 285–288, 290, 292–296, 331

Glinz, Gustav A.   662

Glubokovsky, Nicholas N.   491–492

Gobat, Samuel   152, 156

Gobel, Jean-Baptiste   55

Göçek, Fatma M.   119n

Goeters, J.F. Gerhard   212n, 223

Goethe, Johann Wolfgang von   483

Goetz, Hans-Werner   1n

Gogarten, Friedrich   372

Gogol, Nikolai V.   105, 189

Goguel, Maurice   465n, 468

Goldin, Claudia   400n

Goldziher, Ignaz   592

Gondicas, Dimitri   113n

Gondon, Jules   146n, 246n–247n, 252

Goodall, Norman   738, 740n, 742

Goodier, Alban   657

Göransson, Nils J.   586

Gorce, Denys   689n

Gore, Charles   283, 288, 292, 394, 403, 416, 420, 552–553, 607,
       633, 637, 650–652, 655

Gorham, George C.   153, 155, 157

Gornall, Thomas   162n

Goslin, Tomás S.   544n

Gottsmann, Andreas   72n, 636n, 713n

Gould, Stephen J.   394n

Gounelle, Élie   448, 538

Goutzioudis, Moschos   565n

Goyau, Georges   446n

Graf, Friedrich W.   372n–373n, 378n

Grafton, Charles C.   621

Gratieux, Albert   193n, 209, 260n, 293, 689n

Gratz, Peter A.   307n

Graumann, Thomas   12n

Gray, John H.   151n

Grbešić, Grgo   249n

Green, Bernard   525n

Greene, Jack P.   43n

Greenfield, Robert H.   158n

Greer, David H.   623

Greeson, Jennifer   48n

Grégoire, Henri   245

Gregory i, Pope   33n, 158, 655, 690

Gregory iv of Antioch   632

Gregory vi of Constantinople   115

Gregory vii (Hildebrand of Sovana), Pope   375

Gregory xvi (Bartolomeo Alberto Cappellari), Pope   253n

Gregory, Adrian   431n, 434n, 439n, 523n

Gregory of Sinai   191n

Greinacher, Norbert   10n

Greschat, Martin   438n, 450

Grey, Charles   277

Griffiths, Richard   431n

Grignion de Montfort, Louis-Marie   50

Grillmeier, Aloys   9n

Grootaers, Jan   81n

Gros, Jeffrey   465n

Grosche, Robert   666
Grossi, Giulia   127n, 444n, 449n–450, 529n, 703n, 711n
Grotefeld, Stefan   525n
Grubb, George C.   544
Grubb, Kenneth G.   542n
Grubb, William B.   548
Grünberg, Paul   442
Grundemann, Reinhold   550
Guardini, Romano   476, 479–480, 485, 494n, 659, 663–664, 666–667, 677, 718–719
Guasco, Alberto   81n
Guasco, Maurilio   77n, 455n
Guéranger, Prosper   475
Guérard, Joseph   432n
Guerriero, Elio   77n
Guettée, René-François (Wladimir)   247
Gugelot, Frédéric   246n, 430, 529n, 703n
Guibert, Jean   248n
Guillemin, Thomas   82n
Guinness, Lucy E.   544n
Guitton, Jean   68, 657
Gunkel, Hermann   385–386, 465
Gunner, Byron   407
Gunten, André-François von   70n
Günther, Johannes   678
Gustaf V of Sweden   597
Guyer, Benjamin M.   265n, 269n, 290n, 299, 619n
Gvosdavo-Golienko, N.   704n
Gwinn, Nancy E.   225n
Gy, Pierre-Marie   453n

Haag, Henri   682n
Haar, Miriam   22n
Haase, Wolfgang   80n
Habermas, Rebekka   330n, 338n
Hajjar, Joseph   69, 77n, 254n, 258n
Hales, John   275
Hálfadanarson, Gudmundur   121n
Halifax, Charles L. Wood II   69, 260, 291–293, 295–296, 622, 630, 640–652n, 656–658, 689, 705, 709
Hall, Arthur C.A.   621
Hall, Francis J.   624–625
Hallencreutz, Carl F.   737
Hallifax, Stuart   529n
Halme-Tuomisaari, Miia   540
Hamacher, Theo   484n
Hamann, Brigitte   524n
Hambræus, Axel E.   592
Hammenstede, Albert   503n
Hämmerle, Eugen   111n
Hampden, Renn D.   155
Hancock, Thomas   403
Handy, Robert T.   391n, 397n, 411
Hanley, Frank   399
Hannay, Alastair   586n

Hansen, Heinrich   504–508, 511–514, 520, 659–660
Hanson, John W.   224n
Haquin, André   453n, 474n, 487n, 652n, 679–681n, 692n, 695n–697n, 702, 726n, 709n
Hare, Julius C.   150, 152–153, 156, 161, 281n
Harnack, Adolf von   29, 38–39, 300, 311–319, 372, 374, 381, 385–386, 398, 438, 442, 453, 455, 461, 524n–528, 534, 585, 592, 597, 599, 610
Harnoncourt, Philipp   484n
Harrington, Peter   528n
Harris, Charles   266n
Harrison, Benjamin   146
Harscouët, Raoul   696
Hartdegen, Stephen   454n
Hartenstein, Karl   738
Hartmann, Felix von   442–443
Hartog, Hans   518n, 521, 661n–663n
Hartwig, Georg   628n
Harvey, John W.   595n
Hastings, Adrian   340n–341n, 358
Hauck, Albert   594
Haudel, Matthias   71
Hauf, Theodor   504n, 521, 660n
Haugh, Richard S.   24n, 32n, 101n–109, 569n
Haunerland, Winfried   474n, 484n
Haustein, Jörg   221n
Haxthausen, August F. von   201n
Hayford, Mark C.   421
Haynes, George   407
Headlam, Arthur C.   636–637
Headlam, Stewart   403
Hébert, Jacques-René   57
Hedin, Sven A.   596
Hegel, G.W. Friedrich   89n–90, 98n, 189, 202n, 301, 377, 594
Heid, Ludger   530n
Heiene, Gunnar   76
Heiler, Anne M.   665
Heiler, Friedrich   75n, 508–511, 517n–521, 600, 605n, 659–670, 672, 677
Heinrich, Gerd   524n
Hell, Leonhard   75
Heller, Dagmar   79n
Hemmer, Hippolyte M.   293n, 650, 652
Hempel, Johannes   461
Hendrickx, Jean-Pierre   70n, 449n, 681n, 701, 708n
Henrietta Maria of Bourbon   148
Henry VIII, King of England   275
Henry, Patrick   206n
Herberg, Lea   475n
Hering, Gunnar   130n
Hermelink, Heinrich   678
Hermes, Georg   307n
Hermle, Siegfried   214n
Herodotus   3, 12n
Herring, George C.   154n

Herring, Hubert   545n–546n
Herriot, Édouard   437
Herrmann, Irène   448n
Herrmann, Wilhelm   592
Herron, George   391–392, 404
Hertling, Georg F.K.F. (Graf) von   531–533n
Herwegen, Ildefons   476, 478, 494n
Herwig, Thomas   71
Herzen, Aleksandr I.   189
Herzog, Eduard   181, 268
Herzog, Rudolf   164n
Heß, Christian   678
Heuclin, Jean   443n
Heufelder, Emmanuel   489
Heylyn, Peter   136
Hilarion (Alfeev)   490n
Hilberath, Bernd J.   167n
Hilborn, David   223, 265n
Hill, Alan G.   146n, 161n
Hill, Christopher   80n, 294n, 298n–299
Hill, Thomas   366
Hill, W. Speed   275n
Himes, Michael J.   301n, 319
Hinchliff, Peter B.   297n
Hirai, Kinza R.M.   232–233
Hirschfeld, Gerhard   523n, 530n
Hitler, Adolf   717
Hjelde, Sigurd   29n, 41
Hjelm, Norman A.   529n, 540, 614
Hobson, Samuel G.   403
Hocart, James   376n
Höck, Michael   670–674, 677
Hocking, William E.   734–735n
Hodge, John Z.   424–425n
Hodgson, Leonard   491n, 496n
Hoekendijk, Johannes C.   739
Höfer, Josef   470n, 677n
Hoffmann, Hermann   635, 713
Hofmann, Georg   9n
Hofstadter, Richard   394n
Hogg, W. Richey   151n, 248n, 220n, 414n, 418n, 429, 529n,
      722–723, 728–738n, 743
Hölderlin, Friedrich   301
Holl, Karl   525n
Holland, Scott   394, 403
Hollenberg, Günter   523n
Holly, James   406
Holmes, J. Derek   565n
Holzbrecher, Sebastian   475n
Holzer, Bernard   73n, 250n
Hook, Walter F.   152
Hooker, Richard   267, 271, 274–280, 283, 285, 287n–288, 290
Hope, James   152
Hopkins, Charles H.   10n, 70, 236n, 320n, 325n–327, 339,
      398n–399n, 529n, 711n, 723n, 724n, 743

Hopwood, Derek   121n
Horne, John   436n, 442n
Hösch, Edgar   112n
Hotchkiss, Valerie   206n
Houghton, Walter R.   224n, 242
Houlihan, Patrick J.   449n
House, Francis   580n, 584
Houtin, Albert   380, 382–383
Howard, John E.   150n
Howard, Thomas A.   166n, 170n, 177n, 186
Howson, John S.   173
Hrabovec, Emilia   250n
Huber, Johann N.   180n
Huber, Victor A.   167
Hübinger, Gangolf   372n, 377n, 383n–385n, 389
Hübner, Thomas   313n
Huby, Joseph   689n
Hudal, Alois   715n
Huerta, Victoriano   556
Hüffmeier, Wilhelm   213n, 223
Hügel, Friedrich von   293, 593, 660n
Hugenholtz, Petrus H.   379n–380n, 389
Hughes, Edwin H.   626n–627n
Hughes, John J.   69n, 294n, 657n
Hughes, Michael   155n, 189n
Hühn, Eugen   458n
Hume, David   597n
Huntington, William R.   161, 237–238, 269–276, 278–281,
      283–284, 288–290, 410, 415, 548, 619
Hürten, Heinz   715n
Hutchison, William R.   222n, 372n, 390n, 411, 564n
Hutton, William H.   296n
Huyghebaert, Nicolas   685n

Ignatius (George Spencer)   142–143, 157, 248, 253
Ignatius of Antioch   23, 35, 37, 302, 497–498
Ignatovič, Natalija   485n
Ihmels, Ludwig   594, 604
Ince, William   162n
Inge, William R.   533
Inman, Samuel G.   555
Innocent (Figurovsky)   206
Ioann II of Kiev   496
Ion, Christina   118n
Ioniță, Viorel   486n, 583n
Ireland, John   226
Irenaeus of Lyons   21, 302, 304
Irvine, Cecilia   368n–370
Isaacs, Ann K.   121n
Iserloh, Erwin   93
Israel, Jonathan I.   12n, 43n
Issawi, Charles   113n
Istavridis, Vasil T.   130n, 539n, 571n–572n, 575–576n,
      578n–580n, 582n, 584
Ivantsov-Platonov, Alexander M.   205

Jackson, Eleanor M.   4n–5n
Jacobi, Friedrich H.   97
Jacobs, Jan   75n–76n, 465n, 467n, 469n–470n
Jačov, Marko   68on
Jacquemet, Gabriel   67, 687n
Jaeger, Lorenz   76, 469–471, 666, 668, 676–677
Jager, Jean-Nicolas   142, 146
Jakim, Boris   187n–196n, 198n–200n, 203n, 209
James I, King of England   136–137
James, William   394
Jansen, Henry   71n
Janssens, Laurent   456n
Janyshev, Ioann L.   172–173, 177, 181
Janz, Oliver   523n, 529n
Jarret, Bede   657
Jaurès, Jean   588
Jebb, John   138
Jedin, Hubert   6, 11n, 77
Jefferson, Thomas   43, 225
Jehle-Wildberger, Marianne   534n, 540
Jenkins, Julian   442n
Jenkins, Philip   434n
Jennings, Michael W.   1n
Jennings, Robert   362–364, 366, 368–370
Jerome   458–459, 463n
Jewel, John   267
Joachim II of Constantinople   252
Joachim III of Constantinople   120–126, 566–569
Joachim IV of Constantinople   114
Joan of Arc   433, 438
Job, G.V.   426n
Johansson, Gustaf   605n
John Cassian   11n, 496
John Chrysostom   257, 494–495, 510n–511
John of Damascus   182, 184
John of Kronstadt (Ivan Ilych Sergiev)   252, 485, 493
John of Syracuse   655
John Paul II (Karol Woytiła), Pope   36, 81
John the Evangelist   352–355, 369, 455, 516, 576, 698
John XXIII (Angelo Roncalli), Pope   11n, 77, 81, 472, 657, 697, 706
John, Emmanuel   345
Johnson, Mordecai W.   405
Johnson, Todd M.   426n
Johnston, James   415n, 418n, 547n, 549n
Johnston, John O.   184n–185n
Join-Lambert, Arnaud   474n
Jones, Jenkin L.   224n
Jones, John P.   425
Jones, Rufus   734
Jones, Tod E.   275n
Jonson, Jonas   11n, 70n, 585n–594n, 598n, 603n–604n, 614
Joos, André   496n

Jørgensen, Knud   734n
Joseph of Volokolamsk   191n
Joshi, S.L.   382
Jossua, Jean-Pierre   16
Joye, Edmundus   437n
Jue, Jeffrey K.   12n
Jungmann, Josef A.   476, 480, 501n
Jürgs, Michael   529n

Kaftan, Theodor   597, 628n
Kahle, Wilhelm   184n, 220n
Kahlefeld, Heinrich   665
Kaiser, Jochen-Christoph   525n
Kalaitzidis, Pantelis   7n, 80n, 131
Kalkandjieva, Daniela   114n
Kallis, Anastasios   130n
Kalthoff, Albert   379
Kampmann, Jürgen   212n–214n, 216n, 223
Kamuf, Peggy   8n
Kant, Immanuel   96–98n, 170, 373–374, 379
Kantzenbach, Friedrich W.   674n, 678
Karakolis, Christos   8n, 17
Karathanasis, Athanasios E.   122n, 126n
Kardaras, Christos   120n–121n
Karlström, Nils   533n, 539n, 540, 601n, 614
Karmiris, Ioannis   36, 111n, 115n, 126n, 574–575
Kartashev, Anton V.   496n
Käsemann, Ernst   21n
Kasper, Walter   7, 10n, 301
Katkov, Mikhail N.   203, 206
Katz, Michael R.   247n
Kaufman, John   453n
Kaufmann, Thomas   528n
Kavelin, Konstantin D.   188n, 189, 193n
Kazamias, Alexander   129n
Keats, John   266, 279
Keble, John   132, 140–141, 157, 268–272, 274, 277, 279
Kechriotis, Vangelis   122n
Keller, Adolf   534, 665
Kenis, Leo   172n, 186
Kennedy, Frances H.   43n
Kent, John   416
Ker, Ian T.   146n, 161n–162n
Keramidas, Dimitrios   129n
Kerensky, Alexander F.   691
Kerfoot, John B.   173, 177, 179, 267n
Kerner, Hanns   483n, 521n, 538n, 540
Kesich, Lydia   492n, 500
Kessler, Jean B.A.   544n
Ketelaar, James E.   228n, 230n, 232n–233n
Keul, István   116n
Keum, Jooseop   734
Keyder, Çaglar   129n
Keynes John M.   612

Khomyakov, Aleksey S.   35, 108n, 156, 187–189, 192–204, 208–209, 499

Kiawanga, Marie M.   352

Kidd, Beresford J.   650–652

Kierkegaard, Søren   585–586n, 611–612n

Kimbangu, Simon   340–364, 366–370

King, Benjamin J.   141n, 147n, 154n, 161n

King, Judson   366

King, Martin Luther Jr.   390–391, 404–405, 410

Kinnamon, Michael   290n

Kinsman, Frederick J.   623

Kintondo   354

Kinzembo   358, 369, 347–351, 353

Kippenberg, Hans G.   595n

Kirby, James E.   223

Kireev, Aleksandr A.   172, 180

Kireyevksaya Arebeneva, Natalya P.   189

Kireyevsky, Ivan V.   187–193, 197, 200, 202–203

Kireyevsky, Pyotr V.   105, 189

Kirkland, Robert   366

Kisker, Ursula   660n

Kisolokela   344

Kitromilides, Paschalis M.   113n, 129n

Kitsikis, Dimitri   131n

Kittel, Rudolf   594

Kizenko, Nadieszda   252n, 485n

Klatt, Johanna   441n

Klee, Paul   1

Kleineidam, Carl   524

Klek, Konrad   502n

Klinger, Elmar   89n

Klöckener, Martin   474n–475n, 511, 521

Klueting, Harm   164n

Knies, Karl G.A.   393

Knight, Henry J.C.   145n

Knight, Jonathan   134n, 274n

Knights, Ben   278n

Knoch, Otto   673n, 676

Knoodt, Franz P.   173

Knox, Alexander   138

Knüppel, Michael   129n

Koch, Jakob J.   477n

Koch, Josef   666–667

Koenig, Christopher   378n

Kofos, Evangelos   120n

Kohut, Alexander   232

Kolmodin, Ioannis   577n

Komninos, Pantoleon   571

Komonchak, Joseph A.   78n, 132n, 471n

Konkel, Michael   479n

Konortas, Paraskevas   121n

Kontzevich, Ivan M.   188

Korff, Gottfried   476n

Körner, Hans   482n

Kornreiter, Josef   673

Korolevskij, Cyrille   74, 257n, 260n, 435n, 684, 687n, 693n, 700, 702, 706

Körtner, Ulrich H.J.   577n

Koselleck, Reinhart   2n, 17

Koshy, Ninan   77

Koslowski, Jutta   529n

Koulomzine, Nicholas   35, 496n

Kourie, Celia   461n

Kraemer, Hendrik   736–737

Kramer, Alan   436n, 442n

Kramnick, Isaac   64n

Kranemann, Benedikt   474–476n, 480n–481n, 500, 511n–516n, 521, 659

Kravetskij, Aleksandr G.   485n, 490n, 495n

Krawczyk, Boleslaw J.   481n

Krebs, Engelbert   443

Križanić, Juraj   205

Kröger, Heinrich   660n

Krug, Wilhelm T.   373

Krumeich, Gerd   434n, 450, 523n, 529n

Kuhlmann, Sebastian   678

Kuhn, Johannes E. von   92n

Kuijpers, Erika   9n

Kümmel, Werner G.   467n

Künneth, Walter   667

Kunze, Gerhard   517n

Kupiec, Kazimierz   206n

Kurian, George T.   426n

Küry, Urs   172n

Kuyowa   368–369

Kwasniewski, Peter   479n

Kwok, Pui-lan   5n

Laberthonnière, Lucien   383

Labonté, Thomas   484n

Laboureyras, Pierre   436n

Lacey, Thomas A.   294n

Lacordaire, Henri-Dominique   146

Ladous, Régis   69, 260n, 293n, 320n, 449n, 658, 689n, 708n

Lafayette, Bernard   405

Lafferty, Eric   146n

LaFontaine, Charles V.   438n

Lagerlöf, Selma   603

Lagrange, Marie-Joseph   456, 460–461, 464, 466, 472, 711

Lagrée, Michel   6n

Lahey, R.J.   70

Lahusen, Friedrich   527, 531

Laible, Wilhelm   605n

Laing, Christine   225n, 243

Laing, Mark T.B.   740–743

Lake, Peter   281n

Laman, Karl   349n

Lamb, Charles   4n–5n

Lamberigts, Mathijs   42, 453–454n, 473

Lambrechts, Antoine   684n

La Mennais, Félicité-Robert de 146
Laminne, Jacques 680
Lamparter, Hanne 71
Lamprecht, Karl 594
Landau, Peter 14n
Landau, Philippe-Efraïm 431n
Landon, William 322
Landry, Stan M. 446n
Lane, Ada 476n
Lang, Hugo 671–672
Langdon, William C. 171–172n
Lange, Dietz 11n, 70n, 317n, 445n, 530n, 585, 589n, 591n, 596n, 614, 620n, 633n, 641n, 703n
Langen, Joseph 173
Langenbahn, Stefan K. 479n
Langénieux, Benoît-Marie 248, 253n, 255, 258
Langlois, Claude 58n
Lanker, Jason 219n
Lankester, Herbert 418
Lanne, Emmanuel 35n, 78, 679n, 686n, 689n, 697n, 700n
Lanternari, Vittorio 341n, 361n
Laros, Matthias 678
La Taille, Maurice de 691
Lathbury, Daniel C. 285n
Latour, Francis 444n
Latourette, Kenneth S. 246n, 423n, 541n–542n, 617n, 722, 729–730, 732n–733, 740n, 743
Latreille, André 51n
Laud, William 135–136, 286
Launay, Marcel 458n–460n, 687n
Laurentie, Pierre-Sébastien 198
Lautman, François 82
Lawson, James 405
Layten, Sarah 407
Leander a Sancto Martino 137
Lebrun, François 58n
Leclerc, Jean 136
Le Courayer, Pierre F. 137, 160
Ledóchowski, Włodzimierz 260n
Lee, Frederick G. 137n, 140n, 143n, 149n, 156–157, 161n, 163
Leest, Charlotte van der 215n
Legrand, Hervé 24n, 82n, 246n, 263, 500n, 706n
Lehmann, Edvard 594
Lehmann, Hartmut 434n, 450, 527n–528n
Lehmann, Helmut T. 264n
Lehmann, Karl 76n
Lehner, Ulrich L. 52n, 65
Lehnert, Christian 475n
Leiber, Robert 469n
Lemarchand, Guy 43n
Lenormant, François 454
Lenz, Martin C. 474n, 501, 509n–510n, 522, 659n–660n
Leo I, Pope 33n
Leo III, Pope 176n

Leo XIII (Vincenzo Gioacchino Luigi Pecci), Pope 69, 72, 89, 93, 122, 178n, 226, 244, 249–250n, 253–261, 291–295, 312, 316, 454–456, 458, 460, 463, 487, 549, 640–641, 645, 679–680, 682–683, 685, 689, 699, 703
Leonhard, Jörn 523n
Leonid (Kavelin) 188n
Leonid (Nagolkin) of Optina 188
Le Pappe de Trévern, Jean François-Marie 137
Leppin, Volker 164n, 166n
Leprieur, François 6n
Lerch, Lea 474n–475n, 484n
Le Roy, Édouard 456
Lerrigo, Peter H.J. 349n–351n, 366n
Lesoing, Bertrand 74n
Lesourd, Jean-Alain 247n
Lesti, Sante 432n
Leustean, Lucian N. 71, 114n, 131
Leuzi 347n
Levant, Marie 607n, 656n, 694n, 703, 707n, 714n, 717n–718n, 721
Levie, Jean 464n
Levillain, Philippe 250n, 680n
Lévy, Alfred 431
Lévy, Louis-Germain 381
Lewis, David L. 394n
Lewis, John 405
Lewis, Matthew G. 266
Liddon, Henry P. 152n, 166, 170–171n, 173–175, 177, 179–181, 184–186, 268, 292
Lilienfeld, André de (Félix-Otto) 492n, 693n, 695n
Lill, Rudolf 444n
Lilley, Alfred L. 372
Limburg, Hans J. 483n, 671n
Lindemann, Gerhard 75n, 217n–219n, 222n–223
Lindsay, Ben 399
Linhart, Paula 671, 674, 678
Linkenbach, Antje 117n
Liubimov, Nikolai A. 203
Lloyd-George, David 536
Lloyd, Noel 297n
Loane, Edward 76n
Locherer, Johann N. 307n
Locke, John 275
Lockhart, John G. 292, 643n, 646n–647, 658
Lohfink, Norbert 465n
Loisy, Alfred 383, 455–457n, 461, 472, 589, 593
Lonergan, Bernard J.F. 7n
Loonbeek, Raymond 11n, 75n, 487n–489n, 500, 679–680n, 687–689n, 691–692n, 694–695n, 702, 706n, 709
López-Tello García, Eduardo 104n
Lorain, Hilaire 146
Lorenz, Robert 441n
Lösch, Stefan 165n
Lossky, André 696n

Lossky, Nicolas   7, 35, 79n
Lot   40
Loughlin, Gerard   457n, 473
Louis XVI, King of France   50, 52, 54, 56
Louth, Andrew   21n, 206n
Lowery, Joseph   405
Loyson Butterfield Meriman, Emilie J.   170n, 380–381n
Loyson, Hyacinthe   170, 380
Lückhoff, Martin   246n
Luckmann, Thomas   68
Luçon, Louis-Henri-Joseph   435n, 443
Lüddeckens, Dorothea   227n, 230n, 232, 235n, 243
Ludendorff, Erich F.W.   530
Ludwig, Frieder   447n
Ludwig, Renate   664n, 666
Luffin, Xavier   129n
Lugari, Giovanni B.   261n
Luke the Evangelist   1, 368
Lukens, Michael B.   12n
Lundström, Herman   593
Luneau, René   82n
Lunel, Frédéric   82n
Lupu, Vasile   118
Luther, Martin   100n, 142, 153, 211, 217, 222, 264, 281n,
        284n, 310, 313–314, 333–334, 379, 400, 402n, 438–439,
        504–505, 516n, 586–588, 590, 597, 602, 608–610, 720
Lüttichau, Siegfried von   515, 518
Luz, Ulrich   8n, 17
Lykourgos, Alexandros   181
Lynch, Frederick   527
Lyonnet, Stanislas   462n–465n, 471n–472

Maas-Ewerd, Theodor   474–476n
Maas, Hermann   10n
Macarius (Ivanov) of Optina   188–189, 191, 193
MacColl, Malcolm   174
Macdonnell, Thomas   143n
Macfarland, Charles S.   399, 527n, 632n
MacGaffey, Wyatt   340n, 342n–343n, 349n–350, 357n, 370
Machilek, Franz   249n
Mackay, Donald J.   343n–344n, 346n, 348n–349n, 351n, 353n,
        355n–356n, 358n–361n, 370
Mackay, John A.   738
Mackay, William P.   586
Mackie, Robert C.   325n, 338
Maclagan, William   293, 295
MacLeod, Roy   528n, 540
Macmillan, Arthur T.   293n
Mafwata   368
Mahieu, Patrice   80n–81n, 440n–441n
Mai, Paul   164n
Mainardi, Adalberto   35n, 104n–105n, 474, 485n, 491n, 659
Maire, Catherine   52n
Maistre, Joseph de   245
Makrakis, Apostolos   486

Makrides, Vasilios N.   35n, 101n, 110, 112n, 116n–117n
Maltsev, Alexei P.   251
Mamalos, Georgios-Spyridon   129n
Mammana, Richard J. Jr.   196n
Mandouze, André   73n
Maniglier, Auguste   691
Mann, Wendy   543n
Manning, Henry E.   140, 150, 153, 158–159, 162n, 267, 269, 287
Manning, William T.   623, 626, 628–629n, 631
Mansi, Giovanni D.   21n, 692
Marchadier, Bernard   206n
Marchant, James   524n, 657
Marchetti Selvaggiani, Francesco   468n
Marcion of Pontus   311
Maréchaux, Bernard-Marie   257n
Marguerat, Daniel   8n, 17
Marini, Niccolò   252n
Maritain, Jacques   1n, 438
Mark the Evangelist   369, 422
Markham, Ian S.   292n
Markschies, Christoph   531n
Márkus, Mihály   216n
Marlé, René   432n
Marmion, Columba (Joseph Aloysius)   461, 680, 697
Marolles, Claude E.F.   55
Maron, Gottfried   111n
Marotta, Saretta   11n, 13n, 75–76n, 78, 469n–470n
Marquard, Odo   2n
Marquardt, Manfred   223
Marrou, Henri-Irénée   2n, 17
Marsh, John W.   543n
Marson, Charles   403
Martano, Valeria   11n, 83n
Martin, Hervé   3n
Martin, Hugh   727
Martin, Marie-Louise   347n
Martin, Victor   77
Martina, Giacomo   179n, 285
Marty, Martin E.   43n, 65, 526n
Martynov, Jean (Ivan Mikhailovich)   201–202, 206n, 247
Mary I, Queen of England   295, 640
Masri, Pierre   691n
Massaux, Édouard   466n
Masson, Frédéric   441
Matalas, Paraskevas   118n
Mateus, Odair P.   220n
Mather, Frederick C.   270n
Mather, Samuel   623, 632
Mathews, Basil J.   325n–326n
Mathews, Donald G.   401n
Mathews, Shailer   391, 395, 399
Matsoukas, Nikos A.   570n, 573
Matthew the Evangelist   354
Matthew, Henry C.G.   285n
Mattone, Antonello   2n

Maubert, Léon 442

Maurer, Sabine 480n

Maurice de Nassau 542

Maurice, Frederick D. 270, 272, 274, 280, 282–285, 287–288, 290–291, 395n, 616

Maurice, John F. 282n

Maury, Jean-Sifrein 56

Maury, Pierre 324

Mausbach, Joseph 442

Maximilian I Joseph of Bavaria 213

Maximilian of Saxony 256

Maximos (Tsaoussis) of Sardis 115n

Maximus the Confessor 192n, 495

May, Gerhard 164n

May, Henry F. 48n

Mayer, Rupert 674

Mayeur, Jean-Marie 42

Maynard, Theodore 46n

Mayoux, Pierre 437n

Mays, Benjamin E. 405

Mazzolini, Sandra 87

Mbadi, Davidi 365, 368–369

Mbandila 363

McBee, Silas 415, 420–421n, 727

McChord Crothers, Samuel 375

McClain, Frank M. 282n

McClelland, Vincent A. 157n, 159n

McCormick, Nettie F. 326n

McDowell, Mary 399

McFarland, Charles 603

McFarland, Samuel 632

McGrath, Alister E. 142n

McGrath, Francis J. 140n

McGrath, Thomas G. 140n

McIntyre, Mary L. 150n

McKitrick, Edyth 270n

McMahon, Darrin M. 52n, 65

McManners, John 50n

McNally, Raymond T. 201n

McNeill, John T. 264n

Meacham, Jon 64n

Mead, Sidney E. 43n, 65

Mede, Joseph 142

Meester, Placide de 684

Mehlhausen, Joachim 504n

Meier, Bertram 164n

Meillet, Antoine 588

Meimaris, Theodoros A. 632n

Melanchthon, Philip 100n, 213, 264

Meletios IV (Metaxakis) of Constantinople 128–129, 580

Mélice, Anne 345n

Melloni, Alberto 1–3n, 9n, 11n–12n, 14n–15n, 17, 78n, 81n, 127n, 216n, 444n, 450, 529n

Melton, J. Gordon 705n

Menozzi, Daniele 2n, 42n, 65, 432n, 704n

Mercier, Désiré-Joseph 70, 449, 459n, 630n, 641–657, 681–682, 686–691, 693–694, 699–701, 705, 708

Merker, Nicolao 434n, 450

Merkle, Sébastien 438

Merle d'Aubigné, Jean-Henri 150–151n, 334n

Merry del Val, Rafael 293, 458–459, 656, 694, 711, 714, 719n–720

Mersch, Emile 681n

Meseberg-Haubold, Ilse 449n

Messbarger, Rebecca M. 52n

Methodius 117, 199, 249, 251, 256

Methuen, Charlotte 290n

Métivier, Yves 443n

Mettepenningen, Jürgen 455n–457n

Metz, Judith 46n

Metzger, Max J. 75–76n, 489, 635, 672, 677, 705, 713

Metzger, Paul 366

Metzing, Andreas 213n

Metzlaff, Paul 489n, 509n, 635n, 659, 714n

Meurers, Heinrich von 476

Mews, Stuart P. 428n

Meyendorff, John 35–36, 41, 101n–105n, 109, 486, 500

Meyer-Blanck, Michael 483n, 503n

Meyer-Rewerts, Ulf G. 441n

Meyer, Robert 186, 223, 539, 701, 720

Meyrick, Frederick 154n, 161, 171, 174, 184–185n

Mezei, Balázs M. 291n

Mfulani, Stanislas 358n

Micara, Clemente 710n

Miccoli, Giovanni 42n, 65n, 704n, 721

Michaud, Eugène 173, 254n

Michel, Ernst 716, 718

Michel, Patrick 82n

Michelis, Friedrich 172

Michels, Thomas 494n

Michelson, Patrick 187n

Middendorf, Johannes A. 443

Middleton, Robert D. 143n

Miethke, Jürgen 30n

Migne, Jacques-Paul 245n

Milbach, Sylvain 263

Milbank, Alison 267n

Mill, William H. 152n

Millar, Andrew A. 722n

Millard, Edward C. 544n

Miller, E. Charles Jr. 140n, 161

Miller, Emmy von 674

Miller, George F. 407

Miller, Rudolf von 674

Milojković-Djurić, Jelena 121n

Milton, Anthony 134n, 136n–137n

Minus, Paul M. Jr. 67

Mishkova, Diana 117n

Misler, Nicoletta 486n

Misner, Paul 142n, 660n

Misonne, Daniel   684n
Mitchell, Edwin K.   311n, 319
Moeller, Reinhard   532n
Moessner, David P.   1n
Moffatt, James   311n
Mogila, Peter   103n
Mohlberg, Kunibert   476
Möhler, Johann A.   89n, 92n, 108n, 165, 167, 208, 286,
      300–311, 318–319
Mohr, Jacob C.B.   385
Mojoli, Giuseppe   258n
Molendijk, Arie L.   224n, 229n, 240n, 243, 371n, 378n
Möller, Christian   10n
Molloy, Gerald   159n–160n
Mommsen, Wolfgang J.   529n
Monnier, Henri   433n–434n, 440
Monod, Wilfred   482n, 448, 535, 537–538, 587, 632
Monroe, James   545
Montagnes, Bernard   459n–461n
Montagu, Richard   137
Montalembert, Charles F. de   146
Montet, Edouard L.   380n–381n, 389
Monteverde, Eduardo   558–559
Montgomery, Henry   549–553
Montmort, Renée de   445
Moody, Dwight L.   230, 322–323, 326, 423, 586–587
Moon, Seymour   366
Moore Ede, William   527
Moore, Laura E.   269n
Moore, R. Laurence   64n
Morehouse, Henry   404
Morel, Léon   344, 358, 360, 368
Morerod, Charles   260n
Morgan, John P.   623
Morozzo Della Rocca, Roberto   73, 434n, 447n
Morris, Jeremy N.   137–138n, 146n, 148n, 253n, 266n,
      282–283, 299, 395n
Morrison, Charles C.   399
Mortiau, Jacques   11n, 75n, 487n, 488n–489n, 500,
      679–680n, 687–689n, 691n–692n, 694–695n, 702,
      706n, 709n
Mosel, Heinrich G.W.   508, 633n, 660–661
Moses   455, 464
Mosse, George L.   430n
Mott, John R.   4, 70, 236, 320, 323–339, 410, 417, 425, 529,
      545–547, 551–553, 558–559, 572, 587, 618, 628n, 632,
      723–725, 727–731, 733, 735–737, 740
Motta, Franco   2n
Mowala, Samuel   354, 356, 358, 361–362, 369
Mozoomdar, Protap C.   234–235
Mpadi, Simon-Pierre   341
Mpegzos, Marios   570n
Mpiodi   361
Mrkonjić, Tomislav   249n
Mrówczyński-Van Allen, Artur   193n, 210

Muck, Herbert   482n
Muck, Otto   92n
Muff, Guido   475n
Mugnier, Arthur   430n
Muhlenberg, William A.   619
Müller, F. Max   229, 239, 242
Müller, Gerhard   212n
Müller, Johann E.   713n
Müller, Julius   215
Müller, Karl F.   502n
Münch, Alo   671
Mungeam Gordon H.   427n
Munitiz, Joseph A.   9n
Munkler, Herfried   523n, 528n
Muñoz, Vincent P.   43n, 48n
Murch, James D.   216n
Murdock, Graeme   12n
Murphy, Francesca A.   291n
Murphy, Richard T.   454n
Murray, Nicholas   279n
Murray, Paul D.   457n, 473
Murray, Pauli (Anna Pauline)   405
Musana   358n–359
Mussolini, Benito   694n
Mützenberg, Gabriel   71, 321n

Nagarkar, Balwant B.   235
Naim, Moisés   14n
Nanakis, Andreas   129n
Narbonne, Jean-Marc   9n
Nash, Diane   405
Nasmyth, George W.   537
Naumann, Friedrich   588
Naz, Raoul   259n–260n
Nduma, Thomas   344, 351n
Neale, John M.   151n–152n, 155–156
Neely, F. Tennyson   224n–226n, 228–236n, 239–241n
Negel, Joachim   447n
Neill, Stephen C.   4–5, 10, 44n, 66n, 76, 100n, 163, 216n,
      223, 238n, 246n, 320n, 398n, 410n, 417n, 428, 527n,
      540–541n, 566n, 571n, 584, 617n, 639, 703n, 729n, 736,
      742–743
Neirynck, Frans   466n, 472n
Neufeld, Karl H.   88n–89, 97n, 311n–312n, 314n, 319
Neufville, Eduard de   523–524
Neuhaus, Andrea   484n
Neuhaus, Richard J.   64n
Neuhold, David   166n
Neuner, Peter   3n, 166n, 170n, 180n, 182n, 184n, 186
Neunheuser, Burkhard   478n
Neuser, Wilhelm H.   212n
Nève, Théodore   488n
Neveu, Bruno   260n
Nevin, Robert J.   173, 175
Newbigin, Lesslie   738n, 740–743

Newenham, Thomas 139
Newman, John H. 132–133, 135, 140–150, 152–163, 166, 184, 198, 206n, 215, 247, 266–269, 271, 274, 281n, 283, 286, 288, 293, 454n–455n, 593, 620n, 624
Newsome, David 280n
Newton, Richard H. 395
Newton, Thomas 142
Nfinangani 344, 347, 351, 355, 356, 358–361, 364, 368–369
Nichola I, Tsar of Russia 200
Nicholas (Nalimov) 493, 496
Nicholas Cabasilas 494
Nicholas II, Tsar of Russia 490
Nichols, Aidan 492n, 496n
Nicoletti, Michele 12n
Niebergall, Friedrich 385
Niebuhr, Barthold G. 280n
Niebuhr, Reinhold 391, 405
Niemöller, Martin 617n, 674
Niepmann, Helmut M. 507n–508n, 522
Nikitas Stithatos 191n
Nikolaos of Nubia 578
Nikolaou, Theodor 568
Nikon of Moscow 205
Niles, D. Preman 7
Nilles, Nikolaus 314
Ninkunda 355
Nipperdey, Thomas 165n
Nippold, Friedrich W.F. 378
Nitzsch, Karl I. 215
Nkuba 368
Nkunku, Samuel 354
Nlemvo (Mantanu Dundulu) 353n
Noack, Axel 214n
Nobel, Alfred 613
Nockles, Peter B. 132, 134n, 136n, 138n–140n, 146n, 149n, 153n–155n, 166n, 215n, 247n, 252n–253n, 263, 265n–267n, 270n, 297n, 299, 504n, 620n
Noel-Baker, Philip J. 523n
Nolan, Fergal 16on
Norbeck, Mark D. 616n–617n
Norgren, William A. 77n
Norman, Edward R. 265n
North, Frank M. 399–400
Nottmeier, Christian 524n–525n, 527n
Nowak, Kurt 444n, 446n, 527n
Ntima 368–369
Ntoni-Nzinga, Daniel 358–361n
Núñez, Emilio A. 564n
Nygren, Anders 465–466n, 665–667
Nyuvudi, Paul 358–362
Nzungu 344, 347, 351, 355–356, 358–361, 364, 368, 370

Oakeley, Frederick 148, 159–160
Oakes, Kenneth 291n
Oakley, Francis 265n

Obolevitch, Teresa 193n, 210
O'Connell, Marvin R. 146n
Oddy, John A. 138n
Oduyoye, Mercy A. 5, 79
Oeldemann, Johannes 575n
Ogereau, Julien M. 8
Ohly, Emil C.W. 531–532
Oldham, Joseph H. 70, 412–413, 416–421, 529, 552–553, 573, 617, 621, 724–726, 729–731, 733, 735, 737
Oldmeadow, Ernest 524n
Oldstone-Moore, Christopher 320n
Olga (Slyozkina) 188–189
Oliver, William H. 138n
Olsen, Robert J. 2n, 17
Oman, John 589n
Orchard, Ronald K. 740n
Origen of Alexandria 9n
Ornsby, Robert 152n
Orsenigo, Cesare 673
Osinin, Ivan T. 172, 181
Osthövener, Claus-Dieter 610n
Ostriker, Alicia 266n
Otte, Hans 164n
Otto of Greece 114
Otto, Arnold 76n
Otto, Rudolf 595, 661
Overbeck, Franz 29n
Overbeck, Julian J. 181–185n
Ovington, Mary W. 408
Owen, Robert 148n
Oxenham, Henry N. 157–158, 161n–162, 170, 174, 177, 179
Oxlee, John 139

Paasch, Kathrin 164n
Pacik, Rudolf 476n, 481n, 484n
Pahls, Michael J.G. 144n, 149, 158n
Paiano, Maria 433n, 450
Palmer, Edwin J. 634
Palmer, Geoffrey 297n
Palmer, William (of Magdalen) 144–146, 155–156, 163, 194n, 196–198, 246
Palmer, William (of Worcester) 144–147, 155n, 285, 599
Palmieri, Aurelio 250, 252
Palmkvist, Carl 363
Pamp, Frederic E. 590n
Pannenberg, Wolfhart 87n, 94–96n, 98n–100n, 109
Panzani, Gregorio 137
Papaderos, Alexandros K. 565n, 577n
Papadopoulos, Antonios M. 130n, 578
Parker, Kenneth L. 141, 149, 158n
Parker, Matthew 178, 183
Parmentier, Elisabeth 216n
Parry, John H. 542n–543n
Parsch, Pius 476, 480–481, 484n, 659, 665–667
Parsons, Edward L. 623, 631–632

Pascal, Blaise 91n
Pasenow, Guido 476n
Patelos, Constantin G. 8on, 122n–128n, 130n–131, 254n
Paton, William 586, 733, 735, 737, 740
Patrizi Naro, Costantino 252
Patterson, William B. 136n–137n
Pattison, Mark 160
Paul the Apostle 29, 33, 303, 331, 364, 368, 454n, 461,
       466n–467, 506, 574, 576, 607, 611, 698–699
Paul VI (Giovanni Battista Montini), Pope 81, 657n–658
Paul, André 67n
Pawley, Bernard C. 8on
Pawley, Margaret 8on, 143n, 163
Peabody, Francis G. 391
Pecherin, Vladimir 247n
Pechmann, Wilhelm von 671, 673–674, 676
Peck, Arthur L. 136n
Pelikan, Jaroslav 264n
Pellauer, Mary D. 401n
Pellegrini, Arsenio 261n
Pemberton, Jeremy 347
Penn, William 44
Pepper, George W. 622–623, 626n
Percy, Martyn 292n
Pereiro, James 132n, 149n, 153n, 158n–159n, 265n–267n, 299
Peri, Vittorio 69
Perin, Raffaella 707n, 711n
Permiakov, Vitaly 496n
Pernot, Maurice 445n
Perrone, Giovanni 208
Pershing, John 439
Peter I, Tsar of Russia 104n, 107, 112
Peter of Damascus 191n
Peter the Apostle 33, 36, 159, 253, 305, 352–355, 369, 442,
       645, 651, 654, 718
Peters, Christian 213n–214n, 216n, 223
Peterson, Eric 12n
Petrà, Basilio 103n
Petrescu, Ghenadie 181
Petri, Olaus 592
Petrou, Ioannis 565n
Pettinaroli, Laura 74, 122n, 244, 250n–251n, 447n, 703n,
       706n–707n, 709n, 721
Petty, Orville A. 735n
Pfeilschifter, Georg 442n
Pfender, Jules 432
Pfleiderer, Otto 594, 377–381, 383–384
Pfyl, Othmar 164n
Pheidas, Vlassios 567n–568n, 570n, 584
Philaret (Drozdov) of Moscow 197, 206, 208
Philaret (Pulyashkin) 189
Phillips, John S. 402n
Phillpotts, Henry 152
Philoteos (Bryennios) 181
Photius II of Constantinople 130n, 486

Photius of Alexandria 632
Photius of Constantinople 8n, 21, 199, 207
Piatti, Pierantonio 72n, 250n, 636n, 713n
Picciaredda, Stefano 345n–346n
Pico della Mirandola, Giovanni 9n
Piedra, Arturo 543n, 552n–553n, 564
Pierard, Richard V. 221n
Pierling, Paul 201, 250
Pietryga, Paul 672–673n
Pietsch, Michael 591n
Pilch, Jeremy 104n, 187, 203n
Pinggéra, Karl 447n
Pinnington, John 136n
Pinsk, Johannes 476, 667
Pinto-Mathieu, Elisabeth 246n, 263
Piovesana, Gino 249n
Piper, Ernst 523n
Pirotte, Jean 68n, 70n, 449n, 681n, 701, 708n
Pite, Alfred 547
Pius a Spiritu Sancto 142n
Pius VI (Giovanni Angelo Braschi), Pope 55, 59, 138
Pius VII (Barnaba Chiaramonti), Pope 59, 61–63, 654
Pius IX (Giovanni Maria Mastai Ferretti), Pope 197–198,
       244, 246–249, 252n–256, 258n, 295, 334, 703
Pius X (Giuseppe Melchiorre Sarto), Pope 69, 244, 250,
       256–257, 259–262, 382, 435, 438, 456–458, 460, 477, 593,
       626n, 656, 679, 682, 716–717
Pius XI (Achille Ratti), Pope 69–71, 73, 257n, 459–461, 487,
       607, 645–646, 648n, 656, 666n, 669, 679, 685–689, 691,
       694, 699–700, 706–708, 713–714n, 719–720n
Pius XII (Eugenio Pacelli), Pope 459n–460, 462–464n,
       467, 471n, 476, 669, 676, 686n, 696, 699, 707, 714–716,
       718–719
Plank, Peter 496n
Plato 22
Platon (Rozhdestvensky) 207, 628
Platten, Stephen 136
Platz, Hermann 715
Plongeron, Bernard 42, 46n, 52n–6on, 63n, 65, 245n
Plummer, Alfred 166n, 170, 172n–183n, 185n–186
Pobee, John 7
Podmore, Colin 134n
Poggi, Vincenzo 73n
Pollard, John F. 458n, 529n
Pompili, Basilio 707
Poncet, Olivier 250n
Pons de La Grange, Antoine de 248
Pontzen, Alexandra 479n
Poole, George A. 147n
Popham, Sir Home R. 543
Porphyrius (Uspensky) 121
Portal, É. Fernand 69, 250–253, 260, 291–293, 449, 622, 630,
       640–643, 646–647, 649–650, 652, 656–657, 689–692,
       705, 709
Porter, Andrew 330n, 339

Porter, David R.   337
Portuondo, Emma J.   617n
Porumb, Razvan   83n
Poschmann, Andreas   481n, 483n
Posthumus Meyjes, Guillaume H.M.   12n
Postic, Fañch   442n
Poswick, Réginald-Ferdinand   680n
Potter, Philip   13n, 325n–326n, 330n, 332n, 335n–336n, 339
Pottier, Antoine   680
Poujoulat, Jean-Joseph-François   246n
Poulat, Émile   704n
Powell, Adam C. Jr.   405
Powell, Adam C. Sr.   391, 405, 407, 410
Power, Maria   76n
Prange, Max   665, 667
Pressel, Wilhelm   434n
Pribilla, Max   607, 665–666, 670, 672, 674–676, 678
Prickett, Stephen   267n, 283n
Priesching, Nicole   76n
Printzipas, Giorgos T.   129n
Prochasson, Christophe   528n
Prodi, Paolo   14–15
Prudhomme, Claude   263
Przywara, Erich   672–673
Pseudo-Hyppolitus   27
Puaux, Frank   439n
Pugin, Augustus W.N.   267
Puglisi, James F.   35n
Puller, Frederick W.   293
Purcell, Edmund S.   142n–143n, 154n
Pusey, Edward B.   140, 146, 151–153, 155, 158–159, 162n–163n,
       166, 168, 170, 174, 177, 184–185n, 267–269, 274n, 292,
       620n, 625

Quisinsky, Michael   469n
Quitslund, Sonya A.   74n, 679n, 695n, 702

Rabow-Edling, Susanna   187n
Rački, Franjo   206
Radcliffe, Ann   266
Rade, Martin   383–384, 524
Rademacher, Arnold   718–719
Rahner, Karl   7n, 12n, 34, 167
Raiser, Konrad   22n, 565n, 573–574n
Rambaldi, Giuseppe   69n
Rampolla del Tindaro, Mariano   261
Ramsey, Michael   76, 282n, 658
Randall, Ian M.   223, 265n
Randwijk, S.C. Graaf van   740n
Ransom, Reverdy C.   391–392, 399, 405, 407–410
Ranson, Charles W.   738
Rapp, Claudia   2n
Raschzok, Klaus   476n, 480n, 483n, 516n, 521
Rasmussen, Anne   528n
Rathje, Johannes   383n, 389

Rau, Gokura S.   382
Rauschenbusch, Walter   372, 391–392, 397–405
Raymaekers, Paul   344n, 347–349n, 370
Reardon, Bernard M.G.   372n
Reckett, Maurice   403
Redtenbacher, Andreas   465n, 480n
Rehbach, August   672
Rehberg, Andreas E.   72n, 636n, 713n
Reid, James J.   119n
Reilly, Michael C.   617
Rein, Harald   111n
Reinhard, Wolfgang   117n
Reinkens, Joseph H.   172–174n
Remarque, Erich M.   612
Rémond, René   6
Rendtorff, Franz   525n, 594, 597
Rendtorff, Trutz   525n
Repgen, Konrad   77
Reusch, Franz H.   166n, 173–183n, 185n–186
Réville, Albert   239, 588
Réville, Jean   377, 382–383
Rhinelander, Philip M.   628
Riccardi, Andrea   73
Ricci, Antonello   361n
Richard, François-Marie-Benjamin   293
Richards, George W.   237n
Richards, Henry   365
Richardson, Cyril C.   23n, 497n
Riché, Pierre   2n
Richter, Gerhard   31n
Richter, Julius   729
Richter, Klemens   474n–475n, 480n–481n
Ricoeur, Paul   31n, 41
Riesenberger, Dieter   524n
Rimestad, Sebastian   115n
Ritschl, Albrecht   311, 397, 586–587
Ritson, John H.   415, 419
Ritter, Karl B.   503n, 514–516, 518, 659, 662–664, 666–668,
       677
Rivière, Jacques   435
Robb, Fiona   521, 677
Robert, André   471
Robert, Dana   421n
Robert, Jean-Louis   431n
Roberts, William H.   629n
Robertson, James B.   165n, 301n, 319
Robespierre, Maximilien de   57
Robinson, J. Armitage   643, 645, 647–652
Robinson, Robert B.   465n, 473
Robinson, Ronald   529n
Robson, George   552
Rodger, Patrick C.   21n
Roey, Jozef-Ernest van   467n–468, 643, 647–648, 652
Rogers, Benjamin T.   622n–623, 631–632
Rogge, Joachim   212n, 222n–223

Rogier, Ludovicus J.   45n
Roguet, Aimon-Marie   696
Rohling, August   454
Rohls, Jan   525n
Rojek, Paweł   193n, 210
Romeo, Antonino   472
Roosevelt, Theodore   399, 401n, 546, 556, 617
Rose, L. de   445
Rosenberg, Arthur J.   442
Rosenius, Carl O.   585
Rosenmöller, Bernhard   666, 677
Rosenthal, Leon G.   617n
Rosis, Zikos   173
Ross, Kenneth R.   539n, 541n, 632n, 722, 743
Rossi, Amédée-Filiberto-Giovanni de   343n
Rossum, Willem M. van   459
Rota, Olivier   248n
Roth, Otto-Reinhard   633n
Rothe, Alfred   671n
Rothe, Richard   384
Rottenberg, Elizabeth   8n
Roudometof, Victor   113n, 131
Rouleau, François   188
Rouse, Ruth C.   4–5, 10, 44n, 66n, 76, 100n–101n, 163, 216n,
    223n, 238n, 246n, 248n, 264n, 320, 322n, 325, 332n,
    335–336, 339, 398n, 410n, 417n, 428, 527n, 540–541n,
    566n, 584, 617n, 639, 703n, 722n, 729n, 743
Rousseau, Olivier   245, 485n, 487n, 489, 500, 683–684, 691n,
    697n
Roussiez, Timothée   439
Routhier, Gilles   454n, 473
Rowell, Geoffrey   136n, 270n
Rowley, Harold H.   466n
Roy, Philippe J.   454n, 473
Royce, Josiah   394
Rozell, Mark J.   48n
Rudin, Waldemar   585
Rüenauver, Josef   482n
Ruffini, Ernesto   714, 717
Ruggieri, Giuseppe   1n, 3n, 9n, 12n, 30n, 81n
Ruhbach, Gerhard   212n–215n, 222n–223
Ruhtenberg, Ralph   171n
Runestam, Staffan   596n, 598n, 613n–614
Ruotolo, Dolindo   462n
Rupp, Gordon   163n
Rupprecht, Tobias   5n
Rusama, Jaakko   76
Rusconi, Roberto   9n
Rushbrooke, John H.   523n, 525
Russell, Charles   149
Rutten, Martin-Hubert   680
Ryan, John   391
Rydell, Robert W.   225n
Rylance, Joseph H.   395

Sabanes Plou, Dafne   541n, 564
Sabatier, Auguste   455, 589
Sabatier, Paul   29, 35, 382, 458n
Sabbas of Belgrade   181
Sack, Friedrich   212
Sack, James J.   137n
Sailer, Johann M.   164, 167
Sakharov, Hieromonk N.   121n, 131
Salachas, Dimitri   80n
Salapatas, Dimitris F.   72n, 111n, 486n
Salaville, Sévérien J.   249n
Salemink, Theo   470n
Salmond, Wendy   486n
Salomon, Dialungana K.   342n
Salvatorelli, Luigi   458n
Samarin, Yuri F.   187, 200–203, 206, 210
Sandegren, Paul   598
Sander, Hartmut   222n
Sanders, Charles R.   275n
Sanders, Frank K.   558
Sandford, Charles W.   181
Sandford, Ernest G.   296n–297n
Sanford, Elias   222
Sanneh, Lamin   542n
Santi Cucinotta, Filippo   101n–103n, 107n–108
Santus, Cesare   259n, 710n
Saresella, Daniela   256n
Sarx, Tobias   12n
Sasse, Hermann   581n, 617n, 635n
Satolli, Francesco   226
Saunders, Thomas B.   313n
Sauter, Gerhard   450n
Sautter, Emmanuel   448n
Savage, Richard H.   231
Savart, Claude   455n, 473
Scarpa, Marco   491n
Scatena, Silvia   6n, 11n, 75, 78n
Schäfer, Christiane   475n
Schäfer, Paula   666–667
Schäfer, Rolf   594n
Schaff, Philip   175n, 236–238, 242, 285n
Schatz, Klaus   179n
Schäufele, Wolf F.   223
Scheeben, Matthias J.   175n, 185n
Scheele, Paul-Werner   165n
Scheidgen, Hermann-Josef   732n
Scheler, Max   448–449n, 715
Schelkens, Karim   78n, 454n, 456n, 464n, 469n–473
Schell, Hermann   719
Schelling, Friedrich W.J.   98n–99, 189, 301
Schenk, Richard   164n
Scherr, Gregor von   168
Scherzberg, Lucia   476n
Schiele, Friedrich M.   384n, 389
Schieler, Caspar   380

Schilson, Arno   478n, 480n
Schirripa, Giuseppe D.   361n
Schjørring, Jens H.   76n, 529n, 540
Schlatter, Adolf   465n
Schleiermacher, Friedrich D.E.   96–100, 212, 215, 301, 309, 374, 379, 502, 504, 589, 591–592, 594, 607
Schlimbach, Guido   480n
Schlink, Edmund   26n, 668n, 678
Schlögl, Nivard   458n
Schlott, René   529n
Schmemann, Alexander   35–36, 486, 500
Schmid-Keiser, Stephan   477n–478n
Schmid, Dirk   591n
Schmid, Josef   459n
Schmidt-Lauber, Hans-Christoph   483n, 503n
Schmidt, Martin   373n
Schmidt, Stjepan   461n, 469n–470n
Schmidt, Walter   633n
Schmidt, William J.   534n
Schmidtke, Friedrich   460
Schmitt, Carl   12n, 715
Schmoller, Gustav von   393
Schmucker, Samuel S.   216
Schnackenburg, Rudolf   465n
Schneider, Carl E.   216n
Schneider, John R.   2n
Schneider, Matthias   477n
Schneider, Robert A.   222n
Schoenig, Steven   655n
Schoeps, Hans-Joachim   167n
Schöfer, Friedrich   667
Scholl, Sarah   219n, 236n, 320, 410n, 529n
Schott, Anselm   483
Schrader, Clemens   681n
Schrader, Karl   381
Schreiber, August W.   531–532n, 633n
Schroeder, Roger P.   100n, 105n–106
Schubert, Jan   11n, 71n
Schücking, Walther   523n
Schulte, Johann F. von   172
Schulz, Friedrich   667
Schulz, Georg   665–666
Schuppe, Florian   31n
Schuster, Ildephonso   683
Schutz, Roger   17n, 75, 698
Schwabe, Klaus   528n
Schwahn, Barbara   76n, 677n
Schwaiger, Georg   164n, 373n
Schwarz, Maria   482n
Schwarz, Rudolf   482
Schweitzer, Albert   29–30, 39, 41, 447, 456, 598
Schwöbel, Christoph   383n, 389
Scofield, Cyrus   545
Scott, George   585
Scott, Walter   266, 279

Scrima, André   486n
Scudamore, John   136
Scudder, Vida   391–392, 616
Seager, Charles   160
Seager, Richard H.   229n, 232–235n, 243
Segbroeck, Frans van   472n
Segerstedt, Torgny   589, 606
Séguy, Jean   68, 81
Seib, Adrian   482n
Seitz, Anton   676n
Sekulovski, Goran   696n
Sell, Alan P.F.   220n, 223
Semeraro, Cosimo   706n, 721
Semler, Johann S.   373
Sen, Benoyendra N.   381
Sepúlveda, Juan   541
Serapheim, Pavlos   131n
Seraphim of Sarov   198, 262
Sergius (Stragorodsky) of Moscow   491
Sertillanges, Antonin-Gilbert (Antonin-Dalmace)   465n
Sesboüé, Bernard   7n, 80n, 109
Seton, Elizabeth B.   46
Setran, David P.   321n–322, 328n–329n, 336–337, 339
Sevenster, Jan N.   467n
Sewell, Gabriel   290n
Sfetas, Spyridon   1122n
Shannon, Richard   285n
Sharp, John   136
Sharp, Richard   270
Sharpe, Eric J.   240
Shea, C. Michael   133n, 147n–148
Shedd, Clarence P.   320n, 322n, 324n, 326n, 329–330, 332n, 339, 398n
Sheehan, Donald   486n
Sheptytsky, Andrey   251, 487, 684, 690–691, 700
Sheridan, Thomas L.   142n
Shine, Cormac   127n
Shkarovsky, Mikhail V.   14n
Shook, Laurence K.   72n
Shuvalov, Augustinus M. (Gregory Petrovich)   248
Sibour, Marie D.-A.   198–199
Sicking, Thom   82n
Sidenvall, Erik   157n
Siebeck, Oskar   385
Siebeck, Paul   385
Siegmund-Schultze, Friedrich   524n–527, 531, 537–538, 627–628n, 633n, 635n
Siemens, Johannes   324
Simeon, Charles   328
Simmerding, Gottfried   671
Simmons, William   405
Simon, Constantin   73n, 261n, 263
Simon, Paul   665–670n, 677
Simonetti, Manlio   2n
Singh, Sundar   602

Sixte-Quenin, Anatole   437
Skinner Keller, Rosemary   401
Skouteris, Konstantinos   567n, 584
Slater, Eleanor   621n
Slater, George   391–392, 407
Slezkine, Hélène   188, 189n
Slotte, Pamela   540
Small, Albion W.   394–395
Smend, Julius   516n
Smend, Rudolf   502
Smit, Peter-Ben   254n, 268n
Smith, David   194n
Smith, Florence E.   544n
Smith, Gary S.   48n
Smith, George   414n
Smith, Harry   415n
Smith, Louise P.   373n
Smith, Lucy   407
Smith, Rodney (Gypsy)   448
Smith, Sandra   73n
Smith, William R.   595n
Smyth, Newman   395, 587, 624–627
Snape, Michael   448n
Snell, Merwin-Marie   239
Snodgrass, Judith   228n, 230n, 243
Snoeck, Laurent   343
Socrates   612
Soden, Hans von   524
Soden, Hermann Freiherr von   385
Söderblom, Jonas   585
Söderblom, Nathan   70, 317–318, 417, 445, 510, 530–537, 539,
        572–573, 577–580, 585–599, 601–614, 618, 620n–621,
        632, 634n, 636–637, 660–661, 665, 667, 670, 675, 705,
        712
Söderblom, Sven   602
Soetens, Claude   69, 255n, 679n, 683n, 702
Sohm, Rudolf   35, 496n
Sokolov, Ivan   121n, 131
Sologub, Fyodor (F. Kuzmich Teternikov)   203
Solovyov, Vladimir S.   105, 189, 192n, 197, 201–210, 247n, 249
Sonnenschein, Carl   715
Soper, Edmund D.   638
Sorsky, Nil   191n
Sove, Boris I.   485n, 492, 495–496
Spadafora, Francesco   472
Speer, Robert E.   399, 541, 545–547, 549, 551–555, 558–559,
        561, 564, 724, 735
Spencer, George II   142–143, 157, 248, 253
Spencer, Herbert   394–395
Spicq, Ceslas   465n, 467n–468
Spiecker, Friedrich A.   444, 525–526
Spiteris, Yannis   486n
Spitta, Friedrich   502
Spry, John H.   134
Spurr, John   281

Spyridon of Antioch   121
Srawley, James H.   494
Stadler, Josip   259n
Staerk, Antoine   252
Stafin, Roman   481n
Stahl, Norbert   671n, 678
Stählin, Rudolf   502n, 517n–518n
Stählin, Wilhelm   76n, 514, 518n–521n, 665–668, 677
Stamatopoulos, Dimitris   114n, 117n, 120n–122n, 126n, 131
Stambolis, Barbara   476n
Stanley, Arthur P.   281n
Stanley, Brian   169n, 218n, 264n, 338n, 412–413n, 417n, 429,
        541n, 621n, 727n, 730n, 743
Stanley, Dean   376n
Starr, S. Frederick   249
Staudenmaier, Franz A.   92n
Staughton, William   414
Stavrou, Theofanis G.   121n
Stead, Francis H.   445
Steely, John E.   311n
Ștefănescu, Melchizedek   181
Steglich, Wolfgang   528n–529
Stehle, Hansjakob   73
Steinmann, Jean   465n
Stelzle, Charles   399
Stephanidis, Vasileios   571
Stephanos of Monastir   440
Stephens, Grace   421
Stephenson, Alan M.G.   290n, 372n, 644n
Sternberg, Thomas   481n–482n
Stetson, Francis L.   623
Stillingfleet, Edward   275
Stirling, Waite H.   534, 547
Stock, Eugene   729
Stöckmann, Hagen   441n
Stodart-Walker, Archibald   331n
Stoedten, H. Lucius von   531–533n
Stoelen, André   691
Stohr, Albert   75
Stojan, Antonín C.   709
Stokłosa, Katarzyna   540
Storne-Sengel, Catherine   446n
Stotzingen, Fidelis von   687
Stouraiti, Anastasia   129n
Strange, Roderick   158n
Stransky, Thomas F.   7
Strauss, David F.   183
Strémooukhoff, Dimitri   203, 205–206
Strobbe, Karel   146n, 247n
Strohm, Theodor   525n
Strong, Josiah   394, 399, 404
Strong, Rowan   157, 159n
Strossmayer, Josip J.   206, 249, 254
Struker, Arnold   528n
Stuart, Elizabeth B.   139n, 154n, 156n–157n

Stubbs, William   296
Studd, Charles T.   323
Studd, Edward   323
Studd, John E.K.   323, 326
Stuflesser, Martin   481n
Stumpfl, Aloys   662
Stupperich, Robert   171n
Suchanek, Lucjan   247n
Šuljak, Andrija   254n
Sun, Anna   228n, 243
Sundelin, Robert   585
Sundkler, Bengt G.M.   70, 425n, 429, 533n, 597n
Suter, John W.   269n, 273n
Suttner, Bertha von   524n
Swedenborg, Emanuel   307
Swidler, Leonard J.   75, 663n, 668–669, 678
Syagrius of Autun   655
Sykes, Norman   135, 265n, 281n
Sykes, Stephen W.   134n, 136, 161n, 274n, 276n, 294n
Symeon Metaphrastis   191n
Symeon of Thessalonica   494, 496

Tabaraud, Mathieu-Mathurin   245
Tackett, Timothy   42n, 50n–51n, 54n–56n, 58n
Taft, Robert F.   249n, 485n
Taft, William H.   616–617
Talar, Charles J.T.   382n
Talbot, Edward S.   173, 416, 552
Talleyrand-Périgord, Charles-Maurice de   55
Tamborra, Angelo   69, 244n, 246n, 249n, 254n
Tandberg, Jens F.   532
Tanner, Mary   7
Taparelli d'Azeglio, Luigi   435
Tatlow, Tissington   417, 548n, 552n, 617n, 623n, 629n, 639
Tavard, Georges H.   67, 135n, 139n, 294n
Taylor, Graham   391, 395, 399
Taylor, Jeremy   275
Taylor, Stephen   137n, 290n
Taylor, William D.   544–545, 564n
Tchertkoff, Vladimir   376n
Temple, Frederick   295, 297
Temple, William   76, 283, 601, 604, 729, 735, 737
Tennyson, Alfred   376
Tétaz, Jean-Marc   313n–314n
Theiner, Augustin   253
Theißen, Henning   216n, 479n
Theobald, Christoph   2n, 89n, 93n, 109, 455n, 473
Thierfelder, Jörg   525n
Thiessen, Gesa E.   22n
Thijssen, Frans   469n
Thils, Gustave   67n
Tholuck, F. August   96, 99–100, 146
Thomas à Kempis   191n
Thomas Aquinas   92–94, 435, 716
Thomas, George   366

Thomas, Hilah F.   401n
Thomas, Norman E.   217n–219n
Thomas, William   527
Thompson, Glen L.   8n
Thompson, Nick   12n
Thompson, Ralph W.   727
Thomson, James   543–544
Thönissen, Wolfgang   7, 17, 75, 79n, 166n
Thorndike, Herbert   286
Thornton, Lionel   496
Thorp, William   546
Thucydides   280n
Thurian, Max   28n
Thurman, Howard   405
Ticchi, Jean-Marc   250n, 680n
Tiele, Cornelis P.   239
Tierney, Brian   14, 17
Tierney, Mark   680n
Tikhon of Moscow   491
Tillard, Jean-Marie R.   31n, 35n, 80n, 178n
Tillich, Paul   513–515, 517
Timberlake, Charles   254n
Tippy, Worth M.   399
Tisserant, Eugène   460n–462, 473, 684, 706
Titius, Arthur   385–386
Titus II Mar Thoma   425
Tolomeo, Rita   69n, 249n–250n
Tolstoy, Lev N.   105, 588
Tolstoy, Nicholas   261
Tondini de' Quarenghi, Cesare   248–249, 251–253n, 256n, 259n
Tornau, Christian   9n
Torrance, Thomas   3n
Tottie, Henry W.   593
Tournay, Raymond J.   465n
Touzard, Jules   458n
Tracey, Gerard   149n
Traer, Robert   379n–380n, 385n
Traniello, Francesco   77n
Tretjakewitsch, Léon   73, 251n, 686n, 702, 705n, 709n
Trial, Louis   433n
Trocmé, Hélène   448n
Troeltsch, Ernst   372, 384–385, 387–388, 523n, 603
Tromp, Sebastian   469n, 472
Trumbull, David   544
Tsetsis, Georges   5, 9n, 566n, 570n–572n, 576n–578n, 582n–584
Tsimbaev, Nikolai I.   187
Tsimbaeva, Ekaterina N.   201n, 210, 247n
Tsompanidis, Stylianos   80, 123n–124n, 127n, 539n, 565, 576n–577n, 584, 632n, 704n
Tsurikov, Vladimir   193n, 196n, 210
Tudorie, Ionuț-Alexandru   250n
Turner, Frank M.   153n
Turner, Henry M.   405–407

Turner, William H.   150n
Turrettini, Jean-Alphonse   136
Tyndale, William   134
Tyrrell, George   593, 719
Tyrrell, Ian   323n, 330n–331n, 339
Tyutchev, Fyodor I.   198, 200–201, 210
Tzschirner, Heinrich G.   373

Ugolini, Romano   260n
Ungern-Sternberg, Jürgen von   441n
Ungern-Sternberg, Wolfgang von   441n
Unterburger, Klaus   715n–716n, 718n, 721
Urbach, Otto   670, 672–673
Urban VIII (Maffeo Vincenzo Barberini), Pope   261
Ustorf, Werner   550n

Vaccari, Alberto   462n
Vadkovsky, Anthony   206
Vail, Thomas H.   619
Valente, Massimiliano   255n, 488n
Valentini, Natalino   485n
Valentini, Rudolf von   531n
Vallotton, Benjamin   325n–326
van Acken, Johannes   482
van Bekkum, Wout J.   378n
Van Belle, Gilbert   453n
van Bühren, Ralf   482n
van Caloen, Gérard   684–685n
Van Cangh, Jean-Marie   485n
van der Veer, Peter   229n, 233–234n
Van Hoonacker, Albinus   466
Van Orden, Emanuel   547
Van Waeyenbergh, Honoré   469n
Vanden Bussche, Jozef   142n, 248n
Vanhoye, Albert   456n
Varella, Evangelia   130n, 567n, 570n, 572n, 575n–577n, 579n,
   582n, 584
Varnalidis, Sotirios L.   126n
Vassiliadis, Petros   105n
Vaughan, Herbert   293
Velati, Mauro   78, 244n, 470n, 500
Velbrück, François-Charles de   52n
Vellut, Jean-Luc   340n–341n, 344n, 346n, 349n, 353n, 356n,
   358n–359n, 361n, 363–366n, 368n, 370
Venghaus, pastor   676
Verbeke, Werner   30n
Verdoodt, Albert   75n
Vereb, Jerome M.   78n
Vergottini, Marco   108
Verhaeghe, Raymond   443
Verhelst, Daniel   30n
Verheyden, Joseph   1n
Verhoeven, Timothy   333n
Vermeil, Matthieu   542
Vervaet, Stijn   114n

Vezenkov, Alexander   117n
Vian, Giovanni   711n
Vickers, Mark   657n, 695n
Vico, Giambattista   280
Vidler, Alec R.   282n, 395n, 416
Viénot, John   388n–389
Vigener, Fritz   318
Vigouroux, Fulcran   459
Vigué, Pierre-Gaston   662
Villain, Maurice   68, 74n, 78
Villegagnon, Nicolas D. de   542
Vincent of Lerins   502
Vincent, Boyd   623, 629n–632
Vincent, George E.   395n
Vinck, Honoré   680n, 702
Vingadio, Timoteo   365–366
Vischer, Lukas   21n, 70n
Viscuso, Patrick   129n
Visser 't Hooft, Willem A.   67–68, 71, 76, 325, 566, 572n–573n,
   576–578n, 580n, 582n, 584, 618
Vivekananda, Swami   233–234
Vivian, Cordy T.   405
Voderholzer, Rudolf   678
Voigt, Karl H.   75–76, 218n–219n, 222–223, 528n, 540
Voigts, Bodo   530–531n, 628
Volk, Hermann   668n, 678
Volk, Ludwig   673n, 678
Völklein, Albrecht   614
Volkonskaia, Elizabeth   206, 253
Volz, Paul   461
von Teuffenbach, Alexandra   472n
Vorgrimler, Herbert   12n
Vos, Lambert   487n, 492n, 682n, 691n, 693n, 697n
Vosté, Jacques-Marie   461–462, 467, 473
Vovchenko, Denis   122n, 131

Waanders, Stefan   479n
Wackerbarth, Francis D.   140, 160
Wagner, Adolf H.G.   393
Wagner, Harald   165n, 301n, 310n, 319
Wagner, Hubert   676n
Wahle, Stephan   480n
Wainwright, Geoffrey   7, 741n, 743
Wake, William   135–137, 139, 158, 265, 275
Walker, William   617
Walls, Andrew F.   729
Walsham, Alexandra   137n
Walter, Peter   469n
Walters, Alexander   399, 405
Wandel, Jürgen   528n
Wang, Marina X.   423n
Ward Howe, Julia   240, 242
Ward, Harry F.   394, 399–400
Ward, Kevin   529n, 540
Ward, Lester   394

Ward, Wilfrid   149n, 158n, 163, 293
Ward, William G.   148–149, 154, 293
Ward, William H.P.   156n
Warnach, Viktor   466n
Warneck, Gustav   418, 420, 549–550, 552, 590n, 725
Warner, Horace E.   325
Warnshuis, A. Livingston   733, 737
Warren, Max   738, 740
Washington, Booker T.   405–408
Washington, George   45, 48
Wasmuth, Jennifer   80n
Wathen, Charles   346n
Watine Christory, Pascale   81n
Watson, Edward W.   296n
Wattson, Paul J. (Lewis Thomas)   249, 257, 438
Weatherford, Willis D.   336n
Webb, Mohammed   231
Weber, Martin   482
Websky, Julius   381
Wedgbury, Daphne M.   12n
Weigelt, Horst   212n
Weinel, Heinrich   384
Weiss, Henry L.   544
Weiss, Johannes   29–30, 456, 610
Weiß, Otto   475n
Weiße, Wolfram   538n, 540
Weitlauff, Manfred   165n–166n, 170, 186
Welkenhuysen, Andries   30n
Weller, Reginald H.   623, 631–632
Wellhausen, Julius   461, 586
Wellings, Martin   221n
Wells-Barnett, Ida B.   405, 407–408
Welte, Bernhard   89
Wendland, Heinz D.   665
Wendt, Hans H.   384
Wendté, Charles W.   237, 242, 371–372, 376n, 379–389
Wenger, Antoine   73, 686n, 702, 705n
Wenz, Gunther   166n
Werighine, Serge   260–261
Werner, Yvonne M.   333n
Wernsmann, Maria   81n
Wesley, Charles   153, 225n
Wesley, John   153, 217
Wessenberg, Ignaz H. von   164
Westman, Knut B.   594n
Weston, Frank   428
Wetter, Gillis P.   494
Wheeler, Robin   145n–146n, 196n, 246n
Wheeler, W. Reginald   544n
Wheelwright, Isaac   544
Wheen, Arthur W.   612n
White, Leila A.   327
White, Lewis B.   150n
White, William J.   407

Whitehead, Henry   425
Whitney, Gleaves   48n
Whittingham, Willaim R.   172
Whyte, Alexander   163
Wicks, Jerard   11n
Wiener, Jürgen   482n
Wieser, Thomas   322n, 325n–326n, 330n, 332n, 335n–336n, 339
Wilberforce, Robert   150
Willaime, Jean-Paul   81n–82
Willebrands, Johannes   76, 78, 469–471
William II, Emperor of Germany   222, 432, 513, 524, 531, 717
William IV, King of Great Britain and Ireland   272
Williams, David   297n
Williams, George   320, 711
Williams, Leighton   395
Williams, Norman P.   266n
Williamson, Eugene L.   279n
Williamson, Geoffrey A.   21n
Williamson, John R.   324
Willis, John J.   427–428n
Wilson, Austin   142
Wilson, Bryan   68
Wilson, Woodrow   439, 556, 630
Windelband, Wilhelm   595n
Winter, Jay   431n, 434n, 523n, 540
Winter, Thomas   711n
Winzen, Damasus   666–667
Wiseman, Nicholas P.S.   147–148, 158, 292n
Wishard, Luther D.   322–324
Witte, Jan   469n
Wittig, Joseph   717–719
Wix, Samuel   139
Woelfkin, Cornelius   403n
Wolf, Gerhard P.   221n
Wolf, Hubert   715n
Wolffe, John   145n, 265n, 333n
Woodbey, George W.   391–392, 407
Woodhouse-Hawkins, Michelle   283n
Woodlock, Francis   654
Woods, Frank T.   604
Woods, Robert   616n
Woolverton, John F.   269n, 391n, 410n–411, 415n, 622n, 639
Wordsworth, Charles   162n
Wordsworth, Christopher   161, 172, 181
Wordsworth, John   295–297
Wordsworth, William   274, 279
Work, Monroe   407
Wozniuk, Vladimir   204n–205n
Wright, J. Robert   269n–270n, 283n, 292n, 299, 620n
Wright, Luke S.H.   277n
Wright, Richard R. Jr.   391, 405, 407
Wulf, Naomi   48n
Wynter, James C.   140n

Yannoulatos, Anastasios   105–106n, 742n

Yarnell III, Malcolm B.   275n

Yarnold, Edward   80n, 294n, 298n–299

Yates, Nigel   139n, 155n, 161n

Yates, Timothy   553n, 735n–737, 742n–743

Yengo, André   344, 346

Yfantidis, Evangelos   129n, 131

Yiannaras, Christos   575n

Yoder, Don H.   44n–45n, 49n–50n, 76, 238n, 410n, 619n

Young, Andrew   405

Young, Robert   549n

Yu, Guozhen   423

Zabriskie, Alexander C.   615n, 617n–618n, 621n, 639

Zabriskie, George   623, 630–631n

Zachman, Randall   12n

Zahner, Walter   482n

Zambarbieri, Annibale   89n, 94n

Zander, Lev A.   496n

Zeilstra, Jurjen A.   11n, 71n

Zelepos, Ioannis   129n

Zeller, Hermann von   628

Zenkovsky, Vasily V.   188, 201n

Zernov, Nicholas M.   101n, 105n, 193, 196, 492, 496n, 498, 566n, 578, 584

Zervos, Gennadios   122n, 124n, 126n, 129n

Zerwick, Maximilian   472

Zhukovsky, Vasily A.   189

Zinzendorf, Nikolai L. von   44, 216–217

Ziolkowski, Eric J.   227n, 229n, 233n, 239n, 242–243

Zippert, Christian   664n

Zizioulas, John   21–22n, 24n–25n, 29n, 31n, 41, 500

Zonara, Joannes   496

Zorn, Wolfgang   212n

Zoroaster   589

Zorzi, Benedetta S.   104n

Zouboff, Peter   203

Zschokke, Heinrich   164n

Zuijdwegt, Geertjan   135n, 150n

Zumstein, Jean   8n

Zurlo, Gina A.   410n

Zussini, Alessandro   444n

Zwingli, Huldrych   213